HISTORY OF MANKIND
CULTURAL AND SCIENTIFIC DEVELOPMENT

VOLUME VI

THE TWENTIETH CENTURY

PARTS TWO–FOUR

THE TRANSFORMATION OF SOCIETIES; THE SELF–IMAGE AND
ASPIRATIONS OF THE PEOPLES OF THE WORLD; EXPRESSION

PUBLISHED FOR THE
INTERNATIONAL COMMISSION FOR A HISTORY OF THE
SCIENTIFIC AND CULTURAL DEVELOPMENT
OF MANKIND

BY

GEORGE ALLEN AND UNWIN LIMITED
LONDON

HISTORY OF MANKIND

CULTURAL AND SCIENTIFIC DEVELOPMENT

VOLUME VI

By CAROLINE F. WARE

K. M. PANIKKAR and J. M. ROMEIN

THE TWENTIETH CENTURY

PARTS TWO–FOUR

THE TRANSFORMATION OF SOCIETIES; THE SELF–IMAGE AND
ASPIRATIONS OF THE PEOPLES OF THE WORLD; EXPRESSION

FIRST PUBLISHED IN 1966

Prepared under the auspices and
with Financial Assistance of the
United Nations Educational, Scientific and
Cultural Organization

Consultants for
Volume VI

Professor E. N. Anderson
(University of California,
Los Angeles, United States
of America)

Professor K. V. Ostrovitianov
(Academy of Sciences of the
Union of Soviet Socialist
Republics)

PRINTED IN GREAT BRITAIN
in 11-pt. Plantin type
BY UNWIN BROTHERS LIMITED
WOKING AND LONDON

CONTENTS

PART TWO: THE TRANSFORMATION OF SOCIETIES

XX. MAJOR CHANGES IN CONCEPTS AND IDEAS   649
    I. Introduction   649
    II. Man's Relation to Society   650
    III. Man's Relation to his Past and Future   656
    IV. Man and Nature   658
    V. Man's View of his Gods   660
    VI. Man's View of Himself   662
    VII. Main Lines of Philosophical Thought   662

XXI. ECONOMIC INSTITUTIONS   674
    I. The Common Base: The World Economy of the Early Twentieth Century   676
    II. The Development of Capitalist and Socialist Economies in the Twentieth Century   679

        1. The capitalist economy of the United States and other advanced capitalist countries, p. 679; 2. The socialist economy of the USSR and other communist countries, p. 696.

    III. The Economies of the Newly Developing Countries   710

        1. The mixed economy of India and other non-communist countries, p. 710; 2. The socialist economy of the Chinese People's Republic, p. 722.

XXII. SOCIAL INSTITUTIONS   742
    I. The Family   742

        1. The urban family in the West, p. 743; 2. The joint family in the East, p. 753; 3. The tribal family in Africa, p. 755.

    II. Social Stratification   758

        1. At the opening of the century, p. 759; 2. Changing patterns of social stratification, p. 761.

    III. Voluntary Organizations   769

        1. Functions of voluntary organizations in modern society, p. 769; 2. Economic interest organizations, p. 770; 3. Mutual benefit organizations, p. 774; 4. Organizations for social activities, p. 776; 5. Civic associations, p. 782; 6. Benevolent organizations, p. 783; 7. Cultural and interest groups, p. 784.

    IV. The Individual in the Twentieth Century   784

XXIII. POLITICAL INSTITUTIONS   788
    I. Forms of the State   789

        1. Monarchy, p. 789; 2. Liberal democracy, p. 790; 3. Authoritarian state forms, p. 791; 4. Communism, p. 792; 5. Colonial systems, p. 792; 6. Associated States, p. 795.

II. Institutions of the Liberal Democratic States   797

1. The electoral system and political parties, *p.* 797; 2. Other expressions of political opinion, *p.* 800; 3. Legislative structure, *p.* 800; 4. Bureaucracy, *p.* 801; 5. Administrative law, *p.* 804; 6. Judiciary, *p.* 806; 7. Problems encountered by new states in adopting democratic forms, *p.* 806.

III. Institutions of the Communist States   813

1. The Communist party, *p.* 813; 2. Organs of the state, *p.* 814.

XXIV. MILITARY INSTITUTIONS   828
   I. Traditional Military Institutions   829
   II. The Armament Industry   833
   III. Transformation of Military Institutions by Total War   834
   IV. Military-Civilian Institutions of the Second World War   838
   V. Military Institutions of the Nuclear Age   840

XXV. RELIGION   846
   I. General Trends in Major World Religions   846
   II. Christianity   855
   III. Judaism   871
   IV. Islam   879
   V. Hinduism   885
   VI. Buddhism   891

XXVI. EDUCATION   897
   I. Introduction   897
   II. Education at Opening of Twentieth Century   903

1. Extent, *p.* 903; 2. Auspices and financing, *p.* 906; 3. Teachers, *p.* 907; 4. Content and method of education, *p.* 907.

III. Extension of Education as a Mass Process   908

1. In countries of high literacy, *p.* 909; 2. In countries of high illiteracy, *p.* 912.

IV. Administration of Educational Systems   918

1. Auspices, *p.* 918; 2. Financing, *p.* 919; 3. Supply and training of teachers, *p.* 920.

V. Changing Content and Method of Education   923

1. Modernization of curriculum, *p.* 923; 2. Introduction of technical and vocational content, *p.* 924; 3. Adaptation of content to changes in student body, *p.* 925; 4. Development and application of pedagogical principles, *p.* 928; 5. Application of new psychological insights, *p.* 933; 6. Use of new technology, *p.* 935; 7. Educational content and the aims of the state, *p.* 936.

VI. International Concern with Education   945

XXVII. USE OF LEISURE 950
    I. The New Leisure 950
    II. Leisure-Time Activities 957

       1. Reading, *p.* 957; 2. The cinema, *p.* 965; 3. Radio, *p.* 972; 4. Television, *p.* 976; 5. Theatre groups, *p.* 978; 6. Popular music and dancing, *p.* 979; 7. Sports, *p.* 981; 8. Travel, *p.* 983; 9. Hobbies, *p.* 984.

PART THREE: THE SELF-IMAGE AND ASPIRATIONS OF THE PEOPLES OF THE WORLD

INTRODUCTION 991
XXVIII. THE SELF-IMAGE AND ASPIRATIONS OF NATIONS 993
    I. Liberal Democracy: The Self-Image of Western Europe 994
    II. Marxist-Leninist Communism 999
    III. Anti-Liberal Authoritarianism 1004
    IV. Racial Superiority 1007

       1. Nazi Germany, *p.* 1007; 2. South Africa, *p.* 1011.

    V. States of Religious Origin or Outlook 1019

       1. Israel, *p.* 1019; 2. Pakistan, *p.* 1025; 3. Religious orientation of other states, *p.* 1028.

    VI. National Independence in the Face of European Expansion 1029
    VII. Emerging Nationalism: Africa 1033

XXIX. DRIVES FOR CULTURAL INTEGRITY AND RECOGNITION 1051
    I. Renaissance of Ancient Cultures 1051

       1. India, *p.* 1051; 2. China, *p.* 1058; 3. Japan, *p.* 1064; 4. South-east Asia and Korea, *p.* 1067; 5. The Arabs, *p.* 1071.

    II. Cultures of Recently Settled Lands 1078

       1. The United States, *p.* 1078; 2. Canada, *p.* 1083; 3. Hispanic American countries, *p.* 1085; 4. Brazil, *p.* 1087; 5. Australia and New Zealand, *p.* 1093.

    III. Cultural Reorientation of Mixed Societies: Mexico 1096
    IV. Minorities Seeking Cultural Autonomy 1101

XXX. DRIVES FOR INDIVIDUAL FREEDOM AND HUMAN DIGNITY 1110
    I. Labour 1110

       1. Aspirations of labour, *p.* 1111; 2. Methods of seeking labour's objectives, *p.* 1113; 3. Rights and responsibilities of labour, *p.* 1124; 4. Achievement of labour's goals, *p.* 1130.

    II. Peasants and Farmers 1132

       1. Farmers' movements in countries of advanced agriculture, *p.* 1134; 2. Peasant movements, *p.* 1135; 3. Community development, *p.* 1140.

III. Women   1142

  1. The goals of women's aspirations, *p.* 1143; 2. Methods of seeking objectives, *p.* 1147; 3. Achievement of goals, *p.* 1151.

IV. Race and Caste Groups Subject to Discrimination   1163

  1. Negroes, *p.* 1164; 2. Untouchables, *p.* 1181.

PART FOUR: EXPRESSION

INTRODUCTION   1193

XXXI. TENDENCIES IN LITERATURE AND THE ARTS IN THE WESTERN CULTURE AREAS   1196

  I. At the Opening of the Twentieth Century   1196

  II. The Years of Innovation   1200

  III. The 1920s and After   1213

    1. Western Europe   1213

    (*a*) The crisis of European culture, *p.* 1213; (*b*) Developments in artistic form, *p.* 1220.

    2. Emerging National Cultures in Other Western Culture Areas   1243

    (*a*) The United States, *p.* 1244; (*b*) Latin America, *p.* 1251; (*c*) The USSR, *p.* 1257.

  IV. The New Mass Media and the Arts   1265

    1. The Cinema as an Art   1265

    2. The Arts of Purveying Information   1271

XXXII. DEVELOPMENTS IN EASTERN LITERATURES AND ARTS   1284

  I. Nature of the Western Cultural Impact and Types of Reaction   1284

    1. General features, *p.* 1284; 2. Interaction in specific areas, *p.* 1286.

  II. Introduction of New Literary Forms   1289

  III. Modification of Literary Content   1293

  IV. The Visual Arts   1298

  V. Architecture   1300

  VI. Music and Dance   1301

  VII. Effect of Mass Media   1302

  VIII. Reaction of West to Culture Contact with East   1303

CONCLUSION

XXXIII. THE CHANGING SHAPE OF THE LIFE OF MANKIND   1309

BIBLIOGRAPHY   1319

INDEX   1365

APPENDIX A. FOREWORD BY THE DIRECTOR-GENERAL OF UNESCO   1380

APPENDIX B. PREFACE BY THE PRESIDENT OF THE INTERNATIONAL COMMISSION   1384

ILLUSTRATIONS

PARTS TWO TO FOUR

(All the plates listed hereunder are to be found between
pages 1190 and 1191)

Plate 21   Painting I:
Pablo Picasso, 'Les demoiselles d'Avignon', 1907

Plate 22   Painting II:
Fernand Léger, 'Three Women' (Le grand déjeuner), 1921

Plate 23   Painting III:
Georges Braque, 'Still Life with Grapes', 1927

Plate 24   Painting IV:
Kasimir Malevich, 'Matinée à la campagne après la pluie',
1911

Plate 25   Painting V:
Piet Mondrian, 'Composition in Red, Yellow and Blue',
1921

Plate 26   Painting VI:
Paul Klee, 'Zwitscher Maschine' (Twittering Machine),
1922

Plate 27   Painting VII:
Pablo Picasso, 'Guernica' (mural), 1937

Plate 28   Painting VIII:
Käthe Kollwitz, Portrait (charcoal), 1943

Plate 29   Painting IX:
Alexander A. Deyneka, 'The Defence of Petrograd',
1927–28

Plate 30   Painting X:
Ben Shahn, 'Handball', 1939

Plate 31   Painting XI:
Jackson Pollock, 'Number 1', 1948

Plate 32   Painting XII:
José Clemente Orozco, 'Zapatistas', 1931

Plate 33   Sculpture I:
(a) Auguste Rodin, Bronze Figure from 'L'Enfer', c. 1900
(b) Aristide Maillol, Bronze, c. 1905–10

Plate 34   Sculpture II:
Henri Matisse, 'Head of Jeannette' (Jeanne Vaderin),
1910–12
(a) Jeannette I   (1910)
(b) Jeannette II   (1910)
(c) Jeannette III   (1910–11)
(d) Jeannette IV   (1910–11 ?)
(e) Jeannette V   (1910–11 ?)

Plate 35 Sculpture III:
(a) Umberto Boccioni, 'Unique Forms of Continuity in Space', 1913
(b) Antoine Pevsner, 'Developable Column', 1942

Plate 36 Sculpture IV:
Alberto Giacometti, 'Chariot', 1950

Plate 37 Sculpture V:
Henry Moore, 'Family Group', 1945

Plate 38 Sculpture VI:
Reg Butler, 'The Unknown Political Prisoner' (project for a monument), 1951–53

Plate 39 Sculpture VII:
Alexander Calder, 'Lobster Trap and Fish Tail' (Mobile), 1939

Plate 40 Sculpture VIII:
V. I. Mukhina, 'Industrial Worker and Kolkhoz Labourer', 1937

Plate 41 Sculpture IX:
Oku Ampofo, 'Animist Slave'

Plate 42 Sculpture X:
Isamu Noguchi, Modern Garden in Japanese Style.

Plate 43 Architecture I:
Walter Gropius, The Bauhaus, Dessau, 1925–26

Plate 44 Architecture II:
Frank Lloyd Wright, Johnson's Wax buildings, Racine, Wisconsin, 1936–49

Plate 45 Architecture III:
(a) Individual homes in a suburban development, South Bend, Indiana, USA
(b) Le Corbusier, 'Unité d'habitation', Marseilles, France, 1952

Plate 46 Architecture IV:
United Nations Headquarters, New York, 1947–50

Plate 47 Architecture V:
(a) P. L. Nervi, The Palazzetto dello Sport, Rome, 1956–57
(b) University College, Ibadan, Nigeria, 1961

Plate 48 Architecture VI:
(a) Oscar Niemeyer, Cathedral, Brasilia, Brazil, 1960
(b) Oscar Niemeyer, Supreme Court, Brasilia, Brazil, 1960

Plate 49 Photography I:
Alfred Stieglitz, 'The Steerage', 1907

Plate 50 Photography II:
Margaret Bourke-White, 'Grief', India, 1953

Plate 51   Photography III:
            Henri Cartier-Bresson, 'Shanghai', 1949

Plate 52   Photography IV:
            Gjon Mili, '3/4 Beat', c. 1942

Plate 53   Photography V:
            The interior of the heart

Plate 54   Information
            (a) News photography: F. Durdin, Bombing in Chungking,
                China, 1941
            (b) Hans Erni, Poster for the Consumers Cooperative Asso-
                ciation of Switzerland, 1942

Plate 55   The Theatre I:
            (a) Auguste Perret, Champs Elysées Theatre, auditorium
                under construction, Paris, 1911–13
            (b) Gerhard Weber, The State Opera, Hamburg, 1955

Plate 56   The Theatre II:
            (a) Constantin Stanislavsky, scene from Act IV of The
                Lower Depths by Gorky; Moscow Art Theatre, 1902
            (b) Elwin Piscator, scene from Flüchtlingsgespräche by
                Bertolt Brecht; Munich, 1962

Plate 57   Motion Pictures I:
            (a) D. W. Griffith, scene from 'Intolerance', 1916
            (b) Sergei Eisenstein, scene from 'Battleship Potemkin',
                1925

Plate 58   Motion Pictures II:
            (a) Charlie Chaplin, scene from 'Modern Times', 1936
            (b) Walt Disney, scene from 'Snow White and the Seven
                Dwarfs', 1938

Plate 59   Eastern Art I:
            Abanindranath Tagore, 'Dacca Stripes'

Plate 60   Eastern Art II:
            Jamini Roy, 'Southal Dancers'

Plate 61   Eastern Art III:
            (a) Amrita Shergil, 'Brahmacharies', 1959
            (b) Zainul Abedin, 'Sharing the Meal', 1943

Plate 62   Eastern Art IV:
            George Keyt (Ceylon), 'Nayika'

Plate 63   Eastern Art V:
            (a) Shunko Mochizuki, 'A Lotus', 1957
            (b) Tano Rigen, 'Old Style Exhibition', 1955

Plate 64   Eastern Art VI:
            (a) Chi' Pai-shih, 'Composition'
            (b) Siu Pei-hong, 'Water Buffalo and Snake'

MAPS

PART TWO

Map VII   ILLITERACY, C. 1950   *Facing page* 934

The maps of Volume VI were prepared by Hallwag A.G., Berne.

CHARTS

Chart XXIV   Books Published, 1957   962

Chart XXV   Books Translated.   963

Chart XXVI   World Production of Motion Pictures   967

All charts were designed for this work by Stella Robinson in collaboration with R. G. Hadlow

PART TWO

THE TRANSFORMATION
OF SOCIETIES

CHAPTER XX

MAJOR CHANGES IN CONCEPTS AND IDEAS

I INTRODUCTION

THE application of scientific knowledge in many spheres of life was interwoven with the impact of ideas concerning the nature of human society and man's place in it, and with changing values which reflected social change and guided social action.

In general terms the twentieth century was an age both of great optimism and of great uncertainty. Optimism arose from the new sense of previously unimagined possibilities which science and technology brought and which the changing structure of power and changing social institutions were opening up to many people. Uncertainty reflected the fact that the spread of science and technology threatened established positions and destroyed established ways, and that inherited value systems and philosophical constructs were inadequate to the conditions of the new age. In these years no sphere of life remained unassailed by questions and doubts, no traditional system of thought stood unchallenged.

In the West the schematic philosophies of the past, together with the materialistic positivism of Auguste Comte, John Stuart Mill and Herbert Spencer, lost popularity and the Aristotelian logic on which these schemes had been erected was itself not free from attack. The twentieth-century study of the subconscious and its influence on human personality affected the continued acceptance of much of the philosophical thinking of the past. As knowledge expanded with great rapidity, covering every field and changing basic conceptions of time and space, of the nature of matter and of the universe, of society and of man's place in it, the redefinition of philosophical postulates and new philosophical interpretations proved most difficult to achieve.

In the non-European world the traditional assumptions on which the social order was based were everywhere subjected to heavy criticism. As profound social changes undermined traditional institutions and relationships, the formulations which sanctioned them lost much of their force. In China denunciation of the familial system of life was one of the expressions of the revolutionary drive which produced the New Tide Movement of 1917. In the thirty years of struggle which followed, the hold of Confucian ethics as the basis for social relations was so weakened as to permit the general displacement of Confucian by Marxian principles when the communists came to power in 1949. Japan throughout the period struggled to reconcile traditional values and those imported from the West or to find an accommodation between them. This struggle assumed special intensity after the second world war under the shadow of defeat and occupation. The challenge to the traditional conceptions of Indian society was perhaps even more fundamental, for Hindu society had identified its hierarchical system of castes, sub-castes and untouchables and many of its social customs with religion. As all these were attacked and finally were changed by legislation in the period after 1947, most of the social doctrines of the Hindus were either discarded or modified under the influence of ideas which had their origin in the West.

Nor were such developments confined to Asia for their counterpart was to be seen in Africa, which had remained practically outside world currents throughout the nineteenth century. In the twentieth century the outlook which underlay the traditional pattern of tribal life broke down under the European impact and by the middle of the century African life was undergoing a radical reconstruction.

Though this was an age of uncertainty and no dominant set of ideas could be said to have guided the life of mankind as a whole, it is possible to distinguish certain beliefs, doctrines and concepts as having found general acceptance, and, in any case, as moving large sections of mankind in their social, political and economic relationships. These may be examined in terms of changes in generally held concepts of man's relation to society, to his past and future, and to nature, his view of his gods and his concept of himself, and may also be viewed in terms of the efforts of philosophical thinkers to organize the experience and observations of mankind during these years.

II. MAN'S RELATION TO SOCIETY

First among the central ideas of the twentieth century were two that were often in conflict, the idea of nationalism and the concept of the unity of mankind. Nationalism as such was not an idea which originated in the twentieth century but this century was the first to witness its spread to nearly all peoples. Its influence on the outlook of peoples and the interrelations among them was overwhelmingly great, as has been pointed out in discussing the impact of nationalism on the flow of political events.* But no less far-reaching and even more distinctive of the twentieth century was the growing view of mankind as one.

In previous ages, though many religions stressed the brotherhood of man, the unity of mankind was not a generally accepted belief. The obvious differences among peoples in physical appearance, material advancement and other aspects of culture stood in the way of a general acceptance of the idea that mankind is one. In the period when Europe dominated most of the world the

* See Chapter II: The Impact of Nationalism and Trend toward International Co-operation.

majority of Europeans and other people of the white races felt that the unity of mankind was a myth. Nor was this idea confined to Europeans. Practically every people believed that they were different and superior, in some sense the chosen of God, or simply *the* people.

It was not without a struggle that the idea of the unity of mankind came to be accepted—at least in a general sense—by the middle of the century. The concept of the master *Herrenvolk* was proclaimed by Nazi doctrine, it continued to receive official approval in portions of the African continent and it survived among reactionary groups in old-established societies. But by the period after the second world war the unity of mankind had become one of the leading ideas of the time.

This idea was a motivating force in many of the more significant activities of the twentieth century: the effort to raise the economic, cultural and physical standards of backward communities; acknowledgement in principle of a general level of rights and privileges for all, as expressed in the United Nations Universal Declaration of Human Rights; the sustained endeavour to eliminate avoidable diseases to which many areas were subject; the administration of trust territories under international supervision. Though no one could claim that all peoples had achieved equality of opportunity, the striking fact of the twentieth century in comparison with previous ages of history was the world-wide commitment to the principle.

Not alone with regard to peoples in different stages of development, but within each nation itself the sense of unity was achieved only in the twentieth century. Even in countries such as Britain, France and the United States it was only in the decade following the first world war, and then incompletely, that the sense of equal entitlement was extended to members of the working class, women, racial minorities, and that the unity of the nation as a single community came to be more fully achieved.

In the countries of Asia the lack of unity within the state was even more pronounced, whether it took the form of the persistence of feudal relationships in Japan, of the almost complete lack of facilities for education, economic betterment or elementary medical care for the masses of the people in China, of India's elaborate system of castes and its 40,000,000 untouchables without primary social rights, or of secluded women and the secondary status of non-believers in Islamic countries. The idea of the totality of the people of a state enjoying equal privileges began to assert itself in Asia in the period following the first world war, at a time when the working classes of western Europe attained political power and the October revolution proclaimed faith in a classless society. One of the most significant aspects of the national struggle in India, Burma, Pakistan, Ceylon and Indonesia in those years was the affirmation of national solidarity by acceptance of the principle that internal inequalities should be abolished.

The communist states embodied the principle of the unity of mankind in the concept that the total population shares in the work of the community and enjoys its benefits. In the initial period of social reorganization the capitalist and landowner classes were to be subordinated to the dictatorship of the proletariat or in case of active resistance eliminated; but eventually the unity of the classless society would be achieved.

A second major idea of the twentieth century stemmed from this doctrine of the unity of mankind: recognition that the welfare of all is the concern of all. In the nineteenth century humanitarians were moved by the sufferings of people everywhere but there was no general recognition that poverty, illness, ignorance and the absence of opportunities in many parts of the world were matters of concern to the world as a whole. If people in Venezuela suffered from malaria, if yellow fever and sleeping sickness took their toll in Africa, if large areas of the world were exposed to chronic famines, these were regarded as the fate of the people involved; except as an occasional expression of charity or in time of disaster, the world in general did not accept responsibility for such a state of affairs.

By the middle of the twentieth century the numerous international organizations set up under the auspices of the United Nations bore ample witness to a changed viewpoint and to the widespread acceptance of the idea that the prosperity and welfare of the world is indivisible and is a common responsibility.

Another consequence of the concept of the brotherhood of mankind was the concept of non-violence as a mode of action in human relations. Non-violence was not a new principle; the Buddha preached it and it was part of Christ's teaching. But it had remained a religious doctrine, cherished and preached by idealists and saints, considered too impracticable in the realm of politics. In the twentieth century Mahatma Gandhi transformed non-violence from a purely religious doctrine into a force in politics, first in his struggle with the South African government in the early years of the century and then in the thirty-year fight which he led for the freedom of India.

In Gandhi's conception non-violence alone could successfully resist the use of violence, for if violence were met by violence it could only lead to destruction. His definition of non-violence was not merely a denial of physical force but a determination not to injure anyone, even those who were using violence, and he relied on strict adherence to truth and on moral force which could not be fought by the essentially amoral method of violence. Although the only widespread use of non-violence as a political method came in India, its success there brought it into the realm of practical, operating ideas and it began to be used to a small extent elsewhere. In the face of the ever-mounting destructiveness which the scientific age made possible it began to be seen as an alternative means of effecting political and social change.[1]

Also special to the twentieth century was the broad acceptance of cultural difference. In the prevalent nineteenth-century view Europe represented the final pattern of culture; civilization had originated with the Greeks and had been inherited through the Romans by modern Europe. The predominance that the West enjoyed in industrial, economic and political spheres gave a verisimilitude to the belief that other civilizations were either immature forms, stunted growths or lower organizations of society.

The view of European civilization as the final pattern of life was undermined from many directions. Archaeological research revealed that civilization did not in fact originate in Greece but that great cultures had been in existence in the Nile, Euphrates and Indus valleys, in China and in South and Central America long before Greece emerged as a centre of civilization; that other civilizations of the world, some of which, like the Chinese and the Indian, claimed continuity with the past, had not only produced cultural forms of abiding value but had contributed their share to the growth of science and to the advancement of thought.

The study of cultural anthropology not only brought a new understanding of the life of pre-industrial people in terms of their own cultural patterns and values, but demonstrated how closely many of the cherished conceptions and habits in civilized societies have their counterparts in primitive life. The twentieth century came to accept the idea that cultures differ in their value systems and cannot be simply dismissed as 'backward' or 'queer'. Modern European society came to be seen not as the inevitable outcome of a rigid process of progress which would automatically and inevitably lead to similar developments elsewhere, but as the product of a particular combination of circumstances; not as a model for all but only as one civilization among others.[2]

The twentieth century was further especially notable for the emphasis it placed on economic and social values as against the purely individual and primarily political values which found their apogee in western society in the nineteenth century. By the opening of the century challenges were coming from a number of quarters to *laissez-faire* individualism and its assumptions that the function of government was to assure the individual his natural and inalienable right to be free, that economic prosperity would result from individual effort and that social welfare should be left to the conscience of individuals. A growing body of opinion saw the untrammelled freedom of the individual as a form of social anarchy leading to the oppression of the weak by the strong and exploitation of the poor by the rich; it held that the freedom of the individual could have meaning for the people as a whole only when they enjoyed a measure of economic security and effective social safeguards.

From the mid-nineteenth century the doctrine of socialism emphasized the importance of collective rather than individual values. The trade union movement substituted collective action for the idea of a free market where the worker could sell and the employer could buy labour according to the law of supply and demand. The Catholic Church, which had consistently opposed the idea of the absolute right of the individual, asserted in the papal encyclical *Rerum novarum* (1891) the principle of social justice as a guide to economic relationships.[3,4] But it was only in the twentieth century that trade unionism and collective bargaining were fully recognized, that the social obligation of the state to look after the welfare of the people and tax the rich differentially for this purpose came to be accepted, and that socialist doctrines were put into practice over large areas of the earth.

The economic and social values of the twentieth century were exemplified in the idea of planning. The conscious organization of production on a planned basis was a natural development of socialist activity, and the communist formulation of successive five-year plans which provided for continuing control of economic development at all stages constituted the most elaborate system of planned economy.

But the idea of planning was by no means confined to the Soviet Union and other communist countries where it was combined with collective ownership of the means of production and the full authority to put plans into action. The Tennessee Valley Authority in the United States was the prototype for the planned development of river valleys in many countries. Town planning was carried to great lengths in the British Town and Country Planning Act of 1945 and welfare planning in that country's Beveridge report of 1942, both implemented after the second world war. From the time of the great depression of the 1930s many countries introduced some measure of planning into the direction of their agricultural production and into the use of fiscal and monetary policy for the maintenance of full employment. And most underdeveloped countries in the decade after the second world war approached their task of national development by means of some form of economic planning; the provision of financial aid by international agencies and from other sources was in fact made in terms of such plans.

The twentieth-century concept of planning—of a conscious, collective design for the actions of individuals—seemed to be in a sense the very antithesis of the nineteenth-century elevation of individual freedom to a central value. It was however not incompatible with the changed concept of freedom which came to prevail.

The Atlantic Charter of August 1941 declared among the 'four freedoms' two which expressed the new concepts of the twentieth century, 'freedom from want' and 'freedom from fear'. The twentieth-century view of individual freedom may be defined as the right of each individual to a healthy life, to a share in the goods of the world, to opportunities for education, to social protection against hazards beyond his control, and the opportunity to work as the fulfilment of his social obligation. The idea of individual freedom was no longer simply the right to do what one pleases within the law; it was the conception of being a member of a free society committed to the welfare of all.

This twentieth-century concept of individual freedom rested on a view of the welfare of society as not being a thing apart from the welfare of the individuals that constitute it. The idea was not new for it had often found expression by religious leaders and others in many cultures; it was a seventeenth-century English poet, John Donne, who wrote the oft-quoted lines,

'No man is an island . . . And therefore never send to know for whom the bell tolls; It tolls for *thee*.' But in the twentieth century the idea became the rationale for much collective action.

The organization of trade unions for example limited the freedom of the individual to bargain, but the purpose of collective bargaining was higher wages and better labour conditions, and therewith a greater degree of freedom for those involved. In the same manner planning by the state which controlled the sowing of crops interfered with the freedom of the individual farmer but its objective was to secure the economic interests of the farmers themselves. Every major social institution was seen to limit the individual's freedom in the interests of his own wider freedom. One of the major problems of the twentieth century was how this concept could be realized without destroying individual initiative, impairing the liberty of action essential to human dignity and the development of human potentiality and without imposing a burden of bureaucracy upon society beyond its usefulness as a necessary instrument for achieving common objectives.

Changed concepts of man in relation to society also modified basic ideas concerning the family, the principal institution by means of which the status and role of the individual in virtually all societies had been defined.

The concept of the extended responsibility of the community for the positive welfare of all its members, expressed through the responsibility of the state for education, health and various forms of social security, narrowed the area and lightened the weight of responsibility carried by the family. Not only were parents no longer wholly responsible for the education and health of their children; they could not reject the requirements which the state imposed. The state relieved children of much of the burden of support for aged parents and lifted from families at least part of the economic burden of illness.

At the same time the individualization of economic roles and the concept of each individual as a unit of society in his or her own right undermined the hierarchical structure within the family. As extended to women, it redefined the relations between husband and wife. The concept of the child as a person in his own right, not merely a chattel of his parents or an undeveloped adult, profoundly affected parent-child relations and the child's place in society; under conditions of rapid social change, the child came to be looked upon as the instrument of a new day.

The family itself, freed of much of its responsibility, with its hierarchical structure undermined and its members integrated by work or other activity into other social units, ceased to be the all-embracing and enduring foundation of the social order. In greater or less degree it tended to become a small personal group where mutual obligations within the group rested upon contract rather than sacrament and the possibility of dissolution through divorce was widely accepted. The family tended to become a planned unit, and the idea of birth control and family planning gained acceptance in ever-

z*

broader layers of society, even where clerical opposition continued; some countries stimulated family planning as a matter of public policy.

The changed concept of the family was most dramatic where such ancient, comprehensive institutions as the Confucian family system or the Hindu joint family were modified in practice or their legal basis was destroyed by legislation. The actual reduction in family functions and development of new patterns of relations among family members went farthest in industrial countries where women had the opportunity to be financially independent. The Soviet Union dissolved the institution of the bourgeois family almost completely in the initial process of social reconstruction and then restored 'a socialist form of home'.[5] The Catholic Church remained unshaken in its conception of marriage as sacramental and indissoluble and in its emphasis on the family as the central institution of human society, but even its great and pervasive influence did not prevent the penetration of other ideas into predominantly Catholic countries. Whatever the form of the family or degree of its modification, the reduced position of the family as an economic unit and basis of social organization was one of the features of the twentieth century.

On the whole it may be stated without exaggeration that man's relationship to society by the middle of the twentieth century was governed by many ideas which would have been considered revolutionary or impracticable in virtually every society in the nineteenth century.

III. MAN'S RELATION TO HIS PAST AND FUTURE

Changing viewpoints toward man's relations with his fellow men extended to new concepts of his own past and possible future. The study of history was extended immeasurably both in time and space. Pre-history opened up the vision of man's movement towards civilization through various ages of technical advancement; archaeology made available the history of great civilizations in different parts of the world—in the Nile valley, in Babylonia, in the Indus valley, in China, in America—giving humanity a better idea of its own past. The story of African peoples was being slowly unravelled.

As these stories unfolded, man's ideas in regard to humanity itself changed. They were no longer so directly centred on special regions to which each section attached special value, but embraced the whole perspective of human experience.

This great expansion in knowledge of the past, coupled with a new attitude toward man's efforts to control his destiny, brought a twofold response. On the one hand it created a certain humility arising from a recognition that the civilization in which man is living may also decay and die, and that there may be growing, unnoticed, forces which may ultimately destroy all that men have painfully built up, as was the case in previous civilizations in the world. On the other hand it offered the hope that increased knowledge of the past might enable man to shape the course of human evolution in a manner which would provide for continuous renovation without allowing the structure to break down. In either case it led to efforts to view the present age as a period in human history and to envisage the processes of human development in terms which could provide a new basis for interpreting contemporary events. It made unsatisfactory the various major formulations which had come down from previous times—the concept of all human life as merely a prelude to eternity,[6] or the view of society as essentially timeless and unchanging, or the vision of endless progress toward inherent perfection or through social evolution.

The great popularity of books such as Oswald Spengler's *Decline of the West* (1918–22) and Arnold Toynbee's *Study of History* (1934–54) were symptomatic of the effort to understand the present in the light of the past. Spengler, in whose view civilization attains maturity only when it has ceased to grow, held that western civilization had already passed its meridian and started on its career of disintegration. According to Toynbee, each of the twenty-six civilizations that preceded the present one lost its impetus after a certain period of activity and achievement, and he saw no reason to think that it would be otherwise in respect to western civilization, though he did not deny in theory the possibility of rejuvenation through a revival in religion. Walter Prescott Webb (*The Great Frontier*, 1952) sought to prove that the conditions which produced and had sustained western civilization since the great voyages of discovery—the untapped wealth of nearly 20,000,000 square miles of fabulously rich land—had ceased to exist and that western civilization consequently had begun to break down. The Marxian view saw the historical process as a dialectic one centring on the forms of material production and leading inevitably to a permanent classless society.

Whatever formulation he might accept, twentieth-century man saw himself as part of an historical process stretching farther into antiquity than his predecessors had imagined and embracing all parts of the human race.

As for the future, this too came to be conceived in terms of the whole of humanity. The rapidity with which scientific discovery and social change altered the life of mankind during these years opened up limitless vistas both for good and for ill—not just for a family, a nation or a people but for mankind as a whole.

For the first time in history the means were at hand to abolish poverty, hunger, disease and other major ills that had beset mankind through the ages. It became possible to think in terms of a society based on plenty, and people throughout the world did indeed come to think in these terms, not nostalgically as of a 'golden age', but realistically as a goal to be achieved. One of the most revolutionary ideas that moved men in the twentieth century was that poverty and misery were not the necessary condition of their children and their children's children.

But against this new optimism loomed growing apprehensions about the future of civilization and of mankind arising from the capacity for destruction which men had developed and were developing. The instruments of violence used in the first world war would have seemed apocalyptic to anyone in a previous age and sufficient to destroy civilization. But compared to what was at the disposal of powerful nations in the second world war, the fire-power of weapons, the aerial bombs, poison gas and underseas craft available to the combatants in the first war were child's play. When the first atom bomb was finally exploded in 1945 it seemed at the time to be the ultimate force of destruction, but it was quickly dwarfed by the far more terrible hydrogen bomb. When men realized that radioactive fall-out from atomic and hydrogen explosions could so pollute the atmosphere as to destroy life on earth, they were forced to think in terms of man's new power to put an end to the human race. Violence shadowed man's destiny; the vision of the apocalypse was of a possible man-made reality.

IV. MAN AND NATURE

The idea which penetrated most widely and about which there was nevertheless great ambivalence was the belief that science could find solutions to human problems. The advance of scientific knowledge and its utilization for human betterment was so great that its potentialities seemed unlimited. In the perspective of what had already been achieved and the accelerating rate at which scientific knowledge was being applied to affect the daily life of people, an endless vista seemed to open before it of achievements capable of solving the problems which faced humanity.

Yet faith in the omnipotence of science was not untinged with doubt and fear. In Europe the simple faith shared by many during the nineteenth century that science would automatically bring human progress was shaken by the destructive uses to which it was put during these years and the evident failure of mankind to develop the social and political arrangements which would ensure that its application would be beneficent. Even the peaceful application of science—to transport and communication, the production of food and the prolongation of life—seemed to some people to bring as many problems as it solved. While science was being accepted ever more widely as holding answers to human problems and human needs, its supremacy was being called into question by some who had put their faith in it in the early phases of its application.

It is to be noted, however, that doubts came principally from certain intellectuals and from people who feared that the progress of science would rob them of their privileged place in the world. They came, mainly in Europe, from those whose personal position rested on the continuance of traditional values, or who could not find or accept a place for themselves in the emerging society, or whose world position depended on continuation of the virtual monopoly of scientific advance by the countries where scientific techniques had first been mastered. Except for Mahatma Gandhi whose attack on industrialism was designed as a political weapon against British imperialism, questions as to the desirability of scientific advance did not come generally from the underdeveloped countries. These recognized that their future depended upon technical progress and the scientific education of their people, though they might denounce western culture as materialistic and reassert traditional spiritual values. Nor did the doubts come from the social classes in the industrially advanced countries that were the beneficiaries of increased productivity and of the improvement in housing, health and levels of living which the scientific age was bringing.

The revolutionary developments in the realm of physical sciences changed man's ideas of his relations to nature in a fundamental manner. This was a cumulative process which had been at work in western society since the seventeenth century and had been greatly accelerated by the scientific and technological achievements of the nineteenth. But only in the twentieth century did men acquire a sense of almost unlimited control over nature, and the spread of an aggressive attitude towards nature to large segments of mankind was a phenomenon of the period.

The general idea in most societies in the past was that nature was simply there, unalterably conditioning man's life; in the face of its overwhelming power he could not seek to bend it in any major degree to his requirements but must adjust himself to it. But man in the twentieth century became more and more aggressive in regard to nature, determined to force its secrets, to exploit its resources and to subdue its more dangerous effects. Could not new materials be created by man's power better than those which nature provides? Could not artificial insemination produce better species? If rainfall was irregular, could not clouds be induced to yield their waters? If heat was too great for man's comfort, could not air be conditioned to a normal temperature? And need man remain earthbound while outer space invited his exploration? Clearly, man's vision of himself in relation to what were conceived as the permanent features of nature changed greatly during these fifty years.

The challenge of man to nature brought a radical change in man's attitude toward fate. In the past every major calamity—drought, famine, epidemic and other avoidable misfortune—had been attributed to fate over which man had no control and against which it was unprofitable to struggle. As men came to know that things which used to be attributed to fate can be fought by human measures, the idea of fate retreated into the background. It remained in many minds, too ingrained a conception to be totally displaced, and it retained a potent influence on human behaviour. But its range became more and more restricted. The change in attitude toward fate was most noticeable in the countries of Asia where the doctrine of fate had great hold. One of the major results was a mounting demand in all these areas for the betterment of social conditions, especially in the matter of health.

Yet while the aggressive attitude toward nature gave man greater confidence in his powers and boundless hope, it raised moral problems that were by no means insignificant. If man himself possessed the means to remedy or prevent human ills, he would be forced to accept responsibility for his failure to do so; since he could no longer dismiss misfortune as the work of fate, he was burdened with a new sense of guilt for his failure to use his new powers effectively.

Man's command over nature moreover confronted him with a new source of uncertainty over the purpose of human life. So long as man accepted his lot as determined by a supreme moral law with divine sanction, he could feel that he was serving a supreme purpose by living a moral life. The elevation of man in relation to nature gave him a great sense of his own power but no source of moral authority for its use.

With each new discovery and invention other and greater dangers to humanity seemed to show themselves, and man was assailed by doubts over the results of his own mastery. The prospects of atomic energy opened out to man like a new and unsuspected paradise, but with it many dangers manifested themselves, even apart from the possibility of the deliberate use of this new power for destruction. Men were beginning to ask whether there is a purpose in life or whether humanity is merely moving forward blindly impelled by its own restless intelligence. What moral principles, what obligation of man to his fellow beings, could guide him in the use of his new powers? How, with these powers, could he choose the path which would lead to the welfare of mankind?

V. MAN'S VIEW OF HIS GODS

These questions were closely related to the place of religion in men's lives. All the basic concepts of religion, such as soul, salvation, efficacy of prayer, came under question, not merely as before by agnostics and atheists but by ordinary men and women who found it difficult to reconcile what science was telling them with their inherited beliefs. Consequently man's view of his gods also underwent a noticeable change.

A major fact of the twentieth century was that a third of the world lived under a system whose basic philosophy had no place for God. According to Marxist–Leninist doctrine dialectical materialism and a materialistic interpretation of history are incompatible with the conception of God; in a communist society religion, whose social role is that of an 'opiate of the people', will eventually disappear. With so large a proportion of the world's people in communist states it may be said that the conception of God lost its universality in the twentieth century.

Even in the rest of the world men's idea of God was modified during the same period, or the concept of God was rejected as a mere projection of man's own drive to transcend the limits of his being. As anthropology made clear the tendency of people to create gods in their own image, many people found it no longer possible to conceive of God in anthropomorphic terms or as a Being who might interfere with normal functioning of natural laws or demand special sacrifices as a proof of loyalty.

Yet though twentieth-century man tended to reject intellectually the cruder forms of anthropomorphism, many people continued to hold to revised versions of earlier formulae. They found ways to retain a personally satisfying structure of faith—by giving a symbolic meaning to what had been believed as a literal truth, by identifying human purposes with those of God rather than expecting God's intercession in response to prayer, or by re-interpreting the concepts of lesser deities or saints through which the sense of the divine was made personal.

A major change in most communities was a weakening of the sense of sin and a narrowing of the segment of the population within which it kept its hold on the minds of men. The conception of sin as an offence against the commandments of God was historically of utmost importance in most societies, not only as a source of moral principle but as a measure of social protection. But growing disbelief in some of the tenets which provided strong religious sanction, such as the doctrine of hell and the day of judgment which once had great reality to masses of mankind, made the conception of sin less potent than it was before. The study of anthropology showed that, while many common values underlie cultural differences, what is considered sin in one society may even be regarded as a virtue in another. The scientific concept of relativity seemed to imply a denial of absolute values. As the doctrine of sin depends on finality of judgment it lost much of its authority over the minds of twentieth-century men.

In the face of mounting disbelief, changing concepts and a weakening sense of sin, two trends were evident within the major religions, one to redefine man's relation to the supernatural in terms consistent with modern thought, the other to reassert in uncompromising terms the truth of estab-lished dogma. Reformed Hinduism, after shedding much of its social trap-pings, provided a basis for reconciling scientific thought with basic religious beliefs. In the Buddhist countries there were attempts to reinterpret the *Dharma* in terms of modern thought. Some Christian thought went far in a similar direction. On the other hand, the Catholic Church reasserted the absolute truth of its dogma and in the world of Islam the Quran remained the source of final truth.

The changes in man's view of his gods was perhaps greater in outward form than in inner sense. In spite of the great advance of science much of man's belief in supernatural power continued to be part of the mentality of non-communist countries. Even in communist countries where those in authority rejected the idea of God absolutely it appeared that a certain proportion of the people continued to adhere to one or another religious faith and to seek the solaces of religion.

VI. MAN'S VIEW OF HIMSELF

Man's view of himself as it was emerging at mid-century reflected his changing sense of his relation with society, with nature and with God. In most parts of the world, and widely through many levels of society, men saw themselves possessed of or reaching for new powers and opportunities. They saw themselves as standing on the threshold of a new era whose features could only be glimpsed, but whose prospects were both exhilarating and terrifying.

Throughout the world men had the sense of being cast loose from old moorings to make their way through uncharted seas. For some this meant a great adventure, for others a bewildering threat. Modern man found himself in a situation full of paradox. The more he mastered his environment, the more helpless he felt before forces some of which he himself had loosed. The more aware he became of the world beyond his immediate ken the less able he was to cope directly with much that affected his daily life. The more that new knowledge undermined old certainties and new social forces changed old institutions, the more he felt the need for some source of security to take the place of those which he had lost.

Perhaps no feature was more characteristic of modern man's outlook and view of himself—whether in a Malayan or a Mexican village, an African 'location' in Johannesburg, or the main street of Chicago, Brussels or Tokyo—than his ambivalence toward himself and toward what was happening to his life and the life about him. Except for those who were deeply committed to one orthodoxy or another, the ambivalence of twentieth-century man was both a reflection of and a factor in the transformation of his societies during these years.

VII. MAIN LINES OF PHILOSOPHICAL THOUGHT

The crises of these years were reflected in the varied efforts of philosophical thinkers to reformulate philosophical conceptions so as to include new knowledge, encompass new experience and sharpen the tools of language and logic. The distinctive outlooks of twentieth-century man and of his changing societies found expression in formal and systematic thought as well as in public attitudes and opinions.

In the West the efforts of philosophers produced a wide range of views, and at the same time much interchange and even mutual influence of seemingly opposite tendencies. The period was one of lively and fruitful philosophical activity, though no common systems of thought emerged and though there was a broad division between those who pursued the philosophical implications of modern science and those who turned away from science to seek the answer to their philosophical questions by other, non-rational methods.

After the collapse of Hegelian idealism in the 1860s scientific positivism had become the dominant philosophical idea in the West. Whereas Hegel saw the universe as a reflection of a World Spirit or Absolute Idea, developing and unfolding itself through history in complex dialectic ways, the scientific positivists focused on external reality, approached through the natural sciences. They saw in the ever-extended application of scientific method the highest form of human activity, the only path to truth, however limited it might be, and the key to principles which could guide action. Both systems rested on the rationalist assumption that man through his reason could know and grasp the full meaning of the universe, although Hegel and his followers rejected the Aristotelian logic of the eighteenth-century Enlightenment and substituted a more complex logic of opposites within which a fundamental unity finally asserts itself through the dialectical process of thesis, antithesis and synthesis.

Neither the system-building of the Hegelian idealists nor the materialism and certainty of the positivists could remain unshaken by the discovery of limitations in the system of Newtonian physics, the undermining of traditional mathematics and, in time, the substitution of probability for rigid causality. Nor did the assumptions of rationality and automatic progress survive the crisis of the first world war and the revelations of Freudian psychology.

The Hegelian view that reality could be comprehended in terms of an Absolute Idea lost ground steadily, though it continued influential among some British thinkers in the early years of the century and Kant's idealism lived on in centres in Germany at Baden and Marburg even after the first world war. Its leading and most influential exponent was the prolific histor-ian-philosopher Benedetto Croce (1866–1952), who explored the realms of aesthetics, logic, economics and ethics in his *Philosophy of Spirit* (1902–17), and saw in the unique unfolding of human history the expression of a purpose with which men could align themselves. For him the direction was toward greater human freedom, and he thus became the voice of Italian liberalism. But the effort to find a universal, transcendent Idea lost its appeal for most twentieth-century thinkers, and idealism declined from one of the dominant forms of philosophical speculation in the mid-nineteenth century to one of the forms least representative of twentieth-century thought.

Positivist thought showed a much stronger development, although in its materialistic and mechanistic form it also suffered an almost complete collapse and although in the course of time it became more and more limited in its focus and in the kinds of philosophical problems which it sought to solve. In the early years of the century it gave rise to the vigorous and influential thought of William James, John Dewey (1859–1952) and their fellow prag-matists and instrumentalists. These thinkers insisted that the only meaning of any term and the only reality of any object lies in what it can and will do, and that this in turn can only be determined by scientific test. Ideas have no validity in and of themselves, but only as they express an observable, verifiable reality; their importance lies in their results, in what happens to the person who acts on the basis of them.

In this view neither absolute origins nor ultimate finalities have any relevance; the reality lies in the process, where means and ends are one, where change is central and where conduct can be purposeful. Applying this approach to the whole range of human problems—biological, political, social—Dewey developed a comprehensive view of how human beings, using to the full their potentialities and guided by intelligence equipped with scientific method, could modify their environment and make life progressively better. In breadth of scope, acceptance of change and uncertainty, and orientation toward positive action, the pragmatic view and instrumental method of thought had far-reaching influence, especially in the field of education.

In the following decades scientific humanists such as Julian Huxley carried the philosophical implications of science still further. They saw man still in the process of evolution, only beginning to use his powers to create the conditions which would permit the fullest development of his potentialities. In this view the flowering of the individual is seen as an end in itself; but since man is an infinitely complex, many-sided creature whose individual fulfilment cannot be realized apart from nature and society, he must use his knowledge and intelligence to develop the type of environment and culture which will continually open the way to new and fuller realizations of his inherent possibilities. The application of scientific method to all fields of human endeavour could provide a means of cultural evolution.

Other positivist philosophers, however, focused their attention more narrowly on the sharpening of analytical tools rather than on broad social issues. The logical positivists of the mid-century abandoned all effort to build systems of philosophical thought in favour of the attempt to know accurately and to communicate precisely the elements of thought and observation out of which systems might some day be built. They concentrated on an analysis of language, symbols and meaning, moving ever farther away from those who sought in philosophical thought either a metaphysical view or a basis for values and guide to action, or both.*

In reaction against both main lines of nineteenth-century philosophical thought, idealism and positivism, and their whole rationalistic way of thinking, some of the most influential and popular philosophers of the twentieth century insisted on the primacy of man's non-rational faculties—his intuition, direct apprehension of phenomena, and awareness of inner experience. They rejected the nineteenth-century scientific approach for its materialism and mechanistic outlook and the new scientific view for its dependence on statistical probability, its concern with mass phenomena and its inability to shed light on the individual, unique case. They were concerned with life and with man, and more particularly with the individual, in the face of the mechanization of life in industrial society and the impersonal preoccupations of science.

* See Chapter VII, Mathematics and Logic.

The effort to approach reality through direct non-rational experience took a variety of forms. Henri Bergson (1859–1941), the most influential and popular of French philosophers in the first quarter of the century, insisted that intuition could penetrate to the core of reality which the intellectual pursuits of science could only surround as with a shell, and he maintained that the will could shape this reality creatively. Like his contemporary, Benedetto Croce, Bergson was an apostle of freedom, but not as the unfolding of the universal Idea; he saw it as the achievement of men motivated by an *élan vital* and changing through time in a process of creative evolution. The German 'phenomenologist' Edmund Husserl (1859–1938) focused his attention on what he called 'phenomena', i.e. the structures perceived by an observer, as when the structure of a cube seen from different angles appears different. He thought that the effort to examine these phenomena could fruitfully be applied to the inner perception of self. Even so scientifically oriented a philosopher as Alfred North Whitehead, co-author with Bertrand Russell of the classic statement of mathematical logic *Principia Mathematica* (1911), insisted in his later years that the body of scientific and logical thought is a superstructure built upon fundamentally intuitive beliefs and ideas.

By the second quarter of the century the approaches which assumed a fundamental irrationality in life came to be loosely called existentialism. The view that man must come to terms with the irrational and the absurd was not new; its exponents claimed as forerunners the nineteenth-century Danish philosopher, Sören A. Kierkegaard (1813–55), the German Friedrich W. Nietzsche (1844–1900) and the Russian novelist Fyodor Dostoevsky (1821–81). It was most systematically expounded by the German philosopher, Martin Heidegger (1889–   ), it became most widely known through the work of the French novelist and playwright, Jean Paul Sartre (1905–   ), and it was given a religious emphasis by the French Catholic, Gabriel Marcel (1889–   ), and the German Protestant, Karl Jaspers (1883–   ). The existentialist view had its greatest popularity on the European continent in the middle years of the twentieth-century, where it met the needs of people who had experienced the physical and moral destruction of the second world war—fascism, resistance, concentration camps, death, defeat. But it spread to many areas—to Britain, to Latin America, to Japan and to the United States.

In the existentialist view, existence itself—without reason, without purpose or direction, without a great Idea—is the only reality; this man must accept, and out of this he must make his life through constant choice. As he looks into himself the individual changes the very self which he tries to understand; by his own conduct and the exercise of his will he determines who and what he is. He has freedom to choose but this is a freedom which is imposed upon him, to which he is 'condemned'. Life is thus a risky enterprise, for by existing man risks his existence. In this view man cannot be passive, he cannot be concerned only to know and understand; he is forced by the very nature of his existence to commit himself, to act.

But there is no logic or system inherent in existence which guides such choice and such action; hence this view led to no common set of principles or beliefs. It led some of its exponents to agnosticism or atheism and others to various religious conclusions and commitments; it was used to justify National Socialism, as in the case of the writings of Heidegger, and to motivate the French resistance to Nazi occupation as in the case of Sartre. In its most positive form it gave a stimulus to action in the face of the collapse of traditional values and the revolutionary fluidity of twentieth-century life, it stimulated direct self-understanding without pretence or the intervention of protective rationalizations, and it led to the effort to establish communication with others not through precision in the use of language or other symbols which the logical positivists sought, but by entering intuitively and imaginatively into the existence of others. As such it promoted human relations and human understanding. At its most negative it detached the individual from systematic and organized life and thought, turned him in on himself in self-centred egoism, and produced 'disengagement' with life rather than the 'engagement' which was the core of the positive expression of the existentialist attitude.

Thus the main lines of philosophical thought in the West in these years led away from the certainties of the past and failed to formulate new systems of ideas which gave order to new experience. Yet in spite of their diversity and contradictions they were marked by some common characteristics which distinguished them from the philosophical systems and analysis of preceding centuries.

Philosophers of all schools tended to view reality, truth, the relation between subject and object, the nature of knowledge, awareness and being, in complex and interrelated terms which made obsolete the sharp distinction between the external object and the thinking subject which had preoccupied many philosophers in the past. Although some followed lines suggested by science while others denied the value of science as a source of philosophical knowledge, there was a widespread acceptance of the idea that simple rationalism is insufficient and that man has the capacity to achieve awareness and understanding through direct experience as well as through logical processes. There was a tendency away from the quest for a single 'truth' toward a pluralistic acceptance of the possibility of many kinds and apprehensions of truths. Attention was focused on process, on 'becoming', rather than on origins, ends or changeless forms—on events in a space-time continuum. Except for those who limited their efforts to refining the tools of analysis, the human person was central—his awareness of self, his relation to others and the implications for his action. Although twentieth-century philosophical thought was pursued by highly specialized thinkers using refined and elaborate techniques of analysis, the flow of communication cut across rigid lines and the ideas which emerged had a fluidity which offered fresh, undogmatic approaches, though no universally accepted response, to the challenges of the times.

Yet along with the ideas which reflected the uncertainties that philosophers and laymen both shared, two major orthodoxies remained intact and continued to offer a degree of certainty to their adherents: the assumptions and beliefs of the Roman Catholic Church, elaborated philosophically with the revival of Thomistic thinking: and the dialectical materialism of Marx and Engels as elaborated by Lenin to provide a body of doctrine and method of thought in the USSR, the people's democracies and the Chinese People's Republic.

The orthodoxy of the Roman Catholic Church continued to rest on the reality of the spiritual world and its primacy over the temporal. In the face of both scientific and social developments which brought doubts to many minds, the Church, broadly and in detail, reaffirmed its dogma. In the form of a revival of the philosophy of St Thomas Aquinas it offered a traditional philosophical as well as religious approach to the understanding of life in the modern age.

Interest in the thought of the great mediaeval philosopher had been reawakened by the encyclical *Aeterni Patris* of Pope Leo XIII in 1879 and by the establishment of a chair of Thomism at the University of Louvain, Belgium, in 1882. Thereafter Thomist studies grew in a number of European centres and interest spread throughout the Catholic educational and scholarly world. Subsequent Popes repeatedly prescribed that the Angelic Doctor should be studied, taught and his method followed.

In its assumptions and methods neo-Thomist philosophy retained essentially the same view of life and reality that St Thomas had expressed in the thirteenth century. As reinvigorated and pursued primarily but not exclusively in Catholic circles, it followed two main lines: the application of Thomist methods to the new materials of twentieth-century thought and experience, and the refinement of these methods in the light of historical and analytical studies of St Thomas's writings.

Neo-Thomist thought continued to use the rigorous formal logic of the schoolmen. It accepted the reality of things perceived directly through the senses and grasped intellectually through rational judgment, and it also accepted the reality of things which could not be perceived but could be inferred intellectually by applying the principles of causality and of non-contradiction—principles which could not be proved but which were known through intellectual insight. In the metaphysical Thomist view all things which exist need not be material; in fact all real events and actions cannot be explained by the laws and properties of material bodies. Actions such as thinking and willing depend on operative potencies different from material powers.

The keystone in the Gothic arch of Thomist metaphysics is the demonstration of the existence of a Supreme Being. In this view the existence and actions of things in this universe cannot be fully explained by secondary causes alone; although it is possible to account for a given event in nature by finding its proximate cause in nature, it is not possible to give an ultimate account of the whole system of natural things and events by reference to other natural causes. The only possible ultimate explanation of why the universe exists and works lies beyond the universe itself, in a first cause, God.

Man in Thomist philosophy is understood as a composite of both material and immaterial being, possessed of an immaterial soul as well as a material body. The parents, it is reasoned, who produce the individual's body cannot produce his soul since their own souls, being immaterial, are indivisible; the individual's soul must therefore be created by God, and since there is no known way in which such an immaterial thing may come to an end it must be immortal.

This view of man provides a basis for ethics and a concept of society. Man is seen as responsible for those acts which are under the control of his reason and will. It follows rationally that the good or moral use of man's power to act is related to the purpose and end of human life, and this can be defined in no other terms than the perfect good, that is, God. The attainment of such an end is reserved for a future life. Acts which are morally bad are those which work against the nature and powers of the individual, whether the self or others. Rules of moral behaviour are conceived as precepts of natural moral law because they grow out of the application of natural reasoning to the data of natural human experience.

Social life also is seen as essential to man's nature and the family as the simplest natural society, resulting not from contract but from the natural tendency to reproduce, love and care for offspring and promote the common good. Thomists insisted on the natural character and origin of the family and opposed whatever threatens its integrity as this kind of unit. Since the family is too small to provide for all man's social needs, civil society is also seen as natural rather than contractual, though the specific forms of the state may vary so long as they do not deny the basic, spiritual purpose of human life, the natural moral law and the natural social unit, the family. On the spiritual side the Church is the corresponding ecclesiastical society devoted to man's future life.

This general view was taught in all Catholic institutions, it was elaborated in thousands of universities and centres of Catholic studies, it was the subject of hundreds of learned articles annually and the basis for specialized Thomist journals which numbered no less than twenty-five in the 1950s, as well as for Thomist organizations and for international Thomist congresses. In terms of numbers it appeared that from the time of the first world war onwards no other philosophical group had so many thinkers in its ranks or so many centres of study at its disposal.

Dialectical materialism, which furnished the framework for all thought and the theoretical and philosophical justification for all action in the Soviet Union and other communist states, was at the opposite pole from the metaphysical system of the neo-Thomists. This system of thought was grounded in the basic doctrine and method of analysis developed by Karl Marx and Friedrich Engels in the mid-nineteenth century. Marx's system of thought was designed not merely to interpret the world but to change it, to be intensely practical in terms of historical necessity.

In his view the essential nature of man lies in his capacity for spontaneous productivity; his true activity is his labour which encompasses his total being and in which he transforms both himself and nature outside himself. Since he realizes his conscious being not through thought but through productivity, it is not consciousness that determines life but social life which determines consciousness. This principle extends not only to the forms of production which give life its basic shape but to the superstructure of economics, law, morality and religion. So viewed, the law and morality of bourgeois society can be recognized as merely the expressions of that society without autonomous character of their own.

Following Hegel's dialectical method of analysis, though rejecting his idealism as the purest form of bourgeois ideology, Marx saw the process of nature, of thought and of history as a dialectical one; reality consists of opposites, of theses that engender their own antitheses, which nevertheless contain a fundamental unity; in time this unity or synthesis comes to the fore to replace the old antithesis. He saw in bourgeois society an antithesis between the forces of productivity and the relations involved in production, for the ownership of the means of production gave the capitalist the power to exploit the workers and to prevent the use of their full and many-sided productive capacities; the synthesis could only be brought about in a society in which the private ownership of the means of production has been abolished and social ownership has taken its place.

In Marx's view the class of the proletariat was destined to play the historic role of overthrowing bourgeois society and thus carrying out the inevitable dialectical historical process. Lenin converted the doctrine of dialectical historical materialism into a practical instrument of revolution; under the guidance of a professional revolutionary group, using the method of dialectical analysis to penetrate to an understanding of the forces of society, revolution would be carried out by a close-knit minority with the tacit approval of a majority of the people. He maintained that the revolutionary will of the Communist party must be able to transcend the economic situation and make the contradiction between economic reality and political power in Russia into a positive, active factor through the method of 'democratic centralism'.

Josef Stalin subsequently carried the analysis forward to the conception that the revolutionary dialectic could be carried out and the synthesis of a classless society achieved within a single country, the USSR. By 1950 he believed that socialism had been realized in the Soviet Union and that communism could come under the leadership of the party without a further revolution, since the major contradictions between the forces of productivity and the relations involved in production had been done away with by the socialization of the means of production; the situation was no longer dominated by the antithesis, which Lenin had utilized as an active force, but by the synthesis which was emerging in the society of the USSR.

These concepts provided a unifying view of life to which all aspects and activities could be referred. The materialistic assumption, the dialectical method, historical necessity, the basic concept that ideas are the product of social experience and their function is to modify that experience in the direction of rational organization of production and full development of human capacities for physical and intellectual productivity, the method of democratic centralism—this core of the doctrine provided consistent terms in which to approach the development of technology, literary and artistic expression, political structure and social organization, the individual's view of himself and the direction of public policy.

The currents of thought which flowed in the West penetrated to the non-European world, bringing new ideas, shaking traditional certainties and stimulating a rescrutiny of concepts and values which had been taken for granted for many centuries. Scientific inquiry by both western and eastern scholars was directed toward the philosophical thought of the East and stimulated the republication of Buddhist, Hindu, Confucian and other texts, their critical study and the consideration of their implications for modern life.* Scientific attitudes and principles, both in their nineteenth- and in their twentieth-century forms, and various western philosophical lines of thought, including pragmatism, dialectical materialism and existentialism, entered the thought of the East through western-educated writers and leaders. No less than in the West, traditional structures of ideas were broken down under the general impact of new experience and new thought, without the immediate substitution of alternative, integrating points of view.

The principal orthodoxy of the East which remained firm was that of Islam. Though it had no central church to interpret doctrine with infallibility or to provide channels for administration and communication, and only the pilgrimage to Mecca and the traditional studies in the great mosques furnished a machinery for maintaining a common interpretation among many and varied peoples, the revealed Book, the prescribed prayers and the rules of daily life kept doctrine and attitudes intact. Yet the finality and comprehensiveness of the Quran still left much room for uncertainty in the area of social organization and conduct and the philosophical ideas of the West had their students and followers in Islamic areas also.

Most of the interaction between eastern and western thought was onesided, the impact of ideas originating in the West upon the thought of the East. The development in the West of non-rational philosophies during these years, however, began to provide a possible bridge to the philosophical thought of the East which had always stressed the use of non-rational faculties to penetrate to the essence of reality and had exacted a profound commitment

* See Chapter XXV, Religion.

in action. These tendencies, together with the new respect engendered by the rise of eastern nations to equality of political status, brought a growing interest in the philosophical thought of the East. Through the middle of the century, however, the gap remained wide as far as any real penetration of eastern thought into the West was concerned. It was indeed a rare westerner who was prepared to submit himself to the discipline which easterners associated with the sort of insight, self-penetration and wisdom which was part of their tradition and which the westerner, too, could only hope to experience from within.

NOTES TO CHAPTER XX

1. In the opinion of Soviet commentators, Gandhi's theory of 'non-violence' is not a new progressive method of effecting political and social changes, with the prospect of development in future. It is a backward moral-religious doctrine, which did the cause of Indian emancipation more harm than good, since it drove the national-liberation movement along the road of conciliation and concessions on matters of principle to British imperialism. It is characteristic that the Indian National Congress never applied the tactics of non-violence without reservations and ultimately renounced them. And even Gandhi himself did not remain true to this idea until the end. The theory of non-violence, which Gandhi tried to push through the Indian Congress as a practical basis for the policy of the Indian state, was a continual source of conflict within Congress and led to numerous political crises. J. Nehru writes: 'when Gandhiji raised in 1940 the question of non-violence in relation to the war and the future of free India, the Congress working Committee had to face the issue squarely. They made it clear to him that they were unable to go as far as he wanted them to go, and could not possibly commit India or the Congress to future applications of this principle in the external domain. . . . In December 1941, however, the same crisis took shape again when Gandhiji insisted on complete non-violence. Again there was a split and public disagreement, and the president of Congress, Maulana Abul Kalam Azad, and others were unable to accept Gandhiji's view. It became clear that the Congress as a whole, including some of the faithful followers of Gandhiji, disagreed with him in this matter. . . . At no other time was this issue raised by Gandhiji in Congress. . . . In later months, leading up to August 1942, Gandhiji's nationalism and intense desire for freedom made him even agree to Congress participation in the war if India could function as a free country. . . . In the conflict between the principle of non-violence which had become his very life-blood and meaning of existence, and India's freedom which was a dominating and consuming passion for him, the scales inclined towards the latter.' (Jawaharlal Nehru, *The Discovery of India*, New York, 1946, pp. 454, 455.) Thus, as this eminent Indian leader testifies, the principle of non-violence and the struggle for the liberation of his country from the colonial yoke were constantly in irreconcilable contradiction. There is not the slightest reason to place any hope in the principle of non-violence as a new progressive method of effecting political change.

   See J. Nehru, *op. cit.*, R. P. Dutt, *The Crisis of Britain and the British Empire* (London, 1957).

2. Academician N. Konrad points out that the 'particular combination of circumstances' on which European culture was actually based was itself a natural link in the chain of developments giving rise to world culture. In the Marxist–Leninist view, the general line of the history of mankind is expressed in the steady development and constant perfecting of progress. Despite all manner of retrogression, zigzags, and 'backward leaps', society proceeds along an upward course. One of the most important features of this objective law governing social progress is the historical continuity existing in the development of

culture. The essence of this continuity, a necessary prerequisite for the development of culture, is an unbreakable organic unity between, on the one hand, the heritage of the past, the cultural values accumulated by past generations, i.e. traditions, and on the other hand the critical analysis and creative re-working of those cultural values, i.e. innovations. The culture of any social-historical formation is the logical product of the very essence of that formation, of the processes and phenomena conditioned by its mode of production. The mode of producing material values determines the social, political and spiritual processes of the life of society as a whole, as well as the transition from one social order, and its culture, to another, higher social order, and the culture to which it gives birth. Culture must be seen as an historical phenomenon, as something in the process of development. Historical continuity in the development of material production is the basis of historical continuity in the development of material and spiritual culture. What is called 'European culture' was a continuation of the culture of the peoples of the Ancient Orient, elements of which can be clearly traced in the 'spiritual life' of the European peoples. And 'European culture' in turn is now being superseded by a genuine 'world culture', which is forming before our eyes with the appearance of a new socialist mode of production. (See (1) N. I. Konrad, 'Zametki o smysle istorii' (Notes on the Content of History), *Vestnik istorii mirovoy kultury*, 1961, No. 2, pp. 3–30; (2) E. A. Baller, 'Problema preemstvennosti v razvitii kultury' ('The Problem of Continuity in Cultural Development'), *Vestnik istorii mirovoy kultury*, 1961, No. 5, pp. 14–29).

3. The most widely known formulations of the Catholic position in regard to social justice and to private property in modern times were made by Pope Leo XIII in the encyclical *Rerum Novarum* (1891), and especially in the two recent encyclicals by Pope John XXIII *Mater et Magistra* (1961) and *Pacem in Terris* (1963).

Pope Pius IX, in the encyclical *Quadragesimo Anno* (1931), elaborated upon the statements in the earlier encyclical concerning the relation between social justice and private property in the words:

'First, let it be made clear beyond all doubt that neither Leo XIII, nor those theologians who have taught under the guidance and direction of the Church, have ever denied or called in question the twofold aspect of ownership, which is individual or social accordingly as it regards individuals or concerns the common good. Their unanimous contention has always been that the right to own private property has been given to man by nature or rather by the Creator Himself, not only in order that individuals may be able to provide for their own needs and those of their families, but also that by means of it, the goods which the Creator has destined for the human race may truly serve this purpose. Now these ends cannot be secured unless some definite and stable order is maintained. . . .

'It follows from the twofold character of ownership, which We have termed individual and social, that men must take into account in this matter not only their own advantage but also the common good. To define in detail these duties, when the need occurs and when the natural law does not do so, is the function of the government. . . . It is plain, however, that the State may not discharge this duty in an arbitrary manner.'

Apart from discussion of practical problems of social justice contained in many of the references cited in the bibliographies of the volume, the reader will gain fundamental insight into the subject from Friedmann's analysis of the development of law in accordance with the changes in twentieth-century society, particularly in Western countries. *Cf.* W. Friedmann, *Law in a Changing Society* (Berkeley & Los Angeles, 1959).

4. Soviet scholars claim that it is wrong to present the Catholic Church as a defender of the rights of society against individualism. The basis of Catholicism is the doctrine of the autocratic powers and absolute prerogatives of the head of the Church—the Pope, in regard to whom individuals, peoples, and society as a whole either have no rights at all or are placed in an extremely subordinate position. Catholicism has been and still is opposed on principle to popular sovereignty—the basis of political justice (see *Konstitutsionnye Akty Gosudarstva-gorod Vatikan* (Constitutional Documents of Vatican City), arts. 1, 3, 4, 7 and others).

As far as 'social justice' is concerned, for which the Catholic Church is said to be striving, it is in fact extremely unjust, for private ownership of the means of production, the basis of every kind of social injustice, has always been and still remains the supreme symbol of the Catholic faith. In the Papal Encyclical *Mater et Magistra* (1961), as in a number of other Catholic documents, private property is considered as an irreplaceable element in a properly-ordered and productive society. Despite its demagogic phrases about 'socialization' and 'public ownership', this Papal Encyclical is, from its first syllable to its last, an attempt to give an ideological defence of the institution of private property. *Mater et Magistra* calls for the immutable rights of private property to be preserved at any price. Only such rights, it is said, can ensure the independence of the individual from the omnipotence of society and the state. In the view of John XXIII such rights provide a guarantee of freedom as well as an incentive to preserve it.

See: (1) Yu. Aseyev, 'Novoye izlozhenie sotsialnoy doktriny katolitsizma' ('A New Statement of Catholic Social Doctrine') *Mirovaya ekonomika i mezhdunarodnye otnosheniya* (World Economics and International Relations) (1961), No. 11, pp. 47–56; (2) L. Gallico, 'Razryv mezhdu vatikanskoy ideologiye i sotsialnoy deystvitelnostyu' ('The Gap between Vatican Ideology and Social Reality'), in *World Marxist Review* (Prague, 1961), No. 12, pp. 38–45.

5. Candidate of Juridical Sciences A. Bovin points out that in the Soviet Union no one specifically 'dissolved' the institution of the bourgeois family. The bourgeois family, with its inequality for women, did indeed collapse in the course of the socialist reforms that were carried out. However, the institution of the new socialist family, based on the full economic, and political equality of both parties, has always been encouraged and supported in the Soviet Union, as is shown by the whole history of legislation on family matters in the USSR.

See G. M. Sverdlov, *Sovetskoye semeynoye pravo* (Soviet Family Law), (Moscow, 1958).

6. Father Emilio Pin comments that: 'According to Christian thinking the idea that human life is a prelude to eternity, far from lessening the importance of life on earth, enhances it. It gives an eternal value to the efforts made by man to bring justice and love between men.' This view is elaborated in the Encyclicals referred to above and in many others. It has stimulated the writings of a great number of volumes treating sociology and other subjects in the social sciences, as well as the sciences and humanities from the Catholic point of view.

The following titles may be consulted for further study:

J. Y. Calvez, *Eglise et société économique* (Paris, 1961–63), 2 vols.

Cyril C. Clump, *A Catholic's Guide to Social and Political Action* (Oxford, 1955).

J. F. Cronin, *Catholic Social Principles: the Social Teachings of the Catholic Church Applied to American Economic Life* (Milwaukee, 1955).

J. F. Cronin, *Social Principles and Economic Life* (Milwaukee, 1959).

T. J. Harte, *Papal Social Principles* (Milwaukee, 1956).

Jacques Maritain, *Man and the State* (Chicago, 1951).

Melvin J. Williams, *Catholic Social Thought: Its Approach to Contemporary Problems* (New York, 1950).

CHAPTER XXI

ECONOMIC INSTITUTIONS

THE economic life of the world during the twentieth century was lived within two distinct sets of institutions and relationships.

A large and growing segment, involving a fifth to a quarter of the world's people at the opening of the century and perhaps a third or more by the middle, formed part of the world-wide commercial economy composed of industrial production, agriculture carried on for sale beyond the immediate family or neighbourhood, the trade through which these products were distributed and the transport, communication, construction and services related to these processes.

Outside this interrelated commercial economy, though increasingly affected by it, were the self-contained village and subsistence economies within which a large part of the world's rural people lived out their lives. There the cycle of most production and consumption was local and immediate. Although the few items which entered the subsistence economies from outside were sometimes of crucial importance—salt, essential tools—and some local produce or work had to enter into the commercial economy to pay for these necessities, the bulk of economic activity was carried on locally for local use.

At the opening of the century the subsistence economies, which took a number of different forms, were subject in varying degrees to the impact of the commercial economy. The more accessible of the Indian villages, whose traditional economy had been based on an elaborate system of mutual responsibilities, had already begun to be invaded by products from British factories which displaced local crafts, and in some areas subsistence agriculture had been replaced by commercial crops such as indigo or tea. The communal tribal villages of Africa at that time had barely begun to send their men to work in mines opened by Europeans. The groups of specialized villages in the valleys of Mexico, the nomadic herdsmen of central Asia and Iran, the subsistence farmers of the isolated mountain areas of Europe and the Americas and the shifting cultivators in parts of Latin America and South-East Asia all lived very largely to themselves.

In the course of the twentieth century the commercial economy expanded and penetrated further and further into the subsistence areas. Roads opened up isolated regions, radio communication brought awareness of life outside the village, more workers were drawn from the subsistence areas to work in industry, industrial activity in the form of mines and factories was established in new localities. Yet at mid-century the dual pattern still remained in large parts of Asia, Africa and Latin America. Where the subsistence economies were touched by the commercial economy they were more likely to be passively subjected to its impact than to become active participants in it, although vigorous efforts for economic development in the non-industrial countries were tending to draw them actively into the broader stream of economic life.

The village-subsistence economies were traditional and static, except as the pressure of population or depletion of the soil brought a deterioration of their condition or they were ravaged by famine or pestilence, flood or other disaster. Only where they came under the impact of the commercial economy were their structure and development materially changed. The commercial economy on the other hand was highly dynamic, not only growing and spreading, but developing new institutions or adapting old and undergoing many alterations during this period.

At the opening of the twentieth century the commercial economy was a single world economy, interrelated in all its parts, carried on through a common set of institutions. Although each industrial country had its unique features, these did not radically differ one from the other, and the mechanisms for international trade based on the gold standard linked not only industrial countries but industrialized segments of non-industrial areas. In the latter those engaged in production and trade came within the common commercial framework, either because this framework had been accepted as a basis for trade and industry by the country, as in the Latin American countries, or by virtue of colonial rule in the areas under the dominion of European powers, or through treaties establishing these conditions within independent nations, such as the treaties of extraterritoriality in China or Turkey.

In the twentieth century the unity of the world economy was broken and two separate economic systems were created by the establishment of a communist state in the USSR and the later incorporation of eastern Europe and China within this sphere. The interrelated capitalist economies and the economies of communist countries, as they developed along separate lines, had many common features, for they shared a common technology which influenced the direction of development, and they grew from a common base which was the historical starting point for many features of both systems. But the features which reflected the difference between communist and capitalist approaches brought two distinct patterns of development, and factors inherent in these developments, as well as in the political relations between communist and non-communist countries, so greatly reduced the economic interrelations between the two economic spheres that by mid-century each had come to be, at least for the time being, largely self-contained.

The common base in technological development has already been discussed. In the pages which follow the common base in the world economy of the early twentieth century will be reviewed, followed by a discussion of the divergent developments of the capitalist and socialist economies and of the patterns of economic development that were taking shape in newly industrializing societies, both in the form of mixed economies and under communist direction.* [1, 2]

I. THE COMMON BASE:
THE WORLD ECONOMY OF THE EARLY TWENTIETH CENTURY

The world economy of the early twentieth century was composed of private profit-seeking enterprises bound together and organized into a functioning whole by the operations of the competitive market. In principle, competition was unrestrained; in practice powerful monopolies dominated some fields and public utilities were coming to be regulated or operated by the state.

As an organizing force the market encouraged the production of those things which were in demand and discouraged those which were not; prices were established through the process of buying and selling and reflected supply and demand; producers decided whether they could operate profitably at the prices which the market offered and adjusted their production accordingly; a drop or an increase in price stimulated or reduced demand. The essence of the market mechanism as the organizer of the world commercial economy was flexible prices.

The market economy depended on money transactions and required a reliable money supply for its operations. This was provided in each country in the form of gold or silver, notes issued by governments and backed by their credit, and money created by banks under the regulation of their respective governments, either through the issue of bank notes or by loans which took the form of the creation of bank deposits. The stability of each country's currency was effected by government regulations as to the conditions for the issue of government notes and the conduct of banking; the relation among national currencies was automatically regulated by the flow of gold upon which the currencies of practically all the commercial countries were based.

The capital for industrial expansion was secured through capital markets which made funds available for the purchase of the machines, buildings and other physical capital required for industrial production. A network of financial institutions gathered up the savings of individuals and routed them to industry; banks and other private lending agencies received deposits and loaned them to business, investment houses marketed the securities of corporations, and stock exchanges or other security markets offered places where shares of stock changed hands. These capital markets, operating under national regulations designed to prevent fraud, provided a channel for the investment of foreign as well as domestic savings in the capital formation of a particular country. Capital moved freely, both nationally and internationally, to exploit natural resources and to take advantage of a cheap or skilled labour supply.

* For the technological aspects of these developments, see Chapter IX, Industrial Production; Chapter X, Transport; Chapter XI, Communication; Chapter XIV, Food and Agriculture.

The market for labour, as for goods and for capital, was open and free and operated by means of the wage system. Within limits set by inertia, high wages drew labour to the places and industries where it was needed. A mobile labour force, not only within the industrial countries but immigrating in large numbers to centres of industrial employment, especially in North America, was 'hired and fired' through the mechanism of the free market. Traditional relationships of paternalistic responsibility between master and apprentice had been quite thoroughly replaced by the cash nexus between the worker and his employer.

In order to route the products of industry to the distant markets where they would reach their consumers, a system of marketing institutions had been developed which included wholesale and retail selling, transport by sea, rail and horse-drawn vehicle, storage facilities, insurance in transit and the advertising of products.

The driving force in the commercial economy was provided by business enterprise. With few exceptions this was in the hands of private individuals or corporations, motivated by private profit or, in the case of traditional business castes or special merchant groups in Asia, by customary sanctions. Entrepreneurs were guaranteed in the enjoyment of their profits by the support for private property provided by the laws of the commercial countries; elsewhere they were protected by colonial rule, extraterritoriality and custom. In the industrial countries business success carried with it power and varying degrees of prestige, depending on the surviving strength of the landed aristocracy. Where no such aristocracy had ever existed, as in North America and Australasia, the successful businessman had no rival. 'Economic man' was assumed to act rationally in quest of profits and therefore to improve production to meet competition in the market.

The framework for enterprise was provided by government in the form of law, regulation, and government activity. A body of commercial law established rights of property, enforcement of contracts, conditions of incorporation, relations between agents and principals, stockholders and corporation, buyers and sellers, debtors and creditors. Although the details differed from country to country, especially as between those whose legal system stemmed from the Roman law via the Napoleonic Code and those based on Anglo-Saxon common law, the basic features of commercial law were common to all areas to which the commercial economy extended.

Regulations established by governments varied more than the basic legal framework, but they generally included the establishment and maintenance of standards for money and for weights and measures, regulation of the rates charged by public utilities such as railways, grain warehouses, or gas and electric supply companies, safety codes for building construction and the use of hazardous products, some protection of labour, especially the labour of children and of women in dangerous trades. Countries differed in the extent to which they attempted by law to preserve competition, as in the United

States, or to permit the formation of cartels, as in Germany, and in their acceptance of labour unions and the substitution of collective bargaining for the individual contract between employer and worker.

The economic activity of government itself was small, though it varied from country to country. In addition to military establishments and the post office, which were universally operated by governments, several European countries operated central banks, the British government operated the telephone and telegraph system, the government of Germany operated the railways, while government operations in the United States were limited largely to municipal services such as water-works and sometimes gas and electric utilities and rapid-transit systems. The expenditures for government services covered a limited range of activities for the maintenance of order and sanitation, fire protection, relief of the poor and provision of education, and they were supported out of taxes, chiefly collected in the form of tariffs and excises, which represented a very small proportion of the national income.

International trade was carried on between the enterprises of industrial countries which exchanged their respective products, and between those of industrial and non-industrial countries as industrial products flowed out and foodstuffs, raw materials and luxury products were received in return. Tariff barriers limited the entrance into some countries of products which competed with local industry. Tariff policies were, however, designed for revenue or for the protection of specific home industries, not to regulate the general volume of trade; the flow of gold, in exchange for imports which exceeded exports and as a return on capital invested abroad, was the standard mechanism for adjusting the international balance of trade.

The world economy had been subject to fluctuations in which high levels of economic activity were followed by more or less severe declines in production accompanied by unemployment, business failures and the collapse of markets for goods. There were prolonged depressions in the 1870s and 1890s and a sharp recession in 1907. While the circumstances which appeared to initiate each period of depression had differed—the aftermath of war, a speculative failure, a gold panic—there was widespread belief that such periodic swings between prosperity and depression were inherent in the system, and they were referred to as business cycles.

In classical economic theory they were assumed to be not only temporary but self-correcting phenomena; a boom which carried prices too high or raised the level of production beyond the ability of the market to absorb the output would be automatically corrected by a recession, while at the bottom of a depression business would recover and employment would rise when prices and wages had fallen sufficiently to make production again profitable in the light of potential demand. Each new period of prosperity was expected to carry the economy to a generally higher level before another peak would be reached at which the corrective of recession would again become necessary.

This had indeed been the case, as over the years the system had provided a rising level of living to a growing segment of the population.

In the Marxist–Leninist theory, however, these periodic depressions with accompanying unemployment were held to be an evidence of the fatal weakness of the capitalist system; they were bound to become more and more severe, producing progressive misery and widening inequality in income, and would ultimately lead to the downfall of the system, though that day might be postponed by resort to imperialistic exploitation of weaker economies to bolster economies which could not sustain a profitable market at home.

II. THE DEVELOPMENT OF CAPITALIST AND SOCIALIST ECONOMIES IN THE TWENTIETH CENTURY

1. *The capitalist economy of the United States and other advanced capitalist countries*[3, 4]

The capitalist economies developed from the base of the early twentieth-century world economy and remained part of a common system, although many new controls intervened to modify the free flow of goods, labour and capital both within industrial countries and in world markets. As these economies evolved they took on features which had not been part of the capitalist system in its earlier forms.

Many of these features were especially pronounced in the United States, and the economy of that country will therefore be used to illustrate major trends among the advanced capitalist economies during these years, although there were significant differences between it and some of the other capitalist economies.

(*a*) *Mass production and mass consumption.* [5, 6, 7] The central feature of the American economy was mass production and mass consumption. By elaborating the devices which the factory system of the nineteenth century had foreshadowed, mass production achieved low costs for great quantities of goods.

The pattern of mass production varied among industries. In some industries such as clothing or textiles the economies of mass production could be achieved with relatively small volume. In others such as automobiles, where an efficient production line came to require a market for some 100,000 cars of an essentially identical model, only a large domestic or foreign market could sustain mass production and only large companies could expect to function successfully.

Mass production would have been of little value without a mass market. It was the presence of a large common domestic market, unhampered by tariff barriers or by significant differences in tastes and ways of living, that accentuated the tendency of the American economy to exploit the possibilities of mass production. While much of the product of nineteenth-century industry, like most goods entering into trade and commerce in the past, had gone to satisfy the wants of a small segment of the population, the unique feature of the twentieth-century economy was production for mass consumption.

The American economy came to depend to a major degree on the purchasing power of the masses of the people, which in turn was made possible by rising productivity from mass-production techniques. The resulting wages and salaries, together with the multitude of available goods, produced a pattern of mass consumption in which what had been the luxuries of the few and the distinguishing features of middle-class life became part of the standard of living of the many. In the mid-1950s, for example, nearly three-quarters of American families had cars, telephones and television sets, and nine out of ten had radios and refrigerators.

The great expansion in consumption came in things beyond the bare essentials for survival, especially in durable goods such as household appliances and automobiles. As these were introduced into the consumer's budget they were accompanied by methods of financing which recognized their character as a form of capital. Instalment selling and hire-purchase plans extended to automobiles and refrigerators the principle of payment during use which had previously been limited to the purchase of housing with the aid of a home mortgage.

The mass of consumers who provided the market for the products of industry also provided much of the capital for its continuing expansion. An increasing proportion of the investment funds which entered industry came from the higher earnings of wage and salaried workers. Individual workers invested in corporate stocks through employee-purchase plans, and provided loan funds through the banks and savings and loan associations where their savings were deposited and through life-insurance funds; labour unions built up large treasuries and special pension or benefit funds which became large sources for investment. At the same time mounting taxes reduced the pool of upper-income savings from which capital had been principally derived in the past. The net result was a shift in the segment of the population upon whose savings the expansion of industry depended.

These tendencies were present in varying degrees in all the developed capitalist economies. Smaller countries which lacked a large domestic market tended to develop mass production in industries where mass techniques were effective on relatively low volume or for simple articles, or else to concentrate on special items for export. Sweden for example gained the advantages of mass production by making special products for export, such as ball-bearings and telephone equipment, thus commanding a large market for mass-produced items which could not be sold in sufficient volume at home. They also made very simple and inexpensive articles for domestic use which met the needs of the lower paid workers in order to tap the home market at its largest extent.

Mass consumption was most marked in the United States, but the trend was everywhere increasingly apparent. And it was the advantages of a domestic mass market which led the European countries in the middle of the twentieth century to take steps toward the creation of a common market on the European continent.

(b) *Large-scale organization.* Mass production and distribution brought about large-scale organization and were made possible by it. Large organizations—corporations, labour unions, government structures—grew in dimension and in relative importance in the capitalist economies. Their presence and growing dominance shifted the character of the economy more and more away from market organization and towards the substitution of administration for the traditional market forces.

For business operations the form of enterprise which gained ascendancy in the United States was the large corporation, a great industrial unit which employed many thousands of people, used the savings of many thousands of shareholders—its nominal owners—served hundreds of thousands of customers and controlled assets and did business amounting to many millions of dollars.

The large corporation was not a new phenomenon; by 1890 it had been sufficiently prominent to lead to the passage of anti-trust legislation designed to preserve competition and prevent monopolistic aggregations of economic power. The distinguishing feature of twentieth-century development was the growth in both size and importance of such corporations. As they became the prevailing form of business enterprise they had an increasing impact on the functioning of the economy by reason of their ability to control their own prices and production.

The 200 largest corporations in the United States, leaving aside the banks and other financial institutions, controlled by the 1930s some three-fifths of the assets of all non-financial corporations and roughly half of all industrial wealth. In the field of manufacturing 100 corporations in 1935 employed a fifth of all manufacturing labour and their products amounted to a third of the value of all manufactured goods. The leading corporations remained at least as dominant in later years. More striking and significant for the development of economic institutions was the extent to which they dominated specific industries—notably the great industries on which the industrial system rested, including steel, oil, automobiles, electrical manufacture, copper refining, aluminium, chemicals, rayon, as well as railways and public utilities. Service activities, agriculture, a substantial proportion of trade and many minor industries, however, were largely outside the sphere of corporate control.

The large corporation was chiefly to be found in those industries where the amount of capital investment per worker was greatest. The accelerated trend toward automation which required heavy capital investment further strengthened the position of the larger corporations. The trend was evident in the automobile industry, where one after another of the smaller companies dropped out or were merged with larger units until the industry was almost completely dominated by a very few very large concerns. The extent of concentration in the market may be seen by the list of industries in which 70 per cent or more of the output was produced by the four largest companies. From the 1930s on, these included, among the large industries, motor vehicles, cigarettes, rubber tyres, tin cans, rayon, together with the makers of a host of lesser products such as typewriters, sewing machines, electric light bulbs, chewing gum, breakfast cereals.

Large corporations also entered the field of distribution to provide mass outlets for mass-produced products. The 200 largest non-financial corporations in 1930 included two mail-order houses, two 'five and ten cent' stores, two department stores, a grocery chain and a chain of drug stores. Chain grocery and drug stores expanded greatly thereafter. These mass-distribution agencies, and also the special sales outlets for mass-produced shoes, ready-made clothing, automobiles or automobile accessories, served primarily as mass outlets for mass-produced goods, instead of performing the retailers' traditional role as intermediaries between the wants of consumers and the range of goods offered by producers.

The large corporations grew in size, with no apparent limit to the enterprise which could be operated as a single structure. The largest of them for example, the American Telephone and Telegraph Company, in 1956 had 787,000 employees, 1,492,000 stockholders, and assets of 11,100 million dollars. In 1900 this corporation was already among the large American enterprises; it then had some 37,000 employees and 10,000 stockholders.

Corporations grew in size by various means. The traditional method was to seek new capital funds through the investment market. Increasingly, however, the large corporations grew by the reinvestment of their own earnings, distributing only a fraction of their profits to stockholders. They also grew by exchanging their stock for that of smaller concerns in order to absorb or control them. The corporations themselves, rather than the investing public or the bankers, thus tended to determine where expansion would take place.

From the 1920s on they relied increasingly upon research to guide their growth and development. Following the lead of some of the pioneers such as the electrical manufacturing and telephone companies, they sought out the best scientific talent and offered resources and considerable freedom for study and experiment. By mid-century no large company was without its research arm, the sums spent on corporate research mounted annually and much of the invention and innovation of the period emerged from this source.

The large corporation was a continuing body with a legal personality, 'owned' by many stockholders who had neither direct knowledge of nor control over the affairs of the enterprise. It was governed by a board of directors, technically elected by the stockholders and representing them but in fact self-perpetuating. In the large corporation control was separated from ownership. Where stockholdings were so widely dispersed that no individual or small group owned a majority or even a substantial minority of shares, as was generally the situation in these companies, control rested in the hands of management; a few large shareholders might exercise influence by virtue of their general position and prestige rather than through a voting majority of the company's stock. In some cases the bankers who handled the corporation's financing were in a position to affect its policy, but the larger corporations tended to remove themselves more and more from bankers' control by using their accumulated earnings to finance expansion instead of distributing all earnings as dividends and then seeking new funds through loans or the sale of stock.[8]

Persons with a financial interest in corporate stock came to include a large proportion of the population. Although large stockholdings continued to be held by a limited group of persons with means, millions of small owners held a few shares each. In 1955 more than 8,000,000 people in the United States owned corporate stock directly, about a third of them from families whose income placed them in the lower half of the population. Many millions more had invested indirectly by placing their savings in an investment trust, savings and loan association, insurance company or trade union welfare fund, which in turn held stock in many different corporations and enabled the small investor to diversify his risk.

This widespread ownership gave the people at large a stake in the prosperity of the corporations but it did not involve them actively, except in the rare instances when an outside interest or rival faction challenged the existing control of a corporation and the votes of the small shareholders were solicited by both sides.

The men who ran the large corporations achieved their positions primarily, and increasingly, by rising through the industrial bureaucracy. They entered the structure as technicians or engineers concerned with production, as salesmen involved with promotion, as lawyers handling the multitude of legal relations in which the corporation became involved, in the personnel department responsible for employment policies and labour relations, or as part of the financial machinery of the enterprise. Though in the 1950s they were still likely to have come from families of moderately good incomes, an increasing proportion were coming from families of labourers or white-collar workers, family connections were less likely to have been responsible for their initial job than fifty or even twenty-five years before, and their advancement was no more rapid whether they were from a rich or a poor family.

As each corporation became a sort of small empire in itself, management tended to come from within the same organization, though sometimes a successful sales manager, production director or other executive was brought from one corporation to another. Twenty-two per cent of the chief executives of large corporations in 1950 had had no business experience outside their own company as compared with only 7 per cent in 1900; in the earlier year three-fifths (62 per cent) had had entrepreneurial experience as against less than one-fifth (17 per cent) in 1950.* Once part of the corporate structure, they might be shifted from one locality to another, like civil servants or military personnel, and the road to advancement frequently led from one department to another or through a series of branch plants and finally to the central office.

Each corporate bureaucracy developed its means of training its promising young men and giving them experience for future responsibility, its methods of seeking to command the loyalty and devotion of its members and to build an *esprit de corps* and of arousing the interest of the wives and families in order to reinforce an executive's devotion to his job and the welfare of the company. Since the objective of these efforts was the success of the corporation rather than the profit of any individual, power, prestige and advancement came to play a larger part than simple profit in the motivation of corporate management, although generous executive salaries and bonus systems based on corporate profits kept direct economic motivation very much alive, and high corporate earnings were the mark of success.

This new group of industrial managers came to replace more and more the representatives of the shareholders in the government of the corporation. In 1950 they composed half or more of the membership of the boards of directors of one-third of the large corporations; for 8 per cent of the companies they made up the entire board. The trend for management to occupy a position where no stockholder, banker or other outsider was influential enough to contest its direction of the corporation led some people to see management as taking over business. Other students of corporate structure thought that such a concept exaggerated the role of this group, but there was no question that the corporation manager was coming to be the main prototype of the successful businessman of the mid-twentieth century.

The large corporation contributed to the rootlessness of urban–industrial communities and made many of them dependent on decisions and events wholly outside their control. It often had plants in a number of different localities, sometimes because these were favourable for various distinct operations, or because the company had acquired the properties of smaller enterprises, or as a result of the extension of the corporation's activities into new areas. Decisions affecting these plants were made in terms of the enterprise as a whole, not the effect on the local community, since the large corporation rarely had substantial investments in local real estate, banks, stores or services which would be affected by what happened to its local plant. It could abandon plants containing obsolete equipment, build new plants in other localities, shift work from one plant to another in order to combat labour demands, move from areas where power rates were higher to more favourable sites, or shift to places which had advantages from the point of view of raw materials, transport or markets. Where the plants of large corporations constituted the principal source of employment in a community, whole

* Mabel Newcomer, *The Big Business Executive* (New York, 1955); W. Lloyd Warner and James Abegglen, *Big Business Leaders in America* (New York, 1955).

communities were subject to the decisions of corporate managements which had no direct stake in the community's welfare. Corporations frequently adopted policies of contributing to the physical and civic development of the communities where they operated, but this did not minimize community dependence on decisions in which the people of the locality took no part.

The separate corporations did not stand as completely independent units but tended to be part of a larger corporate community. Many of the large corporations were linked by interlocking directorates, with directors of one corporation sitting on the board of another, or they formed loose groupings of corporations with mutual interests. Bankers on the boards of several companies whose finances they handled used their influence as board members to make the policies of each contribute to the development of the others, as for instance in insisting that the site for a new manufacturing plant should be located on a railway with which they were also connected. Two or more companies frequently joined to establish a new concern for the manufacture of something which both companies needed, as when several oil companies set up a company to manufacture the chemicals which they all used. A common climate of opinion and norms of behaviour for the corporate group grew out of the use of common accounting firms and legal counsel, the activities of the financial agencies engaged in supplying funds and marketing and trading securities, and from personal contacts at lunch, on the golf links or at social gatherings.

In other capitalist countries large corporations played an essentially similar role and took on essentially the same characteristics, sometimes but not always in a less pronounced form. They were somewhat less dominant where co-operative enterprise was extensive as in Sweden, or where a larger proportion of economic activity was carried on by government. In Europe they often formed cartels to divide up the market—a practice legally prohibited in the United States. Some, such as the giant Unilever, were international in organization as well as in operation.

Yet although the large corporation flourished everywhere and became the dominant form of American business enterprise, small business did not disappear during these years. The individual entrepreneur conducting a small venture for direct private profit remained the principal economic unit in agriculture, in much retail trade, in the service industries and in many manufacturing activities.

The great bulk of commercial agriculture in the United States was conducted on family farms. Although a few crops, mainly cotton and sugar, were produced on large plantations, even the largest of the plantation enterprises were responsible for so small a proportion of total production of the particular crop that they did not occupy the kind of controlling position that characterized the industrial corporation.

In the field of distribution a multitude of individually operated retail establishments continued to function in communities or neighbourhoods too small to support mass outlets and in larger communities where some customers were willing to pay for additional retail services which chain stores, mail-order houses and other mass distributors failed to supply.

Small manufacturers survived chiefly in the making of speciality items, the development of new products and in supplying specific small mass-produced articles which either required little capital and relatively small volume in order to gain the advantages of mass production, or which constituted parts to be used by large manufacturers. Many thousands of new enterprises were started each year by individuals or groups who saw a chance for a profit in some new or old line of production. In the 1950s new manufacturing enterprises were being set up at the rate of about 25,000 a year; in addition, new enterprises in construction, trade, service and other non-manufacturing activities averaged 325,000 annually. Some of these efforts failed and old enterprises were discontinued for one reason or another almost as frequently as new ones were started. But many survived, some to remain small, others to grow to considerable proportions and in time to become large-scale enterprises themselves. There was no tendency either for the number of new enterprises to diminish or for fewer small enterprises to continue to function.

Ninety per cent of all manufacturing establishments continued to employ less than 100 workers, and the numbers of such establishments, not always of course operated by an independent company, was more than a third greater in 1954 than it had been twenty-five years before—264,000 as compared with 193,000. Small establishments were to be found in nearly every type of industry.

The existence of an economy of mass production and consumption itself favoured the survival of small enterprise. As the masses of the people acquired higher incomes and more leisure they had more scope for expenditure on things other than basic necessities—on entertainment, sport or hobbies, on things to decorate the home and to embellish its surroundings, on extra clothing, special foods, travel, enjoyment of the arts. Basic products, especially those involving heavy industry, offered little scope for small enterprise, for they were controlled by the large corporations and they required much capital and large expenditures on advertising to reach the mass market. Small enterprise survived as an integral part of the basic industries mainly in the specialized manufacture of machinery and in the mass manufacture of special parts to be used in the machine processes. But the speciality fields remained open and attracted the efforts of ambitious entrepreneurs who took advantage of the growing capacity of consumers to diversify their purchases.

The small enterprise had another advantage which contributed to its survival, its adaptability. It could adopt innovations without undergoing the high cost of revamping an elaborate production process or the delays of bureaucratic decision-making. Although small companies did not have the resources which enabled large corporations to maintain research laboratories, they were less hampered in putting new methods into practice since they did not have such heavy investments in existing processes.

The flexibility of the economy was thus maintained in two ways: by the research and development activities of the large corporations, and by the small companies whose multiplicity, adaptability and ability to enter new fields favoured innovation. The latter in fact exercised a certain pressure to keep the big corporations alert and to prevent their strong economic position from leading to stagnation.

The continuing vitality of small enterprise was even more marked in capitalist countries other than the United States. Notably in France, small enterprises depending on high levels of engineering and other technical skills kept the French tradition of speciality production very much alive.

The growth and power of large business organization were met by large-scale organization of labour. Until the 1930s most American labour organizations were craft unions which flourished especially in industries where small enterprise prevailed, while the large corporations successfully resisted the organization of their workers.

Thereafter collective bargaining was established in principle in the mass-production industries and was achieved in practice by the time of the second world war, although resistance on the part of some employers and in some industries was not dead. Collective contracts, negotiated with large corporations for all their operations and, increasingly, for entire industries, set wages and working conditions for one, two or as much as five years.

The large labour organizations had their own bureaucratic structures, much like those of the corporations. In form they were democratic, with elected officers; in practice the extent to which the structure functioned democratically varied markedly from one union to another.

The position of the union leader had certain unique features, for he was at one and the same time an elected head, a bargaining agent and a recruiter of union members. So long as he was successful in securing the union's demands the membership had little inclination to risk replacing him with someone who might achieve less. There was consequently almost as strong a tendency for the existing union leadership to remain in control of the mass unions as for the existing management to remain in control of the corporations. In some unions, in fact, there was little pretence of offering a choice to the members, and a fight for a change in control of a union tended to become as rare and dramatic as a fight for a change in control of a major corporation.

In addition to acting as bargaining agent for their members, labour unions shared responsibility for carrying out collective contracts. The structure of the corporation and plant was matched by the organization of the workers, with shop stewards to match the foremen and local union officers or business agents to match the higher levels of management. Under the terms of the collective contract, grievance machinery was ordinarily established to handle any question of the failure to carry out the terms of the contract, and union representatives dealt with their opposite numbers at whatever level the matter had to be settled. After the second world war labour unions also came

AA*

to play an important part in community life. As representatives of large segments of the population they were in a position to give or withhold both approval and financial support for civic and welfare projects.

The tendency for labour organizations to become large bureaucratic structures and to participate in the administration of industry was even more marked in other capitalist countries. In some European countries they participated in the administration of certain social benefits or in plant decisions relating to some aspects of production and were sometimes included in boards of directors.

(c) *Government intervention.* The growing power of large economic organizations brought increased intervention in the public interest by the only body with sufficient strength and scope to match corporate power, the central government. Government intervened to regulate the conduct of corporate business in order to prevent fraud against the stockholder, the competitor or the buyer, to prevent the abuse of a monopoly position and to protect labour.

From the early years of the century, the individual American states, and later the federal government (1934), enacted laws to shield investors against fraud. They stipulated the information which must be disclosed to prospective investors when shares of stock or bonds were offered for sale and in the reports of corporate earnings which must be made public. Other laws offered some protection to the buyer, although they only modified to a limited extent the principle of *caveat emptor*—let the buyer beware—which was the accepted legal basis for commercial transactions in general. They required that packaged foods, drugs and cosmetics bear information as to the contents and forbade false or misleading advertising (1906, 1938). Legislation outlawing unfair competitive practices attempted to give the honest producer a chance to compete with the unscrupulous (1912). Checks on the exercise of monopoly power took the form of public utility regulation, laws against combinations in restraint of trade (1890, 1914), limitations on the formation of holding companies to control competing corporations (1935) and the establishment of government enterprise as a yardstick, i.e. a basis for determining whether the costs on which utilities asked approval for their rates were reasonable (1934).

Labour legislation covered hours of work, minimum wages, conditions of safety, child labour and the right of workers to form unions, strike, picket peacefully, and to bargain collectively through representatives of their own choosing (1935, 1938). Social security legislation required contributions from employers for the protection of workers against lack of income (1935).

The government thus provided a framework for the conduct of economic activity which sought to make it serve the public interest. Administrative agencies established to carry out the provisions of this legislation developed a large body of administrative law and procedure relating to the conduct of economic life which went far beyond the principles of commercial law that had provided the legal basis for economic activity at the opening of the century.

The manner in which governments intervened to regulate their respective economies differed from country to country, but the scope and general character covered essentially the same fields and evolved in an essentially similar manner. So also did the direct participation by government in economic activity. Other capitalist countries were more inclined toward government operation than was the United States, especially Britain in the years after the second world war when the Labour party was in power, but the difference among countries was one of degree. Even the reluctant governments undertook hydroelectric and atomic energy developments, built a network of roads, expanded health, education and other services and enlarged their military establishments. The countries which were more inclined to extend government operations entered the same fields of energy production, transport, services and military establishments and left the majority of manufacturing activities in corporate or private hands.

(d) *Breakdown of market mechanism.* The dominant role which came to be played by large organization—the corporation, the labour union and government enterprise—brought a basic change in the character of the American economy and other developed capitalist economies by undermining the market mechanism. The market as an overall regulator was not formally superseded by any alternative structure, as it was in the communist countries by the adoption of central planning. But administration replaced bargaining in many areas and as a result the functioning of the free market was impaired where it continued to serve as the regulator of economic activity.

The market mechanism had depended on adjustment by means of flexible prices. The large corporation which dominated its industry or faced a limited number of competitors set its own price in terms of its costs and the effect which it expected its price policy to have on the market. It fixed its prices for a period of time, revising them only when it deemed a revision to be in its interest. Instead of adjusting to demand by raising or lowering price, it adjusted by increasing or decreasing production, since it was in a position to hold its price and to vary its output. Wages likewise were fixed through collective contracts for periods of time and were as little subject to change in response to fluctuation in the market as were prices; if anything they became even more rigid as labour unions sought security and stability for their members and pressed for contracts extending over longer periods.

In these circumstances the corporation tried to sell as many cars or cigarettes or tons of steel as it could at its established price by capturing as large a share of the market as possible and by expanding the demand for its particular product. This meant high-pressure advertising and the use of brand names and other distinguishing marks to identify the product of the particular company in order that the customer might know and demand it. Mass advertising served the necessary purpose of bringing the products of mass industry to the attention of distant consumers; in the presence of administered prices it took on the additional function of pressing sales, a function which had been accomplished by price adjustment under more competitive conditions.

The importance of this development was not its novelty, but its extent. Industrial concerns making products which could be identified, or supplying local markets where there were few if any competitors, had long set their prices and given their products a distinguishing name; but in the early years of the century these formed only a small part of total output. At that time agricultural products and raw materials, whose prices conformed to market conditions and fluctuated with supply and demand, accounted for a large proportion of the goods which entered into trade, and many manufactured products such as common cotton cloth were made by many producers and were sold without distinction as to their source. What gave the administered prices of the twentieth century their profound impact upon the operation of the economy was the greatly increased proportion of all economic activity represented by industry and, within the industrial sector, by those economic units which were in a position to establish their prices.

The effect of price and wage administration was greatly to increase the instability of the economy. Economic depressions had plagued the industrial economies from their early years, but none had been so severe as the depression of the 1930s. In the economic collapse of these years the prices of manufactured goods produced by large American corporations which dominated their industries, such as automobiles, steel, electrical and farm equipment, fell only a small amount, and wages in these industries remained relatively stable; production, however, dropped as much as 80 per cent, creating tremendous unemployment.

In the face of falling demand, corporations clung to their prices and laid off their workers, uncertain that a lowering of price would increase sales, and preferring the safer road of limited output at a profit to the risk of expanded output at a possible loss. Corporations in other countries followed a similar course, except as they were prevented from doing so by dependence on prices in the world market. Labour unions for their part hung on to their wage structure to protect those of their members who were still employed, preferring to guard what they could control, though it meant loss of membership and protected only the workers who retained their jobs.

Meanwhile in the agriculture sector price flexibility prevailed and the farmer faced declining markets and declining prices. Unable to control his prices his only recourse was to keep up or increase his production in the hope of making something, however little, from the sale of his produce. While industrial workers were idle, farmers worked harder than ever for little or no returns. The fact that the agricultural sector of the economy continued to operate on the basis of the free market may be credited with saving the industrial countries from starvation during the depression, for food continued to be produced and was sold for what it would bring; but it did not save the farmer from bankruptcy and often foreclosure of the mortgage on his farm.

(e) *Measures for economic stability.* Faced with the evidence that the historic mechanism of adjustment had broken down so severely as to endanger the whole society, governments intervened with measures designed to achieve economic recovery and to maintain economic stability.

In the United States these measures included an effort to rescue agriculture by means of a programme to support farm prices, in part by limiting the production of major crops. In order to reduce speculation in the stock market, which had brought heavy losses to many investors, requirements were raised as to the proportion of each purchase which must be in the form of cash. Expanded programmes of public works were undertaken to provide employment to the unemployed. Extensions of unemployment insurance, economic assistance and other social security measures helped to maintain incomes.

As these and other measures were undertaken in the effort to bring economic recovery, it became clear that the government would have to assume positive responsibility for maintaining economic stability once full employment was obtained. In the Employment Act of 1946 the Congress of the United States declared it to be the continuing policy and responsibility of the federal government to promote maximum employment, production and purchasing power by all practical means and placed responsibility directly upon the highest executive and legislative authorities. European governments made similar commitments.

By the middle of the century a wide range of stabilizing devices existed to counteract the threat of economic instability. Some of these were structural and acted as built-in stabilizers. Agricultural price supports, restraints on stock-market speculation and expanded social insurance and assistance programmes, once introduced to combat depression, became permanent features of the economy; high progressive tax rates on individual incomes and corporate earnings provided for an automatic drop in tax collections when incomes fell. Increased general government expenditures for expanded services and for the civil and military establishments, however, did not respond automatically to business fluctuations.

A number of other factors increased the likelihood that the actions of both business and government would contribute to stability. Information on which business, labour and government could plan and act was being collected in a more extensive and systematic fashion, including data covering prices, living costs, employment, unemployment, wages, earnings, investment and money supply. The spread of automation involving large capital investment made uninterrupted high-level production more vital to success, and the recourse of reduced production to maintain profits became less feasible.

Governments had the means to control the money supply so as to permit the creation of additional money when needed, and to adjust fiscal policy in order to expand purchasing power either by increased government spending or decreased taxes or both. For control over the money supply, the United States government strengthened the central financial institution, the federal reserve system, and entrusted it with responsibility and power to keep the money in the country at a volume to sustain a high level of production and employment. Although many government expenditures could not be postponed or expanded to help stabilize economic activity, spending for public works such as roads, public buildings, harbour improvements or parks could be increased if a depression threatened, construction of hydroelectric or other major projects could be speeded up and there was some flexibility in the operation of government services. At the same time tax rates could be reduced and additional purchasing power could be provided by financing expanded government expenditures through borrowing from the banks rather than by withdrawing spending power from the public in the form of taxes. The reverse procedure might be used to check inflation when this arose from excessive demand.

The measures undertaken by other capitalist countries, either their built-in stabilizers or those designed to counteract tendencies toward depression, differed in detail and were affected by the relative independence of the national economy or its dependence on foreign trade. But all were designed to sustain demand when it threatened to drop and thus to prevent a reduction in production from creating serious unemployment and setting in motion a downward spiral which could not be counted on to reverse itself. All involved control over the volume of money and the use of government fiscal policy. Adjustment of government spending could be an even more potent device in European countries than in the United States, for government expenditures in the 1950s amounted to a third of national income in Great Britain and to a quarter in France and Sweden as compared with a fifth in the United States.

At mid-century it had not yet been established whether these controls would in fact be applied with the necessary skill and judgment and whether they would be effective against depression if put to a severe test, for they faced no such real test in the years after the second world war. During the 1950s the United States economy experienced several small recessions which slowed its rate of growth and occasioned some unemployment. The European economies grew steadily and rapidly after their post-war recovery. In any case it was clear that no government was prepared to allow a major depression to descend upon its people as it had in the past, and all were prepared to take the positive measures which they thought would be effective in preserving stability and sustaining a high level of economic activity.

(f) *Adjustment of international economic relations.* As countries controlled their internal currencies and took measures to combat unemployment and to guard against its recurrence, the mechanism of international trade had to be rebuilt. In the presence of these internal controls, the traditional means of international economic adjustment no longer sufficed and the free market forces were partially replaced by devices to manage the flow of trade, monetary payments and capital.

During the first world war the measures taken by the several countries to finance war activity had completely disrupted the pre-war relationship among the currencies of the industrial countries. The resulting disparities were so great that the attempt to restore the old pattern seemed out of the question, and countries abandoned the effort to return to the international gold standard. Although they retained gold as a means of paying for imports which exceeded their exports, they adopted managed currencies whose quantity was not proportionately affected by the flow of gold in or out of the country. The depression of the 1930s brought a tendency for countries to seek to make their economies more self-sufficient in order to insulate them from fluctuations taking place in other countries. This trend toward autarchy was most marked in the countries which were also engaged in a vigorous military build-up, Nazi Germany and Japan, but even Britain abandoned its traditional free trade policy, raised tariffs and worked out a plan of empire preference.

The impact of the second world war further shifted the relations among the economies of the industrial countries and left them at the close of the war even further than they had been at the end of the first world war from the possibility of using the traditional free flow of gold as a mechanism of adjustment. Countries retained their wartime powers to set quotas on imports and exports, to restrict the spending of their currencies abroad and to limit capital movements, using these powers to prevent their internal programmes for economic reconstruction and stabilization from being undermined by an adverse balance of payments.

As new international economic relationships emerged and new techniques for international economic adjustment were developed in the period following the second world war, these unilateral protective controls were gradually relaxed, though they did not wholly disappear. The new techniques consisted in the establishment of the International Monetary Fund and the International Bank for Reconstruction and Development and in a series of intergovernmental arrangements involving economic aid, mutual exchange and the creation of common economic communities of interest.

The International Monetary Fund was set up in 1945 as a mechanism for adjusting imbalances in international payments that might arise. For this purpose it was given authority to work out with the countries concerned the relationships among their several currencies, and it was provided with funds to assist in maintaining the relationships which were established. The Fund maintained a pool of the currencies of member countries and was thus in a position to lend the currency of one country to another in order to tide a country over a temporary inability to meet its international payments without exhausting its reserves of gold and deposits in foreign banks.

The International Bank facilitated the international flow of capital by lending to governments the funds deposited with it by member countries and those secured from private sources through the sale of its bonds; later, plans were made for the provision of risk capital through international channels.

The capital funds required for the reconstruction of the European economies proved too large to be supplied through any mechanism which required their repayment. To meet this situation the United States established what was known as the Marshall Plan for intergovernmental economic aid and collaborated with the European countries in the rebuilding of their economies. These countries, in turn, found their historic separateness an obstacle to their respective efforts to regain the economic position from which wartime destruction and the loss of colonial possessions had dislodged them and to restore a basis for the full employment and rising living standards of their people. Step by step they drew their economies closer together through a series of mutual adjustments in trade, quotas, tariffs and monetary relationships, through the establishment of the European Coal and Iron Community to develop these basic industries for the continent as a whole, and, finally, in 1957, through the agreement to create a Common European Market and a common means, Euratom, for exploiting the economic potentials of atomic energy. By these measures the European economies, restored to vigour, began to be reoriented toward the economic potentials of a common European domestic economy.

In the economic relations between the industrialized and the non-industrial countries, governmental action to provide economic aid and to direct the flow of capital was added to the old pattern of profit-seeking foreign investment. Private oil and mining companies continued to invest in overseas ventures and manufacturing companies established branch plants to assemble automobiles, produce synthetic fibres or process local foods. But the position and role of these enterprises were altered as the developing countries erected barriers to the foreign exploitation of their resources and made positive efforts to bring foreign funds into their development plans. Capital-supplying countries supported these efforts through United Nations technical aid and loans by the International Bank, and through assistance and loan programmes of the United States and countries co-operating through the Colombo Plan.

(g) *The capitalist ethic.* [9, 10] Although the institutions of the capitalist economies underwent major changes during these years, many of the basic drives that sustained early industrial development continued to operate in the capitalist industrial countries. The 'capitalist ethic' continued to sanction and give dignity to work, the quest for material success and the accumulation of wealth, and to condenm idleness, waste and indifference to material goals. In the United States, as well as in other countries such as Germany, the Netherlands, Sweden and Great Britain where capitalist economies were highly developed, it not only permeated the business community but entered the viewpoint of the farmer, or of the mechanic who looked for an opportunity to set up his own enterprise, or of the professional man who was expected to combine economic success with the performing of his professional service. Although the desire for security was intensified by the great depression, and drives within the industrial bureaucracies were often for power or prestige rather than simply for personal profit, the capitalist societies continued to regard the undertaking and conduct of profit-seeking enterprise as normal behaviour, and to accord respect and prestige to those who were successful in it.

The imperatives of this ethic were modified in form by changes in economic structure and social conditions. The American business community generally accepted the concept that profit could best be sought by producing and selling a large volume with a small margin on each unit rather than by a large mark-up on each of a small number of units. Elsewhere this principle was somewhat less generally accepted, especially where, as in France, there was a tradition of quality production for a limited market. High wages linked with high pro-ductivity were recognized as the source of a mass market. The goal of con-sumption, a high standard of living, became central for labour and for all segments of the public. Thrift and saving for its own sake lost some of its virtue as the notion spread that spending keeps the wheels of industry turning and as social measures provided minimum economic security. Much saving was invested in durable goods for current use rather than put away against a rainy day. Advertising played on every sort of desire and emotion in the process of stimulating consumption.

Goals of consumption themselves took new shapes as the economy became more productive. They were no longer expressed in terms of survival but in terms of sharing the fruits of modern industry. Many of the patterns of con-sumption which had distinguished the middle and upper classes from the lower no longer set them apart. The masses of the people ate much the same nourishing food, wore clothes in the street which made them virtually indistinguishable from all but the most elegant of the well-to-do, lived in houses which had many of the same comforts and household conveniences, drove similar cars, travelled and enjoyed holidays, sports and cinemas and had gardens, cameras or other hobbies. The levelling effect of high consumption patterns was most marked in the United States but it was at work in all the advanced capitalist economies.

Although couched in material terms, the goal of a high standard of living which motivated individuals and received the sanction of society had more than a material meaning. For it meant acceptance of the concept that poverty was unnecessary and that man by his efforts had achieved the means to con-quer this ancient enemy. It carried the idea that to free man from material want was to free the human spirit and release human potentialities. And it meant that this freedom and release was not the privilege of the few but the birthright of all.

In this vision, the productivity of industry and the social institutions for the common welfare combined to create the conditions for a life of greater human dignity and satisfaction. This concept was expressed in a study of freedom and welfare in the five Scandinavian countries, sponsored by the welfare ministers of these states: 'The living standard of any nation depends primarily upon the volume of goods and services which it produces. Social benefits, whatever their description may be, are part of this living standard. . . . The goal pursued by the Northern peoples is simple. They want to make their countries a place worth living in for free men and women. . . . To realize this goal requires work and increased productivity; and it requires cooperation in a spirit of practical solidarity.'*

In the words of Britain's Labour prime minister, Clement Attlee, 'the new privileged class is everywhere in the perambulators'. Its members were the new generation of children born into societies which had achieved the means, adopted the determination and developed the institutions to offer material well-being to all their people.

2. *The socialist economy of the* USSR *and other communist countries*

The economic system of the USSR represented the first attempt to build a modern economy in a communist state. It provided an example which other states under communist control could follow in the development of their economic structures.

Only the most general principles for the design of such an economic structure were provided by Marxist theory. Marx described in detail what he considered the weaknesses and evils of the capitalist system and made it clear that a socialist economy would eliminate these features, most especially private ownership of the means of production and repeated economic crises. But on detailed guide-lines for alternative forms of organization Marx was silent. He regarded the new social–economic formation as having two phases, the first and lower phase being socialism and the second and higher phase complete communism. He saw the state as a necessary instrument during the first phase and expected it to wither away in the higher phase with the development of a communist society.

Marx lived in a time when most industrial activity was carried on in relatively small enterprises and he formulated his general expectations in terms of the direct control of production by workers. Lenin, confronted with large and complex economic units, thought of the economy as functioning like a single centralized economic enterprise. His major theoretical contribution to the development of the Soviet economy was his concept of the socialist state as the main instrument of the working class in building a national economy based on socialization of the main means of production. He conceived of the Party as the revolutionary spearhead which should not only assume disciplined direction of the seizure of power, but should continue to play the same role in the organization and operation of the socialist society. In assigning the Party this role, he entrusted it with political and economic generalship and expected that it would be able to work out the structure and operation of the economic system. Moreover, he believed that the modernization of industry was the indispensable condition to achieve socialism,

* *Freedom and Welfare, op. cit.,* pp. 517, 521.

expressing this view in his oft-quoted dictum 'electricity plus soviets equal socialism'.

(a) *Condition of the Russian economy*. The structure built by Lenin and his associates in the early years of the Soviet state and the devices which they created were pragmatically designed to meet the situations with which they had to cope. These situations were difficult and exacting. The country's economy was broken by the destruction and disorganization of the first world war, the Revolution, and the years of intervention and civil war. As a result of these catastrophes the output of large-scale industry in 1920 was scarcely one-seventh of the pre-revolutionary rate and the level of national income was reduced to little more than a third; the burden of homeless, ill, orphaned, uprooted and unemployed was tremendous. The pressing task of putting the pieces together was the first which confronted the Soviet leaders as they sought a way to build a viable economy, and it required six or seven years to accomplish this task after the end of the civil war and intervention.

The second condition faced throughout the forty years following the October revolution was the constant expectation of war. Communist doctrine, and the experience of intervention during the civil war, taught that the capitalist world would not permit a communist society to grow in peace. Although after Lenin's death in 1924 leadership passed to the faction led by Stalin who thought it possible to build socialism in one state without its being sustained by world revolution, the belief persisted that such a state must be prepared to withstand attack from its inevitable enemies. By definition the communist state under these conditions must be a defence state, and the socialist economy must be a defence economy, while it developed the basis for expansion and met the minimum needs of the population. The Nazi invasion of June 1941 justified the expectation of attack and the second world war repeated on a huge scale the destruction of the first. Loss of the main industrial areas to invading armies forced the removal of industry to the east beyond the Urals and required an intense effort to make up the loss and to rebuild the destroyed area as rapidly as possible after the war. Continuing international tension in the period following the second world war kept military defence a major aspect of the economy.

The institutions of the Soviet economy were thus designed under conditions of two major periods of disaster and reconstruction and a continual state of fear and expectation of the need for military defence. The need to establish an industrial base as advanced as that of major capitalist countries to enable the communist system to compete with the capitalist was reinforced by the overriding importance of defence.

Defence, in turn, was seen in relation to Russia's experience of repeated military defeat by more industrially advanced countries, by Sweden in the eighteenth century, France in 1812, Britain and France in the Crimean war of the 1850s, by newly industrialized Japan in 1905, by the invading German armies in the first world war. It meant not merely a strong military establishment but the industrial potential to sustain modern warfare. The drive to expand heavy industry rapidly and at all costs reflected the conviction that only thus could the defence needs of the régime be met and survival be ensured. The development of heavy industry was also urgently needed to provide agriculture with modern machinery and to modernize the light industries, food processing and transport.

The natural conditions upon which the Soviet economy rested were the enormous and varied resources of the great Russian land-mass, many still unexplored, and the rigorous Russian climate, excessively cold in moist regions to the north and excessively dry in many warm areas. These provided the potential and set some of the limits for economic development.

When the communist régime came to power the economy was predominantly agricultural—about 80 per cent of the population was still engaged in agriculture—but the industrial segment had been growing very rapidly in the previous fifty years and included large enterprises. From 1861 on, the tsarist government had taken a variety of measures to encourage industrial expansion: railway construction had opened up the country and linked European Russia with the Pacific; the Donbas-Krivoy Rog coal and iron complex had been developed; Baku oil resources had been brought into production. During several periods between 1885 and 1913 the rate of industrial growth in Russia had exceeded the current rate in the United States, Britain or Germany; from 1890 to 1900 the annual rate of expansion in industrial production had reached an estimated 8 per cent. Russia's relatively late start, however, meant that the extent of industrialization, even before the destruction of the first world war and the civil war, was much less than that of the major industrial countries.

A large proportion of the industrial expansion under the tsars, notably in mining, chemical, metal fabrication, woodworking and textile industries, had been achieved with foreign capital. Half of all the capital in Russian joint-stock companies in 1900 was from foreign sources, about 90 per cent French, British, German and Belgian, while loans from France, Holland and elsewhere had financed much of the railway construction. The vast natural resources of the country had made tsarist Russia an attractive field for foreign investment. A great deal of the machinery and equipment came from abroad, and numbers of foreign technicians supplemented the competent but small group of Russians trained in high-quality Russian technical institutes or abroad. After the October revolution a large part of the organizational, financial and technical resources which had contributed to pre-Soviet industrial expansion was thus not available to facilitate continued growth.

The labour force consisted of a large body of peasants, many of whom were underemployed and therefore available for transfer to industry, and an industrial proletariat of which an estimated 20 per cent retained rural roots and worked part of the year in agriculture while the majority had become permanent urban workers.

From the time of the emancipation of the serfs in the 1860s until 1905 the majority of the peasants had been collectively responsible through their communes (*mir*) for redemption payments entitling them to the lands released to them on emancipation. They were thus held more or less closely within communal groups and were subject to communally established planting patterns. Under the Stolypin reforms of 1906 redemption payments were no longer exacted and individual peasants could demand their share of the land, to cultivate according to their own design or to sell. By 1915 more than half of the peasant households held their land in hereditary tenure, but only a tenth of them cultivated land which had been consolidated into independent farms. The vast majority of all peasants were engaged in subsistence farming by primitive methods, they were in debt to landowners and even if they acquired title to land they often lost it. They generally farmed in collective groups, whether they owned strips individually or worked land which still belonged to the village community. There was profound discontent among the peasants and a constant struggle for land. Industrial workers for their part had repeatedly been subjected to repressive measures against the formation of unions and efforts to improve working conditions.

Both peasants and urban workers were generally uneducated. Three-quarters of the total population over 9 years of age was illiterate; among women only about one out of ten could read and write. A large number of independent artisans, who provided many of the consumer goods especially in rural villages, possessed craft skills. A few able members of the lower classes, including some of the revolutionary leaders, had been able to enter the system of higher and technical education which served primarily the members of the upper classes. The Soviet economic leaders thus had available an under-employed and undertrained agricultural labour force, accustomed to restraint and collective responsibility, from which had already been recruited a smaller but considerable body of industrial workers.

(*b*) *Initial steps in socialization.* In the initial stages, the period of war communism, 1918–21, when the main problem was to meet the emergency and to bring some kind of order out of chaos, the state acted rapidly to nationalize land, banking, industrial enterprises, wholesale and retail trade, and most urban housing, as well as continuing to control former state enterprises such as railways and communications systems. Grain was requisitioned to feed the urban population. In the factories, works councils guided by Party members began to direct production. The Supreme Economic Council, created in 1917, was at first mainly engaged in trouble-shooting—breaking bottlenecks as they arose in order to keep the factories somehow supplied with materials and equipment; thereafter it began to devote itself to the work of directing national enterprises.

Production however declined disastrously in the face of continuous warfare and inexperience in economic administration. The system of requisitioning affected grain production unfavourably. With the end of civil war and intervention it appeared to Lenin and his associates in 1921 that individual incentives, especially for the peasantry, would have to be employed for the time being in order to achieve the momentum for expansion and to allow time for planning processes to be developed to the point where they could effectively guide the economy. The New Economic Policy (N.E.P.) therefore introduced a considerably lighter tax in kind, permitted private trade and allowed peasants to sell a substantial proportion of their produce.

During the next seven years these relaxations of the principle of socialist production and distribution served as a stimulus to the agricultural production needed to feed the growing urban industrial population and for export to purchase machinery essential to industrial expansion until Russia's own machine-making capacity could be increased. The N.E.P. however was never regarded as part of a permanent structure but only as a temporary device. As soon as the rehabilitation of the national economy began to bring an increase in the production of commodities and in state and co-operative trade, private traders were subjected to unfavourable taxes, difficulties in securing supplies and transport and intensified competition from the expanding network of state stores and wholesale agencies. By 1928 the share of retail trade in the hands of private traders had been reduced from approximately 72 to 22 per cent; in 1932 private trading by merchants was forbidden.

At the same time that the N.E.P. was inaugurated the first large-scale attempts at planning were undertaken, in recognition of the fact that the crucial problem of permanent economic organization was how to substitute planning for the free market which acted as the regulator of capitalist economies. In February 1921 the State Planning Commission (later renamed State Planning Committee) or Gosplan was set up. A special commission had already been created to make a comprehensive proposal for the development of electricity. The electric development plan as adopted in December 1920 not only called for the construction over a ten- to fifteen-year period of some thirty electric power stations, but set output goals for coal, iron ore, pig iron, steel and other basic products. It was subsequently incorporated into the first five-year plan when the latter was formulated.

By 1928 the planning mechanism had been developed to the point where it could serve as the major instrument of economic policy and direction. The first five-year plan, developed under a directive of the fifteenth Congress of the Communist party, December 1927, came into effect in September 1928. The planning system involved both the design of a plan and its execution, with mechanisms for checking the conformity of practice to the plan as laid down and measures to bring the execution into line when goals were not being met.

(c) *Collectivization of agriculture.* In such a system all major areas of the economy needed to be subject to unified direction. The backward, scattered, individual peasant households which under the N.E.P. remained outside centralized control were out of line with the growing, concentrated industry. The lack of centralization in agriculture and the very low marketable surplus offered a threat to the success of the programme and led to the determination to undertake the remaking of agriculture by uniting individual small households into co-operative collective farms. The first five-year plan called for a large increase, from $2 \cdot 7$ to $17 \cdot 3$ per cent, in the proportion of farming to be carried on by collectives or state farms. During the following years, an intensive drive to liquidate the class of individual capitalistic farmers known as *kulaks* brought agriculture within the system of control much more rapidly than the plan had envisaged. By 1931 two-thirds of the crop land and more than half of the people engaged in agriculture had been brought within the system of collective and state farms; by 1936 collectivization of agriculture was very nearly complete.

The cost of this operation was so high both in terms of production and in loss of life that the government took steps to slow it down temporarily, and to check the pressure of over-zealous Party workers and poor peasants impatient for land. Peasants who resisted collectivization often slaughtered their livestock, cutting both draught animals and other livestock by more than half; the famine which resulted and the rigours of expulsion and work camps claimed over a million lives. It was, however, considered essential to the overall structure of an economy organized and operated through the mechanism of central planning.[11]

(*d*) *Development of planning mechanism and techniques.* The development of the planning mechanism, its continuous extension into more and more details of economic life, and the elaboration of devices for control and adjustment of the enormous and endlessly complex economy of the Soviet Union was a feat of economic organization hitherto unparalleled in the history of mankind. The disappearance of private property in the means of production did not remove any of the basic problems of administration and co-ordination of enterprise, of relating cost to return, of securing supply and of co-ordinating the volume and flow of production so that the output of myriads of products would be in balance and the output of a piece of machinery would not be held up for lack of a screw or switch or other necessary part.

The first five-year plan, 1928–32, covered in practice only some fifty industries as compared with more than twice that number covered in much greater detail by the second five-year plan. Its method was to set a series of minimum targets which industries were to meet, or if possible to exceed, within the prescribed period. By setting targets for the most crucial industries and by designating some of these as 'leading links', it established a set of priorities in the supply of fuel and raw materials and in financing. If certain industries lagged behind but the leading links met or exceeded prescribed goals, the main objectives of the plan would not be vitiated. It was triumphantly announced that the plan had been fulfilled ahead of schedule in gross production on the basis of over-fulfilment of goals for items such as machinery and electrical equipment, although a number of other products fell short of the objectives set.

Successive plans expanded the number of industries covered—branches of transport, agriculture and trade—and the detail with which sub-targets as well as major goals were spelled out. By the fifth five-year plan, applying to the period 1951–55, the technique had been so fully elaborated that the total plan covered in considerable detail virtually all parts of the economy and culture and approached a balanced programme calling for the meeting of exact goals, or co-ordinated acceleration, rather than spotty overfulfilment of parts.

In the development of planning techniques two approaches initially vied for favour. One group of planners favoured a method which projected past performance into the future in terms of what might prudently be expected to happen, and set modest and 'realistic' goals. This method did not envisage high tempos. The alternative approach was to set goals in relation to the needs of the Soviet state, however difficult of achievement they might seem, and then to marshal every possible resource and every possible effort to overcome difficulties in growth and to reach the objective.

By the time of the first five-year plan the second approach had received the approval of the Party leadership as a revolutionary, progressive approach; those who advocated the more conservative procedure had been removed from an active role in the planning process, and the Russian economy was mobilized for the priority task of developing heavy industry and of creating an expanding base which would provide the military potential and permit a future expansion in consumer goods and food.

During the dictatorship of Stalin nothing and nobody was allowed to stand in the way of what Stalin regarded as the only course which would meet the political conditions of these years.[12] Those who advocated an alternative course became 'enemies of the State'. If something had to be given up somewhere in the economic programme and plan, on the fulfilment of which the country's independence and life depended, it was given up. This generally meant cutting the production of consumer goods and services, except for those such as education and public health which were essential to provide the literate, well-trained and efficient labour force which industrial development and cultural progress required.

The planning process was headed by the State Planning Committee which drew up not only the periodic five-year plans but annual, more detailed plans adjusted in the light of the progress toward fulfilment of the overall plan. From the time of its formation the Gosplan gradually built up a technical staff, not only at the centre but for geographic subdivisions and for separate industries and branches of production. A reporting system headed by a central statistical administration was also established in order to provide the essential tools for designing a plan and observing its execution. In time every industry and geographical area down to the smallest unit developed its planning mechanism, some as part of the Gosplan organization, others under one of the many ministries, others as a part of the party machinery.

National plans were formulated through a continual process of interaction and negotiation between the higher and lower authorities, those at lower levels commenting on goals proposed from above and offering counterproposals. Every effort was made to encourage lower units to offer to fulfil higher goals than those originally proposed. Final decisions taken by the higher authority became the required objectives for all. Frequent reports on fulfilment, made from lower to higher units and reaching the statistical administration, were designed to provide a continuous record of progress and to make it possible to detect and avert impending difficulties. In crucial industries details of plans were sometimes revised from month to month or more frequently in the effort to meet contingencies that might arise.

(e) *Organization and administration.* The administrative structure for conducting the various segments of the economy in line with the plans consisted of ministries at the top and enterprises at the bottom. Some major enterprises were directly responsible to a ministry; many were linked in combines or trusts which in turn were responsible to a ministry. The number of ministries and their scope varied from time to time as policy alternated between consolidating functions in a few ministries and distributing them on a more specialized basis. Under the central ministries the major heavy industries were directed on a nation-wide basis without regard to the administrative political divisions of the country; other industries, such as building materials, cotton or timber and paper, were conducted by union–republic ministries, with major direct responsibility resting in the hands of the ministries of the separate republics, co-ordinated by the corresponding central ministry. In 1957 the decision was taken to decentralize a larger proportion of the responsibility carried by the central ministries and to place it in the hands of agencies of the component geographical units—local councils of national economy.

The structure of economic administration was integrated with the overall administration of the state. At the highest level the Council of Ministers and its Presidium directed both the economy and all other state activity. For the union–republic industries, ministries of the several republics working with the corresponding central ministry carried responsibility within their area. Throughout all levels of the economy, as in all other areas of Soviet life, the Communist party acted as a spearhead to organize and take the lead, ever alert for the fulfilment of objectives. At the centre the Presidium of the Central Committee of the Communist Party and the party congresses established or accepted the goals. Party organs down to the factory and trade-union level assumed responsibility for watching and stimulating the execution of the plans.

Organs of both state and Party at all levels functioned as mechanisms of control, to keep track of development and to hold responsible those who might fall behind. The Gosplan through its representatives throughout the country kept constant check; the Ministry of Finance, through the State Bank and also through the tax collection officials, kept a check on the financial aspects; the Communist party, through its production departments directly subordinate to the Central Committee of the party and through party units at every level down to the factory cell, made special investigations or kept a running record of success or failure in meeting prescribed levels of output.

Trade unions after 1930 had as their main function helping to achieve production goals. During the 1920s there were differences of opinion as to the proper function of trade unions, Leon Trotsky insisting that they were properly arms of the proletariat state for achieving common economic objectives while the head of the trade unions, Mikhail Tomsky, maintained that their function was to represent the workers *vis-à-vis* the state, their employer. Lenin termed the trade unions 'the school of government, the school of communism' but insisted that they should not assume direct functions of government. In 1930 at the sixteenth Congress of the Communist party, the view represented by Tomsky was officially held to be a carry-over of trade-unionist thinking, appropriate to employer–worker relations under capitalism rather than to the conditions of a communist society, and the unions were made responsible for stimulating their members to reach production goals, organizing shock brigades and otherwise sustaining a high level of worker effort, discipline, competence and conformity to party policy and programme.

The ministries, trusts and enterprises constituted, necessarily, huge and complex bureaucracies. Major enterprises and trusts were comparable to the largest of the American or European corporations in size and complexity of structure; the ministries responsible for groups of trusts and enterprises were of course far larger. The immediate and continual problems of economic organization were thus the problems inherent in the structure and functioning of all bureaucracies.

Within the general framework of planning and direction each enterprise had a semi-independent status and identity. Although it was a government entity it operated under a separate charter, not unlike government corporations in non-communist countries. Its operations were expected to show at least the 'planned profit', except where an essential enterprise was planned to operate at a loss with the aid of a government subsidy. The enterprise's account at the State Bank, consisting of whatever capital funds were provided for it under the plan and a revolving fund for current operations, served as a device for financial recording and accounting. Relationships between enterprises were conducted as between independent buyers and sellers, within the physical limits set by the allocation of materials and the assigned quotas and goals, and with the wages, prices and turnover tax rates fixed by the control bodies. Each enterprise was required to achieve a financial as well as a physical balance and to meet its production goals within a framework set by fixed prices and wages and by the physical programme for related enterprises.

Up to the mid-1950s the primary instruments of planning were the physical goals and quotas; adjustments in prices were used to facilitate the realization of these physical objectives but were not in themselves the main means of controlling output. Wholesale prices for use between enterprises were set at a level calculated to encourage the production of needed commodities and to put pressure on enterprise managers to reduce costs. They were based on the costs which the planning agency considered reasonable, average or attainable for the entire industry, plus a planned profit. Sometimes they were set for regional segments of an industry where costs might differ, as for example between high and low-cost coal- or oil-producing areas. Managers of enterprises whose costs exceeded those calculated by the planners were thus under pressure to lower their costs.

Prices of some products were set below reasonable costs in order to stimulate other industries for which they constituted raw materials, as for example low prices set for metals and other materials essential to the machinery industry during the early 1930s, and reduction in the price of building materials in order to lower building costs in 1950. Where prices were held down for the benefit of other industries, losses were made up by government subsidy. When a broad revision of many industrial prices and freight rates was put through in 1949–50, the stated principles on which the new prices were based were: to enable enterprises, practically, to operate profitably according to plan and to avoid the need for subsidies; to stimulate output of deficit or especially necessary products and simultaneously limit their consumption in production; to discourage unnecessary transport, use rolling-stock efficiently, encourage water transport and enable railways to operate without loss.

(f) *Capital formation.* From the beginning the aim of the Soviet system was a self-contained economy independent of the capitalist world. The vast Russian territory with its rich natural resources provided the physical basis for such development, and high priority was immediately given to geological exploration and prospecting in order to discover the unexplored mineral wealth on which a major industrial development could be based. Until Russian heavy industry could be developed, however, much foreign equipment was needed in order to speed up the exploitation of these resources and to lay the basis for self-contained growth. The extremely rapid industrial development of the late 1920s and the 1930s was greatly facilitated by the use of equipment and techniques developed abroad.

Little foreign capital, however, was available to finance imports of mining machinery, electric generators and other equipment, although in the 1920s some foreign companies received concessions to operate mining or manufacturing concerns. A communist state dedicated to the elimination of private ownership in the means of production was hardly in a position to attract extensive foreign investment, even if it had wished to do so. Some foreign credits helped slightly to finance machinery imports, but these debts were liquidated by 1938. Most imports were purchased with the major product available for export, grain. In the early 1930s grain was also exported, even from famine areas, to purchase large numbers of tractors to provide the basis for collectivized agriculture and to replace the horses which had been slaughtered by peasants resisting collectivization.

In the absence of foreign sources the capital for industrial expansion came from the Russian people in the form of restraints on consumption. The major source was a turnover tax levied on all goods at the point where they changed hands. Roughly three-fifths of all the state revenue for financing both economic development and governmental administration was generally provided by this tax. The biggest part of this, amounting to more than two-thirds in 1939, was paid through the several ministries responsible for agriculture and food, and thus came largely from the peasants. It was reflected in the wide difference between the low prices paid to farmers for grain and the high prices charged to urban consumers for food. Most of the remainder was paid on other consumer goods. In addition to the turnover tax a share of the profits of each enterprise was allocated to the state investment fund. Some 10 per cent of the state budget came from this source and additional amounts from state loans and direct taxes on the population. These taxes and loans furnished the capital for industrial expansion.

Emphasis on fixed capital creation and the development of heavy industry and military resources set physical limits on the amount of goods available for consumption, as for example urban housing which remained in very short supply throughout these forty years, and other consumer goods which because of their low priority often fell below their production goals. Restraints on consumption offered a feasible method of securing the capital needed for expansion because they were accompanied by effective incentives and controls.

(g) *Incentives*.[13] The motivations relied upon for the operation of the Soviet economy were a combination of rewards and threats, of positive stimuli, both material and non-material, and of direct controls. The full impact of the state's instruments of propaganda was brought to bear to give prestige, emotional satisfaction and recognition to those who overfulfilled their quotas or otherwise demonstrated co-operation with economic objectives. Posters, wall newspapers, radio appeals and slogans exhorted the workers; publicly posted records permitted comparison and stimulated competition among them; public recognition through the awarding of prizes and titles of commendation, as well as the fundamental attitudes which the entire educational system was designed to build up, provided stimuli for the kind of effort required to keep the economy functioning and growing.

More tangible rewards took the form for managers of advancement through the bureaucratic hierarchy, and perquisites of office such as comfortable homes or cars in a society where these remained scarce. For workers they consisted in piece rates or other forms of incentive pay to stimulate and reward superior effort and to encourage workers to seek additional training in order to qualify for higher paid employment. A director's fund, consisting of a small percentage of planned profits and a larger proportion of profits over the planned amount, was set aside in each enterprise for extra expansion of plant and construction of workers' housing and for special bonuses or other recognition of outstanding workers. The increased pay and prestige received by the

Stakhanovites who exceeded production norms encouraged workers to increase their productivity.

Positive incentives, which played the main role in increasing the productivity of labour, were supplemented by a system of sanctions—demotion, transfer to an undesirable locality, or more severe penalties for those whose failure was judged to constitute sabotage—applied to negligent workers who violated decisions and orders of organs of the state. The security police were expected to detect this as well as all other forms of suspected disloyalty or failure to support the aims and objectives of the state. Direct restraints took the form of limitations on the right of workers to leave their employment, for which they required permission of the manager of the enterprise in the years 1940 to 1956. A large proportion of the youth were drafted into the labour reserve which was established in 1940, given technical training and assigned to specific industries and tasks. Other graduates from technical or other schools were placed in employment where they were needed, with little choice of where they would work. Finally, those who resisted the state provided a supply of forced labour for the most distasteful tasks in remote areas or under exceptionally harsh conditions.

In difficult situations the balance of motivations might lead to conduct which sometimes impeded the progress of the economy rather than promoted it. Some managers who felt themselves too much pressed and feared the consequence of failure to meet what seemed to them to be unrealistic objectives, might resort to hoarding of material or workers and other wasteful practices by which they sought to protect themselves against the danger of being unable to fulfil their quotas. Where some of an enterprise's products could be more profitably produced than others, managers were tempted to shift the proportion of production in favour of these, though the needs of the economy might call for a larger proportion of the less profitable items. There was a temptation to cut quality, especially on consumer goods which enjoyed a low priority and for which it was often difficult to secure the necessary materials. Examples of such practices were reported and discussed from time to time in the press. But the preponderance of evidence indicated that in the industrial sector the positive motivations which were invoked were successful in identifying the efforts of the great majority of the people with the requirements of rapid economic development.

In the agricultural sector the response was less satisfactory. Agricultural productivity was increased sufficiently to permit the recruitment from the rural areas of a large labour force for industrial expansion. Up to the mid-1950s, however, the expansion in agricultural production over the level of 1913 only slightly exceeded the increase in population. Agricultural production, especially livestock, received severe setbacks during wars and the period of collectivization. The problem of guiding and supervising many thousands of scattered units, even when organized as collectives, of providing the necessary incentives and of integrating the whole with the rest of the economy proved one of the most stubborn problems in the organization of the Soviet economy.

Various devices were adopted from time to time in the effort to meet this situation: peasants were allowed to cultivate personal plots in addition to participating in collective farm operations; selected urban workers were sent to collective farms to impart their drive and enthusiasm toward meeting goals. Major scientific efforts were made to expand production. Scientists developed strains of grain which would mature in colder areas with shorter growing seasons. Artificial insemination was extensively used to improve the quality of the livestock. Shelter belts of trees were planted to protect farms on the steppes from hot drying winds. Ambitious projects were launched to irrigate desert regions or to extend grazing areas by providing water for stock.

In spite of these efforts production data disclosed after the death of Stalin revealed a continued failure of agriculture to advance. New efforts to raise agricultural production were then launched by offering better rewards and increased responsibilities to collective farmers and by a vast programme to bring under cultivation virgin lands in the east. All these measures were designed to overcome the obstacles presented by the unfavourable Russian climate, and to raise the volume and efficiency of agricultural production to a point where it could offer an improved level of living to the people of the USSR and could continue to provide a supply of workers to the ever-growing industrial segment of the economy.

The centrally directed economy developed by the USSR demonstrated its strength and flexibility by its rapid industrial growth and its recuperative power following the tremendous losses during the second world war. The balance in the economy differed markedly however from that which characterized other countries which had undergone industrialization, including the deliberately industrialized economy of Japan. The direction of major resources into heavy industry and military equipment resulted in a much larger proportion of all economic activity in these sectors as compared with those producing consumer goods, and in a level of general consumption in most lines below that of countries with a similar *per capita* level of overall economic activity, though substantial resources were devoted to the provision of social services which supplemented private consumption.

It provided however a broad and strong basis for expansion of all sorts, as was evidenced in the late 1950s when the Soviet Union announced its intention of surpassing the advanced capitalist economies in the production of consumer goods. The output of food products was increased, together with many other items of consumption, and wages and pensions were raised, enabling workers to take advantage of these available supplies. At the same time the USSR expanded its export of capital goods to eastern Europe and China and to the newly developing countries of Asia and Africa.

With the exception of Yugoslavia which followed its own line of socialist experimentation, the Soviet economic structure provided the general pattern of economic organization for the countries of eastern Europe after 1945, and Soviet experience provided a guide for much of their economic activity.[14] Within a relatively short period, and with less need for experiment than the Soviet economy had experienced during the 1920s, these countries rapidly nationalized their industries and reduced the private area of trade and handicraft to an insignificant proportion of their total economy. Collectivization of agriculture was established as an objective. The nature and functions of trade unions were defined in terms which corresponded to their role in the USSR. Techniques of planning were introduced with the refinements which had been developed in the Soviet Union.

In contrast to the USSR, however, these east-European countries were not self-contained as the Soviet economy had been in very large measure from the start, but were linked among themselves and with the economy of the USSR. The areas which had been enemy territory during the second world war—East Germany, Hungary, Rumania, and to a lesser extent Bulgaria—paid substantial reparations in the years after the war in forms which assisted in the rebuilding of the Soviet economy and modified the productive capacity of the countries themselves. The Soviet government also took over German assets in these countries and directly operated the economic units which they represented. These enterprises, together with technical aid contracts, agency agreements and a growing number of joint enterprises in which the USSR became a part owner, linked the economies of the east European countries with the Russian. Joint planning was facilitated in specific fields by such bodies as the organization for railway co-operation. Imports and exports were governed by a series of trade agreements between each country and the USSR and among countries, especially Poland, Czechoslovakia and East Germany, which had formerly traded extensively with western Europe.

At the same time each country developed a national plan looking towards a high degree of self-sufficiency. During the first decade of their existence as communist states, two tendencies thus appeared, one to expand the economy of each country as a unit and the other to develop the combined communist area of Russia and eastern Europe as an interrelated whole.[15, 16]

The Yugoslav economy, after the break in 1948 between Yugoslavia and the USSR, developed along quite different lines and outside the interrelated structure of the economies of the USSR and her east European neighbours. Convinced that their form was truly 'socialist', the Yugoslavs based their economic design on social ownership of the means of production and control by those directly engaged in each productive enterprise.

In place of central operational planning, Yugoslavia used the central planning process only to allocate major investment funds between the central government, the governments of the constituent republics, and the pool of funds available to separate enterprises; to establish broad priorities and guidelines for the use of these funds; and to direct those segments of the economy, such as transport and utilities, which were under central government operation. Direct control over enterprises, which competed in domestic and international markets in much the same manner as capitalist firms, rested in the hands of workers' councils with powers similar to those of a corporate board of directors over production, prices, borrowing and disposal of earnings remaining after payment of taxes.

The socialist economy of Yugoslavia thus shared with other socialist economies social ownership of the means of production and a measure of economic planning, and with the capitalist economies a high degree of enterprise initiative, competition and the separation of ownership from control as in the large capitalist corporations. As such it offered an alternative system which was of interest to some of the newly developing countries as they sought economic forms appropriate to their situations and needs.

III. THE ECONOMIES OF THE NEWLY DEVELOPING COUNTRIES

In the years after the second world war economic development became a central objective of the countries emerging from colonial rule or semi-colonial status, and much of the thinking and activity of international bodies was couched in terms of the problems of assisting newly developing countries in their efforts to catch up.

The concept of economic development was not sharply defined but, as used for example by the International Bank for Reconstruction and Development, it meant an advance in national and *per capita* income, increased industrial and agricultural production and productive capacity, increased productivity of labour and a rising level of living for the people in the present or the future. Measures to promote economic development were adopted as people and governments became convinced that positive, constructive steps could hasten the process and as they feared that, without such efforts, levels of living would deteriorate in countries with low productivity and rapidly growing populations.

1. *The mixed economy of India and other non-communist countries*

In undertaking programmes of economic development, countries outside the communist-dominated areas devised a variety of mixed-economy systems in which free enterprise and central direction, private initiative and public responsibility, were variously combined. The mixed economy of India, which drew freely on the thinking and experience of both capitalist and communist countries, afforded a laboratory in which measures to achieve economic development under democratic guidance were being tested and worked out.

For 150 years the colonial economy of India had been shaped to the needs of Great Britain. This had meant the development of those economic activities which furnished raw materials for British industry, such as jute, cotton or indigo, or which supplied the British market with tropical products such as tea. It had meant that the flow of commerce, the transport system and the structure of trade and finance had been oriented toward the port cities. And it had meant the inclusion of the Indian economy within the free trade area and thus its exposure to the impact of European industrialism when machine-made goods entered the Indian market.

In these circumstances India had experienced the successive destruction of once flourishing handicrafts as European imports replaced many local urban industries that supplied the upper-class market. Even the village industries had suffered as imported kerosene replaced locally crushed oils, metal products competed with those locally forged and, above all, machine-spun yarn and machine-made cloth undercut the products of village spindles and looms. Even some of the new industries developed locally by Europeans had been destroyed in their turn, such as the extensive indigo production which collapsed with the development of chemical dyes in Europe at the end of the nineteenth century.

At the time of independence the Indian economy was predominantly agricultural. Roughly three-quarters of the labour force were engaged in agriculture and half the national income came from this source. Perhaps a third of the cultivated land was in large estates, raising commercial crops such as cotton, jute, tea, coconuts. The remainder, mostly in tiny holdings farmed by primitive methods, provided peasants with a bare subsistence, often at a level of permanent hunger. Throughout the period of British rule there had been a tendency to substitute commercial for subsistence crops whenever improvements in transport made it possible to send produce to market, in order to meet the taxes or rents required of the cultivators.

Yields for food crops were generally low, less than half those of Japan and for the staple food, rice, less than a third. Cultivation methods rather than poor soil were generally responsible but irregular rainfall was a major hazard outside the irrigated areas. If the monsoon failed the historic result had always been famine, against which the famine relief system developed by the British had provided only a partial defence. The death toll from the Bengal famine of 1943 amounted to some 1,500,000 lives. During the latter part of the nineteenth century the area of land under cultivation had been substantially expanded, helping to balance some of the depressing and dislocating effects of other economic developments. In the twentieth century, however, little expansion of cultivated land took place and there was a tendency toward subdivision into excessively small plots as a means of sustaining, at successively lower levels, the rural population for whom other outlets were not available.

The Indian agricultural village had, historically, been almost wholly self-sufficient, isolated by lack of roads and organized by a system in which the village craftsmen and the untouchables performed the functions needed by the village as hereditary obligations in exchange for subsistence provided in kind by the farmers whom they served. As factory-made goods gradually seeped into the village and farmers turned to cash crops, the hereditary system of mutual exchange was undermined, though it survived in part in less accessible areas. The village had also been self-governing, but under British administration village self-rule had broken down, as the judicial and revenue functions of the village councils (*panchayats*) were taken over by district judges and administrative officers.

Though the Indian economy was predominantly agricultural there had been substantial industrial development, particularly in the cotton textile and jute industries which employed three-quarters of the factory workers. Although the free trade policy had tended to push the Indian economy towards supplying raw materials rather than towards manufacture, and taxes on Indian-made cloth to prevent its competing with British were not abolished until 1926, the cotton textile industry had surpassed that of Britain by the time of the second world war and was second only to that of the United States. First developed by British firms, the industry had been expanded by Indian capital from the 1870s on. At the time of independence most of the mills were in Indian hands. The jute industry, composed of large mills employing an average of over 2,500 workers, remained in European hands until the establishment of the first Indian mill in 1921, but by independence nearly half the mills were Indian-owned. The nucleus of an iron and steel industry was present in the large steel works built by Indian capital from 1907 on, drawing on India's ample resources of iron ore and coal. Mining, however, especially coal, remained largely in the hands of British companies.

The labour supply consisted of a mass of rural people, distributed through more than a half-million villages, a large proportion underemployed by reason of the smallness of their holdings or the decline of their crafts. Except for agriculture in which all castes participated, both village and urban occupations were linked to caste and were hereditary, but factory and general labour in the urban areas was performed by people of various castes who sought escape from rural poverty in the industrial and service occupations of the city. Such workers came to the cities faster than jobs developed and much faster than housing was constructed. Urban unemployment became chronic, as was underemployment in the villages, and the pavement population of Indian cities mounted into the millions. Among Bombay's pavement dwellers many had jobs, as did those who camped beside roads or on vacant land under low improvised shelters of tin, cardboard or gunnybags, but many had neither jobs nor homes. After partition the number was augmented by millions of refugees.

Until about 1920 the population of India showed little increase. High birth rates were offset by high death rates and were cancelled periodically by famine and epidemic. Deaths numbering many millions from famine in the 1870s, famine and plague in the 1890s and the influenza epidemic of 1918 held the population down to its mid-nineteenth century level. Emigration of plantation labour within the British empire—to Fiji, Malaya, Ceylon, Burma, Africa and the West Indies—also had drawn off some workers, though not in very large numbers. After 1920, major epidemics and famine were brought under control, the changed political situation made large-scale emigration no longer even a minor alternative to unemployment, and the population increased more or less steadily at an annual rate of something over 1 per cent. Although this was not as high a rate of natural increase as that of many other economically underdeveloped areas in the second quarter of the twentieth century, an increase of some 4,000,000 a year was a substantial number for the Indian economy to absorb. In the decade after independence the rate rose to some 8,000,000.

Transport was provided by an extensive railway system, exceeded in mileage only by the railways of the United States, the USSR and Canada, with workshops capable of producing most of the rolling stock and keeping it in repair. Originally constructed and operated by private British companies whose profits were guaranteed by the British government of India, the railways were taken over and operated directly by the government after the 1920s. Railway lines and trunk roads, however, were designed for military purposes and foreign trade not for internal communication, and thus ran to the ports and frontiers rather than providing an interconnecting network throughout the country. Foreign and coastwise shipping travelled almost wholly in British bottoms, except that carried by sailing craft; the only Indian shipping enterprise was established after 1921.

Indian industry came to depend increasingly on Indian capital and Indian management in spite of the economic ties to Britain. The proportion of the factory workers in European-owned establishments dropped from a half to a third, from before the first world war to the eve of the second. Indian trade, moreover, became less and less concentrated on Britain. The percentage of India's imports coming from Britain dropped from a height of 80 per cent in the 1870s to 31 per cent on the eve of the second world war, in part as a result of the Indian nationalist movement to boycott British goods. Exports to Britain dropped from half to less than a quarter before 1932, when the proportion was raised somewhat under the Ottawa agreement which gave a preference to British empire products and which was applied to India over the opposition of the Indian legislative assembly.

The structure of economic organization was compounded of an Indian core and a superstructure of English institutions and practices. The Indian core was provided by the *banyas* or merchant castes, or by merchant communities such as the Marwaris, which carried on trade, banking and moneylending as an hereditary calling. Up to the time of independence, the principal Indian commercial and industrial enterprises which were not in the hands of Europeans were in the hands of these Hindu castes or of the non-Hindu Parsees.

British institutions and practices relating to trade, commerce, industry and banking were introduced into India with only a few adaptations required by local conditions. Except for personal law relating to family relationships and inheritance, which continued to follow Hindu and Muslim practices, British civil and commercial law and legal procedures were applied in their entirety. These recognized ownership in real estate and in tangible and intangible property, regulated contracts and defined agency and trust relationships. The joint-stock company with its concept of limited liability was superimposed on the Indian pattern of family enterprise. European firms in India operated on the joint-stock principle and Indians not only invested in them but formed joint-stock companies of their own.

Banking operations and currency control were well developed. Foreign trade was financed almost wholly through British-operated exchange banks. Four of the five large banks which together did about half the domestic banking business were Indian institutions. A reserve bank, established in 1935, exercised control over the lending operations of member banks, regulated the formation of new banks and exacted standards of banking safety from their member institutions. For more than a hundred years a single currency had been in use for commercial transactions throughout the many political divisions of the country.

The financial principles and legal system introduced by the British had strengthened the Indian class of merchants and moneylenders, who from pre-British times had conducted elaborate and large-scale financial operations. Enforceable contracts which carried the legal right to take possession of property to satisfy unpaid debts brought land into the hands of moneylenders when peasants defaulted on their mortgages. They contributed to the break-up of the joint family by enabling creditors to claim a portion of the joint estate in satisfaction of a debt incurred by a member of the family group.

A unique feature of the Indian economic structure was the managing agency system. In the days before rapid communication British companies had found it impossible to manage their Indian enterprises by long-distance from Britain, and had placed the management in the hands of agents who operated the companies for the owner, reserving a commission for themselves. At first the managing agencies were British firms, but during the twentieth century many Indian firms were formed, often on a family basis. Managing agencies, which frequently took on a number of concerns on a permanent or long-term basis, came to command great wealth and power and to provide much of the initiative for economic expansion. The system furnished a useful device for separating the functions of management from beneficial ownership, but such agencies could become powerful vested interests whose activity would not necessarily correspond with the interests of society.

The policy of the British government of India, in line with *laissez-faire* principles, had been non-intervention in economic affairs beyond the maintenance of a stable currency and other conditions favourable to trade. Not until 1921 was an Indian fiscal commission appointed which recommended a policy of protection to selected Indian industries. Approximately half of the government of India revenues went to the support of the Indian army, which served as the Asian arm of the British army. Although this army was supported by India, it was used outside the borders of India no less than nineteen times between 1838 and 1920. In addition to the army and the civil administration, public funds were used in the operation of railways, irrigation and communication systems and royal teak forests, in some hydroelectric schemes started after 1921 and for limited programmes of education and public health, mainly for the higher levels of education in urban areas, for the control of epidemics and for famine relief.

The government of India was little affected by the changes in economic and political thought that marked Britain's own transition to a welfare state. Indian leaders educated in Britain, however, became imbued with these ideas and sought to apply them to their emerging nation. The Indian National Congress attacked the policy of *laissez-faire* and called for positive measures to promote economic development. Impressed by the adoption of planning in the USSR, it created a planning commission under the chairmanship of Jawaharlal Nehru in 1937 to bring this approach into the preparations for the future Indian state.

The Indian government after independence faced the double economic task of reorienting a colonial economy to domestic needs and developing a more productive economy which could lift the Indian people from extreme poverty to a level of living closer to that of more prosperous and developed countries. It confronted these long-run needs while having to cope with emergency problems arising from partition, integration of the multitude of Indian states, and the threat of famine from floods and droughts during the first years of the régime.

The Indian constitution provided the democratic framework within which the processes of economic development were to be worked out, and set forth the economic objectives of the Indian state (Article 39):

To ensure the right of the citizens, men and women equally, to an adequate means of livelihood; to ensure the distribution of ownership and control of material resources of the community as best to subserve the common good; and to prevent concentration of wealth and means of production to the common detriment.

The state thus took on positive responsibility for economic welfare, on the assumption that this responsibility could be carried out through democratic procedures.

Three years after independence the Indian government created a planning commission to give attention to the broad problems of economic development and the permanent structure of the Indian economy. The commission adopted the approach of setting up goals by means of successive five-year plans, the first covering the years 1951–56, the second designed for 1956–61. In the formulation of the plans the democratic principle of open discussion was fully applied. Divergent economic views were aired, alternative priorities proposed and differing judgments expressed as to how fast the economy could grow.

In the course of these discussions, objectives were clarified: to increase the real income of the people sufficiently rapidly to maintain stability in the society and to match popular demand; to achieve what the leaders termed a 'socialist pattern of society', which meant that extremes of wealth would be reduced, centres of private power would be eliminated or not allowed to develop, and the machinery of the state would be used for such economic purposes as might be appropriate in a democratic system; to seek balanced economic development, which should minimize the vulnerability of the economy to outside influences but not seek autarchy; and to provide for such defence expenditures as the political situation might require, with the assumption that in time these could be made less necessary.

India possessed ample resources of water power, minerals and soil to sustain a developed economy, though little of the water power had been harnessed, much of the mineral wealth was unexplored and much of the soil had been depleted by exhausting methods of cultivation. Its major problems lay elsewhere, in the realms of public attitudes, economic leadership and technical know-how.

The first necessary condition for economic development was the desire for change. In the days before the western impact, Indian society like other Asian societies had been essentially static; it assumed continuity as a central principle of life rather than change. The joint family was a static institution; its members came and went but the family itself remained. Hereditary status and relationships defined the destiny of each; religious ritual punctuated the cyclical events of life. Even the reformers of the nineteenth century had insisted that they were not calling for change but only for a restoration of a state from which society had strayed.

During the years of British rule the idea of change became part of the outlook and thought of the western-educated middle class. It was confined to the educated *élite*, however, until Mahatma Gandhi aroused the masses of the people with his call for the regeneration of Indian society and resistance to the British *raj*. But though his crusade loosened the hold of custom and raised the eyes of the villagers to new potentialities, its economic expression was couched in terms of a return to the spinning wheel. The first question which confronted the Indian leadership after independence was how extensively the acceptance of change could be aroused at the village level and canalized into productive effort.

The leadership itself, while imbued with the principle of change and eager for economic development, had little of the experience, training and habits which characterized the economic leadership in the West. Their western education had been overwhelmingly literary and theoretical rather than technical. They came predominantly from the Brahmin and other upper castes for whom money-making had not been an acceptable career. They had however engaged in management and administration. The problem of developing the necessary economic leadership thus involved modifying traditional attitudes toward economic enterprise among higher castes, or designing an economic structure which would use their managerial ability without requiring them to develop a profit-seeking or money-making motivation. The alternative was to continue to depend primarily on the Parsees, Marwaris and members of the former merchant castes to come forward with sufficient enterprise to create the momentum needed for the whole economy.

The lack of sufficient technically trained personnel reflected the fact that the British, while encouraging the highest literary and theoretical education for the Indian *élite*, had provided technical training chiefly for the lower ranks on the railways, irrigation projects, civil service and army, filling the higher posts with British personnel. While India was better off than areas such as Burma and Ceylon where virtually no technical training reached the local population, the number of technically trained Indians was far below the needs of a developing economy. There were outstanding mathematicians and physicists but limited numbers of trained and experienced engineers, except in the field of irrigation.

Emphasis on theoretical training, moreover, had associated prestige with intellectual as against practical activity, confirming the traditional attitude of the Indian upper castes in this respect, and it had offered a powerful impediment to the development of technicians who would not hesitate to soil their hands in the course of their jobs. In the traditionally status-conscious society of India, the problem of technical know-how was thus not only to train a sufficient number of technicians but so to modify the prestige structure as to overcome traditional negative attitudes toward all but intellectual work.

The first and second five-year plans provided guide-lines for government activity. They did not attempt to cover the entire economy. Since government in India was responsible for only some 8 per cent of the national income, in contrast to some 20 per cent in the United States and considerably more in a number of the capitalist countries of Europe, plans for government action were far from a comprehensive plan for the total of Indian economic activity. Rather, they were plans as to how government could use its instrumentalities to further economic objectives and stimulate growth in the private as well as in the public sector of the economy.

The government's instrumentalities were of five main sorts: its own operations in providing services such as education, constructing public works such as hydroelectric dams, operating enterprises such as railways, and developing basic industries such as shipbuilding, fertilizer production, machine tools, atomic energy; promotional activities, as in stimulating village efforts and reviving responsible village councils through a community development programme or encouraging hand-produced textiles by a special price subsidy; providing a legal framework for the activities of individuals through protection of property, labour legislation or such measures as the abolition of caste; direct restrictions on permitted activity, through licences for certain types of equipment or construction, prohibition of certain types of manufacture such as cloths reserved for hand-looms, or control of foreign exchange; and coercion, primarily through the use of the taxing power or, in some of the states, by the compulsory redistribution of land.

Execution of proposals contained in the plans was left to the appropriate department of government, co-ordinated through the cabinet under the prime minister and responsible to the Indian parliament. Planning thus became a means of co-ordinating and focusing the separate efforts of government agencies and the private efforts of individuals, both through promotion and regulation and by providing goals to which private as well as public agencies could aspire and efforts could be directed.

The first five-year plan focused primarily on agriculture, the basis of the Indian economy, with two major and related objectives, to stimulate the villages to pursue their own development and to improve agricultural techniques in order to provide a better economic base of village and national life. A large-scale community development programme reached 125,000 villages during the first five-year plan. It proved even more effective than had been expected in motivating villagers to accept change: once the interest and initiative of the villages were aroused, their demands for technical and other help in development projects threatened to outrun the ability of the government to make good its offers of aid. Helped by favourable monsoons the campaign for improved cultivation of rice stimulated a sufficient increase in agricultural production to reduce the need for food imports and thus to release foreign exchange for the purchase of steel and industrial equipment.

The first five-year plan also included measures to increase the production of chemical fertilizers and for hydroelectric flood control and irrigation projects designed to regulate the water supply and permit two or three crops on land yielding only one crop under the system of drought and monsoon. The programme thus looked toward the revitalizing of agriculture within the existing framework, with improved techniques, improved communication and irrigation where needed. It recognized the need for changes in landholding to overcome the evils of absentee landlordism and the fragmentation of land into too small plots, but left this matter to be worked out by the separate states, either through legislation or through the voluntary surrender of lands by large holders. The latter programme, initiated by a follower of Gandhi, Vinoba Bhave, resulted in the voluntary redistribution of a considerable amount of land in the 1950s, at first by dividing donated land among peasants, later by giving it to the village for co-operative cultivation.

The second five-year plan was more concerned with the development of industry than was the first. When it was published in tentative form, its stated purpose was 'rapid industrialization, with particular emphasis on the development of basic industries', but after a year of public discussion, the final plan made the development of industry only one part of a balanced programme 'to rebuild rural India, to lay the foundations of industrial progress, and to secure to the greatest extent feasible opportunities for weaker and underprivileged sections of our people and the balanced development of all parts of the country'. While the necessity and opportunity for the development of heavy industry was recognized, it did not dominate planning in these years.

The first two plans thus steered a middle course between two diametrically opposed views held by segments of the population. One group, basing its position on Gandhi's opposition to modern industry in the form experienced under British rule, wanted a policy of return to handicrafts and an effort to avoid industrialization. The opposite extreme was represented by those who saw in rapid industrialization the only hope for overcoming India's widespread poverty and proposed that every sacrifice be made toward that goal.

The counsel which prevailed in the first decade after independence followed neither of these lines, but sought both to strengthen the villages and to lay the foundation for industrialization. The second five-year plan expanded the community development programme, with the aim of reaching all 600,000 villages; it called for the enlargement of fertilizer, hydroelectric and irrigation projects and added two special schemes to strengthen the village and town economies. As a temporary measure, to fill the gap while the groundwork for industrialization was being laid, the hand-weaving of cloth was to be encouraged, and to a lesser extent the spinning of yarn. The objective was to provide employment to a large underemployed class of workers and to increase the supply of consumer goods without the necessity for capital investment to expand machine spinning and weaving. With a more permanent objective, small machine industries were to be promoted in villages and towns, either to produce for local consumption, or to make small articles for sale or as parts to be used in manufacture. The aim was to create a dispersed pattern of industrialization rather than to uproot people from their homes, in the hope of avoiding the creation of huge cities, such as Bombay, where industry had been concentrated in the past and where urban growth rapidly outstripped the ability of the municipality to cope with the housing and other needs of an expanding population.

At the same time the major increases in governmental expenditures called for by the second five-year plan were for industry and mining. While the total plan somewhat more than doubled the outlays included in the first plan, those for mining and industry were increased eightfold. Capital expenditure to enlarge the steel industry accounted for a large part.

The second five-year plan called for the expansion of the public sector of the economy beyond the public utilities to which government operations had been largely confined in the past. In so doing it began to define the respective roles of the public and private sectors and to shape a mixed economy that would aim toward a 'socialist pattern of society'. The policy of state operation of basic industries, such as mining, steel, atomic energy and machine tools, was adopted. Some of these were to be developed wholly by state enterprise and others through a combination of public and private enterprise, with the public sector assuming increased responsibility.

BB*

This policy reflected the thought that private industry would not expand with sufficient rapidity and, more importantly, that since these industries hold the key in industrialized societies, the concentration of economic power in private hands could best be avoided if government assumed responsibility in these crucial areas. The approach was a flexible one, however, and in the initial phase the steel industry was expanded under both private and public auspices. Where an important activity, such as shipping, was in the hands of powerful European companies, the government entered the field in the expectation that no private Indian enterprise would be strong enough to compete.

The problems of attitudes, economic leadership and technical adequacy remained central. Technical training was stepped up sharply, both through foreign study by large numbers of Indian students and through emphasis on facilities for technical training in the programme of educational expansion. In the meantime persons with special technical skills were brought from abroad for temporary jobs, either directly by the government or enterprises, or through the technical assistance programmes of international and national governmental agencies.

Motivation appeared less of a problem at the village level than many had assumed. But in the industrial sector there were problems of economic leadership. The merchant and industrial castes and communities which had furnished the private initiative in the past could be counted upon to continue to do so, and it would not be difficult to make conditions more favourable than they had been under British rule. But the Indian state wished neither to favour nor to depend upon any single group or groups. The agency system permitted a partial solution of this problem, if it could be prevented from creating vested interests, for it disassociated management from investment and enabled a wider group to participate in the management process. But one of the reasons for looking to public enterprise, and to co-operative organization in the private sector, was the opportunity which these forms of organization presented to use the talents of those whose traditional attitudes made them more likely to perform successfully as administrators or managers than as entrepreneurs.

Some outside observers thought that the ability of India to develop an expanding and vigorous economy would require the adoption of many attitudes associated with enterprise in the West. In the absence of the desire to take risks and invest for gain, the necessary drive would, they thought, not be generated. Others thought that motivations different from those to which the western world was accustomed might prove effective under conditions of Indian life, such as the desire to achieve non-material objectives, the motivation of disinterested service to society which was central to the Hindu revival and to which Gandhi gave great currency, or the readiness to follow a leadership which could inspire and show the way. In the initial stages the spirit of nationalism certainly played a role, as well as the sense of being on trial in competition with communist China to prove that economic development could be achieved by democratic means.

The most pressing problem was whether the Indian economy could achieve a rate of growth sufficiently rapid to keep ahead of population increase, to reduce unemployment, to improve the economic situation in villages and towns and prevent rural–urban migration from exceeding the expansion of opportunity in urban areas, and to maintain social stability in the face of the inevitable impatience engendered by high national hopes. The crux of this problem appeared to lie in the rate of investment which could be generated. The second five-year plan was presented to the public with a substantial gap between the expenditures called for and the visible means of securing the required funds. Loans or other financing from abroad were implied, and these proved essential in the event. But the principal need was for new sources of revenue at home. The government took over the life insurance companies and launched a campaign to encourage small savings. Even the full amount of the plan, however, called for a rate of investment below that of most developed countries. But this was more than the Indian economy had sustained in the past.

The crucial question was whether a country of low *per capita* income such as India, which had renounced the centralized methods and coercive techniques of the communist states, could engender through democratic means the level of investment needed for economic growth.[17]

Other countries of Asia, Africa and Latin America which faced the problems of economic development also sought to meet them with mixed economies in which state effort and private enterprise both played a part. The patterns which were evolving at mid-century differed in different regions and countries and were affected by many factors—by the balance of resources and population, the economic history and structure of the country and the orientation of the government. The problems of economic development in the oil-rich kingdoms of the Middle East were very different from those of the crowded valley of the Nile, or from the rice economy of Thailand, or the countries on the high plateau of the Andes. Countries which had experienced colonial exploitation from abroad, as in much of Asia and Africa, were in a different situation from those whose economy was mainly dominated by a local wealthy class, as in much of Latin America, or which had experienced a social revolution, as in Mexico. In some, land was held in *latifundia*, in others by peasant proprietors. Yet in one way or another virtually every underdeveloped country sought to use the conscious intervention of government to accelerate economic growth, and the economic institutions which it developed combined features of different economic systems.

These countries attempted to use the technique of economic planning in some way. In Latin American countries, where the tradition of private enterprise was strong, programmes of economic planning were at first limited to special projects for valley development such as the valley of the Cauca in

Colombia, or for agricultural improvement, or for foreign credits and control of international trade. Most Asian countries adopted some variant of the five-year plan. Some, such as Burma, formulated elaborate goals although effective means of working toward the goals remained to be developed. Others, such as Iraq, concentrated on plans for major public works, such as dams and irrigation projects, and the investment of government revenues which were already in sight. The planning mechanism devised by the commonwealth of Puerto Rico used a continuous process of replanning each year for the next six years ahead, instead of setting a five-year goal and then starting a new plan for the next five-year period. It also sought to combine central planning with local initiative by reserving a portion of the public funds covered by the plan for allocation in response to local interest and effort, rather than according to established priorities.

These countries in greater or less degree included social measures as part of their economic plans. Some, such as Puerto Rico, started with planning for physical construction and gradually included planning for social services as well. Others, like India, included social components from the start. Opinions differed widely as to the proper relationship between expenditures to promote social well-being and those which were more strictly economic in intent. In one view, social expenditures competed with economic and were a luxury which could only be afforded when the economic base had been expanded and national income increased. An alternative view insisted that expenditures for such things as health and education were sound economic investments, for they increased the productivity of the population and removed the costly burdens of dependency, ineffectiveness and early death. Where they resulted in an increase in the population more rapid than the rate of economic expansion, however, they could threaten to cancel out the gains, unless they helped to lay the basis for a future spurt in economic growth.

The conscious effort to accelerate economic development on the part of countries containing a large proportion of the world's people was unique in the history of the world. So too was the technological and political situation within which these efforts were being made. A leading international economist, Gunnar Myrdal of Sweden, reviewing the situation in 1956, concluded that the developing countries should not assume that the economic thinking formulated in the older industrialized countries necessarily had relevance for them. In the light of the new situation of the mid-twentieth century the process of industrialization might bring very different experiences from those which the previously developed countries had known.*

2. The socialist economy of the Chinese People's Republic

While India and most other formerly colonial or industrially underdeveloped countries were pursuing their goal of economic development by means

* Gunnar Myrdal, *An International Economy: Problems and Prospects* (New York, 1956), p. 313.

of mixed economies which retained much of the framework of their existing society, the Chinese People's Republic launched the most drastic movement for industrialization undertaken by any country at any time, by means of a total transformation of Chinese society.

When the communist régime came to power in 1949, the Chinese economy was not only largely undeveloped industrially, with much of what existed in foreign hands or oriented to foreign treaty ports or foreign-concession railways; it was in a state of chaos and disruption as the result of decades of civil wars and Japanese invasion and of the patterns of corruption which had come to operate all along the line under these conditions. In 1949 agricultural production was only about 75 per cent of what it had been during the 1930s, light industry about two-thirds and heavy industry only 30 per cent of former levels.

The Chinese economy was basically agricultural, producing primarily for subsistence, although the principal exports, such as tea and silk, were agricultural products. It provided a bare subsistence to the peasant population; rice and other food grains were imported into most areas, few districts raised a surplus, and famine threatened constantly and occurred periodically. Yet traditional Chinese agricultural techniques were highly developed. Chinese rice yields per acre were double those of India, but only two-thirds as great as the Japanese.

Such industry as existed was mainly light industry, chiefly textiles; only the beginnings of steel and related heavy industry had been made by the Japanese in Manchuria. The natural resources of the country remained largely unexplored. They were presumed to be adequate for a substantial industrial development, but the question remained largely speculative until after 1949. Inadequate transport facilities presented a serious obstacle to economic development. Goods were mainly shipped by water via rivers and canals, but river flows were uncontrolled, floods were periodic and many of the canals had fallen into disrepair. There was no general network of railways, only a few small systems leading to principal ports in the east. Roads were even less adequate, such as existed being mainly unpaved.

The reconstruction of the Chinese economy was carried out by means of the intensive utilization of China's major resource, her great manpower which had been only very partially employed under previous conditions. The labour of peasants in off seasons and of those who could be released by a more rational organization of agricultural production, the labour of women, the labour which could be made available by substituting other means of transport for the carrying pole, even the labour of children who could be mobilized for communal tasks and of older women who could release the more able-bodied by caring for children—these were the major resources which the communist leadership undertook to organize into an effective instrument for remaking the Chinese economy.

In organizing these resources for an effort designed to industrialize the country with unprecedented speed, the Chinese leadership undertook to apply Marxist–Leninist principles with pragmatic flexibility, in the light of Chinese conditions, and to make the most of the prior experience of other countries. In particular China drew upon the experience of the USSR in developing techniques of planning and of large-scale operations, as well as on some of the experience of Japan in achieving economic expansion with a minimum of capital. It carried on its massive reconstruction in an atmosphere of intense nationalism and patriotism, as the nation threw off a century of weakness and humiliation at the hands of western and Japanese imperialism, and it thus had available an emotional resource of great magnitude to focus common effort and maintain the feverish pace set by those in command.

In its first three years, the communist régime restored the chaotic and shattered Chinese economy to productive levels well above those which had been achieved in the past. It organized the country administratively under effective centralized direction and control and rooted out the graft and corruption that had debilitated economic life. It reoriented the economy in its foreign relations toward the Soviet Union and the rest of the communist bloc.

Thereafter it used the technique of formulating five-year plans with ambitious targets which were repeatedly revised upward, as stimuli to bursts of national effort brought overfulfilment at earlier dates. In 1956 it projected a twelve-year plan for agrarian development, comprising agricultural production, industrialization of the countryside and improvement in the farmers' way of life, to be financed principally from local sources and to be carried out side by side with the centrally financed five-year plans.

Developments were in two main areas, the transformation of the agricultural economy upon which some 80 per cent of the people depended and the creation of a base for industrial development, in heavy industry, transport, mining and the construction of physical plant and machinery.

The transformation of Chinese agriculture in the first decade was the most crucial element in the change-over, and both the drastic nature and the relative smoothness of the process made the experience of China unique. Mao Tse-tung had made the peasantry the core of the revolution, not merely one of its supporters, and he had promised them land. First in the north-west area during the war and then in the country as a whole, land was distributed to the poor peasants with small holdings or none who made up 70 per cent of the peasant population. Party cadres and committees in each village classified the peasants and assigned the available land, with a minimum of resistance from the landlords and rich peasants and with the support of the middle peasants who were generally undisturbed in their holdings.

No sooner had the land been distributed, however, than a campaign was launched to encourage the voluntary formation of co-operatives among the peasants whose holdings were small and generally scattered. By 1953 some 40 per cent of the peasants had already become members of agricultural co-operatives or mutual aid teams. The next step was to convert these co-operative associations into collective farms similar to those of the USSR with common operation and common administration. In marked contrast to the USSR and eastern Europe, Chinese peasants showed little resistance to the rapid liquidation of private ownership in land. By 1957 Chinese agriculture was almost completely collectivized.

At this point, the Chinese leadership took a further jump which carried the process of collectivization beyond that which the USSR or any other socialized state had attempted, the conversion of groups of villages and collective farms into communes. Again reorganization of the rural economy proceeded with fantastic speed. In a matter of months whole provinces reported the communalization of their rural society, with administrative centralization, common eating halls, work brigades and the direct provision by the commune of the necessities of life for the members. After the initial rush to establish communes during 1958 there was a momentary period of relaxation; some individual cultivation of garden plots and sale of produce from them was permitted, and use of eating halls, nurseries and other collective facilities was made voluntary but strongly encouraged. The basis had been laid, however, for a fully communalized rural society and for the management of rural production in a manner which permitted the maximum organization of the labour force for work in the commune, for the assignment of task forces to large-scale construction projects elsewhere, or for removal of groups to settle new lands, extend rail lines or develop industrial, mining or oil centres.

Thus in ten short years the ancient peasant economy of China was converted into a highly organized structure. The aim was to raise production, not only to reduce the threat of famine, but to provide the exports with which to purchase machinery and equipment abroad while the foundations for domestic machinery production were being laid. This transformation, in contrast to the Russian, was accomplished virtually without mechanization. Improved ploughs and other simple equipment were distributed to some communes and collectivation permitted the fuller use of the available animal power to replace some manual labour. But the very substantial increases in agricultural production achieved during these years did not result from the establishment of tractor stations or any other form of mechanization. The main factors, in addition to the better organization of production on larger units instead of fragmented plots and the opening of some new lands, came from the same sources as those which Japan had found effective—seed selection, irrigation and more intensive measures for pest control and fertilization.

The industrial and commercial segments of the economy, like the agricultural, were converted from private to state enterprise gradually but rapidly, and with a minimum of resistance. Large-scale industry and trade had been mainly in the hands of Japanese and other foreigners or of the ruling clique of the Kuomintang and was readily taken over. The smaller factory-owners, handicraftsmen and merchants were offered inducements and persuasion to join co-operatives or to turn their businesses over to the government in return for a fixed payment on their investment. As it became increasingly difficult and unprofitable to operate independently, most entrepreneurs found it advisable to turn over their business to the state, often themselves staying on as managers. Here too the process of socialization was completed within a short period and without substantial resistance.

Thus, although in the initial stages it appeared that China might be evolving an economy that would retain some individualistic and capitalistic features, this apparent conservatism was in fact a means to a more rapid and complete socialization, centralization and communalization than any other country had hitherto attempted.

Restoration, extension and improvement of the transport system was the first essential for industrial development, as well as for national unification and administration. Millions of workers, mainly peasants in slack periods, but also some urban workers, intellectuals and soldiers, tackled the tremendous tasks of restoring the old canal and irrigation systems, constructing new waterways, rebuilding and extending the inadequate railways, laying out and surfacing a road system, and beginning the long process of damming and taming China's great, fierce rivers. Again the major resource was manpower, organized to function under central direction. Although earth-moving and other equipment from the USSR and east Europe was used on some of the projects, men and women with shovels and baskets dug most of the canals, laid up the dikes and roadways, levelled and ballasted the railway tracks and worked on the dams.

In line with the objective of laying the basis for industrial expansion, main energies were directed toward the build-up of heavy industry and of the electricity and fuel resources on which such industry depends. Coal mining was expanded rapidly, oil resources in Kansu and Sinkiang were probed and then exploited with the construction of more than a thousand miles of railway and the recruiting of hundreds of thousands of workers for this new frontier. The Anshan area became the centre of a rapidly expanding iron and steel complex. When in 1958 steel working capacity ran ahead of iron supplies, a nation-wide campaign to melt down scrap in backyard furnaces, and in some areas to dig and smelt local ore, made it possible to maintain the breakneck pace of expansion and gave people throughout the country the sense of participating in laying the industrial foundations of the new China.

Although most technology was pre-industrial at the time of the communist take-over, and much of it remained so during the first decade of development, the leadership was determined to place China as rapidly as possible in the front ranks scientifically, and to take full advantage of the scientific developments which had been made throughout the world. Very highly qualified Chinese scientists who had been trained in Europe, the US and the USSR, although relatively few in number, formed a nucleus which was supplemented by several thousand scientific and technical advisers from Russia, by Chinese sent to Moscow for training, and then by the graduates of the technical and research centres established in the country. Although at one end of the scale the campaign for technical improvement took such elementary forms as substituting the wheelbarrow or bullock cart for the carrying pole, at the other end it involved an atomic reactor, and Chinese factories were turning out jet planes.

The stated goal of national efforts was to make China a great industrial nation, moving immediately into the front ranks in scientific development and achievement, surpassing other industrial countries as rapidly as possible, starting with Britain and reaching ultimately a level of production commensurate with China's immense population and large resources.

The results of these efforts, measured in terms of production, were noteworthy. With due allowances for over-optimism and inaccuracies in reporting, including a substantial downward revision in the figures previously announced by the régime in 1959, the rate of economic expansion achieved in the course of ten years exceeded that of other countries in comparable stages of industrial development—Britain in the early nineteenth century, the United States, Germany and Japan in the late nineteenth century, the USSR after the October revolution. It substantially exceeded the rate of economic growth achieved by India or any of the other newly developing Asian countries during these same years.

In terms of consumption, the increases in production were not reflected in levels of living, for they were devoted to laying the basis for expansion in heavy industry rather than to the satisfaction of consumer wants. The extension of education and health services, the improvement in sanitary conditions and in facilities for child care, and greater probability that a minimum of food would be available for the many who had lived under the recurrent threat of starvation must be reckoned as net additions to living standards. But the great efforts called forth from the people during these years were for the sake of the future, not for material benefits in the present.

The Chinese economy was operated under central direction. Ministries, with their provincial and local subdivisions, were responsible for their respective segments of the economy. The party structure, with its cadres at every level, provided the direct stimulus for carrying out plans and directives and for reporting results. The methods of planning, administration and party control which had been tested in the USSR were put into operation. Radio communication provided a means of reaching and mobilizing the entire country immediately with each new phase of the programme and each new appeal for common action, a resource which the Soviet Union had not had at its disposal to the same degree in the early stages of its organization and development.

No aspect of Chinese life remained unaffected by the organization of the Chinese people into a vast instrument of production which could be focused at will on national objectives. Old institutions were discarded and new ones created; the authority of the family was replaced by that of the Party; women's subordination was replaced by equality of status and work outside the home, with institutional provision of meals and child care to relieve the women of former responsibilities; young people were raised to positions of trust and authority; age-old social distinctions were eroded by requiring intellectuals to do manual labour.

The skilful leaders of the Party and the state during these years followed a policy of using persuasion and stimulus to achieve results with as little resort to direct coercion as possible. Alternately heightening the pressures for achievement and relaxing them when they appeared to be creating too great a strain or to have served their purpose—as in the prescription that all should have eight hours of sleep when pressures to achieve new production goals appeared to be producing fatigue—or relaxing controls only to tighten them again, as when the 'hundred flowers' period during which criticism was encouraged was followed by stern measures against those who had gone too far, choosing successive slogans, such as the 'great leap forward', to focus the people's mind and spirit, and offering an outlet for pent-up animosities in hatred of 'western imperialists', especially the United States, they kept up the momentum during these years. But whatever devices were used to arouse public co-operation, to mobilize and canalize the latent vitality of the people and to make the Chinese economy function with increasing productiveness, the structure of control was complete. Nowhere in the world was there so thorough a regimentation of the life of a whole people potentially in the institutional structure developed during this decade, and actually in the daily routines of communal life.

NOTES TO CHAPTER XXI

1. Professor A. A. Zvorikine points out that international comparison of economic indicators is as complex a matter as it is important. The differences in the national statistical methods used make it difficult to compare such general indicators as national wealth, product, and income, etc., which give a highly compressed notion of the countries compared. If such indicators are to be compared properly, their economic basis has to be closely investigated, and special methods of comparison elaborated. In the Soviet Union, considerable methodological work is being done on this problem, and numerous calculations are being made on comparative data for a large number of basic economic and cultural indicators of socialist and capitalist countries. Some of the results of this work can be found in such publications as 'The Scientific Conference on the Methodology of Comparing Basic Economic Indicators in the USSR and the USA', *Vyestnik statistiki* (1963), No. 6, pp. 29–73; 'Statistical Law Patterns. Indexing Methods of Analysis. International Comparison of Statistical Indicators', *Uchonie zapiski po statistiki*, USSR Academy of Sciences, Department of Economic Sciences (Moscow, 1963).

    Significant errors are made in American statistics in defining the indicators for the distribution of the national income, particularly in respect of the share distributed among the workers. The comparison of the living standards of the workers cannot be confined to wages alone: it must take into account pensions, benefits, allowances, free education and medical treatment, the length of paid holidays, and other advantages and payments from public funds; the existence or absence of unemployment, the life-span, birth and death rates, the population growth, the spending pattern of the workers, and other such factors.

One or other statistical method is capable either of disclosing a long list of phenomena, or of presenting a distorted picture. This explains why statistical centres of the government and of business and trade unions in capitalist countries, while often working parallel and selecting data on the same problem, arrive at quite different conclusions. In the United States, for instance, the cost of living in the period from 1939 to 1961, according to the official Labour Bureau statistics, rose by 115·2 per cent, while the figure of the Heller Commission (University of California) for the budgets of working families was 210·4 per cent, and the index produced by the methods of the electricians' union gave 239·4 per cent (see, A. I. Katz, *Polozheniye proletariata S.Sh.A. pri imperialismye* [Moscow, 1962], p. 197).

The use of an indicator such as the average income per head of the population in capitalist countries in which the incomes of workers and employers are mixed, gives a false impression as to the prosperity of the mass, whereas the distribution of families according to the level of the annual income reveals the true material situation of the classes and social groups.

A comparison of the distribution of the mass of personal income among families and single people in the United States for almost half a century gives the following results:

NUMBER OF FAMILIES AND INDIVIDUALS WITH THE LOWEST INCOMES, EXPRESSED AS PERCENTAGES OF ALL PERSONAL INCOMES EARNED IN THE USA in 1910–1959

Families and Individuals with the Lowest Incomes

Year	less than 10%	10–20%	20–30%	30–40%	40–50%	50–60%	less than 40%	less than 60%
	Figures supplied by the National Industrial Conference Board							
1910	3·4	4·9	5·5	6·0	7·0	8·0	19·8	34·8
1918	2·4	4·4	5·7	6·9	7·2	7·7	19·4	34·3
1921	2·0	3·2	4·6	5·9	6·5	7·4	15·7	29·6
1929	1·8	3·6	4·6	5·5	6·5	7·9	15·5	29·9
1934	2·1	3·8	5·3	6·2	7·3	8·2	17·4	32·9
1937	1·0	2·6	4·4	6·0	7·2	8·5	14·0	29·7
	Figures based on a selective survey carried out by the Federal Reserve System							
1947	1·0	3·0	4·0	6·0	7·0	9·0	14·0	30·0
1950	1·0	3·0	5·0	6·0	8·0	9·0	15·0	32·0
1953	1·0	3·0	5·0	6·0	8·0	9·0	15·0	32·0
1956	1·0	3·0	5·0	6·0	8·0	9·0	15·0	32·0
1957	1·0	3·0	4·0	6·0	8·0	9·0	14·0	31·0
1958	1·0	3·0	5·0	6·0	8·0	9·0	15·0	32·0
	Department of Commerce figures							
1944	4·9*	10·9*		16·2*			15·8	32·0
1947	5·0	11·0		16·0			16·0	32·0
1950	4·8	10·9		16·1			15·7	31·8
1953	4·9	11·3		16·6			16·2	32·8
1956	4·8	11·3		16·3			16·1	32·4
1957	4·7	11·1		16·3			15·8	32·1
1958	4·6	10·9		16·2			15·5	31·7
1959	4·5	10·9		16·2			15·4	31·6

* Data for groups including 20 per cent families and individuals.

Source: A. I. Katz, *Polozheniye proletariata S.Sh.A. pri imperialismye* (Moscow, 1962), p. 108; National Industrial Conference Board (NICB), *Enterprise and Social Progress* (New York, 1939), p. 125; Federal Reserve *Bulletin*, 'US Income and Output' (1958), p. 161; and *Survey of Current Business* (July, 1961).

In the tables there are three groups of data which differ not only in respect of the criteria used in determining the incomes, but also in respect of the nature of the statistical material used as a basis for them. The summary series from 1910 to 1937 was compiled at different times by a number of authors using different methods, chiefly based on data for a given period, on wages distribution and fiscal statistics. The results (from 1910, see W. King, *The Wealth and Income of the People of the United States* [New York, 1923]; from 1918, F. Macauley, *Income in the United States* [New York, 1923]; from 1921–29, M. Leven, H. Moulton, and C. Warburton, *America's Capacity to Consume* [Washington, 1934]; and from 1934–37, the National Industrial Conference Board) are compared in varying degrees with the work of the National Industrial Conference Board, which is the scientific organization of the National Association of Industrialists. The data of the Federal Reserve System present the results of an annual selective survey, while the material of the Department of Commerce is made up of the totals of the synthetic calculations, based partly on information from fiscal statistics and correlated with summary calculations for the national income. However, in spite of the overall differences, the data on the distribution of the mass of personal income between groups of families and individuals with the lowest incomes, display on the whole a striking resemblance in respect of the scale and constancy of the trend, which is better than a mutual check. The approximate conclusion is that the share of 40 per cent of families and individuals with the lowest incomes in the general mass of personal income, fell from 19·8 per cent in 1910 to 15·5 per in 1929 and 14 per cent in 1937, and was then 14 to 16 per cent in the period from 1947 to 1959. The share of 60 per cent of the families and individuals with the lowest incomes accordingly dropped from 34·8 to 29·9 and 29·7 per cent, and was equal to 31–32 per cent in the period from 1947 to 1959. With regard to the lowest paid 10 per cent of families and individuals, their share in the overall mass of personal incomes fell catastrophically from 3·4 per cent in 1910 to 1 per cent in the 1950's, while the share of the next 10 per cent fell from 4·9 per cent to 3 per cent in the same period.

Without needing any other comment, these figures demonstrate the significant deepening of the chasm between the incomes of the rich and the poor in capitalist America in the last fifty years, the process of relative impoverishment to a great extent affecting precisely the most impoverished sectors of the proletarian population.

Cf. also notes 5 and 13 *infra*, by A. A. Zvorikine.

2. *The Author-Editors have included few comparative economic statistics in the text because of the difficulty of making meaningful comparisons. The United Nations have assembled some comparative figures for recent years (see Author-Editors' supplementary notes 3 to Chapter III and 2 to Chapter IX), but they point to the differences in the bases for the national figures and urge caution in the use of the tables.*

Different results will be obtained from the choice of different indicators. A comparison of trends in agricultural production and productivity in the USA and the USSR, for example, yields quite different results from the corresponding industrial comparisons. Industrial comparisons will vary according to the indicator, e.g., value added by manufacture, persons engaged, man-hours worked, and agricultural comparisons will vary according to product, or productivity per hectare or per worker or per man-hour. The period chosen for comparison also greatly affects the results. For a general discussion of the problems of Soviet–United States economic comparisons, the reader is referred to: Joint Economic Committee of the Congress of the United States, Comparisons of the United States and Soviet Economies (Washington, D.C., 1959), Part I, pp. 1–30, and illustrations of these difficulties throughout the studies in this publication.

Unemployment data are misleading when they do not take into account hidden unemployment in the form of excess numbers of workers on the land or large numbers of persons engaged in petty trade on too small a scale to yield an adequate income. Comparative wage data are affected by the presence of supplementary benefits. Countries in different stages of economic development show differing patterns, notably where major effort is directed toward laying an industrial base through the development of heavy industry, electrification, etc., as compared to those where greater emphasis is placed on consumer goods and services. Relative rates of growth will be affected by the relative size of the base from which growth is calculated. Fiscal data will reflect differences in the extent of government participation in economic life and the proportion of the gross national product which involves the government. Countries use different categories in their economic statistics or include different elements in similarly named categories, and apply different statistical procedures.

The following data are added to give a more complete picture of the economy of the United States. These data are internally consistent, but their use for comparative purposes, like the use of data relating to other countries, should be guided by awareness of the complicating factors listed above. See also the Author-Editors' supplementary Note 3 to Chapter III for data on occupations, income distribution, and earnings of industrial and professional workers, and Note 7 below for data on labour productivity, earnings, and hours of work.

NATIONAL PRODUCTION AND PERSONAL INCOME IN THE UNITED STATES

	Gross National Product		Per Capita Disposable Income (1)			
	Current dollars	*Constant dollars (1963)*	*Current dollars*	*Constant dollars (1963)*	*Index of Industrial Production*	*Index of Agricultural Production*
	(1000 millions)				*(1957–59=100)*	*(1957–59=100)*
1929	104·4	214·2	682	1254	38·4	62
1930	91·1	194·6	604	1162	32·0	61
1931	76·3	180·3	514	1110	26·5	66
1932	58·5	153·8	390	953	20·7	64
1933	56·0	149·9	364	923	24·4	59
1934	65·0	164·2	411	979	26·6	51
1935	72·5	179·8	458	1067	30·7	61
1936	82·7	204·9	516	1193	36·3	55
1937	90·8	215·6	551	1224	39·7	69
1938	85·2	206·3	506	1152	31·4	67
1939	91·1	223·2	537	1235	38·3	68
1940	100·6	242·0	576	1309	43·9	70
1941	125·8	281·8	697	1483	56·4	73
1942	159·1	323·2	871	1659	69·3	82
1943	192·5	364·4	976	1704	82·9	80
1944	211·4	391·1	1061	1756	81·7	83
1945	213·6	383·1	1075	1717	70·5	81
1946	210·7	332·0	1136	1680	59·5	84
1947	234·3	331·3	1180	1578	65·7	81
1948	259·4	344·4	1291	1632	68·4	88
1949	258·1	345·5	1272	1622	64·7	87
1950	284·6	374·0	1369	1720	74·9	86
1951	329·0	404·9	1475	1737	81·3	89
1952	347·0	420·8	1521	1756	84·3	92
1953	365·4	440·1	1582	1806	91·3	93
1954	363·1	431·4	1582	1790	85·8	93
1955	397·5	464·9	1660	1870	96·6	96
1956	419·2	474·7	1741	1928	99·9	97
1957	442·8	483·9	1803	1941	100·7	95
1958	444·5	476·7	1825	1928	93·7	102
1959	482·7	508·4	1904	1987	105·6	103
1960	502·6	521·3	1937	1993	108·7	106
1961	518·2	531·2	1983	2028	109·8	107
1962	554·9	563·6	2060	2087	118·3	108
1963	585·0	585·0	2127	2127	124·3	112

Source: Economic Report of the President, *1964, and Board of Governors of the Federal Reserve System.*

(1) *Income received by individuals after taxes.*

DISTRIBUTION OF INCOME PRODUCED BY AMERICAN CORPORATIONS

(in 1000 millions of dollars)

| | Income Produced by Corporations | | | Distribution of Corporate-produced Income after Corporate Taxes | | | | | |
| | | | | to Labour | | | to Capital | | |
	Total	Corporate Taxes	Income After Taxes	Wages and Salaries	Supplements	Percent to Labour	Interest	Profits	Percent to Capital
1947	104·7	11·3	93·4	77·3	3·9	86·9	0·6	11·6	13·1
1948	120·4	12·5	107·9	85·9	4·1	83·4	·3	17·5	16·6
1949	115·5	10·4	105·1	83·4	4·4	83·5	·4	17·0	16·5
1950	132·3	17·9	114·4	91·7	5·7	85·1	·2	16·8	14·9
1951	153·3	22·4	130·9	106·2	7·1	86·5	·3	17·3	13·5
1952	158·5	19·5	139·0	114·1	7·5	87·5	·3	17·1	12·5
1953	169·0	20·2	148·8	124·2	8·2	89·0	·4	16·0	11·0
1954	163·3	17·2	146·1	121·9	8·5	89·2	·5	15·1	10·8
1955	184·2	21·8	162·4	132·5	9·7	87·5	·5	19·8	12·5
1956	195·2	21·2	174·0	143·8	10·9	88·9	·3	19·0	11·1
1957	202·9	20·9	182·0	150·6	12·2	89·4	·4	18·8	10·6
1958	195·8	18·6	177·2	147·4	12·1	90·0	1·0	16·8	10·0
1959	220·8	23·2	197·6	160·4	14·1	88·3	·9	22·2	11·7
1960	227·4	22·3	205·1	167·5	15·6	89·2	·6	21·4	10·8
1961	230·0	22·0	208·0	169·7	16·0	89·2	·9	21·3	10·8

Source: U.S. Department of Commerce, Survey of Current Business, *November 1962*, and Economic Report of the President, *1964*.

ECONOMIC CHARACTERISTICS OF UNITED STATES AGRICULTURE

| | Farm Population as per cent of total Population | Index of Farm Output (1947–49 = 100) | Index of Farm Output per Man-hour (1947–49 = 100) (1) | Tenure of Farm Operators (per cent) | | | | Level of Living Index of Farm Operator Families (1945 = 100) (2) |
				Full Owner	Part Owner	Manager	Tenant	
1900	39·3	56	—	55·8	8·0	1·0	35·2	—
1905	—	—	—	—	—	—	—	—
1910	34·9	61	45	52·8	9·3	·9	37·0	—
1915	32·4	68	49	—	—	—	—	—
1920	30·1	70	49	52·2	8·7	1·0	38·1	—
1925	27·0	70	49	—	—	—	—	—
1930	24·9	72	53	46·3	10·5	·9	42·3	—
1935	25·3	72	57	—	—	—	—	—
1940	23·2	83	67	50·5	10·2	·6	38·7	79
1945	18·1	96	84	56·3	11·3	·7	31·7	100
1950	16·6	100	112	57·5	15·3	·4	26·8 (3)	122
1955	13·6	112	149	57·4	18·2	·4	24·0 (4)	143
1960	11·4	129	205	57·1	21·9	·5	20·5	—

Source: U.S. Department of Commerce, Historical Statistics of the United States *and* Statistical Abstract of the United States, *1961*; U.S. Census Technical Paper, No. 3, Farm Population, 1880–1950.

(1) *These figures differ somewhat from those given in Note 7, below, 'Labour Productivity',*

by reason of slight differences in the composition and weighting of the indexes by the reporting agencies.

(2) *Index based on per cent of farms with electricity, telephones, and automobiles, and average value of products sold or traded. Figure for 1955 is average of 1954 and 1956. In 1956, the percentage of farm families having the following was:*

	per cent
Electricity	94
Telephone	52
Automobile	74
Running water	64
Mechanical refrigeration	90
Television	53

(3) *Figures for 1954.*
(4) *Figures for 1959.*

SOCIAL WELFARE PAYMENTS UNDER PUBLIC PROGRAMMES IN THE UNITED STATES, 1935-60

(in 1000 millions of dollars)

	Social Insurance	Public Aid	Health and Medical	Other Welfare	Veterans' Benefits	Education	Public Housing	Total	%Gross National Product	%All Government Expenditures
1935	0·4	3·0	0·5	0·1	0·5	2·2	—	6·7	9·8	51·2
1940	1·2	3·6	·7	·1	·5	2·8	·004	9·0	9·3	48·6
1945	1·4	1·0	1·9	·2	·9	3·4	·01	8·9	4·2	8·2
1950	4·8	2·5	2·3	·4	6·5	6·5	·01	23·0	8·7	36·3
1955	9·9	3·0	2·9	·6	4·4	11·3	·09	32·0	8·5	31·7
1960	19·3	4·1	4·3	1·2	5·1	18·2	·2	52·3	10·6	37·5

Source: *US Department of Commerce, Statistical Abstract of the United States, 1963.*

3. Academician E. S. Varga points out: The capitalist society of our times is the same imperialism that existed at the beginning of the twentieth century; its inherent inner laws of development have not changed. Under the conditions of contemporary capitalism there are incomparably greater opportunities than there were at the beginning of the century for the concentration of production and capital in the hands of monopolies, and particularly for the financial oligarchy to dispose of the capital of others. The monopolies and the financial oligarchy have become much stronger.

At the beginning of the century a factory with one thousand workers was considered a large-scale enterprise. Nowadays a factory with one thousand workers is considered a medium-sized enterprise. A large capitalist enterprise today is one which has at least 10,000 to 20,000 workers and employees. At the beginning of the century a concern with shares worth one hundred million dollars was regarded as one of the largest. Today the Standard Oil group has shares of which the total value amounts to approximately ten million dollars, while the American Telephone and Telegraph Company has shares worth eight million dollars. Share values of several million dollars are also possessed by Royal Dutch Shell, United States Steel, and many other monopolies. At the beginning of the century monopolies had already become the decisive force in the imperialist countries. But they were by no means so powerful as they are at the present time when, for example, three companies control the market for aluminium and automobiles in the USA. (E. S. Varga, *Kapitalizm XX veka* (Twentieth-century Capitalism), Moscow, Gospolitizdat, 1961, pp. 99–100).

Academician D. Kosev writes: The authors' view is based on the assumption that the difference between the firms of the late nineteenth century and the monopolies of the present day is purely one of quantity, that a monopoly is simply a concern that is larger in size. But in proceeding from this assumption they are in effect unable to give a qualitative analysis of twentieth-century economic phenomena (we have in mind the economy of the non-socialist countries). The authors constantly hover around this question, or give it relatively superficial treatment, in connection with the concentration of production (isolated from the concentration of property), but fail to point out what is qualitatively new about monopolies. In this instance the authors refrain even from calling things by their proper names, preferring to speak of 'large-scale organizations'. It can scarcely be considered right to avoid economic categories that have become firmly established in writings on economic theory, and to refrain from a full explanation of what these categories actually imply.

In this connection it may be added that in Marxist works the term 'capitalist monopoly' implies such a high concentration of capital and production that, within certain limits, it is possible to fix prices systematically, obtain a super profit, and secure economic and political supremacy.

4. *The Author-Editors have avoided the use of the term 'monopoly' for two reasons: because of the different senses in which the term is used, and because, in the sense used in classical economic literature, the significant developments of the period in the capitalist and mixed economies do not involve monopoly and the elimination of competition as such but rather the presence of large-scale enterprise with consequent changes in the character of competition and other economic relationships.*

In classical economic literature, the term 'monopoly' is applied to a single producer in an industry, especially where no other industry produces a close substitute for his product, or a single seller in a market (cf. Paul A. Samuelson, Economics: An Introductory Analysis, *5th ed., New York, 1961, p. 518). Large enterprises in industries where there are a few major producers, such as the principal American automobile manufacturers, steel corporations, or oil companies, do not qualify as 'monopolies' by this definition. Public utilities, such as telephone or electric companies, which are granted exclusive franchises for a given area and are consequently subject to government regulation, constitute 'regulated monopolies'. Government enterprises such as postal services are 'government monopolies'. In Marxist literature, the term 'monopoly' is used in a much more general sense to apply to private enterprises which are large enough or so strategically placed as to exercise considerable power over the means of production.*

5. Professor A. A. Zvorikine thinks that in certain countries and in certain historical periods the workers manage to secure for themselves a certain improvement in welfare standards, but on the whole capitalism places them in an increasingly disadvantageous position so far as their share in the growing social income is concerned. As a result of improvements in technology, there occurs a growth of the organic composition of capital, i.e. in the total sum of capital; the share of the fixed capital expended on means of production relatively increases, but the share of the variable capital, expended on labour power, decreases.

Thus, according to official American statistics, the share of the wages paid to workers in production, expressed as a percentage of the value of the products of manufacturing industry, is steadily declining. In 1937 it amounted to 40·2 per cent, but in 1958 to 36·7 per cent. This trend becomes particularly striking when one compares it with the tendency for the profits earned by capitalist concerns to grow: after making allowance for taxes, these rose from 4·7 milliard dollars in 1937 to 18·9 milliard dollars in 1958. The declining share of the total national income received by the working class means that the number of the workers declines in relation to the total population, that there is growing unemployment, that there is an increase in the number of dependants per wage-earner, that the worker increases his labour productivity, and much else, which puts the worker at a disadvantage *vis-à-vis* the employers.

As a clear example of the way in which the workers are losing their gains in regard to a minimum subsistence wage, we may take the 1930s, when an exceptionally grave crisis broke out in the USA. According to data of the US Department of Labour, the nominal weekly wage of workers engaged in manufacturing industry in 1938 was 11 per cent lower than it had been in 1929—and that in conditions of growing unemployment. Official statistics show that the number of unemployed between 1930 and 1940 did not drop below 7·7 million, and that between 1932–35 and 1938 it rose to more than 10 million.

Nor does the growth of productivity of labour, as a result of technical progress and automation, improve the position of the working class. For this growth is turned to the interests of the employers. Thus, according to American statistics, labour productivity in manufacturing industry rose by 25·8 per cent between 1953 and 1959. If we take the nominal wage of workers in manufacturing industry, we find that it rose by 21·4 per cent per worker. It would appear, therefore, that the employers are sharing with the workers the extra income gained by mechanization and automation. But if we check this with the price index we find that the real income per worker during this period increased only by 12·3 per cent. If we take the index of real wages and the index of labour productivity and compare them, we find that the 'relative position' of the worker is constantly worsening. Thus, if 1935 is 100, for the first quarter of 1959 the figure would be 39·3 per cent.

There is a growing disproportion between changing minimal needs required to reproduce labour power and the extent to which these needs are satisfied. The minimum limits of wages under capitalism are fixed by the cost of the means of subsistence necessary to enable the worker and his family to survive and to reproduce labour power, i.e., to raise and educate his children in accordance with the requirements of production. The minimum cost of labour power and the wages that determine living standards are not a constant quantity: they vary from one country or period of history to another. The deterioration of the condition of the proletariat also manifests itself in the direct lowering of living standards below the level historically necessary for a particular country and a particular period. In the monthly bulletin, *Labour's Economic Review*, published by AFL-CIO, it was pointed out that in the middle of 1960 seven million American citizens were living from hand-outs. Furthermore, over 35 million people had such low incomes that they were unable to maintain 'an American standard of decency'. This Bulletin also stated that more than 20 per cent of Americans, i.e., over 40 million, did not have the opportunity to satisfy their growing subsistence needs. They 'still live at a substandard income level today'. (*The Handbook of Basic Economic Statistics*, Vol. XIV, No. 1, January 1960, p. 24; No. 4, April 1960, pp. 94, 101–2; *Economic Notes*, May 1959, p. 2; *Labour Economic Review*, Vol. V, No. 8, August 1960, pp. 45, 47.)

For a more detailed study, cf. J. Kuczynski, *Die Geschichte der Lage der Arbeiter unter dem Kapitalismus*, t. 1, Berlin, Acad. Verb., 1960—see the material describing the twentieth century; *Labour Fact Book*, prepared by the Labour Research Association, 1–15 (N.Y., Inter. Publ. 1931–61); A. I. Katz, *Polozheniye proletariata SShA pri imperializmy* (The Condition of the Proletariat in the USA under Imperialism) (Moscow, USSR, Academy of Sciences, 1962).

6. Professor E. N. Anderson notes that non-Marxist economists and policy makers in non-communist countries regard a certain amount of temporary unemployment as necessary to a society in which workers may leave or change their jobs and employers are free to expand or contract the number and kind of their employees. They contrast this attitude with the economic system of socialist societies. There is difference of opinion among economists in capitalistic countries as to the volume of temporary unemployment necessary for flexibility. Practices also differ among countries as to the amount and the nature of assistance which should be given to facilitate re-employment. Sweden, for example, has demonstrated the ability to maintain flexibility with a very low rate of unemployment, less than 1 per cent in recent years, and has gone further than most countries in measures to facilitate labour mobility. In the United States 2 per cent has been assumed generally to be a probable minimum, and some economists have regarded a higher figure as normal. It is widely agreed that some form of unemployment compensation should be available to workers who have become unemployed involuntarily during the period required for them to find new employment. The cost for this is regarded as a proper one upon industry, and employers are taxed to support unemployment benefits schemes.

The kind of unemployment which represents the flexibility of a free economy is regarded as distinct from massive unemployment accompanying economic depression, such as occurred in the 1930s. Scholars and statesmen in capitalist countries generally agree about the means of preventing massive unemployment flowing from a major economic depression. The governments of these countries since World War II have assumed responsibility for assuring that such condition will not recur and have adopted policies toward prevention. The economic stability of European and American economies during these years is considered evidence of the soundness of such policies. Although there have been fluctuations in economic activity during this time, especially in the United States, small recessions have shown no signs of becoming deep depressions; the rate of expansion has soon been resumed.

Disagreement with respect to both theory and practice within capitalistic economies focuses upon the complex interrelations among employment, productivity, income distribution, consumption, investment and price stability, and on the means of achieving economic growth while avoiding serious inflation. Variations among capitalist economies in the 1950s are cited as indicating the complexity of the technical problems involved and the fact that these problems have not been fully solved; several European countries, for example, have had minimal unemployment; the Japanese economy has shown an exceedingly rapid rate of growth; in the United States, however, productivity has outstripped general economic growth, with the result that the rate of increase in production has exceeded that of employment, and unemployment has persisted at a level above that which reflects flexibility in the economy.

With increase in automation a further problem has begun to appear, the simultaneous existence of labour shortages and unemployment because the kinds of new jobs which are developing call increasingly for education, and the displaced workers lack the necessary education and training to fill available jobs.

Literature on the subject is voluminous; only a few works will be cited:

Sir William H. Beveridge, *Full Employment in a Free Society* (London, 1944).
Douglas Hague (ed.), *Stability and Progress in the World Economy: The First Congress of the International Economic Association* (London, 1958).
Daniel Hamburg, *Economic Growth and Instability* (New York, 1956).
Income, Employment and Public Policy: Essays in Honour of Alvin H. Hansen (New York, 1948).
Money, Trade and Economic Growth: In Honour of John H. Williams (New York, 1951).
Bertil Ohlin, *The Problem of Employment Stabilization* (New York, 1949).
United Nations, Report of a Group of Experts, *National and International Measures for Full Employment* (New York, 1949).

7. *The Author-Editors would like to supplement the text with the following table:*

LABOUR PRODUCTIVITY, REAL EARNINGS, AND HOURS OF WORK IN THE UNITED STATES, 1899–1963

		Index of Output per Man-Hour		Average Real Weekly Earnings in Manufacturing Industries (1963 prices) $	Average Weekly Hours of Work in Manufacturing Industries
	Total Private Employment	(1929=100)			
		Agriculture (1)	Non-agricultural Industries		
1899	54·7	87·9	52·8	—	—
1904	58·5	89·4	—	—	—
1909	65·6	88·1	64·7	—	51·0
1914	64·7	92·7	—	33·16	49·4
1919	79·0	88·4	79·7	38·60	46·3
1924	91·7	90·0	—	42·35	43·7
1929	100·0	100·0	100·0	44·23	44·2
1934	104·5	101·0	—	41·65	34·6
1939	122·2	119·5	(116·4) (2)	52·07	37·7
1944	152·6	134·0	—	79·48	45·2
1949	162·7	165·9	156·3	69·25	39·1
1954	195·4	232·7	179·7	80·38	39·6
1959	225·0	289·9	203·9	92·81	40·3
1963	254·6	362·4	227·7	99·38	40·4

Source: *U.S. Department of Commerce, Bureau of the Census,* Historical Statistics of the United States, Colonial Times to 1957; *U S Department of Labor,* Employment and Earnings Statistics for the United States, 1909–1962; Economic Report of the President, 1964.

(*1*) *These figures differ somewhat from those given in Note 2 above, 'Economic Characteristics of United States Agriculture' by reason of slight differences in the composition and weighting of the indexes by the reporting agencies.*
(*2*) *Figure for 1937.*

8. *The Author-Editors stress the point that within the large corporation, the separation of ownership from control is to be distinguished from the separation of ownership from management. The latter has long been a familiar phenomenon in the form of the absentee landlord whose bailiff or manager is subject to his orders, or the owner of a business who hires a manager, or the owner of the majority of the stock in a corporation who controls the corporation and its management by voting his stock.*

Separation of ownership from control occurs when no one owns a sufficient proportion of the stock of a corporation to exercise control by virtue of such ownership. This is typically the case in the large corporation in the USA and elsewhere, where the capitalization is so great and the number of shares so large that no single stockholder owns more than a small fraction of the total. In the US Steel Corporation in 1957, for example, the largest stockholder owned less than two-tenths of 1 per cent of the outstanding stock and all the members of the Board of Directors and principal officers in combination owned only approximately two-tenths of 1 per cent.

Although individual holdings, in and of themselves, may represent considerable wealth, they do not represent control. The latter resides in the self-perpetuating board of directors which can maintain itself in power indefinitely by means of the proxy system under which it uses company funds to solicit the proxy vote of shareholders. Only a shareholder or group of shareholders in a position to spend very large sums of money to solicit proxies from thousands of shareholders for a rival slate of officers can hope to unseat an established management. On the basis of the experience of large American corporations, a company management could not anticipate such a challenge on the average more frequently than once in 200 years. (See Joseph A. Livingston, The American Stockholder, *Philadelphia, 1958.) This independence of corporate management from those who own beneficial shares in the corporation breaks up the attributes of property—the right to receive benefits and the power to determine use—and thus introduces a new set of relationships unknown to traditional economic theory, either classical or Marxian. (See Adolf A. Berle, jr., and Gardiner C. Means,* The Modern Corporation and Private Property, *New York, 1933; Adolf A. Berle, jr.,* Power Without Property, *New York, 1959; Gardiner C. Means,* Pricing Power and the Public Interest, *New York, 1962.)*

The divorce of control from ownership is not confined to capitalist countries and their large corporations. Yugoslavia has sought to apply this principle in its version of a socialist society by distinguishing between ownership which is social and control which is vested, without ownership, in the workers' council of each enterprise. In the view of Yugoslav economists and outside observers, this is one of the features which distinguish Yugoslav socialism from that of the Soviet Union where ownership of the means of production is assumed to carry control and the state operates, directly or through subsidiary organs, the enterprises which it owns. (See Calvin B. Hoover, The Economy, Liberty and the State, *New York, 1950; George W. Hoffman and Fred W. Neal,* Yugoslavia and the New Communism, *New York, 1962.)*

9. Professor E. N. Anderson thinks that the Author-Editors have not made it sufficiently clear that the capitalist ethic is not an isolated phenomenon but an integral part of a social outlook and value system which pervades democratic societies. Its basis is the belief that multiple centres of decision-making contribute to the health of society and constitute the soundest condition for stability, flexibility and progress, as well as for the development of creative and responsible individuals. According to this fundamental belief as applied to the economic sphere, the value of initiative, creativity and responsible judgment on the part of all types of entrepreneurs at all levels far outweighs the economic waste which may arise from overlapping or unco-ordinated efforts. Furthermore, since the same qualities of individual responsibility and widespread decision-making are of the essence of political democracy, they are part of the very fabric of the society.

With the growing complexity of modern life, these basic principles encounter problems of application in both the economic and political spheres, which have led to the development of large-scale institutions and kinds of regulation that depart from earlier and simpler forms of economic enterprise and political participation. The paramount considerations remain the same, however, and such forms of economic planning and extensions of political administration as are introduced are designed, not to substitute authority for responsibility, but to provide a framework within which initiative can be exercised and the pluralistic concept of multiple centres of decision-making can find effective expression.

For a theoretical discussion and for an analysis of concrete examples the reader may consult the following:

Walter Eucken, *The Foundations of Economics: History and Theory in the Analysis of Economic Reality* (London, 1950).

Walter Eucken, *This Unsuccessful Age, or the Pains of Economic Progress* (New York, 1952).

Frank Knight, *The Economic Order and Religion* (New York, London, 1945).

Frank Knight, *The Ethics of Competition and Other Essays* (New York, London, 1935).

Milton Friedman, *Capitalism and Freedom, Essays in Economic and Social Philosophy* (New York, London, 1947).

10. Academician E. Varga writes: The Soviet scientists' point of view is quite different from the authors' as far as the question of capitalist ethics is concerned. The main stimulus of the capitalist production is the pursuit for the highest possible profits, rising exploitation, and bitter competition. These factors form anti-social ethics of capitalism, justifying the aspiration for enrichment by any means, including unscrupulousness, duplicity, and the cult of force.

11. Soviet historians cannot agree with the appraisal of collectivization given by the authors of this chapter. Lately a profound study has been made in the USSR of the processes of collectivization, and the results of this study have been briefly set forth in the recently published *History of the CPSU* (2nd ed., enlarged, Moscow, Gospolitizdat, 1962, pp. 426, 429–31, 435–51, 462–7).

The urge towards a collective economy came from below and was felt by both the poor and the middle peasants. The vast extent of industrial development and the labour achievements of the workers made a strong impression on the broad masses of the peasantry. They saw how the Soviet power, the workers, surmounted difficulties to build plants for the production of tractors and new agricultural machinery, ever greater numbers of which came to the villages. The Soviet government helped the peasantry by organizing stations for renting machinery, tractor units and machine-and-tractor stations. Numerous peasant delegations visited factories and construction sites, attended workers' meetings and became infected with their enthusiasm. Upon their return to the villages, the advanced representatives of the peasantry became initiators of the organization of *kolkhozes* (collective farms). The turn of the peasant masses towards the *kolkhozes* was also influenced by the stimulating experience of the first *kolkhozes* and *sovkhozes*. The peasants became convinced in practice of the advantages of large-scale economies and collective work over individual farms. The *kolkhozes* and *sovkhozes* were the centres of advanced agrotechnical practices. They helped the surrounding peasant population with machines, pedigree cattle and high-quality seeds. By the beginning of 1930 in a number of districts in the country the *kolkhoz* movement had led to all-round collectivization. Entire villages joined the *kolkhozes*. The poor peasants were followed by the middle peasants. However, the achievements of *kolkhoz* construction in that period were accompanied by grave errors. In view of the attachment of the peasants to their individual, private economies; in view of the considerable number of *kulaks* (about 5 per cent of the peasant households) who resisted collectivization and the socialist reconstruction of the countryside; and in the absence of any historical experience of such reconstruction, the transition of the peasantry to a collective economy was the most difficult and complicated problem of socialist construction. V. I. Lenin understood all the difficulties connected with collectivization and in his time called for great discretion in approaching this objective. He warned that allowance must be made for the attachment of the peasant to his farm and, hence, that he was not to be forced, that too much haste was harmful. The practice of collectivization in the first two months of 1930 proved that these well-warranted warnings had not been heeded, that the Leninist principle of voluntarism in *kolkhoz* construction had been violated. Stalin called for the speeding up of collectivization. His under-estimation of the peasant's attachment to his small private holding, his refusal to listen to the rational proposals of the party workers in the countryside was the greatest miscalculation and the source of many errors at the inception of the mass *kolkhoz* movement. However, by the spring of 1930 the Party realized what the situation had come to in the villages, and took the path of liquidating the errors committed. The main attention was directed to the organizational-economic building up of the new *kolkhozes*. The errors of *kolkhoz* construction had not shaken faith in the correctness of Lenin's co-operative plan, in collectivization as the only way of saving the toiling peasants from enslavement by the *kulaks*, from poverty and ignorance, the only way to a free and happy life.

12. In the opinion of Soviet scholars, one should not identify the personal policy of Stalin during the period of his cult with the policy of the Communist party and the Soviet government. In the resolution 'On Overcoming the Personality Cult and its Consequences' (1956) the Central Committee of the CPSU wrote: 'Fulfilling Lenin's behests, the Communist Party undertook the socialist industrialization of the country, the collectivization of agriculture, and the accomplishment of a cultural revolution. . . . J. V. Stalin, who for a long period occupied the position of General Secretary of the Central Committee of the Party, together with other leading figures actively fought for the realization of Lenin's behests. . . . However, incorrectly all our great victories became associated with his name . . . successes in the construction of socialism, the strengthening of the USSR, were ascribed to Stalin as a consequence of the cult of the personality.' 'The Twentieth Party Congress and the entire policy of the Central Committee after the death of Stalin show convincingly there was a well-knit Leninist nucleus of leaders, who correctly understood the needs of the moment both in domestic and in foreign affairs. It is impossible to say that there was no resistance to the negative phenomena associated with the personality cult, which were acting as a brake upon the forward march of socialism. Moreover, there were certain periods—for example, during the war years—when Stalin's one-man rule was confined within narrow limits, and when the harmful effects of illegal and arbitrary acts were felt much less severely. It is well known that precisely during the period of the war members of the Central Committee, and also leading Soviet army commanders, took into their own hands certain spheres of activity at the front and in the rear, took independent decisions, and together with local Party and Soviet organizations, by their political, economic and military work assured the victory of the Soviet people in the war. . . . Immediately after the death of Stalin the Leninist nucleus of the Central Committee embarked upon a resolute struggle against the cult of personality and its grave consequences. . . . It would be a serious mistake to conclude from the existence in the past of the cult of personality that changes of some sort took place in the social structure of the USSR, or to seek the source of the cult in the nature of the Soviet social system. This would be absolutely wrong, since it would not correspond with reality, would go against the facts.

Despite all the harm which the cult of Stalin as a personality did to the Party and people, it could not alter and did not alter the nature of our social system. No cult of a personality could alter the nature of a socialist state based on public ownership of the means of production, the alliance of workers and peasants, and the friendship of people. . . .' (*KPSS v rezolyutsiyakh i resheniyakh syezdov, konferentsiy i plenumov TsK* [The CPSU in the resolutions and decisions of its congresses, conferences, and Central Committee plenums], 7th ed., Pt. IV, Moscow, Gospolitizdat, 1960, pp. 227–31).

Indeed, even at that time, despite Stalin's distortion of many Leninist principles of Party and Soviet leadership, the CPSU and the Soviet state were carrying out a policy that accorded with the interests of the Soviet people. As a result of this correct activity the USSR was able to emerge victorious in the second world war, and also to restore its economy rapidly after the war.

'Despite the personality cult, and in conflict with it, the popular masses, led by the Communist Party, the product of our system, showed tremendous initiative, performed their great historic task, and overcame all difficulties that faced them in the building of socialism. . . . The very fact that the Party itself boldly and frankly raised the question of liquidating the cult of the personality, of the impermissible errors which Stalin committed, is convincing proof that the Party stands firmly on guard over Leninism, the cause of socialism and communism, that it observes socialist legality and the interests of peoples, and that it safeguards the rights of Soviet citizens' (*ibid.*, p. 233). Cf. Note 17 to Chapter XXIII.

13. Professor A. A. Zvorikine observes that the authors of this chapter do not have a clear

idea of the specific features of the Soviet economy; they picture the development of this economy as the result of measures taken to reward those who work well and to punish those who work badly. The very attitude to work has changed in the USSR. The early years of the Soviet power already saw the rise of socialist emulation, which became a powerful stimulus in the development of the socialist economy. It began in the years of the Civil War when the workers of the Moscow–Kazan Railway organized the first communist subbotnik* on May 1, 1919, and became widespread in the years of the first five-year plan (the shock-workers and Stakhanovite movements). Socialist emulation continued to develop in the years of the war and during the period of rehabilitation of the national economy in the postwar years. Today it has become a powerful movement for communist labour, in which millions of working people participate. A testimony to the changed attitude towards work is the urge of the workers themselves to find ways of improving technology—as expressed in the rise of industrial invention and innovation. In 1961, 2,594,000 persons offered 4,152,000 inventions and rationalization proposals, and of this number 2,676,000 were recommended for application in production. One can cite examples, unthinkable in capitalist society, of Soviet workers making material sacrifices for the sake of improving production records. Valentina Gaganova, a worker of the Vyshnevolotsky cotton goods factory, volunteered to lead a lagging brigade in order to teach its members advanced techniques although for her, personally, this meant a material loss. Gaganova's act met with the approval of public opinion in the country, and many others followed suit. It would be a vulgarization to regard such acts as a response to reward which is an external stimulus. Their roots reach much more deeply, for they are connected with the growth of the people's consciousness, with the development of new socialist ethics. The selfless labour of the Soviet people is based on the deep inner conviction, on the realization that they are working for themselves, inasmuch as the means of production have passed from private hands into the hands of the working people themselves. The abolition of private ownership of the means of production and the establishment of social ownership were the decisive factors in changing the attitude towards work in the USSR. At the same time great importance is attached to material and moral incentives. People who achieve high labour productivity, give excellent quality of production, reduce the cost of production are accorded respect and honours in the USSR. The finest of them become national heroes; the newspapers write about them, there are radio broadcasts about them, their portraits are prominently displayed in the towns and villages of the Soviet Union. The Soviet system of wages which is based on the principle of socialism—from each according to his abilities, to each according to his work—is so organized that people are materially interested in quantity and quality of their output. Socialism does not deny material incentives, to which it adds moral incentives. In addition to the system of incentives there are also measures of reprisal which are applied to idlers and those who violate labour discipline and take the form of reprimands and public censure. In the case of a malicious breach of discipline the offender may be discharged. However, discharge is resorted to only in exceptional cases and then only with the sanction of the trade union organization. The authors of the chapter confuse the punishments meted out to law-breakers with measures for organizing production. Restrictions on the right of workers to leave their employment were introduced in the years of the second world war when there was already the threat of an attack upon the USSR and it was necessary to mobilize all forces to resist the enemy. When the rehabilitation of the national economy was completed after the war, these restrictions were lifted. They were always regarded as an extreme measure called for by extraordinary circumstance, and were not considered the norm for Soviet society. As for the assigning of specialists to jobs upon graduation from educational institutions, this cannot be regarded as a form of compulsory labour. Soviet youth who receive free education and material aid during their course of study consider it their honourable duty upon graduation to work for two or three years in those enterprises and organizations, and in those parts of the country, where there is a need of specialists. In general, recruitment of the labour force for work in any part of the country is carried out exclusively on a voluntary basis. During the Soviet years millions of young people volunteered to work on the new construction projects of the Urals, Siberia, the Far East and on the virgin lands. The methods of organizing the

*Subbotnik—labour freely given to the state on off days or overtime.

socialist economy, far from impeding economic progress, prompted it. The facts reported in the Soviet press about the hoarding of surpus reserves on some enterprises and about other anti-social acts are not characteristic, and by no means a result of the socialist form of organization of production.

Reference:

V. I. Lenin, *Kak organizovat sorevnovaniye* (How to Organize Competition) *Collected works* (4th Russ. ed.) (Moscow, Gospolitizdat, 1949), Vol. 26, pp. 367–76.

V. I. Lenin, *Oscheredniye zadachi sovetskoi vlasti.* (The Immediate Tasks of the Soviet Government) *loc. cit.* (Moscow, 1950), Vol. 27, pp. 230–3).

V. I. Lenin, *Velikii pochin* (A Great Beginning) *loc. cit.* (Moscow, 1950, Vol. 29, pp. 377–400).

(The works of V. I. Lenin are available in all the main languages.)

V. I. Gershberg, *Dvizheniye kollektivov i udarnikov kommunisticheskogo truda* (Movement of Communist Labour, Collectives and Shock Workers) (Moscow Gospolitizdat, 1961).

U istokov kommunisticheskogo truda (At the Sources of Communist Labour) (Moscow, Sotsekgiz, 1959).

I. I. Changli, *Sotsialisticheskoye sorevnovaniye i noviye formy kommunisticheskogo truda* (Socialist Competition and New Forms of Communist Labour) (Moscow, Sotsekgiz, 1959).

14. Academician E. S. Varga writes: 'Even prior to the end of the war serious disagreements arose between the Soviet Union and its allies, particularly Great Britain, in regard to the social order and system of government in the countries that had been liberated from the Hitlerite yoke. The allies wanted to ensure in advance the maintenance of the capitalist system, and to hand over power in Poland and Czechoslovakia to the leaders who had emigrated to London and had proclaimed themselves to be the governments of these countries. The Soviet Union considered that the peoples of these countries themselves should settle the question whether they wished to establish a regime headed by their former leaders or introduce a new regime led by those who had fought against fascism within their own country. The question whether the countries of central and south-eastern Europe should preserve a capitalist system or form a new socialist system, became one of the most important issues in the development, after the war, of the "Cold War".'

By liberating the countries of central and south-eastern Europe from the Hitlerite occupation forces, the Soviet Union paved the way for the activity of the forces that had organized the resistance movement against fascism and its internal allies. There developed a prolonged struggle between the capitalist and anti-capitalist forces which, after three or four years, ended with the victory of the latter and the transition to socialism in all countries of central and south-east Europe, with the exception of Greece where British forces intervened. On the former territory of Germany two states came into existence: The Federal Republic of Germany and the German Democratic Republic.

15. The treatment of Eastern Europe in the text for the period following World War II has been criticized by scholars who think that the 'satellite' relationship between these states and the Soviet Union has not been shown adequately. Among those expressing this view are Professors Oscar Halecki and Robert Strausz-Hupé (United States).

16. *The Author-Editors point out that they have made no attempt to characterize by any single term the complex economic, political and military relationships between the Soviet Union and the states of Eastern Europe.*

17. Academician S. G. Strumilin notes that the stability of the economy of the socialist states is not based on methods of coercion, as the authors maintain, but on the planning of the economy on a national scale. One of the chief advantages of the socialist system over the capitalist system is the possibility of carrying on the entire economy according to a single plan. The planned character of our economy implies conscious observance and consistent implementation of the principle of proportional development of all branches of the economy.

S. G. Strumilin, '*Planirovaiye: nashe reshayushcheye preimushchestvo*' (Planning: Our Decisive Advantage'), in *Molodoy Kommunist* (The Young Communist), 1957, No. 3, p. 12.

CHAPTER XXII

SOCIAL INSTITUTIONS

T HE changes of the twentieth century left no institution untouched and scarcely a relationship unmodified. This included the basic unit of all societies, the family, as well as the various systems of social stratification which gave to the individual his status outside the family group. As these traditional institutions changed their character and as new situations altered the individual's place in society, many relationships came to be determined through voluntary associations based on common economic situation, on common political views, or on age, sex or common interest. In the mobile and constantly changing societies of the twentieth century, however, no substitute was found for the relatively stable relationships which gave security of status and role to most members of most societies in the past. The modern individual thus faced a uniquely difficult task of making his own place amid the complexities of modern life.

I. THE FAMILY*

During the twentieth century the family underwent major changes in its composition, function and structure in virtually every part of the world, whatever had been the family's traditional form and role in the culture of each area.

At the opening of the century family forms varied widely. In the West the traditional rural family, closely identified with the land and maintaining its continuity in relation to it, retained its characteristics both among peasant proprietors and landed gentry. This family was generally patriarchal and authoritarian; typically it included three generations and a more or less extended group of relatives; marriages were where possible designed to improve the position of the family as a landholder. Where primogeniture prevailed, as in Britain, one branch of the family remained intact and related to the land while younger sons, and daughters who failed to marry into a land-inheriting family, made their way to towns and cities or emigrated. Where, as in France, the system of inheritance led to the division of lands among family members, subdivisions into uneconomic units sent those who could not make a living on their small plots to seek employment in the towns or, as frequently in Italy, to seek new opportunities overseas.

In urban communities of the West, the two-generation family of parents and children had become the norm. This nuclear family was generally strongly

* For the application of social science to family life and child rearing, see Chapter XVII, The Home.

patriarchal, the authority of husband and father being supported by both Anglo-Saxon and Napoleonic law, though in practice the strength of paternal authority varied from dominance, as in most German and Italian families, to more limited authority, as in many urban families of the United States. Where the heritage from days of slavery had left its mark on family structure, as in the Caribbean and among many Negroes in the United States, both rural and urban families often tended to be matriarchal in actual form, for slavery had negated family life, generally accorded children the status of their mother and allowed the father neither authority nor responsibility.

Outside the western culture areas some form of the joint family owning its property in common, or of the extended family of mutually supporting but not co-owning members, was usually though not universally the base of the social structure. In China the joint family was further extended by concubinage and by family societies beyond the joint household. The Indian joint family was predominantly patriarchal, though some communities alsc had a matrilineal system of joint family, and it retained as common property the wealth of members who had taken up city pursuits as well as those living within the rural family group. The Muslim family, strongly patriarchal, followed generally the extended family form; its female members were secluded in the home or veiled from the eyes of other men and their first responsibility was to bear sons to carry on the family line; unless the particular marriage contract specified otherwise, they could be divorced by their husbands at will and additional wives could be brought into the household. In tribal Africa and among tribal peoples elsewhere, usually polygamous families were integrated with tribal institutions to provide the social structure of these areas.

During the first half of the twentieth century each of these family forms was modified by the social changes of these years.

1. *The urban family in the West*[1]

Under the impact of industrialization and urbanization the two-generation, nuclear family tended to replace the more extended families of predominantly rural areas. This urban family in turn was affected by changing economic conditions, the changing status of women, changed attitudes toward children, the democratization and individualization of social relations and, perhaps most fundamentally, by a growing sense that man could in some measure control his destiny and need not bow wholly to fate. As a result the urban family was reduced in size, modified in function, individualized and democratized in structure and became increasingly unstable as a social group.

(a) *Change in family size.* The trend in western urban society, and in rural societies where urban influences and values spread, was toward a decrease in the family size. Under the urban conditions of the twentieth century children became economic liabilities rather than economic assets as child labour laws and compulsory education postponed their economic contribution and lengthened their period of dependency. The cost of rearing and educating children mounted as years of schooling increased and the standards of what was essential to the full development of the child rose. Congested urban housing presented a further deterrent to large households.

At the same time the concept grew that children are a responsibility to be assumed positively, not merely accepted as fate, and that parents should be able to ensure them a good upbringing. Families of two or three children became the urban norm, and parents planned their families accordingly.

The idea that the size of the family was a matter for conscious planning and control had grown during the last quarter of the nineteenth century and it spread widely during the twentieth century. The movement for birth control was motivated originally by several distinct considerations: concern of the neo-Malthusians over the possibility of over-population, the desire of reformers to help workers to limit their families to the number of children they were able to support, and the belief of those seeking to defend the welfare and rights of women that they should have some choice and not be subjected to continuous or undesired child-bearing.

The first bureau set up to offer advice on how to prevent unwanted pregnancy was established in Amsterdam in the 1880s by the first Dutch woman physician, Dr Aletta Jacobs, as part of her effort to promote maternal health. But it required a vigorous struggle to bring the issue of birth control into the open and to make knowledge of contraceptive methods generally available. Laws relating to the distribution of obscene or pornographic literature were applied to the dissemination of contraceptive information; Mrs Annie Besant was brought to trial in England in 1877 on such a charge. Her trial gave impetus to the spread of contraceptive information, however, and stimulated the formation of Malthusian leagues in many European countries. The first international neo-Malthusian conference was held in Paris in 1900, followed by others during the next twenty-five years. Famous trials over this controversial subject took place in Belgium, France, Australia and India.

In the early years of the twentieth century the efforts of Dr Marie Stopes in Britain and Nurse Margaret Sanger in the United States emphasized the health aspect of the problem and drew the support of many doctors, as well as of women leaders such as Mrs Ottesen Jensen in Sweden. Their efforts were reflected in the formation of the Birth Control League in the United States in 1914 and the establishment of birth-control clinics in London and New York in the early 1920s. Mrs Sanger travelled abroad in 1922, arousing interest in Japan, China and India. The matter began to be actively discussed in Central and South America. The movement grew in spite of the opposition of many groups, especially the Catholic Church which firmly resisted the relaxation of laws and the extension of clinical facilities; it was not checked by repressive measures enacted in Italy and France in the 1920s in the effort to stimulate an increase in the birth rate.

In the second quarter of the century the movement changed its emphasis from the negative one of preventing unwanted pregnancy to the positive one of family planning. The shift was made realistic by the reduction in infant and child mortality and the consequent expectation that those born would generally survive. The Birth Control League was replaced by Planned Parenthood, whose objective was to help families to have the number of healthy children which they desired and thought they could care for. Clinics offered help in overcoming sterility as well as in using effective methods of contraception to space children and limit their number. By the middle of the century conscious determination of family size had become a widespread practice in the industrially developed countries.

The decline in family size was most marked in the larger cities and among the more educated and higher occupational elements in the population. Differences in family size between urban and rural areas and between upper and lower classes thus tended to be in inverse ratio to the ability of the family to provide for its members. In all western countries, average family size in most of the larger urban areas had dropped by the second world war below the level at which the city population was maintaining itself through natural increase, and urban growth depended on migration to the city from rural areas where families continued to be large. This trend was less marked in Latin America where the pattern of larger families persisted. But in Europe in the inter-war years a number of countries adopted measures, such as family allowances, special subsidized housing for large families and other public benefits, in order to reduce the burden of child rearing. The objective was to encourage larger families among those who took their parental responsibilities seriously, practised family planning, and were more likely to have fewer children than the less responsible elements in the population.

In the years following the second world war trends in family size were somewhat modified. On the one hand the small-family pattern spread to more elements in the population as knowledge of contraception became more general and as workers and farmers aspired to a manner of living and to opportunities for their children similar to those of the families who had practised family planning in the past. On the other hand the tendency toward extremely small families on the part of the more educated, urbanized elements was modified under the psychological and economic conditions of these years and the three- or four-child family became the norm among some groups which a generation before had tended toward a norm of two or three. This trend was apparent for example in France, which had gone furthest in the direction of very small families. As a result the differentials between social groups—urban–rural, class differences, and ethnic differences where these had prevailed—were diminished, though in the decade after the war they did not wholly disappear.

(b) *Modification of family functions.* The developments of the twentieth century stripped the urban family in the West of many of its traditional functions. It retained few of its economic features as a unit of production when it became part of an urban economy. Urban employment was predominantly on an individual not a family basis. To an increasing degree large-scale enterprise took the place of craft production, where father and son had often worked together at the same bench. Although much retail trade continued to be carried on by family businesses—grocery stores, tobacconists or dress shops—the trend toward chain stores, department stores and supermarkets reduced even this form of family enterprise. Some productive activity did remain in the home, and tended to increase with the development of home appliances as, for example, home laundering after the advent of the washing machine. But this did not counterbalance the much more general shift of former home activities, such as the making of clothing, bread and prepared foods, to factory production.

The small family continued, however, as an economic unit for purposes of consumption and mutual support. The extent to which the earnings of individual members working for wages outside the home were pooled to sustain the family group varied considerably with the culture of the country and the practice of the individual family, but the responsibility for mutual support between parents and children, brothers and sisters, grandparents and grandchildren not only was strong but generally had the sanction of law. Even as a unit of consumption, however, the family lost some of its scope with the growth of public eating places which partly replaced family meals, and with forms of recreation, entertainment and social activity enjoyed by individual family members with age-mates or people with common interests rather than with the family group.

The role of the family as educator was also diminished in proportion as the training which the child received became more and more remote from the content of family life and the range of parental experience, and as the task of education was assumed by the state through the extension of publicly supported schools or by the Church. Where the son had been expected to follow in his father's footsteps and the daughter in her mother's, instruction in agriculture, crafts and household duties could be imparted by parents in the home. But in the urban societies of the twentieth century the child needed to acquire a rapidly expanding body of scientific, technical and literary knowledge, of which the school rather than the family was the repository.

In many situations, in fact, the school functioned as an agency of the community vis-à-vis the parents as well as the child, both determining what the child should learn and influencing parental behaviour. Among immigrant families whose children were moulded by the schools to the culture of the country of adoption, or among rural–urban migrants whose children learned city ways, or in countries which were engaged in bringing about rapid social change, children not only learned at school many things that their parents had never known but often acquired attitudes and values at variance with those of the home.

The mobile urban family also lost much of its function as a means of giving status to its members. At the highest social levels and within some limited groups, the individual's place continued to be defined by his family connections. He was primarily *who* he was rather than *what* he was. But for the majority of people, especially in the bigger urban centres, the family largely ceased to give status to its members. The urban individual, in his many kaleidoscopic relationships at school, at work, in a neighbourhood, in the pursuit of interests or recreation or in casual daily contacts, was known by what he did much more than by who he was. Personal attributes—occupation, education, wealth, talents, personality—became the principal determinants of status; while family connections still might contribute to advancement, opportunity or marriage, they tended to play a supplementary rather than a primary role.

But while the family's traditional economic, educational and status-giving functions were diminished, its central role in the formation of personality and as a source of affection and security was enhanced. The small urban family had to equip its children to meet the strains, pressures and anonymity of modern life and to cope with constant and threatening change. Psychologists called attention to the importance of the child's earliest experience to his whole mental and emotional development and to the inner security essential for his effective functioning as a mature individual.

A major problem for the twentieth-century urban family was therefore how to perform this key function. Anxious parents, impressed with the ill effects which according to Freud and his followers might result from too rigorous or unsympathetic an early training, sought guidance in the multitude of best-selling books on child rearing and articles which filled the popular magazines. Much of the rising tide of juvenile delinquency in urban areas and some mental illness were attributed to failures originating in the family.

The very conditions which brought emphasis upon the family's emotional role made the performance of this role progressively more difficult. The ambitions which families with middle-class standards sought to realize for their children often set up strains in view of the family's inability to supply directly the means for satisfying such ambitions, since these depended upon social factors and the individual's own achievement. Working-class parents in their turn were sometimes too unsure of their economic future, their present status, and the values appropriate to the society of which they found themselves a part, to transmit firm values and exercise confident authority over their children. In successive generations, as these children became parents in their turn, their own insecure childhood could make them even less well equipped emotionally than their parents had been to provide their children with a stable home. As they took on the more apparent middle-class values, these were often grafted on to a very uncertain base. The twentieth-century urban family thus became an uneasy unit, far more self-conscious about its role than its predecessors had been.

In these circumstances conscious efforts were made to strengthen the family in its continuing role. Studies, symposia, institutes and conferences on family life abounded. Schools concluded that preparation for family life could not be left wholly to the home, and introduced classes in sex education, human relations and child care. Instruction in home economics was expanded from the practical household tasks of food preparation and clothing to include 'family life education'.

(c) *Individualization and democratization of family structure.* Many of the same forces which modified the family's size and its functions altered its internal structure and relationships. The individualizing influences of the money economy, urban milieu and social values of the West were reflected in emphasis on the personal as against the interfamilial aspect of marriage, on romantic love and on the priority of individual interests over those of the family group. The changing status of women affected the balance within the family and the roles of its members. The general trend toward democratization in social relations had repercussions in the home, altering the relative positions of parents and children. These trends combined to loosen traditional family bonds, to undermine the authoritarian position of the family head and to substitute for a sternly hierarchical structure a pattern of more equal relationships.

The foundation of the twentieth-century urban family was generally marriage based on romantic love, although marriages for money or to further the interests of the family continued to be arranged. In such a family system courtship took on central importance, since young people had to find their own mates rather than to depend upon their parents to do so for them. When the need to provide opportunities for courtship was reinforced by the popularization of Freudian psychology, it led to the relaxation of many of the traditional restraints and taboos concerning the relations among young people, to changed patterns of sexual behaviour and to the development among adolescents of a virtual sub-culture of their own. Once the family was formed, romantic love continued to be relied upon as the principal cement to hold it together, and dissolution of the marriage bonds when this cement failed became increasingly acceptable except in the Roman Catholic Church.

Freedom of association between boys and girls replaced the separation during adolescence and strict chaperonage which had been the norm followed more or less rigorously in different countries in the past. The clearest evidence of this trend was the spread of coeducation, whose principal objective besides that of economy was to encourage boys and girls to know each other and to share common interests in order that they might have a basis for judging character and for establishing relationships not limited to those based on sexual attraction alone.

Free association among adolescents produced new patterns of behaviour to which teenagers were under pressure from their peers to conform, and often conflicts arose between parents and children over the limits which the adults attempted to place on the social activities of the young. These tendencies were particularly marked in the United States, but by the time of the second world war they were to be seen in many other urban communities in the West.

A freer attitude toward sex was part of the new pattern. The line between the good girl whose virginity was her most carefully guarded possession and the bad girl who made a profession of sex became less sharp. With the aid of flourishing cosmetics industries and designers of clothing and bathing suits, respectable girls adopted ways to make themselves alluring which had been reserved for the professionals or semi-professionals in the past, and glamour became one of the major industries of the twentieth century. The cinema played its part in accentuating this trend, not only by making sexiness the principal stock-in-trade of the movie stars but by developing the stereotypes of the 'good-bad' and the 'bad-good' girls who largely replaced the pure heroine and unpure vamp as stock characters.

Patterns in adolescent behaviour changed with the times. The post-war generation of the 1920s earned the name of 'flaming youth' or the rebellious generation. In the years which followed, the freedoms which had been shocking in the 1920s became commonplace. The generation of young people which grew up during the depression of the 1930s and the war years of the '40s took their freedoms for granted and were more concerned with achieving a measure of security and stability than with shocking their elders.

After the second world war two quite opposite tendencies were apparent, one toward early marriage and the establishment of a stable home, the other toward capricious anti-social behaviour. The first of these patterns, characteristic of the majority, reflected the eagerness of young people to find some security in marriage in a world full of insecurities; though such marriages often took place while both partners were still pursuing their education, they were not generally entered into experimentally in the manner advocated by the *avant-garde* of the 1920s, but with the intent to establish a home and start to rear a family.

The patterns of wanton violence in which a conspicuous minority engaged, sometimes marking themselves off by a distinctive style of dress, baffled parents and authorities on the European continent, in Britain and in the United States, for the boys and girls who broke windows, tore up flowers in parks, killed animals in the zoo, raided farms, assaulted passers-by and showed general disrespect for life and property did not fit the stereotype of the juvenile delinquent as the victim of poverty, broken home or other form of deprivation. These children and young people belonged to all social levels and some came from homes where they lacked no opportunity for education or material well-being, as well as from the opposite type. The widespread appearance of the phenomenon of vandalism led educators and responsible citizens to ask what features of modern life were producing such conduct. Did it reflect a breakdown of traditional family authority without the successful substitution of a basis for responsible behaviour? Was it the uncertainties of the adult world or the unusually wide gulf between the generations in a period of rapid social change? Had a misinterpretation of the principle of individualized education led to abandonment of standards and discipline? Or did the very affluence of the society itself give parents and children alike a sense of ease and leave them without the need to struggle and without challenging goals?

The family based on romantic marriage was not expected wholly to supersede the interests and ambitions of the individual members but to contribute to them or to permit their independent development. Most especially it was expected to give the children the best start in life that it could. The main line of responsibility ran from the family to the child; the child was not expected to subordinate his personal goals to those of the family group.

In the urban milieu, influences and interests outside the family were many and tended to pull it apart. The urban community, paying little attention to family identity and unity, offered a variety of other bases for association. Where space was at a premium and apartment dwelling the usual form of housing, family members tended to seek companionship and interest outside their often crowded dwelling. Children and young people were exposed to school, club, street, movies, television, comic strips and other outside influences whose standards, shared by the child's age-mates, competed with and often took precedence over those of the home. Such influences tended to lessen the family's coherence as a social group.

One of the indications of these individualizing and loosening influences was the increase in the proportion of marriages that ended in divorce. In recognition of marriage as a personal union which might be dissolved when its affectional base disappeared, laws with respect to divorce were liberalized in most countries during the period under review, and divorce became more socially acceptable. Among those who took their standards from the behaviour of movie stars, it even became fashionable, though in the decade after the second world war the number of divorces dropped sharply from the immediate post-war peak.

The increase in divorce was generally regarded as evidence that the family had become a more unstable institution than it had been in the past. It was not wholly clear, however, that the divorce trend reflected in fact a great increase in broken homes, for desertion and separation had long been common, and continued to constitute the 'poor man's divorce' and a means of terminating unsatisfactory relationships where divorce was not provided for by law or was forbidden by religion. Some of the apparent increase in family instability may have reflected only a larger proportion of legally recorded break-ups and the conspicuousness of divorce among people in the public eye.

Meantime, the Catholic Church remained firm in its position that no divorce was permissible, some countries provided no legal grounds for divorce, the British royal family backed by the Church of England refused to countenance it in its ranks, and divorce laws in many places required legal subterfuge or considerable indignity on the part of those who sought to free themselves from their marriage bonds. On the other hand there was a broad trend toward the principle accepted by the Scandinavian countries which regarded divorce as an honourable and dignified way to terminate a relationship, once the basis in mutual respect had been lost.

Within the great majority of families, which remained intact, relationships among the members became less rigidly defined. As women acquired the possibility of economic independence through job opportunities outside the home, and as they received political recognition through the extension of voting rights and the right to hold public office, their dependent and subordinate position in the home was inevitably modified. In most areas under Anglo-Saxon and Napoleonic legal systems, family law was revised to remove many, sometimes all, of the traditional disabilities of married women—their obligation to provide their husbands with their services or their earnings, their inability to handle their own property where they could not enter into contracts or sue and be sued, their ineligibility to be made legal guardians of their children. At mid-century some of these traditional legal limitations survived in some countries, but the trend was toward their abolition.

A practical factor contributing to the changing relationships within the family was the disappearance of a cheap servant class. This was most pronounced in the United States but spread with the social revolutions of the period. In the small nuclear family without servants' help and without the extra female relatives generally present in extended families, the full burden of caring for the children and performing the household tasks rested on the mother. In spite of the household appliances and factory-produced food and clothing which lightened her load, these responsibilities were heavy and exacting. Under the force of circumstances fathers and husbands were called on to share many tasks of the home and the lines between the roles of husband and wife in the household became less distinct.

The growing emphasis on democratic social and political values helped to undermine the exercise of strict paternal authority. A new concept of family relationships envisaged the family as a more or less democratic group in which there was mutual understanding of family problems, the child was expected to assume responsibility, decisions were shared and the father's word was no longer the supreme law.

The most extreme breakdown of traditional authority came where the roles of parents and children were reversed under conditions of rapid social and cultural change. Children of immigrants often broke sharply with the traditions of their parents and, on the basis of their superior knowledge of the adopted language and culture, told their parents how to behave in the new milieu. Revolutionary societies counted on the indoctrination of the young and the development of their energies and leadership to effectuate change.

All these tendencies to loosen family bonds and democratize the family structure were carried to great lengths in the measures taken by the Soviet Union in the years immediately following the October revolution. In its initial effort to destroy what it considered the exploitative features of the bourgeois-capitalist and patriarchal families, it equalized the duties and rights of men

CC*

and women, established institutions to assume or share child-rearing functions, abolished virtually all forms of inheritance, permitted unrestricted divorce and legalized abortion. Children, educated by the schools to the communist way of life, often came into conflict with their conservative parents and were encouraged to take the initiative in guiding the family along new lines.[2]

As non-authoritarian family patterns developed and spread, they were challenged by critics who reasserted traditional values. Easterners in contact with the West were often struck unfavourably by the individualism within the family group and the diminished role of the family head; the relative merits of eastern and western family forms became a frequent theme of Asian writers. Within western societies, some doctors, psychiatrists, writers and parents expressed concern lest the modern western family become dominated by the selfish demands of the young. They insisted that the democratizing trend had gone too far when cartoon strips in the United States presented fathers as slightly ridiculous and rather helpless figures, easily manipulated by daughters, wives and ingenious young children. These critics insisted that children needed the support of authority and that too much freedom could be as damaging as too little in equipping them to make choices and assume responsibilities in adult life.

Toward the middle of the century some of the trends toward family instability appeared to be in process of modification in favour of a larger, more cohesive and more stable family group. The increased size of urban families, the trend toward early marriages and the eagerness of young people at mid-century to establish stable homes has already been noted. For some whose loose family structure had been historically associated with low social status, as among Negroes in the United States, achievement of a stable family and home was the mark of social advancement.

Suburban living set the pattern for a growing proportion of urban families. In one respect the influence was divisive, for the breadwinner who commuted to his job had interests in the central city while his wife and children lived most of their lives in the suburban neighbourhood. But in contrast to the city where there was little except television to hold family members in the home, the suburban home itself became for many families a focus of effort and a common venture. Whether it was a matter of gardening, cutting the lawn, making household repairs, engaging in household decoration or pursuing a hobby at home, suburbanism tended to focus activities of the family around the business of living. Separated from the attractions and distractions of the metropolitan centres, suburban families tended to find more of their resources within the family group and their participation in suburban community life was often as a family or in relation to family interests. For those who married young and lived in small family units, this could be limiting in outlook and scope.

In the Soviet Union, too, the family was strengthened. By the 1930s the Soviet family, based on full equality of man and wife and on a community of their interests, had come to be regarded as a firm unit within the system of social relations, and the state took a number of measures to ensure greater stability. Divorce and abortion were made difficult, family duties and respect for parents were emphasized and the family was supported as an integrating force in the society. Motherhood was honoured with a medal for mothers who had brought up five or six children and the orders of Glorious Motherhood and of Mother Heroine for those who had reared eight or nine and ten or more children respectively.

2. *The joint family in the East*

The joint or extended family which for centuries had been the central social institution of eastern societies, notably in China and India, and in many other parts of the world, was altered and in many cases broken up as a result of developments of the twentieth century. In its traditional form the joint family provided a kind of social security for its members, for no one was wholly dependent on his own resources, and any misfortune befalling a member of the family group was shared by the total body. The joint family encompassed the individual's principal personal relationships and defined his status. Only a relatively few members in the course of their lives experienced the role of family head; most—younger brothers and sisters, and younger generations—lived throughout their lives under the direction of father, grandfather, grandmother, uncle, older brother or husband. Nor did the individual experience control over something that was distinctively his own property or a room of his own in the family home. He was, as it were, a transient member of an on-going institution.

Many factors brought a modification in the traditional joint family, some operating gradually and partially, some suddenly and drastically. Commerce and industry brought income and property to individuals, not always to a family group. In general, the legal instrumentalities of the western colonial powers tended to individualize. British, French and Dutch administrations recognized individual ownership in land, and individual contractual relationships and obligations, and placed demands such as taxation or labour service upon individuals. Employment was on an individual basis, whether as a plantation worker or a factory hand or a civil service employee. These economic and legal factors did not, however, automatically destroy the joint family, for individual earnings could be pooled and individually owned land could be claimed as joint or family property.

A second factor tending to break up the joint family was the changing position of women. In the joint family women generally had no rights of inheritance or independence of action. But as the idea of the emancipation of women spread around the world it brought restlessness within the joint family structure. The movement for individuality and equal rights for women paved the way for their equality before the law with rights of inheritance as well as opportunity for education and the right to vote.

The joint family structure was also weakened by rapid social change which tended to undermine the authority of the elders. Where westernization was challenging ancient ways, and young people were acquiring new standards and bodies of knowledge at variance with the knowledge and the values of which their elders were the repository, it was not easy to maintain filial loyalty and respect in the traditional degree.

The joint family in some cases survived the process of urbanization; in both China and India extended urban families living together in compounds had long existed in ancient urban centres. But the movement of individual members to the city tended to erode the joint family, even when it remained as an institution in its village and on its land. Urban housing, with its small dwellings and crowded conditions, made it difficult to accommodate an extended family group.

Although these factors tended to undermine the joint family, it was not until the revolutionary changes of the years after the second world war that the institution was dealt a direct blow in some of the areas of its principal strength. Under the constitution and laws of the Indian republic, the breaking up of joint families was accelerated by taxation, inheritance laws and laws according rights to women. Although joint families had been able to partition their joint property by agreement in the past, the new system of taxation and inheritance placed pressure on families to convert themselves into small single-family units. Partition of joint families did not, however, necessarily mean the adoption of the western family form, for most marriages continued to be arranged and the western pattern of romantic courtship and marriage remained unacceptable to most Indian groups.

In China the traditional joint family and the institutions which contributed to its functioning, already under attack during the Republic, became major targets of the communist régime. In place of arranged marriages, virtual selling of daughters in many cases, concubinage and other features of the joint family structure, the communist régime stressed marriage as a matter of personal choice and responsibility. Confucian ethics, with their stress on filial respect and the family as the focus of social and personal relationships, were rejected as obstacles to the attitudes and activities which the communist régime sought to build up. Collective ownership of land and enterprises replaced family units.

In the Islamic countries the Muslim family was a focal point in the conflicts relating to social reform. Except in the most conservative areas, there was some trend toward monogamy, emergence of women from purdah and increased independence on the part of children. This was especially true of urban areas, and in countries such as Egypt where there had been greatest interaction with the West; but even in such countries as Saudi Arabia, Yemen or Afghanistan there was some tendency toward a weakening of the traditional family system in the cities by the middle of the century. Up to the 1950s, however, Turkey was the only Muslim country which had directly adopted the western family form; and even here the change in law was by no means universally followed in practice.

The experience of Turkey well demonstrated the kinds of problems encountered in the attempt to transplant the family institutions of one society into another. Although Ataturk replaced Muslim family law by the Swiss code in 1925, only a fraction of peasant marriages during the following decades conformed to legal requirements, and the Turkish state found it necessary to pass legislation in 1933, 1945, and 1950 legitimizing children of unregistered unions.

Practical difficulties in applying the Swiss procedure in Turkish villages were partly responsible for the persistence of traditional forms—the need to produce birth certificates where none existed, or the requirement of a medical examination where no doctor was available. But in addition, peasants were reluctant to enter a form of marriage which appeared to them not to fulfil the requirements of their situation. The new form precluded the established practice of marrying any additional unattached female who came to live in a household, as an agricultural worker or because a widowed relative was without a place to live, and the Swiss system of inheritance, which excluded parents from inheriting if the deceased had descendants, seemed to the peasants to leave old people unprotected in a country where social security had not yet replaced family responsibility for the aged. Divorce was made difficult, though equal for men and women, and it required a distasteful inquiry into the personal life of the couple.

Yet such objections as these were overcome and the new form was adopted when direct benefits were involved; members of the armed forces, for example, hastened to bring their marriages into conformity with the law in order that their families might receive allowances.

3. The tribal family in Africa

The disruption of the African tribal family as a result of European contact and urban industrial development brought perhaps the most drastic change to which any family system was subjected during the twentieth century. The family and kinship systems, which in most parts of tribal Africa provided the essential structure of relations among individuals and the integration of the society, were radically undermined where European influences were felt.

While the traditional structure of the African tribal family varied among different tribal groups, each specific form was strongly sanctioned by custom, and kin groups largely defined the social roles of the members of the tribe. In one of the usual forms, encountered with variants in many areas, the family was polygamous, each wife with her children forming a unit. The family group might live in an enclosure where wives and other members of the extended family might have their separate huts, assigned in accordance with their age or their relationship to the head of the household and to each other; groups of enclosures linked by kinship formed larger social units.

In most tribal communities the family or the larger kinship group was a self-contained economic unit for purposes of production and for consumption in which all shared; when times were good all benefited and when they were bad all were affected; division of labour was based on the functions traditionally assigned to persons of the appropriate age, sex or position in the family. It was also generally a unit for purposes of child rearing. The authority of all elders in the family group extended to all children, so that the immediate parents did not have full and unsupported responsibility for their young.

The marriage upon which the family relationships rested, arranged within whatever limits might prevail in the tribe, was in the nature of a union of families or households rather than of individuals, and was generally entered into on the basis of some reciprocal arrangement, sometimes a gift of cattle by the husband to the bride's family. Women often remained in the status of minors, first in relation to their fathers and then to their husbands, but in some tribes older women enjoyed freedoms and responsibilities not accorded them as young wives.

Whatever its forms the family largely determined the status of the individual; but each had his defined relationships, from the head to the first and later wives, the older and younger children, male and female, relatives on the father's or the mother's side. With each status went a corresponding role, and clearly defined conduct attached to it. Children had their established roles during childhood and their passage to adulthood was marked by initiation rites in which they learned the duties and responsibilities which went with their new status.

Ultimate responsibility for the actions of individual members of the family was generally borne by the head of the household who must answer for their misdeeds, protect them when in trouble, represent them in tribal courts or councils, and intercede on their behalf with the ancestral or other spirits; he enjoyed full authority commensurate with his responsibilities. The family contributed to the structure of government through a system of chieftaincies, councils or other forms of authority based upon lineage and kinship. It often also played a religious role, for the responsibilities of the family head and other appropriate family members frequently included performance of religious rituals and were no less spiritual than material.

In the course of the twentieth century, under the impact of European domination, the tribal family structure was largely negated in the cities and was weakened in many parts of the country. Even in rural areas it felt the effect of missionary teaching; since the great bulk of the education carried on during the twentieth century in all parts of tribal Africa was by missionaries, this influence was considerable. Christian missionaries attacked the polygamous family; for their church members they insisted upon monogamy and upon dependence upon the rites of the church rather than the marriage bargain as the marriage sanction. Muslim influence was less disruptive, for polygamy was not contrary to the precepts of the Quran and religious teachers did not seek to put a stop to it.

Colonial administrations generally left customary family institutions intact, except as they were indirectly affected by measures designed to deal with commerce or administration. But occasionally the latter had the actual result of undermining the family form which held the tribal society together, as in the classic case of the effort of the British authorities in Nigeria to reduce excessive litigation among the Tiv people. In the process, they disqualified the form of marriage which had not only provided family stability and continuity but had been essential to the rites to make fertile the land and protect the society against evil, and they in effect legalized only the form which had been used by the Tiv for impermanent unions and for ones involving the purchase of slaves.

The principal disrupting influences, however, were industrialization and urbanization. Men who went away to work in the mines left their family group impaired—in its self-sufficiency, its occupational structure and its structure of authority. Even when their absence was temporary and they returned home after a period or intermittently for parts of each year, the pattern of family life was broken. The major breakdown came when women accompanied their men to the mining towns or the cities and established urban family units in the African 'locations' of Johannesburg, in Broken Hill, Kampala or Nairobi, in Dakar or Brazzaville, in Lagos, Accra or Leopoldville.

From one end of Africa to the other, the ever growing number of urban African families represented a break with virtually every element in their traditional structure, even though they often retained close ties with their relatives in the country. Their economic self-sufficiency based on the contribution of all and shared consumption by all was gone; each individual wage-earner was expected by his employer and by the urban authorities to be economically responsible for his immediate family of wife and children, though the members of his extended family might still expect him to share whatever he had as he would have done in the tribal community. If he found himself in difficulty from unemployment, illness or other misfortune, no head of an extended group was at hand to mobilize the resources of all for the protection of the unfortunate member. The loss of this family function was only very partially made up by the formation of voluntary associations for mutual aid. Numerous savings associations, burial societies, co-operative organizations and occupational groups, sometimes cutting across tribal lines, offered a measure of economic protection and also some common sense of belonging, as when members of a burial society might wear the same colour cloth to commemorate a deceased member.

The structure of authority also was undermined. No compact body of elders reinforced the parents' authority over their children; yet by training and experience parents were not equipped to carry the responsibility single-handed. This lack was doubly serious, for expectations with respect to behaviour were no longer agreed upon and understood. Neither a man's own status and role nor that of his wife, his children, his relatives or his neighbours, was any longer clearly defined and universally recognized. From a society in which the structure of the family ensured that no one should experience uncertainty as to who he was or what was expected of him, the urban African found himself in a society in which these certainties had been swept away.

The urban African family was thus forced to reconstitute itself almost from the ground up and with no source of guidance, especially in the many cases where religious and political authority had also been vested in the family and exercised through the structure of the family group. In fact the very circumstances which made the reconstruction necessary intensified its difficulty, for at the same time that the African was pulled into the new society he was to a greater or less degree denied full participation and status in it.

The situation was clearest in the Union of South Africa where the largest number of urbanized Africans were to be found and where their exclusion from participation in the life of the community was most systematic. Here the urban African encountered the congestion and squalor of the 'locations', the indignities of police passes, exclusion from types of employment carrying prestige and bringing higher incomes, denial of political participation and constant exposure to the contradiction between the principles of European society taught in school or Church and the application of European authority to Africans in their daily life. This environment offered little on which the detribalized African might construct an alternative social system to replace the family-tribal structure whose basis had been destroyed.

The situation was somewhat less harsh and negative elsewhere, but the essential problem remained unresolved. In the Belgian Congo, where a colonial policy of training Africans for responsible participation in economic life distinguished the area from other parts of colonial Africa, the price was detribalization and the destruction of the tribal family. In its extreme form this took the shape of boarding schools where children, removed from their families at an early age, were brought up wholly outside of the structure of tribal life. As the African territories moved toward self-government and independence, the growth of an urban society and the extension of its influence into the hinterland brought similar kinds of breakdown in traditional authority, problems of status and role and uncertainty as to the basis for a new family form throughout the rapidly changing African continent.

II. SOCIAL STRATIFICATION[3]

The twentieth century saw a change in the social stratification of virtually all societies, a change which in general made less sharp the lines of division, expanded the middle group, however that group was defined, introduced new bases for social groupings and provided new means of social mobility.

1. *At the opening of the century*

At the opening of the century most of the world's societies were fairly rigidly stratified along class lines, although nineteenth-century industrialization had upset many of the old relationships and the settlement of new lands had created societies which had never had the hierarchical structure of the traditionally feudal societies from which their settlers were drawn.

In the countries of Europe, with the exception of a few places such as Norway where the feudal system never enjoyed a firm hold, and some of the older cities with long-established merchant traditions, remains of the feudal structure provided a continuing framework of relationships. This was particularly the case in Russia and eastern Europe. Paralleling and partially interlinked with the remnants of feudalism was the class structure of the capitalist economy, an upper or middle class of employers and independent entrepreneurs and a proletariat of industrial workers. Where the landed upper class remained substantial it held a social position above that of the families whose wealth, though often greater, came from the less honoured occupations associated with trade and industry. A professional class, drawn principally from the landed and business classes, generally occupied the lower levels of these upper groups, while the intelligentsia of scholars, writers and artists, also derived from the same social groups, moved in related circles, though with greater inter-class freedom than was enjoyed by others. The beginnings of a white-collar class of clerical workers and minor bureaucrats occupied a position below the business and professional level and above that of urban workers and rural peasants.

In the new lands overseas, especially in North America and Australasia, the absence of a feudal tradition and the geographical and social mobility attendant on the filling up of a new continent produced a much less sharply defined class structure. Wealth rather than an inherited social position tended to define class, no landed aristocracy outranked the captains of industry, and people of nearly all economic and occupational levels regarded themselves as middle class, or aspired to such a status if not for themselves then at least for their children.

In areas which had been peopled by a succession of immigrants from different countries, stratification tended to follow ethnic lines at least in the first generation, with immigrants of an earlier period occupying a more secure and favoured position while later immigrants filled the lower socio-economic ranks. As members of each group rose in the occupational scale, acquired wealth which put them on a par with earlier migrants and moved out of the neighbourhood settled by their compatriots, ethnic lines tended to be replaced by those based on economic or occupational position. Where there was a heritage from days of slavery, divisions were perpetuated on the basis of colour or race. In extreme situations, as in the southern states of the United States, stratification along racial lines was supported by laws requiring racial segregation.

The structure of the Latin American countries, based on large-scale land-holdings or other exploitative industries such as mines, was closer to the feudal pattern of Europe than to the societies composed of family homesteads and middle-class entrepreneurs in North America, Australia and New Zealand. A small Europe-oriented upper class and a mass of Indian, *mestizo* and Negro peons characterized these countries, their proportions varying from such predominantly Indian areas as Bolivia and Guatemala to almost wholly European populations in Argentina and Uruguay, with the Negro element prominent along the Caribbean littoral and the north-east coast of Brazil. Inter-class distances were very wide, nowhere was there a large and prominent middle class, and a sharp line was drawn culturally between those whose lives were led within an indigenous cultural milieu as 'Indians' and those who were culturally European, the *blancos* or *ladinos*. The colour line, though present, was not sharply drawn or supported by law but was associated with class differences— the darker skinned being concentrated for historical reasons in low occupational and income groups—and with the presence of indigenous tribal organization.

South Africa, in the aftermath of the Boer war, presented a complex ethnic pattern. Two mutually hostile groups of Europeans, the predominantly rural Afrikaners chiefly of Dutch extraction, and the predominantly urban British, were working out relationships between themselves and the non-Europeans. The latter included the Coloured of mixed racial ancestry who followed a Europeanized way of life, the East Indians, most of whom had been brought in as labourers in the late nineteenth century and who carried on trade and business, and the African population which continued to live in tribal villages but was being drawn more and more into work in the mines, as farm labourers and as servants in the growing towns.

All these western societies at the opening of the century, both in Europe and overseas, were in varying degrees mobile, fluid and changing under the impact of expanding commerce and industry and large-scale migration.

In other parts of the world most societies at the opening of the century still maintained their ancient systems of stratification, subject to modification almost exclusively at the points where they came into direct contact with colonial powers or through trade and missionary activity. In colonial areas an upper class of Europeans, distinguished by both position and skin colour, was superimposed on the class system of the locality. In some areas, especially in south-east Asia, middle-stratum functions of trade or administration were carried on by a Eurasian element or by distinct ethnic communities, frequently Chinese. In all the largely illiterate societies, the *literati* formed a special class, most notably in China with its history of scholar-administrators and India with its Brahmin caste, but also in such forms as Muslim *ulemas* and some Buddhist monks. Religious and ethnic communities often functioned as discrete entities within the overall social structure.

In most parts of the Middle East a small wealthy landholding upper class was separated by an unbridgeable gulf from the poor peasants who worked their lands and from the nomadic peoples, generally living in tribal groups, who made the deserts their home.

Indian society was one of the most complexly stratified in the world by reason of its elaborate caste system, which provided in some instances a basis for hereditary occupations, and by the division of the society into religious groups with separate institutions and personal law. Elsewhere in south Asia the stratification was less complex. Relatively equalitarian village societies formed the base; a small *élite* made up the top—the royal family with its many ramifications in Thailand and Cambodia, petty aristocracies in the Malay States.

In China wealth and landholding in the country and merchant wealth in the cities provided the basis for an upper class while peasant proprietors or tenants on infinitesimally small holdings and a mass of urban and rural coolie labourers made up the bulk of the vast population. Under the traditional system of civil service examinations which prevailed until the beginning of the twentieth century, however, opportunity to enter the ranks of the bureaucracy was open in principle to any who could meet the test of scholarship, and a road to advancement was thus available for the few talented peasant boys who might manage to secure instruction in classical Chinese learning. In Korea similar examinations were open to the sons of bureaucrats and landed gentry. In Japan the remnants of a feudal structure not only continued to set the pattern for rural life but were to a considerable extent transferred into the growing industrial system, where relations between employers and workers followed a semi-feudal pattern.

Social stratification in tropical Africa followed complex tribal patterns which had begun to be cut across by European-imposed political divisions and uprooted by movement to cities and towns. British colonial policy tended to support the existing tribal structure by delegating administrative authority to certain of the tribal chiefs. In French, Belgian and Portuguese areas the tendency was to draw the few 'assimilated' Africans into the superimposed European structure. In the Union of South Africa the African population was being converted into a permanent substratum of labour.

2. *Changing patterns of social stratification*

During the twentieth century in all parts of the world the growth and spread of industrialism expanded the middle class which commercial capitalism had created or brought a new middle class into being. The technology of industrial production and organization brought this tendency, whatever the political and cultural orientation or the stage of industrial development, and however much the character of the middle group might change.

(a) *In industrial societies.* In the early period of European and American industrial development much commercial and industrial activity had been carried on by small entrepreneurs who constituted the backbone of the original middle class. As the economic structure became more complex, a new middle class emerged composed of the administrators of large-scale enterprises and the host of technicians upon whom modern industry and trade depended. Managers, engineers, accountants, advertising men, lawyers, salesmen, bank managers swelled the upper ranks of the middle class; clerical workers, who filled the lower middle-class ranks, increased more rapidly than production workers, for machines were constantly replacing men in the plants while clerical operations became more and more elaborate as economic units grew in size and complexity.

Production workers, in turn, began to move into the technical middle class as mechanization took over routine tasks, and the industrial proletariat was gradually replaced by a growing class of technicians—mechanics who could keep the machinery in working order and various levels of engineers. Finally, even the less skilled took on some middle-class characteristics as higher wages, made possible by increased productivity, enabled them to share the consumption patterns of the middle class. What some people referred to as the 'nouveau riche proletariat' provided the market for mass-produced goods and were able to afford some of the houses, cars, clothes, travel, entertainment and education for their children which had been the prerogatives of the professional, commercial and managerial groups that made up the old middle class.

The new middle class drew recruits from still other sources—from the expanding bureaucracy which carried out the ever increasing functions of government and industry and from the wide range of professional or semi-professional services which highly productive societies could afford. Though marked cleavages remained among these elements, and terms such as 'blue-collar', 'white-collar' or 'black-coated' worker, or 'man in the grey flannel suit', were used to distinguish these categories, the major effect of the spread of industrial technology was to expand the groups whose functions required a measure of education, skill and responsibility and whose income permitted common patterns of consumption above the level of subsistence.

As the middle class grew from all these sources, the lines of stratification which had characterized earlier industrial societies became less marked. Measured in terms of income, the tendency toward a reduction in class differentials was clear, though income alone did not fully reflect the factors of prestige and power that also affected the status of individuals and groups. In addition the extension of public services and educational benefits greatly reduced the gap in real income even where differences in money income were marked.

The transformation came earliest and most completely in the fluid societies of North America and Australasia, but it was remaking the class structure of European countries also. In London in 1930 a survey committee reviewing the changes in 'life and labour' during the forty years since the first London survey in 1890 noted that class differences were no longer clearly visible to the naked eye in distinctions of dress between residents of the fashionable West

End and the slums. By the decade after the second world war the services of the welfare state combined with a high level of employment, heavily graduated taxes on inherited wealth, and scholarships for promising students were making Britain into a middle-class society. Similar trends were swelling the middle-class ranks of other northern and western European countries.

Yet although the general effect of industrial development was to enlarge the middle class and to blur traditional lines, some conflicting tendencies had the effect of heightening stratification rather than of undermining it. The long and costly training required for advancement in an age of specialization could handicap the child whose family was unable to support him through a prolonged period of training or, because of its own social and cultural level, did not see the necessity. Studies in the United States showed that many children from lower-class homes dropped out of school when they reached the legal age because they did not see their own future in terms of the fruits of further training; Dutch universities at mid-century were still drawing only a tiny minority of their students from the homes of labourers. The increase in the size of the industrial enterprise and the concentration of industries in the hands of powerful corporations or the state made it increasingly difficult for new entrepreneurs to enter the market in many industrial lines, and enhanced the advantage enjoyed by those whose wealth and contacts gave them a head-start. Where a single large industrial concern replaced many small units, the number of places at the top became much fewer and the power of those at the top was immensely increased.

In the USSR the October revolution effectively destroyed the upper classes —landowners, capitalists, kulaks—by means of expropriation and, for some who resisted, exile or execution. The Soviet state created a new intelligentsia of technical and professional workers by training scientific personnel and cultural workers drawn from the ranks of workers and peasants and by re-orienting members of the old intelligentsia who threw in their lot with the revolution. Educational policies at first aimed to give priority to the children of workers and peasants, who came to form the bulk of the new technical class; later, restrictions imposed on the non-working classes were withdrawn. Membership in the Communist party was considered an indication of active, conscious, purposeful participation in the building of communism and carried with it prestige and influence.

After an initial period of equalization, policies of differential pay and incentive rewards provided stimuli for working people to raise their technical, educational and cultural levels. The range in income, including supplements such as housing and extended holidays, between upper officials, scientists or artists and the less skilled of the industrial workers and peasants was similar to the range of salaries and wages in other industrial countries, though artists and scientists generally stood higher in the scale. Such differences, however, did not provide a basis for hereditary class differences since inheritance, though not abolished, was strictly limited and educational opportunities were open to all. Inequalities in accumulated wealth thus tended to be reduced. It was the policy of the state, moreover, in line with Marxist–Leninist theory, that the distinction between manual and intellectual work should disappear. Toward this end, educational programmes were modified to provide direct work experience, and progressive mechanization and automation was expected to break down the line between the ordinary factory worker and the technician.

In both capitalist and communist countries bureaucracies which operated large structures, whether industrial or military or governmental, produced their own hierarchies. The importance of this development was noted by some observers in both societies in spite of their respective theories to the contrary. James Burnham (*The Managerial Revolution*, 1940) in the United States described the growing power and organization of industrial bureaucracies as the creation of a 'managerial class'; Milovan Djilas in Yugoslavia (*The New Class*, 1957), applying what he considered a Marxian analysis to the conduct of the communist upper bureaucracy and the logic of their behaviour, thought that he saw the characteristics of a new class.

Stratification along ethnic lines persisted among mixed populations of diverse origins, although the trends which were blurring class distinctions tended to diminish ethnic differences as well. Such differences were most tenacious where reinforced by religion or by colour. Job discrimination and other practices which prevented upward social mobility had the effect of converting ethnic difference into class distinction, or perpetuating class difference by resort to colour or religious prejudice. A variety of group institutions—fraternal societies, churches, clubs, restaurants, grocery stores, newspapers, sometimes radio programmes in the language of the group—tended to sustain ethnic distinctions.

Changes with respect to ethnic stratification were brought about in part by general economic and social tendencies and in part by public policies which varied markedly from one country to another. The decline of white supremacy around the world, both in fact and in theory, put those who practised racial discrimination on the defensive. In some countries ethnic separateness was formalized in law; in others it was expressly discouraged. Canada, where the French population had retained its identity after the area was transferred from France to Britain in the eighteenth century, had pursued a policy which encouraged immigrant groups to settle in national units. In the twentieth century this policy of group settlement was replaced by one of assimilation, but some institutions, notably the school system, helped to keep alive the divisions which had grown out of the earlier policies. Brazil followed a somewhat similar course, first accepting group settlement which produced ethnic colonies of Germans and others, then, in the second quarter of the twentieth century, reversing the policy. In Australia the large numbers of new Australians who immigrated from Europe in the decade after the second world war were systematically integrated into the economic life of the country in a manner designed to prevent their forming ethnic islands or becoming a lower class.

The United States had never pursued the Canadian policy of group settlement but had expected what was commonly referred to as the 'melting pot' of American life, aided by an English-language public school system, to produce generic Americans out of polyglot foreigners. It was with some shock that Americans discovered at the height of the mass immigration before the first world war that the touch of American soil had not immediately transformed Italian and Polish peasants into 100 per cent Americans, in the image of the dominant Anglo-Saxon, Protestant middle class. In actual fact each successive wave of immigrants entered the society at the bottom of the socio-economic ladder, filled the poorest paying and least skilled jobs, lived in the poorest housing among neighbours who spoke the same language, and were looked down upon by those who were already well-established and who had separated themselves from the newcomers by superior jobs and place of residence. When restrictive immigration laws cut off the flow from Europe after the first world war, the familiar process of ethnic stratification was repeated again as low-paid jobs drew to the slums of industrial centres, and the low social status of newcomers, American 'hill-billies' from isolated mountain hollows or worn-out lands, Mexicans from over the border, Negroes from the rural south and Puerto Ricans from their crowded island.

Where colour differences set the group apart, social stratification on the basis of ethnic differences persisted most strongly. In the United States the principle of the melting pot was not expected to apply to Negroes, for there was presumed to be a colour line between 'white' and 'Negro'. Throughout the first half of the twentieth century the colour line continued to act as a bar to opportunity, but in the course of these years, and at an accelerating pace, barriers were lowered, the gap in levels of income, occupation and education was narrowed and segregation as a legal principle was outlawed by the courts. By mid-century grandchildren of slaves along with children of immigrants had entered the ranks of the expanding and levelling middle class.

In other areas where the colour line was less sharply drawn, notably in the countries of Latin America and in the Caribbean, the same tendency existed toward lowered barriers and increased social mobility. As it affected the indigenous Indian population of these regions, the trend was toward the incorporation without discrimination of those who became part of the national life; the line based on ethnic identity was converted into one based on the cultural isolation of tribal groups. Migration of West Indians to Britain in the 1950s introduced the colour factor for the first time there, and large numbers of Algerian workers in France placed a strain on the tolerance of colour differences which had been traditional in that country. The migration of Eurasians to Holland at the time of Indonesian independence presented a problem of assimilation. But only in the Union of South Africa did the colour line become sharper and the policy of *apartheid* gain in strength while it was weakening in other parts of the world.

(*b*) *In non-industrial societies.* In the stratified hierarchical societies of the East and of Africa, a major instrument of change was the body of western-educated individuals who were in a position to challenge the traditional *élite* of the old society.

The nature of the westernized element and its position differed markedly from country to country. In China the western-oriented constituted a group apart, drawn largely from the merchant classes of the port cities who dealt with foreign traders, and from students at mission schools who commanded the western languages necessary to permit them to study abroad and were in line for scholarships. In their efforts to remake Chinese society they came in conflict with those who represented tradition and power, and they were out of touch with the masses of the people. When the communist régime came to power it could readily reject the western-oriented element as 'foreign' and could discredit them by reasserting traditional Chinese cultural values while themselves remaking Chinese society with technology and institutions derived from the West.

In Japan, on the other hand, westernization was not confined to a distinct group which separated itself from the rest of the population but permeated the society to a greater or less degree. Rather than creating a new social stratum, it produced a conflict within the minds and behaviour of a large proportion of the population, leaving the structure of the society essentially unchanged. In Korea the limited influence of missionaries remained the principal source of westernization until after the second world war, when all segments of the population began to share in a rapid process of modernization. In Thailand westernization came through the pursuit of western education by the royal family and court-centred aristocracy, and thus did not create a new social class but modified the conduct and attitudes of the existing *élite*. In the Arab areas, where the class gulf between peasants and landowners was extreme, virtually all educated elements were drawn from the upper class.

Colonial governments depended for the extension and operation of their rule upon a local element trained for certain tasks. The policy of the Dutch in Indonesia was to develop the Indo-European element as the principal adjuncts to the Dutch administrators while providing little western education for Indonesians; this produced a westernized class which was ethnically distinct. When the Indonesians secured their independence they directed their indignation against this privileged class with such force as to drive a large proportion of them from the country; only a tiny group of western-trained Indonesians was available for the development of the Indonesian state. The British in Burma used Indians for most technical and civil service posts not filled by British, while the Burmans who attended English schools became almost completely identified with European culture and interests. Leadership in independent Burma came from men who had remained closer to the people. In India the development of a westernized element through an extensive system of English education designed to provide for the civil services was accompanied by a series of strong movements for the reform of the society from within and by the movement of Indian nationalism. As a consequence the western-educated elements were not separated from those who remained part of the traditional structure, but acted as a leaven in the total body politic.

The most conscious and determined efforts to change the class structure in Asian countries came in Japan and India and in the revolutionary society of communist China. Elsewhere measures to improve the lot of the peasants, the beginnings of industry, the expansion of the bureaucracy and of the educated professional groups pointed the direction of change, but by mid-century these influences had hardly made a dent on the basic social structure.

Japan introduced a series of reform measures following the second world war in its conscious effort to remake its society on a democratic basis. These affected land tenure, access to education, the status of labour and the position of young people and of women. In their initial impact, these reforms modified outward aspects of the society. But it remained a question how deeply they affected the highly structured pattern of relationships which were entrenched in and reinforced by modes of speech and address and by countless details of prescribed daily conduct.

In India the hereditary caste system had been under attack by reforming movements of the nineteenth century. The most westernized had attacked the system directly, while the Hindu reformers had insisted that the fourfold division of Vedic society did not imply that distinctions should be passed on by heredity but rather that they should reflect personal character and natural capacity. In the 1920s, under the leadership of Mahatma Gandhi, the movement against caste distinction and untouchability gained momentum and became part of the nationalist movement. In Gandhi's own *ashram,* untouchables—whom he renamed *harijans,* meaning 'beloved of God'—lived on a basis of equality with others; he encouraged inter-caste marriage and through constant preaching hammered away at the caste structure. *Harijans* themselves organized to demand the removal of disabilities.

By the time of independence a strong public sentiment against untouchability had been built up and the practice had broken down at a number of points. The Indian constitution abolished it outright and made the enforcement of any disability arising from it a penal offence. Barriers to inter-caste and inter-faith marriage were also removed by the Hindu Marriage Validating Act of 1949 and subsequent acts in 1954 and 1955. These measures took away all legal sanction from the maintenance of caste on an hereditary basis.

Many aspects of the caste system survived in practice when it had been abolished by law, however, and untouchability could not be destroyed overnight. In some respects castes gained a new *raison d'être* from the introduction

of democratic suffrage, for candidates seeking support for political office naturally turned to their own group, and this meant their own caste. But political
parties cut across caste lines, and the longer effect of suffrage was to give the
advantage to the groups which were more numerous rather than to those
which had been more influential and thus to establish a new basis for relations
among social groups.

The most potent factors in breaking down the rigidity of traditional caste
stratification were the growth of modern industry, the development of new
professions which cut across the traditional occupational lines that coincided
with caste, and the mobility, juxtaposition and public activity which characterized life in urban communities and in industry. Taxation, land reform, the
break-up of the joint family, the presence of millions of refugees all made it
impossible to maintain a traditional status and contributed to the development
of new social forms.

Stratification on the basis of ethnic and religious distinctions was even
more ingrained in Asia than in the West, for until the idea of the national,
secular state made its way into Asia the concept of common citizenship was
foreign to the traditions of Asian society. Religious and ethnic groups were
expected to retain their identity and distinctive institutions, including their
law and the practices enjoined by their culture. In the multi-cultural societies
of Asia, therefore, national citizenship was slow to erase, or even to lessen, the
divisions between ethnic or religious communities.

There was scarcely a country of Asia, with the exception of Japan, Korea
and China, where this problem did not present itself sharply. It was perhaps
most dramatic in Malaya, where under British rule the Malays enjoyed certain rights not shared by citizens of Chinese or Indian extraction, though these
numbered more than half of the population of the Malay state at the time of
independence. But it was present in the separate status of the Chinese populations of Indonesia and Thailand, and in the Tamil language issue in Ceylon.
A crucial question confronting India and Pakistan was whether India
could succeed in incorporating its Muslim minority as citizens of a secular
state, and what status would ultimately be enjoyed by the Hindus who
constituted 10 per cent of the population of the avowedly Islamic state of
Pakistan.

Ethnic stratification was complicated where these divisions coincided with
economic class lines, as they often did. This situation existed in Turkey,
where the liquidation of the Armenian population and the expulsion of the
Greeks largely deprived Turkish society of its merchant and artisan classes.
The Chinese in Indonesia, and to a considerable extent in Thailand and
Malaya, were similarly an economic as well as an ethnic group.

Ethnic distinctions thus remained of vital importance to the structure of
society in Asia and the Middle East up to the middle of the twentieth century.
Events tended both to intensify and to mitigate these distinctions. The rise of
nationalism accented ethnic identity, as did the fierce communal strife atten-

dant upon the break-up of the Ottoman empire and the partition of the Indian sub-continent. In the years after the second world war the existence of the Chinese People's Republic made the Chinese in the non-communist countries politically suspect as well as the object of economic envy, and the creation of the state of Israel brought an exodus of Jews from their ghettos in eastern lands.

But there was a tendency for ethnic lines to lose their importance wherever the process of urbanization was accompanied by the loss of distinction in dress, by entrance into unaccustomed occupations and by the substitution of new identities for those associated with an ethnic past. Everywhere there was a tendency to produce what the sociologists termed the 'marginal man', who enjoyed a dual cultural orientation or was in the process of losing an old cultural orientation and seeking to acquire a new one. Though ethnic minorities clung fiercely to their separate loyalties, the new nationalism, with its universal education and indoctrination into the language and culture of the nation-group, tended to make Indians, Iraquis, Indonesians, Malays, Pakistanis and Lebanese out of the multi-cultural units which composed these new and proudly self-conscious nation states.

III. VOLUNTARY ORGANIZATIONS

1. *Functions of voluntary organizations in modern society*

As the family shrank in size and in the range of social functions which it performed, and as class stratification and ethnic groupings lost much of their sharpness and ability to define the status and role of the individual, voluntary organizations came to play an ever increasing part in giving shape to modern society and in defining the identity and status of its members.

Voluntary organizations were of many types and were based on many kinds of common interest. The largest and most pervasive were political parties, of growing importance to the operation of the modern democratic state.* Among the most ubiquitous associations were those formed to promote or protect the economic interests of their members—labour unions, organizations of businessmen into trade associations, employers' associations and chambers of commerce, farmers' organizations, professional associations, associations of consumers or taxpayers. As organizations of this type grew in influence, they sometimes tended to become monopolistic bodies, largely controlling the practice of certain professions, opportunities for certain types of employment or access to certain markets and sources of supply, and thus to lose some of their voluntary character.

Some associations offered their members the opportunity to engage in a variety of social activities with age-mates, especially among youth, or in women's organizations on the basis of sex; some were dedicated to civic or

* See Chapter XXIII, Political Institutions.

benevolent activities; others permitted their members to pursue a common hobby or cultural interest.

These many and varied organizations were spontaneous reactions to the need to find means of participating in complex urban life, for they provided the groupings through which social contacts were maintained, interests pursued and influence exerted. The individual who could no longer define himself wholly in terms of his family had to define himself in terms of his occupation and of the groups with which he was identified—his church, his political party, his trade union, his club, association or fraternal order, or the civic or benevolent society to which he belonged. When he met another person, it was often in terms of an association with one organization or another that he might form his expectations of the new acquaintance, beyond the identification provided by his job.

The voluntary organization, moreover, was an increasingly essential instrument for the operations of liberal democracy. Modern democracies could not depend on the direct forms of communication that characterized the village, the Greek city state or the New England town meeting. Some channels were essential for the thought of the populace to take shape and to be expressed. Voluntary organizations offered more intimate and personal sources than the mass media for formation of opinion and attitudes and provided people with a means of group expression through which they could participate actively in the democratic process.

In the socialist societies also voluntary organizations played a special role. In line with the conception that all people should participate in the long run in the administration of public affairs, organizations such as trade unions, professional associations and similar bodies exercised public functions; they were entrusted with appropriate powers and responsibilities, and settled many questions on their own. Moreover, they embraced virtually the entire population; trade union membership, for example, included practically all factory and office workers, while youth organizations covered the bulk of the young people.

2. Economic interest organizations

(a) Business organizations. Associations of businessmen to promote their interests took the form of trade associations for separate industries, employers' associations with which to confront labour, and chambers of commerce to promote the business interests of a particular locality. All these organizations had their prototypes in mediaeval craft and merchant guilds, as did also the labour unions, but their existence in relation to modern industry dated from the second half of the nineteenth century, and in the period during and after the first world war their number increased and their functions were extended.

Trade associations originated in efforts by producers to modify unrestrained competition and to strengthen their position against manufacturers of alternative products. They engaged in research, promoted the publication of trade data, and sought to influence public policy in respect to such matters as tariffs and freight rates in favour of their products. In competition between industries, they engaged in institutional advertising, promoting the products or services of a whole industry rather than those of a single company.

The first world war gave a strong impetus to the growth of trade associations when industries were called upon to make a concerted effort to meet the demands of the governments for war products. In the years after the war they extended their activities to the development of standards for products, such as uniform sizes for screws and bolts or safety standards for electrical equipment. They were made the instruments of experiments in economic organization, in Mussolini's corporate state where they were entrusted with governing powers over industry and in the short-lived American effort to bring the economy out of the depths of the depression of the 1930s by means of codes drawn up by trade associations to cover wages, prices and business practices in each industry.

Trade associations performed social and educational as well as economic functions, for they enabled businessmen to identify themselves with producers in a common field and to maintain social contacts within the group. Their publications, in addition to informing of matters strictly related to their business, contributed to the formation of opinion and the spread of general information.

Employers' associations were sometimes formed explicitly to cope with labour relations; elsewhere trade associations included this role. In their initial form most employers' associations were aggressively anti-union, and engaged in activities designed to prevent the formation of unions, to oppose their demands and to develop a climate of opinion unfavourable to their existence or operation. As unions gained in strength employers' associations generally dropped their extreme belligerency and became instruments for negotiating agreements with labour or, as in several European countries and in Australia and New Zealand, for representing the employers' interest in government machinery for the adjustment of wages or of labour disputes. Some anti-labour employers' associations survived in the United States after they had lost their belligerency in most other countries, and were found in the 1930s to be engaged in violence, intimidation, the maintenance of private police and the conduct of high-powered public relations campaigns to discredit organized labour. It required the enactment of national legislation and skill in its administration to detect and check the many devices by which such associations sought to nullify the workers' legally assured rights to bargain collectively through unions of their own choosing. Whatever their position, employers' associations did much to form the attitudes of their members and thus contributed to the climate of opinion within which labour relations were conducted during these years.

Chambers of commerce overlapped trade and employers' associations in membership but constituted a distinct class of voluntary organization composed of the members of a local business community—not only the merchants as their name, commerce, implied, but manufacturers, bankers and other business interests as well. Their chief *raison d'être* was to promote conditions favourable to the economic interests of the locality—to maintain a tax policy or a labour market favourable to the needs of local business, to stimulate the industries or trades which flourished in the area or which they hoped to attract there, to sustain the purchasing power of their customers. Chambers of commerce frequently acted as the spokesmen for their communities. In the sprawling and anonymous cities it was often the chamber of commerce which defined the city to itself, and which articulated the interests of 'the community' and the manner in which they should be pursued. In so doing they tended to identify the interests of the community with those of the business group and to contribute to the dominance of the business element.

These business organizations, whether based on trade or locality, were bound together in national federations which constituted the voice of business on a national scale. The national associations of manufacturers and national chambers of commerce exercised informal leadership in some countries and rigorous control of their member units in others. Their presence in every country on a truly voluntary basis was assumed when the International Labour Organization was formed in 1919, and they remained one of the bases for the tripartite representation of each country by labour, employers and government in the structure of that organization.

Business associations were not only linked on a national basis but internationally, both according to trades, and through the International Chamber of Commerce formed in 1919, which served as a channel of informal interchange between business groups in different countries.

(b) *Professional bodies.* Professional organizations became increasingly important as the number of specialized professions grew. Many of these organizations were bodies of long standing, such as the national associations of doctors and lawyers in most countries. Subdivisions of specialists within these broad professional categories, such as psychiatrists, formed separate associations as the speciality became distinct. New professions, such as social work, set up their associations as they acquired professional standing.

The general function of professional associations was to establish, promote and often to police the profession. They prescribed criteria for membership in terms of training, established codes of professional ethics and withdrew the privilege of membership, and with it the right to practise the profession, from those who violated the ethical principles laid down by the body, and they undertook to keep their members abreast of the developing body of knowledge in their fields. The part played by the professional association in licensing for practice and in inspecting and qualifying training institutions varied from country to country. In some these functions were performed by public agencies, in others by professional associations and in still others by the professional organization acting on behalf of the state. Professional associations also provided a channel for their members to voice their views on matters of public concern. In the field of health, for example, the organized medical profession had great impact on the development of health services, both in raising standards of service and in supporting or opposing specific health measures.

(c) *Labour unions.* Labour unions, organized to provide workers with bargaining power *vis-à-vis* the employer, offered industrial workers a means by which to identify themselves with a struggle, and a body in which they could assume responsibility and learn to function in a social group. As unions became more firmly established and more a matter of routine which workers joined automatically in order to hold their jobs, and as they assumed responsibilities before labour courts or in the administration of agreements or of social security benefits, they lost some of their old meaning for the individual worker. Instead of being an association which the worker regarded as his own, the union sometimes became merely a large organization with which he must deal and to which, like the state, he must pay his quota. Yet the labour union remained the largest voluntary organization, apart from the church and the political party, with which the people of industrial countries were identified.*

(d) *Farm organizations.* Farmers and peasants formed voluntary organizations less generally and less durably than did workers and businessmen. Voluntary organization among farmers was sporadic and partial, with some notable exceptions such as Denmark where from the third quarter of the nineteenth century economic, political, and cultural organizations of farmers were a major element in the structure of the state. In countries of advanced agriculture farm organizations were mainly geared to the improvement of their economic operation. In still-feudal peasant societies they were a part of political movements for social reform.†

(e) *Other economic interest associations.* Other kinds of common economic interests afforded a basis for association. Associations of local taxpayers or ratepayers or owners of homes and real estate frequently represented the interests of existing residents or investors in local land or business in efforts to prevent changes in the character of their neighbourhoods or to avoid the burden of supporting new public services. In France in the 1950s, these small investors were roused into a political movement known as *Poujadisme* by their resistance to taxation. The need for buyers of complex industrial products to have an independent check on the claims of manufacturers led to the formation in the United States in the 1930s of membership organizations to test products offered on the market and to report the result of such tests in order that consumers might know what they were buying. So valuable did this service become that by the mid-1950s one such organization counted well over 100,000 members.

* See Chapter XXX, pp. 1110–1132, Labour
† See Chapter XXX, pp. 1132–42, Peasants and Farmers

(f) *Co-operatives*. Individuals banded together into co-operative societies to protect their interests as consumers. The co-operative movement, which had originated in England in the mid-nineteenth century among poor workers who saw a chance to stretch their pennies by returning to themselves the middle-man's profits, grew slowly in most countries. In Britain co-operative societies developed virtually as arms of the labour movement; in Belgium they promoted and became part of the socialist movement; they were active in the Scandinavian countries.

Co-operative organizations of consumers generally played a relatively small role in the total economy. Although in many places there were credit unions, co-operative stores, housing co-operatives or group-purchased medical care, consumer co-operatives rarely included a large proportion of the public or accounted for a substantial part of their purchases.

Even where co-operatives were few and small, however, they tended to have importance for their members beyond their economic effect, for the principles established by the original co-operative at Rochdale prescribed a course of education and discussion before members should launch any co-operative endeavour and required that a portion of the group's annual income should always be devoted to social and educational objectives. In a few places, notably among the fishermen and poor farmers of the province of Nova Scotia in Canada, the co-operative movement became the means of reinvigorating a depressed economy, as it had raised the depressed rural economy of Denmark in the latter part of the nineteenth century. It was one of the forms of organiza-tion for rural communities in Israel, alongside of the communal *kibbutz* and the settlement with individual landownership. By mid-century a number of countries with newly developing economies, notably India and to a lesser extent Indonesia, had taken steps to facilitate the formation of co-operatives in the hope that their citizens might choose this means to advance their well-being. In the communist countries the co-operative was sometimes used as an intermediate step on the way to collectivization or state operation.

3. *Mutual benefit organizations*

Mutual aid in time of distress continued to provide a basis for voluntary organization, although the extension of social security and the benefits of the welfare state reduced the need for such associations as a means of protection.

The fraternal orders which spread from Britain to the overseas British dominions and to the United States during the second half of the nineteenth century were outgrowths of the Friendly Societies formed by working men in British industrial centres for mutual aid in case of illness or death. They had both protective and social features—as insurance societies, often badly man-aged at first but in time operated on a sound actuarial basis, and as lodges patterned on the Freemasons, with secret rituals to which their members were initiated. When health insurance and other social insurance measures were adopted, the fraternal orders were either registered as agents through which a part of the public programme was administered, as under the British health insurance scheme of 1911 or, as in Australia, their activities were limited to those benefits which the state system did not provide.

Their principal importance in the twentieth century, however, was in their social role. 'Lodge night', when members went through secret rituals, addressed each other by elaborate titles and shared a sense of fraternity, offered an escape from the monotony of industrial tasks and the anonymity or urban life. When a lodge member moved to a new community he could count on finding 'brothers' there. In the second quarter of the twentieth century the importance of fraternal orders declined somewhat, as cinema and television offered some of the escape entertainment which the lodge had furnished and public social insurance made mutual insurance less necessary. Yet fraternal orders continued to provide means by which otherwise anonymous individuals could establish social links and a claim to social kinship with others.

Wherever recent immigrants congregated, they too formed mutual aid societies, to stand by each other in sickness and death and as a means by which people in a strange land could enjoy together the customs of the homeland they had left behind. With the decline in mass immigration from Europe after the first world war, immigrant societies declined in importance, for association based on the country of their parents' origin had little appeal to the second generation, especially where societies had been formed on a village or provincial basis as were, for example, most of the Italian immigrant associations. Several of these societies changed their purpose from mutual aid to relief for their former compatriots during and after the second world war, and some immigrant associations that had been on the wane revived on this basis. In the urban communities of Africa a wide variety of mutual aid societies were the principal social units which began to give shape to the life of Africans uprooted from their tribal homes.

Voluntary associations along ethnic lines went beyond mutual aid to promote the interests and improve the status of disadvantaged groups. The National Association for the Advancement of Colored People acted as a spearhead in the efforts to improve the status of Negroes in American society; the All-India Depressed Classes Association acted as spokesman for the untouchables of India.

The most extensive ethnic group organizations were those maintained by Jews. In the centuries of their life as enclaves within other societies, the Jewish people had developed an almost complete set of social institutions through which their separate life was conducted. Where they no longer led a ghetto existence, they continued to sustain ethnic organizations for a wide variety of functions—for the relief of Jews abroad and the support of Zionism, for the provision of welfare services to the Jewish community, for defence against discrimination and for civic participation with other elements in the population.

Other factors of common experience provided the basis for associations devoted to furthering the interests of their members. In a period which saw two world wars involving large segments of the population, organizations of war veterans sought the extension of benefits and privileges, and renewed from time to time some of the camaraderie of the past.

4. Organizations for social activities

Voluntary organizations were by no means limited to associations to promote the direct interest of their members. They offered a means of association for a multitude of purposes—social, recreational, civic, benevolent or the pursuit of a common educational or cultural interest. Voluntary associations based on age and sex proliferated in most countries during this period.

(a) Youth. The conditions of urban industrial society made organization important for youth. Longer schooling and child labour laws combined to raise the age at which young people started to work, to sharpen the distinction between the adult world and the world of the child and to prolong the period of adolescence. In the urban milieu, with its highly individualized relationships and multitude of cross-currents, the small family unit could not provide the basis for status and social relationships which the young person required and had generally found in an extended family group within a stable rural community. For urban adolescents and older children, clubs, gangs or societies composed of contemporaries met their need for something to which they could belong and from which they could derive status, a sense of identity and an opportunity for social life. Youth organizations, whether street corner gangs, boy scout troops, church clubs or political youth movements all served this basic function for their members.

In the many parts of the world where revolutionary political and social changes were taking place, youth organizations performed an additional role. Either spontaneously or under the direction of political leaders, they served as spearheads for movements to bring about change and as instruments for reorienting the values and relationships of their society and for consolidating new structures of power.

The multiplicity of youth organizations which proliferated in number and expanded in membership during the twentieth century had their roots in several quite distinct developments of the nineteenth century: the politically oriented youth movements, represented by Mazzini's 'Young Europe' and corresponding liberal revolutionary movements in Germany, Poland and elsewhere; the spontaneous organization of youth in revolt against adult authority; the efforts of political, religious, labour and other organizations to rally the youth in their ranks; and the efforts of civic, religious and welfare leaders to meet the social needs of working-class youth in the growing industrial communities.

The political youth movements were chiefly composed of university students and other young intellectuals, except for the socialist youth movements which drew from the working class. These young people were in conscious revolt against established institutions and they pitted their idealism and vision of a new political and social order against the attitudes and leadership of the older generation.

In the years before the first world war youth movements of this type in many countries acted as the spearheads for a variety of political movements, staging demonstrations and engaging in both propaganda and direct action in support of their political causes. In the countries where social and political tensions were at a minimum and existing institutions permitted orderly and continuous change, such as Britain, Denmark, Canada or the United States, such politically oriented youth movements were absent or of little significance. But wherever revolutionary tensions were present and the social and political structure was under fire, from the countries of Latin America to those of Asia, spontaneous movements by students and their associates played a part in the struggle to bring radical change. The Young Turks who undertook to remake the Ottoman empire and the Chinese student movement which provided much of the support for Sun Yat-sen and for the revolutionary cultural-political movement known as the New Tide were but two of the more conspicuous examples. Indian students in the 1930s and 1940s were an active element in the struggle for independence, and in the 1950s students took part in the overthrow of the dictator in Cuba, and in many demonstrations elsewhere.

Alongside of the primarily political movements, and also independent of the educational, recreational and character-building organizations founded and governed by adults, autonomous self-governing youth organizations arose in a number of European countries, notably among the Germans, Czechs, Scandinavians and Dutch. These groups went hiking and camping and engaged in sports; sometimes they took part in movements, such as temperance, or acted as the advance guard of the socialist movements.

The most considerable of these groups was the German youth movement, or *Wandervögel*, which originated shortly before 1900. It was in revolt against all forms of traditional authority, in the home and in the rigid, half-militarized, half-paternalistic system of German education. The movement reflected the desire for a new way of life, for greater liberty, sincerity and beauty as opposed to the materialism and conventionalism of the time. It revived romantic German traditions, folk songs and dances and folklore, and formed groups drawn together by the warmth of emotional life and trusting in the leadership of older comrades. Although it fought against all established authority, it had no clear or definite political or social aims as an alternative to the existing order, and it longed for a new authority, a real *Führer*, in place of the established authority of the father in the home and the bureaucratic leadership in the state. Its 'wandering' represented the old, traditional German unrest and the new unrest of dissatisfied youth, involved in a deep conflict that was changing the relations between parents and children, and it constituted a sentimental expression of the striving for freedom within the political and social structure of pre-war Germany.

In the years after the first world war, both the politically oriented youth organizations and the autonomous romantic youth movements were taken over by dictatorial régimes and converted into instruments to consolidate the power of the leader and to remake the society along lines dictated from above. The Italian fascists' *Ballila* and the Nazis' *Hitler Jugend* were not spontaneous expressions of youth directed against the established adult leadership but, rather, tightly organized and disciplined arms of adult organizations. Instead of being composed largely of students and intellectuals, they were drawn predominantly from those social groups which had not exercised social or political power. Although they rejected the authority of their elders more completely than the spontaneous youth movements had done, they acted at the behest of a new ruling adult leadership.

Following the October revolution, the Young Communist League in the USSR became the Communist party's assistant in all fields of social activity, including industry, culture, the upbringing of children and youth, public education, sports. Its members took the lead in many campaigns, such as the opening up of new farmlands, Komsomol construction projects, campaigns for industrial economy, for safeguarding public order. It undertook to train its members as well-educated self-disciplined individuals capable of displaying creative initiative in every undertaking. It guided the work of the Young Pioneers whose purpose was to help the school and the parents in the bringing up of children of school age with a view to their becoming active full-fledged members of the community.

Where youth organizations were enlisted either as followers or as partners in the remaking of societies, they not only offered to their members an active social role and a group to which to belong but they developed in them an intense sense of dedication and identification with the interests of the people and the state. Elsewhere, youth organizations which played an active part in bringing about political revolution and social change often lacked a clearly defined role after these objectives were obtained, as was the case among Indian students whose continued outbursts of passive resistance in the years after independence were regarded as 'student indiscipline' by some of the same people who had urged such conduct during the fight against the British *raj*.

Far different in origin and purpose, but serving some similar functions for their members, were the multitude of youth organizations which reflected the efforts of adult society to meet the needs of urban youth. From beginnings in the Sunday School movement to take factory children off the streets in Birmingham and Manchester and to give them instruction, churches provided organized activities for young people as part of their regular function, and as a means of attraction or to hold them within the church. Through countless clubs, guilds and societies attached to churches of every denomination in most urban areas, young people found opportunities for social contacts and group activity and a channel through which they could render a service to their community, express neighbourly concern for their fellows or establish contacts with other young people across class, ethnic or geographical lines.

Voluntary organizations with religious orientation supplemented those directly affiliated to churches. The Young Men's Christian Association, and its counterpart, the Young Women's Christian Association, established in London in 1844 and 1855, became world-wide in scope with total memberships in the 1950s of over 4,000,000 men and half a million women. These organizations did not confine their membership to Christians, or to any specific denominations, yet their Protestant origin and continuing leadership gave them larger memberships in predominantly Protestant than in Catholic or non-Christian areas. Catholic youth organizations in many countries claimed large memberships composed of parish youth groups and organizations of students in Catholic and non-Catholic colleges and universities. Similar organizations were formed among Jewish youth.

The groups which participated in church-sponsored or religiously oriented organizations differed in age between countries and among individual churches or local communities. The programmes of some churches were primarily for younger children; in some countries the Young Women's Christian Association was composed almost wholly of young adult working women. In combination, however, they included a wide range of children, adolescents and older youth.

Though the churches were first in the field, non-religious organizations initiated by welfare workers and civic leaders became numerous and large. Boys' clubs began to be organized by welfare workers in the 1860s, especially in the United States. The Settlement House movement spread rapidly in the last decade of the nineteenth and early years of the twentieth century from its beginning in London to many cities in Britain, the USA and northern Europe, devoting much effort to the formation of clubs for the boys and girls of the crowded city slums.

Several organizations whose separate units followed a standardized pattern of activity were formed early in the twentieth century and numbered their members in the millions fifty years later. Boy Scouts and Girl Guides founded in England in 1908 and 1910, were organized throughout Europe, the USA and the British Commonwealth countries before the first world war, and in Latin America, Asia and Africa during the next two or three decades. By 1955 the Boy Scouts, with national organizations in nearly every country outside the communist areas, estimated their world membership as 6,500,000 the Girl Scouts or Guides numbered over 4,000,000 members in 35 countries. Boys' club federations, following the pattern established in 1906 in the United States, were formed in other countries and linked in an international organization. Junior Red Cross societies after the first world war followed similar programmes in many countries and were internationally affiliated. Innumerable sport and athletic clubs engaged in team competitions and tournaments.

All these organizations tended to bridge the gap between generations rather than to accentuate it. In one way or another they had an educational character-building objective. They afforded opportunities for the development of personality, social responsibility and leadership while providing recreation and activities designed to develop skills. Through such activity as camping, they enabled predominantly urban young people to acquire some experience in dealing with nature. By giving their members a chance to manage their own affairs responsibly, they offered a training ground for democratic citizenship. Through their national and international affiliations they established communication between young people of different background and nationality, promoted identification across social and national lines and provided their outstanding members with opportunities to take part in national and international conferences or assemblies.

Membership in formal youth organizations was drawn primarily from the middle and professional classes and from the more stable ranks of the industrial population. It was the widespread, if not universal, experience of the Boy Scouts and Girl Guides, the Young Men's Christian Associations and the Young Women's Christian Associations, the Boys' clubs, athletic leagues and clubs at settlement houses, churches and community centres that they attracted chiefly boys and girls with active interests and ambitions from families which could afford to buy a uniform or which encouraged church attendance or were concerned for the education of their children. Although the welfare-oriented youth organizations had been originally established to counteract the disorganizing influences of the city upon the children and young people whose families had the least to offer, few of the socially unstable elements found their way into any of these organizations. For such young people wholly autonomous neighbourhood gangs, sometimes anti-social and often in violent conflict with other groups who might threaten to invade their territory, provided a basis for identification, loyalty and the assertion of their personalities.

Although street corner gangs, Scouts, boys' and girls' organizations, and clubs sponsored by welfare and religious agencies were chiefly to be found in urban areas, organization of rural youth also became well established in a number of places. In contrast to the private origin and support of most urban youth organizations, governments frequently sponsored clubs for rural youth as part of their programme for raising the level of agricultural technology and rural life. Many countries followed the pattern developed by the Extension Service of the United States Department of Agriculture which inaugurated its 4-H club programme in 1914. With technical guidance these clubs for boys and girls built their programmes around agricultural and home-making projects which stimulated their members to learn and use the best agricultural and home-making techniques and to develop their capacities for leadership.

Whatever their character, purpose, or auspices, youth organizations in the twentieth century reflected the changing social conditions which brought them into being and determined their form: reduction of traditional parental authority, increase in social freedom, greater association between the sexes. They operated, too, to develop norms of conduct to which they exacted conformity from age-mates and, ultimately, acquiescence from their elders.

(b) *Aged.* The organization of older people was far less widespread and purposeful than that of youth, but in the second quarter of the twentieth century, and with growing momentum after the second world war, the movement for old people's associations grew. In the United States the tendency to organize on the basis of old age received a major impetus during the depression of the 1930s when a quasi-political movement led to the formation of Townsend clubs, named after their founder, to agitate for old age pensions and incidentally to enjoy social activity. With the provision of old age insurance and assistance in 1935, much of the political effort was dissipated, but the social impetus continued, and took the form of the establishment of 'golden age' or 'silver age' clubs in many communities. Elsewhere retired persons organized to seek improved pensions or to form social groups.

Clubs for senior citizens, however, could be regarded only as a beginning toward finding a means by which older people could retain a functional place in a society where life expectancy was greatly extended but in which the small family of parents and young children constituted the active family group, in which many lines of employment gave preference to the young and in which emphasis on youthfulness tended to make older people feel on the shelf. In some places in the USSR groups of retired persons met this situation by undertaking projects on behalf of the children of the community.

(c) *Women.* Women's organizations were ubiquitous and grew in number and scope. Feminist organizations to promote the cause of women's rights lost much of their importance as rights were achieved, but the role of women in civic affairs expanded. Women organized for mutual support and assistance, as for example university women who joined together to provide a means for continued self-education, to raise fellowships for women scholars, to strengthen standards of women's education, to promote the employment of qualified women and to facilitate interchange and intercommunication among women of common interests in other countries. An international federation formed in 1919 linked university women's associations of fifty countries by the 1950s. Business and professional women organized for comparable purposes.

Some women formed civic organizations, for specific purposes such as the women's temperance societies which were numerous in the nineteenth century and continued in some countries in the twentieth, or for more general purposes. A common religious affiliation provided the basis for some organizations, such as the associations of Catholic, Jewish or Protestant church women. The basis of some organizations was ill-defined and their purpose vague, as in many women's clubs or women's guilds which might have any number of interests, from gardening to adult education, and which were often linked into national federations. Some were formed primarily for welfare purposes, to sustain a particular charity such as the care of unmarried mothers or the provision of workshops for the handicapped.

Apart from the women's auxiliaries of some labour unions or corresponding farm groups and women's divisions of political parties, women's organizations drew most of their members from the middle classes. They represented the efforts of women with some leisure to use their leisure constructively and at the same time to enjoy the society of others. In addition they provided a means, in the highly mobile urban society of the twentieth century, by which women could establish social contacts in new communities to which the vicissitudes of their husbands' jobs or their own might take them.*

5. Civic associations

Voluntary civic bodies of various sorts were indispensable to the structure of the local community in many parts of the world. Much of the business of local government was done on a voluntary basis, or at least by persons whose professional job lay outside local government and who received only expenses or minor fees for the services which they rendered to their community. Local magistrates and local councils in Britain, for example, consisted of volunteer citizens; in the United States the entire school system was governed by local volunteer school boards, generally elected by the locality. While the increasing complexity of local administration brought the professionalization of many municipal services, it also multiplied the areas in which citizens were called upon to give voluntary service as members of boards and committees to oversee, advise or supplement the work of public officials. This form of civic activity drew most heavily on members of the middle and upper classes, but with the growing importance of labour organizations, civic committees and boards included more and more representatives of workers' groups.

In addition to voluntary bodies which carried direct responsibility for local government or services, organizations of prominent citizens set the civic tone of their communities. Some of these, such as the Rotary clubs composed of one representative of each of the major professions and business activities in a community, the Kiwanis clubs, and the Lions clubs, were international in scope, as were their women's counterparts, Zonta, Soroptimists. Rotary International was formed in 1910, five years after formation of the first club.

These clubs met regularly for sociability and to discuss community affairs, welcomed to their meetings members from other communities who happened to be in town, offered hospitality to distinguished visitors, and provided a sort of community leadership. Sometimes called 'service clubs', they stressed the responsibility of their members toward the civic advance of their communities, though they were sometimes accused of being merely a front for the business interests, unsympathetic to labour, and inclined to be conservative in the matter of civic improvements which might involve the raising of taxes. They generally sponsored some welfare projects, varying with the state of the community's social development. In towns with poorly developed welfare services, they might undertake an elementary piece of philanthropy or they might

* See Chapter XXX, pp. 1142–63, Women.

inaugurate efforts to develop a needed service. In large metropolitan areas with a multitude of power groups, the influence of these service clubs was less than in smaller cities and towns where they comprised a larger proportion of the professional and business element. They were however one more example of the voluntary organizations which gave shape and leadership to otherwise amorphous societies.

In many newly developing countries after the second world war, voluntary civic activity received a great impetus from the community development programmes. In Jamaica an extensive programme was built very largely on the basis of voluntary planning committees; in India the government used its influence to stimulate the formation of voluntary organizations as an indispensable means of developing a democratic structure; in the Philippines, Pakistan, India and elsewhere the main task of the village workers who staffed the community development programmes was to stimulate the organization of citizens for voluntary civic activity. Ceylon's rural development programme was based wholly on the formation of voluntary village societies.

6. Benevolent organizations

Benevolent organizations to support an endless range of welfare services, and to promote such causes as the protection of children, the prevention of cruelty to animals, better care and treatment of prisoners and their rehabilitation upon release, were among the most numerous of voluntary organizations. Many of the voluntary agencies had their origin in the late nineteenth and early twentieth century, when the social conscience was aroused against the ills of industrial society and the services of the welfare state had not yet been developed. Frequently they had a religious base; in some instances they were maintained by religious orders which provided nursing services, worked as teachers or provided a refuge for unmarried mothers or juvenile delinquents. Virtually every country had its Red Cross or Red Crescent organization ready to mobilize voluntary effort in case of disaster or emergency.

Innumerable associations were formed in the field of health to promote public health, combat tuberculosis, cancer or heart disease, prevent blindness, promote care for crippled children or the hard of hearing, aid the victims of infantile paralysis or cerebral palsy, or stimulate research on one or another unconquered disease. Such associations were generally formed at the initiative of professional personnel working on the problem and persons who had been victims or were relatives of victims. They provided means by which the leadership of professionals and the participation of interested members of the public could combine in seeking a common social goal. They enabled lay people in a highly complex and specialized society to direct their efforts toward objectives which they sensed in general terms but with which they personally had no technical competence to deal.

In spite of the extension of public welfare services, voluntary welfare agencies continued to function where they had been established in the past. Often

DD*

they changed their role in order to supplement rather than duplicate the services of public agencies, or were used by public agencies to carry out publicly supported programmes. Voluntary welfare efforts were important, too, in countries which were newly developing their social services. Although such countries established welfare services as a public responsibility, they also sought to arouse in their people a spirit of self-help. States where the masses of the people had been neglected for centuries confronted the danger that those who had long been passive under the whip of adversity would wait passively for the new benefits which they now expected to receive. Wherever developing countries envisaged their role in terms of a modern welfare state, they included among their central objectives the promotion of voluntary mutual effort on the part of their citizens.

7. Cultural and interest groups

Finally, voluntary organization provided a basis for the pursuit of any number of cultural interests. Literary, musical and art societies, and private organizations to support the arts, to engage in amateur dramatics, to form community orchestras or to provide art classes and hang each others' paintings were to be found in many cities. Garden clubs, stamp collectors' clubs, organizations of radio amateurs, movie enthusiasts, anglers, or others joined to pursue common hobbies. Amateurs of sports of all sorts were organized into teams and leagues, to maintain playing fields, conduct tournaments and uphold the standards and rules of the games. With the tremendous increase in the amount of leisure enjoyed by men and women and young people in the twentieth century, the growth of organizations to pursue cultural interests was without limit.*

IV.   THE INDIVIDUAL IN THE TWENTIETH CENTURY

The twentieth-century individual, in virtually all parts of the world, thus found his identity, his status and his role in society less and less simply and clearly defined by the agencies which had traditionally given him identity and status—his family, his social class, his parent's occupation, his ethnic identity. All these factors continued to operate in the social life of the period, but the mounting complexity of social relationships and the great increase in geographical and social mobility reduced their relative importance. The individual derived his identity, his status and his role from many different components in his life—his nationality, his occupation, his membership in a trade union or a political party, his religious affiliation, his place of provenance, his educational achievement, his ethnic background. In the many circumstances in which he found himself, one or another of these identifications might, for the purpose in hand, be the major determining factor in his status and relationships.

* See Chapter XXVII, Use of Leisure.

In the fluid anonymous life of the modern city he constantly had to establish his identity anew, to the strangers with whom he dealt, and often even to himself. He was less and less likely to wear his identification in the form of distinctive dress, although at a United Nations gathering it was not difficult to recognize the members of the 'sari bloc' or the 'sarong bloc', though class distinctions were clearly apparent on the streets of Cairo where men of the lower classes continued to wear the long galabieh, and though there were even some villages in Holland where Catholic and Protestant farmers still wore their caps in a distinguishing fashion. He was less and less likely to spend his life in contact with people who could place him by his father's name.

Even when he had found terms in which to establish who he was and to discover the identity of others, he often was still without a reliable guide as to the conduct appropriate to his status and role, nor could he count on others to interpret their relationship to him in the same light as he did and to expect the conduct which he might expect of himself. The difficulties arising from this situation were particularly great where changes in social status were rapid and threatened the position of superior groups. Changing relations between classes in Britain, between Negro and white in the United States, between Indian and *ladino* in central America, between Asian and European, between employers and workers—everywhere the uncertainties of such new relationships were reflected in hypersensitiveness, aggressiveness or other expressions of insecurity among members of the rising group, and in self-consciousness, prejudice or other reflections of uncertainty or resistance among those unable to readjust their conception of their own superior role.

The mobility and the social change of the twentieth century thus placed millions of individuals under kinds of strains that past societies had rarely imposed on large numbers of their members. Where the strains were too great, the individual might find an external object on which to project his inability to cope with the confusions of his age, or he might turn his uncertainty in upon himself. It was no accident that the twentieth century saw, along with a great and general acceptance of the essential unity of mankind and respect for cultural differences, a vicious tendency to seek a scapegoat and to persecute fanatically—witness the sadistic fury of the Nazi effort to exterminate the Jews, the unexpected violence of communalism in Turkey and India, the outburst of suspicion against 'subversives' in the United States or the British 'teddy boy' attacks on inoffensive Jamaican immigrants. Nor was it an accident that psychiatrists found that the point of breakdown in many of their mentally ill patients was in the sense of self.

Only a minority of people felt certain and secure—the minority of convinced religious men and the minority who identified themselves wholly with a new ideal. The former, whatever their religion, held securely to old patterns; the latter, certain of a new vision—the coming of a communist society or the development of one of the new nations—felt themselves securely embedded in a new pattern. But for the great majority of mankind, the individual in the twentieth century faced unprecedented demands on his ability to organize his personal social world and to relate himself flexibly and securely to it.

NOTES TO CHAPTER XXII

1. It is the view of the commentators from the Italian National Commission that the treatment of the family overemphasizes comparatively unimportant aspects, and that it proceeds from a relativistic premise which causes the authors to 'forget the distinction between that which is truly changing and that which is constant'. The position of the Catholic Church with regard to matrimony and the family was restated by Pope Pius XI in the Encyclical *Casti Connubi* (1930). Excerpts from this letter follow:

   '5. . . . let it be repeated as an immutable and inviolable fundamental doctrine that matrimony was not instituted or restored by man but by God; not by man were the laws made to strengthen and confirm and elevate it but by God, the author of nature, and by Christ our Lord by whom nature was redeemed, and hence these laws cannot be subject to any human decrees or to any contrary pact even of the spouses themselves. . . .

   6. Yet, although matrimony is of its very nature of divine institution, the human will, too, enters into it and performs a most noble part. For each individual marriage, inasmuch as it is a conjugal union of a particular man and woman, arises only from the free consent of each of the spouses; and this free act of the will, by which each party hands over and accepts those rights proper to the state of marriage, is so necessary to constitute true marriage that it cannot be supplied by any human power. . . .

   11. Thus among the blessings of marriage, the child holds the first place. . . .'

   Further readings in this field are:

   British National Conference on Social Work, Bedford College for Women, 1953, *The Family; Report*. (London: National Council of Social Service, 1953).

   Famille d'aujourd'hui, situation et avenir. Compte rendu in extenso. (Lyon: Chronique sociale de France, 1958.)

   Robert D. Hess, *Family Worlds: A Psychological Approach to Family Life* (Chicago, 1959).

   John L. Kane, *Marriage and the Family: A Catholic Approach* (New York, 1952).

   Clifford Kirkpatrick, *The Family, as Process and Institution* (New York, 1955).

   Talcott Parsons, *Family, Socialization and Interaction Process* (Glencoe, Ill., 1955; London, 1956).

   John Ryan and Alan Keenan, *Marriage, a Medical and Sacramental Study* (New York, 1955).

   F. J. Sheed, *Marriage and the Family* (New York, 1957).

   Carle C. Zimmerman and Lucius F. Cervantes, *Marriage and the Family* (New York, 1956).

2. Candidate of Juridical Sciences A. Bovin asserts that in the Soviet family children were never encouraged to 'defy' their parents. In the early period of Soviet power there occurred in individual families conflicts which were due to the divergence between the new ethical idea of children brought up by school and society in the spirit of Communist morality, and the backward views and outlook of members of the older generation. These conflicts sometimes became a subject of discussion among wide segments of public opinion. (See G. M. Sverdlov, *Sovetskoye semeynoye pravo* (Soviet Family Law), Moscow, 1958; pp. 13–16.)

3. In the eyes of Soviet scholars this section does not indicate the essential facts about mankind's social structure, since the authors take as the basis of social divisions all manner of derivative differences (way of life, type of employment, incomes, ideas, consciousness, education, etc.) and give a very nebulous and confused picture of 'social stratification'.

   The basis of the social structure is the diverse status of men *vis-à-vis* the means of production. In modern capitalist society there exists, in the status of men *vis-à-vis* the means of production, an opposition that has developed to the pitch of contradiction. This has led to the division of that society into two fundamentally antagonistic classes, the bourgeoisie and the proletariat.

By 'bourgeoisie' is meant the class of capitalists, the owners of the means of social production, employers of hired labour. Closely connected with the bourgeoisie is the class of large landowners. The main source of income of such landowners is the land rent which they receive from agricultural capitalists farming their lands. The bourgeois class and the class of large landed proprietors together form one pole of modern capitalist society.

The other principal class of capitalist society is the proletariat, or working class. The 'proletariat' is the class of modern hired workers, who have been deprived of means of production of their own, who sell their labour power to capitalists and are the direct producers of surplus value, capital, for these capitalists.

Thus one pole of capitalist society consists of the bourgeoisie and large landed proprietors and the other of the proletariat, including both industrial and agricultural workers. However, the capitalist social structure does not manifest itself in a pure form, in the form of these two poles alone. Capitalism is characterized by a network of social relationships and transitional stages between one class and another. The social groups situated between the two poles of the social structure, taken together, form the middle social strata of society. The middle strata do not form a single homogeneous whole economically, socially and politically, as the social classes do. Their representatives occupy different places in the system of material relationships, and consequently stand in a different relation to the means of production; they occupy different places in regard to one another in the process of production and in the sphere of distribution.

(See V. Semonov, *Problema klassov i klassovoy borby v sovremennoy burzhuaznoy sotsio-logii* (The Problem of Classes and the Class Struggle in Modern Bourgeois Sociology), Moscow, 1959, pp. 76–7, 82–3.)

CHAPTER XXIII

POLITICAL INSTITUTIONS

C HANGES in political institutions in the twentieth century were intimately bound up with the changing role and expanding scope of the state under conditions of modern industrial society. They reflected, too, changes in the state's form, most notably the development of new political institutions in the states which adopted communism. The focus of the present chapter is on changes in the state as an institution and on the instruments through which the political machinery operated. It deals primarily with the changing political institutions of the liberal democratic states and the new institutions of the communist states.[1]

A number of states operated under a variety of authoritarian forms during these years, but with the exception of Fascist Italy and Nazi Germany their political institutions did not represent a new development. They are to be described primarily in negative terms—the rejection or discarding of democratic institutions. In positive terms they may be said to represent government based upon and supported by military force.[2, 3]

The Fascist and Nazi states went beyond mere reliance on force, to proclaim alternative conceptions of the shape which the institutions of the state should take. Mussolini, in addition to permeating the state with military, para-military and quasi-military forms, conceived of the organization of the state on a corporate basis, with bodies formed along functional lines exercising authority over their members. Toward this end he gave to associations of companies in a particular industry administrative responsibility with respect to the affairs of the industry. The Nazi régime was built on the leadership principle and the mystical unity of the state. Its institutions were designed to weld the entire society into a single unit, responsive through all its organs to the leader's will and his vision of the purpose and nature of the state. During the period of Hitler's ascendancy that purpose was the remilitarization of the state and its whole-hearted dedication to military objectives.

Both of these states went down to defeat and destruction in the second world war after a brief period during which their institutions remained in a formative, provisional or emergency state. Some features of these systems penetrated into other states and many forms of authoritarianism, old and new, continued to assert themselves in the years after the second world war. But the institutions of Fascism and Nazism as such were abortive, and during the period under review they did not become consolidated into a lasting alternative structure of political life.

Many of the new states which came into existence after the second world war—in numbers which virtually doubled the world's independent political units—lacked the tradition and experience of liberal democracy yet did not directly follow the communist pattern. In their efforts to find institutions appropriate to countries of high illiteracy and varied cultural traditions, which needed to achieve rapid economic development under conditions of the modern age, they introduced a mixture of political forms. By the end of the 1950s it was not yet clear what direction these developments would ultimately take and whether new political systems would eventually evolve.

I. FORMS OF THE STATE

1. *Monarchy*

At the opening of the century monarchs ruled throughout the greater part of the world. The republics of North and South America, Switzerland and France were almost alone in having a non-monarchical form of government.

By the middle of the century a mere handful of monarchs remained. Most of the powerful hereditary rulers were gone—the Hapsburgs, the Romanovs, the Hohenzollerns, the Manchus, the Ottoman sultans, the ruling houses of Spain, Portugal and Italy. Monarchy survived as a form in Europe only where the effective power had long since passed out of the monarch's hands and he functioned mainly as the symbolic head of a parliamentary state, as in Britain, the Low Countries and Scandinavia. It survived in the few small states of Asia and Africa which had never come under direct colonial rule—Ethiopia, Thailand, Afghanistan and Iran—and in Japan, though the nearly divine emperor had become little more than a respected symbolic figure. A few of the new states of Asia and Africa—Libya, Morocco, Jordan, Iraq and Saudi Arabia—adopted monarchical forms at the time of their establishment, but most chose a republican form and set themselves up under some adaptation of a liberal democratic constitution.

By the middle of the century autocratic monarchy may thus be said to have become an anachronistic form of government. Over most of the world, people in their political aspects were citizens, not subjects, and the totality of the people were seen as constituting the state.

The first world war marked the turning point in the history of monarchy as a state system. Though even before the war Portugal had expelled its king and become a republic, and revolution in China had put an end to an imperial tradition of over 2,000 years, it was the disappearance of the four great empires which represented the tradition of autocracy—the Russian, Austro-Hungarian, German and Ottoman—that marked the downfall of the monarchical ideal.

In the following years other monarchies fell and those that survived underwent change. The loss of the British monarch's major colonies was signalized by the abolition of the title of emperor. The last major claimant to monarchy by divine right, the Japanese emperor, gave up the claim under pressure from the victorious Allies. At least in theory, the remaining kings or emperors reigned as a result of national will or with the consent of the people, except perhaps in Ethiopia, Yemen and Saudi Arabia.

Even where monarchy survived only in a symbolic role and the royal house was warmly regarded by the people, the hierarchical social system which the institution of monarchy perpetuated was out of tune with the equalitarian tendencies of the times. Criticisms levelled at the monarchy in Britain and efforts of the Dutch and Scandinavian royal families to behave in a democratic manner were indications that people recognized an incongruity between monarchy as an institution and the social trends of the mid-twentieth century.

2. *Liberal democracy*

In the great majority of states where monarchical authority was unseated its place was taken by some form of what may be termed liberal democracy.[4, 5] This term is here used to denote states where political authority rested in the people acting through elected representatives, and where an elected executive was responsible to the expression of popular will. The term is used in preference to 'parliamentary democracy' which connotes the system of executive responsibility to the parliamentary majority, or 'republic' which excludes the parliamentary democracies with nominal royal heads, or 'representative government'. The term liberal democracy is not used in the nineteenth-century sense of *laissez-faire* liberalism, but rather to distinguish a broad group of states with a parliamentary or representative political tradition from the communist states which designated themselves as 'people's democracies'.[6, 7]

Most generally the form followed by the liberal democracies was the parliamentary pattern with executive power vested in a cabinet responsible to parliament and drawn from the majority party or combination of parties. In some instances the structure approximated the United States pattern of an independently elected executive separated from the legislative authority. But whether parliamentary or presidential, old or new, all democratic states changed much of their inner form during the twentieth century. To meet the needs brought by urban industrial society, the state enlarged its scope of activity to provide a more adequate framework for economic life, to control economic power and to provide common services.

In the first place it became a legislating state to a degree previously unknown. The great expansion of state activity and extension of state services involved a new view of legislation and its role in society. It was no longer merely to protect the state, to assure its revenue and to define and safeguard the rights of the citizen. The traditional concept of law as mainly codifying and interpreting customs and usages which had already become part of social practice was supplemented by a more active concept. Law came to be looked upon and used as an instrument to promote the well-being of the people and to carry out the purposes of the state.[8]

With this new concept the volume of legislation increased immensely. It was estimated that the British Parliament enacted more legislation in the first half of the twentieth century than in all its long previous history, and other legislative bodies showed a similar trend.

In the second place the doctrine of popular sovereignty upon which the democratic states rested became all-inclusive as the franchise was extended to classes formerly excluded and, with few exceptions, to women. From the years following the first world war, and stimulated by the total participation called for in the war, the doctrine that the total people was vested with effective sovereignty became the basis for the functioning of the democratic states.[9]

With this final expansion of democracy came its claim to the totality of powers. No sphere of human activity was recognized, in principle, as lying outside the scope of the democratic state. The distinction between what ought to be directed by public wisdom and what ought to be left to the discretion of the individual or to spiritual authority all but disappeared. Except as limits were explicitly set forth by bills of rights in democratic constitutions and recognized in practice, the state claimed the right to control every aspect of human life, according to the dictates of the popular will.[10]

This gradual but fundamental change in the nature of democratic institutions was one of the outstanding features of the political life of the twentieth century.

3. *Authoritarian state forms*

In a number of states democratic institutions proved unstable or unable to cope with the crises of the time and they were replaced by some form of authoritarian rule which discarded the institutions based on the principle of popular sovereignty but retained and intensified the principle of the totality of state powers. In some instances monarchical authority gave way directly to a dictatorial régime; the Kemalist revolution in Turkey, for example, set up from the beginning an authoritarian régime into which some democratic features were later introduced. Elsewhere dictatorial régimes took over democratically organized states, notably in eastern and southern Europe in the years between the two world wars, in new states of Asia and Africa in the 1950s and sporadically in Central and South America. Thus, though there was a continuing trend toward liberal democracy, and the victory of the democracies in both world wars gave prestige to the system and impetus to its spread, the tendency toward a revival of autocracy was as real a feature of the development of twentieth-century political institutions as was the predominance of liberal democratic institutions and the rise of communist state forms.

The structure of authoritarian government everywhere showed three principal characteristics: a head of state or leader with exceptional powers, with a party or a special group to support him; a legislative body elected generally by a system which proscribed parties or groups opposed to the régime or considered dangerous to the philosophy of those in power; and a bureaucratic administration which maintained no pretence of being subject to popular control.

The authoritarian states differed markedly in the extent to which they interpreted the totality of state power as implying the moulding of every institution within the state in conformity with and as a part of the state structure; in the extent to which they required uniformity of outlook and negated all civil rights; and in the degree to which the state became an end in itself. The extreme position on these points was taken by Hitler's totalitarian National Socialist state, while some dictatorships went so far in the other direction as to declare their ultimate purpose to be the development of effective democracy. But the same features were present to some degree in all the states under authoritarian rule.

4. Communism

The democratic and authoritarian states were not new forms of political organization, though they took on new content in the twentieth century. The new development in state form was the structure of the communist states.

All the communist states, whether federal in structure like the Soviet Union or with centralized constitutions, had certain distinctive characteristics in common. From the lowest unit—a Russian village soviet or its Chinese counterpart—to the highest, every organ of the state was elected on a pyramid basis, with power centralized at the top. Each elected body exercised its authority subject to the supervision and control of the immediately higher one, with final authority in all matters vested in the supreme organ.[11]

Equally distinguishing a feature of the communist states was the role played by the Communist party. As the repository of the interests of the people, the Party held the ultimate authority although it exercised power indirectly. It acted as the formulator of policy and watched over its execution at all levels and in all spheres of activity.

5. Colonial systems

In the case of European nations exercising imperial authority over colonial people—the British, French, Belgian, Dutch and Portuguese—the state had a dual aspect, the first relating to the mother country and the second to the colonies and other dependent areas. The colonial empire headed by a liberal democratic state was a type of state organization which combined two contradictory principles, self-government and freedom at home, autocracy and denial of freedom outside. It was characteristic of all imperial states in the twentieth century that the basic conceptions of government were different in the metropolitan and colonial areas.

Not only was the organization of government different but so also were the administration of justice, policies in relation to education, the rights of the individual *vis-à-vis* the state. Two different standards were applied even in the administration of law. The overriding consideration in colonial government was the prestige and authority of the ruling power. In most colonial territories a gradual change, often more of form than of substance, became visible from the period after the first world war, but the dual nature of colonial rule persisted until colonies became independent states.

The actual structure of colonial government differed among the colonial powers and in different parts of the same colonial empire. The British empire presented the greatest variety of patterns. In the areas settled by European immigration the democratic institutions of the mother country had been transplanted and self-government was the rule, although it was not until 1931 that Canada, Australia, New Zealand and the Union of South Africa formally ceased to be dominions of the British empire and became associated states of the British commonwealth. The Indian empire, which comprised Burma and Aden as well as what became the independent states of India and Pakistan, occupied the special position of an empire within an empire. Operating under a special secretary of state responsible to the British Parliament, the British government in India maintained its own foreign office and entered into treaty relations with states on its border and in the Arabian peninsula; its prestige and authority entitled it to consultation in the shaping of imperial policies affecting Asian states. It maintained a large military establishment out of its own revenues and a civil service whose higher posts were generally filled from Britain.

The remainder of the British empire was administered as a series of crown colonies under the Colonial Office, the manner of governing each area varying with the historic tradition and the social and economic conditions of the area and the principal objectives of imperial rule. Especially in parts of Africa outside the regions of white settlement the system used was that of indirect rule, according to which the local ruler or tribal chief continued to exercise authority, but on behalf of the colonial power.

In addition to the areas which were actual parts of the British empire, Britain exercised effective authority over certain 'protectorates', such as Egypt from 1914 to 1923, or the Sudan; in these the local government remained intact and control of policy was achieved by means of a system of advisers on foreign relations, financial and military matters. In addition, Britain enjoyed spheres of influence through treaty concessions in parts of the Middle East and China.

The French colonial structure was also adapted to differences in local conditions and in the relations of the area with the mother country. In French Indo-China the states of Cambodia, Annam and Laos remained under subordinate monarchies, the French government utilizing the machinery of indigenous administration for the exercise of its authority; Tonkin and Cochin

China were directly administered as colonies. In North Africa Tunisia and Morocco were both administered as protectorates through their local rulers, with the French population settled in the area entitled to special political rights; Morocco, however, enjoyed an international position, while Tunisia did not. Algeria by contrast had the status of three departments of metropolitan France with representation in the French Parliament; until the late 1950s the electorate was composed principally of French settlers. French possessions in tropical Africa until the mid-1950s were under direct administration from France; under the principle of 'assimilation', those who acquired French culture also took on the status of French citizens, with representation in the French Parliament at Paris.

The Dutch, Belgian and Portuguese colonial structures were even more authoritarian than those of Britain and France. The Portuguese system was distinctive in that after 1933 the areas outside the metropolitan country were not organized as dependencies but as provinces of the metropolitan state. Within these areas, however, only a tiny element of Portuguese and 'assimilated' natives enjoyed the status of citizens. The masses of the population in Portuguese Africa constituted a subject people without citizenship rights. Portuguese rule differed, too, from that of the other imperial powers in that the metropolitan government itself did not rest on the application of democratic principles at home, and the disparity between internal and external political structures was therefore not so great.

With the rising tide of anti-colonialism during the twentieth century and the struggle for national self-determination on the part of colonial peoples, colonial powers found it expedient to grant concessions to their dependent territories and the latter tended to take on some of the features of their metropolitan states. In India the British had already begun to introduce British criminal and commercial law in the middle of the nineteenth century as part of their administrative system and to incorporate Indians into the lower ranks of the civil service; in the 1880s they began to introduce a small measure of local self-government. Through successive reforms in 1909, 1919 and 1935 undertaken in response to Indian pressure, the British government extended institutions of government which followed the pattern of the British domestic system, though with limited scope, at the provincial and then at the national level. When it became clear during and after the second world war that colonialism was doomed, Britain accelerated the process of preparing other parts of the empire for self-government and independence, extending in each case the institutional forms developed at home.

France, too, offered its domestic institutions as a legacy to its colonial peoples. Until the close of the second world war the prospect of ultimate independence or self-government had not been part of the French colonial system; rather, the ultimate stated objective, at least for the African territories, was incorporation into the French Union, and as late as 1944 the idea of autonomy, self-government and any possibility of development outside the

French empire was excluded. But it was France's practice to extend its institutions as completely as possible to those who became 'assimilated'. When after the second world war France undertook a vigorous programme of road building and education in its African colonies, it duplicated in Africa the institutions of France. And in 1957 when France finally conceded a measure of self-government under the *loi cadre*, the African ministers who put the system into effect were men who had gained their political experience as members of the French Parliament.

In a similar way the limited Dutch concessions to the demands for political participation in Indonesia, beginning in 1916, were based on Dutch parliamentary forms. The Belgian government, which did not begin to offer self-government in the Congo until the 1950s, started by introducing the institution of the Belgian commune as a basis for local self-government.

By the middle of the twentieth century, however, the efforts to keep colonial structures intact were in the nature of rearguard actions. Britain divested itself systematically of one territory after another—Ghana, Malaya, with the British West Indies and others scheduled to follow—while at the same time holding tenaciously as long as possible to territories which it continued to regard as holdable and as vital to its national interest, such as Cyprus, East Africa, Gibraltar, and protectorates on the Arabian coast, only to relinquish in turn such of these as could no longer be held. France was forced to abandon her vision of Africa as a land of black Frenchmen as the tide of nationalism rose in her territories. The Dutch empire was virtually gone, although Holland continued to claim West New Guinea (Irian Barat) and retained some small territories in the West Indies. In its effort to keep out disturbing influences, Portugal practically closed its African territories to the outside world. By the late 1950s colonialism as a state system was virtually dead; the question which remained was only whether any relation other than that among separate and sovereign nations would be retained among former members of the onetime colonial empires.

6. *Associated States*

While colonialism declined as a basis for aggregating political units into a common structure, there emerged several patterns of associated states, more closely linked than by mere alliances yet not integrated into either a single state or an imperial structure. The most noteworthy of these associated structures was the British commonwealth.

The Commonwealth evolved as a special form of state organization by successive stages. At the beginning of the century, only such overseas territories of the British empire as had a population predominantly of British stock—Canada, Australia and New Zealand—enjoyed the right of self-government, but even they did not enjoy sovereign status, for the British Parliament still claimed the right to legislate for them and they had no diplomatic relations with other countries. The first major change came in 1910 when the

Union of South Africa Act added the first self-governing dominion which did not claim a common inheritance with the British. The political arrangement incorporating the Boer people opened the door to multiracialism, though still in terms of a population of European origin, for the Boer republics excluded non-Europeans from political participation.

The second major change came as the aftermath of the first world war, in which the United Kingdom had depended heavily on the dominions and India for carrying on the war and these in turn claimed the right to share in the determination of foreign policy. After a decade of negotiation and discussion, the principle of equal independent sovereignty was finally agreed to in 1926 and enacted in the Statute of Westminster in 1931, and the self-governing dominions became, with Britain, the British Commonwealth of Nations.

A further constitutional change became necessary after the second world war when India became a republic and agreed at the same time to remain within the Commonwealth. By the inclusion of India, Ceylon and Pakistan, the Commonwealth had already ceased to be exclusively of European origin. With the acceptance of republican India as a member, what had previously been considered the uniting bond, allegiance to a common sovereign, also vanished. In the middle of the twentieth century the Commonwealth thus presented a picture of an international, multiracial, political association. In its evolution it had provided a means of relinquishing control while retaining association. It remained to be seen whether it would continue as a durable political form or would serve only as a bridge between empire and complete separation.

There were other efforts to transform former possessions into associated states. France until the late 1950s hoped to create some form of French community which would provide a basis for continued association with those parts of her former empire which might wish to retain some kind of tie with France. The effort of the Dutch to work out a basis of association with Indonesia failed, however, and the tentative relationship established at the time of independence was abrogated by the Indonesians six years later. The former United States possession of Puerto Rico, rejecting both independence and incorporation as a state of the American union, chose to constitute itself, by compact, the Associated Commonwealth of Puerto Rico, remaining within the customs union of the United States and retaining American citizenship for its people but conducting its own internal affairs.

In the years after the second world war patterns of association were being developed among states which had no former colonial relationship. India maintained a special relationship with the small state of Nepal on its northern border, assuming responsibility for its military defence. The states of eastern Europe which joined the communist camp, Poland, Czechoslovakia, Hungary, Bulgaria, Rumania, Albania and Eastern Germany, were linked to the USSR through aspects of their economic structure, partial integration of their military forces, and the operation of their Communist or People's Democratic party. Western Europe created supranational instrumentalities—legislative, administrative and judicial—to operate its Coal and Iron Community, its Common Market and Euratom, modifying the functions of related national agencies. The North Atlantic Treaty Organization not only involved an integration of parts of the armed forces of the member states but the creation of common institutions.

The international organizations were themselves a form of association, although they were based on the principle of the equal sovereignty of all member states. The Arab League attempted to provide some kind of institutional base for association among the Arab states in the Middle East. The Organization of American States established machinery which was used successfully to intervene when armed conflict threatened among its members. On a world scale the United Nations provided judicial machinery, although the submission of disputes to the Permanent Court of International Justice was voluntary, and it was the means of uniting military forces, albeit only on an *ad hoc* basis during the first dozen years of its existence.

In spite of the strength of national sentiment and the multiplication of national states, these many forms of association, and the constant enlargement in the scope of the activities of international agencies, were all evidences of the strong tendency in the middle of the twentieth century for the wholly independent national state, as well as the wholly dependent colonial empire to be modified by forms of association which better fitted the complex, interdependent patterns of world society and the needs and aspirations of the world's peoples.

II. INSTITUTIONS OF THE LIBERAL DEMOCRATIC STATES

1. *The electoral system and political parties*

The electoral system was at the heart of the structure of liberal democracy, for it was the basic machinery by means of which popular sovereignty was exercised.[12]

Political parties provided the mechanism for selecting candidates and mobilizing support at the polls. They varied significantly in different countries, but all had certain common features. They were voluntary organizations, generally national in scope, composed of people who agreed at least to some degree on desirable public policies. Their purpose was to capture the legislative and executive organs of the state by the method of popular election in order to get their policies accepted and to give effect to them. The work of party organization was carried on to a very large extent on a non-paid voluntary basis, though a nucleus of paid workers was generally necessary.

The enlargement of the electorate increased immensely the importance of party organizations in political life, for it made it practically impossible for individuals to get elected without the support of a party organization. The variety of the issues arising from the enlarged functions of the state greatly complicated the problem of creating and maintaining an informed electorate which could use its franchise responsibly. In addition the methods of influencing popular opinion through new techniques—the cinema, radio, television and other mass media—became too complicated and costly for individuals to undertake. Candidates continued to appear at public meetings, to answer questions and to shake hands with the voters, but the influencing of public opinion on a mass scale became a specialized technique. Mobilization of political support was planned and carried out at high cost on a nation-wide scale, in a manner which required nationally organized and well-financed parties. Party organizations thus came to occupy a pre-eminent place in the functioning of liberal democracies.

Parties were integral parts of parliamentary structures. The role of the opposition as well as the responsibilities of the majority were recognized and the offices of both majority and minority leaders were commonly financed by funds provided for the operation of the legislative establishment. Relations among parliamentary parties were such, moreover, that in spite of opposition the minority gave sufficient support to the policies voted by the majority to provide essential continuity, it functioned as a 'loyal opposition' until it in turn succeeded in becoming the majority. Much of the process of policy formation took place within the parties, which maintained research bureaux and publications and established liaison with press and citizen groups. Through these means the political parties developed information and thinking on major issues and cast the results into legislative form.

Although political parties were thus indispensable to the exercise of popular sovereignty under the conditions of modern national states, they functioned quite differently from country to country.[13] In Britain, the United States and the commonwealth states of British origin, parties were few and stable, and each party tended to embrace a wide range of views and interests. The democratic institutions of these countries operated on an essentially two-party system, with the parties sufficiently balanced to permit the minority party to become the majority by gaining a small additional share of the votes. Major parties might split or a third party might gain sufficient support to displace one of the major parties, as the British Labour party displaced the Liberal party, first as the opposition and then as the government. The essential feature of these parties, however, was their comprehensive character and their ability to endure by adjusting to changes in circumstances and in public opinion.

Since in this type of party system each major party sought to attract to itself a majority of the voters, it necessarily included in its platform policies which had wide public support. Although the major parties retained sufficient difference in emphasis to appeal to different groups of voters and to offer alternatives to the independents who did not vote purely on the basis of party allegiance, the tendency was for party platforms to approximate each other; popular issues introduced by one party were taken up by the other and programmes introduced when one party was in power were carried on by its successor. Retention by the British Conservative party when it came to power in 1951 of many of the social policies with which the Labour party had undertaken to create a welfare state was a case in point. Under this type of party system issues were rarely deeply divisive, party organization did not reflect fundamental cleavages in the society and political institutions were characterized by a high degree of stability.

The situation was quite different where parties corresponded to deep cleavages in the society or where the issues which they were organized to promote involved fundamental questions of the nature of the state and the form of government. In Austria, for example, socialist and Catholic parties tried to pull the state in opposite directions for twenty years, until what was left of democratic government collapsed in the Nazi take-over; after the war these parties worked as a coalition for more than a decade and thus maintained stability, but they sustained a working relationship only by filling all types of public jobs proportionately from each party. A somewhat similar pattern was followed in Holland and Belgium after the second world war. In Colombia a system of 'parity' and an agreement to alternate the presidency was adopted jointly by the two major parties in 1958 in an effort to bring to an end a decade of political conflict and disorder verging on civil war. Where the Communist party had a large following, as in Italy and France, party issues involved the basic form of the state. In republican Spain after 1931 the cleavage was so deep as to prevent the state from functioning and it led to civil war.

Still another role was played by parties in those countries where a multitude of small parties reflected a range of opinion from left to right. France offered an outstanding example of this type of party structure. In contrast to the British and American parties whose main objective was to secure the support of as wide a segment of the population as possible in order to get elected to office, each French party expressed a particular shade of opinion. No French government had behind it the organized strength of a majority party, but always had to depend upon the collaboration of several units, each ready to pull out whenever policy veered away from its particular position. Much of the instability of the French parliamentary system during the twentieth century was a product of a party system which fragmented voters rather than consolidating them into practical and responsible majorities. The Fifth Republic came into existence in 1958 as a reaction against this system.

But whatever the particular system, the presence of competing parties which organized voters and contended for their support on the basis of issues freely discussed was and remained the prime essential of the liberal democratic state.

2. *Other expressions of political opinion*

Although political parties were the principal agencies for developing and reflecting public opinion on political issues, they were by no means the only institutions which contributed to the exercise of popular sovereignty. The multitude of voluntary organizations which brought people together around common interests—occupational, civic, religious, educational, avocational, benevolent—provided common ground for the discussion of public issues and the shaping of a common outlook among their members.

Some of these had direct links with or formed integral parts of political parties, as did the trade unions in several European countries. Some went to great lengths to influence the opinion not only of their own members but of the general public on issues which they regarded of particular importance to themselves, as did the American Medical Association on the issue of compulsory health insurance in the United States. Some were formed for the express purpose of promoting certain measures, such as minimum wages or child labour laws or disarmament. Some merely discussed public issues among themselves; others adopted positions as a group and made their positions known.

Amid the complexities and conflicts of interest in industrial societies, these voluntary associations played an indispensable role in giving shape and voice to opinion. With few exceptions political representation was by geographic areas; yet interests cut across geographical lines and political districts were apt to be far from homogeneous. Voluntary organizations provided one means by which such interests could find political expression. In the intervals between election campaigns, moreover, they afforded a channel for registering voters' views.

A more sensitive instrument for registering public sentiment between elections was the public opinion poll which was used extensively in the second quarter of the century. Taken on the basis of carefully developed sampling techniques, these polls gave legislators an insight into the public mind, and showed party leaders some of the trends in voting which they might expect, although polls did not generally bring out differences in intensity between views which were lightly held and those which reflected strong convictions.

3. *Legislative structure*

The development of the legislating state with its expanded functions, brought an alteration in the institutions through which the legislative bodies themselves functioned. While procedures traditional to each such body generally persisted in respect to voting and debate, the major work of legislatures moved more and more from the floor of the house to the committee room. This was especially the case where there was a separation of legislative and executive functions, as in the United States, or a multi-party system as in

France. In two-party systems with cabinet responsibility, as in Britain, there was less tendency to use parliamentary committees in the ordinary course of preparing legislation and more reliance on study and drafting by the party in power, but some legislative committees functioned here also.

Committees were in no sense new features of the parliamentary structure, for legislative bodies had always delegated responsibility for special inquiries to committees or used them to review aspects of proposed legislation in advance of general debate. It was simply the enlargement of these functions which gave legislative committees their new importance.

The enormous volume of proposed legislation could not be adequately studied, absorbed and evaluated by each and every legislator. In the United States Congress, for example, as many of 15,000 bills might be introduced in a two-year session. The subject matter of legislation, moreover, became increasingly complex and technical, so that only an expert could recognize issues of policy embedded in seemingly minor differences in phraseology. The committee system enabled a few members of the legislature to become thoroughly familiar with each particular area of legislation and thus permitted the body as a whole to act more responsibly on the basis of committee study and recommendation. In addition, committees familiar with legislation in a specific field could provide a measure of oversight in respect to its execution, and thus could help to give reality to the overall responsibility of the legislative body to the electorate for the conduct of the state.

In these circumstances the operating units which carried the main burden of legislative work became increasingly the legislative committees. Where their procedures for reviewing proposed legislation included the taking of testimony from citizens or citizen groups with special knowledge or interest in the subject, as was the case in the Congress of the United States, they provided a direct channel for the expression of public opinion. As they developed professional staffs they came to provide the legislators with an independent basis for expert judgment on technical matters with which legislation had to deal.

4. Bureaucracy

The major institutional development in the democratic states, however, was not in the electoral and legislative machinery but in the executive arm with the growth of bureaucratic administration. Though the roots of modern bureaucracy lay in the nineteenth century when the system of civil service came to be organized in the democratic countries of Europe and America, its emergence as a major factor was a characteristic of the twentieth century. A few figures will indicate the magnitude of the change. In 1855 in the United Kingdom the number of so-called civil servants, including postmen, office keepers and messengers, was less than 18,000; a hundred years later the same categories numbered over 700,000. In 1900 the federal government of the United States employed some 200,000 persons; at mid-century the number exceeded 2,000,000.

The change in the character of the state was responsible for the growth of bureaucracies. From a political state concerned with legislation on broad policies and the maintenance of peace and order, it became an administering state concerned with the detailed effectuation of policy on an ever increasing range of subjects. This required a vast army of trained personnel at all levels, capable of seeing to the execution of government decisions in every corner of the country, and it called into being an immense machinery which no state in the past had ever had the means to create or control. The extended activity of the state involved two major types of function, regulatory and operating. In order to contain the mounting power of great industries, to carry out protective legislation, to control traffic or indiscriminate building or many other aspects of modern life, the state intervened with regulations and set up administrative bodies to make them effective. These bodies performed not only administrative but quasi-legislative functions of rule-making within the framework established by the legislature, and also the quasi-judicial functions of determining whether or not violations had occurred.[14]

Government agencies also carried on direct operations in many fields— in the physical construction of dams, roads and countless types of public works, in a widening range of government enterprises in such lines as transport and communication, mining, shipbuilding, the generation and distribution of electric power, in maintaining hospitals, clinics and many welfare institutions, and in enormously expanded military establishments with their concomitant activities in scientific research and weapons production.

The enlarged bureaucracies for these purposes required not only high competence in administration but a multitude of specialized skills related to the new and specialized activities and services. The civil service systems inaugurated in the nineteenth century had sought to place administrative posts outside the arena of partisan politics and favouritism and to fill them on the basis of competence. The most famous of these civil services, the British, made a broad liberal education, intelligence and integrity the qualifications for most posts, on the assumption that the nature of public administration was such that a person with these qualifications would be equipped to execute established policy faithfully, to handle all types of situations that might arise, and to develop on the job whatever special knowledge might be required.

But the highly specialized and technical fields into which the state penetrated required more than general education, intelligence and integrity. They required engineers and physicists, economists, physicians, statisticians and a host of other specialists. As the new bureaucracies came to be filled with technical specialists engaged in new kinds of tasks, new problems of organization and functioning arose. Public administration itself took on the character of a special field of knowledge in which principles were developed to guide the relationship between those concerned with the technical aspects of a particular activity and those responsible for maintaining the organizational structure and making administrative decisions.

New organizational forms were also devised for carrying out specific activities. In part the expansion of the bureaucracies took the form of enlargement of the regular administrative departments and the creation of new departments as required. But where government engaged in economic activity or entered various other spheres of operation, the normal government department, however well administered, did not seem an adequate structure. The result was the creation of special autonomous corporations or other semi-autonomous units for these special purposes.

The most widely used form was the autonomous corporation established by statute, with extensive but defined authority, functioning more or less as a subordinate arm of the state with a bureaucracy of its own. Under the broad lines of policy laid down by the legislature it functioned without interference. The Tennessee Valley Authority in the United States and the British Overseas Airlines Corporation were examples of this kind of enterprise. In addition semi-autonomous government bodies, not given formal autonomy by statute but in fact practically independent of other branches of government, had charge of specific functions, as in the case of the Coal Board and the Electricity Board in Britain and numerous similar bodies elsewhere. This pattern was widely followed for the operation of nationalized industries. A third type was the independent corporation, set up like a private corporation under company law but with the majority of shares, sometimes the entire stock, owned by the government.

Whatever the form, two features stood out in regard to all these institutions. In the first place a delegation of authority from the state was the basis of these new bodies. They constituted in effect a division and decentralization of the state's functions along functional lines. Secondly, these organizations themselves developed large-scale bureaucracies, thereby reproducing the same tendencies noted in the direct administrative arms of the state.

The changes in the structure of governmental administrative institutions followed the lines along which industry itself developed, that of mammoth corporations. The change-over from comparatively small industrial units to large corporations has already been noted. In its economic and industrial activity the state followed similar principles and reproduced a similar organizational form, giving to the modern state in many areas the appearance of a collection of big corporations, with the traditional political authorities co-ordinating their work, maintaining law and order and managing international relations.

At the same time the autonomous or semi-autonomous bodies were one of the means by which the democratic states sought to preserve a measure of the variety and freedom of action which was fundamental to their principles as states and societies. Large and bureaucratic though these units might be, they were far smaller than the immense administrative organization of the total state. These bodies, entrusted with a measure of independent authority and initiative, were devices by which the liberal democratic states in spite of the enormous extension of their activities avoided a monolithic structure and the regimentation of their people.

The bureaucracies, whether departmental or semi-autonomous, acted in theory under the ultimate authority and control of the political organs of the state, which were the repository of the sovereign will. In states with a parliamentary form this control was exercised directly through the responsibility to the parliament of the cabinet which headed the administrative structure. Where the presidential system prevailed and the executive branch of the government, headed by a president elected by and responsible to the people, was independent of the legislature, the latter still exercised substantial control through the terms of legislation, the legislative intent expressed in debate, the power of investigation and especially through the appropriation of the funds on which the administrative agencies depended.

Nevertheless, the growing independence of the bureaucracy was a major feature of the twentieth century. In the course of these years, it became in practical effect no longer the servant of the state, passively carrying out policies determined elsewhere, but an active element sharing in the making of state policy and the exercise of state authority.

The reasons for this development were not far to seek. At best no legislative body could give attention to the immense amount of detail involved in the administration of a welfare state, yet the actual impact of state policy upon the citizen was embodied in decisions on just such matters of detail. Such attention was even more impossible where services or activities were highly technical; here the technicians who manned a service tended to become its proprietors. Wherever there was some measure of economic planning, even many major policy decisions were of so technical a nature that they had to be made by the planning agency rather than by the political body. The factor of defence added a further barrier to political control. As modern warfare came to involve all aspects of life—most industries, the pursuit of science, many forms of training—large sections of national activity had to be entrusted to a specialized bureaucracy. Even apart from work specifically involving military secrets, the shadow of defence fell over a wide range of activity, and the political state, whatever the theory, could exercise only limited control.[15]

5. *Administrative law*

A major aspect of this development was the growth of a large body of administrative law, formulated and interpreted not by judges but by administrative departments. More and more of the parliamentary legislation in all liberal democratic countries left the rule-making powers—such rules having virtually the force of laws—to administrative agencies, the rules themselves to be interpreted and administered not by courts but by civil servants. Whether in respect to income tax or building regulations or currency control or labour standards and labour relations, the receipt of social insurance benefits, economic assistance or public services, citizens found themselves confronted by decisions taken by anonymous officials who established their own procedures, made their own interpretations of fact and merit, and handed down decisions that had much of the force of judge-made law without going through the 'due process of law' which was generally established in these countries as a citizen's right.

The possibility that this development of administrative law might lead to abuse of bureaucratic power and seriously impair civil rights was well recognized. Yet the impossibility of legislating all the rules and of entrusting their enforcement to the slow procedures of already overburdened courts was equally clear. In these circumstances efforts were made to set bounds to administrative decisions, to prevent arbitrary action by developing standards and procedures, and in some cases to create special courts or to provide for review of administrative decisions by the regular courts.

A dramatic example of the effort to keep the scope of administrative decision within bounds was furnished by the action of the Supreme Court of the United States in 1935 when it declared the legislation for economic recovery enacted at the depth of the depression to be unconstitutional and therefore void because Congress had delegated what were in effect legislative powers to administrative agencies without sufficient expression of policy and without adequately circumscribing the administrative authority. In Britain, in respect to city planning, principles regarding the remuneration of property owners whose property was affected by the action of administrative bodies were laid down by a leading jurist in 1942* and were made the basis for legislation and a guide for the action of administrative agencies. Special courts were created in a number of countries to deal with such matters as labour disputes or tax appeals.

Two general principles entered into the development of administrative procedures, the principle of eligibility and the right of appeal. Wherever entitlement to any sort of service or benefit was involved, uniform publicly announced standards of eligibility were the first safeguard against arbitrariness and favouritism. Some machinery for appeal from an administrative decision was generally provided, either to a special board within the agency itself, or under some conditions to the regular courts.

In these ways liberal democratic countries sought to prevent the vast range of administrative activity from turning into a new despotism. But not a few thoughtful persons expressed a genuine fear that the spreading tentacles of the welfare state would destroy the individualism and initiative which had given European civilization much of its dynamic quality. The full significance of what some people liked to describe as a system of 'parliamentary bureaucracy' and the full impact of the growth of administrative law on the citizens of democratic states was still not yet realized at the middle of the century.

* *Final Report of Expert Committee on Compensation and Betterment* (1942).

6. *Judiciary*

Meantime the judiciary continued to play its traditional role of regulating relations among individuals on the basis of civil, commercial and family law, of safeguarding society and the state through the application of the criminal code, of guarding individual rights *vis-à-vis* the state through such institutions as *habeas corpus* and other elements of 'due process of law', and in some countries acting as guardian of the constitution against the whim of the majority.

In performing this continuing role under the conditions of the modern state, courts of law were constantly confronted with new situations not covered by specific precedent and by the need to take into account factors outside the frame of reference formerly regarded as the domain of law. The new relationships created by the large corporation could not be encompassed within the traditional concepts and principles relating to property and legal personality. Employer-employee relationships could not be fitted into the strait-jacket of a commercial contract for the purchase and sale of labour. Courts found themselves forced to include in their considerations the economic reality as well as the legal form, the social implications of the issues before them, and even the meaning of such concepts as 'equal protection of the law' in psychological terms.

In spite of the great extension of administrative law, the independent judiciary remained a bulwark of the liberal democratic state. At times it functioned as a conservative force, slow to encompass and give legitimacy to new social trends. But it was no accident that wherever democracy was supplanted by totalitarianism, the judicial system was one of the first institutions to be altered. Nor was it an accident that a judicial system, inherited from a colonial power or voluntarily adopted from the West, was one of the corner stones on which the new states which adopted democratic constitutions sought to build a structure to fulfil their democratic hopes.

7. *Problems encountered by new states in adopting democratic forms*

The new states of Asia and Africa with few exceptions adopted some form of parliamentary democracy upon their establishment as independent states. With local variations, they modelled their constitutions on those of the older democracies and they established electoral procedures, parliamentary institutions and administrative structures designed to put these principles into effect. In so doing they encountered formidable problems of government, intensified by their basic problems of economic and social development. One after another they found that the system which they had adopted was not working effectively; several, with the conspicuous exception of India, suspended or abrogated features of their original constitutions, generally under the leadership of the military, in an effort to evolve new forms suited to their experience and needs.

In these countries neither a republican form of government nor democratic institutions based on elected representatives had a genuine local tradition behind them. In most cases, both the experience and the psychological background for putting such institutions into operation were lacking; the full implications of the parliamentary system, with cabinets, legislative bodies and all the other paraphernalia, were imperfectly understood not only among the masses of the people but often by the leaders themselves.

The central problem which they faced was the problem of obedience. The authority of the monarch or his deputy had been well understood; it had been in fact virtually axiomatic. The monarch had been hedged about with 'majesty'; in the formula with which the emperors of China had ended their orders, the populace was expected to 'tremble and obey'. But authority in a democracy, the will of the people, or more particularly the will of the majority as expressed through parliament, was not clearly understood and accepted; obedience to the majority was far from axiomatic. Occasional or chronic rebellion, seizure of power by non-constitutional means, dismissal of parliamentary bodies or cabinets by governor or president to override majority action in one after another of the new states during the first decade of their existence, were evidence that the principle of democratic obedience had yet to become a working basis for many of the new states.

The problem presented itself in acute form in the issue of the supremacy of civil authority over the armed forces. The supremacy of civil over military authority in a democracy depends on a widespread and ingrained democratic spirit among the people. Even in many old and well-established democratic states, the military had at one time or another in their history challenged civil authority; where democratic institutions had functioned imperfectly it had offered a chronic threat. In the new states whose people were long used to accepting authority based on effective power, the threat was very much present and the danger to the survival of democratic institutions was great.

The operations of a democratic state depend upon a series of institutions which were alien to the experience and habit of thought of the new states. Chief among these was the institution of the 'loyal opposition', a party or parties whose opposition to the policies of those in power was freely expressed, who could seek to win a majority to their view and who if successful were in a position to accept power and assume responsibility for government. In many of the new states where opposition had traditionally been synonymous with sedition, it was not easy for those in power to accept organized opposition or for those out of power to seek it in a responsible manner.

Democratic institutions, moreover, require the association of people with government at all levels; a parliamentary system which tries to operate only at the centre, with no experience of democratic functioning at the local level, can have little reality for those going through the motions of casting a ballot. In this respect the countries which had formed part of the Indian empire had an advantage over other new states, for some measure of local government had been introduced in the 1880s, and people had thus become familiar with democratic assumptions and procedures and had learned to operate them locally before being called on to make them work on a larger scale. But elsewhere this sort of experience was generally lacking. Even in Pakistan the initial effort to establish nation-wide democratic institutions was short-lived and these were replaced after a coup by an administrative structure under military leadership. With the declared purpose of developing the basis for a functioning democracy, the new leadership partially re-established local democratic elections as a training ground where Pakistanis could acquire the experience which in time would permit the restoration of democratic institutions at the national level.

Lacking, also, was a process for the generation of ideas and the formation of public opinion. Parliamentary institutions are designed to carry out ideas generated throughout the society, not to be the fountain-head of thought. In the established democracies the vast and varied programmes of national welfare and public policy were shaped by the voluntary intellectual activity of dynamic groups in which intellectuals provided an arsenal of ideas and public discussion hammered out views and issues.

But institutions of higher education were absent or very young in most of the new states, and in the period of colonial rule such intellectual centres as existed could not engage freely in political study and debate. Parties had been built up prior to liberation in order to carry on the struggle for independence. The problem was whether these parties could transform themselves into continuing organizations for participation in democratic government and whether a widespread interest in public affairs could be sustained among a large enough group in the population to keep the democratic machinery functioning.

The most fundamental problem of all arose from the fact that democracy is not simply a set of political institutions but a total complex, a way of life. In each of the older democracies distinctive political forms were related to other aspects of national life; the differences among such countries as Switzerland, France, the Netherlands, Britain and the United States amply indicated the extent to which specific democratic institutions were integral elements in a total structure of society. It was of the essence of democracy, furthermore, that its conceptions and institutions should constantly change as the society changed—that freedom and equality should acquire different concrete meanings in the twentieth century from what they had had a hundred years before.

The problem in the new states was that democracy might remain merely a borrowed ideology—a sort of textbook democracy. The specific forms of democratic institutions which most of these states adopted were patterned on those of their respective metropolitan powers and bore little or no relationship to the social structures on which they were imposed. To the extent that countries accepted political forms without interpreting democratic values in terms of their own life, they faced the danger that their democratic institutions would remain imitative and artificial and would be but a façade behind which a dictatorship or an oligarchy or disorder and instability would rule. There were signs in some of the new states during these years that this danger might be real.

The bureaucracies which the new states inherited from the period of colonial rule, and on which in the first instance they were forced to rely, varied in number and quality, but in all cases they had to be greatly expanded and revamped to provide the necessary machinery of administration. In the colonial civil services, including the most highly developed of them, the Indian civil service, superior posts had been filled almost entirely by personnel from the metropolitan country; in the little-developed services, as in the French colonies or the Sudan, few people from the locality had occupied even the lower posts. The scope of colonial administration, moreover, was extremely limited, involving generally little more than the collection of revenue, the maintenance of law and order and the promotion of favourable conditions for trade. The immense range of functions and services which had to be performed in the newly independent states lay almost wholly outside the sphere of the civil services of the colonial period.

The new states thus faced a threefold task if they were to sustain their state structures and bring about the economic and social changes essential to their development: they must find or develop persons with sufficient competence, training and integrity to fill superior posts, they must enlarge their total civil service enormously and rapidly, and they must develop a body of technicians with a wide range of specialized technical and managerial skills to carry through the specialized operations of a modern state.

In the countries where the educated class was extremely small at the time of independence it was necessary to rely heavily on the temporary device of recruiting administrative personnel from abroad, as was done for example, in the Sudan. Elsewhere, notably in India and to a lesser extent Pakistan, there was a sufficiently large number of educated persons who could be recruited for the public service to permit a very great expansion of the total number and an effective system of promotion to fill the higher posts. But even in the latter countries the problem of finding and training sufficient technical and managerial personnel was formidable. India, which more than doubled the number of its engineers in the ten years after independence, calculated that it would need to achieve a fourfold increase in the next five years to staff the enterprises and services called for in its development plans. Most other countries were much more deficient in needed skills. The stability and progress of the new states thus depended greatly on the rapidity with which they could build up a competent, trained and honest administration which would provide their governments with the necessary stability and with the instruments to implement national policies.

At the same time the scope of activities in which the new states had to engage was far greater than that required in the older democracies, for in the absence or insufficiency of many of the private enterprises and voluntary services which existed elsewhere they had no choice but to do through government many things which were at least partly done by non-governmental agencies in other countries.

The economically backward countries were caught in a vicious circle: the productive capacity of the community was not sufficiently developed to enable the public to look after its own welfare; and without welfare services to improve the standards of life productive capacity could not be expected to increase. So the state had simultaneously to see that the welfare services were undertaken on a nation-wide scale and that industrial and other production increased. This involved the state in every form of activity, from family planning and nutrition to the creation of modern industries and an active role in production. It required not only the provision of better health, education and housing but changes in social structure, in attitudes, in the distribution of land and other wealth.

In the newly independent countries the state had thus to be all-inclusive in its activity, dealing with marriage laws while it encouraged the latest scientific research, promoting preventive medicine along with the modernization of transport, attempting to provide for universal education and to plan for the development of rural life, concerned with large-scale industrialization and with the encouragement of art and literature. The creation of new life in the rural areas, for example, involved not merely the organization of a new machinery of government capable of operating on an extensive scale, but the creation of non-official leadership in the areas concerned; training institutions for village-level workers became as necessary as institutions for the training of technicians. The success of schemes for large-scale industrialization depended not only on the latest technicial knowledge but on the development of a managerial element with trained executive ability. Management of money and credit at national and inter-national levels, the ability to fight inflationary tendencies that were unavoidable where large-scale expenditure was necessary—these too required special training and ability. The skills and capacities needed for these purposes, moreover, were of the highest order, for on every side the problems to be met were of infinite complexity and difficulty.

A special feature of the political institutions of the new states was the part played by law. By the middle of the twentieth century at least some legal principles and institutions based on European law, either on the Napoleonic Code or on the Anglo-Saxon common law, had been incorporated into the legal systems of all countries except the extremely conservative Muslim states such as Yemen and Saudi Arabia, and the communist countries. By one means or another western law was superimposed on the customary or religiously based law of non-western areas or it was combined with it or it replaced it.

The introduction of western law into non-western areas was most complete in respect to commercial and maritime law, which by the nature of trade and commerce tended toward universality. Penal codes tended, by a process of borrowing, to approximate either the Napoleonic or the Anglo-Saxon systems of criminal justice with their related procedures. The area of personal and family law, which involved the heart of the social structure, was least or last to be affected. Law with respect to land, both in the matter of inheritance and transfer, often presented a special area of uncertainty and of conflict between old and new legal principles.

Western law reached non-western areas in various ways. From the sixteenth century on, European commercial law had gained a foothold wherever trading companies had established bases, and other aspects of European law had spread from these footholds by treaty, example and the exercise of colonial authority. Under the system of 'capitulations' Europeans within the Ottoman empire were judged by European law in extraterritorial courts. Similar privileges were secured by Europeans in other Muslim countries, including Persia, Egypt, Morocco and later Iraq, and in China, Japan, Siam and Ethiopia. This extraterritorial jurisdiction extended generally not only to disputes among Europeans but to those between a foreigner and a national, and even to some nationals in the employ of Europeans.

Although extraterritoriality was bitterly resented and its abolition became a focus of national effort, it made European legal principles and practices familiar to numbers of people in these areas. By the time that the system was abolished, first by Japan in 1899 and virtually everywhere else in the 1920s and 1930s, the legal systems of the countries involved had come to approximate those of Europe.

The adoption of western systems of law by non-colonial countries was part of their conscious efforts at westernization or modernization. Japan was the first Asian country to promulgate a new code of laws based on western conceptions. It adopted a penal code modelled on the French in 1882 and a civil and commercial code modelled on the German and English in 1899. Siam subsequently took over a considerable portion of the German code.

The most dramatic and complete substitution of a European system came in Turkey following the Ataturk revolution of 1923. A considerable amount of European law had already been adopted in a piecemeal and unsystematic fashion in the course of the nineteenth century, including codes of criminal, commercial and maritime law and procedures for criminal, commercial and civil courts. In a drastic move to secularize the state, westernize the country and bring social reforms, as well as to bring order into the Turkish legal system, Ataturk promulgated new penal, civil, commercial and maritime codes and codes of civil and criminal procedures based on Italian, Swiss and German legal codes. The Swiss civil code was adopted for the hitherto untouched area of private and family law, and religious courts and Muslim law were wholly replaced.

Quite a different process was followed in Persia, where the effort was to combine western and Muslim law and to adapt them to each other rather than to effect a complete substitution. The first steps, in 1912 and 1914, were to set up a judicial administration along European lines and a system of commercial courts, but the religious courts continued to function. In 1926 a penal code based on the French was adopted. Two years later a civil code was introduced which was based upon the Muslim *sharia* but with adaptations from the French code. Codes of procedure based on the French were adopted for civil, criminal and commercial cases. The modified Muslim law was to be administered by the civil court as a uniform system throughout the country, not according to the individual interpretation of the local *mujtahids* or Muslim judges, and all marriages and divorces were to be registered in the civil courts.

In the areas under colonial rule the legal institutions of the metropolitan power became part of the system of colonial administration, although in Indonesia they were applied only to Europeans and other non-Indonesians. The results of this introduction of western law were most notable in the countries which composed the Indian empire, where for a hundred years the principles of British commercial law, criminal justice and civil and criminal procedure were built into the political structure. The nature of Anglo-Saxon common law had a bearing on the results of this process. In contrast to the civil law embodied in the legal systems of the European continent, it was not a code of legal rules but a set of procedures for determining fact and for settling disputes according to either custom and precedent or on the basis of legislation. As such it introduced basic concepts such as equality before the law, and basic procedures such as *habeas corpus* and rules of evidence, but it modified customary relationships only where legislation was involved. The family law of Hindus and Muslims remained almost wholly unaffected.

The states under former British rule thus acquired a set of legal principles and procedures and the idea of legislation as a means of establishing new relationships which by the time of their independence they had already learned to use. It is noteworthy that the Indian constitution of 1949 in its articles on the judiciary specifically enumerated the various writs such as *habeas corpus*, *quo warranto*, *mandamus* and *certiorari* which were parts of British legal procedure, and that the Islamic constitution of Pakistan in 1956, while stating that no law should be repugnant to the injunctions of Islam, also specified that its high courts should have the power to issue these same writs for the enforcement of the fundamental rights guaranteed by the constitution or for other purposes. These and other new states, moreover, saw their power of legislation as an instrument for changing customary law, and used it to bring further reforms to their society.

The legal concepts and procedures adopted from the West were essentially those of nineteenth-century Europe. The ancient codes of customary laws and the legal institutions which had religious sanction were modified by the impact of the liberal ideas of the nineteenth-century European jurists. Whether they were adopted deliberately in an effort at westernization or absorbed during the period of colonial rule, they were major instruments of social reform and the principles and relationships which they established and the procedures which they created were fundamental to the operation of these states as liberal democracies or related forms.

III. INSTITUTIONS OF THE COMMUNIST STATES

1. *The Communist party*

The most distinguishing feature of the communist state, for which the Soviet Union may be taken as the prototype during this period, was the role played by the Communist party. The Communist party regarded itself as the embodiment of the will of workers and peasants and, as such, as the true vehicle for the expression of the popular will. The formal machinery of the state provided a complex of organs for carrying out the sovereign will expressed in and through the Party. In this sense the Party was superior to the state; the Party congress was the supreme body and the Party leaders who composed the Central Committee functioned as permanent executives. Identifying itself thus with the people, the Party claimed complete and all-embracing authority—in laying down domestic and foreign policies, determining the correctness of theories, planning and directing political strategy, leading, guiding and overseeing every organ of the state.

The Party consisted of the most active elements among the people. It was a dedicated vanguard trained in the doctrines of communism and subjected to a period of probation. Recruitment to the Party was not merely by enlisting those who accepted its general programme. A candidate must prove himself in the various work groups of the state—factory, collective farm, union of intellectual workers or other body—demonstrating his theoretical and his practical capacity and his loyalty and orthodoxy in order to become a full member of the Party. The Party numbered perhaps 1 to 4 per cent of the population, an estimated 8,000,000 in the Soviet Union and 10,000,000 in China in the mid-1950s.

The functions performed by the Communist party differed in essential respects from those performed by political parties in liberal democratic states. Since the Communist party itself acted as the repository of the popular will, the general electoral machinery was not a device for registering a choice among rival candidates and between alternative views on public issues. The function of public elections in the communist state was merely to re-confirm public confidence in the Party and its decisions as the embodiment of the people's will. Voters were therefore simply asked to vote 'yes' or 'no' on the slate of candidates offered by the Party.

Although the Party comprised only a small part of the population, it was the means by which a very large number of people were constantly and responsibly active in the formation and execution of public policy. Every Party cell, local committee or higher Party unit was expected to engage in continuous discussion and to exercise constant vigilance. Every unit was part of the transmission belt for policies determined at the top, part of the reporting system for registering the implementation of policy and keeping upper echelons informed, and part of the mechanism to permit issues to be raised and debated at successively lower levels and opinion to be transmitted to the higher organs engaged in the process of policy formation. Subject to control by the higher unit, which might remove an officer of a lower unit for failure to carry forward the responsibilities of his office, choice of leadership within each group was by election, and higher organs of the Party were composed of delegates selected by the lower units.

The Party not only provided most of the cadres for government work but also the membership of the political bodies within the state. It thus provided the key personnel for all the organs of the state. In addition it functioned at all levels as a guardian, not merely to prevent irregularities and to secure efficient action from the very bottom upwards, but to ensure a uniformity of approach, to see to it that policy was uniformly understood throughout the state and that changes in policy were followed uniformly. It was in fact the Party that gave the monolithic character to the communist state. In these circumstances, the organs of the state were in some respects less important than those of the Party for the weight carried by members in the government depended less on the office they held than on their position in the Party.[16]

2. *Organs of the state*

The central function of the state in a communist society was the development of communist ethics and a superstructure which applied the principles of the society. Since in Marxist-Leninist theory society derives its character from the processes of production and the means of production must be in public hands, the conduct of economic affairs was a central activity of the state and its major organs were therefore the organs of economic life. In this respect the communist state was sharply distinguished from the liberal democratic state, whose central function was to provide a framework of orderly society within which economic and other activities could be carried on independently and which took on direct economic responsibilities only as this action appeared necessary for the general welfare.

The communist state was an enterprise state. Its goals were conceived in economic and social terms and in terms of its world position. Its prime function was to carry on direct operations. From top to bottom—from the overall state to the smallest factory, farm, clinic, school or army unit—the communist state was a great enterprise. As an enterprise it was all-inclusive and highly organized in every aspect of life. Its administrative organization inevitably dwarfed that of any less inclusive state in size, extent and complexity and its structure was designed to further the success of the enterprise —to build a socialist, and ultimately a communist, society.

The first principle of organization was that of 'democratic centralism'. As conceived by Lenin, the institutions of the state were to operate according to a two-way process. Central direction and control were to be combined with widespread public participation through functional organizations and lower state organs from which opinions would rise and reach the centre. After Lenin's death a struggle among his principal followers resulted in the accession of Josef Stalin to the Party leadership, and for the next three decades the machinery of the Party and the state was operated by Stalin as a stern dictator whose excesses were later deplored by his successors. Under the conditions of these years—revolution, industrialization, collectivization, war and reconstruction—the features of central control and domination of all agencies and all aspects of life from the centre were accentuated.

During Stalin's régime, the method used to handle opposition or potential opposition was the 'purge', or removal from office. In serious cases persons thought to be dangerous to the state were arrested, induced to make a public confession of their guilt, and sent to labour camps or executed as the gravity of their offence and the importance of their position seemed to require. This method served the double purpose of removing opposition and of making very clear the line of Party policy.[17] In the major purges of the mid-1930s large numbers of persons who had favoured some of the alternative policies among which the Party had had to choose in the years since the revolution were eliminated and the unity of both policy and organization under Stalin's policies and leadership was assured. Stalin in fact sought to make these features of domination and repression permanent. While the 1936 constitution established in principle many features of socialist democracy—greatly extending the powers of the Supreme Soviet, calling for a more democratic electoral system, providing for the democratization of the judiciary—most of the newly established political forms remained inoperative in the face of mounting fear of fascist aggression and the conditions produced by the second world war.

After Stalin's death in 1953, and in the changed circumstances of the time and the stage of industrial and social development of the USSR, his successors sought to reduce extreme centralization and discontinue harsh measures of control. Transfer to lesser posts served in most cases to remove opposition and to consolidate the policies of the dominant element in the Central Committee of the Party, while public acknowledgement of error or guilt continued to serve as a device for keeping Party policy before the public and making its meaning clear in uniform terms. Steps were taken to decentralize a measure of authority to the several Soviet republics and to place greater responsibility on functional organizations such as trade unions, writers' congresses or youth groups in the conduct of their affairs, thus seeking to bring the state more in line with the balance between central direction and widespread participation which Lenin had conceived.

The general administrative structure of the Soviet state followed functional lines in relation to the economy. The principal ministries were entrusted with

EE*

one or another economic area—heavy industry, electricity, textiles. The basic unit of organization was the productive unit—factory, collective farm, hospital. Intermediate organizations included enterprises and sometimes groups of enterprises formed into trusts, which might be highly centralized or partially decentralized. Geographical organization was supplementary to functional organization. Geographical organs such as town or district bodies had direct responsibility for those activities which did not depend principally on their link with other areas, such as local handicrafts and for the provision of some local amenities and cultural activities. Their indirect responsibility was to further the success of enterprises within their area.

The responsibility of the lower organs was based on the delegation of authority from the centre. The USSR was organized as a federal union with separate governments in each of the republics. Within this federal structure, however, the responsibilities carried by ministries of the republics were determined by the central authority. The federal structure had been established in the USSR in part because of the multi-national character of the country, and the structure included a series of organs based on nationality, centred in a Congress of Nationalities; but this structure, too, was supplementary to the functional structure.

After 1957 the decision to decentralize some of the activities which had been controlled from the centre placed new responsibilities on the institutions of the several republics. A considerable number of factories previously in the charge of central government agencies were transferred to republic and regional organizations. The central agencies relinquished the function of drawing up codes of law, which they transferred to the competence of the republics. National ministries of justice and internal affairs were dissolved, greater powers were assigned to the lower courts and the militia was subordinated to district and regional soviets.

The central organ of the state was the state planning agency. The activities of the state, at all levels and in all fields, revolved around the formulation and the execution of the Plan. The state as an enterprise, and all its component parts, were directed and carried forward through the setting of production goals—whether of tons of steel to be produced or numbers of children to be taught or hospitals to be built or hectares to be planted; performance of each organ or each official was judged by fulfilment of goals. Planning thus became the major administrative instrument for organizing and carrying out the purposes of the state.

Various devices were developed to stimulate the initiative and responsibility of individuals and to avoid the dangers associated with bureaucracy while at the same time maintaining supervision and control. In the USSR each enterprise operated as a separate unit, engaging in contractual relationships with other enterprises from which it secured its materials or to which it supplied its products, and it was accountable financially as well as physically for exceeding or at least being sure to meet goals set by the Plan. Within each enterprise the accountant, quality-control officer, chief of maintenance and trade union leader each carried independent responsibility and was accountable to superiors in the higher organ for the aspect of the enterprise with which he was involved. The Party group in each enterprise was responsible directly to the Party organization for vigilance in the fulfilment of the Plan. In addition, the central authorities maintained a system of inspectors to check on enterprises where there was reason to suspect irregularity or inefficiency, and the organs of state security were also available to intervene if sabotage or other serious offence was suspected.

Because the communist state required the involvement of all the people toward a common, active goal in line with uniformly understood and applied policy, the instruments of propaganda were essential instruments of the Party and the state. The difference between the communist and the liberal state in their concepts of popular sovereignty led to quite different concepts relating to the formation of public opinion. The parliamentary state assumed the existence outside government of independent centres where ideas on political issues would be generated and whence they would find their way to the governing body, to be reflected in public policy. In communist theory and practice the Party itself, as the embodiment of the sovereign people, was the organ for the formation of opinion, the guardian of theory, the leader and shaper of thought. It was therefore its function to stimulate widespread popular discussion within the framework of issues and policies determined at the centre, to control the instruments for the formation of opinion and attitude and to use them fully and systematically both in order to create and maintain public opinion in line with the policies of the Party, and to provide the Party with knowledge of public reactions which it might consider in formulating policy. The press, the radio, the artistic and literary professions, were therefore regarded and treated as arms of the state.

A special feature of the communist state was its use of law as an instrument of both administration and education.[18] In their initial periods communist states discarded the structure of law which had formerly existed. The USSR replaced the legal system in existence under the tsars and the Chinese communist state scrapped the code of law which the former republic had developed with the help of legal advisers from the West. In theory it was initially expected that correction of economic conditions would correct the conditions which in capitalist society led to crime, and would make law in the sense used in capitalist countries unnecessary. Treatment of deviant behaviour was to be through education rather than punishment and offenders were subjected to an intensive process known as 're-education', often administered by the culprit's own social group.

In the course of time complete reliance on re-education was found insufficient and penalties related to the gravity of the offence were introduced. These were however more in the nature of administrative tools than the application of legal principles. Offences were primarily those which impeded the operation of the state as an enterprise—negligence in the pursuit of production goals, waste or damage to state property. Punishment for failure to co-operate fully and effectively in the national effort was the obverse of the premiums, honours or other recognitions with which fulfilment and over-fulfilment were rewarded.

The judicial system thus did not operate in the manner conceived in liberal democracies, as an independent branch of government with rules and principles of its own. Court procedures were not hedged about by the rules of evidence, writs for bringing persons to speedy trial, or other paraphernalia which gave the court systems of the liberal democratic states their basic character. Although a system of legal warrantees was developed in time which gave persons brought to trial a defined status, the legal and judicial institutions continued to be considered as political and educational organs rather than instruments of justice in the traditional sense used in the liberal states.

The communist states functioned during these years under conditions of revolutionary change. Their Party and state structures were the instruments of that change—of the liquidation of former proprietors as a class, of the industrialization of non-industrial or partially industrialized societies, of the immense expansion in economic activity called for by such a change, of extreme efforts exacting heavy sacrifices, and of consolidating national communist states in a world, the greater part of which was hostile to their aims and efforts. The particular form taken by the institutions of the communist states during this period must therefore be seen not only as the application of communist theory but as practical means of implementing revolutionary social change.

While the principal development of communist institutions took place in the Soviet Union, and it is primarily in these terms that the political institutions of communist states have been discussed, some variations in structure were appearing in the other states which adopted the communist political form in the years after the second world war.

The most divergent institutions were developed in Yugoslavia, which though a communist state remained outside the international communist movement after 1948. Here the key principle was decentralization, through workers' councils responsible for the conduct of each enterprise, and local councils with a large measure of responsibility for each locality. In contrast to the Soviet Union where centrally organized production planning provided the directives for the efforts of each unit, planning in Yugoslavia during these years was used only to furnish a framework and climate for local effort, to formulate economic objectives, not to provide the instrumentalities for carrying them out. Indirect methods such as favourable or unfavourable rates on loans were used to stimulate or discourage the capital expenditures called for by the plans.

The institutions of communist China, on the other hand, moved in the opposite direction. In the course of its first ten years the Chinese People's

Republic introduced successively more and more instruments of central direction and control, including the organization of communes to replace peasant family units, villages and collective farms, and control over the movement of people from one place to another. These institutions permitted the state to mobilize millions of workers for major tasks and to carry forward a programme of staggering proportions to remake the economic life and the society of this ancient land.[19]

NOTES TO CHAPTER XXIII

1. Several critics regret the absence of material which is ordinarily associated with the traditional political treatment in a work of this kind. Professor Lynn M. Case writes about Chapter XXIII, 'Political Institutions': 'There should be a little more of the *why* to go with the *what*. . . . There is no explanation for the rise of fascism, nazism, or other totalitarian states. All the political institutions seem to occur in a vacuum.'

2. Candidate of Juridical Sciences A. Bovin points out that at the present time governments 'based upon and supported by military force' do not only exist in countries with fascist regimes. Militarization of the state apparatus is nowadays a characteristic feature of some 'liberal democracies' as well. This has been commented on by many Western public figures and scholars—sociologists, philosophers, and political scientists (see *A Symposium: Disarmament and the American Economy*, ed. H. Aptheker, New York, 1960). The prominent American journalist F. Cook, in his popular book, *The Warfare State: Juggernaut* (New York, 1961), gives a number of examples to illustrate the fact that militarism has penetrated into all branches of the American economy and that the American militarists have captured key positions in the country's state apparatus. Similar processes can be observed in the Federal Republic of Germany, Great Britain and France.
   See:
   (1) Fred Cook, *The Warfare State: Juggernaut* (New York, 1961).
   (2) John P. Davis, *Corporations: A Study on the Origin and Development of Great Business Combinations and of Their Relation to the Authority of the State* (New York, 1961).
   (3) E. Khesin, 'Militarizm i voyenniye kontserny Anglii' ('Militarism and British Arms Firms'), in: *Mezhdunarodnaya zhizn* (International Affairs) (1962), No. 1.
   (4) N. Tsygichko, 'Zapadnogermansky militarizm i yego doktrina' ('West German Militarism and Its Doctrine') in: *Mirovaya ekonomika i mezhdunarodnoye otnosheniye* (World Economics and International Relations) (1961), No. 9.
   (5) E. Fajon 'Nastuplenie monopolii na prava frantsuzskikh trudyashchikhsya' ('The Onslaught of the Monopolies on the Rights of French Workers') in *Mezhdunarodnaya zhizn*, No. 9, 1961; Y. Ostrovityanov, A. Sterbalova: 'Yest li vykhod iz tupika voennoy ekonomiki?' ('Is there a way out of the blind alley of war economy?') in *World Marxist Review* (Prague, 1961), No. 4.

3. *The Author-Editors have treated as a category governments 'based upon and supported by military force' having in mind those governments brought to power by military action and/or maintained in power by this means, in defiance of or in the absence of other established procedures for giving a government legitimacy. The use of this category does not preclude recognition of the influence of the military in time of peace as well as in time of war within states of various forms with legitimately established governments. See Chapters XI and XXIV for a discussion of this influence.*

4. Candidate of Juridical Sciences A. Bovin thinks that it is incorrect to say that the main tendency in the evolution of political institutions during the twentieth century has been in the direction of liberal democracy. At the present time this form of political organization is on the decline; out of the liberal democracies that existed in the Europe of 1918 only fifteen still remain today. And even in these countries various forms of restrictions of the democratic liberties proclaimed in the eighteenth and nineteenth centuries are

being introduced. (See D. E. Brown, *The Growth of Democratic Government*, Washington, 1959, p. 3.)

The democratic countries that have arisen in the former colonial and dependent territories cannot be regarded simply as copies of Western models. They are something radically new. The peoples of the former colonies and dependencies are at different stages in their struggle for complete emancipation, for national independence, the liquidation of the consequences of domination by foreign capital, and development along the road of social progress.

All these tasks can be successfully accomplished by establishing and developing states of national democracy. A national democracy is a state which consistently defends its political and economic independence, fights against imperialism and its military blocs and military bases on its territory. A national democracy is a state in which the peoples enjoy broad democratic rights and liberties, are able to carry through agrarian reform, and realize other demands for democratic and social reforms. (B. Ponomarev 'O gosudartsve natsionalnoy demokratii' ('On the National-Democratic State'), in *Kommunist* (Communist), No. 8, 1961, pp. 36, 41.)

5. *For a discussion of newly independent states, the Author-Editors refer the reader to pages 806–813.*

6. Candidate of Juridical Sciences A. Bovin points out that the definition given here of the term 'liberal democracy' does not indicate the qualitative difference between this form of democracy and other forms.

The People's Democracies, which the authors oppose to 'liberal democracy', also have representative political institutions and traditions. It is precisely these representative organs of state power, both national and local, that constitute the basis of the entire state apparatus of the People's Democracies. In the European People's Democracies such organs include People's and National Assemblies, State Assembly, Seym, People's Chamber, and People's Skupshchina (Parliament); and at the local level People's Councils or National (or People's) Committees. The People's (or National) Assemblies and People's (or National) Councils (Committees), as the most democratic organizations of the working people, with the strongest mass basis, are formed as a result of democratic elections held by the working people themselves and are fully sovereign organs of the state power of the working people in the cities and the countryside.

So far as democratic traditions are concerned, they exist and are rooted in the People's Democracies in the specific historical development of these states. It is well known that the People's Councils (Committees) were set up already during the war in clandestine conditions, as organs for carrying on the struggle for popular emancipation from the invaders and their allies within the country, as embryonic organs of the people's democratic power. Those who took part in setting up such organs included the democratic parties, public organizations, and also certain political groups that advanced the platform of uniting all the democratic forces in the struggle for freedom and independence. The working masses saw in the People's Councils the prospect not only of national liberation but also of the realization of their democratic aspirations, since the power of the People's (National) Councils (Committees) is the power of the people themselves, i.e. of the workers, peasants and all working people. [See (i) *Gosudarstvennoye pravo zarubezhnykh sotsialisticheskikh stran* (The State Law of Foreign Socialist Countries), Moscow: Academy of Sciences of the USSR, Institute of Law, 1957, pp. 83–5; (ii) *Konstitutsii zarubezhnykh sotsialisticheskikh gosudarstv* (The Constitutions of Foreign Socialist States) Moscow, 1956.]

The differences between 'liberal democracy' and People's Democracy is much more fundamental. The heart of the matter is that 'liberal democracy' is bourgeois democracy, i.e. one of the varieties of political organization of society that is based on private property, the competitive struggle, and exploitation. In contrast to 'liberal democracy', the People's Democracy is the political form corresponding to a society of a different type: a socialist society based on public ownership of the means of production, a planned economy, and freedom from exploitation (see *Gosudarstvennoye pravo zarubezhnykh sotsialisticheskikh stran*, Moscow 1957, pp. 7–14).

This point of view is shared by the Hungarian scholar Vilmos Peschka. He writes as follows:

(a) Section II on the 'Institutions of the Liberal Democratic States' occupies—disproportionately and at the expense of Article 3, dealing with the institutions of the socialist states—by far the greater part of the chapter.

(b) Never, in discussing the institutions of the socialist states, is the term 'democratic state' used in connection with the socialist states.

(c) The chapter is built upon the categories and concepts of liberal democracy, and it examines, primarily, the traits of liberal democracy. It should be noted that what the author advances is an apologia of the institutions of liberal democracy. For should the author evaluate even the data and circumstances adduced in the respective part of the chapter, the conclusion would inevitably be reached that the so-called liberal democratic states are no longer liberal democratic in the original sense of the term.

It is the traits and institutions of liberal democracy that the authors are looking for in the authoritarian and socialist states; and inasmuch as they fail to discover them in the state they scrutinize, that state is declared to be, not a democratic, but either an authoritarian or a socialist state. This method of analysis is incorrect, so far as the socialist states are concerned, as it distorts the facts and leads to false conclusions. Socialist democracy cannot be explained in the terms of liberal democracy: socialist democracy is democracy of a new type, that is built on institutions and embodies organizational principles which, in respect of their mass basis as well as the wide scope and fullness of democracy, are far superior to the real democratic principle of the liberal state—democracy that does not accord with what is set forth in this chapter.

7. *The Author-Editors explain that they have not treated People's Democracies (or, in the case of China, People's Republic) as a separate category from 'communist states'. As is pointed out in the note by V. A. Tumanov (Note 6 to Chapter III), 'the basic features of the Soviet and People's Democratic forms of government are the same'. The authors have used the term 'liberal democracy' in Chapters III, XXIII and XXVIII rather than simply 'democracy', or any other term, to identify those states which fall within the democratic tradition of Western Europe and America or follow this model.*

The text presents the institutions of the liberal democratic and communist states as separate wholes. The Author-Editors note that these systems could also be analysed in terms of their corresponding institutions for performing the common functions of governance in modern, complex industrial societies.

Any governmental system must provide institutions: (1) to relate the governing body to the governed, (2) to establish policy, (3) to maintain a measure of continuity of policy and procedure and also to accept and guide change, (4) to execute the functions of the state, and (5) to resolve conflicts among citizens and between the individual and the state. The institutions for performing these functions and their manner of operation tend to be similar by reason of the similarity of function, and to differ by reason of the differing state orientations, in this case between a system of government designed to enable a pluralistic society to change itself through the free interplay of its component parts and one whose role is to lead the society to the goal of communism.

8. Candidate of Juridical Sciences A. Bovin underlines that the reflection in the modern bourgeois legislation of measures directed to the defence of workers' interests is the result of the struggle of workers' organizations and progressive forces, and does not arise from the nature of the bourgeois law itself. On the contrary, in the system of bourgeois legislation there are plenty of legal regulations that have been adopted against the people's will. Such is anti-labour legislation (e.g. the Taft-Hartley Act), anti-democratic legislation (of the type of the McCarran-Wood Act), and militaristic legislation, which has assumed grandiose proportions in Western Europe and the USA since World War II.

(1) *Sovremennoye trudovoye zakonodatelstvo imperialisticheskikh gosudarstv na sluzhbe monopolii* (Contemporary Labour Legislation in the Imperialist States in the Service of the Monopolies) (Moscow, Institute of Law of the USSR Academy of Sciences, 1962).

(2) M. V. Baglay, *Zakonodatelstvo S Sh A v borbye s zabastovochnym dvizheniem* (The US Government in Its Struggle with the Strike Movement) (Moscow, 1960).

(3) S. A. Ivanov, *Mezhdunarodnaya organizatsiya truda i profsoyuznie prava v kapitalisticheskikh stranakh* (International Labour Organization and Trade-Union Rights in the Capitalist Countries) (Moscow, USSR Academy of Sciences, 1959).

(4) S. L. Zivs, *Krizis burzhuaznoy zakonnosti v sovremennykh imperialisticheskikh gosu-darstvakh* (The Crisis of Bourgeois Legality in the Modern Imperialist States) (Moscow, USSR Academy of Sciences, 1958).

(5) S. L. Zivs, *Razvitie formy prava v sovremennykh imperialisticheskikh gosudarstvakh* (Development of Legal Forms in Modern Imperialist States) (Moscow, USSR Academy of Sciences, 1960).

9. Candidate of Juridical Sciences A. Bovin points out that the doctrine of popular sovereignty is not 'all-inclusive' by the middle of the twentieth century, as asserted by the authors in the text. Not all 'liberal democracies' recognize the people as the sole source of authority in the state. Of twenty-three European bourgeois countries, complete popular sovereignty is proclaimed only in eleven (Austria, Andorra, Great Britain, Ireland, Iceland, Italy, Luxembourg, Norway, the Federal Republic of Germany, Finland, and France). In the remaining countries it is enunciated only in part, i.e., legislative authority is shared by the people and a hereditary monarch who is not elected. This is the case in Belgium, Greece, Liechtenstein, the Netherlands, and Sweden. The map of Europe also features states where the principle of popular sovereignty is not recognized at all. These are: Spain, Portugal, Monaco, and the Vatican City. In the Swiss Confederation the principle of popular sovereignty is still the privilege of the stronger sex alone in most cantons.

In addition, even in those bourgeois states where the principle of popular sovereignty is proclaimed in full, in practice it is very often merely a fiction. In modern states of liberal democracy the electoral law incorporates a whole system of limitations (qualifications) which, to a significant extent, curtail the proclaimed general, equal, and secret suffrage. Thus, in the USA in various States there are more than sixty kinds of electoral qualifications, including those of literacy, residence, 'good behaviour', payment of electoral tax, and so on. The result of all these limitations is very often a distortion of the will of the electors, i.e. defiance of the principle of popular sovereignty. See: *Konstitutsii burzhuaznykh gosudarsv Evropy* (The Constitutions of European Bourgeois States) (Moscow, 1957); L. Dadiani, 'Kak prokhodyat vybory v kapitalisticheskikh stranakh' (How Elections are Run in Capitalist Countries), in *Kommunist* (Communist) (1962), No. 4, pp. 111–12.

10. Candidate of Juridical Sciences A. Bovin stresses that in the socialist countries, where the sovereignty of the state coincides with that of the people, there is taking place not a consolidation of the power of the state over society, but a strengthening of the influence of public organizations and the role they play in social life, the encouragement of citizens to take an active part in administering the state, and an extension of the rights of local self-government. Participation of the working people in the state administration is an immutable principle of socialist state organization, which bears witness to the profoundly democratic character of the Soviet system. The administration of the country's affairs is not the exclusive privilege of the group of citizens who specialize in the techniques of administration (Soviet state employees), but is genuinely the affair of the people as a whole. An active and direct part in the state administration is also played by Soviet citizens who occupy no official positions in any of the existing state organs or institutions. Consequently it is the overwhelming majority of the population, without any direct association with the state apparatus (i.e. not working in it) which takes part in administration.

The number of persons involved in the administrative apparatus in socialist countries is clearly decreasing. (See *Sovetskoye gosudarstvo i obschhestvennost v usloviyakh razvernutogo stroitelstva kommunizma: sbornik statey* (The Soviet State and the Soviet Public in the Conditions of the Extended Building of Communism: A Collection of Articles), Moscow, 1962.)

11. Candidate of Juridical Sciences A. Bovin points out that in the socialist countries the system of subordination of the lower organs of authority and administration to higher organs presupposes, firstly, full realization of the principle of popular sovereignty in all representative organs, and secondly, broad autonomy for local institutions within the limits of their competence.

The highest organ of authority in socialist countries is a representative body, elected by the whole population on the basis of universal and equal suffrage, by a secret vote, for a period of 4–5 years. All citizens, men and women, who have attained a certain age (generally 18) have the right to vote, and there are no restrictions with regard to race, nationality, social class, etc. A specific feature of the electoral system in the socialist countries is the right to recall deputies. It is exercised by electors in case a deputy should fail to justify their confidence. Although this right is not exercised very often, its mere existence has a tremendous significance. It ensures constant control by the masses over the actions of their chosen representatives, enhances their feeling of responsibility to their electors, and the energy with which they perform their duties.

Local organs of authority are elected by the population of the area concerned on the basis of universal, equal and direct suffrage, by secret ballot. In accordance with the idea of popular sovereignty these local bodies' powers derive directly from the people, and not from higher organs of authority. Their powers are sufficiently extensive to enable them to guide all aspects of the life of the area concerned. (See: (1) *Constitution of the Union of Soviet Socialist Republics* (Moscow 1961); (2) *Vysshiye organy vlasti stran narodnoy demokratii* (The Higher Organs of Authority in the People's Democracies) (Moscow, 1960)).

12. Candidate of Juridical Sciences A. Bovin thinks that it is only with grave reservations that the electoral system in the liberal democracies can be called 'machinery by means of which popular sovereignty was exercised'. A large number of Western political scientists and public figures have noted that the electoral systems presently in force in bourgeois countries are organically incapable of expressing the will of the majority, as the principle of popular sovereignty requires. Thus, the well-known American jurists, C. B. Gosnell, L. W. Lancaster and R. S. Ranklin, hold that, in view of the inadequacy of the American electoral system, 'popular sovereignty' has been reduced to a sort of 'moral right of veto' (see C. B. Gosnell, L. W. Lancaster, R. S. Rankin, *Fundamentals of American National Government*, New York, 1955). The British political scientists E. Lakeman and J. Lambert, in their work *Voting in Democracies* (London, 1956) take the view that the British electoral system leads to a situation in which the House of Commons does not reflect the feelings of the nation. Leading French political figures also consider that, on account of the electoral procedure now in force in their country, the French Parliament after the 1958 elections 'does not reflect the views of the people' (V. Rochet, Polozhenie vo Frantsii i politika frantsuzskoy kompartii', in *Kommunist* (Communist), 1962, No. 3, p. 85). In general the electoral systems in modern Western democracies are far from perfect. They may be classified into two basic types: proportional and majority systems. Majority electoral systems (such as exist in the USA, Great Britain, France and elsewhere) afford very wide scope for various manipulations with the electors' votes. The proportional system is more democratic, but it is not very widespread and also suffers from major shortcomings. A critique of the electoral systems currently in force in Western countries is given in the following works:

(1) E. Lakeman and J. Lambert, *Voting in Democracies: a Study of Majority and Proportional Electoral Systems*, London, 1956.

(2) R. J. Ross, *Parliamentary Representation*, London, 1944.

(3) I. D. Levin, *Sovremennaya burzhuaznaya nauka gosudarstvennogo prava* (Contemporary Bourgeois Science of Public Law), Moscow, USSR Academy of Sciences, 1960.

(4) L. M. Belson, *Sovremennoye burzhuaznoye gosudarstvo i narodnoye predstavitelstvo* (Contemporary Bourgeois Government and Popular Representation), Moscow, 1960.

13. Candidate of Juridical Sciences A. Bovin points out that the political parties represented in the parliaments of the Western countries are no better able than the electoral systems to express the principle of popular sovereignty. In the largest liberal democratic countries the parties in power, which have a preponderance of seats in Parliament, are as a rule parties of a minority of the population that is most powerful economically. Thus the British Conservative Party, the party of the wealthy strata of the population, for which only 38 per cent of the total number of votes was cast on October 8, 1959, nevertheless remained the party in power and obtained more than 57 per cent of the seats in the House of Commons.

On the other hand, the French Communist Party, which is a democratic mass party, obtained about 4 million votes, i.e. 300,000 more than the Union for the New Republic

(UNR), the party of the bourgeoisie. Yet in the National Assembly there were only 70 Communist deputies and 220 deputies of the UNR. (See V. Rochet 'Polozhenie Frantsii i politika Frantsuzskoy kompartii' ('The Position in France and the Policy of the French Communist Party'), in *Kommunist* (Communist) (1962), No. 3, p. 85.)

14. Candidate of Juridical Sciences A. Bovin points out that the assumption of legislative functions by executive organs is not a positive aspect of the development of political institutions in the twentieth century. The mass of legislative acts issued by officials which regulate in detail the life of society is in the first place evidence of the decline of parliamentary control over the actions of the executive power and in general indicates the decay of the system of liberal democracy itself.

Parliamentary control over governments was one of the bourgeois-democratic institutions which the progressive forces of bourgeois society always sought to establish and perfect. But at the present time the bourgeoisie is attempting by every means in its power to limit the capacity for the popular masses to express their political will through the electoral system, and is taking important steps to restrict the powers of parliamentary bodies. Hence the tendency to strengthen executive governmental-administrative power *vis-à-vis* representative institutions, and the enormous increase in the amount of so-called delegated legislation issued by various governmental departments and committees. Delegated legislation is uncontrolled legislative governmental activity which bears witness to the colossal authority concentrated in the hands of senior officials. Very frequently this uncontrolled activity by the executive is directed against the interests of the democratic strata of the population. Many western scholars have expressed alarm at the growth of 'delegated legislation' at the expense of constitutional rights, and have pointed out that such a state of affairs constitutes a serious 'threat to freedom'. (See C. B. Gosnell, L. W. Lancaster, R. S. Rankin, *Fundamentals of American National Government*, N.Y., 1955, p. 247.)

See the following works on this question:

(1) I. D. Levin, *Sovremennaya burzhuaznaya nauka gosudarstvennogo prava* (The Contemporary Bourgeois Science of Public Law) (Moscow, 1960), pp. 334–6.

(2) B. S. Krylov, 'Kritika sobremennykh burzhuaznykh teoriy parlamentarizma' (A Critique of Modern Bourgeois Theories of Parliamentarism), in *Sovetskoe gosudarstvo i pravo* (Soviet State and Law) (1962), No. 1, pp. 111–15.

(3) S. L. Zivs, 'Osnovnye tendentsii v razvitii sovremennogo imperialisticheskogo gosudarstva' (Basic Tendencies in the Development of the Modern Imperialist State), in *Sovetskoe gosudarstvo i pravo* (Soviet State and Law) (1961), No. 10, pp. 177–8.

(4) S. L. Zivs, *Krisis burzhuaznoy zakonnosti v sovremennykh imperialisticheskikh gosudarstvakh* (The Crisis of Bourgeois Law and Order in the Modern Imperialist States), Moscow, 1958.

15. Candidate of Juridical Sciences A. Bovin points out that correctly noting the tremendous size of the bureaucratic apparatus in modern democracies, the extent of its functions, and its independence of parliamentary control, the authors incorrectly present such a state of affairs as necessary for the effective management of the complex affairs of the 'welfare state'. Actually the process of bureaucratization of the economic, political and entire social life of modern capitalist states is in the direct interests of monopoly capitalism. The basic trend of this growth of bureaucracy is set by the private corporations. The bourgeois parties, reactionary organizations and the state copy the forms and methods of bureaucratic control elaborated by the monopolies.

The bureaucratic inflation of the bourgeois state machine is manifested in the first place in the creation of departments and organizations serving to enhance the economic and financial power of the private corporations at the workers' expense. Secondly, the development of the bureaucratic state apparatus is closely connected with the policy of militarization. The reality of life in modern capitalist countries is characterized by a sharp increase in the role of the military element which interferes in all spheres of activity: in economics, politics, in science and education, in the propaganda system. The military bureaucracy, as is known, is distinguished by the frank crudity of its methods of command, its lack of even an appearance of democracy. In general bureaucratization is a manifestation of the characteristically imperialist tendency to renounce the forms of bourgeois democracy. See:

(1) M. Lerner, *America as a Civilization* (New York, 1957).

(2) C. W. Mills, *White Collar* (New York, 1956).

(3) S. L. Zivs, 'Osnovnye tendentsii v razvitii sovremennogo imperialisticheskogo gosudarstva' ('Basic Tendencies in the Development of the Modern Imperialist State') in: *Sovetskoye gosudarstvo i pravo* (Soviet State and Law) (1961), No. 10.

(4) Yu. A. Zamoshkin, 'Byurokratizatsiya burzhuaznogo obshchestva i sud by lichnosti' ('The Bureaucratization of Bourgeois Society and the Fate of the Individual'), in *Voprosy filosofii* (Problems of Philosophy), No. 4 (1961).

16. Candidate of Juridical Sciences A. Bovin asserts that the Communist party was never 'superior to the state' and is not at the present time 'the supreme authority in the state'. It cannot take the place of state organs. (See *Constitution of the Union of Soviet Socialist Republics*, Moscow, 1961, Art. 30; *Statute of the Communist Party of the Soviet Union*, Moscow, 1961.) In the socialist countries parties are voluntary associations of like-minded individuals who have united to ensure the triumph of communist, socialist and democratic ideals. They determine their policies by taking into account the opinion of the non-Party masses, and put this policy forward for examination by state organizations elected by the entire people. The Communist party of the Soviet Union acts as leader in the whole system of democratic organizations. This role is not imposed upon society. Society itself, or to be more precise its overwhelming majority—workers, peasants and intelligentsia, in a word the toiling masses—put the Communist Party forward as their leader. This is to be explained by the fact that the Party has shown itself the most consistent and active defender of the nation's interests. Everywhere and at all times it fought so that the people should come to power. After conquest of power by the working people, when the Communist Party has become the ruling party, it sets about implementing a programme for the rapid development of productive forces in order to bring about on this basis a radical improvement in the wellbeing of the people, their culture, and their lives generally.

The Communist party seeks to exercise a decisive influence on the activity of all other organizations, including organs of authority and administration. This task is eased by the fact that communists are members of all or almost all organizations. It is through them, in the first place, that the Party realizes its programme. The Communist Party is constantly enlarging its membership by attracting the most conscious elements of the population. The Party consists of approximately 6 per cent of the population, i.e. over 9 million persons in the USSR. It is a genuinely popular party.

The fact that the country is led by such a goal-oriented and disciplined force as the Communist party gives the whole of society a monolithic quality, so that it successfully withstands attempts at intervention from without and solves immense problems in the spirit of Communist ideals. This of course does not mean that the Party takes upon itself the functions of other organizations. On the contrary, the Party is interested in encouraging the broadest possible initiative by each link in the political system, seeing in this a guarantee of the successful solution of the tasks facing the people as a whole. (F. M. Burlatsky, 'Rastsvet sotsialisticheskoy demokratii' (The Development of Socialist Democracy), in: *Vestnik istorii mirovoy kultury* (Review of the History of World Culture), No. 5, 1961, pp. 5–61.)

17. Candidate of Juridical Sciences A. Bovin points out that the anti-Party, anti-Leninist methods of leadership practised in certain cases by J. Stalin should not be presented as methods which served to make the practice of the Party 'very clear'. These were methods that discredited the Party's policy, which did no small amount of harm to the clear line of the Party, and which were condemned with all severity by the twenty-second congress of the CPSU in October 1961.

However, the cult of the personality could not alter either the social-economic essence of the socialist system or the democratic nature of its political system. Precisely on account of the socialist character of its social and political system, which was alien to the cult of 'a chosen personality', on account of the fact that the working masses remained the decisive force under all circumstances in the construction of socialism and communism, under the leadership of the Communist party, linked by the closest bonds to the people, it proved possible to limit very materially the damage done by the personality cult, and then to overcome it and its consequences. ('Sovety i stroitelstvo kommunizma' ('The

Soviets and the Building of Communism'), leading article in *Kommunist* (Communist), No. 2 (1962); pp. 4–5.)

See also Note 12 to Chapter XXI.

18. Candidate of Juridical Sciences A. Bovin points out that the Soviet judicial system was never 'an instrument of administration' but an organ of justice.

The administration of justice in the USSR is an independent function of the state, separate from the general administration. The lower links in the judicial system are elected by the population, the medium-level and higher ones are organs of authority. The courts are independent and subject only to the law. Legislative activity is carried on in such a way as to leave a certain scope to the courts, which include as well as permanent judges, who have no other duties to fulfil, people's assessors—workers in some branches of production or culture, pensioners, etc.

The principle of controversy, the right of defence, recognition of the presumption of innocence, the widest right of appeal up to the Supreme Court, and active participation by the public both on the side of the defence and of the prosecution—these and other principles ensure discovery of the truth in the course of a trial.

Moreover, Soviet jurisprudence proceeds from the principle that the activity of the court has an educational as well as a penal function. Wide use is made of various kinds of penalties that do not involve deprivation of freedom, such as suspended sentences, public censure, etc. Increasing importance is coming to be attached to the practice of handing over minor offenders for trial by their collectives at their place of work. This measure is as a rule more effective than punishment under the penal code. (See *Constitution (Fundamental Law) of the USSR*, Ch. IX: The Courts and Procurator's Office); F. M. Burlatsky, 'Rastsvet sotsialisticheskoy demokratii' ('The Development of Socialist Democracy'), in: *Vestnik istorii mirovoy kultury* (Review of the History of World Culture) No. 5, 1961; p. 9. For a detailed examination of the section 'Institutions of the Communist States', see Volume VI, Tome II, of the *History of Mankind: Cultural and Scientific*.

Bulgarian scholars consider that the chapter 'Political Institutions' suffers from a major defect: the tendency to consider forms of government, legislative activity, etc. by themselves, in isolation from the class struggle in society, the development of productive forces and social economic phenomena—the factors and causes that give rise to them and eliminate them.'

19. Professor E. N. Anderson notes that the Author-Editors fail to make clear one of the outstanding characteristics of the first half of the twentieth century, that of the widespread use of brutality, torture and other forms of violence. Brutality has been present in all human societies and in all historical periods, and it would be strange not to encounter it in an age described as that of 'cultural crisis.' The special features of violence in the present period have been its mass character, the variety of its forms and uses, and its spread among peoples of the highest level of education and technology, as well as among backward areas, among all classes and among groups of strong religious faith along with those devoid of religious affiliation. Brutality has been adopted as official governmental policy, it has been legally disclaimed but officially tolerated or condoned, and it has been invoked in defiance of authority. In many countries violence has become so much a part of the mores that it is difficult to set criteria by which to distinguish between the amount and kinds of violence that are normal to most societies and are subject to the controls of criminal law, and the amount and kinds that stretch far beyond the norms of organized society.

Although it may be impossible to categorize the major forms of violence of this half century, the attempt to do so may clarify the significance of the phenomenon. There is illegal or non-legal violence that reflects racial, national or religious hatred at local, voluntary, informal levels. A second kind concerns opposition by force of arms to a new organization of society. Another category includes the type of individual and of movement analysed by Albert Camus in *The Rebel*. Hatred of existing society and its organization and lust for power in order to remake society led to arson, assault, murder, and the endless harassments of private and public personages flowing from total contempt of opposition. Still another type consists of the legal and official organization of violence. Psychological torture, brain-washing and similar pressures belong in this category.

Systems of law and a judicial organization are frequently introduced to give all these forms of violence the appearance of legality. Thus secret police pervade society, secret arrest and trial and, if the regime regards it is advisable, secret punishment receive the sanction of law, and governmental control of food rationing and officially implemented starvation become essential instruments for dealing with potential opponents. Into this category of official action must be entered the endeavour to wipe out an entire people, the best known example of which is the treatment of the Jewish minority by the National Socialists in Germany. Threat of a reappearance of this type of violence led the United Nations to identify and condemn it as the crime of genocide. National Socialists added a further example of state-directed cruelty in putting to death the mentally deranged or mentally retarded, the physically misformed, the incurable and socially unproductive and of sanctioning experiments for so-called scientific purposes upon enemies of the regime. Still another category of violence closely related to the preceding is that of the forced flight of millions of people from their homes, the brutality connected with exchange of populations and the expulsion of refugees.

The list of categories could no doubt be extended and refined. Suffiicent data have been given, however, to support the judgment that this century has been, and continues to be, a period of ruthless animosities and of varied means of committing physical and mental violence upon individuals and upon masses. It is possible that the extent of brutality is unique in world history.

The literature on this subject is extensive, especially for Europe.

CHAPTER XXIV

MILITARY INSTITUTIONS

MILITARY institutions came to occupy an increasingly important place in the societies of the twentieth century as the character of warfare changed and affected more and more deeply the life of every modern state.

In all periods military institutions have reflected the overall structure of society and in turn have affected it. This was doubly true of the establishments which came to reflect the structure of modern industrial society and to accentuate many of its features. Twentieth-century methods of warfare brought a reintegration of civilian and military institutions which the trends of the nineteenth century had tended to separate. The process of industrial mobilization involved the redirection of civilian institutions to military purposes and the reorientation of the military to make them able to utilize the machinery of industrial production.

The importance of military institutions has always been enhanced by periods of warfare. The occurrence within a period of twenty-five years of two wars of world-wide scope, as well as an almost continuous series of lesser military operations, kept military leadership and organization more or less constantly to the fore. As warfare became more and more total, it required the conscious planning, co-ordination and control of the multitude of separate but mutually interdependent elements of which industrial societies are composed. It was thus the most potent force making for comprehensive large-scale organization. In the centrally administered states it merely intensified the peacetime organization. In other states it required the creation of new instrumentalities which did not wholly disappear after hostilities were ended.

The military institutions of the twentieth century were also instruments of social change. Although they were usually conservative, with strong traditions and dedication to the maintenance of the *status quo*, the nature of modern warfare made them powerful innovators. In some circumstances, moreover, military institutions became the conscious spearheads of social change. The Soviet Red army after 1917 and the People's Liberation army of China were direct instruments of revolution and reconstruction. The military provided much of the leadership for revolution and modernization in such countries of the Middle East as Turkey, Iran and Egypt. In some of the industrially underdeveloped countries, such as Thailand after the second world war, the armed forces were one of the agencies through which modern technology reached into a country. The armies of India and the United States contributed to the integration of disparate social groups.

I. TRADITIONAL MILITARY INSTITUTIONS

In the early years of the century the military establishments of most countries had many common characteristics, although the detail of their form and their role in national life varied considerably from place to place. The German army, from the time of its victory over the French in 1870 to the opening of the first world war, provided a model, or at least an inspiration, to the professional military groups in most other countries, very notably in Turkey and Japan.

All the countries of continental Europe, and also Japan, had conscript armies composed of a permanent officer group, a nucleus of army regulars, chiefly non-commissioned officers, and a large reserve of manpower which had experienced military training, usually for two years. At any given time the forces in being consisted of the permanent elements plus the young men, generally 18–20 years of age, who were doing their compulsory military service. Elsewhere, notably in Britain and the United States, volunteer armies were the rule. Navies depended on volunteer recruitment, although in some countries a certain number of conscripts could choose navy duty.

A sharp gulf separated officers from men. Officers were generally drawn from the upper strata of society and an officer's career was looked upon as a high calling. In some volunteer regiments with special reputations and traditions, most frequently cavalry or guards units, enlisted personnel also enjoyed a special prestige, though they were still separated from the officer class by an unbridgeable gulf.

In many countries a special social group, usually the large landowners, provided the core of the officer personnel—a heritage from feudal society in which the two functions of landowning and fighting were combined. Among the Prussian Junkers, British landed gentry, estate-owners of Russia, the Austro-Hungarian empire or Latin America, at least some member of the family—a second son perhaps—was expected to enter a military career. For many, especially the Prussian aristocracy, these careers were practically hereditary. Professional classes also furnished many officers in these countries and the majority of officers in countries without an aristocratic tradition, such as Switzerland.

Since military leadership tended to be drawn from the upper strata of society and from the agricultural rather than the urban–industrial segment, military institutions were apt to reflect the outlook of these elements. This outlook was not only conservative, *élite* and generally opposed to policies based on commerical interests but, with some outstanding exceptions, it tended to be indifferent to scientific knowledge. German officers objected to having the least competent of their sons excluded from military schools, while their British counterparts insisted that it was a boy's performance on the playing field rather than in the classroom which revealed his fitness for a military career. Navies were on the whole more scientifically oriented than armies because by the opening of the twentieth century they were already more mechanized, although those responsible for the vessel's operation did not enjoy officer status.

The officer group was everywhere organized in a strict hierarchical structure within which position defined not only responsibility but status. Sea and land forces were separately organized with their respective hierarchies, neither subordinate to the other, and with separate training institutions, traditions, administration, and relation to the structure of government. Advancement to higher officer ranks was open to all within the group, and the desire to provide opportunities for promotion often led members of the military bureaucracies to recommend policies which would make this possible. Speed of advancement depended upon the rate of expansion of the service. Friction sometimes existed between the younger men in the lower ranks and the older men at the top, and systems of early retirement were introduced in some services to keep the leadership fresh and the lower ranks filled with new men capable of rising.

While an open system of promotion existed within the officer group there was, prior to the first world war, virtually no access to this group from below. An enlisted man could be elevated to a non-commissioned position—army corporal or sergeant or naval petty officer—but there was rarely any possibility for him to qualify for entrance into the officer corps.

The rigid separation characteristic of military structures and reinforced by difference in social origin contributed to the authoritarian nature of military establishments. In essentially authoritarian societies military institutions were in keeping with the general social pattern. The Prussian and Japanese armies, for example, might be described as exaggerated versions of the pervasively authoritarian and persistently feudal structure of those societies. The German army had in fact helped to stave off the growth of liberalism in that country during the nineteenth century.

The Japanese army combined a strong feudal tradition and complete loyalty to the emperor with features of military structure and organization learned from Germany. Japanese military leaders occupied at all times a strong position from which they sought with fluctuating success to dominate national policy.

In Great Britain the military structure reflected the continuing class divisions but its authoritarianism was not in keeping with the trend toward democratic political forms. The fact that the British armed forces were, in the early years of the century, mainly stationed overseas and were chiefly engaged in maintaining the British empire, however, minimized the possible conflict between authoritarian and democratic attitudes, for the latter did not extend to the relations of the British with their colonial subjects, and it was these among whom the armed forces chiefly lived. In countries such as the United States, the Scandinavian countries or Holland the authoritarian military institutions were at odds with the democratic ethos of the society and were the object of general suspicion on the part of civilians.

In the Latin American countries military organizations were in effect a part of the structure of government. In spite of the fact that most of these republics lived under constitutions which called for free elections, only a few, such as Uruguay, had followed constitutional procedures consistently. Many governments were in fact maintained and changed by the intervention of the army.

The major colonial powers organized and trained some of their colonial peoples and formed native regiments, chiefly for use within the colonial territory. The principal colonial military bodies were the Indian army and the French African legions. The Dutch also trained Indonesian troops, as well as 'colonials' from the home country who signed for service in the Netherlands' Indies. Spain recruited Moroccans and the British enlisted a number of Africans.

The British maintained two distinct military bodies in India, both with British officers, one composed of units of the British army stationed there, the other made up of regiments recruited and trained in India. The Indian army was the arm of the British empire in non-European areas, and was used in Burma, the Persian Gulf and Africa, as well as on the frontiers of India and to maintain British authority in the sub-continent.

French colonial troops were recruited as part of the main French army, to fill manpower deficiencies in the French forces. After the defeat in 1870 of the more highly trained but smaller French army by the more numerous German forces, France sought to keep up with its rival in number of men under arms. The small French population and low birth rate, however, set limits on the capacity to keep up the race, even though in the years before the first world war the French were calling up 83 per cent of those bound to serve while the German army called up only 53 per cent. The French army therefore drew on its colonial and overseas areas. On the eve of the first world war nearly a tenth of France's effective troops were African, largely Senegalese. The officers of these troops were all French and remained so with only a few exceptions up to the second world war.

Military establishments were self-governing and aspired to as much independence of action as they could achieve. In the liberal democracies they were subject to civilian control of funds and determination of policy, but even in these countries such controls were rarely effectively extended into either internal structure or the making of military decisions.

The overall body responsible for military policy and strategy was the general staff. This institution was developed in the German army, taken over *in toto* by the Japanese, and adopted in various modified forms by the armies of other countries, especially Russia. In Germany those who became members of the general staff were selected from among the officer corps solely on the basis of competence and were subjected to intensive training for three years in the War Academy. The small proportion of the entrants to the Academy who completed this exacting training then served a two-year apprenticeship under existing general staff officers. The training covered all aspects—operations, intelligence, transport, supply—together with historical and theoretical studies of techniques of warfare, with the objective of equipping the staff officers to understand and think imaginatively, in strictly military, non-political terms, about overall strategy and military planning.

The German general staff, thus trained and distinguished by a special uniform, was a small select group, numbering 276 at the outbreak of the first world war. Relationships among the members were based on a strong *esprit de corps* and were personal rather than bureaucratic. The concept of the German general staff was of a group rather than of a line of command.

A general staff officer was placed in each headquarters from the divisional level up to the supreme command and functioned as the close adviser of the commanding officer, sharing his decisions and issuing orders in his absence. Communication between general staff officers was direct, without passing through the commanding officers. The whole general staff was expected to have a common knowledge, understanding and view of the complete military strategy and thus to provide unity of purpose and direction to the military effort. It planned and functioned as a virtually autonomous power within the state.

Among the various general staffs developed in other countries, none followed their German model in making the group small, *élite*, permanent and bound together by essentially personal ties, though the pattern was most closely approximated in Japan, both in the closeness of the group and its identification of public policy with military objectives. Elsewhere the general staff was large—the French general staff at the opening of the first world war was more than three times the size of the German for an equivalent number of troops and it was bureaucratic in its interrelationships. Sometimes, as in the United States where the whole idea of a special *élite* group found little favour, it was composed of a changing membership. In Britain the idea of competence in all fields was replaced by a division between operations and intelligence on the one hand and transport and supply on the other. But within every military structure there was a body which had the function of providing the intellectual co-ordination and leadership of military planning and endeavours, and which spoke for the military *vis-à-vis* the civilian authorities and population.[1]

The military establishments in the early years of the century were primarily concerned with men and only secondarily with equipment. Since few military leaders were drawn from the urban–industrial parts of the population, their mentality tended everywhere to be pre-industrial. Their values and relationships were strongly personal. The habit of economic calculation, the tendency to substitute machine for human power, the patterns of industrial organization were all foreign to their experience. They were not in a position to project in their imaginations the importance of industry or its possible relation to military operations or objectives. Almost completely lacking in knowledge or experience of scientific or industrial methods, the military left the initiative in weapon production to private industry.

II. THE ARMAMENT INDUSTRY

By the opening of the twentieth century the production of munitions was a highly organized, independent activity. While the military establishments themselves clung to an essentially feudal-agrarian outlook, the weapon makers were transforming the nature of warfare and ultimately the nature and role of the military itself.

A group of great private munitions firms, each the result of a series of mergers and expansions, dominated the fields. The Nobel Dynamite Trust Company Ltd., which constituted an amalgamation of the dynamite and smokeless powder interests of the Swedish magnate, Alfred Nobel, was at the centre of the international trade in explosives. The Vickers-Armstrong merger in England in the 1890s had made this giant concern the largest armaments company in the world, producing ordinance, armour plate and naval vessels for a world market. It had branches in Spain, Italy, Russia and Japan and an affiliate in Germany. The German Krupp works had absorbed in the 1890s smaller firms with specialized productions and had added naval vessels to its former line of armour plate and guns. Together with its enterprising competitor, Erhardt, it largely monopolized the German market and had extensive markets abroad. Schneider-Creusot in France, one of the oldest of the munitions enterprises, was the leading designer of field guns. The Austrian Skoda works in Bohemia, manufacturing mainly artillery pieces, armour and vehicles, used some of the Krupp patents. The Putiloff concern in Russia operated with the collaboration of British, French and Austrian firms.

In the United States armament production was never a distinct branch of industry, although there were specialized producers such as the Dupont Chemical Company. Output for military purposes was an outgrowth of already existing industrial production and was scattered among many firms. There were no armament kings and no great American combine which entered the world armament market. In Japan the development of heavy industry itself was to an important extent aimed at military production, and from the start it had a large measure of government backing and participation. The smaller powers generally purchased their weapons from the major producers, though some had facilities for making certain munitions or constructing naval vessels.

The great munitions makers were not wholly divorced from civilian production. Most of them had grown out of enterprises making civilian goods, such as iron and steel and various kinds of tools. On the eve of the first world war 60 per cent of Vickers' production was for non-military orders. Krupp remained a major producer of steel for German industry, and of industrial products, especially railway equipment.

Yet the thrust of these companies was to expand the market for munitions wherever it could be stimulated, and in the interest of profits to use every device known to the commercial or political world to help create the appetite for more and better arms. They were the developers and promoters of new designs. Collectively they were often referred to as the 'merchants of death', and the dramatic cloaked figure of Basil Zaharoff, chairman of Vickers-Armstrong, moving in sinister fashion from chancery to chancery became the symbol of the malign role of the munitions makers.[2]

III. TRANSFORMATION OF MILITARY INSTITUTIONS BY TOTAL WAR

Both the nature of military establishments and their place in the total society changed with the coming of total war. The first world war made obsolete nearly everything which linked military establishments to the feudal past. Cavalry went out in the face of mechanization, except in Russia where extreme cold and deep mud made the use of motorized vehicles at certain times impracticable. The special guard regiments which were the pride and ornament of several armies proved of little value. The exclusive officer class gave way, though only partially, to men of different backgrounds as armies were expanded during the war. Mechanized warfare called for technical knowledge and skills and required the organization of many more auxiliary services and for calculations based as much or more on war material as on personnel.

The new character of warfare also changed the relationship among the several military services. Armies and navies had been under separate commands. The rise of air power introduced a third service. In every country air forces had to struggle for status against the efforts of the older services to treat aviation merely as an adjunct to their operation, not as a separate arm. Nowhere were the three services integrated or even fully co-ordinated. The traditions of self-government, loyalty to the particular service, secrecy, the difficulty faced by anyone who tried to think in comprehensive terms about the overwhelming complexities of modern warfare and the orientation given by each military person's training and experience all combined to keep the three services independent of each other, and often in competition. Technical developments however continually thrust the air force into a more and more central position.

The new military establishments took on many of the features of great industrial enterprises. Modern business methods, office organization, systems of record keeping, the use of duplicating, sorting and communications equipment and all the paraphernalia for carrying on large industrial operations gave military institutions many of the characteristics of their civilian counterparts.

In order to deal with industrial mobilization, special branches or units were set up. The usual pattern was for the general staffs to continue to deal with military operations while distinct bodies were created to deal with industrial and supply aspects, such as the Ministry of Supply in Great Britain, the Army Industrial College in the United States, the Economy and Armaments Office in the German Supreme Command. These bodies were responsible for assess-

ing the industrial potentials of their respective countries, developing procedures for dealing with civilian firms and setting up economic mobilization
schemes.

Where central economic planning was developed in the years after the first
world war, as in the Soviet Union, military planning became an integral part.
In Soviet Russia, under the successive five-year plans, requirements of the
Red army were handled through the same machinery for allocating resources
and setting priorities as were those of other commissariats such as those for
electric power, agriculture or transport. The five-year plan was in essence a
plan for rapidly increasing the industrial potential of the Soviet Union; when
war objectives replaced those of peacetime it could be quickly converted into a
'war economy plan', as was done in August 1941. The German four-year plan
of 1936, while originally designed primarily to meet raw material deficiencies,
became the framework for economic mobilization for the second world war.

In countries such as France, Britain and the United States, where general
economic activity remained unco-ordinated, the plans for industrial mobilization formulated by military authorities took the form of outlines which were
used, especially in Britain, to guide the industrial aspect of rearmament in the
1930s and which were intended to furnish an administrative blue-print for the
direction of resources in time of war. In Japan a series of industry-wide control associations provided the machinery through which in the decade after
1931 an eighteenfold increase in military expenditure shaped the Japanese
economy for war.

The munitions industries also underwent a transformation. Prior to the
first world war the armaments trusts had been extra-national private ventures
producing and selling instruments of war on the open market. That each of
the munitions trusts was the principal supplier of the armed forces of its own
nation was no more than was the case with the output of most industrial concerns whose first buyers were in the home market.

When the first world war made it apparent that a few munitions firms could
not meet the needs of a mass army and governments began to draw on all
their industrial resources, the munitions firm lost its central role and became
only one among many producers of military supplies. In particular the initiative in military design began to pass from the industries engaged in making
products to armies and navies looking for new weapons.

Furthermore the new total war—the war of peoples and of total involvement—made the independence and private character of the munitions makers
no longer consistent with the character of warfare and the nature of the
national interest. When a nation was embarked on a great collective effort
which required all its united energies and when the nation's military capacities
came to be defined in terms of productive capacity rather than military
manpower, the national munitions maker became a national military asset, not
an independent entrepreneur. The sale of armaments to another country, in
which the old munitions-makers had freely engaged, became a political move

not a business transaction. Although the great munitions works continued to flourish and expand they lost both their key position as armament producers and their independence of action outside the country. In place of the symbol of Basil Zaharoff seeking to boost his sales by pitting one country against another in competitive bidding for the arms which Vickers-Armstrong had to offer, the new symbol was the long procession of industrialists negotiating with their own governments for an endless variety of military orders that might represent anywhere from 5 to 90 per cent of their peacetime and 100 per cent of their wartime production.

The concept of the total economy of each state as one overall national war production machine was expressed most completely in the autarchy sought by Nazi Germany and to some degree by other powers. Recalling the effects of blockade during the first world war, Hitler attempted to make the German economy independent of trade with other countries and set scientists to the task of developing substitutes for the materials which had been imported from abroad. Japan's programme of expansion sought to build a self-contained economic area in which the resources of Korea, Manchuria, the Chinese mainland and south-east Asia, especially those essential to military production, would be integrated and the densely populated islands of Japan with their limited resources would no longer depend on the hazards of international trade. Under the actual conditions of the second world war, however, the British economy which had not attempted to become self-sufficient was more completely mobilized and integrated into the war effort than was that of Germany.

Changes in military organization reflected changes in the surrounding society as well as changes in methods of warfare. The structure of the Soviet army and the relationships between officers and men reflected the structure of Soviet society and the role played in it by the Communist party. Since the Party directed all aspects of state activity, the political commissar representing the Party was an essential part of the military organization. His position varied with organizational changes in the army and navy and with the need to enhance Party influence at definite periods.

The sources from which the Soviet military leadership was drawn were also the reverse of tsarist days, except for those tsarist officers who threw in their lot with the new régime. New officers came primarily from among the sons of workers and peasants, who rose through an intensive educational system designed to single out the ablest for advancement; in time many were the sons of Red army officers themselves. Academic brilliance in scientific and technical subjects, together with Party reliability, were the keys which opened a military career. Within the military structure, too, the old gulf between officers and men was replaced by more easy social relations and an open path to advancement for those in the ranks who qualified for training as officers. In the course of time, when general Soviet policy shifted from broad egalitarianism to higher pay for those who performed greater service to the state, the officer corps became a highly paid group, and rank, titles and insignia again came to the fore. The Red army was a microcosm of Soviet life.

The Chinese People's Liberation army became a unique body. Militarily it was organized both for guerrilla fighting and for organized warfare. As an instrument of social revolution it reformed the peasant villages in the areas under its control, making the peasantry almost part of the army itself.

In the fascist states military organization was the pattern and ideal for the organization of society. As expressed by Alfred Rosenberg, the philosopher of National Socialism, the permanent style of life which Germans were finding under National Socialism was 'the style of the marching column, regardless of where and for what purpose this marching column is to be used'.* The conversion of all institutions into military institutions was carried furthest in Nazi Germany and in Japan after 1931, but it was central to the principles and structure of fascist Italy and falangist Spain, and coloured the military dictatorships of eastern Europe.

The pervasive military organization of civilian life was in part an expression of the concept that war is the essential purpose of the state. In the words of Benito Mussolini in his article on 'The State' in the *Enciclopedia Italiana,* 'only war brings human energies to their highest tension and ennobles those peoples which dare to undertake it'. Beyond this, however, the military style constituted a way of life in itself.

In Nazi Germany the totalitarian principle was everywhere clothed in military forms. All organizations which rested on a democratic base were replaced by quasi-military bodies. The labour unions became the Labour Front, each factory a military unit in which the management occupied the relationship to the workers of officers to enlisted men. Youth was enlisted in Hitler Youth organizations, women in the Women's Front, and each profession had its official organization in which military structure prevailed. Military terminology pervaded the language of all human activity.

Amid the quasi-military institutions of this militarized society the armed forces themselves took central place, both as models to others and in the authority which they represented. They combined the characteristics, personnel and attitudes of the traditional military class with new features reflecting the new mechanized warfare and the social changes which accompanied the Nazi régime. Although the officer corps continued to come from the old groups—in 1936 five of the six top officers and nearly a quarter of those from the rank of colonel up were members of the nobility—some new talent was being drawn in; the colonels and major-generals in that year included five Ph.Ds, all with non-noble names. The regular army was supplemented, and its position challenged, by Hitler's personal forces, the storm troopers and especially the Waffen S.S., composed of young men from all classes whose brown and black uniforms gave them status and authority.

* *Gestaltung der Idee* (1937), pp. 303 ff.

IV. MILITARY–CIVILIAN INSTITUTIONS OF
THE SECOND WORLD WAR

The second world war completed the transformation of the military establishments into central institutions of industrial societies, sharing and often leading in technical and scientific development. The much more complete economic mobilization and mechanized operation of that conflict led to the incorporation of civilians with special knowledge and skills, such as production engineers, administrators, scientists and technicians of all sorts, into the armed services with ranks which reflected their civilian experience, not their progression through the military hierarchy. The global logistics problems of supply were met by the formation of elaborate organizations overshadowing even the largest of the industrial corporations. Except in communist states where central administrative bodies functioned continuously, wartime administrations had to be created by the expansion of existing agencies, as in Germany, France, Italy and Japan, or by setting up new agencies as in Britain and the United States.

To design and describe millions of war items, establish standards, secure production and arrange for delivery at the right time and place required enormous staffs, elaborate systems of accounting and reporting and a knowledge and understanding of industrial processes which greatly exceeded that necessary for normal peacetime functioning. The complexity of these processes made largely inapplicable the traditional concept of a general staff which could comprehend and direct all phases of the war effort. General staffs everywhere tended to have their scope limited to field operations while manpower mobilization and industrial expansion were placed under the direction of such bodies as the British Ministry of Supply with a staff expanded from 5,000 to 68,496 or the American War Production Board with 300,000 employees.

Mass production and delivery introduced a serious problem of rigidity since most industrial products require one to two years from initial design to actual mass output, yet improvements in weapons came so rapidly that a new model would often be planned before the old one had started to come off the assembly line. In the United States, in order to avoid further delays in production, 'modification centres' were established to remake completed products. Once supplies had been shipped, they flowed toward their destination in the order and with the timing established at the point of departure, and only by maintaining extensive records and establishing diversion depots along the line could they be re-routed when needed elsewhere.

The balancing of competing demands for manpower and the expansion and utilization of the labour force involved a continuous complex process of recruitment, replacement, training and retraining. As much as two-thirds of the total labour force might be directly engaged in military service, war production and civil defence; the estimates for Great Britain were 22 per cent in military service, 33 per cent in war production and perhaps 10 per cent in civil defence, leaving to the remainder the task of producing civilian supplies. The labour force was expanded by using women, youth below military age, and in Germany some 10,000,000 forced labourers from occupied areas or war captives.

The traditional system whereby the able young men went to the fighting front while others remained at home conflicted with the need for specialized skills in war production, as the French discovered when they seriously disrupted their industrial mobilization process by calling up their military manpower on this basis in 1939. Some system of exemption from military service for those in critical jobs had to be worked out.

As skilled civilians were drawn into military activity, persons of less skill had to be up-graded with the aid of special training, while those of still lower skills or new recruits to the labour force had to be trained to fill the places of the latter. In the United States at the peak of the war effort, 22 per cent of the total labour force was involved at a single time in one or another of the training programmes developed to meet this situation and a fifth or more of the entire population migrated in the process of adjusting manpower to wartime needs. In countries subjected to bombardment or invasion the problems of manpower adjustment, with attendant problems of housing, transport and community facilities, were even greater.

The manpower requirements of total war forced a radical expansion of the concept of national service. In the French National Organization Act adopted in 1938 after fourteen years of discussion and experimentation, the principle of 'universal military service' was replaced by the concept of the 'duty of national defence' which embraced all citizens, whatever wartime duties and peacetime preparation they might be called upon to undertake. The British Emergency Powers Act of 1940 expressed the same principle in stipulating that all persons might be called upon to place 'themselves, their services and their property' at the disposal of His Majesty. A similar principle was applied even more thoroughly in the Soviet Union. It was applied less systematically in Germany, Italy and Japan.[3]

Economic stabilization in the face of intense inflationary pressures required the substitution of administrative judgment for the market forces through which most peacetime economic relationships in the non-communist countries were determined. Large administrative organizations reaching into every single community had to be built up to administer systems of price and wage control, rationing and the allocation of materials. To maintain the active support of the population and to undermine enemy morale, extensive propaganda and morale agencies sought to strengthen the civilian front at home and to carry psychological warfare to the opposite civilian camp.

The problems of co-ordinating all these aspects of warfare, both within the military structure and between military and civilian segments, became more intense as warfare absorbed national energies more completely. While every country set up some machinery for these purposes, the traditional autonomy of each military service generally proved too strong to be submerged. The British wartime administration was one of the few which managed to develop a picture of combined military and civilian requirements and total resources to meet them, and to make and carry through the decisions necessary for the most balanced use of manpower and materials. In the USSR the peacetime administrative direction of the total economy embraced all military and civilian requirements and their interrelations and was thus in an advantageous position to co-ordinate national military efforts.

V.   MILITARY INSTITUTIONS OF THE NUCLEAR AGE

As warfare after the second world war became an intense contest for scientific advance, the military establishments added to themselves great scientific bodies engaged not only in applied but in basic research. Especially in nuclear physics, where research required enormously large and expensive equipment, military funds were used to provide facilities. The work of laboratories operated directly by the military establishments, such as the Naval Research Laboratory in the United States, was supplemented by a large volume of research carried on under contract for the armed forces in universities and other institutions.

While the fields selected for study were initially inspired by military problems, such as the need to know the basic structure of metals or more about the ionosphere upon which radar depends, they led to research at the most basic scientific level. The nature of warfare had become such that the most fundamental scientific discoveries were directly applicable to military purposes, and in the anxious era after the second world war science, in its turn, was dependent for much of its further advance on large funds which the military were in the best position to command and supply. The possible threat of this relationship to the future creativity of science had become a matter of grave concern to many scientists.

In the field of military production the role of the military establishments continued to expand until they became inextricably interwoven with the civilian economy. In a close working partnership between industry and the armed services, the military defined the problem to be met and often proposed the designs. Producers, especially the larger ones and those specializing in particular products, worked out improved models, competing among themselves in the effort to meet the military's requirements and to secure orders for manufacture, and vying to attract the best engineering minds.

In general, orders for military supplies tended to go to the larger firms in spite of much discussion of the value of scattered and flexible resources not so vulnerable to a concentrated attack. The large firms could best meet the demand for large volume and uniform specifications. With hundreds of thousands of items to be procured, it was easier for the military to deal with a large contractor than with many small ones, and if the productive resources of the latter were needed they could be tapped by letting the main contractor make a sub-contract with the smaller firms. The result was to strengthen the larger concerns, and it was with these that the military establishments became most closely interrelated.

The extremely rapid technical and scientific developments that made each new device obsolete almost before it could be produced presented the problem of whether the military should accumulate stockpiles of weapons or should concentrate their effort on assuring that industrial capacity was ready on a stand-by basis to be converted to war production if needed. Prior to the first world war most military leaders had assumed that modern wars must be short and decisive and that any war which might break out would be fought principally with weapons already in being at the opening of hostilities, though British strategists, relying on sea-power, had thought in longer terms. In the long-drawn-out conflict of the first world war the outcome depended on the ability of the belligerents to keep a huge stream of newly produced materials flowing to the front. Thereafter, military preparation took the form not simply of armaments but of plans for the mobilization of industrial and scientific resources. With the coming of nuclear weapons, supersonic flight and guided missiles, the question again presented itself whether to think in terms of a short, decisive conflict or a prolonged struggle and whether therefore to rely on weapons in being or on the capacity to produce additional ones.

At mid-century the question was unresolved and most nations were following both courses. Their factories were kept partly busy filling existing military orders, while their equipment used to make civilian goods was geared for immediate conversion to war production if this should be required. The inter-penetration of the military and civilian economies was so close at every level, from the placing of current orders for supplies to capital equipment and finally to the financing of fundamental scientific research, that it was no longer possible to draw the line between one and the other.

Military service, which was required of most or all of the young men in most countries, provided a common experience to all segments of the population, acted as at least a temporary melting pot for the diverse groups of each nation's young citizens, and exposed them all to the attitudes which prevailed in military circles. In all modern armies this training included some degree of political indoctrination and defence against psychological warfare. The youth in training, plus the permanent military establishments, constituted a large drain on productive resources. In the countries which were most reluctant to accept conscription as a peacetime institution, notably Great Britain and the United States, the question was persistently raised as to the value of mass reserves compared to a highly trained specialized force equipped to handle specialized modern weapons.

The military for their part participated actively in many civilian roles. They filled political, diplomatic and administrative posts and high officers frequently headed business enterprises when they retired from active service. The military services offered a field for the development of a number of essentially civilian activities such as engineering, medicine and psychiatry. As military services became more and more technical the training which they supplied prepared young men for a number of civilian occupations such as electronics or aviation technician, civilian aircraft pilot and countless other trades. In some countries specific civilian training was included in the military service, as in El Salvador, Central America, where recruits from rural areas received training in modern agricultural methods during their military service as part of the national programme for agricultural development. In India one-fifth of the places in the military academies were reserved for civilians not in training for an army career.

In some cases the army served as a positive instrument for change in civilian life. The armed forces of the United States, which had used Negroes prior to the second world war mainly in services of supply, gradually admitted them to full participation during the war, first in separate regiments officered increasingly by Negroes, then in technical services not limited to Negro units, and finally in mixed units in all ranks without distinction. In the years during and after the war, when racial segregation was being slowly abandoned in American life, the armed forces served as a spearhead and model. The Indian army served the new Indian state as one of the important instruments for binding the nation together and furthering the policy of breaking down caste lines. The Indian government encouraged enlistment from all parts of the country and all groups in the population and created new all-India regiments where men of all backgrounds and castes would share a common experience.

Military institutions also cast their long shadows into civilian life by way of the special position enjoyed by war veterans. In every country some form of benefit was received by those who had seen active service in time of war, at the least by those disabled by their war service and sometimes by all who had served.

The outlook of youth was also affected, not only through the expectation of a period of military service but also through the presence of cadet corps or military-type youth organizations that oriented children and young people to types of military behaviour and attitudes. Military institutions thus came to play a pervasive role even in those societies with the strongest civilian, democratic and even anti-military tradition.

In countries where the military had traditionally played an important role within the state, they continued to exercise their customary influence. Armies in some of the Latin American countries continued to use their power to support or unseat governments of various types, always maintaining their own position of influence. It was the army which enabled Juan Perón to overthrow Argentina's constitutional system and rise to power in 1942 and which in turn threw him out and promised to restore free institutions in 1955. It was the army in Bolivia that brought in the first Latin American government outside Mexico which seriously undertook major land reform. It was the army in

Venezuela which heard that country's first elected president, Ramón Gallogos, declare in his inaugural address in 1948, 'the army shall be the servant, not the master of the people', and in less than a year drove him out of office and into exile because he had given the military insufficient place. Dictatorships in Spain and Portugal continued to rest on a firm military base.

In some of the countries of the Middle East and Asia the army was the instrument of political change. It was the army in Egypt which ended the monarchy and established a revolutionary government in 1952, the military group in Thailand which executed a political coup in 1951, and military leadership which took over in Pakistan and Iraq in 1958.

In the liberal democracies the tradition of civilian control remained strong. The parliaments of Britain and the Commonwealth countries and the Congress of the United States retained control of military budgets and of basic policies with respect to the military establishments. The chiefs of staff were subordinate to a civilian ministry or council. Nevertheless, the huge size of the military budgets, the inability of legislators to understand the intricacies of modern warfare, and the insistence of the military that they could not reveal budgetary details without revealing military secrets made it ever more difficult for civilian legislators to exercise effective control. Many thousands of millions of dollars, amounting to 30–40 per cent of the budgets of the various major powers, and to some 10–14 per cent of the gross national income of the NATO countries, were turned over to the military with fewer limitations on how they should be spent and less thorough systems of accounting for their use than generally prevailed for civilian outlays. In the communist countries civilian and military institutions were part of a common all-embracing national structure in which the Communist party maintained effective leadership.

Military organization was also developed at the international level. It had taken rudimentary form with some integration of the allied forces towards the close of the first world war and had reached extensive proportions among allied forces in the European theatre during the second world war, though not in the Pacific or on the eastern European front. After the second world war permanent structures were erected under the NATO alliance and the Warsaw pact. In North America a joint United States–Canada defence organization practically merged the forces of the two countries in respect to early-warning systems and air patrols. For the British commonwealth the Imperial War College provided a machinery for exchange of information among the military leadership of commonwealth countries. International military organization under conditions of modern warfare involved not only the incorporation of military units into a common command but the more difficult integration of supplies, with attendant problems of standardization of design and the dovetailing of delivery schedules.

The NATO organization was the most elaborate permanent international military structure which was developed in the decade after the second world war. It included a high command, with a general staff or military committee composed of officers from each country under a rotating chairmanship, and a series of commands for specific areas, each held by a land or naval officer of a particular country commanding the combined forces of several countries. It maintained a staff college, the NATO Defence College, to develop a body of officers trained in methods of international military co-operation and it set up agencies for the standardization and co-ordination of procedures, communications systems, aviation training and supplies. In its initial stages the organization made substantial headway in standardizing administration, communications, weapons design and training, but the multitude of supplies that rested on the whole fabric of civilian production could not be standardized short of an overall co-ordination of the total economies of the member states.

Integration of the military establishments of Russia and the east European communist countries under the Warsaw pact was achieved by means of Red army specialists placed in staff positions within the several armies to provide an integrating structure under a central high command.

The idea of a permanent international force which would help to keep the peace was conceived by the founders of the League of Nations as a possible outcome of the formation of that body. But no such force took shape under the League, or during the first decade of the United Nations' existence. The forces brought together loosely under the United Nations flag in the 1950 Korean conflict were organized on a purely *ad hoc* basis. The police force created to keep the antagonists apart after the Suez Canal intervention in 1956, though hardly sufficient to be regarded as a military force, pointed to the possibility that a permanent force might in time become a reality, perhaps drawing, as did this body, on the forces of the small nations instead of on the great powers as the founders of the League of Nations and United Nations had envisaged. But there was little thought in the middle years of the century of any world military organization which could stand against the national forces of the major powers.

NOTES TO CHAPTER XXIV

1. Professor N. Talensky points out that the description of the German and Japanese General Staffs, given in the text, is incomplete. From the moment it came into being the German General Staff was an organizer of aggressive wars; it played a decisive role in the conduct of military operations and exerted great influence on the foreign and domestic policy of Germany. Like the German General Staff, the Japanese General Staff was a focus for the most aggressively disposed elements in the army and the navy, obsessed by an unquenchable thirst for conquest. It is here that the wild schemes for the creation of an empire of Greater Japan were hatched, and here that the actual strategic plans for the acts of aggression committed by Japan in the first half of the twentieth century were worked out.

2. In the opinion of Professor Talensky, it should be added that the heads of the armaments firms and monopolies mentioned, as well as of many others, are amongst the men who

bear the immediate guilt for the unleashing of the first and second World Wars. He considers it useful to mention that in its day the world press commented extensively on the out-and-out betrayal of their countries' interests of which the heads of these firms were systematically guilty by supplying, through a third party, to an enemy in wartime arms and ammunition which were later used against their own armies.

3. Professor N. Talensky underlines that the text clearly underestimates the degree of militarization of the population in Germany, Italy and Japan prior to, and during, the second world war.

CHAPTER XXV

RELIGION

I. GENERAL TRENDS IN MAJOR WORLD RELIGIONS

IN the twentieth century every great religion reasserted its vigour and renewed its inner core in the face of the strongly secular tendencies of modern life, the challenge of science and rationality to non-rationalistic systems of belief, and the growth and multiplication of non-religious institutions. In some cases such reassertion expressed resistance to new knowledge and new social forms and a retreat from the modern world; in others it involved the discarding of what to modern eyes appeared to be anachronistic trappings, the stressing of social content and an effort to help modern man to re-examine and renew his values in the face of the new potentialities and threats which science had brought. For many of the peoples of Asia and some of Africa, revitalizing of the traditional religion was associated with the new self-image and nationalistic expression. In areas dominated by communism traditional religion was rejected or decried and communism itself constituted a comprehensive system of thought and belief.[1]

At the opening of the twentieth century the world's major religions and their principal subdivisions were distributed over the globe much as they had been at the end of the seventeenth century after the expansion of Europe overseas, the retreat of Moors and Turks from Europe, the halting of Muslim expansion in India and the termination of the religious wars in Europe. Some slight changes had occurred in the intervening centuries: Christianity had been carried by missionaries into Buddhist and Hindu areas of east and south Asia where it acquired numerically small but sometimes influential groups of converts. Arab traders had left a widening trail of Muslim converts along the trade routes of the east coast of Africa and the slave routes of the south Sahara, and Christian missionaries were beginning to penetrate that continent. The Eastern Orthodox Church had accompanied Russian expansion into Siberia. Mass immigration of European Catholics and Jews to the United States had begun to modify the strongly Protestant character of that country.

In the course of the twentieth century relatively little change occurred in the distribution of the world's religions, whether by proselytizing, persecution or migration, with some important exceptions. A large proportion of the Christians were eliminated from the Turkish areas of the Near East by the massacre and deportation of Armenian people during and after the first world war and the exchange of Greek and Turkish populations of Asia Minor and Macedonia in the early 1920s. The Jewish population was largely eliminated from its main centre in central and eastern Europe and became concentrated in the United States and Israel, through migration in the early part of the century, systematic extermination by the Nazis in Germany and in the areas of eastern and western Europe which came under Nazi control during the second world war and migration to Palestine before and especially after the war. The Muslim and Hindu populations of India were partially separated from each other by the establishment of Pakistan and the emigration during partition of some six to eight million Hindus and a roughly corresponding number of Muslims. The separation was by no means complete, however, for nearly forty million Muslims remained in India and some eight million Hindus in Pakistan, constituting approximately a tenth of the population of the respective countries. The emigration of Indians to such areas as Mauritius, Fiji, Malaya, South and East Africa and the West Indies spread Hinduism outside the area to which it had historically been confined. Continued immigration from Catholic regions of Europe, French Canada, Mexico and the Caribbean made the United States an important Catholic area.

Christianity, the only religion to engage in extensive, organized missionary activity, made little headway in Asia in the face of mounting nationalism and the revival of Asian religions, but both Christianity and Islam continued to recruit new followers in Africa. The religions of tribal peoples in Africa, Asia, the Pacific and the Americas were, generally, progressively undermined wherever tribal isolation broke down, although some of the pressures against tribal religions were relaxed as anthropological studies revealed a higher philosophic basis than specific religious practices had led outsiders to suppose.

While the geographical distribution of religious groups remained relatively stable, their political status changed in several areas. The Roman Catholic Church was restored to temporal power by the Lateran treaty of 1929 with the government of Italy under Mussolini, which re-established the Vatican City as a political territory. This treaty recognized the right of the Pope, who had considered himself a 'prisoner' in the Vatican since the Papal States were incorporated into the kingdom of Italy in 1870, to rule as a sovereign and to exchange diplomatic representatives with the nations of the world. The Eastern Orthodox Church, by contrast, was displaced by the October revolution from its position of partner with the rulers of the autocratic Russian empire and became a restricted institution in an anti-religious state. It retained a strong position however in Greece, and remained an important segment of the Christian community.

With the dissolution of the Ottoman empire and the creation of a secular Turkish state, Islam was disestablished in the principal area where Muslims had been free from foreign rule at the opening of the century, and the caliphate was abolished in 1924. But in most of the areas of north Africa, the Middle East, south and south-east Asia where Muslims had lived under non-Muslim rule at the opening of the century or after the fall of Ottoman power, Muslims became politically dominant. In central Asia they came under

FF*

communist rule which disparaged all religion. Hindus in India and Buddhists in Ceylon, Burma and the states of Indo-China, who had also been under Christian colonial rulers at the beginning of the century, became masters in their own houses. The withdrawal of colonial rule, and in China and Turkey the abrogation of treaties of extraterritoriality, removed from Christian missionaries the special protection which the extensions of European political power had brought. Jews, who had occupied the position of a precariously tolerated or persecuted minority in most of the lands of their dispersion for nearly 2,000 years, acquired the state of Israel as a national home in 1948.

The status of Catholic and Protestant churches in various Christian countries changed somewhat during these years. In the main the established churches continued to enjoy state support and official recognition, with freedom of religion enjoyed by other Christian sects and non-Christians. The Catholic Church was, however, disestablished in France and Mexico and both Catholic and Protestant churches were repressed by the Nazi régimes in central and eastern Europe and their position was restricted when eastern Europe came under communist control. In the few countries where the principle of the separation of church and state prevailed at the opening of the century—the Netherlands, the United States, Canada except French Catholic Quebec, Australia, New Zealand—the influence of religious bodies on matters of public concern, particularly that of the Roman Catholic Church, increased somewhat during the period.

Outside the anti-religious communist-controlled areas, the position of the several religions was thus stronger at mid-century than at the beginning, and most peoples were living under régimes where their own religion predominated.

In all the great religions during the first half of the twentieth century some forces undermined while others strengthened the hold of the religion on its followers, the position of religious institutions and the part played by religious leadership. As these forces interacted, the net effect was to enhance the influence of all the major religions except the Eastern Orthodox Church.

In the years before the first world war factors which tended to lessen the influence of religion generally predominated. The rising tide of secularism and materialism threatened to swamp religious attitudes, especially in the western culture areas and among westernized elements in other parts of the world. Rationalism challenged faith and science threatened to destroy the bases of revealed religion. Many of the intellectual currents of the nineteenth century had led to agnosticism, and not infrequently to conflict with religious authority. To the author of the classic *History of the Warfare of Science with Theology in Christendom*, Andrew D. White, writing in 1896, it appeared that every forward step in the quest for knowledge had been fought in the name of religion.

The scientific spirit penetrated increasingly into the sphere of religion itself, as it had been doing since the eighteenth century, leading to critical study and historical investigation of the religious texts of Christians, Jews, Hindus and Buddhists. Through a mass of historical and archaeological studies, the Old Testament gradually took shape as an historical record of the Hebrew people, fitted into the rough chronology which excavations in Mesopotamia, Egypt and Asia Minor revealed. The evidence with respect to the life of Jesus was scrutinized in the effort to determine its historical validity. Literary and anthropological studies examined the poetic and prophetic books and traced the myth and symbolism which they contained. Sanskrit scholars applied similar methods to the sacred literature of Hinduism. The discovery and interpretation of Mahayana texts and the translation and critical editions of Hinayana texts gave a new interpretation to Buddhism. The virtual absence of similar critical and historical study of the Quran distinguished Islam from other major religions.

Although many people ultimately found that the scholarly criticism of the scriptures, and the re-evaluation of religious beliefs which such study required, strengthened their understanding and provided a new basis for accepting their historic faith, the immediate effect was undoubtedly to lessen the influence of those religions to which it was applied.

The apparent conflict between religion and scientific rationalism had its principal impact on the religious attitudes of educated elements in the populations. Masses of common people, meantime, especially the urban proletariat, were turning away from religion or becoming indifferent to it because they were convinced that it did not help them in their struggle for a more decent existence, and often obstructed their efforts. At a time when social ferment and democratization were spreading over the world, the complacency of the *élites* of various societies who stood nominally in the forefront of religious as well as social life marked religious institutions as bulwarks of the *status quo*. This was equally true of the Brahmans of India, the scholar-officials of China, the Catholic *élites* of Latin America and Europe, the Russian Orthodox hierarchy closely associated with the court, the upper and upper-middle class Protestant churches in Britain, America, and the Low Countries, the Muslim landlords backed by the *ulema*. All these elements often appeared to stand for selfish interests and indifference to the welfare of the masses of the people.

In some countries the reaction of workers was vigorous anti-clericalism, as in France and Spain, or in Mexico where the revolution which started in 1910 overthrew simultaneously the Church, the political régime and the landed aristocracy. More generally it took the form of indifference to religion among the urban working classes.

The pattern of working-class alienation appears to have been already well established in Europe by the end of the nineteenth century, according to the scattered evidence from industrial parishes. In England Benjamin Disraeli is reputed to have replied to the Archbishop of Canterbury in 1860, when the latter complained that the Church had lost the towns: 'Your Grace is mistaken, the Church never had the towns.' In the mobile, impersonal city, paced by rapid social change, the Church could not re-establish the central social position which it occupied in stable and simple rural societies; the idiom of the Church, its images and symbols, were remote from industrial experience and most of the clergy remained aloof from the social and industrial struggle; a doctrine which accepted earthly suffering did not meet the temper of those who sought to change their lot by means of their own organized efforts. Wherever Marxian socialism gained strength, Marx's dictum that 'religion is the opiate of the people' intensified the workers' indifference to or rejection of religion. As the urban industrial population grew, religion ceased to be supported by the social milieu and came to figure mainly in the lives of those who were moved by personal devotion rather than by the place of religious institutions in the life of the whole community.

The sense of religious certainty was also being undermined by growing culture contacts around the world. To the extent that each religion rested upon an ethnocentric belief in the rightness of a particular doctrine embedded in a particular culture, awareness of different peoples through intercommunication and from anthropological studies tended to arouse a wider appreciation of the possibility that truth might take many forms and to weaken the sure sense that the religion and culture of a particular group was the only right one. This tendency was still in its infancy in the early part of the century, for belief in the superiority of western culture as well as of the Christian religion still motivated missionary efforts, and the revivals of Asian religions which accompanied mounting nationalist resistance to missionary activities asserted rival claims. But although these attitudes had not by mid-century wholly given way to mutual respect, the developing sense of cultural relativism tended to make the views of others more comprehensible to the followers of each religion.

Against these trends which reduced the influence of religion in many parts of the world, some contrary developments must be noted, not strong enough at first to offset the weakening tendencies but mounting in force until they produced a broad revival of religion in the mid-twentieth century. Against the faith in science and the growing materialism was an increasing bewilderment in the face of the power and complexity which science had brought. As science penetrated beyond the easy certainties that had appeared to be within reach, some scientists themselves stressed the uncertainty of scientific knowledge and the mystery which continued to lie beyond the bounds of scientific discovery. Scholarly criticism was turned by some people into a basis for an intellectually tenable faith.

Movements to stress the social content of the faith and its implications for the reform of social ills in some Christian, Hindu and Muslim circles countered the charge that religion was preoccupied with ritual and other-worldly matters while men suffered here and now. For some people, too, the evidence of anthropology and the knowledge of alien religions emphasized the function of religion in all societies and thus reinforced its place at home. More emphasis in missionary efforts on the provision of educational and health services brought continued support from some who could no longer encourage proselytizing.

Especially, religion tended to gain strength and vitality wherever it was associated with the sense of nationalism. Catholic Poles and Irish, for whom religion was a rallying point for the maintenance of cultural integrity and national aspirations against the alien rule of Anglican British, Eastern Orthodox Russians or Lutheran Prussians, were more intensely Catholic than for example the people of Italy, where the dominant religion was taken for granted, and they carried this difference in loyalty with them even when they migrated to the United States and elsewhere. Indian nationalism both stimulated and was fed by the revival, reinterpretation and reassertion of the Hindu religious tradition. Zionism was from its beginning often associated with intense adherence to the Jewish faith, but the persecutions of Jews in the 1930s led many to seek or to support a Jewish homeland for primarily humanitarian and political reasons. Resistance to British rule in Burma and Ceylon took the form of efforts to re-establish Buddhist education which had been largely destroyed. Japanese nationalism was embodied in the Shinto cult. Islam found its most dynamic expression in the efforts to free Muslim peoples from alien domination.

After the first world war religion suffered a number of heavy blows in some parts of the world but elsewhere the forces of revival gathered strength. The most severe blow was dealt by the Bolshevik revolution which dethroned religion over a wide area. Communist Russia not only disestablished the Orthodox Church but engaged in active anti-religious propaganda. Turkey, once the greatest and most extensive Islamic empire, not only abolished the caliphate but discarded Muslim law in favour of legal codes of the West and substituted western customs for those associated with Islam. The New Tide Movement in China developed a strongly anti-religious programme. The Nazi régime deprived religious bodies of their independence in order to bring all independent institutions in line with the party and state.

The forces which had brought religious indifference or alienation in the early years of the century continued to operate. Secularist tendencies remained strong and spread to non-western areas with the extension of scientific knowledge, education and western cultural influences. Although the certainties of the mechanistic science of the nineteenth century gave way to scientific relativity and uncertainty, science penetrated into more and more of the areas which religion claimed, as biologists and chemists pressed closer and closer toward understanding the nature of life, astronomers gained new insights into the probable origins and future of the universe, and psychologists, penetrating the realms of emotion and the subconscious, explored the area of religious experience. The ever expanding industrial city provided a religiously unfavourable social milieu for more and more of the earth's people. In the communist-dominated areas scientific knowledge about the universe and society was disseminated as one means of fighting against religious beliefs, and the institutions of religion were regarded as a cloak for bourgeois exploitation which had no place in the new society.

Yet at the same time powerful tendencies were strengthening religious sentiment. The crisis of European civilization arising from the first world war undermined faith in science and progress and threw many people back on traditional sources of value and support. The Roman Catholic Church, which since 1864 (encyclical *Quanta cura* and *Syllabus of Errors*) had set its face resolutely against doctrinal concessions to the learning or spirit of the time, reasserted the basic elements of mediaeval church doctrine and the superior values of the age of religious civilization. The encyclical *Quadragesimo anno* in 1931 renewed the social teachings of *Rerum novarum* (1891) and again made the concept of social justice the key to social reform. The restoration of the Pope to temporal status, the encouragement of Catholic education and the growing wealth of the Catholic population of the United States brought new strength to the Church and renewed its prestige. Young Catholic worker movements sought to keep working-class youth within the Church. Catholic Action mobilized lay groups to promote religious observance among their neighbours and to support the work of the Church. A movement for conversion among a section of the intelligentsia, including prominent European writers who called for a return to mediaeval values, helped to usher in a Catholic renaissance in Europe and Latin America.

The great spiritual leadership of Mahatma Gandhi became a world-wide force in support of religion. By demonstrating the power of non-violence, by his successful attack on the caste system and other social ills and by his acknowledgement of spiritual kinship with other faiths, he had an impact far beyond the borders of India and outside the Hindu religion from which he drew his major inspiration. As the movements for national liberation among Muslim, Buddhist and Hindu people grew in intensity and approached fruition, the religious aspect of each movement became more prominent, most notably among the followers of Islam. The impact of the Nazi persecutions forced Jews all over the world to study their traditions anew and generally strengthened adherence to the faith even among some who had drifted far from religious observance.

By the years after the second world war the forces supporting religious institutions and religious leadership appeared to be ascendant in the parts of the world outside communist control. In the troubled and dynamic years after the war religion, linked with triumphant and emerging nationalism, played a role in the achievement of cultural and political self-realization, it offered a haven and source of stability amid strain and change and, against the spread of anti-religious communism, it took part in the world contest for the command of men's minds.

The Hindu revival contributed to the vitality and spirit of the new India even though the state was established on a secular basis. Buddhist philosophy gave orientation to the new Burma and Ceylon. Pakistan undertook to create a viable modern state in Islamic terms, the Egyptian constitution of 1956 declared Islam to be the religion of the state, and two out of the four largest political parties in the new Indonesia were Muslim parties. In some parts of Africa reassertions of native religion accompanied African nationalism. Christian Democratic parties provided much of the leadership for the reconstruction of Europe after the second world war.

In these years, religion offered to many people a sort of sanctuary against the evils of a time with which much of mankind felt hardly able to cope. Fifty years before, when societies had appeared more stable and progress more sure, such a refuge had seemed less necessary. But in a world torn by two world wars within a generation, wracked by a decade of economic collapse, filled with people uprooted from their base by voluntary or forced migration, over-shadowed by the fear of atomic and hydrogen bombs, degraded by methods of police states and shaken by social disorganization which followed in the wake of social change, religion seemed to many people to provide an anchor and an escape from present ills. Amid the anonymity, confusions and conflicts of modern life it offered a sense of identity and basis for group solidarity. Especially in Europe and America where indifference to religion had been most widespread, the revival of religion appeared to reflect a desire to rediscover some inner core of integrity which seemed lost, and to recapture values and concepts which once reigned supreme in western culture.

In this resurgence of religion, both religious liberalism and religious orthodoxy played a part. The effort to reconcile science and religion continued to be carried on by a small segment of those concerned with religion, and the task seemed less difficult than it had seemed fifty years before. Non-dogmatic attitudes became increasingly widespread among conscientious churchgoers. But the principal vitality came from the dogmatic churches, such as the Roman Catholic which rejected Modernism in matters of dogma and from those Protestant sects and religious leaders which offered an apocalyptic vision, a non-rational appeal to emotion, or a path to personal fulfilment outside the realm of rational thought and secular concern.

Among the followers of eastern faiths religion did not offer the same sort of haven in these years that it did in the West, for there had not been the same degree of secularization. But in Hindu, Buddhist and Muslim areas it provided a stabilizing force, and many leaders supported religious institutions as a means of holding their societies together under the stresses of moderni-zation, industrialization and the processes of rapid social change. In these areas, too, conservative religious elements appeared to be strong during these years.

Religious organizations played a growing part in the years after the second world war in the world contest for power. The most highly organized and potent of the world's religious bodies, the Roman Catholic Church, placed itself in the forefront of the opposition to communism, seeking to rally not only its own adherents but non-Catholic Christians and even non-Christians to resist the spread of a materialistic doctrine. Wherever its following was large it enhanced its influence in the total body politic. In Latin America, where the Church had shown little vitality in the early years of the century, it manifested renewed vigour and made a new bid for influence which had slipped away from it. In Europe it reversed the anticlerical trend in such countries as France and Spain and it brought back to the fore in Holland, Belgium and France the issue of public support for religiously operated schools, making gains in each country in respect to the education of the young. It sought to take full advantage of the growing size and wealth of the Catholic population of the United States and the position of that country in the world.

Protestant churches took a more restricted part in the power struggles of these years. They too presented themselves as part of the defence against atheistic communism and they achieved a new degree of unity through the formation of the World Council of Churches in 1948; but they remained deeply split along sectarian lines and further divided among various modernist and fundamentalist factions, and their basic individualism limited the scope of concerted action. They usually lent their support to the cause of internationalism against extreme nationalistic and isolationist forces, and generally, but not universally, defended the liberal principles of freedom of thought, conscience and expression against the encroachments of the modern state.

Next to the Catholic Church the major religious body to become involved in world issues was Islam. With no centralized structure like that of the Roman Catholic Church, its force rested on the acceptance by its followers of the authority of the Quran, the respect accorded to the learned scholars, the *ulema*, who interpreted it, the basic concept of the unity of Islam and the principle of *jihad*, the holy war or struggle, which might be invoked in case of danger to give common direction to the efforts of Islamic peoples. Strategically situated between Europe and Asia and extending into both, astride the greatest known deposits of oil in a world become dependent on motor power, occupying the southern border of much of the communist world, and with strong and growing influence in the awakening continent of Africa, Islam had become by the mid-twentieth century a greater factor in the world than at any time since the expansion of Europe began.

Yet while the major religions increased their active role in other parts of the world, the communist system, in which 'worship, though legal, is unworthy of Soviet youth', consolidated its power, was extended into eastern Europe and China, and offered its appeal elsewhere. The intensity of the early antireligious propaganda in the USSR was somewhat relaxed in later years, but religious institutions were not allowed the privilege of imparting religious instruction outside the home, and religion was excluded from every aspect of the highly organized public life of the Soviet Union. In this officially nonreligious milieu, Eastern Orthodox, Roman Catholic, Protestant, Jewish and

Muslim leaders, as well as devout parents, strove to keep religious feeling and knowledge of the faiths alive in the new generations. The people's democracies of eastern Europe, especially Poland, showed more readiness to allow the Church a larger role.

Time alone would reveal how on the one hand the communist system would succeed in its effort, unique in the history of mankind, to relegate all religion to the place of outworn superstition and to satisfy the spiritual as well as the material needs of people through building a socialist society; and how on the other hand the world's major religions would fare in the face of the continuing changes in man's way of life brought by the inexorable impact of science and technology.

While the broad picture presented above holds for the world as a whole and for the general similarities and dissimilarities in the trends of the world's major religions, a more detailed examination of each faith will show more fully the development of its religious institutions and their response to the conditions and currents of the age.

II. CHRISTIANITY

Christianity felt the full brunt of urbanization and industrialization, and of the other factors which undermined the hold of religion and the place of religious institutions during the twentieth century. At the same time its fundamental spirit was in line with the social drives of the age, for the emphasis on the worth, dignity and individuality of each human personality was the spiritual essence of democracy, and the Christian conscience, guided by the precept to 'love thy neighbour as thyself', found secular expression in the welfare state.

Christianity suffered most directly from the apparent conflict of science with revealed religion and the application of critical scholarship to sacred texts; from the secularization of thought and the mechanization of life; from the failure of the Church to speak the idiom of industrial society and, in spite of its social doctrines, from what often appeared to be an indifference to the misery of industrial workers; from the positive denunciations of Marxian socialism and the degrading of religion in the Soviet Union. As the missionary faith of dominant European nations it suffered from the growth of Asian and African nationalism which often identified Christianity with colonialism. Yet in the course of these years the Christian churches met and survived many of these challenges, and except for the Eastern Orthodox Church they appeared to be stronger at the middle of the century than at the beginning.

The widespread alienation of the European urban proletariat was the most serious quantitative loss to the Christian churches outside the Soviet Union. Careful historical and sociological studies of a number of European cities showed a clear and consistent pattern.* Church attendance was much lower in

* Rev. Joseph N. Moody, 'The European Workers and Organized Religion', paper presented to the American Historical Association (December 1956), citing *Essai de la sociologie religieuse*, Secrétaire du centre d'études des complexes sociaux (Grenoble, 1954), F. Isambert, *Cahiers internationaux de sociologie*, Vol. XIV (1953), and a large number of other studies.

working-class than in middle-class parishes, it declined with socio-economic status and it was very low among manual workers. The class contrast was even more marked among devout practitioners than among mere conformers; a Paris study in 1955 found ten times as many 'devout' in a middle-class as compared with a working-class parish and five times as many 'conformists'. For urban communities as a whole, those practising their religion were in the minority, ranging from 10 to 35 per cent of the adult population attending church on any one Sunday in most of the European cities studied, and the proportion tended to be lower the larger the size of the community. The situation in two French cities and a predominantly working-class parish in Paris illustrated these general trends:

PERCENTAGE OF POPULATION ATTENDING CHURCH, c. 1950*

Small industrial city (*St. Etienne*)		*Large industrial city* (*Nancy*)	*Paris working-class parish* (*St. Hippolyte*)
Management and engineers	50-60	43	13
Liberal professions	40		10
Employees	30	22-35	4·5
Artisans and skilled workers	20	9	4·5
Manual workers and miners	5-10	6	2·5

The phenomenon of working-class indifference was not new in the twentieth century, for it had been well established during the initial period of industrialization; but there was every evidence that it increased during the period as cities grew in number and size, and the new urban-born industrial populations failed to recreate the rural social structure in which the Church had occupied a central place. In the Netherlands, where data on religious affiliation were reported by the decennial census, 17 per cent of the population claimed to be without religious identity in 1949 as compared with 2 per cent fifty years before. For many European workers who retained a strong sense of class difference, the Church tended to be identified with the bourgeois class of employers from whom they felt separated by a wide gulf; among socialist and communist workers it was commonly regarded as an instrument of the opposing class.

Alienation of the workers from the Church was greatest in France where anticlericalism was traditional and nineteenth-century Catholic leaders had

* Moody, *The European Worker and Organized Religion, op. cit.* The occupational categories used in the separate studies were not identical and permit only rough comparisons.

been generally unsympathetic toward efforts of French workers to improve their conditions. Elsewhere the gulf between workers and organized religion was less. Catholic trade union federations drew a substantial proportion of the organized workers in Belgium and Holland; in Germany, where Catholic leaders in the nineteenth century had set a more sympathetic tone, a third of the members of the pre-Hitler labour movement were in the Catholic unions. In Britain evangelical Methodism, the moral leadership of Christian socialists and the occasional prominent Anglican who raised his voice in the workers' cause gave the British labour movement a broadly Christian orientation, though it did not make the organized church an important factor in the lives of most working people.

In the European industrial area as a whole, the anticlerical element constituted a militant minority, amounting to perhaps a fifth of the industrial population where it was most active; a nucleus of personally devout workers, amounting to perhaps as much as a fifth in the centres where the Church was strongest, continued to practise their religion actively; a broad pattern of indifference characterized the great majority.

In the United States, on the other hand, religious indifference did not appear to be as general or to follow class lines as clearly as it did in Europe. Although American religious observance was not subjected to the same careful study as in Europe, the evidence pointed to essentially different patterns which may have contributed to the strength of religion there in the middle of the century.

Basic to the American situation was the separation of Church and state, guaranteed by the constitution and reflecting originally both the country's traditional Protestantism and the attitude toward religion of the eighteenth-century Enlightenment. Every religious sect was free to flourish or languish, without the need to fight an established church that claimed universality or enjoyed official support. The variety of religious institutions thus could reflect the variety of the population and meet its diverse needs. In view of this religious fluidity and the lack of identification of the Church with the employing class, American workers had no reason to develop the anticlerical attitude which reflected the workers' situation in Europe.

Historically, immigrant populations brought to America their respective religious affiliations. As successive waves of population entered an area, the church of the earlier settlers became the church of the more prosperous and established *élite*, while that of the newer and poorer arrivals reflected their lower position in the social structure. In the twentieth century the majority of new immigrants came from Catholic areas, and made the Roman Catholic Church the church of the urban masses. For some of these uprooted people migration meant a loss of religious affiliation, as it did in the cities of Europe. But for many, especially those such as the Irish, Poles and French Canadians for whom religion had been a cherished mark of identity, the Church offered a link with the culture which they had left, a rallying point and a defence against the alien environment. In contrast to the European Catholic Church, which was generally identified in the minds of workers with their capitalist opponents, the Catholic Church in America was not infrequently seen as the church of the workers, for large numbers of its parishioners were workers while the employers were more apt to be members of well-established Protestant churches.

New religious denominations in America had repeatedly arisen or spread by appealing to the masses of the people when older ones had become associated with more conservative or socially select groups. By the opening of the twentieth century the largest Protestant religious units were the major evangelical bodies, Baptists and Methodists, which had enrolled the poorer rural populations and the Negro slaves in the eighteenth and early nineteenth centuries; other denominations with substantial memberships had developed on the westward moving frontier of settlement.

In the twentieth century new churches which appealed to the uprooted urban masses grew up and spread. Some were offshoots of older bodies, others the creation of a charismatic leader such as 'Father Divine'. Calling themselves by such dramatic names as Jehovah's Witnesses, Pentecostals or simply The Church of God, carrying on their activity in empty buildings or wherever they could find shelter, generally scorned by the clergy of well-established denominations, making a strongly emotional appeal against the materialism and rationalism of the age, they offered their followers a haven and sense of personal identity. Although they constituted a small minority of all church membership, their significance lay in the fact that they reflected the disorientation and met the needs of a segment of the urban population which the traditional churches could not hold. They were the urban twentieth-century counterpart of the evangelical and frontier churches which had arisen to serve the masses in earlier periods of America's history.

In the fluid and mobile society of the United States religious observance had never been a universal practice, or in many communities even the practice of the majority, but its vitality had been periodically renewed by the institution of the 'revival', an emotional appeal to entire communities which caught up large groups of people and stimulated public declarations of faith and dedication to a renewed quest for salvation. The emotional revival, originally conducted in the open air or a tent in rural areas, was aimed at urban audiences and used the facilities of mass communication. The most successful of mid-twentieth century revivalists, Billy Graham, refined the techniques which had been well developed by his predecessor Billy Sunday, the leading dramatic evangelist of the early 1900s. Carefully organizing the co-operation of the Protestant clergy to whom the names of all who responded to his appeal were given for follow-up, utilizing all the techniques of mass appeal through press, radio, television and other media, expending over a million dollars on his campaign in a single major city, he called nightly on the packed crowds who filled the largest auditorium available to come forward and 'declare for Jesus'.

He carried his message and his technique to cities in Christian and non-Christian countries around the world.

Thus while religion was losing much of its popular support among the industrial populations of Europe, these various factors gave it a continuing mass base in the United States.

The principal response of the churches to the loss of following among the urban industrial masses was to stress the social content of the Christian gospel and to enlarge the churches' social role. The papal encyclicals on labour, *Rerum novarum* (1891) and *Quadragesimo anno* (1931), and similar calls to promote social justice from Protestant leaders, sought to use the influence of the churches to restrain the selfishness of employers and to arouse a moral urge to improve the lot of industrial workers. Christian teachings calling for dedication to the Kingdom of God on earth and responsibility for and service to one's neighbour received new emphasis. Seminaries for the training of the clergy introduced social studies into their curricula, first in the seminaries of the more liberal Protestant denominations and then in others, both Protestant and Catholic.

Concern with social conditions was not new, for a strong social conscience had permeated, especially, certain Protestant groups and had provided much impetus for nineteenth-century social reforms, including the abolition of slavery, improvement of factory conditions, humane treatment of the insane and the spread of general education. Under conditions of the twentieth century the social emphasis helped churches to hold their own among the multitude of urban institutions and to compete with schools, fraternal bodies, improvement and charitable societies, labour unions, political parties and a wide range of other organizations, all of which claimed the interest and allegiance of urban individuals.

Churches developed welfare programmes which offered a channel of service to some of their members and social aid to others and lent religious support to social action. Home missions sustained centres to provide health and recreation services, vocational training and adult education, day nurseries, libraries and other facilities in poor and congested neighbourhoods and many city churches developed a wide range of social activities for their members. The function of the Christian pastor, unique among the clergy of major religions in that the priest's role was not only to perform the rituals and serve the deity but to minister to the needs of the flock, was expanded to include more aspects of the life of the congregation. Jesuit educational institutions sponsored programmes of labour education for workers and training in industrial relations for workers and employers. Youth organizations such as the YMCA and YWCA spread in many countries. All these activities strengthened the institutional position of the churches; in Europe they helped to reduce the antagonism between socialist and Christian elements and to pave the way for close co-operation between Christian and socialist trade unions.

The social gospel did not come to dominate either Catholic or Protestant churches in their entirety. One Catholic priest might construct a community centre attached to his church on the ground that 'my people should be able to find whatever they need in the church' while his counterpart in the next parish might scornfully declare: 'If the Word of God through the ages has not brought people to Him, my taking the boy scouts for a picnic will not do so.' The Catholic Church, moreover, showed that there were definite limits beyond which it would not go. In 1954 it suppressed the *prêtres ouvriers* in France who for ten years had lived and worked as industrial workers in order to minister to their fellow workers more directly and to help them to voice their needs.

Protestant ministers, also, were very far from unanimous in their concern for social issues. Some were conservative or indifferent; others in their zeal overstepped the bounds deemed appropriate by their superiors or the laity of their congregations. Many in Europe followed the influential Swiss theologian Karl Barth (1886–   ), who turned back to the traditional Protestant theocentric and christocentric preoccupations of Luther and Calvin after an initial period of religious socialism. Yet in spite of Barth's insistence on an intensely personal form of religion—the obligation of man to engage in a constant dialogue with God—his followers were drawn into the social and political arena, for he became a principal spiritual and intellectual leader of the Confessing Church which protested against the unchristian and inhuman spirit of National Socialism.

On none of the major social issues of the twentieth century, however, did the Christian churches provide consistent leadership for social change, though some churches in some places made substantial contributions to such causes as international co-operation and racial equality. As the concept of the welfare state came to be widely accepted, the social conscience became broadly secularized.

While the indifference of the working classes meant the loss of numbers of active followers, it was the apparent conflict with science, rationality, secularism and materialism which undermined the church's intellectual leadership and its influence on the thought of the western world.

In the early years of the century the mechanistic world-view drawn from the physical sciences presented an unsympathetic face to the claims of religion, while those who subscribed to a form of Christianity which rested on revelation and a literal interpretation of the scriptures could not accept scientific attitudes and methods if these touched the realm which religion claimed for itself. Efforts to 'reconcile' science and religion took the form of a retreat by religion and a tendency to discard much of the traditional content which scientific evidence seemed to deny. The alternative appeared to be a head-on clash. As late as 1925 a school teacher in a small isolated American community dominated by fundamentalist religious thought was brought to trial in a court of law for teaching the theory of evolution, in one of the *causes célèbres* of the century.

But later developments of both science and religion changed the frame of reference for their reconciliation, co-existence or conflict. Twentieth-century science became easier for religion to live with as it abandoned its earlier certainty and arrogance and accepted uncertainty as a basic principle. Yet it also became harder for religion to escape as its fields of exploration widened and it penetrated to phenomena which could not be directly observed but only inferred. Religion on its side moved away from the literal-minded position which brought it most strongly into conflict with scientific rationalism, and it found a variety of ways to accommodate new scientific knowledge without abandoning basic tenets of faith.

A number of individual scientists disavowed the presumed conflict between science and religion. Such physicists, biologists and astronomers as J. A. Thomson (*Science and Religion*, 1925), James Jeans (*The Mysterious Universe*, 1930), J. B. S. Haldane (*The Sciences and Philosophy*, 1929), A. S. Eddington (*The Nature of the Physical World*, 1928) and Robert A. Millikan (*A Scientist Confesses his Faith*, 1923) expressed their sense of the inadequacy of science alone to reveal the ultimate mysteries of the universe and of man.*. Some drew a boundary between science and religion; others agreed in essence with Alfred N. Whitehead that 'there were wider truths and finer perspectives within which a reconciliation of a deeper religion and a more subtle science will be found'.† The Jesuit naturalist, Père Teilhard de Chardin (1881–1955), expressed the view that 'religion and science are the two conjugated faces or phases of one and the same act of complete knowledge—the only one which can embrace the past and future of evolution so as to contemplate, measure and fulfil them'.‡ Although during his lifetime he was forbidden to teach in France and to write on philosophical subjects, his *Phenomenon of Man*, published immediately after his death, aroused widespread interest among scientists, religious leaders and the general public.

Some of the churches met the rationalist critique half way, with a reinterpretation of dogma which left room for historical, symbolic or rational explanations of the meaning of the scriptures, articles of faith, rituals and the nature of religious experience.

The Roman Catholic Church set its face squarely against efforts to seek a basis for dogma outside the tradition of the Church. It wholly rejected the Modernist movement which arose within the Church among both clergy and laymen at the end of the nineteenth century and which sought to adapt the teaching of the Church to the conclusions of modern scientific and critical research. By the decree *Lamentabili* and the encyclical *Pascendi dominici gregis*, Pope Pius X in 1907 condemned Modernism as substituting purely subjective criteria in matters of faith and morals for the authority of the

---

* For similar expressions of some continental European scientists, cf. B. Bavinck, *Das Weltbild der heutigen Naturwissenschaften und seine Beziehungen zu Philosophie und Religion* (1933, 2nd ed. revised by K. Otte, Iserlohn, 1952).

† A. N. Whitehead, *Science in the Modern World* (New York, 1925), p. 265.

‡ Pierre Teilhard de Chardin, *The Phenomenon of Man* (London, 1959), p. 285.

Church, and in 1910 required all priests to swear an anti-Modernism oath. The position remained unchanged, and set the limits within which inquiry was permissible. The encyclical *Humani generis* in 1950 reaffirmed the absolute truth of Catholic dogma and condemned other opinions as false.

In the matter of liturgy, however, the Catholic Church looked with favour upon scholarly study into the origins of existing practices and accepted the possibility of revision in the light of new historical evidence. Work in this field, for which the Benedictines in Minnesota, USA, provided a world centre, focused on worship, and the results of historical research were regarded as possible bases for additional rites which would be conducive to religious experience under conditions of modern life.

The Protestant churches, on the other hand, lacking the same authoritarian structure and source of infallibility in matters of faith, did not sweep aside movements to bring their dogma in line with modern thought. While some sects countered these tendencies by reasserting fundamentalist dogma, most of the larger denominations were characterized by a range of views among their membership and their clergy. The modernist view was energetically sustained by some of the seminaries which trained clergy for the liberal churches of various denominations. Most denominations however also contained a fundamentalist element. By mid-century the general public acceptance of the scholarly critique of religious texts was manifested by the enormous interest expressed in the discovery of the Dead Sea scrolls and the light which might be cast by these documents on the Christian gospel. Books on the scrolls were published in pocket editions for mass reading and even appeared on best seller lists in the United States in the late 1950's.

From the Modernist controversy at the opening of the century the Catholic Church emerged more integrated than before. The Protestant denominations, however, continued to include both modernist and fundamentalist elements, though the distinction between the two approaches tended to become less clear and the conflict of views less sharp as the years passed.

Meanwhile, the deep sense of uncertainty with which western man faced his changing world nourished a growing trend toward irrationality. A succession of European schools of philosophy moved further and further away from a strictly rationalistic base. Conspicuous literary figures who found the modern world a waste land turned to religion, seeing the Church as the repository of essential tradition and experience without which life would lose its meaning, as did T. S. Eliot, or, like Jacques Maritain, reasserting the values of mediaeval Christianity as superior to those of the day. The most ambitious and widely read mid-twentieth century historian, Arnold Toynbee, made religion the key to the success of civilizations through the ages. The stress laid by Sigmund Freud on the irrational component in human behaviour was widely interpreted by his followers as providing a scientific justification for irrational attitudes and beliefs, although Freud himself had sought to apply scientific methods to the study of irrationality.

The anti-rational trend with its many manifestations changed the intellectual climate of twentieth-century western society outside the communist areas. Many who had sought to reconcile science and religion gave up the effort and returned to a neo-orthodoxy, omitting science or even rejecting it, and fundamentalist sects or segments of Protestant churches were among those which made the greatest gains in membership. While the change in intellectual climate did not restore religious observance where it had ceased to be general, it sustained those who continued in their religious faith, aroused fresh interest in many who had become indifferent and, by making the practice of religion respectable again, cut the ground from under those who had found it popular to scoff. Fear of communism added a further stimulus.

The renewed interest in religion did not, however, redound wholly to the benefit of the established churches, for much of it was highly subjective. It led to the popularity of writers and preachers who used the devices of modern advertising to offer religion as if it were packaged merchandise, to explorations into Vedanta and forms of eastern mysticism, to a wide variety of cults which seemed to offer religious satisfactions which the organized churches failed to provide, and to such widespread movements as Moral Rearmament which used religious revival to counteract secular tendencies toward social change.

While the swing to neo-orthodoxy at mid-century appeared to be strong, some scientists, laymen and men of religion, fearful lest a society dominated by science but unable to come to terms with it in the realm of values would lose its bearings, continued to press for a meeting-ground upon which an integrated scientific–religious culture could be built. Some found support for the view that the revelations of science confirmed and might further enrich the fundamental insights of religion. Others saw two kinds of reality, accessible through the two distinct processes by which man can know—the scientific method of observation, conceptualization and verification and the religious process of direct experiential perception and intuition. Still others saw the meaning of religion in the role which it plays in human life and not in the truth or falseness of any theological construct.

Christianity, moreover, by virtue of its emphasis on the worth of the individual, contained a strong component of humanism in spite of its God-centred creed. The humanistic view, which had shown itself in the period of the Renaissance and in the eighteenth-century Enlightenment, gave spiritual meaning to man's own striving and made human integrity in its fullest sense an essentially religious goal. In the mid-twentieth century a small number of people, largely unorganized but often individually influential, gave expression to a deeply humanistic faith. Inheritors of both the scientific and the religious traditions of the Christian world, they faced the scientific age without despair, accepted religious insight without retreating to non-rational beliefs, and drew from the spiritual heritage of Christendom compassion, hope, dedication and faith toward mankind. In making a place for such views as these, liberal

Christianity showed its ability to accommodate currents of scientific thought and to offer meaning to scientific minds.

By the opening of the twentieth century the Christian missionary movement, which had accompanied the extension of western dominance in the nineteenth century was meeting resistance from the aroused Asian nationalism and self-awareness which these same western contacts had stimulated. A revived Hinduism not only countered the claims of Christianity in India, but attracted the interest of many people in the West. Japan integrated the Shinto cult with patriotism and education, and presented a national front to missionary endeavours. Repeated violence against missionaries in China, culminating in the Boxer rebellion of 1900, revealed a deep hatred of the 'foreign devils' and of the 'secondary devils', their Chinese converts.

Christian missionary efforts continued, however, although the prospect of bringing large numbers within the Christian fold appeared more remote as the tide of western imperialism receded from Asia and Africa. The mission field drew many devoted workers whose major efforts often came to be directed toward combating disease and illiteracy and whose activities made substantial contributions to health and education. The most noted of these, Dr Albert Schweitzer, enlisted world-wide support for the hospital which he established in Africa, and many people who had little interest in missionary efforts were moved by his insistence on 'reverence for life'.

In both Asia and Africa missionaries were encouraged by the colonial powers, which depended upon them to provide social services—except in Korea and other Japanese colonial areas where the Christian missions were a rallying point for some of the anticolonial sentiment. In the Portuguese dominions the Church was entrusted with full responsibility for education and for imparting Christianity and Portuguese culture simultaneously. In the British and Dutch areas missions provided many of the educational and health services; only in the British dominions in Asia were substantial provisions made for these services by secular agencies prior to the second world war.

From the point of view of the Christian churches, however, the greatest mission field was not any of the colonial areas but China, where the size of the population, the absence of a vigorous entrenched religion, the weakness of central government and the obvious need for health and other social services made this a most attractive area to missionaries of every denomination and every country. Support for Christian missions throughout the world, moreover, was never confined to the colonial powers and came to be provided increasingly from the United States.

By the 1930s the assurance with which Christian missions carried their western culture and faith to what they regarded as the 'backward heathen' had been shaken. A thoughtful review of missionary activity by a distinguished and respected group of Protestant laymen, published in 1932 under the title *Rethinking Foreign Missions, a Layman's Inquiry after One Hundred Years*

(New York, 1932) offered the conclusion that Christian missions might have something to learn from those whom they sought to serve and that mutual interchange rather than one-way indoctrination might well become their goal. Yet conscientious church-goers, who continued to support Christian missions with annual budgets running to many millions of dollars at mid-century, assumed that their voluntary contributions were helping to spread the true faith; members of forty-four Protestant denominations in the United States contributed 59,000,000 dollars to foreign missions in 1954. They were among the last to recognize how deep and widespread was the resentment which their attitude of superiority had aroused.

The history of Christian missionary effort in China revealed in accentuated form the characteristics and problems of such efforts throughout the world. Under treaties imposed on China in 1853 after the wars to open the country to western trade, missionaries had enjoyed freedom to travel and preach and the right of extraterritoriality for themselves and protection for their Chinese converts, who thus became a privileged group under the protection of European powers. During the anti-foreign Boxer rebellion of 1900, Christian churches and schools were destroyed and Chinese Christians massacred. But the hope of converting large numbers continued and missions were re-established with the aid of indemnities imposed for Boxer damages.

The Roman Catholic Church regarded China as so important a field for the extension of its great influence that the Pope personally consecrated the first two Chinese to be made bishops, in 1925. At that time more than a million and a half Chinese were attending some 30,000 Catholic schools, including 1,000 in five institutions for higher education, and Catholic missions maintained approximately 700 hospitals, 2,000 dispensaries, 1,500 orphanages and 80 leper asylums. By the time that the communist government took over the country, Catholic schools were attended by some 5,000,000 pupils, health services were reaching an estimated 30,000,000 people, and the native Chinese clergy numbered 4,000 priests and 12,000 members of Catholic religious orders.

Protestant missions, especially from Britain and the United States, were correspondingly numerous and varied in scope, but they ceased to expand after the first quarter of the century when the movement for nationalism and cultural revival gained force. Many of the western-trained young Chinese who led the revival had been nominally Christian, but they now showed themselves to be anti-religious, anti-foreign and anti-Christian. A distinguished Chinese historian, looking back at mid-century on the role of Christian missionaries in his country, summed up the reaction of this group. He had attended missionary school in his village as a child, been a youth at the time of the Boxer uprising, studied abroad, been rector of a leading Chinese university, and had followed the Nationalist government to Formosa. 'We liked the missionaries because they fixed our water pumps and cured our malaria', he said; 'but they told us that their God was a jealous God, and we did not want any *jealous* gods in China.'* When the communists came to power, Christian missions were among the first institutions to be liquidated.

Nowhere did the extensive missionary activity of the nineteenth and twentieth centuries bring a substantial proportion of the population into the Christian fold. The best estimates of the numbers of Christians in various non-Christian countries, including members of the Church of South India which dated from the early Christian era, ranged from less than 1 per cent of the population in China to something over 4 per cent in Indonesia and parts of tropical Africa and 6 per cent in Indo-China.

The small proportion of Christian converts did not of course wholly reflect the total impact of Christian missions during these years, for missions numbered among their converts many who became national and international leaders, such as Sun Yat-sen at one time, Chiang Kai-shek, Toyohiko Kagawa. Leaders who did not embrace Christianity were to some extent influenced by Christian thought, as were Rabindranath Tagore and Mahatma Gandhi, and its impact produced reform movements among other faiths, such as the Bramo Samaj in India. Mission schools trained many of the men and women who provided the leadership for the modernization of their countries.

The largest proportionate results were secured in parts of Africa, notably in East Africa where an estimated 6 per cent of the population was counted as Christian at mid-century; but here Christian missions often met severe and successful competition from the missionary activities of Islam, as they had at an earlier period in south-east Asia where Islam had offered a means of protest against western supremacy. It was easier for many Africans to believe that the Islamic doctrine of racial equality was genuine and to accept the religion of Arab traders and slavers than to understand what European missionaries could mean by Christian brotherhood when European administrators were enforcing differential wages, Native reserves and police passes for Africans. And although Islam required its converts to change some of their tribal ways, it did not challenge many traditional practices, such as polygamy, which Christians did not accept. Yet Christian missions offered education and medical care which many Africans strongly desired, and they continued to play an important role in African development when their influence had been greatly reduced elsewhere.

For the Roman Catholic Church missionary activity was part of the Church's never-ceasing effort to extend its dominion and to realize its concept of the Church Universal. At mid-century, having weathered the storm of secularism in its old centres, it was prepared to withstand the current of anti-colonialism by developing local clergy and indigenous leadership for its young churches in other lands.

Protestant missions were more vulnerable when the assurance of western superiority was undermined and they encountered self-conscious opposition from those whom they hoped to convert. Since Protestantism rested on the

* Interview with Chiang Monlin, February 1955.

assumption that each individual must, in the last analysis, find his own way to God, it was a small step to concede to the non-Christian that he too might have found a path. In the new situation of the mid-twentieth century many older missions lost much of their proselytizing character and concentrated on providing technical services of health, education or agricultural improvement, in co-operation with the local community. The most generous support for new missions came from some highly evangelical groups such as Adventists, Mennonites, Jehovah's Witnesses, Pentecostals, who regarded their fellow-Christians as needing to heed their call to repentance quite as much as non-Christians and who were among the most ardent critics of much of western civilization rather than its proponents.

Most generally, however, the Protestants, like the Catholics, shifted from the role of alien intruders to that of supporters of the local Christian churches which a hundred years of missionary activity had produced. Missionary activity thus was converted into a means of co-operation between old and new churches. Although these new Christian churches in non-western lands constituted small minorities in relation to the total population, some of them formed substantial units. As they took their places in the structure of their societies and in the councils of Christendom, Christianity became less characteristically the religion of the West and more a part of multi-religious societies around the world.

The Christian churches sought to strengthen their position through organization. In this the Catholic Church achieved considerable success. Under a series of strong Popes who commanded wide respect outside as well as within the fold, the Papacy provided the Church with vigorous leadership. The celebration of jubilee years in 1925, 1933 and 1950 brought multitudes of the faithful to Rome and enhanced the sense of the Church as a world community. Codification of the Canon Law reaffirmed the integrity of the Church's system of jurisprudence.

In spite of severe setbacks the Catholic Church consolidated its position in most countries. It lost its official position in France by the separation of church and state in 1905 and the expulsion of the religious orders, but after the first world war a *modus vivendi* favourable to the continuance and extension of Church influence was established, the conversion of several famous French authors added to its prestige, and the canonization of Jeanne d'Arc cemented the bond between the Church and France. The temporary loss of influence in Spain in the 1930s under the anticlerical Spanish republic was followed by the complete entrenchment of the Church in the régime of General Franco. The position of the Church in Poland was strengthened when that country regained its independence after the first world war, for it had been associated with the national identity and aspirations of the Polish people against their Russian Orthodox and German Protestant rulers. It lost ground there, however, when the communists came to power after the second world war, though it established a working relationship with the communist régime. After the re-establishment of temporal power the Vatican City served as a diplomatic centre.

The Catholic Church came to terms with each reactionary government in the period of its ascendancy—with Mussolini, Hitler, Franco, Perón—accepting governments of the right as bulwarks against threats from the anti-religious left. When totalitarian excesses appeared to leave no room for the independent authority of the Church, it stood up to these same dictators and offered Catholic leadership to the democratic governments which followed the dictators' downfall. In spite of severe criticism from Catholics in democratic countries against the Church's policy of temporizing with fascist and Nazi dictators, the proportion of Catholics and their influence grew in such democratic countries as Holland, Britain and Belgium during these years.

In Latin America the Mexican revolution dealt the Catholic Church a hard blow, but after its initial repression it was allowed to revive under severe limitations and without the restoration of its wealth and status. In other Latin countries religious indifference was widespread, but countries differed markedly; in Venezuela great areas were almost wholly without religious services while in neighbouring Colombia the Church played a vigorous part in national life. By mid-century there were many signs of a Catholic revival in most of the Latin American areas. The traditional distance between priests and people was beginning to be bridged as individual priests launched social programmes in their parishes and seminary training began to include instruction in social issues and in methods of working with people on their social problems. Catholic Action developed a vigorous lay apostolate for the faith in several countries.

The greatest source of the Catholic Church's renewed strength, however, came from its growth in the United States, where it became the largest and most powerful single religious denomination, including in its membership about a fifth of the total American population and a majority in many of the large cities. The traditional separation of church and state in predominantly Protestant United States gave full opportunity for the Catholic Church to develop its activities and institutions. Its growing wealth as the nation prospered and its followers rose in the socio-economic scale enabled it to take advantage of the opportunity. Under a system which permitted the establishment of private schools, the Church set up parochial schools wherever a parish was able to support a school from parents' fees and donations, and by missionary funds in poorer parishes. By the middle of the century the question of public financial aid for parochial schools had become a live issue, in spite of the firmly established American principle of support for public schools alone, and the use of public funds had been allowed for auxiliary services such as school buses, health services and school lunches, and for scholarships and text books for students attending non-public schools.

Profiting by the American tendency to form organizations of all sorts, the Church reinforced its ecclesiastical organizations and religious sodalities with a multitude of other bodies—organizations of Catholic men, women, youth, boy scouts, Newman clubs for students in non-Catholic institutions. A host of welfare agencies reaching out to influence many facets of American life co-ordinated their efforts through the National Catholic Welfare Conference.

From America's position and resources, the Church drew the means of extending its influence in the rest of the world. By the Legion of Decency, a quasi-official Catholic agency set up to evaluate films for the benefit of the Catholic segment of the audience, it made its point of view felt in the film capital of the world and ensured that its concepts and its representations would always appear through that medium in what it considered an accurate form. Whatever resistance Protestant Americans might have offered to the rising influence of the Catholic Church was undermined after the second world war by the fear of communism, for by claiming the role of champion of the free world against communist atheism and tyranny, the Church placed itself beyond attack from its ancient critics. The influence of the Church of Rome in the mid-twentieth century reached more widely, though it penetrated less deeply, than it had done even in the Middle Ages when Christendom extended over only a small segment of the globe.

Neither the Eastern Orthodox nor the Protestant Christian churches could claim the same organizational and political success. For the Eastern Orthodox Church, the virtual destruction of its most influential patriarchate following the strongly anticlerical October revolution constituted the worst defeat for Christianity since the rise of Islam. The complete secularization of the state, the anti-religious teaching in the schools, the failure for some time to appoint a new patriarch after the death of the Patriarch Tichon in 1928, and the requirement that religious groups must apply to the State Council for Religious Affairs for all church building, printing or other needs, reduced the Russian church to virtual impotence. Although freedom of religious worship, as well as of anti-religious propaganda, was guaranteed by the Soviet constitution of 1936, the Church had no standing and religion was officially considered to be a product of the system of exploitation which the socialist society of the Soviet Union had abolished. The Eastern Orthodox Church had no weapon against secularism except its continuing belief that man is by nature religious, and the hope that the Russian people would one day seek to renew their faith.

The organized response of the Protestant churches took two opposite forms: the proliferation of new religious groups in response to the unmet needs of disoriented and uprooted urban people, and the oecumenical movement which sought to unite the Protestant churches and to find their common ground. The first of these developments, most noteworthy in the United States where the multiplication of sects was traditional, had no great effect on the institutional position of the churches. The second, which centred originally in Europe, was a direct attempt to increase the influence of organized Christianity.

The oecumenical movement grew out of efforts to strengthen foreign missions which drew several of the Protestant churches together, and out of the broad tendencies toward internationalism which led the national churches of individual denominations to establish closer ties with their fellow religionists in other lands. It may be said to date from the international missionary conference held at Edinburgh in 1910 which established the International Missionary Council as a permanent body. Meetings in Switzerland and Holland in 1914 and 1919 led to the first world conference of churches in Stockholm in 1925, attended by Protestant church representatives from seventeen countries. A second oecumenical organization, 'On Faith and Order', was formed in Lausanne in 1927. In 1938 the two groups joined to draft a constitution for a single world council, but it was not until after the second world war, in 1948, that the constitution was ratified at Amsterdam and the World Council of Churches established.

This loose body, styling itself a 'fellowship of churches which accept Jesus Christ as God and Saviour', brought together more than 130 of the major church organizations of Christendom, including the Eastern Orthodox, but not the Church of Rome which never relaxed its claim to be the only true Church. The World Council of Churches offered a means by which the non-Roman Catholic Christian churches could reinforce each other in their moral influence, in their stand against secularism and the anti-religion of communism and in the conduct of foreign missions. As a union of churches whose most common feature was the fundamental individualism of Protestantism, however, it could do little to unify doctrine or create common organization.

At mid-century supporters of Christianity were claiming that never in history had it or any other religion 'been as widely extended geographically, as deeply rooted among as many peoples, and as much a force in the life of all mankind'.* They could point to the fact that its principal revival and a growing proportion of its support came from one of the most technologically advanced countries of the mid-twentieth century, the United States. There, a larger proportion of the population was reported to be church members than at any previous time, expenditures for church buildings, benevolences and foreign missions were at an all-time high, church attendance was on the increase and appeared to be as high in large cities as in village and rural areas. The majority of those questioned in a national survey in 1954, reported by the National Council of the Churches of Christ in its *Yearbook*, attributed the growing interest in religion to fear, uncertainty, reaction following the war and renewal of faith. The very conditions which had seemed most to threaten the hold of religion appeared to be providing a fertile soil for its renewed vigour.

* Kenneth S. Latourette, *Challenge and Conformity: Studies in the Interaction of Christianity and the World of Today* (New York, 1955), p. 10.

III. JUDAISM

Judaism in the twentieth century was profoundly affected by the events which befell the Jewish people, as well as by the currents of thought and knowledge which impinged on all religions during these years. At the opening of the century the Jewish population was centred in eastern Europe, where Jews were largely isolated from the surrounding culture and lived a life which was intensely permeated by the spirit of Judaism and organized to permit its daily practice. Most of the centres of Jewish learning and the spiritual leadership of Judaism, as well as the numerical preponderance of the Jewish people, were to be found there.

Under the Nazi programme of systematic extermination, east European Jewry was virtually destroyed. Of an estimated six and a half million Jews in countries which came under Nazi domination, less than a million remained at the close of the war, while another million survived as refugees. In the centre of the east European Jewish community, Poland, where 3,300,000 had been living in 1939, a mere 80,000 were left. By mid-century principal centres of Judaism had been transferred to the United States and the new state of Israel.

This shift in centre had a twofold impact on religious developments: in America Judaism had to provide for the religious life of Jews who were fully participating members of a modern, predominantly Christian, society. In Israel it had to resolve the relationship between Judaism as a religion and Israel as a Jewish state, and meet the religious needs of people who brought a wide variety of experience and expectation to their new national home.

In the Jewish communities of eastern Europe up to the time of their destruction, Judaism furnished the structure and content of the way of life. The tradition of Jewish learning in which all shared provided the basis for respect and authority in the community; the learned scholar was listened to, whatever his economic position or other basis for rank; the child who showed diligence and prowess in the Hebrew studies which were the core of his education earned parental and community approval and even deference; community resources were used to provide stipends for poor students so that they could devote their time to study, and the men of the community spent their time in study and discussion of the Torah and the Talmud, in a room which every synagogue provided for this purpose.

The lives of the people were filled with an elaborate body of ceremonial observance in synagogue and home. These included prayers and blessings daily and on many personal occasions; weekly observance of the Sabbath, from sundown on Friday to sundown on Saturday, with ceremonies in the home and the synagogue and with rigid abstention from every kind of work including household tasks such as lighting fires or cooking; observance at home and in the synagogue of frequent holidays throughout the year, some extending over a number of days; and observance of dietary laws which prescribed the kind of food which might be eaten, the manner and supervision of slaughter, permissible combinations of foods, and separate sets of dishes. The isolation of Jewish life from that of the surrounding milieu was forced on the Jews of ghetto and Pale, and was reinforced by the Jewish community's indifference to the often uneducated population of the area, by language differences between Yiddish-speaking Jews and their neighbours, by rigid restrictions against marriage outside the group and by generations of self-contained Jewish life.

In the west European communities this pattern of intensely Jewish life had been modified before the opening of the twentieth century, for Jews had there achieved toleration, emancipation from externally imposed restraints and, finally, in the liberal movements of the nineteenth century, full status as citizens. In western Europe Jews attended secular schools and universities, shared the currents of contemporary thought and not infrequently inter-married with non-Jews. Especially in Germany, secularization spread and movements for religious reform appeared. These tendencies toward integra-tion into the total society, secularization and religious reform became even stronger in the United States, as the Jewish community in that country grew from under 10,000 at the opening of the nineteenth century to over a million at its close.

By the opening of the twentieth century the pattern of the American Jewish religious community had been established as the result of the efforts of Jewish leaders to arrive at a basis for the religious life of American Jewry. Leaders of one group, Reform, who sought to adapt Jewish practice to the condi-tions of American life, and of another, Conservative, who insisted that traditional or historic Judaism was the only basis for continued vitality, had given up the effort to find a common ground by 1885, and had formed two wings with separate theological seminaries, rabbinical organizations and federations of congregations. A third division, calling itself Orthodox, had come into existence in the 1890s, distinguished from the Conservative group primarily by the fact that its congregations were composed of new immigrants from eastern Europe. The third wing, organized into the Union of Orthodox Jewish Congregations, established in 1898 a Yeshiva, in the manner of east European communities, for the study of the Torah for its own sake. The seminaries of the Reform and Conservative groups undertook to train rabbis in the manner of American specialized institutions of higher learning; they included secular studies or arranged for their students to receive such studies elsewhere, while the Yeshiva originally was unconcerned with secular knowledge.

The three divisions were not separated from each other on matters of basic doctrine, but primarily on matters of practice. The Reform movement, in its platform and prayer book, departed from traditional Judaism in abandoning the dietary laws, simplifying many of the ceremonies, substituting English for Hebrew, seating women and men together in the synagogue, and relaxing the observance of the Sabbath, particularly where people had to work on Saturday to earn their livelihood; it even went to the point of shifting Sabbath worship from Saturday to Sunday. It rejected Zionism and looked upon America as the promised land where the life of Israel should be built. The Conservative and Orthodox wings firmly retained the traditional practices, though the practical conditions of American life made strict adherence to daily ritual, dietary laws and Sabbath observance extremely difficult, if not very nearly impossible.

In the early years of the twentieth century no religious body felt the impact of secularism more strongly than the Jews in western Europe and America. Immigration and interaction with the surrounding culture detached large numbers of the younger generation from their religious roots; for many of the young people growing up in the United States, Americanization meant secularization. In addition, substantial numbers in western and eastern Europe joined socialist parties and adopted a Marxian anti-religious attitude. At the same time the Orthodox element in the Jewish community was greatly reinforced by the flood of emigration from eastern Europe which brought many east European Jews to west Europe and a million and a half to the United States, where the Jewish population nearly trebled between 1900 and the outbreak of the first world war.

After the war Judaism in the United States became increasingly American in leadership and composition although it continued to draw scholars from the main centres of Jewish learning in Poland. With the cutting down of immigration, first during the war and then by restrictive legislation, the Jewish community ceased to be reinforced annually by large new groups of east Europeans with their intellectual and spiritual leaders. Immigrant neighbourhoods, where the synagogues were the centres of life, shops were closed on the Sabbath and kosher food was sold, began to dissolve as their residents moved to less poor and congested areas and no new immigrants took their place. Like the children of other immigrant groups, American-bred Jewish children tended to reject their parents' foreign ways. Orthodox as well as Reform and Conservative congregations took on an increasingly American outlook and, by force of circumstance, many American practices.

The Americanization of the Orthodox wing was strikingly evident in the field of education. In 1928 the Yeshiva abandoned its effort to reproduce the traditional centre for informal rabbinical studies characteristic of the east European Jewish communities and became Yeshiva University, offering a formal course for the training of American rabbis which included general as well as rabbinical subjects. At the elementary school level a movement was started in 1938 to establish parochial schools similar to those maintained by the Catholic Church, where children would receive a general education along with instruction in religion, Hebrew and Jewish history.

On the other hand the Reform movement returned to some aspects of the traditional pattern which it had discarded as inconsistent with modern life. Concluding that the core of belief and ethics alone was insufficient to hold its people against the inroads of secularism unless it was supported by some of the traditional forms, it reintroduced a number of practices which it had dropped, revised the prayer book to restore prayers which had been omitted, and encouraged the many traditional ceremonies in the home which had been very largely abandoned by most Reform families. A new statement in 1937 to replace the original platform of 1885 represented a partial victory for those who maintained that only by the intensification of Jewish practice would the vitality of Judaism be maintained.

The Reform wing also abandoned its firm opposition to Zionism, though it did not as a body espouse the Zionist cause. When some of the outstanding Reform rabbis embraced Zionism, the issue split the Reform group. In the face of United States immigration restriction and Nazi persecution the negative position lost more and more adherents, until a declaration in 1935 that Reform Judaism was neutral on the subject officially recognized the disagreement within the Reform ranks. As the Jews of America watched the destruction of east and central European Jewry, more and more of the Reform element joined in the demand for immigration to Palestine and the establishment of a Jewish homeland but, in contrast to the Orthodox Zionist organization, they supported a political haven rather than a religious centre for the world's Jews.

The major growth in American Judaism came in the Conservative congregations. Adhering to basic traditional practices, the Conservative wing discouraged deviations but did not condemn those congregations which introduced them; accepting the idea of change and development as characteristic of any vital religion, it refused to try to reduce to an official statement the complexity and fluidity which it regarded as the essence of a living faith; ready to reach out into the community and to find a common meeting ground between the ways of American society and the ways of Judaism, it developed synagogue centres with activity programmes similar to those of American churches and quite different from the east European synagogues where men gathered to study and dispute.

The three branches of American Judaism never regarded themselves as separate sects, but rather as different directions of development of a common faith and common religious body. In the second quarter of the twentieth century each sought to put its stamp on the total body and to take each new congregation under the wing of its organization. From 1926 on, the three groups worked together through the Synagogue Council, their representatives joining in such efforts as collaboration with non-Jews in inter-faith bodies, sponsorship of Jewish chaplains to serve the American armed services, preparation of exhibits of Jewish history and tradition, and relief for Jewish communities in Europe and in Palestine. The differences which persisted tended to become more and more organizational rather than religious and to reflect social differences arising from national origins and time of immigration. As leadership of all groups passed into the hands of the American-born generations, these distinctions too became irrelevant.

The unity of the Jewish community was strengthened by the large number of agencies for immigrant aid, Jewish education, welfare, recreation and relief which were set up outside the synagogues and cut across the divisional lines. These many organizations, applying traditional Jewish principles of charity and mutual aid, made the Jewish community one of the best organized and best served segments of American society, as an integral part of the American social structure, not isolated from it. The trend at mid-century was to try to give the programmes of these organizations 'Jewish content' rather than to allow them to become indistinguishable from secular organizations performing the same functions. But Jewish leaders were by no means agreed as to what this content should be.

It had been the distinction of the Jews through the ages that they had accepted only the authority of conscience. Firm in the sense that they had committed themselves to follow the path of righteousness by the repeatedly renewed covenant of their ancestors with God, they stood for the ultimate freedom and moral responsibility of the human spirit against all external authority. Their religious practices kept vividly alive the history of the Hebrew people, in which their responsibility toward God was manifested. Judaism was expressed in no declaration of faith but rather in the acceptance of its discipline; it constituted a way of life, comprehensive and complete.

The problems confronting twentieth-century Judaism in America arose from the difficulty of following the traditional discipline while living in a milieu whose rhythms were geared to the demands of industrial society and to non-Jewish patterns of life. Little conflict arose in the realm of thought, for the Jewish tradition of unrestricted inquiry and intense, logical analysis was fully consistent with a scientific mentality, although scientific and other secular fields of learning competed for interest and attention with traditional rabbinical studies. And the essential spirit of moral responsibility and human dignity was in line with the strivings of the time.

The broad revival of religious interest which swept the United States in the years after the second world war was shared by the Jewish community. For some Jews this was a form of self-identification. Shaken by the evidence from Germany that assimilation might offer them no surety in time of crisis and that they might be thrown back on the resources of their group, they felt that they could ill afford to be cut off from their cultural tradition and many sought to renew their allegiance to their historic faith.

In the other major centre of Judaism, the state of Israel, the mere fact that for the first time in nearly 2,000 years the Jewish people had an opportunity to build a Jewish society did not resolve all questions as to the place of religion and the forms of religious practice. And in Israel, as in the United States, Judaism faced the problem of how far traditional practices were in line with the conditions of life inherent in a modern industrial society.

The Zionist movement, which created the state of Israel and shaped its ideology, was itself the product of diverse and antagonistic points of view. As the movement gathered momentum after the opening of the twentieth century, it attracted men of widely varying religious ideologies ranging from the strictly Orthodox to the violently atheistic, so that no one attitude toward religion could ever be considered the official standard of Zionism.

For some, resettlement in the ancient Jewish homeland meant political autonomy, for others a cultural—though not necessarily a religious—revival, and for still others a re-gathering of all Jews into one state and the abolition of Diaspora Jewry. Some desired the establishment of a country in which Orthodox law could reign supreme, while yet others hoped that this resettlement would break the so-called rigidity of traditional Judaism and cause a newly creative and vitalized religion to spring forth.

The one religious position common to all branches of Zionism was that the Jews are not merely a religious body but are a people, a nation. In this sense Zionism was a reaction not only against the ravages of anti-Semitism, but also against the view of the Jewish enlightenment, *Haskalah*, which had 'denationalized the religion'.

By attempting to solve the problem of the Jewish people through its national regeneration, Zionists saw themselves as modern prophets of the ancient Messianic conception of Judaism. Rejecting the doctrine which asked that the Jewish people wait for supernatural intervention and bear its burden of exile with patience, Zionism called for immediate action through the agency of the Jewish people itself. Since, in the opinion of many, traditional Judaism was responsible for the passivity of the Jews in the face of persecution, the Zionist movement also included a revolt against this traditional Judaism as well as against the past history of the Jewish people. The exilic ghetto and all things associated with it were objects of Zionist hatred and contempt. Religion, being so closely connected with such life, could not escape this contumely and became for some the symbol of that which most hindered Jewish efforts to be free.

While many Zionist pioneers were convinced that a break with the past was necessary to ensure the survival of the Jewish people, they still retained a strong nostalgia for the customs and folk patterns of European Jewish religious life. The extent to which observances such as holy days were secularized and nationalized varied sharply, but only among the actively Orthodox did they completely retain their traditional religious aspect. With few exceptions, the pioneers longed to continue the chain of tradition from generation to generation, but for many the Land was substituted for the Law. They looked to the country, and to social ideals such as the dignity of labour for their binding principles, and not to the traditional religion which, they felt, had kept the people alive in Exile but had outlived its usefulness.

Those who brought the state of Israel into existence thus ranged in ideology from the deeply religious, through the central group of General Zionists who were sympathetic to religion, to the left wing who rejected ritual observance and dogma but retained a kind of dedication to the Land.

In the state of Israel during the first ten years of its existence, many traditions of religion, such as the festivals, were observed in public celebrations as official holidays, while dietary laws and certain Sabbath regulations were also matters of municipal observance, and the Sabbath was the official civic day of rest. As for individual observance, each person had the choice of following his own path. For some this meant the acceptance of a few regulations and observances, for others virtually none. In general, governmental, social and economic conditions were favourable for the practice of Judaism and the schools provided children with a knowledge of the Bible, Jewish history, literature and traditions—a necessity for Jewish religious life.

Traditionally religious Israelis raised their children to follow firmly their religious beliefs, with the aid of excellent religious schools which were part of the state school system. The ranks of religious families were swelled by the huge influx of religious Jews from Arab lands, but the folk customs of these newcomers, unfamiliar with western civilization, made it difficult for them to hold their children. The transition to secular Israeli life involved a clash of eastern and western cultures, and stimulated young people to revolt against parental values, including religion.

Communal settlements determined their community observances according to their ideological position. Some of the *kibbutzim* were strongly anti-religious, others strongly religious. By virtue of its membership and position, the religious *kibbutz* became one of the most positively active religious groups in the country. Fully Israeli in the national sense, educated and modern, the young people in these religiously oriented pioneer farming communities succeeded in demonstrating the compatibility of religious life with the demands of modern existence and in integrating the ideals of the state with the ideals of their religion.

Over the years calls for a renewal of religion began to come from both religious and non-religious elements. Among the Orthodox some advocated reconsideration, within strictly traditional methods, of certain Jewish laws which make life in a modern industrial society difficult if not impossible, or suggested that a Sanhedrin be reintroduced to deal with all questions of Jewish law. Among the non-religious, appeals for a return to religious values appeared with some frequency in speeches and publications. Much of the active antagonism toward formal religion on the part of the original settlers disappeared among the native-born generation whose lack of institutionalized religious upbringing generated indifference in place of their parents' attitude of rebellion.

The majority of the population occupied an indefinite position, non-religious but not atheistic, between the Orthodox and the few extreme leftists to whom religion appeared a stumbling block in the path of social progress. They discarded the binding character of the complete traditional system of Jewish law and theology, but not the concept of God as interpreted by Orthodox Judaism. The non-Orthodox population accepted the results of scientific scrutiny of the Bible as well as of religion in general. The findings of Biblical criticism were taught in the secular schools, and the foundation of Orthodox life, a supernaturally revealed tradition, thus ceased to be assumed by the average Israeli. In the absence of any other satisfactory basis for formal religion, Judaism remained a general belief and observance of certain customs which were aesthetically or nationalistically appealing.

Furthermore, the oft-repeated contention of the Orthodox that only the person who observes each detail of the traditional regulations can be termed religious contributed to the feeling that no midway position in belief and observance was possible. The few attempts at Reform or Conservative synagogues, the product of German or English-speaking elements, were not indigenous and had little attraction for the native Israeli.

The rabbinate in this period, moreover, offered little spiritual leadership in reinterpreting Judaism which could attract the new generation. Its major function appeared to be its official duty under the government to administer certain areas of personal law such as marriage and divorce, which in the Middle East had traditionally been under the jurisdiction of the religious leadership in each community. This stirred up some antagonism amongst the anti-religious who were compelled to acquiesce to rabbinic regulation and disturbed some liberals who felt that such matters should be under lay not religious authority and who felt that the principle of a secular state was being subverted. Moreover the involvement of religion with party politics undermined some of its prestige. As a participant in the political arena it became merely one more ideology alongside others.

Nor did the synagogue in Israel assume a function similar to that of the American synagogue-centre. Social needs were filled by other agencies, while Jewish education was the province of the government schools. There was no need to express one's Jewishness by congregational affiliation, as living in a Jewish country provided for such a tie in everyday life.

The knowledge of the Jewish heritage possessed by every Israeli, however, kept alive the interest in Judaism, though the basic impetus behind such learning was interest in the history of the Jewish nation. The country was filled with sites of religious interest, the national classical literature was religious, and the language was infused with the terms of religion which even the ardent secularist must use to express himself. Non-religious Israelis who were committed to a continuation of Jewish tradition and peoplehood thus had basic knowledge of Judaism, and they were familiar with religious forms, many of which they accepted in a secular version. Some among them hoped for a dynamic leadership that could combine traditional Judaism with modern scientific and philosophic concepts, and find a religious way which would offer religious guidance without rigidity or control, and which would spring from the needs of the nation and its people.

In both its major centres the central issue confronting Judaism at mid-century was how far, and in what forms, the religious component was essential to the continuing vitality of the Jewish tradition which had given the Jewish people their power of survival in the past and which served them still in the lands of their adoption and in the development of their national home.

IV. ISLAM

Islam in the twentieth century was inextricably involved in the political and social developments of the time. As a religion which encompasses the law and way of life of its followers, it was inevitably a factor in the movements to liberate Muslim peoples from non-Muslim rule and in the spread of social changes into the Muslim world. On the other hand it was less affected by currents of scientific thought and historical criticism than were other major faiths. And though some areas were strongly affected by the secularizing influences of the times, the main tendency through most of the Muslim world appeared to be an intensification of religious loyalty.

The major expressions of Islam in the twentieth century, and its major problems, came in the political sphere. The Islamic revival was part and parcel of the political and social ferment among Muslim peoples. In providing a spiritual source of cultural as well as political nationalism Islam gave to the struggle against western dominance some of the quality of a religious conflict. As a guide to political conduct its uncompromising insistence on equality among the faithful was in line with modern democratic trends, but some of its other commands and practices appeared to challenge or diverge from the tendencies of the time. Its principle of universality within the ranks of Islam was at variance with the trend toward national states but in line with tendencies toward internationalism, though its sharp distinction between believers and non-believers was a potential bar to both national and international unity.

Even what appeared as a major blow to the status of Islam, the dissolution of the Ottoman empire, and the abolition of the caliphate in 1924, indirectly enhanced Islam as a political force for it released Arab nationalism in lands which had been under the control of the sultanate. In these areas, and in the lands from Indonesia to Morocco where Muslims had lived under non-Muslim colonial rule, movements for political liberation brought new nations into being. A number of independent Muslim states thus gained the opportunity to govern themselves in the light of the principles of Islam, while the abolition of the caliphate had little effect on the structure of Islamic authority since real religious power rested in the *ulema*, the learned religious leaders throughout the Muslim communities.

Islamic nationalism as a religio–political movement had been stimulated in the second half of the nineteenth century by Jamal ad-Din al-Afghani (1839–97) who, from one end of the Muslim world to another, preached a Pan-Islamic revival linked with local nationalism as a first step. As the movement, under local leaders, grew in vigour during the twentieth century, Islam

GG*

provided a dynamic force for movements of liberation, anti-imperialism and resistance to western domination from Morocco to Java. The Islamic republic of Pakistan was the most distinctive product of the movement, but in a sense Arab nationalism was an even more direct political expression of a movement with deep religious roots. The Arab area was the centre of the Muslim world and Arabic was the language of the Quran. Although Arabs constituted only a fifth of the strength of Islam and were greatly outnumbered by two other groups, the Muslims of India and Pakistan and those of Malaya and Indonesia, it was in the Arab lands that the faith had had its historic centre and period of greatness. It was here that the holy city of Mecca was located and the language of the faith was spoken and printed.

Yet though Islam found expression in national self-rule during these years, the sense of the Islamic world community and the firm line drawn between believers and non-believers were at variance with the trend toward political nationalism and the exaltation of the geographically based political state. And the traditional Islamic law, the *shariah*, shaped in an earlier and far different society, appeared in conflict with many social trends in the modern world.

In its thought and theology Islam remained virtually untouched by modern developments. The authority of the Quran as a revealed Book remained unchallenged, as it had throughout the history of the faith. The *ulema* retained the prestige which enabled them to continue to perform their role as the interpreters of the sources of the Islamic faith.

Various sects and religious orders, with their leaders and following, functioned within their particular area or group, some growing and others declining. The puritanical reform movements such as the Wahhabi, which called for a return to the purity and unity of early Islam and rejected both the theological elaborations of the mediaeval schoolmen and the mystical experience of the Sufi religious orders, remained influential, especially in the Arabian peninsula, and the idea of a direct return to the Quran and the Sunnah continued to offer the main direction of thought for both progressive and reactionary reformers.

The two sects whose growth and impact was greatest during the twentieth century were the Ahmadiya and the Ismaelis, followers of the Aga Khan. The orthodoxy of the Ahmadiya, who acknowledged a later religious leader and accepted his interpretation of Islamic doctrine in terms of modern life, was questioned by most other Muslims, but the sect was strongly organized to carry on missionary activity in the name of Islam, as well as to proselytize among fellow Muslims. The Ismaelis grew from a minor group to a wide-spread sect, emphasizing social and economic development, abolishing purdah, and ensuring education, hospitals and other social services to their members by means of trusts sustained by the collection of tithes. Both the missionary Ahmadiya and the Ismaelis had their main influence outside of the principal Muslim areas; their greatest growth was in Africa and they accounted for much of the spread of Islam in that area. None of the sects or religious orders, however, exerted a major influence over the main currents of Islamic thought.

The impact of western contact and education brought efforts in the late nineteenth and early twentieth centuries to integrate western and Islamic thought and led to the development of what might be termed Islamic modernism in Egypt, India and Turkey. In Egypt Mohammed Abduh (1849–1905), convinced that no conflict would be found between western science and Islamic thought if each were pursued to its fullest meaning, undertook to restate the doctrines of the Quran in contemporary terms. In India Sir Sayyid Ahmad Khan (1817–98), acting on the hypothesis that the essential quality of Islam is its conformity to nature and the laws of science, founded a modern Muslim university in order to strengthen the faith and confidence of Indian Muslims by bringing them abreast of modern thought. The Indian jurist Sayyid Amir Ali, in his influential book *The Spirit of Islam* (1891), invoked the authority of the Quran to support contemporary social ethics in such matters as slavery, polygamy and divorce by repudiation, and he stressed Islam's role as a progressive civilizing force. He found sanction in the Quran for the vigorous pursuit of secular learning, and claimed that modern scientific thought was natively Islamic since its foundations came to Europe by way of Arab scholars in the Middle Ages.

These and other modernists and reformers, with their acceptance of modern scientific knowledge and their concern for social reform, had an important social impact on Muslim society which they sought to revitalize and they enabled young men with western education to remain within the faith and take pride in Islam. Their main impact was on the social aspects of Muslim life for they encouraged the idea of social change and helped to provide the urge for movements for women's rights, education and labour organization which grew in most Islamic areas during the twentieth century. But they had no effect on the structure of religious authority or the content of the faith and they made no attempt to bring modern scholarship into the realm of doctrine.

Religious authority continued to reside in the *ulema*, who clung strictly to the traditional mediaeval presentations of Islam. Dedicated to traditional learning, the *ulema* of the great mosques of al-Azhar in Cairo and az-Zaytunah in Tunis, and their counterparts elsewhere, remained outside the currents of secular study and thought. Few others concerned themselves with religious questions or had any influence even on *élite* groups. The kind of scholarly historical criticism and archaeological study to which the Hebrew and Christian scriptural texts were subjected did not reach into Islamic theological and religious studies. The modern universities established in Muslim lands contained no theological schools or departments of religion comparable to those of the West. Modernism nowhere took shape as a definite school of Islamic thought. Such modernist ideas as were advanced, limited in extent and partial in content, were no match for the orthodox conservatism of the *ulema*.

In the first quarter of the twentieth century Islamic nationalism and modernism appeared to go along together. Mohammed Iqbal in India (1873–1938) drew on the ideas of Nietzsche and Bergson in elaborating his conception of Islam, as well as on the early liberal intellectual tradition of Islam itself; it was he who projected the concept of the Islamic state of Pakistan. In Turkey Ziya Gökalp (1875–1924) applied the positivist thought of Comte and the sociological doctrines of Durkheim to the analysis of Muslim religious institutions and concluded that these were symbols of the collective will and cultural values of Turkish society; he became the proponent and spiritual godfather of Turkish nationalism. Mohammed Abduh's follower, Shaikh Rashid Rida (1865–1935) of Syria, edited a journal, al-Manar, which carried both reformist and Pan-Islamic ideas through the Muslim world. Most Muslim leaders, whose energies were devoted to the struggle against western political and economic domination, assumed that the useful aspects of western scientific thought could be readily absorbed by a liberated Muslim society.

But in the second quarter of the twentieth century a strong fundamentalist revival took form in many areas. The secularization of the Turkish state, with its substitution of western legal code for the law of Islam and the mandatory discarding of fez and veil, seemed to show that reform, modernism or any acceptance of western ideas could only lead to secularism. The reformist journal al-Manar became ardently fundamentalist, rejecting all westernism and regarding every deviation from the most strict observance of religious prescriptions as a threat to the integrity of Islam. The ulema, never having accepted either the efforts of reformists to discard tradition and return to the purity of the Quran or the modernists' assumption that western knowledge was compatible with Islamic doctrines and mentality, insisted on the rigour of their authority and secured the dismissal of university professors and public officials who ventured to introduce new lines of discussion, such as the Egyptian writer Taha Hussein. Muslim activist movements with mass appeal, of which the Muslim Brotherhood in Egypt, Syria and Iran and the Ahrars in Pakistan were the most noted, were prepared to go to any lengths to free Muslim people from foreign ideas as well as foreign domination and to bring about a return to the most literal application of Muslim orthodoxy.

A number of factors contributed to the vitality of religious conservatism. To a degree, the reformers themselves were responsible. They generally shared an attitude of anti-intellectualism, considering theological controversy an impediment to the social reform and spiritual awakening to which they gave priority, and their very insistence that all essential thought could be found within Islam reinforced the sense of orthodoxy. As modern transport made it possible for more and more people to make the pilgrimage to Mecca, increased numbers of hajis returned home to exert their prestige and swell the conservative ranks in every part of the Muslim world. For all factions the battle for the liberation of the Muslim community called for intensity of faith rather than concern as to its content. The very strength of the emotional commitment to political goals consolidated the psychological rigidity of conservatism. A questioning mind or less-than-full acceptance could be readily interpreted as a sign of defection from the active struggle to which the tightly organized fundamentalist groups contributed a fierce vitality.

Although the Muslim extremists were opposed by the moderate elements which generally furnished the dominant political leadership and though their organizations were repeatedly suppressed or their leaders imprisoned, their hold remained strong, for they asserted in positive terms the religion to which the state was committed and they insisted that the development of self-rule was an act of religious fulfilment. The fundamentalists could thus put all others on the defensive. In the difficult years after the second world war during which the Muslim states struggled to establish themselves and to tackle their immense problems of poverty and need, inevitable frustrations invited the search for a scapegoat. Extremists could use the 'western' taint to damn their opponents and the fundamentalist appeal could command a practical monopoly of the emotional drive which had brought liberation and continued to seek expression. Liberal tendencies continued, but the extremists tended to force the issue into a choice between fundamentalism and secularism.

While religious revivalism was following a fundamentalist direction, the practical march of events and pressures of the time were bringing many adjustments which appeared to the fundamentalists to be contrary to the prescriptions of the faith. Pressures for the social reform of Muslim society, both from within and from without, brought successive modifications of Islamic law and custom. Apart from personal law relating to such matters as marriage, divorce and inheritance, British criminal and civil law replaced Muslim law in the Muslim-administered native states of India as well as in the rest of the sub-continent; Egypt adopted the Napoleonic code in 1884. By the middle of the twentieth century the Muslim *shariah* was the law of the state only in Afghanistan, Saudi Arabia and Yemen. Except for these extremely conservative states there had either been some modification of the personal law or proposals looking to its modification were under serious study, although Turkey remained the only Muslim country to replace Muslim personal as well as civil and criminal law with law derived from the West.

As most Muslim areas in the twentieth century became testing grounds for the integration of Islamic principles into the governance of a modern state, two areas, Turkey and India, offered tests of Islam's ability to function in a secularized society, either as the faith of the majority or where its adherents were in the minority.

In Turkey in the 1920s Kemal Ataturk, who carried out his social reforms with the support of a westernized urban *élite*, not only secularized the state and discarded Muslim law but deliberately sought to sever the Turks' connection with the Arabic roots of Islam by discarding the Arabic script in favour of the Latin and by prescribing that the prayers should be said in

Turkish. Thirty years later a political party favourable to the restoration of some religious influence came to power, and took the first step of reintroducing the teaching of religion into the elementary schools. Perhaps more significant was the establishment of a faculty of divinity within the secularly oriented University of Ankara. It remained to be seen what, if any, contribution to the future of Islam would come from this first attempt to bring together Islamic and modern studies at the highest level.

In India 40,000,000 Muslims remained after partition, enjoying full citizenship in a secular state composed predominantly of Hindus. Historically, Indian Muslims had resisted integration into Hindu society under the pre-national, pre-modern conditions where caste determined status and relationships, citizenship in the western sense was unknown, and family and religion formed the basis of communities. The constitution of the Indian state abolished caste, secularized the law and guaranteed freedom of religious practice and democratic rights and responsibilities to all citizens. Those leading Muslims who remained in India in the belief that a satisfactory life for Muslims could be developed on this basis became active participants in government and other fields. They were committed to demonstrating that Islam could exist and flourish as a personal faith within a multi-religious democratic society without being reinforced by the legal or political structure prescribed in the Quran.

For the substantial Muslim populations in central Asia, the impact of communist rule minimized the role of Islam. Muslims were directly subjected to anti-religious pressures, particularly intense during the period of the first Soviet five-year plan, 1928–32, when there was widespread destruction of mosques, deportation of religious leaders, suppression of religious literature and the Arabic alphabet, and settlement of non-Muslims in Muslim areas. Since Islam was associated with minority status and often, especially in the case of nomads, with a way of life which was being radically modified, the processes of modernization and integration into Soviet society tended strongly to orient people away from Islam. Similar forces were at work among the Muslims of Chinese Sinkiang.

Throughout Islam the conditions of the second quarter of the twentieth century presented conscientious Muslims with what some acknowledged to be a 'soul-scorching' problem of how to integrate, or choose between, the demands of the faith and the pressures of the modern world. The problem was present in Pakistan for those who staked their lives and futures on the creation of a separate Muslim state; in the Arab lands for those whose guiding force was Arab nationalism; in India for those who were committed to achieving a satisfactory pattern of Muslim life as citizens of a secular democratic state; and in Indonesia for those engaged in bringing 'unity in diversity' to their far-flung, culturally varied archipelago. The issue in Islam was whether and how the new vitality which it had shown in the preceding decades could give expression to an absolute, revealed, religio–political faith, within the pressures, the mentality and the necessities generated by the world conditions of the mid-twentieth century.

V. HINDUISM

Hinduism provided much of the spiritual dynamic for India's revival in the twentieth century. Reinterpreted and revitalized, it renewed its ancient core and became converted from a doctrine of renunciation to one of activism and from a sanction for rigid custom to a force for social reform. In so doing it reasserted its hold on the Indian people.

During the nineteenth century Hinduism, under the impact of Christian thought and European authority, was generally on the defensive and its more significant movements were sectarian, influenced directly by missionary teaching or resulting from resistance to such influence. They were primarily movements of reform, accepting in the main the western criticism of Hindu thought and attempting to work out adjustments which were considered necessary to make Hinduism modern. Of these, the most important was the Brahmo Samaj, founded by Ram Mohan Roy (d. 1831), which based itself on ancient Hindu teachings but was markedly influenced by liberal Christian thought.

But during the second half of the nineteenth century a new spirit began to manifest itself within the fold of orthodox Hinduism, as new voices were heard emphasizing the necessity to preserve the spiritual heritage of Hinduism. Two quite distinct movements emerged. The first was a militant, revivalist form of Hinduism known as Arya Samaj, founded by Swami Dayananda Saraswati (1824–83) and based on faith in the revealed nature of the *Vedas*. The Arya Samaj opposed the orthodox Hindu organization of caste and untouchability, it emphasized social service and it carried on a militant campaign for reconversion to Hinduism of those who had turned to other religions. Adopting the methods of Islam and Christianity to combat them, it insisted that the Vedas were comparable to the Quran and the Bible as a sacred text, it introduced rigid organization unfamiliar to Hinduism in order to serve the function performed by the church among Christians and, in line with Muslim and Christian practice, it sought individual conversion, in contrast to the tradition of Hinduism which provided for conversion only to incorporate whole groups as separate castes. Thus the Arya Samaj was combative, it entered into competitive activities with Islamic Christian missions and it built up a large and extensive educational system in the Punjab meant to withstand the influence of the mission colleges.

The central figure of the second movement, Sri Ramakrishna (1836–86), mystic *yogi* and a saint in the traditional style of Hinduism, made a deep impression on the Bengali society of his day, especially among the younger generation. He not only arrested the movement among the intelligentsia for a general break-away from Hinduism, but revived their faith and provided them with a dynamic view of life.

The most notable among his disciples, Vivekananda (1863–1902), became the apostle of a new Hinduism, fired by revivalist zeal. A prolonged visit to America and a tour of England influenced his patriotism and his desire to rejuvenate Hindu society and to give to Hinduism a social purpose. His fervent declaration that he did not 'believe in a religion that does not wipe out the widows' tears or bring a piece of bread to the orphan's mouth' expressed the changed temper. His own mission he described as 'to find the common bases of Hinduism and to awaken the national consciousness to them'. That common basis he found in the Vedanta which he interpreted in popular phraseology and preached untiringly all over India. In addition he trained up a body of missionaries, men of education, pure life and religious zeal, to carry this message to the villages. Innumerable other *sanyasis* and learned men, belonging to no particular sect, were preaching the same message in many different places.

The Theosophical Society, under its American founder and organizer Colonel H. S. Olcott, and later Mrs Annie Besant, also was active in the promulgation of Hindu religious ideals among the educated classes in the first two decades of the twentieth century. Through Mrs Besant's translation of the *Gita* (1895) and the society's educational work, it did much to strengthen the faith of the Hindus in their own religion.

It was the reinstatement of the *Bhagavad Gita* as the supreme scripture of Hinduism that enabled the leaders of thought to cast the new spirit in terms of Hindu orthodoxy. Since at least the third century AD the *Bhagavad Gita* had been one of the authoritative texts of the Hindu doctrine, a scripture to which every political writer or apologist turned for arguments in support of his thesis. In the last decade of the nineteenth century and first quarter of the twentieth it was the subject of commentaries by nearly all the major political and religious leaders and it became the most influential single book providing inspiration for a social, ethical and spiritual regeneration of the Hindus.

The political activist B. G. Tilak (1856–1920) was the first to insist that the message of the *Gita* was not renunciatory and other-wordly, as others had taught, but was essentially a scripture preaching a dynamic social ethic, a doctrine of social activism, where action for human good without personal attachment was the first imperative. In his *Secret of the Gita* (1915) he based his interpretation on the *Gita's* description of the ideal man as one who, with a mind which has attained equability, performs his duties in this world without desiring selfish ends and solely for the benefit of the world, and considers such action as dedication to God.

The *Gita's* teaching on sacrifice, he pointed out, emphasizes the *Brahma yajna*, or dedication of all action to the welfare of the world, in contrast to the ritualistic sacrifice, or *yajna*, of the Vedas. This conception that it is the duty of the individual actively to uphold a world order was directly opposed to the renunciatory creed which had dominated much of Hindu thought for hundreds of years.

Tilak maintained that the social order which the *Gita* contemplates is a structure based on *swadharma* or the duty of an individual to act according to the law of his own nature and to hold fast to his own righteous way. This interpretation rejected the meaning that doctrinal teachers had given the word *swadharma* in terms of caste society—that man must be content with the station in which he is born. The *Gita*'s view of society as an hierarchical organization based on functions and qualities, he insisted, has nothing in common with the caste system where division is based on birth. In declaring that the fourfold division was divinely ordained and represents a permanent feature of social organization, the *Gita*, in Tilak's interpretation, denies birth as the basis of the social orders and emphasizes quality and action as the grounds for differentiating the several functions. In this view all persons, including the lowest, are entitled to equal development so long as they cultivate the equable mind, work unceasingly with the sole object of general good and dedicate their works to God. The *Gita* thus was seen as essentially a scripture of democracy.

Even more significant was the interpretation of the *Gita* as offering a doctrine of the rejuvenation of society. Krishna declares: 'Whenever and wherever *dharma* declines and unrighteousness prospers, I shall be born in successive ages for the purpose of destroying evil-doers and re-establishing the supremacy of the moral law.' In the new interpretation the *Gita* foresees the inevitable decay of all institutions and the necessity of revolutionary changes to restore the harmony of life.

To a static society held down by custom and tradition and suffocated by the accretions of ages, the teaching that change is divinely ordained when society has decayed came as a life-giving revelation. No stronger weapon could have been put in the hands of those who desired to reshape Indian society and give it purpose and vitality. The new doctrine of the *yoga* of action not only gave religious fervour and vigour to political action but transformed Hinduism itself from a static organization to a dynamic force. A partial attempt to break the renunciatory tradition had already come from Vivekananda whose lectures on the *Karma Yoga* showed that renunciation need not be identified with a withdrawal from the world and its activities. The monastic order of the Ramakrishna Mission, too, had been an attempt to reconcile the doctrine of the welfare of the world with worldly renunciation, for the monks of that order did not retire into the forests or secluded *asramas* but pursued a career of service in all fields of social activity. But it was Tilak who furnished a more positive statement of the gospel of action by his emphasis on Krishna's call: 'Therefore arise, and fight the battle of *dharma*.' He viewed all the doctrinal teaching of the *Gita* as having the sole purpose of energizing the righteous man into action.

It was easy for Tilak to arouse the young men of India by appealing to the *Gita*. In *The Secret of the Gita* he expounded the doctrine of energism with a wealth of scholarship and an unimpeachable orthodoxy, and with no direct allusion to politics. But the political meaning was clear, for Tilak was the recognized leader of the extremists of Indian nationalism who considered it their duty 'to rise up and fight' the foreigners on Indian soil. To Tilak India was the field of righteousness, and only through the message of the *Gita* could India save herself.

If activism was what Tilak emphasized, it was the doctrine of selfless service that Gandhi taught by his commentary on the *Gita*. He was in fact the embodiment of the *Gita* ideal of the man of equable mind, the *sthitiprajna*, who, unmoved by anger or by fear, had his feet planted firmly in the world and directed all his action to the benefit of the world. His commentary on the *Gita* was therefore a statement of his personal credo.

Gandhi's special contribution to the integral teachings of the *Gita* was the emphasis which he placed on the means. To him it was not sufficient that the ideal should be the welfare of all, the means must be ethically right. His doctrine of *ahimsa*, or non-violence, expressed the concept that the force of action should not be such as to injure the true nature of another's law of life.

The most comprehensive interpretation of the *Gita*, in the sense of being the most integrated in its spiritual values, was that of Sri Aurobindo (1872–1950). Raised in the classical tradition of the West, Aurobindo first appeared as the inspirer of the terrorist movement in Indian politics, but he underwent a spiritual transformation during his incarceration in jail and for nearly forty years, from 1911 to his death in 1950, he was one of India's great spiritual teachers. In view of his training and background, his commentary had wide social significance. He emphasized the ethical nature of the *Gita's* teachings, tore down mercilessly the obscurantist interpretation that polemical writers had given to its social message and helped the Indian public to understand its teachings in terms of life's problems.

The *Gita* thus became the scripture of the new age, the main foundation on which its ethic, its social doctrines and even its political action depended. Its message was carried daily to the common man in a thousand popular versions, as the number of books on the subject published every year in every Indian language amply testified. It was the inspiration and guide of modern Hindus.

Other factors and personalities contributed directly to a universalization of Hindu thought and to a general awakening of social conscience. Rabindranath Tagore (1861–1941) revived the tradition of devotionalism and offered a poet's interpretation of the universalized doctrines of Hinduism. Dr Ananda Coomaraswamy (1877–1947) interpreted its symbolism; Sir John Woodroffe (1865–1936), a British judge of the Calcutta High Court, redeemed the *tantra* forms of worship of the mother goddess from the extravagances to which many of their practices had fallen; Sister Nivedita, an English convert to Hinduism, was responsible for emphasizing the social value of many Hindu institutions.

The contribution of the West to the Hindu reformation was considerable. The *Gita* itself became popular with the educated classes mainly through

English translations. Mahatma Gandhi's first introduction to the teachings of the *Gita*, for example, was through Sir Edwin Arnold's poetic translation entitled *The Song Celestial* (1885). For over a generation Mrs Annie Besant's prose translation of the *Gita* text under the title *The Lord's Song* was the companion of every Hindu student. Though Tilak's commentary was written in Marathi and Gandhi's in Gujerati, it was through their English versions that they came to have all-India influence. The main literature of modern Hinduism was in English. It would be no exaggeration to say that it was the universality of the English language in India that made an all-India movement for the reformation of Hinduism possible.

So long as the great Hindu scriptures were available only to those who knew Sanskrit, their knowledge was confined to a small group of people, mostly Brahmins. Translations of the *Vedas* and the *Upanishads* were not available in India's popular languages; nor were the great commentaries on which the philosophic structure of Hinduism was based. *The Sacred Books of the East* (1875 ff.), published in English in the last quarter of the nineteenth century under the scholarly editorship of Professor Max Müller, made these texts available to the modern western-educated Indians. The interpretation and popularization of Hindu philosophy was also through the medium of English. Vivekananda's discourses and speeches, Aurobindo's *Essays on Gita* and his *Life Divine* (1916–19), Dr Radhakrishnan's *Indian Philosophy* (1927) and most other classics of modern Hindu religious literature were written in English. The political unification of India and the existence of a language which, though foreign, had become a vehicle of national expression reaching every part of India were essential prerequisites of the Hindu revival.

One result of all the movements emphasizing the general philosophical and ethical background of Hinduism was the decline of sectarianism. From the time of the first Muslim invasion to the middle of the nineteenth century, reform movements in Hinduism had generally led to the foundation of new sects. The process of unification which followed the revival of Hinduism was so marked that even the most differentiated among the new sects, the Brahmo Samaj, was practically absorbed into general Hinduism.

A further phenomenon connected with the revived Hinduism of the twentieth century was the large number of genuine saints and holy personalities who, by the spiritual greatness they achieved and the great moral influence they exercised, stemmed the tide of unbelief and provided inspiration for the new generation. The great figures of Sri Ramakrishna, considered by many to be an incarnation and worshipped as such, Sri Aurobindo and Sri Ramana Maharshi were in a sense canonized by universal consent. There were numerous others in the same tradition. In practically every part of India many such holy men and women, by their mere lives, without teaching any doctrine or preaching any philosophy, bore witness to their faith; they were sought out by people of all ranks from within and outside of India and exerted great influence on large masses of men. Revived Hinduism found its support in the lives of these dedicated men and women who, having renounced the world, still lived among the people, practising unattached action for the welfare of the world.

Thus, armed with a scripture of undisputed authority interpreted in terms of modern social needs and based on a philosophical doctrine which provided an answer to the challenge of other religions, Hinduism in the twentieth century could be applied to the problems of social adjustment.

Popular Hinduism continued in the old way, sectarian, devotional and holding fast to a variety of traditional practices, but it also underwent major changes in respect to the social customs which had had religious sanction. Social disabilities based on caste declined, many temples were thrown open to untouchables and, in the most orthodox province of Madras, Hindu religious endowments were placed under the control of public bodies. Popular Hinduism displayed a more vigorous life than it had in recent times, but it lost much of its conservative character and temper while keeping many of its forms.

Although the social institutions of Hinduism, which in a large measure had become identified with religion itself, were deeply ingrained in law and custom, they did not claim divine sanction nor were they sustained by an organized ecclesiastical authority. They could therefore be changed by legislative action. When the legislating state came into existence in India after the first world war, central and provincial governments passed fundamental legislation affecting Hindu practices. The Civil Marriage Act of the Central Legislative Assembly in 1923, making possible marriages between men and women of different castes, struck at the very root of the orthodox Brahminical conception of caste. The Age of Consent Act of 1929, raising the marriageable age of girls to fourteen, made illegal the custom of child marriage which had been traditional for over two thousand years and was considered compulsory at least for Brahmins. Independent India made the modernization of Indian society one of its primary objectives and formulated as an essential part of its constitution a comprehensive system of fundamental rights enforceable by law, which provided for the absolute abolition of untouchability and gave women equal status with men. The Hindu social legislation which followed was the consummation of a hundred years of effort to reorganize Hindu society on a modern basis.

Essential to the ability of modern independent India to achieve its objective of transforming Hindu society was the removal of religious sanction from outworn social institutions and the reform of religious beliefs so as to provide a sanction for change and a common background to the community. This was the achievement of the Hindu reformation which, acting through many channels and deriving its inspiration from many sources, national and foreign, brought a religious revival which provided the Hindu people with a sense of unity and urge for social welfare. The modern Indian state found the ground ready and prepared, for the victory of social reform had already been won in the public mind even before the legislators gave it statutory recognition.

VI. BUDDHISM

At the opening of the twentieth century the religion of the Buddha was nearly everywhere in a low state of prestige and effectiveness. This was especially the case among the Buddhists of China, Korea, Vietnam and Japan. The disestablishment of Buddhism had been one of the first acts of the Meiji restoration in Japan in 1868. In China, though the Manchu emperors gave their patronage to a form of Lamaism, Buddhism as a religion had little standing; the intellectuals devoted themselves to Confucian studies, while the function of the Buddhist clergy was limited chiefly to the performance of ancestor rites, primarily for the peasants.

In some of the areas of south-east Asia which followed the Hinayana or Theravada Buddhist tradition, as distinct from the other major tradition, the Mahayana, followed in China, Korea, Japan and Vietnam, the position was a little better. In Cambodia, Laos and Siam, where the monarchy continued to uphold the faith, the tradition of religious life remained fairly vigorous and unbroken. But when Burma ceased to be independent Buddhism lost its special position in that country; without central direction or discipline, the Sangha, or church, ceased to be a vigorous force, especially as the official patronage of the British government went to Christianity, and Christian missions became active. In Ceylon, the heart of Theravada, centuries of foreign occupation and the conversion of a considerable section of the higher classes to Christianity left Buddhism depressed. Only in the isolation of Tibet could Buddhism be said to have been in a flourishing state.

By the middle of the century the situation had greatly changed. The celebration of the 2,500th anniversary of the death of the Buddha in 1956 found his religion vigorous and mounting in strength. The revival came principally in the Theravada area, where it was associated with nationalist movements. It was stimulated by the researches of western scholars, which made the classic religious texts of Buddhism available to the educated youth, and which led to the development of critical Buddhist scholarship not only in the Theravada area but also in Japan.

In Thailand the religion had never fallen to so low an estate as elsewhere, and the rulers had historically supported and aided the Buddhist church. In 1888 the Siamese monarch Rama V assumed the title of Defender of the Buddhist faith. Among the many steps which he took to carry out his mission were the publication of a new edition of the *Tripitaka* in 1893, reorganization of the Buddhist religious order and the establishment of a Buddhist school.

As the official religion of Thailand, the Buddhist church continued to be organized nationally under a Sangharaja or Supreme Patriarch appointed by the king, and the state, through its Ministry of Religious Affairs, promoted the interests of religion. The Buddhist temple remained the principal institution of the villages, a repository of wealth and often the only source of education and medical treatment; in towns, where public education came to replace or supplement the education supplied by the monks, the temples acted as hostels for students from a distance. All Buddhist young men in Thailand were expected to spend some period of their life as a monk, if only a few months. In the years of change and uncertainty after the second world war, a Buddhist youth organization sought to help young people to find their path among traditional and western ways.

In Ceylon the decay of Buddhism had gone deep during the more than 400 years of foreign occupation. Many people under the Portuguese and the higher classes during the Dutch and British periods, had accepted the forms of Christianity and at the beginning of the twentieth century the Buddhist religion was followed mainly by the lower classes. Many who had not become Christians had become indifferent to a religion which had no prestige in the country and was not favoured by the government. Buddhist temples had fallen into decay and the system of Buddhist education had been destroyed.

The recovery of Buddhism was part and parcel of the revival of the Ceylonese national spirit. It centred around the revival of Buddhist education, and the founding of the Ananda College in 1886 by Colonel Henry S. Olcott may be taken as the first step toward the re-establishment of Buddhism as the national religion. Under the leadership of Sir Baron Jayatilaka, who was also active in the formation of the Ceylon National Congress, the college became the centre of a Buddhist revival, and a generation of young people grew up after the first world war in the conviction that a genuine Sinhalese tradition was inseparable from Buddhism.

Since Buddhism has always welcomed converts, reconversion was at all times a normal process, and many of the younger leaders who started life as Christians reverted to the Buddhist faith. Those who aspired to work for the nation soon recognized that without going back to the religion of the Buddha it was not possible to gain popular hearing or influence. The men who were to become chief political leaders and high officials of independent Ceylon were among those who returned to their ancestral faith and became ardent advocates of Buddhism. The Buddhist religious orders themselves were spearheads of nationalism. After independence, political parties looked to them for organized support, and they remained a major factor in developing the policies and guiding the destinies of the new state.

In Burma Buddhism was no less a part of the national movement and a factor in the new national state. Its influence there was more continuous than in Ceylon, for it was only with the imposition of British rule in the second half of the nineteenth century that the Buddhist hierarchy was abolished and the religion lost its official position. Even then, the monasteries continued to provide a system of elementary education all over Burma and to act as the upholders of Burmese culture. Though the discipline among the monks became lax when the central organization was destroyed, the religion never lost its position among the common people.

When the national movement began to take shape, it was the Buddhist priests—the *pongys*—who carried its message to the villages. Gradually the nationalist movement became associated with a Buddhist revival and a public affirmation of Buddhist conformity became necessary for those who aspired to local or national leadership. Immediately after independence the prime minister, U Nu, himself a lay monk who periodically retired to the monastery, restored the Buddhist hierarchy, re-established stricter discipline among the Buddhist priesthood and drew upon the inner strength of Buddhism for the reorganization of national life on which the new state was engaged.

The elaborate arrangements made in Rangoon for a World Council of Buddhism in 1956 were an indication of how much Buddhism was identified with Burmese national development. The conciliar tradition in Buddhism was ancient, dating from the period immediately following the Buddha's death, but it had been in abeyance for many centuries. Its revival under the auspices of a modern state was a major event in the religious history of Asia. The object of this council, attended by representatives of all Buddhist countries, was not as on previous occasions to settle points of dogma but rather to discuss the discipline of the monastic order and to take steps to reinvigorate the religious life of Buddhist countries.

Marked interest in Buddhism was also revived in India, its original home. Here again it was nationalist sentiment that led to a new appreciation of the Buddhist tradition and its increasing acceptance as one of the major aspects of Indian life. The study of Indian history revealed Buddhism as an important historical trend in Indian life and thought; a large number of Buddhist texts in Sanskrit, originally written in India, were rediscovered and recovered from China and Tibet, and it became apparent that Indian influence in east Asia was to a large extent based on the spread of Buddhism in those areas.

In recognition of the place of Buddhism in Indian life, the Indian government encouraged the establishment of institutions of Buddhist studies at various centres of importance, and arranged for the repatriation of Buddhist relics from Britain. The 2,500th anniversary of the death of the Buddha was celebrated as a great national Indian festival. It was not difficult to accord this recognition, for Hinduism had at no time considered Buddhism as something separate, like Islam or Christianity, and the Buddha himself had always been recognized as a Hindu divinity. Though conversions to Buddhism were not very numerous, apart from some mass conversions of former untouchables, Buddhism ceased to be looked upon in India as an heretical sect. It came to be seen as a great and valuable tradition in Indian life which should be reintegrated with the national culture of modern India.

Buddhism experienced a much less vigorous revival in the countries which followed the Mahayana tradition than it did in the Theravada areas.

Throughout the twentieth century Chinese Buddhism was under constant attack. Both its popular form as practised by the peasantry, and its philosophical interpenetration with Confucianism and Taoism, came under fire from a succession of movements. From the beginning of the century a movement to expand education called for the appropriation of temple property and its use for the support of schools. In 1917 the Chinese renaissance movement, the New Tide, opposed Buddhism in all its forms. Strongly secular and scientific in its emphasis, it denounced popular Buddhism as superstitious and regarded Buddhist philosophy, together with Confucianism, as unscientific and a backward social influence. In the 1920s the Nationalist party struck at popular Buddhism by ordering the systematic destruction of images in the temples, with the declared purpose of purifying and reforming the religion. In self-defence the Buddhist monks initiated some educational activity and introduced some educational reforms. But although the movements for the confiscation of temple property and the destruction of images were carried out only sporadically and often in the face of opposition from the local peasantry, the Buddhist religion was placed on the defensive throughout these years.

With the coming to power of the communists, Buddhism in China found itself in a relatively favourable position, though the fundamentally secular character of communism left little place for any form of religion in the long run. The major targets of the Chinese People's Republic were the Christian missionaries, who were expelled, and the system of Confucian ethics, which was denounced. Buddhism, however, presented no comparable threat to the objectives of the régime and could be accepted as a link with China's past, and a way of rejecting the foreign bourgeois influence of recent years. Many temples were restored with public funds as historic monuments, and scholarly research into the early history of Chinese Buddhism was promoted. It may be said in fact that here too it was the link with nationalism which gave Buddhism such renewed standing as it enjoyed at the middle of the century.

Buddhism in Japan never fell to so low an estate as in China, although after the Meiji restoration Shinto became the state cult, and people were no longer required to be members of a Buddhist temple under a priest who also played the role of inspector. A number of Buddhist universities were maintained by the various sects into which Japanese Buddhism was divided and these served as centres for Buddhist study and preserved traditional dogma and practice.

At the turn of the century, the impact of western Buddhist scholarship reached Japan through the work of Japanese scholars who studied in Europe and returned to preside over Buddhist studies at the national and Buddhist universities. The emphasis of these scholars was on the original Buddhist texts and on a return to purity of the religion which had been obscured by later elaboration and by the development of sects. This movement, however, was mainly among the Buddhist laymen and youth; it did not meet with favour among the priests in the Buddhist universities. These retained their sectarian interests and clung to their traditional dogmatic methods, expelling those among the younger priests who adopted the methods of critical scholarship.

Although Shinto served as the state cult, the organized Buddhist church lent itself to the support of the emperor system and to the programme of the militarists in the decades leading to the second world war; during the war it became a part of the official propaganda organization. After the war Buddhist leaders sought to make the religion independent of politics, and during the period of defeat and confusion numbers of people turned back to their original Buddhist faith.

The six Buddhist universities continued to carry on traditional Buddhist teaching; Buddhist studies were also conducted in a number of other institutions, and national organizations were formed to promote research on Buddhist subjects. The formation of federations of young Buddhist groups and of Buddhist women's organizations attested to a widespread interest. Japanese Buddhism asserted its continuing vitality before the world by acting as host to the second Buddhist World Conference in Tokyo in 1952.

Thus it may be seen that there was a strengthening of Buddhist tradition and a revival of religious life in the countries of south and south-east Asia where the religion became identified with national regeneration. The religion showed continued vitality and capacity to survive under the much less favourable circumstances of China and Japan, and in its homeland, India, it came back not as a religious revival but as an element in India's varied culture. Like other major religions the religion of the Buddha thus revealed new vigour in the middle years of the twentieth century.

NOTES TO CHAPTER XXV

1. The treatment of religion is commented upon from directly opposing positions, that is for failure (1) to recognize the inner spirituality of religion and to give it a central place in the cultural development of mankind; (2) to regard religion as a mere self-defence of capitalist society. Three Italian scholars, Mario Bendisciolo, Silvio Golzio, Vincenzo Cappelletti, ask 'why the religious component of the history of humanity should be treated under the practical heading of social transformations, whereas religious thought should be considered along with philosophy and science, as providing the intellectual and spiritual horizon of twentieth-century history'. They regard as 'intransigent scientism' the manner in which 'the authors have traced the outlines of science and religion'.

Another scholar, Professor Dhanis, finds that:

'An exposition of a very complex reality is presented in this chapter with solicitous attention to objectivity and on the basis of reliable information. However, the great religions are considered from a point of view rather exterior to the subject. Without taking a position in favour of one doctrine or another, it would have been possible to indicate what each of the great religions wishes to offer mankind—in particular, to men of our own days—to describe the moral and spiritual ideals which they propose, and the inner vitality they possess. Instead of this, religion is considered primarily from the point of view of its relationship with cultural and social progress. This is an important aspect, but not the primary one.

'More could have been said about the results which the Christian ideal of justice and charity has achieved in our times. The firmness with which the Catholic religion has maintained its supernatural message against rationalist denials, is rightly noted; but the progress and the vitality of the philosophical, theological and biblical sciences in modern Catholicism are not sufficiently taken into account.'

Communist commentators take an opposite view. Mr Imre Revesz writes:
'The opening sentence strikes the key-note of the whole chapter: it is said that in the twentieth century each of the major world religions has regenerated in its "inner core . . ." However, there is no hint—or almost none—as to the actual spring of this great religious revival. It is in fact a desperate act of self-defence on the part of capitalist society (riddled as it is with feudal survivals, or, in some places, blended with them altogether) in the face of the triumphant march of socialism and its final goal—communism. The great religions are still, to this day, the mainstays of capitalism (and, broadly speaking, of social antagonism), which they reflect ideologically. If, today, every now and then, they appear more sympathetic towards social and cultural progress than they were, say, a hundred or a hundred and fifty years ago, that sympathy is as yet far too feeble to counterbalance tendencies inherent in *each* established religion. It is too weak to break religious and ecclesiastical *autotelism* (which can have no place in future society) in general, or, in particular, the drive of the major religions and churches for political power, and their material, economic, independence (in which the trait of exploitation—open or concealed —is always recognizable).'

Three commentators from the USSR (I. K. Grigulevich, E. A. Belaiev and G. F. Ilyin) explain the communist attitude as follows:
'Communists fight against religious prejudices by disseminating genuinely scientific knowledge about the universe and society among the population and by building a new socialist society, in which the exploitation of one individual by another has been eradicated, and in which the spiritual and material needs of people are being satisfied to a greater and greater extent.'

Additional readings for Roman Catholicism may be suggested:

J. Y. Calvez, *Église et société économique* (Paris, 1961–63), 2 vols.

Joseph Folliet, *World Catholicism Today* (Westminster, Md., 1961).

Joseph Nestor Moody (ed.), *Church and Society: Catholic Social and Political Thought and Movements, 1789–1950* (New York, 1953).

Papal Encyclicals, like that of Pius XII, *On the Sacred Liturgy* (1947).

For religion under communism may be suggested:

Cyril E. Black, *The Transformation of Russian Society* (Cambridge, Mass., 1960).

Robert Pierce Casey, *Religion in Russia* (New York, 1946).

John S. Curtiss, *The Russian Church and the Soviet State, 1917–1950* (Boston, 1953).

Constantin de Grunwald, *La vie religieuse en URSS* (Paris, 1961).

Boleslaw Szczesniak, *The Russian Revolution and Religion: A Collection of Documents concerning the Suppression of Religion by the Communists, 1917–1925* (Notre Dame, Indiana, 1959).

For studies of world religions consult:

Marcus Bach, *Major Religions of the World* (New York, 1959).

C. J. Bleeker, *Anthropologie religieuse; l'homme et sa destinée à la lumière de l'histoire des religions* (Études publiées sous la direction de C. J. Bleeker, avec l'aide de l'Unesco et sous les auspices du Conseil International de la Philosophie et des Sciences Humaines (Leiden, 1955).

Johnson E. Fairchild, *Basic Beliefs; the Religious Philosophies of Mankind* (New York, 1959).

V. T. A. Ferm, *Living Schools of Religion* (Ames, Iowa, 1956).

Sir Julian Huxley (ed.), *The Humanist Frame* (New York, 1961).

Benson Young Landis, *World Religions: A Brief Guide to the Principal Beliefs and Teachings of the Religions of the World and to the Statistics of Organized Religion* (New York, 1957).

Guy S. Métraux and François Crouzet, eds., *Religions and the Promise of the Twentieth Century* (New York: New American Library [Mentor Books], 1965).

Paul Ramsey, *War and the Christian Conscience* (Durham, North Carolina, 1961).

Kenneth Thompson, *Christian Ethics and the Dilemma of Foreign Policy* (Durham, N.C., 1959).

H. F. Vos, *Religions in a Changing World* (Chicago, 1959).

Charles C. West, *Communism and the Theologian* (Phila., Penn., 1959).

CHAPTER XXVI

EDUCATION

I. INTRODUCTION

EVERY current of the times, whether intellectual, social or political, had its impact on education. It is in the nature of education that this should be the case, for the educational system of every society embodies and transmits the values, attitudes and norms of the society, hands on a body of tradition and knowledge and seeks to equip the new generation for what it may meet in the future. As an instrument both of conservation and of change, education is thus inevitably affected by changes in social structure, by new bodies of knowledge, by changing technology and by changing social and intellectual attitudes.

The outstanding influence on education in the twentieth century was change itself. In a world where changes of all sorts came at a staggering rate, education was forced to serve more as an instrument to facilitate and cope with change and could not function mainly as an institution for conserving and perpetuating old ways. This was most clearly apparent in the societies which were undergoing conscious revolution, where education was used as a deliberate means of carrying through revolutionary objectives, as in the USSR, Turkey and the new states of former colonial peoples. But science and technology were remaking all societies during this period, while shifts in world power and changing social patterns cast all manner of people in new roles. Rapid change was the basic factor in educational development in virtually every country in the world.

The central component of the changes which directly affected education was science and its application, both as the spread of the scientific attitude affected the objectives and methods of education, and as science constantly augmented the body of knowledge which it was the task of educational institutions to transmit. Pedagogy itself became a field of scientific study; the fruits of scientific research in biology, psychology, sociology and anthropology provided new bases for many educational procedures; the range of devices available to the educator was immensely increased by new techniques of communication. Modern education had to develop individuals with inquiring minds and with a scientific outlook toward life in terms of which to respond to the new experiences and new knowledge which they were bound to meet. And it had to transmit ever growing bodies of knowledge in the natural sciences and in wide areas of social, anthropological, archaeological and historical inquiry, not only as theoretical knowledge but in relation to a vast and complex range of applications.

In broad terms it may be said that education in the twentieth century was extended and redesigned to meet the requirements of industrial society.

As industrialism spread, no areas remained free from its imperatives and no people could persist without its tools. The twentieth-century individual required a kind of training which would enable him to grow with the times, to shift his job, to recast his thought, to modify habits relating to food, health, child-rearing, to understand and cope with new social situations, to establish new relationships, to absorb the impact of mass communication. Less and less of what he had to have could be provided by parental instruction and practical apprenticeship.

Every country, from the most highly industrialized to those just embarking on industrialization, needed a public equipped with knowledge, skills and the capacity to handle new information and ideas; all needed an expanding supply of technicians, experts and professionals at all levels and in all fields of human endeavour. Neither mass literacy nor the traditional training of the liberally educated *élite*, nor any combination of these, could meet the demand for engineers, mechanics, nurses, aircraft pilots, managers and thousands of other occupations which rested upon specialized knowledge and skill; nor could they keep a country abreast of the scientific developments of the age. The educational systems of all countries were subjected to tremendous pressure for a great variety of training for more and more people.

The needs of industrial societies for trained personnel were paralleled and reinforced by the needs of democratic states for educated citizens. As democracy in the traditionally democratic states came to embrace all the people and as democratic principles spread to other parts of the world, education inevitably followed in the wake. The educational requirements of workers and peasants, women, racial minorities and others once regarded as of the 'lower orders' changed with changing aspirations and status, from those which would have been sufficient if these people had 'kept their place' to those due to them as equal citizens of a democratic society. National self-assertion redefined the educational needs of 'backward peoples'. In the twentieth century education came to be regarded as the birthright of all the people—as much education as they could absorb and as society could manage to provide.

The main responsibility for the ever expanding volume and range of education designed to reach more people for longer periods, and in greater variety, rested on the state, by reason of the state's expanding functions and its expanded power. Among the first responsibilities of the welfare state was the provision of education for its citizens. In addition education was one of the most direct ways by which the state, with its enlarged powers and intensified national objectives, could achieve its aims. This relationship was clearest in the countries experiencing revolution or seeking rapid economic development. But education bore a close relation to the aims and purposes of the state in other countries as well, both those with highly centralized educational systems such as France, and those with local administration of education such as the United States.

The impact of these factors brought common trends in educational practices throughout the world, however different the cultural background, level of economic development, political system or class structure might be. Education spread to the masses of the people, including women. There was a universal tendency to lengthen the term of schooling for each child, until secondary and even some form of higher education also became, in many places, accessible to broad segments of society. The costs of education mounted steadily as years in school were increased, the pay of teachers was raised, and costly buildings, laboratories, libraries and other equipment came to be required. There was a world-wide trend to professionalize the task of the educator, to equip the teacher with special training in educational methods in addition to a knowledge of his subject, and to study the educative process systematically with a view to providing the educator with scientifically based knowledge as part of his professional equipment.

In line with the demands of industrial society, the purposes of the state and new insights into the processes of learning, there was a trend to bring the content and methods of education closer to life experience and to give a more practical cast to school activity. Education tended to be concerned with the total development of the child, to enlarge its scope to take in every facet of his growth, and to view the educative process less in terms of the information to be imparted than of the individual as a person and his ability to function in the society of which he was a part.

Everywhere there was a tendency for education to extend beyond the child in the classroom, both to encompass extra-curricular activities during his school years, and to continue the educational process in later life; further education of youth and adults became part of the educational programme of nearly every country, whether in the form of fundamental education, workers' education, adult education, university extension, correspondence courses or training and retraining on the job.

The democratization of education narrowed the traditional gulf between the possessors of knowledge and the ignorant masses and opened the door to large-scale vertical social mobility. In so doing it both aroused and sustained the aspirations of people toward individual and social change. Mass education also provided a mass audience for literature and the arts and for the mass media, thereby affecting the level and quality of literary and artistic expression. While it offered the means of developing an informed citizenry, it also provided a channel for the indoctrination of people by centralized states.

Education during these years tended to produce a multitude of people equipped with much, but often fragmentary, knowledge drawn from beyond their direct experience. As a result societies came to be composed of a great mass of semi-informed people instead of a small *élite* highly endowed with learning and a basic population equipped by practice and example to deal primarily with the concrete content of their daily lives.

These world-wide trends were not without counteracting tendencies which left unresolved many issues of educational theory and practice. In fact there was scarcely a country in the world at mid-century where education was not a central public issue and where questions of objectives, methods and costs were not the object of intense discussion, study and often controversy as nations and communities sought ways to equip their rising generations to live in the modern world.

Though the trend was to recognize and use the educational system as a means of adjusting to or furthering change, more or less strong elements in many countries resisted the trend and sought to emphasize the conservative function of education as the preserver of traditional values and knowledge. In view of the rapidity of technological and social change during this half-century, it is perhaps as remarkable that educational systems in Europe, the Americas and Asia changed so little in structure, content and method as that they changed so much.

There were counter-trends, too, to the tendency to incorporate scientific materials and a scientific attitude and to expect the educational system to meet the needs of industrial society. In particular the tendency to introduce vocational material into general education was strongly resisted by those who insisted that this subordinated the spiritual, moral and intellectual development of the child to material objectives. Such resistance was especially strong in those societies which placed a relatively low value on action as compared with philosophical thought; educators in the Latin American countries liked to contrast their societies with North America on this score and to attribute to this difference in value systems the lesser tendency to include practical content or methods in their schools.

Nor was the trend toward the democratization of education equally strong everywhere, or unopposed. Where feudal or quasi-feudal relationships and attitudes survived, as they continued to do in Spain and in parts of Latin America and the Middle East, mass education was at best a matter of indifference on the part of the controlling element in society; at worst it was flatly opposed. The persistence of very high rates of illiteracy in many of the Latin American countries up to the middle of the twentieth century is to be explained, at least in part, on this score. In conservative Muslim countries the negative attitude toward mass education was particularly strong with regard to women. The virtual prohibition of the education of women outside the home which continued in Saudi Arabia into the 1950s was an extreme example of this counter-trend. Colonial powers, too, through most of the period were indifferent or opposed to education for the mass of their subjects, though a movement for general education in some of the remaining colonial areas developed after the second world war, building on earlier voluntary efforts which had originated in the metropolitan countries.

The trend toward state responsibility for education also did not go un-opposed. The most effective and organized opposition came from religious bodies which claimed the right and responsibility for educating the young. Of these the Roman Catholic Church was most vigorous,[1] but there were some challenges to secular education from other Christian denominations and from Buddhist and Muslim sources. Less formal opposition, primarily to the mono-poly of education by the state, came from groups and educators who rejected the idea that the interests of society were paramount over those of the indivi-dual and who feared the use to which the omnipotent state might put the educational system were it completely in its hands.

The common educational trends brought common problems throughout the world which remained unsolved during these years. The most practical of these were the cost of education and the difficulty of finding and training teachers fast enough to keep pace with the growing demand. Where expansion was relatively slow and where resources were many and the backlog of edu-cated persons available for teaching was large, these problems were least severe. But in the years after the second world war pressures from mounting birth rates and from the expansion of mass education at the secondary level brought crises in many educational systems. Even in the richest and most economically developed countries, alternative demands upon the public treasury and alternative fields of employment made the problem of school financing and recruitment of teachers very real. At the opposite extreme, these problems were critical and acute in the new states which were pressed by the circumstances of their establishment and the nature of the times to develop with great rapidity both a literate population and a sufficient body of educated and trained people to advance their society.

The expansion of education and the tendency to make it universal at higher and higher levels brought a major pedagogical problem of how to combine quality with quantity—how to preserve a high quality of intensive education for the professionals and scholars, who once were the only candidates for education above the primary level, while extending educational opportunities to large numbers of students whose academic interests were less strong, in-tellectual capacity was often more limited and educational needs were different. There was widespread complaint that standards had been lowered, though few doubted that the best students were as good as the limited group which had once constituted the entire student body.

Educators struggled everywhere with the problem of how best to combine the two processes of mass and intensive education, from the point of view both of pedagogical effectiveness and of the disposition of available educational resources. Like the practical difficulties of educational costs and recruitment of teachers, this problem was especially acute in the countries which had to use limited resources to cope simultaneously with mass illiteracy and the need to train highly qualified personnel. In these countries it was further complicated by the additional problem of language, for the vernacular which served as the vehicle for mass education could not give access to advanced bodies of knowledge, and higher levels of education had to be carried on in a foreign tongue.

Beyond the pedagogical problem of how to balance mass education with the training of an educated *élite* was the intellectual problem arising from the presence of the half-educated. Intellectuals could no longer monopolize the realms of thought and expression, for they found themselves confronted by those whom they could not continue to ignore but who yet did not belong to their old world. Whether this was a source of lament or congratulation depended upon the outlook. The Spanish writer, Ortego y Gasset, representing the aristocratic intellectual tradition which was nowhere stronger than in his native Spain, deplored what he called the *Revolt of the Masses* (1932) as a degrading, levelling-down influence which substituted for independent rational thought the tendency to follow emotional impulses and to accept uncritically the ideas of others. But from another point of view it was a levelling-up, and it provided a new mass base whose potentialities were yet to be fully revealed.

The common trends and problems in education took distinct forms in different educational systems, and these systems in turn varied in importance during the twentieth century according to their influence and the numbers of people affected by them. The British and French systems were extensively followed outside Britain and France. The general British pattern prevailed throughout the British commonwealth and its dependencies; the London Matriculation examination, for example, was widely used as a university entrance or school finishing examination. French education not only was applied to French residents and 'assimilated' natives in the areas of French domination, but was a model for much of the education developed in the Middle East. The German system was influential throughout eastern Europe, and during the early years of the century German institutions, especially in technical and scientific fields, attracted students from abroad and provided a pattern for the technical institutions of several countries. The educational system of the United States embodied and emphasized many of the trends which were general during the first half of the twentieth century, and the influence of some of its leading educators and pedagogical institutions was felt in many parts of the world.

By the middle of the century the educational system of the Soviet Union was attracting widespread attention, for the USSR offered the outstanding example of a country which had made a well-supported educational programme one of the pillars of its national development; it had rapidly overcome mass illiteracy and had trained very large numbers of persons at all technical and scientific levels.[2] For the countries still facing the dual problems of mass illiteracy and the need of rapid economic development, the educational methods employed by the Soviet Union held special interest. General interest also attached to the developing systems of both India and the Chinese People's Republic, for together these countries comprised roughly a third of mankind, and the distinctive manners in which they were meeting the problems of modernizing their vast populations could not fail to be of concern to the rest of the world.

It would not be possible in the pages which follow to delineate the separate developments in these and the many other distinctive national systems. The educational experience of particular countries will therefore be considered only as illustrative of broad developments common to many places.

II. EDUCATION AT THE OPENING OF THE TWENTIETH CENTURY

The main framework for twentieth-century education was already in existence at the opening of the century and it must therefore be reviewed in order that the changes during these years may be understood.

1. *Extent*

At the opening of the century the idea of universal, free and compulsory elementary education was generally accepted as an objective in western countries, and literacy had been achieved for the majority of the people of northern and western Europe, North America, New Zealand and Australia. It had been adopted as an objective which was well on the way toward fulfilment in Japan, and to a lesser degree in eastern and southern Europe. But even where the principle was most fully accepted many practical obstacles stood in the way of its implementation.

Universal education sprang from the need of industrial society for a literate population and the conviction in the countries committed to democratic principles and representative government that an informed citizenry was essential to the effective functioning of that system. In countries where Protestantism predominated, the need to be able to read the Bible or religious texts had stimulated the establishment of common schools before the demands of industry added a secular motivation. Universal education was generally added to an older system designed for an educated *élite* who made up the liberal professions, the priesthood, the scholars, administrators and men of cultivated tastes.[3]

Among western countries national systems of education, well-developed by the opening of the century, provided the educational structure for their respective populations and had begun to influence other parts of the world through colonial administrations, missionary efforts or cultural impact. The systems of Great Britain, France and Germany followed similar but distinct lines while that of the United States differed in basic structure; educational institutions maintained in many lands by the teaching orders of the Roman Catholic Church adapted their special point of view and method to a variety of local conditions.

In the British and continental European systems, mass education and education for the *élite* were separately organized and followed separate lines. An elementary system, generally state supported, led to a terminus usually at the end of six years; in some countries, notably in Germany, Holland and Russia, students completing the primary school could receive additional technical or commercial education in special schools. A system of secondary schools, overlapping the primary system and generally charging fees, led to the university.

The two systems were based upon and perpetuated class differences, for while elementary education was available to all who lived within reach of a school and was generally free and compulsory, secondary education was available chiefly to those who could pay. Determination of whether or not the child would enter the secondary system was usually made at the age of 10 or 11 years or even earlier. University education was enjoyed chiefly by those prepared in fee-charging schools, sometimes privately supported, especially in the case of those attending the older British universities. Some exceptional students, however, were able to secure higher education in all these systems and some of those who later became leaders of social change had taken advantage of such opportunities.

In contrast to the European, the American system was a single continuous structure of free education from primary to secondary and university years. Without either the intellectual class or the aristocracy of Europe, with a strong Protestant tradition and a frontier society, the United States relied heavily on this open system of public education to realize its goals of republican government, national progress and individual opportunity, and to serve as a melting pot for the children of its immigrants from many lands. How far the individual was able to go through the system depended in part on his financial ability to stay out of the labour market and to receive family support during the years of his secondary and higher education; but ambitious students were expected to work their way through school and college, earning money from any job, however menial, which they might be able to secure.

Private fee-supported schools and universities existed alongside the publicly supported institutions, enjoyed prestige and were patronized by those who preferred what they had to offer and possessed either financial means or the exceptional qualities which commanded scholarship aid. For children in rural areas, schooling was often less available or extensive than for urban children, and in the southern states Negro children attended separate and generally inferior schools. Yet the principle of general education, democratically available to all, had been adopted as a guide to educational development in the United States.

The Latin American countries, on the other hand, followed the traditional European system of education for an intellectual élite. Only a few, notably Argentina and Chile, had begun to add the concept of mass education.

Education of adults as well as of children was already a recognized part of the educational systems of western countries at the opening of the century. Mechanics' institutes had grown up in many countries in response to the impact of industrialization in the middle of the nineteenth century, and although these had lost some of their vogue, workers' education movements, closely related to the growing trade unions, were beginning to take shape. All manner of informal educational programmes reflected the widespread desire of people to pursue educational interests during their adult years, through correspondence schools, university extension classes, such forms of popular education as summer camp meetings, lecture circuits and reading circles, and a growing number of public libraries which catered to the general reader rather than to the scholar. In the United States, where great numbers of immigrants presented the double problem of illiteracy and ignorance of the local language and culture, night schools had been organized in major cities.

By the opening of the century the educational principles, practices and, frequently, the personnel from western Europe and North America were penetrating to other parts of the world. In Japan universal elementary education along western lines, first modelled on French and then on German patterns adapted to Japanese objectives and cultural norms, was 'designed to give children the rudiments of moral education and of education especially adapted to make of them good members of the community, together with such general knowledge and skill as are necessary for practical life'.* A limited system of middle schools and of higher schools for boys led to the university.

In the largely non-literate areas of the Middle East, Asia and Africa, well-established missionary schools and some institutions provided by colonial administrations were offering a western type of education for a growing westernized *élite*. Colonial powers in the main furnished such education as they required for the administration of their dependencies. British educational activity was most extensive in India, where the government maintained some primary and secondary schools and subsidized others under missionary or private auspices. These schools went somewhat beyond their principal task of training for the civil service, for various technical government operations such as railways and irrigation systems and for the lower ranks in industrial establishments in India and nearby Burma. In Indo-China and north Africa French culture was being imparted to a segment of the population largely through Catholic mission schools. The Dutch administration of Indonesia, almost completely in the hands of Europeans, rested on a limited educational system designed primarily for European residents, the Chinese and Indo-European middle classes, and some members of the local aristocracy.

Missionary education, chiefly from Britain, France and the United States, was extensive in China and among the subject peoples of the Ottoman empire. In Korea it was modifying the position of women and introducing new knowledge and social ideas. French cultural influence was felt in the higher educational circles of Iran as well as in Syria, while the educated *élite* of Egypt and Turkey drew on French, British and German sources. Among the non-literate peoples of Africa, missionary education, far more limited than that which had become well established in Asia, was beginning to modify the outlook of some members of some African tribes and to provide a bridge to the outside world.

* Imperial Ordinance No. 215, relating to elementary schools, 1890.

Missionary and colonial education at the beginning of the century did not, however, represent mass education as did elementary education in Europe and America.

Nor were there widespread indigenous systems of education in these countries. Some traditional elementary education was provided by Buddhist monks and Hindu religious and charitable establishments. Quranic schools in Muslim countries offered a very limited form of education for boys, often confined to oral memorizing and reciting of the Quran text with such explanatory comments as the mullah might offer. For the rest, the rigorous training of the limited numbers of scholars, monks or priests in the traditional religious and classical learning of Confucian, Buddhist, Hindu or Muslim scholarship and devotion constituted the prevailing form of education, apart from the training provided to apprentices in the shop and children in the home. Each of these systems produced a small key group of literati. The Chinese system of classical scholarship was the most noted, providing as it did for access to civil and military posts through examinations on classical subjects open to any man who could acquire such knowledge. At the turn of the century this examination system was abolished, the University of Peking was established (1898) along western lines, and students were returning from study in Japan and the United States imbued with western educational concepts.[4]

2. Auspices and financing

The principle of state responsibility for the provision of at least basic education had been generally accepted in western countries during the nineteenth century. A large proportion of schools, however, remained under religious auspices. In Europe the state's educational obligations were largely fulfilled through confessional schools, as in the Scandinavian countries with an established church where state schools were confessional or in Germany where the majority of state school inspectors were members of the clergy. Britain and the Netherlands maintained an integrated system of state schools and religious schools which received state aid. In the Austro-Hungarian empire the state supported schools of different denominations, as well as schools for segments of the population using different languages.

Only France among European countries maintained a wholly state-supported and publicly controlled system after the secularization laws of 1882; the suppression of the religious orders in 1905 substantially reduced the number of schools in the voluntary system of Catholic education which functioned independently. In the United States the constitutional principle of the separation of church and state was the basis for a wholly state-supported and state-controlled system of public education, but privately supported schools were permitted and large numbers of denominational schools existed without public support. In colonial areas, with the partial exception of India and Indonesia, education was provided chiefly through religiously administered schools, with or without state support.

In line with the claim of the Roman Catholic Church that education of its communicants is the responsibility of the Church and that it is the duty of Catholic parents to send their children to church schools, Catholic schools were to be found in all countries where there was a substantial Catholic population. In the Iberian peninsula and Latin America, where the population was predominantly Catholic and the state had assumed little independent responsibility for education, Catholic schools provided the principal or sole educational system; elsewhere they flourished, with or without state support, in proportion to the size of the Catholic population and the vigour of the prevailing interest in education. Catholic schools, maintained by Jesuits and other teaching orders, were designed to provide an education infused with religious doctrine and a religious outlook, but they followed local educational patterns in respect to the secular content of instruction. Although several Protestant denominations also maintained educational institutions, especially at advanced levels—witness the multitude of denominational colleges in the United States—they rarely sought to enrol all their followers except where they constituted, in fact, the state system.

3. *Teachers*

In order to supply teachers for the large number of schools required for universal elementary education, teacher training had been systematically organized in western countries. Each of the northern and western European systems provided for two distinct groups of teachers, drawn from and fed back into the elementary and secondary school systems respectively. In the United States, too, in spite of the absence of the two-system structure for pupils, elementary school teachers were trained in normal schools patterned on those for European elementary teaching, while secondary school teachers, as in Europe, were usually drawn from the universities.

4. *Content and method of education*

The objectives and consequently the content of education in the several western systems at the opening of the century were far from uniform, but they followed certain common lines. In all the European systems primary education was designed to provide the basic tools of literacy and ability to compute which had become essential for an increasingly urban society, and to impart in addition such attitudes and skills as each country's educational organizers deemed essential. In the main the secondary and higher educational systems passed on a traditional body of classical learning, though there was a strong and growing movement for acceptance of science and modern languages on a par with classical studies. Universities prepared chiefly for the liberal professions and the responsibilities of government.

Within this general pattern emphasis and structure varied. In Great Britain the elementary schools provided the basic tools for living in an industrial society while secondary and higher education were designed to train persons to a level of high competence, largely through humanistic studies, thus equipping them to enter the flexible and responsible civil service and to pursue the arts and professions. French education, highly centralized and formalized, provided uniform, rigorous minimum training in and knowledge of French language and culture, with competitive access to higher levels of classical academic study and specialized advanced instruction, limited by posts open or expected to be open to those completing various degrees. The German and Russian systems offered vocational and technical training to those not entering secondary and higher schools, and thorough training for research in a chosen field to the intellectual *élite*. The open school system of the United States still furnished a predominantly classical education beyond the elementary years, but it had begun to accept the elective principle and to offer a variety of content in line with the wide range of students' interests and society's needs.

Prevailing methods of elementary education relied heavily on learning by rote and made little effort to adjust to the individual capacity or needs of the children, although a body of education theory, notably the work of Pestalozzi, Froebel and Herbart, had been developed during the nineteenth century to support such an approach.

Universities everywhere served as centres of traditional learning and of preparation for liberal professions, but technical institutions offering courses of university grade in agriculture and engineering had been established in Europe and North America.

III. EXTENSION OF EDUCATION AS A MASS PROCESS

During the twentieth century mass education was extended everywhere, at secondary and higher levels in countries of advanced industrial development, at elementary levels in the rest of the world, and everywhere for adults who needed to keep pace with constant change. In every part of the world more and more people received more and more education, systems for providing formal education grew in size and complexity, and education absorbed an increasing proportion of the wealth, energy, time and personnel of the community.

The pattern in each country depended on various factors: the cultural traditions of the country, its changing social system, the degree of industrialization, the economic resources available for educational expansion, the extent to which the society was dedicated to the principle of equal opportunity, and the determination with which the country was consciously pursuing economic development and sought to use education as a tool in this process. The extension of education thus reflected both the needs of the individual and the needs of society.

Much of the history of educational development in the twentieth century involved the interrelation between the systems designed for mass education and those for training an educated *élite*. The ever mounting demands of industrial society called for a constant increase in knowledge and competence on the part of the masses of the people. The problem of how to meet these quantitative, practical needs while still developing intellectuals of high quality was present in one form or another in virtually every country, at every stage of educational development and in respect to every aspect of education.

1. *In countries of high literacy*

(*a*) *Democratization of secondary education.* For countries which had already achieved a base of universal elementary education by the opening of the century, extension of mass education meant expansion at the secondary level until education beyond the elementary stage was envisaged or achieved for the whole population. In these countries a combination of the increased productivity of industrialized labour and a decline in the ratio of children to adults in the population made child labour unnecessary and provided the resources to support children during adolescence and to finance their schooling. As it became less possible for the uneducated to function effectively, parents demanded more education for their children to enable them to make their way in the world.

In the United States the single, continuous school system, based on the principle of equal opportunity for all and the development of the individual to his fullest capacity, could be readily expanded at the secondary level. High school enrolment grew by leaps and bounds, until it embraced the great majority of the adolescent population. In one state after another, the compulsory school age was raised to 16 until by 1950 all the forty-eight states required attendance to that age and ten had higher requirements. By the opening of the second world war secondary education in the United States had become mass education. In 1952, 82 per cent of the children between the ages of 14 and 17 were attending school.

European countries took various steps to increase the number of students receiving education at the secondary level and they modified their separate systems for mass and *élite* education in the process.

In the first quarter of the century and especially after the first world war there were strong movements in each of the European countries to make a longer period of general education available to all, to provide additional technical education at the secondary level, and to make it possible for children to advance from one level to another and to higher education without having the door closed and the child's future finally determined at 10 or 11 years of age. It was only after the second world war, however, that elementary and secondary systems were more closely integrated and that efforts were made to provide a range of educational opportunities which would fully utilize the capacities of all the children and would make it possible for them to advance through the system without regard to their economic and social status. At mid-century the trend in this direction was very marked; by 1950 some 50 to

80 per cent of the children between 14 and 17 were attending school in all the west European countries except Spain, Portugal and Italy.

In the Scandinavian countries middle school education was made widely available; Denmark in 1937 adopted the principle of 'secondary education for all' for its urban schools and made the middle school an automatic continuation of the elementary system. Great Britain enacted legislation in 1918 raising the school-leaving age as soon as facilities could be made ready, establishing continuation schools, and providing increased grants to finance secondary education. As a result secondary education for both boys and girls expanded sharply, as did university education, but it was not until after the second world war that the new school leaving age of 15 years was made compulsory. Under the British Education Act of 1944 which provided for three types of secondary education—academic, technical and general—the child usually chose his course at the age of 11, but there were opportunities for transfer from one course to another on the basis of interest and quality of performance.

In France there was a strong though unsuccessful agitation after the first world war for the establishment of *l'école unique*, a common, single school system in place of the separate free elementary schools and fee-charging secondary schools. Passage from the elementary to the secondary system was facilitated when the curricula of the overlapping last years of the primary and the first years of the secondary schools were made more similar. School fees were finally abolished in 1933, though the two systems remained under separate administrations. The German Weimar republic established a single *Grundschule* for all children—though with separate, state-aided Protestant, Catholic and Marxist units—and provided financial aid to promising students so that their choice of further education would not depend on financial status.

None of these measures, and similar steps taken by other European countries, fully democratized European education, nor did they wholly discard the basic two-part structure or make secondary education as completely mass education as in the United States. But they did reflect a common trend in this direction.

The Japanese system, in which attendance up to the sixth year was made compulsory in 1907, followed the European pattern of mass elementary education, with access to higher education only for boys who could attend the limited number of higher preparatory schools. After the second world war the Japanese system was recast and followed the American model of continuous progression from bottom to top according to the capacities and interests of the individual, with a resultant great increase in secondary school and university enrolment.

With the momentum of Soviet development, the USSR expanded all aspects of its educational programme at a dramatic rate. Inheriting a European-type two-track system in which mass education reached only a fraction of the population, it created a single, basic general school system, made four years compulsory in 1930, seven years for urban children in 1947, and eight years of general polytechnic training for all in 1958. It insisted that only where all education is publicly supported can a system be considered democratic.

The number of pupils in general schools more than trebled in the dozen years between the launching of the first five-year plan and the outbreak of the second world war. In addition institutions offering technical training and those for higher education were enormously increased and every sort of facility was offered to adults to increase their training or to make up past deficiencies—through trade unions, factories, night schools, correspondence courses, special schools to enable those who had failed to receive regular schooling to enter institutions of higher education. The Soviet government estimated at mid-century that one out of every four persons in the entire population was going to school at least by correspondence.5

(b) *Extension of higher education.* After the second world war higher education also began to take on the character of mass education, most conspicuously in the United States. The provision of educational benefits to war veterans, including subsistence while studying for as many years as the veteran had been in military service—usually four—brought higher education to many thousands who would have terminated their education at an earlier stage.

None of the European systems went as far as the American in opening education at the top to large numbers, but university enrolments increased by as much as 50 per cent or even 100 per cent over pre-war levels and specialized higher-level institutions continued to be established. Access to higher education, moreover, ceased to be limited primarily by ability to pay or to attend fee-charging preparatory schools and became increasingly dependent on ability to compete successfully for stipends awarded to the abler students.

University-level education in Japan, which had been expanded markedly after 1918, was still further enlarged in the reorganization after the second world war. Educational expansion in the Soviet Union included a great multiplication of institutions of higher education, and a similar situation existed in the people's democracies of eastern Europe.6

(c) *Adult and informal education.* Mass education was also extended to adults. In a world where new knowledge was continually opening up and new occupations were becoming available, people did not outgrow either the need or the desire to go on learning when they left school or university. Schools offered night classes and universities conducted extra-mural, extension and correspondence courses to meet the demand. Mounting numbers of people continued their general education from the point where their formal schooling left off, or studied to prepare for a new or better paid occupation, or to bring themselves up to date in their own field. Many large employers, whether in industry or government, offered in-service training to enable their employees to advance. In some countries special programmes of vocational rehabilitation offered retraining to persons whose skills were made obsolete by technological change or who were prevented by accident or disease from continuing in their original occupation.

HH*

Workers' education in a number of countries helped workers to function more effectively as trade unionists and citizens. In co-operation with schools and universities, trade unions developed educational programmes for their members which included economic and social subjects, labour history and trade union methods. Some special schools for workers were set up, either independently or in connection with educational institutions. Workers' education associations, notably in Britain, Sweden and the United States, developed educational methods and materials, sponsored courses, and provided leadership for the workers' education movements. As labour gained political power and community influence, the content of workers' education programmes was expanded to equip their students for greater responsibility. The folk high school, developed in Denmark in the nineteenth century as part of the movement for national regeneration, spread to neighbouring countries, offering the village young men and women intellectual and cultural stimulus, social experience and economic perspective.

Programmes of social and civic education reached many other adult groups, through community forums conducted by educational institutions or organizations, and through countless study groups organized by voluntary associations such as the British Women's Institutes, Canadian film groups, or reading circles organized by libraries.

Any discussion of the extension of education would take a very narrow view if only formal education were included. An enormous amount of education was carried on, consciously and incidentally, through the many organs of mass communication to which the twentieth-century citizen was exposed. In most countries radio was regarded and consciously used as an educational tool; where it was operated commercially, as in the United States, Canada and Latin America, its programmes designed for entertainment were embellished by many educational features. The same was true of the cinema and television. The daily press and the weekly or monthly magazines offered information and instruction on a very wide range of subjects. News, entertainment, political propaganda, even advertising, played an important part in the education of twentieth-century man.*

2. *In countries of high illiteracy*

(a) *Extension of basic education.* Outside the United States, Europe, the British commonwealth, the USSR and Japan, mass education spread slowly before the second world war and with great rapidity and intensity thereafter. In the 1920s and 1930s Mexico and Turkey followed their revolutions with determined efforts to bring schools to their largely rural populations, and Egypt started to put its primary education on a mass basis.

Mexico centred its programme on the development of realistic rural education; it also modified its urban schools to make them more practical and less verbal, and established a variety of technical and vocational schools at all

* See Chapters XI, Communications, and XXVII, Use of Leisure.

levels. Rural cultural missions, composed of specialists in public health, agriculture, construction, trades, industries, rural mechanics, music and recreation, focused on the improvement of rural life and foreshadowed the many similar rural programmes developed in other countries two decades later. Serving first as travelling institutes for cultural awakening and the training of practical rural teachers, the missions later became devices for community education. Through these and other educational efforts, Mexico succeeded in bringing its illiteracy rate down to 23 per cent by mid-century, although half the children were still without schools.

Other Latin American countries expanded their primary education—Argentina and Chile building on the base already laid at the opening of the century, Brazil making an effort to provide for the development of its wide territory, and small countries such as Uruguay, Costa Rica, Cuba and Panama gradually reaching a large proportion of their children.

But many obstacles stood in the way of the spread of mass education in a number of the Latin American countries. Political instability hampered the creation and continuous support of educational systems. The upper-class *élite* of landowners, merchants and intelligentsia supported private education for their own children and felt little necessity to assure schooling for all. In countries with large indigenous Indian populations the isolation of these groups and their language differences were additional deterrents. Where education was traditionally the responsibility of the Church, the impetus for state-supported education was often weak. A very strong literary tradition discouraged the development of practical types of training. Extreme poverty presented an ever-present problem.

By mid-century only a little over a half the children of primary school age in the Latin American republics were in school. Five countries—Haiti, Nicaragua, Honduras, Bolivia, Guatemala—reported two-thirds or more of their children out of school, and nine countries still estimated their illiteracy rate at over 50 per cent. Similar factors impeded the spread of mass education in the Iberian peninsula and, prior to the second world war, in southern Italy and some parts of eastern Europe.

In the colonial areas most of the administering powers followed a policy of substantial but limited expansion of educational opportunities, especially in later years as the demand for education mounted with growing self-consciousness. In the territories under British administration the usual pattern was elementary vernacular schools and English-language secondary schools, the latter leading to matriculation examinations for British or local universities. Especially in Africa, schools continued to be conducted largely by missionaries, with financial aid from the colonial government. French colonial education was patterned directly on that of France and produced a small colonial *élite* grounded in French language and culture. Belgium, after a period of almost complete neglect, introduced a programme of technical education in the Belgian Congo, conducted in the French language and designed to equip

Africans to participate at increasingly high levels of skill and responsibility in the industrial development of the area.

The Dutch in Indonesia, while still offering secondary and advanced education to relatively few non-Europeans, embarked on a popular education movement which involved translation into the vernacular of numbers of books and encouragement of literacy education; in addition, nationalist leaders and intellectuals inaugurated 'garden' schools to reach the Javanese people who were virtually without educational services and taught there with little or no pay. In the Philippines under American administration the 'community school' became the centre of social development. The system introduced by the Japanese in Korea was similar to that in Japan but on a more limited scale, and compulsory education was not put into practice. Education of Africans in Portuguese areas was very limited before 1940. Thereafter it was wholly entrusted to the Church, with state aid, while both state-operated and state-aided or supervised schools served the European and 'assimilated' local populations.

In most of these areas, education of an *élite* preceded mass education. The Belgian Congo offered a conspicuous exception, for basic education and practical training were extensively provided there before virtually any opportunity was offered to Congolese to acquire higher education. More typically, Britain followed the colonial policy of training a leadership group, leaving to a later stage the broadening of education among the masses of the people. This policy was clearly expressed at the close of the second world war when the British government, faced with rapidly mounting pressures for self-rule, established or enlarged eight universities in its colonial areas 'to produce men and women who have the standards of public service and capacity for leadership which the progress of self-government demands, and to assist in satisfying the need for persons with the professional qualifications required for the economic and social development of the Colonies'.*

In a number of countries there were special efforts to spread literacy among the adult as well as the child population. The experiments with methods for doing this which attracted widest attention had in common the idea that the spread of literacy cannot depend on the work of formal teachers alone, but must enlist the co-operation of any and every person who can read and write. In China Jimmy Yen inaugurated a literacy programme in the 1920s which used school children to teach groups of adults in after-school hours, and which stimulated group enthusiasm by singing and other activities. A former missionary in the Philippines, Frank Laubach, raised hopes that a short cut to literacy might be found, but his rapid method and programme of 'one teach one' proved superficial and ineffective, and his followers often left discouragement in their wake. The widespread efforts to conquer adult illiteracy made it fully apparent that the task was a complex and difficult one and that success was

* *Report of the Commission on Higher Education in the Colonies* (H.M.S.O., June 1945, reprinted 1954), p. 104.

closely linked with continuing use of the new skill; merely teaching people to read did not make them effectively literate.

The decade following the second world war was as revolutionary for education in areas of high illiteracy as the late nineteenth century had been for establishing the principle of universal elementary education in Europe, North America and Japan. For the vast populations of the newly liberated countries of Asia and the Middle East, for Africa and the aspiring peoples of Latin America, education became a magic formula for social reconstruction and for national self-realization.

Pressures for the spread of mass education were intense. Adult franchise, the need for new skills at all levels to achieve economic advance, and the world-wide idea that education was a basic right which every modern state must guarantee to its people, made universal education an inescapable imperative upon the new states. But it presented problems of staggering proportions. With their enormous backlog of illiteracy, with the majority of their children without access to school, and with the population growing by leaps and bounds each year, they had to expand educational facilities rapidly merely to prevent the situation from deteriorating.

The dimensions of the task could be seen in India where, in the decade after independence, the enrolment of primary school pupils virtually doubled, while admissions to technical schools increased fivefold and to engineering training threefold. This meant some fifteen million more primary pupils and an additional fifteen thousand technical students and six or seven thousand engineering candidates for whom teachers, buildings, books and equipment must be provided. But even an average expenditure per child of less than I per cent of the amount spent in the United States severely taxed the country's resources.

(b) *Balance between mass education and education of élite.* Even more than in the older democracies, moreover, the new states faced the problem of how much of their educational energy to devote to mass education and how much to the training of an educated *élite*, and how to balance educational efforts so that they would contribute in a sustained way to the total advance of the country. These countries urgently required a well-educated class to man the services and conduct the affairs of the state, and to provide the leadership for the economic and social development which would ultimately bring jobs, incomes and increased well-being for the masses of the people. In addition they had to train technical personnel and to develop men and women who could contribute to scientific advance, for without the capacity for scientific development they could only fall further and further behind as the scientifically advanced countries leapt further ahead.

But the problem of finding and developing professors who could assure high quality to the institutions of higher learning was even more difficult than to find and develop the resources for mass education. Local resources could be supplemented to some extent by personnel from abroad, but one of the chief sources of such personnel in the past, missionary education, became less acceptable. Most countries took steps to facilitate foreign study by promising students, and to make use of opportunities offered by national and international agencies. But these measures could only mitigate, not resolve, the problem of developing the scientific, technical and administrative leadership which they required. Traditional prejudices in favour of legal, literary or philosophical studies in preference to technical fields and ambitions for the career of an official rather than that of a technician further complicated the task of attracting and training personnel of high quality.

Egypt well illustrated the struggle to increase both *élite* and mass education when resources were limited and the need great. Egypt's western-oriented education derived from the institutions established by Mehemet Ali after 1836 to train engineers, doctors and other experts who would put the country on a footing with western powers, and from the fee-charging secondary and primary schools, conducted in French or English, set up to prepare students for these colleges. The education available to the masses consisted of instruction in the Quran and the Arabic language provided free by the mosques. When Egyptians took control of their own domestic affairs in 1923, they looked on education as the road to social reform and devoted increasing percentages of their national budget to improving both mass education and the training of specialists.

Successive Egyptian governments put their emphasis on different phases of the programme: one endeavoured to make available to all children six years of primary education on a level similar to that which had previously been open only to those who could pay the fees of the western-type preparatory schools; another accented the development of leaders and expanded secondary and higher education; still another focused on the creation of technical schools to reduce the pressure on secondary schools with an academic curriculum and to provide minor technicians. Primary school fees were abolished in 1944 and free school lunches and textbooks were also prescribed in the 1949 constitution. In 1951 the Egyptian parliament made primary education compulsory between the ages of 6 and 12.

In order to speed up the spread of schools and reduce costs, educational authorities appealed to notables in the provinces for donations of land and buildings. The number of children receiving primary education in government schools increased four and a half fold from 1925 to 1950 (222,761 to 1,030,486). By the 1950s the government was attempting to expand mass education above the primary level by establishing three-year higher primary schools offering practical studies—rural skills in the villages, industrial and commercial training in the towns—and technical schools at the secondary level for training assistant engineers and other technicians. From 1944 on it sponsored literacy campaigns to bring basic education to adults; landowners, factories, social centres, co-operatives, trade unions and benevolent societies organized classes designed to teach reading and writing, religion, and Egyptian national aims.

At the same time Egypt expanded and strengthened higher education for the training of specialists. In 1925, 8,059 boys and 41 girls were attending government secondary schools; by 1950 there were 80,957 boys and 12,810 girls. The number increased so fast that after 1949 entrance requirements were stiffened and scholarships were provided for able students who could not pay, in the effort to secure the best talent. At the university level the same expansion was in progress. The first university along modern lines, the University of Cairo, was established in 1925; by 1952 there were three modern-type universities with a fourth in the making, serving a total of 33,000 students, double the number enrolled in 1945.

Each country met the problem of balancing mass and *élite* education in its own way. While India was striving to meet its primary school needs, its university enrolments swelled to enormous proportions. It is perhaps an indication of the effort to move forward on both fronts that the ratio between students enrolled in institutions of higher education and those in primary schools in India and Egypt in 1950 was comparable to the ratio in European countries. In spite of their own great needs, both of these countries supplied teachers and technical personnel to other countries of Asia and Africa where the educated element was even less sufficient.

(c) *Fundamental education and community development.* One of the most distinctive developments of the years after the second world war was the approach to mass education of adults which was at first called 'fundamental education'. In contrast to the literacy movements of previous decades, which stressed learning to read for its own sake with little attention to the use which could be made of the new skill, fundamental education regarded literacy as a means rather than an end and concerned itself with vital learning directly related to daily life. The Mexican rural cultural missions furnished one of the models for the development of fundamental education programmes, but many other methods were used to put into effect the basic purpose of enabling people to learn to live better and the basic principle that in spite of a lack of formal education people can learn from materials which have real meaning for them and from experiences in which they are directly engaged.

Greatly stimulated by Unesco, which directed much of its energy toward developing this field, fundamental education brought to the masses of people outside the industrial areas basic modern principles of good health, good nutrition, good agriculture, family living, techniques of work and civic responsibility. Co-operative, self-help and community development activities provided learning experiences through community projects for construction, sanitation, soil conservation or child care. From one side of the world to the other, mass education in the form of fundamental education and community development reached non-literate rural people, modifying the outlook, spirit, health and competence of millions in Asia, Africa and Latin America and helping to canalize newly aroused vitality. Yet in large areas of the world illiteracy remained at mid-century a still unconquered problem.[7]

IV. ADMINISTRATION OF EDUCATIONAL SYSTEMS

1. *Auspices*

Support of mass education and consequently the control over education came more and more into the hands of the state. The trend reflected the expanding concept of the role and responsibility of the state, as well as the very practical consideration that only the state was in a position to finance the expanded educational programme which modern industrial society required. Where the state undertook the positive role of moulding its citizens, especially in countries involved in revolutionary change, education offered a major instrument to achieve defined objectives. In nearly all countries the extension of education by the state was seen as the fulfilment by the government of a responsibility which it owed to its citizens.

Countries differed considerably in the extent to which state-supported schools were administered directly by public agencies—either a central or a local authority—or were conducted by non-governmental agencies with support and a measure of supervision from the state. France maintained a highly centralized system in which every state school followed the schedule, syllabus and other details laid down in the state plan. The pattern in most democratic countries, however, tended to be one of administration either by a local public authority or by non-governmental bodies.

British local educational authorities had primary responsibility for administering the schools, within a general framework of school structure and advisory standards of teacher pay set by the central government. General education in the United States was the responsibility of local school districts acting through elected school boards, with the states setting standards and furnishing financial and technical aid and the central government providing only advisory services or assistance to special categories of students such as war veterans or to special programmes such as vocational and agricultural training. In the Netherlands the policy of leaving confessional or other groups free to conduct their own schools produced a system under which nearly two-thirds of the educational funds spent by the state for general education went to support schools which were privately administered and subject only to government inspection in respect to buildings, equipment, training of teachers and curriculum, and to government-administered examinations for government-conferred diplomas. Where privately supported schools maintained a separate existence without financial aid from the government, as in the United States, the mounting costs of education tended to make their position precarious.

The extension of state control in virtually every educational system did not go unchallenged. Religious bodies continued to regard education as their function and to assert the priority of their responsibilities *vis-à-vis* the state; the Catholic Church fought in every country which contained a Catholic population for the maximum authority over education which it was able to achieve.

In the first quarter of the twentieth century the general tendency toward secularization and the extension of state power and responsibility seemed to mark a trend away from religiously controlled education but, except in communist countries, the Church gained in influence over education in the second quarter of the century. After the second world war it made a determined bid for the restoration of public aid to religious schools, and succeeded in making the matter a live political issue in France and Belgium and in gaining concessions in the form of state funds for school health or school bus services even in the United States where the principle of separation of church and state was most strongly entrenched. In multi-religious societies such as Canada, the United States or the Netherlands the presence of religiously dominated education, with or without state support, tended to divide the society and to counteract the effect of the public schools as a 'melting pot' for the children of different backgrounds.

Religious control of education was an issue not only in the areas where the Catholic Church, and to a much lesser extent some of the Protestant denominations, asserted prerogatives, but in Muslim and Buddhist countries in relation to the schools maintained by the mosques and by the Buddhist monks. Since neither mosques nor Buddhist monasteries were in a position to provide the mass education required, however, and since they had traditionally taught only boys, they tended to become peripheral to a general system of state education.

2. *Financing*

Education became constantly more costly and harder to finance. As standards rose it was no longer sufficient to provide a poorly paid teacher in a bare room with only a blackboard, slates and a handful of books in order to have a school. The cost per child rose with the longer period of schooling, more individualized instruction and more elaborate equipment required by newer content and methods. For the total educational system, costs mounted through the increase in the number educated, the need for better prepared and therefore better paid teachers, rising standards of adequacy for buildings and equipment to keep pace with general technological change and standards of life, and the addition of services such as school health and feeding not formerly included within the scope of education. Where schools were consolidated into larger units in order to permit a wider range of educational offerings and more extensive equipment, costs of transport to and from school were also added.

In a few places elementary education continued to be financed by the parents of those who could pay and offered as charity to the poor. Religious schools were maintained by the various religious orders dedicated to teaching, with contributions from parents and other members of the parish or from donors to missionary efforts. But as school attendance was made compulsory, state financing of elementary education became general, for all except those who chose to avail themselves of private educational resources in preference to public. Where the financing of education depended on local resources, however, the poorer communities, even with greater than average effort, could offer to their children less adequate educational opportunities than those enjoyed in richer localities.

Before the first world war secondary and higher education in most countries was generally supported by fees and private endowments, supplemented by scholarships to permit able students to continue their education beyond the limits set by their family's means. In the United States, however, the publicly supported secondary schools and universities were providing education without charge to a growing proportion of the population.

After the first world war the problem of how to finance education became acute. The spread of secondary education required a more than proportionate increase in the investment of tax funds or private resources, for the need to provide more laboratory and library equipment and to pay higher salaries to teachers usually made secondary education more costly per pupil than primary. Where secondary as well as primary education came to be publicly financed, education became one of the largest items in the budgets of educationally advanced countries. Central governments were called upon to supplement the resources of poorer communities in order that children in those places should not be disadvantaged by the inability of the locality to afford the kind of education to which all parts of the country aspired. The issue of public support for religiously administered schools was intensified as the costs of providing education increased.

In virtually all countries after the second world war population increase placed additional strains on educational resources, both in the countries of relatively low birth rates where a sharp upturn in births brought unexpected millions to the school doors and in those whose rapidly increasing child population reflected increased rates of survival. Education had to compete with other items in the budget for national and local funds—with expenditures for physical or economic development, for the protection of health and safety, for social services and for military establishments.

3. *Supply and training of teachers*

The rapid increase in the volume of education outran the supply of teachers, both in countries which already had mass education at the opening of the century and those which were trying to achieve universal elementary education at mid-century. In addition the alternative opportunities for employment in expanding industry and government made it difficult in many places to hold teachers in the profession or to attract able people who could secure higher salaries in other lines of work. As a practical matter, throughout most of the world primary teachers were paid on about the level of unskilled workers, secondary teachers that of skilled workers, and university teachers no more than junior executives. In many countries it was particularly difficult to secure qualified teachers for rural areas because of low pay and lack of amenities in rural communities.

At the same time that additional teachers were needed and alternative employment opportunities were making recruitment difficult, the qualifications for teachers increased, making it harder to train an adequate supply. In teacher training institutions the trend was toward raising the professional level and expanding the content of training, because teachers required greater competence in order to cope with the wide range of new materials introduced into the school curriculum and to apply new knowledge of child behaviour and the learning process in skilful teaching.

Where the supply of teachers had to be expanded more rapidly than was possible through regular methods of teacher training, countries resorted to a variety of improvisations in order to meet immediate needs while preparing a more solid basis in teacher training for the future.

The Turkish programme for rural teachers offered an example of such improvisation. With schools in only about a tenth of its villages at the time of the Ataturk revolution, Turkey needed some 40,000 new teachers but was adding only about 400 a year through its regular normal schools. Since the success of its social revolution obviously depended upon bringing educational opportunities to the 75 per cent of the population which lived in villages, the Turkish government in 1936 evolved a scheme for using *eğitmen* to spread schools rapidly to rural areas.

Eğitmen were drawn from among peasants, usually with a primary education, who had distinguished themselves during their military service and had risen to the rank of sergeant. They were given an intensive eight-month course, taught by former village teachers and instructors from the School of Agriculture, to consolidate their knowledge of reading, writing and arithmetic and to give them some idea of history, geography, the sciences and teaching methods, together with theoretical and practical lessons in agriculture and building. Each *eğitman* was sent to a village of less than 400 population to teach a three-year primary school and also to help adult villagers with agricultural and building problems. He was supplied with a house, a strip of land, grain, machines, a loom and medicines and directed to teach by example as well as in classes and village meetings. By the use of *eğitmen* as a temporary expedient, the number of children in primary schools was doubled in ten years.

As a second step the Turks established rural institutes, set up like villages, for the general and practical training of rural teachers. In a five-year course, village young people with primary schooling were trained not only to teach in the classroom but to build their school, take care of its garden and its arable land as examples to the villagers, make the school's workshop of use to people of the village, direct the general education of the children and instruct them in health education, and to participate in various agricultural, artistic and technical projects designed to raise the economic and cultural level of the community. By 1952, 21 village institutes were training about 2,000 teachers a year to replace the *eğitmen* and extend the basic primary course to five years, and 55 per cent of rural children were attending primary school. After 1943 the institutes and the university offered an advanced three-year course to train inspectors whose duty it was to help rural teachers to keep in touch with new educational developments.

Since the greatest deficiencies in education were in rural areas, many countries concentrated especially on this aspect of teacher recruitment and training. Some followed the principle used in Turkey of recruiting rural young people who, it was hoped, would be willing to continue to work outside the cities. Egypt launched a programme of centres for rural services, including education, with adequate housing and other amenities and a large enough group of professional workers in various fields to provide some of the qualities of living found in the towns. The Organization of American States made an inter-American rural normal school, located in Venezuela, its major form of technical assistance in the field of education in the 1950s.

Institutions and methods for the training of teachers paralleled the development of the systems in which they were to operate. The tendencies toward democratization of education were reflected in steps to raise elementary school teaching to the level of a profession and in some efforts to break the closed circle of normal school training which prepared the products of elementary schools to teach in the elementary systems, while secondary schools were manned by university graduates. In some countries, such teacher training institutions were raised to higher levels, while some colleges and universities introduced courses to equip their students as teachers for the elementary schools.

At the beginning of the century the principal content of teacher training related to what to teach rather than how to teach. The development of educational theory and methodology brought a new emphasis on training teachers to understand the child and to design learning situations which would be in line with what was known of the process of learning. The specialized training institutions for primary teachers undertook to equip them with pedagogical methods, and to supplement the knowledge of subject matter which they had derived from their general schooling.

Teachers in secondary schools and technical institutions had been expected to be able to perform adequately if they had a command of their subject matter and in many places, notably in Latin America, this assumption continued. As pedagogical theories and techniques were elaborated, however, these were no longer thought important for elementary school teaching only, and special pedagogical training began to be given to secondary and technical teachers also. Where the shortage of teachers persisted, however—and it was widespread in the years of high general employment and expanding secondary and higher education after the second world war—the specialized training of teachers was hampered and teachers were often employed on the basis of emergency training or preparation below the standard which had been set.

The status enjoyed by the teacher had an important bearing on the successful performance of his duties and on the recruitment of people to the profession. Somewhat contradictory tendencies were to be noted in most countries in the first half of the twentieth century. On the one hand there was a trend toward giving greater professional status to the occupation of teacher, through higher qualifications and specialized training and through raising the level of teacher pay. On the other hand, as societies became more mobile and open, the teacher no longer enjoyed the prestige which had been his in a stratified society with few professions. Rising living costs which tended to mount faster than teachers' pay made it increasingly difficult for teachers to maintain the style of living which their position demanded, while industrial wages and salaries in other fields rose more rapidly and offered attractive alternatives in employment. In the United States, for example, the rapidly rising level of average manufacturing wages crossed the line of slowly rising teacher salaries in 1941 and the disparity continued to increase in the following years. In some fields, such as science and mathematics, the higher prestige of alternative occupations, along with higher salaries, accentuated the crisis in teacher recruitment.

The need for good teachers was the most pervasive of all problems in the school systems throughout the world.

V. CHANGING CONTENT AND METHOD OF EDUCATION

Along with increased schooling for more and more people went changes in the content and method of instruction. These changes involved: modernizing the curriculum to incorporate new bodies of knowledge or to direct education toward aspects of the modern world rather than the classical tradition of the area—Greek and Latin in the West, Arabic, Sanskrit or Chinese in their respective cultures; providing technical competence required by modern society; meeting the range of interest and capacities represented in a cross-section of the population; applying the results of pedagogical study and of psychological knowledge and theory as to individual growth and development; and carrying out the purposes of the state.

1. *Modernization of curriculum*

In the early years of the century European classical secondary education began to be supplemented by modern subjects, that is, by more study of modern languages and science and some social studies. The highly centralized French system, in which courses for each grade were prescribed, began to provide a course for 'modern' municipal secondary schools (*collèges*). In time the number of such modern schools grew, and modern content was introduced into the so-called 'classical' schools until by mid-century 40 per cent of the secondary schools were classed as 'modern'; the distinction had lost importance, however, for both classical and modern curricula were generally offered in both classical and modern schools.

Holland established modern high schools alongside the classical gymnasia, as did Germany also. After 1917, when the Dutch high school diploma was made a basis for taking university examinations, gymnasium and high school programmes overlapped. The classical gymnasium diploma was required for admission to the faculties of theology, literature and philosophy and the non-classical and non-scientific high school diploma gave access only to the faculties of economics or social science. But both the gymnasium and the high school offered a modern diploma admitting to the faculties of medicine, mathematics and physics, as well as law, economics and political and social sciences.

In other European countries traditional classical subjects were similarly supplemented or replaced by modern languages and literature, science and social studies. The trend was even more marked in the United States, where classical studies were crowded further and further aside both at the secondary and at the university level. By the 1940s few American universities still required a classical language for admission or for receiving a degree.

Outside the western culture area, modernization of education meant westernization as distinguished from such classical systems as the Chinese, Hindu or Muslim. The content of westernized education, however, generally followed the traditional academic lines of education in the metropolitan area. Schools in French-dominated territories received the same syllabuses from the ministry of education as those in France. Elsewhere schools designed to make it possible for students to attend metropolitan universities had to offer the classical subjects required for admission. The educational systems of independent non-western countries gradually developed curricula which combined the mathematics, science, modern languages and history characteristic of modern western schools with some traditional local elements, adapted to the current interests and needs of their people.

2. *Introduction of technical and vocational content*

The incorporation of technical, vocational and other practical content brought a more radical departure from tradition than did modernization. Germany led the way in the nineteenth century with the establishment of special technical schools at post-primary and higher levels. Some countries such as Holland developed a great range of special technical schools at elementary and secondary levels for many different fields: wood and metal trades, fishing and navigation, agriculture, commerce, fine and industrial arts, home economics, midwifery. Others such as the United States included a wider and wider range of technical and vocational material in the programme of the general school. Britain's educational reorganization after 1944 attempted to place technical secondary education on a par with general secondary education and academic grammar school training.

The rapidity of technological change complicated the problem of technical education. Although the number of occupations and professions requiring specialized training multiplied, techniques and skills learned in school were likely to become obsolete by the time that the child was ready to use them, or might cease to be useful in the course of his working life. While the schools were under strong pressure to teach techniques, educators agreed that what the modern urban child needed was a basic understanding of scientific principles, adaptability and the capacity to learn new ways and to respond to change. The introduction of an increasing number of technical subjects into general education was thus balanced by the tendency to make technical training more basic and less a matter of specific skills.

The inclusion of vocational content raised a question as to the purpose of education which divided the opinion of educators; was it the task of general education to provide the community with trained personnel and to equip children to earn a living when they became adult, or was its function to pass on the cultural heritage and to develop the individual's personality, capacity for growth, and social adjustment? Especially in the United States where the line between general and vocational education was less clearly drawn than in Europe, grave concern was expressed lest the educational system produce only competent technicians, not individually developed and socially aware personalities. In the USSR, on the other hand, practical training and experience in productive activity was regarded as essential to the aims of Soviet education, 'to develop versatile, active and conscious builders of a communist society.'*

3. *Adaptation of content to changes in student body*

As secondary education reached a wider segment of the population, its content had to be enlarged to correspond to the varied capacities, interests and objectives of the pupils. The concept of secondary education for all imposed on the schools a far more complex task than that confronted by schools which served a limited group selected on the basis of social status or intellectual level. Since all adolescents could not be expected to have intense intellectual interests, mass secondary education was virtually forced to include a broad range of subject matter. The presence of a majority of essentially non-intellectual pupils in the school population, moreover, tended to tip the scales in favour of the more practical subjects.

Some school systems met this situation by adjusting the whole programme to a cross-section of the school population, allowing room for flexibility and choice within it, as was usually the case in the United States. Others tried to provide separate programmes for distinct groups, divided according to capacity and interest. The British, after 1944, tried to select the intellectually inclined children on the basis of tests, school performance and interest and route them into grammar schools or grammar school courses in combined schools, preparatory for the university. Children who showed a mechanical bent or technical interest were routed into technical schools or courses. The majority of children were provided for in secondary modern schools in which the

* M. Deineko, *Forty Years of Public Education in the USSR* (Foreign Language Publishing House, Moscow, 1957), p. 8.

attempt was made to combine academic and practical subjects and to adapt programmes and methods to the variety of needs, interests and capacities of the students. In Holland, the problem of student diversity was met through the system of specialized technical institutions.

Within the various systems educational and vocational counselling was provided to help the individual choose from among the offerings in the light of his interests and talents and the likely opportunities for employment. Aptitude and personality tests were developed to help to give a basis for such counsel and to supplement the evidence from the child's performance in the classroom. Schools recognized, too, a responsibility to equip all students with social knowledge, regardless of their special field of training. The social content of all courses tended to be expanded to include psychology, human relations, social institutions, modern history and some knowledge of economics and government.

The extension of education to women raised the question of whether the content should be the same for them as for men. At the elementary level the tendency was to place boys and girls together in the same school with a common body of studies, although some separate schools for boys and girls continued, especially in Muslim and Roman Catholic areas. Even at the elementary level, however, schools which introduced practical activities and physical education had to resolve the question of whether girls should be taught to sew and cook while boys learned to handle tools and whether their physical training should be the same. At the secondary level the problem was sharpened by the inclusion of vocational subjects and material relating to daily life, such as home economics and child care. In school systems where variety and flexibility of courses was provided to meet the needs of a range of students, as in the high schools in the United States, such flexibility made it possible to offer subjects of special interest to boys or girls without excluding either from courses where the other sex predominated.

Universities followed the path of the secondary schools, expanding their fields of study in response to the increase in the number of students receiving university education, to the development of new areas of knowledge, and to the multiplication of professional fields requiring higher education. The traditional European university consisted of faculties of theology, law, medicine, philosophy and letters, and the natural sciences. British universities offered degrees in classics, law, modern history and literature, medicine and the sciences. American universities contained four-year liberal arts colleges with departments corresponding to each field of knowledge, plus graduate schools offering advanced degrees in these fields and professional schools for medicine, law, engineering and other professions. As subject matter was enlarged, European universities added new departments or whole faculties, such as psychology, sociology, economics, political and social science or engineering. British universities offered degree examinations in additional fields, and American universities established new departments both in academic areas and in applied fields such as home economics, business administration or public health. In addition separate technical universities or institutes specializing in the newer fields were set up in many countries.

The character of the university student body also changed and, like that of the secondary school, began to reflect the total society. Students who came from educationally limited homes often did not bring to their university study the richness of cultural background which had been the common property of former student bodies. Partly for this reason there was a tendency to broaden the liberal content in the education of engineers, lawyers, doctors or scientists, who would be called on to use their professional knowledge and influence in a social and cultural context which they needed to understand. As the number of women enrolled increased, they showed some tendency to concentrate in certain courses, but they were not excluded from less usual areas such as engineering, and a few women entered these fields even in places such as the Muslim or Latin American countries where the participation of women in many aspects of public life and employment was recent and limited.

At both secondary and university levels the diversification of content to suit a cross-section of the population and the need to reach average students as well as those of exceptional ability presented the problem of how to prevent the presence of large numbers of heterogeneous students from so diluting the quality of instruction as to keep the able few from developing their highest capacities.

Efforts to resolve the problem took various forms: special schools or classes, 'A-streams' for gifted children, acceleration of the best students through the system, the individualizing of instruction within a common classroom or school in such a way as to enrich the programme of the able student without setting him apart. Each of these approaches had its supporters and detractors. Some educators thought it desirable to separate intellectually superior children from the mediocrity and the distraction of their fellows and group them for mutual stimulation, while others insisted that segregation bred snobbery. Some wanted to encourage the bright child to go forward at his intellectual pace, but others objected that acceleration pushed the child beyond his social maturity. Some maintained that flexible, individualized teaching could bring out the child's full intellectual potentialities without sacrificing his democratic social development.

The immense variety of subject matter offered to students, moreover, presented what might be termed the problem of 'half-knowing'. Mass education exposed large numbers of people to a wide range of knowledge, but it could provide them with only a very partial and limited command of it. The proliferation of specialized fields virtually precluded the kind of integrated and comprehensive grasp to which intellectuals of the past had aspired. One of the most challenging problems brought by mass education was how to live with and interrelate fragmentary parts of the world's vast, increasingly complex body of knowledge.

4. Development and application of pedagogical principles

Changes in both content and method were dictated by developments in pedagogical principles and by the results of scientific study in fields related to learning.

Twentieth-century pedagogy followed the broad line of development marked out by the pedagogical pioneers of the nineteenth century—attention to the child as a learner. In the phrase familiar to all readers of text-books or treatises on pedagogy, the verb 'to teach' governs two accusatives: the subject matter, and the person taught. Following the lead of such influential writers and experimenters of the late eighteenth and the nineteenth century as Johann Heinrich Pestalozzi, Friedrich Froebel and Johann Friedrich Herbart, twentieth-century educators focused their attention on the second of these, the person taught. They brought to bear increasingly refined techniques of observation and tools of theoretical analysis in their efforts to understand the child's growth and development and the elements which enter into the learning process.

Some of the significant developments in educational method in these years grew out of work with handicapped children, for the attempt to meet the special needs of these groups led to an appreciation of the needs of normal children. This was true of the work of Maria Montessori who began her teaching with sub-normal children in Rome in 1898. She insisted that the child must be free to learn for himself, and she designed teaching materials from which the child could learn, with a minimum of interference, if he followed the activity which interested him. The principles of her system were widely adopted in many countries of Europe, especially for children of kindergarten age. The Belgian educator, Ovide Decroly (1871–1932) also developed his educational principles from his work with mentally defective children. He, too, built his educational method around the child's own interest, and sought to design learning opportunities and to identify centres of interest which could be pursued actively and practically in an informal atmosphere, and which were suited to the needs of the child at successive ages and to the differing needs of individuals.

The most pervasive principle of twentieth-century education, which affected methods within many different systems, was that education is not something apart from life but is, rather, life itself. Closely related to this principle, though resting on an independent psychological base, was the idea that learning is a total process, not merely something that goes on in the mind, and that learning by doing, or to satisfy an aroused curiosity, has more dimensions and a more enduring meaning for the learner than merely learning about something which he may use later in life.

The leading exponent of this view, probably the most widely influential educational thinker of the period, was the American pragmatic philosopher and educator, John Dewey. Dewey insisted that education is life, not merely a preparation for life, and that as long as growth continues education continues. The school in a democratic society—and he predicated his thinking on the principles of such a society—must itself be a democratic community where children may gain social experience. The modern child will continuously face new situations and problems throughout his life, and must therefore develop a problem-solving way of thinking. Believing deeply in human potentialities and the possibilities of human development, Dewey maintained that education must preserve and enhance the child's creativity, for as he grows he must select and reorganize his cultural heritage, recasting it to suit his needs in an ever-changing world.

The educational principles enunciated by Dewey were most congenial in countries such as his own United States which had a tradition of democracy and of continuous social change and which accorded high value to action as compared to thought or contemplation. But they made some inroads in most parts of the world, even where, as in Latin America, intellectualism was traditionally regarded as superior to practical sense, or in imperial Japan where society was highly structured and authoritarian.

Similar pedagogical theories which stressed the creativity, freedom and activity of the child, and which came to be known as 'progressive' or 'new' education, were developed by educators in other countries in the first quarter of the century, and these reinforced tendencies set in motion by Dewey and his followers. The Swiss educator Adolphe Ferrière sought to put the movement for 'activity' schools on an international basis by establishing the International Bureau of New Schools at Geneva in 1899. Bertrand Russell in England, with his concept of *Education and the Good Life* (1926), stressed the development of qualities of courage, vitality and sensitiveness, as well as intelligence, through a school in which the child could actively practise self-expression, engage in co-operative activities and take part in free discussion.

Such German educators as Berthold Otto (1859–1933) and Ludwig Gurlitt (1855–1931) rejected the formalism, coercion and standardization traditional in German education and sought to provide activity to stimulate the child's curiosity, as well as to introduce self-government into the school. The Viennese art teacher Franz Čižek demonstrated in his work with gifted children how the child's natural powers could be released through creative expression. His success reinforced the tendency to substitute the child's free expression for the teaching of formal techniques. Stanislas Shatsky (1878–1934) in the USSR converted the idea of activity for its own sake into the concept of socially useful labour and he stressed the relationship of the total and integral development of the child to the requirements of the society of which he is a part. Even within the centralized and formal system of French education, some experimentation was carried on under the stimulus of the New Education Society, organized in 1921 by Roger Cousinet to promote progressive education in France.

The wide spread of these pedagogical principles was reflected in the establishment of 'child-centred' experimental schools. Educational experimentation was of course not new, and the well-rounded personality had been familiar as an educational objective from the time of the Renaissance. The distinguishing feature of the experimental schools of this period, however, was the application to an unselected school population of the concept of the total development of the child, not merely of his intellect, the individualizing of each pupil, and the effort to develop his creative ability and emotional maturity through activity programmes carried out with a minimum of formal discipline.

The methods of progressive education and the principles ascribed to John Dewey, Maria Montessori and others, like any system, were subject to abuse in the hands of those who understood them only imperfectly or lacked the necessary skill to put them into practice. Some critics in fact insisted that these methods required exceptional qualities of sensitivity and creativity on the part of the teacher which the majority of teachers could not be expected to possess, and as such they were impracticable for application on any large scale. These critics insisted, too, that it was too much to expect of most children that they would be motivated by inner drives and interest, without such external stimuli as formal grades, competitive achievement, rewards for excellence and blame for failure. The inexpert application of these principles in fact frequently brought the whole idea of progressive education under attack on the score that it discarded discipline, it looked for creativity in the child without giving him anything to be creative about, produced people who could only work if they were interested and gave students fragmentary rather than systematic bodies of knowledge.

There were counter-movements to 'get back to fundamentals' in the course of these years, but the leaven of the ideas and principles of school reform worked at least to modify educational methods, where they did not revolutionize them. Health and physical education, work and manual activity, music and the arts to stimulate and release the child's creativity, and social experience and study to develop his social maturity all became widely accepted as appropriate and essential features of the modern school. Initially this reorienting of education was principally applied to very young children, but in time it was extended to older children and adolescents and entered into the planning and thinking of entire school systems in many countries.

Closely akin to progressive education, but distinct in its origin, emphasis and certain aspects of its method, was the system of 'basic education' developed in India by Rabindranath Tagore and Mahatma Gandhi. Their educational principles were formulated in response to the conditions of their country where extreme poverty was pervasive and where manual work was held in low esteem by the educated classes or was associated with low status in the caste hierarchy. Both Tagore and Gandhi broke through the barrier between education and labour; they sought to dignify manual labour and to make it a basis for the training of hand and mind and for the regeneration of Indian society. Toward this end they gave central place to the learning of a craft.

In Gandhi's formulation, a handcraft, taught in such a way as to stimulate and enrich the mind as well as to discipline the hand, offers a means of teaching many subjects—mathematics, geography, general science, language—and at the same time it enables the student to engage in useful, productive work. To him, activity itself was not enough; it should be useful activity. The craft must be learned and performed efficiently, to create habits of efficiency and to develop self-reliance and self-respect. He thought, moreover, that by engaging in useful work, students could make their school at least partially self-supporting—an attractive idea in a poor community desperately pressed for the resources to provide general education for all its children.

The specific crafts which Gandhi introduced were spinning and gardening, selected because they were related to the basic human needs of clothing and food and because they required a minimum of costly equipment and supplies. In addition, spinning directly symbolized Gandhi's campaign to free India from dependence on British manufacture. His principles were applicable, however, through any craft which met the criteria of social usefulness. Although it was clear to Indian educators that Gandhi's emphasis on crafts was as much political as pedagogical, that the scope of what could be imparted through craft training was limited and that the effort to make the school pay its way threatened to turn it into a child labour centre, some of the activity principles developed by Gandhi were incorporated into the basic educational system of India.

Soviet education, in its initial phase following the October revolution, drew ideas from progressive education and sought to adapt them to socialist objectives. After the early years of experimentation, however, it was guided by distinct pedagogical principles of its own, within the framework of Marxist-Leninist ideology. A number of teachers and public figures contributed to the development of Soviet pedagogy, among them N. K. Krupskaya, M. I. Kalinin and F. E. Dzerzhinsky. One of the chief formulators was A. S. Makarenko (1888–1939) who tested his ideas in the colonies of homeless children which he directed from 1920 to 1934. He considered the most important pedagogical principle to be 'how to combine with the most exacting demands upon the pupil the utmost respect for his personality'.* He rejected the theory of 'free' education as leading to laxity, lack of initiative and the inability to meet difficulties, and he discarded the use of intelligence tests and other procedures which assumed or implied that the child's personality was predetermined by heredity or a fixed environment.

According to his biographer, 'His entire pedagogical system is imbued with Bolshevik confidence in man's vast potentialities, with great optimism, and faith in the creative powers of people organized in a collective'. He

* A. S. Makarenko, *Road to Life* (Moscow, 1951), p. x.

thought that man must have something joyful ahead of him to live for, which meant, in pedagogical terms, that 'in the first place, the joy itself has to be organized, brought to life and converted into a possibility. Next, primitive sources of satisfaction must be steadily converted into more complex and humanly significant joys'.* He considered the collective to have great educative power and elaborated in detail the manner of using it educationally. He set great store by the effect on the student of engaging in socially useful work, and developed in his own institutions a combination of schooling with productive labour, designed to develop the total child through mental, character, physical and aesthetic education and polytechnical instruction.

The principles formulated by Makarenko were incorporated into the Soviet educational system in the years following the inauguration of the first five-year plan. They were reflected in the exacting demands placed upon students, the system of rewards, the group stimulus to individual achievement, and the combination of schooling with socially useful labour, the effort to maintain a buoyant atmosphere, and the integration of physical, aesthetic and vocational training with other aspects of general education.[8]

Standing firmly against all these modern secular trends represented by progressive education, Gandhian principles, Soviet pedagogy and other forms of experimentation was the system of Catholic education, which remained unshaken in its principles though it might adjust its methods in detail.

Catholic pedagogy rested squarely on Catholic doctrine: on the concept of the dual nature of man, both natural and supernatural, the fall of Adam which deprived man of his supernatural life, man's redemption through Christ, the mission of the Church and of Christian education to enable man to realize his supernatural destiny. The unchanging objective of Catholic education, as stated in the papal encyclical on *Christian Education of Youth* (1929), was 'to co-operate with divine grace in forming the true and perfect Christian . . . the supernatural man who thinks, judges, and acts constantly and consistently in accordance with right reason illumined by the supernatural light of the example and teaching of Christ. . . . It must never be forgotten that the subject of Christian education is man whole and entire, soul united to body in unity of nature, with all his faculties, natural and supernatural . . . . Since education consists essentially in preparing man for what he must be and for what he must do here below, in order to attain the sublime end for which he was created, it is clear that there can be no true education which is not wholly directed to man's last end. . . .'

The enduring principles of Catholic education did not imply specific methods, and there was considerable range in those employed. Though teaching orders like the Jesuits continued to apply their well-developed teaching techniques, some Catholic schools adopted devices, such as the project method, associated with other types of education. The distinguishing feature of Catholic education was that it kept spiritual values always to the fore. It

* Y. Medinsky, Introduction to *Road to Life, op. cit.* pp. xvi, xvii.

insisted that no education could exclude the religious factor, and that secular schools could give only an incomplete and distorted form of education from which the most important aspect, the religious, was missing. It was this insistence on 'man whole and entire' and on man's supernatural end which made the Church hold tenaciously to the proposition that the education of its children could be in no other hands.

5. *Application of new psychological insights*

The development of educational methods was affected during these years by developments in the field of psychology, especially as these related to the processes of learning and to the nature of human growth and development.*

Before the turn of the century, mounting interest in the psychology of the child had led to the founding of child study associations in Great Britain, Germany and France and the introduction of courses in child psychology into some university departments. In the years before the first world war efforts to devise means of differentiating children according to their innate capacity, notably the so-called intelligence tests developed by Alfred Binet in France and carried forward by E. L. Thorndike in the United States, laid the foundation for a scientifically oriented approach to individual differences. Psychologists were first appointed to the staffs of school authorities in London in 1913 and Los Angeles, in the United States, in 1912. Their initial function was to differentiate the children of subnormal intelligence who were unable to profit from the regular school programme. In time their role expanded with the elaboration of testing techniques to detect differences in aptitude, personality characteristics and emotional balance and development.

Better diagnosis of the child's needs and capacities provided a basis for directing his education more effectively. Most of the tests, however, were developed in western culture areas and for urban children. Although they were variously adapted and efforts were made to design tests which would be as independent of cultural factors as possible, they remained inadequate for determining the 'intelligence', aptitudes, potentialities and emotional adjustment of rural and of non-western children.

The issue of how far education itself, or other experience, could modify what were assumed to be innate capacities also remained unresolved. Substantial evidence, however, accumulated in the fields of nutrition, infant care, public health and mental illness, indicated that the child's ability to respond to education might be severely reduced by deficiencies in his nutritional status, by emotional deprivation in infancy or by poor physical or mental health, and that improvement in these respects might, conversely, increase his educability; 'nature' to some extent appeared to depend on 'nurture'.

The growth of experimental psychology, with its emphasis on stimulus and response, perception, association and conditioning, revealed some of the

* See Chapter XVI, The Scientific Approach to Human Behaviour and Human Relations, and Chapter XVII, The Home.

components of the learning process. *Gestalt* psychology stressed the point that new facts or ideas are not grasped in a vacuum but as part of a total concept in the mind of the individual into which each new observation is incorporated. These findings called into question the old pattern of rote learning without reference to a structure of ideas and the assumption that something learned in one context would necessarily be remembered or even recognized in another context.

Through developments in the field of psychiatry, educators also became aware of the emotional element in learning and of the consequent need to be concerned with the child's readiness to absorb material, his motivation for learning and the emotional factors which might block his ability to understand. As it became apparent that the individual must be positively involved in the learning process and not merely a passive vessel into which knowledge is poured, a psychological basis was provided for learning by doing as an educational method and for relating learning opportunities to the child's aroused interest. Greater emphasis was placed on adjustment in early childhood, with a resultant growth of the nursery-school movement. For the mounting proportion of young people who went through the emotionally difficult period of adolescence at school rather than at work, schools sought to design programmes which would help them grow to maturity.

Understanding of social factors, particularly of the role of culture in shaping personality, provided an additional basis for interpreting the child's behaviour and gearing education to his needs. The school had to recognize and deal with the child's social maladjustment as well as with his mental retardation or physical malnutrition. It had to distinguish when a child was deviating individually from his group norms and when his behaviour was that of a conformist to norms which might be at variance with those of school, home or other elements in the community. The modern school recognized that so-called 'behaviour problems' might be reflections of social conflict in the community, or the child's effort to deal with situations beyond his scope, or symptoms of personality disorders. Child guidance services, at first primarily associated with juvenile courts, were gradually extended into the schools and teachers were trained to recognize early symptoms of emotional maladjustment and to refer the child for specialized help. The child who was failing in his school work was studied to determine the reasons for his failure; he was not simply punished, kept back or otherwise disciplined in the effort to force him to learn, but was treated with whatever resources the school and community could provide.

Rapid social change often produced a disparity between the knowledge and values of the school and the home, and the school was forced to seek methods to enable the child to handle such disparities as he might encounter. This was a major undertaking in countries where the school population consisted of the children of immigrants from many lands, in those with a complex of shifting class and value systems, in the rapidly developing countries where schools

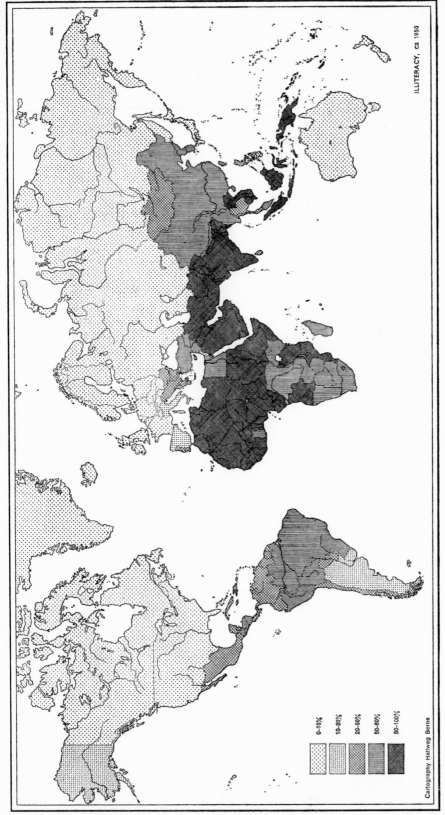

Illiteracy c. 1950

ILLITERACY, ca 1950

Cartography Hallwag Berne

0–10%
10–20%
20–50%
50–80%
80–100%

were instruments of radical social change, and in the urban settings where a constant stream of rural–urban migrants were experiencing a transformation of their lives. Schools organized programmes of parent education and encouraged parent-teacher associations or parents' councils in the effort to bring school and home closer together in their education of the child. The Unesco study, *Education and Mental Health* (Paris, 1955), concluded that the school's methods must sustain the child's relation to the home while helping the home to move in the direction in which the child is developing, and at the same time they must enable the child to cope with difference and conflict in the complex society of which he is a part.

New insights into the processes of learning were applied to the teaching of special skills, notably reading and the fundamental operations of mathematics, although there was sharp and continuing disagreement over method. Experiments with the use of audio and visual materials were designed to permit greater effectiveness of educational effort.

Needs of special types of pupils were also recognized. Special methods were devised and classes established for retarded children in larger schools or for groups of schools, and for children with defective sight, hearing and severe health handicaps. The European educators who reviewed the need for such special provisions in 1952 concluded that, on the basis of the most conservative estimates, 'it seems likely that no less than one child in five or six needs some kind of special educational or psychological help if he is to stand a fair chance of satisfactory and happy growth and if he is not to act as a brake upon other children in the normal class'*. They found that children with some types of special needs were recognized in most countries but that provisions for them were rarely adequate and that children with other kinds of problems were often overlooked.

6. *Use of new technology*

Educational methods were also affected by technical developments. The gramophone, motion picture, tape recorder, radio and television served as educational equipment, along with blackboards, pencils, desks and books. The new media offered great possibilities for enlarging the student's experiences beyond that which the teacher or the library could make vivid, and they could bring the best music into the classroom. Recording devices let the student of foreign language hear his own pronunciation. Closed circuit television enabled a particularly effective teacher, or a special demonstration, to reach many classrooms simultaneously. While none of the mass communication media could take the place of direct contact between teacher and pupil, they greatly extended the teacher's resources and scope.

Schools were slow to take advantage of these media, which did not fit immediately into the classroom pattern of instruction; but their use became progressively more widespread. In part, schools adopted mass communication

* *Education and Mental Health, op. cit.,* p. 249.

techniques for economy; in part they did so in self-defence, recognizing that the child was bombarded in his out-of-school hours with the sound of radio and the visual images brought by the cinema and television, and that they must compete for the child's attention and sense of reality. In countries where the mass media and the educational system were under a common control, the media afforded a powerful reinforcement to the impact of the school.

7. Educational content and the aims of the state

The content of education was strongly affected by political developments and by the purposes of the state. The first world war enhanced its nationalistic tone in nearly all countries, heightening the emphasis which had been present since the state assumed responsibility for universal education. As new countries emerged, or where revolutionary forces established a new order, education was redirected to support the new régime and build a loyal and dedicated citizenry. Countries which felt threatened by national rivals without or revolutionary forces within used their schools to strengthen national sentiment as a bulwark against such threats.

Where liberal democratic principles were reflected in educational policy, one of the major aims of education was to develop each individual for his own sake, according to his capacity and regardless of his social origin. This concept of education was fully expressed in the educational philosophy of John Dewey, who based his thinking on the American Declaration of Independence and the political assumptions of Thomas Jefferson. It implied that education must address itself to the needs and ambitions of all the people and that facilities must be expanded and adapted to assure equality of opportunity.

The course of education in the United States during the twentieth century reflected this basic orientation—in the constant expansion at higher and higher levels, the enormous proliferation of subject matter offered in schools and colleges, the child-centred school for the development of the whole child, and the emphasis on the school's contribution to the child's social adjustment. The many extra-curricular activities carried on in connection with schools and by out-of-school youth organizations had the same objectives. Such organizations as Boy and Girl Scouts, YMCA and YWCA, 4–H clubs for rural children and countless recreational, church or sport groups, all undertook to build character and to develop individual responsibility and the capacity for effective participation in community life.

European education also moved in a similar direction, with marked differences among countries in their educational organization and emphasis. In each country, school reforms were introduced which tended more or less strongly in the direction of the democratic, child-centred school which sought to stimulate the child's creative activity, concerned itself with his total development, included physical education and programmes of school health and school feeding, and which made special provision for children with mental, physical or emotional handicaps. To meet the demands for trained personnel at all levels, countries expanded the technical or vocational content of their education in one way or another, either through specialized schools or through diversification of subject matter in general schools. But at the same time that European systems went far toward accepting the principle of education for all in accordance with capacity and interest, they sought to maintain the values of limited-access, high-grade education for those who were to fill positions of high authority and responsibility and those who required high professional competence.[9, 10]

The content of education reflected state policy most clearly where states were engaged in swiftly remaking their societies. Each revolutionary government used education in its own way. To reorient the Turkish people, Musta-apha Kemal Ataturk used drastic educational measures. By substituting the Latin for the Arabic script in the preparation of all teaching material, he made traditional literature and thought largely inaccessible to the ordinary student and directed his mind toward the future. In Italy Mussolini first concentrated on using out-of-school youth organizations and after-work activities for adults to remould the Italian people to the fascist state. When, as a second step, he sought to bring both religious schools and secular instruction under full state control, the Church stood firm in reasserting the primacy of Church and family in the education of youth. Hitler's educational measures were inspired by his need to destroy centres of independent thought. Since the Nazi régime rejected both rationalism and religious instruction and wished to use mass education to inspire devotion to the Leader and to train men for military life and women for the home, it recast the schools to this end and entrusted the task of indoctrination to the politically faithful.[11]

The Soviet Union made the most far-reaching, ambitious and thorough use of education for the remaking of a people and a state. Its educational task was to develop the kind of people who could create a socialist society, to imbue the rising generation, as well as the adult population, with communist ideology, morality, loyalty to the Party and dedication to the Soviet state, to transform a largely illiterate, predominantly peasant people into competent producers in industry and mechanized agriculture, to replace the class of bourgeois intellectuals with a new body of intellectuals drawn from the ranks of workers and peasants, and to train the technical personnel needed to achieve rapid industrialization and to administer the state and the economy.

In the decade following the October revolution the elementary schools were converted into a system of 'unified labour schools' with a curriculum focused on 'socially useful labour'. In these schools, organized as collectives of pupils, teachers and other school workers, 'socialist competition' between brigades of children took the place of the traditional examination and grading of individual students. The authority of the teacher was minimized, since the growing school system had to be staffed with many old teachers who lacked understanding of or sympathy with communist ideology and new recruits who lacked training and experience. Party control and the teaching of communist principles through the school was achieved in part through the activity of the communist youth organizations—the Young Pioneers and League of Young Communists.

The education of adults was pressed simultaneously. Every centre—trade union, factory, agricultural tractor station—was used as a channel for education, to teach literacy, raise the occupational competence of the men and women at the work benches and in the fields, and develop a capable body of industrial and agricultural workers. In the effort to build a new class of intellectuals drawn from workers and peasants, the Soviet leaders opened the doors of all institutions of higher education to all men and women over 16 years of age without tuition fees or educational requirements for entrance. Since those who lacked preparation could not follow university courses, special preparatory schools known as *rabfac* were established to enable students of worker or peasant origin, and especially members of communist youth organizations, to make up their educational deficiencies quickly and to acquire training at higher levels.

By the time that the first five-year plan was launched in 1928 with its tremendous need for all sorts of technicians, engineers, scientists and administrators, a new intellectual class drawn largely from worker and peasant backgrounds had been created, and a new body of teachers, devoted to communist principles, had been trained. Thereafter the Soviet educational system could concentrate on the fullest development of the Soviet citizen and the training of personnel at every level to participate in the great national effort of building a highly productive communist society.

Emphasis was placed on the mastery of knowledge. School discipline and the authority of the teacher were restored, together with rigorous examinations and grading of individual pupils. Standard textbooks, continually revised to incorporate new knowledge and state policies as they developed, provided the subject matter to be covered. The teacher was required to teach his subject systematically and clearly, using various methods, and to check systematically on the retention of material taught.

Competitive examinations admitted to the various institutions of higher education; stipends to provide a subsistence allowance permitted those who qualified to continue their training. After 1940, when tuition fees were reintroduced into the higher schools, the stipends were granted to the ablest students. An elaborate system of awards and honours to those who did well stimulated student effort and academic achievement. Every medium—press, radio, public occasion—was used to give prestige to the educated person and to inspire the Soviet citizen with zeal to achieve as much education as he could get.

The curriculum of the general school placed great emphasis on mathematics and the physical sciences from the earliest grades. Revisions of the curriculum gave more place to physics and chemistry, increased the amount of time in the laboratory and made additional provision for manual labour and practical work. Nearly half of the school time in the ten-year general schools, which became standard in the larger cities in the early 1950s, was devoted to scientific and practical subjects. The rest was spent on Russian language and literature, history, geography, a foreign language and physical education. After the revisions of 1958 which sought to co-ordinate education more closely with productive work, the time devoted to direct vocational training and productive work was further expanded, amounting to nearly half the school time by the eleventh grade. The Marxist-Leninist ideology provided a framework for the study of all subjects. The curriculum was uniform through the USSR, except in the non-Russian speaking republics where Russian was taught as a second language.

Schools of all types formed part of a unified system, and state guidance ensured not only unity of curriculum but succession in the work of schools and other educational institutions and the proper distribution of educational resources. A variety of schools at different levels provided specialized content related to the fields for which they prepared. The *tecknikum* was designed to produce middle-trained technicians for industry and also for medicine, education, music and the arts; its graduates were assured employment upon completion of the course and had to work for three years in the field for which they had been trained before applying for admission to the university, except for the top-ranking students who could go directly to a higher institution in their fields. Youth between 14 and 17 drafted into the labour reserve, after this practice was instituted in 1940, received six months to two years of industrial training in special labour reserve schools, after which they worked in state enterprises for a period of four years.

Specialized higher education was provided through universities, in technical, medical, legal and other institutes, and in pedagogical institutions for teacher training. Students entered by competitive examination, except for the top graduates of the ten-year schools and the *tecknikums*. The number of places open to students in each field was determined by the requirements of the economy, and the tendency was for courses to become increasingly thorough and specialized. Graduates worked for at least three years in the posts to which their ministries assigned them.

Advanced degrees beyond the university, the first requiring three years of further study plus examinations and defence of a thesis and the second requiring an original and significant contribution to science, drew the ablest scientists on to still further efforts. Military and naval academies, with specialized preparatory boarding schools leading to them and special schools for the training of Party personnel provided specialized training in these areas. Middle technical schools were reported as turning out specialists at the rate of 312,000 a year and higher specialist institutions 224,000 during the period of the fifth five-year plan, 1951–55.

The Soviet educational system, supplemented by press, radio, a network of public libraries and other cultural institutions, was thus designed to give the entire population a scientific outlook, basic understanding of the processes of production and dedication to the principles of the communist society, to create socially oriented citizens and to produce the well-trained personnel required for the rapid economic, social, political and military development of the Soviet Union.

The reorganization of the Japanese educational system after 1945 offered a dramatic example of the redirection and reshaping of education to serve a changed objective of the state. In the years prior to the second world war the highly centralized Japanese system was dominated by the military leadership —military officers were attached to all secondary and higher schools after 1925—and was focused on the duties of the individual to the state which he must serve. During the war most of the secondary and higher educational institutions were closed to release their students for productive or military service and many were physically destroyed.

After the war, acting on the principle that defeat had proved the old ways wrong, Japan set out to build an educational programme which would sustain a democratic rather than an autocratic state and society. The curriculum in all schools put more emphasis on social studies, applied mathematics, science, health, sports and recreation, in an attempt to build sound minds in sound bodies and good citizens of a democracy. Schools provided school lunches and health examinations. A system of general secondary schools similar to those in the United States, open to both boys and girls, replaced the limited number of higher preparatory schools, open only to boys, which had formerly provided virtually the only access to the universities.

In the large number of colleges and universities which offered higher education in science and liberal arts and gave professional and teacher training, students received a broadly cultural education in the humanities, social sciences and natural sciences, in addition to their specialized fields. Both vocational training and social education for adults were also expanded, through extension courses from universities, libraries or museums and in citizens' public halls which were constructed in towns and villages with some aid from the central government. In these halls general cultural courses were offered, library services were provided and recreational and organizational activity was carried on.

Through these measures, and the informal channels of radio and press, Japan sought to make its educational institutions contribute to the development of a general culture 'rich in individuality' and to offer equal opportunity to all according to their ability. A decade after the inauguration of this educational reform, the number of secondary school and university-level students had increased substantially and several thousand women were taking advantage of their new opportunities for higher education. Some educators felt that the change was resulting in less adequate command of certain subject matter than had resulted from the old system and feared that the added numbers would drag down the quality of education at the higher levels. Others, however, noted a greater 'elasticity of mind' and other attributes more in line with the new objectives of post-war Japanese society.

In its tremendous drive for modernization and socialist construction, the Chinese People's Republic used education as a vital instrument to help the country to 'leap ahead'. Even before the communist régime came to power, while the Eighth Army was building up its base in the north-west provinces, the movement placed great stress on education. With few resources and under war conditions the communists undertook not only to teach communist principles, but to develop literacy among soldiers and peasants and to conduct schools and colleges even of university level. Once in power, the communist régime launched a vigorous campaign to overcome the mass illiteracy of the peasants, spread schools as fast as possible throughout the country, and to strengthen the technical and scientific institutions in order to prepare the technical personnel essential to the tasks of economic and social development.

In less than a decade one province after another was able to report that its literacy campaigns had reached nearly the whole of its non-literate population, that whole families from grandparents to young people were enrolled in literacy classes, and that people were painting newly learned characters on walls, trees, tools and furniture to help them to learn and remember. In order to make literacy education feasible on a mass basis, as well as to facilitate intercommunication through the country, measures were taken to establish the use of simplified characters and to make the pronunciation used in the region of Peking standard throughout the country.

To supplement the schools furnished by the state, co-operative farms as well as factories were stimulated to set up their own schools, constructing the buildings and furniture with their own labour and recruiting teachers from every source—government functionaries or technicians sent out to work on the farms, demobilized soldiers and young members of the co-operatives who were school graduates. As the number of schools increased most co-operatives came to have some members who had been to school and could teach others. The more advanced co-operatives went on to set up middle schools and then secondary schools. Meantime, the number of institutions for higher education were multiplied many times over in every major centre, and their enrolments shot into the millions. At every level up to the highest scientific institutes, the expansion of education followed the line laid down by the Communist party for all endeavours—'more, faster, better and more economically'.

The immense expansion of education was at the heart of the technical and cultural revolution which was training new working-class intellectuals and which aimed to eliminate the difference between physical and mental labour. Education was closely integrated with production, and the tie became progressively closer. Factories established schools in which their workers spent part of their working day, receiving partial pay for the hours spent learning new skills; schools organized and operated factories where their pupils learned by doing and at the same time contributed productive labour. Some classes on co-operative farms were conducted in work breaks. Students in technical institutes worked on designs for machinery or buildings for local factories, reservoirs, agricultural equipment, the control of a locally serious diseases or other real and practical problems directly related to production. Scientific institutes developed projects designed to bring China to the level of international scientific standards, or above, in as many fields and as quickly as possible.

For the new states which emerged from colonial status the content and method of education presented a major challenge. The education inherited from colonial administrations was not well designed to meet the needs of a modern state. It was mainly literary, it was imbued with material and points of view more related to the culture of the colonial power than to that of the area, and higher education was carried on in a foreign language which tended to cut off the educated element from the masses of the people who did not command this medium. It provided neither incentive to practical work—the educated *élite* were above soiling their hands in toil—nor training for the technicians and scientists required by any modern society, most especially one aspiring to rapid industrialization.

In India Gandhi had broken through the barrier between education and labour with his educational programme based on the dignity of work. But even the momentum provided by his immense prestige did not make it easy to overcome the prejudice against practical activity. Moreover, his emphasis on handicraft, if literally applied, could impede technical education for the urban child rather than promote it. In other countries, where no Gandhi had shown the way and given work his blessing, the task of developing a positive attitude toward work and technical skills was even more formidable.

Education in the new states had not only to develop a positive attitude toward work, but to create a new social ideal and a new kind of self-esteem. Under colonial rule schools had tended to place the local culture in low esteem, to exalt outside values, to discourage zeal for reform, and to do little to enhance and much to undermine the self-confidence of the people. The educational system of the new states had the problem of developing such a sense of social purpose as would predispose young people to serve the community and of building sufficient self-confidence to enable people to use their capacities effectively without either withdrawal or aggressiveness. The problem was well illustrated in Korea where the Korean language had been banned from the schools during the Japanese occupation and the country's history and arts disregarded. The immediate task of Korean educators was to recover their cultural heritage while at the same time working to readjust the traditional culture to the new democratic ideal.

It was a difficult task to adapt the content and method of education to the new situation. Old teachers, with a literary background, rigid methods and traditional attitudes, often could not command the pupils' interest or respect, and new teachers of the calibre required for the creative task of cultural reorientation were not attracted to a profession where prestige could no longer compensate for meagre pay. Students who inherited traditions of protest from the days when they took part in the struggle for liberation were restless and critical. A number of countries had to deal with what Indian educators termed 'student indiscipline', as many young people, impatient to reach new goals, found their studies irrelevant and their teachers unimpressive, and expressed their unrest in indifference to study, disorder or passive resistance. In the many countries of Asia, the Middle East and Latin America which were seeking to bring rapid social change by democratic means, it was not easy to use the educational system for the purpose of reorientation and change without resorting to methods inappropriate to their goals and the structure of their societies.

The new states faced an acute problem in the matter of language. Mass education in Europe and America had developed in countries with fairly uniform, well-developed languages. When it was extended to Asia, Africa and the Pacific, to many of the peoples of the Soviet Union and to the Indians of Central and South America, it reached peoples whose spoken tongue was sometimes unwritten, sometimes at variance with the literary language and sometimes written but with a very meagre literature.

Universal education had to be carried on in the local language. Pedagogues agreed that the child's initial instruction should be in the language of his home, and local and national pride was also involved. Multi-language countries had the additional problem of the need for a unifying means of communication, to be taught to the newly educated. At the same time modern subjects were accessible only in the major European languages. In time a local langugage might through use become a language for scientific work, as French and English had supplanted Latin, and as German and Russian had later replaced French for scientific work in German- and Russian-speaking areas. Japan went far toward demonstrating that an Asian language could be transformed into a vehicle for modern scientific study and thought, but the process was slow and the need for highly trained scientists and technicians was immediate. The new states had little choice but to carry on at one and the same time the process of developing mass education in the vernacular, the elaboration of a national language as fast as possible, and the continuing use of a European language as a vehicle for the immediate training of the highly educated personnel essential to the development of the state.

India undertook to strengthen its mass education system in local languages, and it redrew its state boundaries with the practical objective of bringing people who spoke a common tongue within the same administrative and educational area. At the same time it sought to make Hindi the official language of the Indian union, introducing it in the third grade in school and aiming to make it ultimately the language of official communication. English was taught as an additional language at the secondary school level to at least as large a proportion of the population as had learned it under the limited educational

II*

system of the past. Some of the universities wished to keep English as their language of instruction in order to retain the advantage of a language which gave access to the world's knowledge without the enormous task of translation and publication involved in developing a comparable body of material in Hindi or in the many local languages.

Indonesia and Burma, with similar yet different problems, turned to other solutions. Indonesia, inheriting schools taught in Dutch and a largely illiterate population speaking a variety of local languages, created a national Indonesian language on the basis of Malay and made it the language of general instruction at all levels in some areas and from the third grade in others. At the same time it substituted English for Dutch as the European language which would be used to provide access to advanced bodies of knowledge and a means of communication with other parts of the world. Burma, inheriting vernacular education which, according to an Education Policy Enquiry Committee in 1946, 'practically ended in a blind alley', plus an English and Anglo-vernacular system which 'led only to the bottleneck of the University', planned to retain English as a language of general use and for secondary and higher education, with early primary instruction in Burmese. It sought to expand the limited literature existing in Burmese, to record traditional oral material, encourage literary expression and translate some world classics, but not to try to make major bodies of knowledge available in Burmese.

In China the educational reformers after 1919 sought to resolve the problem of disparity between the formal literary medium and the many spoken dialects by adopting a written vernacular which permitted colloquial expression. The communist régime took the further steps of standardizing the pronunciation of the 'common speech' and developing simplified script. Israel made Hebrew a spoken language through which to integrate its immigrant population with many backgrounds and tongues.

The language problem was perhaps most acute in the education of Africans who spoke a multitude of unwritten tribal languages. Since strong forces were at work breaking down tribal bonds, the value of reducing many of these languages to writing and building a literature from scratch seemed questionable. The trend appeared to be toward the increased use of a few African languages in certain areas, such as Swahili in Tanganyika, and the use of English and French in West Africa, with Arabic competing for place in the Sudan.

Two factors facilitated the carrying out of educational objectives in states of high illiteracy, the availability of the media of mass communication and the educational aspect of community development programmes. Educational programmes in many countries were carried by radio to the village store or some other place where local people could gather to listen and discuss. In one such programme in Colombia, South America, parish priests organized groups to follow courses in agriculture and other practical subjects. The priests and their assistants acted as discussion leaders and monitors for those attending this radio 'school', and the central office furnished those enrolled with seed, fertilizer or other material called for in the course.

Such illustrations could be multiplied from many areas. In all such programmes, however, it was recognized that information received via the mass media was no substitute for active learning by the person himself. The training centres for fundamental education sponsored by Unesco in Mexico for the Latin American republics and in Egypt for the Arab states, and other centres elsewhere, emphasized the principle of using the person's own experience as the basis for his learning.

Community development programmes offered ample opportunities for learning. Designed to arouse village people to a sense of their own potentialities and to stimulate their co-operative efforts to raise the level of village life, these programmes were basically educational in their approach. In fact the relation between 'community development' and 'fundamental education' was so close that they were sometimes regarded as merely different names for the same basic process.

The community education programme in Puerto Rico offered an example of an educational programme which used both mass media and community development techniques to achieve the fundamental education-community development objective of raising the level of life within the rural community. In this programme 'group organizers', equipped with jeep, loudspeaker system, motion-picture equipment, posters and mass-produced pamphlets, worked in villages and hamlets. First they read and discussed a pamphlet with a group of citizens and arranged for its distribution in the village. Then they returned with a motion picture on the same theme, which always carried a suggestion for community self-help, and with a loudspeaker through which both organizer and citizens could comment on the film or on matters of common interest. When the people of the village, stimulated by these educational activities, expressed an interest in undertaking some community project, the organizer helped them to mobilize their own resources, to tap the technical and other sources available in the area and to develop the capacity to work toward common objectives.

VI. INTERNATIONAL CONCERN WITH EDUCATION

Although education in each country was closely related to national institutions and objectives, its common features and its overall importance made it a matter of international concern and co-operation. A series of international congresses dating from the eve of the first world war brought together individuals interested in the interchange of educational experiences and views. Education became the subject of intergovernmental concern in the 1920s with the establishment of the League of Nations Commission for Intellectual Co-operation and the transformation of the International Bureau of Education, established at Geneva in 1925, into an intergovernmental institution in

1929. At the first intergovernmental conference on public education held in Geneva in 1933, governments reported on their educational systems and received recommendations from the international gathering.

The main lines of international activity in the field of education were in the exchange of information and in the conduct of comparative studies of school administration and organization and of educational content and methods. *The International Yearbook of Education,* published by the International Bureau of Education from 1933 on, made available to each country the trends in experience and thought in other countries of the world.

Unesco, established in 1945, expanded the exchange of information and international documentation and organized international conferences around specific educational problems. Together with the United Nations and the other United Nations specialized agencies, it fostered the exchange of students and teachers. In response to requests from member governments it offered technical assistance in administration, teacher training and the preparation of educational materials. With the co-operation of other United Nations agencies and the Organization of American States it maintained fundamental education training centres for the Latin American countries and the Arab states.

Thus at every level, from the smallest village to the world community, education became a major preoccupation of twentieth-century societies throughout the world.

NOTES TO CHAPTER XXVI

1. Father François Russo, SJ, supplements the Author-Editors' statement about education with the following remarks:

The Roman Catholic Church maintains that responsibility for education rests in the first place with the family and in the second place with the Church, though the State has the right, and indeed the duty, to concern itself with education on the national scale and to set up non-denominational schools. It is the duty of the State to make it possible for the children attending such non-denominational schools to be given religious instruction if their families so request.

The Roman Catholic Church asks parents to send their children to a Catholic school whenever the educational system of their country allows of this. The Church considers that a child cannot receive a satisfactory, all-round education except in a Christian educational environment, since religious teaching, though of fundamental importance, is only one among a number of elements contributing to the Christian upbringing of children.

It is sometimes suggested that in accepting Catholic schools, one is setting up an obstacle to national unity. This view seems very short-sighted.

Far from jeopardizing national unity, a Catholic school does much to foster it—by its broadminded teaching, and by the devotion to the commonweal which is a direct result of Christian education. There is, moreover, ample opportunity for different categories of children to meet together, even if they are attending separate schools. The Roman Catholic Church, while remaining firmly attached to the principles set forth above, recognizes that present-day problems of instruction and education are such that they call for much more State intervention, both in organization and in finance, than was needed in the past, and that Catholic education can no longer be planned independently of the general national educational system. But while the Catholic schools are thus prepared to accept a considerable measure of integration in the national educational system, they declare that it is possible to allow them to retain their spiritual independence.

For other statements of the Catholic position consult:

John D. Redden and F. A. Ryan, *A Catholic Philosophy of Education* (Milwaukee, 1956).
Kevin J. O'Brien, *The Proximate Aim of Education* (Washington, D.C., 1958).

And for other views consult:

M. F. Ashley Montagu, *Education and Human Relations* (New York, 1958).
Aubrey E. Haan, *Education for the Open Society* (London, 1962).
Max Lerner, *Education and a Radical Humanism* (Columbus, Ohio, 1962).
Frederick Meyer, *Philosophy of Education for our Time* (New York, 1958).
National Educational Association, American Education Research Association, *Philosophical and Social Framework of Education* (Washington, D.C., 1958, 1961).
David Riesman, *Constraint and Variety in American Education* (New York, 1958).
Ephraim V. Sayers and Ward E. Madden, *Education and the Democratic Faith: An Introduction to the Philosophy of Education* (New York, 1959).

2. I. Ekholm underlines that the establishment of a single democratic school system in the USSR has made it possible to realize the principle of universal and equal education in an exceptionally short space of time. Many other countries are now following in the path of the Soviet Union which in its work in the field of education incarnates the aspirations of the peoples of the world.

3. I. Elkholm reminds that from the very outset, laws making education compulsory were difficult to put into effect and in fact did not become a reality in some countries, mainly owing to the depressed material situation of the masses and because states which made universal education a statutory requirement did not always provide the necessary backing for legislation in the form of financial appropriations for the expansion of the network of schools, for their equipment and maintenance, for the training of teachers and so on.

4. I. Ekholm writes: The vigorous national liberation movement at the beginning of the twentieth century in colonies and in countries which were not independent led to some democratization of life which was expressed in a certain expansion of the school network and in the training of indigenous administrative, technical and military staff.

5. Professor E. N. Anderson thinks it important to stress the relation between education and national leadership. Writers on the history of education note that the nature of secondary and higher education basically conditions the character and achievements of a society by determining the kind of training that the leaders receive. They tend to regard primary education, although essential in itself, as a reservoir from which the ablest pupils are chosen for advanced training as members of the future policy and decision-making groups. The question must be posed as to whether the Author-Editors have brought out sufficiently the impact of developments in secondary and higher schools in Europe on the achievements of their countries, especially in the economic and social areas of life.

The main problem which Europeans faced in education in the first half of the twentieth century lay in the field of secondary and higher training. Countries entered the period with a record of achievement in developing primary education, whereas the secondary schools in many states had received modest adjustment to meet the needs of the great increase in population and of the emergence and expansion of industrial and technological economy. The character and limitations of secondary training set limits to the achievements of the universities, for the nature of the preparation of the entering students conditioned the kind of education which the latter could instil. The class basis of secondary and higher education in most countries—peasants and workers being largely excluded—was maintained, among other ways, by continuing to offer a curriculum aimed at transmitting a knowledge of the humanities and at preparing young males for the bureaucratic career or for the professions. In most countries, facilities for training engineers, scientists and business men were neglected; Germany and the small states of north-western Europe offered the main or only exceptions, and Germany suffered from denigration of secondary and higher education during the regime of the National Socialists.

When the new states were created after World War I, they followed the educational example in this respect not of pre-Nazi Germany but of France and Italy. The result was that after the positions in the bureaucracies of these new states were filled, there quickly appeared a very high rate of unemployment in the learned professions, with a consequent drift of these persons into radical rightist or radical leftist movements. New professions or occupations which industrialism had made essential lacked social appeal in countries that had not yet achieved substantial industrialization; these countries found themselves expending a disproportionate amount of their incomes supporting a bureaucracy which did not take the initiative in establishing an educational system to prepare personnel at a high level to create an economy capable of sustaining the new state and its apparatus of government. Nor was this condition restricted to Eastern Europe. Spain and Portugal were in a similar situation, and Italy, France and Great Britain, at the mid-century, were still debating the issue. Their educational systems were still not of the kind to train personnel —engineers, scientists, business administrators and other business leaders—in sufficient numbers to man expanding industry. The nature of the demands was acutely revealed by the experience of war, when scientific and technological ability and leadership in production and distribution were desperately sought.

In the years since World War II, European countries have attempted to speed, on a scale varying from country to country, adjustment of secondary and higher education to the needs for trained personnel in non-traditional areas of endeavour, and to break with the old restrictive relationship between social class and the system of education. They have begun to seek out and to train ability irrespective of social origin. However, resistance within the educational system to innovation remains strong. Whether secondary and higher schools will expand and adjust to meet demands or whether centres for training personnel will be set up outside the established institutions is a question which France, for example, has not yet answered, and certain other countries are even further away from facing the issue.

Bibliography for this subject is understandably extensive in today's world. Useful for any especially interested reader are the reports issued by UNESCO in its *World Survey of Education*, for example, the report *Secondary Education* (London, 1961). Important reports have been issued in Great Britain. Examples may be cited in the Newsom Report by the Central Advisory Council for Education, *Half Our Future* (Her Majesty's Stationery Office, 1963), and in the Robbins Report, *Higher Education* (HMSO, 1963). One should also consult Stephen R. Graubard (Ed.), *A New Europe?* (Boston, 1964), for its several articles on education in Europe today. Consult also:

Margaret A. Clapp, *The Modern University* (Cornell University Press, 1950).
W. R. Fraser, *Education and Society in Modern France* (London, 1963).
George F. Kneller, *Higher Learning in Britain* (Berkeley, 1955).
W. M. Kotschnig, *The University in a Changing World* (London, Oxford, 1932).
W. M. Kotschnig, *Unemployment in the Learned Professions* (Oxford, 1937).
Donald W. Miles, *Recent Reforms in French Secondary Education—with Implications for French and American Education* (New York, 1953).
OECD, *Forecasting Manpower Needs for the Age of Science* (Paris, 1960).
Jean Thomas and Joseph Majault, *Educational Problems Common to European Countries*. Report to the Third Conference of Ministers of Education (Rome, 1962).

6. I. Ekholm adds that in the Chinese People's Republic a reform of higher education has also been carried through. The teaching of the reactionary scholastic disciplines has been abolished and the study of Marxist theory and of the history of the Chinese revolution introduced. Great attention is given to the furthering of technical education.

7. I. Ekholm adds: The problem of school education in rural areas which was the subject of special discussion at the Twenty-first International Conference on Public Education is of particular urgency. As the UNESCO material showed, there are still 250,000,000 children in rural areas of the world who have no possibility of attending a school. In many countries there is a noticeable insufficiency of school buildings and teachers. Often the children of poor peasants leave school without completing the primary education course and start working on the family holding. The problem of rural schools is complicated in some countries by the survival of vestiges of feudalism, by a lack of religious and national unity in the population, by serious economic difficulties and by the existence alongside state schools of private schools—missionary, Muslim, Jewish, etc.—most of which

belong to religious bodies or are under their influence. The extremely low rate of remuneration of teachers' work is a substantial obstacle in the way of the development of rural education. The problem of the rural school is being successfully solved in countries which have started on the road to socialist development, and there it is an organic link in a single state system of education. See N. K. Goncharov, *Narodnoe prosveshchenie v SSSR* (Public Education in the USSR), Report submitted to the International Seminar in Tashkent (April 1961), Moscow, 1961. (Parallel texts in French, English, and Spanish.)

8. I. Ekholm writes that in 1958 when the USSR entered the phase of detailed construction of communism, and life confronted the schools with new tasks, a large-scale programme of educational reconstruction was elaborated which, after nation-wide discussion, received its confirmation by the Supreme Soviet of the USSR in the form of a law. The main point in this programme, the realization of which has been successfully begun, is the consistent application of the principle of instruction coupled with productive labour and of productive labour coupled with instruction. One of the principal means for putting this principle into effect is the system of polytechnical education.

9. I. Ekholm points out that the period under review was characterized by new forms of organization of children which to a considerable extent affected their education. With the strengthening of the mass revolutionary movement under the influence of the October Socialist Revolution democratic organizations of the children of workers began to be set up. First came the communist groups in Germany which set up the 'Spartacus' children's organization. Soon after the October Revolution similar bodies began to come into existence in Soviet Russia. In May 1922 the All-Russian Conference of the Russian Young Communist League took a decision to set up an organization of Young Pioneers. In the twenties and thirties children's democratic organizations were founded in many countries including the USA, United Kingdom, Belgium, Switzerland, Austria and Sweden. After the second World War this movement embraced more than thirty countries in Europe, Asia and Latin America. It is in fact an effective means for inculcating into children and young people the best human virtues.

10. See further material on youth groups in Chapter XXII, pp. 776–81.

11. I. Ekholm points out that even the representatives of pre-Nazi pedagogy, whilst verbally asseverating their concern for personality and pretending to safeguard its interests, emphasized the formative significance of religion and race, lauded nationalism and championed the education of youth in a spirit of militarism and chauvinism. It was precisely these highly reactionary ideas which were developed when the Nazis came to power. The concept of the racial superiority of Germans and their rights to world domination, the cult of the Führer and blind obedience—all misanthropic ideas—became the basis for the education of children and young people. Courses in racial studies were given in the schools and an intensified military training of youth was carried out.

CHAPTER XXVII

USE OF LEISURE*

I. THE NEW LEISURE

No aspect of modern industrial society was more distinctive than the new leisure enjoyed by the masses of the people. The ways in which this leisure was spent and the institutions which grew up in relation to it led to the development of mass culture which became more and more pervasive with each decade, placing its stamp on the habits and outlook of industrial societies and spreading with the extension of modern technology and industrialization to many parts of the world.

For the first time in history the masses of the people in the industrial countries were free during a substantial part of each day and each week from the activities necessary for survival—the daily labour in the field or at the bench and the endless routines of household life. Leisure, which had been the privilege of the rich who could command the labour of others, became the common lot of the ordinary citizen.

The very concept of 'leisure' which emerged during these years embodied a new idea and a new attitude toward living. In pre-industrial societies such leisure as the masses of the people had enjoyed took the form of many religious holidays—literally holy days—of family celebrations connected with weddings and other family events and of festivals celebrating the rhythm of agricultural work, especially planting and harvest festivals common to agricultural societies.

The early factory system reduced the free time of workers, for the continuous hours of work in the factory up to fourteen hours a day, six or seven days a week, week in and week out, offered none of the flexibility of agricultural labour or the seasonal periods when work was slack, and the time allowed for the celebration of religious holidays was strictly specified and usually cut down to the minimum. But by drawing a sharp line between time at work and 'free' time, industry laid the basis for a division of life into 'work' and 'leisure', and for an attitude toward leisure or leisure time as something which was desirable in itself, something which men could acquire and 'use'. It established the concept of the annual holiday—a period wholly free from work—and the idea that people could be entitled to such an interval as part of the pattern of living.

Basically, the new leisure was the product of modern technology. Machine production so increased the productivity of the worker as to enable him to

* Dr Dorothy Jackson collaborated in the preparation of this chapter.

earn enough for a livelihood in a reduced working day and work week, and even to earn sufficient in this shorter time to have money to spend on the enjoyment of his non-working hours.

It was not without a struggle, however, that industrial workers gained an increasing measure of leisure for themselves. At first, trade unions had demanded shorter hours on the grounds of health and the need of time for home duties, but by the early twentieth century, when the ten-hour day had become general, the demand for shorter hours was couched in terms of the desire for leisure. Workers associated it with upper-class privilege and in the age of democracy they intended to have it, along with other tokens of equality. They demanded, and step by step achieved, successive shortenings of the working time, then annual holidays with pay and overtime pay for work on Sundays and public holidays. Employers meantime came to recognize that a quota of leisure contributed to workers' efficiency.

By the 1950s the general concept of shorter working hours and holidays with pay, outside agriculture, had been accepted in all western industrialized countries, barring economic pressures such as wars which brought long overtime hours, or slumps which brought unemployment and enforced free time. The forty-hour week was general in the United States and Canada for industrial and white-collar workers, while forty-two to forty-eight hours were usual in most other areas, with a tendency toward further reduction. By 1960 the average for factory and office workers in the USSR was under forty; in Japan, however, it was still more than fifty hours per week.

For many housewives, too, the new technology meant new leisure. Household appliances and the industrial production of baked, canned and frozen foods released women from many hours of washing, cleaning and cooking; the old saying 'woman's work is never done' was no longer so true. For middle-class women whose leisure had formerly been made possible by servants, the new devices helped to redress the balance when their former servants went to work in factories where they could earn enough money to afford some of the new leisure for themselves; for women who had never had the help of servants, the new machines and new products brought some leisure for the first time.

Young people also enjoyed more leisure time, both because the additional earnings of their parents enabled an increasing proportion of them to remain out of the labour market and in school through adolescence, and because labour-saving devices lightened some of their household chores. Many had spending money of their own instead of having to help support their families. This development, in conjunction with the new freedom of association widely allowed to adolescent boys and girls, provided the basis for what came to be virtually a mass sub-culture among the urbanized teenagers of the industrial countries.

Once leisure became available to the masses of the people, the question arose how it would be used. The answer lay in part in modern technology itself, for the means of mass communication and transport gave access to new forms of entertainment and enjoyment. In part it depended on the facilities provided by public or commercial agencies and the choices which people made as to how to use their time and energy.

In the advanced industrial countries an ever larger amount of economic activity was devoted to the production and distribution, the repair and the advertising of products and services which provided for men's leisure-time pursuits rather than for the necessities of food, clothing and shelter. Where productive activity was guided primarily by consumer expenditures, the interaction between consumer demand and the effort of producers to market their wares resulted in a pattern of leisure-time activity which reflected the public tastes and the influence of commercial interests.

The public was eager for entertainment of all sorts, for information along many lines and for the opportunity to engage in a multitude of sports and hobbies. Mass entertainment industries took advantage of the new instruments of communication and developed them for the mass market in the form of mass magazines, the production and distribution of motion pictures and, in countries where radio and television were commercially controlled, entertainment over the air. The vast industrial complex involving pleasure vehicles and their use grew larger and more ubiquitous with every year, while the manufacture of equipment for sports and hobbies flourished and expanded.

The entertainment industries with their ready-made audiences offered a powerful medium for advertising all manner of products and came to depend for much of their support on companies willing to pay for access to this potential market. Advertisers, in turn, adopted entertainment patterns to catch and hold attention and they even sought to make the entertainment itself into a vehicle for selling their wares. Producers and advertisers thus helped to form tastes as well as catering to them, and the patterns which developed resulted from the constant interplay between producer and public.

Nowhere however was provision for the use of leisure left entirely to the operation of the market and the initiative of commercially motivated enterprise. Everywhere some responsibility for the citizens' leisure was assumed by the state and by co-operative, religious or philanthropic agencies. The public provision of parks, playgrounds, museums, zoos and libraries was already a well-established feature of urban communities before either the shortened work-day or the attitudes associated with the welfare state made further provisions for leisure seem necessary and appropriate.

When the eight-hour day began to make substantial amounts of non-working time available, many employers, leaders and welfare workers in industrial countries expressed the fear that working people would not know what to do with their spare time and would use it in drinking and idling. Historically, the major development of industrialism and capitalism had come in those societies which regarded work, savings, accumulation and prudent investment as moral virtues and feared that free time would be spent in frivolity or idleness which would corrupt the population and undermine its moral stamina. When leisure began to become a mass reality, communities where these attitudes prevailed saw a need for people to be taught to use leisure fruitfully and to be provided with the means of doing so. At the same time a widely expressed concern lest the monotony of factory work should destroy the industrial worker's humanity led to efforts to promote activities which would provide a substitute for the old satisfactions of craftsmanship.

The outcome, in the 1920s, was a great extension of organized recreation in the form of sports facilities, handicraft classes, opportunities for amateur dramatics, music, dancing and discussions. Some of these recreational activities were sponsored by governments, others by private organizations. In Britain for example they were often maintained by such organizations as the Women's Institutes, the Workers' Education Association, the British Drama League or by welfare agencies such as settlement houses.

Most countries, either on a national or community basis, experimented in ways of bringing books, arts, music and theatre to a wider public by expanding their library systems and museums, and by establishing orchestras and a variety of art and theatre projects. School programmes were enlarged to include a wide range of sport and other extra-curricular activities designed to develop interests and skills that might lead to the creative use of leisure. Organized recreation was included in the social planning of the depression years and in efforts to maintain morale during wartime. Depression, war and acceptance of the role of the welfare state brought increased provisions by governments in those countries where much recreation was privately sponsored, and stimulated the further enlargement of public parks, playing fields, gardens, zoos, swimming pools, golf courses and the like.

Industrial enterprises and labour unions also concerned themselves with the workers' use of leisure time. Many large corporations provided athletic facilities for their employees and backed company teams, choirs, orchestras and art exhibits. Labour unions secured the co-operation of educational agencies in union education programmes and encouraged their members to make good use of their time in further study or by engaging in sports and hobbies.

With time at their disposal and a variety of commercial and public resources at hand, people chose to spend their time in ways which reflected a range of attitudes toward leisure itself, as well as a multitude of tastes and interests. Persons who wanted to use their time for self-improvement, and those for whom the line between vocational and avocational interests was not sharply drawn, tended to spend their leisure time in ways which increased their skills and supplemented their working life. Others used their leisure chiefly to enhance their enjoyment of life. They were positive in their approach to pleasure, and they did what seemed enjoyable without regard for its effect on their position or the improvement of their personalities.

Some used their leisure time simply for relaxation or to escape from the drabness or strain of their surroundings, to forget what was worrying them and to live another life at least in their mind's eye for a moment; the cinema, radio and television fulfilled this purpose successfully and so gained immensely in popularity. Others, by contrast, devoted many of their leisure hours to the service of their communities, filling posts of responsibility in civic organizations, volunteering their time for such activities as boy scout leadership or as hospital aides, or engaging in activities which promoted a cause, through their trade union, political party, church or other body.

The need for sociability and the immense range of interests which could be pursued under modern urban conditions produced an endless variety of clubs, teams or informal groups formed in communities or at places of work or in connection with a school, church or recreational institution. The list of no less than twenty-one special interest clubs formed in the 1950s by employees of the United Nations at its headquarters in New York was representative of the kinds of association that might be open to people. Such clubs provided a means for people with like interests to get together and enjoy themselves without reference to where they lived, who they were or what position they held, and they served as the nuclei around which many people built their social activities. Common interest took the place of status in providing a basis for a sense of belonging to those exposed to the impersonality and anonymity of urban life.

These ways of using leisure time fell into two broad categories, passive and active: those which entertained people as spectators or listeners and those which involved active participation. The line between the two types was not always sharp, for in the 'passive' forms of entertainment there were degrees of passivity, from the keen interest and informed attention of the music or sports enthusiast who listened to each note and recognized the fine points of each play, to the inactivity of the person who kept the radio going for little more than the noise and who went to a ball game just to follow the crowd. But in all types of passive entertainment the individual depended on the performance of someone other than himself.

By the middle years of the century the factors which affected the use of leisure were producing a common mass culture. Its development had gone farthest and could be seen most conspicuously in the United States, where conditions were especially favourable. But all the essential features were present elsewhere—shortening of working hours, rising incomes, the blurring of old class lines, the development of entertainment industries. *Per capita* movie attendance was higher in Britain in the 1950s than in the United States; Paris set aside an area in the Bois de Boulogne where motoring French campers could pitch their tents; the Scandinavian countries developed special low-cost holiday facilities not only for workers taking their paid holidays but for holidaying housewives as well; Japanese periodical and book output was among the largest in the world. Mass culture was taking on common qualities in all the industrialized regions.

In the socialist economies the trends which characterized the countries where producers were free to cater to and influence public desires were subjected to controls in the interest of the socially advantageous use of resources and the development of what were considered to be socially desirable activities. In these countries the government, either directly or through the participation of public bodies such as trade unions, supplied the kinds of facilities for the use of leisure which were generally provided by public agencies in other countries.[1] They made no provision for types of activity not deemed of social value, or which represented a claim on resources which could not be met in the light of other national needs. The development of unacceptable tastes was directly discouraged and the means for satisfying them from abroad were curbed by censorship and the regulation of imports.

In these societies, planning with respect to the use of leisure was viewed as an integral part of national planning. The USSR included at all stages in its development the provision of local facilities for the use of leisure, it converted the homes and estates of the rich into sanatoriums and holiday rest homes for workers, and it encouraged activities positively designed to promote the physical development and raise the cultural level of the people.

Parks of 'culture and rest' in cities and towns served the combined purposes of providing places where families could relax outside their crowded homes, of furnishing play-space for a variety of activities and of offering a wide range of exhibits and informal educational displays. Athletic stadiums, sports grounds, playing fields and gymnasiums provided facilities for sports and other physical activities. Clubhouses or other meeting rooms in factories and collective farms became the scenes of a wide range of cultural activities carried on by informal groups, with the stimulus and often assistance of the local Party unit. Wall newspapers, magazines, study circles, discussion and writing groups were encouraged and musical, dramatic and sports groups were formed.

At all levels Soviet workers were encouraged to use their leisure time in study in order to improve their skills or train for a higher job, and many types of educational facilities were provided to make this possible. Cinema, radio and television were regarded as educational instruments and were used directly through documentary films or educational broadcasts, and indirectly through dramatic presentations.

The USSR and the people's democracies, which pursued an essentially similar policy with respect to provisions for the use of leisure, thus sought to guide the development of the mass culture and to produce values, tastes, habits and personalities consistent with their image of the society which they were building.

In the course of these years both the new leisure and mass culture spread to the newly industrializing areas. To a certain extent leisure and mass culture spread independently. Where industry developed it brought leisure. The norms which had been reached in the industrial countries over a period of a hundred years were taken over bodily along with factory organization and machine processes. Standards established by the conventions of the International Labour Office, including the eight-hour day, were adopted in principle and were more or less fully applied. Although for the bulk of the population which remained in agriculture and related activities leisure continued to be a matter of religious and family festivals, for those who came within the sphere of industrialization it became part of their new way of life.

At the same time, and to an even greater degree, mass communication brought elements of mass culture to all people, both those with leisure and those without. Films in the major Indian languages, for example, became a favourite form of entertainment in that country, not only in the cities where cinemas were chiefly located but in many rural areas, where several hundred touring cinemas exhibited in tents. Radio entertainment, too, was not limited to industrialized elements in the population of underdeveloped countries but reached all manner of people in towns and villages.

Popular music was widely spread by radio and cinema. Indian films popularized what came to be known as 'film music', light music with some of the flavour of traditional Indian music but without its rigour. Similar popularizations based on Arab musical modes were sung and played over the air in Arab countries. Turkish popular music might be heard almost anywhere in the country—in a coffee shop, outside a store or in a public square.

The principal active use of mass leisure in newly industrializing countries was in sports. Whereas such sports as polo or horse-racing had long been the hobbies of the rich, the growth of popular sports was a twentieth-century phenomenon. The particular sport varied, and some areas were more active than others. Wherever British influence extended, sports were especially encouraged; Indian, African and West Indian football, cricket and hockey teams took part in contests within the Commonwealth. In Latin American countries, soccer or baseball was played on any vacant lot. Successful teams and individuals brought prestige to their community and their nation.

The pattern of mass leisure remained more pronounced in the industrialized countries, it was carried much farther there, and the way of life was more deeply affected by it. But the essential trends in the use of leisure and in the development of mass culture which were well developed in the industrial countries were becoming world-wide by the middle of the twentieth century.

In the account which follows, the several ways in which large numbers of people used the new leisure are discussed both in terms of the development in the activity and of the ways in which related facilities were provided, commercially or by public agencies, in the capitalist areas and as part of planned national development in the socialist societies.

The use of leisure and the shape of the mass culture were intimately related with other aspects of technological and social development and with the development of literature and the arts. The following pages must, therefore, be read in conjunction with the chapters on Communications* and Transport†

* Chapter XI.   † Chapter X.

which present the technologies which revolutionized much of leisure-time activity, and the chapter on Education* which traces the spread of mass literacy on which the vast development of popular literature rested. It should also be read in connection with the chapters on Literature and the Arts,† for no sharp and clear line can be drawn between popular expression, enjoyment of leisure or entertainment on the one hand and literary expression and the arts on the other.

II. LEISURE-TIME ACTIVITIES

1. *Reading*

For many people reading was a favourite form of relaxation, both as an end in itself and as an aid to the pursuit of other interests. This had long been true of the educated classes, but now the higher general level of education for the masses of people combined with increased leisure to provide a great new potential reading public. Publishers responded with mass-circulation newspapers and magazines and a great variety of paper-bound books, in addition to their customary publications. As a result, by mid-century about 90 per cent of the populations of the leading industrial countries read newspapers every day, the circulation figures for magazines went on climbing year by year, and paper-bound books were beginning to be available in neighbourhoods and shops where books had not previously been in demand. Libraries spread in urban communities and many rural areas.

With the widening of the reading public the character of the material offered changed, and new types of newspapers, magazines and books appeared alongside older types modified to meet new demands. The new types ranged from tabloid newspapers to digest and picture magazines, and to paper-backed editions of classics, self-education texts, and an infinite variety of detective, science fiction and adventure novels. Both old types and new included many accounts of travel in remote areas, much biographical or auto-biographical material and a wide range of reports on developments in the sciences and arts.

(*a*) *Mass-circulation newspapers and magazines.* Newspapers, from their beginnings in the seventeenth century, had been chronicles of events for the use of merchants and politicians, and means of political propaganda; in the twentieth century they came to be also vehicles of entertainment. Nineteenth-century readers had demanded financial and political coverage, local news and reviews of cultural and sporting events. Twentieth-century readers wanted all these, reports on scientific discoveries, more complete sports coverage, reports on the weather, and a variety of columns devoted to leisure-time activities. Papers began to add to their news-coverage advice on gardening, photography and other hobbies, sample bridge hands and notes on how to play them, crossword puzzles, travel news, radio, motion picture and television reviews,

* Chapter XXVI. † Chapters XXXI, XXXII.

recipes and suggestions for meals and parties, and fashion sections. Many introduced cartoons and cartoon strips or 'comics'.

The new mass-circulation magazines, like the newspapers, sought to be both vehicles of entertainment and purveyors of information and interpretation of developments in science, technology and a wide variety of other fields. They appealed to all strata of society, all age groups and to people with all kinds of interests and tastes. Magazines of this type were particularly strong in the United States. After the second world war publications in this style began to circulate widely in other countries.

Presenting information and entertainment at various levels of sophistication, these magazines took for granted a common stereotype with which their readers could identify themselves. They assumed a progressively higher standard of living with more and more labour-saving devices and the latest or best in clothes, houses, cars, cosmetics, vitamins and wonder drugs. The image which they conveyed featured romantic love, family life, children brought up according to the latest principles of child psychology, ample leisure and an air of perpetual youth.

Though these magazines were filled with information, they were not primarily designed to stimulate thought or question values. They catered to unfocused curiosity about current events, nature, remote parts of the earth, the workings of machinery and of the mind, medicine, religion, sports, outer space, and the daily lives of film stars, sports heroes and other celebrities. Some offered vicarious violence in standardized forms or escape into fantasies of glamour, sex, crime and adventure.

Much space in the mass magazines was devoted to advertising, upon which they depended for a large part of their revenue. In the hands of highly paid craftsmen skilled in making forms designed to produce immediate attention, interest and action, advertising was a source of information and a constant generator of new desires. Some of the finest photography and use of the graphic arts were to be found in the advertising pages, along with paintings reproduced to suggest the prestige of a product, striking colours, superlatives in language and other attention-drawing devices with emotional impact. Advertising thus often became in itself a form of entertainment.

Within the general pattern the quality of presentation varied, and the points of particular attention were chosen by editor and publisher according to specific audiences and their presumed interests.

A number of general magazines, such as *John Bull* in England and *Saturday Evening Post* in the United States, printed well-written stories, informative articles on many timely subjects and cartoons making fun of everyday problems of living; they appealed to moderately well-read audiences which ran into millions. At first these magazines appeared in varying degrees of taste, but gradually they became more uniformly well-printed and colourful.

The most popular of the general magazines, *Reader's Digest*, had the biggest circulation in the world. From its beginning in 1922 it grew to a circulation of nearly 12,000,000 in the United States in 1956 and 3,000,000 in twenty-eight foreign editions. Every month it printed abridgements of articles chosen from many other magazines of the preceding month, a condensation of a best-selling novel, and stories of individuals who had overcome some difficulty with heartening dignity. It told the story of progress in a thousand fields with sustained and earthy optimism. In such a field as bringing up children, it explained problems in terms of the most advanced psychological research; but in its analysis of business enterprise it reiterated many of the values of early capitalist society. It was followed by other digest magazines in many specialized fields, for even the new leisure contained too little time for anybody to read the informative articles in all the periodicals and many people came to depend on getting information or literature in capsule form.

The powerful American publishing empire of Time, Inc., which included *Time* (1923), *Fortune* (1930), *Life* (1936), *Architectural Forum* (acquired 1935), *House and Home* (1952) and *Sports Illustrated* (1954), set standards of popular knowledge at the sophisticated level and defined the meaning of success. *Fortune* was the first magazine to dramatize the giant corporations—their world-wide scale, their use of science, the men who ran them—and to present twentieth-century industry as 'a world of art comparable to sky-scrapers'.

News weeklies, such as *Time* and its imitators, which covered the main events that an up-to-date citizen wanted to know about, included a broader range of subject matter than the older journals of opinion and assumed less basic knowledge on the part of their readers. They thus appealed to newly educated mass audiences and their circulation figures kept rising.

Pictorial journals used all the resources of modern photography to meet the needs of widening audiences for news which could be quickly grasped, and they satisfied the craving for swift, dramatic impact. Magazine publishers had used pictures for illustrations for many years—the *Illustrated London News* and *l'Illustration* dated from 1842 and 1843. But with the immense improvement in cameras and films, permitting action shots, close-ups and candid pictures of people at crucial moments, the photographs themselves became the core and the illustrated magazine gave way to the pictorial journal. The many magazines of this type, such as *Life* which took its format from the French *Vu*, told their stories in pictures and used text only to give continuity and explanations when needed. They commented on events by means of the pictorial essay, an arrangement of photographs in a pattern which highlighted points that the editor specially wanted to bring out.

Women's magazines kept increasing in circulation throughout the period, and by the 1950s ranked with the pictorial journals among the most popular types of periodicals. The general women's magazines had a little of everything that might be of interest to women: articles on education, labour-saving devices, politics or community affairs; beauty hints, special sections on fashion, homemaking, architecture and interior decorating; short stories, poetry, a film review and a condensed novel. Standards of these magazines varied widely, more noticeably in Britain and other European countries than in the United States because publishers in those countries aimed at providing magazines for different social levels. As a group, they grew in popularity and influence. When the largest of these magazines, the United States *Ladies Home Journal*, put out a retrospective volume in 1956 commemorating its 75th year, many non-readers were astonished to find that with great consistency it had published stories, articles and poems of writers who came to be considered the best of their time. These writers had found the *Journal* a good place in which to appear because of the price it had been able to pay to its contributors and because its circulation placed it third among popular magazines in the United States.

Other popular magazines were those having to do with the entertainment world, including periodicals such as the best-selling British *Radio Times*, which gave the radio and television programmes for the coming week and news and comment about them, and the widely read magazines in many countries given over to gossip about screen, radio and television personalities.

Many low-level mass magazines, sold by the millions of kiosks, tobacconists, drug stores and other news-stands, played up the crudest aspects of sex and violence in extreme forms. Confession magazines, westerns, lurid crime and horror stories depended on sensationalism to attract and sell. Some of the crudest and most violent adopted the cartoon or comic strip form widely used for simplified presentation of stories and information. When this occurred, parents and teachers became aroused and agitated for the banning of horror comics. The agitation came up against the principle of freedom of the press, but it served to focus attention on the results of mass literacy in providing a market for crude sensationalism. It caused much thought about how to get people beyond a juvenile mentality and how to deal with commercial incitement to cruelty without resort to authoritarian controls over expression.

The mass-circulation magazines existed side by side with an infinite variety of periodicals produced for special interest groups. A few literary reviews, political journals and society magazines, inherited from the nineteenth century, managed to hold their own. So did professional and technical journals and semi-educational publications like the geographic magazines and the popular, interpretative scientific monthlies. These were joined by a host of new periodicals. All kinds of occupational groups and even corporations began to put out their own weekly, monthly or quarterly reviews, and the great publishing houses produced new magazines aimed at reaching age groups, social groups or interests not previously thought large enough or rich enough to warrant separate publications. For example, high-fidelity enthusiasts, gourmets and teenagers acquired their own handsome glossy reviews, some with circulations of more than a million. Science fiction and detective story magazines had their devotees in many parts of the world and in all levels of society. A large proportion of these special publications, learned journals and popular-appeal magazines alike, were purveyors of information for people pursuing hobbies or for those who used them to keep up with new information in their professional field of interest.

Among the special-interest magazines were the journals of opinion and the literary reviews which raised questions about values within the mass culture and about industrial and political forces. Weekly journals such as the *Spectator*, the *New Statesman* and *The Economist* in Britain presented the news with a definite and well-understood set of political assumptions—right, left or centre—and with analysis designed, as *The Economist* put it, 'to appeal to thinking people everywhere'. In addition to the old-style literary review, a new type, represented by the *Saturday Review of Literature* in the United States, tried to encourage a widening audience of newly educated people to some critical discrimination in their approach to books and theatre and to the new forms of film, radio, television and records. These magazines had increasing difficulty in surviving because their specific appeal and questioning attitudes meant limited circulation and they did not therefore draw large advertising revenues, while rising publication costs were too large to be met only by increasing rates of subscription.

Indeed powerful economic forces were tending to concentrate the publishing of mass magazines in the hands of a few large houses. The vast range of materials from which selection was to be made, the possibilities of swiftly printing editions running into several millions, and the increasing use of colour made immense capital investment necessary; world-wide networks of correspondents and photographers and teams of research workers collected materials; distribution became a major operation in itself. All these factors made it difficult for the isolated publication to survive and led to the formation of 'families' of magazines which could command, in combination, sufficient resources to serve the mass market.

Mass-circulation magazines in the socialist countries, where magazine publication was a public enterprise, differed from those in countries which enjoyed a free commercial press in the absence of advertising and sensational appeal, but they resembled them closely in other respects. The tone and content of the magazines, designed as they were to raise the cultural level of the people, were unaffected by the presence of tastes and interests among the readers to which commercial publishers elsewhere found it profitable to respond. In so far as they dealt with products and their use, it was as these were brought on to the market in a planned manner and their most appropriate use indicated. In place of the latest appeals of advertisers, the readers of mass magazines in the Soviet Union and people's democracies found the latest forms of official propaganda, and in place of sensationalism, material condemning amoral behaviour and crude, primitive interests.

Like mass magazines elsewhere, however, these publications were purveyors of information to people with a wide range of general curiosity and special interests, and their style followed a similar course, with pictorial journalism, the use of colour, fine printing and skilful layout. General magazines assumed that their readers wanted to know about many things. Specialized magazines of all sorts abounded—for women, young people, farmers, metal workers and every type of professional and technician. Journals covering social and political life and literary reviews were also popular.

(*b*) *Popular books.* The continuous flow of books from the world's presses was ample evidence that periodicals were not supplanting them as reading matter. Unesco's survey of book production in 1952 found seven countries producing over 10,000 titles annually—namely USSR, United Kingdom, India, Japan, German Federal Republic, United States and France, in that order—and sixteen others publishing more than 3,000 titles.

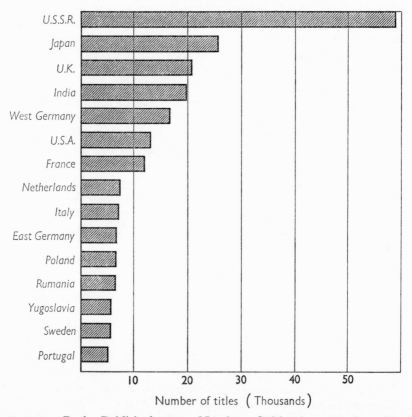

CHART XXIV. Books Published, 1957. Number of titles by countries with the largest book production (countries differ in what they include as 'books'; e.g. pamphlets, government reports, etc.).

Source: *U.N. Statistical Yearbook*, 1960.

The movement for establishing public libraries which had developed in the nineteenth century was greatly extended, and libraries became not only custodians of books but promoters of their use. In many countries city libraries opened neighbourhood branches, put on exhibits, offered lectures, organized discussion groups, provided special reading rooms for children,

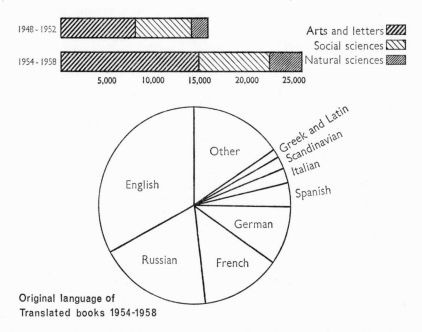

CHART XXV. Books Translated. Annual average world output by subject matter 1948–52, 1954–58; and by original language, 1954–58.
Source: *U.N. Statistical Yearbook*, 1960.

and employed reference librarians to help people find their way to the information which they sought. From the 1920s on, central libraries in cities and in some rural areas sent out travelling bookmobiles which penetrated into regions which had previously been quite cut off from supplies of books, making weekly or bi-weekly visits and enabling readers to request books they especially wanted.

Library coverage was much more complete in some countries than in others, but everywhere library services made more and more books available to more and more people. Sweden was one of the countries whose *per capita* facilities were among the greatest. The Ministry of Culture in the USSR maintained a network of public libraries which extended down to the district level and operated neighbourhood lending centres and itinerant lending libraries and supplied books to libraries established by club-houses, cultural centres, collective farms and other groups. The United States system of public libraries, comprehensive in some cities and regions and less extensive in others, was supplemented by many thousands of school and university libraries and by the specialized libraries of public agencies and organizations, which members of the public could arrange to use. The British public library system was supplemented by a system of ubiquitous low-cost rental libraries.

Book purchase clubs gave their members the opportunity to receive each month, at a greatly reduced price, a book selected by a panel of judges from among current publications. By 1951 there were seventy-four such nation-wide book clubs for adults in the United States and eleven for children, and the number in other countries was growing. Some were general 'book of the month' clubs, others specialized in history, art, new editions of the classics and a multitude of other subjects. The clubs made books available to a wide public, many of whom lacked the discrimination or opportunity to make their own selection. They helped to reduce the cost of publishing by providing a large, guaranteed market, and they filled a gap caused by the concentration of bookshops in larger cities and central locations.

The kinds of books which caught and held public interest ranged from romantic novels, especially those with an historical setting, to semi-scientific reports on the latest battles with nature. Books such as Sir John Hunt's *Ascent of Everest* (1953) enabled people, vicariously, to pit themselves against snow and mountain and to learn something of the techniques involved in planning great expeditions. Travel books and anthropological studies of primitive societies achieved huge circulations during these years as they satisfied the desire for insight into other people's lives. Books on wild life, such as Konrad Lorenz's *King Solomon's Ring* (1952) or Henry Williamson's *Salar the Salmon* (1948), which revealed to readers the habits of animals, birds and fish, appealed to young and old. Biographies and autobiographies of all sorts became best sellers among readers who wanted to know how important people reacted to the problems they faced and among those who enjoyed the role of amateur historian and liked to compare various accounts of the same happenings. Also popular were books which aroused nostalgia for childhood or a remembered way of life and those which offered reassuring answers to common personal problems.

Whatever the subject, whether historical, geographical, biographical, psychological or scientific and whether fiction or reporting, readers demanded authenticity of detail and a sense that their reading was adding to their information and to their insight into reality, past or present.

Books became easier to acquire with the appearance of cheap paper-backed editions on magazine and newspaper counters and in all kinds of retail outlets. The attempt to provide inexpensive books was not new; from the middle of the nineteenth century German Tauchnitz editions had made English and German authors available in cheap printings. But the great expansion came when publishers discovered that by printing books as they did magazines, on high-speed rotary presses, and selling them in quantity they could make a profitable business. Following the lead of the British Penguin series, publishers reprinted standard works and published new ones in inexpensive pocket editions. Since the paper-backed book trade depended on wide circulation, books began to appear not only in bookstalls and on tobacco counters, but in department stores and even grocery shops.

The paper-backs covered a multitude of subjects. The earliest ones were either well-known books, reprinted on the assumption that people would buy paper-backed editions because they were cheap, or else 'penny dreadfuls'. Later, publishers began to offer a mixture of detective, adventure, and science fiction, reprints of famous novels and plays, guides to birds, minerals, stamps, psychoanalysis, and treatises on subjects varying from political theory to the great religions and from archaeology to music—in fact, any and all subjects which appeared likely to have public appeal. The immense range of interest to which the ever-changing array of new titles was addressed bore witness to the fact that, though expressions of mass culture were often garish, fragmentary and crude, they also reflected a new awareness of the world beyond the tiny circle of any one person's circumscribed life and a lively effort to encompass at least some part of its meaning.

In the communist countries where every effort was made to develop a nation of readers out of the newly literate workers and peasants, millions of cheap books were published and distributed and libraries were established in factories, farms, schools and other centres. Editions of Russian classics, the works of Soviet writers, and foreign works from Europe, America and Asia were put out in editions of more than 100,000 copies; they appeared in Russian and in the various languages of the Soviet republics. At the Brussels World's Fair in 1958, the State Publishing House of Fiction and Poetry of the USSR received the Grand Prix for the wide range of the books which it published.

2. The cinema*

Of all the kinds of entertainment available in the twentieth century probably the one that most people had in common was the cinema. From the 1920s on, more and more people went to the pictures, some occasionally, and some often. Figures for 1952 showed the British to be going on an average of 25 times a year, New Zealanders 18 times, Australians 16, and Americans 15; but whatever the nationality—French, German, Japanese, Indian, Mexican or any other—people all over the world shared a taste for the movies. They shared too the personalities and the stories which went to make up this world of illusion created by the twentieth century's 'story-teller of the people'.

The development of the cinema reflected the constant interaction between the producer, testing out his medium and his market, and the public, res-

* For discussion of the cinema as a form of art, see Chapter XXXI, Literature and the Arts, pp. 1265-71.

ponding to the spectacles which it was offered and having its outlook shaped by them. In no other form of leisure-time activity was the role of the producer so important and the nature and quality of the entertainment so dependent on the circumstances and exigencies of production. The making of films was a complex and costly affair and their distribution required elaborate organization and equipment. The motion picture as a medium lent itself to use at all levels of entertainment and art, but the economics of film production required a mass audience. Film producers strove constantly to find formulae which would ensure a mass appeal, and they repeated each successful pattern until a drop in box office receipts showed that it would no longer attract the public.

As a form of entertainment the cinema was dominated throughout the period by Hollywood except in the communist-controlled areas, where these films did not penetrate. Up to the second world war Hollywood provided 70–80 per cent of the films shown in the non-communist countries and even in the 1950s it continued to supply as many as two-thirds of the films exhibited in these areas. A review of the cinema as a form of entertainment during these years, therefore, must give major place to the phenomenon of Hollywood and its impact in the shaping of mass culture, although producers in other countries made greater contributions to the development of the film as an art form and although in the years after the second world war growing national film industries, especially in Asia, were supplying audiences at home and were entering world markets.

The American motion picture industry was built up by men who shared the background and tastes of the masses to whom they appealed. The initial entrepreneurs included a number of former fur workers and salesmen who operated bright, cheap little penny arcades where people from crowded city neighbourhoods could find a variety of machines that provided amusement, including peep-hole motion pictures for a penny a look. The most successful of the arcade owners made enough money to open small theatres which showed short films for a small admission fee, or vaudeville houses which included moving pictures among their acts. When these entrepreneurs became the major Hollywood producers, they continued to think in terms of the recent immigrants and other city workers who had crowded the penny arcades, and they learned only gradually that the public would respond to more sustained, sophisticated and artistic entertainment.

In Europe, by contrast, films were initially an extension of the theatre, and after the first experimental stages the theatre producers who developed them thought in terms of theatre audiences and the film as a form of art.

Until the first world war the centre of the film world was in Europe, but after 1915 it shifted to the United States because the industry there had audience and financial backing unequalled elsewhere. By that time the American 'penny arcade' men had acquired chains of theatres around the country and had organized large producing companies. Representatives of some of the biggest and richest corporations in the United States sat on their boards of directors. In short, the films had become part of big business.

After a period of intense competition the major American motion picture companies emerged as combinations of producing, distributing and exhibiting units. In the early years producers made films and rented them on the open

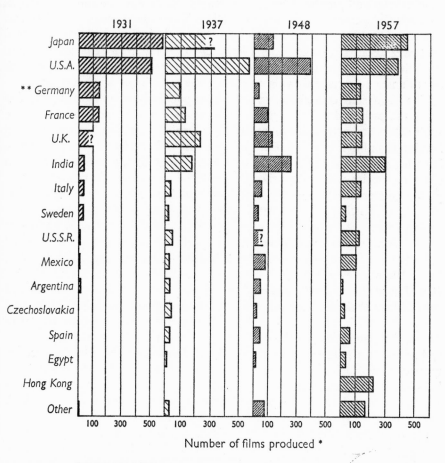

Number of films produced *

* Excludes short films
** Both German Federal Republic and East Germany for 1948, 1957

CHART XXVI. World Production of Motion Pictures.
Source: *U.N. Statistical Yearbook, 1951, 1960.*

market to exhibitors but, as the industry grew, some of the richer producers began to collect theatres in order to ensure places to show their films. Owners of big theatre chains in their turn collected producing studios in the effort to have some control over charges and to ensure films for their theatres. The resulting combinations had large resources at their command and, by the nature of their struggle for survival, were intent on pleasing a mass public.

For years both producers and exhibitors underestimated what the public would take. They developed the custom of making a few first-rate pictures aimed at attaining the highest standards while relying for the bulk of their programmes and profits on 'B class' pictures which they were able to market through the outlets which they controlled. These were made at lower cost than the 'A class' pictures and had the sole object of entertaining, with no pretences about art. Nevertheless, in order to get the greatest public support possible for such pictures, producers experimented widely with stories and actors and never ceased trying to perfect the techniques of picture making.

The star system contributed greatly to the popularity of all motion pictures. From the earliest days of the films, audiences had reacted more favourably to some actors and actresses than others. The Danish star, Asta Nielsen, was the heroine of millions of young Europeans during the first world war. Recognizing this, producers began to vie with each other for the public favourites, choosing stories which they thought could be particularly appealing to the person concerned and offering ever higher salaries. Big studios adopted the practice of putting the favourites under long-term contracts which meant paying them even when they were not actually making pictures, and each studio spent large sums in advertising its own particular stars.

By the 1920s patterns of attendance had become established. People went to see the films which the industry classed as its best efforts, spectacles like *Ben Hur* or the *Four Horsemen of the Apocalypse*; they went to see certain stars: Mary Pickford, 'the girl with the golden curls'; Rudolph Valentino, the handsome idol; Douglas Fairbanks, the hero of romantic action; the great lovers, the glamorous and the seductive heroines, the villains, the comedians, and above all Charlie Chaplin. A considerable number also went to specific types of films, such as westerns, for the sheer joy of the action involved. The halls where the films were shown became elaborate 'palaces' with luxurious décor, uniformed attendants and brightly lit entrances. By now Hollywood had become the symbol of glamour, extravagance, adventure and romance and it provided the public with images for imitation and fantasy.

The powerful American film industry, based on its domestic market where two-fifths of the world's motion picture houses were located, expanded its operations abroad. By 1925 American films were being shown in seventy countries, with their subtitles translated into thirty-seven languages. Eighty per cent of all the feature films shown in Britain were American and 60 per cent of those shown in Germany, which ranked next in total film production. Yet despite the predominance of Hollywood, the European industries continued to make film history, and pictures by the great producers in Germany, Russia, France, Denmark and elsewhere won world renown.

In these circumstances European producers appealed to their governments for aid on the ground that the cinema was a national interest as much as any other form of art or communication. The British Parliament passed an Act in 1927 requiring that a percentage of all films shown must be of British origin and putting limitations on imported films. Other countries made similar attempts to foster their own film industries by means of differential taxation, import regulation, or requiring their exhibitors to show a proportion of the home product.

In 1926 came sound. Although the technical means to achieve it had existed from the early years of the century, it was not introduced until rapidly declining American attendance figures made Hollywood aware that the public wanted something new. The first films with a synchronized musical score and with dialogue were immediate successes and the industry recognized that it must make whatever adjustments a changeover to sound might require. Pictures began to depend on dialogue as well as action and spectacle for their appeal; witty social commentaries and pleasant films about everyday life proved unexpectedly popular. Fine actors with especially effective voices, such as Greta Garbo, rose in favour.

Once sound had been accepted and mastered, the cinema developed the world patterns which existed until after the second world war. The United States, France and Britain dominated the world's screens during these years. The American industry produced many excellent feature pictures, a high percentage of the world's newsreels and animated cartoons, but it also went on producing great quantities of second- and third-rate love and adventure stories. Its mastery of technique made these pictures acceptable to audiences around the world when nothing else was available, but some of Hollywood's leaders warned that it must improve the general calibre of its pictures if it wanted to keep public favour.

The French achieved international pre-eminence in the realm of artistic films. The best of the French films always aimed at select audiences, though the industry also made ordinary films for commercial distribution. Russian films of the 1920s and 1930s were noted for their realism, their close-up studies of human types and the dramatic intensity with which they conveyed their message. The British developed a school of documentary film-making which won critical acclaim and proved most useful during the second world war as an instrument of propaganda and reporting. They also had a sizeable world audience for the best of their feature films, especially those which combined humour and suspense, or such a dramatic masterpiece as *Henry V*.

After the second world war, the world film situation changed, as new and expanding local film industries reduced Hollywood's pre-eminence and television provided a competing source of entertainment. American films underwent a gradual transformation which led to the production of a smaller number of pictures annually, but these generally of a higher standard. During the war years people had gone to see virtually anything; but when television came the public stayed home. In an effort to regain favour Hollywood exploited colour and the wide screen to the limit of their possibilities; it made more pictures on location, thus achieving authentic background and local colour; it produced fewer cheap Class B pictures; it did more social reporting, and it began to try to cope with the reality of human emotions, as distinguished from its earlier largely external approach. Yet though it cut down the number of films, it continued to be the largest producer until after 1955 when Japan and India surpassed the United States in the number of pictures produced.

Britain and France continued to make and export high-quality films, and other nations also began to gain recognition. Italian films attracted attention, both those with bitter realism and those which gave a more suave and humorous treatment of society. Swedish films had a high reputation generally and a few, like the nature film about an otter, *The Great Adventure*, were considered among the most beautiful films made. More Mexican films also began to appear abroad. Canadian documentaries, produced by the National Film Board and translated into five languages, went all over the world. The USSR used films extensively both for instruction and entertainment, and developed regional film industries with the languages and materials of the Soviet republics. In the 1950s vivid Russian films, such as *The Cranes are Flying*, reappeared on the world market, as did some from West Germany. Asian film industries followed the general lines of those in America and Europe, developing their own patterns of glamour, romance, and extravagance, their favourite stars, their musical entertainment, their spectacles and their dramas of daily life. The pace was closer to the long, diffuse forms of entertainment to which Asian audiences were accustomed than to the fast pace and dramatic tension of American and European films.

The most highly developed of the Asian film industries, the Japanese, dated from the early days of the cinema, but it was only after the reorganization which followed the second world war that Japanese films entered the world market. Then their few outstanding art films won prizes in international contests and received world-wide acclaim for their exquisite photography and sensitive portrayals. Most Japanese films continued to offer their people romances out of the past, gay scenes of modern life, sensitive views of nature and highly popular romantic dramas involving the conflict between personal love and family duty.

Indian films relied heavily on music, dance and costume effects for their appeal. They also included romance, the portrayal of high society, and historical drama and biography. An Indian film enquiry board in 1951 complained that the films pandered to a low level of taste and principle and failed to serve as an instrument to promote attitudes in line with the social and cultural development of the country. The Indian government itself produced newsreels and short documentary or educational films which exhibitors were required to show along with each commercial film. After 1955 a few Indian films containing realistic portrayals of daily life received international recognition and were widely shown abroad. The main export of Indian films was to places where there were Indian audiences in Africa, south-east Asia and the Middle East.

In the years after the second world war other substantial film industries producing for the Asian market developed in Singapore, Hong Kong, Manila and Formosa. Those of Singapore, Hong Kong and Formosa made chiefly musical pictures and comedies; the Filipino industry followed the Japanese and Indian in presenting costume dramas based on early history and legends. For films about modern life, family problems were the key themes, especially harsh in-laws, a perennial subject in Asian literature. The Chinese People's Republic used the cinema extensively to carry communist principles throughout the country, frequently using a modified form of the traditional Chinese opera.

Although Hollywood and European pictures continued to be shown in Tokyo, Bangkok and Bombay in the 1950s, Asian films were providing the principal motion picture fare for the audiences in Asian countries. They were creating their own images for fantasy and imitation and were helping to define the mass culture which was taking shape in these lands.

As film producers and film audiences throughout the world interacted upon each other, some forces tended to debase and others to elevate the quality of the product and therewith its influence on the cultural life of the people. Over the years these pressures tended to raise the level of the mass entertainment which the films offered.

The world's literary classics, both great novels and great plays, became the common property of all viewers, as they never would have been in written form, and their presentation on the screen stimulated viewers to become readers. As audiences developed more discrimination and were less ready to flock to anything which might be offered, film critics writing for newspapers and popular magazines became more influential. From 1929 on, the Motion Picture Academy of America presented annual awards, known as Oscars, based on a combination of the critics' and the people's choice, which carried prestige and were a way of attracting audiences to the films named. The popularity of some films of outstanding excellence was further evidence of the level to which popular taste had risen by the 1950s. The picture which broke all records by the length of its run in a major New York theatre was the British film, *The Red Shoes*, a distinguished work of art combining all the special expressiveness of films—shifting scenes, colour, dance, music—in a drama of a ballet dancer's conflict between her profession and her love, which played continuously to capacity audiences for two years.

The result of the wide diffusion of films, both nationally and internationally, was to introduce new ideas and new approaches to life to many people otherwise insulated from such variety of experience. It brought a sense of the cultural diversity of the world, however distorted the view which was often conveyed. In the words of the British committee which investigated the films in the 1920s, the cinema was 'undoubtedly a most important factor in the education of all classes of the community, in the spread of national culture and in presenting national ideas and customs to the world. Its potentialities moreover in shaping the ideas of the very large number to whom it appeals are almost unlimited.'* No other medium had quite the world spread, nor reached as many different kinds of people, as the cinema.

3. Radio

Radio and, later, television were the instruments which brought entertainment and mass culture into the home. They made both the world of reality and the world of make-believe a part of the daily lives of men, women and children, intimately, continuously, insistently and without effort on the part of the listener. From early dawn until far into the night, the housewife in her kitchen, the father home from work and the child home from school had but to turn a knob to bring music or news, drama, sports or information to where they were. These sounds would travel with the motorist along the highway or go with the holiday-maker to sea; they filled the air in eating places, stores, public squares, factories, buses. They were the constant accompaniment of everyday life in the second quarter of the twentieth century.

Broadcasting of entertainment and news did not begin until the 1920s, though wireless had been used as an instrument of communication from the opening of the century. It was inaugurated in 1920 when a radio station in Pittsburgh, USA, broadcast the result of the American presidential election before the newspapers had had time to print the news. The public was immediately interested, and it only remained to build on this interest with further experiments. Stations in the United States and Britain began to transmit regular programmes and soon stations elsewhere followed suit.

The earliest programmes were made up of news, music and novelties— the magnified heartbeats of a butterfly or voices from a submarine—but shortly sports reporting and other popular programmes appeared. At first stations broadcast for only a few hours at a time, but before long they had programmes extending from early morning exercises through news and music, sketches and jokes to keep housewives entertained while they did their chores, to afternoon programmes for children, and sports and variety programmes for the evening hours. People began to look to the radio for the latest news—some even suggested that the new medium would supplant newspapers altogether—and for the latest melodies from new musical shows before the sheet music or the records were on sale in local shops—and for a continuous flow of free entertainment such as never had been known before.

The sale of radio sets went up by leaps and bounds as people became increasingly interested in what they could hear over the air-waves. In the United States, where the radio very soon began to seem indispensable, the number of

* Quoted in *The British Film Industry*, a report by P.E.P. (Political and Economic Planning, London, 1952), p. 13.

homes with radio sets rose from 60,000 in 1922 to 3,500,000 by 1925, and 9,000,000 by 1929; the number of broadcasting stations increased during the same years from 30 to 57 to 618. In other countries the rate of expansion was less rapid, but everywhere the new communications medium, with its almost unlimited potentialities, grew in popularity. The United States had half of the world's total, but the number of sets ran to many millions in the USSR, the United Kingdom, other European and Commonwealth countries and Japan, and to many thousands in virtually every country in the world. However remote the region and whether the reception was in homes, gathering places or the open air, radio was providing entertainment and ideas for people in all lands.

In the course of the 1920s and 1930s, three general patterns of organization and financing evolved which affected the manner in which the radio would be used and the programmes heard over it: the private enterprise system with active competition among stations and a minimum of government control, characteristic of the United States, the Latin American countries, Japan and, in part, of Canada and Australia; the public corporation system exemplified by the British Broadcasting Corporation; and the system of direct government ownership and control of broadcasting operations characteristic of the communist countries, of most new Asian and African states and, in combination with one of the other systems, also used in European and British commonwealth areas.

In the United States, with its multitude of radio stations, broadcasting was financed by advertisers who paid for the privilege of announcing their wares to listeners attracted by an entertainment programme, while listeners paid nothing directly for the entertainment they received, beyond the original cost of their receiving sets. Under this system radio was regarded as a source of entertainment and only very incidentally as a means of education. Most programmes were light; if they were informative, they were varied and dramatic. They were short, or were broken up into a variety of music, dialogue and comment, with frequent interruptions for advertising. Advertising itself became a form of entertainment in order to hold the attention of the listener. Since the federal law required that a certain amount of time be devoted to public service programmes as a condition of receiving a licence to use the air-waves, there were always a certain number of programmes devoted to serious music, discussions of public issues or presentations of information on such subjects as farming or child care, as well as to the latest news and weather.

Even more than the mass magazines, the radio was under pressure to interest the largest possible audience, for the programme to which people listened was the one which advertisers were willing to support. The types of programmes which made up this all-appeal mass entertainment contained variety shows combining comedy skits and the latest popular songs, quiz programmes, sporting events, serialized stories of ordinary people and their emotional crises, mystery dramas, westerns, interviews with public figures and quantities of music, some live and much recorded. Advertising itself, moreover, became part of radio entertainment as advertisers couched more and more of their appeals in entertainment forms.

The main programmes throughout the United States were those provided through four major networks supported by national advertising, although large numbers of local stations operated in most cities of any size, supported by local advertisers and presenting local performers or local interviews, along with recorded music. The large sums paid by advertisers to the networks made it possible to hire the best dramatic, musical and newscasting talent for these programmes, but the listening public could enjoy them only at the cost of constant exposure to a stream of advertising and a tendency toward sameness at the level of maximum popularity. As a result, various educational institutions began experimenting with stations of their own which attempted to programme on the basis of different interests or tastes. So also did local 'good music' stations established in a number of major cities in the 1940s with programmes made up chiefly of classical and serious modern music.

In other countries where radio broadcasting was supported by advertising, a similar pattern and type of mass-appeal programme resulted, with some variation in the extent to which time was set aside for educational broadcasts and in the way in which such time was used.

Where broadcasting was carried on by a public or semi-public agency, it was not necessary to aim all programmes at the widest possible audience, and programmes were designed for distinct bodies of listeners. Even in these systems, however, some of the same pressures toward popular types of programmes were at work.

The British Broadcasting Corporation, operated as a publicly authorized monopoly subject to parliamentary review, made a definite attempt to interest audiences at three different educational levels: the Light Programme, primarily for entertainment, offered variety shows, popular music, popular drama and human interest stories; the Home Service, also designed to attract a wide audience, gave programmes dealing with the arts, science and world affairs at levels which did not demand specialized knowledge, symphony concerts, dramatizations of famous novels, talks, discussions and children's programmes; while the Third Programme was deliberately experimental without regard for popular taste. Started in 1946 with the hope that it would in the long run raise the level of all British programmes, the Third Programme attracted an unexpectedly wide range of listeners. Offering new music, experimental plays, lectures presenting new knowledge and thought-provoking analyses of current events, it proved so successful that Italy, Spain, Greece, Germany and France all devised similar programmes, and educational stations in the United States, British commonwealth and Latin American countries made use of its transcriptions for some of their broadcasts. Even so, the BBC in the late 1950s reduced Third Programme time and offered instead the more popular and practical Network Three programmes designed for listeners interested in specific hobbies or in learning languages.

The state radios of the communist states were used primarily for educational purposes as well as to give people throughout the country a common outlook and interpretation of events. The USSR developed its broadcasting services under the auspices of the ministry of education, which provided national programmes and supervised the programmes of regional and local stations. It built redistribution facilities to give overall coverage to rural areas and provided millions of wired receivers and loudspeakers in public places to ensure that as many people as possible could listen to broadcasts. Radio Moscow regularly broadcast three simultaneous programmes for listeners throughout the USSR, a programme of general interest, a programme for specialized groups such as agricultural and industrial workers, and a programme of formal educational broadcasts. In the decade after the second world war the Moscow radio, together with more than a hundred local committees of radio information located in the capitals of the Union republics and other administrative centres, provided programmes of these types throughout the Soviet Union in some seventy languages. All these programmes informed the working people about the latest in science and technology and popularized the finest works of Russian and world literature, music, fine arts. The popular 'universities of culture' and 'universities of artistic training' programmes devoted to science and engineering, agricultural science and other subjects offered opportunities both for use of leisure and for raising the people's educational and cultural standards. Great importance was also attached to children's programmes.

In other countries with state or public corporation systems, radio was used educationally. The Indian government designed its publicly operated radio programmes for a variety of purposes, including promoting the use of Hindi as a national language and familiarizing the public with traditional Indian music. About 75 per cent of all Australian schools subscribed to that country's school broadcasts in the 1950s. Norway experimented with short-wave educational programmes beamed to its merchant fleet plying the seven seas. But even government-operated radio systems were under some pressure to adapt their programmes to popular tastes in order to hold the attention of the listeners.

Whatever the character of its programmes, radio tended to provide its listeners with a common set of images and body of experience. The styles of speech and patterns of entertainment of New York or Hollywood, London, Paris, or Moscow were heard uniformly throughout the areas to which the broadcasts were beamed, whether in rural areas or cities, in the homes of the rich or the poor, of educated or uneducated. Naturally, there was a certain amount of listener choice, and some receiving sets stood silent much of the time while others operated constantly. But the choice was limited and the radio was ever present in the home, the car, the workshop, constantly speak-

KK*

ing the words and playing the music heard in other homes and shops across the land. The radio came to people; they did not have to go out to seek it, as they did the cinema, or the books and magazines which they borrowed or bought or the sports events which they attended. Thus the radio was one of the most potent instruments giving a common content to mass cultures throughout the world.

4. *Television*

Television, introduced after the second world war, threatened both the cinema and the radio. People no longer had to go to the cinema for visual entertainment; it was theirs for the turning of a button in their homes. And with the added dimension of the picture, television produced a richer fare than the radio could offer with sound alone. The immediate effect was to cut down attendance at the cinema and cause many of the most popular radio programmes to shift over to the new medium. After a time, however, it became apparent that the small television screen placed limitations on the range of visual presentation, while the radio could continue as an accompaniment to other activity without demanding the full attention and fixed position which television required.

Since 1930, broadcasters in the United States, United Kingdom, USSR, France and Germany had experimented with ways of exploiting the addition of sight to sound broadcasting, but regular television programming did not begin till the late 1940s. Once it was introduced, television spread like wildfire. All over the world people were ready to adopt it and incorporate it into their way of life, for they had become thoroughly accustomed to the ever-present radio in the home and to turning to the cinema for entertainment, while the industrial structure present in these industries was readily adaptable to the new device.

By 1955 television was operating on a regular basis in 34 countries, was being developed in 12 others and was in the planning stages in another 19. The United States took a strong initial lead with an estimated 80 per cent of the world's sets in 1955, but everywhere the number of receivers skyrocketed. The number of sets did not fully reveal the extent of television's influence, moreover, for many sets were located in taverns, waiting rooms, clubs and other public places.

The organizational pattern of the television industry in most countries tended to follow that of radio, with some modifications. In the United States most television programmes, like radio, were supported by advertising. The British Broadcasting Corporation introduced a television programme, but in 1955 in answer to public pressure an independent television system was added, financed by commercial advertising. In most European countries television broadcasting was operated under state control. In Latin American countries it was commercially sponsored. In the USSR and the people's democracies it was widely extended as part of the state system.

Television programming resembled that worked out for radio except that it had a smaller proportion of music, more drama and used moving picture films as a major resource. In Russia all motion picture features were automatically shown on television, but elsewhere films only became available as studios released their old cinema libraries. Mostly these were films made a number of years before, but some proved a tremendous hit on television and revived the names and fame of many former favourites.

Variety, quiz and human interest shows were consistently popular everywhere, as were sports events which could often be witnessed in the home more clearly than in the arena as the camera brought a close-up of each play. Drama ranged from fine performances of well-known plays to the general run of serialized romances, westerns and mystery dramas. Documentaries reconstructed past events, pictured phases of contemporary life or recorded the processes of nature. Leading figures were brought to the screen for interviews or to take part in discussions of public issues.

A distinctive feature of television was that it enabled the public to witness directly many public events—a political convention, the coronation of a Pope, a meeting of the United Nations. Millions of people felt intimately acquainted with public figures, for they had watched their expressions and mannerisms during a debate or when they were not the centre of the stage as well as when they were addressing the public through the television medium. Public figures, in their turn, consciously strove to cultivate their 'television personality' and to arrange their television appearances according to the techniques required for dramatic success.

At the start television carried over directly the forms of radio and cinema, but all programmes were not equally appropriate to the new medium. After an initial period of imitation and experiment, certain types of programmes began to emerge as particularly well adapted to television presentation in a small space with a small image and in the intimacy of the home—plays, panel discussions such as the 'Brains Trust' programme presented weekly by the BBC, informational programmes which involved exploration or demonstration, quiz programmes where the audience could identify with the person questioned.

A major problem of television broadcasting was how to get enough talent to occupy all the time at the broadcaster's disposal. The costs of a production for one short showing on television were tremendous. Even where stations broadcast only five or six hours a night, it proved difficult to get enough first-class material. More and more American programmes were filmed rather than presented live, and their production was carried on in Hollywood studios closely associated with those of the film industry.

International programme co-operation helped to meet this situation. From 1954 on, Europe had an exchange relay network known as Eurovision which grouped eight countries—Belgium, Denmark, France, the German Federal Republic, the Netherlands, Italy, Switzerland and the United

Kingdom. Its first telecast showed the 1954 world football championship matches from Switzerland. Programmes of this type continued to be especially popular but in the course of time, besides sports and entertainment, Eurovision provided intimate glimpses of life as it was lived by ordinary people in each of these countries, thus helping viewers to gain understanding of people in other lands. From 1953 on, the United States provided filmed television programmes for Latin America and later began to make them available to Japanese and European stations.

Although the sheer volume of television programmes tended to limit their average quality, there were signs that audiences which had become accustomed to seeing or hearing first-rate talent at the cinema and over the air would not readily be satisfied with second-rate performances on television, once the novelty had worn off. Some of the same factors that were tending to raise the level of mass entertainment in the cinema and radio were thus at work in this new medium as well.

5. Theatre groups

Amateur dramatics remained a popular form of leisure-time activity, in spite of the ubiquity of films and television. The quality and seriousness of amateur performances ranged from the near-professional levels attained by some community and university theatre groups to simple skits for the self-entertainment of clubs or school plays which combined education and entertainment. In the 1920s and 1930s there was a strong movement to establish 'little theatres' with community support, sometimes to provide an outlet for local dramatic talent, sometimes to show plays which did not find a place on the professional stage. As cities expanded their public recreation services they included dramatics among the activities offered.

Outside the main urban centres repertory theatres provided a principal source of dramatic entertainment. Such theatres, which often served as proving grounds for both dramatists and actors, were sometimes closer to the amateur community theatre and at others to the professional stage. They received support from private organizations and public bodies interested in the arts.

In the USSR and the people's democracies workers and peasants were encouraged to enjoy and appreciate music, theatre and ballet, both as spectators and through amateur participation. Professional theatres, ballets and orchestras were maintained in cities and towns of all sizes—some 500 repertory theatres in the USSR in the 1950s—while amateur musical groups or people's art theatres rehearsed and performed in factories, collective farms and educational institutions. These professional and amateur groups drew on the rich background of Russian music, ballet and theatre and also on the traditional folk expression of the different regions. Where there was no theatre tradition the art was developed, as in the Uzbek republic which had no indigenous theatre but by the 1950s was maintaining twenty-six theatrical companies which presented performances of all types. Regional and national arts festivals stimulated these developments.

6. *Popular music and dancing*

Especially for young people, listening to popular music and dancing were favourite ways to spend leisure time. It was in fact chiefly the adolescents who gave successive styles of music and forms of dancing their popularity, supplying the market for popular records and sheet music, and much of the audience for popular music over the air. The current styles in these forms of expression were often of no interest or even distasteful to most adults but were central features of the adolescents' sub-culture.

Popular music in the twentieth century had three principal origins, musical shows, jazz bands and hit songs which caught the public's fancy when sung by a radio entertainer or night club singer. With the aid of radio and television, new songs or tunes could become the favourites of millions overnight. New hits were heard over and over again on radio programmes, sales of records and sheet music soared and then, generally, as quickly dropped. The songs could be simple and even crude and the rendering poor by any musical standards, but if the singer was the current idol of the adolescent listeners or if the song successfully expressed a current mood, the song became for the moment a part of the mass culture.

Musical shows proved extremely popular with audiences which could see them and supplied a large proportion of the popular music which was played constantly over the air and on gramophones in the home. The European type, referred to as the Viennese operetta in recognition of the master of light music, Johann Strauss (1825–99), was gay, tuneful and romantic. These operettas had their heyday in the years before the first world war, and tunes from some of the favourites of that period by the Strausses, the Hungarian Franz Lehar (1870–1948), and others retained their popularity or were revived repeatedly in the following decades.

After the first world war the type of musical show which had the greatest vogue and provided much of the popular music was the American musical comedy which took shape as a distinct entertainment form on Broadway. It had its origin in the tradition of the vaudeville stage and the accident of a fire in 1866 in a New York theatre where a French ballet troupe was to perform. When the manager of the troupe put his ballet on to the vaudeville stage in order to avoid a financial loss and interspersed a miscellany of song and dance, he inaugurated a type of entertainment which depended on a combination of catchy songs and the attraction of 'girls, girls, girls'.

In the course of time the thread on which these features were strung became firmer and musical comedies included more semblance of plot, characterization and dramatic structure. Shows depended less on the attraction of scantily clad, shapely chorus girls and more on costume and stage effects, humour and gay or elaborate dance routines. Well-constructed musical scores and clever lyrics, both romantic and satiric, became the basis for a show's popularity. Some shows came to be based on full-scale plays, like the hit of the 1955 Broadway season, *My Fair Lady*, based on George Bernard Shaw's play *Pygmalion*.

The best of the musical comedies were consistently the leading theatrical attractions on Broadway, and some of them ran to packed houses for years while their songs were heard over every radio and records of the hits or the entire score reached tremendous sales. In time the most popular shows were filmed and they played to millions of people who already knew and relished many of the tunes. By the 1950s this popular form of entertainment appeared to be moving toward a distinct art form. It remained a show that was assembled out of disparate parts, rather than an integral whole that was composed; it was still essentially theatrical entertainment made up of music and dance and spectacle, strung on a story. But some critics saw the best of the musical comedies as commentaries on life which derived a unity of form from the common attitude expressed by the décor, the music, the dance, the lyrics, the performers, the direction. And the particular outlook which the musical comedy expressed theatrically, extravagantly and exuberantly, was a sense of the ridiculousness of cherished institutions combined with a warm affection for the very institutions which the show held up to satire.

While musical comedies provided most of the popular songs, jazz bands furnished the popular dance music. As a musical form, jazz traced its origin to West African rhythms combined with melodic and harmonic forms and musical structure derived from European marches, hymns, work songs and popular ballads. Sociologically it was the music through which New Orleans Negroes released their pent-up energy, anger, nostalgia, sadness, sense of irony and exuberance. When it invaded the night clubs and dance floors of the rest of the United States at the time of the first world war, it brought shock to most adults who were attuned to the suave romanticism of the popular music of the time, and a welcome release to the young.

The essence of jazz was improvisation, so it could never be wholly dissociated from the men who made it. Famous bands had their followers whom they drew to the cafés and dance halls where they played regularly and to dances elsewhere for which they provided the music. Their several styles became familiar through recordings played over the air or on the gramophone, and jazz enthusiasts relished the virtuosity of their favourite performers.

In the course of the years new bands developed new styles, and a succession of distinct types commanded popular favour. The original jazz style of the years before 1914 was heavily accented and lively, exciting to dance to. From the mid-1920s the jerky New Orleans rhythms gave way to smoother and more sophisticated tempos known as 'swing'. By the years after the second world war jazz had ceased to be primarily music to dance to; it had become music to hear and composers were beginning to give serious study to the jazz idiom and to write jazz compositions. The adolescents of the 1950s no longer found jazz exciting to dance to, for it had become, for them, intellectual and sophisticated, the subject of critics' attention and of formal festivals which drew large and serious adult crowds.

Both as dance music and music to listen to, the various forms of jazz spread around the world and groups of young people in many lands danced to it, listened to it, discussed it and imitated it.

A succession of popular forms of dancing caught up each successive generation of young people. Lively dances to jazz rhythms such as the Charleston were popular in the 1920s, the slow fox trot in the 1930s. South American rumbas and tangos won wide favour, followed by variations of them like the samba. 'Jive' was the dance form of young addicts of fast jazz; consisting of elaborate improvisations of a simple basic step, it represented each individual's attempt to express his own reaction to the savage beat of the music. By the mid-1950s, 'rock and roll' was being danced with energetic abandon to a thumping, formless mixture of western cowboy songs, South American dance music and popularized jazz.

Where folk music remained alive, as it did in much of eastern Europe and among many of the peoples of the Soviet Union, traditional melodies and rhythms formed the basis for popular songs and dances. It was part of the policy of these countries to encourage the appreciation and use of folk culture, as in Hungary where the composer, Zoltan Kodaly (1882–   ), worked unceasingly to introduce folk music into the schools and to stimulate the development of choral groups which became well-known throughout the region.

7. *Sports*

Sports provided the people of the twentieth century with much of their entertainment, many of their heroes, a means of personal development or relaxation and, for some, an avenue of advancement. The vast majority of people played only as amateurs, but in the role of spectators they provided the opportunity for professional athletes to achieve a status akin to that of the great popular entertainers.

Large numbers of people in all the western countries liked to spend their Saturday or Sunday afternoons at football or baseball games or at the races. Others liked to go in their free evenings to prize fights or to hockey games, basketball games, ice skating contests or wrestling matches. More than sixty million Americans turned out each spring and summer for a succession of major and minor league baseball games, and fifteen million for high school, college and professional football games. Their British, French, Italian and South American counterparts went in proportionate numbers to football games or the races. The enormous interest in sports was reflected in the space devoted to sports reporting in the press.

Television brought the best of the spectator sports events into the home, and at first had the effect of reducing attendance. A 1950 survey in the United

States, however, showed that people who had owned their television sets for more than a year or two not only watched games on television, but also attended sports events more than non-television owners. Regardless of the impact of television, spectator sports went on drawing huge crowds for whom the excitement of a race or a competitive game was intensified by actual attendance at the arena, and the opportunity to join actively in the betting.

Personal participation in sports grew markedly with the greater amount of leisure time. People had always hunted and fished, bowled and played games. More and more people joined in these and other activities, stimulated by a growing enthusiasm for physical fitness and aided by the provision of playing fields, tennis courts, golf links, pools and skating rinks by munici-palities, schools, private clubs or commercial enterprises. Schools and clubs encouraged team sports because of their value in teaching co-operative effort as well as for the fun they gave participants and spectators.

Sports held an important place in the planned use of leisure in the socialist societies. With the goal of positive health and harmonious physical develop-ment, active participation in all manner of sports was encouraged for both men and women. Teams from thousands of factories, farms, schools and towns competed in many fields, and successful athletes were honoured as local and national heroes. Every effort was made to send champion per-formers to international contests.

Each country had sports it particularly loved: the British played cricket, Americans baseball; Germans hiked, Norwegians and Swiss skied, Italians cycled. But varied activities were popular everywhere. Water sports attracted a large and growing body of people. Swimming became increasingly popular and public pools came to be accepted as a part of normal recreational facilities. But swimming was only the beginning. Especially after the second world war, numbers of people took to water-skiing or donned flippers and oxygen cylinders and went exploring in the underwater world which had previously been known only to professional divers. Some speared fish, others observed the habits of marine life or photographed the weird and beautiful world they had so recently discovered.

Millions bought boats. Boating had long been a widespread holiday pastime in Scandinavian countries, Britain and Australia, but in other countries it had been looked on mainly as a rich man's sport. In 1957, however, a New York paper noted that America's outstanding shift in recreational habits had been from highways to waterways, as yachting, the sport of millionaires and princes, had come down to more democratic size and become 'pleasure boating'.

But if millions headed for rivers, lakes and seaside to spend their leisure hours in or on the water, other millions were land lovers who preferred to walk rather than swim, climb rather than dive, and to investigate the habits of animals instead of fish. Some walkers were amateur geologists or botanists. Others bought field glasses, rose early and went out to watch and listen to the birds. The most vigorous pitted their strength against mountains, and blazed trails and built hostels to accommodate themselves and others in all the great mountain chains of the western countries.

Young and old became outdoor campers. City children in mounting numbers learned to live in the open in summer camps conducted by youth organizations and welfare agencies or as private enterprises. Families packed camping equipment into their cars and pitched their tents on the camp sites supplied with water, sanitary facilities and fireplaces in public parks or private camping grounds, or in farmers' fields. The number of persons camping for a week-end or longer holiday on the camp sites provided by national and state park services in the United States rose by leaps and bounds from the 1930s on, reaching a million or more before the interruption of wartime petrol rationing and at least doubling every five years in the decade following the war.

Winter sports, especially skiing, gained ever larger numbers of devoted adherents, and newspapers began to carry detailed reports on the condition of the snow in various ski resorts as a guide to city dwellers who were planning week-ends or holidays. For those who preferred skating, many cities had rinks where the ice was carefully swept and controlled and people could indulge their fancy for either speed or figure skating without dependence on outside weather. In the cities, bowling alleys and roller-skating rinks, squash courts, swimming pools and gymnasiums provided winter exercise and a release from tension to men and women who were confined in offices or factories for the greater part of their working days.

National and international competitions were held in all lines of sport, amateur and professional, both among teams and individuals. The most famous of the international contests, the Olympic Games, were revived in the 1890s by a Frenchman, Baron Pierre de Coubertin, who was interested in fostering the amateur spirit in sports in order to preserve those characteristics of nobility and chivalry which distinguished sports in the past. The first successful games took place in London in 1908 and thereafter they were held every four years, except in wartime, in major centres around the world. Athletic organizations in the competing nations spent the years between the games in competitive elimination matches to choose the best teams and individuals to represent their nations at the next Olympics. The intensity of this preparation and the support given to it by organized bodies, facilitated, especially in the communist countries, by the state, aroused serious discussion of the line between amateur and professional in sports and questions as to whether the amateur spirit was in fact being fostered and preserved.

8. *Travel*

With the aid of automobile and aeroplane, travel became a well-nigh universal way to spend week-ends, annual and public holidays. If the weather was propitious, the first question in more and more families was 'where shall we go?' A little trip in the family car might mean visiting some place of special interest, exploring unfamiliar territory or a picnic at a favourite spot, but the result was the same everywhere; roads full of traffic.

Foreign travel came to be possible and attractive for increasing numbers of people. Some travelled to the Olympics or other major sporting events, others to musical events like the Edinburgh or Salzburg festivals, or to special art exhibitions or to international trade fairs. Some travelled for scenery and some for historical monuments. Gourmets went to France to eat, mountain climbers to Switzerland to conquer the Alps. All manner of coach tours offered people opportunities for inexpensive holiday trips. Whatever people did for their main relaxation during the working months of the year was likely to influence their choice of place and event when they planned their travels.

As more and more people travelled and came to know the countries closest to them and had made the traditional 'grand tour' of European centres, their desire to get further afield grew. If money permitted they began travelling to parts of the world where tourism had not been common, and thus began to learn about cultures and regions quite foreign to their own. In this way travel, like so many of the other leisure-time pursuits which people enjoyed, acted also as a form of education.

In the USSR travel took the form mainly of trips to museums, historic sites, festivals or major cities, and of holidays to the many rest homes and holiday resorts available to workers in the Crimea, Caucasus and other parts of the country. Trips of special interest were enjoyed as rewards for superior productivity on the job or for outstanding performance in sports or the arts.

9. Hobbies

For many—perhaps most—people, one or more of an endless variety of hobbies constituted an area of interest which supplemented, and sometimes competed with, their major occupation. Occasionally a hobby even led to a change of profession, as in the case of the amateur pet-fancier who became the head of one of the world's largest zoos; more often a hobby provided the basis for an occupation after retirement. Since hobbies required the individual to be active and to become expert to at least some degree, they served an educational as well as a recreational role and were the means of developing people's tastes, knowledge and capacities.

(a) *Gardening.* Gardening ranked as the number one hobby of all groups in Britain, the United States and most of western Europe, except for city dwellers who had no outdoor space, and even some of these indulged their taste through window boxes or plots in community gardens. The Dutch bulb growers were able to make a fortune out of supplying improved varieties of bulbs to other nations and the business of improving and adapting seeds, plants and fertilizers for the use of amateur gardeners proved lucrative in many countries.

Some gardeners gave their greatest attention to the design of their gardens, others to growing perfect roses or dahlias or even vegetables, others to special herb or rock gardens or to collecting wild flowers. All these special interests provided a basis for community, regional and national flower shows, for books and magazines about how to attain desired results and news of what other people with similar interests were doing, and for garden clubs, which existed in most towns or suburban communities to provide social activities and an opportunity to exchange specimens and information on gardening techniques.

(b) *Arts and crafts.* All manner of arts and crafts were immensely popular. Art classes and study groups in drawing, water colour, oil painting, modelling and in crafts such as weaving, woodworking, enamelling or pottery flourished. Sometimes the classes were neighbourhood or shop groups, working for pleasure under a semi-professional teacher; sometimes they were organized units of adult education courses offered by an educational or welfare agency. Amateur artist societies in communist countries received special state encouragement. Everywhere members of classes or groups exhibited their work in neighbourhood displays held in social halls, public squares, schools, shops, museums, libraries and public buildings, and entered those judged to be the best in city-wide and national exhibits, in addition to using them to decorate their homes. All this activity not only gave people a chance to express themselves creatively, but it also helped to raise the general level of taste, for people learned basic principles of art as they experimented with design, colour and technique.

The home itself, especially under suburban living conditions, often provided an opportunity to apply old craft techniques such as carpentry and metal working, which were revived for pleasure when they were no longer necessities of existence. Many householders enjoyed decorating their houses or repairing the structure, equipment or furnishings. In the 1950s 'do-it-yourself' became a craze in many areas where the high cost of labour added a practical consideration to the delights of developing manual or artistic skills and acquiring new knowledge.

(c) *Photography.* Photography was one of the most distinctive of twentieth-century hobbies. Camera addicts bought finer and finer cameras and experimented with faster and faster film as it came on the market, and with colour film. Amateurs and professionals joined camera clubs and held exhibitions in which the prizes went to those who had produced the most effective studies, judged in terms of art as well as technique. To get the best results possible, serious photographers read up on chemistry and the theory of light and processed their own films. They studied photographic magazines, camera annuals, and books representing the best work of the world's most famous photographers, and then experimented with their own studies of people and places, animals and flowers. By the 1950s millions of people were recording home events and travel scenes in amateur motion pictures.

(d) *Music.* Music, always a favourite hobby in some circles and among those with musical talent, became widely popular as radio and gramophone made all types available in the home and as tape recorders enabled amateurs to experiment with sound.

At the beginning of the century, when people suggested an evening of music they usually meant gathering around a piano to sing popular songs or, if they were serious musicians, playing in a string or wind ensemble or singing in a choir. In the following years people with musical talent still played musical instruments and joined choirs and quartets, or school, community or shop orchestras for the pleasure of making music themselves as well as enjoying that of others. In many cases radio and television acted as stimulants, for when individuals or groups were good enough they might find opportunity to be heard on local programmes.

The gramophone won great new audiences for both classical and popular music. Still only a scientific toy at the beginning of the century, it came into its own when musicians began to use it to document their work and commercial companies started to offer presses of Artur Rubinstein playing Chopin or Enrico Caruso singing Italian opera. At first only a few people collected these records, but as radio broadened the musical taste of its audience more and more people began to collect records—and as the market expanded the selection grew more varied. After the invention of high fidelity systems, long-playing records and unbreakable light plastic discs, the popularity of record collecting grew still greater and people began to buy their discs not only in terms of the particular music or the artist but of the technical quality of the recording. Record collectors became expert in their chosen field, broadening their knowledge through radio programmes and reading, and deepening it by listening to their own records.

The tape recorder permitted people to make records themselves. Some people used it merely to record outstanding radio performances or to record their own musical efforts, but others used it as a means of experimenting with sounds and combination of sounds: car horns, church bells, train whistles, the crashing of surf, the howling of the wind. The most elaborate experiments came from France in what the French called *musique concrète*. By slowing sounds and quickening them and by combinations of all kinds, experimenters achieved in music something similar to surrealist experiments in art.

(*e*) *Mechanical hobbies*. The many gadgets of the machine age provided a series of hobbies to those who grew up surrounded by them. Automobile engines held great fascination, especially for young people, who delighted in taking old machines to pieces, recombining parts, rigging them so as to provide extra power, and converting a broken-down old car into a high-speed vehicle.

Radio, from its start, became a favourite hobby of hundreds of thousands of men and boys who experimented with sending out messages and receiving signals from the most distant points which their homebuilt equipment could reach, establishing contacts and participating in human dramas far away. Judging from the number of 'radio hams' who secured licences and the increase in their average age in later years, this was a hobby which did not depend for its appeal on the novelty of the invention or the youth of the experimenters. Other electronic equipment also lent itself to experimentation, particularly high fidelity sound systems which were among the most popular of the gadget hobbies in the 1950s.

Thus the use of the new leisure in all these ways modified the manner of life and affected the outlook of the people. In a sense it might be said that the twentieth century, with all its devices permitting people to have and use leisure, was making it possible for the masses of people in industrial countries to do what leisure classes had always done—enjoy themselves and develop their personalities through self-education of whatever kind pleased them most. But the forms of the mass leisure went beyond the kind of personal development and individual enjoyment associated with the use of leisure by a privileged few. No less than other major features of twentieth-century life—new occupational patterns, urban living, mobility, the prolongation of life by medical science—the new mass leisure and its many uses were re-making the cultural life of a growing proportion of mankind.

NOTE TO CHAPTER XXVII

1. Soviet commentators call attention to the following point: An important part is played in the planning of leisure in the USSR by state and public institutions, by trade union and youth organizations and by sport, artistic and other voluntary bodies which are autonomous in their activity and not subordinated to state control.

The radio, television, cinema, professional theatres and orchestras, museums, gardens and parks, part of the clubs and libraries, and most publishing houses are under the direction of state institutions. Sanatoria, holiday homes, tourist excursion bases and many clubs and libraries are run by the trade unions. The programmes of the People's Universities of Culture and the public lecture halls as well as amateur art activities, athletics and some museums and publishing houses come under the control of public bodies.

PART THREE

THE SELF-IMAGE AND ASPIRATIONS OF THE PEOPLES OF THE WORLD

INTRODUCTION

A MONG the factors which helped to shape the cultural development of mankind in the twentieth century were the aspirations of nations and groups, which gave direction to their efforts to bring the actuality of their lives into line with their ideals. In the atmosphere of constant change, the sense of new possibilities moved men both to dream and to act. Drives toward self-realization in one form or another were part of the dynamics of these years.

The three chapters which follow examine some of the principal self-images in terms of which nation-states and other groups with a sense of common identity visualized themselves and voiced their common aspirations. These chapters are not concerned with the economic forces or power factors affecting the course of historical events or the institutional changes taking place,* but rather with the outlooks of groups of people and the manner in which these helped to focus the conscious efforts of individuals and groups. The validity of these self-images and aspirations is not examined according to any independent criteria; except for some indication of their relation to broad currents such as nationalism, each of these views is examined in its own terms, on the assumption that an understanding of the cultural developments of any period requires an appreciation of how people appeared in their own eyes.

In this era of nationalism, collective aspirations were shaped and expressed in national terms. The internal policies of states and their external relations embodied the views which the people of each nation-state held of their collective destiny. These national formulations were both political and cultural. In a world which entered the twentieth century dominated culturally as well as politically by Europe, drives for cultural expression and recognition were no less real than those for the achievement of political aims. The assertion of cultural independence and uniqueness was a motive force for colonial peoples seeking political independence and others whose political independence was assured but whose cultural expression was undeveloped or overshadowed. Drives for cultural reorientation within countries were associated with changes in the position of ethnic or social groups. In a number of regions, multi-cultural societies faced the problem of how to achieve a cultural *modus vivendi* in the conflict between intensified nationalism and drives for cultural autonomy.

Any attempt to present the self-images of nations and the aspirations which guided their public policies encounters the difficulty that each nation was unique, the aspirations of nations were not static, and no single attitude permeated all sections, classes, occupations, ethnic elements and personal outlooks even in the most centrally administered or totalitarian states. In this

* See Chapters I–V and XXI–XXIII.

and the following chapter it will be possible to touch on only the major features of the aspirations of nations and peoples which contributed to the cultural development of mankind during these years.

In each case the national self-image which had been noted has been that of the dominant element which provided articulate leadership. To avoid an endless catalogue of more than eighty nations, countries have been grouped together on the basis of certain common features. It must be remembered, however, that the basis chosen is only one of the groupings which could have been made, that the outlook of the dominant element in one state was often shared by non-dominant elements elsewhere, and that the divisions and conflicts of view within nations were no less significant than the differences among nation-states.

Within each society, moreover, individuals belonging to disadvantaged categories sought the opportunity to participate as full members of the societies of which they were a part. Most notably, workers whose labour had been treated as a commodity sought bargaining power and status as human beings, peasants yearned for their own land, women strove for a more equal status with men, and racial minorities or castes subject to discrimination struggled for full citizenship. Such groups resorted to organization and launched a variety of efforts to gain for themselves the same measure of freedom and respect as was accorded to those who enjoyed a favoured position in their societies.

Whether as nations or as culture groups or as individuals seeking first-class citizenship, people in the twentieth century made conscious efforts to bring about the social changes which would enable them to achieve their aspirations and to realize the self-images in terms of which they projected their hopes.[1, 2]

CHAPTER XXVIII

THE SELF-IMAGE AND ASPIRATIONS OF NATIONS

To a degree rare in previous ages, the nation-state of the twentieth century, with its demand for supreme, collective loyalty, provided the terms in which its members defined their outlook and desires.

The process of formulating national aims, as well as the nature of the formulation, varied from centralized authoritarian states to those with a looser structure which provided more channels for reflecting the popular view. But everywhere there was in some degree a reciprocal interaction between the people and the state, even where a small element imposed its will on the majority and sustained it by dictatorial means.

The most common ingredient in the national aspirations of peoples was the drive for equality of national status. As the great empires broke up after the first world war and colonial peoples became nations in their own right after the second world war, states large and small saw themselves as autonomous units legally on a par with others. The more than eighty nations which composed the United Nations in the late 1950s shared a sense of their identity as nations, the assumption that their voice, however weak, would be heard and that their integrity, however precarious, should be respected. Although the great powers dominated the United Nations as they had the League of Nations and the world before the first world war they moved among a growing number of others who enjoyed, at least technically, the status of equally responsible members of the family of nations.[3]

At the heart of the idea of equality of national status were two concepts, self-determination and self-realization. The first of these was an essentially political idea, derived from the doctrines of liberalism and democracy and the view of man as a rational being capable of determining his own fate and entitled to do so. In the form inherited by the twentieth century, it had not been applied outside the political arena. It was, moreover, at least partly a negative concept, implying primarily freedom from outside interference and asserting national independence and sovereignty.

The self-realization of peoples was a broader concept which involved not only independence from alien rule or domination but the positive cultural orientation of a people and their development in accord with their systems of values. It could mean very different things according to each nation's image of itself. For the liberal democratic states, historically committed to self-determination in its more limited, political sense, it meant a widening of the concept to encompass economic and social as well as political aspects of life;

for those who saw world history in Marxian terms, it meant the identification of a people with the historical process of dialectical materialism and a unified all-out effort to build a socialist society; in the hands of romantic nationalists, such as Mussolini, it became an effort to recreate the greatness of a distant past; to those such as Hitler or the Afrikaans leaders of South Africa, who saw their race endowed with a mission, it could mean a drive for dominance over 'lesser' peoples within and without the state; for those committed to a religion which made religious and political life coterminous it might mean, as in Pakistan, the effort to define a state in religious terms or, as in Israel, to create a homeland for members of a religious faith; for non-European countries in the days of European expansion, such as Japan or Afghanistan, it might mean such adoption of European ways or such insulation from European impact as would provide the strength to resist; for the peoples of Africa, emerging from tribalism and European domination, it could mean a groping for terms on which to enter the modern world. But whatever the form, the drive for self-realization could be summed up in the simple answer of Prime Minister Nehru to the question of what he regarded as major trends in the twentieth century: 'I think that people want to be themselves.'*

I. LIBERAL DEMOCRACY:
THE SELF-IMAGE OF WESTERN EUROPE

The countries of western Europe saw themselves as the bearers of the great liberal tradition which had come down from the Greeks by way of the Renaissance and they assumed that they were in the vanguard in the evolution of human society. The liberal tradition had provided the cultural milieu within which science and technology had taken root and a dynamic industrial civilization had grown and flourished. Western Europeans and those who represented the extension of western European culture in other lands assumed that the values of their society and the institutions of liberal democracy were favourable to this development and that these values could fruitfully be adopted and applied throughout the world.

The liberal tradition of western Europe was essentially the product of a series of historical events: the fourteenth-century defeat of the French knighthood by the Flemish burghers and the death of the Duke of Burgundy at the hands of the Swiss in the fifteenth century; the Dutch wars of independence in the sixteenth century, which were at the same time a social and economic revolution; the English social, economic and political revolutions of the seventeenth century and the French and American revolutions of the eighteenth century. The main intellectual roots were in the Renaissance, the scientific revolution of the seventeenth century and the eighteenth-century Enlightenment. In economic terms it rested on the destruction of feudalism

* Interview, January 12, 1956.

and the rise of commerce and industry together with the middle classes which were the products and instruments of these developments.

European liberalism was rooted in the idea of human nature which had been part of European thought from the time of the Renaissance, and especially from the period of the Enlightenment—that man is rational, responsible and capable of exercising control over his own affairs. In this view the fullest development of the individual is the aim of society; it is also the means of achieving that aim and the measure of success. The initiative and enterprise of the individual and the process of free inquiry bring benefit to all. The individual is endowed with essential and inherent rights which must be protected and respected. These rights were historically defined in terms of freedom—freedom to enjoy life, liberty and property except as restrained by due process of law, freedom of association, freedom of thought, speech and religion. The history of mankind was seen in terms of the progressive emancipation of the human spirit from ignorance, superstition, and authority and from submergence of the individual in the group.

It was a Europe conceived on these lines, theoretically convinced of the equality of man while in practice maintaining the right and duty to rule and guide the 'less advanced' parts of the world, that had partitioned Africa and established dominion over most of Asia. This lofty ideal of a world in progress led by Europe was a reflection of the self-consciousness of European civilization. From the time of the Roman empire and the spread of Christianity, Europe had seen itself as guarding the heritage of Rome, Greece, Egypt and the Near East and as confessing the only true religion. This self-image of Europe as the bearer of world culture, a view which was even shared, perhaps subconsciously, by many who opposed colonialism, reconciled in the European mind the principles of liberalism and the practice of imperialism.

The classic statements of rights and freedoms which expressed basic liberal principles had been contained in the British Bill of Rights, the American Declaration of Independence and the Bill of Rights of the American Constitution, and the French Declaration of the Rights of Man and of the Citizen. Restated by President Woodrow Wilson as the war aims of the Allies in the first world war, the principles were essentially unchanged, and enjoyed high prestige at victory; they were embodied in the political institutions of the successor states in eastern Europe and in the German Weimar republic.

When a President of the United States again formulated the aims of the liberal democracies aligned in war, the formulation had changed. The 'four essential human freedoms' enumerated by President Franklin Roosevelt included a new freedom, 'freedom from want'. This was the formulation, with its implication of economic measures on behalf of all the people, that was adopted by the new states which emerged after the second world war, when victory had again raised the prestige of liberal democracy. And these were the terms in which the United Nations Charter declared its purpose 'to promote social progress and better standards of life in larger freedom' and the UN

Universal Declaration of Human Rights defined the rights of 'all human beings'.

The newer formulation of liberal democracy was often far from clear, for it was not easy to reconcile the essentials of individualism with the realities of economic organization and the administration of welfare services. But however imprecise their concepts and uncertain their practices, the liberal democracies retained their faith in human capacity and in the rational potentialities of man, in spite of evidence of his irrationality, and they sought to strengthen these capacities in order to enable him to function more fully, more rationally and more humanely.[4, 5]

Although western Europe shared in many ways a common civilization, it was sharply divided by the boundaries between national states each of which maintained its own form of European culture. In the course of the twentieth century the conflicting interests of European national states, reaching all over the world, were sufficiently intense to lead to two disastrous world wars. Each European nation saw itself as unique, and projected its self-image not only in terms of its special emphasis within the liberal tradition but in terms of identification with its historic past. The elements of which liberal principles were compounded—British legal and parliamentary institutions, French rationalism and egalitarianism, and bourgeois economics often reinforced by Protestant ethics—carried different weight in different places. In some countries two or even more competing self-images persisted through the years and found expression during this period in alternations of policy or the domination of one self-image over the other.

For the British the main focus of democratic liberalism was on the parliamentary processes, the common law and non-interference in ordinary daily life. In spite of an aristocratic social structure and authoritarian colonial role, liberal principles were very deeply engrained in the British outlook; according to their own self-image they were the bearers of these principles to other parts of the world where their influence extended. With this view they carried the legal and political institutions of liberal democracy to areas under their rule, and when it became clear that they could no longer hold these areas in subjection they tried to help them to become liberal democratic states. At home British society moved toward its democratic ideal at an accelerated pace, taking on the shape of a welfare state, and it found no difficulty in assimilating many of the principles of democratic socialism to its basic liberal institutions and point of view.

In France, by contrast, the main components of liberalism were the rationalism of the Enlightenment and the belief in human equality regardless of race or position, rather than any set of political institutions. Successive changes in constitutional forms and weakness and confusion within the parliamentary system did not negate the basically liberal orientation of French society. At the same time, France saw herself as the heir of Charlemagne, Louis XIV and Napoleon. Her sense of power was expressed in terms of *la gloire*, the glory of a great nation, rather than in dominion, although she assumed, far more completely than did Britain, that she would place the stamp of her own culture on her subject peoples. The self-image of France was always more intellectual and cultural than it was political, and she viewed her 'civilizing mission' in terms of the rationalism and humanism of the French view of life.

Even more clearly than did the French, the Germans saw themselves in two distinct and opposing terms, both of which were the fruit of a conscious effort to create a self-image. The Germans saw themselves on the one hand as *das Volk von Dichter und Denker*—the people of poets and thinkers—and on the other hand as *das Herrenvolk*—the master race. Both these self-images originated in the eighteenth century and were in a measure a reaction to a sense of frustration. The German middle class, excluded from a political role in the feudal structure dominated by the princes of some hundred petty states and by the Prussian monarchy, turned to literature and philosophy and produced the Germany of Lessing, Goethe, Schiller and Heine, of Kant and Hegel and the other great 'poets and thinkers' of the era. Meanwhile the self-image of the *Herrenvolk* grew from the frustration of the princes, and especially of the Prussian Hohenzollerns, whose desire to play a prominent part in European politics was not realized until the late nineteenth and early twentieth century, and was then lost again in the self-evoked catastrophe of 1918, to be revived for the short period of the Third Reich and lost again in its collapse.

In the smaller countries of western Europe where liberal democracy was rooted and strong, liberalism rested on a firm historic base of owning farmers and capitalist enterprise and it developed a strong welfare component in these years. Each of these countries, too, saw itself both as the bearer of a common European culture and in terms of its unique history and the quality of its life.

After the second world war a series of motives led to the idea of a united Europe, not only in the traditional sense of a common European culture but as an economic-defensive unity in the face of the new strength of the United States and the Soviet Union. In the initial phases the steps taken involved only part of the western European area, they revealed the persistent strength of national interests, and even the most comprehensive proposals stopped at the line which set off from western Europe those sections of central and eastern Europe which had become part of the communist system.

Outside western Europe the liberal tradition formed a more or less important part of the national self-image in four areas: the overseas communities created by western European migration—the United States and Canada, Australia and New Zealand; the republics of South and Central America which won their independence from Spain and Portugal in the first quarter of the nineteenth century; the states of eastern Europe that took shape after the first world war; and the new states that came into being with the break-up of the colonial empires after the second world war.

The most complete assumption that liberal democracy defined the character of national life was in the countries of North America and Australasia. In these new societies, created by people who had sought new homes in their quest for one or another form of freedom or opportunity, there were no remnants of an earlier feudal society, of monarchical or other authority, of religious orthodoxy or of a rigid social system which could offer an alternative to the conception of the liberal society and state. So completely and exclusively were liberal principles embedded in these societies, in fact, that they became a kind of orthodoxy in themselves. Other possible social and political values lacked reality, or appeared more as aberrations than as serious alternatives. Canada relied on these principles to sustain a working union between her French-speaking and English-speaking peoples, to hold together small population groups separated by great, empty distances, and to regulate her relations with a neighbour ten times her size across 3,900 miles of unguarded frontier. Australia and New Zealand were the first countries to extend the franchise to women. Though such expressions as the first world war slogan 'make the world safe for democracy' or the term 'free world' applied to non-communist countries might sound hollow to others, for the people of the United States they carried a sense of reality. Pragmatic modifications of institutions and practices might be adopted and assimilated, but the essential image remained.

In the course of the years some of the old meanings for the terms of liberalism and democracy became less and less clear, especially for the growing urban populations in these countries. In the United States uncertainty expressed itself after both world wars in hysterical waves of suspicion which were levelled ostensibly against those who rejected liberal principles, but which actually expressed authoritarian attitudes and sometimes even attacked those who stood for liberal ideals. The issue was confused by the fact that in other countries both fascists and communists had shown themselves prepared to take advantage of liberal democratic freedoms and rights, only to destroy those rights and freedoms once they had gained power.[6] In the divided world of mid-century, moreover, even the subordination of the military to civil authority began to seem less important than national security. But however uncertain the evolving forms, however indistinct the image and however strong the self-criticism, the peoples of these countries saw themselves in no other terms than those of the basic liberalism which had always provided the outward formulation and the inner drive of their societies.

The states of South and Central America had inherited their institutions and attitudes from Spain and Portugal, where the principles of the English Bill of Rights, the commercial revolution and the Enlightenment had never been an integral part of the culture. At the time of their independence each of the formerly Spanish areas had formally adopted the principles of liberal democracy, modelling their constitutions on that of the United States; Portugal's former dominion, Brazil, eventually followed suit. For all these countries liberal democracy remained a stated ideal. Some such as Uruguay made it a dominant component of their self-image; Mexico used it as a pragmatic guide for realizing, over the years, the fruits of a political and social revolution; others came back to democratic principles repeatedly after periods when the authoritarian, paternalistic, *élitiste* values which were deeply rooted in their Iberian traditions had been in the ascendant; some, at mid-century, had not yet found the means to make liberal democracy a substantial reality in their societies.

For the states of eastern Europe established after the first world war liberal principles were one of the components in their self-images. The tradition of Jan Hus was alive for the Czechs, of Kosciusko for the Poles, of Kossuth for the Hungarians. But other traditions associated with the continuing feudal societies were stronger elements in the nationalism which emerged, and in the years of crisis these were evoked by the leadership of each of the new states except Czechoslovakia. Under Thomas Masaryk and Eduard Beneš, that country, the most industrially developed in the region, identified itself with the liberal democratic tradition of western Europe until it, like its neighbours, was subjugated by the Nazis. When all of these states emerged again after the second world war, their leadership soon passed into the hands of the communists, and it was in terms of revolutionary socialism rather than of liberal democracy that they overthrew the institutions associated with feudalism, clericalism and the types of social structure and authority which had been dominant in much of the area.

In the new states which came into existence after the second world war, the concept of a secular nation-state, with equality of citizenship and civil rights, was an essentially new idea. For most of the new states liberal democratic principles were not an integral part of the new nationalism, even though they were expressed in the first constitutions of each of the states. Asian traditions tended to identify peoples in terms of the religious community to which they belonged or to rely on authoritarian rule; communism offered an obvious alternative to liberalism, especially after the communist régime took over in China and launched a vigorous programme of development. In these circumstances India looked upon itself, and was looked to by others, as the major test of whether liberal democracy could be realized as a national ideal in Asia and Africa. For only in India was liberal democracy an essential part of the self-image, at least of the leadership and the educated elements, and not merely a newly adopted state form scarcely related to their conception of themselves.[7]

II. MARXIST–LENINIST COMMUNISM[8]

The USSR and the states which acquired communist governments in the years after the second world war regarded themselves as the results and the instruments of the dialectical historical process, described by Karl Marx and Friedrich Engels and elaborated to cover new circumstances by Lenin, which inevitably and irreversibly was leading mankind towards socialism and ultimately communism. They saw themselves as the inheritors of the great cultural traditions of the past and the creators of a new day in human history in which man, having conquered nature, would be freed from the 'empire of necessity' where nature had held him in her grip. In this view all history prior to the achievement of communism is the 'pre-history' of human emancipation.

According to the concept of the historical process set forth by Marx, the determining factor in the development of human society is the process of production. The forces inherent in industrial production must ultimately work themselves out into the classless society, for capitalism breeds within itself the means of its destruction and its inner contradictions lead eventually to revolutionary change. The instrument of revolution and the builder of the classless society, once the exploiting classes have been suppressed, is the proletariat.

Marx had assumed that the revolution would come in countries which had reached an advanced stage of capitalism and that the socialist society would follow the capitalist as a later stage in historical development. He had expected the leadership in the world revolution to come from advanced industrial countries—Germany, Britain. He had seen the common bond among the workers of the world as closer and more binding than unity of the workers with the exploiting classes within the same nation.

In the light of conditions at the opening of the twentieth century, however, when the major capitalist countries were enjoying both rising productivity and profits from colonial areas, and workers in these countries were organizing to share to some extent the returns from these sources rather than to overthrow their régimes, Lenin extended the Marxian analysis to envisage the possibility that revolution would come in industrially backward areas. In Lenin's view capitalism in its advanced stages maintained itself at home and brought relative prosperity to its own workers by exploiting the weaker economies abroad, either within colonial empires or in other less-developed areas. In so doing it set in motion two forces, the antagonism of the colonial and industrially weaker peoples against their exploiters, and the conflict among the capitalist-imperialists for markets and sources of raw materials. These conflicts, Lenin believed, would lead inevitably to wars which would weaken the capitalist economies and bring about their ultimate downfall.

Lenin also designed an instrument which could bring about revolution in the absence or immaturity of a revolutionary proletariat. This was the centralized Party, the vanguard of the working class, which would formulate the will of the proletariat and would activate it. It would also activate the peasants. Whereas Marx, thinking in terms of the revolution in an advanced stage of industrial development, had focused on the industrial proletariat, Lenin included peasants in his concept of the revolutionary potential of countries where peasants made up the vast majority of the population.

The successful October revolution validated Lenin's formula for the revolutionary leadership by a select, centralized Party, and showed the possibility of enlisting the support of the peasants for the revolutionary action of the urban proletariat under the Party leadership. It confirmed the fact that revolution could start in a relatively backward country, although Lenin and his associates hoped and expected that revolution would follow in the advanced countries, and that these would provide the USSR during the period of its economic weakness both with a shield against capitalist powers and the advanced technology for industrial development.

When the abortive German revolution of 1918 failed, it became apparent that for the time being revolution was not going to spread to the industrial countries and that the USSR would stand alone in a capitalist world. Although the leaders of the USSR believed that the contradictions of monopoly capitalism would eventually lead to self-destructive conflict among the capitalist economies, they faced the immediate situation of the USSR as the sole embodiment of the historical process of revolutionary change toward a classless society, forced to pursue a strategy of 'socialism in one country'.

In this situation the state assumed a much more positive role than had been envisaged in the original Marxian view. Marx had regarded the state as the instrument of class oppression in bourgeois society and had expected it to 'wither away' once class oppression had been terminated and a socialist society achieved. This concept remained as part of the ultimate picture of the final stage of society, following the ultimate world revolution. But so long as the USSR stood alone or communist societies existed in a divided world, the state was a necessary agency for administering the society and conducting the strategy of internal development and external policy.

Throughout the first forty years of its existence, this was the basic self-image in terms of which the leaders of the USSR shaped policy and guided the outlook and motivation of the people. Tactical changes in internal and external policies and the cruel exigencies of war did not alter the fundamentals. In this self-image the Soviet Union and all its people were building a socialist society in competition with the capitalist world. So long as this society was weaker than that of capitalism, it believed that it was threatened by what it presumed to be the need of capitalism to try to prevent the successful development of a socialist society. The USSR therefore must give priority to heavy industry and scientific advance as the basis for achieving a level of productivity equal to or surpassing that of the most advanced capitalist economies.

In the drive to realize this self-image all available resources were focused on the common objectives. Stalin saw the state as the main instrument to organize the society, to maintain unity, to exact necessary sacrifices and to resolve or suppress conflicts, and he built up its machinery for administration, police, propaganda, censorship and economic operation.

The full apparatus of education and training was dedicated to producing a people who were scientifically and technically equipped to operate a technically advanced and highly productive economy and who were oriented to the task of building a socialist society. Man was viewed as a rational being full of capabilities which were realized in relation to society. The resources of the arts and of mass communication were enlisted to project the reality in terms of the socialist ideal, on the assumption that if people thought in terms of the goal, they would act, under the leadership of the Communist party, in ways which would help to bring it about.

The Marxist–Leninist philosophy was a philosophy of action, designed to change the world, not merely to interpret it. Although it regarded the direction of the historical process as inevitable, it called for conscious action by the revolutionary class or group. Men who were aware of the historical process could align themselves with it and accelerate it. It was thus appropriate that socialist society should be continually pictured as it should be, or with emphasis on its constructive features, in order that present contradictions or imperfections might not confuse the sense of direction and impede action. Similarly capitalist society was to be seen in terms of the contradictions leading to its downfall in order that these might be enhanced. This manner of viewing the present in terms of the desired future was termed 'socialist realism'.

So the Communist party taught the Russian people to look upon the successful building of socialist society as an essential stage in the historical process of the world revolution inaugurated in October 1917. In order to carry out numerous socialist reforms it was first necessary to establish certain economic and cultural prerequisites by attaining an adequate level of industry and agriculture. With the main instruments and means of production in the hands of the proletarian state, enabling it to interfere actively in the country's economic life, much more favourable opportunities could be provided for the speedy setting up of these prerequisites than would be possible under the capitalist system. The historical experience of the Soviet Union was seen as demonstrating that the proletarian state could guide the activities of the working people and the working intelligentsia in the task of prompt, effective and expedient creation of an advanced industrial society.

After forty years of communist rule the Soviet people saw themselves as beginning the task of building the foundations for a communist society. The tremendous economic and political achievements of the Soviet Union in such a brief span of time ensured the complete and conclusive triumph of socialism in that country in the sense that the USSR felt itself fully guaranteed against the possibility of forcible restoration of capitalism. The new task was to create conditions of life, both material and cultural, which would encourage the desire of working people in all countries to remake life on the basis of new, communist principles. The Soviet Union invited capitalist countries to compete in attaining a higher standard of living for working people and in setting up the most favourable conditions for all-round harmonious development of all their forces and abilities, confident that it would win in this competition for it believed its economic system to be by far the more progressive of the two.

The USSR thus saw world events from 1917 on as confirming the Marxist–Leninist view of history. Success of the October revolution demonstrated that the period of transition from capitalism to socialism had acutally set in and must be effected through revolution and not evolution. The victory of revolution in backward Russia confirmed Lenin's prediction of revolution in countries with weaker economies. They saw the strength and growth of capitalist economies during the period as a temporary stabilization which merely made the contradictions of capitalism less apparent, while the world wars and the breaking away of colonial peoples were seen as demonstrations of Lenin's concept of the declining course of capitalist imperialism. The success of revolutions in eastern Europe and China after the second world war seemed to indicate that it was only a matter of time before the working people of more and more countries, led by the Communist party, would bring about change in their countries and become part of the world revolution.

In short, despite all of history's zig-zags the Soviet people saw the main process outlined by Marx—the process of transition from capitalism to socialism on a world-wide scale—as making steady progress and as constituting the dominant trend of the modern age. Whatever variety in form the transition might take, the essentials were identical and followed the theory elaborated by Marx, Engels and Lenin. The people of the Soviet Union were sure that the future belonged to the system whose foundations were being laid in the USSR and the people's democracies.

As the USSR ceased to be the only communist state and as it approached its goal of high productivity and displayed prowess in scientific fields, it saw itself moving to a new position as the leader of the expanded and expanding communist segment of the world. And it saw itself, in line with Lenin's prediction that the rising of the peoples of the East would be decisive in the world struggle for communism, as stimulating the underdeveloped peoples of the world to choose the communist path and align themselves with the course of history.

The communist countries outside of the USSR followed essentially the same Marxist–Leninist self-image. Yugoslavia rejected the Leninist principle of democratic centralism and saw the proletariat as carrying out its revolutionary role through workers' councils and other decentralized organs. Mao Tse-tung gave the peasants an even more important role in bringing communism to China than Lenin had envisioned in his concept of the peasants as supporting the efforts of the industrial workers. But wherever Marxism–Leninism furnished the basis of the national self-image, the people believed that in building a socialist society they were carrying out the irreversible and irrevocable laws of historical development.

III. ANTI-LIBERAL AUTHORITARIANISM

In the states where an authoritarian tradition was strong and liberal democracy never effectively replaced the remains of feudalism, anti-liberal authoritarianism reasserted itself and, in its extreme form, became intensified into totalitarianism.

During the years when liberal democracy had become integrated into the thought and action of northern and western Europe, North America and Australasia, the monarchies of Germany, Austria-Hungary and Russia continued to provide an alternative pattern which retained much of its force. Even after the fall of the monarchies themselves, the system which they had represented and the attitudes on which their system had rested furnished the basis for a resumption of authoritarianism when liberal democracy appeared inadequate to meet crises of inflation, depression and defeat. In Spain, Italy and Greece authoritarianism associated with economic and social inertia persisted behind a parliamentary façade. The concept of man as active, responsible and guiding himself rather than being guided by others, which was basic to liberal democracy, had never been widely accepted in traditionally authoritarian societies, especially where prevailing attitudes were conditioned by the Catholic Church's time-honoured view of man's weakness and its hierarchy of authority for his guidance.

In the pattern of the monarchies inherited by the twentieth century, an authoritarian ruler administered a power state through a bureaucracy, drawn from the ruling class, with the aid of the military, officered by members of the same class. In the late nineteenth century some parliamentary machinery had been added as an appendage to, rather than as the law-making body over, the ruler, bureaucracy and army. The growth of nationalism had furnished an emotional and ideological force which strengthened the authority of the state.

With the spread of liberal and socialist ideas, the traditional authoritarian rule had yielded to new forms, but in such a way as to preserve the essential authority. The rulers of central, eastern and southern Europe had used the power state to support the social and political structure of the old régime; but the spirit of nationalism called for the inclusion of the total population, not merely the ruling class, in the benefits of the state. Bismarck had shown the way by a combination of nationalism and social legislation which expanded the beneficiaries of the state and the basis of its power, without seriously undermining the dominance of the ruling class, or the authority of the monarch and the position of bureaucracy and army. In the process there was no weakening but rather an enhancing of the power of the state *vis-à-vis* the individual.

When the old structure of authority broke down in these societies, there was no effective transfer to popular sovereignty. Before the leaders of the successor states which followed the dissolution of the Hapsburg and Hohenzollern monarchies had more than begun to develop a democratic structure for the exercise of power, new pressures forced them to surrender authority to dictators who claimed to act for the benefit of the people. Throughout southern, central and eastern Europe parliamentary institutions appeared inadequate to deal with urgent problems requiring vigorous state action, and authoritarian habits were readily invoked by a charismatic leader—a Mussolini, Pilsudski, Horthy, Metaxas, de Rivera, or Hitler.

Authoritarianism as a positive principle of state organization received a twentieth-century formulation with Mussolini's accession to power in Italy in 1922. The symbol chosen by Mussolini, the *fasces* borne by Roman lictors as symbol of authority and of the binding together of all elements in the state, gave the name fascism not only to Italy's authoritarian régime but to similar patterns throughout the world.

The essence of the fascist state was unlimited authority. In the words of Mussolini: 'Our programme is simple: we wish to govern Italy. They ask us for programmes, but there are already too many. It is not programmes that are wanting for the salvation of Italy but men and will power.'

Fascism rejected completely and uncompromisingly the principles of liberalism and democracy as foolish and ineffective. For the conception of equality it substituted a permanent, beneficial, hierarchical order of society; for the rights and liberties of the individual, it substituted the rights of the state, a mystical entity to which the individual was subordinate; for the concept that the leaders should be the elected representatives of the people, responsible to them, it substituted the opposite concept that the people were responsible to their superiors who in turn were appointed by those above. As conceived by Mussolini, military discipline and obedience must permeate civilian life, for he exalted war as the highest function of the state and military activity as the highest duty and fundamental virtue of man. The objectives of the state were couched in terms of national greatness. In the case of Italy, Mussolini evoked a vision of the rebirth of the Roman empire.

The imperatives of fascist society were the imperatives of action; parliamentary and other institutions of liberalism were condemned as merely contributing to irresolution of the will. Only a leader was capable of making the swift and bold decisions called for by the 'inexorable dynamics' of the factual situation. Only unqualified obedience could translate the leader's decisions into effective action.

As a doctrine of authority, fascism implied that there could be no alternative foci of power and no alternative bases from which the leader's authority might be questioned or challenged. Since the leader knew intuitively what was best for the nation, he was beyond criticism even though national welfare was theoretically the overriding consideration. The doctrine implied the single party, the alignment of all instruments of education and propaganda—schools, press, radio—the suppression of independent associations, whether trade unions or other groups, and the bringing of every type of organization under the ultimate direction of the state. It rested on a view of human nature which denied the concept of man as a rational being capable of guiding his own destiny and asserted the view of man as weak and irresponsible, needing the guidance and direction of those with superior resolution, knowledge, courage and wisdom.

The revival of authoritarianism and the direct rejection of liberalism in principle and in practice spread during the 1920s and 1930s throughout eastern and southern Europe, and had its echoes in the strengthening of authoritarian tendencies in other parts of the world, notably in parts of Latin America and in Japan. The dictatorships which assumed power in one after another of the successor states of the Austro-Hungarian empire, in Greece and in Spain varied in the degree to which they were committed to the full implications of fascism as Mussolini had formulated them, but all had in common a conception of the power state, headed by undisputed authority which subordinated or suppressed individual rights, political parties and parliamentary institutions as inconsistent with the safety of the state, and all linked authoritarianism to nationalism.

In general, the dictatorships retained and strengthened the ruling classes of landowners and industrialists, and received the active support of these groups who hoped thereby to retain their position and power. They varied in the extent to which they involved militarization, but they were generally brought to power and headed by military men, or men who assumed a military pose, and their immediate followers adopted military trappings and symbols—black, brown or green shirts, and some form of the fascist salute. Each drew on the attitudes and symbols which were part of the national tradition and all invoked some vision of historic greatness projected into the future to define the national aspirations for which the people were called upon to make sacrifices.

The authoritarian states differed, too, in the relation between religious and secular authority. In Spain and in Austria clerical forces joined the secular, reinforcing each other. Where they did so the principle of corporatism—of syndical bodies with a measure of law-giving and executive authority over their members in the manner of mediaeval guilds—received support from the papal encyclical *Quadragesimo anno* in 1931. Mussolini at first received clerical support, along with that of the king and other conservative elements, but when he attempted to bring all education under his control, the Church challenged his power.

In each of the countries which adopted authoritarian systems during these years, the Church initially associated itself with the régime, or came to terms with it. But it was a potential source of dissension and of challenge to the tendency toward totalitarianism, for clerical authority derived from an alternative, supernatural source, not from the mystique of the state or the leader's will. Where the state carried through the integration of all institutions into a monolithic structure under the leader, as in Nazi Germany, the Church became an opponent of the régime.

The fascist states thus gave a new and intensified form to traditional views of human nature, of hierarchical society, of authority and of the place of military activity and military virtues. They drew upon religious as well as secular patterns of subordination. And they offered the appeal of a charismatic leader who embodied the national image and a vision of national greatness to lift the spirits of people who were confused or dismayed by the events of the inter-war years and had no commitment to the liberal principles which had seemed axiomatic to those who had tried to make them the basis for national life.

Authoritarianism in its fascist form met defeat in the second world war as monarchism had gone down in the first world war. Liberal democratic institutions were restored in Italy, Austria and Germany. The states of eastern Europe came under communist régimes. Authoritarianism survived only in the Iberian peninsula and for a time in several of the Latin American republics. But though the image of the authoritarian state lost its hold, the problem remained of how much authority is required to make a modern state effective and how people accustomed to authority may develop the degree of independence and responsibility which modern conditions demand. There remained the possibility of the resurgence of authoritarianism wherever the tradition of authority was strong or liberal democracy might fail to meet the problems of the modern age.

IV. RACIAL SUPERIORITY

1. Nazi Germany

While the fascist elaboration of the authoritarian state originated in Italy, it was Hitler's Germany which carried the idea to its farthest extent and which not only provided the strongest element in the fascist axis but imposed its image on other countries with authoritarian régimes.

The distinguishing feature of Nazi Germany, which at first set it apart from the merely authoritarian countries, was its racial dogma. In the hands of Adolf Hitler, authoritarianism, fascism and the leadership principle became racialism; the drive for a greater Germany was a drive to subject to the *Herrenvolk* not only the Jews, but the 'lesser' peoples of the European continent, especially the Slavs.

Like Mussolini, Hitler found a fertile soil for the development of his National Socialist movement in the disorder and disillusionment following the first world war. In defeated and occupied Germany, racked by runaway inflation, the effort of the Weimar republic to implant liberal democracy in place of the defeated Hohenzollern monarchy was fraught with immense difficulties. Many attitudes inherited from the nineteenth and early twentieth centuries provided a background for the acceptance of fascist principles and of racialist ideas.

Authoritarian habits were deeply ingrained in German society, and hierarchical status was recognized in modes of address and in patterns of education and occupation. The German romantic tradition, which had found expression during the nineteenth century in political theory and philosophy,

LL*

literature and the arts, fostered the idea of a ruling *élite* and exalted the heroic leader. In this tradition German culture was endowed with special qualities of emotion and dynamic originality, in contrast to the 'artificial' intellectualism of western Europe; in its extreme forms it was anti-rational and anti-intellectual.

Nowhere in the world, except perhaps in Japan, was the military tradition stronger or were military virtues more highly regarded than in Prussia; leading political writers had repeatedly held that might is right. Nowhere did romantic nationalism have a stronger hold. The German state which achieved unification in 1871 was conceived as more than a political structure; it embodied the mystic unity of the *Volk*. As such, its mission was to carry German culture, and not a few voices had been raised calling for a pan-German unification of people of German stock, wherever they might be; still more had called for *Lebensraum*—living space—for the vigorous, expanding German people.

The doctrine of Nordic superiority had received support from many quarters during the nineteenth and early twentieth centuries, and not alone in Germany. Richard Wagner had glorified the ancient god-like heroes, conceived as the true type of German and the true embodiment of the German soul. Racial theorists, such as Count de Gobineau, a Frenchman, and Wagner's English son-in-law, H. S. Chamberlain, had ardent followers, and similar views aroused popular interest even in the United States where they influenced the immigration laws of the 1920s. Many people believed that the German *Herrenvolk* was destined to rule.

The concept of Nordic superiority and of racial purity had been linked with anti-semitism. To Wagner, to the Prussian polemicist Eugen Karl Dühring and to many others, the Jews had seemed to personify the antithesis of the qualities which were prized as 'German'. The conservative, aristocratic, romantic and nationalist elements had identified the Jew with Marxian socialism—Marx was himself a Jew—with cosmopolitanism, with urbanism and capitalism as against love of the land, and with rationalism as against 'blood and soil'.

The components of National Socialism were thus available from German tradition and experience when at first defeat, then inflation and finally economic depression offered the opportunity to someone who would integrate them into a movement through which a proud and defiant people could canalize its frustration and hate and could reach out for self-respect.

To this situation Hitler brought a ruthless intensity which galvanized the German people into action. The focus was his passionate anti-semitism. Although Jews had appeared to have been integrated in German society, and the restricted ghettos and recurrent pogroms which continued in eastern Europe had long since ceased to be part of the pattern of Jewish life in Germany, the undercurrent of anti-semitism proved extremely strong when Hitler identified all the evils which he attacked with the Jews. He had seen anti-semitism at work in Vienna during his struggling days before the first world war, where leaders of extremist parties had combined violent and scurrilous attacks on the Jews with both anti-capitalist and pan-German appeals. In his book *Mein Kampf* (1924) he recorded his view that 'it is part of a great leader's genius to make even widely separated adversaries appear as if they belonged to but one category', and the category in terms of which he focused all his own hate and that of his followers was the Jew.

In so doing he aroused the German people to share his passionate conviction that the Jews were in fact the embodiment of evil—whether as Jewish capitalists, or Jewish internationalists, or Jewish trade unionists, or Jewish intellectuals—and he led the nation first to degrade and then to exterminate all with Jewish blood. In time his view that the Jews were a sub-human category fit only for the gas chamber was not only imposed on the areas overrun by the Nazis before and during the second world war, bringing death to the vast majority of European Jews. It spread to fascist movements which had had no racial content originally, to turn Italian fascist policy against the small, assimilated Jewish population of Italy and to make anti-semitism one of the hallmarks of fascism the world around.

Hitler voiced especially the outlook and frustrations of the lower middle class from which he came, a class which felt itself despised by those above and threatened by those below. Before the first world war the upper *bourgeoisie* and the landholding aristocracy had shared the leadership of political, economic, military and social life and had filled the upper ranks of the civil service. The lower ranks of the bureaucracy and the petty tradesmen and artisans had found their position deteriorating as the industrial proletariat became organized and articulate and pressed for workers' rights. The post-war inflation struck them with especially devastating force. National Socialism was aimed against both the upper *bourgeoisie* and the 'Jewish' Marxist trade unions. Its anti-intellectualism rejected the intellectual classes and appealed to the romanticism so strong in German minds.[9]

In glorifying the military ideal in a disarmed Germany Hitler gave an outlet to one of the deepest frustrations. He offered this source of self-satisfaction and self-respect, moreover, to the little people who had not been privileged to enjoy it under the Prussian military system in which the officer cadres were recruited almost entirely from the upper classes of landed gentry and professional men. His brown-shirted storm troopers and *élite* black-shirts could enjoy the sense of identity with the military caste and the power of military force, while at the same time depending for their status wholly on Hitler who hence became indispensable to them as leader and symbol.

Since Hitler appeared to represent each of a number of different aspirations, he received support from many quarters. The regular army—*Reichswehr*—supported him for his military emphasis and intent to rearm the German Reich. Industrialists supported him as a bulwark against trade union organization and Marxist thought. Conservative and reactionary elements supported his attack on the liberal principles and parliamentary procedures of the Weimar republic. Many who felt threatened by the presence of Bolshevik Russia to the east, and who remembered the 1918 effort of the German communists to seize power as it fell from the Kaiser's hands, saw him as a defence against communism. And even those who opposed his methods and many of his ideas welcomed his reassertion of German nationalism, his repudiation of the treaty of Versailles, his vision of a Greater Germany, his renewal of the demand for *Lebensraum*. Each group thought that he spoke for them and none believed that he would have the desire and ultimately the power to subordinate their own interests—the regular army, industry and the established social classes—to his system and his will.

Hitler's appeal and his ability to surround himself with men who carried out the various aspects of his programme came in part from the very fact that he discarded all the rules of established society and gave free rein to his imagination and that of his associates. In one field after another his lieutenants with unrestrained zeal laid out the lines of the new order which, he said, was to last for a thousand years.

Alfred Rosenberg projected the outward extension of the Reich in geopolitical terms to take in the plains of Russia and the Middle East and to make the overseas Germans, loyal to their 'blood' rather than the state of which they were citizens, instruments of a global strategy of domination. For Joseph Goebbels propaganda was an equally open field. Hitler was in no sense the inventor of propaganda, for it had been well developed by all the belligerent countries during the war and it was skilfully and consciously used for advertising in capitalist countries and in the USSR as one of the techniques for building a socialist society. But his bold exposition of the technique of the 'big lie' gave his propaganda minister full scope to destroy the capacity for critical response and to use all the force of the mass media to produce desired action. Heinrich Himmler was free to develop the secret police—the Gestapo —and to direct them in unimagined brutalities, unrestrained by legal procedures or citizens' rights. Julius Streicher could go to all lengths to discredit and eliminate the Jews. Doctors could experiment on human beings in concentration camps as they would on rats in the laboratory. Economists had the challenging task of operating an autarchic economy. Lawyers could have a free hand in working out criteria and procedures which would give effect to the established concept of National Socialist justice—'Right is whatever profits the German nation; wrong is whatever harms it'. Educators were called upon to design a new education which would train the emotions and develop the character and attitudes that would make people dedicated followers in the Nazi state.

For the leader and his associates, National Socialism thus offered a challenge to the imagination and the opportunity for action. For the German people it offered a sense of mission. The basis was a precarious one, for in a society where everything stemmed from the leader there was the ever-present danger of intrigue and of the capricious exercise of power. Many fled from the terror or chose exile and the chance to live as free, critical-minded human beings rather than to become part of a system which extolled 'thinking with the blood'. Others remained submerged and unhappy with the course of events. But for those who shared in some measure the sense of adventure which National Socialism offered, its dangers seemed a small price to pay for release from the humiliation of defeat and the bewilderment and hunger of depression.

With failure in the second world war National Socialism as such came to an end, its leader dead and its doctrines discredited. The German nation, divided by the occupying powers at the close of the war, set two courses, as a liberal democracy in the west and a communist state in the east, both segments making vigorous but not wholly successful efforts to purge themselves of Nazi ideas and personnel.[10]

Yet though Nazism was destroyed, it had showed some of the forces latent in society which could be set loose and which another leader might exploit in another time or place if the situation should become ripe. Such a situation did exist, though in a very different form, in the Union of South Africa.

2. South Africa[11]

In the years after the second world war the Union of South Africa stood against the world current which was bringing equality of status to formerly subject and depressed peoples. Rejecting the principles proclaimed in the Universal Declaration of Human Rights, it took a firm position in support of the idea of a permanent master race and took drastic steps to translate its position into the institutional structure of its society. Its attitude and policy were expressed by the Afrikaner Nationalist party, which came to power in 1948, as *apartheid*.

The situation in South Africa was unique: a nation of some twelve and a half million people in the mid-twentieth century of whom two and a half million were Europeans.* The Europeans were divided in the ratio of three to two between Afrikaans-speaking descendants of the Dutch who originally settled the southern coast in the seventeenth century, and English or English-speaking Europeans who came first as traders, then as masters, after the Cape of Good Hope became part of the British empire during the Napoleonic wars, and then as miners and industrialists after 1870 to exploit the fabulous riches of diamond mines and gold.[12]

Eight and a half million of the non-Europeans were native Africans of the Bantu tribes who had migrated south into the area north of the coastal range at the same time that the Afrikaners were reaching it in their trek up from the south. They had first fought among themselves and then with European

---

* The following discussion relates to the self-image and aspirations of the dominant European minority, not the African majority. For the latter, see *Infra*, pp. 1033–44, 'Emerging Nationalism: Africa'.

settlers for the empty land, and had finally in the nineteenth century settled among the Europeans and in tribal areas known as 'native reserves', whence they emerged in increasing numbers as farm labourers and then for the heavy and menial occupations in the mines and cities.[13] A million 'Coloureds', located principally in the Cape Province, were of mixed blood; most traced their ancestry to early settlers and either Malay slaves or the Bushmen and Hottentots who occupied the area at the time of original European settlement; few were the product of mixture in recent times. Some half million Indians, mostly in Natal, were the descendants of indentured workers brought in between 1860 and 1911 to work sugar plantations in that province and of merchants who followed in their wake.

In the Union of South Africa in the twentieth century, a small divided European element thus confronted a large population of native Africans and other non-Europeans. A wide cultural gap separated Europeans and Africans, they were in constant conflict over possession of land, and the Europeans had established an economic and social pattern based upon the exploitation of cheap labour and a master–servant relationship between the races.

The principle of *apartheid* by which the Afrikaner Nationalists sought to meet the immense problems of such a society had two aspects: the permanent superiority of the European within a European society which the African was to enter only to contribute his labour; the physical, social and cultural isolation of African from European, and the cultural development of African society on the basis of their own traditions and skills, not those of European society. At the time when it was enunciated, however, an estimated two million Africans had already become permanent urban dwellers and many more had been exposed to European industrial practices and manner of life. The number which had acquired western education was exceedingly small; less than half of the African children entered school, and of these only 5 per cent completed the primary grades; only a handful reached the university entrance level. But several generations of missionary efforts, and increasing public provision for the education of Africans since the establishment of the South African Union in 1910, had created a detribalized population which had come to share European values and to aspire to the way of life which Europeans enjoyed.[14]

The most striking feature of *apartheid* was the intensity with which the policy was pursued. That intensity was a product of the Afrikaner mentality, rooted in the history of the Afrikaner people. It was a reflection of a self-image which had been formed in the seventeenth century and had retained its force into modern times, to such an extent that those who held it were prepared to breast the major tides of world developments in the fierce determination to make it survive.

The Afrikaners of South Africa had lived in isolation from the time of settlement, and had preserved in their isolation the seventeenth-century Calvinist outlook which they had brought with them. This was a stern doctrine which placed on those whom God had 'elected' responsibility to live according to their understanding of His precepts and to make these prevail among the non-elect. It carried the spirit of hard righteousness which had ruled in Calvin's Geneva. The North American colonies had shared a similar heritage but there it had been tempered by the admixture of settlers of gentler faiths, by life in a less hostile environment which had enabled many to stray from the fold, and by continuous reinforcements from Europe which had brought a flow of developing ideas, until the eighteenth-century Enlightenment had found in North America a receptive home.

But in South Africa each successive experience had hardened the religious and cultural attitudes of seventeenth-century Calvinism. Armed with sturdy resolve and the sense that they were God's elect, working out His will, the Afrikaners had struggled to bring under cultivation the coastal plain, the more difficult hinterland and then the dry and empty veld. They had trekked north *en masse* in the early nineteenth century to preserve their doctrines in purity and to escape the domination of the British into whose hands the fortunes of European wars had brought the Cape of Good Hope; beyond the mountain barrier they had formed their own republics of Orange Free State and Transvaal. In their expansion they had encountered the Bantu peoples migrating south, and it had seemed still part of God's work to battle with them for the unclaimed wastes, to withstand their raids, and to set them to work tending cattle and tilling fields.

They were still following their God-fearing way of life when the Kimberley diamond strike of 1870 and the discovery of gold in the Transvaal in 1884 exploded the industrial revolution in their midst. This opened the floodgates to European immigrants—*uitlanders*—introduced the heterogeneity and disorder of urban life into the rural society which the Afrikaners had built, and brought British economic imperialism in its most ruthless form. Economic penetration and resort to military force finally culminated in the Boer war of 1899–1902 between the British and the Boer republics of Transvaal and Orange Free State.

From the opening of the twentieth century the Afrikaner mentality, which had never lost its seventeenth-century Calvinist ethos, was deepened and embittered by the sense of aloneness and the resentment of defeat. Although the Boer leadership accepted the Act of Union in 1910, including the idea of partnership with fellow South Africans of British extraction and the prospect of working out their destiny within the British empire, the feeling of apartness was intensified. Two years after Union, one of the leaders, General Hertzog, formed the National party on the ground that true partnership would only be possible when Afrikaners were on a par economically and culturally with the British. He looked towards a future merging of two separate streams, British and Afrikaner, rather than the immediate integration of a single South African people as the party led by General Jan Smuts proposed. Hertzog led a successful movement to resist the policy of anglicization and to substitute

Afrikaans for Dutch as the second official language. The Afrikaner nationalists, later led by Dr D. F. Malan, never relinquished the hope of regaining the independence which had been lost and of an Afrikaner state in southern Africa.

The Afrikaner nationalists saw themselves as occupying a special place in the world. In their eyes British South Africans were members of a world-wide English-speaking community, with a cultural home, Britain, and brothers in Australia, New Zealand, Canada and the United States; if they should lose their identity, their culture would still survive. But Afrikaners were a people apart. They were no longer Dutch: not in language, for their own speech had become distinct; not in affiliation, for this link had been broken more than a hundred years before; nor yet in sense of identity, for few immigrant reinforcements had come from Holland in the 300 years since original settlement. They were only themselves, one and a half million of God's elect, precariously located at the tip of a vast continent filled with blacks, faced with an economically aggressive, culturally strong and politically reinforced British element which, though outnumbered three to two, had the self-confidence of imperialists, entrepreneurs and victors.

The nationalists were determined that Afrikaners should survive as a people. Their secret society, the Afrikaner Broederbond, formed in 1918, had as its declared objective: the abolition of inferiority of Afrikaners and their language; strict segregation of all non-Europeans; an end to exploitation of South Africa and its people by 'aliens'; and the Afrikanerization of public life and education in the Christian National sense. According to its general secretary: 'The Afrikaner Broederbond is born from a deep conviction that the Afrikaner nation was planted in this country by God's hand and is destined to remain as a nation with its own character and its own mission.'*

In the troubled decades after Union, the leadership of Jan Smuts, Jan Hofmeyr and others managed to keep tensions within bounds. In spite of intense and unreconciled opposition, South Africa joined Britain in both world wars. In the depression of the 1930s, the major parties joined, subordinating differences of policy with respect to group separateness to the urgent need of coping with economic developments, though when the second world war broke out the parties again fell apart. Gradually the economic division between the rural, farming Afrikaners and the urban, industrial British and *uitlanders* became blurred as Afrikaners learned industrial skills and took urban jobs. A common educational system, though separately conducted in the two languages, offered common content and maintained a common standard.

But the Afrikaner current of nationalism and separateness ran on, compounded of cultural separation from the British and racial separation from the Africans, and it contained for many years the still living dream of political

* Quoted in G. H. Galpin, ed., *The South African Way of Life* (New York, 1953), p. 138.

independence. Political hopes for a restoration of the Boer republics dwindled as Johannesburg in the Transvaal became a bustling modern centre, not only for the gold to which it owed its birth but for the growing industrial complex of South Africa's expanding economy. But on the cultural issue Afrikaners made constant gains as Afrikaans became the language of instruction in schools for Afrikaner children and an Afrikaans literature began to appear. And on South Africa's number one problem, relations between European and African, their unswerving position of separation seemed to more and more people to provide an appealing answer to a gnawing problem which no one else saw a way to solve.

The constitutions of the Boer republics had reserved the franchise and all other political rights to the Europeans and had stated unequivocally that the native population was to have no part, now or in the future, in either church or state. Boundaries had been drawn between native reserves and European areas, excluding each from acquiring land within the other's domain. African workers in the European areas were treated as temporary sojourners for the purpose of work, without the status or any of the rights of citizenship. The ban was extended to Indians who were forbidden to enter the Orange Free State or to acquire land in the Transvaal. In their unyielding separateness from Africans and Asians, Afrikaners were intent on retaining their racial integrity. Stern Puritan *mores* helped to maintain the separateness of racial stocks.

In the Cape Colony on the other hand, where the population at the time of Union consisted of roughly a fifth European, a fifth Coloured, and three-fifths Native, a more inclusive pattern prevailed. All who could meet residence, property and educational qualifications, regardless of race, were enrolled on the voting lists, though only Europeans were eligible for election to public office. Under the terms of the Union, each province kept the franchise which it had at the time, and the rights enjoyed by Coloured and Native in Cape Province were entrenched by the provision in the Act of Union that they could only be modified by a two-thirds vote of the combined membership of both houses of the legislature.

English-speaking South Africans no less than Afrikaners, however, took for granted their superiority over the native Africans. As a body, they went along with the assumption of a privileged European society, resting on an African labour base. Trade unions composed of white workers insisted on apprenticeship regulations and other measures to exclude all except European workers from skilled occupations and thus to protect their wage levels, based on scarcity of labour in an expanding economy, from African competition. In Natal the discriminatory conditions imposed on Indian labourers were so severe that they led Mahatma Gandhi to develop the techniques for protest which he used successfully after his return to India in 1914. But British South Africans, with an easy-going feeling of racial superiority toward Africans and cultural superiority toward Afrikaners who could boast no Shakespeare, or

Newton or Adam Smith, lacked the intensity and the sense of 'election' which enabled the Afrikaners to make *apartheid* an article of faith.

There were some members of both British and Afrikaner groups who could not accept the assumption of permanent superiority over the majority of South Africa's population. In the Afrikaner ranks such individuals were few; among the British the number was substantial. Members of the Anglican clergy tried to apply the concept of Christian brotherhood; the Dutch Reformed Churches of the Afrikaners clung to the doctrine of the 'elect' and equated it with the distinction between themselves and Africans, though some individual ministers dissented. Missionaries, welfare workers and teachers tried to prepare individual Africans for participation at higher levels in South African society and co-operated with the small group who received training in their efforts to secure broader rights.

In the course of the years the Afrikaner attitude came to prevail more and more over the less restrictive policies of the Cape. The effort of General Hertzog in 1926 to get the Natives removed from the rolls in the Cape Province failed for lack of the required two-thirds vote, but it succeeded ten years later, with the support of the moderate leader, General Smuts. At that time the parties of the two leaders were brought together into a United Party by Hertzog accepting Smuts's position on the integration of British and Afrikaner as South Africans, and Smuts accepting Hertzog's position on permanent exclusion rather than gradual incorporation of the non-European populations. The British gradually lost influence within the political institutions which they had devised and, when the Afrikaner Nationalist party came to power in 1948, they found themselves taking second place in a state dominated by Afrikaner extremists.

The triumph of Afrikaner nationalism and the policy of *apartheid* bore down upon the Coloured and Indian, as well as on the native African. The Coloureds, mainly located in the Cape Province, were culturally a part of the European society; no tribal ties or alien ways set them apart. In language, religion and cultural values—in all except colour—they were indistinguishable from the Europeans among whom they lived. As the principle of *apartheid* took hold, the Coloureds found themselves shoved into becoming a separate community. Finally, they were put off the voting rolls after successive efforts to do so were held unconstitutional by the Supreme Court.

The Indians were regarded as alien and unassimilable. Although all but a handful were South African born, often of South African parents and even grandparents, the declared *apartheid* policy was to seek their 'repatriation'. But it was they who furnished the basis for bringing the whole question of South Africa's racial policy before the United Nations, for the Delhi government championed their cause and repeatedly insisted that the issue was an international one and not merely a matter of domestic policy as the Union of South Africa maintained.

The South Africa of the 1950s was thus the expression of Afrikaner nationalism. What once had been a drive for separation of the Boer republics from the Cape had become the domination of the whole nation, and its orientation to the Afrikaner mentality. The principle of *apartheid* was not alone a device for the permanent subjugation of the African majority to the European element. It was the means by which the Afrikaners set themselves apart, defined themselves as a people and sought to guard their identity and their survival.[15]

World events both played into the hands of the nationalist extremists and undermined their base. The waning prestige of the British empire and the emergence of new powers from colonial rule made British dominance in South Africa seem less inevitable. Nazi Germany contributed the terminology and the institutions to assert racial superiority and apply totalitarian methods. The Nationalists admired them openly, adopted some of their terminology, opposed South Africa's participation in the war and voiced their sympathy with the Nazi cause. The intensification of nationalism all over the world reinforced the nationalistic sentiment and its extreme expression. The earlier, moderate leaders, Smuts and Hertzog, had condemned the Afrikaner Broederbond; Smuts had excluded its members from the civil service. Many of the leaders of the Nationalist party at the time when it came to power were known to be members of the Broederbond.

But while rising nationalism around the world stimulated the expression of Afrikaner nationalism, it also threatened it, for the native Africans were not immune to its appeal. The independence of the Sudan in 1955 and of Ghana in 1957 converted the vague aspiration among various African peoples into concrete demands and timetables for independence. African nationalism within the Union of South Africa, however, did not take the form of separatism or of revival of tribal cultures, for moves in these directions were regarded with suspicion as measures designed to deny to Africans the advantages of modern civilization. Rather, the Africans of South Africa demanded a place in the society and the right to learn the skills which would enable them to enter the modern age. World opinion, as incorporated in the Universal Declaration of Human Rights, supported such aspirations. International communism was ready to capitalize on these aspirations if they continued to be frustrated.

Most directly affecting the course of *apartheid* was the march of industrialism, inexorably complicating its application and negating its premises. When industry first came to South Africa the Afrikaners had shunned it, although the main mining strikes were in their territory—the Transvaal. British and other European capital had opened up the mines; European immigrant labour had exploited them, aided by native Africans on heavy unskilled jobs. At first the Africans came as transient workers, returning to their tribal areas when they had earned enough to pay their taxes in cash. They had lived in labour camps and carried passes which permitted them to come and go. In time more and more of the African workers became part of a permanent labour force. But they still lived in labour camps, called locations, which were bad enough as temporary makeshift accommodation for transient workers, but were appalling slums for permanent workers and their families. And they still carried passes permitting them to go about their business on sufferance.

After the first world war the sons of Afrikaner farmers began to learn city trades and to enter industry. The process was accelerated by the rapid expansion of industry and the mounting labour shortage during the second world war and in the following years. South African industry ceased to be financed from abroad; local capital, including some from Afrikaner sources, sustained the expansion. Nor could it depend on foreign labour—more and more native Africans were drawn into industry to fill the labour requirements. But, as in other parts of the world, industrial labour increasingly required skills as machines took over routine tasks. Yet limitations on jobs and training for non-Europeans barred the way.

In many ways industrial expansion and *apartheid* were in direct conflict. *Apartheid* called for separation, for drawing boundaries between Europeans and Africans as in the days when tribal reserves were set apart from areas of European farms; but industry demanded more and more workers, to work on the spot, not in isolation. *Apartheid* called for restricting the African's level of skill; but industry called for a wider and higher range of competence. *Apartheid* called for encouraging the development of tribal African cultures; but the inevitable exposure to modern industry, to the daily characteristics of urban life, and to the penetration of ideas which no barrier could exclude ensured that the process of transforming tribal people into modern citizens would go on. In the vivid and realistic words of a former South African historian: 'Every inhabitant of the Gold Coast who casts a free ballot, every native of the Congo who drives a locomotive, every native of Uganda, or Tanganyika who independently raises and sells cotton or coffee in the world market, every native worker in a Northern Rhodesia copper mine who strikes against his company, becomes unconsciously and remotely a critic of South Africa's racial policies, establishing contradictions and alternatives which all the world may observe and which no frontier patrol can prevent from entering into the minds of South Africa's own native population.'*

Perhaps the most crucial question was whether seventeenth-century Calvinism would continue to give to city-bred and industrially trained generations the intensity and moral sureness required for a people determined to maintain continuing dominance over the restless and rising masses by whom they were overwhelmingly outnumbered, in the face of the world-wide revolution in race relations of the twentieth century and of the newly independent nations of the African continent.

* C. W. de Kiewiet, *The Anatomy of South African Misery* (London, 1956), p. 8.

V. STATES OF RELIGIOUS ORIGIN OR OUTLOOK[16]

While the major drives of the twentieth century were toward some secular form of national consciousness, two states came into existence whose basic unity and definition were religious—Israel and Pakistan. The former had been the constant dream of a scattered people which had never lost the sense of identity with its 'homeland'. The latter was the product of Asian communalism, and came into being in the crisis of liberation. Both Judaism and Islam offered a basis for many aspects of secular life, for they provided systems of law and prescribed the values and relationships of daily life. Both Israel and Pakistan aspired to develop modern, democratic, economically effective national states and considered their religious origin and identification wholly consistent with this objective.

Certain other countries retained a traditional religious orientation into the middle of the twentieth century, notably those such as Saudi Arabia, Yemen and Afghanistan which had remained largely isolated and relatively free from the impact of the West. Elsewhere national movements against western dominance were identified with religious reassertion, especially among Muslim peoples and in such Buddhist areas as Burma and Ceylon.

1. *Israel*

For nearly two thousand years the Jewish people, dispersed through many lands, included in every synagogue service a prayer for the welfare of Palestine, the Holy Land, and for the return of God's presence to Jerusalem. Through centuries of persecution, when one place after another that seemed to offer a haven turned into a place of torment, expulsion and death, the dream of a return to the Jewish homeland remained always as a ray of hope. Throughout Jewish history a few dedicated people, from all over the lands of Exile, made their way to Palestine.

In the last two decades of the nineteenth century and the years before the first world war, when a great flood of Jews were pouring out of pogrom-ridden eastern Europe, the trickle to Palestine grew, and Zionist organizations of Europe and America lent support to those who made their way there. When the Balfour Declaration of 1917 stated that the British government viewed with favour the establishment of a Jewish national home, and the door of free immigration into the United States was closed in 1921, Palestine became a principal place to which immigrants from eastern Europe turned their course. In the 1930s it offered a refuge from destruction at the hands of the Nazis. In 1947 the land of Palestine was partitioned by recommendation of the United Nations and on May 14, 1948, Israel emerged as an independent state.

The background of the 'return to Israel' thus lay in the continuous history of the Jewish people; its conversion into the reality of an integrated Jewish state was the product of world conditions in the twentieth century and of the efforts of the Jewish people in these years.

At the opening of the twentieth century two-thirds of the Jewish population of the world lived in east and south-eastern Europe, especially in the region which had been Poland; the remainder lived in western and central Europe where they had been gradually readmitted, mainly after the Peace of Westphalia in 1648, in the Muslim lands of North Africa and west Asia where they had settled when expelled from Spain and Portugal after 1492, and in the United States where their numbers were increasing rapidly from the great tide of immigrants that had been pouring in from east Europe since the 1880s.

The Jews of western Europe, outside the Iberian peninsula, had generally come to enjoy full civil and political rights as one country after another during the nineteenth century had removed the religious qualifications which prevented their political participation, opened the doors of schools and universities and removed restrictions on entering the professions. Their recently achieved security had been shaken after 1880, however, by an ominous growth of anti-semitism, especially in Germany and Austria, directed against Jews as a 'race', not against their religion as in previous periods.

Conditions in eastern Europe were much less favourable. Restrictions on landholding, limitation of areas of settlement, extreme poverty, pressure of population and frequent pogroms had set in motion a westward migration that brought poor immigrants into the well-established Jewish communities of west Europe and the flood of immigration to the United States. The rate of Jewish migration rose from an average of 5,400 a year between 1840 and 1880 to 38,200 a year from 1880 to 1900 and 114,500 annually from 1901 to 1914. The United States and Canada admitted immigrants freely and accorded them full civil and political rights.

Since the middle of the nineteenth century, Jews of western Europe and America had been organized to assist their fellow Jews of the east and to intervene wherever the freedom and status of the Jews appeared to be threatened. Organizations such as the Alliance Israélite Universelle established in France in 1860 and similar bodies in England, the United States and Germany, were set up to give educational and philanthropic aid abroad. Support for Jewish settlement in Palestine was one of the forms of such help, and leading individuals in Europe and America responded to appeals from groups in the east European ghettoes who managed to organize for settlement.

It was at the turn of the century, however, that Zionism became an active movement. Though the Conservative Jewish congregations in America supported the return to Israel in principle and immigrants brought with them their 'Lovers of Zion' and 'Seekers of Zion' movements, it took the publication in 1896 of Theodor Herzl's Der Judenstaat to precipitate Zionism as an active Jewish world movement.

During the first decades of the twentieth century many events continued to build up a sense of Jewish nationalism and contributed to the growth of Zionism. The Dreyfus affair in France, which involved the espionage trial of the first Jewish army officer to be appointed to the French general staff, his conviction and imprisonment, retrial, pardon and final vindication, revealed violent anti-semitic sentiments as it divided France and focused the attention of the world for a decade. In Germany and Austria vigorously anti-semitic political groups continued to secure seats in central and local legislative bodies and violently anti-semitic newspapers circulated among the populace.

The growing nationalism of the peoples among whom many of the Jews lived threatened the status of minority groups. Minorities which had lived comfortably within the Ottoman empire found their position precarious as Turkey became a nationalist state; the intense nationalism of the new states of east Europe after the first world war boded ill for their Jewish minorities. In the effort to protect the Jewish communities within the new states, representatives of European and American Jewish organizations appeared before the Peace Conference at Versailles to secure the adoption of minorities treaties designed to guarantee the rights of such minority groups. At the same time the Balfour Declaration of 1917 converted the dream of the Jewish state into a positive hope.

When the United States closed its door to free immigration by its restrictive laws of 1921 and 1924, the flood of Jewish emigration was sharply checked. By the late 1920s Jews were coming to the United States at only one-fifth the rate at which they came when emigration was renewed after the war. Although numbers going to South American countries rose, total Jewish emigration in these years was cut by 60 per cent, from 426,930 in 1921–25 to 172,908 in 1926–30. The 'Jewish homeland' began to look like more than a centre for Jewish religion and culture and to take on the character of a haven. When the Nazi terror struck and exterminated an estimated 6,000,000 of Europe's 8,000,000 Jews, it was Palestine which received the greatest number of those who escaped.

In spite of the growing strength of the Zionist movement in Europe and America, support from the Jewish communities was far from unanimous, and those who lent the movement support differed fundamentally in the kind of 'homeland' which they envisioned. Jews of west Europe and America were divided along complex ideological and social lines. Some of the intensely religious and orthodox supported Zionism ardently, and the Orthodox wing maintained a special arm of the Zionist movement dedicated to Israel as a religious centre where the precepts of Orthodox Judaism could be carried out to the full. The branch of Judaism in the United States which called itself Reform, however, took a firmly anti-Zionist stand in 1869 from which it did not retreat until 1935. Many of the more secularized and indifferent had little emotional attachment to the Holy Land of Israel and were likely to be anti-Zionist. Yet there were outstanding political Zionists among the non-religious who saw the Jewish homeland in national rather than religious terms.

Differences among Jews on the question of assimilation also affected their attitude toward Zionism. Assimilationists sought the integration of Jewish people into the general culture of the country of their residence, retaining their distinctive religious faith and engaging in group activities within the framework of a multi-religious democratic society, but taking their places as individual citizens, associating with others on the basis of occupation or interest, residence or responsibility in the total community. Against this view stood those who maintained that the Jewish heritage was too precious to be discarded, that only intensive Jewish life could provide the milieu for it to flourish, and that Jews should maintain a separate identity as a community. The assimilationists were on the whole opposed to Zionism. But the rise of Hitler, the imposition of the Nuremburg laws and similar laws in fascist Italy, excluding from the privileges of citizenship what had appeared to be the most completely assimilated of Jewish populations, and finally the campaign of extermination, cut the ground from under the assimilationists and made many converts to Zionism.

A third line of cleavage within Jewish communities was between the strongly socialist workers' groups and economically conservative elements. Marxian socialism drew strong adherents from among the Jews of both Germany and Russia, and both groups brought their interests and attitudes to the United States. Religious Zionism had little appeal to these indifferent or anti-religious elements, but among the workers' groups were many who looked to a Jewish homeland as a place in which to build a socialist state.

These different concepts of the Land of Israel within the Jewish communities were reflected in the schools for Palestine settlers supported by the respective wings of the world Zionist organizations. The schools supported by the general Zionist organization were essentially secular; they provided a place for the Bible and Rabbinical literature in the curriculum but they offered no formal religious teaching. The schools supported by the Orthodox Mizrachi wing were religiously oriented and devoted much time to Rabbinical literature and the Bible. The Labour and left-wing Zionists maintained non-religious schools with a vocational emphasis which included virtually no Rabbinical literature in the curriculum.

All who supported Israel agreed on one feature, its role as a centre of learning, so vital to the life of Jewish society. The Hebrew University of Jerusalem, for which ground was broken in 1918 and which admitted its first regular students in 1924, became a centre not only for Jewish studies but for general fields of knowledge. The Hebrew Institute of Technology founded in 1912 at Haifa became the leading school of engineering in the Middle East.

While the factors which underlay the creation of the state of Israel and determined its character and policy lay deep in Jewish history and experience, its shape was forged by those who committed their own lives and direct efforts to the venture. From the closing years of the nineteenth century the groups of settlers who made their way to Palestine set to work at the hard task of rebuilding an agricultural economy in the unfriendly desert. In 1885 there were some 23,000 Jews in Palestine, living mostly in four cities; by 1947 there were 643,000, living in 330 Jewish communities and settlements of which 302 were agricultural. Constituting some 27 per cent of the Palestine population, they produced some 50 per cent of the citrus fruit of the area, 89 per cent of the fodder, considerable amounts of greens and a small proportion of the grains, and were responsible for approximately 85 per cent of the country's industry and trade.

Settlers came from many different places—Hungary, Russia, Poland, Lithuania, Rumania, Bulgaria—aided by money from their own communities and from other countries—Germany, France, Britain, the United States, Turkey. Distinguished leaders from many countries—lawyers, professors, members of parliament, ambassadors—intervened with the Turkish government on behalf of the Jewish settlers. Every sort of Jewish group contributed financial support—charitable and mutual aid organizations, youth groups, fraternities, clandestine and revolutionary bodies.

The Jewish settlement of Palestine was thus the product of the collaboration and the expression of a very broad cross-section of world Jewry and it drew its character from the whole Jewish people rather than from any one of the many facets of Jewish life and thought. Each new wave of immigrants, composed of people who felt that they were going 'home' to the land which they already knew intimately, reinforced those who had gone before. In spite of the tremendous diversity of background and viewpoint, the tensions inherent in the relations among groups and the gap between the dream and the reality, the people who hammered out a nation were integrated through struggle and dedication to a common historic ideal.

The varied settlements were unified by a common language, Hebrew, which was developed from a language of scripture and prayer into a living language of daily use, the language of the school, the culture, the science, the learning and the public life of the people. The earlier settlements were separated from each other by language and cultural differences and retained their respective ties with the places from which they had come. The spoken Hebrew was unique to Palestine, but it was the common heritage of all. It won final acceptance in 1912 when the pupils and teachers of the newly founded Hebrew Institute of Technology, backed by the Palestine community, succeeded in making Hebrew the language of instruction over the opposition of many of the Institute's founders who wished the teaching to be in German.

When Israel became an independent state it opened its doors to Jews from all countries, however difficult it might be to assimilate them rapidly. By the Law of Return, every Jew was given the right to settle in Israel. The number of immigrants during the first four years, 688,000, exceeded the total population of the country at the time of independence. In the next five years some 150,000 additional settlers arrived. Although some continued to come from eastern Europe as they could escape from those countries where their position remained insecure, more than half of the total, including the bulk of the later immigrants, were from the Arab lands of Africa and west Asia where Jews had lived for centuries in enclaves within the Muslim communities, largely isolated both from the surrounding culture and from the Jews of Europe and America. The assimilation of these populations into a common culture offered a further problem of integration to the young Jewish state.

In its initial form Israel took the shape of a modern democratic nation-state of which any Jew could become a citizen by immigration and in which the existing Muslim and Christian citizens enjoyed rights identical with those of Jews, both individually and as communities. Except in matters of personal law such as marriage and divorce, its institutions were secular; for personal law it retained the separate ecclesiastical courts for Jews, Muslims and Christians which it inherited from the Ottoman empire and the British mandate. The practice of the Jewish religion was facilitated, for example, by making the Jewish Sabbath the weekly day of rest and observing the Jewish dietary laws in the armed forces, but both Jewish and non-Jewish religious establishments received support from public funds. It was by its existence as a homeland for the Jewish people rather than by its Jewish institutions and practices that Israel fulfilled its purpose as a Jewish state.

The Jewish settlement in Palestine and the establishment of a Jewish state took place in the face of strong opposition. Up to the first world war the Turkish administration tried to forbid entry into Israel, claiming readiness to admit Jews to any other part of the Turkish dominions but resisting what they recognized as the Jewish settlers' sense of coming 'home'. In spite of the Balfour Declaration, the British government of the Palestine mandate pursued an uncertain policy of admission and restriction in the face of conflicting pressures from Arab and Jewish populations. The surrounding Arab countries would not accept the establishment of Israel, and the state came into existence only after war with her neighbours.[17]

To the neighbouring Arab states Israel, with its modern economy and western outlook, was a beachhead of the West, a trespasser on Arab soil, a temporary phenomenon which must be destroyed. Whether in the violent language with which President Gamel Abdul Nasser of Egypt encouraged border raiders, or in the scholarly tones with which a professor at the American University of Beirut concluded that the only possible future for Israel was the fate which befell the Latin Kingdom of Jerusalem, or in the song of the girl scouts in an Egyptian village, 'Go away bad Israel, you shall not have our dear Palestine', the intention was the same. The state of Israel must not live.

For the Jews of the world, whatever their previous attitude toward Zionism had been, Israel was a heartening reality. More, it was a fulfilment of the age-old dream from which even the non-religious were not far removed and which the religious repeated constantly in their prayers.

For the people of Israel, their mission was to survive, not alone for self-preservation or patriotism to the country which they had made, but because they believed themselves to be the instruments of an historic destiny, the keepers of the Covenant, the means of realizing the prayer, repeated through the years in every synagogue, that God's presence might return again to the Land of Israel.

2. Pakistan

Although Pakistan came into existence only seventeen years after the first proposal for a Muslim state in the Indian sub-continent, its roots went deep into history. From their advent into the sub-continent the Muslim population had been unique among the succession of invaders in resisting the process of absorption into Hindu society. Equalitarian, monotheistic and proselytizing, Muslims would not be fitted into the caste-structured, polytheistic and tolerant Hindu culture. In spite of much intermingling and interaction of Muslims and Hindus through the centuries, the two societies never merged. Under the Mogul emperors, especially after the rule of the sternly puritanical Alamgir who attempted to restore the purity of Islam in the late seventeenth century, the gulf between the two communities widened.

From the beginning of British influence and rule in India, the position of the Muslims fell and that of the Hindus rose. Regarding the Muslims as the main obstacle to the expansion of their authority, the British at the beginning of their rule adopted the policy so often used by conquerors of favouring the non-dominant element, and deliberately encouraged the Hindus. Furthermore, the commercial character of the British intrusion made the Indian class of merchant-bankers, the *banyas*, allies and beneficiaries of the process while the Muslims, who in Bengal were engaged principally in agriculture, administration and minor crafts, suffered economically. In a generation the Muslim population was reduced from the dominant element to an impotent minority.

When the British in 1833 introduced a system of western education in the English language in order to train for the ranks of the civil service, Hindus took advantage of the opportunity while Muslims held aloof. By the time of the uprising of 1857, Hindus were already becoming integrated into the British administration, and although both Hindus and Muslims participated in the rising, the stern punitive measures of the British were directed primarily against the Muslims.

The Hindu revival which grew in strength through the nineteenth century intensified the Muslims' sense of exclusion and depression. European historical and cultural studies of the Hindu-Sanskrit religious literature and the pre-Muslim history of India fed the revival and made the reawakening of India essentially a rebirth of Hinduism. As the Hindus became dominant, Muslims found their social position intolerable; with the loss of Muslim political authority and in the face of Hindu caste exclusiveness, they felt that they were being looked upon as an alien element in society.[18]

Against this background, the Muslim revival which led to the creation of an Islamic state followed the only course which seemed open, to rebuild the Muslim community as a distinct entity within the modern framework established by British rule. Convinced that the policy of aloofness from western education would have to be reversed if the Indian Muslim community was to rise from its depressed state, Sir Sayyid Ahmad Khan founded in 1875 the college which became the Aligarh Muslim University and launched the training of a new leadership for the new Muslim community of India. By the time that Britain was ready to extend self-government at the local level to the Indian population through the Morley–Minto reforms of 1909, the members of the organized Muslim community were convinced that they could only hope to function politically in the face of the Hindu majority if they established themselves as a separate electorate. In securing recognition of the principle of communal voting—Hindus for Hindus and Muslims for Muslims—the Muslims expressed and the British accepted the concept that the people of India constituted in effect two nations. From separate electorates to a separate Muslim state was a short and logical step.

As the Indian nationalist movement against the British gained momentum, however, many Muslims made common cause with the Hindus in the movement for national liberation. The Indian National Congress, though predominantly Hindu, numbered prominent Muslims among its members, including for a period Maulana Muhammed Ali and Muhammed Ali Jinnah, who later became the leader of the Muslim League and the moving spirit in bringing about partition. Mahatma Gandhi appealed to Indians of all faiths to join the movement of passive resistance. But the very terms of Gandhi's appeal revealed the deep Hindu roots from which his thought and expression came, and even those Muslims who joined the movement did not feel that his voice was theirs. The opposition of the Indian National Congress to the principle of a multiple society made up of separate electorates and its insistence on a society in which the basic unit was the individual appeared to the Muslims to mean simply that majority votes would always be against them.

As it became apparent that British power would soon be withdrawn and as the ferment of Muslim nationalism spread throughout the Islamic world, the concept of an Islamic state took shape. First formally proposed by the Muslim poet and influential religious philosopher, Mohammed Iqbal, at the session of the All India Muslim League in 1930, then given a name to suggest the area envisaged for such a state by three students at Cambridge University, England, it was finally made the fighting goal of the Muslim League under the vigorous leadership of Jinnah.

In its original conception the Muslim state was to be composed of the north-western provinces indicated by the name 'Pakistan', Punjab, Afgania, Kashmir, Sind, Beluchistan. Its relation to other parts of the Indian subcontinent was not fully envisioned, for it was by no means clear whether British power would devolve upon a unitary Indian state or some looser federation. But as the movements for independence and partition rose to a climax and tension between Muslim and Hindu mounted, the demand grew for the inclusion of the densely Muslim area of East Bengal as well as the north-western area. When partition came, and the furious violence revealed

how intense were the latent antagonisms among people who had been neighbours for centuries, millions of people streamed across the borders to participate, by choice or by fear, in the creation of the new state. Yet of approximately 100,000,000 Muslims in undivided India, only about two-thirds
became part of the Islamic state, while the other third remained as citizens of
the secular state of India.

The leaders who brought Pakistan into being and directed the shaping of
the new nation were the product of western education and the Aligarh
movement, not of religious fanaticism. They had absorbed many of the
political, economic and social concepts of the West and were convinced that
these were consistent with the basic principles of Islam.

In the ten years after independence they undertook to provide the structure
for a democratic, modern, economically sound Islamic nation. The enormous
practical difficulties which confronted the country almost overshadowed the
effort to define a modern Islamic state. The government of Pakistan had to be
built virtually *de novo*. The relatively small numbers of Muslims in the old
civil service left Pakistan far less well supplied than India with experienced
administrators at all levels. The problem of absorbing nearly 8,000,000
refugees into a total population of 80,000,000 placed a tremendous burden
on the community, and the difficulty of uniting two areas separated by more
than a thousand miles was enhanced by differences in language, economic
conditions and local loyalties. The disruption of normal economic relationships by partition increased the already difficult problems of economic
development while international tensions required the formation and support
of a military establishment. To these and other practical problems was added
intense disagreement as to how far a Muslim state should be 'Islamic' and what
that would mean. It took nine years of deliberation to frame the first constitution, which attempted to embody the principles on which Pakistan had
been founded.

In the constitutional struggle, the Islamic extremists accused what they
called the 'westernized ruling group' of being ignorant of the Law (*sharia*)
and of the true principles of Islam, of being able to see 'only through the
coloured glasses of western thought', and of wishing to establish not an
Islamic but a 'national democratic' state. They called for an ideological rather
than a national state, in which authority would be derived from God, not
from the people, and for the creation of a thoroughly Islamic society, the
complete replacement of prevailing law by the Muslim legal code, and the
enforcement of every prescription of the Quran and Sunnah. 'Indeed, if
secular and Godless instead of Islamic Constitution was to be introduced and
if the British Criminal Procedure Code had to be enforced instead of the
Islamic Shari'ah what was the sense in all this struggle for a separate Muslim
homeland ?'*

* Syed Abul 'Aka Maudoodi, *Islamic Law and Constitution*, ed. by Khurshid Ahmad
(Karachi, 1955), p. 17.

The extremists rejected the principles of the parliamentary system with a cabinet responsible to the majority party. They wished to exclude women from active politics and public office and to establish two classes of citizenship, Muslim and non-Muslim, placing the non-Muslims in the traditional status of *zimmis* under the guarantee of protection by the state.

The constitution as adopted in 1956 established the principle that sovereignty resides in God alone, with governmental powers to be exercised within the limits set by the Quran and the Sunnah. But it provided only that the state should endeavour to facilitate the practice of Islam by Muslims, not that it should require or enforce such practice; it reserved for Muslims no position except that of president; it made no legal distinction between Muslim and non-Muslim citizens, except that only Muslims would be taxed to support Muslim institutions, and precluded discrimination in access to the public services, including defence; it left open the question of whether voting should be as common citizens for a single electoral roll or separately, by religious or other communities; it provided for a parliamentary system of the British type, and reserved a number of seats for women to assure their participation.

The constitution declared that 'the principles of democracy, freedom, equality, tolerance and social justice as enumerated by Islam, should be fully observed', and it guaranteed to all citizens a list of fundamental rights which corresponded closely to those enumerated in other democratic constitutions. The Islamic provisions specified that 'no law shall be enacted which is repugnant to the Holy Quran and Sunnah' and called for setting up an organization for Islamic research 'to assist in the reconstruction of Muslim society on a truly Islamic basis' and for a commission to make recommendations on how to bring existing and future legislation into conformity with the Quran and Sunnah. The 'Islamic' provisions could not affect the personal laws of non-Muslims or their status as citizens, or any of the fundamental rights and other provisions of the constitution.

The Islamic state of Pakistan thus took shape in terms which sought to integrate the spirit and practice of Islam with the requirements of the modern age and the institutions of parliamentary democracy. Only two years after its adoption, however, the constitution was set aside in favour of military rule. It seemed to General Ayub Khan and to the president who handed over power to him that the urgent tasks of organization and development required firmer and more positive leadership than the parliamentary system was providing. But he declared his intention of laying a basis for effective democracy by developing it first at the local level, and his reforms were dictated by the practical needs of a modern state for strong and efficient administration rather than by the demands of the Muslim extremists or the ideology of Islam.

3. *Religious orientation of other states*

Although Israel and Pakistan were unique in the twentieth century in that religion was the rationale for their coming into being as national states, the outlook and institutions in some other countries were more predominantly religious than in these. The traditional Muslim states of Saudi Arabia, Yemen and Afghanistan remained far more religiously oriented than the new Pakistan with its history of western contact and its inheritance of many western institutions. The ruler of Saudi Arabia, as Imam of the Wahhabi sect, combined a political and a religious role, while the Islamic authority, the *ulema*, continued to serve as his chief political advisers. In Yemen, law and custom remained within the prescription of traditional Islamic law.

Elsewhere in the Muslim world national self-assertion against western dominance was infused with a strong Islamic feeling which interacted with and tended to support these political movements. This was notable in the expression of Arabism, both in the Arab states of the Fertile Crescent and Arabian peninsula and in the Arabic-speaking areas of North Africa. Arabism was nourished by a sense of historic greatness based on the rise and spread of Islam and by the memory that the western powers against whom their current nationalistic aspirations were directed had once taken up arms against Islam in religious crusades. Throughout the Arab world three factors were interwoven: local nationalism in the form of attachment to a national unit such as Egypt, Iraq or Morocco, Arabism expressed in identification with the loosely related peoples from Morocco to the Persian Gulf who were linked by a common language and sense of history, and Islamic unity, of which the Arab segment of the Muslim world formed the religious, historic and linguistic core. In the charged climate of the twentieth century, especially its second quarter, these potentially competing identifications, unities and self-images tended to reinforce each other, especially when threatened from outside, and to intensify religious feeling, as well as to be intensified by it.

A somewhat parallel situation obtained in certain Buddhist areas, with Tibet, geographically and culturally isolated, preserving into the mid-twentieth century its religious structure and orientation, and with the reassertion of Buddhist principles and authority in the drive for liberation and the outlook of the new states of Burma and Ceylon. The absence of an authoritative scripture and body of law, however, and other basic differences between Buddhism and Islam, made religion in these modern Buddhist states more a factor affecting the temper of the society than a driving force for the shaping of political and social institutions.

VI. NATIONAL INDEPENDENCE IN THE FACE OF EUROPEAN EXPANSION

The few states of Asia and Africa that successfully resisted European dominance in the period of western expansion did so by a variety of means: Afghanistan and Ethiopia by isolation and resistance, Thailand and Iran by negotiation and by balancing off one European power against another, Japan by adopting western methods and competing with western powers in their own terms. In each case continuous independence and national integrity were central aims which coloured the otherwise diverse outlook of these countries.

Throughout its long, continuous history, the Coptic Christian kingdom of Ethiopia in the mountainous highlands of east Africa had had few contacts with Europe and had stood out against the spread of Islam from neighbouring areas. In the partition of Africa it was the only area on the continent, except the American-created state of Liberia, which remained unclaimed by the European powers. Its access to the Red Sea was cut off by Italian occupation of the coastal strip which formed the colony of Eritrea, but when Italy tried to move inland by force, her armies met defeat. From the time of the battle of Adowa in 1896, at which the Ethiopians turned the Italians back, Ethiopia became a symbol of successful resistance, the first sign that non-Europeans might stand against European aggression. Forty years later it again became a symbol when its emperor appealed unsuccessfully to the League of Nations for protection against Mussolini's imperial ambitions.

Ethiopia's independence was the independence of cultural as well as physical isolation. Its traditional priesthood retained a virtual monopoly of education and learning. Abyssinian herdsmen in the east and tribesmen from the Sudan in the western regions had little communication with the centres of priestly and aristocratic culture, and these in turn had few contacts with cultural currents in the outside world. Until after the second world war very few persons left the country to study abroad. Foreign trade was minimal. The Italian occupation of 1936–41 brought the country its first network of roads and the first beginnings of industry.

Like Ethiopia, Afghanistan maintained its independence by struggle and by isolating itself as far as possible from European influences. From the first half of the nineteenth century its independence was threatened by Britain, which sought to dominate the area in order to protect the north-west frontier of India through which invaders had repeatedly entered the sub-continent in the past. Britain's efforts, together with counter-moves by Russia, brought recurrent fighting to Afghan territory during the nineteenth century, destruction of forts and cities, the presence of foreign troops and intervention in the conduct of foreign affairs. The constant efforts of Afghan rulers to preserve or regain full control continued until 1919, when Britain finally recognized the full independence of Afghanistan.

Few modernizing influences entered the country during its years of isolation and the struggle to maintain its independence. Outside ideas and foreign investment were regarded with suspicion as a possible cloak for foreign domination. Conservative religious leaders opposed social change. Even after 1919 innovation was opposed and the ruler was forced to abdicate in 1929 because of the unpopularity of his educational and other reforms.

In the years after the second world war both Ethiopia and Afghanistan were eager to bring the benefits of modernization to their people. Both had to develop their economy and their basic services, such as education and health, virtually from the ground up, with an acute shortage of trained personnel and of capital. Ethiopia's emperor Haile Selassie undertook an ambitious programme of reform in government and administration, education, finance, social structure, the army and relations between church and state. Afghanistan launched a major programme of hydroelectric and irrigation development, aviation, road building, education and health services. But in both countries leaders working to bring about change sought to do so within the framework of their traditional societies. As expressed by the ambassador of Afghanistan addressing Afghan students in the United States in 1958, the ability of the educated leadership to integrate the new programmes into the national life would determine whether these measures would 'constitute progress or a mere superimposition of an alien culture'.

In contrast to the countries whose defence was associated with isolation, Thailand and Iran preserved their independence by negotiation rather than by armed resistance, and by taking advantage of the rivalry between European powers. For Thailand, her location between the French-dominated states of Indo-China and the region of expanding British control in Malaya and Burma brought her the support of both of these powers in her role as a buffer between their colonial interests. Similarly, the interests of Britain and Russia in Iran set limits to the influence which either would permit the other to exercise over that country. In both countries western influences were considerable and the process of modernization was well under way before the impetus for national development spread to all countries after the second world war.

From the time that the Thai monarchs began to open their doors to western contacts in the middle of the nineteenth century, they welcomed western ideas and knowledge while at the same time they reinforced and renewed their traditional Buddhist culture. During his long reign (1866–1910), King Chulalungkorn introduced western manners at the court, modernized the legal system, abolished slavery, reformed the state administration, police and army, and sent his many sons and competitively selected 'king's scholars' to study in Britain and on the European continent. His successor promoted westernization even more vigorously, in education, recreation, literature, law, and he led Siam to participate in international organizations. The royal patronage and example gave prestige to western practices, which then seeped down through the population. But these monarchs were equally zealous in promoting the Buddhist faith, they encouraged the development or revival of Siamese culture, and the traditional way of life was followed in the country-side. In the middle of the twentieth century Thailand continued to see itself in the process of developing a modern society in its own manner, with a minimum of stress, through the gradual integration of old and new.

Iran during the twentieth century took a succession of steps to raise both its internal conditions and external status from the depressed state and scarcely more than nominal independence to which the country had declined. The revolution of 1906 introduced parliamentary institutions. The *coup d'état* of

1921 was followed by reforms in government, education, public health, in public and private law, the position of women and the place of the religious courts, as well as by developments in transport, communication and industry. Oil, which was discovered in quantity in the Persian Gulf in 1908, brought wealth and foreign economic influences into the country. After the second world war Iran asserted its determination to control its own resources when it nationalized the oil industry and forced the foreign investors to accept terms for the exploitation and sale of Persian oil which would safeguard the national interest.

The non-European country which met the challenge of European expansion most vigorously was, of course, Japan. From the time of the forceable opening of the Island Empire to outside contact in 1853, Japan set out to learn from the West and to compete with it. In little more than a generation, it moved from an isolated, self-contained island to a vigorous position in world trade; it gained military superiority over its huge neighbour, China, and was ready to challenge successfully a great western empire, Russia. Then, becoming itself a conquering and colonial power, it took on the features of western imperialism, following the lead of a comparable island people, the British, who, with a smaller population, had demonstrated the possibility of acquiring and ruling world-wide dominions.

Japan accomplished this transition by mastery of western technology, introduction of universal education and the modernization of its economic and political structure along western lines. But it did not follow a single, direct course, for western ideas often involved divergent concepts. The relative strength of different Japanese leaders and power groups determined the influence of ideas of democracy as against military force, of capitalism or of its Marxian alternative, of racial superiority or of human equality and brotherhood.

Increasingly the military leaders gained predominance and made the drive which had started as Japan's effort to catch up with the western nations into a drive for the extension of Japanese power. They defined national aspirations in terms of an Asian empire under Japanese hegemony which would provide the raw materials and markets for her economy, would reduce her desperate dependence on foreign trade and would relieve the pressure of population in her crowded islands. They interpreted the ancient Shinto myth that the emperor was destined to rule the 'world' of the Japanese islands as promising his rule over the global world.

When the great gamble of the second world war failed, Japan in defeat had no alternative goal to which to turn or return. At mid-century the Japanese people were seeking to redefine their place in a world which had changed drastically in the half century since the aspiration to become a great military empire had been in line with the pattern established by the nations of the West.*

* See Chapter XXIX, pp. 1064–67, for cultural renaissance and adaptation of Japan.

VII. EMERGING NATIONALISM: AFRICA

Latest of the nationalist movements to emerge was that of the African peoples south of the Sahara. Rumblings of incipient nationalist feelings began to be heard after the first world war, with the formation of the National Congress of British West Africa by European-educated Africans, and these rumblings grew in volume during the following years. In West Africa, Nnamdi Azikiwe of Nigeria and Wallace Johnson of Sierra Leone published anticolonial articles, deemed to be seditious, in Azikiwe's *African Morning Post* (1936). In East Africa Jomo Kenyatta appeared before royal commissions to voice the protest of his people, the Kikuyu, against the taking of their lands for white settlers (1928–29, 1931–32), and he declared in his book on the culture of his tribe that: 'The African is conditioned, by the cultural and social institutions of centuries, to a freedom of which Europe has little conception, and it is not in his nature to accept serfdom for ever.'*

But it was only in the years after the second world war that African nationalism spread throughout the continent and assumed the proportions of a major movement. Then it gathered momentum rapidly. In the area of its first major triumph, the British West African colony of the Gold Coast, only ten years elapsed between Kwame Nkrumah's return from his studies in the United States and Britain to lead the struggle for 'freedom *now*' and his celebration of independence. In 1951 he was in prison on charges of attempting to coerce the colonial government; six years later his application for admission of Ghana to the United Nations was immediately accepted as the nations of the world hastened to welcome a new state from tropical Africa.

The focus of African nationalism was anticolonial. Whether leaders and nationalist groups aspired to a modern welfare state or reasserted the values of traditional African culture, whether at any moment they were seeking full independence, self-government or equality of political rights, all opposed foreign domination and made colonialism the centre of their attack. None of the nationalist movements reflected a traditional national unity, for the political divisions of the African continent in the twentieth century were the creation of the European nations which had carved up the territory without regard to those who occupied it, splitting some tribes and grouping others with their traditional enemies. Each movement developed pragmatically in its particular area, subject to many cross-currents of European and local origin. The broader identification was with Africa and fellow Africans, but Pan-Africanism remained a vague and relatively small component of African nationalism until after Ghana's independence.

African nationalism was a reaction to racialism as well as to colonialism. Pride of race which ran like a thread through most movements was a response to the discrimination and the implication of inferiority to which Africans had long been subjected.

* Jomo Kenyatta, *Facing Mt Kenya* (London, 1938), 1953 ed., p. 318.

The European impact on Africa set the framework within which the aspirations of African peoples were formulated and pressed. For the colonial powers the area was a vast region of physical resources to be exploited for trade, profit and the needs of the industrial economies. Tropical climate, malaria and the tsetse fly made the African continent far less suitable for European settlement than the continents of America and Australia where such settlement had spread. Certain areas, however, were attractive for settlement, most notably the veld of Southern Rhodesia and the highlands of Kenya, as well as the Union of South Africa. There European settlers pioneered farming communities and came to look upon the area as their own.

Everywhere, the relations of European to African was that of the 'superior' culture to 'inferior'—representatives of a technological society in contact with isolated, non-literate, tribal peoples for whose way of life they had only an anthropological concern. Cultural 'superiority' was reinforced in most areas by racial discrimination, uncompromisingly in the Union of South Africa, very generally in British areas, much less in French possessions and least of all in Portuguese territory, where there was considerable intermarriage and the sharp distinctions were cultural rather than racial.

Wherever European contact spread the effect was to undermine the structure of African society and the traditional pattern of African life. Commercial crops tended to supplant or intrude upon the subsistence economy of African communities, and not infrequently reduced the available food supply. Recruiting of African labour for mines and plantations drew men away from tribal villages. Taxes which had to be paid in cash forced them to seek employment for wages. The appropriation of African lands cut away the foundations of tribal life. Railways and roads opened up lines of communication and contact between areas and groups. The growth of urban centres around points of administration, mining or trade introduced Africans to an urban milieu where traditional relationships and controls were largely inoperative and the individual had to function under strange, competitive conditions without the extended family and group relationships which had defined his role and sustained him in carrying his responsibilities. As the twentieth century progressed, fewer and fewer of the African peoples remained undisturbed in their tribal life.

Few Africans however were entirely cut off from their tribal roots. Many of those who worked for wages returned to their villages each year as soon as they earned the cash which they required, and their places in mines or on plantations were taken by others for a temporary period. Wives and children remained in rural areas, or city-born children were sent home to relatives to be brought up. But the number remaining in permanent urban employment grew continually as cities expanded. Some enterprises made special efforts to create conditions which would hold a stabilized labour force, and education or personal or family circumstances intervened to cut off tribal contacts and to produce a detribalized urban population.

Even the detribalized Africans, however, rarely became incorporated in any complete way into European culture, for the conditions of European impact generally offered the African no version of European life which he could adopt in place of his own. Forced to labour in the white man's mines by the white man's taxes, required to carry a pass or observe a curfew and subject to arrest by the white man's police, excluded from the white man's buses and residential areas and from the white man's jobs, offered the principles of brotherhood by the white man's religion but refused them in practice, deemed by the white man to be 'unready' for responsibility, the African was in a position to admire and covet the white man's goods but hardly to see or appreciate the bases of his society and to make them his own. The outstanding exceptions, such as M. Félix Houphouët-Boigny of the Ivory Coast, a minister in three French cabinets, only served to underline the general situation.

In urban communities and centres of employment, Africans generally lived apart from Europeans in locations where housing and other facilities often met neither the African's standards for the village nor the European's standards for the city. Classification of 'European' and 'African' jobs placed a ceiling on ambition. Opportunities for secondary and advanced education were severely limited. Where Africans had an opportunity to observe the Europeans in their midst, what they saw was often far from representative of the manner of life which the same people would have followed within their own cultural milieu. Some Europeans in fact had chosen Africa in order to escape from the standards of social responsibility and democratic conduct which their own societies imposed. The gulf between European and African life was narrower and the barrier less complete in some areas than others. After the second world war the trend everywhere except in South Africa was to offer Africans increased access to the education, manner of life, occupations, status and values which Europeans enjoyed.[19]

The impact of European domination varied considerably, according to differences both in local conditions and in the policies and practices of occupying powers. Geographical conditions and natural resources produced such different types of economic development as copper mining, plantation cultivation of sugar and cotton, cocoa growing on individual farms, and the collection of palm oil and ivory from the bush. They also determined the vital question of white settlement. African tribes differed in their form of organization and manner of traditional life, and hence in the basis for their adaptation. Large Muslim populations in some areas had their distinctive outlook, organization and behaviour.

Quite different colonial policies resulted in distinct patterns of development in the areas ruled by each of the European powers.

Britain's policy of 'indirect rule' left much of the structure of African society intact and made local chiefs into agents of British administration. British law prevailed mainly in matters relating to trade. Missionaries provided education and health services, with government subsidies supplemented later by direct government services. A sharp division in status, occupation, area of residence and privileges distinguished the European from the African, but the growing number of educated Africans were conceded a considerable measure of responsibility and opportunity.

British policy was not uniform, however, as between the regions of West Africa and Uganda where climate and terrain offered few attractions to white settlers and the temperate regions of the Kenya highlands and Rhodesia where white settlement was encouraged and became extensive. Where the population was almost wholly African, Britain applied its generally stated colonial policy of preparing colonial peoples for self-government when they were 'ready', though up to the second world war the 'readiness' of African peoples was assumed to lie in the distant future and even in 1950 African leaders working for independence were being arrested and jailed. After the second world war the timetable was revised sharply, programmes of education, welfare and economic development were pushed vigorously, Africanization of the civil service was accelerated and the colonial administration made every effort to assist these regions to become independent African states.

In the areas where there were white settlers, however, Britain supported the settlers and followed a repressive policy toward the African population. In spite of the declaration by the Colonial Office in 1923 that the interest of the African population must be given first consideration, the best lands were made available for European development while Africans were confined to 'reserves' and were restricted in movement, employment, use of public facilities, educational opportunity and political participation. When this policy met violent resistance in Kenya after the second world war in the outbreaks of Mau Mau terrorism, while South Africa moved to strengthen its policy of *apartheid* and West Africans moved toward independence, colonial policy was caught between opposing pressures. Settlers in Kenya and Rhodesia sought independence for 'their' colonies from Britain, with the clear objective of maintaining the supremacy of the small European population over the vast African majority; Africans demanded equality of political rights. British policy in these areas was to resist both settler pressure for continued dominance and African efforts to achieve majority control, to try to develop a 'multi-racial' society in which there would be some sort of balance among racial groups, and to retain colonial authority until a pattern should be established which would prevent the white settlers from trying to follow the course of South Africa.

French colonial policy initially followed a different course from that of Britain, but after the second world war it moved in a similar direction. France viewed its large African domain as an area to be made French. The education which it introduced was identical with that provided in France—African children learned about 'Charlemagne, our great ancestor'—and the 'assimilated' African became a French citizen. African communities where such citizens were sufficiently numerous sent representatives to the National

Assembly in Paris. This French policy drew no racial lines. It produced a small group of highly cultivated 'Black Frenchmen', separated by a wide cultural gulf from the mass of the population most of whom acquired no education or training in even elementary technical skills. The policy did not look toward ultimate African self-government but to the incorporation of African areas into the French Union. As late as 1944 a formal resolution of the French Colonial Conference at Brazzaville stated: 'The attainment of self-government in the colonies even in the most distant future must be excluded.'

The French constitution of 1946 inaugurated a new policy, for it pledged France to lead her dependent peoples toward 'freedom to govern themselves and to conduct their own affairs democratically'. Under this policy facilities for general education were greatly extended and the *loi cadre* of 1956 provided for universal suffrage and a measure of self-government. Two years later, African territories were given the option of withdrawing from the French Union and Guinea was the first to choose independence.

Belgium's policy with respect to the Congo focused on the development of the area's resources rather than on the political development of the area's people. This vast resource-rich region in the very heart of Africa, originally brought under European domination by a private association headed by the king of the Belgians became notorious in the early 1900s for the way in which it was being exploited. Africans were deprived of their land, forbidden to leave their villages, and forced to work under conditions of virtual slavery.

When the Belgian government assumed jurisdiction over the territory in 1908, it abandoned these practices and adopted a paternalistic policy toward the Congo people designed to treat them humanely and to make them into efficient workers. Congolese were given technical training and were employed in skilled and responsible jobs in mines, transport and communication which elsewhere were reserved for Europeans. Living conditions for Africans in areas to which European influence extended were generally superior to those in neighbouring colonies, although racial segregation was clearly maintained. Health services were extended throughout the territory and community centres offered training to women in nutrition, home economics, nursing and child care. The people enjoyed no political rights, however, for the area was governed directly from Brussels by a centralized administration.

In the years after the second world war Belgian policy also changed. In the words of the governor-general addressing the government council of Belgian Congo in 1955: 'We have decided in future to substitute a regimen of trusteeship for the paternalism which we have practised up to now'. The new policy rejected in principle both segregation and assimilation and adopted the concept of a 'partnership' with reciprocal rights and duties between the whites plus the *évolués*—assimilated Africans—on the one hand and the general population on the other. Wage differentials between Africans and Europeans were reduced by introducing common standards, the structure of the Belgian commune was adapted to urban communities and rural districts in order to permit local self-government, and training in administration was offered to the sons of chiefs and others destined to wield authority in tribal areas.

The policy of partnership on Belgium's terms was, however, short-lived. Faced suddenly with violence and demands for independence in 1959, Belgium responded swiftly with the offer of almost immediate independence. In 1960 this vast area, rich in resources, which had been regarded in purely economic rather than political terms, embarked on self-government, although its people had had practically no political experience and there was virtually no European-trained leadership comparable to the *élites* in French and British areas who had been educated in the universities of the metropolitan countries.

Portugal remained committed to a policy of assimilation, coupled with a restrictive policy in respect to political rights and labour which was even more repressive than the authoritarian system in force at home. Portuguese public law distinguished between fully responsible citizens and persons of 'colonial status' who were not subject to Portuguese laws and, in the language of the tribal populations statute, were 'not deemed liable to fulfil obligations which they could not reasonably have foreseen or have been deemed willing to accept'. 'Assimilated' individuals, who declared their intention of coming fully under Portuguese civil and criminal law and who met established qualifications of language, education, occupation, age and good character, enjoyed equality of Portuguese citizenship without racial or other distinction. Catholic missions were entrusted with full responsibility, aided by state subsidies, for such education as was provided to the African populations.

Persistent reports of the systematic use of forced labour led to efforts within the United Nations to require Portugal to report to the United Nations Trusteeship Council annually, as did other colonial powers, on the administration of their dependent areas. Portugal, however, maintained that under a law enacted in 1951 these were not dependent areas but full provinces of the Portuguese state, and the Portuguese government refused to report to the Trusteeship Council or to permit representatives of the United Nations to visit the areas.

In addition to the possessions of the four major colonial powers, the former German territories—Tanganyika, Ruanda Urundi, Togoland and Cameroons—were placed under mandate to Britain, Belgium and France at the end of the first world war and became United Nations trust territories administered by the same countries at the end of the second world war. The Trusteeship Council periodically evaluated their progress toward self-government in terms of: steps taken toward the exercise of the elective franchise; elimination of racial discrimination; extension of education; protection of the African population in their claims to their lands; and measures to increase economic potentials and to expand the base of the economies.

Within the broad framework of European domination and the distinctive pattern applied to each colonial area, a group of African leaders emerged who voiced a growing sense of Africanism. Educated Africans, studying abroad in London, Paris, the United States or India, became aware of world trends and formed African student associations. When they returned home they established organizations to voice the problems of their respective territories or of all Africa. African leaders everywhere aspired to freedom from foreign domination, but at first they differed in the process of African development which they envisaged.

African aspirations were formulated in terms of modern western life and values by Kwame Nkrumah as he led Ghana to independence. Educated in the United States and Britain, calling himself a 'non-denominational Christian and a Marxian socialist', detached from his tribal roots and rejecting the traditional authority of the chiefs as 'feudalism', yet very close to the masses of his people and able to speak directly to them, Nkrumah conceived of his new country as a modern welfare state, based on the principles and structure of parliamentary democracy and the use of modern technology. The leaders of the much more populous neighbouring state of Nigeria held the same view. The nationalist movements of the two areas were in fact closely linked from the 1920s on.

Nkrumah's speech to the legislative assembly in 1953 when he offered his independence motion expressed this position. Rehearsing the history of the region from the time of the ancient empire of Ghana which fell to the Moors in the eleventh century, he asserted that 'throughout our tortuous history, we have not been docile under the heel of the conqueror'. He recalled the resistance of the Ashanti nation to the British, the 'earliest manifestation of Gold Coast nationalism' in the Fanti Confederation of 1868, the National Congress of British West Africa which came into being at the end of the first world war in response to the wartime slogan of the Allies who declared that they fought for freedom, and the succession of organizations after the second world war leading to the formation in 1949 of his Convention People's party with its programme of 'freedom *now*'. His people, he said, knew 'that freedom is not something that one people can bestow on another as a gift. They claim it as their own and none can keep it from them.'

The task of an independent African state, he said, was to create a new society which would benefit from the technology and institutions of the West but would not 'sacrifice unheedingly in pursuit of material progress' the values of its pre-technological society. 'We have to work hard to evolve new patterns, new social customs, new attitudes to life, so that while we seek the material, cultural and economic advancement of our people, while we raise their standards of life, we shall not sacrifice their fundamental happiness.'*

Opposed to the goal of a modern western-oriented state was the traditionalist reaction against European ways. Jomo Kenyatta asserted most dramatically the superior virtues of tribal culture (*Facing Mt Kenya*, 1938); the Mau Mau terrorists in Kenya in the 1950s gave this view a distorted and violent form.

* Kwame Nkrumah, *Ghana: Autobiography of Kwame Nkrumah* (London, 1957), Chapter 17.
MM*

Educated in Britain, where he studied under the great British anthropologist, Bronislaw Malinowski, Jomo Kenyatta resented the condescension of European scholars toward tribal societies, and he was moved to present his own description of the culture of his tribe, the Kikuyu of east Africa. He described family and kinship, age groups and initiation ceremonies, religion, magic, warfare and, especially, the use of the land as vital institutions, providing a rich life for his people. This life would be destroyed by undermining any of its integrally related parts. 'It is all these different aspects of life together that make up a social culture. And it is the culture which he inherits that gives a man his human dignity as well as his material prosperity.'*
He expressed only bitterness and contempt toward those who would break the integrity of this culture on the pretext of 'civilizing' the Africans and giving them 'the benefits of European progressive ideas'.

The feeling expressed by Jomo Kenyatta was shared by Africans of many sorts. Not only tribal chiefs whose position and authority were at stake, but educated Africans who had acquired western training or had embraced Christianity or had achieved a modicum of economic success in the white man's world, yearned for the 'good old days'. Out of a deep sense of chaos and frustration, their own society damaged or destroyed and no decent alternative anywhere in sight, they tried to renew the values and practices which their European contacts had taught them to reject and often to despise.

Throughout the continent, movements of Africans took a modernist or a traditionalist form, or some combination of the two. Prior to the second world war most of those who received western education were western oriented and sought African progress in terms of the development of a western-style society, while traditionalism was represented by some of the hereditary chiefs who continued everywhere to retain a very substantial measure of prestige and respect, from educated and uneducated alike.

In the years after the second world war the clear division between the western and traditional orientations was modified by the neo-traditionalism of some of the educated *élite* and the modernism of some of the tribal chiefs. In the Belgian Congo some of the western-educated elements began to seek to strengthen the authority of the traditional chiefs, to provide them with training for their expanded tasks, and to reorient cultural associations toward African lore and history instead of, or in addition to, European culture. Some of the traditional chiefs, in turn, sought westernization, especially those who had embraced Christianity. Some students and educated Africans from French West and Equatorial Africa, in contrast to their pre-second world war predecessors, turned against the French policy of assimilating Africans into French culture. They sought to revive African culture, exalting 'negritude' and affirming the existence of common Pan-African elements; they wished to reinterpret the history of Africa from the perspective of the African

* Kenyatta, *Facing Mt Kenya*, *op. cit.*, p. 317.

people and to use the knowledge and insight which their western training and exposure was giving them to develop an African ideal. Some envisaged a process of cultural blending, such as that presented by an African dance troupe which toured Europe and the United States in the 1950s with a programme that combined traditional dances and songs, current popular music and dramatizations of such events as the introduction of a mulatto wife to the rites of the tribe.

The development of African trade unions gave the nationalist movements a new mass base. In the British and French areas where union organization was permitted, though often harassed, Africans and whites formed separate unions, and the African unions became strongly nationalistic. They formed substantial components of people's political parties, as in Ghana, and their leaders in West Africa, Kenya and the Rhodesian copperbelt became important political figures. It was the secretary of the Kenya Federation of Labour, Tom Mboya, one of the first group of Africans elected to the Kenya Legislative Council, who acted as chairman of the first conference of Africans from non-self-governing areas, held in Accra in 1958.

As African states moved toward independence, the positive goal of 'development' came to supplement the attacks against colonialism and racialism which had furnished the main emotional drive.

After Ghana's independence in 1957, the nationalist movement throughout the continent gathered great momentum. Everywhere the tempo of change was accelerated, moderate proposals were replaced by more drastic ones before they could receive full consideration or be carried out, and any alternative to independence became unacceptable. The *loi cadre* had been expected to satisfy French African demands for at least ten years, but in a short two years the march out of the French Community had begun. Timetables reckoned in months were set for the independence of one area after another—Nigeria, Uganda, the trust territories of Togoland, Somaliland, Cameroons. In the trust territory of Tanganyika, where the administering authority in 1955 had opposed the idea of even a twenty to twenty-five year target date for self-government, a commission appointed in 1959 to propose limited constitutional steps went beyond its instructions and proposed full-scale elections and responsible government in a matter of months, stating that it knew that if it stayed within the terms of reference which it had been given at the time of its appointment its report would be obsolete before it could be read.

For the areas which contained white settlement, intensified nationalism meant mounting tension and rejection by Africans of efforts to develop a so-called 'multi-racial' society. Proposals for restricted suffrage based on educational qualifications, which would severely limit the number of Africans eligible to vote while allowing the franchise to whites, were regarded by African leaders as a mere device for perpetuating white rule. So were separate voting lists for white, Asian and African voters and representation according to racial groups which gave an equal or smaller number of representatives to

Africans than to the tiny European minority and to the somewhat larger group of Asians. Racial 'parity' which took the form of an equal division of educational funds in Tanganyika between the three racial groups—25,000 Europeans, 70,000 Asians and 8,000,000 Africans—convinced African leaders that the intent of 'multi-racialism' was to maintain Africans in permanent subjection. They insisted that there was only one basis on which a genuine 'multi-racial' society could exist and a workable system for participation of non-Africans be developed: acceptance of the principles of democracy—one man, one vote—and recognition of the basic fact that these were African countries.

Within a short time nationalism invaded the areas where the possibility of future independence had not been contemplated by the colonial powers. The outbreak of nationalist violence in the Belgian Congo in 1959 came as a shock to those who had assumed that the Belgian system was proof against such anticolonial developments; a year later the issue was whether the nationalists would wait four months for elections or would insist on independence on the spot. Disturbances in neighbouring Angola indicated that the fire of nationalism was spreading even to Portugal's 'tribal provinces' where access to and from the outside world was severely restricted.

In the Union of South Africa, Africans who in spite of repression and discrimination had participated most extensively in urban industrial and modern agricultural life and were the most Europeanized of African populations, aspired to equality of status within the mixed society of which they were a part. But the success of nationalist movements elsewhere in the continent and the hardening of *apartheid* policies at home brought mounting tension and the threat of open conflict.

African nationalist movements took on a Pan-African tone. One of the objectives stated in the constitution of Nkrumah's Convention People's party at its inception, was 'to support the demand for a West African Federation and of Pan-Africanism by promoting unity of action among the peoples of Africa and of African descent'. Nkrumah himself lost no opportunity to press toward his vision of united African peoples; he acted as host to the first meeting of independent African states and to the first conference of representatives of the non-self-governing African territories in 1958. Immediately after Guinea became independent, the prime ministers of Guinea and Ghana announced a projected linking of their two countries to form a nucleus which other African states would be invited to join as they became independent.

African peoples, however, faced many problems and difficulties in realizing their aspirations. As the leader of the Tanganyika nationalist movement, Julius K. Nyerere expressed it in 1957: 'We do not seek freedom so that our people may remain in poverty and ignorance or revert to primitive savagery.'* But African economic life was almost wholly dependent on European capital and management. With a few exceptions, such as coffee growing in Tangan-

* Letter to M. Springer, n.d.

yika and cocoa in Ghana and the Ivory Coast, commercial agriculture was European-operated, as were mining, industry and trade.

Without capital, managerial experience and technical knowledge, neither African individuals nor African governments were in a position to exploit the continent's resources for the benefit of the African people. Economic colonialism threatened to remain after political colonialism was gone. Moreover, against the background of the traditional authority and wealth of the chief and with the example of European enterprises using low-paid African labour, there was a real temptation for those Africans who might gain some wealth and power to entrench themselves personally at the expense of the masses of the people.

Tribal rivalries complicated the development of self-governing, viable states, for ancient antagonisms did not disappear overnight and tribal boundaries rarely coincided with political divisions created by European powers and inherited by African nationalists. The difficulties of applying democratic principles were immense, especially on the part of those who had little experience in their operation. Nkrumah, who had shown himself a master of democratic principles and parliamentary processes during his struggle for independence, soon resorted to repressive measures to restrain opposition which he believed was endangering his new state.

The basic problem faced by all new states, the limited number of technically qualified and educated people on whom the burden of development rested, was nowhere so acute as in Africa, though the lack was much greater in some areas than in others. The situation was sharply illustrated in the French territories after the introduction of the *loi cadre* which provided for the partial self-government of the territories by local African ministries and a 50 per cent Africanization of the civil services. In one after another of the territories, the same man served as a member of the French National Assembly in Paris and as the chief minister in the colony or the mayor of the principal city, while scarcely a beginning could be made in the programme of Africanization of the civil services for lack of available personnel.

The rich resources of the continent were potential sources both of salvation and of danger. They provided a basis for productive economies capable of sustaining the African people, but in a resource-hungry world they were coveted by foreign governments and enterprises for their own purposes. Pressures were great to exploit the deposits of copper, uranium, bauxite, iron ore and other materials at a pace and in a manner dictated by outside forces and interests rather than by the tempo at which African society could make use of these sources of wealth. Vast, thinly populated parts of the continent, moreover, offered possibility for settlement, not only in the areas which enjoyed a healthy climate, such as Angola, but in regions which would become habitable as the tsetse fly and other disease carriers were brought under control.

Africans could not hope to be allowed to work out their destiny without interference, as the people of the Americas had been able to do in the years after their independence. They were caught at the moment of their emergence as independent peoples in the midst of a world in conflict, where distance no longer isolated or protected and where so rich a prize as a vast continent could not remain outside the world struggle for power. Though Africa could no longer be simply carved up without regard for the people, as it had been in the nineteenth century, it was the target of the many pressures which powerful states and groups had the resources and skill to apply. Africans might repeat their slogans of 'Hands off Africa', 'Free Africa We Keep', but these were scant protection against determined efforts to draw them into the orbit of one or another of the world's power groupings.

In this struggle the main protagonists were the communist and non-communist worlds. But a pull came also from Islam. A belt of Muslim people stretched from east to west along the border of the Sahara and down the Niger valley, making up more than half the population of the French territories and most of the people of northern Nigeria; substantial numbers of Muslims were also to be found in the east, not only in the Sudan but down the coast, and in most areas Islam was tending to spread. Addressing these populations, the Cairo radio sought to link African nationalism to Islam and to the nationalism of the Arabs, and to induce Africans south of the Sahara to make common cause with the Muslim peoples of North Africa. The Islamic revival of these years and the increased facility for Africans to join the pilgrimages to Mecca made Islam a factor of growing importance in determining the direction of African development.

Under the impact of the long struggle between French and Muslims in Algeria and the use of the Sahara for atomic tests, Muslim states of North Africa traditionally oriented toward the north and east made common cause with African states across the Sahara to the south. From one end of the great continent to the other, leaders began to talk of an African identity, an African personality, the future of Africa—not just of the individual states—and the place of Africa in the world.

At best the African's task of cultural integration between a non-literate, tribal culture and a modern technological one was as difficult a transition as any people had had to make. Under the most favourable circumstances it would place severe strains on the social structure and heavy demands on the creativity, stability and adaptability of the people. Africans brought to this task attitudes and experience built up in the face of colonial rule, racial dominance, and economic exploitation. Moreover, in the cultural atmosphere of the mid-twentieth century, they were exposed to no single accepted version of technological culture but to fundamental conflicts and many uncertainties among its representatives.

The African people, seeking to enter the modern world, faced heavy odds indeed in their struggle for self-realization and development.

NOTES TO CHAPTER XXVIII

1. Professor Radim Foustka (Czechoslovakia) considers that the survey of 'the self-image and aspirations of nations' given in this chapter shows the radical difference which exists between the authors' viewpoint and that of Marxist critics: The very term 'self-image' cannot but evoke an attitude of scepticism. . . . This concept, it would seem, reduces itself to the general idea that nations as a whole formulate their 'aspirations' and 'aims' and carry them into effect both at the political level (through their state and within it) and at the cultural level. This is a completely unscientific assertion and the authors themselves have been compelled to admit that 'in formulating national aims' there is always 'in some degree a reciprocal interaction between the people and the state even where a small element imposed its will on the majority and sustained it by dictatorial means'. How is it possible to discern any self-image of a nation in such a case? . . .

The evolution of mankind in the twentieth century is seen solely from the angle of the ruling class of the bourgeoisie or its leaders . . . There is not the slightest allusion to the great struggle of the working class for democracy and no mention of the fact that on this issue the opinions of the workers were significantly different from those of the bourgeoisie. Of questions as important as this the authors make short work, mentioning only that the national self-image has been 'that of the dominant element which provided articulate leadership', and noting that there were other views 'shared by non-dominant elements'. Thus the artificial concept of 'national self-realization' was designed only to bolster up the ideology of the ruling bourgeoisie and to give a false notion of the general body of national aims and aspirations. . . . The concept is so artificial and unreal that quite naturally the term 'self-image' breaks down. . . . The authors would be in a position to eliminate the contradiction and offer a scientific solution to the problem only if they were to accept as a premise the class system of states and the class system of politics and culture as formulated and realized by the ruling class. Naturally it is impossible to ask for, or expect, from them such an approach to the question, and it is therefore evident that the resultant divergency of views cannot be resolved whatever comments are made on the text submitted by the authors.

The same viewpoint is upheld by A. E. Bovin who considers that people's ideals can find a real expression in life only when there is an effective socialist force behind them. In a class society this force is represented by classes, in other words by major groups of people having one and the same relationship to the means of production. The ideal embodied in the form and substance of a government is always a class ideal, the realization of the interests and requirements of the economically preponderant class.

A. E. Bovin also takes the view that the authors have passed over facts which give a pointer to the basic aspirations of the nations of the world in the twentieth century:

(1) More than a thousand million people in twenty-three countries have put an end to the exploitation of man by man and are building a classless society. These same aims inspire the workers' and communist movement which exists in all countries of capitalist civilization.

(2) Millions of people have definitely finished with colonialism. In the period since the second World War alone some forty independent states have come into existence in Asia and Africa.

(3) The movement of the partisans of peace has become a most important element on the contemporary stage and an active political force in all continents of the globe.

2. *The Author-Editors call the reader's attention to the exact language of the text, including the following statements: '. . . no single attitude permeated all sections, classes, occupations, ethnic elements and personal outlooks even in the most centrally administered or totalitarian states. . . . In each case, the national self-image which has been noted has been that of the dominant element which provided articulate leadership. . . . It must be remembered, however, that . . . the divisions and conflicts of view within nations were no less significant than the differences among nation-states . . . workers whose labour had been treated as a commodity sought bargaining power and status as human beings. . . .'*

3. In the opinion of Professor E. N. Anderson, the Author-Editors may be criticized for identifying the self-image with the national state. They are transferring to the rest of the

world an ideal which is essentially western in origin and general acceptance. Even in Europe, however, there exist minorities which lack all prospect of achieving independence in a national state and yet which have an image of themselves as national groups. The term nation is as yet scarcely applicable to the peoples of Asia and Africa, where national bonds have not subsumed or supplanted caste, religious, tribal or other loyalties. On these continents political unity does not imply cultural unity, and the major problem facing the new states of the world lies in the need to develop a common culture that will assure the continued independent existence of the political state, or that will at least make it possible for a people to decide what the political form and scope of their life should be. Upon the basis of present evidence one cannot assume that the peoples of these continents will follow the example of Europe and everywhere introduce the nation-state as standard. There are alternatives, for example, in federal structures like those of Switzerland and the United States, as Professor Lynn M. Case has remarked in a comment on the text of the Author-Editors, and there are many kinds of agreement among independent political units under the United Nations which offer prospects of a greater variety of self-images than the West has developed up to now.

4. Professor Radim Foustka notes that the authors ignore the fact that liberal democracy took shape in the progressive capitalist countries in the nineteenth century, i.e. in the period of pre-monopoly capitalism. Since then it has undergone, and is continuing to undergo, substantial changes in the direction of a limitation of the classical liberal (bourgeois) democracy. Typical examples of such changes are to be found in the USA legislation (the Taft-Hartley Act, the McCarran-Smith law, etc.) The authors regard faith in the reasonable basis of human nature as being an element only of the liberal democratic view of life ('to function more fully, more rationally and more humanely'). This is tantamount to tacitly denying that the ideology and practical activity of the socialist states is also based on this principle.

See also Note 4 of Chapter XXIII.

5. *The Author-Editors' position has been explicitly stated in Chapter III, p. 64: 'They [the communists], too, viewed man as a rational being whose judgment, in the long run, could theoretically be trusted, and they regarded the state as the product of rational action, not as a mystical entity.'*

6. Candidate of Juridical Sciences F. M. Bourlazky notes that the assertion by the authors that communists when they come to power reject democratic rights and liberties is contrary to the facts. Socialist democracy not only does not reject, but on the contrary gets the best out of, the principles and forms which were elaborated by earlier types of democracy. Social justice and freedom, equality of citizens before the law, freedom of conscience, universal suffrage, the system of representation—all these ideals acquire a special value with socialism and are weighted with a real content. Thus the old principle of democracy—government not only for the people but by the people—gains a new significance in the context of the socialist system. The state makes it its aim to ensure that in the final analysis every individual should be able to take part in the administration of public affairs; and not only by participating in the election of deputies, giving them instructions and listening to their reports, but also directly in day-to-day life.

One aspect of this is the new role assigned to voluntary organizations (of trade unions, young people and so on) and the gradual transfer to them of state functions.

This role of the public organizations is all the more significant in that they have increased enormously in size so that to all intents and purposes they cover the whole population.

The direct participation of the workers in the solution of state problems is achieved, among others, by such original methods as the preliminary discussion of laws and of plans for the national economy. Forty to fifty million people, more than half the adult population of the country, have been involved, for example, in the USSR in such consultations on economic planning. For more details on this point see F. M. Burlatzky 'Rastsvet sotsialisticheskoy demokratii' ('The Development of Socialist Democracy') in *Vestnik istorii mirovoi kultury*, 1961, No. 5.

7. Professors E. Gathier and G. Masson object to the minor role attributed to Christianity in the discussion of the self-image of western Europe. They state that the Author-Editors'

discussion of liberal democracy ignores the fact that the idea that 'man is rational, responsible and capable of exercising control over his own affairs' is also 'an essential part of the Christian message, Catholic as well, and very often asserted by the Popes, defended by the "social Catholics", chiefly in our century'. In general these scholars believe 'that the image of the Christian faith and of the Catholic Church which emerges does not conform to reality and would hurt Christian sensibilities'. They believe that the self-image of Western Europe should not be identified with liberal democracy but with the older Christian tradition still carried by the Catholic Church.

The comments of Gathier and Masson may be elucidated by citing, for example, the encyclical *Atheistic Communism* of Pope Pius XI (1937). It reads, in part:

16. If we would explain the blind acceptance of Communism by so many thousands of workmen, we must remember that the way had been already prepared for it by the religious and moral destitution in which wage-earners had been left by liberal economics.
29. . . . Society is for man and not vice versa. This must not be understood in the sense of liberalistic individualism, which subordinates society to the selfish use of the individual; but only in the sense that by means of an organic union with society and by mutual collaboration the attainment of earthly happiness is placed within the reach of all. In a further sense, it is society which affords the opportunities for the development of all the individual and social gifts bestowed on human nature. These natural gifts have a value surpassing the immediate interests of the moment, for in society they reflect the divine perfection, which would not be true were man to live alone. But on final analysis, even in this latter function society is made for man, that he may recognize this reflection of God's perfection, and refer it in praise and adoration to the Creator. Only man, the human person, and not society in any form is endowed with reason and a morally free will.

The following titles may be suggested for the liberal point of view:

John Dewey, *Liberalism and Social Action* (New York, 1935).
R. M. McIver, *Democracy and the Economic Challenge* (New York, 1952).
J. Roland Pennock, *Liberal Democracy: Its Merits and Prospects* (New York, 1950).
Karl G. Popper, *The Open Society and Its Enemies* (Princeton, 1950).
Massimo Salvadori, *Liberal Democracy* (New York, 1957).

8. Professor Radim Foustka notes that the section 'Marxist–Leninist Communism' gives a quite distorted idea of Lenin's development of Marx' teaching and of the reasons responsible for this. The authors consider that Lenin advanced the view of the possibility of revolution in industrially backward areas 'in the light of conditions at the opening of the twentieth century when the major capitalist countries were enjoying both rising productivity and profits from colonial areas, and workers in those countries were organizing to share to some extent the returns from these sources rather than to overthrow their regimes'. This assertion is absolutely divorced from reality. At the end of the nineteenth century the onset of the age of imperialism, characterized by an extremely uneven development of capitalism, made it apparent that under those conditions the socialist revolution could not be victorious simultaneously in all capitalist countries. Concretizing the general concept of Marx and adapting it to changed historical conditions Lenin, the leader of the Russian Marxists, came to the conclusion that the socialist revolution could and must triumph in one country, taken separately. Imperialism with its highly uneven development and its exploitation of less developed countries by more developed countries, of colonies by their possessors, brought with it a form of mutual dependence between the countries belonging to the world system of imperialism in which some capitalist countries succeeded in reducing their contradictions at the expense of others and temporarily reinforced their positions in the world. Lenin therefore drew the inference that in this new period the contradictions of capitalism might be aggravated precisely in the backward capitalist countries at whose expense the more developed ones temporarily alleviated (or, more correctly, 'repressed') their own economic and political conflicts. This means that there is every likelihood in the assumption that a revolution can and must begin in an economically more backward capitalist country on which its more fortunate competitors shifted part of the load of their contradictions and where, accordingly, capitalism was less solidly entrenched. These ideas found their most systematic development in Lenin's theory of imperialism and in his theory of proletarian revolutions in the age of imperialism which were fully confirmed by the triumph of the October revolution in Russia in 1917.

K. Marx and F. Engels, in equipping the proletariat with a most logical and coherent scientific philosophy, showed that the only way to arrive at a solution of the historic problem of the proletariat—the creation of a communist society—lay in the establishment of a dictatorship of the proletariat. Their teaching on the dictatorship of the proletariat was further developed by Lenin. After studying the experience of the struggle of the revolutionary class in Russia he reached the conclusion that the best form of dictatorship of the proletariat is not a parliamentary democratic republic but a republic of Soviets. He discovered Soviet power as the state form of the dictatorship of the proletariat and defined the dictatorship of the proletariat as a special form of the class alliance of the proletariat with the exploited masses of the non-proletarian classes, under the direction of the working class, and particularly emphasized the fact that the dictatorship of the proletariat and its highest principle was the alliance of the working class with the peasantry. His treatment of the peasant question, which is in effect the question of the allies of the working class in its struggle for power and for the construction of a socialist society, had already begun on the eve of the Revolution of 1905–7. The opportunist leaders of the Second International and the other enemies of revolutionary Marxism were indifferent in their attitude to this issue and claimed that the peasantry could not be an ally in the struggle of the working class for power. In combating the enemies of Bolshevism Lenin revealed the revolutionary potentialities of the peasantry and the possibility, and the need, for an alliance of the working class with the peasantry in its struggle for power and for the victory of socialism. Thus since it is a part of the general question of the dictatorship of the proletariat the peasant question represents one of the vitally important issues of Leninism.

Lenin's presentation of the national question differs radically from the way in which the problem was posed by the parties of the Second International who viewed it out of its context and divorced from the major issue of power and the proletarian revolution. He considered it to be a part of the general question of the proletarian revolution and of the dictatorship of the proletariat. Leninism first connected the national question with the question of colonies thus transforming it from a special intra-state problem into a general international problem, a world problem involving the liberation of the oppressed peoples of dependent countries and colonies from the power of imperialism.

9. The Soviet scientists think that the fascist regime is not the ideology of petty bourgeoisie, but that it is a reactionary and overtly terrorist dictatorship of the imperialist upper bourgeoisie. Its aim is to stifle completely and utterly the resistance of the working class and all progressive forces within the country.

10. Candidate of Juridical Sciences U. P. Ouryas objects to the authors' comparison of the Federal Republic of Germany and the German Democratic Republic in terms of struggle against Nazi ideology. In the German Democratic Republic the former Nazi may live and work only if he fully rejects the Nazi ideology: there are no social strata or groups which are interested in Nazi ideology. The situation is quite different in the Federal Republic of Germany where the Nazi and revanchist sentiments are rather strong—as has been acknowledged even by some official representatives of the government.

11. Candidate of Economic Sciences I. P. Yastrebova notes that in the section devoted to the Republic of South Africa the part played in the national life by the Africans who make up 67 per cent of the population is ignored. It is by their toil that all the wealth of the country has been created. A British publicist who has long been studying the country's problems takes the view that 'without Bantu labour the farms and factories of South Africa would become a desolation within five minutes'. (B. Davidson, *Report on Southern Africa*, London and Cape Town, 1952.)

The authors say nothing about the liberation struggle of the non-Europeans, particularly the African peoples. (See in this connection A. Luthuli, *Freedom in the Apex*, Johannesburg, 1959; W. Alphaeus Hunton, *Decision in Africa*, New York, 1957; and other works.)

The remark made by the authors at the beginning of the section advising reference to 'Emerging Nationalism: Africa' does not invalidate the criticism we have just made, more particularly since there is no mention of the liberation struggle of the Africans in the Republic of South Africa.

12. I. P. Yastrebova underlines that the policy of *apartheid* is not something entirely new or distinct in its nature from the policy practised towards the aboriginal population of the country both in the former English colonies of South Africa (Cape Colony and Natal) and in the former Boer republics (Transvaal and Orange Free State) which in 1910 were incorporated as provinces into the South African Union. Nor does it differ greatly from the policy pursued irrespective of party allegiance by the governments of the Union throughout its existence. All the bourgeois parties of the Union (later Republic) of South Africa, whatever their programmes, form a united front in the matter of their policy towards the non-European population. Here for example is what W. K. Hancock noted: 'Although native policy is the fundamental political question in the Union (or perhaps because it is so) it has not determined the party divisions in parliament and the constituencies. The leaders of all parties, including the Labour party, professed their allegiance to the principles of racial segregation.' (W. K. Hancock, *Survey of British Commonwealth Affairs*, London, 1942, Vol. II, Part II, pp. 12–13.)

13. I. P. Yastrebova calls special attention to the fact that at the moment when the Europeans arrived in South Africa the country was not an empty, uninhabited space. Even the first Portuguese travellers and later the Dutch found here a considerable African population. The earliest inhabitants of this area were Bushmen and Hottentots and later the Bantu tribes. The forward movement northward of the Boers and the English was accompanied by savage fighting with the African peoples not for 'empty land' but for the land held by the Africans. The 'native reserves' were not the result of a process of natural settlement of African tribes. They were transformed into special reservoirs of cheap manpower from which the Europeans drew the workers they needed and to which they sent them back when their labour was no longer required; thus the whole life of the Africans was subjected to innumerable restrictions and regulations.

14. I. P. Yastrebova underlines that the process of detribalization is not a consequence of the well-meaning educational activity of certain groups of Europeans but the objective result of the social and economic changes that have taken place in African society (growth of the urban population, process of differentiation in the African village, etc.). See also L. D. Yablochkov, 'On detribalization and urbanization in Africa South of the Sahara' in *Vestnik istorii mirovei kultury*, No. 3 (21), 1960.

15. I. P. Yastrebova considers it a great mistake to describe *apartheid* as a 'means by which the Afrikaners set themselves apart, defined themselves as a people and sought to guard their identity and their survival'. The South African nationalists in the Republic express the interests of the classes *who hold in their hands the levers of command in the economic and political life of the country*. In the first place apartheid is directed against the native African, i.e. against that part of the population which is exploited and deprived of its rights.

16. Professor Zurayk observes that 'Nowhere in this section ['States of Religious Origin or Outlook'] is it observed how this establishment of states on a religious basis runs contrary to modern ideas and tendencies. Although this chapter purports to describe the 'self-image and aspirations' of peoples—without consideration to their soundness or validity—is it right in a book whose subject is the twentieth century not to express a judgment on a phenomenon which is so much out of line with the basic tendencies of this century?'

17. Candidate of Historical Sciences V. B. Louzky in his works shows that the aspiration of the Jews for establishment of their national state was used by the Great Powers in their own interests. Thus, Great Britain from the moment of the proclamation of the Balfour Declaration (November 2, 1917) supported the Zionist movement to weaken the Arab national movement in Palestine which was turned into a British mandate in 1918.

18. Candidate of Historical Sciences L. R. Gordon-Polonskaya notes that in the first half of the nineteenth century the Muslims in fact suffered rather more from individual measures by the British authorities in India than the Hindus. However, after the insurrection of 1857–59, during which Hindus and Muslims waged a common struggle for the liberation of India, the British colonial authorities, particularly in the seventies of the nineteenth century, began to turn their main attention to setting the so-called Muslim revival against

the Hindu revival and strengthening the Muslim community in an endeavour to direct its activity towards resisting the Hindu domination with which it was allegedly threatened.

In this connection special significance attaches to the publication in 1871 of a book by Sir William Hunter, who was both a senior official of the British colonial service and an historian (W. W. Hunter, *Our Indian Musulmans*, London 1871), in which he analysed the course of British and Muslim interactions in India and came to the conclusion that it was necessary to build up support for British colonial power within the leadership of the Muslim community. The same ideas were expressed by another leading official of colonial India, W. S. Blunt (*Ideas about India*, London, 1885). In 1885 the colonial authorities took a decision to extend the participation of Muslims in the colonial administration. In the eighties the British instigated a series of clashes between Hindus and Muslims all over the country which culminated in 1893 in large scale Hindu-Muslim pogroms in which many lives were lost. From that time onward the fomenting of disputes between Hindus and Muslims became a regular element in the arsenal of the British policy of *divide et impera*.

19. Candidate of Economic Sciences I. P. Yasterbova underlines that the principal reason for the political changes in Africa after the second World War is the development of the mass campaign of the African peoples in favour of independence. It was this struggle, and not the general attitude of the colonialists, that induced the colonial powers to make concessions to the liberation movements.

Between 1945 and 1959 a series of local events reflected throughout Africa the agitation in favour of independence: there were strikes, demonstrations and protest movements in the Belgian Congo, Nigeria, Madagascar, the Gold Coast, Uganda, South Africa, Nyasaland, Northern Rhodesia, etc. repressed by the authorities. In Southern Rhodesia there was a strike by African workers employed in the building of the Kariba Dam. See also Kwame Nkrumah, *Autobiography* (Edinburgh, 1957), Sekou Touré, *L'action politique du Parti democratique de Guinée pour l'émancipation africaine* (Conakry, 1959, several volumes); Sekou Touré, *L'action politique du PEG-RDA pour l'émancipation et l'unité africaine dans l'independence* (Canakry, 1959); and other works.

CHAPTER XXIX

DRIVES FOR CULTURAL INTEGRITY AND RECOGNITION

T HE self-image and aspirations of peoples were couched not only in political forms but also in terms of more or less articulate goals of cultural development.[1]

I. RENAISSANCE OF ANCIENT CULTURES

During the twentieth century the peoples of Asia and the Middle East reasserted the traditions of their ancient cultures and related them, in one way or another, to the cultural currents of the modern day. The process ranged from traditionalism to revolution; it involved both the revival of orthodoxy and the reform of religion; it brought a sense of history and a renaissance in the arts. In whatever form, there was a reawakening and a new vitality of cultural expression among all these peoples.[2]

1. *India*

The self-image of India as she struggled to nationhood and independence evolved during a century of interaction with the West. It was compounded of the rediscovery of a great national past, a newly forged sense of unity, a renewed religious spirit, the incorporation of western liberal ideas and institutions and a commitment to social reform. Alone among the peoples subjected to western colonialism, Indians were exposed to western liberal thought in sufficient numbers and over a sufficient period of time for them to make it their own, apply it to their own traditions and integrate it with the other elements in their view of life. In addition the long, active struggle for independence under the leadership of Mahatma Gandhi consolidated both goals and methods and gave a unique character to the Indian experience.

The absence of an Indian historical tradition had long prevented the emergence of a self-image glorifying the past political achievements of the Indian people. But the revival of Sanskrit studies in Europe in the nineteenth century and the recognition of Indian cultural achievement had helped to create the image of a golden age during which the Hindu mind had achieved a superiority over the rest of the world. 'Hindu superiority' was the theme of many writers who emphasized the spiritual qualities of Indian life and extolled her philosophers and her classical literatures and art. But the current weakness of Indian life and India's political subjection emphasized the unreality of this view.[3]

The result was a great movement for national independence, Hindu reformation, social reform and revival of cultural life which sought to make the facts of Indian life more nearly coincide with the image of its greatness. By the second quarter of the twentieth century the uncertainty and ambivalence had gone and independent India saw itself clearly as a modern state resting on a rich and vital tradition from the past.

The rediscovery and reassertion of Indian culture and its dynamic integration with ideas derived from the West was the fruit of the interaction during the nineteenth century of European scholarship, British administration and the work of Indian scholars, religious figures and practical leaders.

When British authority was established in Bengal at the beginning of the nineteenth century, Hindu society was freed from the Muslim authority which had dominated it for five hundred years, but it found itself confronted by a basic challenge from English civilization and culture. The first effect was astonishment in the face of a new world of ideas, forms of art and literature, new ways of thinking and great political and social doctrines. The youth of Bengal, overwhelmed by European civilization and appealed to by missionary tracts which derided the Hindu religion, were led to question the very foundations of their social and religious life.

A positive response to this situation came in successive movements for the reform of Hinduism.* These followed several courses: some elements of the Christian religion and of the thought and attitude of the West were Indianized by the Bramo Samaj; Ramakrishna reaffirmed the essential spiritual nature of Hinduism; the Arya Samaj, while insisting on the purity of primitive Hinduism, accepted the weapons and methods of its adversaries— sacred text, church organization, individual conversion; the English language gave unity to the revival. By the end of the nineteenth century the feeling of inferiority which Hindus had suffered at the opening of the century had entirely disappeared. In the following period, Hinduism not only developed with revived faith, but with a sense that all the problems posed by society could be resolved within its framework; a Hindu outlook inspired the national upthrust which India experienced in the twentieth century.

Among Indian Muslims, a similar movement centring around the Aligarh Muslim University brought revitalization and a modern outlook. Although in time the dominant Muslim view became separatist and led ultimately to partition and the creation of Pakistan, it played a part during most of the period in the modernization of the Indian view and contributed directly to the nationalist movement.

In the course of the nineteenth century the Indian people came to recognize that they possessed a common tradition, a common history and a common conception of life. The unity of the Indian people had long been apparent, as was reflected in the common terms used by Chinese, Persians

* See Chapter XXV, Religion, pp. 885-90.

and other neighbours for all Indians, regardless of the political divisions from which they came; but the idea of the unity of India as a nation did not exist. All historical works before 1800 were in the form of local chronicles or were written from a dynastic point of view by Muslim chroniclers for whom the history of India began with the Muslim invasions.

A series of discoveries created a sense of Indian history, beginning with the identification by European scholars at the end of the eighteenth century of the Sandro Cottus of the Greek historians with Chandra Gupta Maurya who founded the first Indian empire after the invasion of the north-west Punjab by Alexander the Great. This furnished a central point for dating other events. The next step was the deciphering in 1837 of the Asoka inscriptions which revealed a great monarch who reigned over the greater part of India for many years and whose proclamations reflected a great civilization and an efficient administration and form of government much in advance of that which existed in most countries.

The discovery of the reign of such a king, who sent missions to other identifiable kings, made it clear that there really was an Indian history; the subsequent publication of many documents and inscriptions provided a basis for viewing in detail the life of India through the ages. One of the results of these discoveries was to bring Buddhism back into the Indian tradition from which by the nineteenth century it had practically disappeared, as had the memory of personages such as Asoka. The effect of all these studies was to give to all Indians a sense of the continuity of their history, of an uninterrupted tradition and of the 'Indianness' of their life.

Moreover, the discovery that India had transformed the life of neighbouring countries came almost as a revelation. Documents which threw light on 'greater India'—Funan, Champa, Siam, Indonesia, central Asia—showed that Indians from all the great regions of the country had played a significant role in the expansion of civilization and the creation of national cultures. Archaeological discoveries in Afghanistan and central Asia brought to light a great and dynamic civilization, where Sanskrit was used not only for scientific and cultural purposes but in a simplified form for personal correspondence. The awareness that Indian influence had extended to many countries and that India represented, so to speak, a mother civilization gave to Indians great pride and a sense of their importance in the world.

European scholarship also contributed to the sense of Indian nationality through the study of Sanskrit. Sanskrit studies had always been carried on in India, but they had been limited to a small class, and even in this class certain books were regarded as secret and were accessible only to certain castes. It was the translation into European languages of the Vedas, the *Upanishads*, the *Bhagavad Gita* and the other fundamental texts of Hindu thought, and studies of them published in western universities, which permitted the new Indian middle classes, drawn from all the castes, to study the sacred texts. This extension of cultural traditions which had formerly been reserved to small groups permitted the Indian people to have the common feeling of being inheritors of Indian culture.

The same evolution took place with respect to Indian art. Up to the end of the nineteenth century the attitude of educated Indians was dominated by what they had learned of European art. It remained for Europeans to discover the caves of Ajanta and other treasures in the jungles and, with the Anglo-Tamil scholar Ananda Coomaraswamy, to bring a new appreciation of Indian art in the early twentieth century.

When Indians became interested in their own artistic tradition, they discovered that there was a unity of Indian art throughout the country and that this had spread to other countries. In the caves of the thousand Buddhas at Tan Huang in the heart of the Gobi desert, paintings were discovered which were clearly influenced by Indian thought and styles, as was true in central Asia, Indonesia, Cambodia and Siam. The striking unity of Indian art was not limited to a particular period; in all epochs the fundamental ideas remained the same, showing again that the Indian spirit possessed undeniable unity.

Thus through more than a century in this India which had formerly been divided into many kingdoms but which had only a single civilization, the sentiment grew that all Indians belonged to a single family, that they represented a single tradition, that they had the same artistic and literary heritage and that, in spite of past conflicts, they constituted a single nation.

The incorporation of western liberal thought into the Indian self-image was profoundly affected by the system of education introduced in 1835 by Thomas Babington Macaulay. Before that date India had had its own system of education which had produced scholars and thinkers in all periods. At first the East India Company thought of subsidizing the existing Indian establishments and of setting up others on the same plan, but this was opposed by the most progressive of the Indians of the period, such as Ram Mohan Roy.[4]

Macaulay, who came to India as minister of justice, insisted that instruction should be given in English and on subjects of European interest. He foresaw a time when Indians would have rejected their own ways of thinking and would have accepted what he regarded as the highest form of life, the culture and the civilization of nineteenth-century Britain. Although Ram Mohan Roy did not want to make Indians into Englishmen, he too desired that they should acquire a modern manner of approaching social and religious problems, cultivate a critical sense and appreciate the new ideas then reigning in Europe.

The subject matter taught in the Indian colleges was the history of England and Europe, political science and economics. Instruction in natural sciences came later. Whatever else may be said about this subject matter, one fact was of central importance: the English language was the language of freedom and independence. From Milton to the end of the nineteenth century, the great poets and the political and social thinkers all insisted upon freedom of thought and expression and the right of man to liberty. The study of these texts had consequences which the British had not foreseen, convinced as they were of the permanence of their rule.

This system was in force throughout the entire country for more than a century and it played a central role in creating the new life of the country. It brought a new dynamism into Indian thought and a new way of approaching problems of all sorts, as Indians began to call into question the validity of their own institutions in terms of the principles and doctrines which they had studied in schools and colleges. It produced in the whole of India an educated middle class which had the same outlook, spoke the same language and thought in a similar manner, and which formed the leading element in administration, politics, journalism and education.

A second major result of the new education was the expression of a new humanistic outlook in the Indian languages. While instruction at the university level was given exclusively in English, much instruction in the secondary schools was in the various Indian languages, and it therefore became necessary to write books in each of these languages which would transmit the new ideas. The Indian languages, which already possessed rich literary traditions, were transformed into effective modern languages and they came to reflect the feelings, ideas, doctrines and emotions which modern India was experiencing. Under the influence of a common education and common experience, the languages were used to express the same kinds of thought, they adopted the same forms and they created, even in their differences, a unity of Indian expression.

By the beginning of the twentieth century, a renaissance of Indian literature was in progress. New writers were appearing who were thoroughly imbued with European traditions and culture, but who turned more and more to the genius of their own languages and cultural traditions. The great figure of Rabindranath Tagore symbolized this synthesis. Up to the first world war inspiration came primarily from western Europe, but after the October revolution a strong and growing interest developed in the literature, doctrines and social ideas of the communists, and these additional influences were felt in literature and in humanistic thought. Indian humanism of the twentieth century was thus neither entirely western nor traditionally Indian, but a new product of the two.

One of the essential results of the critical spirit introduced by the new education was to separate the religious from the social. For the first time people realized that caste was not a religious institution, and that untouchability was not an integral part of Hinduism—that in fact all the great Hindus from the Buddha to Mahatma Gandhi denounced it. The separation of the merely social from the truly religious represented one of the most fundamental changes brought into India and made it possible to legislate on all sorts of social matters—marriage, inheritance, caste—since these institutions had lost their religious sanction.[5]

At the same time that Lord Macaulay introduced a system of modern education he introduced a penal code for India which embodied the basic principles of British jurisprudence, including the principles that all men are equal before the law, no one is held guilty until he has been judged so by a competent court, and procedures should be public. Indian law had never admitted the principle of equality, whether in Hindu law where different punishments were applied to different castes or Muslim law where the word of an unbeliever was not accepted as against the word of a believer; the principle of inequality had been in fact part of the structure of Indian society. Now the evolution which began with the introduction of the code of law had the effect of rooting the principle of equality in a permanent fashion in the Indian spirit. The fact that for more than a century all men had been equal before the law permitted the constitutional assembly of independent India to proscribe untouchability, and the parliament to make its practice a crime.

The Indian self-image of the twentieth century was imbued with the spirit of nationalism, which too had evolved through the nineteenth and early twentieth centuries, incorporating first political, then social and finally economic objectives.

The uprising of 1857 had been simply a protest against alien rule; the political ideas of the rebellious princes had been merely to restore the ancient régimes and re-establish the political anarchy of innumerable princedoms under a puppet emperor. By contrast the Indian National Congress established in 1885 was founded by a group of men who had been educated by western methods and who spoke the language of modern history and politics. These were members of a new class who cited the speeches of Mazzini, based their arguments on the logic of Burke and drew their inspiration from the Declaration of the Rights of Man. The national movement was not an association of the dispossessed. It was directed by lawyers, journalists, doctors, industrialists who were the fruit of the contact between East and West.

The first leaders of the Congress did not envisage a free and independent India, for they thought that continued British rule was essential for India to progress. They saw too many difficulties to think in other terms, and they contented themselves with trying to secure changes which would enable them to participate in government. But by the end of the century new ideas intervened and a new generation came to believe that a country cannot progress without independence and that the struggle for independence is one of the first duties of a people.

At the turn of the century Bal Gangadhar Tilak gave the nationalist movement a doctrine of political activism. He believed that the nation should draw its strength from its history and own traditions and not let itself be diverted by modern philosophy and foreign thought. He justified his call for direct action by his interpretation of the *Bhagavad Gita*, in the light of which revolution could be regarded as orthodox and sanctioned by religion itself.

But although Tilak began to give the national movement a mass base by identifying it with traditional religion, it did not become fully a mass movement until Mahatma Gandhi assumed the leadership.

Gandhi believed and declared that political liberty could not be separated from social emancipation.[6] He insisted that India should carry out a social revolution before attaining political independence; he maintained that the new national movement must be based on the whole people and not just an educated class; he associated himself with the activist section of the Muslims represented by the Khilafat movement and by leaders such as Maulana Abul Kalem Azad, and he made Hindu–Muslim unity one of the conditions of national development; he insisted on labour as the way of human redemption; he held firm to his fundamental principle that political action should avoid all violence and even hostility toward those against whom India was struggling.

Gandhi introduced into the Indian national movement the conception that national fulfilment involved not only political independence but basic changes in society itself—the abolition of untouchability, modification of castes, extension of rights to women, a secular state. He incorporated all these elements into the national struggle, strongly urging the participation of women in his non co-operation movement, obliging his followers to spin as a qualification for political work, encouraging inter-caste marriages and making the abolition of untouchability one of the great points of his programme. He developed the movement in the villages, carrying the doctrine of social integration to the masses of the people and arousing a new sense of national unity.

If Mahatma Gandhi had been able to achieve independence within five or ten years, his social objective might not have been realized. But the length of the struggle, which started in 1920 and did not end until 1947, ingrained his views. The entire country received the stimulus of thousands of people accustomed to work hard and to sacrifice and of the sense of unity created by this enormous movement; a whole generation grew up within the framework of a strict national discipline. The long struggle was itself an instrument for eliminating many customs and practices which had been blindly accepted in the past and for putting into effect the social ideas which the leaders had already grasped on an intellectual plane. By the end of the period a new outlook had been created among the masses of the people and the ideas which had been entertained only by the intellectuals became part of the Indian outlook.

Prior to the Soviet revolution nationalism in India was conceived in political terms, in relation to authority, power and the direction of the state. The basic modification brought to Indian thought by the October revolution was the idea that in order to avoid economic collapse and a peril to its future the state would need to intervene in the economic sphere. The Soviet experience played an important role for India in creating a conviction among the leaders that the ideas of political progress gained from contact with the West must be united with a doctrine of economic progress, founded on planning on a national scale.

Thus the contact between East and West in India may be regarded as a process of fertilization which gave a new life to a very ancient people, to transform it and to create a new and dynamic civilization based on its past. India had never had a prejudice against borrowing ideas from abroad. In every period of Indian history Indian humanism borrowed from and gave to others, never hesitating to receive what it thought enriching. If Indian writers formerly borrowed from the Persian language or the traditions of Persian poetry and in modern times borrowed European techniques and cast their works in the form of novels, sonnets or dramas, they did not thereby lose their Indian character. It was wholly within the tradition of Indian history to borrow from the USSR the idea of planning and of economic equality without taking over the idea of the dictatorship of the proletariat or limitations on individual freedom.

It was the inherent strength and flexibility of Indian civilization that permitted the adoption and assimilation of ideas coming from the West. And it was the force and the value of the ideas, social objectives, scientific outlook and economic conceptions of the West which played a part in bringing about the transformation of the Indian outlook.

In this amalgam which constituted the self-image of independent India, the several components had greater or less meaning for different segments of Indian society. For the Muslim minority which made up about a tenth of the population of independent India, the liberal component was the heart of the modern Indian self-image. The Muslim leaders who chose to cast their lot with a secular India rather than with an Islamic Pakistan expressed their confidence in the force of liberalism within the Indian synthesis. More, they thought that the principles of democracy and essential unity which they drew from their Muslim tradition, in combination with the liberal principles which they had imbibed, could make a positive contribution toward the evolution of the new India.

All elements in India saw the new nation as creating a new civilization, deeply rooted in its own past but renewed and modified by ideas from the West, a synthesis which should be of value to the whole world.

2. China

At the opening of the twentieth century China saw itself humiliated and impotent, a chained dragon able only to lash out in ineffectual fury at the foreigners who were extending their influence with force and arrogance further and further into the Celestial Empire. In the middle of the century its leaders could declare that 'bright new China stands like a giant in the East'.

The awakening of China and the reassertion of its historic place in the world followed a very different course from that of India. On the one hand

China had never lost its sense of identity as a nation and a people and it had retained a continuous record and knowledge of its long history. On the other hand China's contact with the West was of a different character. Western influences never entered into the structure and outlook of the entire country, as they had penetrated India through its uniform system of western education and law. Western culture in China remained apart from, and rarely integrated with, the Chinese tradition. Western liberalism neither revitalized the Chinese spirit as it had the Indian, nor stimulated the reassertion of a basic tradition stripped of the accretion of custom. Most of all, no social renovation had begun to modernize the basic structure of Chinese society until the communist forces built their strength on the revolutionary aspirations of the peasants and brought a radically new order of life to the Chinese people.

China's experience with the West during the nineteenth century had been most unfavourable to a synthesis of Chinese and western cultures. When in the 1830s British efforts to force the opium trade on the Chinese people had made it necessary for the Chinese empire to modify its age-old practice of treating the rest of the world as vassal states or as barbarians, the emperor's representative had appealed to Britain in terms of moral principles. The reply—armed attack, vandalism and the imposition of unequal treaties granting a privileged position to foreigners on Chinese soil—established the pattern of relationships which persisted for a hundred years.

In the course of the years the Chinese reluctantly concluded that it would be necessary to acquire western knowledge and to design western methods of defence. Throughout the nineteenth century, however, they did not see this as involving the adoption of western attitudes but only as applying western techniques to Chinese purposes, though there were those who thought the distinction between 'substance' and 'function' unsound since western techniques were in fact the foundation of their government.

In contrast to the Indians who acquired western liberal attitudes before they acquired western scientific techniques, Chinese interest was at first almost wholly in the technical aspects; four-fifths of all the works translated into Chinese in the second half of the nineteenth century were on scientific and technical subjects.

The acquisition and application of western knowledge for 'self-strengthening' was, however, half-hearted, for the ruling group of scholar-administrators, selected through the imperial examinations which had been used for two thousand years, were reluctant to admit new bodies of knowledge or to share their power with men educated in missionary institutions or abroad. Nor were they prepared to adopt an institutional structure which would facilitate the development of modern industry, and such industrial developments as were initiated were treated by the officialdom chiefly as a source of tax revenue and perquisites.

Through the nineteenth century Chinese society continued to be composed of a great mass of peasants and a small group of landowners from whose ranks the scholar-administrators were largely drawn. The imperial régime was weak, but the *literati* under the authority of the emperor still held a monopoly of power and organization. As in the past, however, popular unrest manifested itself in the form of peasant rebellions and in the activities of secret societies. In the middle of the century the Tai-Ping rebellion, led by Hung Hsu-chuan who had borrowed from the Christian missionaries the idea of a Messiah, aroused much of the interior of the country and for a period maintained a rival government until the rebellion was finally suppressed. At the close of the century the Boxer outburst directed against foreigners again revealed the presence of widespread unrest and the precarious base on which the central authority rested. A movement for reform was stimulated by the rivalry of Japan and the example of its modernization; many Chinese were attracted to Japan to learn new ways.

The first effort at social reform, the 'hundred days' of 1898, failed disastrously. At the insistence of a group of scholars led by Kang Yu-wei, the emperor was persuaded to issue a series of decrees designed to set in motion a process of modernization, but the dowager empress nipped in the bud this threat to the old régime, tightened the reins of power in her own hands, and consigned the leaders of the reform movement to exile or death. Yet Kang Yu-wei's vision of a new China was not blotted out. Though he lived in exile and died in obscurity in 1927, his pupils kept alive his concept of the successive stages through which China should progress toward 'the Great Commonwealth' in which there would be no distinction of high or low, rich or poor, race or sex, and in which all men would share property in common; they published after his death his design for a community where the state would assume responsibility for the livelihood and welfare of all, a design which bore a close resemblance to the communes actually established by the communist régime.

Two aspects of the reform movement, moreover, had immediate effect. The old examination system for public office was abolished, and with it the monopoly so long held by Confucian scholars in the leadership of the state. Education along modern lines was instituted with the establishment of the University of Peking, and later of other universities in the western style. From these universities, and from the students returning from study in Japan, the United States, western Europe, and finally Moscow, came a new leadership which first abortively and then decisively revitalized Chinese society and gave it new direction.

By 1911 the structure of Manchu rule was so weak that it was overthrown in 1911–12 almost without a struggle. But the republic set up in its place with Sun Yat-sen as its first president rested on no firm foundation of popular understanding and support. The years of imperial impotence and western penetration had left great social disorganization; missionary education had undermined the social structure and disparaged traditional values without providing an effective alternative, while the missionaries themselves had been identified with the extraterritorial and other privileges enjoyed by western economic interests on Chinese soil. There was as great popular bitterness against the West as against the Manchus, and although Sun Yat-sen drew his own inspiration from the West there was no general understanding of western constitutional principles on which to base a republican structure.

The revolution was carried out centrally and its principal effect was to destroy what remained of central authority while it inherited much of the weakness of the old régime. The provincial war lords only awaited the downfall of the emperor to strike out on their own. When the new government sought foreign loans to bolster its position, the foreign powers demanded further concessions in return. The new régime faced the opposition of military men who rallied many scholar-administrators of the old order. It had no mass support, for the gulf between peasants and intellectuals was unbridged and the traditional hold of the landlords over the villages remained unbroken.

When Sun Yat-sen saw the success of the October revolution in Russia and the fact that the other western powers, instead of supporting his revolutionary effort, continued to take advantage of China's weakness, he concluded that the Russian people were China's best friend and that their methods of revolution and organization had much to teach. To carry forward his own revolution, he organized the Kuomintang party, accepted communists as members and sent his lieutenant, Chiang Kai-shek, to Moscow to study the methods of the Red army. He formulated the steps by which his party was to transform China in terms of his Three People's Principles—*San Min Chu I*: Nationalism, to build China as a free, independent and equal member of the family of nations: Democracy, through a gradual process involving defeat of the warlords, tutelage under the Kuomintang party and finally an elective constitutional government; and People's Livelihood, through 'land to the cultivator' and capital development by the state.

But after Sun's death in 1925 Chiang Kai-shek expelled the communists from the Kuomintang and concentrated the efforts of his party more and more on the military unification of the country. He made no effort to enlarge the scope of democratic activity in order to bring to an end 'tutelage' by the party and to reach the stated goal of constitutionalism. Nor did he make any significant effort to carry out economic reform. By the time that the Japanese invasion began in 1937, the Kuomintang had lost its revolutionary direction and the revolutionary initiative had passed to the communist movement which tapped the energy of the peasants and set in motion a mass drive for social change.[7]

The political changes initiated by Sun Yat-sen were paralleled by a literary movement, the New Tide, which broke sharply with the traditions of Chinese society. Its principal leader, the dean of the College of Letters at Peking University, Chen Tu-hsiu, saw no meeting ground between Chinese and western methods, and he called on the new generation in China to choose 'independence not servility, progress not conservatism, aggressiveness not timidity, world-mindedness not narrow nationalism, practical attitude not ceremonies, scientific approach not speculation'.* The young intellectuals who took part in this renaissance rejected, as equally superstitious, traditional Confucian principles and Christianity which many of them had embraced.

The movement spread with great rapidity and vigour among the younger intellectuals, and it brought a first major step toward bridging the gap between the intellectuals and the people by insisting that books be written in the language of common speech, *pai hwa*, and not only in the literary language which no one spoke and only the educated could read. It focused the attention of Chinese writers on the actual conditions of contemporary Chinese life and developed a school of realistic writing which spared no institution of Chinese society.

The most scholarly of the leaders of the New Tide, Hu Shih, remained true to the liberal principles which had inspired the original movement, but more and more of the writers soon moved to the left. Chen Tu-hsiu together with Li Ta-chao, the earliest popularizer of Marxism–Leninism in China, and others founded the Communist party in 1920, and a series of leftist writers' organizations were established. As the communist movement grew in strength, these writers played an active part in giving the movement its Chinese form.

The communist movement in China thus developed in a society in which the age-old division between the masses of the people and the landowning, literate *élite* had not been bridged, and in which no substantial social measures had been taken to relieve misery and poverty, though these conditions were well-known and were constantly depicted by writers; the sanctioning institutions of Confucianism had fallen into disrespect under the impact of missionaries and Chinese liberals, but no alternative set of values had been incorporated into Chinese thought; the tradition of central authority remained strong but a hundred years of weakness had brought near-dissolution; hatred and scorn of the foreigner and an abiding sense of the unique greatness of the Chinese people had never been lost.

The achievement of the communists, under the leadership of Mao Tse-tung and with the support of many of the intellectuals, was to reach the peasants and to provide the means by which they could identify themselves with the nation. Wherever the communist armies appeared, they organized the villages until the Japanese invaders in the northern provinces found themselves no longer confronted merely by armies but by a people in arms; after the war the Kuomintang could offer no effective resistance to the communist forces based on wide popular support. Once in power, the communists rejected as a foreign intrusion the western liberalism which had always remained an island in Chinese life, and they provided the Chinese

* *La Jeunesse*, September 1915.

people with new terms in which to reassert and re-establish their greatness.

In the first decade of its existence the Chinese People's Republic moved with immense energy and great speed toward its goal—to make China once more one of the greatest, if not the greatest, of the world's peoples. It converted the corrupt bureaucracy which had long provided the structure of Chinese government into a highly centralized administration and it cut the ground from under potential war lords by the organization of the people's army. It set the people from one end of the country to the other at the task of making a great 'leap forward' on every front—in agriculture and industry, in irrigation and construction, in education and science, in transport and mechanization, in health and in the culture of the people.

As this effort was projected, all the resources of the people and the country were to be tapped, from the greatest to the least. Large-scale industrial organization and advanced technology must seek to equal and if possible out-strip the West, but local efforts were to be made to adapt traditional crafts and improvise forms of partial mechanization; hundreds of thousands of workers were organized to build canals and dams, while young people were sent into the mountains to hunt for springs which might supply water for local irrigation; in a land where famine had long been endemic and population was mounting, new methods of farming and farm organization were intro-duced in the effort to raise more food with less labour; schools were organ-ized at all levels with whatever resources there might be at hand.

Although Marxism-Leninism furnished the theoretical guide to the creation of the new China, the Chinese People's Republic regarded itself as the inheritor of the wisdom of the Chinese sages, the inventiveness of the Chinese people and the greatness and unity of the Chinese empire. While the Confucian family system as it had been practised was discarded, leading Chinese scholars found a basis in the writings of Confucius for revolutionary and democratic principles. Alongside modern medicine, which was practised and taught, the practice of traditional Chinese medicine was encouraged. Operas on new themes were composed in the old Chinese style. People in all regions were urged to collect folk songs and to compose new songs in familiar manners. Newly literate people were stimulated to form writing groups and to tell the stories of their factories or farms. Famous Buddhist temples were restored and historical and archaeological discoveries were made widely known.

The task of modernization was gigantic and fantastically difficult. The hectic pace of change in the first years did not conquer the ancient ills of hunger and misery overnight and it brought new strains and problems in its wake. But in the new China nothing seemed impossible to a people of 600,000,000, with four thousand years of recorded history behind them, now that the interlude of weakness was over and they were once more on their way.[8]

3. *Japan**

In Japan, the Asian country which most consciously and zealously sought to adopt western ways, new patterns of thought were incorporated into a basically different culture which nevertheless remained in many respects unchanged. The cultural orientation of Japan during these years was the result of the interplay between traditional habits and imported western attitudes and practices, under the conditions of self-assertion, national expansion and military defeat that made up Japan's history in the twentieth century.

More than virtually any other nation, Japan contained a homogeneous people sharing a common traditional culture. Self-contained, self-centred and at peace through the two and a half centuries of isolation before the opening of Japan by the West, it had been neither interfered with nor stimulated by alien ways, ideas or conflicts. The Japanese image of the world was the image of Japan.

In the closed and ordered Japanese society, basically feudal and familial, each person's status and every relationship was carefully defined and expressed in modes of speech and conduct. Compassion and benevolence were high virtues. Man's relation with nature, too, was clearly defined. It involved an intimate intuitive harmony with the fruitful earth, the gentle climate and the beauty of the changing seasons, together with helpless fear in the face of raging typhoons and calamitous earthquakes. Nature was not as in the West a challenger to be conquered and bent to the service of man. According to religious concepts which endowed living objects with spirit or souls, mankind was part of a natural continuum which included animals and gods. The individual's goal was to maintain self-discipline, fortitude and inner peace within an assigned status and in the face of the stresses and trials of life and death.

This was the cultural base upon which western culture, so fundamentally different in many respects, was eagerly superimposed. Not only did the Japanese people master western technology and put it to work; they imported and translated countless western books on all subjects, coined words to cover new materials and ideas, introduced western music, sports, dancing and other forms of recreation, and made western philosophical thought the framework for academic study.

Many intellectuals devoted themselves with such energy and ability to the study of western thought, literature, science and the arts that they came to be more at home in western ideas and ways of thinking than in those traditional to Japan. Listening to western music, discussing western philosophy, even celebrating such western holidays as Christmas, they began to feel that Japan belonged to the culture group of the West rather than with the 'backward' cultures of Asia toward which modernized Japan looked with scorn.

* For other aspects of Japan's development see Chapter IV, pp. 88–9, and Chapter XXVIII, p. 1032.

The masses of the people, for their part, saw daily life enriched by the fruits of industrialization which raised the level of living, although earnings remained meagre and major industrial efforts were directed to heavy industries and war production. Rapid economic expansion constantly broadened opportunities; no former class of handicraftsmen feared the machine for it largely replaced the labour of already overburdened housewives or entered new fields which were not a part of pre-industrial production. Confusions or conflicts between traditional and western ways seemed transitional, easily borne as part of the process of assimilating new knowledge and making it their own.

Yet western thought and practice did not wholly replace traditional Japanese cultural values and attitudes. Private life—the house and garden and the manner of living in them, the family structure and personal relationships—remained traditionally Japanese; chairs and western clothes were used at work, but straw-matted floors and kimonos in the home. Agriculture retained its traditional form, gradually improved by the pragmatic application of new knowledge. So also did the multitude of small family enterprises where a few machine processes supplemented or replaced handicraft methods. Large-scale industry, banking, commerce and merchant shipping created new institutions and ways, which were added to rather than substituted for older forms. In the arts and in recreation the same pattern prevailed. Western plays and movies flourished, alongside the rigorously maintained traditional drama; western music, dancing and baseball competed with traditional forms of entertainment.

Westernization, in short, meant the incorporation of western knowledge and ways into the existing structure and basic values of Japanese society. The ideal was often expressed as 'Japanese spirit, western talents'. Although the old feudal structure was replaced by political and educational institutions drawn from the West, the feudal texture of the social fabric remained. It continued to condition all relationships—between employer and workers, landlord and peasant, old and young, masters and servants, and superiors and inferiors in every professional, economic, social or family hierarchy.[9, 10]

Moreover, western institutions were modified in the process of being adopted. Although parliamentary forms were introduced, the Japanese government remained essentially an executive system, centralized in the emperor, and designed to carry out the process of rapid capitalist development and military build-up. The Japanese Diet, chosen by restricted suffrage to represent functional economic and social groupings, lacked many of the essential features of western parliaments—an effective party system, cabinet responsibility, full control of the purse, supremacy of civilian over military authority. Universal education was initially imbued with the western concept of equality of opportunity, but it was soon redirected to emphasize responsibilities and duties, on the basis of traditional principles: honour to Japan's historic past, the emperor system as the centre of Japan, Confucian ethics as defining the status relationships of a semi-feudal society.

The self-image and aspirations with which the Japanese people entered and fought through the second world war were thus compounded of western technology, military organization and educational methods, a traditionally Japan-centred view of the world, traditional patterns of loyalty and acceptance of status focused on the state and the emperor, and a traditional attitude toward death as man's last and greatest opportunity to meet the vicissitudes of life with courage and fortitude.

The great defeat brought this self-image down in ruins. Nothing coherent remained, neither the western nor the Japanese components, and least of all the amalgam into which they had been formed. In the years after 1945 the Japanese people, with the same self-conscious endeavour with which they had deliberately sought westernization seventy-five years before, turned their efforts to finding a new viewpoint, social structure and national goal. In the initial phase of this effort they were subjected to the anomaly of a conquering, occupying power attempting to introduce democratic institutions and concepts from the vantage point of its authoritarian position. They experienced too, for the first time in many centuries, large-scale intermingling with and exposure to an alien people. At mid-century the process of reshaping a new self-image and re-charting national objectives was still in flux, but some of the component elements were emerging.

The component of democracy, basic to many of the institutions adopted during or following the period of occupation, was much featured in the revised system of education and was being applied tentatively and experimentally in some areas of personal relationships. But it was not clear how far the concept of democracy would prove viable in this society. For people had been conditioned by tradition, language and experience to conform to prescribed rules and status relationships and they had not been called upon to assume the kind of individual responsibility for decision and choice that was basic to western democratic concepts and institutions.

As Japan faced the new world of the mid-twentieth century, she found to her surprise that the peoples of Asia whom she had formerly despised—India, Indonesia, China and others—were rising as nations. For the first time since the start of modernization, the Japanese could feel in good company among the peoples of Asia and no longer had to try to identify themselves with the West.

But more basic than their reappraisal of other peoples of Asia was the reappraisal of their own Asian heritage. In their process of reorientation, educated Japanese began to re-evaluate the non-western bases of the Japanese mentality and feeling which lay below the surface of conscious, westernized thought. The new self-image could acknowledge these qualities, seek their development and use them as a basis for selecting and incorporating whatever might come from abroad.

Among younger men and women—those who had been forced to rethink their attitudes toward their native tradition and toward the West during the war while facing death in suicide squadrons, or who as school children had seen all that they had been taught crash around them—the effort to rediscover a native base led them to explore popular Japanese culture. It seemed to them that neither rootless westernism nor formal intellectualized traditionalism possessed vitality for a new age. And so they sought to discover the outlook and values of the common people, the sources of their strength and endurance, the nature of their aspirations, and ways to release their potential creativity. This was their answer to the challenge which democratic principles offered to a society which had accorded the intellectual a place apart and had exacted self-discipline but not self-expression from the masses of the people.

4. South-east Asia and Korea.

Prior to the second world war the region of south-east Asia remained firmly under colonial rule, with the exception of Thailand which had maintained its independence and the Philippines which had received self-government in 1935 with the promise of independence in ten years. Korea, which had come under Japanese influence after the Sino-Japanese war, had been annexed in 1910 and made subject to direct administration by Japan. In the decade after the war, east and south-east Asia became a region of independent states and by the time that Malaya joined the family of nations in 1957 only a few small remnants of colonial authority were left in the area.

Compared to most parts of the world south-east Asia, which had been a great meeting-place and crossroad of civilization during most of its history and was the source of considerable wealth, remained relatively secluded and static up to the war though it was not untouched by the currents of thought which were arousing other peoples to self-consciousness and to action. Colonial administrations made few concessions toward self-government and extended western education to only a small fragment of the population. The traditional ruling groups had generally lost their power and position, except as they were sustained by the colonial power, as were some of the Indonesian princelings who served as functionaries for the Dutch.

Throughout the region economic enterprise and public administration were mainly in the hands of Europeans, while the local populations carried on subsistence agriculture and fishing, and worked as plantation labour or in the exploitation of forest and mineral resources such as teak, petroleum or tin. The economic and administrative direction by Europeans was supplemented in some areas by a class of Chinese merchants, Indo-European administrators or Indian moneylenders and technicians; Indian and Chinese workers supplied the labour for some plantations and mines. Though conditions varied within the region, they were nowhere favourable to the growth of effective nationalism.

Yet there were some stirrings of nationalist sentiment in the region and the beginning growth of a new class of potential leaders. Though the colonial atmosphere and social pressures tended to make the educated Burman,

Indonesian or Cambodian into an Englishman, Dutchman or Frenchman and to draw him away from his roots and his people, some with western training were taking on a national outlook.

In Indonesia from 1908 on, there were occasional demands for rights, chiefly for participation in activities reserved to Europeans. The first evidences of anything suggesting revolt came with communist-led disturbances in 1926, a mutiny of sailors in 1933 and the formation of a youth congress which pledged itself to work for 'one Indonesian nation, one Indonesian country and one Indonesian language'. The image of 'one Indonesia' extending for 1,500 miles over a sprawling archipelago, inhabited by people in every stage of economic and cultural development, speaking some 250 languages and dialects, was indeed a bold one; it seemed little short of fantastic when put forward by a group of young intellectuals whose number was very small and who lacked organization and support.

Burma, which was administered until 1937 as a province of India, benefited from the concessions of local self-government secured for India by the Indian National Congress. On the other hand technical posts not filled by Europeans were largely filled by Indians and the Indian army provided for defence. Under colonial administration the pattern of Burmese life based on Buddhist attitudes and institutions had been seriously undermined and disorder and confusion were widespread. The expansion of rice farming in the delta had led to the creation of large estates in the hands of absentee landlords, unstable tenancy and seasonal labour and the establishment of new villages many of which did not even have a pagoda. Indian and some Chinese immigrants supplied much of the labour for plantations, industries and mines; the greater part of the population of the larger towns before the second world war was non-Burmese. There was considerable unrest and repeated expression of opposition to British rule, especially in the 1930s.

The units which composed the loose federation which the French called Indo-China had distinct populations, religions and histories and were subject to different forms of administration. Signs of unrest were evident in the serious rebellion of 1930, which was violently repressed, and in the growth of religious sects which formed themselves into semi-military bodies under strongly nationalist leaders.

Fewer signs of nationalism were visible before the second world war in Malaya than elsewhere in South-East Asia. The Malay peninsula, with its resources of tin and rubber, contained a Malay population mainly engaged in farming and fishing, a large Chinese population many of whom worked in the tin mines owned by Europeans or Chinese, and Indian farm labourers who worked on the rubber plantations mainly owned by Europeans. Colonial policy favoured the Malays, especially the princely class. The people of this communally divided land, living under a colonial economy in the shadow of the great imperial naval base and entrepôt of Singapore, had little basis for a sense of national identity and unity.

The turning point in south-east Asia came swiftly and drastically with the Japanese invasion and rule during the second world war. The rapid collapse of the forces of the colonial powers destroyed in one quick blow the prestige which had sustained their authority in the area. There was no restoring colonial rule once the Japanese were driven back, though the Dutch tried desperately to do so, unable to believe that a people with so little experience could organize and hold together the vast and scattered Indonesian archipelago, and though the French waged a costly war for eight years to try to hold Indo-China.[11]

The Japanese occupation not only broke the hold of the colonial powers. In one way or another it contributed both to the creation of the new nations and to the disorganization with which these nations had to deal.

The Japanese set up a puppet régime in Burma to which they granted 'independence' in 1943 and one in Indonesia to which they promised 'independence' on the eve of their own defeat. They conducted their administration in Indonesia in Japanese, which the Indonesians did not understand, and in the Malay-Indonesian language which the Indonesian nationalists had hoped to make the national language, thus displacing Dutch. In Burma they trained and armed a contingent of Burmese to fight against the British, providing the Burmese with their first military forces. In time the Burmese army units turned against the Japanese and helped to drive them out, and then they became part of the people's movement which demanded freedom from Britain. Independent Burma, recognized by Britain in 1947, was the first of Britain's possessions to withdraw from the Commonwealth.

In these and similar ways the Japanese helped to launch as independent nations the countries of south-east Asia which they had sought to prepare for an 'Asian Co-prosperity Sphere' under Japanese hegemony. At the same time their occupation tended to disorganize the life of the region. The trail of physical destruction left in Burma made it difficult for the post-war Burmese government to re-establish communication and control the countryside or restore the economy. In Malaya, workers were conscripted at the rate of 20 for every 250 persons in the population; of 74,000 such workers sent to work on railway construction in Thailand, only 12,000 were reported as having returned to their homes. Some 300,000 people were shipped as forced labour from Java.

The new countries of south-east Asia, plunged thus swiftly into the responsibilities of statehood through the disorganizing experiences of war and occupation, saw themselves first of all as nation-states. In some the nation was identified with a pre-colonial unit, in others with an entity created by colonial rule. In still others divisions were imposed in terms of the conflict between major power groups. The small kingdoms which the French had brought together into Indo-China re-emerged as the states of Cambodia, Laos and Vietnam. By contrast, the multitude of islands over which the Dutch had exercised authority not only declared their common identity as a nation, but laid claim to Western New Guinea on the ground that it had been part of the Dutch empire and the Indonesian state was heir to all that had composed this unit, as well as to the thirteenth-century realm of Madjapahit.

The collapse of the Japanese empire also left Japan's own colony, Korea, free to join the family of nations. In spite of Korea's long history as an independent entity loosely linked to China by political and cultural ties, Japan undertook to extend Japanese language and culture to the area, as well as to develop its economy as part of her own industrial development. The Japanese surrender offered the Koreans the opportunity to reverse the process of incorporation into Japan, to restore the Korean language, replace the Japanese who occupied most posts of responsibility at all levels, and to reassert a national identity.

But all these countries were caught up, to a greater or less degree, in the global conflict to extend communism or to contain it, and their development was conditioned by their role in this contest. Before Korea had more than begun to establish its national identity, it found its soil converted into a battleground, and after three years of destruction it emerged as two states, divided along an arbitrary line drawn not by the Korean people but by the powers. Like Korea, Vietnam was partitioned by international agreement when the French were finally forced to leave Indo-China after defeat by communist-led armies supported by peasant guerrillas; a northern unit became a communist-controlled state while South Vietnam retained its non-communist orientation. The governments of the other new states of the region, often with outside assistance, resisted internal movements led by communist elements during the initial difficult phases of national organization.

With the exception of North Korea and North Vietnam, the new states all saw themselves in some way as liberal democracies and drew up their constitutions either as republics or as constitutional monarchies; Vietnam, which initially established itself under personal rule, voted almost immediately to do away with its monarchy and to create a republic. All faced immense difficulties in their task of achieving productive and viable economies. The region contained considerable natural resources, not only in the varied islands of Indonesia but in rice-rich Burma and Cambodia and in Malaya with its tin and rubber. Every country was, however, woefully short of the essentials for economic development—technical, scientific, administrative and entrepreneurial personnel, capital and organization. Yet they saw themselves, somehow, as creating modern societies and serving the welfare of their people.

In seeking a basis for their identity and existence, they drew on their traditions in various ways. Burma turned to the Buddhist tradition on which the stability and well-being of its society had formerly rested and it rededicated itself to the values which the Buddha had proclaimed. The personal conviction of its first premier, U Nu, made these values alive in public policy:

the great Buddhist conclave in 1955 in honour of the 2,500th anniversary of the Buddha's death lent them added prestige. The problem was whether this renewal could serve to invigorate and guide the new state and to provide adequate motivation and control, not only with respect to the non-Buddhist minorities but in the less stable of the rural areas and in the cities.

Buddhism was important, too, in Cambodia, Laos and Vietnam—it was in fact officially declared to be the religion of the state in the constitution of Laos—but the special sects, such as the Cao Dai, and the substantial numbers of Christians made the Buddhist tradition somewhat less central to the self-image of these states.

For Indonesia the problem was to achieve 'unity in diversity'. In a first effort to cope with this problem, the new government established a strongly centralized state, but it soon became apparent that the several islands had retained a strong sense of their individual identity and that the slogan of the youth of 1928—'one Indonesian nation, one Indonesian country, one Indonesian language'—would not become a reality overnight. Although Indonesia adopted the principles and forms of liberal democracy, the difficulties of organizing the country economically and politically were great and the wide gap between village and central government was bridged only by personal loyalty. President Sukarno, who commanded such personal loyalty from the early days of the struggle for liberation, looked for some form of 'guided democracy' in terms of which to design a workable state.

For Malaya the problem of 'unity in diversity' was also very real, for communalism was traditional, economic divisions were sharp, and at the time of independence the Malay, Chinese and Indian populations, the farmers, tin miners, rubber workers, mine and plantation owners and merchants, had a long way to go before they could subordinate their separate identities and regard themselves fully as 'Malayans'.

Thus, in all south-east Asia the swift conversion of dependent people into independent states created nations which faced great problems of political organization and economic and social change without having developed a common outlook through a long nationalist struggle, and without possessing a substantial group of educated and experienced men equipped to lead their technical and political development. Flanked on either side by the two giants of Asia, China and India, each driving with great energy to create a powerful modern society in its own terms, these smaller and less firmly established states had, perhaps, only one common guiding aspiration: 'Merdeka'— Freedom.

5. The Arabs

Arab nationalism in the twentieth century was the expression of a people who shared a common language and a sense of common identity with a great past, whatever the political units within which they were to be found. The sense of Arab identity and the aspirations of people who regarded themselves

NN*

as Arabs were built up gradually through the century, reaching a high emotional pitch a decade after the second world war.

Arab nationalism absorbed or overrode other loyalties that offered alternative bases for identification and dedication among Arab peoples. It overshadowed emotional attachment to the nation-state and identification with other than the Arab phase of the long history of the ancient lands of the Middle East and North Africa. Although Egypt set up the gigantic statue of Rameses II in the centre of Cairo and made the most of tourist interest in the great pyramids and tombs, it was the Arab rather than the Pharonic tradition upon which modern Egypt built its sense of mission and identity. The effort to focus on Egypt as a nation-state rooted in the past of the Pharaohs declined as Arab nationalism rose. Finally the Arab identification triumphed with the creation of the United Arab Republic by the union of Egypt and Syria in 1958, and the abandonment of Egypt as a name, with the historic associations which it evoked.

Arab nationalism also transcended loyalty to Islam, though the sense of Arab greatness was bound up with the sense that Islam was authentically Arab. The centre of Islam, the holy city of Mecca, was an Arab city; Arabic was the language in which the Quran was written and continued to be read or recited by all believers; historically it was the Arabs who carried Islam to the East and to the West. Yet Arab nationalism served as a counterweight to the Pan-Islamic movement of the early twentieth century which sought to bolster the authority of the caliph, and the nationalist movement included among its leaders Christian and Druse Arabs who placed national identity above religious affiliation. Arab nationalism tended, too, to overshadow dynastic and other personal loyalties which had been the main form of affiliation known in the region and continued to characterize the relations within the Arab world to the middle of the twentieth century.

Arab nationalism drew much of its strength and emotional intensity from the fact that it became more and more a rallying point for antagonism against the colonial powers of the West. Nowhere was anticolonial sentiment stronger or more charged with resentment and distrust. Nowhere was there a more bitter sense of betrayal. In the climate of the mid-twentieth century, the efforts of western powers to protect their interests in the area seemed an especially intolerable affront to the dignity of a proud people, and Arab nationalism offered an outlet for this indignation.

The initial impetus for Arab nationalism came from the Islamic revival of the late nineteenth century, inspired by the nationalist, Pan-Islamic spirit of Jamal ad-Din al-Afghani and the liberalism of Mohammed Abduh, who believed that a purified Islam could assimilate modern technical and social ideas and could renew the strength of Muslim society. Ideas of secular nationalism, in the western sense, were stimulated by missionary education; some of the most vigorous members of the Arab nationalist movement were graduates of the American University at Beirut.[12]

The Young Turk movement of 1908, with its call for 'Liberty, Fraternity and Equality', appeared to the Arabs to offer an outlet for their awakening self-consciousness. In the multi-cultural Ottoman empire, where administration was carried on by Turkish pashas but the nationalities within the empire retained their identity, the Arabs supposed that they would gain greater autonomy under the constitutional government which the Young Turks proposed. But the Young Turks envisaged a nation-state which should be Turkish in culture and national loyalty, not merely in rule.

The Arabs came to realize that there was no place for them in a movement leading to Turkification, and they turned toward organizations of their own, forming a series of secret societies between 1908 and 1912. The aim of these societies was still not separation from Turkey, but full political rights and an effective share in the administration of the empire. The first all-Arab congress, called in Paris in 1913 on the initiative of a group of Arab students abroad, formulated similar demands.

The most practical encouragement to Arab nationalism came from the western powers who sought to use Arab ambitions to achieve their own military objectives in the first world war. As Turkey became involved in the war and it appeared that the Ottoman empire might be crumbling, the aspirations of the Arabs gradually shifted from participation within the empire to independence. Arab leaders sought and received Allied encouragement for their aims and in 1916 Husain, the sharif of Mecca, raised the standard of the 'Great Arab Revolt' against the Turks. In the name of Arab nationalism the Muslim Arabs thus turned against another Muslim power and hastened the downfall of the sultan who was also their caliph.

But the powers not only mobilized the Arabs and gave them a sense of their potentialities; they created among them a common sense of betrayal and indignation which gave new direction and a new bitterness to their nationalism. During the negotiations through which the British encouraged the Arabs to rise, the Arab leaders understood that they were being promised support for independence. When they joined the Allies' cause, they thought that it was their own battles rather than those of the Allies that they were fighting. But in the peace settlement which divided the Arab lands of the Fertile Crescent between Britain and France as mandatory powers under the League of Nations, they saw themselves as mere pawns in the game of European power politics.

From that time forward the emotional fervour of Arab nationalism, which had hitherto been vague, anti-Turkish or compounded with dynastic ambition, became passionately anti-western. The sense of betrayal was accentuated and the anti-western feeling exacerbated by the Balfour Declaration of 1917 which declared that Britain would look with favour upon the establishment of a Jewish national home in Palestine. A Jewish homeland appeared to the Arabs as an intrusion into what they regarded as *their* land, and in the context of alien rule imposed through the mandate system it took on the character of a beachhead for the colonially-minded West.

The discovery of oil introduced a new factor affecting the aspirations of the Arabs. From the opening up of the immense oilfields in Iraq in the 1920s and in the Arabian peninsula in the 1930s, the politics of the western powers in the Middle East became the politics of oil. The Arabs were subject to the effects of agreements among the powers and between the powers and Turkey which disposed of territory and carved out oil interests. But, as owners of the land where oil was pumped and across which it was carried by great pipelines they could exert pressure on the powers in their turn. Especially after the nationalization by Iran of the Anglo-Iranian oil properties in 1951, which led to a general raising of the share of oil profits received by local states throughout the Middle East from around 10–15 per cent to approximately 50 per cent, the undreamed-of riches which oil revenues brought to the treasuries of Iraq, Saudi Arabia and the sheikhdoms of Kuwait and Bahrein gave these governments the financial means to pursue their ambitions, either for themselves or for the Arab cause. In the years after the second world war their command over these coveted oil resources placed them in a position to play off rival power blocs against one another.

In the inter-war years the exercise of European authority in the Arab countries was vigorously and repeatedly resisted throughout the area. There were armed revolts against the establishment of British authority in Iraq in the early 1920s and even more violent resistance to French rule in Syria. In Palestine violence was almost continuous. Egypt succeeded in throwing off the British protectorate in 1922. The extension of European rule in North Africa had been resisted by tribal chiefs and religious sects during the nineteenth and early twentieth centuries, and such resistance continued to appear, as when the Riff in Morocco waged a five-year campaign from 1921 to 1926. Some of the resistance was Arab-oriented, some expressed tribal or dynastic ambitions, some focused on religion. Especially in North Africa, nationalism during these years was intensely religious; the strong revival movement for the rigorous adherence to orthodox Islam was often scarcely distinguishable from the nationalist movement against European domination. In one form or another nationalist movements became a driving force in the Arab lands.

As these movements grew in intensity, the common opponent—the western colonial powers—was clearer than the common bond of unity. Many factors tended to divide the Arab peoples and to stand in the way of transforming the sense of identity with others who called themselves Arabs into any more substantial form.

The level of social and economic development ranged widely, from Egypt and Lebanon, which had relatively high rates of literacy and a substantial middle class, to the Arabian peninsula where, outside the foreign oil installations, virtually all modern facilities for the population were lacking. Tribalism and nomadism were widespread; the strongest Arab tradition in fact was the nomadic one. Over half the population of the Arabian peninsula and the Fertile Crescent, and much of Arab North Africa was composed of

Bedouins or other nomadic peoples. With the development of modern transport and military weapons, many of the nomads lost their sources of livelihood as caravan drivers and fighters. But though their economic and military function declined, they remained oriented toward their traditional way of life; they were still, at least psychologically, men on horseback or camelback, men of the tents, not of the village or town. Their independence and pattern of personal loyalty tended to stand in the way of national integration, though the trends of the times were driving them towards a settled mode of life.

The peasant villages, in turn, were almost universally part of a feudal pattern, dominated by large landowners who rarely had any but a remote and limited concern for the welfare of 'their' peasants, or encouraged them to expect or seek social change. Arab nationalism, in contrast to the nationalist movement in India, was not fundamentally a movement for social reform.[13]

Dynastic rivalries continued to be a divisive factor. Constant petty wars among neighbouring rulers remained the pattern in the Arabian peninsula through the first quarter of the century, until Ibn Saud, head of the Wahhabi sect, overcame one after another of his rivals and extended his authority over most of the peninsula. In the course of establishing his rule, Ibn Saud displaced the Hashemite sharif of Mecca, Husain, who had led the Great Arab Revolt. When Britain placed Husain's two sons on the thrones of Iraq and Jordan respectively, the rivalry between the two dynasties shifted from control of the Holy City to leadership of the Arab cause.

In addition to the persistence of dynastic rivalries, the Arab peoples were divided into separate national states, more or less arbitrarily defined by outside powers. Iraq was established under British tutelage in a region containing nomadic tribes and urban centres, Sunni and Shi'ite Muslims, a majority of Arabs and a large minority of Kurds. France divided its mandate into half-Christian Lebanon where French influence had long been strong and Syria, where intense devotion to Islam became linked with national resistance. Britain, caught in Palestine on the horns of the dilemma it had created by professing support to the cause of both Arabs and Jews, carved out the desert kingdom of Transjordan as an Arab state.

In each of the mandate territories, as well as in Egypt which had been under British tutelage since 1882 and became a protectorate in 1914, and in North Africa, the nationalist struggle was carried on by separate political units which sought and gained successive measures of self-government, constitutional rights and finally independence. When a comprehensive movement for Arab nationalism reasserted itself during and after the second world war it encountered vested interests identified with the states which had come into being.

It encountered, too, competing claims to Arab leadership. Syria's location made it the keystone of the Arab arch and some of its leaders entertained the idea of a 'greater Syria' extending south-east and south-west from Damascus.

Iraq had the advantage of greater freedom during the inter-war period, and wealth derived from oil. Egypt had the largest population, published the newspapers read most widely throughout the region, and furnished teachers and technicians to other Arab countries.

The first concrete move toward some form of political unity came at the encouragement of the British early in the second world war when it was apparent that the Allies could not count on Arab support such as they had received in the first world war, and that in fact they might find the Arabs among the supporters of the Axis, as an abortive anti-British outbreak in Iraq showed. In May 1941, the British foreign secretary, Anthony Eden, declared that the British government would give full support to any scheme for Arab unity that might command general Arab agreement, for it seemed 'both natural and right that the cultural and economic ties between the Arab countries, and the political ties too, should be strengthened'.*

On the initiative of Egypt the League of Arab States was formed in 1944. But the separate nationalisms, the rivalries for leadership, the cultural disparities and other divisive factors made the league merely a loose organization of sovereign states. In the aftermath of the second world war it was the individual states of west Asia and north Africa that were the beneficiaries of the wave of nationalism which swept across the world. By 1957 ten separate Arab states were members of the United Nations; Sudan, with one foot in the Arab world and one in tropical Africa, might be counted as an eleventh.

But Arab nationalism was not submerged by the separate nationalisms of the Arab states, and it was soon called into new vigour by the continued intervention of the European powers, in one way or another, in the Middle East. As colonialism came to a virtual end in Asia, its remnants in the Arab lands appeared even more intolerable than when Arabs had shared with much of the rest of the world their subordination to European rule. Britain retained certain special rights in Iraq as well as its protectorate over Aden and some of the sheikhdoms of the Arabian peninsula; the Suez Canal was under foreign administration; Algeria was administered as part of metropolitan France. Above all, Israel appeared as a spear thrust by the West into the side of the Arab body.

The humiliation of the defeat by Israel in the Palestine war of 1948 stimulated the sense of Arab unity and of the need to stand together against a common threat. But it was not until a leader emerged who could focus Arab sentiment and harness it to his own ambition that Arab nationalism became more than a discontent, a binding attitude among the Arab states within the United Nations, and a constant threat to the continued existence of Israel.

Initially Gamal Abdul Nasser was the leader of an Egyptian revolutionary movement which threw out King Farouk in 1952 and launched a programme for economic and social reform. Within a short period he became the outstanding figure in the Arab world, voicing most uncompromisingly and per-

* *The Times*, May 30, 1941.

sistently the Arab hatred of Israel. When Britain and France intervened with force in Suez in 1956, Nasser became the target of the kind of gunboat diplomacy that had been the mark of colonial tactics in the past. Thereafter he was the symbol of the Arab stand against the colonialism of the West.

The constitution which Nasser promulgated for Egypt at the beginning of 1956 proclaimed that Egypt was both an Arab state and an Islamic state.

As an Arab state, Nasser saw Egypt as the centre of an Arab union or federation: the first step was to attempt to effect a union of Syria and Egypt. It was fully indicative of the triumph of Arab nationalism over the nationalism of the separate states that the name 'Egypt', with its long history and many associations, was discarded in favour of 'United Arab Republic'. As the champion of Arabs still in subjection to western powers, he offered support to the rebels in Algeria and a home to the Algerian nationalist government created in exile. In bidding for Arab leadership, however, Egypt faced rivalry from Iraq, and it was not immediately apparent whether the spirit of Arab nationalism could bring the various parts of the Arab world together on a political basis.

In proclaiming Egypt an Islamic state, Nasser sought to keep the centre of Islam with the Arabs as it had always been, in spite of the emergence of Pakistan as an Islamic state and the numerical proponderance of non-Arabs in the total Muslim population of the world. Yet this concern was secondary to the focus on Arabism, for the provisional constitution of the United Arab Republic (1958) proclaimed only that: 'The United Arab state is a democratic, independent, sovereign republic and its people are part of the Arab nation.' It made no mention of Islam.

Nasser also declared Egypt to be an African state, and entered a bid on behalf of the Arabs for the leadership of Black Africa as it emerged from colonialism and tribalism. Islam was strong in parts of the African continent and was spreading; the Sudan, though rejecting union with Egypt in favour of independence, announced itself as one of the Arab states; Cairo radio beamed its special programmes constantly to the south and south-west; representatives of the United Arab Republic were on hand to take as important a part as possible in any gathering of African states or groups.

These moves were part of the power politics of the mid-twentieth century, when politicians talked of a 'power vacuum' in the Middle East, oil was vital, the communist and non-communist worlds were at odds, and anyone who might succeed in organizing and modernizing the Arab area could play a strategic role. But beneath these hard political realities lay the vague dream of an Arab 'homeland' stretching from the Persian Gulf to the Atlantic and a strong emotional feeling of Arab identity. In spite of technical backwardness, lack of economic development, much poverty and ignorance, and every problem that beset the underdeveloped countries of the modern world, the Arab people had the sense that they were experiencing a spiritual renaissance and were standing on the threshold of a new era of Arab greatness.

II. CULTURES OF RECENTLY SETTLED LANDS

In contrast to the ancient societies which drew on their historic past to renew their life in the twentieth century, the countries which had been settled in relatively recent times—in the Americas, Australia, New Zealand—were culturally oriented toward the future. These new countries had been created by people who had deliberately turned their backs on the past and had ventured into a new life in an empty continent or a new society. They were based on hope and the expectation that the lot of the children would be different from that of the father, and better. The pioneer spirit of these countries was constantly renewed by streams of immigrant newcomers and by the recurrent movements of older settlers into new regions of undeveloped land or into new fields of endeavour.

In all these countries in the twentieth century there was some nostalgia for the 'old world', some seeking for roots in the cultural heritage of Europe and some sense of cultural inferiority which they were still striving to outgrow. But such backward pulls were more than balanced by the sense that these were peoples who had taken fate into their own hands and whose eyes were on the future, for their children and their children's children.

1. *The United States*

The familiar terms often applied to the United States reflect the orientation of its culture toward the future, 'the land of opportunity', the immigrant's dream of 'gold in the streets', the injunction 'go west, young man'. The legend on the Statue of Liberty in the harbour of New York proclaimed a land dedicated to a future to which all could aspire, whatever their past: 'Give me your tired, your poor, your huddled masses yearning to breathe free.'

From their beginnings as a nation, the American people were self-conscious about the historic experiment which they were living out. In their 'land of promise' they saw themselves as building a new kind of life and a new kind of society which would stand as a model for the rest of the world. They never ceased to take for granted that the United States was a unique experiment and suitable for imitation, that their approach to life in a society composed of all manner of men could well be used by all manner of men elsewhere.

The 'American dream'—the social myth which drew millions of Europeans to American shores—was compounded from the rationalism and optimism of the eighteenth-century Enlightenment and the rigours and rewards of peopling a continent; the heritage of British institutions provided the equipment and a Calvinist ethic much of the original drive. The dream rested on the basic assumption that man, by his own striving, could advance toward an earthly goal; he could overcome the obstacles presented by nature, which could be subdued, and by the faults of man, which could be remedied. Society could remake and renew itself and bring itself closer to the conditions for ideal life.

In this permanent revolution, where the individual's own striving was backed by the social conscience of the successful and the social effort of voluntary groups, work had supreme value, success was a measure of individual worth, material well-being was a social objective, and freedom the favourable condition. These were not purely materialistic goals, as they often appeared to others. At its core, the American drive for material well-being was an expression of the refusal to accept poverty and misery as the necessary condition of man. In the American view, material well-being, health and education freed men to lead lives of human dignity. Because Americans believed profoundly in men's potentialities, they insisted that opportunity should be open to all who would work to achieve a better life for themselves and for their children.

Throughout the American experience, this fundamental vision was taken for granted, however far it was from realization in practice. There were sharp conflicts over how it might be realized; the simple faith in automatic progress wore thin and came to seem naïve; the shibboleths of individualism, freedom and enterprise were abused and made to sanction corporate power; prejudice and discrimination, especially against Negroes, mocked the principles of equality of opportunity. The small, indigenous Indian population, displaced in the process of settlement and relegated to reservations, was largely forgotten. In the process of eliminating the contradiction of slavery from a society committed to democracy and equality, civil war during the 1860s tore the country apart regionally and left an aftermath of regional poverty, bitterness and nostalgia that still continued to act as a drag on the realization of national ideals in the middle of the twentieth century.

But only small groups of extremists seriously questioned the basic tenets, while the people as a whole clung stubbornly to the faith that had brought them or their fathers or grandfathers to American shores. Even in the depths of the depression of the 1930s, radical alternatives had small appeal. Although Marxism attracted a number of intellectuals and some workers' groups, and fascism rallied some 'hate' groups, the great mass of the people at all levels remained confident that a way would be found within the framework of the democratic constitution and the enterprise system to re-establish the conditions within which they could live progressively fruitful lives.

Historic experience gave substantial reality to the social ideal. Initially it rested firmly on an agrarian tradition built up in the process of settlement. The land and climate, by and large, were friendly to man. Though the forests were dark and the prairies wide, the hills stony and the rivers dangerous in flood, the soil for the most part was fertile, rainfall was sufficient, mountain barriers could be crossed and the climate included neither the cold of the Arctic nor the tropical heat of jungle or desert. In such a land men of sturdy courage, endurance and ingenuity could carve out a livelihood for themselves. With the aid of favourable provisions for landholding, families cleared the land, established homesteads and either stayed to farm or again moved on. From the 1840s squatters could buy the land which they occupied at a minimum price; from the 1860s, the settler could claim a homestead of 160 acres merely by living on it and cultivating it. By this process of land settlement, democracy and individualism were firmly grounded in an agrarian base; in fact some historians attributed the genius of American political and social life to the repercussions on the total society of this moving frontier.

Simultaneously with the settlement of the continent, industry took root and grew, under conditions which made labour scarce and placed a high premium on mechanical ingenuity and labour-saving techniques. Through most of the nineteenth century the urban population grew even more rapidly than the rural, and after 1870 industrial expansion proceeded at an accelerated pace. Both land and industry drew a constant stream of peasant immigrants from every part of Europe, to mingle and form the American population.

These and other conditions of American life combined to sustain the basic self-image. America had no feudal heritage, and although class differences were marked, such classes as developed were of recent origin, and anyone could aspire to enter them. The 'self-made man' was a favourite American stereotype; successful politicians, business men, writers and professional men pointed with pride to their lowly beginnings. The class system was in continual flux; the saying, 'from shirtsleeves to shirtsleeves in three generations' expressed the assumption that class position was not static, but could only be kept by constant effort.

Americans took it for granted that they were in tune with the times and an example to others because the major tendencies of the modern world—industrial technology, capitalist enterprise, democratic principles and institutions—were the basic ingredients of their tradition. These were held in check by no previous pattern or structure, nor was there the need to repudiate conflicting elements of tradition in order to establish them on a revolutionary basis. The 'American system' had the full and continuous sanction of the American tradition and could thus be assumed to be in its essentials beyond question or debate.

But a society built on the sense of promise was bound to fall short and there were always many gaps between the dream and the actuality. From the start Americans were self-critical, for denial of the basic principles brought a sense of guilt and failure. Self-criticism and defensiveness—even violent expressions of prejudice—were reflections of the discomfort that Americans felt over the contradictions between ideals and daily life.

Moreover, the individualistic, competitive, open society, with its emphasis on success and its constant influx of new people, placed heavy psychic demands on the individual. In the wilderness or in the world of strangers, each man had to make his own place; he could not simply accept it. Self-reliance was a hard and lonely precept. It is not surprising that those from whom it demanded too much should have projected their anxieties on to others. As successive groups of immigrants filled the lowest paid jobs and occupied the poorest housing, each in turn—Irish, French-Canadian, Italian, Mexican—

met a recurrent stereotype which attributed the conditions of poverty and ignorance to supposedly inherent characteristics; as each group became established, its members joined in applying the stereotype to the latest arrivals. From time to time demagogues exploited the anxieties that lay beneath the surface and turned latent fears into bursts of hate.

American society was, by choice as well as geography, self-contained. The American people, in emigrating, had rejected the lands of their origin and cast their lot in the New World. They might feel sentimental toward the 'old country' or send money to relatives, but they did not want to look back or to become involved in Europe's affairs. Isolationism was the expression of people who saw their 'manifest destiny' within their own continent and whose aspirations took the form of a future for their children, not a place of power in the world.

In the course of the twentieth century the American self-image was subjected to many strains. In the first decades the flow of immigrants reached a peak and placed a heavy burden on the process of integration. The traditional assumption had been that anyone who came with the intention to make the United States his home became an American as soon as he landed, or at least as soon as he had taken out his naturalization papers. But at the height of the mass migration it became apparent that the 'melting pot' had not worked as rapidly and completely as some people had expected, though millions of peasants from many different countries, quite unaccustomed to democratic processes and urban industrial life, had learned to function effectively within the institutions of American society.

A wave of anti-immigration sentiment led to restrictive legislation after 1920 which brought to an end a long chapter in the history of both Europe and the United States. This legislation set quotas which discriminated against south and east Europeans—the most recent immigrant groups—on the charge that they were less 'assimilable', attributing to them the familiar stereotypes of poverty and ignorance. The quota system was to prove embarrassing in later years, when many of the children and grandchildren of Italian and Polish immigrants had risen to positions of prominence and leadership, but it remained for decades on the statute books, a monument to the uncertainty that beset a mixed people striving to be one.

The persistent failure to accord full equality of opportunity and status to racial minorities and even to ensure to Negro citizens their elementary rights remained a thorn in the American conscience and a source of conflict whose bitterness was enhanced by the underlying sense of guilt. Systematic attacks on discrimination slowly reduced obstacles to employment, education, political participation and the enjoyment of the amenities. Negroes never ceased to believe that American principles would ultimately be applied to them. But racial discrimination remained the major blot on American life in the eyes of Americans themselves.

The two world wars drew the United States out of its isolation and into world affairs.[14, 15] After the first conflict, the old desire to reject Europe reasserted itself with such strength as to prevent American participation in the League of Nations, though many people felt that the country was sufficiently mature to assume a share of world responsibility. But after the second world war the United States could not withdraw as it had before. Reluctantly the American people looked beyond their own preoccupations to world problems, taxed themselves to provide financial aid to other parts of the world, spent immense sums for military defence, and tried to play a role commensurate with the position in which they found themselves.

Economic development raised questions as to the adequacy of principles and methods formulated in other times. During the 1920s there was much self-criticism and discussion of the effects of machine civilization. Amid the speculative prosperity of the period, many people began to wonder whether equality, democracy and independence were compatible with the monotony and regimentation of factory life. The depression of the 1930s shook the faith in the American dream. Where was liberty, with no place to go? Where was the American standard of living, with no job? Especially, where was self-respect, with no work? Since success was the culturally established goal, its absence left people without a sense of direction and with the awful weight of failure. The experience was particularly shattering to the many children of immigrants who came of age in these years, for they had learned to identify Americanism with a high standard of living and success, yet they found the door of opportunity closed to them. It left a deep mark upon the American outlook and aroused the desire for security in a society which had hitherto been mainly concerned with opportunity.

But one of the most persistent components in the American tradition was the spirit of reform which kept Americans always working at the unfinished business of removing the injustices and imperfections in their society. The New Deal of the 1930s, which refashioned many institutions in response to the depression, was in this tradition. It was a pragmatic effort to make American institutions work better, not to discard them, and it sought to meet the problems of a modern capitalist economy within the framework of freedom and democracy. It restored to the American people the sense that their own fundamental principles and habitual approach to problems gave them the means to pursue their course under the new conditions of modern economic life.

The growth of large-scale organization brought further problems. Bureaucracies in government, industry and labour organization replaced much of the individual enterprise which had had its roots in the small shop and family farm. In the years after the second world war, Americans became conscious of the 'organization man' and of a tendency for people to rely on others for their ideas and sense of direction rather than on themselves. Sociologists found some signs of greater class rigidity, but under pressure of heavy progressive taxation lower economic levels rose faster than upper, closing the gap in patterns of living. Initiative and enterprise retained high cultural value and continued to be expressed in business and community life. The aspirations of people in all walks of life were increasingly defined in terms of common standards of consumption and welfare.

The continuing proof to Americans of their way of life was the success of the American experiment. Although they recognized that good fortune had brought a continent into their hands at a crucial time in world history, the American people nevertheless regarded their prosperity, the stability of their society in an unstable world and the progressive extension of their democracy as evidence of the validity of their principles. In the nineteenth century they had seen their experience as unique because they were engaged in establishing a democratic way of life in an untamed continent. In the twentieth century they still believed it to be unique, for they were the first to develop an economy of plenty on the basis of modern technology—the first major society which did not rest on a substratum of exploitable poor.

At mid-century many Americans were asking themselves whether, in achieving affluence, they were in fact attaining their goal. Did highways crowded with private cars, generously stocked supermarkets, ever extending suburbs, and countless forms of convenience, comfort and entertainment add up to the good life? Did the persistence of unresolved social problems—bad housing, over-crowded schools, water pollution—reflect too great a preoccupation with private satisfaction at the expense of public responsibility? Were people becoming soft and losing their sense of purpose? Yet even in asking themselves these questions Americans continued to assume that their way was not merely right for themselves but a valuable example to others.

Abraham Lincoln remained America's most authentic voice. The millions of Americans who climbed the steps of the Lincoln Memorial in the nation's capital to stand before the gaunt, compassionate figure of the Great Emancipator felt that here, more than anywhere, they were in the presence of America's spirit. It was Lincoln's vision of human dignity in freedom that they too, however awkwardly, sought to realize. And though they could accept intellectually the fact that other peoples in other cultures might pursue other values, in their hearts they believed, with Lincoln, that 'the spirit which prizes liberty' is the heritage of 'all men, in all lands, everywhere'.

2. Canada

Canada, which shared the continent with the United States, shared also the same pioneer spirit. It, too, was a democratic society on the upgrade devoted to work, committed to the principle of equality, composed of immigrants striving to make good, pragmatic in its approach to life and proud of its material achievements.

But Canada had much that gave it an outlook quite distinct from that of its more populous neighbour. Its land and climate were harder to tame and to endure. A large part of its vast territory lay north of the Arctic Circle, and in much of the rest the climate was severe. Only a narrow strip from east to west could be peopled by the kind of frontier settlement that spread across the United States. Canada's frontier lay to the north, and here advance depended on science and technology—on new strains of wheat that could mature in the short growing season, on magnetic aerial prospecting and the new demand for uranium and cobalt, on airlifts to sustain Arctic settlements.

Canada's was a bi-cultural society. The majority of its population was English-speaking and predominantly Protestant. Its French population had been allowed to retain 'the benefit and use of their own laws, usages and customs' when Britain acquired the area from France in the eighteenth century, and French Canada never ceased to insist on the right to its characteristic way of life. It was an essentially peasant society, conservative, and deeply devoted to the Catholic Church which played a central role in the community's life. The Canadian outlook and virtually every aspect of Canadian society were affected by the need to accommodate distinct cultural groups, to tolerate wide disparities and to maintain an atmosphere of mutual respect which would enable all elements to move forward together as Canadians. Canadians became masters of the art of creating and sustaining a working partnership.

The British empire provided the framework within which Canada worked out its difficult problems of geography and population. In this relationship, too, the key was partnership. Within the flexible structure of the empire, Canada moved toward autonomy and independence without ever breaking with the mother country and it made a nation out of small, widely separated islands of population. In the process, it had the effect of transforming the British empire into the Commonwealth, for each step in this transformation from the Durham reforms of 1838 to the Statute of Westminister in 1931, was worked out to accommodate the situation and meet the demands of Canada, the most politically developed and independent unit of the empire, and the other dominions became the beneficiaries of the process.

With a small and slowly growing population and an enormous, difficult terrain, Canada's schemes for development and her institutional structure generally ran ahead of the actualities. Whereas in the United States people were repeatedly breaking out beyond the bounds, in movement of population and in all manner of activities, so that formal institutions and orderly processes of government kept having to catch up, Canada repeatedly developed the institutional framework before the people were there to use it. The symbol of Canada's frontier was the Royal Canadian Mounted Police—the red-coated 'Mounty'—in contrast to the image of the 'wild west' in the United States. Individual initiative was prized, but Canadians took it for granted that public action was necessary to create the conditions where it could be exercised.

As the smaller partner in close working relations with the United States, Canada was at some pains to preserve her interest and identity. The sheer size of the United States and its prior industrial development made it a magnet attracting Canadians in search of opportunity. Large numbers of rural–urban migrants crossed the border to the growing cities of the United States. From 1850 to 1950 emigration from Canada practically equalled immigration into the country from abroad; nearly a million Canadian-born were living in the United States in 1950, as compared with a total Canadian population of 14,000,000. Canadians and Americans were linked through common organizations—labour unions, professional bodies, religious, business and voluntary groups—with Canadians, of course, habitually in the minority. Here again, Canada's ability to maintain integrity within a partnership relationship kept her identity and inner drive intact.

In the middle of the twentieth century Canadians saw themselves as just beginning to unlock the unlimited wealth of their frozen north, with the aid of science, with their capacity to develop the necessary institutions and with a people undeterred by hardship. As a leader within the British commonwealth and an increasingly strong member of the North American partnership, Canada was in a position to benefit and draw strength from both associations. On the basis of their success in accommodating a bi-cultural society and in adjusting their internal and external relations, Canadians believed that they had a unique contribution to make to a world in which nations and peoples desperately needed to find practical ways of living and working together.

3. Hispanic American Countries

The countries of South and Central America fall into two groups, those with a basically Indian and mixed population, such as Mexico, Guatemala, Ecuador, Peru and Bolivia and those which, like Canada and the United States, were essentially the product of European settlement, although minorities of indigenous populations might remain as islands or have contributed substantially to the racial composition of the general population. The latter countries included Spanish-speaking Argentina, Uruguay, Colombia, Chile, Venezuela, Paraguay, and some of the countries around the Caribbean, as well as Portuguese-speaking Brazil.

Each of the Hispanic countries had its distinctive history and character. They shared a common language and expression, a similar layout of their cities and towns according to the pattern prescribed by their Spanish ruler in the sixteenth century, and the beginning of their national histories in the period of liberation from Spain around 1820. The identity of the several countries after independence had corresponded in part to Spanish administrative jurisdictions, but boundaries were uncertain and conflicts between neighbouring states were part of the history of most countries during the first hundred years of their existence; the great statue of the Christ of the Andes, erected in 1902 on the border between Chile and Argentina, symbolized the termination of one of these long conflicts. The formation of the Organization of American States in 1948 with its mutual security system did much to reduce inter-American tensions and to promote co-operation in meeting common problems in the mid-twentieth century.

Most of these countries found the principal market for their products in the United States and this country was the major source of foreign investment, though much Argentine wheat and meat went to Britain. Inevitably they resented this dependence on their larger and richer neighbour while at the same time they felt a common bond with it, for the American republics from the start had maintained an identity of interest *vis-à-vis* any European power which might seek to establish or re-establish dominion in the western hemisphere. Culturally they looked to Europe rather than to the United States, except in respect to economic affairs. This ambivalent attitude toward the United States fluctuated with changing circumstances, changing leadership and changing policies on the part of the United States. In the nationalistic, anticolonial atmosphere of the mid-twentieth century, anti-United States sentiment was often an expression of the growing national aspirations of the Latin American peoples.

Among the individual Hispanic-American states, Argentina was the most economically developed and drew its population from the most varied European sources. During the first quarter of the twentieth century it became one of the world's important food producers, not only for the meat raised on its broad pampas but, as dry farming permitted the extension of grain cultivation into its southern plains, for wheat as well. Industrial development received a stimulus during both world wars and from the vigorous efforts of the régime of Juan Perón in the 1940s and 1950s to achieve economic self-sufficiency.

In time, the cattle-raising *gauchos* were overshadowed by the growth of large cities peopled in substantial part by Italian, German and other immigrants. Especially after the United States closed its doors to free immigration in the 1920s, Argentina was a principal destination for European emigration, and its rapidly growing population of varied European origins distinguished the country from those on the Pacific coast whose people remained predominantly of colonial origin, as well as from the countries which rested on a broad Indian base. Its size, wealth and vigour gave it a position of leadership among the Hispanic-American republics, not only in economic development but in intellectual fields through a lively press and publishing industry. This leadership was lost in the 1940s and 1950s when for a dozen years the country came under the only fascist-type dictator to rise in the western hemisphere, Juan Perón; but after Perón's fall in 1955 Argentina again took its place as a vigorous member of the Latin American family of nations.

Chile went far toward developing the features of a welfare state and provided both an example to other countries and trained personnel to man their services. From the 1920s it developed an elaborate system of social insurance which grew in the 1950s into one of the most comprehensive health services in the world. It took the lead in the training of social workers and in placing the expanding social services on a professional basis. It was in the forefront in national economic planning with the establishment of the Chilean Development Corporation in 1939 to provide an approach to overall national development.

Others of the Hispanic countries had their distinctive characteristics and roles. Uruguay proudly maintained a continuous record of stable democracy; it was so intent on guarding against one-man rule that it placed the executive power in a nine-man presidential council instead of in a single president. Colombia retained a particularly strong Catholic tradition and prided itself on the purity of its Spanish speech. Cut into a series of high plateaux and valleys and little affected by recent immigration, it developed strong regional differences focused in a number of vigorous urban centres. Partisan cleavages with deep historic roots, however, broke the political stability which the country had enjoyed until 1948 and created a state of uncertainty which stood in the way of efforts to take advantage of large, undeveloped territory and resources and to raise the economic and social levels of its people. Venezuela, rich in oil and minerals which were exploited mainly with foreign capital, drew on these sources to provide an ample public treasury, but long years of dictatorship left a backlog of limited social development which the country was vigorously striving to overcome in the late 1950s.

4. *Brazil*

Much the largest of the basically European countries of Latin America and one of the most rapidly growing was Brazil. With a territory equal to the entire continent of Europe or to the United States, and distinguished by its Portuguese language and colonial history from the Spanish-speaking republics, Brazil saw itself as a culture and people in the making.

Up to the middle of the twentieth century vast areas of the country remained unsettled, and the majority of Brazil's more than 50,000,000 people were still concentrated on the coastal plain and in the central coffee-growing and mining plateau regions. Much of the Brazilian terrain was unfriendly and difficult of access, with its untamable tropical jungles and immense menacing rivers. It was filled with dangers—from poisonous snakes and insects, tropical diseases and attacks by nomadic Indians.

Yet most parts of the country had already been penetrated by the end of the eighteenth century. At a time when North American settlers had spread only a sixth of the distance across their continent, Brazilian frontiersmen, *bandeirantes*, had been driving their herds from pasture to pasture or founding wilderness settlements in nearly every region. But unlike frontier settlements in the United States which retained contact with centres of population and culture and thus constituted the forward line of an advancing civilization, those of the Brazilian hinterland lived an isolated, self-sufficient life of their own, out of touch with the people of the coast.

The main segment of the Brazilian population, economy and society was made up of large estates, slave-owning until the last decade of the nineteenth century, devoted to sugar or coffee cultivation or to mining. Plantations—*fazenda*—raising sugar in the tropical areas and coffee in the uplands, with their patterns of big house and slave quarters, provided the basis for a rural aristocracy which furnished the wealth of the country and its patriarchal upper class. Considerable racial mixture partially bridged the gulf between Europeans and the Africans who continued to be brought as slaves until the middle of the nineteenth century and remained in slavery until 1888. In 1872 the mulattoes were estimated at a fifth and slaves at a seventh of the total population. In the middle of the twentieth century, a third of the population was estimated as of mulatto or Negro stock.

In no other country of the old world or the new was the process of racial amalgamation so fully achieved as in Brazil. The heritage of slavery continued to be reflected in the low economic status of the darker elements of the population; prominent persons of mixed ancestry seldom if ever boasted of their African heredity, though they might often point with pride to Indian elements in their background; immigration policy in the twentieth century encouraged European immigrants rather than those from the Caribbean or Africa—or, after a brief period when Japanese immigration was welcomed, from Asia. But the relatively little racial prejudice which Portuguese settlers generally displayed had laid a basis for racial amalgamation and for the racial attitudes of Brazil in the twentieth century.

The rural aristocracy of the coastal region constituted a small cultivated *élite*. This type of *élite* was characteristic of all the countries of Latin America, where a quasi-feudal economic system provided little or no means for the basic population to partake of the cultural life of the country.

The back country was another world. Here, neither big house nor slave, neither riches nor such wide social distance characterized the frontiersmen, herders, ranchers or the people of the small towns which served as market centres for the nuclei of population in the hinterland. Here, in the plateau of the back country, ethnic and social mixture went on constantly, and Brazilian popular culture gradually took shape during the years of colonial rule and of continued feudal dominion in the nineteenth century. It was from this popular culture and native base that much of the vitality for the definition of a distinctly Brazilian outlook and self-image emerged in the twentieth century.

The distinctive course of Brazil as a new country in process of defining itself was partly conditioned by the relations which had existed with the mother country in the period of colonial rule and the half-century after independence. In contrast to Spain, which had poured much cultural energy into its empire in the New World, designing cities, establishing universities and developing centres of rich living and high culture, Portugal's interest in her Brazilian colony had been chiefly economic. The first professional schools in Brazil were established at the beginning of the nineteenth century more than 350 years after the founding of the University of Mexico and the University of San Marcos in Peru. While many cities of the Spanish colonial empire had been centres of wealth and culture, Brazilian cities had been poor towns of petty merchants; the real wealth and culture had been centred in the big houses of the rural aristocracy. The small Brazilian intelligentsia had been trained in Portugal.

Separation from the mother country was achieved in 1823 without the kind of heroic struggle which characterized the Bolivarian wars of independence against Spain; the regent himself declared the country to be independent. And during much of the nineteenth century, while many of the Hispanic republics were experiencing great political instability, Brazil enjoyed the continuous fifty-year reign of her emperor, Dom Pedro (1840–89). Throughout the period, the old social structure remained virtually unchanged, while the available education perpetuated the traditional literary-juridical mentality and did little to develop the outlook and skills to cope with the Brazilian milieu.

The downfall of the empire in 1889, like the earlier separation from Portugal, was brought about from the top, by the very elements which had enjoyed prestige and power—the Church, the army and the rural aristocracy. The Catholic Church, which occupied the status of state church under the constitution of 1823, objected to the disciplining of clerics who were outspoken against the régime; the military resented the fact that they were kept out of politics; and the rural aristocracy turned against the régime when it replaced the gradual, compensated emancipation of the slaves by outright, unrecompensed abolition. A military coup established a republic and set Brazil on a course of modernization.

The republican constitution adopted in 1891 was modelled essentially on that of the United States in its provision for a federal system, a bicameral legislature and periodically elected president, the separation of church and state and the declaration of certain civil rights. Much of its spirit was provided by the positivist philosophy of Auguste Comte, whose words 'Order and Progress' appeared on the Brazilian flag. Although this political orientation and structure was repeatedly threatened by the military, which tried to intervene when the operation of the political system did not seem to its liking, it provided the framework for a vigorous approach to industrialization and to encouragement of economic development.

The doors to immigration were opened wide, and Brazil received a substantial portion of the great flood which poured out of Europe in the last decades of the nineteenth and early part of the twentieth century. Two-thirds of the white population in 1940 were of other than Portuguese stock, mainly Italian and other south European. Many of the immigrants were settled on the land in colonies established under the supervision of the government or on large estates, where they retained their language, educational institutions and cultural patterns, and mingled little with Brazilians of other origins.

After the formation of the republic the cultural ties with Europe were not broken, but the chief cultural link was with France. Paris, the 'city of light' which attracted so many painters, writers and students from Europe and the New World, became a main source of cultural influence on the intelligentsia of the new Brazil. Major economic ties were with the United States.

The first world war gave an impetus to Brazil's process of coming of age. Although its direct participation in military operations consisted only of a medical mission and a few ships, the decision to participate was a reflection of its sense of status, and it earned Brazil a place at the peace table and a temporary seat on the Council of the League of Nations. It thus, in a sense, marked the début of Brazil on the international scene outside the western hemisphere.

Brazil's new sense of identity was strongly reflected in the modernist movement in art and literature which began in 1922 with an exhibit of modern arts in São Paulo in that year. This movement was not simply an extension of the literary and artistic movements which had taken shape in Europe before the first world war and were being taken up throughout the occidental culture areas, including various movements in the Hispanic countries of Latin America which called themselves 'ultra-modernist' or 'vanguardist'.

The central characteristic of the Brazilian modernist movement was that it was bitterly and violently anti-European. However much it might owe to currents of thought and style which originated or were nourished in Europe, its spirit was one of rebellion and protest not simply against tradition but against European dominance. It was an intensification of the same spirit of Brazilian nationalism which had found expression before; at the time of independence it had taken the form of romantic treatment of native Brazilian themes—nature, the idealized Indian, the romantic figure of the *bandeirante*; after the establishment of the republic, it was reflected in the acclaim accorded to Euclides da Cunha for his novel dealing with a rebel fanatic of the back country—*Os sertões* (1902).

Up to the 1930s, however, the course of Brazilian development had still not broken through the old social structure and pattern of life, though the great new centres of urban society had already grown spectacularly. Rio, freed of yellow fever in the first decade of the century, became one of the world's great capital cities, and São Paulo, in addition to serving as the prosperous port for the coffee country, took on the characteristics of a thriving industrial centre. By the 1930s industrial production exceeded agricultural in value, although industrial activity was still largely limited to the processing of agricultural products in the food and textile industries. The prosperity of the country from the late nineteenth century on still flowed almost entirely into the hands of the old patriarchal upper-class *élite*, except for the largely self-contained agricultural prosperity of some of the colonies of immigrants, notably some of the German settlers in the state of São Paulo. Illiteracy remained widespread and poverty characterized the lot of the vast majority of the population, on the land and in the urban slums. Even in 1950 hardly more than half the children of primary school age were in school.

From the 1930s on, national efforts were directed toward the development of a distinctively Brazilian, modern society, capable of realizing the potentialities of the vast country, exploiting its material and human riches and building for Brazil a distinctive culture and place in the world. A series of educational reforms laid out an extensive system of primary, secondary, normal and university education. In the next two decades some twenty universities were established—public universities in the capitals of most states, and Catholic universities in five of the principal cities. Key members of some of the faculties were recruited abroad, chiefly in France, Italy and Germany.

Numbers of technical and specialized schools in all fields were set up with great rapidity, often in advance of the availability of teaching personnel. More than a third of all the schools of social work in the Latin American republics, for example, were located in Brazil in the 1950s. The first school of public administration in South America was instituted in Brazil in 1955. In one field after another Brazil, which had been late to start, forged ahead, proliferating institutions and organizations, initiating new efforts, giving vent to its ambitions during these years. Education and the related fields of publishing, press, radio, bookselling, and the beginnings of active social research were only a few of the directions in which Brazil showed the vigour of a young country shaping its outlook, its people and its culture.

The older policy of group settlement, which encouraged or resulted in the maintenance of national minorities with their own languages and institutions, gave way to a policy of Brazilianization. The educational reforms of the 1930s required all teaching of basic subjects to be carried on in the Brazilian language. Immigration policy was adjusted with a view to bringing in immigrants who would contribute directly to the building up of the country and the open policy of the early part of the century was modified to achieve this purpose.

A series of political changes were reflected in the revision of the Brazilian constitution to provide among other things for greater centralization and for the assumption of economic responsibilities by the state. Social legislation of an advanced character was enacted. Brazil was the first of the Latin American republics to attempt to extend the benefits of its social security and other welfare programmes on a large scale to the rural population. From the 1930s on, a strong national Catholic revival brought the Church more actively into the process of shaping modern Brazilian life, with the founding of a series of pontifical universities, a successful campaign for religious education in the schools and active participation in welfare programmes.

In the middle of the twentieth century Brazil was still in the process of defining itself, seeking to find its own ground in the midst of conflicting world tendencies. It was committed to democratic principles by its first republican constitution in 1891, but actual practice and later constitutional revisions revealed uncertainty as to the extent and nature of this commitment. The dictator, Getulio Vargas, seized power in 1930 in contravention of the constitution and held it with military support for fifteen years; eight years later, he was returned to power by a democratic election. In the constitutions of 1934 and 1946, individual rights were assured in less complete terms than in the constitution of the United States and of other democratic countries; freedom of speech, for example, was specifically limited. Voting was not universal, but was confined to those who could read and write, a substantial limitation in a country where, in 1950, adult illiteracy was still estimated at 52 per cent. In the economic sphere principles of capitalism and private enterprise were generally accepted and assumed; but the constitutions of 1934 and 1946 included specific statements of the power and responsibility of the state to intervene, not only in order to supply basic services, but to break any monopoly in private hands.

Brazil was clear in principle on the issue of racial integration and amalgamation; one of the constitutional limitations on freedom of speech was directed against the expression of racial prejudice. But even this wholehearted principle was qualified by the policy of encouraging European immigration and limiting that of other racial elements. Religious liberty was clearly established in principle, and the presence of a substantial Protestant minority attested to the reality of the religious guarantees; but the traditionally Catholic character of the culture, strengthened by the Catholic revival, tended to convert Catholic attitudes into public policies; in response to strong Catholic pressure the complete prohibition on divorce was retained in the constitution of 1946.

The conflict was still unresolved between the traditional society—aristocratic and personal, patriarchal, literary and juridical—and the modern trends toward a democratic, practical, scientific, industrial way of life.

As Brazil looked toward its role as a growing state and a potential large power, it sought to open up and exploit its remaining territory and to build an internally integrated economic and political structure—a far easier task in the modern days of motor roads, aeroplanes and the extension of railways than in the time of the *bandeirantes* whose frontier settlements had lost touch with the coastal areas. But it brought in its wake severe inflationary pressures that threatened to undermine efforts to lay the basis for economic expansion.

The ultimate evidence of the determination to base its national development squarely on its land and the masses of its people was the decision to move the seat of government away from the bustling, cosmopolitan coastal city of Rio de Janeiro and to build in brilliantly modern style a new capital, Brasilia, in the interior of the country.

With its vast territory and resources, its varied ethnic stocks, its rapidly growing population and its immense vitality, Brazil asserted its leadership increasingly within the system of American states and it looked forward to taking its place in the coming century as one of the major nations of the world.

5. Australia and New Zealand

Australia and New Zealand were outposts of the British empire. In contrast to the United States with its mixed population and Canada with its French minority, the lands 'down under' were British in population, in culture and in their dependence on the British empire for their existence. Until the second world war they assumed that the British empire was a permanent institution and the basis for their survival. Their identification with the empire and sense of dependence upon it were well reflected in their contributions to its preservation. In the first world war Australian casualties practically equalled those of the United States, although the population of Australia was hardly more than 5 per cent as great; in New Zealand some 40 per cent of men eligible for military service volunteered, and a large proportion failed to return.

It was not until after the second world war that these countries emerged as self-reliant entities. With the British empire in Asia gone, they found themselves on their own, small countries, far from the parent to which they had been linked. The role of Australia in the United Nations showed the change. In the early formative days of that organization it was the Australian delegate, Dr. H. V. Evatt, who led the movement to give a larger role to the Assembly in order that the voices of the small nations might be heard. Australia thus stood as a spokesman for the small nations, no longer merely as a segment of the British empire.

The history of Australia in the nineteenth century was the history of conflict among economic groups over the kind of society to be established on the continent. Because of the distance and the cost of emigration, most settlers came with governmental assistance rather than by the sort of free, undirected immigration which peopled the United States and Canada. Settlement, therefore, always involved public policy and the issue of what kind of country was being built, while the harsh, arid continent set severe limits to the kinds of settlement which were possible beyond the areas along the coasts.

For more than sixty years Australia was used as a penal colony, but before transportation of convicts was finally discontinued in 1853 free settlers had introduced sheep raising and had begun to make Australian wool famous. In contrast to the homesteaders who opened up the United States, Australian ranchers acquired large areas of arid terrain for grazing operations. Under a policy designed to keep a labour supply available by preventing the easy acquisition of land, lands were offered for sale with no limit on the size of the holdings and half of the proceeds were used for assisting further migration. When a short-lived gold rush in the 1850s left many diggers seeking homesteads after their diggings failed, there were pressures on behalf of small settlers. But measures to permit homesteading in the 1860s and after brought conflict with the ranchers and the climate made homesteading difficult if not impossible in all but a small part of the country.

Australia thus developed as a country not of small farmers but of large operators and labourers—of large ranchers, mining companies and shipping firms rather than of small enterprises, and of migrant sheep shearers and ranch workers, miners and maritime or other workers in the coastal cities rather than independent cultivators. In this situation strong labour unions were formed early. Men with union ideas and experience from Britain organized sheep shearers, miners and dock workers into large unions which extended beyond local political divisions.

In the second half of the nineteenth century the issue was joined as to whether the country should be developed for the big owners of ranches, mines, sugar-cane plantations and shipping companies or whether it should be developed for the workers. Owners sought to exploit the resources of the continent with whatever labour they could secure; workers insisted that the continent should be developed for the benefit of the common man under conditions which would offer a decent standard of living. The 'white Australia' policy emerged from this struggle, originally directed against the Chinese brought in to work in the mines and then broadened into a general opposition to the importation of labour from Asia and the Pacific. Organized workers fought and finally outlawed the system by which plantation labourers for the sugar-cane fields were being recruited from the Pacific islands under conditions closely approaching forced labour. In time the 'white Australia' policy came to be used as a broad limitation on the free immigration of Asians to Australia.[16]

During the 1890s the big owners scored a temporary victory when they beat down massive strikes of sheep shearers, miners and maritime workers by force and with the aid of the police and the courts. But their victory was short-lived, for labour, defeated on the economic front, turned to political action and formed the first Labour party to achieve power in any country. It set up a unique system of labour arbitration and enacted a body of social legislation which put Australia in the forefront of the movement toward the welfare state.

In the twentieth century Australia saw itself as a new society committed to maintaining for all the people, through organized effort, a high minimum standard of living which would give an opportunity for all, not to become rich but to live decent lives. Self-critics in the middle years of the century complained that Australia was not keeping up with other countries—Britain, the Scandinavian countries, New Zealand—in the welfare field which she had pioneered in the years before the first world war. But the system of minimum wages, union organization, social insurance and social services provided the means for absorbing large numbers of penniless immigrants after the second world war at the levels already established for Australians, without permitting their influx to undermine wage levels, place an undue burden on social services or disrupt the pattern of life.

Australia did not see itself as a land of individualism, in spite of the lonely sheep stations and the self-reliance of the people. Its very distance from Europe made it especially conscious of the importance of world ties. Its history of economic conflict made it conscious of the need for collective action. Its uncompromising terrain and climate, which required more than endurance and ingenuity to make headway against drought, soil deficiency, pests and disease, made Australians especially conscious of the dependence of man on the applications of science.

One scientific conquest after another changed the agricultural outlook on a grand scale. Intensive research developed drought- and rust-resistant strains of wheat which made Australia one of the world's great bread-baskets; the rabbit pest was conquered by the spread of a disease, the prickly pear cactus which was taking over land at the rate of a million acres a year was driven back by the release of a moth, and the identification of trace elements missing from the soil virtually doubled the land area which could be brought under cultivation. Equally spectacular results were envisaged in the development of mineral resources and industry.

In the mid-twentieth century Australia was still a land which was building a society in terms of a decent standard of living for all. But by then it could take for granted its old tools of labour organization and social security which had become permanent features of its social and governmental structure, and it was placing major emphasis on the contributions of science. The heart of its development programme after the second world war was a nation-wide organization for scientific research and development, and it was indicative of the light in which Australia saw itself that the young university at Canberra should seek to develop a centre for the physical sciences which would be second to none and would attract the ablest and most creative scientific minds that could be found anywhere in the world.

New Zealand's short history since the beginning of European settlement in the 1840s and its population of only 2,000,000 by the mid-twentieth century, made it very much aware that it was young and small in relation to the position in which it found itself in the world. Some of its spokesmen attributed to this situation New Zealand's great concern with education and welfare, for every individual counted and must be developed and protected —and also its special combination of individualism and governmental support.

On the basis of its favourable soil and climate, New Zealand attained a high level of productivity—it claimed the highest *per capita* agricultural productivity in the world—and a commensurately high level of living for its people. With few extremes of wealth or poverty, it could insist that its high *per capita* income more truly reflected the condition of all the people than did the high average incomes of some other countries which covered wider disparities. Its social welfare system was one of the most comprehensive in existence.

But as a small, isolated people, New Zealanders faced central problems which were driven home to them by the collapse of world markets in the 1930s, the war in the Pacific and the constant emigration of many of their ablest men. How far should New Zealand try to develop a self-contained life, and how far should it continue to produce meat and other foods for world consumption and depend upon imports for many of its needs? What was involved in sustaining its high living standards in a crowded world? And could so small a country develop a rich cultural life which would hold its highly educated people, or must it continue to expect its distinguished sons, such as the great atomic physicist Ernest Rutherford, to find better opportunities to make their contribution away from the land of their birth?

III. CULTURAL REORIENTATION OF MIXED SOCIETIES: MEXICO

In the regions of Central and South America once dominated by the great empires of the Aztecs, Incas and Mayas, a European overlay rested on a broad Indian foundation. Here, developments of the twentieth century took the form of a cultural reorientation and a movement toward integration which brought to prominence the Indian heritage. The process involved a social revolution through which depressed classes and isolated peoples moved toward full citizenship.

Mexico led the way in this process, which was still very far from complete at the middle of the century. The Mexican revolution of 1910 set in motion both a social revolution and what has been termed 'the reconquest of Mexico by the Indian'. The result was not only to alter the class structure but to change racial and cultural values until it was no longer a source of prestige to be 'European' but an expression of pride to call oneself 'Indian'. The impact of the new self-image which the revolution brought to the people of Mexico did not stop with the country where it originated but penetrated throughout the Indian-based societies of Central America and the Andean region.

The population of these countries was composed of three main elements, European, Indian and *mestizo*. The small European overlay consisted of the descendants of European conquerors and later settlers. Since much of the European migration had been of men alone, a very large proportion of the population was *mestizo*, of mixed Indian and European ancestry. But at the opening of the twentieth century large Indian populations in Mexico, Guatemala, Ecuador, Bolivia and Peru, and smaller ones in other countries had been barely touched by European ways and were isolated from the national life. In 1950 estimates placed this culturally Indian population still at 20 per cent in Mexico, 40 per cent in Ecuador and Peru, and 55 per cent in Bolivia and Guatemala.

In each of these countries, at the opening of the century, a small, wealthy Europeanized *élite* ruled over an illiterate and impoverished people, enjoying virtual monopoly of land and other wealth, political and military force and social prestige. Although the cities which had been great centres of culture in the colonial period had lost some of their imperial baroque splendour in the stormy years after independence, the old landowning families still made up an aristocratic society. They identified themselves culturally with Europe and lived a cultivated life in their town houses facing the central plaza or in the 'big house' on their estates, sending their sons to officer the army, to manage the sugar estates, to enter the liberal professions and fields of learning, and to man the upper ranks of the highly personal bureaucracy.

The masses of the people who remained outside this cultural milieu were divided into two main elements, those who continued to live as Indians within the structure of their traditional communal culture, geographically isolated, on islands within the Europeanized society, and those who lived and worked as peasant-labourers, often in a state of quasi-serfdom on the large estates, or in the mines, or as industrial workers in the towns. The small middle class of merchants, foremen and urban artisans were generally made up of *mestizos* and such special groups as Jews or Syrians, some of whom had recently immigrated to the area.

The racial, economic and cultural elements of this divided society were variously defined in different regions. The *ladino* might be distinguished from both Indian and white, as in much of Central America, or the general category of 'white' might embrace all who were not clearly Indian or Negro; 'Indian' might mean, specifically, those who lived within the Indian communal village structure, or it might simply mean 'poor, rural and backward' and be applied without limitation of race. Whatever the pattern, however, the Indian was depreciated as culturally inferior; 'European' carried prestige and these attitudes were everywhere reinforced by strong class feeling.

Although the constitutions of the Latin American republics, drawn up at the time of independence, were democratic in words and were generally modelled on that of the United States, the social reality was thus inconsistent with the political formulation. The wide gap which separated the upper *élite* from the mass of the people was bridged only by the paternalism of master or quasi-feudal landlord. The Catholic Church discouraged racial discrimination but sanctioned the class division and bade the lower classes accept their status and respect the authority of their masters.

The Mexican revolution which began in 1910 cut through this pattern. It was started by intellectuals with democratic ideals but little interest in social reform who attacked the political tyranny of Porfirio Díaz and the denial of democratic processes by his dictatorial régime which had been in power for more than forty years. In the years which followed the dictator's fall, it was joined by other groups who pressed the leaders to include their demands in the revolution's aims, and it became an economic and social revolution against the quasi-feudal structure of society.

The groups which rose to take advantage of the revolution and to make it the expression of their hopes were first of all the peasants, under Emilio

Zapata, who demanded land and an end to the *latifundia* system. They were joined by the urban workers whose unions took shape within political clubs and whose military battalions organized the workers in each town where they were victorious. Workers' participation in the revolution led to the inclusion in the Mexican constitution of 1917 of the most advanced labour law in the world at that time. Since most of the industrial expansion under Díaz—mines, transport, industries—had been developed with foreign capital, the workers' movement had a strongly nationalist, anti-foreign character and drew to it other nationalist elements.

The Mexican revolution was led by no disciplined party or group and followed no single ideology. Only after seventeen years did a National Revolutionary party take shape, secure election to office and undertake to institutionalize the revolution. The course of the revolution and the policy of its leaders veered in different directions from time to time, accelerating or slowing down the process of land distribution, intensifying or relaxing the antagonism to foreign investors, becoming anticlerical or tolerating the Church. But it never lost its popular methods and intent.

The direct effects of the revolution were many. It destroyed the *latifundia* system, releasing the peasants from their dependence on and bondage to the semi-feudal landlord. It reduced the position of the Church, excluding it from the field of education, nationalizing Church property and restricting the activity of the clergy. It initiated a wide range of social and educational reforms. It gave a place to organized labour. It brought a renaissance in the arts which combined the use of indigenous forms and the expression of modern social themes, to make Mexican mural painting one of the outstanding forms of creative expression in the twentieth century. And it made the Indian no longer a debased drag on Mexico's progress but an authentic representative of its people and its spirit.

At mid-century Mexico still had a long way to go to reach the goal of economic and social reconstruction and cultural integration. Although the incorporation of the Indian into Mexican national life was greatly accelerated by the revolution and much national effort was devoted to programmes designed to enable the Indian population to raise its living standards and move out of its isolation, an estimated quarter of the Indian population in the 1950s was still living in extreme poverty. Though the *latifundia* system had been broken, great contrasts of wealth and poverty persisted, and the rate of economic expansion barely kept ahead of population increase.

It was the new sense of dignity which Mexicans found in the reintegration of their Indian heritage which made the contribution of Mexico's revolution unique. The drive toward integration of cultures and peoples had appeared recurrently in Mexican history—initially in the attitude of the conquerors toward the Indian as a soul to be Christianized and the acceptance of intermarriage, at the time of independence in the concepts of political equality formulated by the *mestizo* leader José María Morelos, and in the mid-nineteenth century in the rise of the Indian, Benito Juárez, to be chief justice and then president of Mexico. Now Mexico offered to the world the first demonstration in modern times that a people could express its self-respect in terms which it had formerly despised. In a world where European superiority was still almost unchallenged, it was an assertion of human dignity for the mixed-blood to be able to boast that he was Indian instead of apologizing for being only partly white. At mid-century Mexico remained an outstanding example of the successful integration and reorientation of races and cultures.

The same reorientation of cultural values which accompanied the Mexican revolution was under way in all the countries with predominantly Indian and *mestizo* populations by the middle of the twentieth century. It had still not broken the hold of the old society in most countries; only Bolivia had effected a major social revolution involving the distribution of land. The Aprista movement in Peru had been repeatedly suppressed and in Guatemala, in spite of a start at land reform, the gulf between Indian and *ladino* was still wide. But the direction of movement was clear and the old *élites* were on the defensive or in retreat. The framework within which national policies were debated and shaped was provided by the Indian heritage and racial stock as well as by the European currents that continued to flow through the life of the continent.

The dynamic for the economic reorganization and cultural integration of these mixed societies, historically fragmented by class and ethnic divisions, came logically from the *mestizo* element. It could hardly come from the *élite*, for they had too high a stake in the preservation of the economic structure, and their own prestige was at issue. Nor could it come from those who continued to live as Indians in small, ethnocentric communities, for it was predicated on some form of participation in national life. But for the *mestizo*, his own status was bound up with a national image which gave equal place to the Indian and the European heritage and defined national well-being in terms of racial and cultural integration. So long as the national ideal was defined in terms of the racial and cultural characteristics of the European, white *élite*, the *mestizo* must take second place. But he need yield to none in a society where Indian blood was a cause for pride and Indian cultural values commanded respect.

The Mexican measures for land reform and education were outstanding examples of attempts at such integration. A unique form of land tenure, the *ejido*, was evolved by the revolution to meet the special tradition, mentality and needs of the landless peasant. It retained many of the elements of the indigenous communal land holding, but secularized and individualized, without the sanction and cohesion of the communal culture. It thus both involved a reinterpretation of the Indian's cultural patterns and permitted him to acquire new attitudes, e.g. an individual and secular instead of a communal and sacred relation to the land, which could enable him to accept change in other aspects of life.

The educational devices included rural cultural missions and rural schools which used the local crafts, customs and modes of expression as a basis for learning, and which encouraged their development. In these schools traditional wisdom and crafts were combined with literacy, arithmetic, and improved health and farming practices, to enable the peasant, whether Indian or *mestizo*, to better his lot in his own terms and also to follow an avenue into the broader society should he or his children have the initiative to do so.

The movement which made the most conscious effort to close the cultural gap and achieve a fusion which would respect the Indian's personal and cultural integrity defined itself as *indigenismo*. Originating in Mexico, it reached an international level by 1940, with the first Inter-American Indian Congress at Patzcuaro, Mexico, followed by the second and third such congresses in 1949 and 1954 at Cuzco, Peru, and La Paz, Bolivia. *Indigenismo* as a movement distinguished itself from *indianismo* on the one hand and *occidentalismo* on the other. It rejected the 'indianism' which occasionally took the form of a nativist movement of rebellion against the surrounding society, and it was equally out of sympathy with the romantic effort to preserve the Indian in his untrammelled state as a museum Indian. At the same time it rejected the glib occidentalism of both left and right, which saw the Indian as possessing no positive values and assumed that his only road to progress lay through accepting, at all costs, western material and intellectual values and patterns, either socialist or individualist.

Those who stood for *indigenismo* sought integration through interaction, reinterpretation and synthesis. They recognized that from the years of the Conquest the changes in Indian culture had been largely on the surface. But they also recognized that the penetrating force of industrial culture was not to be checked, and that it had the power, unless its impact was mitigated, to produce disorganization in Indian communities. They sought means which would be based on respect for the Indian personality and culture but would not hesitate to intervene to facilitate the adjustments inevitably produced by cultural change.

The principles of *indigenismo* were set forth in the declaration of the third Inter-American Indian Congress in 1954. Within the framework of the Universal Declaration of Human Rights, it claimed for the indigenous American the full exercise of his economic, political and social rights. These it defined as rights to land, liberty, suffrage and education; the right to properly remunerated work and the protection of social legislation; the right to organize on a communal, labour or co-operative basis; the right of freedom from racial discrimination and of respect for his cultural traditions, and the right to the incorporation of his cultural traditions with modern techniques.[17]

These claims for the indigenous American expressed the goals of the societies of which he was a central part.

IV. MINORITIES SEEKING CULTURAL AUTONOMY

In many parts of the world nation-states included populations which differed in culture from the dominant element and which yet sought to retain their identity as peoples. They generally comprised a minority in the population but, where the dominant element was itself numerically small, the majority of the people might be identified with groups which occupied the status of minorities.

The minorities problem in this sense was in large measure a by-product of nationalism. In traditional Asian societies, under the Ottoman empire, and to a degree under the Austro-Hungarian and Russian empires, many cultural groups submitted to a common rule and often lived for generations in neighbouring areas, while retaining their cultural identity, their language and customs, their distinctive dress, their religion, their system of education and sometimes their personal law. The growth of nationalism destroyed this situation, for it made all members of the state into nationals—Frenchmen or Dutchmen, Canadians or Mexicans, Brazilians or Lebanese. Wherever the population of a nation-state was not culturally homogeneous, nationalistic aspirations and a desire for self-determination on the part of non-dominant segments might conflict with the nationalism of the dominant group.

The minorities problem was already present before the opening of the twentieth century in the irridentist claims of nation-states to neighbouring territory inhabited by people of the same culture, such as the Italian claim to Trentino and Trieste and the French claim to Alsace-Lorraine. It was also present in the restiveness of the subject peoples of the Austro-Hungarian, Russian and Ottoman empires who sought the restoration of their former independence, as did the Poles, or demanded a measure of autonomy combined with full economic and political rights and opportunities. Where a minority was culturally related to another state or identified with it on the basis of religion, its aspirations might become an excuse for international intervention and it might find itself a pawn of international politics. The German minorities in eastern Europe and the Slavic populations in the Balkans were the bases for Pan-German and Pan-Slavic movements, and the Eastern Orthodox and other Christians within the Ottoman empire were brought under the 'protection' of Russia and France respectively. Where the minority was related to no outside state, its aspirations did not bring involvement in international politics; the Irish stood alone in their effort to secure autonomy from Britain, as did the Catalans in their similar demand from Spain; Jews in each country had the support only of their fellows who were also in a minority position in some other land.

During the nineteenth century the right of minorities to cultural autonomy had been recognized in principle by Austria, whose constitutional law of 1867 provided that every nationality had an inviolable right to preserve its national character and the use of its language in education, administration and public life. No such policy was followed, however, in the Hungarian part of the Hapsburg empire or with respect to minorities by Russia or Germany. Precedent for protection of minorities by international treaty had also been set by the treaty of Berlin in 1878 in respect to the newly established Balkan states, but there were no means of enforcement; Rumania, for example, continued to refuse citizenship to its Jewish population until after the first world war.

During the early years of the twentieth century the issue of the status of minorities was intensified by the mounting drive for national independence and self-determination and by the extension of suffrage, mass education and other pressures for the identification of all citizens with the state. The Irish pressed unremittingly for home rule; the effort to improve the position of minority peoples contributed to the Russian revolution of 1905 and to repeated disturbances within the Austro-Hungarian empire. At the same time the intensified nationalism of such groups as the Young Turks or the Prussians placed their minorities under new pressures designed to make Arabs into Turks or Poles into Germans.

In the peace settlement after the first world war the application of the principle of self-determination, 'as far as practicable', resulted in independent status for some of the former minorities of eastern Europe. The creation of new states, however, did not remove the problem of minorities and their status. Culturally distinct populations were so interspersed that boundaries could not be clearly drawn on ethnic lines. Furthermore, other factors, such as strategic boundaries or efforts to create viable economic units, left cultural minorities along several borders.

The Versailles Conference recognized the dilemma arising from the conflict between the principle of national self-determination and the presence of cultural minorities and undertook to deal with it in respect to the new and enlarged states. With these and with the defeated states of Austria, Hungary, Bulgaria and Turkey, the Allies concluded treaties requiring that minorities should enjoy full civil and political status and have the right to receive elementary education in their own language, to use their language for publication and before the courts, and to establish their own social and cultural institutions. The 25–30 million people covered by the minorities treaties made a fifth of the total population of the thirteen countries involved; in Czechoslovakia and Poland they were approximately a third and in Rumania a quarter of the population. Much the largest groups were Germans, Ukrainians and Jews. The treaty obligations with respect to these minorities were placed under the guarantee of the League of Nations. No similar internationally sanctioned obligations were imposed on other members of the League, however, with the exception of Iraq which agreed to them as a condition of admission to League membership in 1932.

During the twenty years when the principle of international protection of minority rights was in effect, the difficulties inherent in minority conflicts were well revealed. The several hundred petitions received by the League of Nations ranged from individual acts of violence to charges of systematic suppression of large groups. Some minorities did not dare appeal to the League for fear of reprisals; others tried to use the League machinery to resist social measures, such as land reform, which penalized the few for the benefit of the many. Some groups refused to accept their status as minorities and sought persistently to undermine the authority of the state or disrupt its operation. German and Hungarian groups, especially, regarded the Slavs to whom they were subject as inferior peoples to whose dominance they were unwilling to submit.

For the many cultural minorities in Russia which had been generally neglected under the tsars and in some cases suppressed, the October revolution brought a marked change. The USSR encouraged the cultural expressions of non-Russian groups, within the framework of the Soviet economic structure and administration, wherever these expressions were consistent with the overall purpose of the state. It developed written languages for peoples who had none, used the local languages for elementary education and for propaganda and promoted literary and artistic activity. In the 1930s educational materials were being published in 104 languages, as were technical instructions and literary works.

Where, however, the cultural patterns and nationalist traditions of certain ethnic groups were inconsistent with the interests of the larger society, they were overridden. The drive for industrialization, collectivization, and for uniform education stressing scientific subjects and Russian history and culture went on throughout the Soviet Union. The settlement of nomadic peoples put an end to their ancient way of life. The anti-religious basis of communist principles undermined the cultural integrity of groups whose traditions were strongly rooted in religion and in religious practices. Under the constitution of the Soviet Union a number of autonomous republics were set up on the basis of the cultural identity of the inhabitants. During the second world war, however, the German autonomous republic on the Volga was liquidated and its population removed to Siberia, and other autonomous republics in the Crimea, Caucasus and Volga disappeared. After Stalin's death, the national autonomy of several peoples was restored.

Over the years the atmosphere in many parts of the world became progressively less favourable to the status of cultural minorities. At one extreme, steps were taken to eliminate them as a group from within the body politic. This approach was first applied in Turkey and Greece under the treaty of Lausanne terminating the hostilities which had continued in the eastern Mediterranean after the first world war. In order to achieve cultural homogeneity, Greeks were expelled from Asia Minor, though many of their families had lived there from time immemorial, in exchange for Turks from Macedonia who had long been resident in that area.

The rise of dictators and the intensification of the kind of nationalism of
oo*

which National Socialism was the most exaggerated example brought régimes to power which were prepared to go to any lengths to rid the state of minority elements or to bring them into conformity with the dominant group. Hitler's policy of ridding areas under his control of Jews and of displacing non-Germans from the Baltic provinces was followed after the war by the expulsion of hundreds of thousands of Germans from Poland and Czechoslovakia.[18] The resettlement in Israel of Jews who had survived in central and eastern Europe and of Jewish communities from Muslim countries —Yemen, Iraq, Morocco—was accompanied by the displacement of nearly a million Arabs most of whom remained for a decade or more as homeless wards of the United Nations relief agency. The exchange of populations in the partition of India brought the largest mass migration in history, although it still left large Hindu and Muslim minorities in Pakistan and India.

The change for the worse in the status of many minorities between the ends of the first and second world wars was reflected in the approach to the problem by the United Nations as compared to the League of Nations. Whereas the League had sought to guarantee the right of minorities to continued cultural existence and the enjoyment of civil rights, the United Nations was concerned with their physical protection. The League's efforts on behalf of minorities petered out before the League itself came to an end. Petitions on behalf of minorities dwindled from 204 in 1930–31 to 4 in 1938–39 and the minorities office in the League's secretariat was disbanded in 1939. The United Nations made no effort to revive this machinery. For non-self-governing territories, it established a Trusteeship Council, and through its Human Rights Commission it concerned itself with the rights of individuals. But when it approached the issue of minorities which wished to maintain their cultural autonomy and identity, it saw the problem not in terms of rights to be guaranteed, but in terms of threats to survival.

The United Nations' contribution was the concept of 'genocide'—acts committed 'with intent to destroy, in whole or in part, a national, ethnical, racial or religious group as such' (Genocide Convention, Article II). The United Nations Genocide Convention applied to such acts as killing, causing serious bodily or mental harm, preventing births and forcibly transferring children.

The conflict between the aspirations of minorities and the drive of the dominant elements to realize their own aspirations for the whole nation was a source of tension in the years after the second world war. There was scarcely a region where this problem was not present in some form. It was not a major problem in most of western Europe, in part because minorities were few and the non-repressive character of state institutions made for accommodation among people of different traditions, but there were unresolved tensions in such areas as Northern Ireland and Catalonia. The problem was most likely to be present in areas where peoples had lived interspersed for many centuries and where new states had been created or borders had changed; but the French minority in Canada was evidence of the persistence of cultural minorities in countries settled in the relatively recent past. In the tangled population pattern of eastern Europe, minority problems were further complicated by the displacement and resettlement of populations as a result of the second world war and its aftermath. In the Middle East the variety of tribal and religious loyalties added to the problems of integrating the several states, while throughout south and south-east Asia separate communities remained distinct. The issue of tribal identity could not fail to be of major importance in the emerging national states of Africa.

At mid-century, minorities which desired to retain their cultural identity found themselves in a variety of situations. In well-integrated, multi-cultural societies, where substantial harmony existed among elements, they occupied a more or less clearly defined and accepted position, though there might be competing efforts to increase the influence or extend the institutions of one or another group. French Canada, for example, remained almost a state within a state, yet its people participated in national life in ways which transcended the cultural separateness of the group.

In less integrated, multi-cultural societies, groups which composed the state maintained a precarious balance while they were in the process of developing institutions, attitudes and a body of experience which would cut across ethnic lines and lead toward a more integrated society. Lebanon, with its evenly divided Muslim and Christian populations, was such a country. Malaya offered a classic example of a precarious balance, for the Malays had been less aggressive than the almost equally numerous Chinese minority, and both the Chinese and Indian minorities could identify themselves with large and dynamic states of fellow-nationals if the process of integration should not become effective in the new state of Malaya.

Some minorities were in situations of active conflict, as were the Tamils of Ceylon who were determined to establish their language on a par with the official Sinhalese, or the Turks in Cyprus who resisted the efforts of the Greek majority to unite the island with Greece. Some found themselves subject to expulsion or suppression. Bulgaria offered its Turkish minority the opportunity to leave the country by a specified date or conform to conditions which the majority of Turkish inhabitants considered unacceptable, and they emigrated to Turkey.[19] East European Jews were alternately prevented from emigrating and encouraged to leave. Groups of foreign traders in a number of areas were the object of resentment by virtue of their economic position and were sometimes subject to attack on ethnic grounds, as were Chinese in south-east Asia and Indians in East Africa.

In parts of Asia and the Middle East where the shift from group to national loyalty was in its early stages, and especially in Africa, minorities were in a state of transition. The Karens whose semi-autonomy was recognized by Burma, the varied peoples of Indonesia who were not immediately prepared to accept centralized government, the tribal peoples of Iran and other tribal peoples throughout the Middle East, were relatively new to nationalism. They had only begun to experience the institutions of the nation-state and the impact of common education, modern thought and modern economic life.

A quite different situation existed where tribal enclaves remained in the midst of highly developed societies. Aborigines in Australia and New Zealand, North American Indians on reservations, hill tribes in north and central India, and indigenous Indian communities in Central America and the Andean plateau lived as islands within modern society and culture. The aspirations of these isolated tribal groups differed and were changing. Among North American Indians, for example, there was great ambivalence between the desire to retain their identity and live their own lives and their recognition that this was necessarily a narrow and limited prospect. Some, such as the Hopi, had such a deep conviction that their way of life was superior that they resisted all influences which might change it. Others, especially after many young men had participated in the second world war, saw their only future in integration into the larger society and the abandonment of tribal life. All such groups faced a radical choice between continued isolation and the virtual abandonment of their traditional culture.

For cultural minorities, whatever their status, a number of issues remained unresolved. The first was the nature and extent of cultural pluralism that was possible within national societies and cultures. There was a trend towards patterns of accommodation based on common national identity combined with acceptance of religious, linguistic and ethnic differences; but the counter-trend toward uniformity and intolerance had shown itself strongly in the 1930s and it could reappear in time of stress, as when Egypt turned against its age-old Jewish population at the time of the Suez crisis in 1956.

The second question was how much cultural diversity would survive the levelling effect of urban industrial culture, with its mobility, industrial discipline, effects of mass production and patterns of conformity. To the extent that cultural identity was associated with a nomadic or an agrarian way of life, industrialization tended to destroy it, though cultural groupings remained within the common urban environment. Identifying distinctions of dress were likely to disappear in the streets of the city, at the work bench and in offices. Movement in search of jobs broke down the isolation which made for cultural separateness, as did the roads which penetrated into remote areas and the common ideas that spread out over the air-waves.

Finally, there was the relation between the drive of individuals for opportunity to function as full-fledged citizens and the drive of minorities for recognition of their separate identity. Were these drives compatible? Or did the insistence upon cultural recognition so set apart the members of a group as to stand in the way of their full acceptance as individuals and therefore their full enjoyment of the citizenship which they claimed? And, conversely, did their acceptance as individuals on the basis of merit so attenuate their sense of identity with the group from which they came that they would no longer share the drive for the maintenance of cultural identity and minority rights?

NOTES TO CHAPTER XXIX

1. Doctor of Philosophy A. I. Arnaldov thinks that it is essential for the authors to stress the point of view of Soviet scholars that this chapter should include a special section on the development of *Communist culture* which has become a significant component of cultural evolution in the twentieth century.

The socialist reconstruction of society is inconceivable without profound changes in the field of culture, changes which can be classed as a true cultural revolution, and whose goal is the creation of a new, socialist culture. The cultural revolution, however, is not to be understood in a vulgar sense as the negation of all past culture. Socialist culture does not arise in a vacuum. It is the heir to the best that was created in the conditions of a society based on exploitation. V. I. Lenin said: 'It is necessary to take the entire culture left by capitalism and to build socialism from it. It is necessary to take all of science, technology, all knowledge, art. Without this we shall not be able to build the life of the communist society.' (V. I. Lenin, *Collected Works*, Vol. 29, p. 52.) Hence, one of the concrete tasks of the cultural revolution is to select from the cultural heritage of the past everything of lasting value and to discard everything that is unnecessary, that is contrary to the nature of socialist society, not to say harmful and reactionary. This is the basis for the development of a culture that is truly socialist in content, i.e. reflecting the life and ideals of the new society, pervaded by its ideology, by the urge to serve the people and to help them actively in the struggle for socialism, and subsequently for communism.

2. Doctor of Historical Sciences A. M. Dyakov underlines that the renaissance of the ancient cultures of the peoples of Asia is in the first place linked with the growth of the national liberation struggle and the creation of independent states. The October Revolution in Russia has had a decisive influence in this direction: 'The national movements in the countries of Asia which finally won their freedom were influenced, and in some cases inspired, by the existence of the Soviet State and the growth of Soviet power.' (K. M. Panikkar, *Asia and Western Dominance*, London, 1954, p. 248.)

3. T. Földessy (Hungary) and candidate of Historical Sciences L. I. Yurevich, noting that the study of India in Europe has undoubtedly played a definite part in arousing in the Indian people an interest in its past, however underline that the renaissance of Indian culture and the reformation of Hinduism were chiefly an expression of the growing national liberation struggle and of the new bourgeois ideology which came to the fore.

4. Dr Dušan Zbavitel writes: Many distinguished figures in Indian politics and cultural life have pointed out that English education in India was too one-sided. It stifled Indian traditions and also prevented Indians having any deep knowledge of Russian, French, German and other cultures. It is enough to refer to Rabindranath Tagore who in his famous letter to Miss Rathbone (1941) gave a fair appreciation of the influence of English education on Indian life. This point of view is shared by T. Földessy and L. Eötvös, who note that describing British policy in India particularly in the cultural and educational spheres, Mr Nehru wrote that the British 'deliberately tried to prevent change, except in so far as this was necessary to consolidate their position and help them in exploiting the country and its people to their own advantage. . . .

'Changes, and some changes in a progressive direction, did come, but they came in spite of British policy, although the impetus for that change was the impact of the new West through the British.

'. . . Even the British government, in spite of its dislike of education, was compelled by circumstances to arrange for the training and production of clerks for its growing establishment. It could not afford to bring out from England large numbers of people to serve in this subordinate capacity. So education grew slowly, and though it was a limited and perverted education, it opened the doors and windows of the mind to new ideas and dynamic thoughts.' (See J. Nehru, *The Discovery of India*, New York, 1946, pp. 312–13.)

5. Dr Dušan Zbavitel underlines that reformist trends for the abolition of the hierarchy of caste and even of the caste system itself existed in India long before the introduction there of English education. The Sikhs for example had very much earlier advocated the abolition of the caste hierarchy.

6. Dr Dušan Zbavitel underlines that Rabindranath Tagore expressed the view that political liberty could not be separated from social emancipation long before Gandhi; Tagore, moreover, declared that the social emancipation of the Indian people was the first condition for the political liberation of India from the British domination.

7. Doctor of Historical Sciences S. L. Tikhvinsky argues that the Kuomintang lost its revolutionary character not in 1937 but in 1927. From the moment that it came to power in 1927 all the progressive elements were excluded from it and its ranks were filled with bureaucrats and representatives of the semi-feudal military class who soon obtained an absolute majority in the party.

   A most important feature of the internal political life of China from 1927 to 1936 was the armed conflict between the reaction personified by the Kuomintang and the revolutionary democratic camp. The Kuomintang government deluged China with the blood of revolutionary workers and peasants. The report of the International Organization for Assistance to the Fighters of the Revolution for 1930 says: 'From the moment when the so-called period of hostilities came to an end in 1928 and up to the all-China session of the Kuomintang in 1929 approximately 450,000 workers and peasants were exterminated. During the last six months of 1930 the number of revolutionaries who lost their lives amounted to 140,000.'

   From the outset of the Japanese aggression against China in 1931 the government of Chiang Kai-shek pursued a policy of concessions to the aggressors: first Manchuria was abandoned to them and then the province of Jehol. And when in the summer of 1933 the Kuomintang forces in the province of Chalhar in defiance of the government's orders resisted the Japanese attack Chiang Kai-shek's crack divisions were sent against them. During the period from the end of 1933 to the beginning of 1934 the Kuomintang savagely suppressed the anti-Japanese uprising in the province of Fukien. In 1935 it admitted the occupation by the Japanese of the province of Hopeh and of the northern part of the province of Chahar. This view is supported by T. Földessy and L. Eötvös.

8. Professor Zurayk has commented: These pages seem to me to carry a eulogy of Communist China, underscoring the brighter aspects and omitting the grim ones. It not only portrays the aspirations and the self-image, but implies more or less an approval of them and of the achievements of the system.

9. Doctor of Economic Sciences H. J. Eydus considers that it is impossible to see the capitalist development of Japan as merely the result of the penetration of Western economic, socio-political and cultural influences into the country. Japan passed from a feudal to a capitalist structure in pursuance of the same objectively ruling laws of historical development as other countries. The survivals of feudalism conserved in Japan are a result of the development of Japanese capitalism and not emanations of the 'Spirit of Japan'.

10. *The Author-Editors call the attention of the reader to the discussion of Japanese industrialization in Chapter IV, pages 88-9.*

11. Dr Min Latt underlines that it is wrong to consider the Japanese occupation as a turning point for the liberation movement in South-East Asia. At the beginning of the war the peoples of South-East Asia already had great experience of the anti-colonial struggle, of which the most important landmarks were the national uprising against Dutch rule in Indonesia in 1926–27, the national insurrection in Burma in 1930–32 and others.

12. Candidate of Historical Sciences V. B. Lutsky underlines that according to the testimony of the missionary Al Smith (*Zeitschrift der deutschen Morgenländischen Gesellschaft*, 1854) the foundation of the first educational society in Syria was due to Arab initiative.

13. Soviet scholars believe that the authors are wrong in saying that Arab nationalism, in contrast to the nationalist movement in India, 'was not fundamentally a movement for social reform'. V. B. Lutsky, a research historian, has stressed the fact that social reforms

were introduced in Algeria, Tunisia, Morocco, Egypt, Syria and Iraq after the liberation of these countries.

14. Doctor of Historical Sciences L. I. Zubok notes that the assertion that the USA remained in isolation up to the first world war and did not participate in world affairs is not in accordance with the facts. See Note 5 to Chapter I.

15. *The Author-Editors call the reader's attention to the exact language of the text.*

16. Candidate of Historical Sciences L. A. Zak underlines that the catchword of a 'White Australia' designed to arouse racial antagonism among workers affected not only the interests of the workers but also those of certain circles of the bourgeoisie. See L. L. Sharkey, *An outline history of the Australian Communist Party* (Sydney, 1944), L. L. Sharkey: *The Trade Unions* (Sydney, 1959), and other works by leaders of the Australian Communist Party.

17. Candidate of Historical Sciences L. A. Zak underlines that the main problem confronting the population of Latin America in the sixties of the twentieth century is still the struggle against the oppression of foreign capital which has entrenched itself in the economic life of these countries. (See for example the work by the Peruvian journalist Yenaro Carnero Checa: *Ensayos latinoamericanos*, s.l., 1959.)

18. Tamas Földessy and Lorant Eötvös observe that there is nothing in common between the Hitlerite policy against the Jews and other nations, and the expulsion of the Germans from Czechoslovakia and Poland after the second world war:

(*a*) The Hitlerite policy was directed against innocent people whilst the Germans in Poland and Czechoslovakia were deeply involved as a fifth column in the preparation of the war against the countries where they lived.

(*b*) Hundreds of thousands of people lost their lives as a result of the Nazi crimes, but there was never any threat to the lives of the Germans evicted from Poland and Czechoslovakia. They were able to go on living and working in their new homeland.

The expulsion of Germans from the territory of Poland and Czechoslovakia was sanctioned by the decision taken by the three allied powers—the United Kingdom, USA and USSR—at the Potsdam (Berlin) Conference in 1945. (See section XIII, of *Report on the Berlin Conference of the Three Powers*. 'Regularized transfer of the German population.')

19. Academician D. Kosev writes: After the establishment in Bulgaria of a People's Democratic Government the Turks intensified their propaganda among the Turkish population in Bulgaria in order to render them disaffected towards the Bulgarian nation and national authorities and to persuade them by demagogic promises to emigrate from Bulgaria. The Turkish mission and consulate played a special part in this agitation as did also some rich Turks who utilized the influence they had enjoyed among the people in the past.

Influenced by many years of agitation and by the demagogic promises of Turkish propaganda, part of the Turkish national minority expressed a desire to emigrate to Turkey. In fulfilment of the wishes of these Turks, and in conformity with the Convention of October 18, 1925, between Bulgaria and Turkey on the exchange of population, the Bulgarian government, following the elimination of the consequences of the post-war economic situation, took steps to issue emigration papers to all Turks who wished to leave. Up to October 1950 about 120,000 Turks who had made declarations attesting their desire to emigrate had been given emigration passports.

However, the Turkish government created a number of difficulties and hindrances for the emigrants and many of those who had sold their property did not manage to obtain Turkish visas but had to stay in Bulgaria. Those who went to Turkey found themselves in a very difficult situation there. Here for example are the impressions of one emigrant as reported by the newspaper *Gercek* on September 20, 1950: 'We thought that in Turkey there was a heavenly paradise. Now we are asking one another where is this paradise? . . . Even in a year or two's time we shall still not be able to find work. We just do not know what to do.'

CHAPTER XXX

DRIVES FOR INDIVIDUAL FREEDOM AND HUMAN DIGNITY

W HILE nations and peoples sought to realize their aspirations as total societies, elements in the population aspired to change their condition and status. Workers, peasants, women and members of minority groups sought to attain the status and opportunities promised for all people by the principles of the Declaration of the Rights of Man, but enjoyed only by the more favoured elements. Their drive was for individual freedom and human dignity, self-respect and the respect of others, first-class citizenship and full participation in the life of their societies.

I. LABOUR[1, 2]

Labour's drive for recognition, status and welfare was the most potent and widespread of these efforts. By the opening of the century 'labour' was well-established as a self-conscious entity in the industrial societies of Europe, America and Australasia. Though aspirations were variously defined and concepts differed as to how best to pursue objectives, labour was an element to be reckoned with in these countries. The major difference in aspirations was between those who hoped to overthrow the existing system and usher in a new social order by revolutionary means and those who sought an improved status within the existing society.

In the older industrial societies it was primarily craftsmen and industrial workers who thought of themselves as 'labour' and organized to secure their rights. Agricultural workers were minor elements in these labour movements, or were not organized at all; white-collar employees only slowly and partially came to identify themselves with labour. In some of the non-industrial and newly industrializing societies, however, almost the opposite situation prevailed in the labour movements which took shape there, for the principal groups of employed workers were frequently plantation labour and government or public utility workers. Moreover, in the very different conditions in which labour consciousness developed and industrialization was taking place, labour movements were often interwoven with nationalist movements and the aspirations of people as workers were linked with their desires for national integrity.

But whatever its form, a self-conscious labour movement was assumed by mid-century to be a normal and integral feature of modern society.

I. ASPIRATIONS OF LABOUR

Workers expressed their aspirations in many ways. In every industrial country, and in non-industrial countries as ideas or industrial practices spread, workers voiced their common interests through trade unions. Their aspirations were also expressed through political channels, by the formation of labour parties or the identification of workers with other political groups which offered promises of meeting their desires. Within organizations based on religious, welfare, racial or other common interest, workers formed sections to identify their aspirations and to enlist the support of the total group.

Workers also expressed their aspirations in many individual, unorganized ways—in the manner in which they spent their earnings, their response to job opportunities and incentives, their quest for education, the effort to give their children advantages which they themselves had not enjoyed, their participation or non-participation as citizens in community life.

The hopes and aims of labour were differently formulated in various countries in relation to the social structure, the manner and time of industrialization and the ideology which prevailed among workers and their leaders, but everywhere they reflected common desires for dignity and decency, for status and participation in the society of which they formed a part and a reasonable share in what it had to offer. In countries with the strong class traditions which characterized most European nations, workers focused on the desire to raise their class status and to function on a more nearly equal footing with other elements in society. Where class lines were less rigid, the objectives were more specifically economic. Where liberal principles had already been established by a vigorous middle class, labour sought the extension of these principles to themselves, and found many allies among middle-class people who saw in labour's aspirations a reflection of their own beliefs. Where they saw only exploitation in the existing order, they sought its overthrow in favour of a dictatorship of the proletariat. Under authoritarian rule they faced charges of insubordination and subversion, and they were suppressed.

Everywhere workers sought a fuller share in the fruits of industrial production and a more adequate income in order to support a higher standard of life. The central demand of labour for increased real wages, present in virtually every contract negotiation or labour dispute, expressed the workers' insistence that they should be the beneficiaries as well as the instruments of industry and be able to enjoy more of the good things of life as these were defined by the standard of living of other segments of society. They sought, too, to establish standards for decent and humane conditions of work, such as shorter hours and protection against accident and industrial disease. They wanted security in the face of the hazards of life and the uncertainties of industrial employment.

Most fundamentally, labour in all countries sought personal dignity—the status of human beings. Challenging the nineteenth-century *laissez-faire* economic concept of labour as a commodity to be purchased and used in the process of production, and also the traditional class attitudes as to what was good enough for workers, they asked to be treated as people and to enjoy the rights and dignity of free men. Towards that end they sought the right to form organizations, to speak with a common voice through representatives of their own choosing, and to withhold their labour through the strike. In a few countries they wished to share in the management of industry. In many they aspired to assume responsibility for the conduct of national governments through parliamentary forms, and to use these governments to take over and operate major segments of basic industry.

In many areas of the world organized groups of workers hoped to bring about a basic change in the economic, political and social structure by revolutionary means, and to substitute worker control for control by those who traditionally exercised privilege and power. In the countries where such revolutionary change did in fact occur, labour organizations assumed responsibility for achieving production goals and for administering protective regulations and social benefits.

In the course of these years the aspirations of labour expanded with the changing society, though the fundamental drive for full economic and social participation remained. In the early years of the century the labour movements were concerned to protect the workers against a variety of ills—low wages, instability of employment, danger of accident and disease and exposure to the unrestrained authority of employers. Unions sought to increase the workers' share in the fruits of industry and to reduce the relative power of the employer. Although these objectives remained central, they ceased to be the sole interest as workers acquired better conditions and greater power. By mid-century labour was also becoming concerned with the maintenance of a dynamic, growing, productive economy, as workers realized that their welfare was intimately bound up with increasing the fruits of industry through rising productivity and economic expansion, not merely with securing an adequate share.

A committee of the International Labour Organization noted this shift of emphasis during the second quarter of the twentieth century. Reviewing the role of its workers' and employers' representatives, it observed that 'the contribution to be expected from the representatives of the employers and the workers is more positive and less negative than it was at the beginning'. When the ILO had been formed in 1919, employers and workers had been represented separately 'very largely for the protection and defence of their respective material interests'. By 1956 this representation had 'taken on a wider content and now represents also a combined interest of the two elements in the productivity of industry and in the function or skill of management in industry'.*

* International Labour Office, *Report of the Committee on Freedom of Employers' and Workers' Organizations* (*McNair Report*) (International Labour Office, Governing Body, 131st session, Geneva, March 6–10, 1956. Mimeo), p. 200.

The broad economic and social changes in these years were at least partially responsible for the realization of many of labour's goals. The rising material level of living of the workers in industrial countries rested basically on the productivity which modern technology brought.[3] The relationship was a reciprocal one: increased wages which greater productivity made possible in turn stimulated employers to use labour more efficiently. Technical change, too, inevitably altered the status of the worker by eliminating much unskilled labour and requiring an educated, alert, technically competent labour force. It tended to create within the ranks of labour a worker-aristocracy of skill and competence, distinct from those who had nothing to offer but their physical effort. The interests of these two segments of labour did not always coincide.

The welfare and position of the worker at any particular time, moreover, was deeply affected by general economic conditions beyond the control of individual worker and organized labour alike. The contrast between the condition of workers at the depths of the economic collapse of the 1930s and in the prosperous decade after the second world war was far greater than any difference which the success or failure of labour's efforts during either of these periods could make. The change in the situation of North American labour in this period, for example, reflected primarily the shift from a desperately sick to a vigorous economy, although during these same years a weak and despised labour movement became a powerful, well-recognized force.

Changes in the place of labour in society, furthermore, were part of the whole process of social change during these years—the breakdown of class structures, the extension of responsibility and authority of the state, rising levels of general education, destruction of old privilege—all hastened by wars, taxation and shifts in political power. The achievement of many of labour's aspirations came about through the dissolution of the social structure which had assigned to labour a place from which it sought to emerge. Finally, the proletarian revolution in Russia provided the rest of the world with a new image which had a profoundly unsettling effect on the old concepts of labour's status.

Yet when the impact of these broad forces has been duly recognized, the part played by labour itself still remains a major factor in the history of the first half of the twentieth century. The struggles of labour unions, the exercise of political power and the constant efforts of countless individuals achieved for workers both material benefits and a new status.

2. METHODS OF SEEKING LABOUR'S OBJECTIVES

The organized ways in which labour formulated and sought its objectives differed from place to place, partly because of the historic shape of social and political institutions, partly in relation to the time of industrial development and its form, and partly because of the ideology prevailing among the leaders and rank and file of workers.

The major difference in ideology was between those who accepted the capitalist system and sought to improve the lot of labour within it and those who repudiated the system and saw their hopes realizable only through its overthrow. The distinction was not, however, clear-cut and simple.

The first group focused its efforts on using collective bargaining to secure higher wages, improved conditions of work, freedom of association and action, and various direct benefits. They generally looked to the state to establish minimum conditions of wages, hours and conditions of health and safety and to provide social security and welfare services, and they used their political influence to bring about legislation to this effect.

Those who rejected capitalism tended to concentrate upon disruptive measures designed to demonstrate labour's strength and ultimately to overturn the existing power structure. They were divided into several camps. Syndicalists and anarchists rejected the state as well as the structure of capitalist industry in favour of the concept of industries run by their workers. Revolutionary socialists sought the dictatorship of the proletariat and saw the labour movement as the instrument of the proletarian revolution and an arm of the dictatorship of the proletariat for the administration of industry.

A large middle group, including both non-revolutionary socialists who followed the Marxian analysis of the weaknesses of the capitalist system and others who accepted capitalism to some extent but distrusted the profit motive for different reasons, favoured the ownership of the principal means of production by the state or co-operatively and they sought to nationalize key industries.

In pursuit of its objectives, labour used both the economic power which it could command through union organization and the political force which it could muster through organized parties. The choice of method and the relation between the economic and political approach varied with the factors mentioned above.

Although the labour movements which resulted all expressed their common conflict of interest with employers in similar ways, they differed in emphasis and in the extent to which they used one or another of the techniques available to organized workers. In some countries, the character of the movement changed with changing situations over the years. The British labour movement was built on the basis of collective bargaining, but it developed in time as a strong political force. Similar movements with emphasis on collective bargaining took shape in the Commonwealth countries and the United States. On the European continent the orientation of labour from the beginning was political and revolutionary, as part of the socialist, anarchist or communist movements, but these labour organizations also engaged in collective bargaining to improve the economic condition of workers. The communist unions played a post-revolutionary as well as a pre-revolutionary role, while the potentialities of the labour movements in the newly industrializing countries in the mid-twentieth century were only beginning to be apparent and their direction was far from clear.

(a) British labour movement

The oldest substantial labour movement, that of Great Britain, evolved its form and method under the conditions which surrounded British industrialization. Britain was the first country to become industrialized; it had a well developed tradition of voluntary association and parliamentary democracy and a Protestant religious ethic which stressed individual and social responsibility; its feudal institutions had been disrupted though not wholly destroyed by an increasingly dominant commercial and industrial middle class.

Against this background British labour adopted the method of voluntary association for collective bargaining, first by crafts and then by industries; it established, in law and practice, its right to organize and to use its economic strength through the strike, peaceful picketing and other orderly practices; it entered political life and functioned through the parliamentary system.These methods were already well established by the opening of the twentieth century; they were guaranteed to workers when Parliament, dominated by the middle-class Liberal party, passed the Trades Disputes Act of 1906 at the instigation of the first Labour party member.

The approach of British labour was always pragmatic. As explained by Margaret Bondfield, first British woman cabinet member and minister of labour in the Labour party government of 1929: 'We learnt from facts and events. Doctrine played comparatively little part in the lives of most of us . . . experience was the main thing.'*

Through the first half of the twentieth century labour extended its influence by these same methods until the Labour party, resting squarely on a trade union base but including in its membership individuals from outside the union ranks, achieved a majority position. At the close of the second world war it assumed office and carried through a programme of public ownership of certain key industries coupled with a widespread system of public social services and educational reforms supported by heavy, progressive taxation. The efforts of British labour played an important part in the modification of British society which resulted in very substantially reducing the gap in real income between rich and poor. British workers secured a new status, level of living, range of welfare services and a measure of power and responsibility.

(b) Labour movements on the European continent

The German labour movement grew up in a country with authoritarian rather than democratic traditions, where industrialization came later and more rapidly than in Britain, and where there was a strong class structure and many remnants of the feudal order. In this setting the German labour movement was the product of political organization.[4]The unions were the creation of the Social Democratic (Socialist) party, and functioned as an appendage to the party until the Mannheim declaration of 1906 placed them on an equal basis

* Margaret Bondfield, *A Life's Work* (London, 1948), p. 10.

of collaboration. Thereafter they continued to regard their political efforts to gain influence in government as of at least equal importance with collective bargaining. The goal of both unions and party, as stated in the Mannheim declaration, was 'the rise of the working class and its equality with the other classes of society'. German Catholic workers, similarly situated but unable to accept the Marxian concept of class struggle, formed separate unions, generally affiliated with the Catholic Centre parties, and following the ideology of the 1891 papal encyclical, *Rerum novarum*.

In most of the other countries of central and northern Europe labour followed the German pattern. Socialist parties sponsored trade union organization and acted as the workers' voice. Collective bargaining was secondary to political action. The central struggle was for elevation of the working class and the ideology was the Marxian concept of the class struggle. The political situation in these several countries largely determined the course of labour's development. Where there was a strong parliamentary tradition, as in the Scandinavian countries, labour organization and methods came to approximate closely those of Great Britain. Where, as in the Netherlands and Austria, a large Catholic population constituted a separate political force, Catholic trade unions corresponded to Catholic political parties. Where communist parties acquired strength, some of the unions passed under their political influence.

In contrast to the socialist labour movements elsewhere on the continent, French and Italian labour prior to the first world war followed an anarchist-syndicalist course. Confronting weak parliamentary systems characterized by a multitude of parties divided along minute ideological lines, labour in these countries called for revolutionary economic change by direct means rather than through political action or party affiliation. Revolutionary goals and direct-action methods made French and Italian workers resort to the general strike or other spectacular work stoppage as a favoured instrument to dramatize the plight and assert the demands and power of labour.

With the rise of international communism after the first world war the French and Italian labour movements were torn between those who thought that communism offered a way to realize their revolutionary hopes and those who tried to avoid the political approach which communism implied. In the years after the October revolution and again after the second world war, the struggle for and against communist control which took place within virtually all labour movements was particularly acute in Italy and France.

(c) Labour movements in newly settled industrial countries

In the countries outside Europe which achieved a high degree of development before the middle of the twentieth century, notably Australia, New Zealand, Canada and the United States, labour followed a course which was closer to that of Britain than to the labour movements of the Continent. In all these newly settled countries, however, the absence of a feudal past and the fact that effective manhood suffrage antedated industrialization profoundly affected the attitudes of labour, their goals and their methods. Workers did not have to fight to destroy long established class privilege or to establish political democracy. Their goals, therefore, were to secure for themselves in the economic field rights and privileges corresponding to those which they already enjoyed as citizens and to raise their level of living and of opportunities for their children to those of the comfortable middle class with which they felt themselves identified.

The labour movements of Australia and New Zealand, however, differed from those of the United States and Canada in their much greater use of legal machinery. In Australia a system of compulsory arbitration was established at the turn of the century after a series of widespread and disruptive strikes. Labour had to seek its practical objectives through this channel and to engage in litigation before arbitration tribunals in order to secure awards of wages, hours and terms of employment that would incorporate the principle of a living wage and security on the job. At the same time it formed its own political party, which held the balance of power in federal and state parliaments from the early years of the century and governed the country during the first world war, in the late 1920s and during and after the second world war.

Australian labour used its influence and power to secure protective factory and mine legislation, free compulsory education, and a comprehensive system of public social services. In addition, Australian labour shared the outlook of the rest of the population—a small, isolated people of European origin seeking to achieve and retain a European manner and standard of living—and vigorously supported the 'white Australia' policy and a protective tariff designed to keep out the products of low-paid Asian labour.

Labour in the United States, on the other hand, and also in Canada, focused its efforts on collective bargaining, first on a limited craft basis, then from the 1930s through mass industrial unions in mass-production industries. Its major struggle was for the right to bargain collectively and to use the weapons of economic power which would make such bargaining effective, without being victimized by employers for these efforts. North American labour evolved methods of negotiation, equipped itself with the necessary technical knowledge to meet employers on their own ground, and developed an elaborate voluntary union–management machinery for carrying out contracts and adjusting grievances or disputes under the contracts.

The main body of North American labour formed no political party. At first labour unions looked with suspicion on all political action and even on social legislation, fearing that government intervention might lead to governmental restriction on union activity, and preferring to keep the exercise of economic power free from political involvement. From the 1930s on, however, after federal legislation had protected the right of unions to organize, bargain collectively and engage in peaceful picketing, and after the impact of the depression had made clear the need for social security and other forms of protection, the labour movement shifted its position. It actively supported social legislation and became an important force in mobilizing public opinion and bringing pressure on legislators. In addition, unions threw their support to friendly candidates of one or the other of the major political parties, and organized committees for the political education of their members and to stimulate their political activity.

(d) Communist labour movement

The communist pattern of labour organization arose under the conditions of tsarist Russia where the rights and freedoms enjoyed by British and west European workers were absent and channels for political expression were closed. Though the concepts of class struggle, revolutionary overthrow and dictatorship of the proletariat owed their origin to Karl Marx, it was Lenin's scheme of organization which shaped communist trade unionism both in its pre-revolutionary and its post-revolutionary stages.

In both phases, the concept of the Party as the essential voice of the working class and the organizational plan of 'democratic centralism' defined the role and procedure of the labour movement. Any and every organization had to recognize the leadership of the Party and submit to it. 'Democratic centralism' meant that a disciplined Party membership, receiving directives from the central committee of the Party, would form cells through which to transmit central Party directives to trade unions under their control, while the unions in turn would extend this influence to workers at large.[5] In the pre-revolutionary state, the pyramid of tightly organized and centrally directed Party cells provided a means of developing and carrying out a strategy of revolution. Once the Communist party gained control and administered the state, this system provided the transmission belt for communicating central policy to workers' groups and for workers' opinion to reach the centre.

In Soviet Russia and the other communist states, the labour unions functioned as organs of government, responsible for carrying out economic policy, achieving production goals and administering social benefits.[6] The preamble to the statutes of the Soviet workers' organizations provided that they 'shall organize a socialist emulation of workers and employees to raise labour productivity to the utmost, to fulfil and overfulfil State plans, to continuously develop all the branches of industry, transport and agriculture, to improve quality and reduce production costs, to make full use of all the reserves of the socialist economy; to take part in planning and regulating wages . . . promote the introduction of progressive technologically substantiated production rates . . .'. The trade unions exercised some responsibilities in the fields of social security, industrial health and safety and labour inspection commonly carried by government agencies in other countries.

In these circumstances bargaining was inappropriate and the collective agreement did not serve the function of establishing wages or other basic conditions, all of which were determined by the planning agencies. 'The purpose of Soviet collective contracts is to ensure the fulfilling and exceeding of production plans, the continuous increase of output and improvement in the organization of labour and the strengthening of the responsibility of economic and trade union organizations for improving the material living conditions of the workers and of the cultural services made available to them.' The collective agreement, which must be in conformity with state plans and which was signed after full discussion within the plant, usually contained the following matters: commitments of the management and works committee in respect of the implementation of the production plan; remuneration; training and upgrading of workers, engineers, technicians and salaried employees; state and labour discipline; protection of labour; housing and living conditions; provisioning of workers and communal catering arrangements, and cultural services.

Differences of opinion between directors and factory committees were transmitted for decision to the competent ministry and central committee of the trade union, and thence to the Central Council of Trade Unions acting in agreement with the competent ministry.

According to the principle of democratic centralism all trade union organs 'from the base to the summit' were elected by the members of the trade union to which they reported on their activity, and all decisions were taken by majority vote. Trade union organizations settled all questions in accordance with the Statutes of the Trade Unions and the decisions of the higher trade union organs. 'Trade union organs of a lower level are subordinate to the organs of a higher level.' Soviet trade unions 'conduct all their activities under the guidance of the Communist party of the Soviet Union, the organizing and directing force of Soviet society'.

With respect to the right to strike, the Soviet government reported to the ILO in 1955 that: 'No provision is made, or has ever been made in Soviet legislation, to restrict or prohibit strikes. In practice, however, no strikes occur in the Soviet Union, because there is no reason for them in a country with a socialist economic and social régime, where the instruments and means of production belong to the workers themselves.' The reports from Bulgaria, Czechoslovakia, Hungary and Poland were similar.*

Although strikes *per se* were not illegal, anyone participating in a work stoppage might be guilty of other offences which carried severe penalties, such as counter-revolutionary activity, or of absenteeism which was punishable by correctional labour at reduced wages in the worker's usual job. Reports of anything resembling strikes were extremely rare, and it appeared that this institution was in fact virtually eliminated in the Soviet Union. Serious large scale strikes did however occur in 1956 in Poland, East Germany and Hungary; these were attributed by the authorities to mistaken leadership, the action of counter-revolutionary elements and the backwardness of certain parts of the working class.[7]

* International Labour Office, *McNair Report, op. cit.* pp. 194–5.

(e) Labour movement in Japan

The conditions of industrialization in Japan were not favourable to the spontaneous organization of workers and their independent expression. A strongly feudal and authoritarian society set its stamp upon both the large-scale enterprises set up with government support for the heavy industries, and the small, paternalistic light-industry shops where family-type relationships were extended to the relations between workers and employers. For many years the Japanese labour movement was less a movement of workers than of intellectuals who had read Marx and knew something of the labour movements in Europe, and who formed a succession of organizations, dividing and re-combining over the central issue of whether to stand for the complete over-throw of the economic system or to work for reforms.

In the periods when the government was anti-democratic and militaristic, the labour movement was suppressed by law, and from the early 1930s to the end of the second world war its leaders were in jail. In the periods when the political climate was more favourable, leaders from among the Marxist in-tellectuals drew their following largely from the civil service, teachers and transport workers and some of the employees of larger factories. Since each union was generally confined to a single enterprise where paternal family atti-tudes continued to prevail and 'temporary' workers did not belong to the same union as those with 'permanent' status, no strong, worker-led, practical-minded trade unions developed. Some slight tendency toward practical union-ism appeared after the second world war under the stimulus of the United States occupation and the co-operation offered by the International Confed-eration of Free Trade Unions, but the chief feature of the Japanese labour movement at this time was the contest for domination between communist and non-communist leadership. To the extent that the workers themselves were articulate, they tried mainly to protect at all costs their hold on their jobs in the difficult and uncertain conditions which beset the Japanese economy in the immediate post-war years.

(f) Labour movements in newly industrializing areas

As industrialism spread to other parts of the world, or even in advance of industrial development, labour movements arose in imitation of those already well-developed in the older industrial countries. These movements grew up in the framework of very different societies from those of Europe or of Euro-pean settlement, under different economic conditions and in a different climate of local and world opinion. In consequence they played a different role in relation to the self-image and goals of the workers of these areas. As bor-rowed rather than indigenous institutions, they did not grow from local roots. Inheriting standards and ideology developed elsewhere and lacking the ex-perience of slow growth, struggle and step-by-step achievement, they seldom developed a sturdy structure or a basis for realism and responsibility. They were even more dependent than European unions had been at a corresponding stage of their evolution on the leadership and participation of intellectuals. At the same time the weakness of the middle classes in these countries increased the importance of labour as a factor in the evolution of their societies.

In the non-industrial areas of Latin America, Asia and Africa where European and North American firms developed mines, industrial enterprises or factory-type plantations, inexperienced local workers were no match for the great corporations. In the early stages of the European labour movements, workers and industrialists had grown up together; many men of small means had emerged as entrepreneurs at the same time that workers entered and found their place in industry. But when workers in non-industrial areas experienced the sudden impact of highly organized enterprises, already fully developed in their home areas, they found themselves separated from the masters of modern industry by a wide gulf of power, knowledge and culture.

In the countries consciously and actively engaged in economic development, state enterprise or other large-scale operations led the way, and the drive for rapid industrialization left no time for the gradual development of labour organization.

Yet the workers and potential workers of these countries were aware of some of the conditions which their fellow workers in industrially developed countries enjoyed. They had before them the success of the 'workers' state' in Russia in achieving rapid industrialization, and much impetus for Asian labour organization came from communist sources, aided by Russia's Institute for Toilers of the Far East. They also saw the high living standards and political responsibility enjoyed by workers in such countries as Britain, Scandinavia, Australia and the USA and desired these benefits for themselves.

They looked to the government, however, rather than to their own direct efforts to define the obligations of employers and to establish standards and conditions of work. It was natural that they should do so. Internationally accepted labour standards were formally accepted by many of the non-industrial countries which ratified International Labour Organization conventions relating to such matters as hours of work, the labour of women and minors, industrial accident and disease. Even dictatorial governments which sternly repressed labour organizations, as in some countries of Latin America, adopted labour codes and social legislation for which European workers had long struggled, though such codes often remained unenforced.

In the older industrial countries labour unions had been formed in response to actual industrial experience and labour and social legislation had resulted from the long struggle of organized workers for decent working conditions, terms of employment and social benefits. In the newly industrializing countries the order was reversed. The first step was the enactment of labour and social legislation for which labour itself did not have to fight—legislation designed by governments to protect their people against foreign exploitation or to bring their countries in line with international standards. This body of legislation, covering such matters as hours of work, minimum pay, child labour, accident compensation, maternity leave, job tenure and social security, provided a very different framework from that within which industry had developed in Europe and America, and placed labour in a very different position.

In these new circumstances the role of labour unions and their appropriate methods of operation were far from clear. Collective bargaining was rarely their central function. In some countries, notably in Latin America, a major activity of the unions was to watch the enforcement of the protective legislation and to help workers to secure their rights under such laws.

In most newly industrializing countries, notably in Asia and the Middle East, labour leadership came almost wholly from outside the ranks of labour itself and was provided by intellectuals or other educated members of the middle class. Such leadership tended to be more preoccupied with ideology than with the day-to-day problems of workers in industry and to reinforce the political character of the unions.[8] Trade unions formed substantial parts of the various political parties, and each union group had its political affiliation. Trade unions played a special role in the emerging African countries because of the virtual absence of a middle class and because the unions offered virtually the only basis for mass organization and leadership outside the tribal structure.

As the young labour movements in these countries gained experience and increased their contact with labour leaders from other countries through participation in the International Labour Organization and the international labour federations, and through technical assistance and the mutual visiting of leaders under international aid programmes, they began to adopt some of the attitudes and procedures which the older unions had developed. It remained an open question at mid-century, however, how far the experience and attitudes gained in the already industrialized countries were relevant to the situations which the new unions encountered.

Among the major factors conditioning the role of the new unions was the level of productivity. In the older industrial countries increased real wages and standards of living for workers had largely reflected, and been made possible by, increased productivity. The success of organized labour in securing advances in real earnings had been achieved within limits set by the advancing level of productivity. In the communist countries the major function of trade unions was to help to achieve production goals and to raise the productivity of the workers as a means of ultimately raising levels of living. In the newly industrializing countries labour productivity was low; but many of the conditions that reflected productivity increases in other countries were claimed as a matter of political right. At mid-century the dilemma of low productivity and high aspirations remained unresolved in the labour movements of this segment of the world.

(g) International labour movements

From the early days of industrialism labour consciousness had a strong international component. This was particularly true of the politically oriented, ideologically dominated movements. The Communist Manifesto in 1848 had called upon the 'workers of the world' to unite, and Marx's followers of all shades of opinion, whether gradualists or revolutionaries, shared in some measure the sense of common destiny and common cause which he enunciated. The more pragmatic labour movements might be narrowly nationalistic in such matters as immigration restriction or tariff protection, but even they often recognized that their gains would in the long run be protected by the success of workers in other countries in raising their wages, and they expressed a common sympathy.

The First International (1864), and especially the Second International (1889) which was composed initially of the socialist parties of Europe and later included those from overseas, provided a meeting ground for the socialist-oriented labour movements. But labour's national loyalties proved stronger than its international solidarity when put to the test by the outbreak of the first world war. The Third International, formed in 1919, became the international centre for communist parties and, through them, for the trade unions which they controlled.

Meanwhile trade unions united internationally on the basis of separate crafts or industries such as miners, typographers, metal trades workers. The main function of these secretariats was to keep their members informed about trade conditions and disputes in different countries and to prevent workers in one country from acting as strike-breakers in another. In 1903 the International Secretariat of National Trade Union Centres was formed, composed of the principal trade union centre in each country; in 1913 it changed its name to the International Federation of Trade Unions. Its primary purpose was to furnish a meeting ground for the discussion of common problems. The national Christian trade unions, whose organization in several countries was stimulated by the papal encyclical Rerum novarum (1891), met in Zurich in 1908 to form the International Secretariat of Christian Trade Unions, with membership open to Protestant as well as Catholic unions. Much the largest membership, on the eve of the first world war, was in Germany.

Following the second world war, unions had to regroup themselves internationally after the European trade unions which had been destroyed or distorted by Nazi and fascist domination had been re-established. The communist unions took the lead in reviving international labour organization by joining with non-communist unions from a number of countries to establish the World Federation of Trade Unions in 1945, but four years later the non-communist unions withdrew to form the International Confederation of Free Trade Unions. The latter did not limit itself, as had the International Federation of Trade Unions, to a single federation or trade union centre from each country and so drew in unions with different political affiliations in Europe and Asia and different wings of the labour movements in the United States and Latin America. The International Federation of Christian Trade Unions continued to be composed chiefly of Catholic unions in France, Belgium, Austria and Canada, and both Catholic and Protestant unions in the Netherlands and Switzerland.[9]

3. RIGHTS AND RESPONSIBILITIES OF LABOUR

The manner in which the labour unions of the several countries were able to function depended not only on the form and intention of the unions themselves but on the legal framework within which they operated and the attitude of employers, government and the public. This framework involved: the right of workers to form labour unions, and of unions to conduct their own affairs; the right of labour to use its ultimate weapon, the strike; and the provision of machinery for carrying on labour–management negotiation, and requirements with respect to its use.

(a) Right of organization

In virtually every country labour had to struggle long and often bitterly in order to establish the right freely to form and join unions without interference by employers or government.

The British trade unions, among the earliest to achieve status and freedom from interference, fought for more than a hundred years to free themselves from legal restraints. They had been subject to prosecution, at first for their very existence and then for most of their acts, until the Trade Union acts of the 1870s gave them legal standing and the right to engage in activities essential to their effectiveness. Nevertheless, a court decision in 1901, the Taff Vale Railway Co. case, had the effect of virtually preventing strikes; the Trade Disputes Act of 1906 was then enacted to confirm this right. Again in 1909 trade unions were restrained from using their funds for political purposes, and it required the Trades Union Act of 1913 to lay down the conditions under which unions could seek political objectives. Australian labour in the 1890s fought bitterly for the right of collective bargaining against intransigent employers in the sheep raising and maritime industries; it was only able to consolidate its position and establish its rights when it entered politics and the Labour party became a political force in the early twentieth century.

The fascist and Nazi régimes of Italy and Germany made the free trade union one of their principal targets.

In the United States many large-scale industries bitterly resisted the formation of labour unions. A public investigation of violations of free speech and the rights of labour in the early 1930s disclosed that some large companies had acquired arsenals of tear gas and other weapons, violence and threats of violence were common, and associations of employers were systematically engaged in building up anti-union public sentiment, preventing labour from organizing, and breaking union strength. From 1934 to 1941 issues connected with labour's attempt to organize, gain recognition and bargain collectively were the most frequent single cause of strikes.

In the 1930s a series of laws enacted by the federal Congress gave labour a new legal charter within which to seek its objectives. These laws guaranteed to workers the right to organize and be represented by 'unions of their own choosing', defined 'unfair labour practices' in which employers were forbidden to engage, established the right of peaceful picketing and forbade the use of injunctions in labour disputes. They established administrative machinery to facilitate the choice by workers of the union through which they wished to be represented, to ensure that employers would bargain in good faith, and to provide an agency to which workers could appeal when they thought that the prohibitions against unfair labour practices were being violated. With these guarantees labour organizations grew rapidly in the mass-production industries from which they had been largely excluded and union recognition and collective bargaining became established and accepted procedures in American industry. In 1947 the new strength of labour organization was restrained by the Taft-Hartley Act, which limited certain union practices relating to the closed shop, boycotts and jurisdictional disputes and which provided that when, in the opinion of the president of the United States, a threatened or actual strike imperilled the national health or safety, workers might be enjoined from striking for a period of eighty days while the government sought to settle the dispute.

German trade unions had enjoyed a favourable legal position from 1890 on, after the expiration of Bismarck's anti-socialist laws which had been used to restrict their activity, and the German labour movement was one of the most vigorous on the European continent. But when the Nazis came to power, strong, independent unions had no place in a totalitarian state; their organizations were dissolved and their leaders persecuted. Under the principle of *Gleichschaltung* and the idea of military organization as the pattern of German life, the Nazi Labour Front was formed as a disciplined body of workers, obedient to the captains of industry and loyal to the régime.

Italian unions had never occupied a secure position; a number of proposed laws to give them legal status in the late nineteenth and early twentieth centuries failed of passage. Unions enjoyed a sort of *de facto* status by virtue of legislation which implied their existence by setting limits to their activity or authorizing their representation on certain bodies. The fascist régime liquidated the independent trade unions and substituted workers' organizations that functioned not as bargaining agents but as arms of the corporate state.

In the years after the war the German and Italian trade unions, and those in other Nazi-occupied countries, had to be rebuilt from the ground up.

Labour's right freely to associate was recognized as a principle internationally in the structure of the International Labour Organization. In this organization, established in 1919, each member country was represented by separate representatives of government, workers and employers, and these delegates voted individually rather than as a national group. This form of tripartite representation permitted the workers' delegates from different countries to join in formulating the position of workers on specific issues. The Universal Declaration of Human Rights confirmed: 'Everyone has the right to form and to join trade unions for the protection of his interests' (Article 23). The International Labour Organization adopted conventions in 1948 and 1949 specifying in detail the conditions which constituted genuine freedom of association for labour. These included the right of all workers, without previous authorization, to form organizations of their own choosing, and the right of these organizations to function freely without control, supervision or danger of dissolution in such matters as drafting their constitution and rules, electing their officers, holding meetings, joining national and international federations and engaging in political activity.

By 1955 these principles of freedom of association were generally part of the legal structure of the industrial countries of west Europe, the United States and the British commonwealth. In these countries unions commonly enjoyed constitutional or legal guarantees of the right of association, not expressly subject to limitations by law. They were not required to register, although in a few cases certain privileges were reserved for registered unions, and there were no restrictions as to which workers were permitted to form labour unions, including those in public employment.

Unions in these countries were uncontrolled in respect to the formation of their constitutions, election of officers, meetings, right to engage in political as well as economic activity and right to join national or international federations. They enjoyed the legal right to strike as well as to engage in collective bargaining and enter into collective contracts. Apart from limitations relating to essential industries or public employees, only an occasional restriction remained, such as the prohibition against jurisdictional strikes in Denmark, sympathetic strikes in Canada or secondary boycotts in the United States.

Outside the industrial countries, however, the legal status of unions was usually more circumscribed. In a number of areas compulsory registration and a measure of government supervision was required and the right to strike was limited or denied.

(b) The strike

The ultimate weapon of the labour union was the strike—the ability of organized workers to withhold their labour. The right to strike was one of the basic rights which the free trade unions enjoyed, but there was a tendency to seek means other than painful and costly work stoppages to secure the benefits which labour sought. Lock-outs by employers to force labour to accept their terms and often to prevent organization were used extensively in the late nineteenth and early twentieth century, but became less frequent as unions gained more general acceptance.

The strike had a different character and served a somewhat different function where labour was oriented toward collective bargaining than where it was geared for political action. In all cases it was a test of labour solidarity and as such had an ethical and emotional meaning for workers who were called upon to make individual sacrifices for common objectives.

As the last resort in collective bargaining the strike represented the workers' ability to inflict direct economic injury on those from whom they were seeking bargaining concessions. Between stubborn bargainers, a strike was a test of endurance—of whether the employers could endure loss of production longer than workers could endure lack of wages. Such bargaining strikes tended to be long drawn out, for they were not usually entered into until the bargaining process had broken down and a difficult impasse had been reached.

Where labour was politically oriented, the strike served more as a demonstration or protest than as part of a bargaining procedure. The object was to impress, to embarrass, above all to dramatize the workers' case. A quick walk-out, a twenty-four hour stoppage was a public gesture, to demonstrate the power of labour or to cause public disorder rather than to injure employers economically or to pit the workers' capacity to sacrifice against the employer's capacity to forgo income. Political strikes tended to be very short, lasting only a day or two or even a few hours.

The general strike, designed to paralyse the economic life of the community was the most drastic of the workers' means of protest. In the early twentieth century the more radical unions regarded it as a principal weapon while the moderates opposed its use. The French anarchist-syndicalist, George Sorel, expressed the belief in his *Reflections on Violence* (1908) that the value of the general strike was not its actual use but its role as a 'social myth' to keep alive the sense of the class struggle.

The general strike was used for political purposes, notably in Belgium in efforts to secure manhood suffrage in 1893, 1902 and 1913. It was used to protest economic conditions, as in Sweden in a month-long general strike in 1909 to protest against the growing use of the lock-out, or in the British general strike of 1926 to protest against a national lock-out of coal miners. It was invoked for revolutionary purposes, notably in the Russian revolution of 1905 and in Germany in 1918.

General strikes were suppressed with great vigour, punitively and with heavy loss of life in the case of revolutionary and some political strikes and with economic and legal penalties when the objectives were economic. The British general strike of 1926 evoked a reactionary Trade Disputes Act which reversed the hundred-year trend toward liberalizing the position of trade unions.[10]

While the right to strike was generally accepted as a basic element in the freedom of workers to organize and seek their objectives, changes in the nature and structure of industry raised complex problems with respect to the exercise of this right. In addition, the development of other methods for securing labour's objectives tended to make the strike somewhat less central, as workers came to depend more upon political or legal action or economic research to press their cause. This was true both of industrially developed countries where the institutional structure for regulating labour relations became more elaborate, and for newly industrializing countries where workers' political influence often exceeded their ability to put pressure on their employers by withholding their labour.

In the course of these years the public sector of the economies of the non-communist countries expanded very substantially, both in response to practical considerations and under strong socialist influences in many countries. The ILO found in its survey of the economies of the seventy member countries in 1955 that the public sector was employing a large segment of the labour force of most countries, regardless of the political structure. In addition to the regular civil services, education, health and welfare, the areas of employment by units of government or by government corporations included generally some or all of the communications services—post, telegraph, telephone, radio; the utilities—electricity, water, gas; transport—railways, city transit systems, air, merchant marine, roads, canals, airport and dock facilities; banking and finance agencies; munitions industries; conservation and exploitation of certain natural resources, such as water power, forests, mines and petroleum; atomic energy; and frequently some government participation in basic chemical, steel, electrical, shipbuilding or automobile industries and in major development programmes such as the TVA in the United States or the Snowy Mountains scheme in Australia. In these circumstances, where as much as 20 per cent of the labour force was in government employ in a country like Australia or 10 to 13 per cent in Canada and the United States, the question of the rights of workers *vis-à-vis* the government became involved.

In addition, the great growth of cities and the extreme interdependence of industrial activity made the entire community acutely dependent on the continuous operation of many industries and the continuous maintenance of central services. Cities of millions of people with only a few days' supply of food were exposed to disaster if transport services were interrupted for a long period; shut-downs in basic materials such as steel or in fuel supply or electric power could paralyse whole areas or economies. Health and safety could be menaced by the cessation of essential services. It was immaterial whether these industries and services were provided by public or private operations; their interruption menaced the public.

In these circumstances the industrial countries where the right of free association and resort to the strike were generally recognized hedged the strike about with limitations designed to protect the public while leaving the basic rights and freedoms of labour unimpaired. At mid-century nearly every industrial country placed some restraints on the workers' freedom to strike when such a strike would result in danger to health or safety or hardship to the community, or when it involved an 'essential' industry or public employees. The only west European industrial countries without one or another of these limitations in 1955 were Denmark, Sweden and Italy. In non-industrial countries restraints on the right to strike were more general. Strikes were permissible only for the purpose of direct economic or social benefits in several Latin American countries and all strikes were prohibited in Turkey, Spain and Portugal.

The line was not an easy one to draw, however, especially in view of the tendency for governments to enlarge the areas of their activity and thus to bring a larger proportion of workers into the category of public employees. To deny to these workers the rights enjoyed by those in comparable types of work in private industry appeared to penalize them for being public employees. Equally difficult was the effort to draw the line between 'essential' and 'non-essential' services or industries.

(c) Machinery for adjusting labour–management relations

The unresolved dilemma was made less serious in most countries by the development of positive means for adjusting labour relations which would reduce the likelihood of resort to the strike. Some form of machinery to facilitate negotiation and collective bargaining was set up in practically every country; in some a strike was legal only if the established procedures had been followed.

Mediation services were generally offered by government where negotiations threatened to break down, and their use was made compulsory in some countries. In the Scandinavian countries the negotiation of industry-wide contracts was set up on a national basis with a fixed schedule for annual preliminary negotiations, the referral of points of disagreement to government mediators, the settlement of remaining unresolved issues by government wage boards in Norway and a joint employer–union board in Sweden, and the adoption of the new agreement at a uniform time each year. Only in the rare instances where agreement was still lacking after the procedure had been followed would there be the possibility of a strike. The principle was also well established that disputes arising over the interpretation or execution of the labour contract were not to lead to work stoppages and labour courts were established to adjudicate such disputes in Denmark in 1910, Norway in 1915 and Sweden in 1928.

In most west European countries works councils were provided for by law and their elections, conducted by secret ballot, were carried on under government supervision. Within the general framework of laws and broad collective agreements, these works councils had responsibility for developing the detailed terms of the work contract and assuring its observance. The most binding structure for the conduct of labour relations was the system of compulsory arbitration established in Australia, New Zealand, the Union of South Africa and Northern Ireland.

4. ACHIEVEMENT OF LABOUR'S GOALS

By mid-century many of the goals which had looked far distant to workers at the opening of the century had been at least partially achieved or had come within sight—in terms of material standards, rights as workers and status as citizens.

As a consequence both of better wages and working conditions and of the social provisions of the welfare state, workers had come to take for granted many of the material benefits of which their predecessors of 1900 had hardly dared to dream—greatly increased real wages, leisure, social security, social services, housing, travel, holidays, pensions, medical services, the education of their children. Such benefits were not enjoyed equally by the workers of all the industrial countries nor by all workers in each country, for great differences in productivity continued to be reflected in differences in levels of living, the gap between rich and poor had been narrowed more sharply in some countries than in others and disadvantaged groups remained. But with all these qualifications, most of the workers of the industrial countries enjoyed a material standard of living well above that of fifty years before, and in the most advanced industrial countries the difference was great. The struggle for higher wages and other benefits continued unabated, however, for the rising aspirations of workers more than kept pace with the rising productivity of industry.

The rights of labour freely to associate and to seek their objectives had become well established in the major industrial countries. In most countries machinery for the conduct of negotiations and the settlement of labour disputes enabled representatives of labour and management to deal with each other without the need for constant militancy or intransigence; in fact it sometimes appeared to the union rank and file that their officials had become so preoccupied with the mechanics of labour–management adjustment that they no longer provided vigorous leadership, and 'wildcat' strikers protested against their unions as well as against their employers.

Yet the memory of the destruction of labour organizations by the fascist and Nazi régimes was still vivid; labour's rights were still limited and trade unionists imprisoned under some of the ruling dictators. Anti-labour sentiment was in fact far from dead even where labour organization was a well-established institution. Labour movements continued to act as the guardians and promoters of labour's rights and to serve as the means through which workers struggled within the social and political framework of their several societies to secure for themselves and their children the status, opportunities and conditions of life which the principles of western society made the goal of all people.

Labour's political role was also generally well-established. Through political parties or pressure on legislatures, labour continued to work for social legislation and it participated responsibly through the International Labour Organization in the formulation of world-wide standards for labour's status and welfare.

In their individual response to widening opportunities, moreover, workers demonstrated both the determination and the capacity to move into a new place in society. Many sent their children to secondary schools and some to universities; they acquired and enjoyed decent homes, travelled, read, enjoyed cinema and radio, developed hobbies and accepted community responsibilities.

By the mid-twentieth century the worker in the industrial countries had thus achieved a status as a human being and a citizen. He enjoyed, for the most part, decent conditions of work. He was far less distinguished than in the past by dress and speech, by the poorness of his housing and his lack of education, by his poor health and that of his children. Nor was he expected to keep his place and to accept as his due inferior standards that were deemed good enough for him. In the words of the report sponsored by the welfare ministers of the northern European countries: 'By joining with his fellows the wage-earner has found a powerful means not only of furthering his economic interests but also of enhancing his general status and dignity as a useful member of the community. The downtrodden labourer of former days standing in wooden shoes and cap in hand before his employer is now but a memory from the bygone past.'*

Nevertheless, the very nature of all industry continued to make the status of the individual worker dependent and insecure. His job was often monotonous and conditioned by the machine; changing technology offered a constant threat to his mastery of his job and to the value of his skills; many factors beyond his control—automation, economic fluctuations, changes of product or plant location—might leave him without work and require him to find a new job or move to a new place; in the calculations of management he remained an item of cost. In their continuing struggle for status, workers made a constant effort to reduce their dependence on the employer's whim, through such devices as seniority and guaranteed annual wages; they sought positive measures to facilitate necessary changes, such as provisions for retraining and the costs of moving to new jobs; they endeavoured to secure a share in determining the manner in which changes affecting workers, such as automation, would be introduced.

The place which labour occupied had become a key to the character of industrial states. In the democratically oriented states labour became a major power element, extending its influence and active participation step by step throughout the period, assuming the political leadership in some countries for periods of time. The status and rights of labour served as symbols of democratic liberalism in constitutions and national policies. In countries where authoritarian forces were strong, labour was a rallying point for challenges to authority and the suppression of the right of workers to organize and express their grievances was a symbol of dictatorship. In the communist countries the interests of labour organizations were bound up with the interests of the

* *Freedom and Welfare, op. cit.*, p. 503.

government and they were responsible for carrying out economic policy, achieving production goals and administering social benefits.

In the newly developing countries labour's self-conscious effort to secure status was inextricably bound up with the political awakening of the people, with their national aspirations and with their efforts to find their identity as citizens in the new societies that were replacing the static and status-bound societies of the past. The conditions which workers faced were often worse and their problems more formidable than those which had confronted labour in the early days of western industrialization. But the workers of Asia, of Latin America and of Africa had before them, in the achievements of the workers of industrially developed countries, a standard of aspiration which their predecessors had lacked.

II. PEASANTS AND FARMERS

While labour was achieving a large measure of success in its struggle for status in industrially advanced countries and a growing self-consciousness elsewhere, the rural masses remained generally less articulate and less successful in their more sporadic efforts to improve their lot.

Both in regions of advanced agriculture and in underdeveloped areas, farmers occupied a relatively disadvantageous position as compared with those engaged in industry and trade. In both types of societies farm incomes were generally below those of corresponding elements in the city. In underdeveloped areas primitive techniques and insufficient land meant low productivity and, consequently, low returns to the cultivator. Where agricultural technology was advanced, the farmer's very efficiency tended to depress his income by bringing a constant threat of glutted markets and falling prices. Rural populations everywhere had higher birth rates than those in the city and the expanding needs of industry for workers were met from the extra hands not needed on the farm. Differential wages in favour of industry reflected this process.[11]

In dealing with other segments of the population, farmers were generally at a bargaining disadvantage, for many small, competitive units often confronted a few strong suppliers of equipment, storage, transport, processing and marketing services. Where cultivators did not own their land but were required to give a substantial portion of their crop to absentee or feudal landlords, they were at an additional disadvantage. Where they were also in debt to their landlords, they might be in a state of virtual peonage.

For his lesser income, the farmer generally worked long and hard, as his crops or his stock might require, rarely able to restrict his hours to a fixed number as did the urban worker. He might be idle in slack seasons and overworked in others. With the high rural birth rate, the cost and burden of child-rearing fell disproportionately on the country people. In addition rural life in many areas lacked the amenities of the town—conveniences such as electricity and running water, facilities such as schools and health services, shops, sources of entertainment.

Though the rural dweller was at an economic and social disadvantage as compared with the city dweller, and though the city exerted a strong pull to attract rural migrants by virtue of jobs and urban attractions, there were aspects of rural life which farmers cherished and wished to maintain. The aspirations of rural folk as they found expression during these years were mainly for means to enjoy these positive rural values. Farming as a way of life contrasted favourably with the kind of life available in the city in that it was geared to the rhythm of the seasons to which men through the centuries had been attuned. It offered to the farmer a measure of self-direction, subject only to the demands of nature, and, except where he worked for another, freedom from the dictates of other men. Although rural tasks were often laborious and of a sameness, they were much more varied than the monotonous jobs which urban workers were often called on to perform, repetitively, day in and day out. Land, in the rural tradition, meant security; the alternative of city employment at the pleasure of an employer meant hazard.

The rural person wanted first and foremost the security which was part of the rural way of life—albeit full of hazards from nature—enhanced by security of tenure or ownership in his land. Secondly, he wanted access to the means of exploiting his land effectively, and in such a way that it could yield him a decent living. This meant access to knowledge, to markets and sources of supply on favourable terms, and to credit for development. Thirdly, farmers aspired to enter fully and freely into the cultural life of the broader society, through access to education, through communication and through the opportunity to enjoy the amenities which had become part of city life, such as labour-saving appliances in the farm home and enlarged social contacts made possible by modern transport and communication.

The situation of the farmer and the character of farmers' movements differed radically from one area to another, but all shared two basic, common aspirations: to reduce the disparity, both economic and cultural, between farm and city, and to realize the positive values of rural life.

Where, as in western Europe, North America, South Africa, Australia and New Zealand, the typical farmer produced crops for market on a family farm which he owned or held in secure tenure, farm organizations were composed of independent producers who banded together to provide themselves with common services, for economic bargaining or to use their political power to gain public facilities or legislation favourable to agriculture. Some organizations were primarily economic in their emphasis, others essentially political and some included social activities, but all sought to strengthen the farmer's hand within the existing structure of agriculture and the existing social order. Where there were class distinctions between well-to-do, middle and poor farmers or farm labourers, farm organizations generally represented the middle and upper groups.

In the very different conditions of essentially feudal landholding in east Europe, Latin America and the Middle East, where tenants or farm labourers were only one step removed from serfdom and lived in poverty and ignorance at the mercy of their landlords, peasant movements had a more or less revolutionary aim. They were composed of the poor or landless peasants who made up the vast majority of the peasant population in areas where the middle-level farmer, so typical of western Europe and North America, was almost non-existent. They sought to recast the structure of agrarian society to give the peasant rights in the land which he tilled and to break the landlords' power.

After the second world war a third type of movement among rural people began to take shape in Asian countries and in other underdeveloped rural areas under the outside stimulus of community development programmes. The objectives of such programmes were to raise the economic and cultural level of backward and often isolated rural areas as a part of the effort for national development; their method was to stimulate self-help among the people themselves. The vigour with which people in many areas responded to these stimuli—in India, Pakistan, the Philippines, Jamaica, Puerto Rico, Africa—indicated that community self-help had the potentialities of a major movement for the reconstruction of rural life.

1. FARMERS' MOVEMENTS IN COUNTRIES OF ADVANCED AGRICULTURE

Farmers of western Europe, North America and Australasia were not a depressed class but were entrepreneurs with a middle-class outlook. Though their status was generally below that of the urban middle class, it was nevertheless that of property owners and business men. There were, however, profound differences in attitude between the farmer in young countries such as Canada, Australia and the USA and peasant owners who were more deeply rooted in the land which had been in their family for many generations. For the former, land was a resource to yield him a living and, although he was often strongly attached to his particular acres, his main interest was in the income which the use of the land might bring. His immediate forebears had moved from one farm to another in the course of a lifetime seeking better opportunities, and many twentieth-century farmers continued to look for additional acres or better land.

In contrast, the European peasant-owner was almost a part of the land which he farmed. He was the temporary custodian of a terrain which had sustained his ancestors and which was his to cherish and to hand on as a heritage to his children, richer if possible but certainly no poorer. The peasant who lived within a family–land continuum could not willingly exploit and exhaust the land, as the farm entrepreneur often did, careless of the morrow. He must practise good husbandry, for his own future and that of his children were bound up with preservation of the fertility of the soil.[12]

Farm organizations in countries where independent farming and commercialized agriculture predominated grew out of technical societies for such purposes as stock breeding, out of scattered fraternal or social unions, and out of sporadic protest movements against conditions unfavourable to agriculture. They tended to become the means through which farmers engaged directly in co-operative economic activity, for agricultural credit as in Germany and Italy, or for co-operative marketing as in Denmark, Switzerland, Canada, New Zealand and the United States. They engaged in political action, sometimes through an agrarian party, more often by political pressure within parties and on governments as in Canada and the United States. As government services to agriculture were extended and countries adopted economic measures to support farm incomes, farmers' organizations frequently became the medium through which these programmes were carried out. Agricultural extension services, for example, were provided in Denmark by government grants to farm organizations and were partially supported by farm organizations in the United States; local farmers' committees participated in the administration of acreage allotment and soil conservation programmes in the United States and much responsibility for the British farm programme rested with local farmers' councils.

Farm organizations tended to be dominated by, and to reflect the interests of, the more substantial farmers, sometimes to the point where the smaller farmers formed a separate organization, as in Denmark. The principal international association which linked national farm organizations, the International Federation of Agricultural Producers formed in 1946, spoke for these substantial groups.

On broad social and economic issues organized farmers tended to be on the side of social reform when issues directly affecting farming were involved; they opposed the power of banks, public utilities and large corporations and called for anti-monopoly measures; they supported cheap power, easy credit, rural electrification, public ownership or regulation of transport, storage and marketing facilities and the extension of roads, education, health and other services to rural areas. On other issues they tended to be more conservative; some farm organizations went to the extreme of being anti-labour and of opposing the various social protections of the welfare state; others made common cause with labour in support of broad social programmes.

In general, farm movements of the twentieth century in the technically advanced countries reflected the efforts of independent farm entrepreneurs to withstand the pressure of, or to get in step with, the modern industrial economy and to make a secure and prosperous place for themselves in it.

2. PEASANT MOVEMENTS

The most articulate and well-organized movements of peasants on feudal estates were those of Russia and eastern Europe. Here, at the opening of the century, land was still held in *latifundia* on essentially feudal terms; the abolition of serfdom in the 1860s had left the peasantry scarcely better off than

PP*

before, for they were burdened with payments for their land and often lost it to the richer landlords. Within the feudal structures, different peasant traditions survived, the village community or *mir* in Russia, the extended family or *zadruga* in some of the Balkan areas and individual proprietorship elsewhere. But everywhere the aspirations of the peasants were the same—to own their land.

Peasant movements of protest and reform had gathered momentum during the late nineteenth century. The Populists in Russia envisaged an agrarian society based on the *mir*, and from 1900 on their successors, the Social Democrats, retained this as their goal for the rural sector while adopting a revolutionary socialist view for industry. Peasant unrest was a major element in the abortive Russian revolution of 1905, and the Stolypin reforms were adopted thereafter in a belated effort to quiet peasant discontent. These reforms were designed to create independent peasant proprietors rather than to strengthen the village community.

Peasant parties and movements in eastern Europe pursued the goal of individual ownership of the land. A number of such movements took shape around the turn of the century, the Czech peasant party, formed in 1896, being one of the strongest and most practical. The movement in Rumania led to a peasant uprising in 1907 which was not suppressed until some 10,000 peasants had been killed.

As against the aspirations of the peasants for an agrarian society of peasant proprietors, Marx and his followers insisted that the proletarianization of the peasants was inevitable and that fundamental improvement in the lot of the peasants could come only as the lower peasants joined the class war and as agriculture was reorganized on a collective basis into large producing units. The socialist parties thus stood opposed in principle to the populist aspirations and movements of peasants.

Lenin, however, saw that the revolutionary thrust of the peasants could be used as a practical aid in bringing the proletarian revolution and that it was in fact essential to the success of the revolution in predominantly agrarian societies such as Russia. His slogan 'land for the tillers' linked the uprising of the peasants to the proletarian revolution and brought under his leadership the peasants who moved on their own initiative to dispossess the landowners once the revolution of 1917 got under way. The October revolution was thus a victory for peasants as well as for workers, and the distribution of land to the peasants was one of its most immediate fruits.

The revolution in Russia gave a tremendous impetus to the peasant movements of eastern Europe. Taking advantage of the extension of the franchise under the new constitutions of the east European countries, peasant parties rose to power in the 1920s throughout the area.

These peasant parties were entirely composed of poor peasants, for there was no peasant middle class comparable to that in west European countries, and they were directed against the landlords. Their programmes reflected peasant aspirations. They stood for the individually owned family farm, both as an economic unit and as a way of life. They supported democratic principles of government.

They were anti-capitalist as far as the ownership and exploitation of large units of land and of large-scale industry were concerned. They favoured state ownership of public services and basic industries and the scattering of small, individually owned industries through the countryside to spread the benefits of industrialization and share them with the peasant proprietors. They favoured the organization of co-operatives where larger operations of either rural industry or agriculture were desirable. They wanted education, health and the other services of the modern state extended to the villages and they opposed what they regarded as the privileged position of the towns. Their image was that of a rural society, based on an educated, independent, landowning peasantry, which would use co-operation as the means of combining the advantages of small property with those of large enterprise.

Although the peasant parties shared a common outlook, they varied considerably from country to country. The well-organized Czechoslovak party was successful in pushing through the most extensive of the programmes of land reform and for introducing the eight-hour day for agricultural labour. Polish peasants formed no single organization but a number which ranged from radical to conservative and from anti-clerical to clerical. In Rumania the peasant party constituted the political opposition until it came to power in 1928 and established the first parliamentary government which the country experienced. The Bulgarian party, in existence since 1901, received a majority of the votes in 1923. The Croat peasant party which became a dominant element in Yugoslavia in the 1920s combined Croatian nationalism with a clearly defined rural ideology.

Moves to link peasant movements internationally came from both right and left. After the first world war a conservative element in Bavaria and Austria attempted to initiate an international organization but failed. A Russian-sponsored Communist Peasant International held its first congress in 1925, but it had relatively little influence on east European peasant movements during the inter-war years. On the initiative of the Bulgarian peasant party, a bureau for agricultural research was established in Prague in 1921 with Czech, Bulgarian, Polish and Serbian peasant parties as members, joined later by some west European groups. The peasant movements never attained a degree of international organization comparable to that of the socialist and communist parties.

Except in Hungary, where the landowning class retained its hold, a very considerable measure of land distribution was carried out throughout east Europe in the inter-war years. Although the agrarian reforms varied greatly in their completeness, in the size of holding left to the former landlord, in the proportion of the poor peasants who acquired land, and in the ability of the peasants to command the necessary means of cultivation, the landlord class was virtually eliminated and a major social revolution was effected. And though the peasant holdings were small, their freedom from obligations to landlords and the opportunity to raise more subsistence crops instead of grain for market enabled numbers of peasants to make some improvement in their condition and to take a step toward their ideal of a prosperous agrarian society.

The tenure of power by the east European peasant parties was, however, short-lived. Reactionary elements, displaced from the land, reasserted themselves politically and broke down the democratic procedures which had enabled the peasants to rise. The murder of the Bulgarian peasant party leaders in 1923 broke up that party; the Croat peasant leaders were imprisoned and some killed; Rumanian leaders were persecuted and the party denied the power it had earned at the polls; in Poland some leaders were imprisoned and others fled. Suppression of the peasant parties ended in dictatorship for most countries of eastern Europe.

Meantime in the USSR private peasant proprietorship of the means of production was replaced by co-operative ownership. At no time did the Communist party accept peasant aspirations to the individual ownership of land as anything except a practical device to get rid of the landowners and to create a partnership between peasants and industrial workers. Collectivization was always the goal. An initial period of collectivization was followed in 1921 by the period of the New Economic Policy when individual peasant operations were permitted; but this was declared from the start to be a temporary slackening of pace, not a basic change in direction. When collectivization was resumed in 1928 it was carried through rigorously, in spite of the opposition of certain categories of landowning peasants.[13, 14]

In the years leading to the second world war and during the war the peasants of eastern Europe were strong elements in the anti-Nazi resistance movements of their countries. When these countries regained their independence at the close of the war, urban-led communist minorities with strong backing from the international communist organization contended for power with the more loosely organized peasant majorities. When the communist parties came to power they expropriated the remaining estates and divided the land with great rapidity, and they organized communist peasant parties in Poland, Bulgaria, Rumania, Hungary and Czechoslovakia in the effort to orient the peasants toward collectivization.[15]

In the face of strong traditional aspirations to individual landownership among the peasants, the communist leaders in each of these countries moved somewhat cautiously toward this avowed goal, in Poland halting and even reversing the process in 1956. But the leadership of the people's democracies was committed to the Marxian view that socialization of agriculture was essential. A socialist society had no place for the vision of a rural democracy of peasant proprietors to which the east European peasant movements aspired in the years when they offered a means of expression to the peasant masses of these areas.[16]

Peasant risings played a part in revolutionary movements in Latin America and Asia. The aspiration of peasants changed the character of the Mexican revolution which began in 1910. Under the long dictatorship (1877–1911) of Porfirio Díaz, more than 90 per cent of the Mexican peasants were landless; in many states the proportion exceeded 95 per cent. Their real income fell steadily, especially in the decade after 1900 when the decline was variously estimated at between 33 and 75 per cent. Meanwhile the mounting wealth of the country flowed into the hands of a small class of rich landholders, the Church and foreign investors. In its initial phase, the revolution, inspired and led by middle-class intellectuals who sought an end to political tyranny and concessions to foreign exploiters, was not a movement for agrarian reform. But when the agrarian leader Emilio Zapata raised the cry of 'land for the landless' and urged his followers to demand and take over lands belonging to landlords and the Church, this became its central drive.

The demand of the Mexican peasants for land expressed two distinct ideologies with quite opposite origins, the traditional Indian concept of communal lands held and worked by the village, and the North American concept of individual ownership of his own land by each farmer. From both points of view the peasants and their leaders rejected the authority of the 'patron' or landowner and the admonition of the Church that they should submit to this authority as from God. Nor were they guided by Marxist principles as a basis for collectivization.

In the successive stages of the continuous Mexican revolution, the peasants achieved freedom from submission and debt-peonage to the landlords and secured the distribution of a large proportion of the agricultural lands—all of the lands in the most populous regions. They combined their traditions of communal holdings and their desire for individual possession in a system of *ejidos* owned in common by the village, but parcelled out to each villager or *ejiditario*, who was entitled to possession of a portion of the land so long as he cultivated it. More than forty years after the beginning of the revolution, the economic condition of the Mexican peasant remained low and the claims of many *ejiditarios* were still unmet for lack of sufficient available land to provide all with farms which would yield an adequate livelihood. But the agrarian basis had helped to keep the Mexican revolution essentially democratic in its values and orientation.[17]

Elsewhere in Latin America, the aspirations of the peasants—*campesinos*—were the basis of revolutionary movements, but with little success in changing the *latifundia* system which prevailed so generally throughout the area. The Apra party of Peru, formed in the 1930s by urban intellectuals, drew its mass support from the rural areas and couched its demands in terms of land for the landless. The movement, however, was suppressed, its leaders were jailed or exiled, and in the 1950s the peasants of Peru, as of most other Latin American countries, had as yet found no means of breaking the hold of the landowners. In other countries the undercurrent of land hunger rose to the surface briefly or locally from time to time, as in Guatemala in the early 1950s. In Bolivia, however, the peasants' aspirations for land achieved fulfilment when, in 1952, a government pledged to redistribute the land took power by force and proceeded to make good its pledge; and land reform was a principal plank in the platform of the revolutionary leader who ousted the dictator in Cuba in 1959.[18] No popular leader could be unaware of the Latin American *campesino*'s desire for land or fail to recognize that, in a world where the remains of feudal landholding had been or were being swept away, agrarian reform in these areas was already overdue.

All over Asia peasants became aroused to seek new rights in the period after the first world war. In most areas, notably India, Indonesia and Burma, the peasant awakening contributed to the nationalist movements. After independence the reconstruction of rural life was part of the process of national development.

In China the communist leadership built the revolutionary movement squarely on the peasants' aspirations for land, for Mao Tse-tung insisted that the peasant, not the urban worker, must provide the revolutionary base in an essentially agricultural country. Under the actual conditions of Chinese agriculture, holdings were infinitesimally small and insufficient to provide a living, even when worked by intensive and often skilful methods.

When the communist leaders, after first redistributing the land, used persuasion, inducements and pressure to encourage co-operative or collective farming, they found Chinese peasants less insistent than Russian and east European peasants had been on retaining individual ownership. Within ten years of the initial land distribution, they were able to take the further step of placing landholding and the whole of rural life on a communal basis.

3. COMMUNITY DEVELOPMENT

In the years after the second world war efforts to raise the peasant masses in all parts of the world came not only from the peasants themselves but from national and international agencies seeking to promote economic and social development. To the men who led these countries in their struggles to function as modern states, peasant populations isolated from the currents of the modern world appeared as a drag on their efforts. The national leaders knew that unless the level of productivity and participation among the rural people could be raised, the economies of their countries could not advance substantially and their political and social structures would rest on shaky foundations. In each of these countries, therefore, means were sought to stimulate the peasants not only to change their agricultural methods but to engage on their own behalf in efforts to improve their lot. This process went under the general term of 'community development'.

Community development meant organized efforts to raise the level of rural community life, primarily through self-help and co-operative activity on the part of the rural community itself, stimulated and provided with technical aid in such a way as to cultivate self-reliance, initiative and common effort. Community development programmes had their antecedents in a variety of related activities: in agricultural extension services, community programmes of health education, co-operative organization, community schools or cultural missions, and various forms of welfare activity. As they took shape in different countries they varied considerably in form and emphasis, but all in one way or another represented a partnership between government and people.

At one end of the scale, in the Philippines where all government was highly centralized, the programme was administered from the office of the president of the republic and was set up as a means by which public services could be carried to remote regions which they had not previously reached. A 'village worker' represented all government services at the neighbourhood level and acted both as a liaison to the combined government agencies to which he was responsible and as an awakener of initiative and guide to village and neighbourhood self-help. At the opposite extreme, the programme in Jamaica, West Indies, took the form primarily of assistance to volunteer effort provided by personnel of what was originally a non-governmental organization, the Jamaica Welfare Commission. It operated only in the communities which sought assistance in carrying out some common effort. The main task of its workers was to advise, assist and train volunteer local leaders and to act as consultants to the groups which gave democratic expression to the interests of the locality.

Between these two extremes were a variety of community development programmes, differently designed to fit different areas. The ambitious programmes undertaken in India and Pakistan aimed to reach all of the more than half-million villages in that vast sub-continent within ten years. The Indian programme grouped approximately one hundred villages in each 'development block'; appropriate rural services were provided at the block centre—veterinary services, health clinics, vocational education, agricultural extension, co-operatives, small industries. A 'village-level worker', living in one of the villages which he served, acted as stimulator and consultant to a group of villages within the area. Government offered a certain amount of financial as well as technical assistance to projects undertaken by the villagers, providing some of the materials for the construction of roads, wells, schools, latrines, drainage pits, or furnishing fertilizer and seed for agricultural demonstrations, or materials and equipment for vocational training.

The Egyptian programme, designed for the large crowded villages of the Nile valley, emphasized the establishment of centres serving several villages where a range of services and activities were united—hospitals, schools, adult education, vocational workshops, co-operative enterprises, social centres. The objectives were both to overcome the disparity between rural and urban areas in respect to services which had been almost wholly confined to the cities and, by bringing these services close to the people, to stimulate their use. In a number of countries, special 'aided self-help' housing programmes provided technical guidance and materials at low cost to enable groups of families, by their co-operative efforts, to provide themselves with improved rural housing.

The philosophy which ran through all the community development programmes was well expressed in the law establishing the community education programme in Puerto Rico in 1948: 'The community should not be civically unemployed. The community can be constantly and usefully employed in its own service, in terms of pride and satisfaction of the members.' While the emphasis in some places was on concrete results—acres planted by improved methods, miles of roads constructed with village labour, wells dug, bridges built, schools built, land reclaimed, and community centres in operation— these were only the outward signs of the change in outlook and habits of rural people.

Community development was, in a sense, imposed on rural people from the outside and was designed to bring them into line with the values and practices of the broader society. Yet wherever such programmes were carried on with vigour and skill, their effect was to release latent energy and uncover latent desires and interests. Those who had started in the role of stimulators soon found themselves facing demands for further aid from villagers whose initiative often far exceeded what the technicians and leaders had been prepared to expect. Governments were hard pressed to make good on the promises of technical and material aid with which they had undertaken to supplement local efforts. Although some efforts to stimulate village initiative were abortive, the picture of apathetic rural people hard to arouse and tenacious of old ways had to be rapidly revised. Lack of energy often turned out to be merely the prevalence of malaria, malnutrition or internal parasites; lack of ambition reflected the long-existing hopelessness of the peasant's lot, and ignorance and conservatism the absence of the opportunity to learn. Ancient peasant societies were not being transformed overnight, for the heavy burden of poverty and ignorance presented a problem of staggering dimensions in all the newly developed countries, and the distance to be travelled was very great. But the impulse to change was unmistakably there. In the mid-twentieth century the peasant peoples of Asia and the Middle East, of Latin America and Africa were beginning to glimpse a new life toward which they were prepared to strive and were beginning to find their voices and means of action as they moved toward participation in the life of the modern world.

III. WOMEN

Many of the major changes of the twentieth century had their sharpest bearing upon the lives of women, who not only shared the new experiences and outlook which affected the whole society but found their own position altered. Every aspect of urban industrial life invaded and modified women's traditional domain, the home, removing most of its economic functions and making its former responsibilities, such as health, housing, sanitation and education, into matters of community concern. Inescapably these forces changed the activities of women, their sphere of operation and their place in society, drawing them into employment and public life, altering their relationships both within and outside the family group, and giving them a new status, new roles, new opportunities and new responsibilities. In large measure the new position of women was an incidental result of broad social trends. But to a considerable degree it was brought about by the conscious efforts of women themselves.

Prior to the twentieth century women in all parts of the world lived within social systems which assigned to them an inferior position and a restricted role. Law, religion and custom in western countries had combined to sanction complete subordination of women to men, though in practice women had always found means to make their influence felt. Under the Anglo-Saxon common law, married women enjoyed no independent legal rights—to property, guardianship of their children, use of their own earnings, determination of their own domicile. In the systems derived from the Roman law via the Napoleonic Code, property and parental rights were almost wholly enjoyed by men, and a married woman could not take legal action or engage in business and enter into contracts, or could do so only with her husband's consent. Religion sanctioned the duty of obedience. With few exceptions women enjoyed no political rights and had very limited access to education.

In eastern countries the position of women was somewhat less restricted by law than it was in the West, but it was far more limited by custom. Under Muslim law women enjoyed independent rights of property, guardianship and legal personality; in practice, except in Indonesia, the system of seclusion was general, women were veiled if they emerged from the home—except as they worked in the fields—and education and political rights were limited to men. Hindu women lived under severe legal and social restrictions, their scope of activity defined by their place in the extended family system. Seclusion was common, child marriage frequent, permanent widowhood the rule and education rare. Buddhist principles permitted general equality in property and personal status, but the strong patriarchal family in China left women little independent scope and the highly structured Japanese society reinforced the subordinate status of women by language, gesture and every detail of life.

I. THE GOALS OF WOMEN'S ASPIRATIONS

In the twentieth century increasing numbers of women throughout the world aspired to a new status and a new life. The status which they sought was one of personal identity as individuals; the new life was one of full opportunity. They wished to share the rights enjoyed by men and to be able to take part in the same political activity, receive the same education, engage in the same professions or other types of work, and be governed by the same code of social behaviour. But they wished, too, for the opportunity to give full expression to their differences without the implication of inferiority. Such aspirations were generally voiced by educated women; it was not always clear that they were wholly shared by others. They were achieved in large measure during the first half of the century by the women of the industrialized countries but were only beginning to be realized at mid-century by most women elsewhere.

In each country women couched their common goals in terms of the ideologies and conditions of their societies. European women had begun to agitate for a change in status at the time of the French revolution when they sought to extend to women the concept of the 'rights of man'. But they had met little sympathy for such expressions as Mary Wollstonecraft's *Vindication of the Rights of Woman* (London, 1792), or the proposal of a group of Frenchwomen that the National Assembly of 1789 adopt a 'declaration of the rights of women'. Nor had anyone taken seriously the warning of Abigail Adams to her husband in the Continental Congress of the rebellious American colonies in 1776: 'If particular care and attention is not paid to the ladies, we are determined to foment a rebellion, and will not hold ourselves bound by any laws in which we have no voice or representation.'* Such ardent exponents of the rights of men as Jean Jacques Rousseau and Thomas Jefferson insisted that these rights did not include women.

In time, however, the concept that 'all men are created equal and are endowed with certain inalienable rights' worked as a leaven until the concept 'man' took on the meaning 'human'. It was no accident that the founders of the movement for women's suffrage in the United States should have been leaders in the anti-slavery crusade, or that the classic text for the women's rights movement in Britain and on the European continent, *The Subjection of Women* (1869) should have been written by the great exponent of liberalism, John Stuart Mill.

These principles of liberal democracy furnished the driving ideology for the women of Britain, the Commonwealth nations and the United States, for many of the women of the European continent and for most of the articulate women of Latin America and the eastern countries. Their concept of themselves and their objectives was based on a view of the individual personality as the ultimate social value. The basic ideological drive toward individualism was bolstered by economic trends, but it often had to contend with the traditional view of the priority of the woman's duty as wife and mother in a patriarchal family and with the new emphasis on the role of the mother brought by twentieth-century psychiatry.

Marxian socialism provided the ideology for women workers who took part in the socialist and communist political movements and in the labour organizations associated with them. In this view equality between the sexes was an integral aspect of a society in which the exploitation of one individual by another would have been eliminated.

Karl Marx regarded the subjection of women as a form of exploitation and an evil of capitalist society, and declared that 'social progress can be measured

* Quoted in C. A. Beard, *The Republic* (New York, 1943), p. 5.

with precision by the social position of the female sex'.* Equality of the sexes was in fact so basic to the socialist concept of a new society that it ceased to be a separate issue. Women enjoyed the same rights and duties as men in common activities within the political parties formed by the working class. Many women such as Rosa Luxemburg (1870–1919) and Clara Zetkin (1857–1933) in Germany, Louise Michel (1830–1905) and Laura Lafargue (1846–1911) in France, and Nadezhda Krupskaya (1869–1939) and Alexandra Kollontai (1872–1952) in Russia played a prominent part in the revolutionary movements. The second International Conference of Socialist Women, held in Copenhagen in 1910, instituted an 'International Women's Day', March 8, as a day of international solidarity of women in the struggle for economic and political equality, preservation of peace and the well-being of children. The principle of equality between men and women was automatically incorporated into law upon the establishment of the USSR.

Some agitation for changes in the position of women had begun in Asian countries before the close of the nineteenth century as a result of contact with the liberal thought of the West. In Japan a few women had been trained abroad and had founded higher educational institutions for women and organizations to seek women's rights. They received little support, however, from the men who led the movement for westernization, even though a freer and more equal status for women was recognized as a feature of western society. In China the influence of missionaries had affected a limited number, especially among the merchant classes whose contacts with the West were greatest, and had set a few women on the path of education. Reform movements in India stimulated by contact with the West, such as the Bramo Samaj, had included emancipation of women from Hindu customs as a cardinal point in their programmes, and Indian women were among the active participants and leaders in nationalist agitation. In Muslim areas there was as yet little sign of movement.

During the twentieth century women's movements grew in nearly all parts of Asia. After the October revolution the equality of men and women in the USSR became an inspiration and stimulus to women in Asian countries, for they saw in this example the first society where women were expected to function according to their capacities and potentialities.

Once the breach had been made in the wall of seclusion and subordination by the impact of either liberal democracy or Marxian socialism, Asian women invoked the equalitarian principles of the Quran and Buddhism and the basic assumptions of Hindu thought to attack the body of customs by which these had become overlaid. Muslim women called attention to the fact that the Quran gave them property rights not enjoyed by the women of the West, that the Prophet had encouraged women's political participation, and that the limitation to four wives with the injunction to take only one if justice could not be done to more had been a great step forward, designed to enhance the

* Letter to Kugelmann, 1868.

position of women. Hindu women had the support of Hindu reformers who regarded such traditional practices as permanent widowhood and child marriage as distortions of Hindu principles. Even in Africa, westernized African leaders began to recognize that their efforts to modernize their countries could be continually dragged down unless women shared the education and the concepts with which they themselves were working.

Women's aspirations were often closely linked with other movements, such as national liberation or the rights of labour, though the efforts of working women to achieve equal pay for equal work did not always receive the full support either of the trade unions or of other women's groups more intent on political rights. By sharing in the struggle against colonial rule, women in India and in Indonesia became part of common efforts and received as a matter of course the same voting rights as men when their countries became independent nations. Similarly it was the participation of Egyptian women, still veiled, in the movement for national liberation in 1919 that gave the initial impetus to their emancipation and brought support to their cause.

In the second quarter of the twentieth century international organizations gave strong endorsement to the aspirations of women. The fifth Inter-American Conference of 1923 recommended that the governments of the American republics modify their constitutions and laws 'in order to obtain for the women of the Americas the same civil and political rights enjoyed by men'. Women of the communist countries and related groups elsewhere worked together internationally through the Women's International Democratic Federation, formed at the first International Women's Congress in Paris in 1945. They joined in celebrating International Women's Day, and in initiating the first World Peace Congress in 1949 and the annual celebration of June 1st as 'Defence of Children Day'.

The Charter of the United Nations affirmed faith in the 'equal rights of men and women' and declared among its purposes the encouragement of respect for human rights without distinction of race, sex, language or religion. The Universal Declaration of Human Rights formulated a clear vision of women's status in the kind of society which the Declaration implied, declaring that 'men and women . . . are entitled to equal rights as to marriage, during marriage, and at its dissolution', that 'everyone' has the right to 'free choice of employment' and, 'without any discrimination, has the right to equal pay for equal work', the 'right to education' with higher education 'equally accessible to all on the basis of merit', the 'right to take part in government' and 'freely to participate in the cultural life of the community'.

By mid-century the women of the world thus had formal world opinion on their side, though a wide gulf remained between the goal envisaged by the Declaration of Human Rights and the actuality of the day. As a goal, it was rarely challenged openly, however much it might be rejected in thought and feeling.

2. METHODS OF SEEKING OBJECTIVES

In the initial stages of the women's movement in each country, outstanding women came forth as leaders, and their names became by-words in their own countries and sometimes around the world. Much of the movement for women's rights in the nineteenth and early twentieth centuries in Europe and America centred in the activity of individual women, such as Susan B. Anthony (1820–1906), Elizabeth Cady Stanton (1815–1902), Lucretia Mott (1793–1880) and Lucy Stone (1818–93) in the United States, the trade unionist, Mary MacArthur (1880–1921) and the militants Emmeline (1857–1928) and Sylvia (1882–1960) Pankhurst in England, Frederika Bremer (1801–65) and Ellen Key (1849–1926) in Sweden, Nina Bang (1866–1928) in Denmark, Louise Otto-Peters (1826–95) in Germany and Aletha Jacobs (1849–1929) in Holland. By the time of the first world war the women's movements in these countries had passed beyond the phase of individual leadership, though distinguished women continued to break ground, as did Margaret Bondfield (1873–1953), first British woman cabinet minister, whose career as a leader of labour rather than of women brought her to political office in 1929.

In the non-western countries individual women exercising personal leadership launched vigorous movements on behalf of women in their countries during the twentieth century. Madame Sarojini Naidu (1879–1949) of India, Madame Saraawi (–   ) in Egypt, Halide Edib Adivar (1875–   ) in Turkey, Baroness Ishimoto (1897–   ) in Japan, Mme Sun Yat-sen (1890–   ) in China, by their personal courage, sacrifice and ability to dramatize the cause of women, focused attention and drew support. They surrounded themselves with followers whom they developed into leaders in their turn and to whom they handed on their role and responsibility.

Outstanding women in every country sought higher education and the opportunity to enter the leading professions which carried prestige and the highest status in the society. They sought these opportunities for their own self-development and the personal satisfactions of professional work, but at the same time they believed that they were demonstrating that women as a class were not the inferior beings they had been assumed to be. Those who achieved distinction and were able to compete successfully with men at the highest level of professional activity, science, scholarship or artistic creation were symbols of their sex. By their achievements they hoped to wear down the prejudice of men and enhance the self-confidence of other women.

From the nineteenth century on, women formed organizations to promote their cause. One of the earliest objectives of their organized efforts was to make higher education freely available for women as a road to the professions and to economic independence and leadership. Institutions for the higher education of women were established in several countries, in the United States in the 1830s and in England in the 1840s; the London Medical School for Women was set up in 1874. In the last quarter of the nineteenth century

European and American universities began to admit women, either in special cases or freely. The first Dutch woman was admitted to university study by special permission of the prime minister in 1870, and selected women secured permission to enter universities in Russia and Switzerland. The publicly supported state universities established in the United States from 1862 on were open to both men and women, as were, generally, the British municipal and dominion universities. Mexico graduated its first woman physician in 1887 and first lawyer in 1898. By the opening of the twentieth century momentum had been created for the full extension of higher education to women.

In the non-western countries where the movements for women's rights did not take shape until after the first world war, the right to enter higher educational institutions was not the important issue which it had been for western women at a corresponding stage of their organized effort. The principle had already been established and the western-style universities which were being founded in these areas generally had no specific bars against admission of women.

Everywhere the main focus of organized movements for women's rights was on securing the right to vote; such an emphasis was natural in the democratically oriented societies of the West which had gone through a long struggle to establish manhood suffrage and had couched their statements of the rights of men in essentially political terms. It was an integral part of the socialist movement for both economic and political equality.

The women's right movements, which drew their leadership and main support from the middle and upper classes, generally involved two groups: a militant element, such as the British suffragettes, who staged mass demonstrations, chained themselves in public to dramatize their cause, courted arrest, went on hunger strikes or engaged in other forms of aggressive behaviour, and a more moderate element who felt that such tactics would not advance their cause but were more likely to alienate the men upon whom they had to depend for legislation. The moderate group urged patience, reason and the demonstration of what women could do as workers and citizens, rather than resort to spectacular behaviour.

The movements for women's rights which emerged later in other parts of the world engaged in a similar struggle for the suffrage, had a similar upper- and middle-class composition, and showed the same division. In Egypt in the 1950s, where women still had no vote, the leader of the militant element went on a hunger strike and courted imprisonment as the Pankhursts had done in their day in Britain, while the more moderate women's organizations worked to encourage women to enter the professions, called attention to their achievements, and tried to secure the implementation of the positive rights of women provided in the Quran. In Indonesia, where suffrage was not an issue, the broad women's organizations were devoted to general welfare, while a small group focused on the promotion of women's legal rights.

Some women sought political office and figured as political leaders. In Europe this was chiefly as candidates of the socialist parties which were almost alone in welcoming women candidates. Elsewhere women candidates were less likely to be confined to particular parties. Rarely, however, did women organize as a political bloc to support candidates of their sex.

Only the most ardent elements in the women's rights organizations of the western countries attacked the legal disabilities of married women with the same zeal that they brought to the struggle for higher education and suffrage. Since the inability to dispose of property, enter into contracts, establish domicile or exercise guardianship of children became important only in time of family conflict or crisis, these matters seemed vital chiefly to those women who had suffered directly and those concerned as a matter of principle. In the United States a militant group sought to prohibit all legal discrimination on the basis of sex by means of an amendment to the federal constitution but they encountered strong opposition from other organized women who feared that the measure would undermine protective labour legislation which the latter regarded as more important than gains in legal status. For organized Muslim women, however, greater rights in respect to marriage and divorce and the application in practice of their stipulated rights of property and guardianship were of central importance.

As women became active in community life they organized for other purposes than to advance their own status, and the group dedicated to women's rights became a small fragment of the whole, either maintaining a separate organization or representing a special interest within broader groups.

In virtually all countries women organized for purposes of social welfare. Religious congregations of nuns had long provided hospitals, orphanages, homes for unmarried mothers and other institutions. Along with teaching, social welfare was one of the earliest types of activity undertaken by women outside the home. In some places it remained the principal way in which women participated in community life. Voluntary organizations took the initiative in establishing welfare services where they were lacking, providing milk stations for babies, clubs, nurseries, playgrounds, homes and hospitals for children, homes for unmarried mothers, settlement houses and a multitude of other services. Women in Pakistan formed an organization to provide schools, handicraft employment and other services to refugees; Turkish women undertook to establish the first institution in the country for juvenile delinquents; women of Thailand supported services for the blind; women in Colombia set up and sustained community centres, clinics, kindergartens and schools; voluntary groups in the United States supported pioneer projects in dental hygiene, travelling libraries, children's dramatics. Where services were already provided by the state or by organized private agencies, women's organizations supplemented professional services, supplying volunteer nurses' aides to hospitals, recreation aides to community centres and filling a host of other posts under professional direction.

These voluntary organizations were chiefly composed of women of the middle and upper classes who had leisure to devote to such activity and were in a position to donate or raise funds. Leadership was often supplied by a prominent figure such as the wife of the president, governor or prime minister, a member of the royal family or of the aristocracy, or a woman of wealth. Participation in such activities was frequently a mark of social prestige. A leading organization in the United States composed of the socially *élite* admitted to membership only those who would dedicate several hours a week to voluntary service in social welfare agencies.

The voluntary welfare activities led by prominent women were particularly characteristic of the early stages of women's organized efforts, although they continued along with other lines of activity. As women extended their activities they formed a wide variety of organizations with many purposes and bases for membership. Some organizations were formed for self-entertainment, mutual improvement or pursuit of a common interest such as gardening. Others were based on religion, nationality or race and sought to promote the interests of their group in the total society, to provide a basis of social solidarity, to engage in welfare activity, or to support broad social objectives in line with the principles of their group or their responsibilities as women. Women's auxiliaries of men's organizations, such as fraternal organizations, professional or labour groups, gave support to their husbands' interests and provided a social group on the basis of their husbands' occupations.

Still others were formed to provide means for the social, educational and recreational activities of women and girls, as through the YWCA, Girl Scouts and Girl Guides, or the Countrywomen of the World. Some were dedicated to a specific social cause, such as temperance, peace or birth control. Others were the women's arms of political parties, or were non-partisan organizations dedicated to a proper use of the suffrage. University women organized to support fellowships and promote education. Women in business and the professions formed associations to strengthen their position, especially where they were still struggling to break down occupational barriers.

All these organizations reflected the active interest and concern of women outside the home. While they drew their membership most heavily from middle-class elements, they included a wide social range and utilized the energies, training, intelligence and time of both employed women and housewives.

Whatever their basis and purpose, most of them developed programmes of study, some form of democratic organization and the means of voicing the views of their members on public issues. They supported legislation and other public measures in line with their objectives, engaging in campaigns of public education, persuading legislators and getting out votes. They worked especially for such things as maternal and child health and the suppression of prostitution, civic improvements, the extension of social services, adequate inspection of food and drugs, better schools. Through these organizations, women's activities came to be more and more directed toward the welfare of the total community rather than the direct championship of the rights of women.

Although women's organizations continued to flourish up to the middle of the twentieth century, both in those countries where they had been in existence for many years and in those where they expressed the new role of women emerging from seclusion, there was a growing tendency for women to function in bodies composed of both men and women rather than in separate groups. As members of professional associations, trade unions, political parties or interest groups, on governing boards of community agencies, in associations of parents and teachers composed of men and women, and in countless other groups, women participated as full members without regard to their sex and performed functions determined by their individual capacities. Where this kind of participation existed and women were accepted on their merits as individuals, they felt that they had achieved the fundamental goal envisaged by the pioneer champions of women's rights.

3. ACHIEVEMENT OF GOALS

In each of the fields in which women aspired to a changed status, their conscious efforts or the broad social and economic developments of the period brought them toward their goals. The United Nations Commission on the Status of Women, reviewing in 1955 the progress toward realization of the status envisioned in the Universal Declaration of Human Rights, found a marked extension of women's political rights, some changes with respect to the legal status of married women but many limitations still to be removed, continued inadequacy of facilities for secondary and higher education as compared with those available for boys, and only a beginning toward implementing the principle of equal pay for equal work. It noted that the rights of women on paper were far more numerous than those in actual practice and that a major task ahead was to help women to become aware of their rights and to exercise them.

(a) Political rights

At the opening of the century women had the right to vote only in New Zealand, in two Australian states and in four states of the USA. By the middle of the century they had secured the vote in nearly all countries. Suffrage advocates achieved few successes before the first world war, adding only Norway, the rest of Australia, Finland and eight more of the states of the USA, plus municipal franchise in Britain and a few other places. But the impact of the war brought large numbers of women into the labour market and gave the suffrage movement the momentum for victory. During and immediately after the war, the British Parliament capitulated and granted the vote to women over 30 (1918), the United States constitution was amended to forbid any state to deny the right to vote on the ground of sex (1920), women's suffrage was included in the new constitutions of the USSR, the states which succeeded to the

Austro-Hungarian empire, and the Weimar republic of Germany, and women were enfranchised in the remaining Scandinavian countries, the Netherlands, Canada and the Union of South Africa.

Elsewhere in Europe, as well as in Latin America, resistance to women's political participation continued up to the second world war, especially where democratic liberalism was weakest and the influence of the Catholic Church was most strongly felt. The first of the Latin American countries which took formal action to give women the vote was Ecuador (1929), followed within the next five years by Brazil, Uruguay and Cuba. In the East, Turkish women who had been agitating for the franchise since 1908 secured it as a result of Ataturk's reforms, but not until 1934, more than ten years after he came to power. During the 1930s Britain extended the right to vote to women in Ceylon, India and Burma, and the United States did the same in the Philippines. Thai women were successful in being included as voters when their country became a constitutional monarchy in 1932. Japanese women, however, failed in their efforts to get women's suffrage written into the Japanese constitution of 1920.

The impact of the second world war and the declaration of the 'equal rights of men and women' in the United Nations Charter helped to bring political rights to the women of most of the remaining independent nations of the world, though in a few cases subject to qualification or limitations not imposed on men. France and Italy enfranchised their women, leaving the Swiss as the only European women still disfranchised in 1955. All of the Latin American republics except Paraguay had granted suffrage by that time. Women were fully entitled to vote in the newly created states of Asia, in China and under the post-war constitution of Japan. Liberia was the first African state to give its women the franchise, followed in 1955 by Ethiopia, and African women voted in the elections leading to the establishment of the Gold Coast as the independent state of Ghana.

In the Middle East, the enfranchisement of women was still in process at mid-century, as the Muslim women who had started in the 1920s to work for political as well as social rights were beginning to achieve success. Women with education received the franchise in Syria in 1949 and Lebanon in 1952. But the eight remaining Muslim countries in the region made up the bloc of states where women in 1955 were still without political rights; besides Switzerland and Paraguay, the only other such states were the tiny territories of Liechtenstein and San Marino. Egyptian women, however, were promised the vote at the time of the adoption of the constitution of 1956, and when Tunisia became independent in 1957 its women received the right to vote in municipal elections.

Although the franchise was sought as a means to secure other things which women desired, there appeared to be little tendency for women to vote as a bloc. Their political behaviour closely resembled that of men, expressing a similar range of opinion and of local, group or class interests. How far their presence in the voting population contributed to the trend toward an increasing volume of welfare legislation could not be readily assessed, since the trend to enact such legislation was strong everywhere.

The number of women holding public office generally remained small, even after the franchise had been enjoyed for some years, except in a few countries, notably the Soviet Union where they made up more than a quarter of the members of central and local soviets. Most countries, including those where the vote had been recently granted, could point to a few examples of women elected to national legislative bodies, serving as cabinet ministers, appointed to diplomatic posts, chosen mayors of cities or serving as judges. In a few instances a certain number of places in legislatures were specifically designated for women in order to ensure their representation, as initially in the provincial legislatures of Pakistan or the system of group representation in the Diet of Japan after the second world war.

Women were rather more likely to be appointed to responsible posts, especially in education, social welfare, labour and cultural affairs, than to be elected to office, and women's organizations often made it their business to see that the names of qualified women were placed before appointing officers when a position was to be filled. The presence of women in high office was not, however, an accurate reflection of the general level of public participation, for some women were appointed to responsible public positions even in countries which had not yet accorded them the franchise. The middle ranks of the civil service offered a better indication of such participation, and women served in great numbers in those countries where they had been most fully incorporated into public life.

(b) Education

Women were generally successful in securing access to higher education. The principal European universities opened their doors in the first decade of the twentieth century, as did those of Turkey and, generally, in Latin America. By the second quarter of the twentieth century the opportunity for higher education was no longer an issue in western countries, although some professional faculties were slower to admit women than others, and subtle forms of discrimination often continued to make women feel unwelcome. In Japan women were effectively barred from the universities in fact, though not in theory, until after the second world war because the higher schools through which the student had to pass on the way to the university admitted only boys, but they attended a number of institutions of higher education for women.

Women were more readily admitted to the higher institutions which prepared for the arts and sciences and the liberal professions than to the technical vocational schools that trained for skilled occupations. A review of the Latin American countries in 1953 found that whereas women were everywhere admitted to universities on an equality with men, they were effectively excluded in every country but one by custom, prejudice or regulation from vocational training for skilled tasks other than those relating to home making, sewing and other traditionally feminine skills.

In the countries where basic education reached the entire population, it included both sexes equally. But where illiteracy remained high, elementary education was usually less available to girls than to boys. Girls made up only 14 per cent of the primary school pupils in India in 1937, 24 per cent in Egypt and 35 per cent in Turkey; by 1950 the proportions had risen to 27, 35 and 38 per cent respectively.

There was a general tendency for school systems to adopt co-education, both as a matter of principle and for practical reasons, although opposition from conservative Catholic and Muslim sources remained strong. Co-education was supported in principle by most of the pedagogical literature of the period, and it was made necessary in practice by the difficulty of duplicating for boys and girls the increasingly complex and extensive facilities which modern education required.[19]

(c) *Legal status*

The legal disabilities of married women with respect to property, guardianship, domicile, legal personality and the right to contract and engage in business were only partially and slowly removed. Where they were modified, it was often as the result of measures designed to limit rights formerly enjoyed by men or to protect the interests of children.

Married women in England in the 1870s and 1880s acquired the right to hold property in their own names, retain their own earnings and share with their husbands in the guardianship of their children, though equal guardianship was not established until 1925. The individual states of the USA began to accord some or all of these rights in the middle of the nineteenth century and by the mid-twentieth century only a few states retained some limitations on guardianship and rights over property. The German civil code of 1900 placed single women on the same basis as men, but for married women the husband retained virtually complete authority over property, children and domicile. These provisions remained unchanged under the Weimar republic, and were not modified until the code was revised in the 1950s to bring it into conformity with the basic law of 1949 which established full equality of men and women before the law and prohibited discrimination on the ground of sex.

The French civil code which gave married women no right to dispose of their property, enter into a contract or sue in court without their husbands' consent remained unchanged until 1938, and these same provisions, in whole or in part, were still in the codes of the majority of the Latin American countries in 1955. Eight of the Latin American countries, however, revised their laws to remove or modify these limitations and several enacted legislation, primarily in the interest of the child, which restricted the authority of the father to dispose of family property and increased the rights of the mother over the children. In the Soviet Union all legal disabilities were removed by the first Soviet constitution, and the constitutions of the people's democracies of eastern Europe also provided for complete equality of legal status.

Except where the principles of the Roman Catholic Church were supported by law, as in Ireland and in some of the countries of Latin America, divorce laws in western countries were generally liberalized and inequalities in the conditions for divorce as between men and women were removed. The viewpoint underlying many of these revisions corresponded to that of the divorce laws of Sweden, Norway and Denmark, enacted between 1915 and 1920 after extensive study by a joint commission. These Scandinavian laws were expressly designed to preserve the ethical character of marriage as a union based on mutual sympathy, love and confidence, and they made mutual consent the basic ground for marriage dissolution where deep and constant discord exists.

In Muslim areas the legal status of women remained unchanged, except in Turkey where the civil code of 1925 replaced Muslim law and put men and women on an equal footing, including the abolition of plural marriage and the equalization of the conditions of divorce. Proposals were made in Indonesia and Pakistan for marriage laws within the framework of the Quran which would safeguard the wife by specifying the conditions in which divorce or second marriage was acceptable and requiring court procedure before either would be legal, but as late as 1956 no such law had been enacted in any Muslim country. The constitution of India and subsequent legislation established complete legal equality for Hindu women in matters of property, marriage rights, parental responsibility and authority.

(d) Economic rights and opportunities

The crux of women's changed position lay in their economic role, since without potential means of independent support their status in industrial society could not be other than that of a dependent. Their employment involved three issues: the chance to train for and enter those occupations which required skill, paid well and carried prestige; equality of pay and absence of discrimination in employment at all levels; and suitable conditions of work and freedom from abuse.

Pioneer women, often at the cost of great personal struggle and sacrifice, succeeded in entering one occupation after another that had been regarded as the exclusive domain of men. In Europe and North America vigorous women paved the way during the nineteenth and early years of the twentieth century. At the middle of the twentieth century distinguished Asian women similarly pioneered by representing their countries diplomatically, serving in their countries' ministries, and practising medicine, law or engineering. These were outstanding individuals who overcame obstacles and gained the inner satisfaction and the outward recognition that comes to the pioneer.

As the initial phase passed, however, and professional women increased in number, their position often became ambiguous. Prejudice and negative social attitudes hung on, and many women found that they had to work doubly hard to achieve the recognition readily accorded to men, without enjoying the status or satisfactions of pioneers. Women's organizations, which had supported and cheered the first women in their fight to break through initial barriers, were indifferent to the difficulties which women continued to encounter in securing favourable employment or promotion. Neither men nor women looked upon the aggressive woman as a desirable personality type.

Professional women themselves became less ready than the pioneers had been to struggle for a career if this meant the sacrifice of marriage and a home, and they generally tried to combine both. At best the professional woman with a home and family carried a double load and required exceptional stamina to be able to give to her career the same intensity of effort that her male counterpart could devote to his. If her husband regarded her success as a competitive threat to his status, her career might endanger her marriage. Often she could not count on servants to look after her home and children as the pioneer women had generally been able to do, for domestic help was no longer plentiful and cheap. Many women with professional training found it necessary to interrupt their careers while their children were young, only to encounter great difficulty in re-entering the field after a lapse of years. Potential employers, in their turn, hesitated to offer the best opportunities to young women because of the expectation that they would remain active for only a brief period. The basic problem of how to combine a professional career with the responsibilities of a home had not been solved by the women of the western countries by mid-century.

In the USSR, where women constituted nearly half of the work force in factories and offices and a still larger proportion of trained specialists and professional workers especially in medicine, various aids and services provided by the state lightened the home burdens of employed women. A system of canteens was steadily extended to lessen the need for housework, and nurseries and kindergartens were available for pre-school children. Increased numbers of boarding schools as well as after-school provisions for supervised study and play reduced the working mother's direct responsibilities. All these facilities made it somewhat less difficult for Soviet women than for those elsewhere to meet the demands of both profession and home. In the Chinese People's Republic the commune system went still further in relieving women of household responsibilities and enabling them to devote themselves to work outside the home.

In all industrial countries, the tendency for a large and increasing proportion of all women to engage in work outside the home during at least some period in their lives was accelerated by labour shortages during the wars. The first world war opened up new fields to large-scale employment of women and the impact of the second world war was even more pronounced. Conditions of full employment during the decade after the second war confirmed new patterns of employment which might have been abandoned if there had been a post-war slump.

In the non-industrialized countries employed women fell into two main groups, a small number of professionals drawn from the educated *élite*, and a large group of factory workers drawn from the poorest and most necessitous elements in the population. The former were pioneers; the latter were often the product of social dislocation—refugees, widows, unmarried mothers or members of a depressed group. The mass of women in respectable homes were not permitted or expected to work or to move freely in the broader society. Only as this last group began to emerge did signs appear of an approximation to the employment pattern which had developed in the industrialized countries.

Except in the Soviet Union and the people's democracies, where equal pay for equal work was a standard policy, women often received lower pay than men. In part, they worked in traditionally low-paid employment—in industries such as textiles with relatively low wage scales, in lower paid unskilled tasks, often excluded from skilled trades by discriminatory apprenticeship rules or lack of access to training, and rarely promoted to supervisory positions. In addition, pay scales established for public employment in European countries and agreed upon by collective contracts between employers and trade unions commonly specified differentials on the basis of sex. Formal pay differentials were rare in the United States, as they never existed in the civil service and were infrequent in collective contracts with trade unions, but they were not uncommon in practice. The rationale of such differentials was that male workers were assumed to have dependents to support but females not. Yet studies of employed women consistently showed that a large proportion of them were supporting children, parents or other relatives.

Change toward greater equality of pay came slowly in European countries. The Swedish civil service accepted the principle of equal pay in 1925 but it was still in the process of removing inequalities thirty years later. Collective bargaining contracts in European countries quite generally continued to provide for differentials. The British government in 1955 initiated gradual steps to eliminate pay differences in the civil service and for teachers by 1961. By 1955 nine countries had adopted the convention on equal pay prepared by the ILO in 1951, and legislation had been enacted by fourteen states of the USA and three Canadian provinces. But French employers complained that France's acceptance of the ILO convention put them at a competitive disadvantage with other countries where inequality of women's wages continued to prevail.

The countries where women were only beginning to enter the labour market in large numbers toward the middle of the century tended to adopt the principle of equal pay but often did not achieve the practice. The experience in Latin America was indicative of the problem. Although a number of Latin American countries had laws requiring equal pay for equal work, the actual earnings of women in industrial employment ranged from 20 to 50 per cent below those of men. Limitations on employment opportunities and technical training, depressed wages in jobs regarded as typically 'women's work', inadequate inspection or lack of a proper system for evaluating what constituted 'equal work' contributed to this situation. Similar factors were at work elsewhere.

Most of the labour codes enacted and extended during this period contained provisions designed to protect women workers against hazardous employment; many required the granting of maternity leave. ILO conventions covering maternity protection (1919), prohibition on the employment of women in mining or other underground work (1935) and prohibition on night work for women (1941, revised in 1948) had been ratified by 18, 35 and 16 countries respectively by 1957.

The largest single group of working women was composed of those employed in domestic service. Traditionally, this was the occupation in which women received the lowest pay, worked the longest hours, were least protected from their employer's caprice and abuse, and were most often excepted from provisions of labour laws and social security guarantees. In the industrial countries the development of alternative fields of employment offered new opportunities which freed many women from the necessity of working in other people's homes and the withdrawal of large numbers to factory or other work improved the bargaining position of those who remained as domestics. Although household workers generally continued to work longer and more irregular hours and to receive less pay than those in other employment, wages rose, hours declined and conditions became more standardized. In the course of time the social legislation which applied to other workers was extended to domestic workers, including social security benefits and minimum wages, and they joined trade unions.

For middle-class women this generally meant the loss of household help since they could no longer have someone at their beck and call for a small sum and they could not afford to pay a decent living wage for a regular day's work. But for millions of other women it meant a chance to live their own lives and take care of their own homes. The progressive elimination of the cheap household servant was one of the most democratizing influences of the century for the women of the industrialized countries.

(e) Maternal health

In human terms the change in the conditions of child-bearing was the most revolutionary development in the lives of women in the twentieth century. For centuries mankind had lived under the assumption that women would bear children, often with great frequency, in pain and danger of death, and that a large proportion of babies and a considerable number of mothers would die. Even during the nineteenth century graveyards were filled with infants' headstones and often the graves of women who had died in childbirth.

Advances in medical knowledge and the spread of maternal and child health services removed most of the risk and much of the pain of childbirth and greatly reduced the likelihood that the child would die. By the middle of the twentieth century women in cities and most rural areas of the West, and wherever modern health facilities existed around the world, could count on a safe pregnancy, barring illness or accident from other sources, and could experience a delivery under hospital conditions which ensured protection from infection and emergency medical aid to save the life of mother and child in case of complications. They had access to knowledge of safe and reasonably sure methods to avoid pregnancy and were thus in a position to plan the spacing of their children and the number that they would undertake to bear and rear. In some areas, such as Japan, they could interrupt an unwanted pregnancy by safe means, although in most countries the practice of abortion was discouraged or forbidden by law and thereby rendered unsafe. With these developments went a change in attitude which brought maternity within the scope of scientific control and removed the process from the realm of fate.

The combined effect of the small-family system and the increased likelihood that children born would survive greatly reduced the number of years which women spent in child-bearing and thus made a larger part of their lives available for other activities. This helped to make possible their wider economic role as well as their participation in other areas of social life.

(f) Social status

All these changes brought women a new social freedom and blurred the lines between the social worlds of women and men.

The early feminists attacked as a major source of indignity the sharp division which made all social activity outside the home exclusively the affair of men, reserving to them the coffee houses, taverns, sports and clubs and permitting them to seek sexual gratification outside the home, while women were limited to home-bound activity and were held to a rigid code of sexual morality. But it was not so much the feminist attacks or their aping of masculine appearance and behaviour that affected women's social status. Rather, it was the schools and the jobs which took women out of the home, the general loosening of formal manners and conduct based on status, a freer attitude toward sex and the narrowed scope of the home.

With the achievement of social freedom and relative equality of status, however, Western women found themselves in an ambivalent situation. The principle of equality was firmly established in the context of democratic individualism. A common system of education oriented girls and boys to the same idea of developing their own capacities and interests to the fullest; the open doors of higher education invited the girl to pursue this development as far as her abilities would lead; employment opportunities offered a choice of occupation and the chance to earn her living; she was expected to understand public issues, vote and take part in public life as an independent person; she associated freely with boys and could choose her mate, or choose not to marry.

But she was expected to marry and to raise a family. The impact of Freudian psychology strengthened the idea that the woman who sacrificed marriage to pursue a career was failing to lead a normal life, and stressed the role of the mother and the importance of the early experience of the child. She was expected to give to her children the love, security and intelligent upbringing that she had learned was their due, and she was far more conscious than earlier generations had been of the damage which she could do to the personality of the child if she bungled her maternal role. She was expected to take her status from her husband's occupation and position and to help sustain it; to further his advancement was one of her first responsibilities.

The inner conflict and uncertainty as to values which this dichotomy set up manifested itself in a frequent cleavage or tension between the career woman and the housewife, each tending to look down on the other in order to express her inner jealousy and both jealous of the women who successfully combined the two roles. For the women who maintained both a career and a home, the double burden was heavy. Opportunities for part-time employment were generally few and there were insufficient child-care centres, housekeeping aides, community kitchens or other devices which might lighten the home part of her task; the inadequacy of such services often reflected the idea that mothers should remain in the home. The conflict and problem were brought out sharply in the 1955 meeting of the United Nations Commission on the Status of Women where statements by some of the non-governmental consultants to the commission precipitated a discussion of whether working mothers could be good mothers and drew from members of the commission a plea for measures to make it less difficult for women to cope simultaneously with their duties as mothers and workers.

For women in eastern countries in process of modernization, the inner conflict was no less sharp than for women of the West, for their problem was how far to follow the pattern of western social behaviour and how far to conform to the pattern traditional to the East. They experienced in a most intense and personal form the cultural ambivalence common to societies in transition. Men in these countries could adopt many western attitudes and ways without seriously modifying their attitudes or behaviour relating to the home, their relations with women of their own culture and their concept of women's position. Many externally westernized men maintained non-western values in their homes, marrying the girl selected by their parents, never taking their wives with them when they went out socially, and keeping intact the traditional pattern of masculine authority and the separateness of the life of men from that of women. Women, however, could not adopt western values without becoming involved in the issue of their own position.

Their dilemma was apparent in every eastern country. In Japan it appeared to some observers that the most durable effect of the changes inaugurated during the period of occupation after the second world war might be a new status for women, yet ten years after the close of the war that change was still very unsure. There was great uncertainty in the relations between boys and girls and considerable reaction against the free association which was encouraged in the immediate post-war period. Co-education at secondary and university levels was still working itself out. Highly trained women were still not readily accepted in responsible posts. Social workers found themselves dealing with family situations in which basic conflicts of values and alternative concepts of family structure and duties underlay family disorganization. The most popular Japanese films, radio programmes and novels were devoted to such themes as the conflict between romantic love and filial duty, the right of the daughter *vis-à-vis* the mother-in-law, the right of the woman to her own decisions and her own life.

For Indian women traditional and Western practices were in direct conflict. Arranged marriages were the rule, with careful consideration traditionally given by the families to caste status, family reputation and economic position and to the horoscopes of the couple, and with no close association between the young people prior to marriage. The Indian woman who aspired to the social independence of the Western woman and the pattern of romantically based marriage was in broad defiance of traditional *mores*. Mahatma Gandhi lent powerful support to those who wished to break through custom by encouraging inter-caste marriages and accepting the individual choice of mates. Nevertheless, many educated women were unsure as to whether to remain with the old, to adopt new ways, or to seek some compromise between basically opposed systems.

On the surface, at least, the easiest transition to a modern social status for women seemed to be taking place in the Buddhist countries of south-east Asia and in Indonesia, although the traditional protected status retained a nostalgic appeal. By the second quarter of the twentieth century women of Thailand enjoyed access to education, easy freedom of movement, varied employment and free choice in marriage. Women leaders were undertaking to make equality of status a reality in practice through a broad programme of social and cultural development designed to enable women to keep pace with their husbands and stimulating their participation in welfare and other activities within their communities. Women in Ceylon formed a larger proportion of the school population than in Hindu and Muslim countries and were the first of the Asian women to vote. Indonesian women inherited traditions of equality and participation, and those with education entered a labour market where trained people of all sorts were few and their services were in great demand.

In some of the Muslim countries the issue of women's social position at mid-century continued to centre around the question of seclusion. In Pakistan a small group of women from educated homes who had themselves enjoyed personal freedom sought by gradual means to further the steady process by which women were emerging from purdah, making the matter an issue at one point and avoiding the issue at another. In the early 1950s the director of the newly established department of social work at the University of the Punjab refused to allow the curtain down the middle of the classroom which separated the sexes in some of the other departments of that university, preferring to recruit only those students who could associate freely with men, while near by the director of a new school for training in home economics had a wall built around the grounds in order to enrol girls who otherwise would not attend.

The Arab states at mid-century ranged from a strongly Westernized pattern in Lebanon, half-Christian and half-Muslim, where free social movement was the general rule and large numbers of women had been educated in local French and American schools, to the complete seclusion which prevailed in Saudi Arabia and Yemen. Many educated Egyptian women had come to move freely in the society of the principal cities in the course of the thirty years after their prominent leader first discarded her veil, but Egyptian feminists were still complaining that the political leaders who talked about the rights of Egyptian women did not appear in public with their own wives. Families were expected to arrange suitable marriages for their daughters; even for girls who were receiving professional training, choice was usually limited to the chance to say 'no' to their parents' selection.

The women of Turkey experienced a drastic change in social status by a revolution from above at a time when the educated *élite*, already Westernized, was ready for it. At mid-century many of the rest were still catching up. Leading Turkish women were occupying important positions and had many achievements to their credit. A larger proportion of the members of university faculties in Turkey were women in 1948 than in any country reporting this information to Unesco except the United States, 15 per cent as compared with 24 per cent in the United States and 3–5 per cent in European universities. But thoughtful Turkish women were reconsidering the meaning of the westernization which they had experienced, determined to be 'western' but wishing to avoid mere imitation. Some saw signs of reaction—a religious revival which might threaten their position, the resumption of the veil in some villages, the possibility of general political reaction. To others it seemed that the revolution had been less complete than had appeared on the surface and that the process was still going on.

Among the Asian women who experienced the most drastic change were those of China. In the first part of the century Western-educated Chinese women found themselves caught between their new aspirations and the strength of the Chinese family system with the filial obligations which it entailed. The conflict was sharpened as the attacks on the Confucian family grew following the New Tide movement. When the communists came to power, they made the liberation of the Chinese women from family tyranny a central objective; personal choice in marriage, independence, education and comradely participation were the declared programme. By rapid steps they relieved women not only of their family subordination but of many of their family responsibilities. The women of the Chinese communes represented as radical a change in status as had been experienced by any large body of women during the course of the twentieth century.

By mid-century women nearly everywhere had thus attained many of the goals which the articulate among them had expressed and their leaders had sought. But their status, role and self-appraisal were still in flux, for throughout the world many of the strains and uncertainties of industrial society impinged inexorably upon their lives.

IV.   RACE AND CASTE GROUPS SUBJECT TO DISCRIMINATION

The drive for individual freedom and human dignity in the twentieth century involved groups in many countries who were the object of discrimination because of race, caste or other social disability and who were frequently accorded less than the full privileges of citizenship. Unlike other minorities who desired cultural autonomy within multi-cultural societies,* members of these groups sought the removal of social stigma and legal restrictions which stood in the way of individual and group acceptance and advancement.

A variety of historic situations had resulted in the presence of such elements and had produced the patterns of relationship with the dominant populations which existed in the twentieth century. Negroes in the Americas were still handicapped by the long aftermath of slavery. Native Africans in South Africa had been subjugated in the unequal contest with European settlers for land, and the other non-European populations of that country—Coloureds and Indians—shared the disabilities imposed by the European element in its efforts to keep the Africans in subordination. Untouchables of India were the product of the long history of migration by the warring peoples in the Indian sub-continent, for whom the Hindu caste system had provided a mechanism for establishing and perpetuating superior-inferior relationships; they had been assigned the most unpleasant work, and the disabilities to which they were subjected were a means of ensuring that tasks necessary to the life of the villages would be performed. The Eta of Japan, descended from a class of untouchables in feudal times, had acquired the legal status of commoners in 1868, but were the object of prejudice and social discrimination. North American Indians had been relegated to reservations in the United States and Canada in the expansion of European settlement, whence some had emerged to seek status as individual citizens while others pressed their claims as tribal groups. Jews had lived for centuries as non-Christians in Christian-organized societies and as enclaves in Muslim areas, and although in Europe they were generally free from former legal restrictions, they faced attitudes generated in earlier times.†

The patterns of advance followed by two such groups, Negroes in the western hemisphere and untouchables in India, are presented here as illustra-

* For a discussion of such groups, see Chapter XXIX, pp. 1101–7.
† See Chapter XXV, pp. 871–9, Judaism, and Chapter XXVIII, pp. 1019–25, Israel.

tive of some of the many forms which the struggle for full and effective citizenship took in various parts of the world. These two groups were selected for their size, for the differences as well as the similarities surrounding their status and its change and because world-wide interest in their fate was felt and expressed during these years.

Under the impact of the world-wide trend toward equality, all such groups pressed their efforts to achieve first-class status within their societies. With the tragic exception of European Jews and of the dark-skinned peoples of the Union of South Africa,* they generally made substantial headway toward this goal during the first half of the twentieth century.

I. NEGROES

The people most subject to discrimination, whose aspirations everywhere took the form of a desire for status on a par with other citizens—'first-class citizenship'—were Negroes. Virtually nowhere outside Africa did they aspire to cultural identity and separateness on the basis of race. Where they developed separate institutions and expressions of identity it was because they were forced to do so, or as a means of working toward full equality, and these institutions, such as churches, press or legal and welfare organizations, took their form from the corresponding institutions of the broader society.

The great majority of the Negro people outside Africa lived in the Americas —North America, the Caribbean islands, and Caribbean littoral of Central and South America, where they had originally been brought as slaves. Their status at the opening of the twentieth century reflected their history in each of these areas.

(a) Caribbean and Latin America

In the islands of the Caribbean, Negro slaves had constituted the mass labour force for sugar plantations worked under the direction of a handful of planters and administrators. In the twentieth century the bulk of the population of most of these islands was made up of direct descendants of Negro slaves and mulattoes of combined Negro and white ancestry. This was most true of Haiti, which forceably threw out its French masters in 1798 and therewith its white population. Here a mulatto *élite* confronted the black masses, and virtually the only whites were Syrian traders who had entrenched themselves in the island's economy. On the other islands, which continued under colonial status, a dominant white element remained; as the islands moved toward and acquired self-government, leadership passed to representatives of the predominantly Negro majority.

In the islands of Cuba and Puerto Rico which had been part of the Spanish empire, the European element had not been confined to a few planters but had immigrated in sufficient numbers to make up a large part of the population. Since racial exclusiveness had never characterized the Spanish, there had been

---

* See Chapter XXVIII, pp. 1011–18, South Africa.

considerable intermingling of white and Negro elements until, by the twentieth century, these populations ranged in colour from black to white with no sharp line of distinction. The darker element, for historical reasons, tended to predominate in the plantation areas of the coast and in the lower economic ranks, while the lighter were more numerous in the interior and generally predominated at the higher economic levels.

The situation was similar in the countries of Central and South America which bordered the Caribbean. From Mexico to Brazil the coastal regions were largely inhabited by dark-skinned people who traced their origin to slavery on local plantations or who had come over as plantation workers from the Caribbean islands in post-slavery times. In some areas people in the interior were predominantly European, as in Costa Rica; elsewhere they were predominantly Indian, as in Guatemala. More generally they were *mestizo*—mixed Indian and European—as in Mexico, or mulatto—mixed white and Negro—as in Panama.

In none of these areas was a sharp line drawn between white and coloured. Either there was simply a gradation or three groups were identified, white, mulatto and black. Colour prejudice was present, expressed in minor and often subtle ways—exclusion of dark-skinned people from the most select clubs, a tendency to show job preference to the lighter of two candidates for the same post, special comment, open or whispered, when dark-skinned persons achieved prominent positions. Venezuela put up a bar against immigrants from the Caribbean islands, and Brazil showed preference for European immigrants. But in none of these areas of Spanish and Portuguese background was the Negro population subject to specific forms of discrimination; nor was it self-consciously engaged in seeking first-class status in the society. Whatever racial and cultural self-consciousness existed in these countries was identified with the indigenous Indian, not the Negro, elements in the population.

(b) Negroes in the USA

Historic position of American Negroes. The situation was very different in the United States where a sharp colour line defined the Negro minority. Here, during the twentieth century, the Negro people carried on a conscious struggle for first-class citizenship. The framework for this struggle was provided by the historic circumstances of their entrance into American life, the legal and ideological basis of American society, the impact of American economic development, and a racial dogma which was originally formulated to reconcile the contradiction between slavery and democracy and which continued to sustain an arbitrary colour line.

In contrast to the situation on the Caribbean islands, Negro slaves brought into North America never constituted a large body of workers managed by a handful of white owners or overseers. Except in a few limited areas—small islands off the south-east coast and, later, some of the rich land of the Mississippi delta—Negro slaves were interspersed with white settlers. They worked farms adjacent to others worked by indentured white labourers, and when the latter completed their term of service they acquired land and, in time, often one or two slaves. At the time of the Civil War in 1860 only a quarter of the slave population was living on plantations worked by fifty slaves or more, while an equal number were on farms with less than ten slave workers. Of the total population of the United States in the twentieth century, Negroes constituted roughly 10 per cent. In no state did they comprise more than 30–40 per cent of the population.

Scattered in small groups, the slaves imported into the North American colonies had no basis for retaining the relationships, language or culture of their African past; on the larger plantations it was generally customary to secure slaves from different regions so that they could not build up solidarity against their masters on the basis of common language or old ties. There was no such transplanting of African culture as among the people of Haiti whose songs and voodoo practices in the twentieth century still recalled their homeland of Dahomey, although some few African traces were found by anthropologists in the speech and superstitions of some areas. American Negroes were culturally the products of the American environment; they took their ideas, values and patterns of behaviour from their white masters and neighbours and adapted them to their own experience as an exploited minority within a democratic society.

The Negro people in America never looked upon slavery as part of the order of nature or a permanent condition. Though for more than 200 years the majority were unable to escape their lot as slaves, though many exhibited strong personal loyalty to individual masters, and though many patterns of outward subservience were developed as protective behaviour, the indignities of slavery never became an accepted part of their outlook on life. They sang of the 'children of Israel' emerging from bondage in Egypt to seek the 'promised land', singing of themselves. And when freedom came individually to the manumitted or collectively with emancipation they grasped it as their birthright and sought to make it fully real.

The obstacles which they confronted, however, were many. Chief among these was the racial dogma developed during slavery to rationalize the existence of that institution in a basically democratic society. Had slavery been an acceptable institution, it would not have been necessary to ascribe natural inferiority to those who happened to be slaves. But in a society which proclaimed that 'all men are created equal and are endowed by their Creator with certain inalienable rights' it was necessary to consider those held in slavery as somehow less than 'men'.

The dogma as developed had two major parts. On the one hand it attributed the dependence, poverty, ignorance and other effects of the conditions imposed upon the Negro to his inherent inferiority. On the other hand it assumed the ethnic integrity of the 'white race'.

Although intermarriage was not countenanced, as it was in the Spanish and Portuguese colonies, much intermingling took place, until the American 'Negro' as a physical type came to range from black to a colour indistinguishable from that of many so-called 'whites'. Since during slavery children took the status of their mother, the slave population came to include many children of white masters. These and all others of mixed ancestry became 'Negro', no matter how closely they resembled whites in appearance or how preponderantly white their ancestry. In contrast to the Latin American countries where the mulatto either represented a part of the gradation from dark to light or a defined middle group, a sharp colour line was drawn between the whites and all who could be identified as having any Negro ancestry. The illogic of this colour line was made ironically plain by the opposite treatment of white-Indian mixtures, for in the latter even a small proportion of white forebears enabled a person to call himself 'white'.

After emancipation, in 1863, the doctrine of Negro racial inferiority and white racial purity, devised to justify the institution of slavery, became a rationale for continued prejudice. Its psychological value in assuaging troubled consciences and permitting behaviour inconsistent with the principles by which other aspects of life were governed embedded the dogma of racial inferiority deep in the popular mentality. Only slowly did it give way to the impact of contrary evidence produced by scientific investigation, to day-by-day experience in a society where mounting numbers of Negroes functioned ably in positions requiring high levels of responsibility and skill, to the broadening concept of liberalism, and to the shifting world situation with its changed relationship between Europeans and darker peoples. Even at mid-century a Negro writer could conclude that 'it still offers more resistance to the Negro's progress than all the practical difficulties of social advance combined'.[*]

The practical obstacles faced by ex-slaves were, however, also very real. In the Civil War which brought emancipation to the Negroes, an essentially agrarian society sought to resist one that was becoming more and more industrially oriented. The two regions, south and north, clashed over the basis upon which the new lands to the west should be developed and on the policy of protective tariffs to encourage industry versus free trade to maintain markets for agricultural products abroad. The victory of the north meant the triumph of industrialism. The agrarian south came out of the war defeated and impoverished.

The southern milieu into which the Negro people emerged from slavery was, consequently, both economically and psychologically unfavourable to their effective integration. The great majority of the Negroes stayed on in the areas where freedom found them, farming the land on shares for owners who were often too poor to pay cash wages, in communities too poor to support good schools, and among people resentful and sensitive in defeat and determined to regain and reassert their self-respect.

[*] Margaret J. Butcher, *The Negro in American Culture* (New York, 1957), p. 18.

QQ*

Nor did the expanding industries of the north offer an alternative, for workers for the factories were recruited among the peasant immigrants from Europe, not the freedmen of America's rural south. The people of the north who had fought to abolish slavery as an institution gave little thought to those whom they had made their fellow-citizens. Some northerners supported missionaries who went south to establish schools for the freedmen and their children, but most were much too preoccupied with the rapid industrialization of their region and the rapid growth of the western states to worry about what was happening to three and a half million ex-slaves. After a brief attempt to impose conditions favourable to the Negroes, they abandoned the effort in favour of political reconciliation and reunion of the divided country. Left to deal with the situation in their own terms, the southern states took whatever measures they could to recreate a subordinate and restricted status for their Negro populations.

The legal basis of the Negro's position was laid down in the constitution of the United States which stated the rights of citizens in terms of the basic concepts of eighteenth-century liberalism. After emancipation, former slaves as well as those born free acquired full citizenship; an 1856 declaration by the Supreme Court that citizenship rights were not meant to apply to persons of colour even when free had been erased by the Civil War. Additional amendments to the constitution in the following years explicitly forbade denial of the right to vote on grounds of 'race, colour, or previous condition of servitude', and forbade the states to deny to any citizen the 'equal protection of the laws'.

The federal structure of the United States, however, greatly complicated the legal problem of ensuring full citizenship rights to Negroes, since the general police power, most kinds of authority over the conduct of individuals, control of education, determination of qualifications for voting, and regulation of conditions of employment fell within the domain of the states. Attempts by the federal Congress after the Civil War to assure to Negroes the unrestricted use of public facilities such as inns, eating places and transport were held by the Supreme Court to be beyond the scope of federal legislation in so far as they applied to the acts of individuals rather than those of official bodies.

Even within the scope of federal authority, moreover, there was the crucial question of whether separation was compatible with equality. The constitution specified 'equal'; it did not specify 'same'. Over the eloquent dissent of one of its members, the Supreme Court in 1896 held that the constitutional requirement of equality might be satisfied by the provision of separate facilities if these were equal in quality to those provided for other citizens. For nearly sixty years this decision enabled the southern states to practise segregation in their systems of education, public parks, public health facilities and the like, and to require that separate facilities be provided in public transport and other services.

By the opening of the twentieth century it was apparent that the struggle for full citizenship would be more complex than it had at first appeared. The elaborate design of subordination developed by the white south confronted the Negro with a pattern of expected and enforced behaviour which placed many practical and psychological blocks in the way of his advance. Southern whites adopted toward all Negroes the manners and attitudes used toward children or servants, always calling them familiarly by their Christian names even, for example, when a school inspector spoke to a teacher in the presence of his pupils, and expecting or excusing childish behaviour, irresponsibility, petty thievery or buffoonery but resenting and even punishing outward evidence of self-respect which could be interpreted as an assertion of equality, such as a well-painted house or a non-servile manner. They established job ceilings which closed most of the middle range of skilled, factory and clerical occupations and supervisory positions and generally restricted professionals to service to other Negroes. Under the pattern of segregation, Negroes had to sit in coloured waiting rooms, travel in coloured sections of trains, use service lifts, walk in coloured parks, read in coloured libraries and attend coloured schools.

In the north segregation was not a matter of principle, but Negroes were simply expected to live in the poorest slums and to fill the lowest jobs. By unsystematic but effective job discrimination, refusal to let or sell housing space, and exclusion from public eating places, Negroes in northern cities were backed into a ghetto-type of existence. And always, south and north, they had to be prepared to meet the stereotype of the lazy, easy-going, irresponsible person of inferior mentality whose slum living, poverty and lack of education were attributed to his 'racial characteristics'. The most industrious, responsible, moral, educated or wealthy Negro individual was not free from the stereotype applied to the group.

The struggle for full citizenship. (i) *Education.* Education seemed to offer the open door to progress. All testimony agrees that the freedmen exhibited an unquenchable zeal for the schooling which had been denied them as slaves and, in some states, as freed Negroes. The thousands who took refuge behind the Union lines during the Civil war begged to be taught; more thousands streamed to the schools established by missionary societies. In the brief period immediately after the war when Negroes enjoyed political power under the protecting guns of the victorious Union forces, they spent public funds on education with what their former masters regarded as financial irresponsibility. Throughout the following years, education continued to be an indispensable element in the struggle for full participation, both on the part of millions of Negroes as individuals and in the organized expression of their aspirations. Institutions of higher education were established for Negroes by the private efforts of missionaries, churches and public-spirited citizens, by the southern states, and in the nation's capital with the aid of the federal government. They played a central role not only by providing a body of educated leaders but by serving as focal points for the formation of opinion, for mutual support and for the development of a Negro middle class.

In the early years of the century two opposing tactics were advocated by Negro leaders. One view, for which Booker T. Washington was the spokesmen, held that Negroes should concentrate on developing their practical skills and earning capacity in order to equip themselves as a mass to function above the lowest economic level of American society. Up from slavery himself (see his autobiography, *Up From Slavery*, 1900), he thought that Negroes should, as a tactical matter, accept for the moment the pattern of segregation, which he compared to two fingers of the same hand. In line with his philosophy, he founded an educational institution devoted especially to vocational training and means to improve living conditions—home economics, public health, nutrition—among the Negroes in the south.

An opposing viewpoint, associated initially with the name of W. E. B. DuBois who came of northern free Negro stock, held that there should be no acceptance, even tactically, of the pattern of segregation and no differentiation of the Negro's education from that received by whites, for to emphasize manual skills in the training of Negroes only played into the hands of those who regarded the Negro as intellectually inferior. According to this view, the most important task was to break down the image of the Negro as inferior, to destroy the habits of segregation and discrimination, and to establish the Negro's legal rights. Negroes should seek nothing less than the best, in their own educational institutions if necessary, or by entering the institutions of the majority, and should distinguish themselves as individuals in the professions and occupations which carried prestige in the society and would earn them respect. This approach came to be referred to as the 'talented tenth'—i.e. the advance of the Negro group through the success of its outstanding individuals. Numbers of able individuals entered the leading universities in the country and distinguished themselves as students and in their subsequent professional careers. In addition, several of the major institutions of higher education for Negroes strove valiantly to offer a level of liberal education on a par with the best in the country, and many less well-equipped colleges did their best to follow suit.

Although these two approaches were advocated as alternatives, they were in fact followed simultaneously. In time Booker T. Washington's viewpoint lost much of its support as new generations of Negroes with more education and wider experience became impatient with the pattern of accommodation to the imposed indignities and felt that a more militant attitude was in line with the times. They rejected the 'Uncle Toms', who knew how to exploit the stereotype of the respectful, subservient Negro in order to secure from whites financial support for education, health services, welfare institutions and other things which the Negro community needed; the younger generation preferred to receive less, but with dignity and as a matter of right, rather than to beg successfully for more.

(ii) *Legal status.* While education remained fundamental to the Negro's striving for equal status, his effort to secure his legal rights was the most dramatic aspect of the struggle. Once freed, his rights as a citizen were those of any other man. Even the 'separate but equal' doctrine was not designed by the courts to be discriminatory in principle, since theoretically it applied equally to whites. In entering the legal battle to achieve in fact what the constitution and the common law guaranteed in principle, the Negro lawyers and their white collaborators knew that eventual victory would come to their side so long as American democracy endured, but that the necessity of combating discrimination point by point and state by state, often community by community and subterfuge by subterfuge, meant a long, discouraging fight. To meet this situation the National Association for the Advancement of Coloured People was formed by whites and Negroes together in 1910 to protect and promote Negro rights. It first sought to secure protection against direct maltreatment, whose most extensive form, mob violence and 'lynching', had too often gone unpunished; then it marshalled legal talent and made it available wherever Negro citizens were prepared to make a test case out of the denial of their legal rights.

Through the years, cases brought by Negroes, generally argued by lawyers supplied by the NAACP, led the Supreme Court to interpret in detail the meaning of the constitutional provision that no state might deny to any citizen the 'equal protection of the laws'. It held that a Negro was entitled to be tried by a jury from which Negroes were not excluded, and that state courts could not enforce private agreements to exclude Negro residents from an area, since such exclusion by direct state action would be unconstitutional. It outlawed one subterfuge after another by which Negroes were prevented from voting—declaring invalid state laws which specified that only those whose grandfathers had been eligible to vote could be enrolled, and the claims by some states that political parties were private organizations whose primary elections to choose candidates did not involve 'voting' in the sense meant by the constitution.

It soon became apparent that 'separate but equal' in fact meant unequal, and the courts so ruled in one specific situation after another, finding the 'equal protection of the laws' denied by unequal pay for teachers, unequal physical facilities for schools, or by the provision by a state of scholarships for Negroes to study in another state instead of admitting them to the state's own institutions of higher education. Finally, after a series of decisions in which it recognized that 'equality' had intangible as well as material aspects, the Supreme Court in 1954 arrived at the conclusion that enforced separation in education, in and of itself, meant inequality, and it reversed the decision which had established the 'separate but equal' doctrine fifty-eight years before. The constant legal struggle not only achieved specific gains in breaking down discriminatory practices, and finally the doctrine of 'separate but equal' itself, but made the Negro people conscious of the law as their potential ally.

(iii) *Equal economic opportunity.* While some Negro leaders and their white associates worked aggressively on the legal front, others directed their efforts toward achieving equal economic opportunity and modifying the social and economic handicaps under which masses of Negro people lived.

The first world war swelled to a flood the trickle of Negroes moving from the rural south to northern cities. With the supply of immigrant labour cut off and industry expanding to meet war needs, factory recruiting agents turned to the south and set in motion a mass migration to northern industrial communities which continued in the following decades. But as they entered northern industry, Negroes encountered negative and discriminatory attitudes on the part of both employers and fellow workers, built up during the years when most factory employment was closed to them and only the unskilled, heavy or menial tasks were regarded as proper 'Negro jobs'.

In the effort to meet some of the problems of inexperienced and often confused people from the backward rural areas of the south who moved into the worst slums, were offered the lowest paid jobs and were subjected to the competitive atmosphere and discriminatory attitudes of northern cities, Negro leaders and white citizens joined to set up welfare organizations dedicated to the promotion of equal opportunity. Such organizations, which by the 1950s had been formed in some sixty cities and were affiliated since 1911 in a national association known as the National Urban League, worked to change the discriminatory habits of their communities. They laboured patiently to modify patterns of employment, prying doors open through negotiation, finding competent workers for new positions, stimulating schools and parents to encourage their children to train for occupations which were not yet available to them, and combating the depressing conditions and frustrations which tended to undermine the Negro's sense of himself and destroy ambition. Prior to the second world war, these efforts produced only limited openings at higher levels of employment, generally much more slowly than people were prepared to fill them.

The extreme shortage of labour in the second world war forced employers to set aside their preferences and prejudices and use any workers they could get—older workers, women, handicapped, as well as Negroes. Even then it required pressure from the government, which adopted a wartime policy of non-discrimination in order to use manpower efficiently, to facilitate the opening up of skilled, technical and clerical jobs on any large scale. By the close of the war the employment pattern had been radically changed. Although in some communities many occupations remained difficult for Negroes to enter or virtually closed, in others Negroes were unprepared and untrained to take advantage of new opportunities as fast as these opened up. In the years after the second world war those who had been working for equality of economic opportunity turned their efforts in two directions, to eliminating job discrimination by securing the enactment of state and municipal laws making such discrimination illegal, and to stimulating the masses of Negro children and young people to raise their occupational sights as the abler and more determined among them had done long before.

In their contacts with organized labour, Negroes found themselves at first on the outside, excluded from most craft unions and, from time to time, brought into mines or mills as strike-breakers by anti-labour employers. As their numbers in northern industry grew, it became apparent to some Negro leaders that the fate of the great majority of the Negro people as workers was closely bound up with the fate of labour. Unions composed of Negroes existed in trades traditionally carried on by them, notably sleeping car porters and baggage carriers, and the leaders of these unions undertook to stimulate unions in other fields to recruit Negro members and helped to build a favourable attitude toward unionization among Negro workers.

A change in the character of American trade unionism facilitated this process. The strength of the craft unions which dominated the American labour movement until the 1930s lay in their monopoly of a particular skill, and restrictions on admission to membership were therefore a part of the union strategy. But when union organization was extended into the mass-production industries, unions formed on an industrial basis virtually had to adopt an inclusive policy on membership, since their strength depended upon complete organization within the industry rather than monopoly of a limited skill. As Negroes entered these industries they became members of the mass unions. Some of the local craft unions still refused to lower their bars, and some antiunion employers in the south successfully appealed to the racial prejudices of their white workers in their effort to prevent labour organization. But on the whole the labour movement in the 1940s and 1950s made an important contribution to the Negroes' economic advancement. Unions insisted on equal pay for equal work, they offered an opportunity for many Negroes to function as responsible members of the organization without having their leadership activity restricted to their own racial group, and the labour movement as a whole could generally be counted on to support the efforts of Negroes to extend their rights in other areas.

The net effect of the broad economic forces, the growth of labour organization and the special efforts to expand employment opportunities for Negroes was marked by a rise in the economic level of the Negroes relative to the whites. Although Negroes remained at mid-century predominantly in the lower economic ranks, the average wage received by Negro workers increased from 38 per cent of the average received by whites in 1939 to 61 per cent in 1958, a period during which the real incomes of whites were rising rapidly.

(iv) *Housing*. Discrimination in housing remained one of the most stubborn obstacles to full integration into American society. As rural Negroes migrated in ever larger numbers to industrial cities, they moved into the slums which those who could afford better homes were leaving. But when they in turn acquired the means to move out of their slum ghettoes as their predecessors had done, they found the way barred by a multitude of restrictive practices—unwillingness of builders, real estate brokers and lending institutions to build, sell or finance except in areas where non-whites already predominated, and agreements among white neighbours not to sell to non-whites. The suburban areas into which cities were spreading were especially hard to enter.

The result of these restrictions was generally poor housing, crowding and higher rents than white families had to pay for similar accommodation. Most seriously, they meant isolation from the broader community, for limitation of housing led in effect to segregation in neighbourhood facilities such as schools or parks. As Negroes made headway in their efforts to break down discrimination in other areas, the right to live wherever their means and tastes might permit became an increasingly central issue in the struggle for equality. In time they began to score some successes in this difficult field.

The Supreme Court of the United States in 1917 forbade as unconstitutional municipal ordinances which sought to designate residential areas on the basis of race. In 1948 the Court further held that restrictive covenants entered into by white neighbours were not legally enforceable if one of the group should choose to sell to a Negro. Practices of the federal government's housing agencies which had tended to reflect restrictive patterns were discarded in the 1950s in favour of a policy of open occupancy. One by one, states and municipalities began to enact laws directly forbidding various forms of discrimination in housing; sixteen states and fifteen cities had taken some official action by 1957. Even with these measures, however, the road to equality in housing was long and difficult and a commission on race and housing aptly reported its findings in 1958 under the title *Where Shall We Live?*

(v) *Political influence.* Political power had been a weapon for Negro advance during a brief period immediately after the Civil War, when the Negroes in the south had been forcibly enfranchised. But as one device after another effectively kept the majority of southern Negroes from the polls, political action ceased to afford a recourse. In spite of successful legal efforts to outlaw many of these devices and of substantial gains in the number of Negroes registered and voting in the southern states, the combined effect of many obstacles up to mid-century left Negroes in the south still politically weak. In the northern cities, however, large numbers of Negro voters went to the polls. They sent only a handful of Negroes to the federal Congress and a limited number to state legislatures, but increasing numbers were elected to city councils, and many persons elected to federal, state and local bodies who were not themselves Negroes were very conscious of the votes of their Negro constituents.

It was never the policy of Negro leadership to try to stimulate or organize bloc voting by Negroes; to have done so would have implied that Negroes constituted a separate community. For many years most Negroes identified themselves with the party of Abraham Lincoln—the Republican; the dominant white element in the south was almost solidly of the opposite party—the Democratic. In the northern cities, they found most of their neighbours Democrats, and under Franklin D. Roosevelt a large proportion of them swung to his party, the Democratic, because of the liberal labour and welfare policies of his administration. In the succeeding years, both parties recognized that the votes of Negroes could be decisive in many closely contested elections and were thus under pressure to identify themselves with the accelerating pace of Negro advance rather than with indifference or with die-hard opposition.

With a single brief exception, Negro chauvinism did not provide a basis for political or other form of organization up to the middle of the century. At the end of the first world war a dynamic West Indian Negro, Marcus Garvey, launched a movement which declared that there was no hope for the Negro in the white man's country, and called for a return to the homeland of Africa. He exalted everything black, proclaiming a black God and black Christ. He conducted mass demonstrations, set up co-operative stores, restaurants, laundries and other businesses for the separate life of black people, formed uniformed corps of Black Cross nurses and military units, and sponsored the organization of a Black Star steamship line to Africa. Appealing to the black masses, and condemning the middle-class Negro leadership as vehemently as they disclaimed him, he raised substantial sums of money and enlisted large numbers of followers—he claimed 6,000,000 while his opponents insisted that he had less than 1,000,000. But after a life of only about three years the movement collapsed, with business failures, legal entanglements and loss of membership. Its main contribution was to demonstrate the unrest in the Negro masses and their readiness to respond to vigorous leadership which offered a basis for self-respect even when combined with a counsel of despair.

During the 1930s the Communist party made a strong bid for Negro members, and some, especially among younger intellectuals, were attracted by the Party's ardent championship of Negro rights, though its proposal of 'self-determination' or a separate state for the area where the Negro population was densest had little appeal. Many Negroes became disillusioned, however, when the Party line shifted. After Hitler invaded Russia the 'imperialist' war became an 'anti-fascist' crusade, and the Party urged them to forget their grievances during the war. Meantime the more conservative Negro leaders told them to press their wartime advantage at the same time that they supported the war effort. After the war the Communist party resumed its support for the Negroes' struggle against discrimination, but it played an insignificant role in the strategy of racial advance.

The full force of Negro political influence was rarely brought to bear on the national government, but its potential effect was demonstrated during the second world war. When it seemed to Negro leaders of all types—labour, legal, clergy, educational, professional—that the government was not taking adequate steps to incorporate Negroes into the war effort, they organized what would have been a nation-wide 'March on Washington' to impress the government with the unanimity and strength of Negro feeling. Under the threat of such a march the president issued an executive order forbidding discrimination in war industries and government agencies and set up a special wartime agency to see that the order was carried out. After the war the policy of non-discrimination was continued in the government service, and extended to the armed forces and to private industries doing work on contract for the federal government.

(vi) *Literature, the arts and sport.* The battle against the stereotype of the inferior Negro was waged on the literary and artistic front, especially from the 1920s on. In 1925 Alain L. Locke, a graduate of Harvard University and the first Negro to have been a Rhodes Scholar at Oxford, published a book which included writings by Negro authors under the title *The New Negro.* In the following decades both white and Negro readers were introduced to a range of talent among Negro writers and to books by both Negro and white authors in which Negro characters were deeply and vividly revealed. These books helped to make Negro Americans as individuals an integral part of the national American image, as other books were doing for other Americans—pioneers on the western prairie, small farmers on worn-out mountain land or children of immigrants in the urban jungle.

Because the arts were loosely integrated into the prestige and economic structure of American life, they were less beset by prejudice and discrimination than most other avenues to success. Especially in the arts of entertainment, many Negroes showed great talent and received recognition, although it required persistent efforts on the part of Negro leaders and liberal whites to overcome the motion picture industry's reluctance to portray Negroes in any roles except those which would seem fitting to southern audiences.

Sports also were relatively open, and Americans became accustomed to cheering Negro sport stars and to being represented internationally by Negroes as Olympic runners and jumpers and world boxing champions. Professional baseball was slow to lower its bars, but once Negro players began to be hired in this highly competitive and popular sport, they pitched, caught and batted their way to distinction. In making their marks in entertainment, arts and sports, Negroes were taking advantage of the same avenues by which other disadvantaged groups such as the children of poor immigrants often found a pathway to the top.

Meantime Negro folk expression was becoming part of the American literary and artistic tradition, along with the lore of other folk elements such as 'hill-billies' and cowboys. Spirituals—religious songs composed in slavery—were first introduced to audiences around the country by singers from Negro colleges who went on tour to raise money for the support of their schools. Work songs, humour and slave biographies were brought together during the 1930s when unemployed writers and musicians were set to work collecting

American folk materials from all sources. Jazz music and dance not only became the basis of America's popular music, especially from the 1920s on, but achieved popularity in many other parts of the world.

The pattern of Negro life. As they struggled to make an honourable place for themselves in the full range of American life, Negroes developed a series of institutions and a range of attitudes that were in part products, in part instruments, of their struggle. Although their objective was to be able to function as ordinary citizens, the circumstances of discrimination led to the development of separate institutions paralleling those of the broader society, not only in the officially segregated south but generally in the north as well.

Oldest and most central of these institutions were the Negro churches which came into being in part because of exclusion from white churches in the south after the Civil War and in part because the church, as a sanctioned institution, provided an opportunity for Negroes to congregate without arousing the fear of the whites and inviting their interference. The church provided a rallying place, training ground and centre of mutual aid and social intercourse; much of the leadership in local communities was provided by Negro ministers.

Within the pattern of segregation, the Negro school became an important institution of the group, even though it was under the supervision of the white school administration and was generally handicapped by poor equipment as well as by the isolation resulting from segregation. Teachers made up the largest group of professionals in the southern Negro communities and hence formed the core of the Negro *élite*. They did much to insulate Negro children from the depressing effects of their environment and to keep alive their ambition and determination in the face of heavy odds.

The Negro press served two functions, as an organ of protest and as a news service, reporting to the Negro community news of its members and of events of importance to it which did not find their way into the pages of the general press. As the one agency which reached out beyond the bounds of local church or school and carried news from all sections of the country, the press conveyed a sense of the total national Negro community and provided an image in terms of which the Negro people could see themselves.

In addition to these major organizations, Negroes formed duplicates of many bodies from which they were excluded—associations of doctors, lawyers, or business men in those communities where local medical societies, bar associations, or chambers of commerce did not admit Negro co-professionals to membership. They also organized a multitude of social and interest groups and fraternal bodies, as did other elements of the population in the typically heterogeneous American communities.

The sharply drawn colour line had the effect of solidifying the Negro group in spite of itself, of forcing its advanced members to identify themselves with the Negro masses and become their leaders instead of simply trying to enjoy personal success, and of keeping dark and light together instead of prizing off a privileged mulatto element. It created the presumption, both within the Negro group and without, that each individual must be preoccupied with the fate of the race—he must study the health of Negroes if he were a doctor or their incomes if he were an economist, he must act as a spokesman if he found himself in a mixed group, and be regarded as a symbol, a test case, a representative of his race wherever he went. By thus taking away the private character from the Negro's life it forced all to participate, willy-nilly, in the common struggle for equality of status and for the right to function as unqualified Americans.

The steady advance in education and economic status produced a growing Negro middle class which by mid-century had assumed substantial proportions. Between 1940 and 1950 the proportion of Negro men who were engaged in professional, clerical, managerial, skilled or supervisory occupations increased from 10 to 17 per cent and the proportion of Negro women in these occupations increased from 7 to 13 per cent. While these percentages were still far below those of the whites, more than half of whom were in these occupations, they reflected a considerable expansion of the middle-class group.

Originally the Negro middle class was drawn principally from those who already enjoyed superior advantages at the time of general emancipation and thus had a head-start over their fellows in the process of integration into American life. These were the descendants of free Negroes who made up an eighth of the Negro population in 1863, of the children of white masters and Negro slaves whose fathers had seen to it that they were given special training as craftsmen, or were assigned to preferred tasks, or occasionally were given land, and the other personal retainers or household slaves whose position set them apart from ordinary field-hands. During the second world war and after, the basis was greatly broadened by the combination of wartime wages and benefits from labour gains which enabled many more families to keep their children at school and the educational benefits for war veterans which enabled large numbers of Negro veterans to attend universities and technical schools at government expense.

Although the Negro middle class was far more privileged than the Negro masses, it was in some ways subjected to greater psychological strains. Because of its precarious status it felt the need to conform to middle-class standards of conduct, morality and patterns of consumption even more rigorously than did other members of the American middle class. It was under great pressure for success and could not, as could members of the lower class, accept defeat from the start in the unequal battle. Members of the middle class, unsure of acceptance in the broader society, were ambivalent in their own attitudes. Struggling desperately to erase the 'Negro' stereotype from the minds of the whites with whom they had to deal, they were under pressure both to dissociate themselves from the masses whose poverty and its accompanying manifestations confirmed the stereotype, and to defend and aid them since they could never wholly escape identification with the total Negro group.

The colour line took its psychological toll in other ways. In a society where 'white' carried prestige, colour prejudice was reflected within the Negro group; the darker child soon learned that in many subtle ways his less dark fellows were likely to receive more favoured treatment—to be cast as hero in a school play, be more popular if a girl, or find the teacher expecting better performance and more ready to recognize it. Constant reminders that he was held in low esteem by others gnawed away at the Negro's own self-respect. Studies during the second quarter of the twentieth century revealed the depth of self-hate which frustration, combined with the negative evaluation of society caused many Negroes to turn in upon themselves. Other psychological studies began to call attention to the equally devastating effect of colour prejudice on the personality of the white person, and the added burden imposed upon the Negro by displacement upon him of the white man's sense of guilt.

The accelerating rate of change in status. By the mid-fifties the groundswell towards full participation had become broad and deep. With each passing year it became less possible for those who resisted the full acceptance of Negroes as fellow citizens, workers and neighbours to maintain that they were not ready for full citizenship, that they preferred to remain apart, or that agitators were stirring up a people who were generally content. When in 1955 a tired seamstress riding home on a bus in the southern city of Montgomery, Alabama, was arrested for refusing to surrender her seat to a white passenger and move to the crowded rear of the bus, the entire Negro population of the city remained off the buses for months, until separate seating of whites and Negroes was discontinued by court order. Led by a young minister, meeting in churches and prefacing their meeting with prayer, they organized an orderly, steady passive resistance.

Before the Montgomery demonstration, the idea of passive resistance as a weapon in the struggle for racial equality had been used only by small interracial groups who sat together patiently in restaurants which refused to serve them; economic pressure had only occasionally been used, as in campaigns under the slogan 'don't buy where you can't work' to force the employment of Negroes in neighbourhood stores. It remained for this episode to establish beyond a doubt that the masses of the people, south as well as north, had decided that the time for patience in the face of discrimination was over, and were capable of spontaneous disciplined expression in ways which could dramatize their cause and have a major impact on the economic interests of the communities of which they were a part. Passive resistance and boycott were used increasingly in the following years, not only to overcome the opposition of die-hards who sought to block execution of the order of the Supreme Court to end segregation in the schools, but to open up all manner of facilities and to tear down the structure of segregation and discrimination wherever it remained.

In the north, meantime, Negroes and their collaborators were using political power to secure legislation making discrimination on grounds of race, religion or nationality illegal in employment, public facilities, education and housing. By 1957 fifteen states had expressly prohibited discrimination in employment, six states had extended the prohibition to all housing which received any form of public aid, and New York City had made it applicable to purely private housing as well. At the same time individual Negroes in all walks of life, especially those in kinds of jobs or responsibilities which few of their race had formerly filled, strove to demonstrate by their competence the ability of Negroes to perform whatever tasks their individual training and capacities had prepared them for. However modest their outlook and however much they might wish to lead personal, anonymous lives, they knew that they could not yet escape the burden of being symbols and champions of their race.

In the changed climate of American society and the altered world situation, the rate of change in the status of the American Negro was greatly accelerated. The transformation of Africa from the dark abode of primitive people into the home of independent nations whose representatives sat shoulder-to-shoulder with the great powers in the United Nations could not fail to have repercussions on the status of Negroes throughout the world. Many American Negroes who had dissociated themselves from their distant African past found the new African states a source of racial pride and self respect, while more and more whites came to realize that the treatment of the Negro minority in the United States was not a purely domestic matter but one which had a major impact on the foreign policy of the country and the nation's place in world affairs.

The very rapidity of change and mounting evidence that the day was past when it was possible to 'keep the Negro in his place' evoked a burst of massive resistance and of typically counter-revolutionary violence from the defeated but die-hard element in the south. As the extremists captured the initiative in reaction against the Supreme Court's school integration decision of 1954, it appeared that the momentum of change was for the moment checked in the southern states. But only the die-hards regarded the set-back as more than temporary. And in the face of renewed indignities the Negro people remained self-disciplined. The vast majority continued to struggle for an integrated society in line with American principles and Christian doctrine, but the growth of a bitterly anti-white organization calling itself 'Black Muslims' showed that white intransigence could evoke a corresponding response.

In spite of violent reaction the process of integration gathered momentum. In the 1950s Negro engineering school graduates had their choice of jobs in major industrial corporations which, little more than a decade before, had refused employment to Negro applicants; there was thorough integration in the armed services, which had been completely segregated at the opening of the second world war, and in civilian branches of the government; Negroes served in growing numbers in the diplomatic service, occupying such responsible posts as that of cultural attaché in Rome or Rangoon; they were appointed as professors in the faculties of major American universities; they were active as rank and file and in many leadership posts in the labour movement and other voluntary organizations; the job aspirations of the nine Negro boys and girls who entered the famous Little Rock, Arkansas, high school in 1957 under the protection of federal troops were representative of any group of high school students—engineer, atomic scientist, dress designer, lawyer, teacher, ballet dancer.

Most important of all, more and more Americans who happened to be Negroes were able to function as individuals outside traditionally Negro roles on the basis of their interest and training, without having to preoccupy themselves with Negro problems alone, or be limited to serving members of their own group, or stand always as a spokesman or symbol of the race.

Throughout the years the struggle to integrate Negro Americans as full citizens and participants in American life was not a struggle of Negroes alone, but of the people of the United States, for it was part of the overall American effort to realize the full meaning of democracy. In the words of one of the dynamic Negro leaders of the 1950s, describing what she called the 'epic achievement' of the Negro in the United States since 1863: 'The Negro's progression from chattel to freedman, to legal citizenship, to increasing equality of rights and opportunities, to accepted neighbor and compatriot represents a dramatic testament to democracy's positive and dynamic character.' Wherever undemocratic inconsistency exists 'the majority stakes in its progressive solution are fully as great as those of the minority'.* The 'American dream' of freedom and equality, of the rights of each individual as a citizen, of his worth and dignity as a person and of his entitlement to equal opportunity to pursue his well-being and development remained basic to American life and thought, however much these principles might be violated in practice. As the Swedish social scientist, Gunnar Myrdal, concluded, after an extensive study of the position of the American Negro in the 1940s: 'The whites have all the power, but they are split in their moral personality. Their better selves are with the insurgents. The Negroes do not need any other allies.'†

2. UNTOUCHABLES

Among the largest groups subject to the most extreme forms of discrimination were India's untouchables, who numbered 50,000,000 according to the census of 1931. These classes were segregated, denied elementary civil rights and confined to occupations like scavenging which were considered unclean. They were present in all parts of India, for every village and town depended on them to do the necessary tasks which no other Hindu would perform; they in turn were wholly dependent, for they could not even draw water from the village well and must wait for their water jars to be filled by others.

Untouchability dated from time immemorial—it existed at the time of the

* Butcher, *The Negro in American Culture, op. cit.,* p. 22.
* Gunnar Myrdal, *An American Dilemma* (New York, 1944), p. 1004.

Buddha, for he attacked it—and it was entrenched in social custom. To many it had the support of religion, for the belief was widely held that the untouchable person had come to his present status as a result of his sins or failures in a previous life. Many untouchables held this view of themselves. They thus found themselves held down by strong sanctions that were practical, religious and psychological.

The revolutionary change in their status, to the point where the practice of untouchability was made a penal offence, was brought primarily by the forces which liberated the country and were reforming the broad structure of Indian society. The efforts of untouchables themselves played only a minor part in the alteration of their position from that of outcast to citizen with full legal rights.

By the end of the nineteenth century movements for the reform of Hindu society brought untouchability under attack. Swami Vivekananda, one of the major figures of the Hindu Reformation, denounced it root and branch. A number of Brahmins and other high-caste persons began to work individually among the untouchables. A few maharajas took steps within their domains. The maharaja of Baroda attempted to abolish untouchability in his state, but was unable to give full effect to his intention; the maharaja of Travancore appointed untouchables as judges and to other public office. These were, however, isolated attacks, and although they grew in number they represented the special interest of individuals rather than a broad movement. Nevertheless, together with other aspects of the reform movements of the time, they began to undermine the public attitude which took untouchability for granted as a permanent, unchangeable institution.

Some outside pressures contributed an impetus toward a change in the treatment of untouchables, notably the danger of large-scale conversion to Christianity or Islam. Christian missionaries in the nineteenth century first appealed mainly to the Brahmins and attracted a number of educated persons, especially in Bengal where British interests were centred and western ways were gaining prestige. But with the movement to reform Hindu society from within, Christianity lost much of its appeal to those whose reason for leaving the Hindu faith had been the rigidity of its social customs. Thereafter many of the Christian missionaries shifted their approach and appealed to the untouchables, to whom they offered equality of status within the Christian community. Especially in certain regions, missionaries were successful in attracting substantial numbers of untouchables, and Hindu leaders saw a threat of large-scale defection unless the lot of the untouchables within the Hindu community could be improved. In addition, there was the ever-present attraction of casteless Islam.

It was Mahatma Gandhi, however, who made the abolition of untouchability a vital national issue. When he returned to India from South Africa in 1915, he visited the families of the untouchables who had provided the main support for his passive resistance in South Africa and, to the dismay of his friends who had endowed an *ashram*—or retreat—for him, he welcomed untouchables to stay with him in the same house. From that time on he made it clear that the eradication of untouchability was one of his primary missions.

Under Gandhi's leadership the national movement committed itself to the abolition of untouchability as a central objective. The 1920 session of the Indian National Congress passed a resolution stating that the removal of untouchability was necessary for the attainment of freedom, and thenceforth the Congress never veered from this position. In 1929 it set up an Anti-Untouchability Committee which worked to get temples, schools and wells freely open to untouchables. Where the Congress party secured control of provincial governments under the constitution of 1935, it secured the enactment of measures on behalf of untouchables, such as free education from primary school through to university in Bihar or the opening of some of the temples in Bombay.

Gandhi himself lost no opportunity to keep the 'sin of untouchability' in the public mind. He insisted that the workers of the Congress party go into the villages and actually practise equality with the people who had so long been considered outcasts. In his own tours all over India he stayed with untouchables in their colonies. For the untouchables themselves he sought to build up their own self-respect. Considering the name 'untouchable' objectionable and likely to confirm a sense of inferiority, he renamed them *harijans*, children of God. He encouraged them to seek their own self-improvement, to adopt conduct, such as not drinking, which would command respect, and to participate actively in the Congress party. To assist them in their efforts at self-improvement he founded and served as president of a society for the service of *harijans* —*Harijan Seva Sangh*—with funds and personnel devoted to education and welfare services.

The *harijan* community itself became active in its own behalf in some places and produced some outstanding leaders, the most notable of whom was Dr Bhim Rao Ambedkar, a lawyer and sociologist educated in London. As the nationalist movement began to use the method of passive resistance against the British administration, *harijans* adopted the same technique for their own ends. In Travancore, for example, a passive resistance movement led to a proclamation in 1932 permitting *harijans* to enter Hindu temples. *Harijan* movements for self-improvement were local and were mostly centred in urban communities, except for a state-wide movement in Travancore which sought to raise the whole community. With the help of local units of the Congress party, there were repeated local efforts to remove disabilities, but in British India these came up against the law courts which upheld local custom in such matters as access to village wells. Even where there was no legal change, custom did break down to some extent in a number of places.

These piecemeal efforts, however, appeared entirely inadequate to Dr Ambedkar, who saw no future for the Depressed Classes within the Hindu fold. He therefore began to organize a political movement with the object of gaining recognition for untouchables as an entity separate from the Hindus, entitled to separate political rights and representation as were other non-Hindu communities, notably the Muslims. The movement received recognition from the British government, whose policy was to encourage separatist tendencies among groups in the Indian sub-continent, and Ambedkar was invited to attend the Round Table Conference in London in 1931 as a representative of the untouchables. But the move to make the untouchables into a separate community was opposed by Gandhi in the strongest terms, and he conducted a 'fast unto death' when the British proposed to put the plan for a separate community into effect in 1932. His fast resulted in a compromise providing for special seats for *harijans* but election from joint constituencies.

Dr Ambedkar's efforts received little mass support from *harijans*, for the majority of them were devout Hindus by religion and they did not respond to his anti-Hindu appeal; those who were ready to dissociate themselves from Hinduism were more likely to seek identity with the Christian or Muslim community than with a community of outcasts whose identity was defined in Hindu terms. More importantly, since what the *harijans* desired was to enjoy the full rights of citizens, their goal was assimilation into the total community and the removal of barriers rather than the perpetuation of a separate identity.

By the time of independence the Hindu public had come to recognize untouchability as an evil and to accept the necessity of eradicating it. More than twenty-five years of Gandhi's propaganda, the commitment of the Congress party, and the awakening among the *harijans* themselves had prepared the ground for a radical solution.

In independent India the legal position was clear. According to the constitution: ' "Untouchability" is abolished and its practice in any form is forbidden. The enforcement of any disability arising out of "Untouchability" shall be an offence punishable in accordance with law.' The Untouchability (Offences) Act of 1955 spelled out in detail types of discrimination and imposed penalties. In addition the Indian government recognized that centuries of disability had placed *harijans* at such a competitive disadvantage even where they were no longer barred that special provisions were necessary to ensure them the opportunity to secure an education and to participate in public life. Accordingly, special scholarships were earmarked for *harijan* students and a proportion of vacancies in public appointments were reserved for *harijan* appointees. Meantime the ablest among them held cabinet offices in the central government and in the several states.

The habits and attitudes of centuries did not vanish overnight in the more than half a million Indian villages and towns, and legal rights did not immediately become social practice. But democratic processes were making the abolition of untouchability effective. The adult franchise brought political power to former untouchable classes in local, provincial and central governments, and the recruitment of *harijans* to all branches of public service helped to give reality to the revolutionary change in status of this most disadvantaged segment of Indian society.

NOTES TO CHAPTER XXX

1. Corresponding member of the Academy of Sciences Ludvik Svoboda (Czechoslovakia) thinks that the section devoted to the workers' movement does not contain a thorough and comprehensive exposition of the problem. It only enumerates facts but does not bring out the essential and definitive phenomena. . . . The main reason for this is that the authors do not grasp the underlying economic realities of the problems. . . . It is characteristic that the authors sympathize only with the economic struggle of the working class and repudiate the political and ideological struggle. It can be inferred from a reading of the text that the authors consider the strike an admissible means of pursuing the struggle only when it does not go beyond the limits of economic demands and that they condemn the political strike. In the authors' view the ideological struggle is something that has been introduced into the workers' movement from outside mainly by the intelligentsia. It is not surprising therefore that the situation of the working class in Western Europe seems to the authors to be quite satisfactory. This point of view is supported by Dr János Jemnic (Hungary), who notes that the authors devote attention mainly to those aspirations of the workers which were directed towards improving the situation of the working class within the framework of the existing social system. Such a narrowing of the field of investigation has brought with it the result that the workers' movement as a whole has been represented in a distorted way: the false impression is created that the welfare of the popular masses can in the main be assured by a reformist movement in the framework of the existing social system. In two places in the text the authors make a brief reference to the revolutionary movement of the working classes in the West, but not nearly enough is said about it.

2. *The Author-Editors wish to draw the attention of the reader to the language of the text, notably to the discussion of the communist labour movement, pp. 1118–19, and of revolutionary unionism in western Europe, p. 1116.*

3. Dr János Jemnic and K. Baginyan underline that the expansion of power resources and mechanization, the rational organization of industry and the growth of labour productivity under conditions of the predominance of private property do not lead to higher living standards for workers, but are mainly exploited in the interests of employers. See Lewis Mumford, *Art and Technics* (New York, 1952), Lewis Mumford, *In the Name of Sanity* (New York, 1954), and other works. The worker gains nothing unless he wins concessions by struggle (for example the strikes in the iron and steel industry in the USA in 1959).

4. Doctor Baginyan notes that it was no mean achievement of the German workers that they were able to utilize the very limited constitutional legality to set up their own organizations—the trade unions, the co-operatives and the party. This latter exerted a great influence on the activity of the trade unions until a resolution was carried at the party's Mannheim session in 1906 which laid down the principle of 'equality of rights' between trade unions and party, and so undermined the position of the revolutionary wing in the trade unions (see Farwing: *Der Kampf um die Gewerkschaften*, p. 219).

5. Dr Baginyan underlines that 'democratic centralism' means not only strict discipline but also the giving of extensive democratic rights to all local organizations and to each member of the party and the exercise of control over the elected organs by the whole mass of the party. Here are the provisions laid down in this connection in the Statutes of the Communist Party of the Soviet Union as confirmed at its twenty-second session in 1961:

The guiding principle of the organizational structure of the party is democratic centralism which implies:

(*a*) the elective character of all the controlling organs of the party from the lowest to the highest;

(*b*) a periodic rendering of accounts by party organs to their party organizations and to their superior organs;

(*c*) a strict party discipline and subordination of the minority to the majority;

(*d*) the unconditional mandatory force of decisions by higher organs for lower organs. (See *Ustav KPSS* ('Statutes of the Communist Party of the Soviet Union'), Moscow, 1961, p. 12).

6. Drs János Jemnic and K. Baginyan write: In Soviet Russia and the other socialist countries the workers' unions have received very extensive rights. Their interests fully coincide with those of the government. The trade unions are not only called on to defend the interests of the workers but they have been given the function of handling social insurance funds and are responsible for occupational health, safety in factories and protection of labour. Under these conditions collective agreements have become bilateral obligations binding both on the administration and on the trade unions, and designed to promote common aims. See for example *Ustav professionalnykh soyuzov SSSR* (Statutes of the Trade Unions in the USSR) as confirmed at the twelfth session held on March 27, 1959 (Moscow, 1959).

7. Candidate of Juridical Sciences A. Bovin underlines that organically strikes cannot take place in the USSR and in the people's democracies as when power is in the hands of the working class strike action loses all meaning. The events which took place in 1956 in Poland, in the German Democratic Republic and in Hungary have nothing at all to do with the struggle of the workers for their rights. These were attempts at counter-revolutionary insurrections directed towards the overthrow of the socialist structure in those countries and were organized by internal counter-revolutionary forces with the active support of international imperialism. The working class in Poland, the German Democratic Republic and Hungary very quickly liquidated those expressions of hostility to socialism since they had not the slightest roots in the working masses. See Note 12 to Chapter II.

8. Dr Baginyan writes: In most newly industrializing countries the struggle for freedom and independence against foreign intervention is of vital importance. Therefore in comparison with political issues the everyday problems of the workers at times temporarily recede into the background.

9. Dr Baginyan underlines that the leaders of the International Confederation of Free Trade Unions took up a schismatic attitude and refused to collaborate with the World Federation of Trade Unions in the struggle for peace. See for example W. Z. Foster, *Outline History of the World Trade Union Movement* (New York, 1956) and also Labour Research Association, *Labour Fact Book* 12 (New York, 1955).

10. Dr János Jemnic notes that the Trade Disputes and Trade Unions Act of 1927 paralysed trade union activity in the United Kingdom for many years.

11. Candidate of Economic Sciences V. P. Tikhomirov calls attention to the fact that the peasantry in itself does not represent a homogeneous mass and therefore the position of the various strata of farmers and peasants in the class society is different.

12. Professor A. N. den Hollander writes: 'The difference between "peasant" and "farmer", as made chiefly by American authors, remains as indistinct in this manuscript as it is in whatever other publication I have ever read.' Although the Author-Editors use the term 'farmer' for the essentially capitalistic type of agriculturalist in Western Europe, North America, Australia and New Zealand, and 'peasant' for the subsistence farmer or farm tenant of Eastern Europe and Asia, a further analysis of criteria may be of use. The distinction between peasant and farmer is cultural, and the difficulty of defining the one type and the other arises from the fact that in modern times, especially during the present century, the transitional stages between the one and the other become so numerous as to blur the outline of each.

The concept of peasant, at least as understood in the West, derives from the caste society of the feudal age and its continuation in the Old Regime, when the peasant as an agriculturalist was stationary. He worked the land in an almost self-sufficient economy; he did not see or think—except in religion—much if at all beyond the limits of his locality, and he was a member of a family as the primary working unit and of the village as a compact, co-operative group. He found little value for his kind of existence in learning, even to the extent of knowing how to read and write, and he had the habits of behaviour of one accustomed to working the soil and associating with livestock as much as with human beings. Whether he owned the land which he worked or had the status of serf did not affect the essential characteristics of the cultural type; in either case he was a peasant.

Whether and to what extent these characteristics persisted into the recent period depended largely upon the availability of alternatives to this way of life for members of the peasantry. Alternatives first became possible on a significant scale with the rise and spread of industrial society, which changed market relations for the agricultural population and thereby brought about a transformation in the attitude of the peasants toward change and time and toward the quickest means of adjusting to the new opportunities, those of education. The process of adaptation to the industrial society included learning something about commercial, scientific agriculture and cost accounting, and these interests entailed the adoption of many social and political mores and interests of the urban population. Rate and extent of adaptation varied according to circumstances, and often in the same region according to personal qualities; but as individuals adjusted to the new society, they acquired characteristics very different from those of the peasantry. In lieu of a better term to refer to the new type of agriculturalist, one may employ the word developed in the United States, where, in the absence of a traditional caste or legally fixed class or status structure, the new type predominated and set the norm. The new type was referred to as 'farmer', a person with middle-class characteristics, whose occupation, a capitalistic enterprise, was not industry or commerce but agriculture. As this occupation became increasingly mechanized and subject to scientific discipline, the agriculturalist tended more and more to share even the habits of work and of thought of the industrial technician, and the distinction between rural and urban society has rapidly faded. At this stage working the soil ceased to be synonymous with the way of life of the peasantry and became a means of earning a living which would enable the practitioners to be as much like the members of urban society as the occupation of agriculture would permit. In the process involved Europe has offered many examples—one thinks of Denmark among others—of the type 'farmer', but most of the agricultural population remains at various stages in the movement from peasantry to farmerhood.

Important reading for this subject is the article 'Farmer' by Professor Rudolph Heberle in the *Handwörterbuch der Sozialwissenschaften*, volume III (edition 1961), pp. 478 ff. (The article and Professor Herbele's bibliography are in German.) Especially to be recommended is the report of a symposium of French scholars in various fields held in Paris in March 1951 on the theme *Villes et campagnes. Civilisation urbaine et civilisation rurale en France*. The report, edited by Professor Georges Friedmann, was published by the University of Paris, École des Hautes Études, at the Librairie Armand Colin (no date).

13. V. P. Tikhomirov notes that the authors give a distorted view of the policy pursued by the Communist Party of the Soviet Union on the peasant question and of the collectivization of agriculture which was carried out in the Soviet Union. At the end of the twenties agriculture in the USSR was lagging very far behind the growth of socialist industry. Industry was centralized and operated on a large scale. Agriculture had remained on a small scale and fragmented. Heavy industry was based on communal, socialist ownership of the means of production whilst private ownership of the means of production was the rule on the small peasant farms. Socialist industry was subordinated to the principle of planning. The small peasant holding was at the mercy of market fluctuations. Large-scale socialist industry could rely all the time on the newest technical advances and was developing at a rapid tempo in obedience to the principle of reproduction on an extended scale. The small peasant holding, based on primitive techniques and manual labour, had no possibility of using up-to-date machines, and was developing slowly, often so slowly as not to ensure even simple reproduction.

By 1927 the small fragmented peasant holding had basically exhausted its potentialities for further increase of productivity. The process of splitting up peasant holdings was continuing in the countryside. These yielded only a minimum of marketable produce, particularly grain. Whilst the gross output of agriculture for 1926–27 exceeded the pre-war level the gross yield of grain, the basic farming crop, amounted in that year to only 95 per cent of the gross output for 1913; the marketable part of the grain harvest was 13·3 per cent against 26 per cent in the pre-war period.

Under those conditions the grain harvest could not satisfy the country's bread requirements which were increasing in proportion to the growth of the urban population and the working class. The backwardness of agriculture was putting a brake on all socialist construction.

In the interest of the construction of socialism it was urgently necessary to liquidate the backwardness of agriculture and to effect a transition from the small privately owned peasant holding to the large-scale socialist farm. In order to build socialism all land had to be transferred to public ownership as socialism could not successfully be constructed if two forms of economy—the socialist economy in the urban sphere and the petty goods economy in the rural sphere—continued to coexist.

The socialist reconstruction of agriculture is based on Lenin's co-operative plan. Lenin had pointed out that co-operation is the most easily accessible way to the socialist reconstruction of agriculture, that in the conditions of the dictatorship of the proletariat the mere growth of co-operation is identical with the growth of socialism, and that when there is state ownership of all the major means of production, and an alliance of the proletariat with the masses of the toiling peasantry, and when the proletariat plays the directing role in this union all the conditions are fulfilled for using co-operation as a means of building the socialist society. Leninism teaches that the peasantry must co-operate on a strictly voluntary basis, and that they must be gradually convinced by practical illustrations, initially in those spheres of co-operation which relate to supplying and selling and then in the sphere of agricultural production, so that there is a progression from the lowest to the highest forms of production co-operation. The creation of a solid industrial basis is an essential prerequisite for the mechanization of agriculture and contributes to the socialist reconstruction of the countryside.

By putting agriculture on a co-operative basis three important problems were at one solved: (a) the units of agricultural production were transformed from small and fragmented peasant holdings to large-size collective farms; (b) the last exploiting class—that of the kulaks (rich peasants) was liquidated; and (c) the conditions required for a decisive rise in agricultural production were created.

In the first years of Soviet rule, the Russian peasantry acquired by personal experience the conviction that only if agriculture were put on a co-operative basis could there be any possibility of raising the standard of living of the peasants as a whole and of liquidating exploitation in the countryside. That is why the overwhelming mass of the poor peasants and middle peasants voluntarily adhered to the collectivization of agriculture.

In the place of twenty-five million small peasant holdings in the USSR there now exist seventy thousand collective farms. The peasantry of the Soviet Union has become a homogeneous class in the socialist society. See also Note 11 to Chapter XXI.

14. *The Author-Editors refer the reader to the chapter on Agriculture (Chapter XIV) and to the references provided in Note 1 to that chapter.*

15. Academician D. Kosev thinks that the assertion that the peasant parties in the countries of Eastern Europe were organized by the communist parties is at variance with the historical facts. Such parties were in existence even before the second world war. Already during the war against fascism a *rapprochement* had begun between the peasant parties and the communist parties and was later transformed into a fighting alliance.

16. Dr János Jemnic thinks that the views expressed on the development of the Eastern European countries since the war proceed from a mistaken concept. The characteristic feature did not lie in the divergencies between the peasant parties and the communist parties. On the contrary the communist parties everywere played a major role in carrying out land reform; and they defended peasant holdings from the big landowners (there is no mention of this).

V. P. Tikhomirov agrees with him and notes that the authors give a wrong idea of the process of collectivization in the people's democracies of Europe. A solid alliance of the working class and the peasantry under the leadership of the communist and workers' parties was established whilst the war for liberation from foreign and domestic reaction was still going on during the second world war. After the collapse of Nazi Germany at the end of the war, people's democracies, which were the expression of a system based on the alliance of workers and peasants, were set up.

The communist and workers' parties were able to adjust their relations with the peasant parties. In regard to the mass peasant parties whose leadership was at the outset strongly under the influence of the rural bourgeoisie the communists began by adopting a policy of unmasking and isolating the reactionary leaders from the masses.

They supported the left wing of the peasant movement and helped to bring about the advancement of genuine representatives of the peasants. The peasant parties expelled the bourgeois elements from their leadership and recognized the directing role of the working class.

Democratic agrarian reforms which did away with the landlord class were carried out in all the European people's democracies between 1945 and 1947.

In Poland and Hungary half of all the cultivated land belonged to the landlords, in Czechoslovakia and Roumania one-third and in Albania the majority. It was only in Bulgaria where at the time of the Russo-Turkish War of 1877-78 the landlords—all Turks by nationality—had fled the country, leaving no more big estates in the hands of their owners, that the agrarian reform was from the outset of an anti-capitalist character. In the people's democracies only a small part of the arable land was nationalized; as the mass of the peasants wanted to get the estates of the big landlords into their private ownership, these were in the first place divided up between peasants who had little or no land.

The masses of the peasantry themselves took part in the appropriation and distribution of the landlords' properties, in securing which they were assisted by the working class. When in 1945 the government of General Radescu in Rumania began to sabotage the land reform the workers called upon the peasants themselves to divide up the land and their advice was followed. At the end of 1944 commissioners were sent by the Polish Workers' party into the villages to apportion the estates, who were assisted in their task by teams from the factories.

The division of the big estates strengthened the union of the workers and of the peasants. Material conditions in the countryside were somewhat improved and in a few years most poor peasants raised their holdings to the economic level of the middle peasants. However this was not a radical solution of the peasant problem. In course of time the peasants convinced themselves by personal experience that there was very little likelihood of a major improvement in the great mass of peasant holdings and that large-scale collective farms must therefore be set up.

By the beginning of 1962 almost all the peasants in the European people's democracies, including even the former kulaks, had voluntarily joined productive agricultural co-operatives. The incomes of the production co-operatives in the European socialist countries are distributed basically in proportion to work done and partly also in proportion to land.

17. V. P. Tikhomirov notes that actually it was only the Cárdenas government (1934-40) that began to implement the agrarian reform in Mexico but this reform was not carried through to the end. The struggle of the peasants for the land still continues in Mexico. Thus in 1958 there was peasant agitation in the north-west part of the country.

18. V. P. Tikhomirov notes that the land reform in Cuba was not just a 'plank in the platform of the revolutionary leader'. On May 17, 1959, a law for agrarian reform was adopted in Cuba. When it was put into effect in 1960 it resulted in the complete elimination of the *latifundia* which represented the main obstacle to the consummation of the Cuban revolution. As stipulated by the agrarian legislation about 125,000 peasant families, mainly selected from among those who previously had been tenants of the big landowners, received plots of land. One special feature of the agrarian transformation was a mass movement for the creation of co-operatives (production co-operatives with joint cultivation of the soil) to which more than half the area of cultivable land was allotted. The co-operatives have been mainly aligned on the sites of the big landed estates which had been granted to the agricultural workers and peasants who previously possessed little or no land.

19. Candidate of Economic Sciences Z. M. Pashetkina notes that the constitution of the Soviet Union specifically lays down that women have an equal right to education. A case in point is the vocational training of women. In 1960-61 out of the total number of pupils in intermediate vocational schools 47 per cent were women. In the 1960-61 session, women formed 43 per cent of the students in higher educational establishments, and 63 per cent of those in higher educational institutions for training teachers; they made up 56 per cent of students in institutions for training staff for the public health service and for the sports and cultural departments. (*Narodnoye khozyaistvo SSSR v 1960 g. Statisticheskiy sbornik* ('Statistical annual of the national economy of the USSR for 1960'), Moscow, 1961, p. 779.)

21 PAINTING I

Pablo Picasso, 'Les demoiselles d'Avignon', 1907. New York, Museum of Modern Art

PAINTING II

Fernand Léger,
'Three Women'
(Le grand
déjeuner), 1921.
New York,
Museum of
Modern Art

PAINTING III

Georges Braque,
'Still Life with
Grapes', 1927.
Washington,
Philipps Collection

24   PAINTING IV

Kasimir Malevich, 'Matinée à la campagne après la pluie', 1911.   New York, Guggenheim Museum

25 PAINTING V

Piet Mondrian, 'Composition in Red, Yellow and Blue', 1921. Amsterdam, Municipal Museum

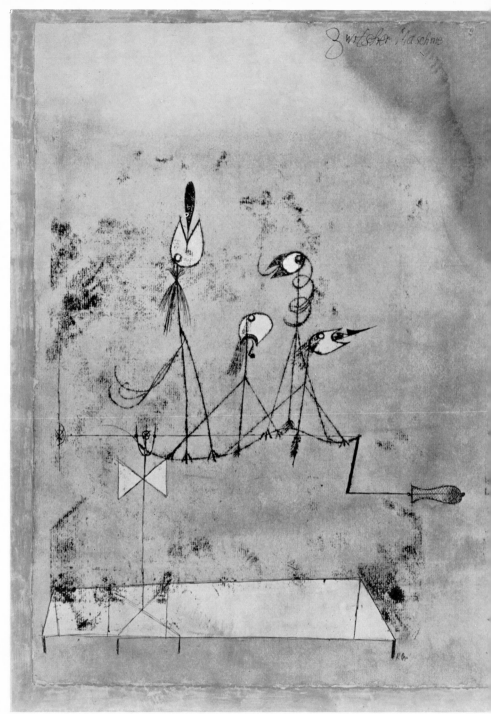

[Mode

26 PAINTING VI

Paul Klee, 'Zwitscher Maschine' (Twittering Machine), 1922. New York, Museum of Modern Art

27   PAINTING VII

Pablo Picasso, 'Guernica' (Mural), 1937. New York, Museum of Modern Art

28   PAINTING VIII

Käthe Kollwitz, Portrait (charcoal), 1943

29 PAINTING IX

Alexander A. Deyneka, 'The Defence of Petrograd', 1927–28

30

PAINTING X

Ben Shahn,
'Handball', 1939.
New York,
Museum of
Modern Art
(Abby Aldrich
Fund)

31 PAINTING XI *Jackson Pollock, 'Number 1', 1948. New York, Museum of Modern Art*

32 PAINTING XII

*José Clemente
Orozco, 'Zapatistas',
1931. New York,
Museum of Modern
Art*

[*Giraudon*

(a)

33 SCULPTURE I

(a) *Auguste Rodin, Bronze figure from 'L'enfer', c. 1900. Poitiers, Musée des Beaux Arts*

(b) *Aristide Maillol, Bronze, c. 1905–10. Poitiers, Musée des Beaux Arts*

(b)

[*Giraudon*

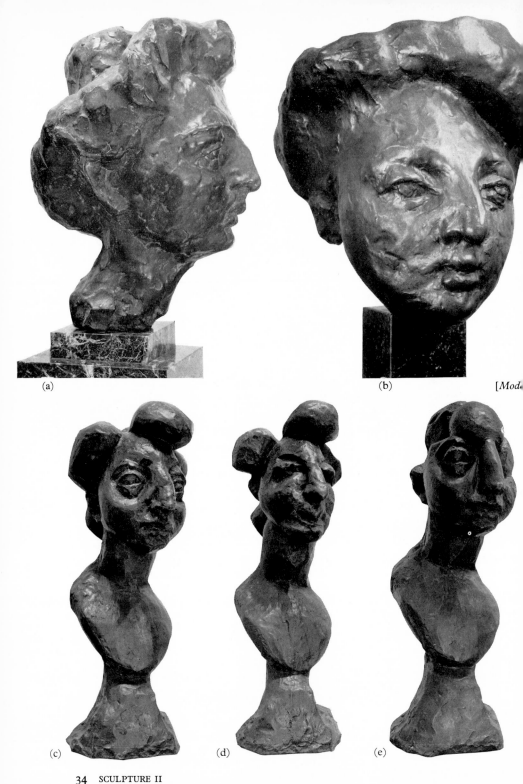

(a)

(b)

[Mod

(c)

(d)

(e)

34 SCULPTURE II

Henri Matisse, 'Head of Jeannette' (Jeanne Vaderin), 1910–12. New York, Museum of Modern Art

(a) *Jeannette I* (1910)   (c) *Jeannette III* (1910–11)
(b) *Jeannette II* (1910)   (d) *Jeannette IV* (1910–11 ?)
                        (e) *Jeannette V* (1910–11 ?)

[Modern Art

[Modern Art

(a)

(b)

35 SCULPTURE III

(a) *Umberto Boccioni, 'Unique Forms of Continuity in Space', 1913. New York,*
    Museum of Modern Art
(b) *Antoine Pevsner, 'Developable Column', 1942. New York, Museum of Modern Art*

[Moder

36 SCULPTURE IV

Alberto Giacometti, 'Chariot', 1950. New York, Museum of Modern Art

37   SCULPTURE V

Henry Moore, 'Family Group', 1945. New York, Museum of Modern Art

38 SCULPTURE VI

Reg Butler, 'The Unknown Political Prisoner' (project for a monument), 1951–53.
New York, Museum of Modern Art

[Modern Art

Alexander Calder, 'Lobster Trap and Fish Tail' (Mobile), 1939. New York, Museum of Modern Art

40 SCULPTURE VIII

V. I. Mukhina, 'Industrial Worker and Kolkhoz Labourer', 1937

41 SCULPTURE IX

Oku Ampofo, 'Animist Slave', Accra, Ghana

42   SCULPTURE X

Isamu Noguchi, Modern Garden in Japanese Style, 1958. Unesco House, Paris

43 ARCHITECTURE I

Walter Gropius, The Bauhaus, Dessau, 1925–26

44 ARCHITECTURE II

Frank Lloyd Wright,
Johnson's Wax
buildings, Racine,
Wisconsin, 1936–49

45 ARCHITECTURE III

   (a) *Individual homes in a suburban development, South Bend, Indiana, USA*

   (b) *Le Corbusier, 'Unité d'habitation', Marseilles, France,* 1952

46   ARCHITECTURE IV

United Nations Headquarters, New York, 1947–50

47　ARCHITECTURE V

(a) *P. L. Nervi, The Palazzetto dello Sport, Rome,* 1956–57
(b) *University College, Ibadan, Nigeria,* 1961

(a)

[*Brazilian Embass*

48 ARCHITECTURE VI

    (a) *Oscar Niemeyer, Cathedral, Brasilia, Brazil*, 1960

    (b) *Oscar Niemeyer, Supreme Court, Brasilia, Brazil*, 1960

(b)

[*Brazilian Embass*

[*Georgia O'Keefe*

49   PHOTOGRAPHY I

Alfred Stieglitz, 'The Steerage', 1907. New York, Museum of Modern Art

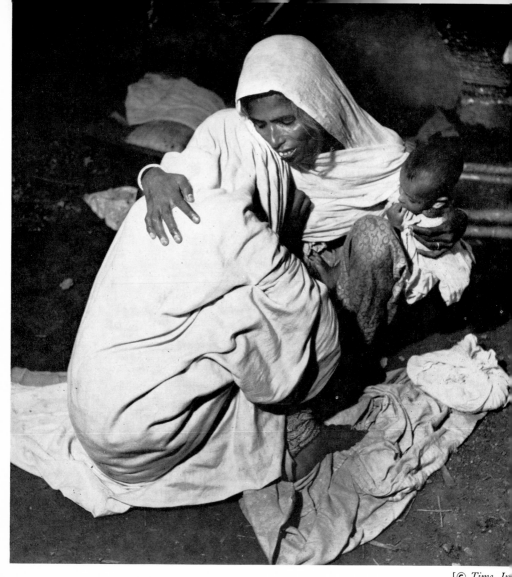

50   PHOTOGRAPHY II

Margaret Bourke-White, 'Grief', India, 1953

51   PHOTOGRAPHY III (opposite)

Henri Cartier-Bresson, 'Shanghai

[*M*

52   PHOTOGRAPHY IV

Gjon Mili, '3/4 Beat', c. 1942

53 PHOTOGRAPHY V

The Interior of the Heart

(a)

mehr anbauen
oder hungern?

...Gartenbau-Aktion des VSK und der Konsumgenossenschaften

(b)

(a)

55   THE THEATRE I

(a) *Auguste Perret,*
Champs Elysées
Theatre, auditorium
under construction,
Paris, 1911–13

(b) *Gerhard Weber, The*
State Opera,
Hamburg, 1955

(b)

(a)

[

56 THE THEATRE II

(a) *Constantin Stanislavsky, scene from Act IV of* The Lower Depths *by Gorky.*
    Moscow Art Theatre, 1902

(b) *Elwin Piscator, scene from* Flüchtlingsgespräche *by Bertolt Brecht. Munich,*
    1962

(b)

a) [CF

57 MOTION PICTURES I

    (a) *D. W. Griffith, scene from* Intolerance, 1916
    (b) *Sergei Eisenstein, scene from* Battleship Potemkin, 1925

b) [CF

58 MOTION PICTURES II

(a) *Charlie Chaplin, scene from* Modern Times, 1936
(b) *Walt Disney, scene from* Snow White and the Seven Dwarfs, 1938

(b)

59   EASTERN ART I

Abanindranath Tagore, 'Dacca Stripes'

60   EASTERN ART II

Jamini Roy, 'Southal Dancers'

[Modern Art, Delhi

61 EASTERN ART III

    (a) *Amrita Shergil, 'Brahmacharies', 1959. New Delhi, National Gallery of Modern Art*

    (b) *Zainul Abedin, 'Sharing the Meal', 1943. Dacca*

[Photo Kafil Uddin Ahmed

62 EASTERN ART IV

George Keyt (Ceylon), 'Nayika'

(b)

(a)

(a) *Shunko Mochizuki, 'A Lotus', 1957*
(b) *Tano Rigen, 'Old Style Exhibition', 1955*

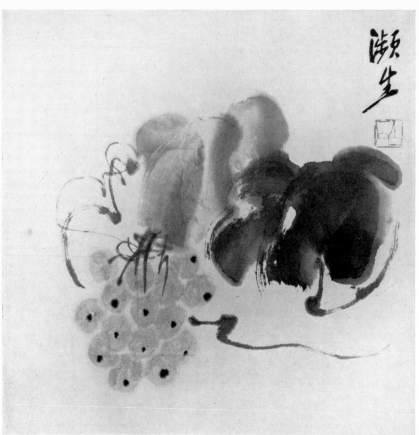

(a)

64 EASTERN ART VI

(a) *Chi' Pai-shih, 'Composition',
London, F. Skinner Collection*

(b) *Siu Pei-hong, 'Water Buffalo
and Snake'. Paris, Musée
Cernuschi*

(b)

PART FOUR

EXPRESSION

INTRODUCTION

THE literary and other arts which gave expression to the developments of the twentieth century reflected the struggles of men all over the world to make order out of the new experiences and conceptions brought by the scientific theories and technological applications, and by the social changes, political upheavals and catastrophes that determined the direction of their lives and moulded their hopes and fears.

In western industrial society the process involved an examination and re-evaluation of society, consideration of the nature of man and his place in the universe and psychological exploration of man's hidden motivation. During the first half of the century all the movements in the arts could in one sense be interpreted as carrying to their logical end forms started in the late eighteenth or nineteenth century. They could be regarded too as negating or dissolving all style and common modes of expression in favour of a multitude of individual, almost private, idioms. Yet in a more profound sense they expressed fundamental re-evaluations of the meaning of life in the face of accelerated, drastic, world-wide social change, and they produced recognizably different, even revolutionary, artistic and literary forms.

When neither scientists nor statesmen, nor yet religious leaders, were clear about the potentialities of order in the universes opened by science, artists alone could not make a complete poetical statement for the new world comparable to the *Divine Comedy* or the cathedral of Chartres for the mediaeval order. But though the outlook and styles of western writers, painters, sculptors, architects and composers remained up to the middle of the century still experimental and often chaotic, they were as different after Marcel Proust and James Joyce, Picasso, Le Corbusier, Debussy and Schönberg as was the outlook of science after the work of Planck, Einstein, Heisenberg, Mendel and Freud.

The centres from which changes in literary and artistic expression radiated were in Europe, but after the first world war the offshoots of European civilization, especially the United States and Latin America, were developing their distinctive forms of expression which interacted with the European but asserted an identity of their own. After the October revolution, revolutionary experience and intent gave new direction to the literature and arts of the USSR and to the interaction of western and non-western cultures within the Soviet Union.

In other parts of the world artistic expression involved a variety of reactions to the aggressively expanding culture of the West, the revitalization of traditional cultural forms and, drawing on both sources, the quest for modes of expression appropriate to the new national experiences which these countries were undergoing.

Most conspicuously in the West, but to a large and increasing extent in non-western culture areas as well, the technology of mass communication, together with mass education, altered the milieu, changed the audience and blurred the distinction between the popular and fine arts. The secular orientation of much of twentieth-century life, the spread of leisure and the development of the entertainment industries shifted artistic expression away from the religious area where much of it had originated into the realm of entertainment or information. Yet the search for poetic truth beyond any single religion, and the function of the arts in revealing human possibilities, opening visions of order, and redeeming pain and failure, remained no less necessary than in the past.

The new tendencies affected the place of the artist in society and broadened the social strata from which artists were drawn. The artist's place, in turn, affected the tendencies taking shape. He might be aloof from the main currents of his society, as were many in the West; he might be drawn into direct contribution to social change as in the revolutionary societies of Russia and China and the active nationalist movements in colonial areas; he might be the guardian of a traditional art such as the No plays of Japan; he might be one of many individuals scattered through many different cultures who combined a functional participation in modern life with the attempt to find and express its meaning. Increasingly he depended upon one or another form of public support for the arts.

By mid-century artists all over the world had begun more self-consciously to recognize that whatever their own culture they had common aspirations and problems. Intensification of nationalism influenced many of them in their experiments with materials and form, yet both in the West and in the East they refreshed themselves by drawing on forms from many parts of the world. More and more, in spite of national feeling, barriers of language and other idioms, and of conflicting political ideologies which extended to different conceptions of the function of the arts in society, they and their audiences became aware of each other on a world-wide scale. Films had a world-wide audience, and were shown at international festivals; the International Society of Contemporary Music presented works of new composers in different countries; international writers' congresses were held frequently. American and Siamese dance troupes appeared simultaneously in Rangoon, while Balinese, Kabuki and Indian dancers were popular on Broadway and elsewhere, and the Chinese Theatre and Russian Ballet played to full houses in London and other capitals, both West and East. An occasional writer, such as the Indian poet Rabindranath Tagore, was able to achieve a unique synthesis which made him an integral part of other cultural traditions as well as his own. With the aid of modern photography André Malraux drew on the ancient and modern arts of many cultures and parts of the world to convey in *Les Voix du silence* (1951) his conception that 'all art is man transcending his destiny'.

Yet expression remained infinitely varied in terms of the multitude of languages and of visual and musical idioms which embodied the world's manifold cultures, and of the individuality of the creative artist. The tendencies during these years cannot begin to be encompassed within the limits of the pages which follow. The works of numbers of writers and artists of first quality have necessarily been passed over, most especially those written in the less widely used languages; only a few have been mentioned to exemplify the trends discussed or because their influence was widespread and profound.[1,2]

CHAPTER XXXI

TENDENCIES IN LITERATURE AND THE ARTS IN THE WESTERN CULTURE AREAS[3]*

I. AT THE OPENING OF THE TWENTIETH CENTURY

By the opening of the twentieth century the social changes brought by industrialism and the intellectual changes engendered by the spread of science and technology were already finding expression in the arts.

The classical Graeco-Roman and the Judaeo-Christian traditions, which had provided the principal formulations for western artists and writers in the pre-scientific, pre-industrial age, had ceased to be satisfactory vehicles for thought and expression.[4] Nineteenth-century theories of the origin of the species made man a part of nature instead of a special creation and turned attention to his actions as expressions of biological drives while questioning the concepts of conscience and sin which were the basis of traditional morality.

Extremes of wealth and poverty, the dehumanizing tendencies of aristocratic landowning, the helplessness of individuals in war, the revelation that serfs were men, the conflict of rationalism, the Church and Christian brotherhood had produced crises of conscience and social changes which were embodied in Tolstoy's *War and Peace* (1864–69) and Dostoevsky's *Brothers Karamazov* (1879); Tolstoy himself had turned his back on his previous way of life and his *Resurrection* (1899) augured a new order and kind of man.

In Britain a line of realistic novelists and critics like Thomas Hardy (1840–1928), William Morris (1834–96) and John Ruskin (1819–1900) had detailed the disintegration of rural society, the ugliness of industrial cities, the loss of craftsmanship and the experience of factory hands as men. The genteel tradition of bourgeois respectability had been relentlessly unmasked by the realism of French novelists after Gustave Flaubert's (1821–80) *Madame Bovary* (1857). It had been shaken to its foundations by the Norwegian dramatist Henrik Ibsen (1828–1906), whose dramas of social criticism and protest revealed the harshness of middle-class domesticity. The life of the slums had been grimly delineated by Émile Zola (1840–1902) in *Les Rougon-Macquart* (twenty volumes, 1871–93) and by the Russian Maxim Gorky's (1868–1936) glimpses into the *Lower Depths* (1902). The coming revolt of workers and their assertion of their right to life was the heart of Zola's *Germinal* (1885) and Gerhardt Hauptmann's (1862–1946) *The Weavers* (1892).

The Dutch painter Vincent Van Gogh (1853–90) had expressed the explosive energy in simple workers and in nature even in its apparently most

* Dr. Helen D. Lockwood collaborated in the preparation of this chapter.

ordered aspects. Paul Gauguin (1848-1903) had offered the French world of art an escape to the freshness of primitive life. The Danish critic and essayist Georg Brandes (1842-1927) had brought Nietzsche to world attention and introduced Scandinavian and Russian authors in western Europe.[5]

In poetry, eloquent descriptions of feeling were replaced by concentrated forms designed to evoke directly the feeling of a unique experience by the use of symbols and new metaphors. The influence of Stéphane Mallarmé (1842-98) and Jean Arthur Rimbaud (1854-91) spread. Mallarmé had sought to purify language of dead metaphors and discursive meanings, and to attain pure music of words. Rimbaud had sought to find forms so free and packed with associations that the full chaos of inner conflicts could be expressed.

In the visual arts, Auguste Rodin (1840-1917) had by 1900 turned sculpture from the static, draped figures of conventional decoration approved by academicians to dynamic characterizations. His combination of strength and mind, of faith in humanity and closeness to nature made him influential. His brilliant reinterpretation of motion and of surfaces related to the inner centre opened the way for the movements of the next decades, even though these movements—neo-classicism (Aristide Maillol, 1861-1944; Charles Despiau, 1874-1946), then Cubism and organic abstraction—broke away from his ruggedness and love of nature. (Pl. 33a, 33b.)

New forms in painting had begun to replace the naturalistic representation and the visual illusion of perspective characteristic of western art from the time of the Renaissance. A succession of French painters from Édouard Manet (1832-83) to Claude Monet (1840-1926), Georges Seurat (1859-91), Paul Cézanne (1839-1906) and others after them approached the problem of form by studying the relationships of impressions made on them by objects; others probed their own inner feelings directly, as did Edvard Munch (1863-1944) in Norway and Ernst Ludwig Kirchner (1880-1938), Vasily Kandinsky (1866-1944) and others in Germany. Whichever the approach, they were all trying to present not the outer appearance but their view of essential reality. Their interpretation thus became itself the object. They moved away from literal imitation to abstracting particular factors—light, lines, colour, planes, symbols of feeling. Thus during the last decades of the nineteenth century the ground was laid in philosophy and practice for the development of abstract art and new interpretations of the human image.[6, 7]

In music Richard Wagner (1813-83) and Johannes Brahms (1833-97) had loyal followings. The nineteenth century symphony was modified and new forms began to emerge. Brahms upheld the classical tradition but enriched the form with a sensuous lyricism partly drawn from delight in German folk-songs and gypsy songs and partly affected by the atmosphere of Vienna where he was living. The influence of Wagner's operas spread over the whole of the musical world—his conception of the unity of the arts, his large orchestra, his complex texture of *leitmotivs* making a continuity of psychological association, his bold freedom in harmony. Indeed it even affected the later orchestration of Nicolai Rimsky-Korsakov (1844–1908), a leader in the rising Russian national school. Opera itself was further varied under the stimulus of nationalism to include national history, legend, folk-song and -dance and to express these with orchestral originality and directness (Modest Mussorgsky: 1839–81: *Boris Godunov*, 1874; a succession of operas by Rimsky-Korsakov). Italian opera modified its traditional form to express first romantically and then more realistically the loves and hates of ordinary people (Pietro Mascagni, 1863–1945: *Cavalleria Rusticana*, 1890 and Giacomo Puccini, 1858–1924: *Madame Butterfly*, 1904); in Giuseppe Verdi (1813–1901) it reached high dramatic skill and clarity of orchestra in interpreting Shakespearian subjects (*Otello*, 1887; *Falstaff*, 1893).

The symphony had developed in magnitude, expressing boundless personal sorrow (Peter Tchaikovsky, 1840–93: *Sixth Symphony*, 1893) or ecstasy of mysticism (Alexander Scriabin, 1871–1915: *Third Symphony—The Divine Poem; Fourth Symphony—Poem of Ecstasy*). Scriabin's radical use of harmonies gave fresh effects to an essentially classical structure. Gustav Mahler (1860–1911) expanded it to include double choirs of instruments and of voices and new percussion instruments in a gigantic effort to convey religious significance (*Eighth Symphony*, 1907). Symphonic poems and rhapsodies of Franz Liszt (1811–86), romantic tone poems and operas of Richard Strauss (1864–1949) using even larger orchestras than Wagner, eastern tales of Rimsky-Korsakov, Finnish legends by Jean Sibelius (1865–1957), lyrical suites by Edvard Grieg (1843–1907) introduced new subjects, precipitated debates about the validity of programme music and fostered national self-expression; they continued a movement toward freeing music from tonal harmonies and introduced changes in structure.

The basis for new architectural styles had been laid with the use of some of the materials that industry had made available. The Crystal Palace which housed an international exhibit in London in 1851 had introduced the possibilities of iron and glass and the first 'skyscrapers' had thrust their heads above city roofs in the 1880s and 1890s. By 1900 Louis H. Sullivan (1856–1924) and Frank Lloyd Wright (1869–1959) in the United States had begun to design office buildings and houses that would change the face of the rising industrial cities.

As literature and the arts broke out of their traditional moulds, they took two main directions which presaged the courses which would be followed in the succeeding years. Many writers adopted a rational approach. George Bernard Shaw (1856–1950) accepted the technological, money-based milieu as the given raw material that had to be civilized and he brought to bear the study of history, economics and biology in developing his conception of social change and human evolution. Anatole France's (1844–1924) interest in philosophy led him to religious scepticism and belief in human progress without intervention of any mythical personal deity. Painters such as Seurat and

Cézanne made experiments applying the physics of light and principles of geometry.

In contrast to these rational efforts to find and express natural truth, varied tendencies gathered up into a trend toward romanticism. In the decades before 1900, under the influence of the English arts and crafts movement started in 1870 by William Morris, a style known as *Jugendstil* (in France *Art Nouveau*, in Britain *Modern*) expressed a conscious revolt against historical styles and the ugliness of industrial technology and rationality. It took many forms in striving for a contemporary vocabulary and for originality, especially in the graphic arts, architectural ornamentation and interior decoration; its decorative element was felt widely in paintings of such men as Van Gogh and Gauguin, Pierre Bonnard (1867–1947) and Jean Edouard Vuillard (1868–1940) and in some architecture.

Similar revolt in literature expressed itself by escape into a world of fantasy or colourful bygone ages and in the exaltation of writers as a separate *élite* having no connection with ordinary society (Maurice Maeterlinck, 1862–1949; Hugo von Hofmannsthal, 1870–1929; Stefan George, 1868–1932; Alain Fournier, 1886–1914; Ricarda Huch, 1864–1947). Other writers who also turned their backs on natural science and rationality but were more concerned with truth of actual life probed unexplored realities of emotion and actions of men in situations of crisis or madness or under the impact of primitive cultures. They sought modes of expressing directly the emotions of men cut off from their social roots and subject to chance and weakness (Joseph Conrad, 1857–1924), or seeking renewal of life by following instinct (D. H. Lawrence, 1885–1930), or oppressed by the sense of perversity, decadence or madness in Europe itself (André Gide, 1869–1951; Jacob Wassermann, 1873–1934; Gustav Meyrink, 1868–1932; Franz Kafka, 1881–1924).

All kinds of literary and artistic expression—books, pictures, serious music —continued to find their audiences among the cultivated bourgeois class of patrons who could afford the arts. It was they and the *nouveau riche* who bought pictures to hang in their homes and supported museums. They bought and read the books and magazines. They made up the audiences and provided the support for concerts, opera, ballet and theatre.[8, 9]

Artists and writers themselves generally came from the same bourgeois class. As in all periods, they performed a number of different functions: as artists in the classical sense of 'fine arts' and 'literature'; as designers of physical objects from cathedrals or skyscrapers to clothing or toys; as entertainers at all levels from grand opera to circuses; and as reporters and interpreters of information, which might range from on-the-spot news to a popular presentation of a scientific theory.

Those who identified themselves with the tradition of the fine arts thought of themselves as dedicated professionals whose sense of calling and skill distinguished them from members of other professions and from amateurs in

RR*

the arts. They saw their role as that of seekers who must therefore be free to probe and express the reality behind the appearances in any way that they could. The artist as a free spirit was a kind of ultimate in a free society. Society could take the results of his quest, gaining enlightenment and providing him with a living; or it could disregard or reject them, leaving him to make his living by teaching his art, doing journeyman's work in it or engaging in some unrelated work, or else to remain poor and lonely.

Those who functioned as designers, entertainers or interpreters had to relate themselves directly to their society, for their expression found its outlets through the agencies engaged in production, entertainment or the spreading of information.[10]

II. THE YEARS OF INNOVATION

The early years of the twentieth century, especially the decade from about 1905 to the first world war, were distinguished by an outburst of experimentation in all the arts. In these years the trends present at the opening of the century were carried forward and virtually all the principles which resulted in distinctively twentieth-century forms of expression were explored.

Until the first world war shattered men's faith in unbroken movement toward peace and progress, the tempo and sense of change brought hope more often than confusion or despair to the artists and writers of Europe and America. The advancement of technology at first seemed to reinforce the faith in progress. It was now possible to conceive a standard of living for all people which should mean that they could have opportunity to use their human qualities and become fully developed free beings, who might even evolve biologically into higher forms of life, more adequate, especially, in the use of reason.

When writers and painters came to look closely at their society, to be sure, they found that great contrasts of wealth and poverty remained and that success itself tended to bring conformity, mechanization, preoccupation with property, deadening fatigue and compensating sensuality rather than freedom of the spirit. Production and machines appeared to be worshipped as new gods while owners, managers and bench workers alike were driven by the tempo required for the market rather than by direct human need. Artists began to feel that science and technology were not great liberating agents after all, and to revolt against the stifling of imagination for the sake of efficiency. Yet playwrights like George Bernard Shaw and novelists like H. G. Wells (1866–1946) believed that educated men would use their intelligence to remedy social ills, once these were exposed, and that creative evolution was part of the process of the universe. In this they expressed a widely held view.

But as changes accelerated and deepened, there was widespread consciousness of loss of standards and need of some vital reassertion of imaginative truth. From the seventeenth century, artists had been in a Europe changing through experimental science, and they had had to discover ways to express an enlarging and shifting variety of orders. There was no longer a leading style, such as Gothic or Baroque or heroic drama.

When in the twentieth century the discoveries of Planck and Einstein brought an even profounder revolution in science, people recognized that something momentous had happened that could shake the world, though they knew that they did not understand it. While physicists were coming to treat their generalizations not as true absolutely but as true within a certain frame of reference, artists were already seeking ways to convey the shiftings of relationships. 'Relativity' became a concept to apply to nearly everything. The apparent implications of the new theories and the confusion of standards pushed artists to ever more revolutionary expression. Time was a dimension to be included in many different ways and needed a relevant language. Motion and lines of force were more important than mass. Values were tested by experience, itself breaking the bounds of tradition.

In psychological relationships, writers and artists continued to follow the line of Jean Jacques Rousseau, William Wordsworth and Feodor Dostoevsky who, by direct, self-conscious observation and imagination, had revealed many aspects of man's nature, from delicate sensing to depths of hidden motivation. Their understanding that knowledge comes by way of sense experience and that environment influences people's behaviour was now beginning to be confirmed by experimental psychology with its demonstrations of conditioned reflexes. Their own psychological probings received further impetus from Freud's evidence that this conditioning goes on at very early stages of life, and that a basic creative drive, the libido, expresses itself in various symbolic ways in daily life and in dreams.

Yet in these times no Leonardo da Vinci or Goethe could comprehend the whole scientific and human revolution of his age, could both experiment scientifically and make great works of art. Artists and writers sensed the impact of scientific thinking, but few were themselves students of the sciences. There were important exceptions, such as the sculptor Naum Gabo (1890–   ) and the painters Vasily Kandinsky and Paul Klee (1879–1940). But the principal influence of the new science was through the climate of change rather than the direct application of scientific knowledge.

Artists of all sorts were caught up in the atmosphere of change. They tried one experiment after another, confident that they would find ways to penetrate to new realities and gain their own fresh vision of life, and they sought evidences of human dignity and man's identity in folk cultures, new strata of society and new psychological depths. Conscious as they were of different kinds of reality, they felt the need for new forms. Cubist painters analysed shapes that could be seen with the naked eye; constructivists looked for the scientific law behind specific observations and derived abstractions mathematically; expressionists abstracted feelings directly without reference to external images. But all selected some essential quality and contemplated it in its own separate context, which was no longer defined, as in the old perspective, by the visual illusion of distance but rather by the field of force and time.

Writers intent on probing immediately and swiftly to the essence of experience rejected the long-winded eloquence of romanticism and its vague feeling of the infinite; they rejected descriptive realism and naturalism. They were preoccupied with techniques for evoking sense impressions freshly, the blurring of senses into each other, and all sorts of fleeting feelings as interest shifted from the actual world to dreams and hallucinations. They used elliptical forms that could be intense and fresh. In the new forms of the novel they aimed to evoke experience rather than to describe or comment on it.

Gifted and energetic young poets, composers, painters and architects knew each other, formed societies, wrote manifestoes and produced their works in the midst of lively interchange of ideas. True, they scorned the *bourgeoisie* which had to be their audience and they did not discover an audience in the industrial masses. Many had difficulty in being heard and at times in subsisting. While some gloried in the possibilities of the age, many felt that the creative imagination was under attack; expressiveness for them became an end in itself. Already overtones of neurosis were present. Some of the most seminal originators saw worlds that had no hope in them. Marcel Proust (1871–1922), who started writing of personal identity eternally alive in memory, came to be more and more deeply disgusted by the decaying upper class among whom he lived, until in the end he saw that even love among them brought only destruction and finally their own oblivion in death and absence from anyone else's memory; the only value left was relentless uncovering of their vanity in a work of art.

The atmosphere for most of the younger men of these years, however, was one of possibility and they engaged with positive vigour in the battle for expression and acceptance. Even the powerful middle class itself was more ready to accept change and to listen to new voices than it had been, partly because it was caught up in the momentum of industrial progress and partly because the conscience of its more enlightened members forced them to see the misery and ignorance of masses of people.

The struggles of artists and writers to find new forms of expression and to reach new levels of reality were dominated by two opposing concepts of man's nature, the rational and the irrational, with correspondingly distinct approaches to life and art.

In these years, as in the previous decades and those to follow, one line of artists and writers grasped the tools which science put in their hands, adopted the scientist's objective viewpoint, applied rigorously a more relevant and psychologically deepened analysis, and sought to find and express new order and relationships beneath and beyond traditional institutions and forms. The systematic experiments of the cubist painters were of this order, as were the plays of social criticism, the theories of such composers as Arnold Schönberg

(1874–1951) and Paul Hindemith (1895–   ), and the work of sculptors and architects who called themselves 'constructivists'.

In the other line were writers and artists of many schools who denied the existence of the rational or saw it submerged by man's irrationality. They rejected the method of science as well as the kind of life which science and technology had produced. They saw man responding to inescapable irrational forces acting within the individual to produce his emotions, and to bring romantic or mystical unity with the universe or regression to a primitive state. They tried to convey such responses in language, colour, tone or shape.

The two viewpoints persisted side by side and interacting in the expression of the twentieth century, one view or the other becoming dominant in a particular place or time, in one or another of the arts, or in the work of a specific artist. The greatest artists, as in the past, combined both views, as did some groups, most notably in the Bauhaus of the 1920s where sculptors and painters of both schools joined architects to develop buildings and furniture, theatre design and display which should be modern in design and human in intent. But generally the two tendencies operated separately and in counterpoint with each other, the contrast between them sharpened and their interplay made more dramatic by the intellectual development of the time which carried both the rational and the irrational to new heights and depths—the magnificent achievements of the scientific mind and imagination and the appalling brutality of war and terror.

Artists and writers in this decade of experimentation used the tools which they were fashioning chiefly to unmask society, to tear away every sort of convention, and to probe for inner meaning and experience. Carrying forward the line of the nineteenth-century realists, writers and artists assaulted one after another of bourgeois society's best established institutions and most cherished values. They attempted to bring the detachment of the natural scientist to their scrutiny of society, as historians were examining the past by means of 'objective' history. Treating all old conceptions of value and ways of describing life as mere conventions, dead and irrelevant, they brought everything under microscopic search for some new interpretation which would coincide with reality and evoke it. They assumed that for man to attain his full development as a human being he must be able to express his full nature, including his biological drives, and they regarded any morality which was not based on these needs as contrary to their conception of human values.

As they looked at their society, they saw two worlds of the poor and the rich, those whose fate was unremitting, repetitive toil, misery and early death, and those who rose to success or enjoyed the fruits of industry and trade. And they saw that this industrial society not only presented grave problems of wealth and poverty but raised serious doubts as to the life values of the successful. So they examined critically the bourgeois family, relations between parents and children, monogamy, prostitution, the professions and the courts, religion, property, women, the masses. They detailed the texture of life in drab industrial towns (Arnold Bennett, 1867–1931); they exposed the possessiveness and sturdiness of men of property in the upper middle class and their complete failure to understand love or the creative imagination (John Galsworthy, 1867–1933: *Man of Property*, 1906; Thomas Mann, 1875–1955: *Buddenbrooks*, 1901); they looked for and found redeeming human values in those whom society scorned, the lowest drunkard, the pitiful failure; they found the nobility of work among peasants tilling the soil (Knut Hamsun, 1859–1952: *Growth of the Soil*, 1917) and factory workers, and also the potential tragedy and grandeur in the rising revolt of these workers (Maxim Gorky, *Mother*, 1907); and they showed up the superficiality of those engaged in social reform who did not recognize the relation between the basic structure of society and human need (G. B. Shaw, *Major Barbara*, 1905).

George Bernard Shaw expressed the point of view which underlay this scrutiny in commenting on the meaning of his play about prostitution, *Mrs Warren's Profession*:

'I must, however, warn my readers that my attacks are directed against themselves, not against my stage figures. They cannot too thoroughly understand that the guilt of defective social organization does not lie alone on the people who actually work the commercial makeshifts which the defects make inevitable ... but with the whole body of citizens whose public opinion, public action, and public contribution as ratepayers alone can replace Sartorius's slums with decent dwellings and Mrs Warren's profession with honorable industries guarded by a humane code and a "moral minimum wage".'*

Yet Shaw believed in life and the evolution of man; his sure comic sense, devastating as it was, did not undermine certainty and open the way to neurosis as did Thomas Mann's classic novel *Buddenbrooks*. For here the child of the decaying German bourgeois family is the one who himself becomes the critic and challenger of his own world, which he sees as crushing creative vitality and artistic sensitivity. With similar disillusionment, Thomas Mann's brother, Heinrich (1871–1950), grimly satirized the fatal German adoration of authority in military, civil and home life (*Professor Unrat*, 1905; *Der Untertan*, 1918).

The conventions which artists and writers attacked most aggressively were the taboos around the subject of sex. What had been the special province of the *risqué* French novel in the nineteenth century became a main focus of attention. Samuel Butler (1835–1902) had not dared to publish his autobiographical novel, *The Way of All Flesh*, when he wrote it from the 1870s on, and it appeared only in 1903 after his death. But in 1891 Frank Wedekind (1864–1918) had broken the silence about sex with his drama *Frühlingserwachen* and in the decade before the first world war the stories and plays of Arthur Schnitzler (1862–1931), who brought a Viennese doctor's detachment

* G. B. Shaw, Preface to *Plays Pleasant and Unpleasant* (London, 1898).

to the subject of sex, became famous all over Europe, and D. H. Lawrence's *Sons and Lovers* was an immediate literary success when it appeared in 1913.

In their exploration of sex a succession of novels, poems, plays and musical compositions analysed the relationship between father and son into its hidden hatred and unrelenting battle; they looked at the relations between husbands and wives, treated marriages as breakable when they had become conventional and hampered the free expression of creative impulse, and assumed that women as well as men were struggling to be free of frustration and were active in pursuit of their need; they viewed the 'eternal triangle' from every angle except that of traditional morality—lyrically, realistically, in terms of new frustrations when lovers found that the satisfaction of their physical attraction shut them off from other relationships. D. H. Lawrence sought always the positive expression of sex and its resulting freedom enhancing all life; he found it, not in people bound up by success, power and high position, but in workers such as miners or gamekeepers, and he searched for this freedom to the ends of the earth.

As they unmasked the face of their own world, a number of writers and artists thought that they saw in primitive society vitality and beauty which civilization had overlaid or destroyed. Stimulated by publications in the growing field of anthropology and aided by the ethnological museums founded in the last quarter of the nineteenth century where African masks and other examples of the art of primitive peoples could be studied, they looked for evidence of the deepest human values among people unrepressed by modern civilization. Sir James Frazer's study, *The Golden Bough* (1890) furnished materials to writers and artists and stimulated their imagination. French and German painters used African masks to convey what they saw in the human face; Igor Stravinsky (1882–   ) drew inspiration from the primitive, ancient Russian folk ways for his *Le Sacre du printemps* (1913); D. H. Lawrence, in *The Plumed Serpent* (1926), glorified the unity of man with nature through the symbols and rituals of the Indians of Mexico.

In their recourse to primitivism, artists and writers borrowed external forms and projected their own longings into their image of primitive life. Few if any in this period, or indeed in later years, recognized the rigorous discipline, rigid traditionalism and complex symbolism of primitive expression or learned to share the vision and emotions of its creators.

When they contemplated the place of man in the universe, they confronted the necessity of accepting emotionally what since the time of Copernicus men had known intellectually, that the pre-Copernican view of a man-centred universe was false and that the heavens did not revolve around man's planet, guided by a beneficent providence ready to intervene on man's behalf or to order the spheres in relation to his welfare.

Faced with the problem of man's place in an indifferent universe, some such as Thomas Hardy saw man as helpless, tossed about like a cork, buffeted by chance and blind fate, overpowered by nature and destroyed by his own passions. In such a world, tragedy reigned. Others, like Maxim Gorky or Martin Andersen Nexö (1869–1954) who followed Karl Marx, saw the destiny of man as inseparable from the society of which he was an organic part, and society itself as the product of inevitable forces operating dialectically to produce successive patterns of action, reaction and synthesis. Those who accepted the concept of the philosopher Henri Bergson that there was a vital force making the world evolve creatively, saw man as an individual part of this *élan vital*.

While most writers and artists found the Christian synthesis inadequate for the twentieth century, a minority of distinguished and eloquent Catholic writers, such as Paul Claudel (1868–1954) in France and others elsewhere, reasserted the continuing validity of the Catholic view. As others became disheartened in their search for a satisfactory new view of man's place in the universe, the sureness of these writers helped to keep their influence alive.

The great upthrust in experiment during these years went on in all the capitals of Europe, and along similar lines in all the arts.

In Paris, which came to be known as the 'city of light' because so many movements of the arts were centred there, an exhibition of new painters in 1905 marked the beginning of twentieth-century painting. These painters were known as *Les Fauves* ('the wild beasts') because of their startling and dramatic use of brilliant colours instead of perspective as forces determining the composition of their paintings. Their use of colour was an example of the principle which was to dominate all twentieth-century painting. Painters were not imitating nature, they were conveying their own awareness. The picture itself thus became the object. They distorted parts for emphasis; they filled the canvas with large blocks of colour to make designs rather than to convey distances and produced an emotional impact by the colour relationships within the design.

The most gifted of this group, Henri Matisse (1869–1954) Georges Braque (1882–   ), Georges Rouault (1871–1958), André Derain (1880–1953), Maurice de Vlaminck (1876–1959), went far beyond the first stages of violent colour. Each created a succession of experimental works in painting or sculpture, exploring the human figure, religious passion and nature. Matisse loved life and expressed it always in harmonious patterns which he worked to make more and more fundamental, as in the five forms of 'Head of Jeannette' (1910–12). In his *Notes to a Painter* (1908), which were read by many young painters, he said: 'What interests me most is the human figure. It is through it that I best succeed in expressing the nearly religious feeling that I have toward life.' He explained that he studied a face until he found 'lines which suggest the deep gravity which persists in every human being'. Rouault, profoundly religious, used the new techniques and principles to make compositions resembling mediaeval stained glass and to probe to depths of hypocrisy, suffering or spiritual insight. Braque became a leader in a new movement which grew out of the feeling of a need for more structure. (Pl. 34a–e.)

The need for structure was crystallized by the retrospective exhibit of Paul Cézanne (1839–1906) in 1906 which presented twenty years of his unknown work. At once he became a central influence, decisive in turning painters to consider planes, cylinders and spheres. A new group emerged who analysed the geometry of objects—a breakfast table including its newspaper, a nude descending the stairs, a machine. They abstracted the crossing and recrossing of planes and the projections of them into space beyond their immediate mass; they minimized the factor of colour and separated it from the structure. They came to be known as Cubists. Braque and Picasso were the leaders and by the 1920s every young artist had to understand their principles if he was to be of his time.

Pablo Picasso's (1881–) 'Les Demoiselles d'Avignon' (1907) embodied the new attitude. Here he abandoned the rounded and slender shapes and delicate bluish colours of the acrobats and clowns whose inner sadness he had painted compassionately, and instead he now painted angular, distorted women, their harsh faces turned two ways at once or shaped like the African masks which he had been studying. Braque began to paint many facets of an object seen at the same time. Juan Gris (1887–1929) developed a style which maintained geometric severity. Fernand Léger (1881–1955), who loved machines and the common vitality of the new age, enlarged and simplified human figures to the lines of force of machines and strongly outlined their bold colours; he thus at once simplified and revealed with arresting clarity such daily rituals as women at lunch ('Le grand déjeuner', 1921). (Pl. 21, 22.)

These painters were rejected by the salons at first, but they exhibited their paintings independently and gradually became a major influence upon the main currents of twentieth century art. They laid the foundation for the new architecture and industrial design.

Similar movements, each claiming its own special principles, flourished in other countries. In Italy a group led by the poet Filippo Tommaso Marinetti (1876–1944) and the sculptor-painter, U. Boccioni (1882–1916) called themselves 'Futurist' and sought an idiom appropriate to modern cities. They came out with manifestoes and works expressing the conception that the dynamic of motion was the essential reality of modern life. Their *Manifesto*, (February 20, 1909), said: 'Everything moves, everything runs, everything is being rapidly transformed.' Boccioni in his sculpture experimented with analysis of the relationship of time and space in his 'Development of Bottle in Space' (1912) and his bronze 'Unique Forms of Continuity in Space' (1913). (Pl. 35a.)

In Germany, as in France, the years 1905–6 were key years in which artists paralleled *Les Fauves* in their insistence that the picture is not a copy of things but an entity in its own right made out of the artist's reactions. Various groups formed in different parts of Germany were influenced, not only by French symbolist poets and post-impressionist painters, but by the expression of passion in the Norwegian painter Edvard Munch whose works were exhibited in 1907, and the stimulus toward intuitive probing of inner experience from such dramatists as Ibsen and August Strindberg (1849–1912), the philosopher Friedrich Nietzsche, and the Viennese school of psychoanalysts.

By 1912, the group known as *Der Blaue Reiter* had formulated and expressed with passionate intensity (*Spiritual Art*, 1912; *Der Blaue Reiter*, 1912) the principles known as German Expressionism, to be applied to painting, music and drama, and Vasily Kandinsky had applied them in the first abstract water-colour. Kandinsky, Franz Marc (1880–1916), August Macke (1887–1914), Alexey Jawlensky (1867–1941) and Paul Klee were the painters who formed the core of the group; Arnold Schönberg spoke for music. Marc was killed in the first world war but Kandinsky and Klee continued as leaders in the movement of abstract painting, Kandinsky relying on intuition and Klee combining with intuition more observation and rational analysis.

These artists had a religious feeling of unity with the universe and conceived of their paintings, in Marc's words as 'pictorial allegories expressing the underlying mystical design of the universe'. They believed that the inner world of feeling could be made immediately visible without resort to the images of the outer world, i.e. that the abstract power of pure colour paralleled the psychological effects of musical tones, and they thought of abstract paintings as symphonic movements. They found in the physicist's conception of fields of force the basis for their forms of kinetic motion and they thought that the new evidence from psychology and biology confirmed their belief that human perceptions are valid reflections of reality. Therefore they conceived of their pictures not as anarchical or disordered violations but as new expressions of the creation of the universe.

In Russia, too, from 1907 on, various groups of young artists were turning away from naturalism. They studied French art and also old Russian ecclesiastical art which interested them because of its tendency to abstraction, its use of line and the way its perspective suggested motion. Their major tendency was toward pure mathematical abstraction, 'the expression of non-objectivity' as the 'suprematist' Kasimir Malevich (1878–1935) described his 'Black Square' on a white background (1913). In 1913 the suprematist group, Malevich, Vladimir Tatlin (1885–   ), and the brothers Antoine Pevsner (1886–   ) and Naum Gabo, with a group of architects, engineers and painters in Moscow, introduced principles of 'constructivism'. Pevsner had worked alongside the cubists in Paris. His brother had gone all over Europe studying art forms, but also he had studied mathematics, physics and engineering at the University of Munich and had made three-dimensional models of mathematical formulae. The constructivists considered both cubists and futurists limited because not scientific enough. They believed that pure representation of beauty could not be found by means that were merely personal and subjective. They aimed for abstraction based on mathematics and an underlying scientific law, and for forms relevant to the expressive qualities of the machine, which they recognized as dominant in the new world. They made constructions in space; they used steel as their medium; the forms were dynamic and partly functional.[11, 12] (Pl. 24.)

Pioneer architects in many countries, such as Victor Horta (1861–1947) and Henry C. Van de Velde (1863–1957) in Belgium, H. P. Berlage (1865–1934) in Holland, Charles Rennie Mackintosh (1868–1928) in Scotland, Peter Behrens (1868–1940) in Germany and Frank Lloyd Wright in the United States, revolted against the false overlay of imitated Renaissance and Baroque decoration on steel structures and began to construct office buildings with smooth walls, and houses fitted to their sites and their human use. Peter Behrens in Berlin insisted that the shape of the building must match the new materials, demonstrating the principle in a turbine factory of steel and glass in 1908 for the Allgemeine Elektrizitäts Gesellschaft. He insisted, too, that the quality of industrial design must be as high as that of the best craftsmen of the past. The three most important European architects of the twentieth century, Walter Gropius (1883–   ), Ludwig Mies van der Rohe (1886–   ) and Le Corbusier (1887–   ), all began by working with Behrens. The Cubist painters' studies of planes, rectangles, cubes and flat colours contributed to development in architecture, especially through the part played by the Dutch cubist painter, Piet Mondrian (1872–1944), in forming and guiding the *de Stijl* group, and through Le Corbusier's association with Léger and his own experiments in painting along cubist lines.[13] (Pl. 25.)

Experiments with musical forms paralleled those in the visual arts. Though they started somewhat later, the new musical idioms of the early twentieth century had much in common with the impressionist painting and the symbolist poetry of the preceding generation. Claude Debussy (1862–1918) renewed music for France and thence for all Europe by bringing into it the techniques of impressionism. His opera *Pelléas et Mélisande* in 1902 marked the end of the dominance of Wagnerian opera, and his tone poem *La Mer* (1905) evoked changes of the sea, the ground-swell, the counterpoint of light and winds playing over the surface and the dark mysterious depths. He used a new scale and rhythms such as those of Javanese gamelans; his open ninths and unresolved chords gave an atmosphere of freedom and his successions of chords conveyed iridescence and shifting motion. He gave music an idiom for expressing directly subtle, evanescent sensations and veiled feeling hitherto inaccessible to it. Other composers learned from him—Maurice Ravel (1875–1937), whose strong sense of structure and astringent dissonance made him most influential among the young French composers, Stravinsky, Bela Bartok (1881–1945), Ralph Vaughan Williams (1872–1958), Gustav Holst (1874–1934) and Jean Sibelius.[14]

Igor Stravinsky showed the influence of Debussy's innovations in his early music; he added a vast orchestra and his own emancipated rhythms based on Russian tradition. He was brought to Paris by the Russian choreographer, Sergei Diaghilev (1872–1929) where he wrote *L'Oiseau de feu* in 1910 and

Petrushka in 1911. These ballets established a new form in which the music and the pantomime of the dance were an integral structure. The brilliant originality of the music combined with the luxurious virtuosity of Diaghilev as director made them a sensational success. *Le Sacre du printemps* shocked its audiences when first performed in 1913 by its daring, barbaric rhythms and the primitive fierceness of the story, but by the end of the first world war it seemed, especially to young people, the very expression of western Europe's regression to blood sacrifice in 1914–18.

In Hungary Bela Bartok was drawn to Debussy in 1907, for he thought his music resembled folk songs. This helped to free Bartok from some conventionality and he wrote an opera (*Duke Bluebeard's Castle*, 1911–18) which was considered an Hungarian *Pelléas et Mélisande*. But then he went on his own way, studying and using the folk songs of Hungary, Yugoslavia and the Middle East, living among the people in order to collect their songs. He transcribed these songs and evolved harmonies for them; he combined them and art music in his major choral work *Cantata Profana* (1930) and made his own melodies for them. He experimented with various ancient modes and with atonalism. By the time of the first world war the direction of his style was clear, though it was not until the 1930s that he emerged as the composer of quartets comparable to those of Beethoven.

Gustav Mahler, composing in Vienna in the line of Brahms and nineteenth-century romanticism, originated the symphonic poem. In *Das Lied von der Erde* (1908) orchestra and voice dramatically interplay with subtle psychological shadings in a series of six episodes based on ancient Chinese poetry and covering the whole destiny of man to the final profound resignation before death. More experimentally, Arnold Schönberg, who had understood and used Wagner profoundly and who had grown beyond him to the need for new principles of composition, composed *Pierrot Lunaire* (1913) using atonality and striking contrasts to express the tension and anxiety that became the characteristic mood of the century. He belonged to the German Expressionists and wrote in *Der Blaue Reiter* along with Kandinsky. He introduced a radically new system of composition with a highly complex, mathematical musical language based on twelve notes used in series. This system came to be influential with composers later in the century and was brilliantly used by his two pupils, Alban Berg (1885–1935), who made it psychologically descriptive, and Anton von Webern (1883–1945) who made it more spare and abstract.

Musical awakening extended to Finland, Czechoslovakia, England and other countries. Sibelius in a series of symphonies from 1900–24 brought Finnish music into the classical line and made significant modifications of symphonic form. In England for the first time in centuries original English music flourished again. It was based on old English themes, folk songs, use of ancient modes and closeness to the temper of the country. Vaughan Williams in *Fantasia on a Theme from Tallis* (1909) took England away from imitation of continental music by his use of modal development of a sixteenth-century English theme, by his original rhythms and by a serious, aspiring splendour and orchestral richness. He and Gustav Holst were leaders in bringing new idioms to many kinds of choral and orchestral compositions. Choral societies and music festivals encouraged young composers who experimented with orchestral instrumentation, cross-rhythms of old madrigals, dramatic choral music, symphonies and opera. Among these Benjamin Britten (1913-   ) was especially successful in bringing into use the traditional English gift of melody.

Writers, not less than painters and musicians, felt the need of new forms. In trying to find ways to strip away the layers of convention and traditional connotation and to express new depths of consciousness that had not previously been exposed, they needed tools to explore the irrational. Marcel Proust, writing his search for identity in memory, analysed parts of a pattern of feeling that would be set off again and again later by recurrence of its key theme. Poets tried free verse and sought newly living possibilities in language itself, either stripping away all ornament and finding the word which conveyed the exact image, or seeking fresh comparisons used as private symbols and aiming at musical effect rather than meaning. Like the painters, symbolist novelists and poets insisted that since there was no reality except that interpreted through their perceptions, the form of the novel or poem was the reality; they too were demonstrating 'art for art's sake', as in the work of Paul Valéry (1871–1945), Proust, William Butler Yeats (1865–1939) or Rainer Maria Rilke (1875–1926).

Artists in all fields, convinced of the unity of the arts, explored together their interrelationships. The musicians set the works of the symbolist poets to music while the painters illustrated the texts. Several of the cubist painters designed the décor for Diaghilev's ballets.

The audiences for the artists' work remained up to the first world war essentially what they had been in the late nineteenth century, and the artists' relation to them continued to be based upon the cash nexus between the detached artist and the middle-class concert and theatre goers, museum visitors and purchasers of easel paintings and books.

The big orchestras in the capitals of Europe, organized to give the public serious music of the great tradition, tended to provide programmes of music that was already known and accepted. Many who attended did so as a sort of ritual to which they exposed themselves while remaining undisturbed. It rested with the conductor, who had emerged as one of the most important figures in making music, and to some extent with the virtuoso, to determine what music would be played.

Some conductors were interested in the new music and either commissioned or found works which they played occasionally, well surrounded with safer pieces, but gradually accustoming the audiences to newer sounds. Choral societies in cities, choirs in churches and musical festivals used new music in similar small amounts, but did provide some outlet and stimulus. But the difficulty of developing their own audience and of earning a living beset all pioneering composers now that the patronage of church and court was gone. Bartok's music began to be played extensively only after his death, and Schönberg never achieved popularity, though his theories kept increasing in influence among younger composers.

Painters and sculptors were in an even more difficult situation, for the middle class which could afford original works wanted paintings for the walls of their houses that were easily recognizable, decorative and pleasant to live with. Neither the artists' view of life nor their experiments with form fulfilled these requirements. Although portrait-painting continued to flourish at the richer levels of society where having family portraits was a snobbish symbol or to honour public figures, the new photography made portraiture less essential to preserve likenesses. In buildings constructed according to either functional or organic principles, decorative features which had been furnished by wall painting and sculpture were provided by the ways in which the structural materials themselves were used. Churches were largely imitative of old styles, conforming to tradition and conventional taste.

So easel-painting and independent sculpture became something personal to the artist, in which he felt himself free to say whatever he could find out about reality. His audience was neither present nor of concern to him. Museums or private collections were the principal repositories of his work. Salons and art dealers acted as intermediaries between artist and owner. Some rising men of property adopted the aristocratic tradition of connoisseurship, partly as a hobby and partly as a sign of success. Some museums showed, and began to buy, new works by contemporary artists. Within this special world, art became a sort of cult for its own sake, the museum a place where works were enshrined, and the artist a dedicated seeker guided by his own inner light.

Writers for their part retained a more direct relationship with those who read and saw their works, the middle-class readers and theatre-goers who saw their own lives depicted and dissected. Audiences were at first shocked by George Bernard Shaw, not knowing whether to take him as a clown or a prophet, but gradually he became popular. The reading public initially repudiated and then came to accept each new level in the uncovering of sex drives. They protested against free verse as well as free love. But they were losing their sense of certainty in the rightness of their own place and the beneficence of their society, and were ready to respond with acceptance and even eagerness to the exposures and insights which writers had to offer.

An increasingly important link between the reading, listening and viewing public and those who produced works of art was furnished by the critics whose dicta filled the columns of many new journals devoted to the arts and appeared increasingly in journals of opinion and the daily press. The critics' judgments often meant for the artist the difference between acceptance with the promise of present or future income, and failure. The less cultivated and independent-minded public learned to take its cue from their views. But sometimes the artists found them ruthless and lacking in understanding; Schönberg at one time founded a society to play new music which should be closed to all journalists.

III. THE 1920S AND AFTER

The first world war brought to a tragic close the period of creative experimentation in the arts and the hope for social regeneration with which the century opened. It shook European society to its foundations and made a mockery of what remained of traditional values. It broke up the groups of artists, writers and musicians who had known each other and worked together. Although Paris remained a magnet which drew artists and writers to its Left Bank, the image of the 'city of light' gradually dimmed. From the time of the first world war on, European artists and writers felt themselves caught in a cultural crisis, heirs of a sick society, uncertain of man's nature but confronted with terrible evidences of its irrationality.

Outside of western Europe, most notably in North and South America, countries which had remained culturally dependent long after they had gained political independence emerged from cultural colonialism during these years. The shock of the war and the European crisis stimulated tendencies already present in the United States and the Latin American countries to explore and voice the richness of their land, their people and their historic traditions and the qualities of their emerging national cultures. The USSR, intent on building a new society established by revolution, enlisted its writers and artists as workers to help accomplish this task, and, on the basis of the Marxist-Leninist conception of society, evolved principles of socialist realism to guide their work. What had been a more or less common western cultural evolution up to the war thus tended to become a series of related but distinctive national developments, which by the 1950s had acquired recognizably different qualities.

1. WESTERN EUROPE

(a) The crisis of European culture

For western Europe the dominant note from the 1920s onward was one of deep uncertainty. Few artists and writers, except those who dedicated themselves to the new architecture or the spread of information or some of the forms of mass entertainment, found ways to relate themselves positively to the main currents of modern life. But in their expression of conflict, absurdity or chaos they often voiced the confusions and anxieties which beset many of their contemporaries. Their honesty took away sham glories and supports and readied the ground for new growth.

Against the background of violent and drastic change wrought by the war and the October revolution, the artists' pre-war attacks on convention which had seemed daring and radical appeared tame, and their new forms became accepted and even popular. They now had the war itself to interpret. Even from the beginning of the fighting, a novelist such as Romain Rolland (1866–1944) protested against it in a series of articles published in 1915 as *Au dessus de la mêlée*. In 1916 Henri Barbusse (1874–1935) dissected the process of war in *Le Feu* and shocked his readers by taking them to the very smell of its destruction. In the decade after the war, novels, plays and poems, based on the invincible dignity of the common soldier, exposed the violation of all human values by trench warfare and revolted against the traumatic division of will in supposedly civilized men engaged in war (Arnold Zweig, 1887–   : *The Case of Sergeant Grischa*, 1921). Titles such as *All Quiet on the Western Front* (Erich Maria Remarque, 1929), *What Price Glory?* (Maxwell Anderson and Laurence Stallings, 1924), *Journey's End* (Robert Cedric Sherriff, 1929) and *Farewell to Arms* (Ernest Hemingway, 1928) came into the common language of the people as ironical comments on the human cost of war.

In the decade following the war, many of the pre-war experiments were put to use in a wide range of expression—in architecture, in the founding of literary magazines and the flowering of criticism, in a flood of novels and dramas, and in the mature work of some of the outstanding composers and painters of the pre-war decade. Freedom to experiment was no longer an issue but a condition so complete as to leave the artist in a state of virtual anarchy in which the burden of freedom could be as unbearable as the restraints of convention.

In the 1930s and 1940s whatever sense of direction the post-war burst of expression contained was again shattered by the collapse of the capitalist economies, the rise of totalitarian states and the horrors and dislocations of the second world war. Writers and artists, cast on to the waste-heap of unemployment or fugitives from the Nazi terror or the dictatorships of Italy or Spain, found the society which they faced ever more confused and intolerable and their isolation from it more complete; more and more of the voices of western European artists and writers were the voices of exiles. After the second world war, the terrible menace of the nuclear age added further evidence of chaos, brutality and madness on an ever more gigantic scale.

(i) *The sickness of society.* As writers and artists looked at the world about them, they saw it as a basically sick society. Many accepted the dictum of Spengler that they were witnessing *The Decline of the West* (1918–22). They wrote war novels which took away all glory and reason from war and left it as only a futile assault on human dignity. They wrote intimate biographies of great men revealing their all-too-human qualities and their feet of clay (Emil Ludwig, 1881–1948; Lytton Strachey, 1880–1932). Rejecting the assumption, which such writers as George Bernard Shaw and H. G. Wells had expressed, that educated man would reform his society, they delineated man's forlorn state with deep pity, as did Käthe Kollwitz (1867–1945) (Pl. 28) or, like George Grosz (1893–   ) mercilessly depicted man's cruelty to man and hit out at society angrily, contemptuously, with a sense of indignity or despair.

They attacked the fragmentation and confusion of city life and showed mass production and the machine as taking away all craftsmanship, subjecting workers to an unnatural, deadening rhythm and turning men into 'robots' (Karel Čapek, 1890–1938: *RUR*, 1920); they aimed their shafts at sophisticated upper-class and complacent bourgeois society (e.g. Aldous Huxley, 1894–   : *Chrome Yellow*, 1921; Jacob Wassermann, *Der Fall Maurizius*, 1928; François Mauriac, 1885–   : *Thérèse Desqueyroux*, 1927); they viewed with irony and horror the prospects for a *Brave New World* (Aldous Huxley, 1932) opened up by science. They adopted T. S. Eliot's (1888–   ) term for the whole cultural scene, *The Waste Land* (1922). In the classic statement of the sickness of European society, Thomas Mann symbolically chose a tuberculosis sanitarium as the milieu in which to conduct his diagnosis, and to point to the unsympathetic, materialistic figure of the engineer as the emerging authoritarian of the future (*The Magic Mountain*, 1922).

Many of the artists and writers felt themselves threatened by the instruments of mass communication—radio, motion picture, telecommunication, recording, the popular press—which created vast new audiences, and broke the boundaries between the serious and the popular arts. They agreed with the Spanish cultural philosopher José Ortega y Gasset (1883–   ), who saw that they faced a *Revolt of the Masses* (1929) and thought that the mass audiences could only degrade taste and debase the arts from the standards called for by the *élite* audiences of the past. The human predicament was epitomized by the German playwright, Ernst Toller (1893–1939), in his play *Man and the Masses* (1929), where the thrust of the masses to power and the ruthlessness of revolution overrode the individual human values which the symbolic woman tried to defend, and where both masses and individual stood against the existing society.

(ii) *The inner search.* Faced thus with uncertainty, irrationality, an oppressive sense of the sickness of society and the threat that the rising masses would overwhelm their world, artists and writers sought anxiously, sometimes even desperately, to find meaning in life. The artist in the classical tradition had always expressed a search for an integrated view of man's identity, his place in the universe and the social values within which he worked out his destiny. Now his quest became nervously intense and it led him in many directions.

The spread of Freudian concepts, which became part of the intellectual climate in the 1920s, stimulated intensive search into man's inner nature. Although some, such as D. H. Lawrence, rejected Freud along with all attempts to substitute scientific inquiry for intuition, most writers and artists used his ideas as they understood them to reinforce their tendency to seek reality in psychological depths, and to concentrate their search on the ramifications of sex. Freud himself had sought to bring rational observation and analysis to bear on the irrational behaviour of men, and to find ways to re-direct irrational impulses. His concept of 'sex' as a central drive was much broader and more general than the narrow physical meaning of the term. But the public at large, and most of the artists and writers, took from Freud only his discovery of irrational behaviour, not his rational approach to it, and they looked for the basis of human action and of man's creativity in the drive for physical gratification of sexual impulses.

Writers and artists, from the 1920s onward, thus carried to further depths the psychological probing and exposure of sex which had been part of the search for reality in the preceding decades. Whereas the earlier works had stripped off the mask of gentility, had shown society hiding its lusts under the institution of prostitution, had attacked conventional marriage and had revealed the shams and inner tensions of the bourgeois family depicted as the enemy of love and art, these had generally been in the nature of social commentary, though they were often couched in psychological terms.

Under the influence of Freud, the psychological novel, play, painting or music now sought motivation in deep layers of experience, especially the frustration from repressions in earliest childhood or, for those who followed one of Freud's disciples, Jung, in inherent archetypes provided by a sort of racial memory. Family conflict, especially the relation of father and son, was viewed and explored over and over again in terms of the 'oedipus complex' by writers and artists who either retold the classic Greek story with modern overtones (e.g. Jean-Paul Sartre) or cast in modern guise the son's love for his mother and murderous feeling toward his father (e.g. Eugene O'Neill, 1888–1953). James Joyce (1882–1941) was but the most gifted and extreme of the many writers who delineated the physical relation between man and woman to the last detail and related this sex drive to his character's whole personality. Proust, Gide and others explored homosexuality until it became commonplace to treat this once-taboo subject. Emphasis on, or pre-occupation with, a deep sexual urge infused much of the painting of Picasso and many others whose work bore the marks of his influence. Alban Berg in his opera *Wozzek* (1923) gave his listeners a direct sense of mad jealousy when he used a structure resembling psychoanalysis to show a military doctor and an officer treating a simple man as sick and uncovering his uncertainties, frustrations and capacity for violence until he is goaded by jealousy to kill his wife and drown himself.

The Dadaists (1916) chose their very name to express their sense of the absurd meaninglessness of life. André Breton, (1896–   ) who led the surrealist movement which followed them, was introduced to Freud's work as a trained medical student, and saw the relevance of psychoanalysis to the chaotic expressions of the Dadaists and to a possible fruitful use of automatic association of images in liberating the human spirit.

(iii) *Search into the lives of other men.* The quest for meaning led some writers and artists to look at the lives of many different kinds of people in different places, strata of society, and circumstances: rural people on the farms of Norway, peasant villages of Poland, the olive fields of Spain, the hills of Sicily; in industrial towns and cities as workers, business or professional men; in areas of cultural conflict and under stress of social change; in primitive societies and others of which the West had been largely unaware. Many found frustration, dullness, futility and pettiness in the lives which they explored, but others saw essential dignity, vitality and compassion. Not many, however, examined the imagination, vision or personality of the most dynamic elements in modern society, the scientists, engineers, industrialists, labour leaders or modern statesmen.

A few novelists began to see with prophetic insight and sympathetic imagination the clash of cultures and the inevitable human tragedy that augured the breakdown of nineteenth-century empires, as in Joseph Conrad's *Heart of Darkness* (1909) where white men were pulled to destruction in central Africa, and in E. M. Forster's (1879–   ) *A Passage to India* (1924) and André Malraux's (1901–   ) *La Voie royale* (1930); Malraux went on to delineate the beginnings of the revolutionary struggle in China in *La Condition humaine* (1933). Joyce Cary (1888–1957) saw similar conflicts in Africa in *Mister Johnson* (1939).

When the economic depression of the 1930s revealed capitalism in an apparent state of collapse and when the rise of totalitarian states threatened all liberties, many writers and artists believed that they had no recourse but to choose between fascism and communism. Only a very few chose the former except as they were forced into acquiescence. A number chose communism, or at least sympathized with it. Some, such as Ignazio Silone (1900–   ) in Italy (*Fontamara*, 1930) and Anna Seghers (1900–   ) in Germany (*Der Aufstand der Fischer von Sankt Barbara*, 1928) became convinced communists. Not a few of the prominent authors and journalists in Germany took sides against fascism, either because they recognized and fought it as the enemy of humanism and culture, as did Carl von Assietzky and Kurt Tucholsky in their *Weltbühne*, or because Hitler's seizure of power struck them like lightning and drove them into emigration. Lion Feuchtwanger's (1884–1958) novels *Erfolg* (1930) and *Die Geschwister Oppenheim* (1933) were revealing attacks on the system. Stefan Zweig (1881–1942), a typical representative of the intellectual *élite* of pre-war Vienna, wrote a series of historical novels as reflections of contemporary developments (*Fouché*, 1931, *Castello gegen Calvin*, 1936). Anna Seghers, a refugee in Mexico during the second world war, published a harrowing tale of escape from a concentration camp (*Das siebte Kreuz*, 1947).[15]

Those who inclined to communism did so in part because it seemed the road to bring them closer to the masses who, they felt, must be more real than their own middle class which they despised; in addition it appeared to offer an alternative to bourgeois capitalism in which man might perhaps find a basis for more humane relations with his fellows. But a number of these writers and artists became disillusioned as they discovered the police methods of the Stalinist state and saw in the Soviet purges of the mid-thirties new means for breaking the human spirit by the state and subjecting the individual to authority (e.g. *The God that Failed,* by Arthur Koestler, Ignazio Silone, Richard Wright, André Gide, Louis Fischer, Stephen Spender, edited by Richard H. S. Crossman, 1950).[16]

(iv) *Search for roots.* Some hoped to find answers to their anxious search in a renewal of tradition. Once they had shaken off the shackles of the immediate past, they reached into their cultural background for roots. For some this meant a return to religion. The poets, T. S. Eliot and W. H. Auden (1907–   ), turned their backs on the 'waste land' and found meaning in the Anglo-Catholic church and the traditions associated with it. The Norwegian novelist, Sigrid Undset (1882–1949) became a convert to Roman Catholicism and wrote warmly of mediaeval life (*Kristin Lavransdatter,* 1920–22) and the French writer, Jacques Maritain (1882–   ), also a convert, was a leading exponent of the values of mediaeval Christian society.

For others the search for roots involved exploration of folk culture. The interest in folk song which had influenced composers from the early romantic period and was part of the growth of nationalist movements, now led to large-scale systematic collecting, the founding of folk song societies, and devoted search by such composers as Bela Bartok and R. Vaughan Williams. For many, especially in France, it meant renewal of identification with the classical tradition of Greece and Rome (e.g. Jean Giraudoux, 1882–1944: *Tiger at the Gates,* 1935; André Gide, *Theseus,* 1946). Stravinsky moved from the primitive theme and rhythms of *Le Sacre du printemps* to the classic myths of *Persephone* (1927) and *Orpheus* (1948). Schönberg found his roots in the old Jewish tradition and left as his last work the unfinished opera *Moses and Aaron* (d. 1951). Thomas Mann, likewise, after dissecting European society turned to the Jewish story of Joseph, conscious that his probing into the past was a search for man in the present, for 'the essence of life is presentness' (*Joseph and His Brothers,* 1934).

Those who rescrutinized the past in order to find some living form to which they could hold sometimes found only fragments, which they expressed nostalgically but could not put together into a meaningful whole, and which they used, in T. S. Eliot's phrase, to shore up their ruins. Sometimes they wholly reinterpreted myths in ways that both renewed the past and interpreted the present.

(v) *Existentialism.* The search for meaning which drew writers and artists in many directions led some who had faith in neither God nor reason to a final sense of nothingness or absurdity. In their view, the only possible attitude of mind must be to confront existence without self-deception.

This attitude of mind had been developing through a line of writers from Sören Kierkegaard and Feodor Dostoevsky (*Notes from Underground,* 1864) through Friedrich Nietzsche and Martin Heidegger. New literary formulations were sought by Franz Kafka and later by Jean-Paul Sartre and Albert Camus (1913–1960), two of the leading novelists and dramatists of the 1940s and 1950s, who became the main literary exponents of existentialism.*

Kafka expressed the ambiguity of existence in *Die Verwandlung* (*Metamorphosis*, 1916) and in the unfinished work, *Der Prozess* (*The Trial*) published after his death (1925). In *Metamorphosis* the schizophrenia of the man turned insect was written with complete lucidity to bring out the logic of each situation. In *The Trial* a little man was accused of something—he was not clear what—tried in what court he did not know, assumed he was condemned but was not clear for what, accepted it all as natural, went on eating, loving and reading his paper, was one day invited by two gentlemen into a wretched suburb where they put his head on a block and executed him.

Jean-Paul Sartre believed that man is what he wills, that he is responsible and that he must understand what his nature is that makes him capable of self-deception. He formulated systematically in *L'Être et le néant* (1943) the vague uncertainty which many others felt, and he expressed it in a series of novels beginning with *La Nausée* (1938). Unlike Kafka's people, his were always aware of the incomprehensibility and loneliness of their existence, and their search for fullness of life was expressed in various, often lurid, ways. But they were not freed of obligation, for they must engage themselves actively as the only liberation possible, without knowing the meaning of their acts in any universal context, but being wholly self-conscious in making their individual personalities.

The writings of Kafka led directly into Camus's interpretation of the human condition as absurd and the only possible attitude towards it that of the rebel who knows. Camus found the myth of Sisyphus relevant to today— the man who passionately loved life, condemned to eternally unfinished work but, each time that he began over again, suddenly experiencing a moment of consciousness in which he knew the whole of the human condition; this lucidity was his torture but it was also his crown of victory for he could scorn his fate and revolt (*L'Étranger*, 1942; *L'Homme révolté*, 1954). In his novels, dread, death, tyranny, conformity and capacity for renewal were gravely explored. *La Peste* (1947) dealt with the isolation of a community smitten with plague and men tested in face of mass death; integrity and decency between friends and devoted and conscientious work, however unavailing it might be, kept the dignity of the individuals authentic.

This general view of life came to be the dominant outlook among a large proportion of the writers and artists of western Europe in the mid-twentieth century. Although it did not define the terms of 'engagement' which would allow the reflective consciousness to be free, it was a view of life which could give courage and strength to those who had survived the horrors of war and concentration camps and must live with the knowledge that men had designed instruments of destruction which could extinguish life on earth. It contained

* For the philosophy of Existentialism see Chapter XX, pp. 665–6.

neither joy nor hope, nor yet the dramatic struggle of tragedy, the detachment of comedy, the irony or exaltation which had been the gift of great artists of other ages to their fellowmen. It was popular, especially in France and Germany, for the honesty with which it tried to face the whole of existence.

While the existentialists were concerned with the chaos of existence, other writers were oppressed by its excessive order. George Orwell (1903–50), in *1984* (1949) delineated an over-organized, inherently authoritarian world in which freedom of the human spirit could not exist. Some young men of the 1950s, inheriting both the existentialist recognition of incomprehensibility and Orwell's sense of the menace of ever increasing organization, refused to become involved, and they made a point of disengagement and of preoccupation with their private worlds and private lives.[17]

British writers and artists did not adopt the existentialist view as generally or completely as did their neighbours on the European continent. Although they had much in common with them, a persistent strain of compassion and sense of human dignity prevented most British writers and artists, for example E. M. Forster or Joyce Cary, from sharing fully the irrationality and nihilism which dominated so many of their fellows across the Channel. The feeling for the English countryside and a lively sense of the continuing past never wholly lost its capacity to renew the spirit. The composer Vaughan Williams could express the horror and nothingness of war, but he could still invoke the healing quality of the land. Some British painters and sculptors rivalled those of the Continent in the nightmares of violence which they called up (Francis Bacon, 1910–), and in their experiments with abstract form (Ben Nicholson, 1894–   ) but many persisted in seeing nature (Barbara Hepworth, 1903–) and in evoking its meaning even in their abstractions. Writers such as Virginia Woolf (1882–1941) tended to hold to some joy in their surroundings; though she saw life as a stream of sense impressions without purpose or direction, she nevertheless loved London's red buses and crowded streets and respected the people whose inner lives she relentlessly explored. And in 1956 the sculptor Jacob Epstein (1880–1959), a Jew, could create a suffering, transcendent 'Christ in Majesty' for the cathedral of Llandaff, Wales, as a testimony of his own sense of common humanity. Among those of the generation of the 1950s who tended to share the Continent's judgment that they lived in a sick society, there was more likely to be compassion, anger and even a call to reawakening rather than despair.

(b) Developments in artistic form

By the 1920s experiments in all the arts had freed artists and writers, as craftsmen, from old forms and had provided tools to express the complexity and immediacy of hitherto unclarified experience. In the decades which followed, the new tools were applied in many new works. Where the vision flagged and only experiment remained, the works came to be esoteric and barren. But where the artists had genius in using their skills to grapple with their need for some concept of the relationship of the individual and the universe and of the individual and society, they produced living works that added to the great tradition of the arts.[18]

For most there was no longer God or Platonic perfection or Kantian imperative; but artists faced and tried to interpret eternity and death, the uncertainties and ambiguity of changing processes of youth and age, love and hate, the relationship of the individual to the universal, the oscillations between the static and the creative, violence and order, light and dark, and men's consciousness of all these. Dread, anxiety and anguish accompanying the consciousness gave a characteristic tone to the expression, and abnormal manifestations were often anatomized as ways to understand the depths of what was usually called the normal. But the vitality of some artists in struggling for form enabled them to transcend chaos and gave them freedom from the authority of a deadening society. They interpreted their personal experience as a type of the universal. Making the work of art and watching the process were inseparable.

For those artists in all fields who felt themselves most out of tune with the world around them and isolated from their fellow men, the forms of their art became a compulsive expression of themselves. Among easel painters and sculptors especially, but also among writers and musicians, there were those for whom form became an end in itself and the world of 'art for art's sake' became the artist's private world, where others might perhaps penetrate but from which the artist made little effort to communicate. Some even made a cult of not being understood. Their audiences were small groups of connoisseurs who read the little magazines or frequented private galleries and workshops.

Meantime, the forms which had been radical a generation before became part of the common mode of expression. Commercial artists used abstraction, surrealist juxtaposition, simplification and stylization of sculpture and geometrical design in their advertising, store displays, furniture or textiles. Even some of the paintings which had been shocking when they were painted became familiar to the point of seeming commonplace. Writing with stream of consciousness technique came to be expected and music which did not use dissonance, new scales and irregular rhythms seemed dull. (Pl. 6.)

(i) *The novel.* In literature this was the end of a long line of exploration of sense experience, association, memory and imagination which had begun with Rousseau and which Wordsworth and Coleridge had turned into great poetry. The new features were the language, the symbols and the attitude.

With the increasing interest in psychology, in unwinding complexes to the last particular, and in varieties of tension in feeling, the novel became more and more the appropriate form. It was used both as direct expression of experience and as illustration of philosophy; it ranged from the discursive to the poetical; it became so varied as to be almost indefinable. It was supplemented by numbers of biographies and autobiographies which were written almost in novel form.

In Henry James's (1845–1916) works at the opening of the century, the interrelationships of inner feelings and the outer world in a stream of consciousness were still expressed by the all-observing author outside the novel or at times by a character who acted as observer. The sentences still kept to the traditional grammatical structure, but they had become involuted and elaborate.

Marcel Proust took the next steps in his *la recherche du temps perdu* (1914 *seq.*). Here the artist had become the work of art. The whole novel is a symbol. The characters have no existence in themselves but are the feelings which they set off in the observer, the 'I' who is the writer imprisoned in his sick-room watching himself in the act of creation. They stand for his desires as they reveal themselves in frustrated love and the social vanities of upper-class society, both among the *nouveaux riches* climbing and the aristocrats declining. They are developed in variations of great complexity, starting with the first volume in which all the main themes are announced as in an overture —the main characters, the places, the patterns of relationships which will recur with mounting complexity of meaning and shifting changes as the adolescent who first experiences them re-experiences them in other times and places. Here they are set against his childhood family background with its kindness and moral values, every one of which will be violated in the course of the development. In the beginning there are intricate sentences of interwoven strands of perception, event and feeling, making patterns that will be touched off as living memory again and again later. But gradually the motion becomes staccato, and the images become harsh and dissociated as the patterns are broken into ultimate disillusion.

Other novelists wrote staccato narrative, sought words for their sound as much as their sense, and conveyed action, motion and tension by breaking the structure of sentences in many different ways or trying to use different words. James Joyce made his own syntax in three novels and explored its possibilities to the limit. In his autobiographical novel, *Portrait of the Artist as a Young Man* (1916), the artist grows up from the beginning of consciousness, expressed in the language of a baby's perception, to his maturing logic of thought, expressed in the language of a Jesuit debate on aesthetics. In *Ulysses* (1922) he used a more complex structure to express the eternal search of man for home and self, and extravagant language to convey its irrationality. In *Finnegans Wake* (1939) he explored the language of sleep in the story of guilt, death and resurrection, and made up words out of syllables from many languages to express his concept that European man's deeply hidden consciousness was drawn from the archetypes of all Europe.

Virginia Woolf made the novel essentially poetry in *The Waves* (1931). She worked with sense impressions much as the painters did, and she used many of their techniques in making time and place and shifts of mood and psychological level.

Writers in the realists' line, interested in the structure of society, were by the 1920s using the techniques of fragmentation and sudden juxtapositions of unlinked detail in conveying the many kinds of experience present in a single outer situation. John Dos Passos (1896–) in *1919* (1932) gave the tone of confusion which is the intent of this novel by juxtaposing without explanation or transition the daily slang and other speech of ordinary people, the lofty eloquence of President Wilson, reportorial biographies of famous people, screaming newspaper headlines. André Malraux in *L'Espoir* (1937) used the interruptions of the radio to give what was happening all over Spain at a given moment of the revolution. In the 1940s Joyce Cary wrote two trilogies each delineating a single person in the round by viewing him in different situations through the eyes of three different characters.

In the later decades, shorter forms of narrative became more important. Ernest Hemingway's (1898–) concentration and action, and his swift, simple sentences were influential not only in his native United States but in Europe. Delight in concentration, together with the needs of magazines, made short stories increasingly popular both with writers and with readers. The form had been chiselled to masterpieces by de Maupassant and Chekhov in the nineteenth century. Now it took on all the varieties of language and mood that characterized novels. Only one rule continued to hold it together: it must make a single effect.

(ii) *Verse.* Verse in the twentieth century was not as important as in earlier centuries, for it was mainly lyrical, to be read privately, and indeed it came to be more and more special with meaning only for the few. Even verse drama approached popularity only a few times, as in the works of J. M. Synge (1871–1909), T. S. Eliot, Christopher Fry (1907–) and W. H. Auden. Younger poets paid tribute to Yeats by commenting that he kept the spirit of poetry alive and gave them courage to be poets by the magic of his music, his starkness in accepting the full range of passion and by his steadfastness in remaining a poet even into old age. Actually many experiments in imagery, cadence and rhythm did find new areas of awareness, and as poets struggled toward an imaginative expression of the shifting sense of reality they extended the bounds of poetry.

The intense poets of pure form carried the exploration of individual feeling, begun by the revolutionary romantics of the early nineteenth century, to a kind of ultimate, for they were not concerned with the interaction of their feeling and their fellowmen, but with the process of their own self-awareness. The subject matter of art was to be found in this process, and giving it shape by making works of art was itself the meaning of life. Such works were written by poets as different as the brilliantly intellectual Paul Valéry in France and the sensuous, passionate Rainer Maria Rilke in Austria. Valéry thought that consciousness was a flaw in the infinite. Thus the form even of pure poetry was a shadow on the vision of infinity and therefore to be rejected as imperfect; but after years of silence following his first poems, he did make exquisitely proportioned musical structures to express the subtle movements of his own disturbing awareness as he watched it in himself. Rilke, starting with a painter's observation of things, felt them always transformed into human meaning; he repudiated science and the mechanical age, rejected responsible social relationships lest his individual creativeness be killed, and dedicated himself to keeping it alive by probing changes in love, sickness and death until the fear and anxiety and pain became endurance of the self alive in infinity expressed in *Duineser Elegien* (1912–22) and *Die Sonette an Orpheus* (1923).

These poets and others freed verse from the traditional alexandrines, heroic blank verse and folk song. They renewed ancient Greek and Latin accents or verse forms of pre-Renaissance writers in their own language, for they were in revolt from the Renaissance. They tried *vers libre* with its varied length of line and freedom from rhyme to give, not the incantation of spells, but the shifting colours of mood and the swift, terse point of an image or movement. They left out links in order to maintain the concentration. Paul Claudel was almost alone in keeping the great dithyrambic effects in *L'Annonce faite à Marie* (1912) and *Christophe Colomb* (1933). When poets used traditional forms as Valéry did in *La Jeune Parque* (1917) or Rilke in *Die Sonette an Orpheus*, they filled them with such freshness of metaphor, starkness of statement or new pauses and rhythms that they made cadences sounding quite different from the past and indeed conveying the universal in twentieth-century terms.

Poets, except those who were defending the disappearing and still loved order by some traditionally descriptive verse (Robert Bridges, 1844–1930: *Testament of Beauty*, 1929) followed one of two lines, the imagist or the symbolist. The imagists laid down the principles that a poet could write about anything he chose, that the exact word for the image was to be used, and that the writing should be 'hard, clear, never blurred or indefinite' (*Imagist Manifesto*, 1913). They tended to limit themselves to separate impressions and, as they refused to evaluate these, in the end diminished into triviality. But their precision was used with skill by the other school of experimental verse, the symbolists. Their influence extended the poetical expression of the senses to include taste, touch and smell, and they were gifted in suggesting subtle transformations.

Since Mallarmé, the symbolists had tried to free language of discursive meaning and use it as pure music. They were preoccupied with the special moment of life, a moment unique to the individual and containing more than external images; they therefore sought fresh symbols to stand for it. Accepted symbols like the Cross were inadequate because they had become stereotypes expressing social conformity and were no longer historically relevant. But the poets of the 1920s and later needed symbols of this magnitude that would either order the chaos of hitherto unexplored reality or bring them closer to the source of life.

Indeed whether writers sought to convey experience directly as the imagists did, or metaphorically as the symbolists did, their problem of language was real. Yeats pointed out its implications when he said that every man has his own symbol. His most ambitious one was a 'Great Wheel' as explained in *A Vision* (1926), his better-known one 'Byzantium' in *Sailing to Byzantium* (1928). Rilke's symbols came from many sources—nature, the arts, Biblical tradition, classical myth, especially Orpheus. In *Die Sonette an Orpheus*, his resolution of fear and pain became finally a gracious music of acceptance and praise; like Orpheus he too was making temples out of the wilderness. He wrote a poetry of intensity and elegance new to Germany. He used a language of new shadings and overtones. French writers accepted him as bringing needed profundity to complement their essentially intellectual expression, and they regarded him as a truly European poet. He himself translated Valéry into German. He was read not only in Europe but in the United States and Russia.

Valéry, basically conceiving of the Creation as a flaw in the universe bringing change into the perfection of its unity, chose symbols of purity of vision: Apollo, the sun which in its brilliance could make men forget the flaw, the dazzling sea at noon, the diamond—a perfect focus of light, its facets reflecting the light back through the same lines as it entered. He symbolized the dark sources of creative energy by forest, trees, the Pytheness.

Such symbols were special to each writer and did not have meaning for the general run of people who still thought of the infinite in terms of the traditional sacred texts or did not think about it at all in their increasingly secularized lives. Indeed these poets of pure form could have meaning only for a literary audience specially ready to accept them on their own terms.

Other poets were searching for new symbols of social struggle or of national life. One of the first of these was Herman Gorter (1864–1927), a gifted Dutch poet who spoke for the heroic phase of European social democracy before the first world war in his *Pan* (1916), a poem in the form of an epic, attempting to reconcile the poetry of nature and Marxian political philosophy even as, centuries before, Lucretius had made poetry of Epicureanism. In Spain Federico García Lorca (1899–1936) used the traditional forms of Spanish folk song and Spanish classical drama to give modern expression to the humanity of the little people of the earth in the face of organized cruelty and to their bitter, tragic dignity in the face of the inevitable frustration of fate. W. H. Auden and Christopher Isherwood (1904–) in *The Dog Beneath the Skin* (1935) and *The Ascent of F6* (1936) dramatized the implications of Marxism and of Freudian psychology. Auden gave a name to his time in the poetry of *The Age of Anxiety* (1947). But Gorter wrote in Dutch, a language accessible only to the people of a small nation; a popular poet such as García Lorca had meaning only within his own Spanish tradition; and Auden became an exile who turned to Christianity and wrote poetry historically.

It was outside of western Europe itself that the poetry of the individual showed its continuing vitality. In America, Robert Frost (1874–   ) found his images and symbols in the daily life about him. From India came the voice of Rabindranath Tagore, whose poetry and plays were eagerly and widely read in Europe and America and who was recognized as bringing to the poetic expression of the West an added quality from his eastern background. And in the Soviet Union the lyric poet, Boris Pasternak (1890–1960), who dedicated his autobiography (*Safe Conduct*, 1931) to Rilke, asserted the essential inner creativeness of individual self-awareness and the necessity that this be kept alive whatever the social and political structure. His poetry was read and loved in Russia, although his lyrical novel *Dr Zhivago* (1957) was rejected as failing to show an understanding of the great social effort of his countrymen and the meaning of their sacrifices, and it found publication and a wide audience only abroad.[19]

But there was no language in the developing urban cultures of the West in which poets could speak to their people. Even if writers tried to bring their language close to the spoken language of the people, they were confronted with the fact that only a highly educated few spoke the traditional literary language and that forces making new language tended to flatten it out as much as to enliven it. In western Europe and America the Bible was the last great body of literature in which the literary and the popular language were combined. The complications and specializations of industrialized society brought out special vocabularies, from the '$E = mc^2$' of the mathematical physicist to the plumber's 'bushings'. Industries, professions, departments of learning all had their own vocabularies, so specialized that they were unintelligible to even highly educated people outside their specific boundaries. Also, these vocabularies were filled with dead or synthetic metaphors, like the sociologists' 'underpriviliged', or the psychologists' 'adjustment', so that if a poet or novelist tried to draw his language from them, it had no freshness of life and tended to call up only classification. The statistics of life expectancy had no resonance such as 'men are as the grass' of the Bible; but the range of experience included in them was no less needing poetical expression.

The language of ordinary use became equally lifeless. Many forces made a babel of the spoken language among the rootless urban populations. Moreover, the common language of general literacy tended to become synthetic, a mixture of that used by mass newspapers, magazines and radio and what people learned in schools attended by everybody, and everywhere debased by advertisers and propagandists who, in the process of identifying their objects with desires, deliberately emptied language of its meaning.

(iii) *Music.* The new tools available to European composers—ideas of harmonic structure, rhythm, melody and tonal colour—enabled them, also, to express new dimensions of feeling. By the time of Debussy's death in 1918 they were free to use melody or not; to break out of tonality and use dissonances juxtaposed for special emotional effects; to leave chords unresolved, and to use successions of them, not in a structure but to give independent harmonic sensations; to draw on oriental scales or ancient modes; to develop the intricacies of chromaticism in series. Debussy himself, having experimented with modulations and chords to give shifting sensory effects, returned in his last works to the traditional dramatic form of the sonata and gave it new force. The way was indeed open to renewal of more sustained structure, with flexibility of expression now taken for granted.

Composers continued to write symphonies, quartets, cantatas and operas. But the symphonies might unfold on a succession of themes rather than dramatize two and develop them symmetrically; they were made more flexible by compressing or rearranging the four movements, the use of dissonances, the use of modes and by experiments with orchestral effects and the addition of voices; they might reflect varieties of national origin as in the works of Jean Sibelius, Vaughan Williams, Sergei Prokoviev (1891–1953) and Dmitry Shostakovich (1906–   ). The quartets used extreme ranges of sound on the stringed instruments, as Bartok's *Third, Fourth* and *Sixth*. The opera limited the range of intonation in the singing and either extended the potentialities of music-drama to express horror, madness and direct characterization or restored the classical tradition of opera with arias, recitatives, choruses and ensembles. Gian Carlo Menotti (1911–   ) used such unfamiliar subjects as *The Medium* (1946) and *The Consul* (1950) and Benjamin Britten dramatized traditional English materials. Stravinsky, in *The Rake's Progress* (1952), gave the classical opera form a new texture by using ambiguous tonality, delicate shifts to fit the exact syllables of the verse and skilfully interwoven quotations from a whole range of traditional music.

Modern ballet, which Stravinsky and Diaghilev had popularized as a form in its own right—an integrated combination of classical ballet, folk dance, pantomime and music with rich orchestral effects—was further developed by some of the French composers in ironical and masterly expression of men as puppets in a meaningless post-war existence (Erik Satie, 1866–1925: *Parade*, 1917; Francis Poulenc, 1899–   : *Les Biches*, 1924). Stravinsky himself changed its character after the first world war by the introduction of a chorus to sing elements of folk song as part of the orchestra (*Les Noces*, first performed 1923), by re-asserting Italian melodic line and classical dancing drawn from French dances of the seventeenth century (*Apollo Musagetes*, 1927; *Orpheus*, 1948), by a mixture of ballet and scenic oratorio (*Persephone*, 1934). Finally, in 1957, he constructed *Agon* in a complicated, highly original, abstract pattern. It was a dance competition with no story and no setting, but pure music and pure dance complementing each other, and a large orchestra, not for crashing blows but for intricate variety, attained by using parts of it in succession so that the music was always light and clean-cut.

Composers were fascinated with problems of the relationship of words and music, and composed music to series of poems (Hindemith's *Marienleben* of Rilke; Webern's songs of Rilke; Stravinsky's *Symphony of Psalms* and *Mass;* Arthur Honegger's (1892–1955) and Carl Orff's (1895–   ) scenic oratorios). Many wrote religious choral works (e.g. Vaughan Williams, Stravinsky).

In the course of the century, music tended to become both more abstract and more emotionally intense. The disquiet of the century went far beyond the pale shimmering of light of Debussy's music or the dim vagueness of doom of his *Pelléas et Mélisande* to the terrifying ominousness of some marches in Bartok's quartets, their sardonic humour, ribaldry and, at the other pole, profound tenderness.

Bartok wrote in the main line of the experience of his people. In the mountains and plains of the Carpathian basin where he lived among them making his collections of their songs, he found them still living as they had for centuries, while war continued to go over them. When he used their folk songs or made his own in similar vein, his curious mixture of East and West came straight from their present and not merely from their history or his own. His originality of form and understanding had a depth of expressiveness transcending any national interest and fruitful for all western music. His works might suggest the transparent mystery on the very edge of the audible as in his 'night music', or the sturdy assertiveness of loud dances; but they were not pictorial music. New forms, such as his *Music for Strings, Percussion and Celesta*, contained the range of feeling within a short, strong architectural form, shaped by concentrated use of every note of the themes, by symmetrical repetition of themes with varied relationships and swift complexity, by the variety and emphasis of the percussion instead of orthodox instruments, and by using five parts in dramatic contrast to each other in rhythm and tempo and mood. Most of the younger composers adopted Schönberg's system of the twelve notes of the chromatic scale used in series, although not all agreed with him, even in theory. Paul Hindemith worked out an opposing theory in his *Unterweisung im Tonsatz* (1937); he suggested a logical revision in tuning the tempered scale and outlined a system of musical construction based on scientific acoustical principles. Among them all there was less tendency to gather monumental orchestras with double brass and more to thin out the sounds and to use new combinations of various instruments.

By the 1950s Anton Webern in Germany stood out as the most influential composer using Schönberg's abstract theories. He wrote short concentrated forms ordered in a rigorously perfected symmetry and used the chromatic series in various groupings, working them out in canon and mirror canon. He separated the notes of the melody and let one instrument after the other trace and retrace them through the orchestra. The individualizing of notes, combined with complex use of long, silent intervals and rapidly changing tempos made a spare, subtle effect. Webern heightened it by new combinations of traditional orchestral instruments or by introducing popular instruments such as guitar, mandolin, harmonium and bells. This music was the expression of a man of great culture and balance of mind, of searching imagination and sensitive ear, and such works as his *Variations for Piano*, *opus 27* and *String Quartet, opus 28* were especially influential. But in less able hands his methods could produce very dry results.

In France the influential composer with whom most of the younger men studied was Olivier Messiaen (1908–   ). His organ and piano music was not abstract, but often very lofty and mystical in character. He was influenced by Debussy, especially in the use of unresolved chords. He explored new effects of polyrhythms, notable for the use of pauses and subtle variations in the lengths of tones.

One of the recurring questions through the first half of the century was what was to be the relationship of jazz with the traditional art forms of music, however revolutionized, for jazz was the widespread popular form. It originated in the USA and after the first world war became popular in Europe. It was even taken up by some of the most advanced composers in Europe and used within their own idioms; Stravinsky quoted jazz along with Vivaldi and Bach in the same piece.

Its mood was always ambiguous—sad under apparent gaiety, sometimes maliciously satirical, sometimes full of longing, and always beating the deep rhythms that reach to the crude nerve centres, thus releasing immense vitality. Its effects were attained by flatting the thirds, fifths and sevenths in the melody and playing it against a straight tonal accompaniment, beating with syncopated rhythms against the continuum. It was especially exciting because of improvisation. Gifted solo instrumentalists in small bands could take one theme after another and improvise unexpected and varied patterns on it, letting their temperaments go freely with the feeling of the moment. They borrowed from old songs or from whatever classical or popular music they knew and treated them all with complete freedom. The principal instruments were trumpet, saxophone, clarinet, piano, xylophone, double bass and drums. The musical tones were closely related to the quality of voices, especially the resonant voices of Negroes among whom jazz started. Some of the mutes in the wind instruments were used to give the effect of the voice in different moods. Many of its outstanding later performers were urban Jewish musicians, and jazz thus came to be expressive of some of the special tensions of twentieth-century urban life.

In the early decades people danced to this music; but gradually it became music to listen to and even took shape in a few concert pieces. In the middle of the century the question was whether it would serve to give new life to the abstract experiments that, in the hands of highly skilled composers who were detached from the stream of popular life, were tending to become purely technical.

(iv) *Visual Arts: painting, sculpture, theatre, photography.*

Painting. The main direction of the visual arts was toward abstraction. Once the picture had become the object with its planes carefully marked out, its space filled with the projections of these planes, painters began to make many modifications of pure Cubism, and by the 1950s had developed new forms of abstraction involving the texture of paint and colour as such and the use of symbols.

The two great leaders of Cubism, Braque and Picasso, developed in separate ways. Braque painted many canvases, always refining his own unique style. He was occupied with subtle aspects of space that Cubists had started to explore; he used more and more complicated techniques of shadows, colour and even representational aspects of objects, of planes overlapping and interlocking to convey the volume of the space he lived in and the quality of life in it. This led to a famous series of large decorative paintings of his studio in which he ordered all the dimensions of a professional painter's life—his tools, his unfinished canvases, his collection of *objets d'art* from all ages of Europe used as models, an image of a bird escaping from one of the canvases and suggesting a free flight of the imagination. It was the artist's experience made universal. (Pl. 23.)

Picasso experimented with many styles. In 1921 he combined Cubism, heightened colour and classical proportion in 'Three Musicians'. In 'Guernica' (1937), a large mural in whites, greys and blacks, he created the drama of brute power symbolized by the man-bull trampling helpless masses of people and a horse; their anguish of unavailing flight he conveyed by extreme distortion of every part of the bodies. In his many paintings characterizing different women and his own children, he drew simplified, heavy outlines of great vigour, often making the features grotesque and giving a fierce, penetrating realism without being literal. (Pl. 27.)

Among the expressionists, Paul Klee sought symbols of the unity of man, the earth and the cosmos, in his words (*On Modern Art*, an address in 1924) 'the one essential image of creation itself rather than the image of nature as a finished product'. He disciplined his mind and his technique to a point where he reconciled the objective with the abstract, the generative process and forces of nature with contemplation of their changing relationships and with free association of dream, fantasy and idea welling up from his subconscious. He was always trying to penetrate to the place 'where primaeval power nurtures all evolution'. His technique was fine-spun and subtle. His shapes were sharply drawn but were wholly non-representational. His backgrounds of colour were shaded delicately to convey the atmosphere of the world in which the figures existed. The figures were composed in precise, humorous caricature ('Zwitscher-Maschine', 1922) or tragic simplification of fear or captivity ('Maske Furcht', 1932; 'Gefangen', 1940), or complex rhythms of colour and motion ('Revolution des Viaduktes', 1937). His vigour and keenness as an original seeker into the relationships between clear exposition, poetical feeling and objective experience made him one of the most sought-after artists in the early periods of experiment. By the 1950s his stature was more and more appreciated. (Pl. 26.)

The surrealists, revolting from science and institutions, talked about the explosion of beauty and painted the explosions of their subconscious as discoveries of this beauty. Two unique painters who belonged to no movements but who fascinated their contemporaries by the new dimensions of their work opened the way for the later explorations of worlds of fantasy and dreams by the surrealists. Marc Chagall (1889–   ), who went from his native Russia to western Europe, startled and delighted the experimental artists there by painting his feelings in free combinations of realism and dream imagery shifting in an imaginary world always wholly his own and always essentially that of a village boy loving home, always original in colour and endearingly lyrical. Giorgio de Chirico (1888–   ) fascinated the same generation by pressing beyond the confines of ordinary dream images to a metaphysical unknown. He used recognizable Italian scenes with well-known forms of classical architecture and traditional Renaissance perspective, but turned them into strangeness by a light unknown on land or sea, by unexpected proportions of buildings, and occasionally by anonymous figures wandering as if lost.

Surrealism itself started as a literary movement with André Breton, Louis Aragon (1897–   ) and Paul Éluard (1895–1952). André Breton and Philippe Soupault (1897–   ) established a review, *Littérature*, in which to practise a new instrument, automatic writing, and they gathered other writers and painters around them. In 1924 in *First Surrealist Manifesto*, Breton wrote his definition of surrealism:

Pure psychic automatism by which it is intended to express whether verbally or in writing, or in any other way, the real process of thought. Thought's dictation, free from any control by the reason, independent of any aesthetic or moral preoccupation . . . . Surrealism rests on a belief in the superior reality of certain forms of association hitherto neglected, in the omnipotence of dreams, in the disinterested play of thought. It tends to destroy all other psychic mechanisms and to substitute itself for them in the solution of the principal problems of life.

In this view, surrealism would liberate the individual spirit. Initially many of these men, surrounded with social chaos and violence, not only rejected bourgeois art but believed that there must first be a change in society and that the proletarian revolution was necessary. Although their revolutionary faith did not survive, their artistic attitude expressed itself for twenty-five years in the works of groups in France and other countries—the United States, Belgium, Czechoslovakia, Yugoslavia, Denmark, Japan, England. Many painters and sculptors were led to extremes in juxtaposing all sorts of objects or fragments in fantastic, incongruous, shocking or apparently meaningless relationships. They attached physical objects—bits of bone, newspaper, rope, cloth—to their canvas and substituted for formal sculpture conglomerations of materials—roots, twisted wire, cement blocks, feathers. They dredged up from the subconscious images of experience hidden deep in the nervous

SS*

system and exalted whatever behaviour would allow these images to swim to the surface—dreams, drink, drugs, madness, infantilism, identification with primitive people. The visions which resulted often conveyed the sense of a nightmare.

Painters like Max Ernst (1891–   ), André Masson (1896–   ) and Joan Miro (1893–   ), and sculptors such as Hans Arp (1888–   ) who exhibited with the surrealists, used their mastery of technique to reveal a reality with more meaning. Arp's polished marble expressed simple biological life. Exquisitely observed shapes of nature were designed into contrasts or angry battle by André Masson or by Max Ernst into fantastic mysteries of cosmic relationships or grotesque and sensual nightmares of human temptations. The witty Joan Miro carried out his own saying that 'one must go beyond form to poetry' in different moods, always with elegance, variety and proportion. 'Catalan Landscape: Hunter' (1923–4) expressed the hallucinations of hunger, the pink sky and yellow sea making an infinite space in bright light in which a little man with a gun larger than himself hunted a still larger rabbit stretched in flight; these were just suggested by finely drawn triangles, circles, open rectangles, solid cones and spheres, and their proportions of size and mass of colour brought the impact of their emotional implications.

After the second world war young painters, influenced by the surrealists and again compulsively seeking something new, became more and more interested in abstract patterns of colour for their own sake, sometimes relationships of coloured squares, sometimes calligraphy, sometimes undefined irregularities of shapes. They liked the grand scale and were preoccupied with the texture of paint itself. They were known as *tachistes* (Nicholas de Stael, 1914–55), 'activists' or as 'action painters'. A group of Americans of this school, most notably Jackson Pollock (1912–56), for the first time interested the Europeans in American painting in terms of pure art by reason of their vitality and brilliance of colour, boldness of technique and confident atmosphere of discovery. Other artists such as the English John Bratby (1928–   ), in some revolt against these abstractions, painted enormous canvases of ordinary commonplace life more or less symbolically. In London in 1957 a full-scale exhibit of works by the Australian Sidney Nolan (1917–   ) opened a real and mythical world of untamed, cruel desert and jungle and of heroes and criminals struggling with it. (Pl. 31.)

Sculpture. In sculpture, abstractions were organic and constructivist. Sculptors of organic forms selected the single essential of motion or growth, elaborated surrealist fantasy by dreamlike juxtapositions, and expressed qualities and relationships by simplified or distorted representation. Constantin Brancusi's (1876–1957) 'Bird in Space' (1919) in polished bronze stripped the form of all detail to give the essential lift of the bird into the air. Alberto Giacometti (1901–66) made tiny surrealist structures in which dreamlike figures moved strangely as if affecting each other by their presence but not communicating ('Palace at 4 a.m.', 1932–33). His tiny bronze men were elongated shadows standing alone ('Man Pointing', 1947) or isolated from each other ('City Square', 1948). Henry Moore (1898–) made monumental reclining figures based on observation of people sheltering in the Underground during the second world war and on primitive Mexican sculpture, using holes of space to dramatize the primitive power in the massive solid bronze parts. His 'Family' (1945) was a classical expression of a central conception of husband and wife holding the child high and cherishing it together, made dynamic not by distortion but by simplification expressing deep acceptance of nature. At the other pole Reg Butler's (1913–) project for a monument, 'The Unknown Political Prisoner' (1952) gave tragic symbolical power to the large mass of stone making the base, and the cage-like mechanism of stairs and ladders suggesting a relentless threat of execution and insurmountable walls within which little men, both prison guards and prisoner, are trapped and anonymous. Ossip Zadkine (1890–) combined elements of cubism, surrealism and primitive art to achieve an expressionistic style; his monument to a destroyed town found a suitable place in Rotterdam. (Pl. 36–38.)

The more geometrically minded constructivists moved from plans for monumental buildings in the early 1920s to smaller statements like Antoine Pevsner's 'Developable Column' (1942), a bronze column using mathematically developed curves. Naum Gabo made many pieces of transparent celluloid, often called 'Construction in Space' (1932; 1951). Alexander Calder (1898–) made mobiles—mathematically proportioned abstractions of shapes in nature, delicately hung together so as to move always in balance and throw shadows of the forms in regular ways. He thought of his form as reflecting the system of the universe, with many detached bodies of different qualities floating in space, in motion or at rest, some near, some immensely distant. In the 1950s other sculptors tried to express astronomical conceptions in such intricate works as Richard Lippold's (1915–) 'Variations on Full Moon' (1949–50), space caught within fine aluminium wires marking planes.

The younger sculptors were all working in metals, using the resources of these materials to express extravagant harshness and satire, or mathematical harmony and strength. Some were seeking a vocabulary through which to communicate the brotherhood of common destiny.[20, 21] (Pl. 35b, 39.)

Theatre. In Europe and the United States the theatre expanded or diminished with the vicissitudes of war and competition with the cinema, radio and television. At times, flourishing repertory theatres took drama to towns far away from the great capitals; at others, only a small percentage of the people had seen a live play. In Russia the revolution in the theatre preceded the October revolution and the theatre was ready as a powerful instrument for interpreting a new world to new audiences.

Serious drama of the liberation of the human spirit, expressing itself in appropriate scenic design and action, had to struggle with the commercial theatre's notions of amusement. Numerous new theatres were organized in revolt, such as the Moscow Art Theatre (1898), the stylized Kamerny Theatre of Tairov (1914), the Deutsches Theater in Berlin (1905), the Abbey Theatre in Dublin (1904), the Vieux Colombier in Paris (1913), the Court Theatre in London (1904), the Provincetown Theater (1916), and Washington Square Players (1911) in New York. Amateur groups in many places were resources for new actors and new beliefs in the theatre. Directors established schools of theatrical training, explaining that the best amusement is akin to the best instruction and that the noblest theatre both amuses and instructs (E. Gordon Craig, 1872– : *On the Art of the Theatre*, 1911; *The Mask* (magazine) 1908 ff.; School for the Art of the Theatre, established at Florence, 1913).

Under the influence of Vaslav Nijinski (1890–1950) and Diaghilev, the dance ceased to be limited to classical ballet; various schools of modern dance followed in Germany and the United States. Composers wrote for the stage— Stravinsky, Prokoviev, Darius Milhaud (1892–), George Gershwin (1898–1937), Virgil Thomson (1896–) Kurt Weill (1900–50) and others. New scenic art emerged. A succession of styles challenged the concept of the unities in drama and even the tragic catharsis.

Up to the first world war the theatre was essentially realistic, in the manner of Ibsen and the Russian drama, producing the plays of Chekhov and the early Shaw. In the 1920s various bold experiments in symbolism, expression-ism and constructivism accompanied the exploration of the psychology of the subconscious and of myths, as in the plays of Eugene O'Neill, and were used in pacifist propaganda by Ernst Toller and in the drama of the masses in the USSR. In the 1930s political and anti-war drama took many forms, especially introducing new ways of interpreting vast social movements and making new demands on the audience.

At the beginning of the century great plays determined theatrical pro-ductions. Ibsen's drama continued to be staged all over Europe. Anton Chekhov's slices of life, with their psychological insight into the sadness and the comic aspects of the decaying and frustrated middle class, determined Stanislavsky's special style in the Moscow Art Theatre. Effectively presented in the Court Theatre by Harley Granville-Barker (1877–1946), Shaw's plays made the modern stage in England with his drama of discussion in which ideas became dramatic forces, intelligence became a dimension of human character and wit unmasked the pretensions of conventional moral complacency.

Before the October Revolution, Constantin Stanislavsky (1863–1938) had brought the Moscow Art Theatre—founded by him and V. Nemirovich-Danchenko (1858–1943) in 1898—to such perfection of realism, in the line from Pushkin and Gogol, that all over Europe it was the symbol of excellence and his method was an influence everywhere; indeed it was significant even into the 1950s in Europe and America. He ranged over different epochs and styles—a play of Gogol, a Russian verse play, Alexey Tolstoy's *Tsar Feodor*, or *Tartuffe* and *Le Mariage de Figaro*. He insisted that the actors live the parts, not merely act them; they must dedicate themselves to the theatre and constantly work on self-development so as to know every human emotion and how to control it. They must be able to execute the physical action of the play perfectly. Stanislavsky invented endless individual and group exercises to bring out the actor's hidden resources and he rehearsed meticulously over and over again until the depths of meaning were exactly expressed in a fused and living work of art. After the Revolution he showed Soviet projects and victories. He gave special attention to the youth who must make the new culture and organized studios for their training. (Pl. 56a.)

In the 1920s the theatre became a director's theatre and remained so through the 1950s. It was true that expressionist plays, such as those of O'Neill and Pirandello, lent themselves to directors' experiments. O'Neill's people in *Great God Brown* (1920) put on and took off masks startlingly as different relationships emerged; in his *Strange Interlude* (1928) two structures were presented visually at the same time, the outside gestures and direct speaking between the characters, and the thoughts accompanying them. Luigi Pirandello (1867-1936) staged the tragic impossibility of anyone's getting outside himself and showing himself to another in his own reality in *Six Characters in Search of an Author* (1921). But the understanding between these dramatists and the directors was never adequate, and the plays were not dominant.

Gifted men, influenced by the new painting rather than by plays, experimented with new forms and audiences and technology, using any plays available—Gordon Craig, Max Reinhardt, Elwin Piscator, Gaston Baty, Louis Jouvet, Jean-Louis Barrault, the futurist and constructivist Vsevolod Meyerhold (1874-1943). Edward Gordon Craig, whose influence had already been effective throughout Europe, looked to the renewal of the theatre through a director who would understand the true nature of the theatre and maintain a high standard, not as literature or as imitation, but as vision—a fusion of action, spoken words, music and scene. The modern theatre restored to its origins in the dance, its scene controlled by changing light creating an ever shifting maze of colour, form and motion, should enchant its audience into a beautiful mental and physical ease. (Pl. 56b.)

His work directly affected Max Reinhardt's (1873-1943) Deutsches Theater in Berlin. Reinhardt created the new stage proposed by Gordon Craig and made it dynamic with his own observation of great national or religious processions and festivals, his own love of the colourful and fantastic, and his own driving power and imagination. His repertory ranged over the whole of the world's dramatic literature, both classical and contemporary. Before and after the first world war he made the expressionist theatre of Germany. Among others he staged plays by August Strindberg (1849-1912) with their sense of unknown and evil power working in the life of man and their search for salvation (*Nach Damascus*) and by Franz Wedekind asserting man's drive for sexual power as an active force in the world (*Erdgeist*). He used every new technical resource—the revolving stage, searchlights to bring out expressionistic shadings, all-embracing masses of actors or small groups bursting out from the audience, and he had a genius for bringing out actors' ability so that they transcended themselves. Exiled in 1933, he went to the United States where his spectacular technique was popularized in plays such as *The Miracle* which he had made famous in Europe and America and he remained an influence during the decade.

In the 1930s, with the depression and the ominous gathering of forces leading to the second world war, a new kind of theatre emerged in western Europe which moved still further away from traditional dramatic structure. Bertold Brecht's (1898–1956) 'Epic Drama' was designed not to enchant the audience or to produce catharsis but to encourage the modern scientific attitude to society, to make an unsophisticated audience aware of conditions causing tensions and ready to apply its understanding reasonably in improving society. He revolted from all the traditional dramatic unities and used episodes, parables, narrative, folk ballads, free movements in space, expression by speech, music, dance, pantomime, slogans motion-picture sequences to make a drama fusing realism and poetic imagination, balancing the effect so that the audience remained interested but not immersed. His genius as writer and his control made these *Lehrstücke* far more than pieces of propaganda for dialectical materialism. His stinging comment on *laissez-faire* in *Threepenny Opera* (1928) with a musical score by Kurt Weill, the outstanding musical comedy in central Europe when it was first produced, ran several years in New York in the 1950s. Exiled from Germany and writing from Finland, he bitterly showed the very victims of war trying to profit by it and sharing responsibility for it in *Mother Courage and Her Children* just before the second world war. He understood the revolutionary force of vital people beyond any specific social structure and at the same time their inescapable human weakness, their malice or even alienation, whether it was the peasant girl struggling to keep the governor's child she had saved and a fantastic judge deciding her case in *The Caucasian Chalk Circle* (1944–45) or the brilliant scientific discoverer in *Galileo* (1938–39).

Other original attempts to dramatize vast structures of power, social relationships or scientific discovery were made by the Federal Theater, 1935–39, in the United States under the direction of Hallie Flanagan Davis (1890–   ). It made a form, the Living Newspaper, in which dramatic lines leading up to a climax of human interest were combined with statistical narrative to show *Power* (the struggles which led to the Tennessee Valley Authority), *One Third of a Nation* (the need of housing), *Spirochete* (the discovery of the tubercular bacillus); $E=mc^2$. These plays went out across the country to people who had never seen live theatre before.

During the 1920s in the USSR the documentary theatre presenting social problems and building socialism produced a flood of plays. In 1927 in celebration of the tenth anniversary of the October revolution, the Moscow Art

Theatre produced *Armoured Train 14–69*, a dramatization of Vsevolod Ivanov's (1895–   ) novel of peasants who captured a train sent by the Whites to destroy them. One of the Moscow plays of the 1930s, *Oil*, set in a realistic scene of machinery for producing oil, showed the sacrifices necessary for this industrial expansion. At the end the players cried to the audience, 'Comrades, will you make this sacrifice,' and the audience roared back its willingness. Other plays celebrated the Revolution, such as *Chapayev* which later was made into a popular motion picture.

After the second world war the theatre retreated from documentation and the poetic drama emerged again briefly in England, France and the United States. In the main, the *élan* of experimental staging had settled into the gloss of theatre in the big capitals; no great dramatist was needing a stage. Little theatres reproduced earlier experiments, some romantic outbursts of angry young men and plays of the existentialists (Sartre, *Les Mouches*, 1943; Camus, *Caligula*, 1944). It was significant that Shaw's *Major Barbara* was filmed with Shaw co-operating with the director. The theatre was actually in competition with the motion picture and plays were often interchanged.

Photography. Photography developed rapidly as an art form which could express not only interpretations of mood and social realities similar to those of painters, sculptors and writers, but could penetrate other worlds. The swift accuracy of the camera could fix events that the human eye could not record— quick motion, momentary emotion, distant, inaccessible or tiny objects.

In the first enthusiasm for the new photography as art, not as the mere mechanical result of clicking a shutter, photographers thought of their compositions as paintings. The technology of the camera and of processing plates and film with the possibilities of using double exposures, retouching, distortions and other manipulations, led them to try angle shots, atmospheric effects, surrealist images, collages and photograms. They were able to suggest hidden mysteries and varied relationships—Alfred Stieglitz (1864–1946), *Venerable Trees*; Frederick Sommer (1906–   ), *Max Ernst*; Arnold Newman (1918–   ), *Igor Stravinsky*; Edward Steichen (1879–   ), *Rodin: Thinker*; Moholy-Nagy (1895–1946), photograms; Man Ray (1890–   ), *Raygrams*. (Pl. 49.)

Such varieties of composition were specially effective in posters for advertising, for they had the necessary instantaneous effect. Moholy-Nagy in the influential group of artists at the Bauhaus during the late 1920s and early 1930s and later as the head of the New Bauhaus in Chicago, taught the use of these devices and himself experimented. The photographic engraving process made production of prints of any size and quantity possible. Advertisers found these compositions especially effective in suggested relationship of desires and by the 1950s they were using a vast range of photographs, at first in black and white, and then in colour as fast as technical development of colour photography allowed.

But romanticism in using effects like painting gave way to use of the special resources of the camera in untouched, unmanipulated photographs. The pioneering Alfred Stieglitz himself and many other photographers aimed at precision of image and richness of texture brought out by light and by exact timing. The beauty and penetration of the picture depended on the special sensitiveness of the artist's perception and swift, sure technique in using the camera. The pictures might be dramatic or abstract; but they were neither decorations nor illustrations. They were records of the meaning of experience made by the artist as seeker. So Eugene Atget (1856–1927) recorded Paris and Walker Evans (1903–) and Margaret Bourke White (1905–) captured the face of the USA (*You Have Seen Their Faces*, 1937), Russia during war *Shooting the Russian War*, 1942), and the new India (*Halfway to Freedom: Report on the New India*, 1949). (Pl. 50.)

High-speed photography with exposures of a millionth of a second, developed in 1930 as a scientific tool for critical observation of rapidly moving (machine parts, permitted a series of exposures on one plate to trace the path of swift motion. This technique, used imaginatively, gave a quite new aesthetis experience of hitherto unseen shapes and patterns of motion, as in Gjon Mili'c (1904–) photographs of a factory worker's hands moving in assembling parts of bolts, his *Ballet Dancer* and his 3/4 *Beat* (Pl. 52). These and other techniques made it possible for the camera to reveal biological shapes hidden under the sea or processes like hatching an egg, or even to capture in a motion picture the working of the valves of the heart (Dr G. Keith Hargett and Edwin C. Udey, *Red River of Life.*) (Pl. 53.) By mid-century, wide-angled astronomical cameras not only gave astronomers an image of the universe far beyond anything previously possible, with which to seek answers to the question of whether the universe is expanding and what is its age, but enabled ordinary people to glimpse the scale and order of the universe and its continuing processes of creation, and to take aesthetic delight in the photographs.

Pictures used in conjunction with writing to increase the impact were the basis of photographic journalism which expanded rapidly after 1936. (Pl 54a.) The big publishers of the photographic journals sent photographers all over the world to cover wars, national crises, ordinary daily lives of remote peoples or of their own people; they published 'photographic essays' by juxtaposing single pictures in a series to make interpretative patterns. Governments made pictures to educate their people, or to interpret their country abroad (e.g. Farm Security Administration in USA and Empire Marketing Board in Great Britain), and many books were made by individual photographers or by editors selecting from far and wide—Walker Evans, *American Photographs*, 1938; Henri Cartier-Bresson (1908–   ), *D'une Chine a l'autre*, 1954; Donald C. Peattie and George Aymer, *This is Living: A View of Nature with Photographs*, 1938. (Pl. 51.)

The scale and development of the art and its possibilities in poetical communication were demonstrated in a photographic exhibit, 'The Family of

Man', 1955, made by Edward Steichen for the Museum of Modern Art in New York, later sent to many cities in many parts of the world, and also reproduced in both a cheap and an expensive book form. The exhibit contained 503 photographs made by 273 photographers in 68 countries, and selected from over 2,000,000 prints. It was conceived as a mirror of the essential oneness of mankind throughout the world as seen 'in the universal elements and emotions in the everydayness of life'; the photographs ranged from birth to death and included the daily relationships of ordinary men to themselves, their families, their communities and the world they live in. The American poet Carl Sandburg (1878–   ) wrote the prologue, and quotations from great poems, proverbs and sacred texts of many races and peoples defined the structure and pointed the meaning. Crowds of people attended the exhibit wherever it went. Here was a dynamic and popular art.

(v) *Architecture*. Architecture became in the 1920s the outstanding form of modern art and the one which most boldly carried forward the experiments which had gone on before the war, both the rational line of development and the exuberant organic school. The nature of architecture, to meet a practical need, required direct involvement in the society which it served and in the use of the new materials and processes which industry was developing. Under the leadership of a group in Holland known as *de Stijl* (1917–25), the Bauhaus in Germany (1919–33), and Le Corbusier's *Esprit nouveau* in France (1921 on), architects and painters evolved what came to be called the 'international style', although the leading architects themselves deprecated the label as suggesting fixed ideas.

Frank Lloyd Wright in the United States established the principles of organic architecture by a long series of buildings, plans for communities, and writings, and his influence spread in Europe and his own country. The Bauhof was started in Europe on the same principles.

Wright in his *Testament* (1959) defined the principles of organic architecture:

Amidst turbulent changes a way of building has brought to our society a new integrity. . . . These simple buildings themselves show architecture to be an *organism*, based upon 'part is to part as part is to whole'. Only such entity can live. Inevitably this nature-concept was individual in architecture as it was individual in the Declaration of Independence and characteristic of the nature of man himself. Wholeness of human expression in architecture is now assured. Never again could successful building be otherwise. 'Such as the life is, such is the form.'

Lao-tze expressed this truth, now achieved in architecture when he declared, the 'reality of the building does not consist in the roof and walls but in the space within to be lived in'. I have built it. When Unity Temple was built, this sense of interior space began to come through: 1906.

Whether the new architect belonged to the organic school or the European international, the essence of twentieth-century style was engineering honesty in the use of material—what looked like supports must actually be supports, not decoration—and 'functionalism' in design of the building. Architects worked in terms of the potentialities of mass production and of the new materials—steel, glass, concrete, aluminium, ceramics, plastics. They constructed houses which should not be boxes but homes or 'machines for living', and schools, office buildings, factories or banks which should provide ample light, efficient arrangement of space, and economy of construction and look like what they were instead of like pseudo-Greek temples, Gothic cathedrals or Baroque edifices.

The first group to be formed, de Stijl, led by the painter Mondrian and the architect Jacobus Oud (1890–   ), worked strictly with cubes, rectangles and flat planes, experimented with the effects of colour—varying the colour of the walls of a single room—and designed furniture to harmonize with their rectangular houses, using new materials such as steel.

In 1919 Walter Gropius established the Bauhaus in Weimar by reorganizing and combining an art academy (the Grand Ducal Saxon Academy for Pictorial Art) and a school for arts and crafts (the Grand Ducal Saxon Academy for Arts and Crafts). As he explained in his Theory and Organization of the Bauhaus, he sought to break down the hierarchy which had divided the fine from the applied arts:

The Bauhaus strives to co-ordinate all creative efforts, to achieve in a new architecture, the unification of all training in art and design. The ultimate, if distant, goal of the Bauhaus is the collective work of art—the Building—in which no barriers exist between the structural and the decorative arts.*

At first every student was taught by a theoretical artist and a craftsman until gradually people were trained who could combine the necessary factors. In spite of bureaucratic indifference and the hostility of an uncomprehending public, Gropius succeeded in bringing together as teachers some of the most outstanding painters, designers and architects of Europe. Students came from a number of countries, besides the main group from Germany. They not only studied theory of design but worked creatively in a range of workshops—carpentry, stained glass, pottery, furniture, metal, weaving, stage design, display and typography. When they moved the Bauhaus to Dessau in 1925, they illustrated both the new style and the principle of a creative group working together in the structure which they designed and the interior which they decorated and equipped. After the rise of Hitler caused the Bauhaus to close in 1933, its influence was dispersed throughout Europe and America as its students and teachers returned home and its directors, Gropius and his

* Museum of Modern Art, Bauhaus 1919–1928, ed. by H. Bayer and W. Gropius (New York, 1938), p. 22.

successor, Mies van der Rohe, went to the United States to head schools of architecture at Harvard and the University of Illinois and to become, with Frank Lloyd Wright, the architectural leaders in that country. (Pl. 43.)

The objectives of the Bauhaus were not only technical but social. Gropius insisted that if the development of industry had economic effects alone, the results would be dehumanizing; there must be some principle of human dignity, freedom, and satisfying relationships fostered by the environment in which people lived. Oud's row houses for workers in the Hook of Holland in 1924 were among the first to give effect to this principle through functional architecture.

Le Corbusier went even further, to think in terms of density of population, of articulating transport, work and living, and of planning whole cities that should be on a human scale and free of the confusion, crowding and gigantism all too prevalent as industry expanded and populations increased. He rejected the romanticism of modern suburbs, for they appeared to him only half city and half country and to solve none of the basic problems of living. Instead, he designed tall, slender flats, set in open spaces so that no family would be without light and air, oriented so that every family should have some sunlight during some part of the day, or be shaded from excessive sun in tropical or semi-tropical climates. He outlined possible plans for individual cities (Paris, 1925; Rio de Janeiro, 1929–30) and for types of cities which he called the Concentric City (1922), the Radiant City (1930), the Co-operative Village (1934), the Linear Town (1942). Areas were classified according to function; factories and homes were spaced so that workers could walk to work. Streets were planned in accordance with man's relationships to the automobile and shopping centres; recreation and education were provided for populations of specific sizes. Plans were open so that if the city expanded new integrated units could be worked out for different sizes of population. (Pl. 45a, 45b.)

Le Corbusier's influence spread widely, through the buildings which he constructed and plans which he laid out in many countries, through the spread of his idea for urban towers set in open spaces which was taken up by builders and housing agencies in such places as New York, Paris and Marseilles, through the leading role which he played in international congresses of architects and of city planners and through his students, many of whom occupied influential posts on planning commissions. His concept of the team of engineers and other technicians within which the architect must work was reflected in the organization of great building firms, which might number several hundred architects, engineers, city planners, designers, economists and other specialists. One such US firm in the 1950s was composed of 9 partners and 322 others, with offices in New York, Chicago and San Francisco.

During the second quarter of the century the new architecture was remaking the face of cities, and simplicity of style and forms adapted to the nature of the new materials became increasingly characteristic of furniture and household goods, the equipment for factories and offices, the layout of the printed page, and all manner of displays. Initially taken up by a few rich individuals who dared to build homes of 'advanced' design, the style came to be applied more and more to the functional purposes inherent in modern life for which the architects had conceived its value—streamlined factories to conserve workers' energy and speed; office buildings lifted from the ground on mushroom pillars, the walls serving only as screens and the interior space capable of being divided flexibly according to needs and easily changed; schools and flats with ribbons of windows rising vertically or cutting horizontally to give full sides of light; theatres with perfected acoustics and cantilevered balconies to be free from blinding posts; and parks designed as playgrounds for city children and adults. Because of its extensive use of glass and the tendency to make the inside of the building and its outer surroundings flow into each other, the style was especially well adapted to tropical and semi-tropical climates, and was adopted very widely in such places as Rio de Janeiro, Caracas, Cuba, Puerto Rico and southern California. (Pl. 55a, 55b.)

As the style matured in the hands of many architects, engineers and designers, it came to be used with increased flexibility. In its initial phase it had no place for decoration, depending for its beauty wholly on the proportions of the building and the panels of flat colour which might be part of the building design, and it clung rigidly to rectangular shapes. By the 1950s buildings began to make use of sculpture and painting as an integral part of the building's design and some curved lines were no longer taboo. Mies van der Rohe designed a fountain for a green space in front of one of his New York office buildings, and used paintings to decorate the executive suites on the top floors. Gropius in his building for the Harvard University Graduate School, used coloured tiles, abstract brick bas-relief, and a tall, tree-like construction. The United Nations Assembly building was decorated by Scandinavian, French and Spanish frescoes and tapestries. (Pl. 42, 46.)

During this process the organic school had considerable influence in emphasizing the human aspect of building and the relation of urban design to social forms; it did battle with gigantism or too narrow functionalism. Frank Lloyd Wright's influence rose and fell, but in the 1940s and 1950s it was high all over the world. His buildings were famous and each was unique—the Robie House (1909) in Chicago, horizontal like the prairies it belonged to, the earthquake-proof Imperial Hotel in Japan (1915–23), the models for Broadacre City designed in 1932, the most extended use of the cantilever principle in the tower of the Johnson Wax Co., in Racine, Wisconsin, the flowing space of the Guggenheim Museum (1959) in New York. He was critical of European architecture as still framing a box. Meanwhile the line of organic architecture was carried on in Europe by the Bauhof from 1920, and by 1951 there was a movement among Dutch and English architects to explore ways of drawing the two schools together, to spread the recognition of the function of form in society so that, without losing the gains of functionalism, more human elements could be included and the community could be beautiful. Neither school could be said to be dominant, and indigenous forms were emerging in different countries combining different elements. (Pl. 44.)

As architects sought to meet the new needs of the industrial age, they found their place in society changing and their scope determined by considerations quite outside of the world of art. They had to work not only in functional terms laid down by the prospective user and in a team with a variety of technical specialists, but within an economic and political framework. They were called on to design large units—whole city blocks, new towns, rebuilding war-shattered cities and obsolete sections of others, new capitals like Chandigarh in the Indian Punjab and Brasilia in Brazil, workers' suburbs, housing estates. They had to think in terms of large-scale construction methods involving prefabrication of standard parts and their assembly at the site. They worked within limits set by government plans for development, building and zoning regulations, real estate and financial practices, the organization of the construction industry and the readiness of those in power to carry out their plans.

At mid-century, although the influence of new architectural ideas appeared in many parts of the world, vast suburban developments around rapidly spreading cities were all too often laid out without reference to the architects' concepts of community design and were filled with trite, conventional dwellings built without regard for standards of excellence or honesty and imagination in the use of materials. Some of the finest buildings lost their effectiveness because of the construction of unrelated buildings around them and some of the most functional housing threatened to turn into new slums as a result of regulations as to who should live in it and the manner of its administration. Some buildings reflected preoccupation with materials for their own sake. (Pl. 47a, 47b, 48a, 48b, 20b.)

Yet architecture remained up to the middle of the century the most vigorous of the traditional arts, and the most fully a part of industrial society.[22]

2. EMERGING NATIONAL CULTURES IN OTHER WESTERN CULTURE AREAS

Outside western Europe three principal new lines of expression were developing within the western culture area in the decades after the first world war. The emerging national cultures of the USA, Latin America and the USSR grew from European roots and continued to be affected by European currents, but during these years they became more and more distinctive and self-conscious in spirit and form. By mid-century similar trends toward distinctive modes of expression were appearing in other young countries of European origin, Canada, Australia, New Zealand, South Africa.

In one form or another the developments in all these countries involved self-awareness as a nation and a people, discovery and assertion of the distinctive quality of national life and the social forms and personal experiences that were part of the shaping and maturing of new societies. These drives for cultural integrity and independence within the western culture area were no less a feature of the twentieth century than the drives for political independence from European domination by subject peoples.

Such movements did not, however, take place in isolation but in constant interaction with developments in Europe. During these years interaction was greatest in the case of the United States by reason of its stage of development, its world position, the constant flow of European immigrants and refugees to the United States and of American writers and artists to Europe, the wealth in the United States available for publication and the arts, the fact that American society was representative of the mass culture toward which European societies were tending and American writers were coming to grips with aspects which Europeans had not yet faced; American names inevitably appear among the representatives of major European trends discussed in the preceding pages.

With respect to Latin America, the distinctive forms of expression that were emerging had not yet entered the main stream of western literature and the arts, with a few noteworthy and distinguished exceptions—the poetry of the Nicaraguan Rubén Darío (1867–1916) and the Chilean Gabriela Mistral (1889–1957), the mural painting of the Mexicans José Clemente Orozco (1883–   ), David Alfaro Siqueiros (1898–   ), Diego Rivera (1886–1957), the music of the Brazilian Heitor Villa-Lobos (1887–1959). (Pl. 32.)

The USSR lived largely as a closed community during these formative years, using its arts to help develop its revolutionary society and to discover and release the creative potentialities of a broad range of its people; apart from the influence of pre-revolutionary figures such as Stanislavsky, Eisenstein, or Prokoviev, who continued to function within the Soviet Union, especially in drama, films, music and ballet, the literature and arts of the USSR were little known beyond its borders.

In all these areas, and in the other countries of European origin from which an occasional writer or painter was beginning to be heard or seen, writers and artists conceived of themselves not as set apart but as contributing to a stream which would in time flow back into the common pool to add to the richness and variety of the great literature and arts of the West.

(a) The United States

When the USA at the close of the first world war found itself thrust into a central position in the world, its arts and expression had only begun to reflect a native view and to use native idioms. Predominantly they remained identified with Europe, mainly nineteenth-century England in literature, the classic and Renaissance art of Italy and France, and German and Italian music. The word 'culture', in fact, meant the European fine arts. The novelist Henry James, who finally became a British subject, revealed this attitude as he analysed the subtleties of inner feeling of Americans searching for refinement in the art centres of Europe and confronting aristocracies in decay.

The close cultural ties with Europe were maintained mainly by the middle class of the eastern seaboard who were educated in the classical tradition and, like their counterparts in Europe, read the books and magazines, supported the orchestras, bought pictures and endowed museums. But beyond them, stretching across the continent, lay vast areas of newly settled land, big, growing industrial cities, large, newly literate immigrant populations, and Negroes only a generation away from slavery.

Before the USA became involved in the war, young critics, such as Van Wyck Brooks (1886–   ) in *America's Coming of Age* (1915) and Randolph Bourne (1886–1918) (*History of a Literary Radical*, edited by Van Wyck Brooks, 1920) called on American writers to grow up out of cultural colonialism, to develop the wide range of new expression needed to convey the variety of the North American continent and mixed cultures, and to speak to other audiences than those for whom Henry James had meaning. They saw in the vigorous native tradition represented by such nineteenth-century American writers as Walt Whitman (1819–92), Ralph Waldo Emerson (1803–82), Herman Melville (1819–91) and Mark Twain (1835–1910) an authentic statement of the dignity of each man and of self-reliance as a part of the vast harmony of nature, viewed lyrically, philosophically, in terms of tragic conflict with evil, or humorously. They saw the expanding country, the wilderness, the forging of new forms of government in the terms defined by Abraham Lincoln 'of the people, by the people and for the people', the problems of industry, the many kinds of people learning to live together.

Some writers and artists had in fact already begun to express the broad American scene. The audiences that read Henry James had been shocked by the ruthless realism of Theodore Dreiser (1871–1945), whose *Sister Carrie* (1900) was at first refused publication. He showed Carrie, full of imagination and vitality, refusing to accept respectable poverty and the factory job that represented 'opportunity' in Chicago, but finding only emptiness in her relations with the successful men who were ready to give up their hard-won respectability for her. The two poets who became authentic voices of the new America, Robert Frost and Carl Sandburg, had published their first volumes in 1915 and 1916; in the 1950s they were still writing out of the lives of the people they knew and were still read and loved. Frost's poetry from *North of Boston* (1915) to *The Masque of Reason* (1945) and *The Masque of Mercy* (1947) had the sharp-edged humour, hard-bitten realism, and terse, bare understatement of his neighbours who farmed stony, infertile land; he wrote of them with love and with sensitiveness to both the terror and exquisiteness of nature, catching the sound of their speech in the distinctive cadence of his pentameter. Sandburg's *Chicago Poems* (1916), *Cornhuskers* (1918), *Smoke and Steel* (1920), *Good Morning America* (1928) voiced the sorrow and joy, the vulgarity, vitality and dreams of the masses of the people, whether in a new sprawling metropolis in the heart of the continent or on the open prairie.

In painting, a group known as 'The Eight' had exhibited their works in

New York in 1908, interpreting the crude forces of cities, the human struggle in villages on the prairie, men wresting a livelihood from the sea, the western desert. Their styles were distinctive and non-derivative; some indeed were in outright revolt from the new Paris. John Sloan (1871–1951) and others like him insisted on baring the harshness of city life ('Roofs: Summer Night', 1906) and were scornfully labelled the 'ash-can school'. The most authentically American among them, John Marin (1873–1953), developed between 1912 and 1922 an original style to express his faith in the turbulent energy which was thrusting up skyscrapers and spanning rivers with suspension bridges and his feeling that these structures were alive. Like Frost and Sandburg he continued through the following decades to express the vitality of the United States.

Two gifted and influential young American writers, the poets Ezra Pound (1885–   ) and T. S. Eliot, however, had turned away from the American reality to the European tradition in which they had been trained. Believing that the only way to cope with the disillusioning present was to recapture the riches of the past, they explored neglected aspects of European literature and also the literatures of the East. Pound published translations of Chinese poetry. Eliot studied Sanskrit and wrote about Dante. He became the high priest of a cult of the seventeenth-century English metaphysical poets, especially John Donne; he rationalized, in terms of a theory of order transcending the natural world of science, nostalgia for a society based on an *élite*, not yet corrupted by egalitarianism or the Rights of Man and the emptiness of increasingly secularized life. The skill and brilliance of both Pound and Eliot in experimental verse-forms fascinated young American writers eager to be in the *avant garde* and turned many of the next generation away from their own people; at the same time they made them aware that the United States was not isolated but was part of a world.

The first world war and the disillusioning peace shocked the people of the United States into realization that they must see themselves more clearly and also that they were in a larger world where their own position of power needed new attitudes. The writers who searched America itself and those who explored the experiments in the arts in Europe, especially in the school of Paris, became parts of interacting movements in the next decades. Unprecedented numbers of fearless, well-made novels, plays, poems, stories, debates in criticism, autobiographies, biographies, books of reporting, magazines and films were published and read and seen. They made the decade of the 1920s and the years that followed a revelation of new self-consciousness, while the new mass audience provided broad support for a wide range of artistic expression.

Americans now expressed themselves as distinct from Europeans. They were more consciously aware of Europe and often more critically. They used the experiments in form and techniques as they liked, and they drew on the tools of both continents provided by the social sciences and by the translation of Freud. They shared the general European trends—toward abstraction, psychological probing, preoccupation with sex, social criticism—but in terms of their own experience.

Yet while American writers and artists struggled for an authentically American expression, they continued to feel the pull of Europe. After the war, T. S. Eliot and Ezra Pound went to live in Europe, and their verse became part of current European expression. Throughout the 1920s American writers and artists flocked to the Left Bank in Paris, trying to turn their backs on the commercialism of society, and lured by the irresponsibility of the 'art for art's sake' school. But in the 1930s the depression forced most of them home and awakened them also to the realization, in the words of the returned poet Archibald MacLeish (1892–   ), that 'here we must live or live only as shadows' (*American Letter*, 1930).

The self-consciousness that now found expression took many forms. A long list of regional novels detailed the varied lives of ordinary people in the middle west, the south, New England, the isolated mountain hollows of the Appalachian ridge, the south-western desert, the mill towns and the mining communities, and made these all part of a common heritage.

Many writers saw the harshness or emptiness of life, as their counterparts did in Europe: the dull materialism of the small prairie town of *Main Street* (Sinclair Lewis, 1920), the flatness of success in the business of real estate in *Babbitt* (Sinclair Lewis, 1922), *An American Tragedy* (Theodore Dreiser, 1925) in which society was accountable for a bell-hop's becoming a murderer, the urban dweller buffeted by *A World I Never Made* (James T. Farrell, 1904–   : 1936, the families of displaced, migrant farm labourers with no home but the roadside in John Steinbeck's (1902–   ) *Grapes of Wrath* (1939), the meagre or decadent personalities with which William Faulkner (1897–   ) peopled the imaginary county in the deep south where his novels were laid.

Behind this criticism was the assumption that America ought to be the country envisioned by Whitman and Lincoln, and faith that if Americans would just see, they would bring its true destiny into being. Babbitt believed that it would be better for his son, and in *Grapes of Wrath* the character of Ma had the earthy vitality to survive and make another home, and her son found hope in the organization of workers in trade unions. Except for Faulkner, these writers were angry that Americans were blindly betraying their own ideals; they did not fundamentally despair of the human condition or believe in the inevitable violence of revolution.

The search for national self-awareness found roots which would give an historical dimension to a fast-moving culture. The western pioneers in their covered wagons, who had stood as symbols of limitless opportunity in the dreams of the American people, became the subjects of a succession of novels which used psychological approaches to deepen the understanding of this part of the epic of America. Conrad Richter's (1890–   ) trilogy took one pioneer woman and her family through successive stages of settlement, *The Trees* (1940), *The Fields* (1946), *The Town* (1950); O. E. Rölvaag's (1876–

1931) story of Norwegian immigrants, *Giants in the Earth* (1929) called up the fears, heroic courage and knowledge of the earth with which men and women faced the limitless stretches of lonely prairie which they were trying to bring to fruitfulness and which could wipe out a man and his work with blizzard, drought, locusts or undefinable chance; Willa Cather (1876–1947) told how death came to the cultivated, sensitive Spanish archbishop at his lonely outpost among simple Mexican and Indian people on the edge of the desert (*Death Comes to the Archbishop*, 1927). The cost of taming the wilderness was reflected in the poetry of Edwin Arlington Robinson (1869–1935).

The Civil War of 1861–65 was exploited in every conceivable manner, most sensitively in Stephen Vincent Benét's (1898–1943) dramatic poem of the lives of people on all sides in the war (*John Brown's Body*, 1929), but also romantically, in careful historical studies, in biographies and in countless novels built around episodes or individuals. Intimate biographies of men who shaped the nation were written from hitherto unnoticed source materials and in a manner to evoke the period and the milieu in which they lived.

The masses of the people were accepted and celebrated in their own idiom, which was becoming a distinctly American speech (Carl Sandburg, *The People, Yes*, 1936). An ever wider range of voices was heard—immigrants speaking through their autobiographies (e.g. Ludwig Lewisohn, 1882–1955: *Upstream*, 1922) and through the picture of life given by their children (e.g. Jerre Mangione, 1919– : *Mount Allegro*, 1942), Negroes in their poetry (Sterling Brown, 1902–   Langston Hughes, 1902–   ), autobiographies, novels (Richard Wright, 1908–60: *Black Boy*, 1945, *Native Son*, 1940) and family history (Pauli Murray, 1910– : *Proud Shoes*, 1956). The range of kinds of people, their interrelations and their personalities widened as the process of cultural integration went on and those who wrote came from more varied backgrounds; all brought to their writing an awareness of other elements in the mobile, fluid American society quite outside the scope of American writers at the beginning of the century.

Painters, too, saw and commented upon the cities and the prairies, industry, the desert and the sea. They were not originators of new styles, though each painted with his own special language. Whatever their differences they all conveyed the clear atmosphere and sharp bright light of the American continent by their use of strong colour. Together they made Americans more at home with their country and the ways of the people—the harshness and loneliness of cities, but also the homeliness of the little houses lighted for workmen to come home to; the tough solemnity and endurance of man and wife who had brought civilization to the wilderness frontier, the harvests, the tree planting, the grand sweep of the land that were all part of converting the wild and dangerous prairie into a bread-basket of the world; they saw machines and industry wittily, lyrically and realistically; they satirized the pompous oratory of their senators. Among them all Ben Shahn (1898–) had an especially original way of simplifying themes, a brave imagination and love of people and cities that threw a clear, strong light on the play of boys in the slums bounded by walls, the fantastic nightmare of devastation of war and, in a mural done for a trade union hall, a better world possible through the organization of workers. (Pl. 30.)

American music showed less development and originality than the other arts, although a few composers drew from American sources and developed styles which lifted their compositions to the level of universal art. Aaron Copland (1900–   ), writing the music of the ballet *Appalachian Spring* (1944) for the American dancer, Martha Graham, used his own idiom in interpretation of regional rhythms. Roy Harris (1898–   ) used thematic material from folk songs of both cowboys and Negroes; his *Symphony for Voices* (1935) written to passages from Walt Whitman expressed Whitman's robust vigour with grandeur, austerity and simplicity. Several composers based operas upon the rhythms, tunes and language of the people, using evangelical hymns, political oratory and the cadence of daily speech and frequently employing American themes, such as the pioneer of women's suffrage in Virgil Thomson's *Mother of Us All* (1947).

The most distinctive American music came not from the composers of 'serious' music, but from the new popular musical idiom of jazz. From its origins in the Negro cafés of New Orleans, jazz spread in the 1920s until people throughout the country were dancing freely and excitedly to its nervous, syncopated rhythms and the wild improvisations of drums, trumpets, piano and saxophones. Famous band leaders became enormously popular, and led a series of changing jazz fashions which were followed by lesser bands. Mounting numbers of jazz enthusiasts became connoisseurs of the different jazz modes, developed a vocabulary of their own, and treated jazz as music to be listened to and not simply for dancing. By the 1950s serious jazz music festivals were being held, attended by appreciative audiences from all walks of life—one of the leading jazz music critics was a Catholic priest—and jazz compositions were being written, not merely improvised. The first serious composer to grasp the jazz idiom as the basis for a distinctive, American musical style was George Gershwin (1898–1937), whose *Rhapsody in Blue* (1923) and his folk opera of Negro life, *Porgy and Bess* (1935) established this new mode at the level of musical art.

In the effort to understand the quality of their emerging society and to define Americans to themselves, writers brought a range of approaches to the meaning of technology, abundance, mass literacy, the accompanying mass culture, the tensions of modern American life. Thorstein Veblen analysed respectable ways with brilliant irony in *The Theory of the Leisure Class* (1899, much read in the 1920s) and introduced the concept of 'conspicuous consumption' into current thought. Henry Adams (1838–1918), after analysing in his influential *Education* (privately printed 1906, published 1918) his immediate and unsatisfying heritage of eighteenth-century Enlightenment and Protestant Christian morality, turned to the cultural synthesis of the twelfth century; but he saw that there was no escaping to the past and that the Virgin of Chartres, the focus of that culture and symbol of compassion, only served to heighten the problem of modern man, who must find a basis for compassion and morality in an age of science, technology and accelerating social change. Walter Lippman's (1889–   ) classic examination of *Public Opinion* (1922) broke ground in exploring the relation of the mass culture and new media to the processes of democracy. The far-ranging news reporter, Lincoln Steffens (1866–1936), traced his efforts to understand crime and corruption in American cities and the men involved until he saw how they were bound up with efforts of people to meet their human needs (*Autobiography*, 1931).

Lewis Mumford (1895–   ) was one of the few writers in any country who analysed comprehensively the impact of science and technology on architecture, literature, painting and the culture of cities and tried to chart new directions (*Technics and Civilization*, 1934; *The Culture of Cities*, 1938). Vernon Louis Parrington (1871–1929) reviewed the quality and range of American expression in politics, press, popular novels and belles lettres, as related to the social and economic history of the continent (*Main Currents of American Thought*, 3 vols. 1927–30). Lillian Smith (1897–   ) brought a fearless understanding of Freudian principles to bear on the back-door sex relations between white men and Negroes, to uncover the nature and sources of racial prejudice and hate (*Killers of the Dream*, 1949).

During the depression of the 1930s the federal government, which had not been a patron of the fine arts as were the governments in European countries, gave great stimulus to the arts on a mass scale by including artists, writers, musicians and actors in its programme of work for the unemployed. Thousands of painters did wall paintings for public buildings or canvases which became available to schools or other public institutions; musicians formed municipal orchestras and played new compositions; experimental theatres tried out new forms; writers collected the life stories of all manner of people, and gathered a wealth of historical records and folklore. Although this aid to the arts was short-lived—a purely temporary depression measure—and was undiscriminating in extending support to unemployed artists without regard for the quality of their work, it uncovered a large reservoir of talent, made the arts a part of daily life outside the metropolitan centres to which they had tended to be confined, and left a residue of continuing interest and municipal or private support when federal funds were withdrawn.

About 1942 a group of young painters in New York turned against the realism and description of the land and people which the Federal Art Project during the years of the depression had encouraged. They adopted the principles of surrealism. They saw themselves as paralleling the discoveries of psychoanalysis. In emotion they felt that the basic fact of the United States to be interpreted was violence. They filled large canvases with great blocks of often subtle colour in dramatic contrasts, with shifting biological shapes and intricate confusions of lines. Although a number of such painters got into the museums in the United States during the 1940s and 1950s and began to be influential in Europe, this painting remained foreign to the general run of people. Alexander Calder's constructivist abstractions—his mobiles—however, were popular in the United States, and he was well known in Europe also.

It was of the essence of American expression during these years that it was the work of people from many lands and many backgrounds, immigrants and the children of immigrants who represented the interaction of two cultures, and older Americans, most of whom traced their cultural roots to Britain but some in the south-west to Spain, some in Louisiana to France, some in Pennsylvania to Germany, and some throughout the country to Africa. Outstanding writers, painters and musicians, who were completely identified as Americans, had been born in or were only a generation removed from Russia and Japan, Italy, Yugoslavia, Germany, China, France, Greece, Poland, Ireland, Czechoslovakia. In addition, the USA during these years was a principal haven for the many European artists and intellectuals who chose exile from the régimes which they could not accept at home. Although still identified culturally with their country of origin, writers such as Thomas Mann, architects such as Gropius and Mies van der Rohe, musicians such as Stravinsky and Hindemith and sculptors such as Naum Gabo and Pevsner lived, worked and taught in the United States.

From these varied and sometimes conflicting trends, in constant interaction with contemporary currents in Europe and among Europeans in exile, no single national style emerged. Europeans tended to identify American expression with violence and primitivism, and to enjoy it for this feature—not only the 'wild west' stereotype of the second-rate movies, but the sophisticated violence of Hemingway or Faulkner or the elemental passion of Steinbeck's barely civilized men. They recognized that the American language had taken on a character of its own, and French translations began to specify on their title page 'translated from the American' or 'translated from the English'. By the middle of the century the American vision and the American idiom had become distinct and had produced a body of works which were taking their place in the great tradition of the West.

(b) Latin America

The literary and artistic expression of Latin America was in some ways closer to Europe than was that of the United States and in other ways more distinct. The difference arose from the nature of the Latin American societies —quasi-feudal in structure, based upon *latifundia* worked by poor and illiterate rural masses and mines or other extractive industries largely exploited with foreign capital, the benefits accruing to the small upper class of landowners and the foreign entrepreneurs. In a number of countries—notably Mexico, Guatemala, Ecuador, Peru and Bolivia—large Indian communities, amounting to from 20 to 55 per cent of the total population, lived on the margin of westernized society, maintaining their language, social organization and cultural values. In Brazil the people of the hinterland were for a long time out of touch with the life on the coast.

Although the constitutions of Latin American countries since their independence in the first quarter of the nineteenth century had established the principle of democratic citizenship, the economics of the *latifundia* system, the cultural isolation of the Indians and the physical isolation imposed by the wilderness, perpetuated a very different reality. Neither rural masses, nor Indians, nor yet the men of the back-country, participated fully in the national life. During the twentieth century the struggles to achieve a fusion and integration of these fragmented societies provided the political and social milieu for the arts and letters of the period.

But while the societies of Latin America offered a less integrated national base from which to develop their forms of expression, they contained elements far more distinct and independent of European origin than any that were native to the United States. In the great pre-Columbian cultures of the Mayas, Incas or Aztecs and in the living continuity of the cultural traditions of the Indian populations lay rich resources quite outside the European line of influence. This substratum of Indian culture was evident in the archaeological remains, the large Indian populations, and the Indian blood in the *mestizos* who constituted a majority of the westernized populations in most countries. In Brazil the popular folk culture drawn from a combination of African, Indian and European origins developed during 300 years of isolation. As these indigenous influences came to the surface, they interacted with European elements to give Latin American expression in the twentieth century its unique quality.

The geography of the continent provided a second major factor shaping a mentality distinct from the European. Far more than in North America, where moderate rainfall, controllable vegetation and traversable terrain invited settlement and permitted the advancing frontier to remain in contact with centres of population, the violence and rigour of nature in many parts of the South American continent constantly challenged those who penetrated beyond the coastal strips.

Especially in Brazil, much of whose immense territory was made up of dense jungles traversed by huge, fierce rivers, man had to learn to live with untameable nature. In the words of the Brazilian writer, Euclides da Cunha (1866–1909), whose novel of the wild, rebellious life of the back country *Os sertoes* (*The Back Country*, 1904) became a classic, 'To conquer the land, we even had to produce a man capable of fighting it—bred in its image with its crudity and its energy in revolt.'* In isolated, self-contained pockets of settlement or wandering as herdsmen from one pasture area to another, the frontier *bandeirantes* and their descendants were deeply conditioned by their physical surroundings.

* Quoted in F. de Azevedo, *Brazilian Culture* (New York, 1950), p. 35.

Elsewhere, men had to come to terms with the limitless pampas of Argentina, to adjust to the rugged, domineering Andes with their steep slopes, isolated valleys and the thin atmosphere of their windswept plateaux, to cope with the *llanos* or plains where engulfing floods alternated with searing droughts, or with unyielding deserts in regions of Mexico, Peru, Chile and northern Brazil. Although parts of Latin America enjoyed a comfortable climate, manageable terrain and adequate rainfall, vast areas presented a constant menace to man. Nearly all were impressive in their majesty, richness and beauty.

In the late nineteenth century Spanish-American writers initiated the Spanish modernist movement which lightened the classic Spanish syntax and introduced a lively rhythm and impressionist style more appropriate to the spirit of the times. The leader and most influential poet of this movement was the Nicaraguan, Rubén Darío. Its precursors had been the Cuban poets José Marti (1853–95) and Julián del Casal (1861–93), the Mexican Manuel Gutierrez Nájera (1859–95), the Colombian José Asunción Silva (1865–96). Darío carried the movement to Spain when he went to live and work there during the early years of the twentieth century.

Modernist writers rejected both classic rhetoric and romantic eloquence and sentimentality. In the manner of the French Parnassians and symbolists, they sought clarity and purity of imagery and used a precise vocabulary enriched from the language of daily speech. They introduced great variety of metric forms in place of the limited number of classical metres.

During the first two decades of the twentieth century poets and writers in most Hispanic American countries followed the general direction set by Rubén Darío, who was recognized as the outstanding contemporary poet in Spain as well as in the New World. Leopoldo Lugones (1874–1938) in Argentina represented the left wing of the modernists; like Stravinsky and Picasso, he remained an experimenter, adopting new stylistic modes every few years. The Uruguayan, José Enriquez Rodó (1872–1917), outstanding among the prose writers, contributed to the positive sense of identity among Latin American writers; like other prose writers, who wrote mainly essays, articles or narratives of travel rather than fiction, he was best known for his critical essays, including his evaluation of the work of Rubén Darío, and especially for *Ariel* (1900) in which he set the idealism and spiritual character of the Hispanic heritage against what he saw as materialism and reliance on force in the culture of North America.

In their reaction against romanticism, with its idealization of the Indian and of local life, the modernist writers at first turned away from American materials and drew on a wide cultural heritage for inspiration—Greek or Scandinavian mythology, Christian legends, Japanese modes. Soon, however, they returned to native materials and themes. The Peruvian poet José Santos Chocano (1875–1934) called the poems which he published in 1906 *Alma América* (*Soul of America*). Lugones's *Odas seculares* (1910) were on native themes. Darío himself, after vigorously rejecting his American surroundings as unpoetical, used American scenes, legends and history in his later work. Short-story writers created distinctively South American characters, and though they patterned their stories on those of de Maupassant, they developed them in local terms.

The major renascence of arts and letters in Brazil did not come until 1920. Cultural relations between Brazil and Portugal had never been as close as those between Spain and her former colonies, for Portugal had done little or nothing to further cultural development during the colonial period. In the early nineteenth century, when the Portuguese government and royal court, fugitives from Napoleon, had been transferred to Rio de Janeiro, the king had imported a French cultural mission to offer instruction in the arts, and thereafter France supplied the chief European cultural inspiration to Brazilian artists and writers. Local literary and artistic traditions remained weak during the nineteenth and early twentieth century; they lost what little support they had had when the fall of the Brazilian empire in 1889 removed the principal source of patronage, the court.

The Latin American writers of the first quarter of the twentieth century constituted a more or less self-contained group, far removed from the general population. A number of them lived for a time in Europe, chiefly in Paris or Spain. Except in Buenos Aires, they could count on neither a well-developed publishing industry not a periodical press; Brazilian publications prior to 1920 were put out in editions of not more than one to two thousand copies. They were more concerned with style than with social content or impact. Their audience was a devoted circle of initiates drawn from the *élite* class to which they also belonged, for a broad public was yet to be developed.

The Mexican revolution which began in 1910 set in motion a major process of cultural reorientation whose effect extended not only to the countries where Indians made up a large proportion of the population but to other areas as well. In the years after the first world war, writers in Argentina, Chile, Colombia, Venezuela and Cuba joined those of Mexico, Ecuador and Peru in drawing their inspiration and their material from pre-Columbian and current Indian sources. Archaeological research brought to light during these years much new evidence of the very great antiquity and the amazing richness of early American civilizations. The influence of the archaeological remains was reinforced by a continuity in identity and in feeling from prehistoric times to the present where Indian populations lived on, tenacious of their way of life.

To this renewed appreciation of the Indian was joined a spirit of social protest. The tone was set by the poem '¿ *Quién sabe* ?' (Who knows ? 1913), written by Chocano while accompanying the Mexican revolutionary army: 'Indian, you who labour to till the lands that others own, do you not know that your blood and your sweat should make them yours?' The famous novel by the Mexican writer, Mariano Azuela (1873–1952), *Los de abajo* (1916, translated as *The Underdogs*) was one of many which dealt with the exploitation of the Indian.

In Brazil the major cultural movement dated from 1922 when a Week of Modern Art in São Paulo brought together poets, critics, novelists and artists. The movement which got its impetus from this event, well represented by the strongly nationalist poet, Mario de Andrade (1893–1945), was vigorously anti-European. Although it derived many of its technical characteristics from European sources, its spirit was that of revolt from tutelage to the older cultures. It marked the efforts of Brazilian writers and artists to speak as representatives of an independent culture, rooted in the physical surroundings, popular spirit and intense vigour of a people struggling to find itself in modern terms.

In the second quarter of the twentieth century Latin America produced clearly defined forms. In spite of local differences, writers and artists who did not know each other personally and were separated by great distances corresponded through the pages of reviews to shape among themselves a common Latin-American culture. There were strongly nationalistic novels and a wide range of interpretations of the essentially American in anthropology, philology, folklore, history and philosophy.

The most distinctive and best known of these forms were in the field of painting. Inspired by the revolutionary struggles of the people and by the forms and feeling expressed in ancient Indian monuments, Mexican painters, most notably Diego Rivera, José Clemente Orozco, and David Alfaro Siqueiros, gained world-wide renown for the quality of their murals. The exteriors of the University of Mexico buildings with their huge, brilliantly coloured figures and designs displayed a modern adaptation of pre-Columbian styles. The work of Cándido Portinari (1903–   ) in Brazil, was comparable in type and quality. Both in murals for public buildings and in single paintings representing ethnic and social types—Indian, *mestizo*, Negro, sharecropper's wife, family group, village at work—he conveyed a sense of the vitality, strength and endurance of the Brazilian people.[23] (Pl. 32.)

Musical expression, too, took on a distinctive character. In this field, it was the popular expression rather than ancient, indigenous styles which provided the basis for the best known work. The most widely known and prolific of the twentieth-century Latin American composers, the Brazilian Heitor Villa-Lobos, drew much of the style and feeling of his work from popular music and dance in which African and Iberian rhythms were ingrained.

Poetry had always been the most characteristic form of literary expression in the region. During these years poets experimented widely. Both the writers in Spanish, who called themselves 'ultraists' or 'vanguardists' and their Brazilian counterparts identified as 'modernists', made free use of metre and syntax, turning to free verse or reverting to archaic forms at will; they called up a great variety of associations by their images; some sought the utmost purity of form while others retained a feeling for the objectively real and specific.

In the poetic movements and expression of these years, the tendencies toward the abstract and toward the essentially native were intertwined. The Chilean poet Vicente Huidobro (1893–1948), representative of those whose search was for new forms of expression abstracted from reality, called himself a 'creationist' to denote the freshness of his approach. The Peruvian poet, César Vallejo (1895–1938) was known as 'essentially Indian' in spirit, for the sense of ancient, enduring sadness which his poems conveyed. Argentine writers named one of their leading literary magazines, established in 1925, after the protagonist in a famous novel of gaucho life, *Martín Fierro* (by José Hernandez, 1872). In this magazine, both native and abstract poetry appeared side by side, each equally a part of the quest for a native idiom, free from dependence on Europe— a quest which had been going on with more or less intensity from the time of independence.

In prose, some writers chose to use the psychological novel, others the novel of social import. The social novels which appeared in mounting numbers revealed not only an identification with the indigenous element but the struggles for the integration of society. They contrasted with European novels in giving nature a determining role; conflicts appeared more environmental and earthy than psychological. They revealed collective tensions between hostile and incompatible groups in great economic and social disequilibrium—Indians and rural masses versus the urban minority, or the spiritual and economic conflict between the native worker and the foreign enterprise. When the protagonist was not struggling against indomitable nature in the form of tropical jungle, forbidding Andes, empty desert or raging rivers, he was caught in the turmoil of societies in the process of fusion.

Novels of Indian life, which had been idyllic in the romantic period of the nineteenth century, became brutally realistic; Ecuadorian writers in particular depicted the Indian's lot as intolerable. The literature of the social underworld peopled by Indians dispossessed, debased and subjected to all manner of frustrations and injustices recalled the bitterest literature of tsarist Russia such as Gorky's *Lower Depths*.

The incorporation of indigenous elements, both human and environmental —even the revolt against European cultural dominance—did not however mean isolation from Europe and its intellectual and artistic influences. Whatever intellectual currents were sweeping Europe also swept the Americas— positivism, Marxism, psychoanalysis, existentialism. Works in other European languages were quickly translated into Spanish or Portuguese and circulated; the cultivated circles of Latin America discussed the same philosophers, playwrights, novelists or poets as were being discussed in the literary circles of Europe and North America. Europe's literature of crisis, failure, resentment and social rebellion had its repercussions on the Latin American literature of social protest. Such techniques as stream of consciousness, explorations of the subconscious and surrealist imagination gave the works of Latin American writers their modern flavour. The influence of Picasso was visible in the works of many painters.

These very currents of modern European thought and art, in fact, made it easier to understand the ancient cultures and to incorporate their spirit. The Venezuelan critic, Mariano Picón-Salas, noted that the

indigenous heritage would not have had so much validity if the spiritual attitude of twentieth century man and certain deep currents in the psyche and the art of the times had not prepared us—better than in other epochs—to comprehend these ultra-archaic forms. The neo-classicists and rationalists of the eighteenth century would not have understood the monumental art of Chichén-Itzá and Palenque, of Mitla, Tula and Teotihuacan as the contemporaries of Picasso could feel and revitalize them. Monsters, symbols, dreams and forms of our anxious and full age are related to those of distant times. As a result of our immersion in the mysteries of ethnology, of the symbolic enigma of the most ancient human cultures, of the terrible cosmic vitality of the germinal myths, of the depths in the subconscious to which contemporary psychology probes, the great sculptures of the Aztecs or Olmecas seem now nearer and more comprehensible. Compared to these, what a banal vision of life would be offered by the contrived portraits of the Rococo or the lightly hedonistic sensuality of the figures of a Renoir.*

Thus, in perhaps no other part of the world did so many diverse currents come together. The ancient Indo-American was still alive and also renewed; the Spanish and Portuguese represented a continuous European tradition; the cosmopolitan immigration of the twentieth century brought other European elements, especially to Argentina, Uruguay, Brazil and Venezuela; the major African influence was on music and dance, but spread thence to painting and literature; the impact of the physical surroundings was always present. In the emerging cultures of the region, the most modern European trends interacted with old traditions; the culture of the cultivated *élite* met the popular culture of the masses. The Spanish and Portuguese languages and the Catholic Church were unifying factors. Economic and social revolution, well under way in Mexico and barely initiated in many other areas, was in process of converting feudal, paternalistic societies into more democratic ones. The literature and arts of Latin America were coming to reflect the complex dynamics of these emerging societies.

(c) *The USSR*

The USSR inherited the literary and artistic traditions of western Europe, of which the Russian component was a major element during the nineteenth century. The works of the great Russian novelists, Dostoevsky and Tolstoy,

* 'El aire cultural en América Latina', *Journal of World History*, I (1954), p. 701 (translated).

the plays of Chekhov and the realistic stories of Gorky were among the works which had the greatest influence upon western writers when they were translated into German and French in the nineteenth century and into English in the early twentieth century. The major Russian composers of the nineteenth century, Tchaikovsky, Mussorgsky, Alexander Glazunov (1865–1936), Rimsky-Korsakov, shared with the German romantics a central place in the musical tradition of the West. The brilliant and creative Russian theatre and ballet were the inspiration of producers and choreographers on both sides of the Atlantic.

In the years before the first world war Russian artists and musicians shared the experimentation in which their western European contemporaries were engaged, in a free flow and interchange of influence and experience; Diaghilev's Russian Ballet used the work of foreign artists and in turn influenced them. Russian artists were prominent among those who carried experimentation with form the farthest, notably Kandinsky in his use of colour alone to express mood and the constructivists with their mathematically based abstractions. The Moscow Art Theatre under Konstantin Stanislavsky took the lead in experimenting with dramatic techniques for making the stage express inner psychological realities. Symbolist poetry was represented in the work of Alexander Blok (1880–1921) and Andrei Biely (1880–1934).

The October revolution gave impetus to these experimentations and an opportunity for pre-revolutionary writers and artists to apply their ideas of freedom from classical traditions to the making of the new Soviet culture. Kandinsky returned from Germany to join Pevsner, Gabo, Malevich, Tatlin and others in replacing the old Academy of Art. Members of the group started a new Higher and Technical Art Workshop which integrated architecture, sculpture and painting.

From 1917 to 1920 their movement expanded. They developed their ideas of art in the new Soviet world and designed projects to express them—a 'Monument to the Third International', to be an office building and a symbol of the new synthesis of art, learning and technical knowledge (Tatlin, 1919), a project for a radio station and a design for a textile town prepared by Naum Gabo. In 1920 they issued a *Constructivist Manifesto*, declaring that art is based on space and time; kinetic and dynamic elements are necessary to express time; art should not imitate but discover new forms, for reality is constantly changing. Vsevolod Meyerhold applied constructivist principles to the theatre and experimented with stylized forms, in staging, acting and the massing of performers until the play became essentially a design created by the producer.

Experimental writers, too, identified themselves with the Revolution. Vladimir Mayakovsky (1894–1930) welcomed the revolutionary spirit which discarded traditional values, and threw his energy into propaganda verse, epigrams on topical subjects in the style of popular factory songs, verse dramas glorifying the Revolution, and poems epitomizing the national aspirations as in *150,000,000* (1920), a poem in which the peasant stands for 150,000,000 Russians. Alexander Blok expressed the spirit of revolutionary Leningrad in his classic poem *The Twelve* (1918), using popular language and rhythms. Musicians formed an Association of Contemporary Music to encourage musical experimentation and to perform works of new, anti-bourgeois west European composers.

After 1920 the climate of free experimentation began to change. The movement of constructivist artists broke up, chiefly on the issue of whether art should reflect a definite ideology. Tatlin accepted the principle that art is an instrument of the socialist state, and remained to take part in the development of the USSR. Gabo, Pevsner and Kandinsky, believing that art must keep itself free of political influence, left Russia and became part of the movements of art in western Europe and the United States. A number of artists in other fields who wished to remain individual and experimental, including the composer Stravinsky, also left, as it became clear that those who remained would be called upon to participate directly in the building of the socialist society, and would be governed by the principles of style deemed appropriate to this purpose. But the theatre, still in the hands of Stanislavsky and Meyerhold, and the cinema under the creative leadership of Sergei Eisenstein, continued through the 1920s to experiment boldly. And some who emigrated, such as Alexey Tolstoy (1882–1945) and Ilya Ehrenburg (1891–   ), returned to their homeland.[24]

The pre-revolutionary writers, painters, musicians, sculptors and architects who remained in Russia or returned, and who went through the difficult process of having to reconsider their artistic doctrines, dedicated their efforts to helping in the struggle to remake Soviet society, to creating a popular art comprehensible to the working people, and to interpreting for them the heritage of the past. Their energies found outlets in dramatic, satirical and rousing political posters which raised propagandist art to a high technical level, as in the pictures and rhymes of the famous ROSTA windows by the poet and artist, Mayakovsky; in monumental propaganda sculpture to honour great revolutionary figures of the past; in the design of hydroelectric stations, factories, public buildings and workers' housing or the laying out of whole communities and new towns; in novels such as those of Alexey Tolstoy who wrote of the decay of the pre-revolutionary society and of his own childhood (*Nikita's Childhood*, 1921) and created fantasies into which he wove revolutionary ideology.

In the years immediately following the Revolution there were those who took a narrow view of the problems and paths of the new art. The group which organized Proletkult in 1917, to train gifted workers in the arts, maintained that the new culture could be created only by the hands of those directly linked with the working class, rejecting the possibility that men stemming from the old intelligentsia could take part; they repudiated Russian and world classics, declaring them to be bourgeois literature and hence utterly alien to the people. Other groups proposed that 'Pushkin be cast overboard from the ship of modernity' or insisted on the purely utilitarian mission of art. Lenin took a definite stand against these views of vulgar simplification, stating that 'proletarian culture must appear as a logical development of those resources of knowledge which humanity had amassed under oppression in capitalist society'.*

Some writers and artists did indeed emerge from peasant or partially peasant backgrounds; more, whatever their background, had participated actively in the revolutionary struggle and wrote with realism and insight drawn from direct experience. Men and women from many different walks of life brought to literature and the arts new material, new problems and new characters. Mikhail Sholokhov (1905–) hailed from a Don Cossack village, participated in the struggle against the kulaks, and after gaining world fame as a novelist continued to live and work in the same village, both as novelist and deputy to the Supreme Soviet. In his epic novel *And Quiet Flows the Don* (vol. I, 1938) he gave full expression to the vitality of the peasant as it showed itself in every relationship—to his land, his horses, his wife and children, his village, the whole Don River basin, and the confusion of armies passing over the land. Alexander Fadeyev (1901–56), who took part in guerrilla warfare in the Far East, showed the civil war in terms of the individual psychology of those who fought in it in *Razgrom* (*The Rout*, 1927). Dmitry Furmanov (1891–1926) was commissar of the legendary Chapayev's division, of which he wrote (*Chapayev*, 1923). Isaac Babel (1894–c. 1938) in *Cavalry* (1926) portrayed the civil war with grim realism.

With the first five-year plan in 1928, artists and writers were involved more directly in the work of socialist reconstruction, for the plan provided for the utilization of their talents, as of other human and material resources, and required their training, development and organization. Many writers belonging to diverse groups set out together for various parts of the country and produced works on the great changes that were being wrought in central Asia, in the north, in central Russia and in the Far East. The Russian Association of Proletarian Writers (RAPP) under Leopold Averbakh (1903–39) became the instrument for enlisting writers in the programme of industrialization and collectivization. In 1932 a more inclusive organization, the Union of Soviet Writers, in which Maxim Gorky, Sholokhov and Fadeyev were influential, brought together writers of all social origins, including many not members of the Party.

The role of writers and artists was, in Stalin's phrase, that of 'engineers of human minds'. As set forth in the statute of the Union of Soviet Writers, they were to create 'works of high artistic significance, saturated with the heroic struggle of the world proletariat and with the grandeur of the victory of socialism, and reflecting the great wisdom and heroism of the Communist

* Quoted in T. Trifonova, 'Soviet Literature', *Journal of World History*, VII (1962), p. 101.

party'. A common creative method, known as 'socialist realism', was approved for all forms of expression. (Pl. 29.)

This style, designed to create understanding, support and a favourable climate for national efforts, called for realistic presentation which would show things not only as they were but for what they represented in the building of a socialist society—figures which were both individuals and social types, such as portraits of 'The Delegate' (1927) and 'The Chairwoman' (1928) by the painter Georgy Ryazhsky (1895–1955), 'The Worker' (1922) and 'The Red Army Man' (1923) by the sculptor Ivan Shadr (1887–1941), or 'Peasant Girl' (1927) by Vera Mukhina (1889–1953); stories in which those who took an active part in the battle for production—workers, peasants, scientists, engineers—played the hero's role; historical scenes which identified valour in the present with the grandeur of the past; the Russian landscape lyrically seen and felt; warmly sympathetic sketches of peasant and industrial life.

In this vein, writers depicted the heroic struggles against nature, in the building of a paper mill in the remote forest of north-east Russia (Leonid Leonov, 1899– : *Sot*, 1930), the drama of mechanization on a massive scale in the huge Magnitogorsk coke-chemical combine (Valentin Katayev, 1897– : *Vremya, vperyod—Time, Forward!*, 1933), the vision and inescapable tragedy in collectivization (Mikhail Sholokhov, *Virgin Soil Upturned*, 1931). Whereas the works of the 1920s had been mainly devoted to the revolutionary struggle and the civil war, with such notable exceptions as F. Gladkov's (1888–1958) *Cement* (1925), major attention was now directed to the labour and efforts of the Soviet people who had become masters of their land and were transforming it. Painters produced documentary representations of the new way of life, the elemental strength of peasants, the vitality in scenes of labour. Sensitive to the human drama and recognizing that their task was to help create the new Soviet man, some writers dealt with the psychological conflict within the individual between the old and the new, and with the coming of age of the new man, as did Konstantin Fedin (1892–) in *First Joys* (1945) and *No Ordinary Summer* (1947–48).[25]

In the 1930s Maxim Gorky's influence was strong in relating new art to the classical tradition and in encouraging the cultures of the national republics. Proletarian writers were stimulated to study the great classics, though not to adopt the negative tone of Dostoevsky. The Union of Soviet Composers, organized in 1932, included in its purposes a reassessment of the classical and romantic heritage and it formed sections in the different republics to develop special national characteristics and the use of folk songs.

A distinctive type of historical novel emerged, devoted to the historical destinies of the people. Thus Alexey Tolstoy's *Peter the First* (Book I, 1929), although named after a tsar, reflected a whole epoch in the development of Russia, embracing all the strata of the Russian society of the time including the unpropertied masses. Novels such as Olga Forsh's (1875–) trilogy devoted to the eighteenth-century revolutionary Russian writer Radishchev

(1954) and A. Chapygin's (1870–1937) story of Stepan Razin (1926–27) depicted individual destinies, recreated decisive periods in the history of the people and showed widespread popular movements.

Writers of the many nationalities which make up the Soviet Union followed a course similar to writers in Russian, treating modern themes, producing regional historical novels such as Mukhtar Auezov's (1897–   ) *Abai* on nineteenth-century Kazakhstan, or drawing on personal experience as in Sadriddin Aini's (1879–1954) memories of youth, *Bukhara* (1948). By the 1950s Soviet literature was being produced in the languages of more than seventy nationalities, some of which had had no written language of their own, and was being translated into all the languages of the USSR so that wide masses of readers in all corners of the land could become familiar with a multi-national socialist literature as a whole.[26]

Continuity with musical tradition was also evident and was maintained into the 1950s in the works of the leading composers. Sergei Prokoviev, who returned to the USSR in 1933 after fifteen years in western Europe and America, made subtle and skilful use of classical forms as well as popular dances and tunes in his ballets, symphonies, concertos and sonatas ranging in theme from lyric to heroic and in mood from witty and gay to dramatic or grand. His music was much loved and played both in the USSR and in western Europe and America. Dmitry Shostakovich, whose work also became well known outside Russia as well as inside, drew freely on the whole classical tradition of European music and used its forms ingeniously and originally in his prolific output of symphonies and other works to celebrate great national efforts of the Soviet people. His *Symphony of 1905 Revolution* (1957) for the fortieth anniversary of the founding of the Soviet state incorporated the revolutionary songs of the people into a symphony in the classical form, combined with a great fugue to give a massive, cumulative effect. Folk themes were used in combination with traditional Russian modes by the Armenian composer Aram Katchaturian (1903–   ): *Gayna Ballet*, 1943; *Spartacus Ballet*, 1954).

Ballet, one of the most popular of the arts, also retained the form which had made it famous before the turn of the century. The dozens of ballet schools (thirty-two in the mid-1950s) taught the classical techniques, and troupes performed both traditional ballets, such as *Swan Lake*, and new ones on modern themes such as the story of the Chinese revolution in *The Red Poppy* (1927, by Reinhold Gliere, 1875–1956), danced in the classical style. Operas also used both legendary and folk materials.

The tone of all the arts was heroic—the five-year plan novels, monumental sculpture, such as Vera Mukhina's huge 'Worker and Collective Farm Woman' (Pl. 40) made for the Soviet pavilion at the 1937 Paris Fair, decorative painting to adorn façades and interiors of public buildings, Shostakovich's solemn and eloquent *Fifth Symphony* (1937), Prokoviev's music for Sergei Eisenstein's (1898–1948) spectacular film of the national hero, *Alexander*

Nevsky (1938). The heroism of the tsarist past was recalled with such figures as Ivan the Terrible. Writers drew inspiration from the personalities of out-standing leaders of the Revolution, most notably Lenin, of whom Mayakovsky created a profoundly human and at the same time monumental image in his poem *Vladimir Ilyich Lenin* (1924). The search for the Soviet hero led to such popular novels as N. Ostrovsky's (1904-36) *That's How Steel was Tempered* (1935), the story of the formation and growth of a young com-munist of working-class origin.

With the second world war artists and writers were mobilized even more completely than before for the common national purpose. In devoting them-selves to arousing patriotic fervour and war efforts they were aware that they must reach deeper psychological levels than had been touched in much of the literature dealing with the struggle for production in the preceding years. The conference of the Union of Soviet Writers in 1942 expressed the view that only through 'psychological realism' and a humanistic and patriotic approach could Soviet literature preserve its most valuable asset: its ties with the masses. Amid the great volume of war reporting, historical and other novels, war plays and biographies of national heroes, some works of literary quality stood out, such as Fadeyev's *The Young Guard* (1945) and Leonov's prize-winning play, *Invasion* (1942).

Socialist realism had been conceived as a form which, while demanding truth and historical concreteness, a clear Party tendency and active participa-tion in the life of the people, would not restrict artistic exploration; the statute adopted at the first Writers' Congress in 1934 stressed that socialist realism gives wide range to creative seekings. But during the Stalin era, literature and the arts suffered from the no-conflict theory and tendencies toward pompous depiction which all too often prevented the reflection of difficulties and contradictions involved in the building of the new society.

After the second world war writers and artists were subjected to a more restrictive interpretation of the state's demands upon them and of the limits of socialist realism than at any time since the early years of the first five-year plan. By resolution of the Central Committee of the Communist party in 1946, two of the leading literary magazines were denounced for publishing ideologi-cally harmful works and one of them was suppressed. The theatre, which retained great vigour and popularity—some thousand theatres played to enthusiastic audiences composed especially of young people—was severely censured for failure to reflect the life of Soviet socialism and was directed to 'train youth in cheerfulness and joyousness, in devotion to their country and in confidence in the victory of their cause'. Under the stern direction of the Party's propaganda chief, Andrei Zhdanov, writers were required to be Party-minded and anti-cosmopolitan.

Following the death of Stalin a number of writers sought to free them-selves from what they felt to be the narrowing and deadening effect of these policies, and in their congresses they expressed the hope that they might be

TT*

allowed more leeway for lyric and personal expression. The veteran critic and writer, Ilya Ehrenburg, ventured a novel, *The Thaw* (1954), in which he treated the human problems of artists forced to choose between their vision and success, a dedicated doctor and teacher whose devotion did not bring full social rewards and a factory manager motivated by bureaucratic self-seeking.

Especially after the twentieth Congress of the Communist party in 1956, there was a marked revival of literary life. A number of new magazines and literary newspapers came into being. Problems such as literature's close touch with modern times, the hero in literature, lyric poetry, were animatedly discussed in the press and in All-Union Writers' congresses (1954, 1959). Stereotyped presentations had given way to more intricate portrayals of individualized heroes with deep roots in the masses, rich spiritual life and complexity of character. Socialist realism remained the method; the arts retained their essentially educational role; works were not acceptable which tended to undermine or disparage the common effort. But Soviet writers and artists were fulfilling their mission in increasingly varied and versatile ways.[27]

The literary and artistic expression of the USSR thus presented a contrast in many respects to that of western Europe. While west European writers looked upon themselves as special and apart, Soviet writers and artists were proud to regard themselves as fellow-craftsmen with those who followed other trades in the interest of society and the state. They functioned as did other workers through their trade unions, which served as channels for receiving the plans and aims of the state and for expressing their views and which were guided by the Party nucleus. Leading artists enjoyed high social status and prestige and some, such as the composer Shostakovich, and the prima ballerina, Galina Ulanova, served as delegates from their districts to the Supreme Soviet. Some of the most politically prominent of the Party leaders at different times headed the ministry of culture which administered the cultural components of the national plans.

Many of the experimental currents so prominent in western Europe were absent in the USSR. The ballet preserved its traditional romantic styles, performed with great skill, and its traditional décor. Architecture retained its massive character and use of decoration, adapted to the technology of cement and the prefabrication of structural elements.[28] Realism prevailed in all the arts in contrast to the European tendency toward abstraction. There was no Freudian probing of the unconscious, or deeply psychological poetry, though sensitive writers did not fail to capture and reveal their characters' inner life; in fact, Soviet expression came closest to that of western Europe, and especially of the United States, when it took the form of imaginative presentations of varied people in human terms.

Doubt and inquiry were discouraged and joyousness prescribed. The note of despair was absent; optimism, heroism or constructive criticism were the pervasive tones. The certainties of Marxist–Leninist ideology provided basic assumptions, in marked contrast to the west European's uncertain search for the meaning of life and the nature of man. In the words of Nikita Krushchev: 'We are against those who hunt only for the dark sides of life and gloat over them, trying to disparage and blacken our Soviet ways of life. Likewise we are against those who create sugar-coated pictures of life, offending the better senses of our people who scorn and cannot tolerate any falsehood.'*

Soviet leaders had no doubt that the literature and arts of the Soviet Union, as integral expressions of the new society, would make as significant a contribution to the world as had the great Russian writers and composers of the past.

IV. THE NEW MASS MEDIA AND THE ARTS

In the course of the twentieth century, and especially from the 1920s on, the media of mass communication greatly expanded the scope of the popular arts, provided the means of mass entertainment, and brought all manner of new information and knowledge within the reach of the common man. They also brought undreamed of means of influencing him by propaganda.

The media of mass entertainment—film, radio and television—offered employment to many more writers, designers and producers than ever before and gave them devices of hitherto unknown possibilities and the opportunity to reach vast new audiences. Many artists of only moderate gifts earned their living by their art in these industries, but artists of first-rate ability could also find new outlets. While many of the serious artists and writers scorned these new tools and left their exploitation to those whose only aim was to entertain, persuade or inform, some saw the film and the press, TV and radio as media of art and eagerly grasped the new instruments.

I. THE CINEMA AS AN ART

Once the Lumières in France had patented their first projection machine and showed a two-minute film to a Grand Café public in 1895, and Edison and Armat had projected narrative scenes for audiences in New York, the new art of the cinema was possible, an art close to the masses of the people and potentially expressive of the new scale of world-wide interests, revolutions of people and scientific discoveries. It began with Georges Méliès, the first poet of the cinema. His *A Trip to the Moon* (1902) was one of a long line of films that he made with inventiveness, technical audacity and careful workmanship; he made scenes of a fantastic world of motion, fairy tales, miracles of speed and the new science. His successors were the makers of animated cartoons which began in 1908.

At the same time the film telling a story appeared in France (Ferdinand Zecca's *History of a Crime*, 1901) and in America (Edwin S. Porter's *Great Train Robbery*, 1903, which ran twelve minutes), using from the start the melodrama of crime and violence that proliferated through the next fifty years. Both kinds of film developed rapidly into more sustained forms with varied

* Quoted in Trifonova, 'Soviet Literature', *op. cit.*, p. 107.

themes. In Italy and France a succession of historical dramas based on literature (*Quo Vadis* 1912; *Cabriria* 1914) sustained the story through several reels, were staged as grandiose spectacles and played by great actors like Sarah Bernhardt (*Queen Elizabeth*, 1912); but the production was limited by being treated as theatre.

D. W. Griffith (1875–1948) in the USA freed the cinema from the theatrical tradition and from literary sources. He told his story by scenes which he made from life. He moved his camera freely from place to place; he moved his characters about so that their motions were not stage-bound but natural; he had a scale of camera shots for focusing on special aspects of the players. Especially, he anatomized each scene into a succession of shots which he then edited by cutting so as to give the intensity required by his taste for melodrama. It was the delicate use of various kinds of motion in this editing that made a new aesthetic medium. Actually the aesthetic pleasure from the patterns of motion might be quite separate from the substance of the narrative material, and this became standard in later films from Hollywood which developed extraordinary technical resources in use of motion, even when the narrative content was immaturely extrovert.

As gifted directors and writers worked in the medium, the combination of story and moving pictures produced increasingly powerful works of art. D. W. Griffith's *The Birth of a Nation* (1915) and *Intolerance* (1916) were the first in the United States to show the possible magnitude of a feature film. *The Birth of a Nation* was hailed far and wide for its beauty of style, in spite of the fact that its narrative content was attacked in the United States and other countries lest it have the effect of renewing the racial hatreds of the Civil War. (Pl. 57a.)

The great Russian director Sergei Eisenstein (1898–1948) appreciated Griffith's successions of shots and his editing. He wrote: 'It is a question of creating a series of images composed in such a way that it provokes an affective movement which in turn awakens a series of ideas. From image to sentiment, from sentiment to thesis. . . . I think the film alone is capable of making this great synthesis, of giving back to the intellectual element its vital sources, both concrete and emotional'* His *Potemkin* (1925), the masterpiece of this kind of film, was a story of revolt of sailors against injustice, brilliantly photographed and using dramatic juxtapositions—the contrasts of calm scenes and the ruthless military; close-ups of a doctor inspecting the food which caused the revolt and of a horrible, squirming mass of worms occupying the whole screen—the symbol of evil and wrong that makes revolt inevitable; long lines of people on the quay passing the bier of the sailor killed in the skirmish; the soldiers' boots marching in relentless order down the steps toward peaceful people's outstretched hands and a common, fragile perambulator left after they had passed. (Pl. 57b.)

* Quoted in Maurice Bardèche and Robert Brasillach, *History of the Film* (London, 1938), p. 273.

During the first world war the Swedish director, Victor Sjöström (1879–1960) created the film of atmosphere—beautiful, poetical compositions closer to painting and music than theatre, such as *The Outlaw and his Wife* (1917) and adaptations of novels of Selma Lagerlöf. He understood the principle of keeping his stories and characters simple and of building up the incidents of ordinary daily scenes to an emotionally moving visual image of the whole life of the people and the nature around them.

The cinema after the first world war developed a variety of forms. The directors of the Soviet Union, confronted with the problem of interpreting the Revolution to the people, crystallized theories and made memorable films in the true-to-life line. The Kíno-eye Group, founded by Dziya Vertov in 1921, worked on the principles of documentation, use of unrehearsed scenes, selection of actors from among ordinary people according to the types needed, and scientific editing, cutting and putting together of the footage of each sequence to make a rhythm in relation to the total length of the film.

Eisenstein was the master of this technique, working mainly from life and in epic narratives (*Alexander Nevsky*, 1938, *Ivan the Terrible*, 1944). V. I. Pudovkin (1893–1953) carried the technique into the studio with controlled setting and light, professional actors trained to realism so severe as to approach life, and use of Vertov's theory of rhythm. He originated a school of films of individual human interest within society. His *Mother* (1926) made from Gorky's novel showed an ignorant, beaten-down peasant woman becoming socially conscious and, in the end, full of new faith, radiantly leading a procession of workers in revolt. The Ukrainian producer, A. P. Dovzhenko (1894–1956), interpreted the themes of nature and the peasant's love of life in *Earth* (1931).

Comedy, derived from the circus and its technique of pantomime, developed through a line of screen actors gifted in the use of symbolic gesture. American burlesque and parodies were translated into visual humour by Mack Sennett. His pupil, Charlie Chaplin (1889–   ) working in this line had by 1917 evolved for the silent screen a film language of great precision. It was, in his phrase, 'the poetry of movement'. His unique genius as actor and producer, and as an observer of life close to the people, lifted the film from vulgar buffoonery to great comedy expressing the grief and bitterness of the universe and bringing release through laughter. He was the little tramp with the bowler hat and cane making the ordinary gestures of life in a world which he did not understand, who always brought startling trouble and always met it with unfailing kindness and gentle courtesy and the detachment of the pure comic. He became the universal hero of his time, in the end always going down the road and out of the picture with dignity intact whatever the defeat or loss.

Chaplin was sensitive to the crises and climate of feeling of his time and expressed them sharply in *Shoulder Arms* (1918), one of the boldest war films, *The Kid* (1921), *The Gold Rush* (1925) parodying sentimental films of covered wagon days, *City Lights* (1931), and the more severe *Modern Times*

(1936) taking the monotony of machine industry to its logical extreme. *The Great Dictator* (1940) demolished the image of Hitler by ridicule. Even after the coming of sound his films kept his great art of pantomime and used sound only sparingly and in well understood relation to the gesture. (Pl. 58a.)

A conception of the aesthetics of motion pictures according to which scenes were treated as successions of paintings or as ballet determined many of the French and German pictures. The Germans especially were interested in the painterly aspects of settings and made films distinguished for these. Emotionally they were preoccupied with the macabre and the occult mixed with science, as in Paul Wegener's romantic *Prager Student* (1913) and Robert Wiene's *The Cabinet of Dr Caligari* (1919), one of the first horror stories and one which used every resource of expressionism. In both countries in the 1920s films were produced by poets and other experimental writers who often used surrealist symbolism; they found the medium especially flexible in conveying dreams, fantasy and in moving from one world to another. René Clair (1898–   ) made a witty, poetical world of his own where delicate irony played over enchanted and absurd romance and stylized characters danced through the vulgar incidents of daily life in ballet form. He might evoke an atmosphere of complete gaiety as in *Le Million* (1931), or he might create a sense of pointed irony in *A nous la liberté* (1931) by setting his romance in a fantastic amusement park and making the monotonous rhythms of industrial workers into those of prisoners walking up and down in the court of their prison.

More popular and widespread use of this conception produced animated cartoons—a series of paintings or drawings of figures in different positions photographed against a moving background. In 1923 Walt Disney began these and used them in a wide range of comedy; his Mickey Mouse was popular all over the world. His first long feature film, *Snow White and the Seven Dwarfs* (1938) dramatized a fairy story with grotesque humour and considerable horror. (Pl. 58b.)

In this development of motion pictures as story and drama, the need of sound was implicit from the beginning; lines of dialogue flashed on the screen had usually been necessary. Yet when it was introduced in 1926 (*Don Juan*) in synchronized music and in 1927 in combined singing and dialogue by Al Jolson in *Jazz Singer*, it seemed at first to divert attention from the natural suitability of film for expression by gesture and motion and to turn film drama into mere spoken dialogue. Regardless of old skills in acting, it called for new actors with voices effective on the sound track. New theories were expressed and practised. In the manifesto *Sound Film* by Sergei Eisenstein, V. Pudovkin and Grigory Alexandrov in 1928, the writers underlined the immense significance of sound and the danger that it might be misunderstood and used in mere 'speaking films' of a theatrical nature, and then defined the positive principle: 'Only utilization of sound in counterpoint relation to the piece of visual montage affords new possibilities of developing and perfecting the montage. The first experiments with sound must be directed towards its pronounced non-coincidence with the visual images. This method of attack only will lead in course of time to the creation of a new orchestral counterpoint of sight images and sound images.'*

A few of the directors of silent films made creative use of sound. René Clair used sound in imaginative counterpoint; the German director, G. W. Pabst turned from psychoanalysis to realistic social drama in *Kamaradschaft* (1932). Walter Ruttman made sound the substance of *Melody of the World* (1929), using screams of mechanical saws, panting of railway engines, howling of derivishes, voices of American orators, African war drums.

Colour introduced new complications of perception and its technology brought various theories for its use in the art of the cinema. Many experimenters delighted audiences who came to demand technicolor more and more, from the first three-colour feature, *Becky Sharp* (1938) to the brilliant subtleties of the Japanese *Gate of Hell* (1956), which combined the sureness of Japanese artistic taste with the technical excellence of film manufactured in the United States after the war.

Sound and colour led to wide use of novels and stage plays—these always in simplified form to make their unconfused impact within the less than two hours' time for their showing—e.g. *War and Peace* (1956), *Henry V* (1946). Among the significant productions made originally for the screen, Italian films in the 1940s and 1950s were outstanding for their neo-realism. Their *Open City* (Rossellini, 1946), *The Bicycle Thief* (De Sica, 1949) and *The Roof* (De Sica, 1958) were stories of the devastation of war and poverty and the struggle for a home. The directors used ordinary people living in the cities where these pictures were shot and thus obtained the authenticity of realism. But the lack of full expressiveness remained, and they found it necessary to experiment with using professional actors to speak the dialogue on the sound track.

By the 1950s a few films were presenting complex themes with penetration and sophistication, such as *Breaking the Sound Barrier* (1952), whose theme was the passionate drive to extend and apply new scientific knowledge and the tests of character involved, or *The Bridge on the River Kwai* (1957), popular wherever it was shown around the world, which told a mature story with complicated inner motivations and counterplots leading to the final irony of self-destruction in war.

Documentary films interpreted actual happenings in the world by direct use of the camera eye and their makers concentrated on photography itself. Robert Flaherty (1884–1951), the father of the documentary, in a series of studies of the daily lives of simple people living far from urban centres, depended directly on his camera for his form. He lived with the people sometimes several years until he knew their lives the year round and they were his friends. Then he shot his story through from beginning to end, studied the pictures, retook them and came out in the end with the poetry of man in his struggle

* Quoted in Bardèche and Brasillach, *History of the Film, op. cit.*, pp. 354–5.

with nature (*Nanook of the North*, 1922; *Moana*, 1926; *Man of Aran*, 1932–34; *Louisiana Story*, 1948). Flaherty's influence was in all the documentaries which followed, whether directly in similar poetical form as in Steinbeck's *The Forgotten Village* (1941), in which modern science comes into conflict with ancient ways in Mexico, or in the works of the group set up under public auspices by John Grierson (1898–   ) in the 1930s to make informational films in Britain.

The members of this group were trying to interpret the reality beneath the surface no less truthfully than Flaherty interpreted the people he knew; but they worked with large and complex ideas and environments—cities, industries, trade, war. Grierson wrote that 'human dignity is easier to see in the "noble savage". But the realist documentary, with its streets and cities and slums and markets and exchanges and factories, has given itself the job of making poetry where no poet has gone before it, and where no ends, sufficient for the purposes of art, are easily observed.'*

The school of gifted young men and women whom Grierson gathered around him worked in different ways, some analytically, some symphonically. Alberto Cavalcanti, from France, in *Rien que les heures* (1926) viewed the city around the clock; Joris Ivens from Holland, in *Zuyder Zee*, (1930) showed the struggle to repair the broken dike and turn back the sea; Basil Wright's *Song of Ceylon* (1934) depicted the life of one member of the British commonwealth and its trade. These and other makers of documentaries were called on by governments, industries, educators and scientists to produce interpretive films on many subjects, which gave them opportunities to experiment. In 1956, in one of the most artistic and scientifically revealing films of all, *The Silent World*, a crew of French scientists sailing through the tropical seas of the world told for the first time the story of underwater life as viewed by their colour cameras.

The cinema by the 1950s had matured into a complicated pattern of production by a skilled team of workers. It was the director who brought into harmony the screen play, the staging of the action, the camera work, editing and cutting, music and sound. Every new technical development involved new possibilities of interplay of these factors. The screen play had developed from the sketchy notes of the director to a completely detailed scenario worked out by the script writer. He and the director gave the substance of originality, meaning and proportion to the final form. The director had to be not only an imaginative artist conceiving his work of art; he had to be a leader of people able to convey shadings of his intent to them so that working together they would produce the unified whole.

Writers had begun to find the screen play a satisfying outlet for their experience of twentieth-century tensions. A few painters found the dynamics of motion more satisfactorily expressed in film than in two-dimensional canvases. Some of the best composers made the accompanying music. Critics

---

* John Grierson, *Grierson on Documentary*, ed. Forsyth Hardy (London, 1946), p. 84.

wrote seriously in newspapers. International festivals in Cannes, Venice, and in Asia selected prize-worthy films for originality and artistic excellence rather than popularity. Little theatres were outlets for works of genuine artistic quality.[29]

Although the finest films did not always require lavish expenditure to produce, at best the cinema was an expensive medium. Films required sponsors, and governments, educational bodies, research organizations, industries and arts councils were increasingly ready to support the development of films within the limits of their interests. The needs of the new audiences were only just beginning to be explored. Much remained to be found out about the camera itself. The TV screen brought new problems of motion-picture composition designed within its terms, specifically the restriction in width, the necessity for motion back into the picture and forward, the effect of diminution of size of figures and the fact that television reaches private audiences at home. But vast possibilities of aesthetic satisfaction were open beyond the forms demanded by audiences and producers thinking only of an evening's entertainment at a theatre.

2. THE ARTS OF PURVEYING INFORMATION

The arts of expressing information through the press, film and radio were extended for new mass audiences at a level of mass literacy never before reached. The scale of world consciousness and the needs of people to understand the forces and events that were changing their society demanded a new kind of writing that should convey accurately and understandably knowledge about happenings among men.

Reporters, seeking to express the reality within the appearances, faced complex problems of communication, for they had to imagine two worlds simultaneously and write in terms of both. If they described events in the terms and with the patterns of expression of the place from which they were reporting, people at home would read with their own presuppositions in mind and might miss the actual human meaning of the report. Writers therefore tried to send news or interpretive reporting in images that would at once conform with the reality at the point of happening and translate it for audiences with preconditioned patterns of thought, who were absorbed in their own lives, often given to quick response to stereotypes and only superficially touched by remote happenings. Public interest in events and the appearance of newspapers daily gave central importance to 'spot news', successive fragments of observation and information with which the public was bombarded day after day, and which *in toto* added up to the images of reality in terms of which masses of people reacted to public policy and to human beings in other parts of the world. Newspaper and radio reporters and commentators sought ways to help their audiences to make intelligible structures out of these fragments while keeping within their responsibility to report the facts.

As purveyors of information, writers and artists had to find ways to express both the magnitude of experiences and their alive, human significance. When they reported such events as the carrying of the mail across a country, the destruction of a city or the struggles of a vast army in the African desert, they were dealing with both individual and national effort or tragedy. Documentary films could show individual workers as representative of all the jobs in the intricate organization for carrying the mail, and could convey the tempo and duration of movement at successive points on the long train journey. They could show marching columns and parades of tanks over the limitless desert contrasted with close-ups of anxious faces as men prepared for immediate battle and with people at home in an ordinary factory listening to the news of battle action. The documentary film of climbing Mt Everest (1953) took the audience through this experience by means of mathematical diagrams, long-view shots of ice-masses and close-ups of their structure and of footsteps chopped in ice, successive scenes of individual climbers struggling to put one foot after the other, conveying the sense of duration, size, danger and the limits of endurance, and by tracing the stages by which the leader first conquered his objective mentally and then, with the others, physically achieved his goal. Writers, too, succeeded in translating overwhelming events into human terms. John Hersey's account of the bombing of Hiroshima (1946) told by taking six survivors through the whole day of the bombing was a classic of such reporting. (Pl. 54a.)

The mass media also brought new forms of mass propaganda which had as far-reaching ramifications for the arts as for politics. Propaganda itself is as old as religion; its new features in the twentieth century were its scale, its widespread use and the techniques which it could employ. Since the aim of propaganda is to produce an attitude or action in line with a preconceived point of view, its central principle is the identification of the audience's desires with the propagandist's goal. New knowledge of psychology—of conditioning and motivation—enabled the propagandist to develop techniques for manipulating attitudes and feelings—by repetition, association playing on hidden fears, evoking acknowledged or unacknowledged aspirations. In the complexities of the modern world, individuals who were constantly exposed to generalizations which they could not check against their own direct experience were vulnerable to emotional manipulation by these means.

Propaganda always required artists to give it form. They often wrote the speeches which public leaders then delivered or articles carefully placed in leading magazines; their painting and photography made the posters, billboards and advertising pages; their songs, their theatre, radio and television productions filled the air; they knew the rituals of mass ceremonies. Whatever the medium or the outlet, the artists' task was to make compositions that had immediate emotional impact leading in the direction the propagandist intended. The compositions therefore always had some images that would appeal to the audience, slogans that pointed the desired meaning of the pictorial or other images and finally the imperative 'do this', with the implication that doing it would satisfy the dreams and aspirations now aroused. Governments, industries which depended on mass advertising to market their products, and public and private bodies which undertook campaigns to promote such causes as improved agricultural or health practices, all used these skills of the artists. (Pl. 54b.)

This was at once an opportunity and a danger to the artists. The demand for their skills and the pay that went with it enabled them to live by their talents in their chosen art and to be successful members of their society. Some of the outstanding artists and writers did such work, not only in totalitarian countries where they were major contributors to national efforts, but elsewhere. Picasso, for example, decorated a salesroom for the Italian typewriter manufacturer, Olivetti; Salvador Dali (1904–   ) designed store window displays in New York. Writers and artists of all sorts contributed to wartime propaganda during the second world war. Many of the art forms developed by the leading artists and writers were taken over by those who were wholly engaged in commercial and propagandist art, and became familiar to wider publics. But there was always the crucial question: how free were artists to carry out their essential task of interpreting the human condition? Their form was determined by the purposes of the propagandist and the medium and outlet to be used. The men controlling both acted with certain assumptions about people, that they were either self-respecting individuals capable of making choices and having a right to know the nature of the choice, or a vast ignorant mass able to respond only to the simplest slogan hammered in by countless repetitions and as ready to respond to lies as to the truth.

The artists found symbols to fit these purposes and assumptions about people. If the purpose and assumptions were also their own, as for example in the documentary film *The River* (by Pare Lorentz and Virgil Thomson 1938), sponsored by the US government to promote flood control, there was freedom and the sincerity and insight which gave the work artistic value as interpretation. But often enough the artists worked insincerely, jaded by the product they were promoting or not believing in the goal of their propaganda, sometimes despising an audience that might respond to false appeals. Those who created the torrential output of vapid or dishonest advertising or propaganda appeals, dividing life into black and white categories and whipping up blind feeling, could only revolt under such conditions or become cynical.

In general the forms of conveying information through the mass media and of persuading people were not conceived of as 'art'. They were produced by men and women working at daily tasks, within large organizations, meeting deadlines, compressing their works into an allowed three or five or ten minutes of radio time, held down by the requirements of events and audiences. Much 'copy' was the merest routine. The purpose was, ordinarily, temporary, an observation of the moment, recorded in the ephemeral press or the still more ephemeral air waves. Yet these practical limitations were not unique to this age, for artists in all societies have worked within the framework of the conventions and pressures of their times. And when these efforts to convey information or attitudes were at their highest, they had the essential qualities of works of art, for they penetrated to realities behind the surface appearances, they sought and communicated deeply human meanings and deeply rooted human values, and they had form.

Most important for twentieth-century expression, those who used the mass media approached reality in contemporary terms, and they spoke not to the traditional, limited middle-class audiences or groups of connoisseurs but to broad masses of people. At mid-century these forms appeared to be the beginning of new modes of expression which opened vistas for the future at a time when self-centredness, rejection of society, uncertainty as to man's nature and preoccupation with form were bringing to a dead end many of the tendencies which had characterized western poetry, painting, sculpture, serious music, and even architecture in the previous fifty years.

NOTES TO CHAPTER XXXI

1. Doctors of Philological Sciences R. Samarin and A. Elistratova think that the text of Chapters XXXI and XXXII requires some preliminary notes:

Belles-lettres and art constitute an important element in the culture of the twentieth century. Being an original form of the reflection of reality they help to give a vision of the world. A rich variety of aesthetic feelings and emotions are generated from the wealth of man's practical experience and as this develops new forms of art such as the cinema for example evolve and display themselves, giving in their entirety a picture of objective reality. The failures, the anxieties and the sickness of our century, its desires and seekings, its discoveries, joys and triumphs, seen through the eyes of the contemporary artist and translated into imagery give a knowledge which cannot be replaced from any other source. But the works of literature and art do not only help us to know the world about us, they exert an influence on it by fashioning a social conscience and through this have an impact on reality. And it is here—in the ideological and aesthetic effect on society, and in the education of society—that the main social function of literature and art lies. People go to the artist to learn what man really is and what are his inner forces and potentialities. The propagandist effect of progressive ideas and moral standards makes art a progressive social force and contributes to its successful development just as, for example, very fine civic virtues such as patriotism, respect for the rights of other nations and deep humanism were inculcated into people by classical Russian literature, wherein lay one of the causes of its profound and universal influence. If we look at the literature and art of the twentieth century from this angle we must admit that there are two cultures in the world: one bourgeois, reactionary and to a considerable extent decadent, and the other democratic and progressive. 'Modern man'—his relation to the world, to society and to himself, the rhythm of his life, his aspirations and hopes—is in both cases the centre of interest but there are differences in the representation of this figure and his pressing problems. In the bourgeois world bourgeois culture rules whilst democratic culture finds itself in an oppressed state: under the conditions of a class society the thoughts and ideas of the ruling class are dominant also in the field of culture. On the other hand the oppressed classes, hostile to this social structure, create their own artistic culture which reflects their conditions of life and expresses their aims and interests. In a socialist society, a democratic culture prevails. In the West there are a number of theories which try to elucidate the essential problems of modern man. The major influence on literature and art comes (as is clearly indicated in Chapter XXXI) from the psychoanalytical school of Sigmund Freud and his followers, and from Existentialism.

In the twentieth century the influence of all the bourgeois schools taken together pales before that of Freud and, compared with it, represents a declining force. Freudian ideas have penetrated into the novel and drama and are now making strong inroads into the cinema. Freud translated into psychological problems all social conflicts; be exteriorized the unhealthy nature of man, declaring it to be the fundamental expression of his entire being. He consequently made what could be called a pessimistic apologia of existence. 'Alas, this is bad but it cannot be otherwise.' This creates a suitable attitude of psychological pessimism as a way of coming to terms with evil reality; and at the same time there is endless prating about a feeling for what is new and about intellectual intrepidity.

At the basis of Freud's theory lies the doctrine of egoism—the psychological emanation of all that is sensual, carnal, biological and erotic in man—which always remains an irrational embodiment of the anti-social principles of personality. Freud rejected the result of preceding historical development—that a higher type of man, a man of lofty principles, could come into existence—since in his view the process of cultural development does not eliminate the wild and primitive in man, it only represses it into the sphere of the subconscious. The rationally human is superimposed on the biological, predatory element, it does not replace it. It is only by constraint that the energy of the sexual urge can be directed towards work and people led to create the conditions for their own material well-being. Everything irrational, vicious and incomprehensible in social life has thus been placed within the individual, within the empire of the subconscious. Only by separating the sexual desires from the whole circle of human interests was Freud able to discern the flow of the impulses which originate in the innermost part of our being and clash with social impacts. But in reality the sexual desires do not possess the full autonomy which he attributed to them.

The realistic novel (L. Tolstoy, J. Galsworthy) showed that any form of egoism in whatever layer of the spirit it may lie, is the result of the social education of the individual, a projection of social relations into his subjective world. When life is viewed through the murky glass of utility and calculation, and a mood of utter tedium spreads abroad, there are far-reaching consequences in the realm of the carnal appetites; desires which are evidence of perversion are aroused. The further we penetrate into the twentieth century the more often we go through the entire gamut of psychological abnormalities, and the realistic novel convincingly illustrates the whole process by which passion is transformed into 'sex' (as a result of the alienation of sexuality from the high motives of spiritual life). The realistic artists regard these pheomena as the specific result of capitalist development. Thus the views of Freud are not a mere invention. They have given expression to that decadence of bourgeois society where love becomes impossible. This is why Freud delivered an attack on art asserting that it reflects only prettified reality, that poetry and real life are not compatible, that genuine pleasure is anti-aesthetic, and so on. To all the other ways devised for providing a basis of legitimacy for the bourgeois order Freudianism added the psychological motivation and therein lies the reason for its popularity.

The popularity of existentialism on the other hand is to be explained by the fact that it poses with unusual clarity the problem of human personality, displaying rather than concealing the crisis of bourgeois culture. No other trend shows so plainly that even the existence of personality is becoming impossible in bourgeois society which is strangling the culture it has generated. In this philosophy of despair and pessimism there is no room for faith in progress, in humanism or in the beneficial role of science and education; it connotes a disparagement of reason, of history and society; and going still further, it leaves no place even for society. The hope of existentialism is real personality, the lone individual opposed to all and to each. Whether the existentialist appears as a critic of the ideas of humanism and democracy (M. Heidegger) or of faith in science and enlightenment (K. Jaspers)—he always criticizes the concept of reason (and particularly the system of Hegel because it does not devote attention to the human personality and insists on the cult of reason). The dominance of this way of thinking—so the existentialists contend—has meant that man in the contemporary world has come to be felt as merely one thing among a number of other things. The actual idea of the depersonalization of man in capitalist society, of his transformation into a cog in an enormous mechanism is quite right but by no means new. As early as in the middle of the nineteenth century Karl Marx had brought this truth to light and had pointed out the inference—that a state of society which does not give full play for the development of personality must be changed. It is along this path that a third of mankind are now proceeding. Existentialism proposes another solution. Not the reconstruction of the social system which has man in thrall, but a realization that reason and science, instead of emancipating him, enslave him—this is the way out offered by the existentialists. 'Reason is the killer of human freedom, the killer of personality', is the dictum of Kierkegaard. In order to free himself man must be conscious of himself in another way. Only the realization of life as 'existence' opens to him a real way of being. He is not content to endure his freedom and responsibility, he endeavours to rid himself of them by flight into commonplace workaday life and seeks to become like others. There exists, however, a means of liberation from the bonds of this workaday life. It is the decision to look death in the face; to evaluate everything from the threshold of the final parting with life. 'Genuine existence' is in effect the structure of thought, the spiritual condition, the assessment of his own place in life that characterize a man 'in the face of death'. Genuine freedom can thus be attained only in the face of death and happiness lies in an awareness of the senselessness of existence. 'There exists no fate which could not be overcome by scorning it' (A. Camus in *The Myth of Sisyphus*). Although this philosophy no longer satisfies a number of existentialists (for example J.-P. Sartre) the idea that knowledge cannot be equated with the liberation of man has penetrated deeply into belles-lettres and art.

Against the background of the twentieth century, a century of wars, destruction and catastrophes (as it is frequently considered in the West) there is a sense of divorce from society and nature, an ever increasing isolation of the individual and a growth of subjectivity. Even the fantastically rapid advances in technology are often regarded as offering yet one more motivation for a pessimistic evaluation of the epoch as a whole; for is not this very technology threatening to turn against humanity? Given such views and the constant, obtrusive reiteration that man is unable to change anything, all that reflects the perdition of humanism, the twilight of reason and the subordination of man to impersonal and inhuman forces, or expresses a mood of scepticism and bitter irony, despair and perplexity, seems to be contemporary. The spirit of innovation in literature and art is regarded by the authors of Chapter XXXI as an aesthetic expression of irrationalism, and spiritual confusion. It is identified with the disintegration of human character, the break-up of language, the atrophy of basic literary genres, the effacement of the picture of reality, the dehumanization of art and the rupture with tradition. But of course there is another view of life—as seen through the eyes of a member of the socialist society—which is in flagrant contrast with it. In this, too, anxieties and complications have their place, but the outlook on the world and its future is joyous; man realizes himself to be a free and equal member of a society in which humanism has reached its zenith and the relation of man to man is that of friend, comrade and brother. The harmonious fusion of the personal and the social magnifies many times an individual's strength: he can and must do much to beautify the world, to improve people's lives and to bring about his own happiness. Literature and art are called on to give a true and historically concrete representation of reality in its progressive revolutionary development. The works of art and literature must provide knowledge, offer a source of joy and inspiration to millions of people; express their determination, feelings and thoughts, and serve as a means of ideological enrichment and moral enlightenment. To fulfil these complicated major tasks the links with the life of the nation must be reinforced in every possible way and there must be a deep penetration into the essence of the contemporary world, a true and highly artistic representation of the rich and many-sided practical aspects of life, an inspired and clear reproduction of something new and genuinely communist, and an unmasking of everything which thwarts the onward movement of society. These ideals serve as an orientation for the method of socialist realism, the main creative method of writers and artists in the socialist countries which, together with critical realism and neo-realism, also finds expression in the creative works of many progressive art workers in the capitalist countries. Its most important principles are its partisanship and strong links with the people, and a spirit of innovation which is connected with the applying and developing of all progressive traditions in world civilization. Interest in, and careful observance of, national form is inherent in the method of socialist realism and is a manifestation of its links with the people. Usually a socialist revolution with its wealth of ideas gives to art a clear, alert, inspired content, and has the significant effect of removing all obstacles that had previously existed between the artist and the nation.

The Stalin cult did a certain amount of harm to the development of the popular spirit in art; it deflected writers and artists from concentrating on the representation of ordinary Soviet people. The popular spirit manifests itself with particular clarity and appropriateness whenever professional art is closely linked with anonymous artistic creation and the mass development of amateur art. One of the most important professional, social and moral obligations of the leaders of culture in the USSR and other socialist countries is to show an interest in new talents and to seek out, develop and train them. Of course it is no mere chance that many significant artistic manifestations in the USSR have owed their origin to amateur art.

The popular character of art goes hand in hand with its partisanship (steady promotion of the communist ideals). Under present-day conditions in most countries it is impossible productively to serve the nation without taking an active share in the conversion of communist plans into living reality. Communist partisanship implies a repudiation of subjectivism in all its manifestations and of the deformation of reality. The 'theory of the absence of conflict' which existed for years under the cult of personality had a baneful influence on the creative work of a number of writers and artists who frankly devoted themselves to embellishing reality and representing in a saccharine, idealized way the complicated processes of the re-education of people.

Adherence to the party spirit demands from the writer or artist profound concern and emotion, and a sympathetic attitude to the individual human being: naturalism and formalism are incompatible with it.

A determination of the outlines of what is new in society and in man, which is required by partisanship and the popular spirit in art, are not only indivisible from the search for new forms and means of expression but directly stimulate them. But one can and must write in a new way not by destroying realism but by developing and renewing it. Finally there comes the problem of traditions, in the break with which many today in the West see the creative strength of modern art. What a profound delusion! Marxist–Leninist theorists have always emphasized the significance of inheritance in the development of culture: only by critical adaptation of all that is best in the legacy of humanity is it possible to achieve progress. The maintenance of genuine standards of beauty on which to build for the future is the most important requirement of the method of socialist realism. But 'conserving the inheritance does not mean restricting oneself to the inheritance' (V. I. Lenin: *Collected Works*, 4th Russ Ed., Vol. II, p. 494). Progressive leaders of culture are therefore confronted with the urgent problem of effecting a reappraisal of traditions. So literature and art must not kill the human features in man but on the contrary must cultivate in him whatever is fair and lovely and humanistic and human.

Professor Svoboda, taking the Marxist stand, makes a similar criticism of the text and considers that the arts are seen from the point of view of the so-called middle class, or to be precise from a section of the middle-class intelligentsia. There is a tendency to write about the 'modern' which caused some sort of sensation but not about the fundamental phenomena which are of a lasting value. As far as the social situation is concerned, it is also seen through an 'intellectual's eyes', from the point of view of those who show a tendency 'from naturalism toward abstraction' . . . Consequently it is clear that the author sees everything from a narrow, bourgeois point of view and evaluates everything accordingly. He prefers of course a non-political attitude in arts.

2. *The Author-Editors draw the attention of the reader to the fact that the chapters on Expression, which come at the end of the volume, are set in the context of the scientific and social revolutions of the period which have been discussed in the rest of the volume. As noted in the text, all the movements in the arts during these years expressed 'fundamental re-evaluations of the meaning of life in the face of accelerated, drastic, world-wide social change' (p. 1193), and reflected 'the social changes brought by industrialism and the intellectual changes engendered by the spread of science and technology' (p. 1196). For trends other than psychological exploration and abstraction which were only two among many tendencies, the reader is referred to sections dealing with 'Search into the lives of other men' (pp. 1216–18), and 'Search for roots' (p. 1218), to developments in Theatre, Photography and Architecture (pp. 1233–43). For the influence of Freud, see pp. 1215–16 and Chapter XVI, pp. 537–9, 546–9, Note 3, p. 567.*

to sections on literature and the arts in the USA, Latin America, and the USSR (pp. 1243–65), and to the discussion of 'The new mass media and the arts' (pp. 1265–74).

3. Commentators differ widely as to whether the major trends have been correctly identified and presented in this chapter. Professor Mario Praz fails to find a 'masterly synthesis', a 'clear outline', a tracing of phenomena to 'their origins', a 'logical trend' in the 'mass of facts'. Professor Jacques Presser, on the other hand, considers it a 'competent and trustworthy guide' to the cultural and artistic developments of the world, in which 'the main currents of modern times as manifested in men and in artists who represent them' are revealed and all the 'principal movements' of this half century are discussed.

With respect to the selection of material, Professor Praz thinks that the space allotted to the United States, Latin America and Russia is 'entirely out of proportion with the other countries' and results in neglect of many important European authors in favour of minor American writers. Professor O. Halecki states that the literature and art of the nations of east central Europe are neglected; Professor Edvard Bull suggests the addition of several Norwegian authors. Professor Presser recognizes that the selecting of persons to be included is 'precarious, especially in territories inaccessible to the authors' and that 'the reality will always be more nuanced than the best reproduction'.

Some commentators question the Author-Editors' evaluation of the main currents of aesthetic development which they discuss. Professor Presser asserts 'not without some scruple and reserve' that

'the text shows us the great currents of our century on the whole in their pessimistic aspects. The forces of disorganization, of decomposition, of dissolution are described here with more lucidity and more detail than the others, giving the reader the impression of a world balancing itself almost constantly on the brink of a precipice. The artists, in expressing the feeling of the life of this period, equally constantly mirror this precarious position—an imminent Last Judgment, expressed in words, sounds, painting, sculpture, architecture, in the theatre, film, and ballet by the most sensitive men of their generation. I wonder if this picture of our age, destined, if I am not mistaken, for all mankind, does not contain an element of too great subjectivity, is not, perhaps one must say, too "occidental".'

Professor E. N. Anderson adds:

In reading the chapters on Literature and the Arts one must bear in mind the authors' purpose of portraying the character of society as expressed in these media. Thus the chapters are not intended to be brief histories of literature and the arts; rather they are to relate literary and artistic expression to the socio-economic developments and currents of thought of society, and their method and approach are of such a kind as to enable the relationship to be clarified. Whether a 'logical trend' as demanded by Professor Mario Praz can be found depends upon whether one is looking for formal development and thematic analysis or whether one is concerned with the nature of the experience which writers and artists have portrayed. If there is one criticism to be made of the volume as a whole, it might be that the emphasis upon constructive action and achievements in the earlier chapters does not prepare the reader for 'the pessimistic aspects' mentioned by Professor Presser as revealed in the literature and the arts. The later chapters, especially the one about the western culture area, afford an essential balance to consideration of the total life of the period portrayed. This period was the most destructive in the history of the world; it was the most upsetting to mores, the most revolutionary in its conception of nature, man, society, and transcendental powers. The Author-Editors rightly emphasize the expression of these profound changes by the members of society most sensitive to spiritual and moral forces, writers and artists. Both those who were aesthetically creative and others as well were searching more or less consciously for identity, for a social order and for a place in that order, and the Author-Editors in their writing offer the results of this search by creative personalities.

It is another question whether the Author-Editors in discussing western culture gauge properly the relative importance of the several forces in it. They introduce them all, but they regard science and its technological expression as fundamental. They bring out the fact that many writers and artists, although aware of and influenced by currents of scientific thought and new technology, tended to reject this main stream of social development. They note that this tendency was by no means universal, that it was less strong in the United States and, of course, in the Soviet Union than in western Europe, and that it was not generally shared by architects, photographers and theatrical producers. They point to the potentials for new and positive developments in the arts offered by the new mass media and new forms of communication.

Although any discussion of degrees of influence quickly becomes subjective, or an exercise in semantics, it may be said with some confidence that aesthetic creators knew far less about science, except at a very popular level, and even about technology than, from personal experience, they did about the effects of power politics, war and revolution, social problems arising in an industrial urban society—crime, delinquency, poverty, pogroms, unemployment and the like, political disturbances, emotional insecurity, or of the profound change in the structure of society since the eighteenth century. These data are those about which writers and artists are concerned, and the question may be legitimately asked whether the aesthetes respond to and express in their work all aspects of experience. That Surrealism was no more fantastic than a Nazi concentration camp or an atomic explosion seems evident. As the Author-Editors point out, new experience evoked new ways and new themes for aesthetic expression, and, one might add, it stimulated some of the finest writers and artists to employ old themes and methods to express their novel experience. In these chapters the illogicality, the variety, the wealth of forms, subjects, methods and materials of aesthetic experience are richly employed in detail to reflect the life of the half century.

The synthesis of the Author-Editors is all the more remarkable because of the absence of monographic literature with the kind of approach they use. Wylie Sypher's excellent book, *Rococo to Cubism in Art and Literature* (New York, 1960), for example, does very little with the social aspects of the history of literature and art, and Pierre Francastel's volumes, *Peinture et société* (Lyon, 1951), and *Art et technique aux XIXᵉ et XXᵉ siècles* (Paris, 1956) are similarly strong in respect to intellectual and ideological analysis and weak respecting social analysis. Sigfried Giedion's volume, *Space, Time and Architecture* (Cambridge, Mass., 1956) has many revealing conceptions, but this work covers only architecture and town planning and is mainly concerned with the preceding century. There is no work which one can recommend as an expansion of the Author-Editors' attempt in these chapters to explore the relations between literature and the arts and society in this period.

4. Professor R. G. Villoslada remarks: To state that social and intellectual transformations have been (only or mainly) engendered by industrialism and scientific progress, will be of course challenged by those who admit in the march of history other more spiritual causes. But what cannot in any way be admitted is that Christian ideology is no longer, for western writers and artists, a satisfying vehicle of thought and expression.

5. Doctors of Philological Sciences R. Samarin and A. Elistratova assert that the development of realism in literature and art continued in the twentieth century in the form of critical realism (Anatole France, Romain Rolland, Roger Martin du Gard, George Bernard Shaw, Thomas Mann, Ernest Hemingway, B. Kellerman, Hans Fallada) and of neo-realism (Alberto Moravia, Vasco Pratolini, Renato Guttuso, the film directors Roberto Rossellini, Vittorio de Sica, Giuseppe de Santis, Federico Fellini, Lucchino Visconti and others).

During these years the method of socialist realism was also evolved (M. Gorky, V. Mayakovsky, M. Sholokhov, A. Tvardovski, M. A. Nexø, Pablo Neruda, Louis Aragon, Bertolt Brecht, Lu Hsün, Henri Barbusse, M. Sadoveanu, V. Mukhina, I. Shadr, S. Eisenstein, A. Dovzhenko, and others).

V. D. Dneprov: *Problemy realizma* ('Problems of realism') (Leningrad, 1960).

Problemy sotsialisticheskogo realizma ('Problems of Socialist realism') (Moscow, 1961).

Sotsialistichesky realizm v zarubezhnikh literaturakh ('Socialist realism in foreign literatures') (Moscow, 1960).

A. Ivashchenko: *Zametki o sovremennom realizme* ('Notes on contemporary realism') (Moscow, 1961).

T. V. Balashova *et al.*, *Sovetskaya literatura za rubezhom, 1917-1960* ('Soviet Literature Abroad, 1917-1960') (Moscow, 1962).

'Khudozhnik i sovremennost' ('The artist and contemporary problems') in *Akademiiya khudozhestv Ezhegodnik* Vol. I (Moscow, 1960), Vol. II (Moscow, 1961).

6. Candidate of arts V. M. Polevoy underlines that the text characterizes only one of the trends of art in the twentieth century, a trend which by no means encompasses all the processes taking place in the art of the time. At the turn of the nineteenth century the realistic trend entered a new stage of development in which it drew closer to social problems and political struggle. As a result, the realistic form acquired a new, pertinent and active content and became more expressive (for example, the work of K. Kollwitz in Germany, political satire in Russia during the revolution of 1905–7, etc.). Thus, the realistic and abstract trends represent two poles in the theory and practice of art in the twentieth century.

   Sovremennoe izobrazitelnoe iskusstvo kapitalisticheskikh stran ('Contemporary pictorial art in the capitalist countries') (Moscow, 1961).

   S. Mozhnyagin: *Abstraktsionism—razrushenie estetiki* ('Abstract art, the ruin of aesthetics') (Moscow, 1961).

7. *The Author-Editors call the reader's attention to the treatment of realism, pp.* 1196, 1202–6, 1214, 1247–8, 1260–61.

8. Doctors of Philological Sciences R. M. Samarin and A. A. Elistratrova assert that it was in the twentieth century that for the first time in history there came clearly to the fore the aesthetic questions of the wide masses who find satisfaction in those elements of democratic and socialist culture which have arisen both in the countries of Western Europe (the works of Romain Rolland, Henri Barbusse, M. A. Nexø, Sean O'Casey, Louis Aragon, Bertolt Brecht, M. Sadoveanu, V. Nezval, A. Seghers, Alberto Moravia, H. Bell, A. Tvardovski, A. Fadeyev, L. Leonov, K. Fedin and many others) and in America (works of Jack London, Sinclair Lewis, Theodore Dreiser, John Reed, Pablo Neruda, Jorje Amado and others).

   In artistic culture for example there are the Mexican monumental painting, the graphic schools of South America and Italian neo-realism which are characterized by forms possessing specific national traits; this art is firmly linked with popular national life and is, in one or another way, based on the tradition of the national artistic schools.

9. *See pp.* 1216–18 *and* 1265–74, *also Chapter XXVII for a discussion of the mass audience and the use of material drawn from broad elements of the population.*

10. Candidate of Philological Sciences T. K. Trifonova asserts that the artist is confronted with the dilemma of whether he is to be a 'free spirit', a 'solitary artist' or a 'journeyman', but there is also at third road which he can choose, that of service to the people; this is the potentiality which is realized in the creative works of a large number of contemporary writers and artists—Romain Rolland, M. Gorky, Rabindranath Tagore, P. Picasso, K. Stanislavsky, G. Ulanova and many others.

11. Candidate of Arts V. M. Polevoy notes that pp. 1206–8, as well as the preceding text, reduce the entire development of the fine arts to the evolution from Les Fauves to abstractionism. This is not true to the facts. In reality, the twentieth century witnessed the appearance of many realists (the Belgian Masereel who worked in France, Kolbe in Germany, Manzu and Guttuso in Italy, Aaltonen in Finland, Epstein and Kent in the USA, Despiau, Bourdelle and Marquet in France, etc.). Whole new schools sprang up, for which the realization of the social significance of art was the basis for the adoption of the realistic method. At times these schools were of a national or international character. Moreover, the history of art in the twentieth century furnishes many an example of artists rejecting their abstract-aesthetic stand in favour of realistic art related to life. This is the natural development of twentieth-century art, contrary to the evolution which, on the above-named pages of the text is presented as the only and all-encompassing trend.

12. *The reader's attention is called, by the Author–Editors, to the pages referred to in Note 7 supra and to the sections on Theatre, Photography, Cinema, and Reporting, pp.* 1233–39, 1265–74.

13. V. M. Polevoy stresses that in his opinion between the creations of Horta, Van de Velde, Berlage and Mackintosh, on the one hand, and those of Gropius, Mies van der Rohe and Le Corbusier on the other hand, despite their continuity, runs an important demarcation line. It is not only of a stylistic nature, but also involves the social problems of architecture, its functional character, a new approach to city planning, the wide utilization of reinforced concrete, the artistic comprehension of new constructions, etc. It is probably in place here

to mention the 'national romanticism' of architecture in the countries of Northern Europe, which was one way of overcoming the eclectic imitation of historical styles.

14. Candidate of Arts B. B. Granovsky supposes that the silence about the creative works of Enescu, Rachmaninoff and some other composers is connected, it would seem, with the authors' basic tendency to regard the history of music in the twentieth century as merely the history of modernism in music. This is the only reason which can explain the relatively detailed description they give of the works of A. Schoenberg, A. Webern and O. Messiaen. For reasons which we fail to understand they have passed over in silence the influence of Rimsky-Korsakov on the young Stravinsky. See Y. Keldysh: *Istoria russkoy muzyki* ('History of Russian music'), (Moscow and Leningrad, 1947–54), parts 1–3; *Istoria russkoy sovetskoy muzyki* ('History of Russian Soviet Music') in four vols.: Vol. I, 1917–34, (Moscow, 1956); Vol. II, 1935–41 (Moscow, 1959); *Enescu* (Bucharest, 1961).

15. Candidate of Philological Sciences T. K. Trifonova thinks that it is necessary to underline that of great importance for the history of civilization in the thirties of the twentieth century are the collective statements made by writers and other exponents of culture as part of the struggle against the threat of fascism and war. Examples of these are to be found in the activity of the international group of writers *Clarté*, in Gorky's address *S kem vy mastera kultury* ('Whom do you side with, masters of culture ?'), in the appeal launched at the initiative of the writers Henri Barbusse, Romain Rolland and Jean-Richard Bloch, in the series of anti-war and anti-fascist congresses (in 1932 in Amsterdam, in 1934 in Chicago, in 1935 in Paris, in 1937 in Valencia, in Madrid, in Paris) and in many other movements.

16. Doctor of Philological Sciences R. M. Samarin notes that whilst discussing writers who left the communist camp (they list the names of Arthur Koestler, André Gide, Louis Fischer amongst others) the authors prefer not to enumerate any of those who went over to the side of communism. Neither Dreiser nor Romain Rolland are mentioned here. But the fact that individual writers became disappointed and abandoned communism only proves that communism was never a conviction with them and that they had sworn fidelity to the ideas of communism only in words and could not grasp the difference between the existence of a new order of things and the distortions which occurred in Stalin's time. The practical experience of life shows that the disappointments and recantations are insignificant in comparison with the successes of the communist movement, the numerical growth of the communist parties, and their influence on the peoples as a whole.

17. Candidate of Philological Sciences T. K. Trifonova underlines that considerable attention is devoted to George Orwell, A. Koestler, F. Kafka and some other writers whilst at the same time the works of such outstanding personalities as Roger Martin du Gard, S. Maugham, Käthe Kollwitz and F. Masereel have not been described.

18. Candidate of Arts V. M. Polevoy notes that the strong ties between the artist and the life of society, and the task of creating works of art that would play an essential role in the spiritual life of society are advanced as the fundamental problems in the art of the socialist societies which emerged in the twentieth century.

19. Candidate of Arts V. M. Polevoy thinks that there are no grounds for including Pasternak in this section. Soviet poetry should be represented first and foremost by Mayakovsky. Mention should also be made of Alexander Blok. The reference in the text is not even to the poems of Pasternak (mention might have been made of the poem *Lieutenant Schmidt*, 1926) but only to his prose. This appears irrelevant in a chapter on poetry.

20. Candidate of Arts V. M. Polevoy underlines that on pages 1229–33 the evolution of the fine arts in the twentieth century is given a one-sided interpretation. Again, only one line of development is shown; phenomena in the history of art are regarded in isolation, unconnected with the important events in the history of countries and peoples. In distinction to the section on the theatre, for example, no account is taken of the new phenomena in the art of Europe evoked by the socialist revolution in Russia.

In the twentieth century, under the conditions of aggravated social and political conflicts, art has reacted keenly to the upheavals of two world wars; it is transformed under the influence of revolutionary outbursts, establishes stronger and more direct ties with social movements. The evolution of forms and the changes in aesthetic views are an expression of this process, which changed the relations of art to life in their broadest aspect and gave birth to new forms of the fine arts, to their new functional trend, etc.

As a result of the 1917 Revolution in Russia a new art was born, which was closely linked with the needs of the popular masses. This led to the strengthening of realism as the method best suited to the social tasks of art, and also to the wide development of such mass forms of art as political posters, book illustrations, etc. A most important indication of the new contacts which were established after the revolution between art and the public was the sharp rise in the number of visitors, mostly workers and peasants, to art exhibitions. The art of Europe was affected by the influence of mural paintings, meant for the masses, which arose in Mexico, partly on the basis of the idea of the revolution. The 1920's saw both the process of isolation of a number of art trends within a range of aesthetic ideas divorced from life; and also the attempts of certain trends—e.g. expressionism —to find points of contact with life. The subjective revolt against the repugnant aspects of life, so characteristic of expressionism, acquired a definite anti-militaristic shape in postwar Germany. The affirmation of humanism, the protest against war and fascism were traceable in the creative work of many artists, and formed the social and political basis of the poignant and intense aesthetic experience of many outstanding artists. One of the most striking examples of this is Picasso's *Guernica*, inspired by protest against the fascists' barbarous bombing of that Spanish city.

The second world war and the Allied victory over fascism freed the art of Germany and Italy. The socialist transformations in the countries of Eastern Europe led to the development of an art whose form and content are determined by its interrelations with the life and requirements of the popular masses. Side by side with the spread of abstract art, and to a considerable degree counterbalancing it, we witness the development of trends based on the affirmation of the value of life, the people, the ordinary man with his thoughts and feelings. The aesthetic value of these categories is expressed by realistic means, making them accessible to the millions. Among these trends, completely untainted by hermetism, mention must be made of neo-realism in Italy and France. Many artists of these trends made the transition to realism from expressionism (Renato Guttuso in Italy), from abstractionism (Cremer in Germany, the creator of the memorial to the Nazi victims in Buchenwald, with its profound plastic and emotional appeal).

21. *The reader is referred by the Author-Editors to pp. 1257–65 for a discussion of Soviet art and literature.*

22. Candidate of Arts V. M. Polevoy considers it necessary to point out that the radical changes in architecture in the twentieth century, brought about by the evolution of styles, the introduction of new materials and designs and their aesthetic comprehension are also connected with major changes in city planning. Among the novel aspects one can mention the construction of satellite towns to solve the problem of urban overpopulation, the zonal development of cities, the construction of neighbourhood units according to a general plan, the creation of building ensembles related to the natural environment, the reconstruction of cities to solve traffic and other problems, etc.

At mid-century the architectural appearance of Europe was greatly changed as a result of the widespread reconstruction of cities and towns destroyed during the war. The crying need for housing led to the development of industrial methods of construction, which in turn affected architectural solutions.

Architecture and building in the socialist countries opened new paths in town planning. The absence of private land ownership, the planned nature of the economy made it possible to solve on a large scale the problems of urban reconstruction, the building of new cities, the development of industrial and public buildings and of housing construction in accordance with the needs of society as a whole.

23. Candidate of Arts V. M. Polevoy notes that another form of the fine arts which rose to prominence in the countries of Latin America with world-wide repercussions was work in black-and-white. In its ideas and imagery it is closely related to mural painting, but it is generally more expressive and dramatic and is practically uninvolved with the renascence of the motifs of pre-Spanish culture. The *Taller de Gráfica Popular* in Mexico (founded in 1937) is the outstanding centre of this form.

24. Candidate of arts V. M. Polevoy points out that the description of the work of Tatlin and other artists on this page should not be separated from the data on the development of the poster and monumental sculpture (p. 1259). A wrong impression is created that first there was a period characterized by the works of Tatlin and Chagall, and then in the 1920's Mayakovsky and a number of other artists began to create posters and sculptors to make monuments. Actually, this occurred at the same time (monuments began to be erected in 1918). These were two simultaneous trends, of which the latter proved promising and enduring.

25. Doctor of Philological Sciences R. M. Samarin notes that the authors of this chapter are very much inclined to stress the break with tradition rather than the succession in the development of culture. 'I therefore should like to observe that in the art of socialist realism based on principles of strong links with the people and the party bold innovation in the artistic representation of life goes hand in hand with the use and development of all progressive traditions of world culture.' See also T. Trifonova: 'A Note on Socialist Realism', *Journal of World History*, VII, 1 (1962), p. 108.

26. Candidate of Arts V. M. Polevoy adds that similar phenomena also characterized other forms of art: music, the theatre, the fine arts. As in literature, new creative forms arose among the many peoples of the USSR: for example, opera, painting and sculpture in Soviet Central Asia, etc.

27. Candidate of Philological Sciences T. K. Trifonova in her papers asserts that the right understanding of innovation is of immense importance for socialist realism. A genuine spirit of innovation is connected in the first place with the ideological content and social tasks of literature and art and with the capacity of the writer and artist to understand and perceive the new in life. What is new in life and in activity determines the new content and the new social role of Soviet literature and art and creates continually new forms for the expression of a new content.

28. Candidate of Arts V. M. Polevoy asserts that from mid-1950's architecture was dominated by the striving to achieve aesthetic comprehension of mass industrial construction, as well as new materials and designs, free from decorative elements.

29. Candidate of Arts V. M. Polevoy says that mention should also be made of the international film festivals in Karlovy Vary and Moscow, where special prizes are awarded to films which promote ideas of humanism, friendship among the nations, the struggle for peace.

CHAPTER XXXII

DEVELOPMENTS IN EASTERN
LITERATURES AND ARTS

I. NATURE OF THE WESTERN CULTURAL IMPACT
AND TYPES OF REACTION

1. *General features*

THE development of literature and the arts in the East during the twentieth century was intimately bound up with the awakening of national self-awareness and with the reaction to cultural contact with the West. Few forms of expression were untouched either by direct influence from the West, or by the stimulus to the development of indigenous arts in response to such contact. By mid-century a similar process of interaction was beginning to be evident in Africa, chiefly in the visual arts, music and dance since traditional African expression was oral and visual rather than written. (Pl. 41.)

The tendencies to assimilate new cultural influences and at the same time to revive old cultural traditions in a period of national awakening both reinforced and competed with each other. Where traditional forms had great vitality, either because they were an integral part of the life of the community, as for example, Balinese dancing, or because they were in the hands of a responsible professional group, as were the No, Bugaku and Kabuki drama of Japan and the Chinese opera, they remained relatively unaffected by western contacts. Where the idiom or spirit of a classical form was incompatible with that of the West, as for example in much eastern music, there was no western impact, or else one form was substituted for the other form, or both continued in competitive co-existence. Where there was a measure of compatibility, as in the literary expression of many countries, notably China, or in the consonance between traditional Japanese architecture, painting and flower arrangement and western functional architecture, abstract painting and surrealist 'collages', a process of synthesis took place in which western forms were used as vehicles for expressing an eastern spirit, or traditional forms became vehicles for ideas and attitudes derived from contact with the West.

Where a form of expression was wholly absent, either because it had never been a part of the cultural tradition of the country or because it had disappeared, western forms were adopted and adapted to provide means for the expression of new attitudes and experiences. This was the case with most forms of prose, and the realistic drama of contemporary life. The coming of the cinema and radio added new and powerful media for the introduction of new forms and for the perpetuation or revival of some traditional modes of expression, such as music and the dance. These media, together with the spread of education, enlarged the audiences and altered their character.

Although the response to European cultural contact differed widely according to the indigenous culture, to the nature of the contact and to the period of maximum interaction, certain broad lines of development appeared in most areas.

The initial effect of the western impact was to stimulate enthusiasm among the western-educated *élite* for the literature and arts of the West. Western works were translated into local languages. Writers and artists began to follow western modes, using their native idioms. In a second phase, they re-emphasized their own classic forms. As the process continued, these countries developed and refined their national literature and arts, making such blend of western and traditional forms and themes as would reflect their emerging life and the role of their artists and writers in it.

The process began in different countries at different times, according to the time and form of western impact. The types of western literature and art which had most direct influence in different areas depended upon their source —British, French, German, Russian—and the time of their penetration. The manner of adaptation was affected by the local idiom and traditional forms and by the social development which accompanied the literary and artistic revival. The quality of the result ranged from weak and imitative stories, novels, poems or paintings to works of power and skill which reflected the genius of their authors and maturity of literary or artistic development. But everywhere interaction produced new vigour, and its effects were not limited to the western-educated elements who provided the initial channel. In fact, the writers and artists who made the most creative use of new concepts and forms were often, and increasingly, those who remained within their national cultural milieu rather than those whose education made them bi-cultural.

On first consideration, it would seem improbable that western expression could exert general influences upon eastern cultures in view of the changes in western literature and art during the period. Many of the problems which most concerned western writers and artists were quite irrelevant to the East, such as the disorders of a once-dominant European society, the impossibility of continuing to think in terms of a man-centred universe—a concept which the East had never entertained—or the liberation from a kind of representationalism in art which had not characterized the arts of the East. Nevertheless, there were enough broad differences between the western and eastern forms of expression for the general impact of the former to produce similar tendencies throughout the very different societies of the East.

While the impact of the West introduced new forms and content and broke the hold of traditional literary and artistic conventions, it simultaneously spurred interest in these same traditions, both by stimulating an awakened national consciousness and by arousing a reaction against the pretensions of the West.

The scorn with which some colonial administrators, missionaries and teachers viewed many aspects of traditional cultures, asserting the superiority of all things western, brought an initial turning away from the forms of local cultural expression by some of the western-educated. At the same time the western scholars who studied and translated the ancient classics, penetrated forgotten areas of history and brought to world attention the archaeological record of Angkor Vat, Mohenjo-daro, the Ajanta caves or the ancient cities of the Tigris–Euphrates valley, aroused a sense of history among the peoples of these areas and brought their cultural traditions alive. Many who had been indifferent or negative toward their cultural heritage reacted vigorously against the western sense of superiority and became determined to reassert traditional values.

2. *Interaction in specific areas*

The circumstances surrounding the western cultural impact in different countries, as well as the distinctive characteristics of the traditional forms of expression, determined the course taken in each country by the process of interaction during these years.

In the Indian subcontinent the process was long, gradual and complex. Literatures of high quality existed in a number of the Indian languages when English education, in the middle of the nineteenth century, brought the educated element in contact with English literature and the European classics in English translation. Western influence aroused its first strong response in Bengal, where in the late nineteenth century, Michael Madhusudan Dutta (1824–73) introduced the sonnet and the European epic forms and B. C. Chatterji (1838–94) introduced the novel. There the poet Rabindranath Tagore achieved a unique integration of western and Indian literary and musical qualities and his nephew, Abanindranath Tagore (1871–1951) made a similar synthesis in painting. In time, other regions experienced comparable developments.

The developments in all fields were closely linked with the political struggle and reflected its successive phases—first enthusiasm for things western; then romantic reconstruction of India's past; then, as the movement for self-rule gained momentum from 1919 to 1936, vigorous realism, optimism and zeal for reform together with the revival of classical arts; a growing spirit of social criticism and the rise of so-called 'progressive' writing from 1936 on; and, after independence, strong public support for the traditional arts, a wide range of individual expression, and the growing influence of popular forms which were developed and spread through the cinema.

In China the impact of western arts and letters came more suddenly, as a part of revolutionary movements. Traditional literary and artistic forms persisted into the early twentieth century scarcely touched by movements elsewhere, although more than fifty European novels were translated into Chinese. Following the political revolution of 1911–12, a literary revolution led by the scholars Chen Tu-hsiu (1879–1942) and Hu Shih (1891–1962), and the writer Lu Hsün (1881–1936), introduced western literary forms and the use of the vernacular, though Chinese painting continued to retain its traditional form.[1]

The leaders of the literary revolution insisted that there must be a clear and complete choice between old Chinese and new western ways, and that the Chinese literary language was completely dead and must be replaced by a comprehensible language based on common speech. Realistic novels and plays of social criticism focused attention on social ills. When the communist régime came to power in 1949, 'socialist realism' in literature and drama produced stories and plays which conveyed the optimism and vigour of social reconstruction and, in painting, provided a new idiom for propagandist art. At the same time traditional Chinese opera was revived and used as a vehicle for new ideas, while interest in folk music and art was stimulated.

Japan's Meiji restoration and self-conscious westernization set in motion two distinct tendencies in the arts, one to study and imitate western modes, the other to purify and reassert traditional forms, notably the formal literary language. In the arts, as in much of Japanese life, the two tendencies remained side by side, the western strong in the public sector and the traditionally Japanese dominant in the private sector of life. Changing political emphases had little reflection in the arts. Choice of western or traditional modes and efforts to integrate them on one basis or another remained largely an individual matter. Completely western types of expression existed parallel to completely traditional plays, music, painting, and flower arrangement, and readers enjoyed independently both western literature and Japanese classics. After the defeat and occupation following the second world war, pressure to find a valid integration and a modern, native idiom became extremely strong and led young writers to explore the popular ethos for a base to which to relate whatever they might draw from the classic Japanese tradition and the varied forms from the West.

Elsewhere in Asia a small western-educated group, by mid-century, had barely begun to reflect western influences in their native idioms. In Indonesia after 1925 an extensive programme of translation began to make western literature available in the local languages, and a small group of writers, using both Dutch and the Malayan which was being consciously developed as a national language, tried out western literary forms, especially the novel of social comment and psychological insight, to explore the problems of the day. Meantime, the rich gamelan music and dramatic dance of Bali and Java retained their vitality and integrity, to be discovered by the West and admired as one of the most highly developed stage cultures in the world, and Balinese painting and sculpture experienced a renaissance in the 1930s.[2]

Western-educated Thais acquired tastes in western literature and the arts, and provided appreciative audiences for western music; a few experimented with these western forms. Some of the most popular of the modern Thai novels revealed the Europeanized to themselves and confronted them with their problem of cultural integration. At the same time traditional literary forms such as short topical verses were put to current use, and the traditional arts of the dance, music and floral creations flourished and received strong official support. In the states which composed French Indo-China a few French-educated writers conveyed a sense of their ancient land in exquisite French verse and a few artists used essentially western forms of visual expression while others refined the traditional modes.

In the Arab countries the impact of western literature and arts resulted neither in as great an assimilation of western forms as in Asian countries, nor so strong a stimulus to the revival of traditional expression. Especially in Egypt, the principal centre of Arab cultural developments during these years, the educated element became familiar with western literature, music and painting, and much western literature, including some modern works, was translated into Arabic. Modern journalism and the prose essay were developed as vehicles for expression, but the western novel, short story and social drama, which were important vehicles of modern expression elsewhere, had not by mid-century overcome the handicap of the literary language, while the traditional Muslim prohibition on representing the human form tended to condition the development of pictorial art.

By the time that western influences became strong in Iran, the rich tradition of Persian literature and exquisite miniature art had lost its vitality, though there were always individual writers of distinction. In the early twentieth century much of modern Persian writing, including a number of magazines, was published outside the country, in Istanbul, London, Calcutta and Berlin. From the time of the revolution of 1905–8 the national movement gave a new impetus to literary expression. Actual forms were often shaped by journalists, for the press provided an important outlet for Persian writers and helped to make the written language simpler, more flexible and closer to popular speech. Historical novels in the western style, drawing on Persian materials, began to be attempted after the first world war and some poets turned to contemporary and public themes as well as to the lyric subjects and forms which were traditional.

One of the results of the changed position of Turkey in the nineteenth century was an effort to develop a national Turkish literature, freed of customary Persian forms ill-suited to the Turkish language, and in tune with Turkey's desire for westernization. The movement became intensified with the nationalism of the Young Turks in the early twentieth century. Drawing both on western sources, mainly French, and on classical Turkish forms and historical themes, writers sought to develop genuinely Turkish modes. Two of the most influential poets in the first quarter of the century, Yahya Kemal Beyatli (1886–1958) and Ahmet Hasim (1885–1933), found their main inspiration respectively in classical Turkish sources and in French Impressionism.

The decisive turning point in Turkish literary development, however, came at the time of the Ataturk revolution of 1923, when the Arabic alphabet was discarded in favour of the Roman script in the conviction that the language of common usage could thus find freer and more accurate expression. The reform turned Turkish students away from Arabic and Persian sources and augmented to a flood the translation of western classics of all sorts—French, English, Russian, German, Italian, Latin, Greek—making the major literary traditions of the West a part of the Turkish heritage. Under this stimulus, Turkish writers refined the vernacular language for poetic purposes and experimented with various verse forms. Novelists such as Halide Edib Adivar and Resat Nuri Güntekin (1892–1956) developed the novel along realistic, social and psychological lines, and many writers, such as Refik Halit Karay (1888–) became adept at using the short story to convey the rich variety of the Turkish country and people.[3]

Until the middle years of the twentieth century, literary and artistic interaction among the countries of the East was less pronounced than with those of the West. However, there was some cultural interaction between China and Japan, and the painting of these countries had a certain influence on the styles of modern painting in India. Only after independence were there the beginnings of literary exchanges among Asian countries and conferences of Asian writers, chiefly under 'progressive' auspices, as at Delhi in 1956 and Tashkent in 1958. There was some effort to bring modern Indian and Chinese literary and artistic circles into communication with each other. Indian writers, both classic and modern, were translated into Chinese. Indians had access to the Chinese classics in English translation; some current Chinese writing was published in English and became available to Indian readers. Visits of dance troupes between Asian countries and the distribution of films were other points of exchange.[4]

II. INTRODUCTION OF NEW LITERARY FORMS

The first aspects of western expression to be absorbed were literary forms—the novel, short story, Ibsen-style drama, essay, lyric poetry, such verse forms as the sonnet. New content came later, once the forms had become naturalized. Where traditional forms required strict adherence to elaborate and complex canons of expression, the western forms released the writer from traditional rhetoric, permitted direct expression and opened the way to new types of writing.

The traditional forms of eastern literature, drama and dance were predominantly poetical. The main body of literature used classical literary languages distinct from the language of speech. Its themes were traditional, telling stories of the gods or heroes, singing praises or invoking God or the gods, or expressing love in the conventionally established manner. Drama was stylized according to the canons of the No or Kabuki plays of Japan, the classical opera of China or the religious dance-drama of India and Bali.

Alongside these dominant forms of expression, however, most countries also had a secular literature which might use less stylized language or forms.

India had a non-religious dramatic tradition; vernacular literatures, using traditional forms and dealing with the familiar epic subjects, had developed in several of the major Indian languages. In these literatures the rigid formalism of classical Sanskrit had never wholly prevailed and their great masterpieces had long discarded many of the canons of Sanskrit poetry. Japan's non-classical literature took the form of semi-popular prose tales, written in the more informal language, and read primarily by women and the merchant class rather than by the samurai and literati. The Meiji restoration, however, had required the use of formal language and strengthened the more classical literary tradition. Prose fiction had been created as a genre in China some centuries before, so that the western novel was a less alien form there than elsewhere. Persian and Arabic literatures were largely devoted to religious and love poetry and some prose tales but did not include the various forms of drama that were central parts of the literatures of other Asian countries. Turkey had no strong literary tradition, for Persian influences predominated until the eighteenth century and by the middle of the nineteenth century efforts to follow French literary forms had counteracted tendencies toward a distinctive Turkish style.

Some form of folk expression was alive in most areas, as in the puppet plays of Indonesia or Turkey or the village dancing and extensive folklore in India, but it had little relation with the more formal literature and the other arts.

The western literary forms most easily and widely adopted were various types of prose, for there was usually less conflict of style in prose than in poetry or else the western prose forms were wholly new and distinct. They were suitable vehicles for realistic expression and social analysis and as such were appropriate to express the process of social change.

The short story and the novel were perhaps the most generally accepted. For the short story, the influences of de Maupassant and Chekhov were paramount. In China and Japan, India and the Arab countries, story magazines were established and flourished. Novels followed several styles. They appeared in large numbers in Japan; they became a popular mode of expression in China after the New Tide movement of 1917 and, with renewed vigour, after the establishment of the communist régime; Indian writers developed distinct styles for novel writing in the several Indian languages. After the first world war Arab writers, mainly located in Egypt though often originating in other Arab areas such as Syria and Lebanon, began to add original novels to the translations of western works which they had been introducing to Arabic readers for a generation. Turkish novels and short stories, drawing their material mainly from the life of the people, were numerous and varied; a bibliography of Turkish women writers in 1955 listed no less than seventy-eight women who had published novels since 1923. Although the numbers of original novels in Indonesian, Siamese, Persian and other non-western languages varied and the quality was uneven, the novel was accepted virtually everywhere as a modern literary form.

In all these areas writers also experimented with the modern drama, chiefly along the lines of the Ibsen-type modern social problem play. The one-act play, used as a vehicle for social commentary, was also popular. In China, Japan and India modern drama took its place alongside the quite different traditional dramatic forms which continued to be played in their classical manner and to retain their great popularity. Western plays in translation or western-style plays by local authors were produced under separate auspices and with an altogether different tone and intent. Some few attempts were made to recombine traditional elements into something closer to the western dramatic form, or to use old forms to present new content, notably in India with some adaptation of the dance-drama and the introduction of some political commentary into traditionally religious plays. Script writing for movies, a completely modern form, drew some of the outstanding writers in countries where extensive movie industries developed, notably Japan, India and communist China.

In countries which lacked the play-going traditions of China, Japan or India, western-style plays were not so generally written or produced. Among the Arabic-speaking countries modern drama was developed only in Egypt, where in the second quarter of the century it took the form of poetic plays, popular comedies and a few serious prose works. In Indonesia, where traditional puppet plays and dancing remained the great sources of popular entertainment, few attempts were made to compose plays in the western form, but new ideas were conveyed through the old medium. In Iran popular semi-religious dramas, traditional or spontaneous, continued to be performed during the month of Muharram, but formal dramatic writing was used primarily for political pamphleteering, in the form of satirical comedies to be read rather than played. Although some Turkish novelists and poets also wrote plays, the dramatic form achieved little popularity in that country during these years.

The growth of journalism was a major factor in changing literary style, for in many countries it was the principle vehicle for modernized prose. It required flexible expression in place of the old, formal, puristic writing limited by the kind of vocabulary permitted and the conventions surrounding its use. Literary journals had already appeared and were beginning to assume importance in India in the nineteenth century. In the twentieth century they proliferated in vernacular languages throughout the country. In the Arabic-speaking countries the press was one of the major vehicles for the modern literary movement, and the prose essay the principal form of modern literary expression. The movement for the nascent modern culture and expression of Indonesia centred in the 1930s in a review, *Pudjangga Baru* ('The New Writer', 1933 ff.), which published essays on such subjects as the significance of traditional literature for the modern generation, the conflict between traditional gamelan music and modern popular music influenced by the West, the aims of education, art for art's sake versus art with a social purpose, and the ever recurring question of the antagonism between East and West. The prose essay lent itself especially to social commentary and analysis of the problems which concerned the writers in these rapidly changing societies.

Although in all eastern countries poetry was the traditional form of most literary expression, and poetic forms were firmly established and very distinct, the western impact had a substantial effect on poetry also. Just as the western poets abandoned established forms in order to experiment with language, cadence and rhythm, eastern poets freed themselves from the far more rigid verse forms which their literary canons required, and in addition broadened the range of poetical themes beyond the prescribed subjects. For some, notably the Chinese after 1917, experimentation meant a sharp break with the past; for others, notably poets writing in the Indian languages, Arabic and Persian, traditional forms were modified through experimentation rather than being discarded.

Everywhere, the western impact, together with the spread of education and the growth of literacy, raised the problem of what language to use. The trend toward realistic writing about the contemporary scene meant a tendency, if not a necessity, to use the language of speech. India enjoyed the advantage of possessing vernacular languages which had already been used as literary vehicles and were well adapted to realistic subject matter. As Japanese writers in the late nineteenth century began to follow western models, they used the less formal language of speech rather than the prevailing literary language (e.g. Futabei Shimei, *The Drifting Cloud*, 1887–89).

In China, by contrast, it was only after the literary revolution of 1917 that a language appropriate to the western style of realism, the spoken vernacular *pai hwa*, was accepted as a literary medium; novels and plays using the vernacular in earlier periods had not been regarded as literature. This movement for the use of the vernacular was intensified with the measures taken by the communist régime to facilitate the use of a popular Chinese idiom and to develop a simplified script. Arab writers, for their part, found themselves hampered in attempting to write realistic novels or stories by the difference between the classical, literary Arabic and the common speech. All movements toward the use of the spoken languages for literary purposes up to the middle of the twentieth century proved abortive, and in all Arab countries the literary language continued to be used for press and radio, schools and mosques and all literary expression.

Whatever the obstacles, however, the same factors which led western writers to experiment with language and sentence structure in order to convey their meaning pushed writers in the East toward a freer use of language and toward efforts to bring the written work closer to the terms of everyday speech.

Many of the western-influenced writers were well grounded in their own classic literature and continued to use its forms while also following western lines. The Indian Malayalam poet, Vallathol (1879–1958), for example, started in the early twentieth century as a writer in the classic style. Under western influence he adopted a realistic approach, and then became one of the 'progressive' writers. Yet at the same time he translated one of the Sanskrit classics, the *Rigveda*, into traditional-style Malayalam. One of the leaders of the Chinese literary revolution of 1917, Hu Shih, was a thorough scholar of the Chinese classics and even the Chinese communist leader, Mao Tse-tung, did not feel it necessary for the Chinese to be limited to the forms of 'socialist realism' but set an example to his followers by writing and publishing poems in the classic Chinese style.

As writers drew on their native heritage for themes and forms of expression, they found two distinct sources, the literary tradition preserved by an educated *élite*, and a folk tradition more or less alive among the people. Between the two, the gulf was often wide.

Various factors tended to enhance the folk aspect. The new realism focused attention on the common people and their forms of expression. Western interest in folk cultures as repositories of common human experience, myths and symbols further tended to elevate folk art. The folk tradition, couched in the idiom of the people rather than a literary language, was often more in line with the modern temper and with what modern writers were trying to express than was the classical. This was most vividly illustrated in communist China, where the traditional, popular picture-broadsides furnished a more usable base for the development of pictorial and written realism and material with didactic and propaganda intent than the traditional artistic and literary media. The combined effect of westernization, the revival of interest in local culture and practical objectives thus tended to narrow the gap between literary and folk expression.

III. MODIFICATION OF LITERARY CONTENT

New content followed the adoption of new forms. Western writing was realistic; it dealt with contemporary society and with live people, living their ordinary daily lives; it was concerned with the personality of many different individuals. It was in sharp contrast to the content of classical eastern writing which treated mythological or historical figures and bygone or imaginary ages in a symbolic, allegorical or stylized manner and presented characters as types, defined by their position in society or in the hierarchy of the gods. It was not so markedly different, however, from the secular or popular writing.

Since western literature differed so markedly from the predominant types of literature in the East, its impact upon content as well as form carried eastern writing in a clearly defined direction. However great the differences among the novels of Scott, Goethe, Dickens, Dostoevsky, Zola, Aldous Huxley, Sartre or Hemingway, the short stories of de Maupassant, Chekhov, Gorky or Thomas Mann, and the plays of Ibsen and George Bernard Shaw, their influence was similar. It strengthened whatever secular literary trends were already present and it stimulated the writers of China and Japan, of India,

Indonesia, Egypt, Lebanon or Turkey to look at the social world around them and to try to depict and analyse its people and its institutions.[5]

Since much of the literature of the West was associated with social change, it offered appropriate models to writers whose own societies were marked by even greater extremes of wealth and poverty and were experiencing even more drastic social upheavals.

The aspects of western literature which appealed in each area and at each period varied with changing conditions. The relation of successive influences to the stages of the political struggle in India has already been noted. Scott and Dumas rather than Dickens or Thackeray provided models for the first of the western-style Indian novels in the latter part of the nineteenth century, for the social urge of the time was to recreate history. Indian nationalism was drawing on the rediscovery of India's past; the historical romanticism of Scott was therefore a welcome model to follow in casting this nationalist historical urge into literary form. The Bengal novelist, Bankim Chandra Chatterji, provided the model for the heroic Indian novel. Modern Indian drama of this period, too, as initiated by the Bengal playwright D. L. Roy (1864–1913), used Indian historical characters.

At a second stage, in a period of self-criticism, Indian writers found models in the western novels and plays of social criticism. Along these lines, Tagore's novels in Bengali revealed the weaknesses of Indian society, and S. C. Chatterji (1876–1938) exposed social evils of Indian life with insight and ruthlessness. Prem Chand (1881–1936), writing in Urdu and Hindi, dealt with village life and the problems of rural India. Similar tendencies appeared among writers in other Indian languages. For Indians in this mood writers such as Dostoevsky had immense appeal. The social drama in the manner of Ibsen and Shaw was used by the leading writers in Marathi (Mama Warerkar), Kannada (T. K. Kailasam, R. V. Jagirdar), Malayalam (C. V. Raman Pillai), Tamil (P. Sambandha Mudaliar) and other languages to examine and expose mercilessly various aspects of political life, formal religion and all manner of social evils.

Then, with the rapid social changes that preceded and followed independence, and with the influence of communist writers reinforcing the realism of the literature of the non-communist West, many Indian writers adopted a 'progressive' approach, writing social comment and criticism in the manner which they regarded as 'socialist realism'. Dramas, short stories and one-act plays were used as vehicles for mass propaganda to depict the breakdown of feudal society, the exploitation of the workers, the misery of landless peasants and the conflict between old and new.

But though these successive influences were followed by leading writers they never produced a uniform trend, for Indian writers at all times drew their inspiration from a wide range of sources, ancient and modern, local and foreign and produced a variety of styles which reflected the complexity of Indian life

China, on the other hand, where the main impact of western literary influence came after the literary revolution of 1917, went through no period of western-influenced historical romanticism, but plunged directly into self-criticism. Lu Hsün's *Diary of a Madman*, which was published in 1918 in the *New Youth Magazine*, introduced the Chinese reading public to vernacular prose, sharp satire and a bitter attack on Chinese social life, and his *True Story of Ah Q* (1923) pilloried the passivity and gloom in the character of ordinary Chinese people resulting from centuries of feudalism, the callousness to suffering and the misery brought by the self-deception of 'saving face'. Virtually all the writers after the literary revolution wrote bitingly of the misery, oppression, chaos and disorder of Chinese society. Yeh Shao-chun (1893–   ), a follower of Dostoevsky, drew his characters from the oppressed and downtrodden; Mao Tun (1896–   ), in his novel *Midnight* (1923) and trilogy *Disillusion, Agitation,* and *Pursuit* (written in 1927–28, later issued as *Eclipse*) portrayed the mental processes of different classes of people in the face of national disorder, economic collapse, the evils of landlordism and foreign aggression; the dramatists Tsao Yu (1905–   ) and Tien Han (1899–   ) dealt with the breakdown of the family system and the effects of the semi-feudal social structure and rising capitalism and dramatized the misfortunes of the common folk as a result of the civil war.

Western literature was of less direct influence in China than in either India or Japan, and of less interest to Chinese writers. Nevertheless, Hu Shih's defence of Ibsenism ushered in the social drama, Dostoevsky provided the inspiration and model for novels dealing with the poor and oppressed, Lu Hsün found inspiration in the works of Gogol and Chekhov and most of the leading writers were also prolific translators; the leading modern poet, Kuo Mo-jo (1892–   ), translated works by such varied authors as Goethe, Tolstoy, Turgenev, Upton Sinclair, J. M. Synge, Shelley, Galsworthy, and the *Rubaiyat* of Omar Khayyam. Once the western influence had broken the traditional Chinese literary mould, writers turned less to western models than to Chinese examples and their own experimentation. The literary renaissance established as respectable the old Chinese novel, such as the fourteenth-century masterpiece, *All Men Are Brothers,* and therewith provided a realistic vernacular model which modern writers could follow.

The close association of Chinese writers with revolutionary movements and the continual political conflict, civil war and foreign intervention which racked Chinese society led them to form a succession of literary organizations which reflected their respective positions. A few remained outside the political currents, such as the essentially romantic Yu Ta-fu (1896–1945), who wrote of the personal confusion of individuals caught in the uncertainties of the changing pattern of marriage and family life, Pa Chin (1905–   ), who pictured the decay of the Confucian family, and Hu Shih, who continued to press for freedom of literary experimentation. But most writers turned increasingly to the left and became spokesmen for the communist cause.

UU*

With the coming to power of the communist régime in 1949, writers who had been part of the original literary revolution came to occupy positions of leadership in the new régime; the novelist Mao Tun became minister of culture, the poet Kuo Mo-jo, vice-premier of the Chinese People's Republic. The tone of the writing changed drastically, though the realism, irony, homely characters and social themes remained. Preoccupation with suffering, despair, chaos and decay was replaced by confident assertions of social progress. Such a writer as Lao Shê (1898–   ) moved from the realism of extreme poverty and despair in *The Horned Moon* (written in the 1930s) and *Rickshaw Boy* (1946) to his propaganda plays during the Japanese war when he headed the National Writers' Anti-Aggression Association; after the establishment of the communist régime he wrote a proletarian play, *The Dragon Whisker Drain* (1951) about the construction of Peking's new sewage system to beautify the capital and improve the living conditions of the workers.

Peasants' struggles against landlords, and their own transformations in learning to work in cadres and expand production in the agrarian revolution were described in novels such as Ting Ling's (1907–   ) *The Sun Shines Over the Sankan River* (1948) and Chou Li-po's *Hurricane* (1948–49), both of which received the Stalin prize in 1951. Chao Shu-li (1905–   ), a writer whose knowledge of peasants and capacity to write their language with realism, humour and zest made him an outstanding popularizer, showed in his *Rhymes of Li Yu-tsai* (1946) the new will among the peasants as they dealt with the landlords and with each other. The theme appeared in many short stories, new forms of traditional opera and new adaptations of folk songs. More and more efforts were made to bring writers to live among the masses and to encourage workers and peasants to become writers

Japanese writers, by contrast, read avidly any and all western literature and followed many different styles. From the 1880s they were stimulated and influenced by English, German, French and Russian authors. Among them, Tsubouchi Shoyo (1859–1935), one of the first promoters of western views of literature in Japan and a reformer of Japanese drama, translated all the works of Shakespeare; Mori Ogai (1862–1922), translator of *Faust*, introduced continental European literature; Natsume Soseki (1867–1916), a student of English writing, became a satirical novelist; Shimazaki Toson (1872–1946) was first influenced by romanticism in his poetry and later, under the influence of naturalism, became a realistic novelist writing of social problems.

Twentieth-century European writers were translated as they appeared. After 1920 some Japanese writers leaned toward Marxism in philosophy and proletarian novels in writing. Many found the doubt and uncertainty of the European writers a basis for their own doubts about their efforts to assimilate western ways, as in Tanizaki Junichiro's (1886–   ) *A Fool's Love* (1925, Nagai Kafu's (1879–1959) *The Tale of America* (1908) and *The Tale of France* (1909). As their own inner struggle reached a crisis, the European cultural crisis took on meaning. At mid-century the existentialists seemed to express their mood, and the writings of Sartre became popular.

The extensive Japanese literature of the twentieth century followed no line. In most instances it was characterized by some form of realism, often meticulous detail of daily life; it did not generally attempt to explore emotional depths; it might or might not express a social attitude; it usually retained the traditional Japanese imagery, which remained alive. Japanese writing reflected both the currents of the West and the vicissitudes of Japanese life. In one sense it might be regarded as an extension of the literature of Europe; in another sense, it was an emerging national expression which by mid-century was still in process of taking shape.

At different periods, in differing atmospheres, and in the hands of people of different political beliefs, social criticism thus took a variety of forms. It was used to expose the misery of rural peasant or urban shopkeeper, to pillory the well-to-do, to portray the class struggle, or to show the efforts of nationalists, revolutionaries or others working for social change. The experience of the writers themselves determined the closeness and realism with which they could enter into the lives of those about whom they wrote. Some, notably in China after the New Tide movement, shared the life of village or market place and knew the peasants or other common people; others were limited by their class position and western education, and could write at first-hand mainly of their own social group.

On the whole, western-influenced writing tended to deal with progressively broader and lower social strata, starting with essentially upper-class material in the early years of the century, and dealing by the second quarter of the century more and more with the peasant, the rickshaw boy, the shrimp fisherman or the pearl diver. Western-influenced writers in the main were in the vanguard of social change and often followed a style of writing and thought strongly influenced by communist philosophy and canons of expression even where communist political influence was not dominant or strong.

Such writing, too, tended to be secular in tone. Much, if not most, of the traditional expression of the East had been religious in origin and some, such as temple dancing in India, retained a religious function. The spirit of modern western literature and art was strongly secular. Whether western forms were adopted or imitated, or whether traditional forms were revived, existing secular aspects were strengthened and the predominant tone and use became secular.

The romantic emphasis in western writing, relating as it did to a society which encouraged the expression of individual preferences and beliefs and in which romantic marriage was the general form, introduced a new set of values to societies where behaviour was closely prescribed by situation and status, and marriage was a matter of family arrangement. Romantic themes, and especially the conflict between romantic and traditional values in marriage and family life, became prominent in the literature of India and Japan. In communist China marriages arranged in the interest of the family were brought under attack and the western-style romantic marriage was given support.

The western literature and art which probed the subconscious, however, found little acceptance and exerted much less influence than did romantic writing or realism and social criticism, although there was experimentation in this area by some of the younger writers. There was no such widespread interest in psychology as in the West, the subject matter of western psychological novels seemed often remote and the attitudes revealed by these writings often incomprehensible or offensive, while the style and vocabulary of writers such as James Joyce acted as a barrier to understanding and acceptance.

Of less influence, too, was the literature which expressed the quest for meaning in the universe and man's place in it. To the Asian mind, the western *malaise* in the face of the implications of modern science, the need for reassurance, or the despair of meaninglessness were strange reactions. On a different plane, however, the acute conflict of values to which western-influenced easterners were exposed stimulated a quest for new values or a new synthesis.

Up to the middle of the twentieth century distinctive literary forms that drew from both traditional and western sources and were modern in spirit had nowhere fully emerged. But some combination of revival, adaptation, and experimentation in every country reflected the national awakening, the cultural interaction, and the cultural vitality of each area. When the Indian poet Rabindranath Tagore received the Nobel Prize for Literature in 1913, it was in recognition of his creative assimilation of western influences combined with a genius for expressing depths of the Indian spirit in forms which could not only be loved and absorbed by the Indian people but understood effectively in other parts of the world.

IV. THE VISUAL ARTS

The impact of the western visual arts upon artistic expression in the East was much more limited than the influence of western literary expression. Whereas the western-educated element everywhere was more or less familiar with western literature, and modern literary expression in eastern countries was intimately bound up with the process of social change, western arts were known to a much more restricted group and played no such general part in the cultural adaptation through which eastern societies were passing. The character of the traditional idiom and the place of the visual arts strongly influenced the manner in which western influences were felt.

In the nineteenth century the traditional visual arts of the Indian subcontinent were in disrepute with the western-educated element which had imbibed the negative attitudes of the puritan-minded British toward art forms which were often sensuous and which they did not understand. The revival of Indian art came at the turn of the century, largely as the result of the researches of an Anglo-Tamil, Ananda Coomaraswamy and the work of an Englishman, E. B. Havell (1861–1934), who headed the School of Art at Calcutta and expounded the beauties of Indian art, and Abanindranath Tagore, who became the founder in Bengal of the first modern style of Indian painting. Trained in western techniques, and also influenced by the techniques of visiting Japanese artists, Abanindranath derived his style from the miniature paintings of the Mogul period, the sculpture of Hindu temples, and the wall paintings from the caves of Ajanta and Ellora. His pupils carried the Bengal style, with its eclectic Indian manner and traditional themes, to many parts of the country, where they directed or taught in the principal art schools. At Bombay, however, a school of art under the direction of western painters remained a centre of western training and influence. (Pl. 59.)

A few individual artists developed their own special idioms. M. A. Rahman Chughtai (1897–   ), who came from a family of artists in the Persian tradition, developed his delicate, flowing, romantic style from Mogul miniature painting; after partition he became a sort of painter-laureate of Pakistan. Jamini Roy (1887–   ) turned to the folk tradition and developed his manner wholly on the basis of the stylized forms, bright, flat colours, and visual conventions of folk art. Amrita Sher-Gil (1912–41), most influential painter after Abanindranath Tagore, freed Indian painters from the effort to conform to the Bengal school or to imitate western modes, by using her thorough western training freely and flexibly to evoke the feeling of the Indian people and scenes which she depicted. (Pl. 60, 61a.)

The most distinctive characteristic of Indian painting as it emerged in the 1940s and 1950s was its eclecticism. With few exceptions, young painters experimented with many modes; in a collection of paintings, often even the paintings of a single man, some element from nearly every school, East and West, could be seen integrated into the painter's personal idiom and used with whatever sensitivity, brilliance, mere derivativeness or lively originality he could achieve. (Pl. 61b, 62.)

In Japan, by contrast, a painting tradition based on an elaborate artistic vocabulary used with great flexibility and economy was very much alive when western influences began to enter Japan, and it continued to flourish along traditional lines. When Japanese artists became interested in western painting, they found themselves confronting a completely alien idiom, oil paint with its opacity and shadings, rounded figures, large canvases, external perspective. These were the complete antithesis of the transparent water-colours, the always decorative, two-dimensional, delicate and small paintings of Japanese art. Japanese painters learned to use the western media and to paint in the western manner, imitatively, sometimes skilfully, but without incorporating any of the feeling or the technique of their own style. Some art scholars who visited Europe after the Meiji restoration (1868) had urged their compatriots to stick to their traditional styles, and had exerted their leadership in this direction. But numbers of Japanese artists studied in Paris or under French influence, and painted French nudes and still-lifes, landscapes and distorted figures that would have been indistinguishable from the work of their fellow students in a European art class. (Pl. 63a, 63b.)

For those who stuck to the traditional medium and essential forms, exposure to western art had a more creative effect. Abstraction could be, and was, successfully absorbed into their works—in designs of decorative papers, textiles, posters, screens; new abstractions could be incorporated into the traditional artistic vocabulary to give flexibility and variety to compositions in the traditional mode. Freedom of line and in the use of colour could give warmth and a less formal atmosphere without destroying the essential quality. All manner of constructions, whether surrealist compositions, constructivist designs or balanced mobiles, could be elaborated by people trained through the art of flower arrangement to apply principles of harmony to the juxtaposition of objects. In contrast to dull imitativeness in the use of oils, the western influences which could be assimilated to the Japanese style itself became part of the idiom and were used with ease and brilliance.

Until the Communist revolution Chinese painters were not seriously influenced by western styles of painting.[6] Modern Chinese painters followed the old masters in their technique—their calligraphy, their inner rather than outer perspective, and the intent of the picture to speak with an inner voice. Under the communist régime art was enlisted as a means of propaganda, and artists were encouraged to paint in the style of socialist realism. Portraits of leaders, scenes depicting the vigorous and happy work of building a socialist state, posters to exhort and inform were turned out as needed, and artists learned to use the unfamiliar medium of oil for this purpose. In the initial stages this work was quite unrelated to the traditional manner in which the artist expressed himself; it was much closer to the popular broadsides which made no pretence to art but which had long served to entertain, and sometimes to inform, the villagers.

Interest in traditional Chinese culture was however great. Study and reproduction of the early Buddhist paintings in the Tun Huang caves of north-west China brought these works to public attention; some of the most distinguished painters in the traditional style were honoured; people throughout the country were encouraged to collect and preserve folk materials of all sorts and to experiment with their own forms of expression. Thus elements were present for a possible integration of traditional and new forms in the expression of a renewed national spirit.[7] (Pl. 64a, 64b.)

V. ARCHITECTURE

Until after the second world war public buildings, commercial structures and factories followed closely the undistinguished styles current in the West, whether they were built by colonial governments or western commercial interests or by local agencies. The main streets and public buildings of Tokyo, Shanghai, New Delhi and Cairo became hardly distinguishable from those of western cities, except where a colonial government tried to adapt some local motif as, for example, when the British in India built railway stations or post offices in a pseudo-Mogul style, as irrelevant as the Greek columns or Gothic windows that were the hallmarks of their public buildings at home.

As the new international style of architecture began to remake the cities of the West, it spread to the East. In Japan it was much more in keeping with the architectural traditions of the locality than earlier European styles had been, for light and space, simple lines, clean surfaces and the union of the interior with its outdoor surroundings were principles of Japanese architecture. Elsewhere it was introduced in eastern cities in occasional buildings, frequently hotels. When the partition of India and Pakistan left the capital of the Punjab, Lahore, on the Pakistan side of the line, the Indian government invited Le Corbusier to construct a new capital for the East Punjab, Chandigarh, and features of Le Corbusier's style began to appear in new buildings all over India. (Pl. 20b.)

By the 1950s the international style had become the symbol of modernism— as much for the main street of Bangkok as for the main street of small cities in the United States. It did not have the same technological *raison d'être* as in the West, for steel and glass were not readily available and mass production did not provide materials for building construction and decoration. It was primarily for stylistic and social reasons, and because its features of lightness and space made it suitable to the tropics, that the international style was being adopted in the cities of the East.[8]

VI. MUSIC AND DANCE

Even more than the visual arts, music and dance in the East retained their traditional form, unaffected by contact with the West. Musical idioms so distinct as to be incompatible prevented the interaction of most eastern music with the music of the West, although the gamelan music of Java, which used intervals not unfamiliar to the West, had been the inspiration for some of the musical innovations introduced by Debussy. Music and dance were integral parts of highly traditional institutions associated with religion, with the court or with carefully preserved artistic forms. As such they were largely insulated from the currents that were modifying others forms of expression. If they were touched at all it was through the stimulus to the revival of cultural traditions which came as an indirect, but powerful, response to the impact of the West.

The revival of the dance in India offers a striking example of such a response. At all times dancing had been a highly developed art in India, closely associated with religious practices, but in the nineteenth century it had come under widespread disapproval among the educated classes, influenced by

British puritanism and the zeal of social reformers. Without patronage, both the temple dancing of south India and the court dancing in the north had fallen into a state of decay and abuse.

The leader of the movement to revive interest in Indian dancing in the second decade of the twentieth century was the poet Rabindranath Tagore, who brought the Manipuri dance form, which he found in a flourishing state in the north-east province of Assam, to his school, Santiniketan, in Bengal. Others followed, establishing schools for the teaching of other forms—the classical Bharata Natyam temple dance of south India, taught by expert masters at a school in Madras (Rukmini Devi, Kalakshetra); and in Travancore the elaborate Kathakali dance-drama, revived and popularized at the centre established by the poet Vallathol (Kerala Kalamandalam). Dancers began to appear on the stage, at private performances and before the numerous dance societies which were formed to arrange dance showings. By the 1930s the dance had not only regained its place within India, but outstanding dancers such as Uday Shankar and Ramgopal had brought the beauty and complexity of Indian dance to European audiences.

Where the dance remained an integral part of the life of the community, it retained its vitality within its own cultural milieu and gained appreciation from outside. Balinese village dancers and gamelan orchestras continued to develop new dances and music and to adapt traditional modes. Siamese dance troupes received government patronage and not only performed for important occasions at home but were sent abroad as a gesture of official courtesy and good will. These and other eastern dancers inspired a few choreographers and artists in the West, and troupes visited western capitals, where their beauty and style became more widely known. Within the Soviet Union, the Asian republics were encouraged to develop their indigenous dance forms, and the participation of performers from these areas in national festivals made their styles familiar in other parts of the USSR.

VII. EFFECT OF MASS MEDIA

The literature and arts of the East, as those of the West, were profoundly affected by the new media—radio, cinema and, in later years, television. These means of mass communication provided vehicles both for the rapid and widespread introduction of new forms and ideas, and for the preservation of traditional forms and their dissemination to the masses of the people. In countries with extensive local motion-picture industries, most notably Japan and India, the new medium was used to convey traditional themes and traditional art forms, such as the music and dance that filled most Indian films.

The cinema also became a vehicle for social commentary, with a far wider audience than the modern play or novel. In rare instances, notably a few outstanding Japanese and Indian films, it became a new and powerful art form. At the same time foreign films, often 'B grade' productions featuring violence or romance rather than those of literary and artistic merit, were widely shown both where a local industry flourished and where none had been developed. Their impact was more widespread and direct than was that of western literature and art. By affecting standards of taste, the cinema stimulated the development of popular art forms in these countries. The so-called 'movie music' in India, scorned by those who cherished the purity of classical Indian music, and also 'movie dancing', offered examples of such popularization, based on traditional forms but reduced to a popular idiom for the new mass audiences which the cinema brought into the literary and artistic milieu.

VIII. REACTION OF WEST TO CULTURE CONTACT WITH EAST

Although the relation between western and eastern forms of expression was chiefly a one-way flow from the West to each of the eastern countries, it was not wholly one-sided. As world communication grew and western peoples lost some of their ethnocentrism and sense of superiority, western writers and artists showed increased interest in, and appreciation for, the arts of the East. Painting, sculpture and the dance were most readily understood without the barrier of language.

With the aid of modern photography, the ancient art revealed by archaeological discoveries and the arts of new cultural areas were brought into world consciousness, such as the paintings in the Ajanta caves and other examples of the art of mediaeval India, the art of Tibet, or the Khmer art of south-east Asia. The artistic expression of Egypt or Persia, Cambodia, China, India or Africa might be seen not only in museums but in articles in popular magazines or text-books for schoolchildren. Only in the twentieth century would it have been possible to discuss the art of the world, past and present, as a common expression of human striving, as did André Malraux in *Les voix du silence* (1951).

Translation set up a two-way flow, also, as Chinese, Japanese, Indian and Arabic classical writings were increasingly translated into western languages. Already in the nineteenth century, eastern philosophy, especially the Hindu classics, was affecting philosophical thought in the West, notably in Germany in the latter part of the nineteenth century, and in the outlook of American thinkers such as Ralph Waldo Emerson and Henry Thoreau. *The Rubaiyat* of Omar Khayyam achieved immense popularity, while *The Arabian Nights* furnished the most common picture of the 'East' in western minds.

In the twentieth century a number of western writers were influenced by the literature of one or another eastern country. Arthur Waley's sensitive translations of Chinese classics into English made these works widely accessible. In time, modern Chinese, Japanese and Indian writings also began to be translated into European languages. Expressions of eastern thought reached a wider and wider range of people in the West. By mid-century almost any news-stand where cheap books were sold offered translations of the *Bhagavad Gita*, the *Analects* of Confucius, the words of the Buddha, or the *Holy Quran*. The poetry of Rabindranath Tagore helped to prepare the way for acceptance in the West of India's right to independence and to enable the West to begin to understand and welcome India's belief that its development could bring to the world a fresh vision of the creative human being.

The images of eastern culture which reached the West, however, were sometimes far from authentic, for what the West liked to think of as the 'wisdom of the East' was often only a romantic projection of a desire to escape from its own *malaise*. In the effort to build a more accurate, fuller and deeper basis for mutual understanding, Unesco set up an 'East–West' programme of mutual interchange in the 1950s and made it an increasingly central part of its international activity.

Yet it still may be questioned whether, up to the middle of the twentieth century, familiarity with non-western forms of expression had more than a superficial influence on the thought and expression of the West.

NOTES TO CHAPTER XXXII

1. Candidate of Arts V. M. Polevoy makes the following addition: However, a number of painters seek for ways of broadening the possibilities of the traditional style, drawing on the experience of European art (Hsü Pei-hung, known under the pseudonym of Shu Peon); the traditional ink painting is undergoing a definite rejuvenation. But it is in the field of engraving that the traditional art makes the most telling effort to break through the medieval imitations and come closer to life. The decisive role here was played by the Lu Hsün Academy of Arts, set up in the 1930's in the Red districts of China. The artists of this Academy made an extensive study of Soviet engraving and created works reflecting the life and struggles of the people.

2. Candidate of Arts V. M. Polevoy thinks special interest attaches to the lacquer painting of Vietnam, which has revived in a new form the traditional medieval techniques. A group of masters in Northern Vietnam have succeeded in raising it to the level of genuine art, combining realistic solidity of image with amazing decorative colourfulness.

3. Corresponding member of Tadjik Academy of Sciences J. S. Braginsky thinks that it is necessary to point out that one of the major writers of Turkey in the twentieth century is Nazim Hikmet (1902–63). His creative work in which brilliant innovations are associated with profound mastery of a number of the best classical and popular traditions of Turkish literature is widely known in many countries. (See R. G. Fish: *Nazim Hikmet*, Moscow, 1960.)

4. See *Tashkentskaya konferentziya pisatelei stran Azii i Afriki Materialy* ('Tashkent Conference of the writers of Asian and African countries—Materials') (Tashkent, 1960).

5. Candidate of Arts V. M. Polevoy thinks that here and in the other pages treating of the influence of European authors on the writers of Asia, the enormous influence of the work of Tolstoy is unjustly passed over. Yet this influence was quite profound by virtue of the ethical-educative impact and depth of socio-psychological penetration into life characteristic of Tolstoy.

6. In this connection Candidate of Arts V. M. Polevoy points out the exception of wood-cutting as observed above in Note 1.

7. Candidate of Arts V. M. Polevoy makes the following addition: Especially striking is the development of the arts among the peoples inhabiting the Soviet part of Asia. After the Revolution of 1917 major changes in cultural life occurred here. The people freed from the double burden of class and national oppression devoted themselves with new energy to the development of literature, music, theatre and fine art in their traditional forms. Folk art received state and public support. Of especial significance was the birth of new forms of art, in which the possibilities of the realistic method developed in the West are applied to the national art forms. Thus, professional painting and sculpture have arisen among the peoples of Central Asia, where they were formerly non-existent; national music drama, ballet and other forms are developed. These innovations are called for by the growing scope of spiritual life, by the necessity for developing those art forms which by virtue of their method are capable of reflecting the people's contemporary life.

8. Candidate of Arts V. M. Polevoy underlines that the new needs of social life in the newly-independent countries of the East stimulate the development of new branches and idioms of architecture. The development of a national industry, public education, the tasks of raising the standard of living—all promote the development of new forms of architecture and building, the destruction of the sharp contrast between the living conditions in the European and native sections, so typical of the colonial countries.

CONCLUSION

CHAPTER XXXIII

THE CHANGING SHAPE OF THE LIFE
OF MANKIND

By the middle of the twentieth century the scientific and cultural developments that had taken place in the past fifty years had already radically altered the life of mankind and trends then apparent were in process of bringing further revolutionary changes.

The dramatic advances in scientific knowledge, the methodical application of such knowledge, and the resulting changes in material conditions were exerting a vast and ever increasing influence on the economic, social and political life of man, as well as on his cultural, ideological and moral development. Within the span of fifty years man's knowledge of the universe had increased beyond all previous experience; power generated from many sources had been harnessed and nuclear energy was further increasing man's control; the ability to break down matter and recombine it had permitted the creation of new materials to serve man's purposes; men travelled at speeds beyond the speed of sound; they had placed satellites in orbit around the earth and sent rockets beyond the earth's gravitational pull to circle the sun, and they were preparing to travel into space themselves.

An unprecedented growth in medical science had brought new and potent means for the control of disease and the virtual eradication of such scourges as plague, malaria, smallpox and cholera which had taken heavy toll of human lives over large areas, while preventive medicine had diminished infant deaths, extended the life span and raised the general level of health. The people of the world had available to them an abundance of riches and a level of well-being which no previous society could have even imagined, much less provided.

The new potentialities were becoming the heritage of all mankind, not merely of the privileged few. The sense of equal entitlement to the means for a decent life had taken hold of all manner of men, within nations and throughout the world community, whether in industrially developed or newly developing countries, in centres of old empires or among peoples emerging from colonialism, in socialist or free enterprise societies, and whether under communist, democratic or even dictatorial rule. Equality of status had become an accepted principle in most of the world, as monarchical, aristocratic and other systems of rank and class had been discarded, disabilities imposed on women had been removed, and measures to implement concepts of equality were being applied with some effectiveness within different social systems. An ever widening range of education, opportunities for recreation, facilities for the welfare of children and the handicapped, and a multitude of other services and amenities were being provided for the entire population in many areas. Remaining limitations on universal suffrage were being withdrawn. Virtually every state was using its taxing power to bring about greater equality by deriving tax revenue from those able to pay and dedicating it to services for the benefit of all.

Racial superiority, so dominant a feature of human society in the past, was declining sharply through all but a very small part of the world. The European white man no longer dominated the darker peoples of the earth. Although in a few places groups fought desperately to hold a superior position on the basis of race, the principle of equality of status was being extended, both within mixed societies and in the world community. The one issue on which there was near unanimity in the United Nations was opposition to racialism.

Literature and the arts were no longer the cultural inheritance of an educated *élite*. They were reaching the people as a whole, who made up the mass audiences and were beginning to participate in creative activity. Men had not yet however found the means to give full expression to their new experiences and the new social forces that were taking shape. They had broken through traditional conventions and forms of expression, to explore new psychological depths, new social forces and man's new relation to the physical universe. The period had been rich in experimentation, but new styles had not yet been developed which would permit a flowering of expression comparable to that which had occurred in great ages of the past.

Cultural expression throughout the world, however, was taking on a quality of universality. Before the twentieth century the literature and arts of each culture area had been set off in compartments; the cultural expression of China and India and of the Islamic peoples was little known or shared by the people of the West, and although the political dominance of the West gave to other peoples a certain superficial knowledge of the culture of Europe, only rarely did this make a deep or lasting impact. By the middle of the twentieth century peoples of all parts of the world were aware of other cultures, and although their understanding and appreciation was limited they recognized that each culture had values of its own which were important for mankind as a whole. Nearly everywhere there was a double tendency—to foster indigenous expression and to seek to understand, appreciate and embrace the expression of others.

A new world society was in fact emerging in which many different people were all playing an active part. The first half of the twentieth century brought to an end four centuries of European expansion and world dominance and reduced Europe to the position of only one among several dynamic centres of culture and of power. At the middle of the century, western Europe was flanked by two great areas, America and Russia, continental in size, with fast growing populations and still unexploited resources, which were developing new, dynamic societies. On the continent of Asia, ancient, populous and historically civilized societies, most notably China and India with a population between them of a thousand millions, were taking their place in the world, impelled by vital urges and mastering and utilizing the new scientific knowledge and its technologies to build up social and industrial strength. Within the Americas the growing importance of the Latin American states gave evidence of their great potentialities, while the stirring of new life on the continent of Africa made it clear by the middle of the century that the emergence of the African people into the world community was a new and vital fact in the history of mankind.

The reduction in the relative position of Europe and the reinstatement of other regions as units in world history restored a balance among societies which had been destroyed by the extension of European power. But now the several centres of dynamic power in Asia, Europe, America and Africa were not self-contained and cut off from each other as they had been in the days before Columbus and Vasco da Gama linked Europe with the West and the East. They were interrelated and interacting one upon the other, for distance was no longer a divider and no society was isolated from the vital currents which flowed from all parts of the world.

Mankind thus enjoyed immeasurably greater prospects for the enrichment of life than ever before, and the benefits of man's new powers over nature were being extended to all manner of men and to all peoples. Yet man also faced graver dangers than ever in the past: on the one hand, a rate of population increase such as even Malthus had not imagined; on the other hand, powers of destruction which could bring annihilation.

The conquest of diseases and better preventive measures had already raised the life expectancy of men in progressive societies to double that of less developed communities, and the spread of medical knowledge was rapidly extending the same trend to other areas. As death rates fell sharply, population mounted ominously in areas which were struggling to shake off their age-old burdens of hunger and poverty. On a world-wide basis, calculations of the earth's potential for producing food gave no cause for concluding that food supply could not keep pace with population growth, and the actual threat of famine had been reduced by increased agricultural productivity and improved transport. But the political organization of the world was not such as to bring together hungry peoples and the vacant lands which remained on the globe, and the anomaly of food surpluses in some areas and chronic hunger in others continued to confront mankind. And even more serious than the question of food was the burden of a rapidly expanding population on all manner of facilities in countries scarcely able to provide the barest minimum in education, housing, water supply, transport and other necessities, especially when they were trying to devote their energies and resources to expanding the base for their economic development.

The explosive force of rapidly expanding population was a factor in the world situation which mankind in the middle of the twentieth century had hardly begun to face. Differential rates of growth were expanding the newly developing areas, not only absolutely but relative to the areas which had been economically dominant, altering relationships among peoples. At the rate at which world population was then increasing, the world would be filled to its maximum capacity, by any system of calculation, within measurable time.

Few nations, within themselves, had made successful efforts to adjust the relation between their people and their resources. Among nations, population pressures were a continuing source of tension. The demand for *Lebensraum* had ceased to be the basis for colonial expansion when colonialism came into disrepute, but the pressure behind the claim had not abated. The open doors of the New World through which millions of immigrants from Europe had poured in the nineteenth and early twentieth centuries were closed and only a trickle of the old stream continued to flow, but an emigrant potential was present in many parts of the world.

Mankind in the middle of the century was more conscious of the threatened destruction of human life than of dangers from its multiplication, for from the moment when the first atomic bomb was dropped on Hiroshima men knew that this was but a portent of the capacity for self-destruction which man had discovered and let loose. No previous generation ever faced the danger to humanity itself inherent in the new weapons of ever greater and more incalculable power. Knowing that wars in the past had been unleashed by men in their pride without counting the cost to humanity, mankind could find little assurance in the often expressed hope that the very magnitude of the danger would act as a deterrent to the use of the terrible weapons and would save man from destroying himself.

The drama of the mid-twentieth century was thus projected on a new scale of almost unlimited hopes and unlimited threats, of high possibilities for the realization of human potentialities and of supreme dangers, of immense powers in the hands of men, far beyond the forms of power known in the past. The power of modern science to alter the conditions provided by nature for the earth changed the situation of mankind as radically as did the discovery of fire, or the movement from the stone to the metal age. The environment within which man lived became increasingly man-made. Man himself had the power to determine whether this environment would increase his survival or terminate it, whether it would foster his physical, emotional, intellectual and spiritual development or restrict and menace it, and which of his many potentialities it would favour and which suppress.

The unprecedented power of science created a new priestly caste, the scientists, who alone could exercise the ultimate power which scientific knowledge conveys. Mankind had become dependent on this class, beyond the dependence of earlier societies on the priests who knew the mysteries. It was deeply affected by the character of the scientists and technicians, their distribution through society, the structure through which they functioned and the factors which determined the uses to which their knowledge would be put.

As among the peoples and societies of the earth, those which rested upon a base of developed science held power over those which did not command scientific knowledge and processes, whether or not they enjoyed political independence and national status. Europe's dominance in the nineteenth century had rested on such a base. In the twentieth century the disparity between the scientific and non-scientific societies increased immeasurably, while at the same time the command of scientific knowledge spread from old centres to new ones, altering in a major way the balance among nations and peoples. The contest among the world's peoples for status or dominance had become inexorably a contest to command this power. Concepts of freedom, independence, sovereignty and status had come to have meaning fundamentally in terms of the mastery of scientific knowledge.

States of continental size, with large populations and with natural resources covering essential requirements had obvious advantages in the technological age over smaller units, however progressive and advanced they might be. Although the twentieth century saw the break-up of the few great empires which had dominated the world and the birth of a multitude of independent, sovereign nations, the tendency was toward the emergence of a few states of great size and power—the USA and the USSR in dominant positions at mid-century, China and India rising, Brazil seeing itself as a future great state of continental proportions—and toward the grouping of smaller units into blocks or closer federations—the Common European Market, the Arab states, the Organization of American States, the moves toward Pan-African unity. In the middle years of the century these trends were pulling the world into parts —communist, anti-communist and neutralist—and the contest among these great divisions was becoming more and more a test of strength through the command and application of the resources of science.

The power which science had placed at the disposal of man could be utilized only with immense and increasingly complicated organization—political, industrial and technical. Without a very great measure of direction, on a scale rarely attempted in the past, the new forces opened up by science could not be harnessed effectively. The entire shape of economic life underwent revolutionary changes, in capitalist as well as in communist and mixed economies. The mammoth corporations which alone could command the resources, technical skills and capacity for continuing scientific research had become huge centres of scientific inquiry, social life and economic dynamism. Over a larger and larger part of the world these vast industrial complexes were coming to constitute the units of which society was composed. The state, in turn, could not fail to assume more and more power, for even if it did not wish to organize production activities itself it had to exercise control in relation to the use of such great powers by others.

Great organizations were thus inescapable and dominant factors in the life of mankind, whether in the form of giant industrial corporations or of the all-pervasive state, or of lesser associations through which men sought to organize their lives and to cope with the new forces. These were the new

Leviathans, and the magnitude of the power with which they confronted the individual far exceeded that which he had faced in the past. Earlier societies had been composed of scattered and more or less isolated units—villages, tribes, cities, regions—separated by distance and geographical barriers, where effective power was confined and limited by lack of communication. Now there was no spot on the globe where men lived in self-contained isolation, beyond the long arm and the insistent voice of power, organized on a gigantic scale.

The inevitable concentrations of power could not fail to affect the status of the individual. The supreme value of the individual, which had been proclaimed in the revolutionary doctrine of 'liberty, equality and fraternity', remained a vital part of the heritage of the twentieth century and a dynamic concept in the political evolution of those years. The modern state, based on universal suffrage, was committed to the welfare of all the people and it offered its citizens a vast array of services and protections which earlier states had not thought it necessary or appropriate to provide. At the same time, the relation of the individual to society was inescapably changed as the modern state entered into every sphere of life, equipped with powerful instruments to compel or induce conformity to its policies and purposes.

There were basic differences in the position of the individual within different systems of organization and authority. Where all power rested in an all-embracing, centrally administered state, the individual derived his role from the policies of the state. These might call for his self-improvement and his active participation in planning and achieving common goals, or at the other extreme they might require his unquestioning acquiescence in the judgment of those in command, devoted subjection to their authority, and sacrifice of individual ends. In all cases the scope of individual initiative was defined by the higher authority and all roles and responsibilities were ultimately related to a common purpose.

Where, however, a number of organizations acted in some measure as independent centres of power, their countervailing forces tended to balance each other and to leave the individual with latitude to exercise a wide range of choice and initiative. The individual retained a considerable measure of freedom and scope in societies where labour organization confronted organized management, corporations competed one with another, religious organization counterbalanced secular authority, military organization was subject to civil powers, organized farmers could influence public policy, an entrenched civil service was secure against political interference, an independent judiciary could apply accepted principles of law, and political parties could compete freely for political control. Yet here also it was through organized groups that the individual must generally function in order to make a place for himself in modern society.

The power of science and the power of organization brought both an intellectual and a moral crisis in the life of mankind. Intellectually, the question was whether men had the capacity to understand the complexities of the forces which they had loosed and to imagine new kinds of order which would replace the orders of nature which they had learned to manipulate or destroy. Morally, the crisis arose from the collapse of many values and the conflict among those which remained, and from the disparity between the power which men held in their hands and the weakness, uncertainty or contradiction in the guides to its use. These had become the great issues of the second half of the twentieth century.

The enormous complexity of the forces which men had let loose defied man's understanding. Patterns of air traffic became so complex that human observation and calculation no longer sufficed to keep speeding jets out of collision paths; electronic devices operating more swiftly and precisely than human senses and thought, were taking over the control of the air from the men in the control towers and the men at the controls of the planes. But these electronic brains in turn depended upon men's ability both to feed them the right information and to keep them in perfect operation. Expanding cities and proliferating highways encroached on each other and on the countryside, creating more problems for every one that they solved. Agricultural surpluses piled up in some areas while hunger stalked in other parts of the world. The conquest of disease and the resulting increase in survival and lengthening of the life span impinged on many institutions. To grasp these complexities, to foresee the impact of each change, to calculate the interaction of innumerable factors demanded knowledge and thought far beyond that demanded by former societies where a much smaller part of life was subject to modification by the actions of man. And it demanded knowledge and thought by more people, for complex forces played upon individuals in all walks of life and few could limit their understanding and guides for action to matters within their direct experience as most men had done in the past.

The changing world conditions challenged men's capacity to envision the desirable and the possible when the old orders would no longer suffice to contain the new powers and potentialities The institutions, relationships and social ideas of the period of the first industrial revolution could not be expected to absorb the changes wrought by the atomic age. New patterns must be conceived. What concepts of the good life were compatible with the new situation and took advantage of the new potentialities? What relations among peoples, nations, groups and individuals could be sustained and could foster the development of human potentialities? What balance of countervailing forces could maintain an essential degree of stability and yet keep open the door of freedom and opportunity for individuals, groups and peoples? What controls could hold in check destructive or overweening forces? Without the vision of new order, man could only fumble with old forms.

The moral issue was whether a new morality for a scientific age was to be found in science itself, or whether any of the historic formulations of moral values and sanctions were sufficient in the new situation. Scientists themselves faced an ethical dilemma. Science had its own morality for the pursuit of knowledge—relentless search, freedom of mind, utter honesty in observing and reporting, mutual co-operation in the common quest for truth. But scientists did not traditionally extend these values to the application of knowledge, for in this area it was not the values of science but those of the society that reigned. Other professions had their ethics for the use of scientific knowledge—the medical profession for healing, the military profession for destruction. But with the terrible possibilities that had been unleashed, scientists began to question their own neutrality in relation to the application of their knowledge and to ask whether they did not have a special responsibility, at least to make the potential effects of their discoveries known to the public and to those concerned with policy.

Value systems inherited from the past were embedded in the social fabric of all societies and they inevitably formed a part of the approach to new situations. In respect to each of these systems, two issues presented themselves: what values might have validity, and who would decide which should serve as guides.

Each of the great religions was asserting itself with renewed vitality in the middle of the century, but it remained a question whether any or all of them furnished a basis for making the kinds of decisions that men were called upon to make in the new age, and whether they offered sufficiently powerful sanctions to give effect to the moral judgments which they might prescribe. The morality of socialism was being invoked in large parts of the world; yet it had been formulated by Marx in the age of early technology and elaborated by Lenin in the beginning period of the scientific revolution of the twentieth century.

In the value system of liberal democracy, the basic principle of individual worth was implemented by dependence upon the self-direction of the individual and the collective wisdom of the people; but however appropriate the concept *vox populi, vox Dei* might have been in pre-technological days when decisions related to things about which people could have direct knowledge, it seemed less likely that wisdom would reside in the collective will in respect to problems of the atomic age. At the opposite extreme the 'leadership principle' placed full responsibility for moral judgment upon an individual whose intuition and personal conviction, whatever its basis, would provide a guide for his followers and relieve them of the moral burden; but the danger in this principle had been revealed by its main twentieth-century proponents, and this danger grew with each increase in potential power over the material universe and the minds of men. Collective leadership by a dedicated group might provide some of the technical knowledge which the people as a whole lacked and avoid the caprice of a single leader; but such leadership, too, required a basis for responsible decision.

Perhaps the central moral challenge to a world in which all people professed adherence to the Universal Declaration of Human Rights was whether man could find human terms in which to build a system of values, whether dedication to the cause of mankind could provide sanctions for such a system, and whether human values could be related to the order found in nature. In a society where great power was inherent and pervasive, what would sustain human compassion and respect for the essential dignity of every man? Once the old, limited concept of 'natural order' had been destroyed, could science yield insight into a deeper level of natural order where unifying principles and relationships might be found which would favour human development and could act both as guides and as sanctions for conduct?

These had become momentous issues for mankind—not for one race or one nation or group of nations, not for one class or one creed, but for all the earth's people.

Faced with these issues, men in the second half of the twentieth century had a new view of progress. Through much of human history men did not think in terms of progress but of fixed orders, timeless and eternal, the stage on which man lived his brief life and other men would lead theirs after him. The fixed social order continued to provide the image of man's life on earth in the societies of Asia and in the tribal societies elsewhere in the world even up to the twentieth century.

In the western world, from the time of the Renaissance, and especially from the scientific revolution of the seventeenth century, men no longer saw society as fixed but as capable of progress—of change for the better. In the eighteenth century progress involved the removal of imperfections which kept human society from the state of perfection inherent in the natural order. With the enunciation of the theory of evolution, progress itself was seen as part of the natural order. In the view put forth by Karl Marx, progress occurs through a dialectical process in which the struggle of two contending systems of production always leads to the victory of the higher one—the feudal form being essentially higher than the form based on slavery which it superseded, the capitalist form higher than the feudal, the socialist than the capitalist, and the ultimate and highest form, communism. When the twentieth century opened, western society saw progress, whether evolutionary or revolutionary, as inevitable; it might be accelerated or retarded by the conscious efforts of man, but it was the sure direction of human development.

The concept of the static society and the concept of automatic evolutionary progress were destroyed by the events of the first half of the twentieth century. Formerly static societies glimpsed the possibilities of change and set themselves on new paths. In Europe, however, there were many people, representative of a wide range of viewpoint, who saw that new powers could be evil as well as beneficent in effect and came to believe that the idea of automatic progress was worse than an illusion. They saw it as a dangerous superstition which prevented men from recognizing the awful threats in scientific and technical development uncontrolled by a parallel development in morality. In part this view was a reflection of the decline in the position of Europe as a result of the shift of power. But in part it was a cry of danger, a warning that men were not fearing atomic destruction enough because they were spell-bound by the traditional idea of progress.

Yet outside western Europe the idea of progress remained as living a concept as it had ever been. It lived in the United States and in other parts of the New World, not so much as an elaborated theory but as the outlook of young societies in the process of achieving material well-being and with great resources at their command. It lived, also, in the new nation-states of Asia and Africa as the mental counterpart of their determined drive for industrialization and modernization. But its stronghold was in the communist orbit, wherever Marxism was a living force, for it was the corner-stone of Marxian thought. Since, in this view, the superstructure of society always follows the basic system of production, man is bound to grow with his self-shaped forces of production and, to the extent that he lives up to the task put before him by history, progress is assured.

In the outlook of mankind at the middle of the twentieth century, progress thus appeared as a possibility which man might grasp. The challenge was one of choice. No society in the past had even begun to give full scope to the potentialities of all its people, and only the great figures of all ages and cultures had shown by their intellectual power, their sensitivity of perception, their spiritual force and their capacity for human relationships some of the possibilities inherent in the human species. Man's new powers had given him some of the means to create a social and physical environment favourable to the richer development of human life on a broader scale than ever before—if, and only if, he would use them to that end. Man might fall by the way or scale new heights, but whichever his destiny he would bring it about by his own use of his new powers.

BIBLIOGRAPHY

The scope of the subject matter treated in this volume precludes the inclusion of a systematic bibliography. Even when limited to the language of the text, any comprehensive and balanced list of references would be monumental and any list of references dealing with contemporary history is bound to become out of date even before it is in print. Furthermore, since material relating to individual countries has been used in the text mainly to illustrate broad tendencies rather than for its own sake, and since technical subjects have been considered in relation to general scientific and cultural developments in non-technical terms for the non-technical reader, bibliographical references may appropriately be limited to these same purposes.

With these considerations in mind, the author-editors have selected items for each chapter as follows:

1. The general bibliography is confined to guides and to world histories which include a substantial consideration of the recent past.
2. Books relating to the general political development of these years are listed with chapters I—III, and those relating to general economic and social developments with chapters IV and V.
3. Books relating to individual countries and specific social movements are listed in connection with chapters XXVIII, XXIX and XXX.
4. Publications relating to scientific thought, the development of knowledge and various forms of expression are mentioned in the text of the chapters dealing with these subjects. Bibliographies for these chapters, VI, VII, VIII, XIII, XVI, XX, XXXI, XXXII, merely add a few works of general reference, where such are available.
5. Chapters on the application of scientific knowledge—IX-XII, XIV, XV, XVII-XIX— and on the transformation of social institutions—XXI-XXVII—are supplemented by brief lists of works which treat the subjects in comprehensive or comparative terms or which approach a limited area or aspect in a manner to illumine the broader field.
6. In general, books referred to in the text are not repeated in the bibliographies.
7. With a very few exceptions the following are excluded:
   (a) Books published since 1960.
   (b) Magazine articles and pamphlets.
   (c) Books not available in English.

BIBLIOGRAPHY—GENERAL

A substantial body of material dealing with cultural and scientific developments on a global scale is contained in the reports, studies and other publications of international organizations, both official bodies, i.e. the United Nations and its specialized agencies, and non-official. The official agencies publish lists of their publications. For the publications of unofficial agencies, consult the *Directory of International Scientific Organizations* published by UNESCO, Paris, which describes the scope of these organizations and lists their publications.

AMERICAN HISTORICAL ASSOCIATION, *Guide to Historical Literature* (New York, 1961).

AMERICAN UNIVERSITIES FIELD STAFF, *A Select Bibliography: Asia, Africa, Eastern Europe, Latin America* (New York, 1960).

MONTAGUE F. ASHLEY MONTAGU, (ed.), *Toynbee and History: Critical Essays and Reviews* (Boston, 1956).

GEORGES BALANDIER and J. F. M. MIDDLETON, (eds.), *International Index of Social and Cultural Anthropology* (New York, 1958).

ERICH H. BOEHM, (ed.), *Historical Abstracts, 1775-1945* (Vienna, 1955–), quarterly

MAURICE CROUZET, (ed.), *Histoire générale des civilisations* (Paris, 1953-59), 7 vols.

LUIS DIEZ DEL CORRAL, *The Rape of Europe* (trans. by H. V. Livermore, London, 1959).

ALOIS FISCHER, *Neue Weltstatistik: Zahlen, Daten, Karten*, (2nd ed., Vienna, 1952).

PATRICK GARDINER, (ed.), *Theories of History* (Glencoe, Illinois, 1959).

A. GRANDIN, *Bibliographie générale des sciences juridiques, politiques, économiques et sociales de 1800 à 1925–26* (Paris, 1926–   ), 3 vols, with annual supplement.

S. HOFSTRA, (ed.), *Eastern and Western World: Selected Readings* (The Hague and Bandung, 1953).

INTERNATIONAL COMMITTEE OF HISTORICAL SCIENCES, *International Bibliography of Historical Sciences* (Paris, 1926–   ), annual.

INTERNATIONAL INSTITUTE OF DIFFERING CIVILIZATIONS, *International Guide to Study Centers on Civilizations and their Publications* (Brussels, 1955).

ANNA et ANDRÉ LEJARD, (eds.), *Cinquante années de découvertes: Bilan 1900–1950* (Paris, 1950).

GOLO MANN and ALFRED HUESS, (eds.), *Propyläen Weltgeschichte* (Berlin, 1960–62), 10 vols.

New Cambridge Modern History (Cambridge, 1957–62), 10 vols.

ROBERT R. PALMER, (ed.), *Atlas of World History* (Chicago, 1957).

ALEXANDER RUESTOW, *Ortsbestimmung der Gegenwart: eine universalgeschichtliche Kulturkritik*, (Erlenbach and Zurich, 1950–57), 3 vols.

ARNOLD J. TOYNBEE, *A Study of History*, (New York and London, 1948–1961), 12 vols.

UNESCO, *International Bibliography of Sociology* (Paris, 1952–   ), annual.

UNESCO, *International Bibliography of Political Science* (Paris, 1953–   ), annual.

UNESCO, *International Bibliography of Economics* (Paris, 1955–   ), annual.

UNESCO, *International Political Science Abstracts* (Paris, 1951–   ), quarterly.

UNITED NATIONS, *Statistical Yearbook* (New York, 1948–   ), annual.

BARBARA WARD, *The Interplay of East and West: Elements of Contrast and Co-operation* (London, 1957).

CAROLINE F. WARE, (ed.), *The Cultural Approach to History* (New York, 1940).

WALTER P. WEBB, *The Great Frontier: an Interpretation of World History since Columbus* (Boston, 1952).

W. S. WOYTINSKY, *Die Welt in Zahlen* (Berlin, 1925–28), 7 vols.

EUGENY M. ZHUKOV *et al.*, (eds.), *Vsemirnaia Istoriia* (Moscow, 1955–   ), 10 vols.

CHAPTER I
THE SHIFT IN WORLD POWER

RENÉ ALBRECHT-CARRIÉ, *A Diplomatic History of Europe since the Congress of Vienna* (New York, 1958).

G. L. ARNOLD, *The Pattern of World Conflict* (New York, 1955).

MAX BELOFF, *The Foreign Policy of Soviet Russia, 1929–1941* (London and New York, 1947–49), 2 vols.

SAMUEL F. BEMIS, *The United States as a World Power: A Diplomatic History*, 1900–1955 (rev. ed., New York, 1955).

MORITZ J. BONN, *The Crumbling of Empire* (London, 1938).

DENIS W. BROGAN, *The Era of Franklin D. Roosevelt* (New Haven, 1950).

EDWARD H. CARR, *The Bolshevik Revolution*, 1917–1923 (London, 1950–53), 3 vols.

EDWARD H. CARR, *The Soviet Impact on the Western World* (New York, 1947).

WINSTON S. CHURCHILL, *The Second World War* (London and Boston, 1948–53), 6 vols.

GORDON A. CRAIG and FELIX GILBERT, *The Diplomats*, 1919–1939 (Princeton, N.J., 1953).

DAVID J. DALLIN, *The Rise of Russia in Asia* (New Haven, 1949).

FOSTER R. DULLES, *America's Rise to World Power*, 1898–1954 (New York, 1955).

ERIC FISCHER, *The Passing of the European Age* (rev. ed., Cambridge, Mass., 1948).

GEOFREY M. GATHORNE-HARDY, *A Short History of International Affairs*, 1920–39 (4th ed., London and New York, 1950).

CHARLES DE GAULLE, *War Memoirs* (trans. by J. Griffin and Richard Howard, New York, 1955–60), 3 vols.

ERNEST B. HAAS, *The Uniting of Europe: Political, Social and Economic Forces*, 1950–1957 (Stanford, 1959).

S. WILLIAM HALPERIN, *Germany Tried Democracy: a Political History of the Reich from 1918 to 1933* (New York, 1946).

HENRY V. HODSON, *Slump and Recovery*, 1929–1937: *a Survey of World Economic Affairs* (London and New York, 1938).

HAJO HOLBORN, *The Political Collapse of Europe* (New York, 1951).

YAMATO ICHIHASHI, *The Washington Conference and After: A Historical Survey* (Stanford, California, 1928).

JOHN H. JACKSON, *The Post-War Decade: a Short History of the World*, 1945–1955 (London, 1955).

OSZKÁR JÁSZI, *The Dissolution of the Hapsburg Monarchy* (Chicago, 1929).

BRUNO LASKER, *Books on Southeast Asia: a Select Bibliography* (rev. ed., New York, 1959).

C. A. MACARTNEY, *Hungary and Her Successors: The Treaty of Trianon and its Consequences*, 1919–1937 (London, 1937).

FRANZ H. MICHAEL and GEORGE E. TAYLOR, *The Far East in the Modern World* (New York, 1956).

K. M. PANIKKAR, *The Afro-Asian States and Their Problems* (London and New York, 1959).

K. M. PANIKKAR, *Asia and Western Dominance: a Survey of the Vasco da Gama Epoch of Asian History*, 1498–1945 (London, 1953).

HARRY B. PRICE, *The Marshall Plan and its Meaning* (Ithaca, N.Y., 1955).

JAN M. ROMEIN, *The Asian Century* (London and Berkeley, 1962).

ROYAL INSTITUTE OF INTERNATIONAL AFFAIRS, *Atlantic Alliance: NATO's Role in the Free World*, compiled by Donald McLachlan (London and New York, 1952).

HUGH SETON-WATSON, *Eastern Europe Between the Two Wars, 1918–1941* (2nd ed., Cambridge, 1946).

HUGH SETON-WATSON, *Neither War nor Peace: The Struggle for Power in the Postwar World* (New York, 1960).

WILLIAM L. SHIRER, *The Rise and Fall of the Third Reich* (New York, 1960).

IVAR SPECTOR, *The Soviet Union and the Muslim World, 1917–1956* (rev. ed., Seattle, 1958).

LEON TROTSKY, *The History of the Russian Revolution* (trans. by Max Eastman, Ann Arbor, Mich., 1947), 3 vols.

DIXON WECTER, *The Age of the Great Depression, 1929–1941* (New York, 1948).

PATRICK G. WILSON, *Government and Politics of India and Pakistan, 1885–1955: A Bibliography of Works in Western Languages* (Berkeley, Calif., 1956).

GUY A. WINT, *The British in Asia* (rev. ed., London and New York, 1954, 1955).

MAURICE ZINKIN, *Asia and the West* (rev. ed., London and New York, 1953).

CHAPTER II
THE IMPACT OF NATIONALISM AND TREND TOWARD INTERNATIONAL CO-OPERATION
Nationalism

ALFRED COBBAN, *National Self-Determination* (rev. ed., Chicago, 1948).

KARL W. DEUTSCH, *Interdisciplinary Bibliography on Nationalism* (Cambridge, Mass., 1956).

KARL W. DEUTSCH, *Nationalism and Social Communication: An Inquiry into the Foundations of Nationality* (Boston and New York, 1953).

RUPERT EMERSON, *From Empire to Nation: The Rise to Self-Assertion of Asian and African Peoples* (Cambridge, Mass., 1960).

CARLTON J. H. HAYES, *Essays on Nationalism* (New York, 1926).

HANS KOHN, *Nationalism, Its Meaning and History* (Princeton, N.J., 1955).

ROYAL INSTITUTE OF INTERNATIONAL AFFAIRS, *Nationalism: A Report by a Study Group* (London and New York, 1939).

PHILIP W. THAYER, (ed.), *Nationalism and Progress in Free Asia* (Baltimore, Md., 1956).

International Co-operation

ROBERT E. ASHER et al., *The United Nations and Promotion of the General Welfare* (Washington, D.C., 1957).

HANS AUFRICHT, *Guide to League of Nations Publications: A Bibliographical Survey of the Work of the League, 1920–1947* (New York, 1951).

ROBERT BERKOV, *The World Health Organization* (Geneva, 1957).

CHARLES G. FENWICK, *The Inter-American Regional System* (New York, 1949).

LELAND M. GOODRICH and EDVARD I. HAMBRO, *Charter of the United Nations: Commentary and Documents* (second ed., Boston, 1949).

HESSEL DUNCAN HALL, *Mandates, Dependencies and Trusteeship* (Washington, D.C., 1948).

GOVE HAMBIDGE, *The Story of FAO* (New York, 1955).

MANLEY O. HUDSON, *The Permanent Court of International Justice, 1920–1942* (rev. ed., New York, 1943).

INTERNATIONAL LABOUR OFFICE, *The International Labour Organization: The First Decade* (London, 1931).

WALTER H. C. LAVES and CHARLES A. THOMSON, *UNESCO: Purpose, Progress, Prospects* (Bloomington, Ind., 1957).

OLIVER J. LISSITZYN, *The International Court of Justice: Its Role in the Maintenance of International Peace and Security* (New York, 1951).

ANDREW MARTIN, *Collective Security: A Progress Report* (Paris, 1952).

AMOS J. PEASLEE (ed.), *International Governmental Organizations: Constitutional Documents* (The Hague, 1956), 2 vols.

WILLIAM E. RAPPARD, *The Quest for Peace since the World War* (Cambridge, Mass., 1940).

WALTER SCHIFFER, *The Legal Community of Mankind: A Critical Analysis of the Modern Concept of World Organization* (New York, 1954).

FREDERICK L. SCHUMAN, *The Commonwealth of Man: An Inquiry into Power Politics and World Government* (New York, 1952).

JULIUS STONE, *Aggression and World Order: A Critique of United Nations Theories of Aggression* (Berkeley and Los Angeles, Calif., 1958).

CHARMIAN E. TOUSSAINT, *The Trusteeship System of the United Nations* (London and New York, 1956).

UNITED NATIONS, *Everyman's United Nations: The Structure, Function and Work of the Organization and Its Related Agencies During the Years 1945–1958* (New York, 1959).

FRANCIS P. WALTERS, *A History of the League of Nations,* (London and New York, 1952), 2 vols.

QUINCY WRIGHT, *Mandates Under the League of Nations* (Chicago, 1930).

ALFRED E. ZIMMERN, *The League of Nations and the Rule of Law, 1918–1935* (2nd. ed., London, 1939).

CHAPTER III

THE NEW ROLE OF THE STATE AND ITS COMPETING FORMS
(See also Chapter XXIII)

The Inclusive State

WILLIAM H. BEVERIDGE, *Social Insurance and Allied Services: Report* (London and New York, 1942).

SOLOMON FABRICANT and R. E. LIPSEY, *Trend of Government Activity in the United States since* 1900 (New York, 1953).

MARY P. FOLLETT, *The New State: Group Organization the Solution of Popular Government* (New York, 1918).

HAROLD J. LASKI, *Authority in the Modern State* (New Haven, 1919).

HAROLD J. LASKI, *Liberty in the Modern State* (London, 1930).

ROBERT M. MACIVER, *The Modern State* (Oxford, 1926).

THOMAS E. UTLEY and J. STUART MACLURE, (eds.), *Documents of Modern Political Thought* (Cambridge, 1957).

Liberal Democracy

CARL L. BECKER, *Modern Democracy* (New Haven, 1941).

JOHN DEWEY, *Freedom and Culture* (New York, 1939).

WILLIAM Y. ELLIOTT, *The Pragmatic Revolt in Politics* (New York, 1928).

THOMAS G. MASARYK, *The Making of a State* (New York and London, 1927).

T. ROLAND PENNOCK, *Liberal Democracy: Its Merits and Prospects* (New York, 1950).

Challenges to Liberal Democracy

G. D. H. COLE, *A History of Socialist Thought*, (London, 1953–56), 4 vols.

G. D. H. COLE, *Fabian Socialism* (London, 1943).

E. F. M. DURBIN, *Politics of Democratic Socialism* (London and Toronto, 1940).

JOSEPH A. SCHUMPETER, *Capitalism, Socialism and Democracy* (3rd. ed., New York, 1950).

GEORGES SOREL, *Reflections on Violence* (trans. by T. E. Hulme, New York, 1914).

Fascism

WILLIAM EBENSTEIN, *The Nazi State* (New York and Toronto, 1943).

HERMAN FINER, *Mussolini's Italy* (London and New York, 1935).

GUY STANTON FORD, (ed.), *Dictatorship in the Modern World* (2nd ed., Minneapolis, 1939).

CARL J. FRIEDRICH and Z. K. BRZEZINSKI, *Totalitarian Dictatorship and Autocracy* (Cambridge, Mass., 1956).

ADOLF HITLER, *Mein Kampf* (trans. under direction of Alvin Johnson, New York, 1939).

BENITO MUSSOLINI, *The Corporate State* (2nd ed., Florence, 1938).

FRANZ L. NEUMANN, *Behemoth: The Structure and Practice of National Socialism, 1933–1944* (2nd ed., New York and Toronto, 1944).

GAETANO SALVEMINI, *The Fascist Dictatorship in Italy* (New York, 1927).

Communism

CENTRAL COMMITTEE OF THE COMMUNIST PARTY OF THE SOVIET UNION, *History of the Communist Party of the Soviet Union* (New York, 1939).

MILOVAN DJILAS, *The New Class* (New York, 1957).

KARL KAUTSKY, *Social Democracy vs. Communism* (ed. and trans. by D. Shub and J. Shaplen, New York, 1946).

V. I. LENIN, *Collected Works* (authorized trans., New York, 1927).

MAO TSE-TUNG, *The Chinese Revolution and the Chinese Communist Party* (Peking, 1954).

ROYAL INSTITUTE OF INTERNATIONAL AFFAIRS, *The Soviet-Yugoslav Dispute* (London and New York, 1948).

HUGH SETON-WATSON, *From Lenin to Krushchev: The History of World Communism* (New York, 1960).

JOSEF STALIN, *Leninism* [*Foundations of Leninism; Problems of Leninism*] (trans. by E. and C. Paul, London, 1928–33), 2 vols.

SIDNEY and BEATRICE WEBB, *Soviet Communism: A New Civilisation?* (London and New York, 1935).

CHAPTER IV
THE TRIUMPH OF INDUSTRIALISM
(See also Chapters IX and XXI)

PAUL ALPERT, *Twentieth Century Economic History of Europe* (New York, 1951).

JULIUS H. BOEKE, *Economics and Economic Policy of Dual Societies, as Exemplified by Indonesia* (New York, 1953).

WILSON BRAND, *The Struggle for a Higher Standard of Living: The Problem of Underdeveloped Countries* (Glencoe, Ill., 1958).

NORMAN S. BUCHANAN and HOWARD S. ELLIS, *Approaches to Economic Development* (New York, 1955).

J. H. CLAPHAM, *An Economic History of Modern Britain:* Vol. III, *Machines and National Rivalries* (1887–1914) *with an Epilogue* (1914–29) (New York and Cambridge, 1938).

COLIN CLARK, *The Conditions of Economic Progress* (3rd ed., London and New York, 1957).

HENRY DAVID et al., (eds.), *The Economic History of the United States* (New York, 1945–), 9 vols.

J. FREDERIC DEWHURST, et al., *America's Needs and Resources: A New Survey* (New York, 1955).

J. FREDERIC DEWHURST et al., *Europe's Needs and Resources: Trends and Prospects in Eighteen Countries* (New York and London, 1961).

MAURICE H. DOBB, *Soviet Economic Development since* 1917, (London and New York, 1948).

S. HERBERT FRANKEL, *The Economic Impact on Under-Developed Societies* (Oxford, 1953).

SIMON G. HANSON, *Economic Development in Latin America* (Washington, D.C., 1951).

EIJIRŌ HONJŌ, *The Social and Economic History of Japan* (Kyoto, 1935).

LLOYD J. HUGHLETT, (ed.), *Industrialization of Latin America* (New York, 1946).

PETR I. LIASHCHENKO, *History of the National Economy of Russia to the 1917 Revolution* (trans. by L. M. Herman, New York, 1949).

WILLIAM W. LOCKWOOD, *The Economic Development of Japan: Growth and Structural Change, 1868–1938* (Princeton, N.J., 1954).

GUNNAR MYRDAL, *An International Economy: Problems and Prospects* (New York, 1956).

SERGEI N. PROKOPOVICH, *L'industrialisation des pays agricoles et la structure de l'économie mondiale après la guerre* (trans. by N. Nicolsky, Paris, 1946).

WALT W. ROSTOW, *The Process of Economic Growth* (2nd ed., Oxford, 1960).

FRED A. SHANNON, *America's Economic Growth* (3rd ed., New York, 1951).

EUGENE STALEY, *The Future of Underdeveloped Countries* (New York, 1954).

INGVAR SVENNILSON, *Growth and Stagnation in the European Economy* (Geneva, 1954).

W. S. WOYTINSKY and E. S. WOYTINSKY, *World Population and Production* (New York, 1953).

GEORGE WYTHE, *Industry in Latin America* (New York, 1945).

MAURICE ZINKIN, *Problems of Economic Development in Asia* (rev. ed., New York, 1954).

CHAPTER V

THE CHANGING SOCIETY

Industrial Society

CYRIL E. BLACK, (ed.), *The Transformation of Russian Society* (Cambridge, Mass., 1960).

G. D. H. COLE, *World in Transition* (New York, 1949).

GEORGES FRIEDMANN, (ed.), *Villes et campagnes: Civilisation urbaine et civilisation rurale en France* (Paris, 1953).

ERIC FROMM, *Escape from Freedom* (New York, 1941).

KAREN HORNEY, *The Neurotic Personality of our Time* (New York, 1937).

SEYMOUR M. LIPSET and REINHARD BENDIX, *Social Mobility in Industrial Society* (Berkeley and Los Angeles, Calif., 1958).

KARL MANNHEIM, *Man and Society in an Age of Reconstruction: Studies in Modern Social Structure* (London, 1940).

ELTON MAYO, *Social Problems of an Industrial Civilization* (Cambridge, Mass., 1945).

DAVID M. POTTER, *People of Plenty* (Chicago, 1954).

PRESIDENT'S RESEARCH COMMITTEE ON SOCIAL TRENDS, *Recent Social Trends in the United States* (New York, 1933), 2 vols.

ARNOLD M. ROSE, (ed.), *The Institutions of Advanced Societies* (Minneapolis, 1958).

UNITED NATIONS, *Report on the World Social Situation* (New York, 1957).

ERNEST WATKINS, *The Cautious Revolution* (London, 1951).

WILLIAM H. WHYTE, *The Organization Man* (New York, 1956).

Changing Non-Industrial Societies

GEORGES BALANDIER, *Sociologie actuelle de l'Afrique noire: Dynamique des change-ments sociaux en Afrique centrale* (Paris, 1955).

SYDNEY N. FISHER, (ed.), *Social Forces in the Middle East* (Ithaca, N.Y., 1955).

BERTHOLD F. HOSELITZ, *The Progress of Underdeveloped Areas* (Chicago, 1952).

MARGARET MEAD, (ed.), *Cultural Patterns and Technical Change* (Paris, 1953).

MARGARET MEAD, *New Lives for Old: Cultural Transformation—Manus, 1928–1953* (New York, 1956).

WILBERT E. MOORE, *Industrialization and Labor: Social Aspects of Economic Development* (Ithaca, N.Y., 1951).

JEROME F. SCOTT and R. P. LYNTON, *The Community Factor in Modern Technology* (Paris, 1952).

EDWARD H. SPICER, (ed.), *Human Problems in Technological Change: A Casebook* (New York, 1952).

UNESCO, 'Social Factors in Economic Growth: A Trend Report and Bibliography', *Current Sociology*, Vol. VI (Paris, 1957).

WILLEM F. WERTHEIM, *Indonesian Society in Transition: A Study of Social Change* (The Hague, 1956).

TAYA ZINKIN, *India Changes* (New York, 1958).

Population Movements and Changes (see also Chapter XV)

HARRISON S. BROWN, *The Challenge of Man's Future: An Inquiry Concerning the Condition of Man During the Years that Lie Ahead* (New York, 1954).

ALEXANDER M. CARR-SAUNDERS, *World Population: Past Growth and Present Trends* (Oxford, 1936).

H. A. CITROEN, *European Emigration Overseas: Past and Future* (The Hague, 1951).

OSCAR HANDLIN, *The Uprooted* (Boston, 1951).

PHILIP M. HAUSER, (ed.), *Population and World Politics* (Glencoe, Ill., 1958).

DUDLEY KIRK, *Europe's Population in the Interwar Years* (Princeton, N.J., 1946).

EUGENE M. KULISCHER, *Europe on the Move: War and Population Changes, 1917–1947* (New York, 1948).

POLITICAL and ECONOMIC PLANNING, *World Population and Resources: A Report* (London, 1955).

DONALD R. TAFT and RICHARD ROBBINS, *International Migrations: The Immigrant in the Modern World* (New York, 1955).

JACQUES VERNANT, *The Refugee in the Post-War World* (New Haven, 1953).

CHAPTER VI

THE NEW SCIENTIFIC THOUGHT

JACOB BRONOWSKI, *The Common Sense of Science* (London, 1951).

HERBERT DINGLE, (ed.), *A Century of Science, 1851–1951* (London and New York, 1951).

xx*

GERALD W. ELBERS and PAUL DUNCAN, (eds.), *Scientific Revolution: Challenge and Promise* (Washington, D.C., 1959).

PHILIPP FRANK, *Modern Science and Its Philosophy* (Cambridge, Mass., 1949).

EDWARD HUTCHINGS, (ed.), *Frontiers in Science: A Survey* (New York, 1958).

International Encyclopedia of Unified Science (Chicago, 1955–   ).

JOSEPH NEEDHAM and WALTER PAGEL, (eds.), *Background to Modern Science* (Cambridge, 1938–   ).

ALFRED NORTH WHITEHEAD, *Science and the Modern World* (New York, 1925).

LORANDA L. WOODRUFF, (ed.), *The Development of the Sciences* (New Haven, and London, 1941).

CHAPTER VII
MATHEMATICS AND LOGIC

NICOLAS BOURBAKI (pseud.), *Éléments de Mathématique* (Paris, 1940–1960), 6 vols.

ALONZO CHURCH, *Introduction to Mathematical Logic* (Princeton, N.J., 1956).

RICHARD COURANT and HERBERT ROBBINS, *What is Mathematics? An Elementary Approach to Ideas and Methods* (London and New York, 1941).

HOWARD EVES and CARROLL V. NEWSOM, *An Introduction to the Foundations and Fundamental Concepts of Mathematics* (New York, 1958).

WILLIAM FELLER, *An Introduction to Probability Theory and Its Application* (2nd ed., New York, 1957).

GODFREY H. HARDY, *A Mathematician's Apology* (Cambridge, 1940).

DAVID HILBERT, *The Foundations of Geometry* (trans. by E. J. Townsend, Chicago, 1902).

STEPHEN C. KLEENE, *Introduction to Metamathematics* (Amsterdam, 1952).

CLARENCE I. LEWIS and HAROLD L. COOPER, *A Survey of Symbolic Logic* (2nd ed., New York, 1959).

PAUL ROSENBLOOM, *The Elements of Mathematical Logic* (New York, 1950).

BERTRAND RUSSELL, *Introduction to Mathematical Philosophy* (London and New York, 1919).

EDWARD C. TITCHMARSH, *Mathematics for the General Reader* (London and New York, 1948).

BARTEL L. VAN DER WAERDEN, *Science Awakening* (trans. by A. Dresden, Groningen, 1954).

ALFRED NORTH WHITEHEAD and BERTRAND RUSSELL, *Principia Mathematica* (Cambridge, 1910–13), 3 vols.

RAYMOND L. WILDER, *Introduction to the Foundations of Mathematics* (New York, 1952).

CHAPTER VIII
THE ELABORATION OF THE PHYSICAL SCIENCES

FRANK D. ADAMS, *Birth and Development of the Geological Sciences* (Baltimore, 1938).

RITCHIE CALDER, *Science in our Lives* (East Lansing, Michigan, 1954).

CARL T. CHASE, *The Evolution of Modern Physics* (New York, 1947).

ARCHIBALD and NAN CLOW, *The Chemical Revolution: A Contribution to Social Technology* (London, 1952).

PETER DOIG, *A Concise History of Astronomy* (London, 1950).

ALBERT EINSTEIN and LEOPOLD INFELD, *The Evolution of Physics* (New York, 1942).

JAMES K. FINCH, *Engineering and Western Civilization* (New York, 1951).

ALEXANDER FINDLAY, *A Hundred Years of Chemistry*, (2nd ed., London, 1948).

GEORGE GAMOW, *Matter, Earth and Sky* (Englewood Cliffs, N.J., 1948).

J. ROBERT OPPENHEIMER, *Science and the Common Understanding* (New York, 1954).

EDMUND T. WHITTAKER, *A History of the Theories of Aether and Electricity* (London and New York, 1951–54), 2 vols.

CHAPTER IX
INDUSTRIAL PRODUCTION

Materials and Energy

SAM H. SCHURR and JACOB MARSCHAK, (eds.,) *Economic Aspects of Atomic Power* (Princeton, N.J., 1950).

DEMITRI B. SHIMKIN, *Minerals, A Key to Soviet Power* (Cambridge, Mass., 1953).

UNITED NATIONS, ECONOMIC COMMISSION FOR ASIA AND THE FAR EAST, *Relationship Between Industrial and Power Development* (New York, 1951).

UNITED NATIONS, INTERNATIONAL CONFERENCE ON THE PEACEFUL USES OF ATOMIC ENERGY, *Proceedings* (New York, 1955–58), 17 vols.

UNITED NATIONS, *Proceedings of the United Nations Scientific Conference on the Conservation and Utilization of Resources, 17 August to 6 September, 1949* (Lake Success, New York, 1950–53), 8 vols.

UNITED STATES PRESIDENT'S MATERIALS POLICY COMMISSION, *Resources for Freedom*, (Washington, D.C., 1952), 5 vols.

ERICH W. ZIMMERMANN, *World Resources and Industries: A Functional Appraisal of the Availability of Agricultural and Industrial Materials*, (rev. ed., New York, 1951).

Technology

AMERICAN MANAGEMENT ASSOCIATION, *Automation and Other Technological Advances* (New York, 1953).

PERCY DUNSHEATH, (ed.), *A Century of Technology, 1851–1951* (London and New York, 1951).

PAUL EINZIG, *The Economic Consequences of Automation* (London, 1956).

ROBERT J. FORBES, *Man the Maker: A History of Technology and Engineering* (London and New York, 1958).

GREAT BRITAIN, DEPARTMENT OF SCIENTIFIC AND INDUSTRIAL RESEARCH, *Automation* (London, 1956).

FREDERICK POLLOCK, *Automation, A Study of Its Economic and Social Consequences* (trans. by W. O. Henderson and W. H. Chaloner, Oxford and New York, 1957).

DICKSON RECK, (ed.), *National Standards in a Modern Economy* (New York, 1956).

ABBOTT P. USHER, *A History of Mechanical Inventions* (rev. ed., Cambridge, Mass., 1954).

A. A. ZVORIKINE, *Sosdanie Materialno-Tekhnicheskoi Basi Kommunisma v SSSR* (Material and Technical Foundation of Communism) (Moscow 1959).

Management and Labour Utilization

JAMES C. ABEGGLEN, *The Japanese Factory: Aspects of its Social Organization* (Glencoe, Ill., 1958).

A. ARAKELIAN, *Industrial Management in the U.S.S.R.* (trans. by E. L. Raymond, Washington, D.C., 1950).

DAVID GRANICK, *Management of the Industrial Firm in the U.S.S.R.* (New York, 1954).

G. B. HURFF, *Social Aspects of Enterprise in the Large Corporation* (Philadelphia, 1950).

INTERNATIONAL LABOUR OFFICE, *Higher Productivity in Manufacturing Industries* (Geneva, 1954).

INTERNATIONAL LABOUR OFFICE, *International Comparison of Real Wages: A Study of Methods* (Geneva, 1956).

INTERNATIONAL LABOUR OFFICE, *Minimum Wages: An International Survey* (Geneva, 1939).

INTERNATIONAL LABOUR OFFICE, *Payment by Results* (Geneva, 1951).

INTERNATIONAL LABOUR OFFICE, *Unemployment Insurance Schemes* (Geneva, 1955).

ABRAM T. JAFFE and CHARLES D. STEWART, *Manpower Utilization* (New York, 1951).

HENRY A. LANDSBERGER, *Hawthorne Revisited. Management and the Worker: its Critics, and Developments in Human Relations in Industry* (Ithaca, N.Y., 1958).

THOMAS M. LING, (ed.)., *Mental Health and Human Relations in Industry* (London, 1949).

FRITZ J. ROETHLISBERGER and WILLIAM J. DICKSON, *Management and the Worker: An Account of a Research Program Conducted by the Western Electric Company, Hawthorne Works, Chicago* (Cambridge, Mass., 1939).

SOLOMON M. SCHWARZ, *Labor in the Soviet Union* (New York, 1952).

FREDERICK W. TAYLOR, *Principles of Scientific Management* (New York and London, 1915).

S. HERBERT UNTERBERGER, *Guaranteed Wage and Supplementary Unemployment Pay Plans* (Chicago, 1956).

LYNDALL URWICK and E. F. L. BRECH, *The Making of Scientific Management* (London, 1945), 2 vols.

CHAPTER X
TRANSPORT

REGINALD M. CLEVELAND and SAMUEL T. WILLIAMSON, *The Road is Yours* (New York, 1951).

CHARLES E. GIBSON, *The Story of the Ship* (New York, 1948).

ADAM W. KIRKALDY and ALFRED D. EVANS, *Transport: Its History and Economics* (6th ed., London, 1946).

OLIVER J. LISSITZYN, *International Air Transport and National Policy* (New York, 1942).

HARRY O. MANCE et al., *International Transport and Communication* (New York, 1943–47), 7 vols.

CARL E. MCDOWELL and HELEN M. GIBBS, *Ocean Transportation* (New York, 1954).

P. HARVEY MIDDLETON, *Railways of Thirty Nations* (New York, 1937).

JACOB SCHENKMAN, *International Civil Aviation Organization* (Geneva, 1955).

LESLIE A. SCHUMER, *The Elements of Transport* (Sydney and London, 1954 and 1955).

CHARLES E. R. SHERRINGTON, *A Hundred Years of Inland Transport, 1830–1933* (London, 1934).

CHAPTER XI
COMMUNICATIONS

EDWARD L. BERNAYS, *Crystallizing Public Opinion* (New York, 1923).

GEORGE A. CODDING, *The International Telecommunication Union: An Experiment in International Co-operation* (Leiden, 1952).

COMMISSION ON FREEDOM OF THE PRESS, *A Free and Responsible Press: A General Report on Mass Communication: Newspapers, Radio, Motion Pictures, Magazines, Books* (Chicago, 1947).

GOVERNMENT OF INDIA, *Report of the Press Commission* (New Delhi, 1954).

ALEXIS INKELES, *Public Opinion in Soviet Russia: A Study in Mass Persuasion* (Cambridge, Mass., 1950).

WALTER LIPPMANN, *Public Opinion* (New York, 1922).

ROBERT K. MERTON, *Mass Persuasion: The Social Psychology of a War Bond Drive* (New York and London, 1946).

VANCE PACKARD, *The Hidden Persuaders* (New York, 1957).

POLITICAL and ECONOMIC PLANNING, *Report on the British Press* (London, 1938).

FRANK S. PRESBREY, *The History and Development of Advertising* (Garden City, N.Y., 1929).

WILBUR L. SCHRAMM, (ed.), *Communications in Modern Society* (Urbana, Ill., 1948).

BRUCE SMITH, HAROLD D. LASSWELL and RALPH D. CASEY, *Propaganda, Communication and Public Opinion* (Princeton, N.J., 1946).

UNESCO, *News Agencies: Their Structure and Operation* (Paris, 1953).

UNESCO, *Press, Film, Radio: Reports on the Facilities of Mass Communication* (Paris, 1951), 5 vols.

UNESCO, *Tentative International Bibliography of Works Dealing with Press Problems (1900–52)* (Paris, 1954).

UNESCO, *World Communications: Press, Radio, Film, Television* (3rd ed., Paris, 1956).

UNITED NATIONS, ECONOMIC AND SOCIAL COUNCIL, *Freedom of Information, 1953: Report Submitted by Salvador P. Lopez, Rapporteur on Freedom of Information* (New York, 1953).

FRANCIS WILLIAMS, *Transmitting World News: A Study of Telecommunications and the Press* (Paris, 1953).

CHAPTER XII
MEANS OF DESTRUCTION

RALPH NORMAN ANGELL, *The Great Illusion: a Study of the Relation of Military Power in Nations to Their Economic and Social Advantage* (London, 1910).

RAYMOND ARON, *The Century of Total War* (Garden City, N.Y., 1954).

JAMES P. BAXTER, 3rd, *Scientists Against Time* (Boston, 1946).

ELIS BIÖRKLUND, *International Atomic Policy During a Decade* (London, 1956).

PATRICK M. S. BLACKETT, *Atomic Weapons and East–West Relations* (Cambridge, 1956).

LIONEL M. CHASSIN, *Histoire militaire de la seconde guerre mondiale* (Paris, 1947).

CYRIL FALLS, *The Nature of Modern Warfare* (London, 1941).

JOHN F. C. FULLER, *A Military History of the Western World* (New York, 1954–1956), 3 vols.

JOHN F. C. FULLER, *The Second World War: A Strategical and Tactical History* (New York, 1949).

VICTOR WALLACE GERMAINS, *The 'Mechanization' of War* (London, 1927).

EDGAR J. KINGSTON-MCCLOUGHRY, *War in Three Dimensions: The Impact of Air-Power upon the Classical Principles of War* (London, 1949).

HENRY A. KISSINGER, *Nuclear Weapons and Foreign Policy* (New York, 1957).

BASIL H. LIDDELL HART, *A History of the World War, 1914–1918* (London, 1934).

WALTER MILLIS, *Arms and Men: A Study in American Military History* (New York, 1956).

JOHN U. NEF, *War and Human Progress: An Essay on the Rise of Industrial Civilization* (Cambridge, Mass., 1950).

GERALD WENDT, *Atomic Energy and the Hydrogen Bomb* (New York, 1950).

QUINCY WRIGHT, *A Study of War* (Chicago, 1942), 2 vols.

CHAPTER XIII
THE DEVELOPMENT OF BIOLOGICAL SCIENCES

RALPH W. GERARD, *Unresting Cells* (New York, 1940).

RICHARD S. GOLDSCHMIDT, *Understanding Heredity* (New York, 1952).

JULIAN S. HUXLEY, *Evolution, the Modern Synthesis* (New York, 1943).

ALEXANDER OPARIN, *The Origin of Life on the Earth* (trans. by Ann Synge, 3rd ed., New York, 1957).

CHRISTIAAN P. RAVEN, *An Outline of Developmental Physiology* (trans. by L. de Reiter, London and New York, 1954).

GEORGE G. SIMPSON, *The Meaning of Evolution* (New Haven, 1949).

GEORGE G. SIMPSON, COLIN S. PITTENDRIGH and LEWIS H. TIFFANY, *Life* (New York, 1957).

CHAPTER XIV
FOOD AND AGRICULTURE

Agriculture

Agriculture in the Twentieth Century: Essays . . . Presented to Sir Daniel Hall (Oxford, 1939).

MURRAY R. BENEDICT, *Farm Policies of the United States 1790–1950: A Study of Their Origins and Development* (New York, 1953).

FOLKE DOVRING, *Land and Labour in Europe, 1900–1950: A Comparative Survey of Recent Agrarian History* (The Hague, 1956).

FOOD AND AGRICULTURE ORGANIZATION OF THE UNITED NATIONS, *Inter-relationship between Agrarian Reform and Agricultural Development* (Rome, 1953).

FOOD AND AGRICULTURE ORGANIZATION OF THE UNITED NATIONS, *The State of Food and Agriculture: Review of a Decade and Outlook* (Rome, 1955).

FOOD AND AGRICULTURE ORGANIZATION OF THE UNITED NATIONS, *So Bold an Aim: Ten Years of International Cooperation Toward Freedom from Want* (Rome, 1955).

LEONARD E. HUBBARD, *The Economics of Soviet Agriculture* (London, 1939).

NAUM JASNY, *The Socialized Agriculture of the U.S.S.R.: Plans and Performance* (Stanford, Calif., 1949).

CHARLES KELLOGG, *The Soils That Support Us* (New York, 1941).

FAIRFIELD OSBORN, *Our Plundered Planet* (Boston and London, 1948).

HOWARD S. REED, *A Short History of the Plant Sciences* (Waltham, Mass., 1942).

ROYAL INSTITUTE OF INTERNATIONAL AFFAIRS, *World Agriculture: An International Survey* (London, 1932).

EDWARD J. RUSSELL, *World Population and World Food Supplies* (London, 1954).

US DEPARTMENT OF AGRICULTURE, *Science in Farming: The Yearbook of Agriculture, 1943–47* (Washington, D.C., 1947).

DOREEN WARRINER, *Land Reform and Development in the Middle East* (London and New York, 1957).

DOREEN WARRINER, *The Economics of Peasant Farming* (London and New York, 1939).

PAUL LAMARTINE YATES, *Food, Land, and Manpower in Western Europe* (London and New York, 1960).

Forestry

FOOD AND AGRICULTURE ORGANIZATION OF THE UNITED NATIONS, 'Ten Years of Forestry in FAO', *Unasylva* II, 2 (Rome, 1957).

STEPHEN HADEN-GUEST, JOHN K. WRIGHT and EILEEN M. TECLAFF, (eds.), *A World Geography of Forest Resources* (New York, 1956).

US DEPARTMENT OF AGRICULTURE, *New Knowledge in Forestry: Report of the Chief of the Forest Service, U.S. Department of Agriculture, 1948* (Washington, D.C., 1949).

ROBERT K. WINTERS, (ed.), *Fifty Years of Forestry in the U.S.A.* (Washington, D.C., 1950).

Fisheries

CHARLES L. CUTTING, *Fish Saving: A History of Fish Processing from Ancient to Modern Times* (London, 1955).

FOOD AND AGRICULTURE ORGANIZATION OF THE UNITED NATIONS, 'Improving the Fisheries Contribution to World Food Supplies', *FAO Fisheries Bulletin*, VI 5 (Rome, 1953).

MICHAEL GRAHAM and G. L. KESTEVEN, 'Biological Possibilities in World Fisheries', *FAO Fisheries Bulletin*, VII, 1, (Rome, 1954).

HAROLD A. INNIS, *The Cod Fisheries: The History of an International Economy* (rev. ed., Toronto, 1954).

G. L. KESTEVEN and G. E. R. DEACON, 'The Contribution of Oceanographic Research to Fisheries Science', *FAO Fisheries Bulletin*, VIII, 2, (Rome, 1955).

JAN-OLOF TRAUNG, (ed.), *Fishing Boats of the World* (London, 1955).

UNITED NATIONS, *Papers Presented at the International Technical Conference on the Conservation of the Living Resources of the Sea, Rome, 18 April to 10 May, 1955* (New York, 1956).

UNITED NATIONS, *Report of the International Technical Conference on the Conservation of the Living Resources of the Sea, Rome, 18 April to 10 May, 1955* (New York, 1956).

Nutrition

FOOD AND AGRICULTURE ORGANIZATION OF THE UNITED NATIONS, Committee on Calorie Requirements, *Calorie Requirements: Report. 12–16 September, 1949* (Washington, D.C., 1950).

FOOD AND NUTRITION BOARD, National Academy of Sciences—National Research Council, *Recommended Dietary Allowances: Revised 1953* (Washington, D.C., 1953).

ANCEL B. KEYS *et al.*, *The Biology of Human Starvation* (Minneapolis, 1950), 2 vols.

JOHN BOYD ORR, *Food, Health and Income* (London, 1936).

MARJORIE L. SCOTT, *School Feeding: Its Contribution to Child Nutrition* (Rome, 1953).

HENRY C. SHERMAN, *The Nutritional Improvement of Life* (New York, 1950).

HAZEL K. STIEBLING and MEDORA WARD, *Diets at Four Levels of Nutritive Content and Cost* (Washington, D.C., 1933).

CHAPTER XV

HEALTH AND POPULATION

Health

BRITISH MEDICAL ASSOCIATION, *Fifty Years of Medicine: A Symposium from the British Medical Journal* (London, 1950).

ARTURO CASTIGLIONI, *A History of Medicine* (trans. and ed. by E. B. Krumbhaar, 2nd ed., New York, 1947).

RENÉ and JEAN DUBOS, *The White Plague: Tuberculosis, Man and Society* (Boston, 1952).

MIKE GORMAN, *Every Other Bed* (Cleveland, 1956).

L. FABIAN HIRST, *The Conquest of Plague* (Oxford, 1953).

DONALD HUNTER, *The Diseases of Occupations* (London, 1955).

JOINT ILO/WHO COMMITTEE ON OCCUPATIONAL HEALTH, *Second Report* (Geneva, 1953).

GEORGE ROSEN, *A History of Public Health* (New York, 1958).

PAUL F. RUSSELL, *Man's Mastery of Malaria* (London and New York, 1955).

RENÉ SAND, *The Advance to Social Medicine* (London and New York, 1952).

RICHARD H. SHRYOCK, *The Development of Modern Medicine: An Interpretation of the Social and Scientific Factors Involved* (2nd ed., New York, 1947).

JAMES S. SIMMONS, (ed.), *Public Health in the World Today* (Cambridge, Mass., 1949).

LUDWIG TELEKY, *History of Factory and Mine Hygiene* (New York, 1948).

NIKOLAI ARKADEVICH VINOGRADOV, *Public Health in the Soviet Union* (3rd ed., trans., Moscow, 1952).

C. E. A. WINSLOW, *Man and Epidemics* (Princeton, N.J., 1952).

C. E. A. WINSLOW, *The Cost of Sickness and the Price of Health* (Geneva, 1951).

Population (see also Chapter V)

F. G. BOUDREAU and CLYDE V. KISER, (eds.), *Trends and Differentials in Mortality* (New York, 1956).

ANSLEY J. COALE and EDGAR M. HOOVER, *Population Growth and Economic Development in Low-Income Countries* (Princeton, N.J., 1958).

RONALD FREEDMAN, P. K. WHELPTON and A. A. CAMPBELL, *Family Planning, Sterility and Population Growth* (New York, 1959).

FRANK LORIMER and F. OSBORN, *Dynamics of Population* (New York and London, 1934).

WILBERT E. MOORE, *Economic Demography of Eastern and Southern Europe* (London and New York, 1946).

GUNNAR MYRDAL, *Population: A Problem for Democracy* (Cambridge, Mass., 1940).

JOSEPH J. SPENGLER and OTIS D. DUNCAN, (eds.), *Population Theory and Policy* (Glencoe, Ill., 1956).

UNITED NATIONS, *The Determinants and Consequences of Population Trends* (New York, 1953).

WILLIAM VOGT, *People: Challenge to Survival* (New York, 1960).

UNITED NATIONS WORLD POPULATION CONFERENCE, *Papers of the World Population Conference, Rome, 1954* (New York, 1955).

WORLD POPULATION CONFERENCE, Geneva, 1927, *Proceedings* (ed. by M. Sanger, London, 1927).

CHAPTER XVI

THE SCIENTIFIC APPROACH TO HUMAN BEHAVIOUR
AND HUMAN RELATIONS

FRANZ G. ALEXANDER and HELEN ROSS, (eds.), *Dynamic Psychiatry* (Chicago, 1952).

STUART F. CHAPIN, *Social Science Research: Its Expanding Horizons* (Minneapolis, Minn., 1953).

GLYN E. DANIEL, *A Hundred Years of Archaeology* (London, 1950).

WAYNE DENNIS *et al.*, *Current Trends in Psychology* (Pittsburgh, 1947).

HOWARD S. ELLIS and BERNARD F. HALEY, (eds.), *A Survey of Contemporary Economics* (Philadelphia, Pa., and Homewood, Ill., 1948 and 1952), 2 vols.

Encyclopaedia of the Social Sciences (New York, 1930–1935), 15 vols.

LEON FESTINGER and DONALD KATE, (eds.), *Research Methods in the Behavioral Sciences* (New York, 1953).

JOHN CARL FLÜGEL, *A Hundred Years of Psychology, 1833–1933* (2nd ed., with developments 1933–47, London, 1951).

GEORGES GURVITCH and WILBERT E. MOORE, (eds.), *Twentieth Century Sociology* (New York, 1945).

Handwörterbuch der Sozialwissenschaften (Stuttgart, Tübingen, Göttingen, 1952–).

PHILIP L. HARRIMAN, JOSEPH L. ROUCEK and GEORGE B. DE HUSZAR, (eds.), *Contemporary Social Science, Volume I; Western Hemisphere* (Harrisburg, Pa., 1953).

R. F. HARROD, *The Life of John Maynard Keynes* (London, 1952).

H. STUART HUGHES, *Consciousness and Society: The Reorientation of European Social Thought, 1890–1930* (New York, 1958).

ERNEST JONES, *Life and Work of Sigmund Freud* (London and New York, 1953–57), 3 vols.

FELIX M. KEESING, *Culture Change: An Analysis and Bibliography of Anthropological Sources to 1952* (Stanford, Calif., 1953).

CLYDE KLUCKHOHN and HENRY A. MURRAY, (eds.), *Personality in Nature, Society and Culture* (2nd ed., New York, 1953).

ARTHUR L. KROEBER, (ed.), *Anthropology Today: An Encyclopedic Inventory* (Chicago, 1953).

DANIEL LERNER, (ed.), *The Policy Sciences: Recent Developments in Scope and Method* (Stanford, Calif., 1951).

GARDNER LINDZEY, (ed.), *Handbook of Social Psychology* (Cambridge, Mass., 1954), 2 vols.

KARL MANNHEIM, *Ideology and Utopia: An Introduction to the Sociology of Knowledge* (trans. by L. Wirth and E. A. Shils, New York, 1936).

FRITZ MORSTEIN MARX, (ed.), *Elements of Public Administration* (2nd ed., Englewood Cliffs, N.J., 1959).

NATIONAL BUREAU OF ECONOMIC RESEARCH, *Economic Research and the Development of Economic Science and Public Policy*, Twelve Papers presented at 25th Anniversary Meeting (New York, 1946).

TALCOTT PARSONS and EDWARD A. SHILS, (eds.), *Toward a General Theory of Action* (Cambridge, Mass., 1951).

MASSIMO SALVADORI *et al.*, (eds.), *Contemporary Social Science, Volume II: Eastern Hemisphere* (Harrisburg, Pa., 1954).

BRIAN SIMON, (ed.), *Psychology in the Soviet Union* (trans. by J. and M. Ellis *et al.*, Stanford, Calif., 1957).

SOCIAL SCIENCE RESEARCH COUNCIL, COMMITTEE ON HISTORIOGRAPHY, *Theory and Practice in Historical Study* (New York, 1946).

SOCIAL SCIENCE RESEARCH COUNCIL, COMMITTEE ON HISTORIOGRAPHY, *The Social Sciences in Historical Study* (New York, 1954).

SOL TAX *et al.*, (eds.), *An Appraisal of Anthropology Today* (Chicago, 1953).

UNESCO, *Contemporary Political Science* (Paris, 1950).

UNESCO, *International Repertory of Social Science Documentation Centres* (Paris, 1952).

UNIVERSITY OF MINNESOTA GRADUATE SCHOOL, SOCIAL SCIENCE RESEARCH CENTER, *The Social Sciences at Mid-Century: Papers Delivered at the Dedication of Ford Hall, April 19–21 1951* (Minneapolis, Minn., 1952).

MAX WEBER, *On the Methodology of the Social Sciences* (ed. by E. A. Shils and H. A. Finch, Glencoe, Ill., 1949).

MAX WEBER, *The Theory of Social and Economic Organization* (trans. by T. Parsons, rev. ed., New York, 1947).

LEONARD D. WHITE, (ed.), *The State of the Social Sciences* (Chicago, 1956).

BARBARA WOOTTON, *Testament for Social Science: An Essay in the Application of Scientific Method to Human Problems* (London, 1950).

CHAPTER XVII

THE HOME

JULIET LITA BANE and MILDRED R. CHAPIN, *Introduction to Home Economics* (Boston, 1945).

ISABEL BEVIER, *Home Economics in Education* (Philadelphia, 1924).

JOHN BOWLBY, *Maternal Care and Mental Health* (Geneva, 1951).

LEONARD CARMICHAEL, (ed.), *Manual of Child Psychology* (2nd ed., New York, 1954).

HAZEL T. CRAIG, *The History of Home Economics* (New York, 1946).

PAULINE NICKELL and JEAN M. DORSEY, *Management in Family Living* (New York and London, 1942).

WILLIAM D. WALL, *The Adolescent Child* (London, 1948).

HELEN L. WITMER and RUTH KOTINSKY, (eds.), *Personality in the Making: The Fact-Finding Report of the Midcentury White House Conference on Children and Youth* (New York, 1952).

CHAPTER XVIII
THE ENVIRONMENT

NELS ANDERSON, *The Urban Community: A World Perspective* (New York, 1959).

RICHARD K. BEARDSLEY et al., *Village Japan* (Chicago, 1959).

LE CORBUSIER (C. E. JEANNERET-GRIS), *Concerning Town Planning* (trans. by C. Entwistle, London, 1947).

DAVID and ISABEL CROOK, *Revolution in a Chinese Village* (London, 1959).

ROBERT E. DICKINSON, *The West European City: A Geographical Interpretation* (London, 1951).

RONALD P. DORE, *City Life in Japan* (Berkeley, Calif., 1958).

SHYAMA CHARAN DUBE, *Indian Village* (Ithaca, N.Y., 1955).

OTIS D. DUNCAN et al., *Metropolis and Region* (Baltimore, 1960).

ORLANDO FALS-BORDA, *Peasant Society in the Colombian Andes* (Gainesville, Fla., 1955).

HERMAN FINER, *The T.V.A.: Lessons for International Application* (Montreal, 1944).

ROBERT M. FISHER, (ed.), *The Metropolis in Modern Life* (Garden City, N.Y., 1955).

FOOD AND AGRICULTURE ORGANIZATION OF THE UNITED NATIONS, *Essentials of Rural Welfare* (Washington, D.C., 1949).

ARTHUR B. GALLION and SIMON EISNER, *The Urban Pattern: City Planning and Design* (New York, 1950).

PATRICK GEDDES, *Cities in Evolution* (London, 1915).

PAUL K. HATT and ALBERT J. REISS, Jr., (eds.), *Cities and Society: Revised Reader in Urban Sociology* (Glencoe, Ill., 1957).

JOINT UNITED NATIONS–UNESCO SEMINAR, *Urbanization in Asia and the Far East: Proceedings*, (ed. by Philip M. Hauser, Calcutta, 1957).

PAUL H. LANDIS, *Rural Life in Process* (2nd ed., New York, 1948).

MAHMUT MAKAL, *A Village in Anatolia* (London, 1954).

LEWIS MUMFORD, *The City in History: Its Origins, Its Transformations, and Its Prospects* (New York, 1961).

LEWIS MUMFORD, *The Culture of Cities* (New York, 1938).

ROBERT E. PARK, *et al., The City* (Chicago, 1925).

WILLIAM A. ROBSON, (ed.), *Great Cities of the World: Their Government, Politics and Planning* (London and New York, 1957).

PITRIM A. SOROKIN *et al.,* (eds.), *A Systematic Source Book in Rural Sociology* (Minneapolis, 1930–32), 3 vols.

UNITED NATIONS, *Second Report on the World Social Situation* (New York, 1959).

UNITED NATIONS, *Urban Land Problems and Policies* (New York, 1953).

CHAPTER XIX
PREVENTION AND TREATMENT OF SOCIAL BREAKDOWN

ERNEST BARKER, *The Development of Public Services in Western Europe, 1660–1930* (London and New York, 1944).

WILLIAM H. BEVERIDGE, *Voluntary Action: A Report on Methods of Social Advance* (London, 1948).

ANNE BOURDILLON, *Voluntary Social Services, Their Place in the Modern State* (London, 1945).

LUCIEN BOVET, *Psychiatric Aspects of Juvenile Delinquency* (Geneva, 1951).

ERNEST W. BURGESS, (ed.), *Aging in Western Societies* (Chicago, 1960).

EVELINE M. BURNS, *Social Security and Public Policy* (New York, 1956).

CYRIL BURT, *The Young Delinquent* (rev. ed., Brickley, Kent, 1944).

ALBERT DEUTSCH, *The Mentally Ill in America* (rev. ed., New York, 1949).

INTERNATIONAL LABOUR OFFICE, *International Survey of Social Security: Comparative Analysis and Summary of National Laws* (Geneva, 1950).

INTERNATIONAL LABOUR OFFICE, *International Survey of Social Services, 1933* (Geneva, 1936), 2 vols.

INTERNATIONAL ASSOCIATION OF GERONTOLOGY, *Old Age in the Modern World* (London, 1954).

GEORGE R. NELSON, (ed.), *Freedom and Welfare: Social Patterns in the Northern Countries of Europe* (Denmark, Finland, Iceland, Norway, Sweden, Ministries of Social Affairs, 1953).

MADELINE ROOFF, *Voluntary Societies and Social Policy* (London, 1957).

CLIFFORD R. SHAW and HENRY D. MCKAY, *Juvenile Delinquency in Urban Areas* (Chicago, 1942).

DAVID STAFFORD-CLARK, *Psychiatry To-day* (Harmondsworth, Middlesex, 1952).

RICHARD TITMUSS, *Problems of Social Policy* (London, 1950).

UNITED NATIONS, *International Survey of Programmes of Social Development* (New York, 1955).

UNITED NATIONS, *Social Progress Through Local Action* (New York, 1955).

UNITED NATIONS, *Training for Social Work: An International Survey* (New York, 1950); *Second International Survey* (1955); *Third International Survey* (1960).

UNITED NATIONS, *Economic Measures in Favour of the Family* (New York, 1952).

BARBARA WOOTTON *et al.*, *Social Science and Social Pathology* (London, 1959).

CHAPTER XX
MAJOR TRENDS IN CONCEPTS AND IDEAS

I. M. BOCHENSKI, *Contemporary European Philosophy* (trans. by D. Nicholl and K. Aschenbrenner, Berkeley, Calif., 1956).

ROBERT N. C. HUNT, *The Theory and Practice of Communism* (rev. ed., New York, 1957).

THOMAS A. JACKSON, *Dialectics: The Logic of Marxism and Its Critics* (London, 1936).

WALTER KAUFMANN, (ed.), *Existentialism from Dostoevsky to Sartre* (New York, 1956).

HERBERT MARCUSE, *Soviet Marxism: A Critical Analysis* (New York, 1958).

JACQUES MARITAIN, *The Degrees of Knowledge* (New York, 1938).

CHARLES A. MOORE, (ed.), *Essays in East-West Philosophy* (Honolulu, 1951).

F. S. C. NORTHROP, (ed.), *Ideological Differences and World Order* (New Haven, 1949).

F. S. C. NORTHROP, *The Meeting of East and West* (New York, 1946).

JOHN P. PLAMENATZ, *German Marxism and Russian Communism* (London, 1954).

SARVEPALLI RADHAKRISHNAN, (ed.), *History of Philosophy, Eastern and Western* (London and New York, 1952–3), 2 vols.

DAGOBERT D. RUNES, (ed.), *Twentieth Century Philosophy* (New York, 1943).

BERTRAND RUSSELL, *A History of Western Philosophy* (London and New York, 1945).

JEAN WAHL, 'Philosophie', in *50 Années de Découvertes: Bilan 1900–1950* (Paris, 1950).

MORTON G. WHITE, (ed.), *The Age of Analysis: 20th Century Philosophers* (Boston and New York, 1955).

PHILIP P. WIENER, *Evolution and the Founders of Pragmatism* (Cambridge, Mass., 1949).

CHAPTER XXI
ECONOMIC INSTITUTIONS
(See also Chapters IV and IX)

SOLOMON ADLER, *The Chinese Economy* (London and New York, 1957).

WILLIAM ASHWORTH, *A Short History of the International Economy, 1850–1950* (London and New York, 1952).

S. S. BALZAK *et al.*, (eds.), *Economic Geography of the U.S.S.R.* (trans. by R. M. Hankin and O. A. Titelbahn, New York, 1949).

ALEXANDER M. BAYKOV, *The Development of the Soviet Economic System: An Essay on the Experience of Planning in the U.S.S.R.* (New York and Toronto, 1947).

BURNHAM P. BECKWITH, *The Economic Theory of a Socialist Economy* (Stanford, Calif., and London, 1949).

ABRAM BERGSON, (ed.), *Soviet Economic Growth: Conditions and Perspectives* (Evanston, Ill., 1953).

ARTHUR R. BURNS, *Comparative Economic Organization* (New York, 1955).

ROBERT W. CAMPBELL, *Soviet Economic Power* (New York, 1960).

THOMAS C. COCHRAN, *The American Business System: A Historical Perspective, 1900–1955* (Cambridge, Mass., 1957).

JEROME B. COHEN, *Japan's Postwar Economy* (Bloomington, Ind., 1958).

ROBERT I. CRANE, *Aspects of Economic Development in South Asia* (New York, 1954).

DAVID J. DALLIN and BORIS I. NICOLAEVSKY, *Forced Labor in Soviet Russia* (New Haven, 1947).

HAROLD U. FAULKNER, *The Decline of Laissez-Faire, 1897–1917* (New York, 1951).

PHILIP SARGENT FLORENCE, *The Logic of British and American Industry* (London, 1953).

DHANANJAYA R. GADGIL, *The Industrial Evolution of India in Recent Times* (4th ed., London, New York, Bombay, 1942).

JOHN KENNETH GALBRAITH, *American Capitalism: The Concept of Countervailing Power* (Boston, 1952).

GOVERNMENT OF INDIA PLANNING COMMISSION, *The New India: Progress through Democracy* (New York, 1958).

GEORGE N. HALM, *Economic Systems: A Comparative Analysis* (New York and Toronto, 1951).

GEORGE W. HOFFMAN and FRED W. NEAL, *Yugoslavia and the New Communism* (New York, 1962).

CALVIN B. HOOVER, *The Economy, Liberty and the State* (New York, 1959).

TREVOR JONES HUGHES and D. E. T. LUARD, *The Economic Development of Communist China, 1949–1958* (New York, 1959).

K. WILLIAM KAPP, *The Social Costs of Private Enterprise* (Cambridge, Mass., 1950).

JOHN MAYNARD KEYNES, *The Economic Consequences of the Peace* (London, 1919).

JOHN MAYNARD KEYNES, *The General Theory of Employment, Interest and Money* (London, 1936).

EDWARD S. MASON, (ed.), *The Corporation in Modern Society* (Cambridge, Mass., 1959).

NATIONAL RESOURCES COMMITTEE, *The Structure of the American Economy, Part I: Basic Characteristics* (Washington, D.C., 1939).

RAGNAR NURKSE, *Problems of Capital Formation in Underdeveloped Countries* (Oxford, 1953).

WILLIAM A. ROBSON, (ed.), *Problems of Nationalized Industry* (London and New York, 1952).

WILHELM RÖPKE, *A Humane Economy: The Social Framework of the Free Market* (trans. by Elizabeth Henderson, Chicago, 1960).

HARRY SCHWARTZ, *Russia's Soviet Economy* (2nd ed., New York, 1954).

W. SOMBART, *Das Wirtschaftsleben im Zeitalter des Hochkapitalismus* (Leipzig, 1927) Part III of *Der Moderne Kapitalismus*, 2 vols.

NICOLAS SPULBER, *The Economics of Communist Eastern Europe* (New York, 1957).

GEORGE A. STEINER, *Government's Role in Economic Life* (New York, 1953).

GEORGE W. STOCKING and MYRON W. WATKINS, *Cartels in Action: Case Studies in International Business Diplomacy* (New York, 1946).

JOHN STRACHEY, *Contemporary Capitalism* (London and New York, 1956).

C. N. VAKIL and P. R. BRAHMANAND, *Planning for an Expanding Economy* (Bombay, New York, 1956).

HENRY C. WALLICH, *Mainsprings of the German Revival* (New Haven and London, 1955).

MAX WEBER, *Wirtschaft und Gesellschaft* (4th ed., Tübingen, 1956).

CHAPTER XXII
SOCIAL INSTITUTIONS
(See also Chapter V)

'AFRICAN ELITES', *International Social Science Bulletin*, VIII, 3 (Paris, 1956).

FREDERICK L. ALLEN, *The Big Change* (New York, 1952).

RUTH N. ANSHEN, (ed.), *The Family: Its Function and Destiny* (New York, 1949).

SHMUEL N. EISENSTADT, *From Generation to Generation: Age Groups and Social Structure* (Glencoe, Ill., 1956).

ERIK H. ERIKSON, *Childhood and Society* (New York, 1950).

DAVID V. GLASS, (ed.), *Social Mobility in Britain* (London, 1954).

INTERNATIONAL AFRICAN INSTITUTE, *Social Implications of Industrialization and Urbanization in Africa South of the Sahara* (Paris, 1956).

INTERNATIONAL INSTITUTE OF DIFFERING CULTURES, *Development of a Middle Class in Tropical and Sub-tropical Countries* (Brussels, 1956).

JOHN J. JOHNSON, *Political Change in Latin America: The Emergence of the Middle Sectors* (Stanford, Calif., 1958).

MARION J. LEVY, *The Family Revolution in Modern China* (Cambridge, Mass., 1949).

REUBEN LEVY, *The Social Structure of Islam* (Cambridge, 1957).

DAVID LOCKWOOD, *The Blackcoated Worker: A Study in Class Consciousness* (London, 1958).

C. WRIGHT MILLS, *The Power Elite* (New York, 1956).

C. WRIGHT MILLS, *White Collar: The American Middle Class* (New York, 1951).

MARY MORRIS, *Voluntary Organizations and Social Progress* (London, 1955).

ALVA MYRDAL, *Nation and Family: The Swedish Experiment in Democratic Family and Population Policy* (London, 1945).

ALICE C. PERCIVAL, *Youth Will be Led: The Story of the Voluntary Youth Organizations* (London, 1951).

UNITED NATIONS, *Slavery* (New York, 1955).

ROBERT VAN NIEL, *The Emergence of the Modern Indonesian Elite* (The Hague and Chicago, 1960).

SIDNEY and BEATRICE WEBB, *The Consumers' Cooperative Movement* (London 1921).

GERHARD ZIEMER and HANS WOLF, *Wandervögel* (Bad Godesburg, 1962).

CHAPTER XXIII
POLITICAL INSTITUTIONS
(See also Chapters III, XXVIII)
Democratic and Authoritarian

HAROLD E. DAVIS, (ed.), *Government and Politics in Latin America* (New York, 1958).

MAURICE DUVERGER, *Political Parties: Their Organization and Activity in the Modern State* (London, 1959).

MAURICE DUVERGER, *The French Political System* (Chicago, 1958).

HERMAN FINER, *Theory and Practice of Modern Government* (rev. ed., New York, 1949).

WOLFGANG FRIEDMANN, *Law in a Changing Society* (Berkeley and Los Angeles, Calif., 1959).

HAROLD R. G. GREAVES, *The Civil Service in the Changing State* (London, 1947).

RICHARD HOFSTADTER, *The American Political Tradition and The Men Who Made It* (New York, 1948).

LIONEL CECIL JANE, *Liberty and Despotism in Spanish America* (Oxford, 1929).

GEORGE M. KAHIN, (ed.), *Major Governments of Asia* (Ithaca, N.Y., 1958).

CARL LANDAUER, *European Socialism: A History of Ideas and Movements from the Industrial Revolution to Hitler's Seizure of Power* (Berkeley and Los Angeles, Calif., 1959), 2 vols.

HAROLD J. LASKI et al., for the Inter-parliamentary Union, *Development of the Representative System in Our Times* (Lausanne, 1928).

HAROLD D. LASSWELL and ABRAHAM KAPLAN, *Power and Society* (New Haven, 1950).

HERBERT LUETHY, *France Against Herself* (trans. by E. Mosbacher, New York, 1955).

HERBERT S. MORRISON, *Government and Parliament: A Survey from the Inside* (London and New York, 1954).

FRANZ L. NEUMANN, *The Democratic and the Authoritarian State* (Glencoe, Ill., 1957).

SIGMUND NEUMANN, (ed.), *Modern Political Parties: Approaches to Comparative Politics* (Chicago, 1956).

AMOS J. PEASLEE, (ed.), *Constitutions of Nations* (2nd ed., The Hague, 1956), 3 vols.

WILLIAM E. RAPPARD, *The Government of Switzerland* (New York, 1936).

WILLIAM A. ROBSON, *Justice and Administrative Law: A Study of the British Constitution* (3rd ed., London, 1951).

HERBERT A. SIMON, *Administrative Behavior: A Study of Decision-Making Processes in Administrative Organization* (New York, 1947).

CARL B. SWISHER, *American Constitutional Development* (2nd ed., Boston, 1954).

Communist

JOHN A. ARMSTRONG, *The Soviet Bureaucratic Elite: A Case Study of the Ukrainian Apparatus* (New York, 1959).

CONRAD BRANDT, BENJAMIN SCHWARTZ and JOHN K. FAIRBANK, *A Documentary History of Chinese Communism* (Cambridge, Mass., 1952).

ISAAC DEUTSCHER, *Stalin: A Political Biography* (London and New York, 1949).

MERLE FAINSOD, *How Russia is Ruled* (Cambridge, Mass., 1953).

VLADIMIR GSOVSKI, *Soviet Civil Law* (Ann Arbor, Mich., 1948–49), 2 vols.

JOHN N. HAZARD, *Settling Disputes in Soviet Society* (New York, 1960).

JOHN N. HAZARD, *The Soviet System of Government* (rev. ed., Chicago, 1960).

CHARLES P. MCVICKER, *Titoism: Pattern for International Communism* (New York, 1957).

LEONARD B. SCHAPIRO, *The Communist Party of the Soviet Union* (New York, 1960).

DEREK J. R. SCOTT, *Russian Political Institutions* (London and New York, 1958).

S. B. THOMAS, *Government and Administration in Communist China* (rev. ed., New York, 1955).

JULIAN TOWSTER, *Political Power in the U.S.S.R. 1917–1947: The Theory and Structure of Government in the Soviet State* (New York, 1948).

Colonial Systems

NTIEYONG U. AKPAN, *Epitaph to Indirect Rule* (London, 1956).

GEORGE BENNETT, (ed.), *The Concept of Empire: Burke to Attlee, 1774–1947* (London, 1953).

THOMAS E. ENNIS, *French Policy and Developments in Indochina* (Chicago, 1936).

JOHN S. FURNIVALL, *Colonial Policy and Practice: A Comparative Study of Burma and Netherlands India* (Cambridge, 1948).

PAUL KNAPLUND, *Britain: Commonwealth and Empire, 1901–1955* (London, 1956).

FREDERICK J. D. LUGARD, *The Dual Mandate in British Tropical Africa* (London, 1922).

HERBERT I. PRIESTLEY, *France Overseas: A Study of Modern Imperialism* (New York and London, 1938).

KATHLEEN M. STAHL, *British and Soviet Colonial Systems* (London and New York. 1951).

JOHN STRACHEY, *The End of Empire* (London, 1959).

AMRY VANDENBOSCH, *The Dutch East Indies: Its Government, Problems and Politics*, (3rd ed., Berkeley, Calif., 1942).

GEORGES VAN DER KERKEN, *La Politique Coloniale Belge* (Antwerp, 1943).

CHAPTER XXIV
MILITARY INSTITUTIONS

WALLACE CARROLL, *Persuade or Perish* (Boston, 1948).

RICHARD D. CHALLENER, *The French Theory of the Nation in Arms, 1866–1939* (New York, 1955).

FRANK P. CHAMBERS, *The War Behind the War 1914–1918: A History of the Political and Civilian Fronts* (London, 1939).

JEROME B. COHEN, *Japan's Economy in War and Reconstruction* (Minneapolis, 1949).

GORDON A. CRAIG, *The Politics of the Prussian Army, 1640–1945* (London, 1955).

D. FEDOTOFF WHITE, *The Growth of the Red Army* (Princeton, N.J., 1944).

RAYMOND L. GARTHOFF, *Soviet Military Doctrine* (Glencoe, Ill., 1953).

CHARLES GIDE, (ed.), *The Effect of the War upon French Economic Life* (Oxford and London, 1923).

WALTER GOERLITZ, *History of the German General Staff, 1657–1945* (trans. by B. Battershaw, New York, 1953).

W. K. HANCOCK and M. M. GOWING, *British War Economy* (London, 1949).

ELIOT JANEWAY, *The Struggle for Survival: A Chronicle of Economic Mobilization in World War II* (New Haven, 1951).

EDGAR J. KINGSTON-MCCLOUGHRY, *The Direction of War: A Critique of the Political Direction and High Command in War* (London and New York, 1955).

HAROLD D. LASSWELL, *Propaganda Technique in the World War* (New York and London, 1927).

BASIL H. LIDDELL HART, (ed.), *The Red Army* (New York, 1956).

ALBRECHT MENDELSSOHN-BARTHOLDY, *The War and German Society* (London and New Haven, 1937).

WALTER MILLIS et al., *Arms and the State: Civil–Military Elements in National Policy* (New York, 1958).

JAMES T. SHOTWELL, (ed.), *Economic and Social History of the World War* (New Haven, New York and London, 1922–1936).

HANS W. SINGER, *The German War Economy* (Manchester, 1943).

HANS SPEIER and ALFRED KOEHLER, (eds.), *War in Our Time* (New York, 1939).

ALFRED VAGTS, *A History of Militarism: Civilian and Military* (rev. ed., New York, 1959).

N. A. VOZNESENSKY, *The Economy of the U.S.S.R. during World War II* (Washington D.C., 1948).

JOHN W. WHEELER-BENNETT, *The Nemesis of Power: The German Army in Politics, 1918–1945* (London and New York, 1954).

CHAPTER XXV

RELIGION

World Religions

CHARLES S. BRADEN, *Modern Tendencies in World Religions* (New York, 1933).

KURT GALLING *et al*, (eds.), *Die Religion in Geschichte und Gegenwart*, Handwörterbuch für Theologie und Religionwissenschaft (Tübingen, 1957–)

KENNETH P. LANDON, *Southeast Asia, Crossroad of Religions* (Chicago, 1949).

SARVEPALLI RADHAKRISHNAN, *Eastern Religions and Western Thought* (2nd ed., London, 1951).

Christianity

DANIEL A. BINCHY, *Church and State in Fascist Italy* (London and New York, 1941).

JOHN S. CURTISS, *Church and State in Russia: The Last Years of the Empire, 1900–1917* (London and New York, 1940).

JOHN S. CURTISS, *The Russian Church and the Soviet State, 1917–1950* (Boston, 1953).

EDWARD DUFF, JR. *The Social Thought of the World Council of Churches* (London and New York, 1956).

CHARLES P. GROVES, *The Planting of Christianity in Africa* (London, 1948–1958), 4 vols.

WALDEMAR GURIAN, (ed.), *The Catholic Church in World Affairs* (Notre Dame, Ind., 1954).

G. L. H. HARVEY, (ed.), *The Church and the Twentieth Century* (London, 1936).

JULIUS F. HECKER, *Religion and a Changing Civilization* (London, 1935).

WILLIAM E. HOCKING, Commission of Appraisal of the Laymen's Foreign Missions Inquiry, *Re-thinking Missions: A Laymen's Inquiry after One Hundred Years* (New York, 1932).

KENNETH S. LATOURETTE, *A History of the Expansion of Christianity* (New York and London, 1937–45), 7 vols.

JOHN L. MECHAM, *Church and State in Latin America* (Chapel Hill, N.C., 1934).

ERICH MEISSNER, *Confusion of Faces: The Struggle Between Religion and Secularism in Europe* (London, 1946).

JOSEPH N. MOODY, (ed.), *Church and Society: Catholic Social and Political Thought and Movements, 1789–1950* (New York, 1953).

ARNOLD S. NASH, (ed.), *Protestant Thought in the Twentieth Century* (New York, 1951).

RUTH ROUSE and STEPHEN C. NEIL, *A History of the Ecumenical Movement* (Philadelphia, 1954).

HERBERT W. SCHNEIDER, *Religion in 20th Century America* (Cambridge, Mass., 1952).

GEORGE STEPHENS SPINKS et al., *Religion in Britain since 1900* (London, 1952).

FRANCIS HERBERT STEAD, *The Story of Social Christianity* (London, 1924), 2 vols.

ANSON P. STOKES, *Church and State in the United States: Historical Development and Contemporary Problems of Religious Freedom under the Constitution* (New York, 1950), 3 vols.

ROBERT TOBIAS, *Communist–Christian Encounter in East Europe* (Indianapolis, 1956).

Judaism (See also Chapter XXVIII)

JACOB B. AGUS, *Guideposts in Modern Judaism: An Analysis of Current Trends in Jewish Thought* (New York, 1954).

LOUIS FINKELSTEIN, (ed.), *The Jews: Their History, Culture and Religion* (2nd ed., New York, 1955), 2 vols.

ROBERT GORDIS, *Conservative Judaism* (New York, 1945).

DAVID PHILIPSON, *The Reform Movement in Judaism* (rev. ed., New York, 1931).

LEON ROTH, *Jewish Thought as a Factor in Civilization* (Paris, 1954).

Islam (See also Chapters XXVIII, XXIX)

CHARLES C. ADAMS, *Islam and Modernism in Egypt* (London, 1933).

HAMILTON A. R. GIBB, *Modern Trends in Islam* (Chicago, 1947).

ALPHONSE GOUILLY, *L'Islam devant le monde moderne* (Paris, 1945).

MUHAMMAD IQBAL, *The Reconstruction of Religious Thought in Islam* (London, 1934).

ROGER LE TOURNEAU, *L'Islam contemporian* (Paris, 1950).

WILFRED CANTWELL SMITH, *Islam in Modern History* (Princeton, N.J., 1957).

JOHN S. TRIMINGHAM, *Islam in West Africa* (Oxford, 1959).

GUSTAVE E. VON GRÜNEBAUM, (ed.), *Unity and Variety in Muslim Civilization* (Chicago, 1955).

Hinduism

JOHN N. FARQUHAR, *Modern Religious Movements in India* (New York, 1915).

KENNETH W. MORGAN, (ed.), *The Religion of the Hindus* (New York, 1953).

K. M. PANIKKAR, *Hindu Society at Cross Roads* (Bombay, 1955).

DITTAKAVI SUBRAHMANYA SARMA, *Studies in the Renaissance of Hinduism in the Nineteenth and Twentieth Centuries* (Benares, 1944).

Buddhism

CHAN WING-TSIT, *Religious Trends in Modern China* (New York, 1953).

EDWARD CONZE, *Buddhism: Its Essence and Development* (New York, 1951).

HIDEO KISHIMOTO, (ed.), *Japanese Religion in the Meiji Era* (trans. and adapted by John F. Howes, Tokyo, 1956).

KENNETH W. MORGAN, (ed.), *The Path of the Buddha* (New York, 1956).

T. R. V. MURTI, *The Central Philosophy of Buddhism* (London, 1955).

CHAPTER XXVI

EDUCATION

ROBERT FREEMAN BUTTS and LAURENCE A. CREMIN, *A History of Education in American Culture* (New York, 1953).

OLIVER CROMWELL CARMICHAEL, *Universities: Commonwealth and American, a Comparative Study* (New York, 1959).

MARGARET A. CLAPP, (ed.), *The Modern University* (Ithaca, N.Y., 1950).

STANLEY J. CURTIS and M.E.A. BOULTWOOD, *A Short History of Educational Ideas* (2nd ed., London, 1956).

STANLEY J. CURTIS, *Education in Britain since 1900* (London, 1952).

M. M. DEINEKO, *Forty Years of Education in the U.S.S.R.: Fact and Figures* (trans. by D. Myshne, Moscow, 1957).

HAROLD C. DENT, *Change in English Education: A Historical Survey* (London, 1952).

JOHN DEWEY, *School and Society* (rev. ed., Chicago, 1915).

ROBERT K. HALL, *Education for a New Japan* (New Haven, 1949).

NICHOLAS A. HANS, *Comparative Education: A Study of Educational Factors and Traditions* (London, 1949).

RICHARD HOFSTADTER and C. DEWITT HARDY, *The Development and Scope of Higher Education in the United States* (New York, 1952).

HUMAYUN KABIR, *Education in New India* (London, 1956).

HUGH L. KEENLEYSIDE and A. F. THOMAS, *History of Japanese Education and Present Educational System* (Tokyo, 1937).

EDMUND KING, *Other Schools and Ours* (London, 1960).

EDGAR W. KNIGHT, *Fifty Years of American Education: A Historical Review and Critical Appraisal* (New York, 1952).

ALEXANDER G. KOROL, *Soviet Education for Science and Technology* (New York, 1957).

INTERNATIONAL BUREAU OF EDUCATION and UNESCO, *International Yearbook of Education* (Geneva and Paris, 1933–).

RODERIC D. MATTHEWS and MATTA AKRAWI, *Education in the Arab Countries of the Near East* (Washington, D.C., 1949).

ADOLF E. MEYER, *The Development of Education in the 20th Century* (2nd ed., New York, 1949).

ARTHUR M. MOELMAN and JOSEPH S. ROUCEK, (eds.), *Comparative Education* (New York, 1952).

WALTER S. MONROE, (ed.), *Encyclopedia of Educational Research* (3rd ed., New York, 1960).

MARGARET H. READ, *Education and Social Change in Tropical Areas* (London and New York, 1955).

ROBERT ULICH, *History of Educational Thought* (New York, 1950).

UNESCO, *Basic Facts and Figures* (Paris, 1952–   ), biennial.

UNESCO, *Education in a Technological Society* (Paris, 1952).

UNESCO, *Humanism and Education in East and West* (Paris, 1953).

UNESCO, *National Programmes of Education for Social Development* (Paris, 1954).

UNESCO, *Progress of Literacy in Various Countries* (Paris, 1953).

UNESCO, *World Handbook of Educational Organization and Statistics* (1st ed., Paris, 1951).

WILLIAM D. WALL, *Education and Mental Health* (Paris, 1955).

HOWARD E. WILSON, *Universities and World Affairs* (New York, 1951).

JAMES Y. C. YEN, *The Mass Education Movement in China* (Shanghai, 1925).

CHAPTER XXVII
THE USE OF LEISURE
(See also Chapters XI and XXXI)

J. FREDERIC DEWHURST and ASSOCIATES, 'Recreation', in *America's Needs and Resources* (New York, 1955).

GEORGE A. LUNDBERG *et al.*, *Leisure: A Suburban Study* (New York, 1934).

HAROLD D. MEYER and CHARLES K. BRIGHTBILL, *Community Recreation: A Guide to Its Organization and Administration* (Boston, 1948).

MARTIN H. and ESTHER S. NEUMEYER, *Leisure and Recreation* (New York, 1949).

G. OTT ROMNEY, *Off-the-Job-Living* (New York, 1945).

BERNARD ROSENBERG and DAVID MANNING WHITE, (eds.), *Mass Culture: The Popular Arts in America* (Glencoe, Ill., 1957).

GILBERT SELDES, *The Public Arts* (New York, 1956).

THE ARTS COUNCIL OF GREAT BRITAIN, *The First Ten Years: Eleventh Annual Report* (London, 1956).

Reading

R. E. BARKER, *Books for All* (Paris, 1956).

MALCOLM COWLEY, *The Literary Situation* (New York, 1954).

JAMES D. HART, *The Popular Book: A History of America's Literary Taste* (New York, 1950).

FRANK LUTHER MOTT, *A History of American Magazines* (Cambridge, Mass., 1938–   ), 5 vols.

Motion Pictures

BOSLEY CROWTHER, *The Lion's Share: The Story of an Entertainment Empire* (New York, 1957).

FILM CENTRE, London, *The Film Industry in Six European Countries* (Paris, 1950).

GOVERNMENT OF INDIA, *Report of the Film Enquiry Committee* (New Delhi, 1951).

MOTION PICTURE ASSOCIATION OF JAPAN, *Japanese Motion Picture Industry* (Tokyo, 1955).

PARKER TYLER, *The Three Faces of the Film: The Art, the Dream, the Cult* (New York, 1960).

HORTENSE POWDERMAKER, *Hollywood, the Dream Factory* (Boston, 1950).

PAUL ROTHA, *The Film till Now: A Survey of World Cinema* (New York, 1949).

MARTHA WOLFENSTEIN and NATHAN LEITES, *Movies: A Psychological Study* (Glencoe, Ill., 1950).

Radio and Television

LEO BOGART, *The Age of Television* (rev. ed., New York, 1958).

BRITISH BROADCASTING CORPORATION, *The BBC Television Story* (London, 1956).

CHARLES A. SIEPMANN, *Radio, Television and Society* (New York, 1950).

Popular Music and Dance

RUDI BLESH, *Shining Trumpets: A History of Jazz* (rev. ed., New York and London, 1958).

MARGARET LLOYD, *The Borzoi Book of Modern Dance* (New York, 1949).

MARSHALL STEARNS, *The Story of Jazz* (New York, 1956).

BARRY ULANOV, *A History of Jazz in America* (New York, 1952).

Sports, Travel and Hobbies

FRANK G. MENKE, *The New Encyclopedia of Sports* (rev. ed., New York, 1953).

NATIONAL RECREATION ASSOCIATION OF THE USA, *Recreation and Park Yearbook, Mid-century Edition: A Review of Local and County Recreation and Park Developments, 1900–1950* (New York, 1951).

CHAPTER XXVIII
SELF IMAGE AND ASPIRATIONS OF NATIONS
(See also Chapters III, XXIII)

Liberal Democracy

JAMES B. BRYCE, *Modern Democracies* (London, 1921), 2 vols.

MICHAEL P. FOGARTY, *Christian Democracy in Western Europe, 1820–1953* (Notre Dame, Ind., 1957).

THEODORE M. GREENE, *Liberalism: Its Theory and Practice* (Austin, Texas, 1957).

THOMAS P. NEILL, *The Rise and Decline of Liberalism* (Milwaukee, 1953).

MICHAEL OAKESHOTT, *Social and Political Doctrines of Contemporary Europe* (Cambridge, 1939).

GUIDO DE RUGGIERO, *The History of European Liberalism* (trans. by R. G. Collingwood, London, 1927).

ARTHUR M. SCHLESINGER, Jr., *The Vital Center* (Boston, 1949).

JOHN A. SCOTT, *Republican Ideas and the Liberal Tradition in France, 1870–1914* (New York, 1951).

THOMAS VERNON SMITH and EDUARD C. LINDEMAN, *The Democratic Way of Life* (Chicago, 1926).

Marxist–Leninist Communism

RAYMOND A. BAUER, *The New Man in Soviet Psychology* (Cambridge, Mass., 1952).

COLUMBIA UNIVERSITY RUSSIAN INSTITUTE, (ed.), *The Anti-Stalin Campaign and International Communism: A Selection of Documents* (New York, 1956).

MICHAEL T. FLORINSKY, *Toward an Understanding of the U.S.S.R.* (rev. ed., New York, 1951).

MALCOLM D. KENNEDY, *A History of Communism in East Asia* (New York, 1957).

NIKITA S. KRUSHCHEV, *Speeches and Interviews on World Problems* (Moscow, 1958).

ANNA M. PANKRATOVA, *History of the U.S.S.R.* (comp. by K. V. Basilevich, Moscow, 1947–48), 3 vols.

G. V. PLEKHANOV, *History of Russian Social Thought* (trans. by B. Bakar *et al.*, New York, 1938).

MIKHAIL N. POKROVSKY, *Brief History of Russia* (trans. by D. S. Mirsky, New York, 1933).

ANDREW ROTHSTEIN, *A History of the U.S.S.R.* (Harmondsworth, Middx., 1950).

ERNEST J. SIMMONS, (ed.), *Continuity and Change in Russian and Soviet Thought* (Cambridge, Mass., 1955).

UNITED NATIONS, *Report of the Special Committee on the Problem of Hungary* (New York, 1957).

GEORG VON RAUCH, *A History of Soviet Russia* (trans. by P. and A. Jacobsohn, New York, 1957).

ALEXANDER S. VUCINICH, *The Soviet Academy of Sciences* (Stanford, Calif., 1956).

Anti-Liberal Authoritarianism

GERALD BRENAN, *The Spanish Labyrinth* (2nd ed., Cambridge, 1950).

CHARLES A. GULICK, *Austria from Habsburg to Hitler* (Berkeley, Calif., 1948), 2 vols.

NICHOLAS HORTHY, *Memoirs* (trans. by F. G. Renier and A. Cliff, New York, 1957).

EDWIN LIEUWEN, *Arms and Politics in Latin America* (New York, 1960).

BENITO MUSSOLINI, *The Doctrine of Fascism* (trans. by E. Cope, 2nd ed., Florence, 1937).

Racial Superiority

ALAN L. C. BULLOCK, *Hitler: A Study in Tyranny* (London and New York, 1952).

GEORGE H. CALPIN, (ed.), *The South African Way of Life: Values and Ideals of a Multi-Racial Society* (New York, 1953).

GWENDOLEN M. CARTER, *The Politics of Inequality: South Africa since 1948* (London and New York, 1958).

CORNELIUS W. DE KIEWIET, *The Anatomy of South African Misery* (London and New York, 1956).

HANS KOHN, (ed.), *German History: Some New German Views* (London, 1954).

DANIEL W. KRUGER, (ed.), *South African Parties and Policies, 1910–1960* (Cape Town and London, 1960).

LEOPOLD MARQUARD, *Peoples and Policies of South Africa* (2nd ed., New York, 1960).

FRIEDRICH MEINECKE *The German Catastrophe* (trans. by Sidney B. Fay, Cambridge, Mass., 1950).

KOPPEL S. PINSON, *Modern Germany, its History and Civilization* (New York, 1954).

HUGH R. TREVOR-ROPER, *The Last Days of Hitler* (3rd ed., London, 1956).

States of Religious Origin

DAVID BEN-GURION, *Rebirth and Destiny of Israel* (trans. by Mordekhai Nurock, New York, 1954).

MARTIN BUBER, *Israel and Palestine: The History of an Idea* (trans. by S. Godman, London, 1952).

ISRAEL COHEN, *The Zionist Movement* (rev. ed., New York, 1946).

J. B. DASGUPTA, *Indo–Pakistan Relations, 1947–55* (Amsterdam, 1958).

JACOB C. HUREWITZ, *The Struggle for Palestine* (New York, 1950).

S. M. IKRAM and PERCIVAL SPEAR, (eds.), *The Cultural Heritage of Pakistan* (Karachi and New York, 1955).

OSCAR I. JANOWSKY, *Foundations of Israel: Emergence of a Welfare State* (Princeton, 1959).

I. H. QURESHI, *The Pakistani Way of Life* (New York, 1956).

WILFRED CANTWELL SMITH, *Pakistan as an Islamic State* (Lahore, 1954).

RICHARD SYMONDS, *The Making of Pakistan* (London, 1950).

Independence in Face of European Expansion

HALIDÉ EDIB, *Turkey Faces West* (New Haven, 1930).

ELIOT G. MEARS *et al.*, *Modern Turkey: A Politico–Economic Interpretation 1908–1923* (New York, 1924).

MARGERY F. PERHAM, *The Government of Ethiopia* (London, 1948).

IKBAL ALI SHAH, *Modern Afghanistan* (London, 1939).

DONALD EVERETT WEBSTER, *The Turkey of Atatürk: Social Process in the Turkish Reformation* (Philadelphia, 1939).

DONALD N. WILBER, *Iran, Past and Present* (4th ed., Princeton, 1958).

AHMED EMIN YALMAN, *Turkey in my Time* (Norman, Okla., 1956).

Awakening Nationalism—Africa

DAVID E. APTER, *The Gold Coast in Transition: A Case Study of Political Institutional Transfer* (Princeton, N.J., 1955).

WILLIAM R. BASCOM and MELVILLE J. HERSKOVITS (eds.), *Continuity and Change in African Cultures* (Chicago, 1958).

GWENDOLEN M. CARTER and WILLIAM O. BROWN, (eds.), *Transition in Africa: Studies in Political Adaptation* (Boston, 1958).

JAMES S. COLEMAN, *Nigeria: Background to Nationalism* (Berkeley, Calif., 1958).

BASIL DAVIDSON, *The African Awakening* (London, 1955).

ROBERT L. DELAVIGNETTE, *Freedom and Authority in French West Africa* (London, New York and Toronto, 1950).

JAMES DUFFY, *Portuguese Africa* (Cambridge, Mass., 1959).

THOMAS L. HODGKIN, *Nationalism in Colonial Africa* (London, 1956).

WILLIAM MALCOLM, LORD HAILEY, *An African Survey: A Study of Problems Arising in Africa South of the Sahara* (rev. ed., London and New York, 1957).

Z. A. MARSH and G. KINGSNORTH, *An Introduction to the History of East Africa* (Cambridge, 1957).

GEORGE PADMORE, *Pan-Africanism or Communism? The Coming Struggle for Africa* (London, 1956).

VIRGINIA M. THOMPSON and RICHARD ADLOFF, *The Emerging States of French Equatorial Africa* (Stanford, Calif., 1960).

CHAPTER XXIX
DRIVES FOR CULTURAL INTEGRITY AND RECOGNITION

India and Ceylon

FREDERICK G. BAILEY, *Tribe, Caste and Nation* (New York, 1960).

A. R. DESAI, *Social Background of Indian Nationalism* (Bombay and New York, 1948).

MOHANDAS K. GANDHI, *Gandhi's Autobiography: The Story of My Experiments with Truth* (trans. by Mahadev Desai, Washington, D.C., 1948).

JAWAHARLAL NEHRU, *Jawaharlal Nehru, An Autobiography: With Musings on Recent Events in India* (new ed., London, 1945).

JAWAHARLAL NEHRU, *The Discovery of India* (New York, 1946).

LEWIS S. S. O'MALLEY, (ed.), *Modern India and the West: A Study of the Interaction of their Civilizations* (London, New York, 1941).

K. M. PANIKKAR, *A Survey of Indian History* (3rd ed., Bombay and New York, 1956).

RICHARD L. PARK and IRENE TINKER, (eds.), *Leadership and Political Institutions in India* (Princeton, 1959).

SARVEPALLI RADHAKRISHNAN and J. H. MUIRHEAD, (eds.), *Contemporary Indian Philosophy* (rev. ed., London, 1952).

B. PATTABHI SITARAMAYYA, *The History of the Indian National Congress* (Bombay, 1946–47), 2 vols.

THOMAS G. P. SPEAR, *India, Pakistan, and the West* (2nd ed., London and New York, 1952).

WILLIAM HOWARD WRIGGINS, *Ceylon: Dilemmas of a New Nation* (Princeton, N.J., 1960).

China

O. BRIÈRE, *Fifty Years of Chinese Philosophy, 1898–1950* (trans. by L. G. Thompson, London, 1956).

CHIANG MONLIN, *Tides from the West, a Chinese Autobiography* (New Haven, 1947).

HERRLEE G. CREEL, *Chinese Thought, from Confucius to Mao Tse-tung* (Chicago, 1953).

CHARLES P. FITZGERALD, *Revolution in China* (London and New York, 1952).

HO KAN-CHIH, *A History of the Modern Chinese Revolution* (Peking, 1959).

ARTHUR N. HOLCOMBE, *The Chinese Revolution, a Phase in the Regeneration of a World Power* (Cambridge, Mass., 1930).

HU CHANG-TU *et al.*, *China: Its People, its Society, its Culture* (ed. by Hsiao Hsia; New Haven, 1960).

KUO PIN-CHIA, *China: New Age and New Outlook* (London, 1956).

JOSEPH NEEDHAM, *Science and Civilisation in China* (Cambridge, 1954–   ).

SUN YAT-SEN, *San Min Chu I: The Three Principles of the People* (trans. by Frank W. Price, Shanghai, 1927; Taipei, 1953).

TENG SSÜ-YÜ and JOHN K. FAIRBANK, *China's Response to the West: A Documentary Survey, 1839–1923* (Cambridge, Mass., 1954).

Japan

RUTH BENEDICT, *The Chrysanthemum and the Sword: Patterns of Japanese Culture* (Boston, 1946).

HUGH BORTON *et. al.*, *A Selected List of Books and Articles on Japan in English, French and German* (Cambridge, Mass., 1954).

HUGH BORTON, *Japan's Modern Century* (New York, 1955).

DELMER M. BROWN, *Nationalism in Japan* (Berkeley, Calif., 1955).

CENTENARY CULTURAL COUNCIL, *A Cultural History of the Meiji Era* (Tokyo, 1955–1958), 10 vols.

KAZUO KAWAI, *Japan's American Interlude* (Chicago, 1960).

E. HERBERT NORMAN, *Japan's Emergence as a Modern State* (New York, 1940).

EDWIN O. REISCHAUER, *Japan, Past and Present* (2nd ed., New York, 1953).

GEORGE B. SANSOM, *The Western World and Japan: A Study in the Interaction of European and Asiatic Cultures* (London, 1950).

South East Asia and Korea

WILLARD H. ELSBREE, *Japan's Role in Southeast Asian Nationalist Movements, 1940 to 1945* (Cambridge, Mass., 1953).

JOSEPH R. HAYDEN, *The Philippines: A Study in National Development* (New York, 1942).

GEORGE M. KAHIN, *Nationalism and Revolution in Indonesia* (Ithaca, N.Y., 1952).

GEORGE M. MCCUNE and ARTHUR L. GREY, *Korea Today* (Cambridge, Mass., 1950).

MAUNG MAUNG, *Burma in the Family of Nations* (2nd ed., Amsterdam and New York, 1957).

VIRGINIA M. THOMPSON, *Thailand: The New Siam* (New York, 1941).

AMRY VANDENBOSCH and RICHARD A. BUTWELL, *Southeast Asia among the World Powers* (Lexington, Kentucky, 1958).

RICHARD OLOF WINSTEDT, *The Malays: A Cultural History* (rev. ed., New York, 1950).

The Arabs

JAMAL MUHAMMAD AHMED, *The Intellectual Origins of Egyptian Nationalism* (London, 1960).

GEORGE ANTONIUS, *The Arab Awakening: The Story of the Arab National Movement* (London, 1938).

EDWARD S. ATIYAH, *The Arabs* (Harmondsworth, Middx., 1955).

CARLETON S. COON, *Caravan: The Story of the Middle East* (rev. ed., New York, 1958).

NABIH A. FARIS, (ed.), *The Arab Heritage* (Princeton, N.J., 1944).

NABIH A. FARIS and MOHAMMED TAWFIK HUSAYN, *The Crescent in Crisis: An Interpretive Study of the Modern Arab World* (Lawrence, Kansas, 1955).

ALLAL AL FASSI, *The Independence Movements in North Africa* (trans. by H. Z. Nuseibeh, Washington, D.C., 1954).

WALTER Z. LAQUEUR, (ed.), *The Middle East in Transition* (New York, 1958).

STEPHEN H. LONGRIGG, *Iraq 1900–1950: A Political, Social and Economic History* (London and New York, 1953).

GAMAL ABDUL NASSER, *Egypt's Liberation: The Philosophy of the Revolution* (Washington, D.C., 1955).

H. ST. JOHN B. PHILBY, *Sa'udi Arabia* (London and New York, 1955).

NICOLA A. ZIADEH, *Syria and Lebanon* (New York, 1957).

United States of America

DANIEL J. BOORSTIN, (ed.), *The Chicago History of American Civilization* (Chicago, 1956–   ), 20 vols.

HENRY S. COMMAGER et al., *Years of the Modern: An American Appraisal* (New York, 1949).

HENRY S. COMMAGER, *The American Mind* (New Haven, 1950).

MERLE E. CURTI, *The Growth of American Thought* (2nd ed., New York, 1951).

RALPH H. GABRIEL, *The Course of American Democratic Thought: An Intellectual History since 1815* (2nd ed., New York, 1956).

RALPH H. GABRIEL, (ed.), *The Library of Congress Series in American Civilization* (Cambridge, Mass., 1951–54), 6 vols.

OSCAR HANDLIN *et al.*, *Harvard Guide to American History* (Cambridge, Mass., 1954).

LOUIS HARTZ, *The Liberal Tradition in America: An Interpretation of American Political Thought Since the Revolution* (New York, 1955).

RICHARD HOFSTADTER, *The Age of Reform* (New York, 1955).

HALVDAN KOHT, *The American Spirit in Europe* (Philadelphia, 1949).

ARTHUR M. SCHLESINGER, Jr., *The Age of Roosevelt* (Boston, 1957–60), 3 vols.

HARVEY WISH, *Society and Thought in America* (New York, 1950–52), 2 vols.

Canada, Australia, New Zealand

GEORGE W. BROWN, (ed.), *Canada* (Berkeley and Los Angeles, Calif., 1950).

JOHN B. CONDLIFFE, *New Zealand in the Making* (rev. ed., London, 1959).

GORDON GREENWOOD, (ed.), *Australia: A Social and Political History* (New York and Sydney, 1955).

ARTHUR R. M. LOWER, *Colony to Nation* (3rd ed., Toronto, 1949).

ALAN G. L. SHAW, *Story of Australia* (London, 1955).

Latin America

RICHARD N. ADAMS *et al.*, *Social Change in Latin America Today* (New York, 1960).

FERNANDO DE AZEVEDO, *Brazilian Culture* (trans. by W. R. Crawford, New York, 1950).

HARRY BERNSTEIN, *Modern and Contemporary Latin America* (Philadelphia, Pa., 1952).

WILLIAM R. CRAWFORD, *A Century of Latin American Thought* (Cambridge, Mass., 1944).

ROBERT A. HUMPHREYS, *Latin American History: A Guide to the Literature in English* (London and New York, 1958).

HENRY B. PARKES, *A History of Mexico* (rev. ed., Boston, 1950).

ANÍBAL SANCHEZ REULET, *Contemporary Latin-American Philosophy* (trans. by W. R. Trask, Albuquerque, New Mexico, 1954).

WILLIAM L. SCHURZ, *This New World: The Civilization of Latin America* (New York, 1954).

T. LYNN SMITH, *Brazil: People and Institutions* (rev. ed., Baton Rouge, La., 1954).

FRANK TANNENBAUM, *Mexico, the Struggle for Peace and Bread* (New York, 1950).

DANIEL COSÍO VILLEGAS, *Extremos de América* (Mexico, D. F., 1949).

GEORGE WYTHE *et al.*, *Brazil, an Expanding Economy* (New York, 1949).

Cultural Minorities

ALBERT H. HOURANI, *Minorities in the Arab World* (London and New York, 1947).

CLAUDE L. INIS, *National Minorities: An International Problem* (Cambridge, Mass., 1955).

CARLILE A. MACARTNEY, *National States and National Minorities* (London, 1934).

JOSÉ CARLOS MARIÁTEGUI, *Siete Ensayos de Interpretación de la Realidad Peruana* (2nd ed., Lima, 1934; Santiago de Chile, 1955).

VIRGINIA M. THOMPSON and RICHARD ADLOFF, *Minority Problems in Southeast Asia* (Stanford, Calif., 1955).

CHAPTER XXX
DRIVE FOR INDIVIDUAL FREEDOM AND RECOGNITION

Labour

MARGARET BONDFIELD, *A Life's Work* (London, 1948).

G. D. H. COLE, *A Short History of the British Working-class Movement, 1789–1947* (London, 1948).

JOHN R. COMMONS et al., *History of Labour in the United States* (New York, 1918–35), 4 vols.

WILFRID H. CROOK, *The General Strike: A Study of Labor's Tragic Weapon in Theory and Practice* (Chapel Hill, North Carolina, 1931).

ISAAC DEUTSCHER, *Soviet Trade Unions: Their Place in Soviet Labour Policy* (London, 1950).

SAAD ED DIN FAWZI, *The Labour Movement in the Sudan* (London, 1957).

WALTER GALENSON, (ed.), *Comparative Labor Movements* (New York, 1952).

LEWIS L. LORWIN, *The International Labor Movement: History, Policies, Outlook* (New York, 1953).

VAL R. LORWIN, *The French Labor Movement* (Cambridge, Mass., 1954).

HILARY A. MARQUAND, (ed.), *Organized Labour in Four Continents* (London and New York, 1939).

H. A. MILLIS and R. E. MONTGOMERY, *Organized Labor* (New York, 1945).

ADOLF F. STURMTHAL, *Unity and Diversity in European Labor: An Introduction to Contemporary Labor Movements* (Glencoe, Ill., 1953).

Peasants

HENRY H. AYROUT, *The Fellaheen* (trans. by H. Wyament, Cairo, 1945).

RONALD P. DORE, *Land Reform in Japan* (London, New York and Toronto, 1959).

ERICH H. JACOBY, *Agrarian Unrest in Southeast Asia* (New York, 1949).

DAVID MITRANY, *Marx against the Peasant: A Study in Social Dogmatism* (Chapel Hill, North Carolina, 1951).

N. G. RANGA, *Revolutionary Peasants* (New Delhi, 1949).

ROYAL INSTITUTE OF INTERNATIONAL AFFAIRS, *Agrarian Problems from the Baltic to the Aegean: Discussion of a Peasant Programme* (London, 1944).

JOZO TOMAŠEVIĆ, *Peasants, Politics and Economic Change in Yugoslavia* (Stanford, Calif, 1955).

RUTH TROUTON, *Peasant Renaissance in Yugoslavia, 1900–1950* (London, 1952).

Women

SOPHONISBA P. BRECKINRIDGE, *Women in the Twentieth Century* (New York, 1933).

VERA BRITTAIN, *Lady into Woman: A History of Women from Victoria to Elizabeth II* (London, 1953).

MAURICE DUVERGER, *The Political Role of Women* (Paris, 1955).

SIDONIE M. GRUENBERG, *The Many Lives of Modern Woman* (Garden City, N.Y., 1952).

FANNINA W. HALLE, *Women in Soviet Russia* (trans. by M. M. Green, New York, 1933).

ASIZA HUSSEIN, *Women in the Moslem World* (Washington, D.C., 1954).

INTERNATIONAL INSTITUTE OF DIFFERING CULTURES, *Women's Role in the Development of Tropical and Sub-Tropical Countries* (Brussels, 1959).

RADEN ADJENG KARTINI, *Letters of a Javanese Princess* (trans. by A. L. Symmers, New York, 1920).

MARGARET MEAD, *Male and Female: A Study of the Sexes in a Changing World* (New York, 1955).

HANSA M. MEHTA, *The Woman Under the Hindu Law of Marriage and Succession* (Bombay, 1943).

ALVA MYRDAL and VIOLA KLEIN, *Woman's Two Roles: Home and Work* (New York, 1956).

ARTHUR H. NETHERCOT, *The First Five Lives of Annie Besant* (Chicago, 1960).

RACHEL C. STRACHEY, (ed.), *Our Freedom and Its Results* (London, 1936).

RACHEL C. STRACHEY, '*The Cause': A Short History of the Women's Movement in Great Britain* (London, 1928).

UNESCO and INTERNATIONAL BUREAU OF EDUCATION, *Access of Women to Education* (Paris, 1952).

UNITED NATIONS, *Legal Status of Married Women* (New York, 1950).

RUTH F. WOODSMALL, *Women and the New East* (Washington, D.C., 1960).

Race and Caste Groups

B. R. AMBEDKAR, *What Congress and Gandhi Have Done to the Untouchables* (2nd ed., Bombay, 1945).

MARGARET JUST BUTCHER, *The Negro in American Culture* (New York, 1956).

JOHN HOPE FRANKLIN, *From Slavery to Freedom* (2nd ed., New York, 1956).

E. FRANKLIN FRAZIER, *The Negro in the United States* (rev. ed., New York, 1949).

GOVIND S. GHURYE, *Caste and Class in India* (3rd ed., Bombay and New York, 1957).

OSCAR HANDLIN, *Race and Nationality in American Life* (Boston, 1957).

RAYFORD W. LOGAN, (ed.), *What the Negro Wants* (Chapel Hill, North Carolina, 1944).

GUNNAR MYRDAL, *An American Dilemma: The Negro Problem and Modern Democracy* (New York, 1944), 2 vols.

KAREL L. ROSKAM, *Interracial Relationships in the Union of South Africa and the International Community* (Leiden, 1960).

CHARLES H. WESLEY, (ed.), *The Negro in the Americas* (Washington, D.C., 1940).

CHAPTER XXXI

LITERATURE AND THE ARTS IN THE WESTERN CULTURE AREA

Visual Arts

ALFRED H. BARR, Jr., *H. Matisse, His Art and His Public* (New York, 1951.)

ALFRED H. BARR, Jr., *Masters of Modern Art* (New York, 1954).

ALFRED H. BARR, Jr., *Picasso: Fifty Years of His Art* (New York, 1946).

Encyclopedia of World Art (New York, 1961–), 15 vols.

GEOFFREY HOLME, (ed.), *Art in the U.S.S.R.: Architecture, Sculpture, Painting, Graphic Arts, Theatre, Film, Crafts* (London and New York, 1935).

PAUL KLEE, *The Thinking Eye: The Notebooks of Paul Klee* (trans. by Ralph Manheim, London and New York, 1961).

JOHN A. KOUWENHOVEN, *Made in America: The Arts in Modern Civilization* (Garden City, N.Y., 1948).

OLIVER W. LARKIN, *Art and Life in America* (rev. ed., New York, 1960).

MUSEUM OF MODERN ART, *Photography 1838–1937* (New York, 1937).

GEORGII V. PLEKHANOV, *Art and Society* (trans. by A. Goldstein *et al.*, New York, 1937).

MAURICE RAYNAL, (ed.), *Modern Painting* (trans. by Gilbert Stuart, Geneva, 1953).

HERBERT READ, *Concise History of Modern Painting* (New York, 1959).

ANDREW C. RITCHIE, *Abstract Painting and Sculpture in America* (New York, 1951).

ANDREW C. RITCHIE, (ed.), *German Art of the 20th Century* (New York, 1957).

ANDREW C. RITCHIE, *Sculpture of the Twentieth Century* (New York, 1952).

G. DI SAN LAZZARO, *Klee: A Study of His Life and Work* (trans. by Stuart Hood, New York, 1957).

EDWARD STEICHEN, (ed.), *The Family of Man* (New York, 1955).

Architecture

HERBERT BAYER, WALTER GROPIUS and ISE GROPIUS, (eds.), *Bauhaus 1919–1928* (New York, 1938).

YY*

LE CORBUSIER (C. E. JEANNERET-GRIS), *My Work* (trans. by J. Palmer, London, 1960).

LE CORBUSIER (C. E. JEANNERET-GRIS), *Towards a New Architecture* (trans. by F. Etchells, New York, 1927).

SIGFRIED GIEDION, *Space, Time and Architecture* (3rd ed., rev., Cambridge, Mass., 1956).

HENRY RUSSELL HITCHCOCK, *Architecture: Nineteenth and Twentieth Centuries* (Harmondsworth, Middx, 1958).

HENRY RUSSELL HITCHCOCK, *Latin American Architecture* (New York, 1955).

PHILIP JOHNSON, *Mies van der Rohe* (New York, 1947).

STAMO PAPADAKI, (ed.), *Le Corbusier, Architect, Painter, Writer* (New York, 1948).

MORRIS WEITZ, (ed.), *Problems in Aesthetics: An Introductory Book of Readings* (New York, 1959).

FRANK LLOYD WRIGHT, *A Testament* (New York, 1957).

Music

MERLE ARMITAGE, (ed.), *Schoenberg* (New York, 1937).

BORIS V. ASAFIEV, *Russian Music from the Beginning of the Nineteenth Century* (trans. by A. J. Swan, Ann Arbor, Mich., 1953).

GILBERT CHASE, *America's Music, from the Pilgrims to the Present* (New York, 1955).

HOWARD HARTOG, (ed.), *European Music in the Twentieth Century* (London, 1957).

PAUL HENRY LANG, *Music in Western Civilization* (New York, 1941).

ADOLFO SALAZAR, *Music in Our Time* (trans. by Isobel Pope, New York, 1946).

HALSEY STEVENS, *Life and Music of Bela Bartok* (New York, 1953).

HEINRICH STROBEL, *Stravinsky: Classic Humanist* (trans. by Hans Rosenwald, New York, 1955).

Literature

ANTUN BARAC, *A History of Yugoslav Literature* (trans. by P. Mijušković, Belgrade, 1955).

E. R. BENTLEY, *The Modern Theatre: A Study of Dramatists and the Drama* (London, 1948).

PIERRE BRODIN, *Présences Contemporaines* (Paris, 1954–57), 3 vols.

E. GORDON CRAIG, *On the Art of the Theatre* (London, 1911; New York, 1956).

RICHARD ELLMANN, *James Joyce* (New York, 1959).

ANGEL FLORES, (ed.), *The Kafka Problem* (New York, 1946).

JOHN GASSNER, *The Theatre in Our Times: A Survey of the Men, Materials and Movements in the Modern Theatre* (New York, 1954).

NIKOLAI M. GORCHAKOV, *Stanislavsky Directs* (trans. by M. Goldina, New York, 1954).

SIMON HALKIN, *Modern Hebrew Literature: Trends and Values* (New York, 1950).

PEDRO HENRÍQUEZ-UREÑA, *Literary Currents in Hispanic America* (Cambridge, Mass., 1945).

MANFRED KRIDL, *A Survey of Polish Literature and Culture* (trans. by O. Scherer-Virski, New York, 1956).

VICTOR LANGE, *Modern German Literature, 1870–1940* (Ithaca, N.Y., 1945).

C. K. OGDEN and I. A. RICHARDS, *The Meaning of Meaning* (2nd ed., London, 1927).

GEORGE D. PAINTER, *Marcel Proust, a Biography,* (London, 1959), 2 vols.

J. B. PRIESTLEY, *Literature and Western Man* (London and New York, 1960).

I. A. RICHARDS, *Principles of Literary Criticism* (2nd ed., London, 1926).

HAROLD V. ROUTH, *English Literature and Ideas in the 20th Century* (3rd ed., London, 1950).

RICHARD SAMUAL and R. HINTON THOMAS, *Expressionism in German Life, Literature and the Theatre* (Cambridge, 1939).

ERNEST J. SIMMONS, *Russian Fiction and Soviet Ideology: Introduction to Fedin, Leonov, and Sholokhov* (New York, 1958).

MARK L. SLONIM, *Modern Russian Literature* (London and New York, 1953).

HORATIO SMITH, (ed.), *Columbia Dictionary of Modern European Literature* (New York, 1947).

ROBERT E. SPILLER *et al.*, (eds.) *Literary History of the United States* (rev. ed., New York, 1953), 3 vols.

GLEB STRUVE, *Soviet Russian Literature, 1917–1950* (Norman, Okla., 1951).

WILLARD THORP, *American Writing in the Twentieth Century* (Cambridge, Mass., 1960).

ARTURO TORRES-RIOSECO, *The Epic of Latin American Literature* (rev. ed., New York, 1946).

RENÉ WELLEK, *A History of Modern Criticism, 1750–1950* (New Haven, 1955–   ).

EDMUND WILSON, *Axel's Castle* (New York, 1931).

Mass Media and the Arts

MAURICE BARDÈCHE and ROBERT BRASILLACH, *The History of Motion Pictures* (trans. and ed. by Iris Barry, London and New York, 1938).

SERGE M. EISENSTEIN, *The Film Sense* (trans. by Jay Leyda; new ed., London, 1948).

RICHARD GRIFFITH, *The World of Robert Flaherty* (London and New York, 1953).

JAY LEYDA, *Kino: A History of the Russian and Soviet Film* (London and New York, 1960).

HERBERT L. MATTHEWS, *The Education of a Correspondent* (New York, 1946).

PAUL ROTHA, (ed.), *Documentary Film* (3rd ed., London, 1952).

GILBERT SELDES, *The Seven Lively Arts* (New York and London, 1924; 1957).

CHAPTER XXXII

LITERATURE AND ARTS IN EASTERN CULTURE AREA

Literature

ARTHUR J. ARBERRY, (ed. and trans.), *Modern Arabic Poetry: An Anthology with English Verse Translations* (London, 1950).

PIERRE CACHIA, *Taha Hussein: His Place in the Egyptian Literary Renaissance* (London, 1956).

CHOU SHU-JÊN, *Selected Works of Lu Hsün* (pseud.) (trans. by Yang Hsien-yi and Gladys Yang, Peking, 1956–1959), 3 vols.

HU SHIH, *The Chinese Renaissance* (Chicago, 1934).

HUANG SUNG-K'ANG, *Lu Hsün and the New Culture Movement of Modern China* (Amsterdam, 1957).

TAHA HUSSEIN, *The Future of Culture in Egypt* (trans. by Sidney Glazer, Washington, D.C., 1954).

MUHAMMAD IQBAL, *Poems from Iqbal* (trans. by V. G. Kiernan, London and New York, 1955).

DONALD KEENE, *Japanese Literature: An Introduction for Western Readers* (London, 1953).

DONALD KEENE, (ed.), *Modern Japanese Literature, an Anthology* (New York, 1956).

KOKUSAI BUNKA SHINKOKAI, (ed.), *Introduction to Contemporary Japanese Literature* (trans. by Kenji Hamada, Tokyo, 1939).

BHARATAN KUMARAPPA, (ed.), *The Indian Literatures of Today* (Bombay, 1947).

YOSHIO OKAZAKI, (comp.), *Japanese Literature in the Meiji Era* (trans. and adapted by V. H. Viglelmo, Tokyo, 1955).

K. M. PANIKKAR, (comp.), *Modern Chinese Stories* (trans. by Huang K'un, Delhi, 1953).

PEGGY RUTHERFORD, (ed.), *Darkness and Light: An Anthology of African Writing* (London, 1958).

SAHITYA AKADEMI, *Contemporary Indian Literature* (New Delhi, 1957).

RABINDRANATH TAGORE, *Collected Poems and Plays* (New York, 1937).

EDWARD J. THOMPSON, *Rabindranath Tagore: Poet and Dramatist* (2nd ed., London, 1948).

WANG CHI-CHEN, (trans.), *Contemporary Chinese Stories* (New York, 1944).

RICHARD OLOF WINSTEDT, 'A History of Malay Literature', *Journal of the Royal Asiatic Society, Malayan Branch*, XVII, 3 (London, 1939).

Arts

FAUBION BOWERS, *Theatre in the East: A Survey of Asian Dance and Drama* (New York and Toronto, 1956).

FAUBION BOWERS, *The Dance in India* (New York, 1953).

MARG (Bombay, 1946–   ), quarterly.

P. R. RAMACHANDRA RAO, *Modern Indian Painting* (Madras, 1953).

MICHAEL SULLIVAN, *Chinese Art in the 20th Century* (Berkeley, Calif., 1959).

ARTHUR WALEY, *The Nō Plays of Japan* (London, 1921).

YUKIO YASHIRO, *2,000 Years of Japanese Art* (New York, 1958).

BERYL DE ZOETE and WALTER SPIES, *Dance and Drama in Bali* (London, 1938).

INDEX

Adams, John Couch (astronomer), 123
Adams, Henry, 1249
Adivar, Halide Edib, 1147, 1289
Adler, Alfred, 537
administrative law, 804–5
adolescent behaviour, 545, 621–4, 748–9
adult education, 904–5, 911–12, 917, 938
Afghani, Jamal ad-Din al-, 879
Afghanistan, 7, 22, 1029–31; nationalism in, 23–4
Africa, 4; moves for independence, 32; labour movements, 1041, 1121–2; minerals and metals, 85, 230, 231; nationalism in, 1033–44; tribal family, 755–8: see also entries for individual countries
Afrikaners, 1011–18 passim
Afro-Asian bloc, emergence of an, 31
aged, 632–6, 781; health problems of, 487 ff.
agnosticism, 848
agriculture, 86, 387 ff., 1132–40; economics of, 690, 732; government support for, 425–7; income from, 82; international measures for, 459–63; management, 410–11; mechanization, 98; 407–11; processing and marketing, 423–5; production organization, 416–22; research, 411–12; training, 412–16; distribution of workers, 86: see collectivization; also under entries for individual countries
Aini, Sadriddin, 1262
air pollution, 493, 583
air transport, 291, 297–302
alcoholism, 629–30
Alexandrov, Grigory, 1268
algebra, 175–6
Algeria, 31, 1077
aluminium, 233
Amanullah, King (Afghanistan), 24
Ambedkar, Rhim Rao, 1183–4
American States, Organization of (OAS), 52, 922, 946
analysis, mathematical, 177–9
Anderson, Carl D. (physicist), 195, 196
Andrade, Mario de, 1255
animal behaviour, 365–7
anthropology in study of human behaviour, 126–7, 142–3, 534, 542 ff., 549, 555–7, 563, 573, 653
antibiotics, 481–3
anti-clericalism, 849, 854
anticolonialism, 22–5, 704–5, 1033 ff.
apartheid (South Africa), 1011–18
Appleton, Edward, 210

Arabs, 1029, 1071–7; and Israel, 1024, 1104; nationalism, 23; League of Arab States, 52, 1076
Aragon, Louis, 1231
archaeology, 541
architecture, 1198–9, 1209, 1239–43, 1301
Argentina, 1086
armaments industry, 339, 833–4, 836
Arp, Hans, 1232
artificial insemination of livestock, 405, 708
arts and crafts as hobbies, 985
Aryanism (Nazi concept), 45
Asia, 7–8; agriculture, 390; industrial development, 12; literature and the arts, 1284–1304; nationalism 23, 43, 651; and League of Nations, 47; changing attitude to progress, 110–11; women's status, 1145, 1161–3
Assietzky, Carl von, 1217
associated states (political system), 795–7
astronomy, 211–17
Ataturk: see Kemal, Mustapha
Atget, Eugene, 1238
Atlantic Charter, 49–50, 654
atmosphere of the earth, 208–11
atom, the
    atomic physics, 130, nucleus of, 130, 187 ff.; structure of, 122, 130
atom bombs, 26–7
atomic energy, peaceful uses of, 245–6
Attlee, Clement, 696
Auden, W. H., 1218, 1223, 1225
Auezov, Mukhtar, 1262
Aurobindo, Sri, 888, 889
Australia, 1093–6; agriculture 389; labour movement, 1117, 1124
Austria, 9, 13, 1006–7; Hitler and, 17
Austro-Hungarian empire, break-up of, 10, 13; minorities, 1101–2
authoritarianism, 791–2, 1004–7
automation, 249, 558, 691
Averbakh, Leopold, 1260
Aymer, George, 1238
Azad, Maulana Abul Kalem, 1057
Azikiwe, Nnamdi (Nigerian minister), 1033

Babel, Isaac, 1260
bacteriology, 378, 465, 468, 472 ff.
Baer, Karl von, 376
Balfour Declaration (Zionism; 1917), 1019, 1073
ballet, 1227, 1262
Baltic States, 13
Barbusse, Henri, 1214

Barnett, M. A. F. (physicist), 210
Barrault, Jean-Louis, 1235
Barth, Karl, 850
Bartok, Bela, 1209, 1210, 1212, 1218, 1227, 1228
Bateson, William (biologist), 357
Baty, Gaston, 1235
Beadle, George (biologist), 358
Beard, Charles A. (historian), 551
Becker, Carl, 551
Becquerel, Henri, 130
Behrens, Peter, 1209
Belgium, 9, 622; and the Congo, 5, 1037-8
Benedict, Ruth, 543
Beneš, Eduard, 14
Benét, Stephen Vincent, 1248
benevolent organizations, 783-4
Bennett, Arnold, 1204
Berg, Alban, 1210, 1216
Berger, Hans, 369
Bergson, Henri, 665
Berlage, H. P., 1209
Berlin airlift, 28
Bernhardt, Sarah, 1266
Berr, Henri (historian), 552
Besant, Annie, 744, 886, 889
Bethe, Hans A., 154, 217
Beveridge report (1942; social welfare, Gt. Britain), 640, 654
Beyatli, Yahya Kemal, 1288
Bhagavad Gita (Indian literature), 110, 886 ff. *passim*, 1053, 1056, 1304
bicycles, 308-9
Biely, Andrei, 1258
Binet, Alfred, 538
biochemistry, 139, 378-82
biology, 124, 137-40, 355-83, 387, 399-402, 405, 465 ff. *passim*
Birge, E. A., 365
Birkhoff, George D., 173
birth control, 109, 518-21
Blok, Alexander, 1258, 1259
Boas, Franz, 142-3, 543, 556
Boccioni, U., 1207
Bohr, Niels, 130, 152, 189-91
Bolivia, 96, 1085, 1098
Bolyai, Johann and Wolfgang, 169
Bondfield, Margaret, 1115, 1147
Bonnard, Pierre, 1199
book publishing and book clubs, 962-5
Boole, George, 170
Booth, Charles (sociologist), 126
Bort, L. P. Teisserenc de, 209
Bourbaki (mathematicians group), 180
Bourne, Randolph, 1245
Bowen, N. L. (geologist), 204-5
Brachet, Jean, 359

Brahms, Johannes, 1197
Brancusi, Constantin, 1232
Braque, Georges, 1206, 1230
Brasilia, 1092, 1243
Bratby, John, 1232
Brazil, 1087-93, 1252 ff.
Brecht, Bertolt, 1236
Breit, Gregory, 210
Breton, André, 1216, 1231
Bridges, Robert, 1224
British Broadcasting Corporation, 321, 329, 332-3, 974-5, 976
British Commonwealth, 15, 795-6: *see also* entries for individual countries
Britten, Benjamin, 1211, 1227
broadcasting: *see* radio; television
Broglie, Louis de, 192
Brooks, Van Wyck, 1245
Brown, Sterling, 1248
Buddhism, 891-5, 1029, 1053, 1071
building industry, 591-2
Bulgaria, 1137-8
Burckhardt, Jakob, 551
bureaucracy, 801-4, 809
Burma, 24, 1029, 1068, 1070; religion, 892-3
Burnham, James, 764
Butler, Reg, 1233
Butler, Samuel, 1204

Calder, Alexander, 1233, 1251
Cambodia, 28, 1069-71 *passim*
Cameroons, 1038, 1041
Camus, Albert, 1219, 1237
Canada, 1083-5; agriculture, 388 ff. *passim*; forestry, 431-3; housing legislation, 589; per capita income, 80, 81; labour movement, 1117
Cantor, Georg, 170
Čapek, Karel, 1215
capitalist economies, 679-96; ethic, 694-6
Cartier-Bresson, Henri, 1238
Cary, Joyce, 1217, 1220, 1223
Casal, Julián del, 1253
Caso, Alfonso, 543
Caspersson, Torbjörn, 359
caste system (India), 761, 767-8, 775, 887, 890, 1055, 1057, 1163: *see aso* untouchables
Cather, Willa, 1248
Cavalcanti, Alberto, 1270
Cayley, Arthur, 169
cell biology, 371-8
Central African Federation, 31
Ceylon, 1029; religion, 891-2
Cézanne, Paul, 1197, 1199, 1207
Chadwick James (physicist), 130, 152, 194-5
Chagall, Marc, 1231

Chain, Ernst B., 481
Chamberlain, Edward (economist), 550
chance, law of: *see* uncertainty
Chandigarh, 1243, 1301
Chao Shu-li, 1296
Chaplin, Charlie, 968, 1267–8
Chapygin, A., 1262
Chardin, Père Teilhard de, 861
Chatterji, Bankim Chandra, 1286, 1294
Chatterji, S. C., 1294
Chekhov, Anton, 1223, 1234, 1258, 1290
chemistry, 122, 139–40, 184–7: *see also* biochemistry; food chemistry
Chen Tu-hsiu, 1061, 1286
Chiang Kai-shek, 25, 1061
Child, Charles Manning, 376
children
 child health, 476–7, 483–7, 628–9; labour regulations, 257; child marriages (India), 890, 1146; child psychology, 747; study and rearing, 571–9; child welfare, 617–24
China, 4, 1058–63; agriculture, 390, 393, 411, 724 ff.; art and literature, 1286–1300 *passim*; class distinctions, 761; communist party, 28; education, 906, 941, 944; European powers in, 25; family life, 649, 743, 753–4; interwar policy, 25; Japan's penetration into, 18; the 'leap forward' policy, 105; the Liberation army, 837; migrations from, 107; peasants, 1140; power production, 239; religion, 893; socialist economy of, 722–8; technological advances, 224–5; transport, 725, 726; exclusion from UNO, 33; women's status, 1162–3
Chile, 502, 616, 1086
Chirico, Giorgio de, 1231
Chocano, José Sanotos, 1253
Chou Li-po, 1296
Christianity and the Christian Church, *see also* entries for individual denominations *and* evangelism; missionaries
Chughtai, M. A. Rahman, 1299
Church, Alonzo, 179
Churchill, Winston, 29, 49
cinema, the, 956, 965–72; as an art, 1265–71; in eastern countries, 1302–3
cities, development of, 101–2, 580 ff.; municipal administration, 607–8; city planning, 594–606
Clair, René, 1268, 1269
class structure, changes in, 100–1, 758–69
Claudel, Paul, 1206, 1224
Clements, Frederick (botanist), 364
clerical and administrative workers, 260–3
Clifford, William K. (mathematician), 169
club organization, 782–4

Cockcroft, Sir John D., 194
collectivization system (agriculture), 390, 419, 700–1, 709, 725, 1138
Colombia, 1087
colonial systems, 792–3
Comenius, Johann, 571
Common Market (Europe), 4, 32, 694
Commonwealth, the British, 15, 795–6: *see also* entries for individual countries
communications, 97, 105, 311–36, 557–8
communism, 28–30, 64–6, 68, 669, 792, 1062, 1123; Marxist–Leninist doctrines, 65, 669–70, 724, 999–1003, 1062; institutions of the communist states, 813–19; communist labour movement, 1116, 1118–19
community development, 642, 917, 945, 1140–2
community services, 606–7
Compton, Arthur H. (physicist), 191
computers, 173–5, 564
Comte, Auguste, 125, 1089
concrete, uses of, 235–6
Congo, 5, 1037, 1040, 1042
Conrad, Joseph, 1199, 1217
conscription, 9, 829, 839, 841
Coomaraswamy, Ananda, 888, 1054, 1299
corporations, industrial, 103, 282, 681–91
Cowles, Henry (botanist), 364
Craig, Edward Gordon, 1234, 1235
Crick, F. H. C. (chemist), 140, 360
criminals, treatment of, 624–6
Croce, Benedetto, 663
Crossman, Richard H. S., 1218
Cuba, 96
culture and human behaviour, 142, 531, 544–6, 991
Cunha, Euclides da, 1090, 1252
Curie, Irene, 198
Curie, Marie, 130
Cuvier, Georges, 204
Czechoslovakia, 13, 14, 419, 709, 1119, 1136–7

Dali, Salvador, 1273
Dalton, John (scientist), 186
dancing, 979–80, 1227, 1262, 1301–2
Darío, Rubén, 1244, 1253, 1254
Darwin, Charles, 124–6, 355, 361, 363, 364, 365
Davis, Hallie Flanagan, 1236
death rates, changes in, 108–9, 469, 518
De Beer, Gavin, 376
De Forest, Lee, 313
Debussy, Claude, 1209, 1210, 1301
Decroly, Ovide, 928

Dedekind, Julius, 170
deficiency diseases, 453, 489
Denmark
   agriculture, 389; education, 912
dental care, 489–90, 497
'depression', the (1930s), 16, 690, 693
Derain, André, 1206
Despiau, Charles, 1197
Dewey, John (philosopher), 663, 928–30 *passim*, 936
Diaghilev, Sergei, 1209–10, 1227, 1258
diet: *see* nutrition
Dilthey, Wilhelm, 552
Dirac, A. M., 195–6
discontinuity, principle of, 144–5
Disney, Walt, 1268
divorce, 1155; increase in, 750; the Church and, 748, 750
Djilas, Milovan, 764
Dokuchayev, V. V., 396
Domagk, Gerhard, 481
domestic servant class, disappearance of, 751, 1158
Dos Passos, John, 1223
Dostoevsky, Feodor, 665, 1196, 1201, 1218, 1257–8
Dovzhenko, A. P., 1267
Dreiser, Theodore, 1245, 1247
Driesch, Hans, 372, 376
Dumbarton Oaks conference, 50
Durkheim, Émile, 127, 535
Dutta, Michael Madhusudan, 1286

earth, nature of the, 203–11
earth satellites, 98, 309–10, 347
earthquakes: *see* seismology
Eastern Orthodox Church, 847, 851, 869
ecology, 364–5
economic institutions, 550–2, 559–60, 674–728
economic organizations, government intervention in, 688 ff. *passim*
economic stability, measures for, 691–2
Ecuador, 1085, 1152
Eddington, A. S., 861
education, 897–946, 1100; technical developments in, 935–6; women and, 1153–4
Egypt, 23, 1072, 1075, 1076–7; education, 916; rural communities, 1141
Ehrenburg, Ilya, 1259, 1264
Ehrlich, Paul, 480
Einstein, Albert, 132, 133, 148, 151–2, 184, 190–3: *see also* Relativity
Eisenstein, Sergei, 1244, 1259, 1262, 1266, 1268
elasticity, theory of, 185
electronics, 174, 218; in industry, 249, 312–14

Eliot, T. S., 1215, 1218, 1223, 1246, 1247
Ellis, Havelock, 546
Éluard, Paul, 1231
embryology, 372–6
Emerson, Ralph Waldo, 1245, 1303
employment, conditions of, 263–8
energy, production and consumption of, 77, 78, 239–46
entertainment industry, 952, 965 ff.
Epstein, Jacob, 1220
'equal pay for equal work', 1157
Ernst, Max, 1232
Esthonia, 13
Ethiopia, 1029–31; and the League of Nations, 48
ethology, 365–7
Euler, Leonhard, 168
Euratom, 694
Europe
   decay in, 13–18; hegemony, 5–9; recovery, 32; self-image, 994–9
European Coal and Steel Community, 32, 694
evangelism, 858–9
Evans, Walker, 1238
Evatt, H. V., 1093
existentialism, 665–6, 1218–20
expanding universe, theory of the, 216

Fadayev, Alexander, 1260, 1263
families, economic aid for, 636–7
family life, 106, 655–6, 742–58
family planning: *see* birth control
FAO: *see* Food and Agriculture Organization
Faraday, Michael, 184
farm management, 410–11
farm mechanization, 407–10
farmers and peasants, 415, 416–17, 1132–40
Farrell, James T., 1247
fascism, 17, 26, 63–4, 788, 1005–7
Faulkner, William, 1247
Fedin, Konstantin, 1261
Fermi, Enrico, 196–9 *passim*
Finland, 49, 645
first world war, 9–13, 339–42, 834; caualties, 10
Firth, Raymond, 543
Fischer, Louis, 1218
fishery, 442–9
Fitzgerald, George Francis (physicist), 132
Flaherty, Robert, 1269–70
Flaubert, Gustave, 1196
Fleming, Alexander, 481
Florey, Howard, W., 481
food and agriculture, international measures for, 459–63

Food and Agriculture Organization (FAO), 4, 326, 388, 393, 414, 441, 447, 459, 460–3
food chemistry, 575
food processing, 284, 423–4
food production and consumption, 387 ff., 394
Ford, Henry (industrialist), 248, 276, 278
foreign investment in industry, 85–7
forestry, 428–42; forest products, 236, 433–4
Forsh, Olga, 1261
Forster, E. M., 1217, 1220
Fortes, Meyer, 543
Fournier, Alain, 1199
France, Anatole, 1198
France, 13–14; birth rate, 14; colonies, 6, 31, 793–5, 1036–7; interwar period, 16; education 908; and Indo-China, 28; labour movement, 1116; military institutions, 831; painting, 1206 ff.; and Spanish Civil War, 14
Franco, Francisco, 17–18
Frazer, Sir James, 142, 1205
Frege, Gottlob, 170
Freud, Sigmund, theories of, 141–2, 536–8, 545–7, 556, 573, 747, 1215–16
Frisch, Karl von, 367
Froebel, Friedrich, 571, 908, 928
Fromm, Erich, 548
Frost, Robert, 1226, 1245
Fry, Christopher, 1223
fuel and power: see energy
'fundamental education', 917
Furmanov, Dmitry, 1260

Gabo, Naum, 1201, 1208, 1233, 1251, 1258, 1259
Galsworthy, John, 1204
Gamow, George, 197
Gandhi, Mahatma, 24, 767, 852, 888–9, 930–1, 1026, 1057; and non-violence, 652; and South Africa, 1015; and the untouchables, 1182–3
Gauguin, Paul, 1197, 1199
Gause, G. F. (biologist), 365
Gauss, Carl Friedrich, 134, 168, 169
Gaza strip police force, 52
Geddes, Patrick, 601
genetics, 137–40, 356–64, 399–402
genocide, 1104
geology, 204–8
geometry, 135–6, 176–7
George, Stefan, 1199
Germany
   art, 1207; education, 908; in inter-war years, 14–15, 17; and League of Nations, 47, 48; military institutions, 831–2; social

Germany—continued.
   sciences, 528; technological advances, 224; trade unions, 1125; and USSR, 21; and first world war, 9, 10, 11, 340–1; and second world war, 26, 28, 32: see also Hitler; National Socialism
gerontology: see aged
Gershwin, George, 1249
Gesell, Dr Arnold, 574
Ghana, 3, 1033, 1039, 1042; independence granted, 31
Giacometti, Alberto, 1232–3
Gide, André, 1199, 1216, 1218
Giraudoux, Jean, 1218
glass-making, 235
Gliere, Reinhold, 1262
Gödel, Kurt, 137, 179
Gold Coast: see Ghana
Goldschmidt, Richard (geneticist), 375–6
Gorky, Maxim, 1196, 1204, 1206, 1260, 1261
Gorter, Herman, 1225
Graham, Billy (evangelist), 858–9
Graham, Martha, 1249
Granville-Barker, Harley, 1234
Grassmann, Hermann, 135
Great Britain
   broadcasting, 972–8; colonies, 6, 793, 1035–6; economic situation, 560, 693; education, 902–18 passim; health programme, 501–2; housing, 586, 588; per capita income, 80, 81; industrial plants, 251; labour movement, 1114, 1115; literature and arts, 1196–1243 passim; military institutions, 830–1; nationalization of industries, 238; social services, 616; trade unions, 1124; town planning 602 ff.; two-party system, 67; unemployment, 16–17
Greece, 28, 48
Grieg, Edvard, 1198
Grierson, John, 1270
Griffith, D. W., 1266
Grimm, Jakob and Wilhelm (folklorists), 142
Gris, Juan, 1207
Gropius, Walter, 1209, 1240, 1251
Grosz, George, 1215
Gruenberg, Sidonie, 575
Guatemala, 1085, 1098
Guinea, 31, 1037
Güntekin, Resat Nuri, 1289
Gurlitt, Ludwig, 929

Hadorn, Ernst, 376
Hague conventions, 338–40
Hahn, Otto (physicist), 131, 199
Haile Selassi (Emperor of Ethiopia), 48, 1031
Haldane, J. B. S., 363, 861

Hamsun, Knut, 1204
handicapped persons, care of, 626-8
Hardy, Godfrey Harold (mathematician), 152
Hardy, Thomas, 1196, 1205
Hargett, Keith, 1238
Harris, Roy, 1249
Harrison, Ross G., 373, 376
Hasim, Ahmet, 1288
Havell, E. B., 1299
health insurance schemes, 500-3: see also public health
Heaviside, Oliver, 210
Hegel, Georg W. F., 126, 663
Heidegger, Martin, 665, 666, 1218
Heisenberg, Werner, 146, 192, 193, 200
Heitler, Walter Heinrich, 193
Hemingway, Ernest, 1214, 1223, 1251
Herbart, J. F. (educator), 908, 928
heredity and evolution, 124-5, 355-64
Hernandez, José, 1256
Hersey, John, 1272
Hertz, Heinrich Rudolf, 123
Hilbert, David, 136, 178
Hindemith, Paul, 1203, 1227, 1228, 1251
Hinduism, 767, 849 ff. passim, 885-90, 1052
Hiroshima, atom bomb on, 26-7, 345, 351
Hitler, Adolf, 14-15, 937, 1007-10; and the Jews, 17; rise to power, 17, 26; League of Nations and, 48
hobbies, 984-7
Hofmannsthal, Hugo von, 1199
Holland: see Netherlands
Holst, Gustav, 1209, 1211
home economics, 575-7
Honegger, Arthur, 1227
Hooke's law (physics), 185, 186
hormones, 377-8, 488-9
Horney, Karen, 544
Horta, Victor, 1209
Horthy, Admiral Nicholas, 15
Houphouët-Boigny, M. Felix (Ivory Coast), 1035
housing, 585-94; for the aged, 635; of Negroes in USA, 1173-4
Howard, Ebenezer, 599
Hu Shih, 1286, 1295
Hubble, Edwin P., 151, 215, 216
Huch, Ricarda, 1199
Hughes, Langston, 1248
Huidobro, Vicente, 1256
human behaviour
    biological and evolutionary aspects of, 368; scientific approach to, 527-67: see also anthropology
Human Rights, Universal Declaration of (UNO), 5, 51, 327, 651, 996, 1126, 1146
humanism, 664, 863

Humphrey, Rufus, 376
Hungary, 13, 15; revolt (1956), 29, 51
Husain (Hashemite sharif), 23, 1075
Husserl, Edmund, 665
Huxley, Aldous, 1215
Huxley, Julian, 366, 376, 664
hydroelectric schemes, 241, 244, 245
hydrogen bomb, the, 27, 346

Ibn Saud, 23, 1075
Ibsen, Henrik, 1196, 1208, 1234
Iceland, 645
illiteracy, and measures for reduction of, 912-17
income
    distribution of, 81, 101; effects of industrialization on, 80-1
independent nations outside European domination, 1029
India, 5, 7, 24, 1051-8; agriculture, 711, 718; child marriages, 890, 1146; class distinctions, 761; and communism, 12-13; economy of, 701-2; changes in family life, 753-4, housing programmes, 590; iron and steel industry, 12; illiteracy, 915; literature and art, 1054, 1286, 1294, 1299, 1301-2; and Pakistan, 1026 ff.; religion, 885-90, 893; status of women, 1145-6: see also caste system; untouchables
Indians (American), 1098-1100, 1106, 1163
indigenismo, 1100
Indo-China, 5, 1068, 1069; and communism, 13, 25; France and, 28
Indonesia, 5, 8, 25, 67, 1068
industrial hazards, 492-3
industrial management and labour relations, 273-83
industrial production, 222-87
industrialism, 75-92; impact of, 97-104
infant and maternal mortality, reduction in, 108-9, 483-6
International Bank for Reconstruction and Development, 51, 693
International Civil Aeronautics Organization, 302
International Geophysical Year (1957-8), 153, 230-2, 347
International Justice, Court of, 47, 52
International Labour Office, 49, 52, 254, 261, 267
International Labour Organization, 5, 227, 1112, 1121, 1126
international law, UNO and, 52-3
International Telegraph (Telecommunications) Union, 46, 326, 331
Iran, 7, 22, 1029-32; nationalism in, 23-4
Iraq, 1074-7, 1102

Ireland, 15
iron and steel production (USA), 27
'iron curtain', the, 29
Isherwood, Christopher, 1225
Islam, 670, 847, 854, 879–85, 1044, 1072:
    see also Muslims
Israel, 877–8, 1019–25; and the Arabs, 1077,
    1104: see also Jews; Zionism
Italy, 15, 16; education, 937; and Ethiopia,
    7; as a fascist power, 26, 1005–7; trade
    unions, 1125
Ivanov, Vsevolod, 1237
Ivens, Joris, 1270
Ivory Coast, the, 1035, 1043

Jagirdar, R. V., 1294
Jamaica, 1141
James, Henry, 1222
James, William (philosopher), 536, 663
Jansky, Karl, 212
Japan, 7, 1032, 1064–7; agriculture, 388–95
    passim; art and literature, 1287–1300
    passim; invasion of Burma, 1069; bid for
    colonial power, 18; and China, 18; as
    copyists and adaptors in technology, 227;
    education, 905, 910, 940–1; feudalism in,
    651; industrialism and industrial plants,
    88–9; 251–3; labour movement, 1120;
    invades Manchuria, 18, 20; military
    institutions, 830, 831; attack on Pearl
    Harbor, 26; religion, 894–5; war with
    Russia, 18; working hours, 951
Jaspers, Karl, 665
Jawlensky, Alexey, 1208
jazz music, 980–1, 1177, 1229
Jeans, James (astronomer), 861
Jews, 1102; Hitler's persecution of, 17: see
    also Israel; Judaism; Zionism
Jinnah, Muhammed Ali, 1026
Johannsen, Wilhelm (geneticist), 356, 357
Johnson, Wallace (of Sierra Leone), 1033
Joliot-Curie, Frédéric, 198
Jolson, Al, 1268
Jordan, 1075
Jouvet, Louis, 1235
Joyce, James, 1216, 1222
Judaism, 871–9
Juday, Chauncey, 365
judiciary, the, 806, 817
Jung, Carl, 537, 1216
juvenile delinquency, 621–4: see also adoles-
    cent behaviour; vandalism

Kafka, Franz, 1199, 1219
Kailasam, T. K., 1294
Kandinsky, Vasily, 1197, 1201, 1208, 1258,
    1259

Karman, Theodore von, 218
Kashmir dispute (India and Pakistan),
    UNO and, 52
Katchaturian, Aram, 1262
Kelvin, Lord, 206, 207
Kemal, Mustapha, 23, 883, 937
Kennelley, Arthur E., 210
Kenya, 31, 1036, 1039, 1041
Kenyatta, Jomo, 31, 1033, 1039–40
Key, Ellen (feminist), 573, 1147
Keynes, John Maynard, 550–1
Khrushchev, Nikita, 1265
Kierkegaard, Sören A., 665, 1218
Kinsey, Alfred C., 546
Kirchner, Ernst Ludwig, 1197
Klee, Paul, 1201, 1208, 1230
Klein, Felix, 169
Koestler, Arthur, 1218
Koffka, Kurt, 535
Köhler, Wolfgang, 535
Kollwitz, Käthe, 1215
Korea, 4, 28, 1067, 1070
Korean War, UNO and the, 28, 51
Kossel, Albrecht, 359
Kroeber, A. L., 534
Kuo Mo-jo, 1295, 1296
Kuomintang, the, 12, 1061–2

labour, status of, 1110–32; supply and
    utilization of, 254–63
labour-saving equipment, 283–4
Lack, David (zoologist), 367
Lagerlöf, Selma, 1267
Landauer, Walter, 376
landholding and land reform, 416–22,
    1132–40
language, 943 ff., 1101–7 passim
Lao Shê, 1296
Lao-tze, 1239
Laos, 28, 1069, 1071
Laplace, Pierre Simon, 127, 150, 168, 169
Lasswell, Harold, 547
Latin America, 47, 66, 68; agriculture, 391;
    class distinctions, 765–6; economic plan-
    ning, 721–2; education, 943–5; energy
    production, 239; housing, 590; land
    reform, 418; literature and the arts,
    1251–7; peasants and farmers, 1139–40;
    petroleum, 225
Latvia, 13
Lavoisier, Antoine Laurent, 186
law, 804–6, 810–13, 817
Lawrence, D. H., 1199, 1205, 1215
Le Corbusier, 601, 1209, 1239, 1241, 1301
League of Nations, 19, 22, 46–8, 392, 458,
    460, 1102
Leavitt, Henrietta, 214

Lebanon, 23, 1075
Lee. T. D. (physicist), 155, 197
Léger, Fernand, 1207, 1209
leisure, use of, 950–87
lend-lease, 27
Lenin, Vladimir, 11, 39, 239, 329, 669–70, 696–7, 699–700, 704, 815, 1000–1: *see also under* communism
Leonov, Leonid, 1261, 1263
Leverrier, Urbain J. J., 123
Lewin, Kurt, 558
Lewis, Sinclair, 1247
Lewisohn, Ludwig, 1248
Liapunov, A., 134
liberal democracy, 59–62, 66–8, 790–1, 806 ff., 994–9; institutions of liberal democratic states, 797–813
Liberia, 1030
libraries, public, 963
life, origin of, 382–3
life expectancy, increase in, 108, 466, 468, 632–3
Lillie, Frank R., 374
limnology, 365
Lincoln, Abraham, 1083, 1245
Lindbergh, Charles, 301
Lippman, Walter, 1250
Lippold, Richard, 1233
Lister, Joseph L., 466
Liszt, Franz, 1198
literature and the arts, 1196–1304: *see also* under entries for individual countries and forms of expression
Lithuania, 13, 16
livestock, 405–7; artificial insemination of, 405, 708
Lobachevski, Nikolai, 169
Locarno pact (1925), 48; Hitler's denunciation of, 14
Locke, Alain L., 1176
logic, mathematical, 136–7, 179, 664: *see also* mathematics
London, Fritz (physicist), 193
Lorca, Federico Garcia, 1225
Lorentz, Pare, 1273
Lorenz, Konrad, 141, 366
Lotka, Alfred, 365
Lu Hsün, 1286, 1295
Ludwig, Emil, 1214
Lugones, Leopoldo, 1253–4
Luxembourg, 9
Lysenko, T. D., 361

Macaulay, Thomas Babington, Lord, 1054, 1056
McDougall, William (psychologist), 536
Macke, August, 1208

Mackintosh, Charles Rennie (architect), 1209
MacLeish, Archibald, 1247
Maeterlinck, Maurice, 1199
Maharshi, Sri Ramana, 889
Mahler, Gustav, 1198, 1210
Maillol, Aristide, 1197
Makarenko, A. S., 931–2
Malaya, 1068, 1070, 1071, 1105
Malevich, Kasimir, 1208, 1258
Malinowski, Bronislaw, 142–3, 543, 1040
Mallarmé, Stéphane, 1197
Malraux, André, 1194, 1217, 1223, 1303
Malthus, Thomas R., 363, 515, 744
Manchuria, Japan's invasion of, 18, 20
Manet, Édouard, 1197
Mangione, Jerre, 1248
mankind, concept of, 650 ff.
Mann, Heinrich, 1204
Mann, Thomas, 1204, 1218, 1251
Mao Tse-tung, 1062, 1140; poetry of, 1293
Mao Tun, 1295, 1296
Marc, Franz, 1208
'March Front' (Hungarian writers' group), 550
Marconi, Guglielmo, 210
Marinetti, Filippo Tommaso, 1207
Maritain, Jacques, 1218
Markov, Andrei A. (mathematician), 134
Marshall Plan (US aid), 349
Marti, José, 1253
Marx, Karl, and Marxism, 126, 515, 549, 552, 669; and capitalism, 696; and religion, 850; on status of women, 1144–5; *see also* communism
Marxist–Leninist theory, 65, 669, 724, 999–1003, 1062
Masaryk, Thomas, 14
Mascagni, Pietro, 1198
mass production and mass consumption, 679–81
Masson, André, 1232
mathematics, 124, 134–6; and logic, 136–7, 166–80; relation between pure and applied mathematics, 170–5
Matisse, Henri, 1206
matter, nature of, 122–3, 130–4, 184–203
matter, theory of 187–203
Mau Mau terrorist movement, 1039
Mauriac, François, 1215
Maxwell, James Clerk, 123, 173, 184
Mayakovsky, Vladimir, 1258, 1259, 1263
Mboya, Tom, 1041
Mead, Margaret (anthropologist), 543–4, 565, 572
mechanics, laws of, 184–5
mechanization of agriculture, 407 ff.; of industry, 75, 81, 222–9, 246 ff.

medical research institutions, 467–8, 503
medical science, 108, 111, 465 ff.
Meissner, Walther, 201
Méliès, Georges, 1265
Melville, Herman, 1245
Mendel, Gregor, 137–8, 172, 357, 361
Mendeléyev, Dmitri, 186, 187
Menotti, Gian Carlo, 1227
mental illness, 467, 493–6, 628–32
Merriam, Charles, 547
Messiaen, Olivier, 1229
metals, minerals, and metallurgy, 85, 229–39
Mexico, 1096–1100; land reform, 1139; oil industry, 237; revolution in (1910), 96
Meyerhold, Vsevolod, 1235, 1258
Meyrink, Gustav, 1199
Michelson, Albert A. (physicist), 131
Michelson-Morley experiment, 131, 184
microscopes, 371
Middle East, 4; nationalism in, 23–4; oil and oil concession terms in, 24, 237–8: see also entries for individual countries
Mies van der Rohe, Ludwig, 1209, 1241, 1251
migrations, industrialization as a cause of, 75, 107
Mili, Gjon, 1238
military institutions, 828–44: see also warfare
military technology, 342–3
Millikan, R. A., 861
Milne-Edwards, Henri, 372
mining and mining techniques, 231, 236–7
minorities seeking cultural autonomy, 1101–7
Miro, Joan, 1232
Mises, Ludwig von, 557
missionaries, 864–7, 880, 905
Mistral, Gabriela, 1244
Moholy-Nagy, 1237
Mohorovičič, A., 207–8
monarchy, 789–90
Mondrian, Piet, 1209, 1240
Monet, Claude, 1197
Montenegro, 13
Montessori, Maria, 573, 928, 930, 931–2
Moore, Henry, 1233
Morgan, T. H. (geneticist), 356, 357, 358, 362
Mori Ogai, 1296
Morley, Edward Williams (physicist), 131, 184
Morocco, 1074
Morris, William, 1196, 1199
motivation, 367, 547, 928, 930
motor vehicles, 291–7
Mudaliar, P. Sambandha, 1294
Muhammed Ali, 1026
Mukhina, Vera, 1261, 1262
Muller, Hermann J. (scientist), 362

Müller, Max (theologian), 889
Mumford, Lewis, 1250
Munch, Edvard, 1197, 1207
Munich pact, 22
Murray, Pauli, 1248
music, 1197–1303 passim; as a hobby, 985–6; popular music and dancing, 979–80
Muslims, 670, 1145; in Africa, 31, 1035, 1044; in Arab countries, 1071–7 passim; family life, 743, 754–5; in India, 24, 847, 1052, 1058; migrations by, 108; and Pakistan, 1025–9; status of women, 1149, 1152, 1155, 1161
Mussolini, Benito, 15, 48, 937, 1005, 1006
Mussorgsky, Modest, 1198
Myrdal, Gunnar, 722

Nagai Kafu, 1296
Nájera, Manuel Gutierrez, 1253
Nasser, Gamel Abdul, 1076–7
national health services, 501–3
National Socialism (Nazism), 17, 45, 63, 666, 788, 1007–11; and military organization, 837: see also racial superiority
nationalism, 22–5, 39–46, 111, 991, 993–1044 passim, 1051 ff.
nationalization of mineral rights, 238
NATO alliance, 843–4
Natsume Soseki, 1296
natural gas, 303
natural resources, 85, 228, 229–39
Nazism: see National Socialism
Negroes, 765, 775; and sport, 1176; in USA and the Americas, 1081, 1163–81
Nemirovich-Danchenko, V., 1234
Netherlands
  agriculture, 389, 394, 413; colonies, 6, 794–5, 1067–71; education, 918, 924
Neumann, John von, 150, 173
New Deal (USA), 1082
New Zealand, 1093–6 passim; agriculture, 388, 1095; labour movement, 1117; social services, 616
Newman, Arnold, 1237
news agencies, 322–3
newspapers and periodicals, 323–6, 957–62
Newton, Isaac, 123, 150, 151
Nexö, Martin Andersen, 1206
Nicholson, Ben, 1220
Nicol, William (physicist), 204
Nietzsche, Friedrich W., 665, 1208, 1218
Nigeria, 31, 1033, 1041
Nijinski, Vaslav, 1234
Nkrumah, Kwame, 330, 1033, 1039, 1042, 1043
Nolan, Sidney, 1232
nomadism, 106, 1074–5

North Atlantic Treaty Organization: *see* NATO
Norway, 445, 645, 1152
nuclear physics, 130–1, 187–203
nuclear weapons, 345–6
number theory, 176
nutrition, 376 ff., 392, 449–59
Nyerere, Julius K., 1042

observatories (astronomy), 211, 215, 216
occupations and professions, 99, 100, 496–9, 644–5
Ogden, C. K., 558
oil: *see* petroleum
Olcott, Col. Henry S., 886, 892
Omar Khayyam, 1303
O'Neill, Eugene, 1216, 1235
Oparin, Alexander, 382
Orff, Carl, 1227
Orozco, José Clemente, 1244, 1255
Ortega y Gasset, José, 902, 1215
Orwell, George, 1220
Ostrovsky, N., 1263
Otto, Berthold (educator), 929
Ottoman Empire, break-up of, 10, 23–4, 1073
Oud, Jacobus, 1240

Pa Chin, 1295
Pabst, G. W., 1269
painting, 1229–32, 1196–1300 *passim*
Pakistan, 25, 1025–8
palaeontology, 204
Palestine, 23, 1075
paper industry, 236
Paraguay, 1085, 1152
Park, Robert E. (sociologist), 548
Parrington, Vernon Louis, 1250
Pasternak, Boris, 1226
Pasteur, Louis, 380, 382, 467–8
patents systems in technology, 226–7
Pauli, Wolfgang, 193, 196
Pavlov, Ivan, 141, 370, 533, 553
Peano, Giuseppe, 170
Pearson, Karl (mathematician), 134
peasants and farmers, 415, 416–17, 1132–40
Peattie, Donald C., 1238
pedagogy, 928–33
people's democracy, 28: *see also* communism
periodicals: *see* newspapers and periodicals
Perón, Juan, 327, 842
Persia: *see* Iran
Peru, 1085, 1139
Pestalozzi, Johann, 571, 908, 928
Petrie, Flinders, 540
petroleum, 237, 241, 243, 294, 1032; pipelines for, 303
Pevsner, Antoine, 1208, 1233, 1251, 1259
Philippines, 8, 1141

philosophy and philosophical thought, 103, 662–71
photography, 1237–8; as a hobby, 985
physical sciences, 122–4, 130–4, 183–219
Picasso, Pablo, 1208, 1216, 1230
Picón-Salas, Mariano, 1257
Pillai, C. V. Raman, 1294
Pilsudski, Marshal Joseph (Poland), 16
pipelines, increasing use of, 303
Pirandello, Luigi, 1235
Pirenne, Henri, 551
Piscator, Erwin, 1235
Pitt-Rivers, A. H., 540
Planck, Max, 133
planning, 654, 700–1, 717–20, 721–2
plant diseases, weeds and pests, 402–4
plant genetics and growth, 399–402
plastics industry, 234–5
poetry, 1223–6, 1289–90
Poincaré, Henri (mathematician), 132, 136
Point Four Program (US aid), 27
Poland, 13, 14, 16, 709; Germany and, 18
political institutions, 788–819
Pollock, Jackson, 1232
Poncelot, Jean Victor, 169
population, 107–11, 512–22;
    of colonial areas (1910–13), 6; increase in growth rate, 108–9, 512; migration as cause of changes in, 107; in urban areas, 101–2
Portinari, Cándido, 1255
Portugal, 16; African territories of, 31, 1038, 1042
positivism, 125, 663–4
Postal Union, 46
Poulenc, Francis, 1227
Poulson, Donald, 376
Pound, Ezra, 1246, 1247
Prandtl, Ludwig, 218
press, 319–26; freedom of the, 326–31
Prokoviev, Sergei, 1227, 1244, 1262
propaganda, 326–9, 1271–4
Protestant churches, 845–70 *passim*
Proust, Marcel, 1202, 1211, 1216, 1222
psychology
    in education, 933–5; and the study of human behaviour, 529, 533–9, 545–8, 553; and the social sciences, 554–61 *passim*
public health, 467–503
public libraries, 963
Puccini, Giacomo, 1198
Pudovkin, V. I., 1267, 1268
Puerto Rico, 8, 722, 796, 1142; health practices, 509–12
Punnett, Reginald (biologist), 357

quantum mechanics, 133, 190–4

racial discrimination, 765–6, 904, 1011–18, 1163–84
racial superiority, Nazi concept of, 45, 1007–11, 1017
Radcliffe-Brown, A. R., 142–3, 543
radio, 311–14, 315–17, 321–2, 331–4, 972–6
radio industry, 226
radioactivity, 130, 188, 197–200, 217
railways, 303–6; underground systems, 307–8
Ramakrishna, Sri, 889
Raman, Chandrasekhara Venkata (physicist), 155
Raman effect (physics), 155
Ramgopal, 1302
Rathenau, Walter, 277
Ravel, Maurice, 1209
Ray, Man (photographer), 1237
Rayleigh, Lord, 129
Razin, Stepan, 1262
reading as a leisure-time activity, 957 ff.
Reber, Grote, 212
recreational facilities for the masses, 953 ff.
Red Cross organization, 486, 491
Reinhardt, Max (impresario), 1235–6
Relativity, 131–3, 148, 157, 1201; General Theory of, 151, 211; Special Theory of, 132, 184, 185, 191
religion, 846–95; and philosophy, 660–71; and science, 848–9, 860–1
Remarque, Erich Maria, 1214
revolution, 10–13, 96, 1139, 1140
Reza Khan, 24
Rhodesia, 1036, 1041
Richards, Ellen H. (food chemist), 575
Richards, I. A. (philosopher), 558
Richter, Conrad, 1247
Rickert, Heinrich, 552
Riemann, Georg F., 136, 169
Riesman, David, 557
Rilke, Rainer Maria, 1211, 1223, 1224, 1225, 1227
Rimbaud, Jean Arthur, 1197
Rimsky-Korsakov, Nicolai, 1197
Rivera, Diego, 1244, 1255
Rivera, Primo de, 15–16
road accidents, 293, 296, 492
road-building, 293–4
Robinson, Edwin Arlington, 1248
Robinson, Joan (economist), 550
Rodin, Auguste, 1197
Rodó, José Enriquez, 1253
Rohrschach test (psychology), 546
Rolland, Romain, 1214
Rölvaag, O. E., 1247–8
Roman Catholic Church, 667–8, 845–70 passim; and birth control, 520–1, 744; and divorce, 748, 750, 1155; and education,

Roman Catholic Church—continued.
903, 907, 918–19, 932–3; and marriage and family life, 656; in Latin America, 1089, 1091, 1092, 1098
Röntgen, Wilhelm Konrad von, 123, 188
Roosevelt, Franklin D., 50; and American Negroes, 1175
Rouault, Georges, 1206
Rousseau, Jean Jacques, 571, 1201
Roux, Wilhelm, 372
Roy, D. L. (playwright), 1294
Roy, Jamini (painter), 1299
Roy, Ram Mohan (religious reformer), 1054
Ruanda Urundi, 1038
Rumania, 14, 237, 1136
rural communities, changes in, 610–11, 1140–2
Ruskin, John, 1196
Russell, Bertrand, 136, 168, 665, 929
Russia, 7, 10–11; colonies (1910–13), 6; and first world war, 12: see also USSR
Rutherford, Ernest, 130, 152, 188–9, 194
Ryazhsky, Georgy, 1261

Saccheri, Girolamo, 169
Saha, Megh Nad (astronomer), 217
Salazar, Antonio (Portugal), 16
Salisbury, Sir Edward, 364
Salk, Jonas, 477
Sandburg, Carl, 1239, 1245, 1248
Sanger, Margaret, 744
Sanskrit studies, 1053
Sapir, Edward, 543, 556–7
Sartre, Jean-Paul, 665, 1216, 1219, 1237
Satie, Erik, 1227
Saudi Arabia, 1029
Scandinavian countries, 428, 431, 585–6, 616, 636, 645
Schnitzler, Arthur, 1204–5
Schönberg, Arnold, 1202–3, 1210, 1212, 1218
Schrödinger, Erwin, 192, 193
Schroeder, Ernst, 170
Schwann, Theodor, 124, 372–3
science and scientific thought, 121–58; and industry, 82–3; elaboration of the physical sciences, 183–219; biological science, 355–83; social sciences, 527–66; and religion, 849, 861; support for research, 153–4
Scriabin, Alexander, 1198
sculpture, 1196–1300 passim
second world war, 25–37, 343–5; casualties 349; military-civil institutions of, 838 ff.
Seghers, Anna, 1217
Segre, Corrado (mathematician), 135
Segre, Emilio (physicist), 203
seismology, 207–8
Sennett, Mack, 1267

Serbia, 9, 13
Seurat, Georges, 1197, 1198–9
sex
 adolescents and, 749; Freudian theories, 536–8; in literature, 1215–16; and psychology, 538, 546
Shadr, Ivan, 1261
Shahn, Ben, 1248
Shankar, Uday, 1302
Shapley, Harlow, 214
Shatsky, Stanislas, 929
Shaw, George Bernard, 1198, 1204, 1212, 1214, 1237
Sher-Gil, Amrita, 1299
Sherriff, R. C., 1214
Sherrington, C. S., 368
Shimazaki Toson, 1296
Shintoism, 894
Sholokhov, Mikhail, 1260, 1261
Shostakovich, Dmitry, 1227, 1262, 1264
Siam: see Thailand
Sibelius, Jean, 1198, 1210, 1227
Sierra Leone, 1033
Silone, Ignazio, 1217, 1218
Silva, José Asunción, 1253
Simmel, Georg, 552
Simon, Thomas (psychologist), 539
Simpson, George Gaylord, 363
Sino-Japanese War, 18
Siquieros, David Alfaro, 1244, 1255
Sjöström, Victor, 1267
Sloan, John, 1246
Smith, G.Elliot (anthropologist), 534
Smith, Lillian (writer), 1250
Smuts, General J. C., 1016
social institutions, 564–6
social sciences, 140–3, 528–66; research on, 554–62
social services, growth of, 613 ff.
social welfare, principles and methods of, 637 ff., 733, 1094–6
socialism, 126, 653, 669–70, 696–710: see also communism; Marx
Socialist International, First, Second, Third, 21, 41, 1123
soil management and erosion, 396–9
solar energy, uses of, 246
Somaliland, 1041
Sommer, Frederick, 1237
Soupault, Philippe, 1231
South Africa as an authoritarian state, 1011–18
South America: see Latin America
South-East Asia, 25, 26, 1067–71: see also entries for individual countries
space travel, 309–10
Spain, 15, 17–18, 1006
Spanish-American countries, 1085–7, 1251–7

Spanish Civil War, 14
speech, freedom of, 329
Spemann, Hans, 375, 376
Spencer, Herbert, 126
Spender, Stephen, 1218
Spengler, Oswald, 551, 657, 1214
Spock, Dr Benjamin, 574
Sport, 953, 955, 956, 981–3, 1176
Stael, Nicholas de, 1232
Stalin, Joseph, 68, 669, 702, 815
Stanislavsky, Constantin, 1234, 1244, 1259
state, the
 forms of, 789–97; new role of, 57–68
Steffens, Lincoln, 1250
Steichen, Edward, 1237, 1239
Steinbeck, John, 1247
Stern, Curt, 358, 376
Stieglitz, Alfred, 1237, 1238
Stopes, Marie, 744
Strachey, Lytton, 1214
Strassmann, Fritz, 131, 199
Strauss, Richard, 1198
Stravinsky, Igor, 1205, 1209–10, 1218, 1227, 1228, 1229, 1251
strikes, 1126–9
Strindberg, August, 1208, 1235
structure, principle of, 143–4
submarines, 306–7
Sudan, 31, 1077
Sudetenland, Hitler's annexation of, 15
Suez crisis, UNO and the, 51
suffrage, universal, 61, 111, 791
Sullivan, Louis H., 1198
Sun Yat-sen, 12, 62, 1060–1
Sunday, Billy (evangelist), 858
surgery, 490–2
surrealism (art), 1231–2
Sweden, 80, 544, 598, 637
Switzerland, 80, 418, 1152
Synge, J. M., 1223
synthetic fibres, 235
Syria, 23, 1072–5

Taft-Hartley Act (USA; 1947), 1125
Tagore, Abanindranath, 1286, 1299
Tagore, Rabindranath, 888, 930, 1055, 1226, 1286, 1302, 1304
Tanganyika, 31, 1038, 1041, 1042
Tanizaki Junichiro, 1296
Tatlin, Vladimir, 1208
Taylor, Frederick W., 276
Tchaikovsky, Peter, 1198
teachers and teacher-training, 907, 920–3
technology
 relation to basic science, 153–5, 187, 211–12, 217–19, 359, 371–2; in industry, 222 ff.
television, 976–8, 981

Teller, Edward, 197
Tennessee Valley Authority, 245
Terman, Lewis M., 538
Thailand, 7, 891–2, 1029–31
theatre, the, 1233–7; theatre groups, 978–9
Thomas, W. I. (sociologist), 549
Thomism, 667–8
Thomson, J. A., 861
Thomson, Joseph John (physicist), 130, 131, 152, 188, 189
Thomson, Virgil, 1249, 1273
Thoreau, Henry, 1303
Thorndike, E. L. (psychologist), 534
Tibet, 891, 1029
Tien Han, 1295
Tilak, Bal Gangadhar, 11–12, 886–9, 1056–7
Tinbergen, N., 141
Ting Ling, 1296
Togoland, 1038, 1041
Toller, Ernst, 1215
Tolstoy, Alexey, 1234, 1259, 1261
Tolstoy, Leo, 1196, 1257–8
town planning, 594–606, 654, 1243
Toynbee, Arnold J., 552, 657
trade unions, 60, 103, 278–9, 653–4, 773, 1110–32; and educational programmes, 912; in USA, 687–8, 1173; USSR and, 704
transport, 97–8, 105–6, 290–310, 584–5
travel as a leisure activity, 983–4
tribalism, 106, 650, 755–8, 775, 1034–5, 1039–40, 1043, 1074
tropical diseases, 472–4, 476, 503–6 passim
Trotsky, Leo, 704
Truman, Harry, 27
Tsao Yu, 1295
Tsubouchi Shoyo, 1296
Tucholsky, Kurt, 1217
Turing, A. M., 179
Turkey, 22, 23, 28; art and literature, 1288–9; education, 921; family institutions 755; law, 811
Tuve, Merle A., 210
Twain, Mark, 1245
Twitty, Victor, 376
Tylor, Edward B., 529

Udey, Edwin C., 1238
Uganda, 31, 1041
Ulanova, Galina, 1264
uncertainty, 145–8, 150; Heisenberg's principle of, 146–7, 192
underdeveloped countries
    economic development, 710–28; education, 912–17, 942–5; energy consumption, 241; health measures in, 505–8; housing problems, 589–90; impact of industrialism, 80–3, 90–2, 105–7; labour movement,

underdeveloped countries—continued.
    1120–2; rapid population increase in, 109, 515–18; welfare services, 641–2
Undset, Sigrid, 1218
unemployment, 16–17, 70–1
UNESCO (United Nations Educational, Scientific and Cultural Organization), 4, 51; and the arts, 1304; and education, 917, 935, 945; functions of, 946; and social science, 556
UNICEF (United Nations International Children's Emergency Fund), 4, 506, 620–1
United Arab Republic, 1077
universal suffrage, 61, 111, 791
universities, 911, 926–7
UNO (United Nations Organization), 3, 4, 28, 32–3, 49–52, 1104: see also entries for UN specialized agencies
untouchables (Indian caste), 107, 767, 775, 1055, 1163, 1181–4
uranium, 199, 219, 231
urbanization, effects of, 102–3, 580–610 passim
Urey, H. C., 195, 207
Uruguay, 1087
USA (United States of America), 3, 18–20, 1078–83; agriculture, 388 ff. passim, 732; child care and rearing, 573–9 passim; class distinctions, 765; colonies, 6, 8; industrial corporations, 681 ff. passim, 732; and depression of the 1930s, 16; average earnings for selected occupations, 115; economic situation, 561; education, 782, 904, 908, 909, 924–6 passim, 936; family income distribution, 101, 114, 732; free enterprise policy, 67; housing, 585, 587; per capita income, 80; industrial plants, 251; industrial production, 27, 223 ff. passim, 292; labour movement, 1115, 1117, 1125; distrust of Japan, 20; labour supply and utilization, 225 ff. passim; literature and the arts, 1197–1304 passim; military institutions, 840; occupational distribution, 113; power production and consumption, 239 ff. passim; production and personal income, 731; psychological studies, 547; social sciences, 528; social welfare payments, 733; space travel, 309–10; technological advances, 224–8 passim; unemployment, 16, 690; in first world war, 10
USSR (Union of Soviet Socialist Republics), 3, 20–2, 29–30; agriculture, 388 ff. passim, 707–10, 1138; army organization, 863–7; broadcasting, 975; child rearing, 577; and class distinctions, 763–4; communist labour movement, 1118–19; condition of

USSR—*contiuued.*
the economy, 697–709; education, 937, 939–40; expansion of electricity production, 239–40; organization of family life, 751–3; forestry, 439; health programme, 502; housing, 585, 587–9; industrialization, 89–90; and League of Nations, 22; literature and the arts, 1213, 1257–65; non-aggression agreements, 22; discards patents regulations, 227; psychological studies, 546–7; and religion, 851; revolution, 10–13, 96; social sciences, 553–4; social security, 616; space travel, 309–10; sport, 955; technological advances, 224; challenge to USA, 30; and Warsaw pact, 844; working hours, 951; status of women, 1153, 1156–7: *see also* Russia

Valéry, Paul, 1211, 1223, 1225
Vallathol (poet), 1292
Vallejo, César, 1256
Van de Graaf, R. J., 194
Van de Velde, Henry C., 1209
Van Gogh, Vincent, 1196, 1199
vandalism by adolescents, 749
Varenne, Alexandre, 11
Vargas, Getulio (of Brazil), 1092
Vaughan Williams, Ralph, 1209, 1210–11, 1218, 1220, 1227, 1228
Veblen, Thorstein, 542, 548, 1249
venereal diseases, 482, 494, 495
Venezuela, 474, 1085
Verdi, Giuseppe, 1198
Versailles, Treaty of, 14
Vietnam, 4, 8, 28, 1069, 1070, 1071
Villa-Lobos, Heitor, 1244, 1255
viruses, 139, 477, 483
vitamins, 378, 452–4
Vivekananda, Swami, 886, 889, 1182
Vlaminck, Maurice de, 1206
Voldemaras, Augustinas, 16
Volterra, Vito, 365
voluntary organizations, 769–84
Vries, Hugo de, 138, 361, 362
Vuillard, Jean Édouard, 1199

Waddington, Conrad, 376, 377
wages, 268–71
Wagner, Richard, 1197–8
Waksman, Selman A., 480
Waley, Arthur, 1303
Walton, E. T. S. (physicist), 194
Warburg, Otto, 380
Warerkar, Mama, 1294
warfare, methods of, 337–51, 834
Warsaw pact, 843

Wassermann, Jacob, 1199, 1215
waste disposal, 583–5
water supplies, 582–3
water transport, 306
Watson, James D. (chemist), 140, 36
Watson, J. B. (psychologist), 535
Weber, Max (sociologist), 539, 542, 557, 614
Webern, Anton, 1227, 1228–9
Wedekind, Frank, 1204, 1235
Wegener, Paul, 1268
Weill, Kurt, 1236
Weismann, August, 361
Weiss, Paul, 376
Weizsäcker, C. F. von, 217
Wells, H. G., 1200, 1214
Wertheimer, Max, 535
Whipple, Fred L., 209
White, Margaret Bourke, 1238
Whitehead, Alfred North, 136, 665, 861
Whitman, Walt, 1245, 1249
WHO (World Health Organization), 4, 272, 302, 480, 487, 493, 501, 504, 572, 630, 631
Whorf, B., 558
Whyte, William H. (sociologist), 558
Wilson, Woodrow, 12, 19, 39, 40
Wittgenstein, Ludwig, 136
Wöhler, Friedrich, 187
women, status of, 1142–63; in China, 727–8; and education, 926; in India, 890; in industry, 256, 258–9; maternal health, 483–7, 1158–9; organizations, 781–8; suffrage, 111, 1151–2; UNO commission on, 51, 513
women leaders, 1145, 1147
wood, 236
Woolf, Virginia, 1220, 1222
Wordsworth, William, 1201
workers: *see* labour; trade unions
working conditions, improvements in, 253–4, 271–3
working hours, 265–8, 951
Wright, Frank Lloyd (architect), 1198, 1209, 1239, 1241, 1242
Wright, Richard (writer), 1218, 1248
Wright, Sewall (mathematician), 363, 376
Wundt, Wilhelm, 127

X-rays, 123, 188, 201, 362, 371, 380

Yang, C. N. (physicist), 155, 197
Yeats, William Butler, 1211, 1223, 1225
Yeh Shao-chun, 1295
Yemen, 1029
Yerkes, Robert M., 534
Young, J. Z. (zoologist), 367
youth movements, 776–80

Yu Ta-fu, 1295
Yugoslavia, 13, 14, 764; economic system, 708, 709–10; and Soviet ideologies, 68
Yukawa, H. (physicist), 55, 202

Zadkine, Ossip, 1233
Zaharoff, Basil, 834, 836

Zecca, Ferdinand, 1265
Zernicke, F., 371
Zhdanov, Andrei, 1263
Zionism, 23, 873–6, 1020–4, 1073
Znaniecki, Florian, 549
Zola, Émile, 1196
Zweig, Arnold, 1214
Zweig, Stefan, 1217

APPENDIX A

FOREWORD*

by the

Director-General of UNESCO

At a time when man is preparing to launch out from this planet into space, it is well that History should hold him in contemplation of his trajectory through the ages.

Never before, indeed, has he shown so searching a curiosity about his past or such jealous care to preserve its vestiges. It is as though in some mysterious way a balance were now maintained in his thought between the exploration of space and that of time, the extroversion of the one being offset by the inwardness of the other.

Be that as it may, never more than now, when man finds himself hurtling at vertiginous speed towards a wondrous future, has there been a great need for the function of memory to ensure for mankind the appropriation of its creative actuality. If consciousness were not thus rooted in such reflection on its own process of becoming, many of the inventions we hail as conquests and advances would be no more than the uncontrollable workings of an alienated destiny.

To evoke this retrospective awareness is the first thing that this work which we now have the honour of introducing to the public sets out to do; it is an attempt to sum up the heritage of civilization to which we owe our present élan.

The ambition to write a universal history is a very old one indeed. Many have tried their hand at it before, particularly in the classical epochs—not without merit, nor without success. The present work belongs to that noble line of great syntheses which seek to present to man the sum total of his memories as a coherent whole.

It has the same twofold ambition, to embrace the past in its entirety and to sum up all that we know about the past. And it adopts the same intellectual approach—that of the interpretative as opposed to the descriptive historian—reducing events to their significance in a universal frame of reference, explicit or implicit.

However, this *History of Mankind* parts company with its predecessors on several essential points. In the first place, it deliberately confines itself to shedding light on one of mankind's many aspects, its *cultural and scientific development*.

In so doing it departs from the traditional approaches to the study of history, which, as we know, attach decisive importance to political, economic and even military factors. It offers itself as a corrective to the ordinary view of man's past. And those who initiated the enterprise may well have thought at first that this was, in itself, sufficiently useful and original for them to dispense with any further aim.

Admittedly, it rests with the science of history to decide objectively, *a posteriori* and according to the case, on the relative importance of the different elements and factors in particular situations. To that extent the approach deliberately adopted in this history may well be said to be an *a priori* postulate. This is the very postulate on which UNESCO itself is based, namely, the conviction that international relations, in their ultimate reality, are determined not merely by political and economic factors and considerations but spring as well, and perhaps even more surely, from the capabilities and demands of the mind.

Nevertheless, even from the strictly scientific point of view, this History, deliberately partial though it be, may well claim that, in restoring to the achievements of culture and science their full reality and significance, it has made an essential contribution to that sum of factual knowledge and right understanding which a complete history aspires to offer.

But the originality of the enterprise does not stop there. In point of fact, that is where it begins. For the facts of which this History treats are no ordinary ones. To put them back in their proper place is not merely to fill a long-standing gap and thus complete the sum, restoring its balance to the whole. It is to discover a new dimension of the historical object, perceptible only when approached from a particular intellectual angle.

Cultural or scientific facts, whatever their subject-matter, means, cause, pretext or circumstances, are essentially thoughts of man about man.

This is obvious in the cultural sphere, every value being a human ideal. But it is no less

* Published in Volume I of *The History of Mankind: Cultural and Scientific Development*.

true of science; for apart from the fact that truth, too, is a value, the essence of science is not knowledge, but the method by which knowledge is gained, the rule the mind prescribes itself in order to attain it; and every rule is a form of reflection and self-discipline; that is, doubled consciousness.

Thus, the history of what has no doubt been too simply described here as 'the cultural and scientific development of mankind' is, strictly speaking, the story of how, through the ages, men—individually and collectively—have conceived of humanity. Or, to be more correct, have conceived of *their* humanity, that is, the universal aspect of their experience. In short, the subject of this work is the gradual development, in its most expressive manifestations, of the consciousness of the universal in man.

As will be seen, great care is taken to describe the exchanges and influences which link the different foci of civilization across space or time. We are shown how this web of reciprocal influences is becoming more closely woven as spatial communications grow more numerous and rapid and relations in time more intensive.* Indeed by no means the least interesting feature of this work is the stress it lays upon this still too little known aspect of historical reality in which the 'intellectual and moral solidarity of mankind' referred to in the Preamble to UNESCO's Constitution can really be seen at work.

Yet even this is not the decisive discovery. That lies not so much in the evidence of inter-relation between the many and varied civilizations as in the fact, manifest in all forms of culture and science, that every civilization implies, produces or invokes an image of man in terms of the universal.

This immanence of the universal in every cultural and scientific experience is what gives its essential character to the spiritual solidarity of mankind. And it is in this form that the solidarity can serve as the foundation for the true peace described in UNESCO's Constitution, whereas the effect of intercultural relations upon the interplay of the forces conducive, in a given situation, to peace is, as well we know, extremely complex and indirect, and therefore contingent. In fact it is because the object of this History, as already pointed out, is the development of the consciousness of this solidarity that UNESCO regards such an understanding as both vital and necessary.

But straightway we are faced with another fact, no less rich in implications. In the actual experience of science and culture, sense and style, which constitute the universal element, remain indissolubly bound up with the singular act of invention or creation from which they derive. It may truly be said both of science and of culture, regarded as experiences, that 'the more one concentrates on the particular, the more universal one becomes'. And it is only by repeating the various operations of the act of creation, reduced to their objective characteristics—which make up what we call method—or by subjective communion with the mental atmosphere of that act—which is what we call intuition—that another person can understand and assimilate this sense and style.

It follows that for a history which aims to keep in constant touch with experience and restore it in its contingent truth, scientific and cultural facts have significance only for certain individuals, namely those who are capable of applying these methods and of exercising this intuition which give access to the secrets of creativeness in its unique aspects. However, to possess this ability, there is no doubt that one must belong to the particular context of civilization in which such unique phenomena occur. Accordingly a concrete history of science and culture can only be written from a plurality of viewpoints corresponding to the variety of civilizations.

To acknowledge the fact that there is more than one civilization is not to deny in any way the continuity or solidarity of human development. On the contrary, the study of the inter-relations, across time and space, of ideas, values and techniques restores this sense of continuity and solidarity, which have never before been so definitely and convincingly established as in this History. Similarly, to be aware of the originality of the works and symbols which make up each civilization is not to gainsay the universality of the human mind. As we have seen, true universality is no more than a dimension of this consciousness of a sense or style, which opens out to the potential totality of mankind only by rooting itself in the particularity of its initial emergence.

* Even in time, relations are reversible—not, of course, through any real causation, but owing to the perpetual reappraisal of the significance of events that take place in the course of man's constantly renewed, and renewing, retrospection.

The classical rationalism of the West conceived the history of the human mind as a process of development in which all scientific and cultural facts are arranged in order with reference to a single, constant subject that is universal by nature. There is no need to plunge into a philosophical discussion on ontological humanism in order to expose this myth. It would be only too easy, now of all times, to show how into this allegedly universal subject has been projected, out of pride or sheer naïveté, the subjectivity, in more or less sublimated form, of certain personalities eminently representative of their epoch, civilization or race.

The work you are about to read represents the first attempts to compose a universal history of the human mind from the varying standpoints of memory and thought that characterize the different contemporary cultures.

But in doing so, its main purpose was not to banish all subjectivity of interpretation. Indeed, such a pretension could not be entertained in a history which seeks to assess the significance of events and which takes as its starting points the positions adopted by the various cultures. For there is a kind of subjectivity, co-substantial, as it were, with culture, which causes the perspective opened by each culture on the universal in man to be a projection of that culture's humanity in its own particular circumstances. The originality of this attempt at a universal history lies in its having taken for its frame of reference the multiplicity of contemporary cultural perspectives and projections. For the first time an attempt has been made to present, with respect to the history of consciousness, the sum total of the knowledge which the various contemporary societies and cultures possess and a synthesis of the conceptions which they entertain. For the first time an attempt has been made to offer a history of human thought which is the product of the thought of mankind in every aspect of its present complexion. A universal history indeed, and doubly so—in both its object and it subject.

This aspiration, which is the essence of the whole undertaking, has determined the choice of method.

The History is the work, not of a team with a homogeneous cultural background, but of an International Commission which, by its very composition and even more by the spirit pervading it, embraces all the varied cultural traditions and modern ideologies which form the spiritual framework of our present-day world. What is more, the International Commission made it a rule that the contributions of the many scholars whose services it enlisted be submitted to the scrutiny of the National Commissions which, in the Member States of UNESCO, group together persons particularly qualified to represent the fields of education, science and culture. Subject always to the overriding considerations of scientific truth, the observations received in the course of these extensive consultations were scrupulously taken into account in drawing up the final text. Never before has what I may call the decentralization of viewpoints and interpretations been carried so far in the science of history.

Accordingly the work is also an act; for this historical study is itself a cultural achievement calculated to influence, by its spirit and its methods, the present trend of culture. And that, no doubt, is its ultimate end. For just as the awareness of mankind's intellectual and moral solidarity to which it stems leads less from the discovery of the interrelations of the past than from the effort of its scientific and cultural heritage, so the essential feature of this effort is not so much the complete restitution of the object which it is designed to achieve as the fact that the whole of the subject as it exists today is taking part in it and thus affirms its own unity in the process of achieving it.

In this humanism, whose universality springs not from a unique abstract nature but is being gradually evolved, on the basis of a freely acknowledged diversity, through actual contact and a continuous effort at understanding and co-operation, UNESCO recognizes both its own *raison d'être* and its guiding principle. The unity of mankind, we believe, has to be patiently built up, through mutual respect for the cultures which diversify it without dividing it, and by the establishment of more and more centres of science which spread man's technological power throughout the world, fostering equality of opportunity for progress and for the genuine preservation of his dignity.

Such, then, are the principal ideas and essential features of this work; they are, at the same time, the very reasons which led UNESCO, as the educational, scientific and cultural organization of the United Nations, to conceive the project and assist in its execution.

The author of this History is not UNESCO; it is the International Commission which, since 1950, has directed this venture in complete intellectual independence. It is to the Commission, therefore, and to it alone, that the full credit for this work is due. And at the same time—allow me to state—it also bears the sole responsibility for its scientific worth.

UNESCO is, however, proud to have organized this work and to have made possible its accomplishment by providing the necessary funds, administrative machinery and international background. In that sense this great venture, without precedent in many respects, is also in some measure its work, too.

It is, therefore, my pleasant duty to express the Organization's gratitude to all those who have, to whatever degree, participated in this undertaking and contributed to its success. Above all, its thanks are due to the distinguished members of the International Commission and to its eminent Chairman, Professor Paulo E. de Berrêdo Carneiro, who for thirteen years have given unsparingly of the wealth of their knowledge and talents, with a devotion and selflessness equalled only by the nobility of their thought. In this concept of scientific and cultural development in which consciousness is an act and all reflection a creation, it may be said without fear of exaggeration that, in presenting this vast panorama of the past history of the human mind, such as never was before, they have made a powerful contribution towards the advent of a consciousness of civilization on a scale encompassing the whole of mankind. With all my admiration, I wish to express to them UNESCO's gratitude.

RENÉ MAHEU

Paris, 1962.

APPENDIX B

PREFACE*

by the

*President of the International Commission
for a History of the Scientific and Cultural Development
of Mankind*

Among the great tasks assigned to UNESCO by its Constitution is the duty to promote and encourage mutual knowledge and understanding throughout the world. While many of the divergences which divide people date from a distant past, an analysis of their historical antecedents discloses links which draw them nearer to one another, brings to light their contributions to a common patrimony of humanity, reveals the ebb and flow of cultural exchanges and emphasizes their increasing tendency to become integrated into an international community.

Beyond differences of race, climate, economic structure and systems of ideas, history shows the fundamental identity of the various human groups, making it possible to discern, in many cases, profound analogies among the transformations they have undergone from the Palaeolithic era down to the present time. If we consider the human species as a whole, we perceive that the course of its evolution has been accomplished from one region and one people to another by way of a series of oscillations, greater or lesser in extent, longer or shorter in duration. The different civilizations which have arisen in the course of the ages correspond to distinct phases and patterns of this general movement. Almost every one of them is to be found somewhere in the world of today. Contemporary society appears as a mosaic in which the most widely-differing cultures adjoin and confront each other.

It was, I think, in order to know them better and to strengthen their solidarity that UNESCO took the initiative of entrusting to historians, men of science and of letters, recruited from all parts of the world, the task of preparing and of publishing this work. This, at least, is how I have understood the mandate of the International Commission over which I have the honour to preside. Our task was not to draw up a philosophy of history in the light of the economic, intellectual and moral laws which may govern social development but to describe, from a universal standpoint, the contribution of each age, each region, each people to the scientific and cultural ascent of humanity.

In the official reports which I have presented since 1951 to the General Conference of UNESCO will be found a detailed account of the steps taken in implementing this project which originated in a resolution submitted to the second session of the General Conference held in Mexico City in 1947. The idea had been put forward in 1946 by Dr Julian Huxley, then Executive Secretary of the Preparatory Commission for UNESCO:

'The chief task before the Humanities today would seem to be to help in constructing a history of the development of the human mind, notably in its highest cultural achievements. For this task, the help of art critics and artists will be needed as well as of art historians; of anthropologists and students of comparative religion as well as of divines and theologians; of archaeologists as well as of classical scholars; of poets and creative men of letters as well as of professors of literature; as well as the whole-hearted support of the historians. Throughout, of course, the development of culture in the various regions of the Orient must receive equal attention to that paid to its Western growth. Once more, UNESCO can help by being true to its many-sidedness, and by bringing men together from all these various fields to help in one or other facet of this huge work.' (UNESCO: *Its Purpose and Its Philosophy* [London, 1946].)

Several preparatory meetings were held and preliminary studies made in 1947 and 1948 with the participation of Professors Carl J. Burckhardt, Lucien Febvre, Joseph Needham, Georges Salles, Taha Hussein, and UNESCO officials, among whom were Dr Julian Huxley, then Director-General, Mr Jean Thomas and Professor Pierre Auger. In 1949, Professors Lucien Febvre and Migual Ozorio de Almeida were asked to prepare general reports on the basis of which the General Conference, at its fourth session, recommended that the work should proceed immediately.

* Published in Volume I of *The History of Mankind: Cultural and Scientific Development.*

In the same year a committee of experts was called to draft the plan to be submitted to the General Conference for the elaboration of a scientific and cultural history of mankind. It included the following scholars: R. Ciasca, L. Febvre, M. Florkin, J. Needham, L. Piaget, P. Rivet and R. Shryock. In opening the proceedings, Dr Jaime Torres-Bodet, at that time Director-General, evoked the spirit in which he considered the work should be accomplished:

'Through UNESCO, humanity must come to realize its common past and understand the significance of the sum total of endeavour, invention and enlightenment which have gone to make up the heritage we seek to serve today. If we can regard this moment in the world's history as UNESCO's hour, it is thanks to the slow and often unnoticed growth of an outlook of Mankind. . . .'

'We seek only to draw up the table of the major cultural events which have shaped Man's existence and slowly brought civilization into being. . . .'

'The important thing is to embark on it with the will to succeed and in a spirit of serene and dispassionate objectivity. . . .'

'Nevertheless, by publishing today a synthesis of our present knowledge of *humanity's scientific and cultural history*, UNESCO, far from lulling the critical spirit to sleep, will spur it to new and eager research. It is my profound conviction that there is nothing in the nature or the present state of historical science precluding the making of such a synthesis; indeed all circumstances invite us to it.'

In accordance with a resolution of the General Conference of 1950, consultations were held with the International Council of Scientific Unions (ICSU) and the International Council for Philosophy and Humanistic Studies (CIPSH) as to the appointment of an international commission to undertake, on behalf of UNESCO, full responsibility for the preparation and execution of the work. The following experts nominated by these two councils were invited by the Director-General to become active members of the Commission: Professors Homi Bhabha (University of Bombay), Carl J. Burckhardt (Switzerland), Paulo E. de Berrêdo Carneiro (University of Brazil), Julian Huxley, FRS (United Kingdom), Charles Morazé (University of Paris), Mario Praz (University of Rome), Ralph E. Turner (Yale University), Silvio Zavala (University of Mexico), and Constantine K. Zurayk (University of Damascus).

The International Commission met for the first time in December 1950 and again in March 1951 in Paris. It decided during these two meetings to invite a number of distinguished persons to become Corresponding Members, and to set up an Editorial Committee, under the chairmanship of Professor Ralph E. Turner, with Professors Constantine K. Zurayk and Charles Morazé as members. The Commission did me the honour of electing me as its President, with Dr Julian Huxley and Professor Carl J. Burckhardt as Vice-Presidents. A Bureau was created comprising the President, the Vice-Presidents and the Chairman of the Editorial Committee, Dr Armando Cortesao, a member of the Department of Cultural Activities of UNESCO, initially responsible for the secretariat of the Commission, was unanimously elected Secretary-General. In 1952 he was succeeded by Dr Guy S. Métraux.

Between 1952 and 1954 new members were added to the International Commission to enlarge its geographical, cultural and philosophical representation. The following scholars were appointed in agreement with the Director-General of UNESCO: Professors E. J. Dijksterhuis (Netherlands), Jacques Freymond (Switzerland), Mahmud Husain (Pakistan), Hu-Shih (China), Erik Lönnroth (Sweden), R. C. Majumdar (India), Percy E. Schramm (Federal Republic of Germany), Ali A. Siassi (Iran), and J. Pérez Villanueva (Spain).

As early as 1952 the International Commission approached scholars of countries which, at the time, were not members of UNESCO but which represented important cultural areas. Invitations were sent to national academies of sciences and arts, but met with no response. It was only in 1955 that the International Commission was able to welcome as new members historians and scientists from the Union of Soviet Socialist Republics and the People's Republics of Czechoslovakia, Hungary and Poland.

Since 1954 the Bureau, acting as delegate of the International Commission with additional responsibilities placed on it by the General Assembly, has been enlarged to comprise the President and six Vice-Presidents as follows: Sir Julian Huxley (United Kingdom), Professor R. C. Majumdar (India), Professor Ralph E. Turner (United States of America), Professor Gaston Wiet (France), Professor Silvio Zavala (Mexico), and Professor A. A. Zvorikine

(Union of Soviet Socialist Republics). Professor Louis Gottschalk (United States of America) was unanimously elected as a further Vice-President in 1961.

The first publication which the International Commission initiated, on the proposal of Professor Charles Marazé, was a quarterly review, the *Journal of World History*. Professor Lucien Febvre was the Editor until his death in 1956, when it came under the supervision of the Bureau, with Dr François Crouzet and Dr Guy S. Métraux as its editorial staff.

The main function of the *Journal of World History* has been to provide the International Commission with material for the final compilation of the History—documentary or biblio-graphical details about problems which have so far remained obscure; translations of documents which may have appeared desirable; contributions to the History itself. This review has also enabled scholars in all countries to take part in an exchange of views on questions of interpretation and the actual presentation of the History.

The *Journal of World History* represents a considerable contribution on the part of the International Commission to historical knowledge and towards a better understanding of historical processes. Comprising articles of the highest scientific quality which bear the signature of scholars from every country and which express the most diverse ideological trends, it foreshadows to some extent the great work for which it has furnished basic materials.

The preparation of the History was examined in detail during the first and second meetings of the International Commission. Several courses of action presented themselves: the Commission could draft the final text, or it could be entrusted to a single editor, or to independent authors. It was decided that, while the Commission would retain the full authority conferred upon it by the General Conference of UNESCO, the wisest course would be to select individual author-editors for each of the six volumes. The author-editors would be fully responsible for the text, but they would work under the supervision of, and in collaboration with, the Editorial Committee and the Commission; they would benefit by the assistance of scholars, designated by them, to deal with certain chapters; and, if necessary, sections could be referred to specialists.

On the recommendation of the Editorial Committee, author-editors for five of the six volumes were at this time appointed. For Volume I, Jacquetta Hawkes and Henri Frankfort, both of the United Kingdom. On the death of Professor Frankfort in 1954, the late Sir Leonard Woolley (United Kingdom) was appointed to write the second part of this volume. For Volume III, René Grousset (France), with two co-authors, Vadime Elisséeff and Philippe Wolff (France). Professor Gaston Wiet (France) took over the author-editorship of this third volume in 1953 on the death of Professor Grousset. For Volume IV, Louis Gottschalk (United States of America); for Volume V, Jorge Basadre (Peru), who afterwards resigned and was replaced later by Professor Charles Morazé (France); and for Volume VI, K. Zachariah (India), who was succeeded in 1956 by Dr Caroline F. Ware (United States of America), H.E. Dr K. M. Panikkar (India), and the late Dr. J. M. Romein (Netherlands).

In 1963 the late Professor Luigi Pareti (Italy) was appointed author-editor of Volume II, with Professors Paolo Brezzi and Luciano Petech of Italy as assistants.

By the spring of 1952 a first draft plan of the History was in circulation. Through the active interest of the author-editors, the members of the International Commission, and scholars consulted throughout the world on the initiative of the International Commission, this plan was slowly revised to constitute a general guide for the elaboration of the six volumes.

At a meeting of the International Commission in February 1954 it was decided, on my proposal, to include in its membership the author-editors of the six volumes and the editor of the *Journal of World History*. This measure was designed to enable those primarily responsible for the text of the volumes to take part in discussions and so to make a more effective contribution to the direction of the activities of the International Commission. In addition it was decided that one single body—the Bureau of the Commission—should be made entirely responsible for the co-ordination of the Commission's work. To ensure the unity of style and presentation essential to a work of such high intellectual standing and covering so wide a field, Professor Ralph E. Turner was entrusted with the task of editing the English texts.

In the course of the execution of its programme the International Commission benefited by the co-operation of UNESCO and of the General Conference which, at several of its sessions, had the opportunity to examine the work plans prepared for the History, and on two occasions took decisions which markedly influenced our work. The Ninth General Conference held in New Delhi in 1956 recommended that the texts of all volumes be submitted to the National Commissions set up in the Member States. The objective was to assist the International Commission in obtaining for each volume additional critical materials to enable the author-editors to revise and to perfect their texts. While not all National Commissions responded, the comments which were received proved most useful. All the author-editors have conscientiously noted the criticisms received and have taken them into account, wherever possible, when revising their texts. Furthermore, the International Commission has sought the advice of experts on several points.

Again at the invitation of the General Conference, following its tenth meeting held in Paris in 1958, the International Commission decided to appoint a number of historians to advise the Bureau and the author-editors on possible modifications of the text of each volume of the History, in the light of comments and criticisms received, and to suggest editorial notes on controversial issues. This step had become necessary as Professor Turner's illness had prevented him from accomplishing the editorial work. In pursuance of this policy, and in agreement with the members of the Bureau and with the author-editors, I selected a number of eminent historians, of different nationalities, particularly qualified to act as special consultants. Thus, at the end of each chapter of all volumes the reader will find grouped together editorial notes and bibliographical references that will provide him with summaries of historical opinions on those questions which can be variously interpreted.

The International Commission plans to issue a supplement to Volume VI, *The Twentieth Century*. While the first part treats of the history of our age in the same way as the history of previous periods was considered in all the volumes, this second tome will be devoted to an open debate on the main trends in scientific and cultural development at mid-century.

The six volumes include line drawings prepared by Mrs Stella Robinson at the request of the author-editors, photographic plates assembled by the Secretariat of the International Commission in co-operation with the author-editors and their assistants, and maps drawn specially by the Swiss firm, Hallwag, A.G.

At the time of publication I must recall with gratitude and regret the memory of those scholars whom the International Commission had the misfortune to lose in the course of its work and who contributed so much to the achievement of its task: Professors René Grousset, Henri Frankfort and K. Zachariah, Sir Leonard Woolley, Professors Luigi Pareti, Lucien Febvre, J. M. Romein, and H.E. Dr K. M. Panikkar.

I must hereby express, on behalf of the International Commission, my gratitude to the General Conference of UNESCO which made this project possible, to the Directors-General, Messrs Julian Huxley, Jaime Torres-Bodet, Luther Evans, Vittorino Veronese and René Maheu, and to the Secretariat of UNESCO which, through ten years, has extended assistance and guidance on every possible occasion.

The International Commission is greatly indebted to the author-editors who, often under difficult circumstances, fulfilled their task with the highest competence and devotion; to its Vice-Presidents, who constitute the Bureau, for assuming with me full responsibility for every phase of the execution of this project; and in particular to Professor Ralph E. Turner, Chairman of the Editorial Committee, for the elaboration of the general plan of the History and for his whole-hearted dedication to the success of the work to which he brought his own personal outlook of an integrated world history. I am particularly happy to acknowledge herewith the co-operation of the Corresponding Members, the consultants and the translators, whose work proved invaluable for the completion of this project.

The International Commission benefited throughout its work by the advice of the official Observers of the International Council of Scientific Unions, Professor R. J. Forbes; of the International Council for Philosophy and Humanistic Studies, Sir Ronald Syme; and of the International Social Science Council, Professor F. H. Lawson.

Lastly, I would like on behalf of the International Commission to thank the Secretary-General, Dr Guy S. Métraux, and his staff for their active and faithful collaboration which has contributed so much to the success of this scientific and cultural history of mankind.

PAULO E. DE BERRÊDO CARNEIRO